D1503065

Guides to Information Sources

Information Sources in

Finance and Banking

Guides to Information Sources

A series under the General Editorship of
M.W. Hill
Ia C. McIlwaine
and
Nancy J. Williamson

This series was known previously as 'Butterworths Guides to Information Sources'.

Other titles available include:

Information Sources in Architecture and Construction (Second edition)
edited by Valerie J. Nurcombe
Information Sources in Chemistry (Fourth edition)
edited by R.T. Bottle and J.F.B. Rowland
Information Sources in Physics (Third edition)
edited by Dennis F. Shaw
Information Sources in Environmental Protection
edited by Selwyn Eagle and Judith Deschamps
Information Sources in Grey Literature (Third edition)
by C.P. Auger
Information Sources in Music
edited by Lewis Foreman
Information Sources in the Life Sciences (Fourth edition)
edited by H.V. Wyatt
Information Sources in Engineering (Third edition)
edited by Ken Mildren and Peter Hicks
Information Sources in Sport and Leisure
edited by Michele Shoebridge
Information Sources in Patents
edited by C.P. Auger
Information Sources for the Press and Broadcast Media
edited by Selwyn Eagle
Information Sources in Information Technology
edited by David Haynes
Information Sources in Pharmaceuticals
edited by W.R. Pickering
Information Sources in Metallic Materials
edited by M.N. Patten
Information Sources in the Earth Sciences (Second edition)
edited by David N. Wood, Joan E. Hardy and
Anthony P. Harvey
Information Sources in Cartography
edited by C.R. Perkins and R.B. Barry
Information Sources in Polymers and Plastics
edited by R.T. Adkins
Information Sources in Economics (Second edition)
edited by John Fletcher

Guides to Information Sources

Information Sources in
Finance and Banking

Ray Lester

London · Melbourne · Munich · New Jersey

British Library Cataloguing in Publication Data
A catalogue record for this title is available from the British Library

Library of Congress Cataloging-in-Publication Data
A catalog record for this title is available from the Library of Congress

Published by Bowker-Saur, Maypole House, Maypole Road,
East Grinstead, West Sussex RH19 1HU, UK
Tel: +44(0)1342 330100 Fax: +44(0)1342 330191
E-mail: lis@bowker-saur.co.uk
Internet Website: http://www.bowker-saur.co.uk/service/

Bowker-Saur is part of REED REFERENCE PUBLISHING

ISBN 1–85739–037–7

Cover design by Calverts Press
Phototypeset by Intype London Ltd
Printed on acid-free paper
Printed and bound in Great Britain by Bell & Bain Ltd, Glasgow

Series editors' foreword

The second half of the 20th century has been characterized by the recognition that our style of life depends on acquiring and using information effectively. It has always been so, but only in the information society has the extent of the dependence been recognized and the development of technologies for handling information become a priority. These modern technologies enable us to store more information, to select and process parts of the store more skilfully and transmit the product more rapidly than we would have dreamt possible only 40 years ago. Yet the irony still exists that, while we are able to do all this and are assailed from all sides by great masses of information, ensuring that one has what one needs just when one wants it is frequently just as difficult as ever. Knowledge may, as Johnson said in the well known quotation, be of two kinds, but information, in contrast, is of many kinds and most of it is, for each individual, knowable only after much patient searching.

The aim of each Guide in this series is simple. It is to reduce the time which needs to be spent on that patient searching; to recommend the best starting point and sources most likely to yield the desired information. Like all subject guides, the sources discussed have had to be selected, and the criteria for selection will be given by the individual editors and will differ from subject to subject. However, the overall objective is constant; that of providing a way into a subject to those new to the field or to identify major new or possibly unexplored sources to those already familiar with it.

The great increase in new sources of information and the overwhelming input of new information from the media, advertising, meetings and conferences, letters, internal reports, office memoranda, magazines, junk mail, electronic mail, fax, bulletin boards etc. inevitably tend to make one reluctant to add to the load on the mind and memory by consulting books and journals. Yet they, and the other traditional types of printed material, remain for many purposes the most reliable sources of information. Despite all the information that is instantly accessible via the new technologies one still has to look things up in databooks, monographs, journals, patent specifications, standards, reports both official and commercial, and on maps and in atlases. Permanent recording of facts, theories and opinions is still carried out primarily by publishing in printed form. Musicians still work from printed scores even though they are helped by sound recordings. Sailors still use printed charts and tide tables even though they have radar and sonar equipment.

However, thanks to computerized indexes, online and CD-ROM, searching the huge bulk of technical literature to draw up a list of references can be undertaken reasonably quickly. The result, all too often, can still be a formidably long list, of which a knowledge of the nature and structure of information sources in that field can be used to put in order of likely value.

It is rarely necessary to consult everything that has been published on the topic of a search. When attempting to prove that an invention is genuinely novel, a complete search may seem necessary, but even then it is common to search only obvious sources and leave it to anyone wishing to oppose the grant of a patent to bear the cost of hunting for a prior disclosure in some obscure journal. Usually, much proves to be irrelevant to the particular aspect of our interest and whatever is relevant may be unsound. Some publications are sadly lacking in important detail and present broad generalizations flimsily bridged with arches of waffle. In any academic field there is a 'pecking order' of journals so that articles in one journal may be assumed to be of a higher or lower calibre than those in another. Those experienced in the field know these things. The research scientist soon learns, as it is part of his training, the degree of reliance he can place on information from co-workers elsewhere, on reports of research by new and (to him) unknown researchers, on data compilations and on manufacturers of equipment. The information worker, particularly when working in a field other than his own, faces very serious problems as he tries to compile, probably from several sources, a report on which his client may base important actions. Even the librarian, faced only with recommending two or three books or journal articles, meets the same problem though less acutely.

In the Bowker-Saur Guides to Information Sources we aim to

bring you the knowledge and experience of specialists in the field. Each author regularly uses the information sources and services described and any tricks of the trade that the author has learnt are passed on.

Nowadays, two major problems face those who are embarking upon research or who are in charge of collections of information of every kind. One is the increasingly specialized knowledge of the user and the concomitant ignorance of other potentially useful disciplines. The second problem is the trend towards cross-disciplinary studies. This has led to a great mixing of academic programmes – and a number of imprecisely defined fields of study. Courses are offered in Environmental Studies, Women's Studies, Communication Studies or Area Studies, and these are the forcing ground for research. The editors are only too aware of the difficulties raised by those requiring information from such hybrid subject fields and this approach, too, is being handled in the series alongside the traditional 'hard disciplines'.

Guides to the literature have a long and honoured history. Marion Spicer of SRIS recently drew to our attention a guide written in 1891 for engineers. No doubt there are even earlier ones. Nowadays, with the information and even the publishing fields changing quite frequently, it is necessary to update guides every few years and this we do in this present Series.

Michael Hill
Ia McIlwaine
Nancy Williamson

About the author

Ray Lester graduated in chemistry, and took a PhD in chemical pathology at Leeds University whilst working as a clinical biochemist in the Leeds General Infirmary. He then worked for Unilever as an information scientist at its Colworth Research Laboratory, before being invited to join Unilever Computing Services as a system analyst. After various posts in the libraries of Bradford University, University College London, and Queen Elizabeth College, he became Librarian at the London Business School in 1981. In 1990 he was asked to take charge of all of the business school's computing, networking and audio-visual services, alongside management of its library and internal and external information services, and later, the voice telephony services. He is currently coordinating within the school a review of approaches to quality management, as well as acting as its Director of Career Management (helping to place in employment graduating MBA and MSc students). Dr Lester has had a wide variety of professional involvements within Aslib, SCONUL, the Library Association and the Institute of Information Scientists – currently being Chair of the latter's External Affairs Committee and a member of its core Management Committee. He has been an external examiner to Thames Valley University and the University of Sheffield. He has produced a number of papers on aspects of strategy and policy in academic library and information services, including a text *Environmental Scanning and Business Strategy* for the British Library Research and Development Department.

Contents

Preface xiii

Notes on Organization of the Book xxi

1 Approaches to Structure 1

2 Legal, Economic and Political Environments 147

3 Value-adding Processes 355

4 Corporations 393

5 Financial Institutions and Markets 421

6 Financial Management and Investment 567

7 Scholarly Research and Study 607

8 The Electronic Imperative 653

Index to Organizations 729

Index to Serial Titles 753

Preface

> No subscriber or other reader should act on the basis of any statement contained in this publication without considering appropriate professional advice. The publisher, and the author and editor, expressly disclaim all and any liability to any person, whether a purchaser of this publication or not, in respect of anything, and of the consequences of anything done, or omitted to be done by any such person in reliance upon the contents of this publication.
>
> (DOGGART, C. **Tax Havens and Their Uses 1993**. *Economist Intelligence Unit*, 1993.)

This book is an introductory survey of the publicly available information sources of finance (and banking). I write the words 'and banking' in parenthesis, because the sources specifically relevant to banking activity I cover are a relatively small subset of the whole. In fact, I consider the subject of 'finance' to encompass quite a broad range of entities and processes. Naturally I make reference to information sources produced by, or about, the entities and processes of central, domestic and international banking, and also to those produced by or about the various participants in the securities industry, and – to a much lesser degree – in the insurance industry. I also cover: the various types of savings institution (credit unions, friendly societies and so on); those entities sometimes collectively known as finance companies (such as venture capital, credit and leasing companies); those companies and organizations concerned with fund management and investment – for instance, mutual funds/unit trusts, and pension funds; and those commercial and non-commercial organizations who are involved with asset-backed finance (especially in the real estate/property industry). As perhaps the reader will already have inferred from this outline, my approach is very much an entity-based, rather than a process-based, approach to categorizing the information sources I list.

However I do not wish to imply that there is not much that is about the processes of finance, as opposed to the entities which carry out those processes: for instance, about the business of personal, corporate, public, international financial management and investment; or about financial market trading; or about scholarly research on the financial system. But my prime concern has been with the entities who produce or influence the production of what I later term the *facts* of the financial system. Indeed, we are preoccupied here particularly with the influencers: the diverse range of national and international official, quasi-official, professional and trade bodies who are such critical components of the finance subject arena: not only determining the characteristics of the finance information that other (trading) entities need, are required, or choose to produce for the public domain, but also making publicly available a significant corpus of finance information in their own right.

So we cover a wide area in this book, including many references which in other contexts might be labelled as being, for instance, about 'trade', 'business', 'commerce', 'economics', 'politics', 'accountancy', 'taxation' or 'the law'. People and organizations in all of these disciplines one might say at one time or another are (also) engaged in 'finance'; or, at the least, they will have an exceptionally close involvement with finance activity.

Obviously, views about what is covered by the term 'finance' vary greatly. What a 'banker' might think that the subject area of finance comprises, will almost always differ from what a 'corporate treasurer' might think are its limits, and this clearly will not be what an 'economist' would say are the boundaries of finance as a discipline, which will in turn not be the same as the view of one or another of the various types of 'accountant' (financial, management, cost, etc), and that will be different again from the definition a lawyer would produce; and so on, and so on. Partly for that reason, it did not seem fruitful to try to delineate the field rigorously in this book, so that, say, the reader might recognise an information source in finance (and banking) when he or she saw one.

But I suppose that if I had to define our scope here, I might write that we are primarily concerned with the complex of entities, processes and systems, which have as their prime working material, those things collectively known as financial assets. The contention would be that entities (individuals and organizations) which regularly engage in substantive activities involving financial assets (or directly or indirectly assist with such engagements), are involved in 'finance'. One of the prime objectives of such individuals and organizations who together comprise the resulting (global) financial system, is continually to try to improve its overall efficiency and effectiveness: whilst at the same time (we trust) ensuring conformation to, and support of, current prevailing national and international legal, economic and political imperatives.

I used the word 'complex' above advisedly, for it is remarkable just how often that word (and similar meaning variants) appears in the literature surveyed in this book, to an extent one hardly remembers happening in other subject areas, say, in science, which surely are just as 'complex'. Over the far, far too long period this book has been in gestation, I have frequently (sometimes necessarily!) wondered why this is.

I believe that there are perhaps four main reasons. Firstly, most of the activity of finance is of a practical rather than a research nature. This then translates itself into a volume of practitioner orientated published output seeking to explain perceived complexities to the non-specialist. Note that such non-specialists will often meanwhile be specialists in cognate disciplines (such as those mentioned above). So, for instance, we have descriptive or prescriptive explanations of the latest thinking on one or another aspect of derivatives-based trading appearing, not just in the generic finance literature aimed at derivatives practitioners, but also in the practitioner literature of accountancy, taxation, law, economics etc.

Secondly, finance, driven particularly by the continuing developments in information technology, is a very fast moving field. So this process of explanation of complex matters has to be a continuing process, too, elucidating for the reader new financial instruments, new institutional processes or new regulatory arrangements, and so on.

Thirdly, this explanation has to occur with respect to a worldwide terrain, since what is happening in the United States is frequently just as important to a finance practitioner there as what is happening in the United Kingdom, Europe, the Far East or in any (emerging or emerged) country internationally engaged in significant finance activity. This would not in itself create an added layer of 'complexity', were it not for the differing legal, economic and political frameworks applicable within each national boundary. (Note also the unique further complexities of the European Union.)

The fourth and final manifestation of complexity in the publicly available information sources of finance is of a different order and soon leads us into difficult waters. Problems of entity, asset and transaction definition abound in this subject field, and these generate the majority of the examples of the three types of complexity just covered. But even when the necessary definitions have been adequately framed and used by those who have prime initial responsibility for the 'generated' information referring to each specific entity, asset, or transaction, there is no guarantee that this will continue to be the case once the resulting information passes to other interested parties. In this semantic domain, we are dealing for example with bankers from all sorts of sectors in all sorts of countries; corporate and public treasurers and other designated financial managers; internal and external accountants, auditors and tax professionals; mergers and acquisitions and divestment specialists; lawyers, registrars and trustees; bankruptcy and insolvency professionals; financial and investment analysts, advisers and planners; financial market traders, dealers and brokers; credit and debt raters; business and public economists; investigative journalists; market researchers and consultants; academic researchers; and the actual personal, corporate and institutional traders and investors for whom in the end all the others primarily exist. Each of these groups is, potentially, a source of information about one or another aspect of the financial system, and the information user ideally needs to know how faithful has this person or organization been to the information originally framed – generated – within the boundary of a particular individual or organizational entity? We will see later that answering this question is complicated by the relatively large amounts of information generated and used in the financial system that have a restricted distribution – so that it often becomes even more difficult to establish exactly what has happened to the information one is interested in, since its original formulation.

Given this fundamental question of evaluating information validity within the world's financial information system, my approach has been purposefully to avoid assessing the value of the sources I list. So the descriptions of some 4,000 organizational and printed and electronic sources of information related to the financial system, which comprise the bulk of the book, almost always simply paraphrase text provided by the organization about itself, or about one of its print or electronic publications. (Very occasionally I quote from an external review of an information source and also very occasionally, my enthusiasm for a specific source leaks out!)

In these descriptions, I have not shrunk from including statements which a moment's thought should reveal are no more than advertising hype! As I stress early on in the opening essay, it is critical for the newcomer to this field to realise that the hard core of reliable financial data available about the world's entities, assets and transactions is in fact surprisingly small; and much of this relatively small corpus must, by law, be (eventually) made publicly available to all who wish and have the opportunity to peruse it in ideally as equitable a fashion as possible. The corollary of this is that the reader must be continually sceptical of published material that appears to offer a unique source of data on one or another aspect of the financial system not available elsewhere. So much of the financial information industry is driven by the desire of specific investors to be 'the first to know' about some investment-sensitive event; alongside, no doubt, another 5,000 or so investors who, surprise, surprise, just happen to be currently subscribing to the same expensive and 'exclusive' newsletter! There is, indeed, an awful lot of published material in finance which seems, to this writer, to add nothing of value to what is already available elsewhere in the public domain.

But, obviously, it is up to the reader to decide for him or herself, the value of specific sources. Information sources are meant to be used, not just read about in books such as this. So I have tried to make locating potentially relevant sources as swift and easy as possible. Firstly, I have thought a lot about structure – both as regards to how the various types of source relate to each other, and also about how they all should be arranged in the book to maximize its usability. Secondly, there are comprehensive indexes to all of the serial titles covered, and to all of the non-commercial organizations that are referenced. Thirdly, I have tried to give full and up-to-date contact details for each source producer (as of early 1995) so that the reader can easily get more up-to-date intelligence on each producer's current portfolio of information products and services. Competitive and, more recently, technological pressures have long ensured the continuing development of information sources within the finance subject area, as this extract from the Preface to Jack Revell's classic text of 25 years ago reveals (a volume with an excellent and still largely valid introduction to many of the problems of institutional classification in this field):

> An author who tried to be up-to-date in this field faces an impossible task: many further changes will have occurred before this work appears in print. This volume was corrected up to the middle of July 1972, and a very few corrections were made in the winter of that year. For changes since that date the reader must find his own way among the sources suggested in the General Notes. I hope that the background knowledge which he has gained from this book will make his task easy.
>
> (REVELL, J. **The British Financial System**. *Macmillan*, 1973)

Partly because the field of finance moves so fast, I have restricted citations in the main body of the text to serial (as against non-serial) print and electronic publications. My reason being that (assuming that the serial still exists) perusal of recent print issues or of up-to-date copies of the database – as well of course as personal contact with organizations active in the area – is then a good way (I suggest, the best way) of quickly getting into the part of the overall field that interests the reader. In my experience, such books as the present text are of most help when one needs rapidly to get going with a few sources as a starting point: these few then, one trusts, leading via citation (or other tracking method) to the information actually needed.

Many of these sorts of leads can be gleaned from the longer descriptions I have reproduced for several of the sources I cover. Thus I have left out of the book a number of points that I might have made in the commentary part of the book, because they are stated or can be inferred from these longer source descriptions. I have also tried to avoid using space to state the really obvious. For instance, I would suggest that we hardly need a book to tell us how important the *Financial Times* and the *Wall Street Journal* are to finance practice and research; in fact neither of those publications are formally cited in this book, though both are mentioned at a number of points in the text. I feel that it is inconceivable that my readers will be unfamiliar with such fundamental sources of finance information.

There is no significance as to which source descriptions are long and which are short. The reader should not conclude that because the entries for the *Federal Reserve Bulletin* and for the *International Securities Market Association* are several times longer than those for, respectively, the *Bank of England Quarterly Bulletin* and the *International Swaps and Derivatives Association*, the former are several times more important than the latter! The last thing that I wish to happen is for the reader to pick up this book and think that they have a totally comprehensive reference work to the information sources in finance (and banking). Frequently, all that is referenced is the title of the serial – where that seems self-explanatory of its coverage. In other cases, I just hint at the 'complexity' of one or another element of the overall subject field.

More generally, I would hope that the structure I have adopted will encourage readers to explore previously unfamiliar or long neglected territory. I would like to feel that the book, whilst not perhaps for bedtime reading, nevertheless will lead the reader to reflect on a wider range of issues than perhaps he or she normally would. Given the awful time pressures most of us have to cope with these days, is it not the case that we are all too frequently constrained within our specific disciplines? Is it not also the case that if we were better able to build links to others coming at the same problems we face, but from different angles, we would be able together better to solve the problems frequently thrown up by the complexity of the global trading environment?

Be that as it may be, having completed what seems to be a first attempt to pull together into a single simple coherent and consistent framework finance information sources across a large number of subsidiary and cognate disciplines of finance, I do find that the printed book – as an information artefact – has a considerable amount to offer for gaining perspective. Despite my final contention that eventually, all of the publicly available data, information and documents needed by finance practitioners will be accessible electronically, personally it still seems to me that an appreciation of the overall structure of a relatively multi-facetted communication system is best gained through a single printed volume. And I offer that thought, despite the considerable advances brought about by hypertextual approaches of systems such as the Internet's World Wide Web. This book in fact deliberately stops at the Internet. This reflects my belief that not only does the Web as an information system not (yet?) provide anything like the universal connectivity, coverage, functionality and performance of such as the real-time electronic systems used by finance practitioners, it also – by definition – is best explored hands-on. You cannot hypertravel in a printed guide (but you can serendipitously browse in this volume to your heart's content!)

On the choice of sources I list, it has only been possible within this single volume to cover in detail the domestic arrangements of the United Kingdom and the United States. To these are added coverage of 'International' material; and material relating to 'Europe' (for which, read 'The European Union'). Within those domains, I would hope that there are entries for all of the public and private information producing organizations who have a major presence and, in addition, entries for a significant number of more minor operations. As regards the latter, again, there is no significance – especially in respect of the commercial information providers – as to who is included and who is not. The prime purpose of this book is not to list all of the information providers operating in one or another area of finance: there are any number of directories (such as those listed at the end of the first chapter of the book) which will provide that. It is to give examples of the range of types of material produced and to explore the relationship of each part of the range to all of the other parts. Similarly, in the Notes, I have purposefully restricted the background reading I cite to substantive non-serial items. Again, it is relatively easy to find recent journal articles on a topic of interest (though regrettably there is no one secondary source which provides the breadth of coverage of the finance discipline reflected in this text). What is more difficult – or is at least less common – is the retrieval of background books and reports.

It is with pleasure that I acknowledge my grateful thanks to the large number of individuals and organizations who have helped this book come to fruition. First must be mentioned the various editors at Bowker-Saur (and before that Butterworths) who have patiently waited for me to deliver: I will especially refer in this connection to Val Skelton and Linda Hajdukiewicz, who with the Series Editors in the event have born the bulk of the editorial work. Next, I must of course thank the information providers themselves, particularly those based in the United States, who have been so helpful in promptly sending me material about their various products and services. Then there are the various librarians who generously allowed me to use their collections or offered such welcome advice and encouragement. Unfortunately, there are far too many of these to list individually, but I must note the sterling contribution of Jules Winterton and colleagues at the Institute of Advanced Legal Studies, Penny Hope and colleagues at the Bank of England Reference Library, Pam and Allan Foster, Ruth Pagell and Sheila Corrall.

Staff of my own Library and of the London Business School more generally, have directly or indirectly been tremendously supportive of this project. Again, one hesitates to single people out individually, but I must thank Dick Brealey and subsequently other staff at the Institute of Finance and Accounting, who have been continually encouraging of the venture, Keith Foreman and Fergus Lynch, who daily do wondrous things with the technology I have used and Gerry Quincey, who has been very understanding of the time and commitment such a book as this consumes.

Lastly, I must thank my various families past and present for their – if not understanding! – at least resignation when yet more time had to be devoted to 'The Book'. I doubt whether it is ever the case that an author's nearest and dearest really think that all of the 'lost' evenings and weekends such a project as this entails is in the end justified by the result. But I do know that three people in particular have not been able to wait for the moment when it was all finished. So I am more than happy now to dedicate this work to them and their futures: my children, Catherine, Richard, and of course, Joanna.

October 1995

Notes on Organization of the Book

a. The majority of the information sources listed are of three types:

(i) *Organizations*—Each non-commercial and commercial organization is numbered sequentially in the format **#n**, and its title appears in **bold type**. In addition, the organizational entries are numbered in brackets sequentially within each numbered paragraph before the entry itself. Subsidiary organizations appear in *italic type*. There is an *Index of Organizations* at the end of the Book covering the non-commercial organizations: that is, it does not include the commercial information providers. Full contact details for each organization listed are given. There is then frequently a summary of the purpose of the organization – usually simply reproducing (rather than paraphrasing) what the organization is currently saying about itself. These statements are given in single quotes (‘’).

(ii) *Serials* The citations for these are indented under an entry for the producer of the serial, are in smaller type, and are numbered in a separate sequence. There is an *Index of Serials* at the end of the Book. Again, in each citation, single quotes indicate quotations from material provided by the producer of the serial. In a few cases it has seemed helpful to distinguish what I have termed:

- *reference works*—Here the compilation is regularly updated by replacement loose-leaf pages, or amended electronically, whilst remaining essentially the same body of knowledge;
- *current awareness*—Here each issue of the serial normally

adds to and is different from what has already been published.

The abbreviations used are:

a.	Annual
bi-a.	Every two years
bi-m.	Every two months
bi-w.	Fortnightly
c.	At least more frequently than daily: up to 'real-time'
d.	Daily
i.	Irregularly
m.	Monthly
s-a.	Every six months
w.	Weekly

Price information—Where this has been gathered, it shows the level of price one might pay for each serial. Such information dates very quickly: but the (rather large) relativities between the prices of different serials should stay constant. Where the frequency of issue of the serial (and its price, where that is given) appear immediately after the title, then that is of the paper-based (or other non-electronic) version of the serial.

Where an electronic designator (*online*, *CD-ROM*, or *diskette* are the main forms covered) appears immediately after the serial title, then the frequency and price details given are of that version. In some cases, both electronic and non-electronic versions for the same title are referenced. I have not named those CD-ROM producers providing access to the electronic versions of specific serials (i.e. the service supplier(s) currently supplying access to that serial online; and whether the CD-ROM or diskette version of the serial is available directly from the artefact's original publisher, or via a different supplier). This information in particular is subject to frequent change: the original publisher will know how to obtain access to electronic versions of the serials they produce.

(iii) *Notes*—These appear at the end of each Chapter.

b. Below is a sample organizational entry.

(a) #A Scope International 62 Murray Road, Waterlooville, Hants PO8 9JL, UK. t: (44 1705) 592255 f: 591975.

With the ever turning tides of fortune it is absolutely essential for the security of anyone of substance or ambition to have at least one other passport and nationality. Dual citizenship can also be thought of as a business proposition. The tax benefits and investment opportunities can be enormous and total financial *privacy can be achieved*...

- *Scope Reports*—'Your personal invitation to discover the secrets of the super rich . . . Revealing a coherent plan for a stress-free, healthy and prosperous life, without government interference, taxes or coercion; including how to:
- Become a 'PT' – a Perpetual Traveller – and avoid taxes, governments, ex-spouses, lawsuits and hassle . . .
- Earn a substantial income underwriting insurance at Lloyd's of London, the safe way . . .
- Make a million or more in three years or less . . .'

a. **Mouse Monitor: The International Journal of Rodent Control**. q. 'A journal of bureau(c)rat control and we are sending it to you free. You can receive it free for life if you wish by purchasing one of *Scope's Special Reports*, which explain how to, and help you to, live your life free from government interference and other constraints – legally.'

b. The **Passport Report**. a. £60. 'How to legally obtain a second foreign passport . . . Most countries now *sell* passports. The wording of their laws describe entrepreneurs, financial benefactors, treaty traders, and special investors in government loan paper as being welcome new citizens. Put up from $10,000 to $100,000 and you can obtain an almost instant passport . . . How dual nationality can be obtained legally is fully explained. In many situations there is no residence requirement. In a few places there is not even any need to *ever* visit.'

c. *Geographical focus*—Categorizing this is not quite as straightforward as one would have thought. Part of the difficulty is common to any attempt at hierarchical classification. But the main problem is in defining what exactly we might mean by the geographical 'focus' of a specific information source: which problem is well illustrated in this quotation:

'Before embarking on the rest of the analysis, it is worth clarifying a few geographical terms. These terms are used to describe markets, economies, products, services, firms, regulators and supervisors, and consumers . . .

Domestic refers to the environment within a single economy . . . Domestic business refers to the business conducted in the same market as the domicile of the firm or customer, for the most part being the place where taxes are paid and where the majority of the ownership lies. It will also usually mean where business is conducted in the same currency as the base currency of the firm. The domestic market is also that which is presided over by the national regulators and government. Terms such as resident and non-resident are used to define differences between domestic and foreign. The end of geography itself blurs the precise boundaries between domestic and other (foreign) business: indeed, all geographical terms become harder to define and at the extreme become meaningless.

International means activities taking place between nations. International finance refers to financial flows or services between nations, although it is regularly used to describe any business that is not wholly domestic. If nations did not exist there would be no '*inter*-national' concept.

Multinational describes activities taking place in more than one nation. A bank or company, for example, may be multinational by operating in more than one nation ... Of course most multinational businesses and banks will carry out international transactions as well as operate in local markets ... Often the whole purpose of the multinational presence will be to operate in other countries, behind national boundaries and barriers, as well as to offer international and cross-border services.

Cross-border is almost synonymous with international and often will be a preferable term, in that it is less likely to be confused with global or multinational. It is another way of expressing the sense '*inter*-national'.

Offshore refers to activities that are outside some specific jurisdiction (albeit onshore somewhere else).

Global should refer to operations within an integral whole, if it is to have a separate meaning from the foregoing terms ... A truly global service knows no internal boundaries, can be offered throughout the globe, and pays scant attention to national aspects. The nation becomes irrelevant, even though it will still exist. The closer we get to a global, integral whole, the closer we get to the end of geography.' (O'BRIEN, R. **Global financial integration: The end of geography**. *Pinter Publishers* for *Royal Institute of International Affairs*, 1992.)

d. However, despite such nuances, which must be pursued in the actual retrieval and use of information sources, for simplicity here, I have tried in the following to encompass under the heading *International*: all organizations and sources which relate to activity in more than one country, or to activity across the boundaries between countries, or which are truly 'global' in the sense defined in the above quotation. (The reader will note examples of all these types of usage in the sub-sections headed 'International'.) In the Chapters concerned with Legal, Economic and Political Environments, and with Financial Institutions and Markets, I have also separately distinguished a number of organizations which have a specifically European Union dimension – using the heading 'Europe'. In addition, in the former Chapter, and in a number of ways cutting across this categorization of 'International' and 'Europe' focused sources – it has been found useful to use a sub-heading 'Trade and Development'. Under this sub-heading, for the most part we reference examples of organizations and serials that deal with 'cross-border' rather than 'domestic' trade and development, but there are also some examples given that deal with the latter, as well.

CHAPTER ONE

Approaches to Structure

Capital markets are markets in financial information. Financial information is both an input into and a product of the decisions that are made in capital markets. How such information is generated, interpreted, and controlled matters greatly to the society at large. Thus the changing patterns of generating and managing financial information – including who has it or controls it, how it is processed, and who uses it – are central to understanding the historical development and regulation of capital markets.[1]*

Despite all the electronic hardware that has been brought to bear on global financial markets, the market is still only a collection of people. It will reflect their moods, their hopes, and their fears. Even the most exactly calculated arbitrage position could be blown out of the water because the rest of the market suddenly goes crazy. For example, I was in a trading room in New York during the early course of the Falklands Islands conflict. The market was tense because no one knew how things might go. A great deal depended on the carrier *Hermes* (the chief British naval asset in the conflict). So when the chief foreign exchange dealer suddenly shouted 'They've sunk the *Hermes*', and began selling sterling heavily, the pound weakened sharply. The market assumed that we had inside information. Then we saw the source of the dealer's fears. At the bottom of the Telerate quote screen, a message flashed 'Carrier lost . . . Carrier lost . . . Carrier lost', to tell users that the line carrying Telerate's signal had been lost. We laughed . . . an expensive laugh.[2]

It would be an exaggeration to claim that the mentality of people in the world of money is fixed in an ethic-resistant style exclusively

* The Notes appear at the end of each Chapter.

by the nature of economic rationality. In fact, what is being claimed is that the nature of financial institutions and City modes of thinking reinforce an ethic-resistant disposition bred from economic rationality and from the original motivations which attracted people to work in the financial sector. At a practical level, the disposition is further strengthened by the volatility factor, which applies not only to the speed of monetary transactions but also to the speed-driven role of the employers in the financial sector. Behind this, of course, lies the electronic technology now used in money markets and the process of 'dematerialisation' which has changed the system for settling transactions. Paper is disappearing. The pace of electronic systems and the need for instant decision-making is not the natural ground for ethical reflection. Indeed, many workers in the City look on the introduction of ethical considerations as an abandonment of professionalism; they distrust the non-quantifiable aspects of the exercise and consider the whole approach as an excuse for unaccountability.[3]

The trading system

1. For the purposes here, we might start by viewing the world as a set of *entities* (individuals and organizations) who need or wish to *trade* with each other. That is, an individual or organization needs or wishes to interact with another individual or organization such that resources are transferred between them. These interactions – or *transactions* – will result both in economic *flows* between the entities; and in changes in the volume, composition or value of each entity's assets or liabilities: in their *stocks*.
2. We shall be focusing primarily in this book on the *financial* aspects of the world's transactions between entities. For instance, to take one important type of 'financial information', we will later give examples of publicly available information sources which reveal the assets and liabilities of entities, and recent changes in those assets and liabilities, expressed in monetary terms (the *accounts* of the entities).
3. However, there will be much coverage also of information sources arising from the *environments* within which trade takes place. The network of official and quasi-official organizations comprising these environments are not only critical in determining the detailed nature of trade itself. But – of even more relevance here – a number of the organizations are charged with specifying what 'financial' and financially related information about such trade shall appear in the public domain – when, where and how. Thus – if only by implication – what can be kept 'secret'. It is not possible to understand the nuances of our chosen field without delving in some depth into the environments of trade. This, indeed,

is a book about *information sources* (generated and used) *in* (the practice of, and research about) *finance and banking*: not just one about finance (and banking[4]) information sources (whatever we might think such would comprise).

4. Before a trade transaction takes place, at the least each participating entity will normally wish to know: first, what resources are on offer: what resource asset or assets will Entity A receive from Entity B, and vice versa? Second, what are the future benefits or economic *return* that will, or is likely to, accrue to the transacting entities once the transaction has taken place? In writing 'or is likely to', we are introducing the notion that there will frequently be a *risk* that an asset will not in the event provide the future return assessed before it was acquired. Given such fundamental uncertainty, it is not surprising that much of the finance publishing industry is concerned with forecast of the outcomes of trading events that are about to happen, in addition to comment on and analysis of those that have already happened. We shall also need to give due attention to this area.

5. In fact, much of the forecasting that goes on is not of trades which are yet to occur (e.g. will sterling sink through the floor?; what will happen to the price of Microsoft's shares?). It is of events that have already taken place, but the details of which are not publicly known (e.g. what have Novell earned in the third quarter?; what are the latest money supply figures?). This has two important ramifications. First, rules and procedures need to be in place to ensure that those *inside* the entity that is about to make publicly available such trade-related – and market sensitive – information, are not able to profit from such knowledge ahead of formal publication. Second, clearly there will be potential advantage to those *outside* of the entity that is publicly releasing a specific piece of information, to know of its details ahead of other market participants. Thus, there occurs the frenetic competition between the commercial information providers to post such released information on to their customers' dealing room screens as speedily as possible. Thus, also, perhaps, the ultimate pointlessness of those of us without access to such 'real-time' systems in trying to 'beat the market'. By the time we get to the information, it will already have been reacted to by the big boys. We will return to this theme too later on. We will find that the theme very much revolves around the economic idea of *efficient markets*.

6. As well as restricting ourselves for the most part to publicly available information relating to the financial aspects of transactions, we will be focusing on transactions in *financial assets*, as against those in *real assets*:

> *Real assets* are those expected to provide benefits based on their fundamental qualities. A person's home provides benefits commensurate with the quality of its construction, its location, and its size. A corporation's main computer provides benefits based on its speed, the size of its memory, the ease of its use, and the frequency with which it needs repair.
>
> In contrast, *financial assets* are those expected to provide benefits based solely on another party's performance – that is, they are *claims* against others for future benefits. A bank savings account will provide future benefits only if the bank continues to operate and to pay interest on the account; the account holder depends on the bank's performance for any benefits from the financial asset. It follows from this concept of financial assets that one party's financial asset is another person's *financial liability* – that is, the latter has an obligation (often a legal one) to provide future benefits to the owner of the financial asset.[5]

This relative concentration on trade in financial assets means that the reader will find here only tangential mention of information sources which might help research of the financial aspects of trade in real assets: for instance, historical trends in the UK imported prices of Tasmanian beer; or a comparison of the average salaries of English and American church organists.

7. *Financial claims* may be issued by *government* entities:

> When the government incurs a budget deficit, it must borrow from the public to pay its bills. To borrow, the government issues bonds, which are IOUs that promise to pay money at some time in the future. The *government debt* (sometimes called the public debt) consists of the total or accumulated borrowings by the government; it is the total dollar value of government bonds owned by the public (households, banks, businesses, foreigners, and other non-federal entities).[6]

and they may be issued by companies – or as we shall more generally term them here *corporations*[7] – of one type or another:

> To carry on business a modern company needs an almost endless variety of *real assets*. Many of them are tangible assets, such as machinery, factories, and offices; others are intangible, such as technical expertise, trademarks, and patents. All of them unfortunately need to be paid for. To obtain the necessary money the company sells pieces of paper called *financial assets*, or securities. These pieces of paper have value because they are claims on the firm's real assets. Financial assets include not only shares of stock but also bonds, bank loans, lease obligations, and so on.[8]

8. Financial claims may of course also be issued by non-incorporated individuals: you might lend me £10 or $20, and I might in return give you a signed piece of paper (a *note*[9]) to that effect. But information in the public domain on such transactions normally is unavailable (for almost all of us thankfully), especially as such claims will hardly be tradeable in a legally recognised *secondary market* (having initially been issued as it were in a *primary market*). Secondary financial markets facilitate the transfer of (already existing) financial claims between trading entities, the prospect of an active secondary market in a specific financial claim often encouraging acquisition of the financial claim when it is first issued.

9. As an aside, it is interesting to note that currency itself is in the widest definition a financial claim, as Sechrest colourfully points out:

> Please note that each country's currency is supported by the 'full faith and credit' of each country's government. In essence, when currencies were 'taken off' gold, silver or other commodity support, the currencies became unsecured notes. . . . In fact, if you read the fine print on any currency, you will discover that every currency is a note. The US dollar bill is described on its face as a Federal Reserve Note and states the following: 'This note is legal tender for all debts, public and private.' The result is if you seek redemption of a dollar bill by the US Treasury, you will, if successful, not receive gold, silver, or any other commodity. Rather, you will receive another dollar bill. A similar result arises with Britain's various sterling notes. For example, the five pound note declares 'I promise to pay the bearer on demand the sum of five pounds.' Turn a five-pound note in, get a five-pound note back.[10]

10. One of our preoccupations here then is with information in the public domain relating to the assets and liabilities of public sector bodies and private sector corporations expressed in monetary terms; and with the financial claims (on the bodies' and corporations' real assets) that those entities issue to investors. It is often not possible for an *ultimate deficit entity* (some person or organization currently in need of 'money'[11]) to find a corresponding *ultimate surplus entity* (a person/organization with, as it were, 'money' to spare) able and willing to accept the transfer of the totality of financial claims of defined characteristics on offer. Thus, a sophisticated array of *financial institutions* has arisen allowing – among a number of other important functions – transformations of the characteristics of financial claims so that there is a matching of ultimate surplus and deficit entity needs. There is now on offer an immense variety of what in this context might often be termed *financial instruments*[12] which facilitate this matching process. As is well known, although much of the world's trading of financial instruments arises from 'real' trading needs, much also is completely divorced from trade in real assets – being a more or less simple *investment* by entities in the hope of future financial gain.[13]

11. The transfer of funds with the aid of one or more financial institutions can either be direct; or it can be indirect. Gardner and

Mills – in their valuable wide-ranging US-based text from which we have already quoted – highlight the differences between the two, at the same time characterizing the practice of (financial) *institutional investment*, and the idea of the *broker*:

> Funds transfer can occur directly between parties, as when an individual lends to a friend or purchases stock in a large nonfinancial corporation. In these cases, the lender/investor has a claim on the friend or on the corporation; that is, the investor is engaged in *direct investment*. Direct investment results in the creation of a primary security.
>
> The transfer of funds from one party to another can also occur with the assistance of a *financial institution*, taking one of two forms. One form occurs when an investor with excess funds purchases a secondary security, such as a life insurance policy or a savings account, allowing the financial institution to determine the ultimate recipient of the funds. For instance, a life insurer may invest the premium payments of its policyholders in corporate bonds, or a credit union may invest the savings of some of its members in home-improvement loans to other members. The policyholder or the saver is engaged in *indirect investment*; his or her claim is on the financial institution, while the institution holds a direct claim on the corporation or the homeowner. The institution has thus transformed a secondary security into a primary security. This transformation is called *intermediation*.
>
> Not all funds transfers involving financial institutions occur through intermediation. Sometimes an institution arranges or assists in the transfer of funds between parties, without issuing its own financial liabilities in the process. When a financial institution acts in this more limited capacity, it is acting as a *broker*. . . . Securities brokers and investment bankers seldom issue secondary securities themselves but rather assist in the transfer of funds from suppliers to demanders. Many financial institutions act as both intermediaries and brokers from time to time.[14]

12. You will notice that the terms *primary* and *secondary* are used in that extract in a quite different sense to our earlier use; and Gardner and Mills helpfully comment in a footnote:

> Unfortunately, like most fields, finance sometimes uses confusing terminology. Readers should be careful not to confuse the use of the terms 'primary' and 'secondary' in this discussion with their use in other contexts. For example, students who have previously studied corporate finance or investments may have encountered the terms *primary* and *secondary markets*; primary markets are defined as those for the original issuance of securities, and secondary markets are for securities resale. In the context of this chapter, 'primary' and 'secondary' are used to differentiate between *issuers* of securities and not to distinguish between changes in securities ownership.[15]

13. As examples of further possible confusion in terminology for those new to this subject field, we can illustrate two quite different

– though clearly related – usages of the term *investment*; and follow that with a range of definitions of its frequent bedfellow, the key term *capital*. In the standard US-based encyclopedia covering our subject field, the emphasis in the definition of the term 'investment' is – as a moment ago – on investment in *financial assets*:

> *Investment*
>
> In a general sense, any employment of capital in expectation of gain, whether in a business, farm, urban real estate, bonds, stocks, merchandise, education etc. In its more specific use in the field of securities (bonds, stocks), investment is contrasted to *speculation* in that investment is primarily for income, whereas speculation is primarily for capital gains; investment is for holding, whereas speculation is for turnover; investment is for the long term, whereas speculation is for the short term.
>
> These distinctions, however, are not fundamental. Investment may be motivated by both types of gain – income and capital gain. Investment rationally should involve turnover whenever the objectives of an investing program have changed or particular selections have reached their full potential or are no longer suitable for particular investing requirements.[16]

14. In contrast, the focus in a major recent (and excellent) UK-originated encyclopedia of the finance subject field, is on investment in *real assets*:

> *Investment*
>
> Investment is capital formation – the acquisition or creation of resources to be used in production. In capitalist economies much attention is focused on business investment in physical capital – buildings, equipment, and inventories. But investment is also undertaken by governments, nonprofit institutions, and households, and it includes the acquisition of human and intangible capital as well as physical capital. In principle, investment should also include the improvement of land or the development of natural resources, and the relevant measure of production should include nonmarket output as well as goods and services for sale.[17]

15. The different – though clearly again related – usages of the term 'capital' are well brought out in a contemporary (UK published) dictionary:

> *Capital*
>
> 1. The total value of the assets of a person less liabilities.
> 2. The amount of the proprietors' interests in the assets of an organization, less its liabilities.
> 3. The money contributed by the proprietors to an organization to enable it to function; thus *share capital* is the amount provided by way

of shares and *loan capital* is the amount provided by way of loans. However, the capital of the proprietors of companies not only consists of the share and loan capital, it also includes retained profit, which accrues to the holders of the ordinary shares. (*Reserve capital* is that part of the issued capital of a company that is held in reserve and is intended only to be called up if the company is wound up.)
4. In economic theory, a factor of production, usually either machinery and plant (*physical capital*) or money (*financial capital*). However, the concept can be applied to a variety of other assets (e.g. *human capital*). In general, the rate of return on capital is called *profit*.[18]

16. Many other examples could be given reflecting the need carefully to define the terms that we use, where that is not clear from the context. For instance, the prefix 'euro', when used within the environment of the so-called 'international capital markets', although it originally focused on events in 'Europe', is now frequently used as a generic term worldwide:

Euromarkets are financial markets that involve instruments either denominated in a currency that is not the local domestic currency or denominated in the domestic currency but sold in nondomestic markets or distributed by an international syndicate of investment bankers or merchant banks. This is a comprehensive definition that describes a multitude of financial instruments and arrangements. The instruments themselves can be placed in four general classifications:

(1) Eurodollars,
(2) Eurobonds,
(3) Eurocommercial paper and Euronotes, and
(4) Euroequities.

Eurocurrencies, particularly Eurodollars, have proved effective in correcting international liquidity imbalances for banks, industrial firms, and sovereign governments. Eurocurrency markets that started in London are now found in other European cities and in Singapore, Hong Kong, Tokyo, the Cayman Islands, and the Bahamas, while London is still the site of most Eurobond issues and active secondary trading. Eurocommercial paper, Euronotes, and Euroequities have all grown rapidly.[19]

17. Here are some examples of recently published or updated terminological dictionaries and thesauri:

Banking terminology. 3rd ed. *American Bankers Association*, 1989. 409 pp. Covers more than 6,000 separate banking-related words and phrases. Includes five appendices: Acronyms and abbreviations; Common bank performance ratios; Addresses of Federal Reserve Banks; Directory of regulatory agencies, congressional banking committees, and other useful organizations; Glossary of economic indicators.

PASS, C. and LOWES, B. **Collins dictionary of economics**. 2nd ed. *HarperCollins*, 1993. 576 pp.

PESSIN, A.H. and ROSS, J.A. **The complete words of Wall Street: The professional's guide to investment literacy**. *Business One Irwin*, 1991. 799 pp.

The credit & lending dictionary. *Robert Morris Associates*, 1990.

FRENCH, D. **Dictionary of accounting terms**. 2nd ed. *Croner*, 1991.

PERRY, F.E. **Dictionary of banking**. *Pitman*, 1992. UK orientation.

ROSENBERG, J.M. **Dictionary of banking**. *John Wiley*, 1993. 369 pp. US orientation.

INGLIS-TAYLOR, A. **Dictionary of derivatives**. *Macmillan*, 1995. 444 pp. Over two-thirds of the book is devoted to *Contract Specifications* for ten exchanges trading derivatives.

WEBBER, A. **Dictionary of futures & options**. *Irwin Professional*, 1993. 240 pp. 'Over 1,500 international terms defined and explained.[1]

BENNETT. **Dictionary of insurance**. *Pitman*, 1992.

HINKELMAN, E.G. **Dictionary of international trade**. *World Trade Press*, 1994. 279 pp. Includes a US-based section *Resources for International Trade*: Books and Directories . . . Periodicals, Magazines and Reports . . . Business & Trade Associations . . . International Trade Organizations.'

ROSENBERG, J.M. **Dictionary of international trade**. *John Wiley*, 1994. 336 pp.

ROSENBERG, J.M. **Dictionary of investing**. *John Wiley*, 1993. 368 pp.

ROBERTSON, D. **A dictionary of modern politics**. 2nd ed. *Europa Publications*, 1993. 494 pp. Includes over 500 extensive definitions/mini essays.

Dictionary of real estate appraisal. 3rd ed. *Appraisal Institute*, 1993. 527 pp. 5,000 real estate appraisal-related terms.

GARWOOD, A.N. and HORNOR, L.L. eds. **Dictionary of US government statistical terms**. *Information Publications*, 1991. 247 pp.

Employee benefit plans: A glossary of terms. *International Foundation of Employee Benefit Plans*, 1993. 202 pp.

RAMSAY, A. **Eurojargon: A dictionary of European Union acronyms, abbreviations and soubriquets**.4th ed. *Capital Planning Information*, 1994.

GONDRAND, F. **Eurospeak: A user's guide. The dictionary of the Single Market.** Translated from the French by Peter BOWEN. *Nicholas Brealey Publishing*, 1992. 296 pp.

KOCH, R. **The Financial Times guide to management and finance**. *Pitman Publishing*, 1994. 426 pp. 'While having the benefits of dictionary format, this is quite unlike any other management dictionary, for eight reasons ... It is up-to-date ... It is chatty and fun to read ... It is practical ... It is also conceptual ... It is opinionated ... It reports and synthesises an overall philosophy of management ... It is global in its vocabulary ... It takes a broad view of management, including finance, culture, technology and psychology, pointing out the public policy implications and the role of industrial policy, while also cutting out broad swathes of academic and useless economic theories that obstruct insight but are all too present in conventional dictionaries and guides.'

FINIS thesaurus of financial services marketing terms. *Bank Marketing Association*, 1991. 367 pp.

Glossary of fiduciary terms. 5th ed. *American Bankers Association*, 1990. 58 pp. The exact definitions, descriptions and/or illustrations of approximately 900 words and phrases likely to be encountered on a daily basis by anyone associated with the trust business.

Glossary of futures terms. *National Futures Association*. Free of charge.

Glossary of insurance and risk management terms. 5th ed. *International Risk Management Institute*, 1994. Defines over 1,300 terms; includes a glossary of over 500 frequently used abbreviations and acronyms.

The glossary of property terms. *ISVA*, 1990.

Glossary of stock market terms. *London Stock Exchange*. Free of charge.

GREEN, T. **The gold companion: The A-Z of mining, marketing, trading and technology**. *Gold Institute*, 1992. 154 pp.

PRYTHERCH, R. **Harrod's librarians' glossary**. 8th ed. *Gower*, 1995. 712 pp. 'To explain and define terms and concepts, identify techniques and organizations, provide summaries of the activities of associations, major libraries, Governmental and other bodies.'

IMF glossary. *IMF*, 1992. 341 pp. Includes titles of international institutions and terms relating to the organization, structure and staff titles of the IMF; also an IMF Organization Chart. English-French-Spanish

Incoterms 1990. *International Chamber of Commerce*, 1990. 215 pp. 'This edition ... clarifies existing terms and brings the overall list of Incoterms fully into line with the needs of the 1990s. The introduction of the new Incoterms ... was an event of major importance to bankers, transporters, exporters, lawyers and everyone with an interest in international trade. To be used in conjunction with the *Guide to Incoterms 1990* (150 pp.) . . . (which) indicates why it may be in the interest of buyer and seller to use one or another trade term. Each explanation is illustrated with easy-to-understand graphics which show the respective responsibilities of the parties to a transaction. All Incoterms are commented on, clause by clause, to draw the attention of seller and buyer to their respective responsibilities.'

Index to legal citations and abbreviations. 2nd ed. *Bowker-Saur*, 1994. Lists 25,000 entries covering the legal literature of the United States, the United Kingdom, the Commonwealth, and Europe.

Index to the standard industrial classification of economic activities 1992. *HMSO*, 1993. 212 pp.

JOHANSSEN, H. and PAGE, G.T. **International dictionary of management**. 5th ed. *Kogan Page*, 1995. 368 pp. 'With more than 6,000 terms, techniques and concepts of use and interest to management worldwide . . . supplies current information on employer and employee organisations, professional bodies, international trade and economic organisations and financial institutions.'

International tax glossary. *International Bureau for Fiscal Documentation*. A regularly updated compilation.

Key words in international trade. 3rd ed. *International Chamber of Commerce*, 1990. 416 pp. 'Contains more than 1,800 business words and expressions, translated into English, German, Spanish, French and Italian.'

KNOPF, K.A. and PARKER, H. **A lexicon of economics**. *Academic Press*, 1992. 262 pp. 'The convenient alternative for in-depth definitions and concepts, this is a one-volume answer to economics, banking, and business questions. It defines a select list of key terms and explains concepts.'

PARKER, R.H. **Macmillan dictionary of accounting**. 2nd ed. *Macmillan*, 1992. 305 pp.

Macrothesaurus for information processing in the field of economic and social development. 4th ed. *United Nations*, 1991.

GREENWALD, D. ed. **The McGraw-Hill encyclopedia of economics**. 2nd ed. *McGraw-Hill*, 1994. 1,093 pp.

GIPSON, C. **The McGraw-Hill dictionary of international trade and finance**. *McGraw-Hill*, 1993. 'Defines and explains more than 4,000 international finance terms used in the global marketplace today.'

BRAY, S. et al. **Mortgage banking terms: A working glossary**.

6th ed. *Mortgage Bankers Association of America*, 1990, 100 pp.

MOYS, E.M. **Moys classification and thesaurus for legal materials**. 3rd ed. *Bowker-Saur*, 1992. 386 pp.

LAIDLER, J and DONAGHY, P. **Multilingual dictionary of financial reporting terms**. *Chapman & Hall*, 1994. 400 pp. Covers English, French, German, Italian and Spanish.

VAN BREUGEL, L., WILLIAMS, R. and WOOD, B. **The multilingual dictionary of real estate**. *Chapman & Hall*, 1993. 408 pp. English, French, German, Spanish, Italian, Dutch.

Numbers guide: The essentials of business numeracy. *Economist Books*, 1991. 237 pp.

GREENER, M. **The Penguin business dictionary**. *Penguin Books*, 1994. 465 pp. 'The objective remains . . . to provide a key to the multifarious rules and regulations which surround and attach to man's behaviour in the market place, whether that market place be the City of London, the local shopping precinct or the country fair.'

BANNOCK, G. and MANSER, W. **Penguin international dictionary of finance**. *Penguin Books*, 1990. 220 pp.

Pensions terminology: A glossary for pension schemes. 4th ed. *Pensions Management Institute*, 1992.

Pocket finance. *Economist Books*, 1994. 214 pp. 'The essentials of the world of finance from A to Z.' Short definitions of about 1,000 terms.

Reuters glossary of international financial & economic terms. *Longman*, 1994. 138 pp. 'Reuters is the world's leading supplier of financial and economic information to the professional markets and produces news services in 17 languages. To maintain consistency in our worldwide coverage there is a need for clear and concise definitions of the often highly technical terms our journalists may encounter or employ.'

Risk management glossary *Risk & Insurance Management Society*, 1990. 82 pp.

AITCHISON, J. ed. **The Royal Institute of International Affairs Library Thesaurus**. *Royal Institute of International Affairs*, 1992. *Volume 1* Classification Schedules. 352 pp; *Volume 2* Alphabetical Thesaurus. 547 pp.

Rupp's insurance & risk management glossary. *NILS Publishing Company*, 1992. Covers 4,500 terms.

The securities law glossary. *American Bar Association*, 1991, 100 pp. Compiled by the *Young Lawyers Division*.

MINARS, D. and WESTIN, R. **Shepard's McGraw-Hill tax dictionary for business**. *McGraw-Hill*, 1993. 416 pp. '6,000 terms for business people who are not tax experts.'

There are also:

KABDEBO, T. **Dictionary of dictionaries.** *Bowker-Saur*, 1992. 256 pp.

LOUGHRIDGE, B. **Which dictionary?: A guide to selected English language dictionaries, thesauri and language guides.** *Library Association Publishing*, 1995.

as well as a regularly updated compilation **Thesauri** available for online searching via the *Commission of the European Union*.[20]

18. Recapping, the phenomena with which we are primarily concerned are the financially interpreted states, and changes in those states, of the world's entities. The financial states will often be formally recorded in the *accounts* of the entities; changes in the financial states occur because of *trade* between entities. One of our objectives is to give examples of the many types of publicly available information artefact which report the financial states of entities, and details of the trade taking place between them.

19. The trading metaphor can in fact be applied not just to trade in real and financial assets; but also to trade in the risk associated with such real/financial asset trading. Kohn, in his well-written text,[21] reflects the overall approach to the subject adopted here with a broad opening statement: *The financial system makes it easier to trade.*[22] He then goes on to distinguish simple trades in goods and services, from more complicated forms – of which he describes three:

> *Lending* is a form of trade. When you lend, you give up purchasing power now in exchange for purchasing power in the future. For example, when you put $1,000 into a savings account for a year, you give up what the $1,000 could buy today in exchange for what the $1,000 plus interest will buy one year from now. . . . On the one hand, we have savers and wealth-holders with an excess of purchasing power now that they wish to trade for purchasing power in the future. On the other hand, we have businesses and households needing purchasing power now to finance investments. Both groups stand to gain from trade.
>
> The world is an uncertain place: businesses and households face a variety of risks. Trade can reduce significantly the economic burden of many of these risks. There are two principal forms of trade in risk – *insurance* and forward transactions . . . With 'reciprocal insurance' (those facing a particular kind of risk agree to share the losses), some will be lucky after the event and others will not . . . With 'external insurance' (an arrangement with others who are not themselves inherently at risk), the diversity lies in the 'exposure' to risk. Those not inherently exposed are willing, in exchange for payment, to accept a small share of the exposure.
>
> Price risk can be mitigated by a form of trade called a *forward*

> *transaction*, a price is set today for delivery and payment at a specific time in the future. . . . Forward transactions provide protection against adverse changes in future market prices. Those participating include speculators and hedgers.
>
> Because of the danger of default, a lender needs to gather and process information on the borrower, negotiate and write a contract, and monitor compliance. . . . Trade in risk involves promises and therefore suffers from many of the same problems as lending.'[23]

20. Let us now imagine that we are wondering whether to engage in a trade with another person, or with an organization. To simplify the presentation we will assume that we have some 'cash' available which we would like to use to purchase something: it does not matter here whether this something, once purchased, would be classified as a real asset or as a financial asset. What might we wish to know *before* the trade takes place? I suggest that we might be asking questions in four areas:

(a) First, what do we know about the entity with whom we are wondering whether to trade? Are they financially sound? Are they trustworthy? Might they run off with the money before the trade is completed? What do we know in a similar vein about any *agencies*,[24] distinct from the principal to the trade, who will provide material assistance with the proposed trade?[25]
(b) Second, what is on offer? What is its price? How is that price to be paid? Perhaps the total payment can be spread out over a period. What will be the anticipated future benefits – financial or otherwise – of our acquiring what is on offer? What, again, is the timing of those benefits? What will be the risk that the benefits will not materialise?
(c) Third, will the trade be legal in all respects? Is it permissable for it to take place? Is the contract (actual or implied) crystal clear and acceptable. What about tax?
(d) Fourth, is this projected trade the best use of our money? Perhaps it would be better to engage in an alternative trade?; or to leave the money to continue 'trading' where it is (provided that the trading location is not a box under the bed!).

21. Let us assume that the answers to all those questions lead to the conclusion that the trade should happen; and that the trade is successfully completed. Let us now take the role of bystander, quite separate from the individuals or organizations who are the trading Entity A or Entity B; or who are agents whom have assisted with this trade between Entity A and Entity B; or who are other 'insiders' who know or would be able at least fairly easily to find out, the details of the trade that has just taken place.

Let us ask: as people who are not involved or implicated in the trade in any way, what would we know about that trade? Well, the answer – which I would invite the reader to dwell upon for a few moments, for it is fundamental to so much that is referenced in this book – is actually obvious! Unless we happened to come upon the details of the trade by accident, we would not know *anything* about that trade: until those in the know about the trade chose voluntarily – or were somehow required, or needed – to reveal to us its details.

22. We should mildly qualify that last statement – though it does not significantly affect the main thrust of the argument. It might be possible to reconstruct the trade by matching routinely recorded changes in the asset/liability positions of the trading parties. I write 'might' because such a reconstruction would only be possible if the trade had taken place directly between the trading entities. If, as is frequently the case with trades in financial rather than physical assets, the trade had taken place via an intermediary (and clearly here I am widening the notion of a 'trade'), it still might just be possible to 'put two and two together': Entity A exchanged something for cash with the intermediary and that same intermediary exchanged the same something for cash with Entity B. This sort of activity is of course the stuff of investigations into suspected fraud, insider dealing, money laundering,[26] and so on.

23. Putting those rather unsavoury topics to one side, it is a fact that the participants in the vast majority of trades will almost always choose *not* to reveal the trades' details voluntarily: certainly not to reveal the trades' financial details. This primarily for two reasons.

(a) Most entities prefer to keep quiet about their financial affairs. The information is too sensitive, too open to abuse. In addition, entities who are commercial trading organizations are constantly aware of the bargaining powers of their suppliers and of their customers if too much is known of the financial details of their trade transactions, and of their current trading position. Private sector corporations must be continually vigilant against their competitors, and against the threat of takeover if they are publicly quoted. Public sector entities – in a democracy – must be vigilant against the electorate, and such a charge as 'wasting public money'.

(b) Second, in almost all trades between entities, there are tax implications; and there will be a temptation – at the least – to give the impression to the tax authorities that this or that trade did not take place, or was somehow different from what actually happened, where this might avoid the payment of some tax.

24. For these and for other reasons to do with *investor protection*[27] and notions of *information equity* there has developed in most countries a large, and it turns out unfortunately rather convoluted, legal, regulatory and supervisory infrastructure which requires . . . *certain* individuals and organizations and other agencies party to trade to reveal the details of . . . *certain* of their trade transactions and of the effects on their assets and liabilities to . . . *certain* authorities: of which information a . . . *certain* proportion is then made publicly available, with a . . . *certain* subset of that proportion made available as soon as is feasible after the trade has occurred with the remainder made available some time later, of which a . . . *certain* amount will relate to specific transactions and specific entity assets and liabilities, whilst a residual . . . *certain* amount will be summaries of groups of transactions or of groups of entity assets and liabilities.

25. No doubt the reader will have already recognised that the prime outputs of the processes just described in a stylized manner are the three key distinct types of financial data and statistics which are publicly available:

(a) those required to be released by corporations (companies);
(b) those emanating from the financial markets;
(c) those released by governments – and by central banks and other national (and international) official and quasi-official bodies – revealing details not just of their own trading activities, but also of the trading performance of elements of the national economies which are in their charge.

26. It is worth continuing to remind ourselves that it is the financial information (and other information 'that would be material to an investor's investment decision or that is necessary for full and fair disclosure')[28] coming from corporations, the data generated by the financial markets, and the information – including policy statements – produced by national and international official and quasi-official organizations, which are the overwhelmingly prime drivers of the public information ebbs and flows of our chosen subject field. In fact, given the need strenuously to try to avoid the random issue of market-sensitive information, surely by definition *all* other 'material' publicly available financial and financially related information relating to corporations, to the financial markets themselves, and to the legal, economic and political environments within which those corporations and financial markets go about their trading activities, must either be pure *surmise* (a word we might use to cover everything from rigorous forecasting to rampant speculation!); or – if it has a basis in fact – that basis must arise from *inside information* of some sort?

27. Stepping aside from that rhetoric, two further points will be made before we close this short introduction to the trading system. First, *taxation*. Although the tax system provides entity financial information to the authorities, it often does so with delay, and such summary information as is subsequently released only appears with further delay. In addition, in many countries – including the UK and the USA – the classification of the various types of income and expenditure can be different in the tax reporting system, when compared to the financial accounting reporting system. For instance:

> UK companies are subject to corporation tax on their world-wide income but relief is given for tax paid in other jurisdictions where double taxation treaties exist. Net profits and gains are taxable by reference to the rules of the tax Acts, and these rules are independent of those determining accounting profit (although there are many similarities). Some of the most significant differences between accounting profit and taxable profit lie in the rules governing the depreciation of fixed assets. The Inland Revenue ignores the depreciation figure and substitutes a capital allowance at a rate determined by legislation. Interest paid is charged for accounting purposes on the basis of the amount due in respect of a period, whether paid or not, whereas for tax purposes only the actual payment is allowed. These tax differences lead to complex accounting procedures in respect of deferred taxation liabilities.[29]

28. Second, much information in the public domain regarding the assets/liabilities and trading activities of *financial institutions* appears there because many of those institutions (though by no means all) are in turn incorporated; and thus are subject to the general reporting requirements of corporations. But, as will become apparent, many types of financial corporation (and often of financial institution in general, whether incorporated or not) are required to disclose much important information additional to that required of non-financial corporations/institutions: particularly to the bodies charged with regulating and supervising those financial corporations/institutions. Some, at least, of this information will subsequently be published – if only in a summarized form.

An economic framework

29. How can we best categorize the various types of entity – particularly 'financial' entity – which exist in the world? One fruitful approach could be to look, first, at the totality of entities which trade; at the complete range of types of assets which they trade with each other; and at all the different types of transactions in which the entities engage. Using the classificatory facets identified in this exercise, we could then focus more specifically on those entities which might be classified as financial entities (ie entities whose primary role relates to trade in financial assets, rather than real assets). With respect to the specific focus of this text, we might then look in more detail at the various classes of such financial assets that are traded, and at the range of financial asset transactions which occur: noting that such transactions can be undertaken by non-financial entities, as well as by financial entities. Finally, having explored in such detail the trading system and its component objects and processes, we could summarize the sorts of information which appears in the public domain about such systems and objects and processes, where, when and how.

30. Such an omnibus approach would be a totally daunting task were it not for the existence of a marvellous recently updated tool to aid us in our quest. This is the *System of National Accounts*, whose importance we have already noted.[30] We will now make a series of extensive quotations from the summary volume describing the System: this, not just because that publication is an authoritative, comprehensive, and internally consistent and coherent introduction to our concerns here; but also, because *1993 SNA* is clearly a key reference with regard to the economic statistics produced both by national authorities, and by the five leading international official organizations who generate such statistics on a global basis: European Union, International Monetary Fund, Organisation for Economic Co-operation and Development, United Nations, World Bank (these being the bodies who cooperated to produce the System).

31. Five quotations can set the scene:

(i) The *System of National Accounts 1993* (1993 SNA) represents a major advance in national accounting. Adoption of the 1993 SNA was unanimously recommended to the United Nations Economic and Social Council by its Statistical Commission.... The Council recommends that member States consider using the 1993 SNA as the international standard for the compilation of their national accounts statistics, to promote the integration of economic and related statistics, as an analytical tool, and in the international reporting of comparable national accounting data. The Council further recommends that international organizations consider the 1993 SNA and its concepts when they review standards for particular fields of economic statistics and endeavour to achieve consistency with the 1993 SNA.[31]

(ii) The adoption of the updated, simplified and clarified, and more completely harmonised SNA is one of the most important events in the field of official statistics in the past 25 years. That its adoption is so regarded is a reflection of the comprehensiveness of its coverage and the breadth of its applicability. Four points may be made about these features to highlight the role the SNA has come to play:

(a) The 1993 SNA provides a comprehensive view of an economy.
(b) The 1993 SNA is expected to provide guidance for national accounts almost universally.
(c) The 1993 SNA recognises the need for flexibility.
(d) The 1993 SNA reinforces the central role of national accounts in statistics.'[32]

(iii) The goal of this publication is to describe the SNA as a conceptual system. This conceptual system is meant to be applicable to economies around the world. The publication therefore recognises differing conditions and institutional arrangements that may be found in developed and developing countries and in newly emerging market economies. Further, it attempts to present the rationale for the treatments applied so that national accountants can, by extension, decide on treatments for new developments and new institutional arrangements in the future.[33]

(iv) 1993 SNA consists of a coherent, consistent and integrated set of macroeconomic accounts, balance sheets and tables based on a set of internationally agreed concepts, definitions, classifications and accounting rules. It provides a comprehensive accounting framework within which economic data can be compiled and presented in a format that is designed for purposes of economic analysis, decision-taking and policy-making. The accounts themselves present in a condensed way a great mass of detailed information, organized according to economic principles and perceptions, about the working of an economy. They provide a comprehensive and detailed record of the complex economic activities taking place within an economy and of the interactions between different economic agents, and groups of agents, that takes place on markets and elsewhere. In practice, the accounts are compiled for a succession of time periods, thus providing a continuous flow of information that is indispensable for the monitoring, analysis and evaluation of the performance of an economy over time. The SNA provides information not only about economic activities, but also about the levels of an economy's productive assets and the wealth of its inhabitants at particular points of time. Finally, the SNA includes an external account that displays the links between an economy and the rest of the world.[34]

(v) The System is built around a sequence of interconnected flow accounts linked to different types of economic activity taking place within a given time period, together with balance sheets that record the values of the stocks of assets and liabilities held by institutional units or sectors at the beginning and end of the period. Each flow account relates to a particular kind of activity such as production, consumption, or the generation, distribution, redistribution or use of income.[35]

32. The reader familiar with corporate – or 'business' – accounts may wonder how such individual entity accounts might link into the national and international accounts produced via the use of the 'concepts, definitions, classifications and accounting rules' described in 1993 SNA. Should not the two types of accounts be directly related? Could not/should not the 'macroeconomic' trading accounts be generated from the constituent 'microeconomic'[36] entity trading accounts? Yes; but no:

> The accounting rules and procedures used in the System are based on those long used in business accounting. The traditional double-entry bookkeeping principle, whereby a transaction gives rise to a pair of matching debit and credit entries within the accounts of each of the two parties to the transaction is a basic axiom of economic or national accounting . . . The sequence of accounts and balance sheets of the System could, in principle, be compiled at any level of aggregation, even that of an individual institutional unit. It might therefore seem desirable if the macroeconomic accounts for sectors or the total economy could be obtained directly by aggregating corresponding data for individual units. There would be considerable analytical advantages in having micro-databases that are fully compatible with the corresponding macroeconomic accounts for the total economy.
>
> Micro-data sets also make it possible to follow the behaviour of individual units over time. Given the continuing improvements in computers and communications, the management and analysis of very large micro-databases is becoming progressively easier. Data can be derived from a variety of different sources, such as administrative and business records, as well as specially conducted censuses and surveys.
>
> In practice, however, macroeconomic accounts can seldom be built up by simply aggregating the relevant micro-data. Even when individual institutional units keep accounts or records the concepts needed or appropriate at a micro level may not be suitable at a macro level. Individual units may be obliged to use concepts designed for other purposes, such as taxation. The accounting conventions and valuation methods used at a micro level typically differ from those required by the System. For example . . . the widespread use of historic cost accounting means that the accounts of individual enterprises may differ significantly from those used in the System. Depreciation as calculated for tax purposes may be quite arbitrary and unacceptable from an economic viewpoint . . . Most households are unlikely to keep accounts of the kind needed by the System. Micro-data for households are typically derived from sample surveys that may be subject to significant response and reporting errors. It may be particularly difficult to obtain reliable and meaningful data about the activities of small unincorporated enterprises owned by households. Aggregates based on household surveys have to be adjusted for certain typical biases, such as the under-reporting of certain types of expenditure (on tobacco, alcoholic drink, gambling, etc.) and also to make them consistent with macro-data from other sources, such as imports. The systematic exploitation of micro-

> data may also be restricted by the increasing concerns about confidentiality and possible misuse of such databases.
>
> It may be concluded therefore that, for various reasons, it may be difficult, if not impossible, to achieve micro-databases and macroeconomic accounts that are fully compatible with each other in practice. Nevertheless, as a general objective, the concepts, definitions and classifications used in economic accounting should, as far as possible, be the same at both a micro and macro level to facilitate the interface between the two kinds of data.[37]

33. Thus the System of National Accounts is built around the broad concepts of *institutional units* (we have used the term 'entities' in this text), engaging in a variety of *transactions* (ie in 'trade'), with respect to a wide range of (real and financial) *assets*. We might then ask three questions:

(a) How might we classify the institutional units – or entities – which trade?
(b) What are the types of transactions in which those entities engage?
(c) In which way would we best gather together into meaningful chunks the immense variety of assets which the entities trade with each other worldwide?

These, clearly, are fundamental questions to be asked – and answered – in any attempt to understand the publicly available finance corpus of trade. It is hardly possible to use with profit – or for profit – individual elements of that information store unless one has a clear definition of exactly what phenomena (objects and processes) those elements represent.

The classification of entities

34. Let us take each of the three elements in turn. First, the classification of *entities*: or, as 1993 SNA has it, the 'classification of institutional sectors':

> Two main kinds of institutional units, or transactors, are distinguished in the System – households and legal entities. The latter are either entities created for the purposes of production,[38] mainly corporations and non-profit institutions (NPIs), or government units, including social security funds. Institutional units are essentially units capable of owning goods and assets, incurring liabilities and engaging in economic activities and transactions with other units in their own right. For the purposes of the System, institutional units that are resident in the economy are grouped together into five mutually exclusive sectors composed of the following types of units:
>
> Non-financial corporations

Financial corporations
Government units, including social security funds
NPIs serving households (NPISHs)
Households

Institutional units that are resident abroad form the rest of the world. The System does not require accounts to be compiled in respect of economic activities taking place in the rest of the world, but all transactions between resident and non-resident units have to be recorded in order to obtain a complete accounting for the economic behaviour of resident units.[39]

35. Looking in a little more detail at each of these five mutually exclusive sectors, we find that the *Households* sector is classified further into:

Employers
Own account workers
Employees
Recipients of property and transfer income
Recipients of property income
Recipients of pensions
Recipients of other transfers

The Households sector is of least interest in this context because of the necessary paucity of 'financial' information available in the public domain relating to such non-legal entities. The *Non-profit institutions (NPIs) serving households* sector[40] for the same reason need not detain us: it is not subdivided further in 1993 SNA.

36. Turning to the three transactor sectors which are of importance here (that is, they generate publicly significant amounts of financially interpreted information representative of their activities), in volume of source material available, the *Government units, including social security funds* ranks the least of the three. This, for three reasons. First, there are fewer government entities about which financial information may be sought, than there are non-financial, and financial, corporations. Second, the amount of financial information produced for the public domain by non-governmental entities is greater than for governmental entities, reflecting the much wider range of their activities. To take two obvious examples: 'incorporated' entities are frequently able and then choose to issue equity stakes to other entities; further, they can be merged with, or acquired by, other incorporated entities. These activities generate a large volume of published material. Third, the amount of information which corporations – especially those whose equity is 'publicly quoted' – must disclose to the public domain, and the frequency with which this must be done, are both much greater than for non-incorporated government entities.

37. However, having noted that governments publicly release relatively little information about their own behaviour as trading entities, we might then remind ourselves that they more than make up any deficiencies as information suppliers to the public domain in other ways! Government entities in fact perform three quite separate information-rich functions:

(a) First, they are indeed trading entities in their own right, their actions for instance in the financial markets having – or attempting to have – a decisive influence on the financial trading activities of private entities. Amounts of information generated by the various organs of government need to appear in the public domain relevant to these activities.
(b) But in addition, second, governments also issue codes, directives, laws, regulations, rules, standards, treaties and so on which – quoting from the beginning of Chapter 2 – 'determine the types of organizational entity which can flourish in each country, what services and products each type of entity can provide, how they will be taxed, and how the whole is regulated and supervised'. These activities of government generate a very large amount of financially relevant information.
(c) Third, following on directly from that determining role, governments are also gatherers and subsequently providers of financial and economic information relating to private and public entities and their trading activities: because, having gathered such information in order to fulfil their regulatory and supervisory responsibilities, they are then frequently also required to keep the public informed of the overall situation in each functional area.

38. Much of this can be implied from this further quotation from 1993 SNA:

> Government units may be described as unique kinds of legal entities established by political processes which have legislative, judicial or executive authority over other institutional units within a given area. Viewed as institutional units, the principal functions of government are to assume responsibility for the provision of goods and services to the community or to individual households and to finance their provision out of taxation or other incomes; to redistribute income and wealth by means of transfers; and to engage in non-market production. In general terms:
>
> (a) A government unit usually has the authority to raise funds by collecting taxes or compulsory transfers from other institutional units. In order to satisfy the basic requirements of an institutional unit in the System, a government unit – whether at the level of the nation, a region or a locality – must have funds of its

own either raised by taxing other units or received as transfers from other government units and the authority to disburse some, or all, of such funds in the pursuit of its policy objectives. It must also be able to borrow funds on its own account;

(b) Government units typically make three different kinds of final outlays:

   i The first group consists of actual or imputed expenditures on the free provision to the community of collective services such as public administration, defence, law enforcement, public health etc., which, as a result of market failure, have to be organized collectively by government and financed out of general taxation or other income;

   ii The second group consists of expenditures on the provision of goods and services free, or at prices that are not economically significant, to individual households. These expenditures are deliberately incurred and financed out of taxation or other income by government in the pursuit of its social or political objectives, even though individuals could be charged according to their usage;

   iii The third group consists of transfers paid to other institutional units, mostly households, in order to redistribute income or wealth.

Within a single country there may be many separate government units when there are different levels of government – central, state or local government. In addition, social security funds also constitute government units.[41]

39. Moving to the second of the three entity sectors we have characterized in 1993 SNA as producing significant amounts of published 'financial' information – the *Non-financial corporations* sector – we find that it is simply subdivided therein into three sub-sectors:

Public non-financial corporations
National private non-financial corporations
Foreign controlled non-financial corporations

40. The reader will note the two divisional facets which are used here. First, there is that between 'public' and 'private' corporations. However, the distinction 1993 SNA is making is not that between a 'public corporation' – one which has 'gone public' (has issued equity to the general public) – as compared with a corporation which has stayed in 'private hands'. It is between corporations which are in 'public ownership', in contradistinction to those that are in 'private ownership'. Public non-financial corporations, as defined in 1993 SNA: 'consist of resident non-financial corporations and quasi-corporations that are subject to control by government units, control over a corporation being defined as the ability to determine general corporate policy by choosing appropriate directors, if necessary'.[42] Yet more opportunity for terminological confusion!

41. The second facet used to produce the three sub-sectors of the non-financial corporations sector is that which distinguishes between resident and non-resident (ie 'foreign') ownership control.

42. It is not difficult to imagine even such a simple threefold classification throwing up significant difficulties in the classification of individual entities. (And, remember, any errors or biases by those who use 1993 SNA for the practical classification of economic entities and their activities will create similar errors/biases in the official statistics subsequently generated and published.) But when we turn to the last of the broad entity sectors characterized in 1993 SNA – the *Financial corporations* sector – the problems of entity classification become far more taxing yet awhile.

43. Let us first give the full financial corporations sub-sector breakdown used in the System:

- Central bank
- Other depository corporations
  - *Deposit money corporations*
    - Public
    - National private
    - Foreign controlled
  - *Other depository corporations, except deposit money corporations*
    - Public
    - National private
    - Foreign controlled
- Other financial intermediaries, except insurance corporations and pension funds
    - Public
    - National private
    - Foreign controlled
- Financial auxiliaries
    - Public
    - National private
    - Foreign controlled
- Insurance corporations and pension funds
    - Public
    - National private
    - Foreign controlled

44. We can immediately note four features of this sub-sector classification (apart from the similar distinction to that already introduced between 'public' and 'private', 'domestic' and 'foreign' corporations):

(a) The notion of financial auxiliaries as an adjunct to the financial intermediaries themselves.
(b) The separate designation of the central bank.
(c) The idea of depository corporations – which is further subdivided into 'depository money' and 'other depository' corporations.
(d) The wish within 1993 SNA to consider insurance corporations and pension funds as a separate sub-sector of the national economy.

We will elaborate on each of these features in turn in the following paragraphs.

45. *First*, 1993 SNA makes some very helpful comments on the overall concept of *financial enterprises*, introducing at the same time that of *financial auxiliaries*:

> Financial enterprises are defined in the System as enterprises that are principally engaged in financial intermediation or in auxiliary financial activities which are closely related to financial intermediation. They thus include enterprises whose principal function is to facilitate financial intermediation without necessarily engaging in financial intermediation themselves. Financial enterprises consist of all those enterprises (i.e. institutional units as distinct from establishments) whose principal activity is classified under Divisions 65, 66 and 67 of the International Standard Industrial Classification of All Economic Activities.[43]
>
> The provision of services that are auxiliary to financial intermediation may be carried out as secondary activities of financial intermediaries or they may be provided by specialist agencies or brokers. The latter consist of agencies such as securities brokers, flotation companies, loan brokers etc. There are also other agencies whose principal function is to guarantee, by endorsement, bills or similar instruments intended for discounting or refinancing by financial enterprises and also institutions that arrange hedging instruments, such as swaps, options and futures which have evolved as a result of wide-ranging financial innovation. These enterprises provide services which border very closely on financial intermediation, but they may not constitute true financial intermediation as the enterprises may not acquire financial assets and put themselves at risk by incurring liabilities on their own account. However, it is becoming increasingly difficult to draw a clear distinction between true intermediation and certain other financial activities. The boundary between financial intermediation and many of the services which are auxiliary to financial intermediation has become rather blurred as a result of continuous evolution and innovation in financial markets.[44]

46. Subject to those qualifications, the definition of *financial intermediation* used by the System pleasingly echoes that given earlier in the excerpt from the Gardner and Mills' book:[45]

Financial intermediation may be defined as a productive activity in which an institutional unit incurs liabilities on its own account for the purpose of acquiring financial assets by engaging in financial transactions on the market. The role of financial intermediaries is to channel funds from lenders to borrowers by intermediating between them. They collect funds from lenders and transform, or repackage, them in ways which suit the requirements of borrowers. They obtain funds by incurring liabilities on their own account, not only by taking deposits but also by issuing bills, bonds or other securities. They use these funds to acquire financial assets, principally by making advances or loans to others but also by purchasing bills, bonds or other securities. A financial intermediary does not simply act as an agent for other financial institutional units but places itself at risk by incurring liabilities on its own account.[46]

47. *Second*, when now turning to allocating within the System the activities of the *central bank* of a nation (and thus, for instance, the nature of the financial data which might be publicly available about such activities) one might have thought that this would be relatively straightforward; but, even here, difficulties can arise:

This sub-sector consists of the central bank together with any other agencies or bodies which regulate or supervise financial corporations and which are themselves separate institutional units. The central bank is the public financial corporation which is a monetary authority: that is, which issues banknotes and sometimes coins and may hold all or part of the international reserves of the country. The central bank also has liabilities in the form of demand or reserve deposits of other depository corporations and often government deposits.

In some countries, some monetary authority-type functions, such as the maintenance of the international reserves or the issue of currency, may be carried out by an agency, or agencies, of central government which remain financially integrated with central government and are directly controlled and managed by government itself as a matter of policy. Such agencies are not separate institutional units from government and must, therefore, remain in the general government sector.[47]

48. *Third*, we find that yet further problems of classification can arise in the sub-sector *Other depository corporations*. These come principally from the need for a more broadly based concept of *money* than that comprising:

an asset which is immediately, universally and legally accepted as a means of payment. Narrow money . . . consists of currency (including coin) plus deposits which are repayable on demand and immediately transferable by cheque, standing order or other means of transferring deposits for the purpose of making payments. In the past, only deposits with certain types of corporations, typically called 'banks', were universally acceptable for this purpose. However, two developments have led to the use of a more broadly based concept of money. The first is that, as a result of increasing competition and financial innovation, banks have been able to offer other kinds of deposits or facilities which are very close substitutes for narrow money and which can be used for payment purposes with little or no delay or financial penalty, without being technically transferable deposits payable on demand. The second is that deposits with other kinds of financial corporations (not necessarily describing themselves as 'banks') which in the past may not have been repayable on demand or used as a means of payment, have become increasingly transferable, again as a result of financial innovation.[48]

49. These problems of defining what exactly we mean by a 'bank' are well described in this extract from a standard reference text written almost ten years ago:

What is commercial banking and what is a commercial bank?

It would be helpful to define commercial banking and to indicate how one recognises such a bank. These questions are neither easy nor trivial. The answers suggest the degree and amount of competition facing the banking industry.

The easiest, most precise, most accurate answer is probably the least helpful. A commercial bank is one that is recognised as such and is called a 'commercial bank' by governmental regulatory agencies. It is not clear, however, that any set of products and services is so unique to commercial banking that one such institution would be instantly recognisable. For example, a major product of commercial banks is the demand deposit, or checking account. However, for more than 10 years, the credit union industry has offered its members (customers?) the share draft.

Notwithstanding legal technicalities, the share draft account is one on which the member may write drafts and transfer funds to a third party. In essence, it is a checking account. Similarly, mutual savings banks and certain savings and loan associations in New England have offered negotiable order of withdrawal (NOW) accounts since the early 1970s. These accounts are checking accounts that pay interest. Consider also the cash management account pioneered by Merrill Lynch. A number of nonbank firms have successfully offered an account in which credit balances are placed in a mutual fund and may be transferred by check or credit card. The list could continue, but these examples show that through legislation, regulatory action, and technology, financial institutions other than banks have come to offer products traditionally thought to be the province of commercial banks.

Some examples in the lending area might also be instructive. For the past 20 or more years, banks have been active in issuing bank credit cards that may be used nationally even though issued by a local bank. That is, an international interchange system is operative, permitting a customer with a bank card issued in Maine to use the same piece of plastic in California. However, several major retailers issue credit cards that are also valid in their stores nationwide. Indeed, Sears Roebuck has a consumer receivables portfolio exceeding that of any bank. Similarly American Express, Diners Club, and Carte Blanche issue travel and entertainment cards that have many of the same features as bank cards. In the area of business lending, a highly developed market now competes with banks. In this market, which is known as the commercial paper market, large, well-known corporations issue unsecured, short-term debt directly to investors. Thus corporate treasurers for large creditworthy companies have the alternative of borrowing from a bank or placing debt directly in the commercial paper market. Commercial paper interest rates are competitively determined in the open market. Banks that lend to such corporations must consider commercial paper rates in setting loan terms.

Similarly, banks have moved into areas traditionally restricted to other financial service providers. One example of this is the provision of stock brokerage services. Several years ago banks began acquiring or establishing brokerage activities. These have been 'discount' brokers not offering the full range of services. Although the securities industry has challenged these new services in court, the banking industry has prevailed and these services are being offered directly by a bank or through a brokerage subsidiary of a bank holding company.

Returning to our original question, the answer must be that commercial banking is what commercial banks do, and banks do what they are allowed to do by law and regulation. In addition, other firms, including but not limited to financial institutions, compete with banks in a variety of product and service markets.

Who gives any individual commercial bank the power to be in the commercial banking business, and who establishes the laws and regulations that determine what commercial banks may do? As mentioned earlier, the answer is less straightforward than it may seem. Basically, except for a small number of private banks, a commercial bank is granted a *charter* by either the federal government or a state government. Under existing law, such a bank may establish branches in only one state, whether federally or state chartered. The process of granting a bank charter is by no means simple, but once a bank has successfully cleared the applicable regulatory hurdles, what can it do? In very basic terms it gathers funds from customers by issuing liabilities on itself. The liabilities are generally know as *deposits* and have a wide variety of price and nonprice terms. The funds so acquired are then used to purchase the liabilities of other organizations and/or individuals. The types of liabilities issued by the other organizations are *loans and investments*, depending on their characteristics and terms. Both the issuing of liabilities to acquire funds and the use of funds by commercial banks are subject to a high degree of regulation.[49]

50. Within the sector 'Other depository corporations', notwithstanding the difficulties of categorization just discussed, 1993 SNA defines the sub-sector *Deposit money corporations* as:

resident depository corporations and quasi-corporations which have any liabilities in the form of deposits payable on demand, transferable by cheque or otherwise usable for making payments. Such deposits are included in the concept of money in the narrow sense, These corporations include so-called 'clearing banks' which participate in a common clearing system organized to facilitate the transfer of deposits between them by cheques or other means.[50]

51. *Other* entities within the group 'Other depository corporations':

consist of all other resident depository corporations and quasi-corporations which have liabilities in the form of deposits that may not be readily transferable or in the form of financial instruments such as short-term certificates of deposit which are close substitutes for deposits and included in measures of money broadly defined. . . . They may include corporations defined as savings banks (including trustee savings banks and savings banks and loan associations), credit cooperatives and mortgage banks or building societies. It must be emphasised that such corporations are described in different ways in different countries and they can only be identified by examining their functions rather than their names.[51]

52. Finally, *fourth*, in this outline sketch of some of the difficulties in classifying 'financial corporations', there are the insurance companies and pension funds. On *insurance*, 1993 SNA naturally distinguishes between 'life' and 'non-life' insurance, but then needs to link both those to the idea of *social insurance*. Here there are a variety of arrangements adopted in various countries:

Social insurance schemes can be operated in a number of ways. They are usually organised either by government for the population at large (social security schemes), by employers on behalf of their employees and their dependents or by others, for example a trade union, on behalf of a specified group (both these cases are here called private social insurance schemes).

Private social insurance schemes may be arranged with an insurance corporation as a group policy or series of policies or they may be managed by the insurance corporation in return for a fee. Alternatively, the schemes may be managed by an employer directly on his own behalf. Schemes arranged via an insurance corporation are always funded. Those managed by employers themselves may be funded or unfunded. An unfunded scheme is one where there are no identifiable reserves assigned for the payments of benefits. In such cases, benefits are paid from the receipts of contributions with any surplus or deficit going into, or being drawn from, the scheme manager's other resources.

Cover other than for pensions may be provided via an insurance scheme or from an unfunded scheme. If an employer manages his own scheme in respect of non-pension cover, it is treated as unfunded because no reserves have to be established as is the case for pensions. On the other hand, employers not infrequently manage their own pension schemes. These may be funded or unfunded. Funded schemes are divided into those that are autonomous, that is they constitute separate institutional units operating on their own behalf, classified in the insurance corporation and pension fund sub-sector, and those where the funds are segregated from the rest of the employers' own funds but are not autonomous. These remain classified in the same institutional sector as the employer. In both these cases, the funds are regarded in the System as being the property of the beneficiaries of the schemes and not of the employers. Schemes where the pension provisions are not even segregated from the employers' own funds are regarded as unfunded pension schemes. In this case there are no separately identified funds to which the beneficiaries can lay claim. Often an unfunded pension scheme will be non-contributory for the employees, but this is not invariably so.

Social security schemes may either be funded or unfunded. Even where separate funds are identified, they remain the property of the government and not of the beneficiaries of the schemes. Schemes set up by government in respect of their employees only are not included in social security schemes but are treated in the same way as other employers' social security schemes.[52]

The classification of transactions

53. I trust that far and enough has been written and quoted to alert the reader new to this field to the difficulties of classifying financial corporations and – to a lesser degree – entities in general.[53] Unfortunately, problems continue when we move to considering how best the types of transactions which the entities enter into should be categorized. As will be well known by the reader – at the least in a preliminary sense (given the wide media coverage in recent years of financial 'derivatives'):

> The identification of financial transactions has . . . become more difficult because of financial innovation that has led to the development and proliferation of new and often complex financial assets and other financial instruments to meet the needs of investors with respect to maturity, yield, avoidance of risk, and other factors. Some of these instruments are tied to prices of commodities, so the distinction between financial and non-financial transactions may be blurred. The identification issue is further complicated by variations in characteristics of financial instruments across countries and variations in national practices on accounting and classifications of instruments. These factors tend to limit the scope for firm recommendations with respect to the treatment of certain transactions within the SNA. A substantial degree of flexibility in presentation is therefore appropriate to meet national needs and to reflect national practices.[54]

54. Pursuing further the *financial derivatives* issue, it is fortunate that there is now a large amount of exceptionally good introductory material aimed at unravelling their apparent mystery. Particularly useful as a start is a compact Report produced by the Group of Thirty in 1993:

> In the most general terms, a derivatives transaction is a bilateral contract or payments exchange agreement whose value derives, as its name implies, from the value of an underlying asset or underlying reference rate or index. Today, derivatives transactions cover a broad range of 'underlyings' – interest rates, exchange rates, commodities, equities, and other indices.
>
> In addition to privately negotiated, global transactions, derivatives also include standardized futures and options on futures that are actively traded on organized exchanges, and securities such as call warrants. The term 'derivative' also is used by some observers to refer to a wide variety of debt instruments that have payoff characteristics reflecting embedded derivatives, or have option characteristics, or are created by 'stripping' particular components of other instruments such as principal or interest payments.
>
> The array of derivatives contracts is not as complex as it first seems. Every derivative transaction can be built up from two simple and fundamental types of building block: forwards and options. Forward-based transactions include forwards and swap contracts, as well as exchange-traded futures. Option-based transactions include privately negotiated, OTC options (including caps, floors, collars, and options on forward and swap contracts) and exchange-traded options on futures. Diverse types of derivatives are created by combining the building blocks in different ways, and by applying these structures to a wide range of underlying assets, rates, or indices.[55]

55. Those specific comments on derivatives can be placed within the context of the whole array of financial instruments, as in this excerpt from a good comprehensive text:

> The financial instruments we will consider may be divided into four broad classes: equities, debt, derivatives, and hybrids. Equities represent ownership interests in a business firm. The most often discussed form of equity is common stock. But other forms exist as well and, from a financial engineering perspective, are at least equally important. For example, limited partnership interests constitute equity in limited partnerships. Equity interests are sold by corporations and partnerships in order to provide the equity financing – a necessary ingredient in any business organization.
>
> Debt instruments represent a debtor/creditor relationship evidenced by some form of promissory note. That is, the borrower (creditor) has signed a binding obligation to repay borrowed principal together with interest under a schedule provided in the promissory note. Failure to make payments as required constitutes default. Debt instruments are sold by business firms, governments, and individuals to finance purchases and to increase leverage.
>
> Debt instruments are often lumped together with preferred stock into a larger category called fixed-income securities. However, with the

rapid growth of floating rate debt, the term fixed-income securities no longer accurately describes all forms of debt. Conventional preferred stock is accurately described as a fixed-income security because its dividend is fixed in the same sense that the coupon on a conventional bond is fixed. But, new forms of preferred stock have recently been engineered that pay a floating or adjustable dividend and, hence, not all preferred stock can accurately be described as fixed income.

Derivative instruments are instruments whose value is derived from that of other assets, called underlying assets. The most important types of derivative instruments are futures contracts, forward contracts, options contracts (including both single-period and multi-period options), and swaps. Futures contracts and forward contracts are contracts for deferred delivery of the underlying asset. While forward contracts are tailor-made to meet the idiosyncratic needs of the end user and trade over-the-counter in dealer-type markets, futures contracts are highly standardized instruments that trade on futures exchanges in auction-type markets. Futures and forwards can be used to speculate on the direction of a price, hedge price risk, and to arbitrage between the cash and deferred delivery markets.

Whereas futures and forward contracts are binding on both the purchasers and the sellers, options contracts are only binding on the sellers (called writers). That is, the owner of an option has the right, but not the obligation, to do something. Most often, this right entitles the option holder to buy or sell some number of units of the underlying asset at a specified price for a defined period of time. Options can be used to hedge downside risk or to speculate on the direction of price. They can also be used to arbitrage markets.

Swaps are relatively new derivative instruments making their first appearance in the early 1980s. In the ten years that followed, the notional volume of these instruments grew so rapidly as to dwarf the growth of any other market in financial history. Yet, swaps cannot and would not exist in the absence of other financial markets including the debt markets and the futures markets. Swaps have also spurred the growth of related instruments including multi-period options and forward rate agreements. As simply put as possible, a swap is an agreement between two parties calling for the first party to pay a fixed price (based on some underlying quantity of assets) to the second party in exchange for the second party paying a floating (market determined) price to the first party. Swaps are widely used to reduce financing costs and to hedge risks, but they have other uses as well.

Critical to understanding derivative instruments are the cash flow diagrams and the payoff profiles associated with them. That is, there is a series of cash flows between the parties to derivative instruments and/or there is a payoff profile associated with a position in a derivative instrument. Understanding derivative instruments is largely a matter of understanding these cash flows and the payoff profiles. For these reasons, any discussion of derivative instruments will rely heavily on graphics to illustrate concepts.

Hybrid instruments are instruments that are not perfectly classified into any of the other categories because they possess properties from more than one category. For example, some debt instruments have option components, others have an equity component, and still others have both an equity and an option component. Hybrid instruments have become a very important category of asset in recent years and much financial engineering has been devoted to it.

There are two categories of assets that have been neglected in the discussion above . . . These are the currencies and the commodities. Currencies were adequately discussed . . . (earlier) . . . and further discussion would be largely redundant. . . . Commodities are another matter. The traditional commodities include such groupings as the grains and oilseeds, foodstuffs, livestock and poultry, industrial materials, precious metals, and oil and petroleum products. Parties holding cash positions in commodities or who have future need for, or supplied of, commodities are exposed to price risk. For some years, it has been possible to hedge these risks in futures, forwards, and options; and, recently, it has been possible to hedge certain forms of commodity price risk in commodity swaps. Rather than devote valuable space explicitly to commodities, we will incorporate our comments on the management of commodity price risk in our discussion of futures, options, and swaps.[56]

56. Returning to the System of National Accounts, we might now for perspective place transactions in financial instruments within the context of the total classification by 1993 SNA of 'transactions and other flows'. We do not reproduce here the complete classification used: much is concerned with recording transactions in real, as opposed to financial, assets. The intention, again, is to indicate the wide range of trading activity in the world – instances of all of which will find their way into financial information sources. Here is the outline:[57]

Classification of transactions and other flows

1. *Transactions in goods and services (products)*

P.1 Output
P.2 Intermediate consumption
P.3 Final consumption expenditure
P.4 Actual final consumption
P.5 Gross capital formation
P.6 Exports of goods and services
P.7 Imports of goods and services

2. *Distributive transactions*

D.1 Compensation of employees
D.2 Taxes on production and imports
D.3 Subsidies
D.4 Property income
D.41 Interest

D.42 Distributed income of corporations
D.421 Dividends
D.422 Withdrawals from income of quasi-corporations
D.43 Reinvested earnings on direct foreign investment
D.44 Property income attributed to insurance policy holders
D.45 Rent
D.5 Current taxes on income, wealth etc
D.51 Taxes on income
D.59 Other current taxes
D.6 Social contributions and benefits
D.7 Other current transfers
D.71 Net non-life insurance premiums
D.72 Non-life insurance claims
D.73 Current transfers within general government
D.74 Current international cooperation
D.75 Miscellaneous current transfers
D.8 Adjustment for the change in net equity of households in pension funds
D.9 Capital transfers
D.91 Capital taxes
D.92 Investment grants
D.99 Other capital transfers

3. *Transactions in financial instruments (net acquisition of financial assets/net incurrence of liabilities)*

F.1 Monetary gold and SDRs
F.2 Currency and deposits
F.21 Currency
F.22 Transferable deposits
F.29 Other deposits
F.3 Securities other than shares
F.31 Short-term
F.32 Long-term
F.4 Loans
F.41 Short-term
F.42 Long-term
F.5 Shares and other equity
F.6 Insurance technical reserves
F.7 Other accounts receivable/payable

4. *Other accumulation entries*

57. Many of the transactions of particular interest in this book occur in the financial markets. Just as there is considerable variety – and some difficulties of classification – in the entities which trade, and in the transactions in which those entities engage, so there are a range of types of securities markets. Kohn gives an excellent cogent summary:

We have seen what securities markets do: they discover prices, provide liquidity, and minimize trading costs. While different organized markets all perform these same functions, they do so in very different ways. Organized securities markets differ along a number of dimensions – whether they are exchanges or over-the-counter markets, whether they are centralized or decentralized, whether they are dealer markets or auction markets.

Examples of *exchanges* include the New York, Tokyo, and London Stock Exchanges (stocks and bonds) and the Chicago Mercantile Exchange (futures and options). Examples of *OTC markets* include NASDAQ and the London International Stock Exchange (stocks and bonds), the market for government securities, the money market, the market for mortgage-backed securities, and the foreign exchange market.

You used to be able to tell an exchange from an over-the-counter market by how traders communicated with each other. On an exchange, traders met face to face on the trading floor; in an OTC market, they bargained over the telephone. In recent years, however, this distinction has been blurred by technology. While some exchanges still rely on face-to-face trading, many have switched to automated trading using computer terminals. Many OTC markets now rely on similar automated trading systems.

The main difference today is in the formality of the structure. With an exchange, participation is more restricted and trading rules more strictly specified. Over-the-counter markets differ in their degree of formality: some are not very different from exchanges; others are very loose structures indeed.

Organized markets differ in their degree of centralization. If you are a trader in one of the Chicago futures exchanges, you see every single trade that takes place. It all happens right in front of you in the trading pit. . . . This is a *centralized market.*

If you are a trader in the government securities market, you are in contact with some of the other participants over the telephone but not with others. It is quite possible that trades are taking place elsewhere in the market that you know nothing about. This is a *decentralized market.*

Many markets are 'semicentralized'. For example, most of the trading in stocks on the New York Stock Exchange takes place on the floor of the exchange, but substantial trading does take place elsewhere.

There are two alternative ways to conduct trading – the dealer market and the auction market. If you want to buy or sell a T-bill, you go to your bank. The bank calls up a government securities dealer and asks for a price. The dealer quotes bid and ask prices for the T-bill in question. The government securities market is a *dealer market.* Dealers are 'market-makers' who quote prices at which they are willing to trade and who stand ready to accommodate traders at these prices. All OTC markets are dealer markets, but so are some exchanges – for example, the London Stock Exchange.

If you want to buy or sell a futures contract, you tell your broker how many contracts you want to trade and perhaps the price at which you are willing to buy or sell. Your broker passes on your order to the trading pit. At the same time, other traders are submitting their orders. The trading pit takes all the orders and matches them against one another.... The futures market is an *auction market*. While dealer markets are quote-driven, auction markets are order-driven. Most exchanges are auction markets – the futures exchanges, most European stock exchanges, and the Tokyo Stock Exchange.

Some markets are hybrids, comprising elements of both auction market and dealer market. The most notable example is the New York Stock Exchange. There, specialists can act either as brokers, matching traders' orders, or as dealers, quoting prices at which they themselves are willing to trade.[58]

Classification of assets

58. Finally, in our last consideration of the 1993 SNA classification, we come to the assets traded themselves. Fortunately, our treatment can be brief and straightforward. We can ignore here the non-financial assets – such as the delightful fixed assets 'Vineyards, orchards and other plantations of trees yielding repeat products', and the tempting 'Precious metals and stones' – and merely note that the classification of the financial assets/liabilities in the System matches exactly the classification of the transactions in such financial assets and liabilities: as one would expect.

National and international official statistics

59. We have outlined how the System of National Accounts (and its predecessors and any variants still being used in specific countries) has been designed to summarize a country's trading activity (of both real and financial assets): such information either being automatically reported to the official national statistical agencies; or being acquired (as a sampling) by those authorities on request. This data, in turn, is used to generate each nation's publicly available *national official statistics* for the respective national economy. Similar statistics are meanwhile being generated in the majority of national jurisdictions of the world. Subsets of all of this data originating in nation–states is then transmitted more or less routinely to one or more of the five international bodies listed earlier: to which should now be added a sixth, the Bank for International Settlements. Each of these bodies – amongst many other activities – combines the national data they receive into series of published *international official statistics*.[59]

60. In the first of our profiles of information providers, we look at the BIS, the IMF, the OECD and the World Bank, following with entries for the two major national official bodies involved with economic and financial statistics respectively in the UK and the

US. (The United Nations and the European Union are profiled in Chapter 2.) In line with one of the major purposes of this book, I have not restricted the presentations here or elsewhere to material that is specifically relevant to the financial aspects of the trading system. Further, to save space and to simplify the layout, serial entries for all of the non-commercial (organizational) and most of the commercial information providers only appear *once* in the book. Occasionally, this means that some of the serials cited would have been more appropriately positioned elsewhere within the overall structure. On the other hand, it can be useful to know of the range of an information provider's involvements. All the way through the book I have been concerned to remind the reader – if only by implication – of the interlocking nature of this subject field: that what happens, for instance, in the financial markets feeds upon – but is also fed by – what happens in their surrounding political, economic and legal environments. In the serial citations themselves, frequently all that we do is to give the reader the briefest reminder of the existence of a specific serial: rather than use up valuable space recounting details which he or she will most likely already know – or could easily ascertain. For example, in the entry for the CSO below I have not felt it worthwhile to detail the content, for instance, of the publication *Financial Statistics.* Its critical importance – if not already known by the reader – will be self-apparent. Its details, as always, are best appreciated by actual use of the publication.

(1) #1 Bank for International Settlements CH-4002 Basle, Switzerland. t: (41 61) 280 8080; f: 280 8100/9100. *Economic Papers*; *Working Papers.*

The Bank publishes a valuable *Annual Report* annually in June. A *Guide to the BIS statistics on international banking* was issued in 1988. 'The general policy with our publications is to release them as soon as they are ready. Much of our work in servicing central bank committees and others is of course confidential, and is not released outside official circles.'

The objects of the BIS are: to promote the cooperation of central banks and to provide additional facilities for international financial operations; and to act as trustee or agent in regard to international financial settlements. The Bank is authorised, inter alia, to accept deposits in gold or currencies from central banks; to buy and sell gold and currencies; to buy and sell a wide range of readily marketable securities; to make advances to or place deposits with central banks. The Bank may deal similarly with commercial banks and international institutions but may neither make advances to governments nor open current accounts in their name. The Bank's Board of Directors is made up of representatives from eight countries: Belgium, France, Germany, Italy, Netherlands, Sweden, Switzerland, UK.

BIS serial publications whose distribution is not restricted are:

1. **Central Bank Survey of Foreign Exchange Market Activity**. t-a. Latest edition issued in March 1993 relates to the survey of April 1992.

2. **Statistics on External Indebtedness**. bi-a. **diskette**. $115. Joint publication with *OECD*. 'These statistics combine two important elements of countries' external indebtedness reported directly to the two institutions from creditor sources – namely the total external claims of banks in the BIS reporting area and the official and officially guaranteed or insured trade-related claims of banks and non-banks in 22 OECD countries, including both short- and long-term claims.'

The regular distribution of two serials is normally restricted to banks or banking organizations, although single issues may be issued to individuals upon special request:

3. **International Banking and Financial Market Developments**. q. 'This provides a quarterly overview of international financial markets, and usually contains special articles on financial market topics. Our statistical contribution is that we aggregate very detailed information on international banking business provided by the monetary authorities of eighteen industrial countries and six offshore centres. This covers currency composition of assets and liabilities; shows reporting banks' aggregate positions vis-a-vis each other country (including of course all the non-reporting countries in the developing world and elsewhere); and provides a breakdown between bank/non-bank sectors. It also provides data on international positions by nationality of ownership of reporting banks.'

4. **Maturity, Sectoral and Nationality Distribution of International Bank Lending**. bi-a.

The Bank has – or is closely associated with – a number of important Committees:

- *Basle Committee on Banking Supervision* BIS provides a permanent secretariat for this informal Committee, established by the central bank governors of the *Group of Ten* countries in the 1970s following the failure of Bankhaus Herstatt. Its initial *Basle Concordat* was revised following the Ambrosiano scandal in the early 1980s – with the goal that no international banking operation should escape effective supervision. *Reports* produced by the Committee have included: 10. Minimum standards for the supervision of international banking groups and their cross-border establishments. (July 1992); 13. Measurement of banks' exposure to interest rate risk. (April 1993).
- *Committee on Payment and Settlement Systems* The Committee have published a number of influential reports, as well as publishing the regular:

5. **Statistics on Payment Systems in the Group of Ten Countries**. a. The eleven Group of Ten countries are: Belgium, Canada, France, Germany, Italy, Japan, Netherlands, Sweden, Switzerland, United Kingdom, United States. Figures for 1993 were published in December 1994.

- *Euro-currency Standing Committee* Monitors developments in international banking and capital markets and considers issues relating to the functioning and stability of financial markets. The Committee has published a number of significant reports: Recent innovations in international banking' (Cross Report, 1986); 'Recent developments in international interbank relations' (Promisel Report, 1992); 'A discussion paper on public disclosure of market and credit risks by financial intermediaries' (Fisher Report, 1994); 'Macroeconomic and monetary policy issues raised by the growth of the derivatives markets' (Hannoun Report, 1994).

The Bank's work is also furthered by a number of specialist groups:

- *Group of Computer Experts* Studies a wide range of computing and networking issues, especially those related to international financial operations.
- *Group of Experts on Monetary and Economic Data Bank Questions* Involved, for instance, in exploring improvements in the timeliness and quality control of central bank statistics; and in broadening the coverage of statistics in the BIS database, particularly through bilateral data exchange arrangements with the central banks of countries outside the Group of Ten.
- *Service for Eastern European Countries and International Organisations* Organizes technical assistance and training – particularly for the central banks in eastern European countries and the republics of the former Soviet Union.
- *Working Party on Security Issues* Has examined, for example, the external links which central banks have established for the purpose of data exchanges outside the framework of payment systems and identified the potential risks incurred by each type of exchange.

(2) #2 International Monetary Fund 700 19th Street, N.W., Washington, DC 20431, USA. t: (1 202) 623 7000; f: 623 4661. Orders for and enquiries about IMF publications should be directed to: *Publications Services*, Catalog Orders, 700 19th Street, NW, Washington, DC 20431, USA. t: (1 202) 623 7430; f: 623 7201. In the UK, IMF publications can be obtained from *HMSO* (and they are listed in the HMSO catalogues); there are agents in many other countries that maintain in stock virtually all IMF publications.

Article 8(5) of the IMF Articles requires members to furnish information on their foreign exchange reserves, balance of payments, trade figures, national income, exchange rate policies etc. 'All Fund documents and research papers are held confidential within the institution and shared only with the authorities of member countries, unless a decision is made to publish or release them.'

The IMF's valuable *Annual Report of the Executive Board*, published in September, and usually of about 200 pp, is available free of charge (and in French, German and Spanish versions). It reviews the IMF's activities, policies and organization, as well as the world economy, with special emphasis on balance of payments problems, exchange rates, world trade, international liquidity, and developments in the international monetary system.*Occasional Papers* For example: 91. Economic policies for a new South Africa; 94. Tax harmonization in the European Community: Policy issues and analysis; 103. Liberalization of the capital account: Experiences and issues; 105. The structure and operation of the world gold market; 107. China at the threshold of a market economy. *Working Papers* About 120 papers are released each year, designed to make IMF staff research available to a wider audience.

Reference works

6. **Annual Report on Exchange Arrangements and Exchange Restrictions**. a. Published in August, approximately 600 pp. The 1993 report covered 178 countries, including for the first time reviews of the Baltic countries and of all the states of the former Soviet Union, with the exception of Tajikistan.

7. **Balance of Payments Statistics Yearbook**. a (in two parts). **online**. Monthly issues, published until April 1991 also in a paper edition, are available on **magtape**.

Balance of Payments Manual. 5th ed. 1993. Contains significantly expanded and restructured coverage of financial flows and stocks, and international transactions in services. Changes in the treatment and classification of balance of payments and international investment position components reflect widespread alterations that have taken place in the nature and composition of international transactions since publication of the 4th edition (1977). Like previous editions, the fifth edition serves as an international standard for the conceptual framework underlying balance of payments statistics. The manual also functions as a guide for member countries submitting rĕgular balance of payments reports to the IMF.

8. **Direction of Trade Statistics**. q. $96. **online**. Covers data for recent periods for about 135 countries and for the industrial countries as an area reported by themselves or by their partners. The *Yearbook* issue (usually published in August) gives seven years data for about 160 countries and two sets of world and area summaries.

Guide to Direction of Trade Statistics. 1993. 33 pp.

9. **Government Finance Statistics Yearbook**. a. Data on government financial operations for about 120 IMF member countries, including budgetary operations, extrabudgetary operations, social security transactions, and consolidated financial operations of central governments. A useful supplement lists the *Sources of Data* for each country used to compile the Yearbook.

Manual of Government Finance Statistics. 1986. 373 pp.

10. **Summary Proceedings**. a. Approximately 400 pp; usually published in January. Record of the IMF's Annual Meeting, containing the opening and closing addresses of the Chairman of the Board of Governors, presen-

tation of the Annual Report by the Managing Director, committee reports, resolutions etc.

Current awareness

11. **Economic Reviews**. Series launched in 1992 containing authoritative economic and financial analysis of member countries. The reviews are based on IMF staff consultations with these countries. At the time of writing, the countries covered are all former components of the USSR.

12. **Finance & Development**. q. Free of charge (on application). **online**. Published jointly with the *World Bank*. Intended for a broad, non-technical audience, covering: 1. the main current international monetary trends and the IMF's role in the maintenance of stability and orderly change in existing world monetary arrangements; 2. the central problems of economic development and the Bank's efforts to help developing countries achieve an acceptable rate of economic growth.

13. **IMF Survey**. bi-w. $79. Report of IMF activities, including all press releases, communiques, and major speeches. There is an annual *Supplement*, published in September, and there are occasional special supplements.

14. **International Capital Markets**. a. 1993 edition was in two parts: I. *Exchange Rate Management and International Capital Fl[illegible]* [illegible]xamined the implications of the growth and integration of international capital markets for the management of exchange rates, with particular attention to the inferences that can be drawn from the currency turmoil that shook the European Monetary System in Autumn 1992. II. *Systemic Issues in International Finance*. Includes coverage of: recent experience with loan losses – especially in real estate – of banking systems in a number of industrial countries; and sources of systemic risk in the rapid growth of off-balance-sheet financial transactions.

15. **International Financial Statistics**. m. **online**. **cd-rom**. The standard source of international statistics on all aspects of international and domestic finance. Reports, for most countries of the world, data on exchange rates, international liquidity, international banking, money and banking, interest rates, prices, production, international transactions, government accounts, and national accounts. Information is presented in country tables and in tables of area and world aggregates. The *Yearbook* issue, usually published in September, contains annual data for 30 years, with some additional time series in country tables and some additional tables of area and world aggregates.

16. **Staff Papers**. q. **online**. Theoretical and economic analyses of macroeconomic issues.

17. **World Economic Outlook**. s-a. Also available in French, Spanish and Arabic. Discusses the problems of balance of payments adjustment by major groups of countries, the key policy options available to them, issues of inflation and interest rates, debt, and capital flows. Also details

scenarios for the evolution of the world economy over the medium term under various policy options.

(3) #3 Organisation for Economic Co-operation and Development rue André-Pascal, 75775 Paris Cedex 16, France. t: (33 1) 45 24 82 00. *Publications Service* f: (33 1) 45 24 81 76; *Electronic Editions* t: (33 1) 49 10 42 65; f: 49 10 42 99. *Also*: OECD Publications and Information Centre, 2001 L Street, NW, Suite 700, Washington, DC 20036–4910, USA. t: (1 202) 785 6323; f: 785 0350. In the UK, via *HMSO*.

The OECD members are: Australia, Austria, Belgium, Canada, Denmark, Finland, France, Germany, Greece, Iceland, Ireland, Italy, Japan, Luxembourg, Netherlands, New Zealand, Norway, Portugal, Spain, Sweden, Switzerland, Turkey, UK, USA – and Mexico, which joined in 1994.

18. **Annual Labour Force Statistics**. a. $88. **diskette**. $635.

19. **Balances of Payments of OECD Countries**.

20. **Bank Profitability: Financial Statements of Banks (Years)**. a. $39. **diskette**. $215. The April 1994 volume refers to the period 1983–1992.

21. **Business Sector Data Base**. s-a. **diskette**. $450. 'Business sector value added, employment, investment, factor prices and capital stocks.'

22. **Code of Liberalisation of Capital Movements**. a. $30.

23. **Code of Liberalisation of Current Invisible Operations**. a. $30.

24. **Competition Policy in OECD Countries (Years)**. a. $40.

25. **Creditor Reporting System: Individual Financial Transactions**. a. **diskette**. $145. 'Contains individual *Official Development Assistance* (ODA) commitments from each *Development Assistance Committee* (DAC) member country to each recipient country by year. The commitments are grants and loans reported by each member country to the *Creditor Reporting System* (CRS), an information system managed jointly with the *World Bank*.... Data are available from 1973 to the present; approximately 6,000 commitments are reported each year.'

26. **Development Co-operation**. a. $26. The *Development Assistance Committee* (DAC) Chairman's annual report. Time series similar to the reference tables in this Report's Statistical Annex are available on **diskette** ($265). Available on **magtape** is the Public Data Base of the Committee ($3125).

27. **External Debt Statistics**. a. $22. **diskette**. $115. The debt and other external liabilities of developing, Central and Eastern European and certain other countries and territories. 'The data are reported to OECD by member countries' governments and credit institutions, and by the main international organisations. As a result of the use of common reporting rules and timely reporting, this volume gives a comprehensive, consistent and up-to-date account of external debt, making it invaluable for

international comparisons and country risk analysis.' The November 1993 Annual Report recorded data as at end-December 1992 and end-December 1991.

28. **Financial Market Trends**. bi-a. $47. **online**. 'Presents commentary and analysis of the major international financial markets including bonds, syndicated credits, and borrowing facilities, as well as the national financial markets.'

29. **Financing and External Debt of Developing Countries**. a. $43.

30. **Flows and Stocks of Fixed Capital**. bi-a. $190. **online**.

31. **Foreign Trade**. m. $153. **diskette**. $1145. *Series A* 'Presents an overall picture of trade of OECD countries including analysis by flows with countries and country groupings of origin and destination. seasonally adjusted foreign trade indicators, and summary monthly tables showing trade by main commodity categories.'

32. **Foreign Trade by Commodities**. a. $425 (five volumes). *Series C* 'Summary information on the value of trade flows of OECD Members with all partners by commodity to the two-digit SITC level.'

33. **Geographical Distribution of Financial Flows to Developing Countries**. a. $63. **diskette**. $265. 'This is the unique source of data on the origin, volume, purpose and terms of the aid and other resource flows channelled to over 130 developing countries. The data show the inflows to each recipient country and territory from member countries of the *Development Assistance Committee* of the OECD, multilateral agencies and Arab countries.'

34. **Indicators of Industrial Activity**. q. $60. **online**. **diskette**. 'Presents up-to-date production, deliveries, orders, prices and employment indicators on an annual, quarterly, and monthly basis for 17 industrial sectors.'

35. **Insurance Statistics Yearbook (Years)**. a. $55. **diskette**. $270. 'Gathers together major official insurance statistics for the 24 OECD countries.' The 1994 volume covers the period 1984–1991.

36. **International Direct Investment Statistics Yearbook (Year)**. a. $52. 'This volume contains the first complete series of FDI statistics in a standardised format combining sectoral and geographical breakdowns for flow and stock data for all OECD countries. Technical notes explain the methodology used in each country.'

37. **International Sectoral Data Base**. a. **diskette**. $1145. 'Unique source of sectoral statistics on a standardized international basis for professional economists and industrial analysts.'

38. **Main Economic Indicators**. m. $220. **online**. **diskette**. $1270. 'An essential source of timely statistics for OECD member countries. Graphs provide a picture of the most recent changes in Member country economies and tables give statistics and/or indicators for GNP; industrial production; construction, prices, etc.'

39. **National Accounts of OECD Countries (Years)**. a. *Volume I* Main Aggregates ($35; **diskette** $265); *Volume II* Detailed Tables ($120). **online**.

40. **OECD Economic Outlook**. bi-a. $44. **online**. The full set of historical time series data and projections underlying the *Outlook* are available on **diskette** at the same time as its publication. 'A major publication providing a survey of economic trends and prospects in OECD countries.'

41. **OECD Economic Outlook: Historical Statistics**. a. $28. The 1992 edition covered the period 1960–1990.

42. **OECD Economic Studies**. bi-a. $48. **online**. 'Features articles in the area of applied macroeconomics and statistical analysis, generally with an international or cross-country dimension.'

43. **OECD Economic Surveys**. $220. **online**. 'Analyses in detail the subject country's economy, supplemented with extensive statistical coverage and short term forecasts. One survey is published for almost every OECD country each year (17 to 19 surveys).'

44. **OECD Financial Statistics**. $320. **diskette**. $935. In three parts: *Part one* covers domestic markets (m.); *Part two* deals with the international markets (m.); *Part three* provides financial accounts of OECD member countries (bi-w.). Two *Annuals* are also included which provide non-financial enterprises financial statements and a methodological supplement.

45. **OECD Observer**. bi-m. $25. **online**. 'The best source to keep informed about the OECD's latest work and forecasts.' The 1994 Edition of a useful *OECD in Figures* was published with the June/July issue of the Observer.

46. **OECD STAN DataBase**. **diskette**. $290. (First edition, 1994.) 'An invaluable tool in international economic research and analysis, the **ST**ructural **AN**alysis (STAN) industrial database provides the most complete internationally comparable data on industrial activity to date for 16 countries and 49 manufacturing industries. This compatible national accounts database, created to fill the gap that exists between detailed data collected through industrial surveys which lack international comparability, reflects trends, highlights the correlation between various industries and captures the relative relationships that prevail between countries.'

47. **OECD Reviews on Foreign Direct Investment**. q. $36. 'Reviews OECD countries' policies on foreign direct investment (FDI) with a country by country analysis of their laws, regulations and policies as well as those of companies that affect foreign investment.'

48. **OECD Working Papers**. $600. 'A new subscription service (began on 1 October 1993). Each year the OECD publishes a large number of working documents which, until now, have had a very limited and guarded circulation . . . Increasingly, the international media are making references to many of these documents. In addition, they are being quoted in the bibliographies and notes of other publications which in turn has increased their visibility. As a result, many people have expressed a desire to receive them on a regular basis . . . This new subscription service will allow the

reader to receive without delay each document as soon as it has been authorised for release to the public. Subscribers will receive documents which are quasi-confidential, alerting them to the latest work of the OECD . . . It is difficult to predict how many documents will be produced each year; the initial estimate is for approximately 150.'

49. **Public Management Developments**. a. $22. Produced by the *Public Management Committee*. 'In addition to examining comprehensive reform programmes, the report looks in more detail at specific organisational and structural changes to the public sector; shifts towards managing for results; and moves towards better service quality and client satisfaction. It also covers initiatives in human resources; financial management; and regulatory processes.'

50. **Quarterly National Accounts**. q. $68. **online**. **diskette**. $470. 'Provides the latest national income accounts for the USA and 11 of the OECD countries.'

51. **Quarterly Labour Force Statistics**. q. $43. **online**. **diskette**. $425. 'Provides current statistics on the short term development of the major components of the labor force in the USA and 12 other OECD countries.'

52. **Revenue Statistics of OECD Member Countries (Years)**. a. $54. **online**. **diskette**. $145. The 1992 edition covered the period 1965–1991. 'This publication provides a conceptual framework for defining which government receipts should be regarded as taxes and how the different types of taxes may be classified.'

53. **Services: Statistics on International Transactions (Years)**. a. $270. **diskette**. 'This information, which was reported by member countries to the OECD and is largely unavailable elsewhere, provides a statistical picture of the growth in international trade in services'.

OECD has a number of influential committees, including:

- *Committee on Capital Movements and Invisible Transactions*
- *Committee on International Investment and Multinational Enterprises*
- *Development Assistance Committee*
- *Public Management Committee*

as well as the:

- *Economic Policy Committee* 'The main organ for the consideration and direction of economic policy among Member countries. . . . This comprises governments' chief economic advisers and central bankers, and meets 2 or 3 times a year to review the economic and financial situation and policies of Member countries with a view to attaining OECD's objectives. The EPC has several major working parties notably one dealing with Policies for the Promotion of Better International Payments Equilibrium (WP3). *Economic and Development Review Committee* is responsible for the annual examination of the economic situation of individual Member countries. An annual report is usually issued on each country, after an examination carried out by a panel of representatives of a number of other Member countries.'[60]

There is also:

(i) *#4 Business and Industry Advisory Committee to the OECD* 13–15 chaussée de la Muette, 75016 Paris, France. t: (33 1) 42 30 09 60; f: 42 88 78 38. *Annual Report*.

Constituted in 1962 as an independent organisation officially recognized by the OECD as being representative of industry.

(4) #5 World Bank [International Bank for Reconstruction and Development] 1818 H Street NW, Washington, DC 20433, USA. t: (1 202) 477 1234; f: 477 6391. (World Bank publications are also obtainable from: *Microinfo* PO Box 3, Omega Park, Alton, Hampshire, GU34 2PG, UK. t: (44 1420) 86848; f: 89889.)

Provides development assistance only to its member nations, which must be requested by an agency of the member government. Most programmes take the form of project loans. The Bank's *Export Credit Enhanced Leverage* [EXCEL] programme is designed as a co-financing scheme to provide export assistance for sales to markets where such financing would otherwise be unavailable even from official export credit agencies.

54. **Commodity Markets and the Developing Countries**. q. $150. Looks at production, consumption and trade patterns to pinpoint why commodities thrive or falter. Checks current market climate for such items as food, agricultural raw materials, energy and fertilizers.

55. **Financial Flows and the Developing Countries**. q. $150. Examines the latest events and trends affecting developing-country access to international capital and looks at the capital markets, emerging stock markets, foreign direct investment, debt flows.

56. **Global Economic Prospects and the Developing Countries**. a. $10.95. 'Very helpful. A fairly long-term projection all in one place. Consistent . . . Saves an immense amount of time' (*Global Business Opportunities*).

57. **Global Outlook and the Developing Countries**. q. $150.

58. **Social Indicators of Development**. a. $24.95. **diskette**. a. $70.

59. **Trends in Developing Economies**. a. $21.90. Two volumes.

60. **World Bank Group Directory**. q. $35.

61. **World Debt Tables**. a. $125. **online**. **diskette**. a. $95. External debt data for some 140 countries.

62. **World Development Indicators**. **diskette**. a. $70. Thirty statistical indicators of economic and social development for 200 countries.

63. **World Development Report**. *Oxford University Press*. a. $19.95. Summary of the state of economic development in developing countries.

Includes a current overview of the world economy, statistics on social and economic development, and a special theme of current importance.

64. **World Tables**. a. $39.95. **diskette**. s-a. $95.

(i) #6 *International Centre for Settlement of Investment Disputes* (1 202) 458 1533; f: 477 1269. An *ICSID Bibliography* was published in March 1992. *Newsletter*.

'Seeks to encourage greater flows of international investment by providing facilities for the conciliation and arbitration of disputes between governments and foreign investors. In addition, ICSID undertakes advisory, research and publications activities in the area of foreign investment law.'

65. **ICSID Review: Foreign Investment Law Journal**. *Johns Hopkins University Press*. s-a. $50. Consists of articles, comments, cases, and documents pertinent to investment law and international business transactions.

66. **Investment Laws of the World**. *Oceana Publications*. l. Ten volumes. $950.

67. **Investment Treaties**. *Oceana Publications*. l. Six volumes. $595.

(ii) #7 *International Finance Corporation* t: (1 202) 477 1234; f: 477 6391.

'Established in 1956, to further economic growth in its developing member countries by promoting private sector development. Although IFC is a member of the World Bank Group . . . it is legally and financially independent, with its own Articles of Agreement, shareholders, financial structure, management and staff. IFC is considered the most experienced supranational organization providing financing and financial services to the private sector in developing countries. It combines the characteristics of a multilateral development bank with those of a private financial institution.'

68. **Emerging Markets Data Base**. **online**. **diskette**. w. Over 1000 time series on corporate stocks from some 20 developing countries.

69. **Emerging Stock Markets Factbook (Year)**. a. Brings together the various time series of fundamental market data on the leading stock markets of the developing world, within the context of their own domestic economies and comparing them to markets in developing countries. Contains data and statistics on both the developing country and developed country markets, including performance with respect to the International Finance Corporation indices – whose methodology is described.

(5) #8 Central Statistical Office Great George Street, London SW1P 3AQ, UK. t: (44 171) 270 3000; f: 270 6190/6085/6019. *Press Office* t: (44 171) 270 6363/6364; f: 270 6019. *Also* Business Statistics Division, Government Buildings, Cardiff Road, Newport, Gwent, NP9 1XG, UK. t: (44 1633) 815696; f: 812863/2949/2599.

'Responsible to the Chancellor of the Exchequer. Encompasses: data collection from businesses; the preparation of macro-economic and social statistics; the central management of the *Government Statistical Service*; and the production of statistical publications and press notices.'

70. **Annual Abstract of Statistics**. a. £22.50.

71. **CSO Macro-Economic Data Bank**. **online**. **diskette**. Over 70,000 monthly, quarterly and annual time series.

72. **Economic Trends**. m. £320. There is a quarterly supplement *UK Economic Accounts.*

73. **Financial Statistics**. m. £245.

74. **Housing and Construction Statistics**. 8/year. £44.

75. **Monthly Digest of Statistics**. m. £113.

76. **Statistical News**. q. £45. Developments in British official statistics.

77. **United Kingdom Balance of Payments**. a. £13.25. 'The Pink Book'.

78. **United Kingdom National Accounts**. a. £15.50. 'The CSO Blue Book'.

BUSINESS MONITORS. MISCELLANEOUS SERIES

79. **Guide to the Classification of Overseas Trade Statistics**. a. £36. Series: MA21.

80. **Insurance Companies' and Pension Funds' Investment**. q. £24. Series: MQ5.

81. **Overseas Trade Statistics of the United Kingdom**. Various series. Note the *Guide to the Classification of Overseas Trade Statistics.*

82. **Overseas Transactions**. a. £23.95. Series MA4.

83. **Price Index Numbers for Current Cost Accounting**. m. £43. Series: MM17.

84. **Producer Price Indices**. m. £80. Series: MM22.

85. **Retail Price Index**. m. £75. Series: MM23.

BUSINESS MONITORS. SERVICE AND DISTRIBUTIVE SERIES

86. **Assets and Liabilities of Finance Houses and Other Credit Companies**. q. £24.

- *CSO Advisory Committee* Membership of 21, appointed with the agreement of the Chancellor of the Exchequer, and comprising representatives of CSO data users and suppliers.
- *Retail Prices Index Advisory Committee* Consists of representatives of employers' and employees' organizations, consumer interests, academic experts and government departments. Members are nominated

by the organizations concerned and appointed by the Chancellor of the Exchequer. The Committee's recommendations are normally published by *HMSO* as Command Papers.

(6) #9 Department of Commerce 14th Street and Constitution Avenue NW, Washington, DC 20230, USA. t: (1 202) 482 2000; f: 377 2592. *Public Affairs* t: (1 202) 482 6014; *Newsroom* t: (1 202) 482 4901; *Freedom of Information* (1 202) 482 4115.

Prime purpose is to encourage, serve and promote US and international trade, economic growth, and technological enhancement. The bi-weekly *Commerce Publications Update* contains a listing of all publications and press releases issued by the Department. The Update also provides the latest data on some 20 areas of economic and business activity.

87. **Commerce Business Daily**. d. **online**. **cdrom**. 'The Commerce Business Daily, CBD, a daily list of US Government procurement invitations, contract awards, subcontracting leads, sales of surplus property and foreign business opportunities, has been made available via the global Internet . . . The Internet is a perfect distribution system for the CBD since so many Internet users depend on the Commerce Business Daily to find funding opportunities . . . (The) service makes the full text of the CBD available to Internet users the day before the paper volume is released . . . The Internet CBD is available to any Internet connected host. Subscribers may choose Gopher/WAIS, NNTP (Usenet News), or FTP.'

(i) *#10 Bureau of the Census Information and Publications* t: (1 301) 763 4100; *Freedom of Information* t: (1 301) 763 5262.

88. **Statistical Abstract of the United States**. a. $24.95. For sale by *Reference Press*. **diskette**. a. $78. 'The standard summary of statistics on the social, political and economic organization of the United States.' Includes the useful *Appendices*: 'Guide to sources of statistics'; 'Guide to State statistical abstracts'; 'Guide to foreign statistical abstracts'.

(ii) *#11 Bureau of Economic Analysis Public Information Office* t: (1 202) 606 9900; f: 606 5310.

Provides basic information on such issues as economic growth, inflation, regional development, and the US role in the world economy. A detailed *User's Guide to BEA Information*, containing also a list of 'Telephone Contacts for Data Users' is available from the Bureau, and is reprinted periodically in the *Survey of Current Business*.

The Bureau's current national, regional and international estimates usually appear first in *News Releases*: a 'Schedule of Upcoming BEA News Releases' appears on the back cover of each issue of the *Survey of Current Business*; such data series include, for example:

- Gross Domestic Product (preliminary or final)
- Corporate Profits
- Composite Indexes of Leading, Coincident, and Lagging Indicators

- Summary of International Transactions

The information in such news releases is available to the general public in four forms:

- Economic Bulletin Board
- Facsimile Delivery
- Printed Reports
- Recorded Telephone Messages

The latter are brief (3–5 minutes) recorded telephone messages summarizing key estimates immediately after their release. The messages are available 24 hours a day for several days following release.

The majority of the Bureau's work is presented in:

89. **Survey of Current Business**. m. Each issue normally comprises:

- *Business Situation* A review of current economic developments.
- *National Income and Product Accounts* The value and composition of US output and the distribution of incomes generated in its production.
- *Business Cycle Indicators* Tables for about 270 series and charts for about 130 series used to analyze current cyclical developments.
- *Current Business Statistics* Tables for over 1900 series covering general business activities and specific industries.
- *Special Articles* e.g. in the March 1993 issue: 'Capital expenditure by majority-owned foreign affiliates of US companies, plans for 1993.'

However, other more specialized statistics are disseminated on diskette or tape; for instance:

90. **Detailed Wealth by Industry**. a. Estimates of gross and net stocks, depreciation, and discards for fixed nonresidential private and residential capital, durable goods owned by consumers, and fixed capital owned by governments.

- *International Investment Division* Collects and analyses data on US direct investment abroad, foreign direct investment in the United States, and selected services transactions with unaffiliated foreign persons. The data gathered are normally published in the *Survey of Current Business*; but because of space constraints, supplementary tables are available in separate publications and on diskette or tape. Enquiries about the latter or about special tabulations or analyses can be directed to the Division's *Data Retrieval and Analysis Branch*.

91. **Foreign Direct Investment in the United States**. a. Information on the financial structure and operations of nonbank US affiliates of foreign direct investors. Data are classified by industry of US affiliate, by country and industry of ultimate beneficial owner, and, for selected data, by industry of sales and by State. *Preliminary* estimates from annual surveys are released as soon as possible; *revised* estimates are released one year later.

92. **US Direct Investment Abroad**. a. The most detailed results of the

Bureau's annual survey of the worldwide operations of US multinational companies. Contains information on the financial structure and operations of both US parent companies and their foreign affiliates. Data are classified by country and industry of foreign affiliate and by industry of US parent. The Tables present: Balance sheets and income statements; Employment and employee compensation; Property, plant, and equipment; Merchandise trade; Sales of goods and services; Foreign income taxes. *Preliminary* results are published as soon as available; *revised*, one year later.

(iii) #*12 Office of Business Analysis* Herbert C Hoover Building, Room 4885, Washington, DC 20230, USA. t: (1 202) 482 1986; f: 482 2164.

Responsible for disseminating economic data from the *Bureau of Economic Analysis*, as well as providing access to:

- *Economic Bulletin Board* Contains the latest statistical releases from: *Bureau of Economic Analysis*; *Department of the Treasury*; *Federal Reserve System*; and other agencies. Also contains a series of files of more general topics, such as: Fiscal and Monetary Policy Data; US Treasury Auction Results. In addition there is a calendar of release dates for major federal data programmes. The Bulletin Board can be reached by direct dial anytime on (1 202) 377 3870 (300/1200/2400 bps), or via the Internet. A free limited-access service is available by typing 'GUEST' at the User ID prompt. Guest users may not download actual files; but are encouraged to read bulletins within several sample files.
- *EBB/FAX* Facsimile-based service that provides access to the *Bureau of Economic Analysis* news releases. Copies of the releases are usually available within one hour of the time of the release. Dial 1–900–786–2329 from a fax machine's touch-tone telephone and follow the simple voice instructions. There is no registration charge or fees (other than the cost of retrieving the fax). The service is available 24 hours a day, 7 days a week: more information on this service is available on (1 202) 482 1986.

93. **National Trade Data Bank**. **cdrom**. m. Over 100,000 data series covering a very wide range of US domestic and international activity culled from fifteen US government agencies, including: *Bureau of Economic Analysis*; *Federal Reserve System*; *US Export-Import Bank*.

94. **National Economic, Social and Environmental Data Bank**. **cdrom**. q. The complete text of a number of key Federal Government publications, including the *Economic Report of the President*, plus a number of *Bureau of Economic Analysis* statistics.

(iv) #*13 Economic Development Administration* 14th Street and Constitution Avenue, NW, Washington, DC 20230, USA. t: (1 202) 482 5113. *Freedom of Information* t: (1 202) 482 4687.

Organized to generate new jobs, to help protect existing jobs and to stimulate industrial and commercial growth in economically distressed areas of the United States.

(v) *#14 International Trade Administration Information and Publications* t: (1 202) 482 3809; *Freedom of Information* t: (1 202) 482 3756.

Established to promote world trade and to strengthen the international trade and investment position of the United States.

95. **US Industrial Outlook**. a.

(vi) *#15 National Technical Information Service* t: (1 703) 487 4650. *Also* c/o Microinfo, PO Box 3, Omega Park, Alton, Hampshire, GU34 2PG, UK. t: (44 420) 86848; f: 89889.

'Each year the United States Government funds billions of Dollars worth of R&D in all fields of science and technology. Additionally, Government Agencies and Departments of State support data collection and research on all kinds of subjects of interest to the Federal authorities, including international business and trade, foreign affairs.... Most specialist material available from US Government sources is published through the Department of Commerce, National Technical Information Service (NTIS) – represented in the UK by Microinfo Ltd.

96. **NTIS Alerts**. bi-w. 'Access to the latest US Government technical studies.' The *Business & Economics* prepackaged NTIS Alert covers: Banking and finance; consumer affairs; domestic commerce, marketing and economics; foreign industry development and economics; international commerce, marketing and economics; and minority enterprises.

- *FedWorld* Centralized electronic marketplace to locate, order, and acquire US Government information. Access to more than 130 Federal online computer systems is free via modem.
- *Global Competitive Intelligence* 'As part of its expansion in the business subject area, NTIS is rapidly increasing its collection of export materials. A publication *International Trade Administration Bibliography* with more than 1000 competitive intelligence-related reports and studies, is now available.'

61. The time from the original trade to the appearance of the data referring to that trade in summary form in international official statistics can often seem unduly long. But the collection and reconciliation of the data is a highly complicated business, given the immense problems of data definition and system specification which we implied earlier. The corollary of this is that many of the economic and other statistics that one sees published by market research and other commercial organizations are more often than not – in the end – based directly on the data released by the national and international statistical authorities. (But note that some of these private organizations – including a number of the leading electronic utilities active in the area – themselves use 'national' statistics to create 'international' statistics, rather than wait for the international organizations to do the job for them.)

62. Despite the national authorities' presumed best efforts, the statistics available can sometimes be very unsatisfactory, as for instance this quotation reveals:

> The Working Party has found that world capital account statistical systems are in a state of crisis. At a time when important developments in international financial markets have occurred, the systems have failed to keep pace and to provide policymakers with adequate information. Problems are widespread. Although 10 industrialized countries account for 85 percent of the total reported capital flows and the solutions therefore lie largely in their hands, other countries must also contribute to the solutions. Improvement is possible, but it will take time; it will require considerably more international coordination than hitherto seen; and it will need additional resources in many countries.
>
> The Working Party's studies have revealed gaps in the data, nonreporting, misclassification of many transactions, inconsistencies, and lack of coordination among countries. Some of these problems have resulted from a failure to adhere to the guidelines for balance of payments accounting specified in the IMF's *Balance of Payments Manual*. The Working Party has also found many examples of poor data quality, and, in some cases, lack of resources for the compilation of balance of payments statistics.
>
> From 1986 through 1989, recorded global capital inflows in each year have exceeded global outflows by an average of $40 billion per year. By making a number of adjustments to improve the past data, the Working Party has been able to reduce this global discrepancy by an average of $23 billion per year. However, substantial gaps remain.
>
> The capital account of the balance of payments is usually broken down into four broad components – direct investment, portfolio investment, other capital, and reserves. World inflows in each of these four components – and in the capital account total – should, in principle, balance world outflows. In practice, reported inflows have not equalled reported outflows in any component. As was previously noted, consideration of only the statistical discrepancies in a component total would hide an important part of the problem because errors in inflows or outflows could be larger than the recorded discrepancy.[61]

63. One should add that although a part of the sorts of problems revealed in that extract no doubt may well be because of faulty data gathering or processing procedures, a part also will be because the data needed to do the job properly are simply not available to the authorities: as is well brought out here:

> Although statistics have improved, nobody really knows how big the world market for foreign exchange really is. All we do know is that it

> is huge. A recent estimate by the Bank for International Settlements . . . put the average daily turnover in the world market at $640 billion in April 1989 (net of double counting), which compares with an average daily turnover on the New York stock exchange of $8 billion for 1988. It also compares with the total foreign exchange reserves of industrialised countries as reported by the International Monetary Fund at the end of 1989 of SDR344 billion (equivalent to $440 billion). In other words, the entire reserves of all industrialised countries, if committed to foreign exchange intervention, could be swallowed up in two to three days' normal trading volume of the market.[62]

64. The relative paucity of reliable publicly available information on the international capital markets has long existed. Dennis, in his extensive and detailed comparative analysis of international financial flows data published ten years ago,[63] in fact only used for analysis a dozen statistical series, which he lists in an Appendix as:

Bank for International Settlements

- Annual Report
- Press Release – 'International banking developments'
- Press Release – 'The maturity distribution of international bank lending'

Bank of England

- Quarterly Bulletin

International Bank for Reconstruction and Development (World Bank)

- Borrowing in International Capital Markets
- World Debt Tables

International Monetary Fund

- International Financial Statistics
- IMF Survey

Morgan Guaranty Trust Company

- World Financial Markets

Organisation for Economic Cooperation and Development

- Development Cooperation: efforts and policies of the Development Assistance Committee
- Financial Market Trends
- Financial Statistics

65. On reflection, this apparent minimal availability of basic source material is what one would expect – particularly bearing in mind the point made earlier about the usual reluctance of entities to reveal details of their trading activities. Who else but the national and international official organizations have the authority to require trading data to be revealed? The only private source analysed by Dennis was that produced by Morgan Guaranty (because of its wide availability at that time) – of which he comments:[64]

> The main advantage of the Morgan Guaranty information in this area (and the reason that it achieves such wide publicity) is the rapidity with which data are published on a regular monthly basis. Therefore, the issue of *World Financial Markets* for any particular month will include new bonds and credits actually announced in that month of publication. With such timeliness and the fact that Morgan Guaranty records these new agreements earlier in their negotiation process . . . this means that these figures are widely quoted as virtual 'leading' indicators of the international capital markets.

66. However, as Dennis later points out,[65] the practice of Morgan Guaranty measuring credit *announcements* in contrast to the OECD and World Bank measuring credit *signatures* created discrepancies between the various series:

> Examples of such discrepancies are easy to locate. For example, credits of $500 million to the Kingdom of Denmark, $400 million to Peugeot-Citroen of France, $850 million to the Kingdom of Sweden and two loans of $300 million each to the Bank of Finland were recorded by Morgan Guaranty in its total for June 1980 but included by the OECD and World Bank in their figures for the second half of that year.

This is just one small example of the care which must be taken in using published economic and financial statistics.

67. Finally, in this brief introduction to national and international economic and financial statistics, we give some examples of the range of commercial serial publications which use such statistics as the basis for comment, analysis, forecast and advice. There are a number of facets that differentiate the differing types of publication. For instance, some concentrate on the economy of one particular country:

#16 Slater Hall Information Products 1301 Pennsylvania Avenue NW, Washington, DC 20004, USA. t: (1 202) 393 2666; f: 638 2248.

SHIP 'The most compehensive and reliable source of government statistics . . . Government statistics can be dauntingly hard to access because they come from many different, sometimes obscure, sources and in a variety of formats. *With SHIP you obtain your data from a single source* . . . SHIP data products are meticulously prepared and guaranteed by the firm's principals, Dr Courtenay Slater, former Chief Economist for the US Department of Commerce and George E Hall, former Census Bureau Associate Director.'

97. **Business Indicators. cdrom**. m. $2200. Includes: US National Income and Product (or 'GDP") Accounts; Income and Employment by State; Business Statistics (data as published by the *US Department of Commerce*

in their biennial *Business Statistics* volumes and updated monthly in the 'Blue Pages' of the *Survey of Current Business*).

Others concentrate on the economies of several countries:

#17 Data Service & Information GMBH PO Box 1127, D-47476 Rheinberg, Germany. t: (49 2843) 3220; f: 3230.

98. **EUROSTAT-CD. cdrom**. s-a. DM 3,000.

99. **International Financial Statistics on CD-ROM**. m. DM 2,000.

100. **International Statistical Yearbook on CD-ROM**. a. DM 5,000. 'Brings together the most important national and international databases on a single CD-ROM.' Includes databases from: *Eurostat*; *OECD*; *IMF*; *UNIDO* and *Citicorp*. The latter 'offers macro-economic data material for the United States of America for planning and analytical purposes. The extremely up-to-date *CITIBASE* database particularly covers the fields of finance (money aggregates, interests, other banking and loan statistics), investment and consumption patterns.'

101. **OECD Statistical Compendium on CD-ROM**. q. DM 4,500. Over 20 sets of OECD statistics including those prepared from: *OECD Economic Outlook*; *National Accounts*; *Flows and Stocks of Fixed Capital*; *External Debt Statistics*; *Insurance Statistics*; *International Direct Investment Statistics*; *Revenue Statistics of OECD Member Countries*.

102. **Short-Term Economic Indicators on Diskettes**. m. 'The DSI diskette service has been established as a direct competitor to so-called online services and is accordingly very efficient: the latest databases received from our suppliers are immediately processed and are hence available to our customers the very next day.' Series include: *EUROSTAT* Main Economic Indicators; Eurostatistics; *OECD* Main Economic Indicators; Leading Indicators and Business Surveys; *Citicorp* CITIBASE.

103. **United Nations Statistics on CD-ROM**. a. DM 500.

#18 Janet Matthews Information Services 19 Hatherley Road, Sidcup, Kent, DA14 4BH, UK. t: (44 181) 300 1003; f: 300 7367.

104. **Quest Economics Database. online**. d. 'QED provides detailed macro-economic, financial and money market-related information for EC and EFTA countries, North America, Latin America, Asia and Eastern Europe, with briefings, market news, round-ups and comment. Statistical data includes summaries of interest rates, exchange rates, inflation, oil, and money supply figures. Long- and short-term forecasts are given for fiscal, monetary and economic policies with analysis of the implications for domestic and international markets and business. Economic and political risk profiles for over 150 countries are included as well as manufacturing, industrial and economic surveys. Information is drawn from weekly, monthly, quarterly and annual reports and reviews supplied directly by the economic research departments of UK and European banks, financial institutions, government agencies and economic research organisations.'

Some are updated relatively frequently:

#19 Argus Vickers 17 Battery Place, New York, NY 10004, USA. t: (1 212) 425 7500; f: 509 5408. *Also* American Equity Research Limited, Royex House, Aldermanbury Square, London EC2V 7HR, UK. t: (44 171) 606 0006; f: 606 0666.

105. **Economy at a Glance**. bi-w. 'This bi-weekly four page report is a pictorial analysis of the US economy. It contains a series of bar charts and graphs portraying various financial, monetary and economic trends, with comments relating to each graph or chart. The back page summarises Argus' view of the economy and includes a calendar of release dates for pertinent economic indicators, consensus estimates and Argus estimates. One of Argus' most popular publications.'

#20 United Communications Group 11300 Rockville Pike, Suite 1100, Rockville, MD 20852, USA. t: (1 301) 816 8950; f: 816 8945.

106. **International Reports**. w. $1190. 'Detailed analysis of the world's foreign exchange, bond and equities markets and advance warnings on economic and political and market risk in developed and emerging economies trends internationally.'

Others are updated relatively infrequently:

#21 John Wiley 605 Third Avenue, New York, NY 10158–0012, USA. t: (1 212) 850 6000; f: 850 6088 and Baffins Lane, Chichester, West Sussex, PO19 1UD, UK. t: (44 243) 779777; f: 775878.

107. **Wiley Business Intelligence Reports**. £75 per report. 'Promise you precise, authoritative and current information. Unlike other reference sources, the reports contain informative editorials and incisive analysis, written by some of the world's leading researchers, journalists and analysts, who contribute to such international media as:

- *Financial Times of London*
- *British Broadcasting Corporation*
- *Latin American Newsletters*
- *The Wall Street Journal*
- *The Guardian*
- *The Observer*
- *Asahi Shimbum*
- *The European*
- *The Age, Melbourne*
- *The Buenos Aires Herald*
- *The Christian Science Monitor*
- *The Washington Post*.'

For some the prime focus is economic data:

#22 NPA Data Services 1424 16th Street NW, Suite 700, Washington, DC 20036, USA. t: (1 202) 884 7634; f: 797 5516.

108. **Regional Economic Projection Series. diskette**. '*ECONOMIC* database provides 52 time series which includes total population, 21 employment series, and 30 income items . . . The current 1994 REPS Series update reflects local economic data through mid-1994, and the new outlook for national and local economic conditions based on information available as of November 1994. This update incorporates new data and projections of the growth of the US economy and population over the years 1995–2015.'

For others, economic data are only one part of a larger picture:

#23 Electronic Publishing Group PO Box 6818, FDR Station, New York, NY 10150–1921, USA. t: (1 212) 980 5146; f: 980 6726.

109. **GlobalVision. cdrom**. s-a. $395. 'The International Trader's Edge . . . Trade statistics on over 14,000 commodity exports . . . (and) 8,000 commodity imports from more than 200 countries . . . 250 full color maps . . . Over 3,000 color charts and graphs . . . Over 4,000 market reports. Includes ratings of the best business opportunities in individual countries . . . Extensive list of useful contacts and government programs . . . Country reports on 249 different countries. Includes data compiled from CIA and State Department Sources . . . Assessments of trade barriers worldwide as well as the effects of the North American Free Trade Agreement . . . Sources of information from finance to small business programs and export insurance . . . Tracks global exchange rates, interest rates, price indices, and stock market indices.'

#24 Europa Publications 18 Bedford Square, London WC1B 3JN, UK. t: (44 171) 631 3361; f: 637 0922. *Also* c/o Gale Research, 835 Penobscot Building, Detroit, MI 48226–4094, USA. t: (1 313) 961 2242; f: 961 6815.

110. **Europa World Year Book (Year)**. a. £310. Two volumes. 'Detailed surveys of over 200 countries & territories. A comprehensive listing of over 1,650 International Organizations. Easy access to the very latest statistics, directory information and current analysis.'

111. **USA and Canada (Year)**. a. £195. "It is difficult to see how any other single volume of comparable size could possibly improve its coverage in terms of comment or information." (*Reference Reviews*)

112. **Western Europe (Year)**. a. £165. 'Presents text, statistics and directory information on more than 30 Western European countries and territories.'

#25 University Press of America 4720 Boston Way, Lanham, MD 20706, USA. t: (1 301) 459 3366.

113. **Freedom in the World**. a. £22.50. 'The Annual Survey of Political Rights and Civil Liberties . . . Political, social and economic snapshots of every nation and territory in the world, and a country-by-country over-

view of the year's most significant political events. Also included is useful data on life expectancy, population and economic indicators.'

#26 Washington Service Bureau 655 15th Street NW, Washington, DC 20005, USA. t: (1 202) 508 0600; f: 508 0694. Same day 10Ks, 13Ds etc. 'Call for our free *Federal Information Primer*.'

114. **Economic Chartbook**. l. 'This book of 76 charts highlights selected economic and financial indicators . . . Charts are updated immediately as new data are released, and revised copies sent to Washington Service clients by first class mail. The same data are also available in machine readable format in two versions: Lotus 1–2–3 or Harvard Graphics.'

115. **Evans-Novak Political Report**. bi-w. 'Covers the inside workings of Washington politics.'

116. **Federal Reserve Releases**. 'The Federal Reserve tracks a wide variety of statistical series which provide data not available elsewhere, including:

- Aggregate reserves of commercial banks
- Balance sheets of the US economy
- Consumer installment credit
- Flow of funds
- Foreign exchange rates
- Money stock
- Liquid assets and debt measures
- Selected interest rates
- Survey of the terms of bank lending.'

This service also covers the Minutes of the *Federal Open Market Committee* and the *Beige Book* report, prepared by district banks in advance of FOMC meetings, commenting on current economic conditions in each of the twelve districts. Summaries of district bank publications and public addresses by Federal Reserve principals are also offered online through *Bloomberg*.

117. **Highlights of Budget Deficit Financing**. m. 'Summary of the unified federal budget deficit and its relationship to Treasury financing plans. Compares forecasts to actual outlays, revenues, and deficits.'

118. **Monetary Policy Scorecard**. m. 'Review of monetary statistics and their relationship to Federal Reserve Board targets for the aggregates and bank credit. A handy guide for determining the *Open Market Committee*'s performance in hitting the Fed's monetary targets.'

119. **Potomac Portfolio Perspective**. w. 'Highlights current developments on policy issues significant to investors. Summarises government policy studies and provides timely analysis.'

120. **Statistical Services. online**. 'Offers all US government releases via fax, Federal Express, first class mail, or electronically on the Bloomberg system.'

121. **US Quarterly Balance of Payments**. q. 'Analysis of the trade and

services balance and its impact on the current account and the means of financing current account deficits.'

122. **Washington Service Calendar**. m. 'Indicates the scheduled release dates of major economic statistics.'

Some concentrate on the past:

#27 Euromonitor Publications 60–61 Britton Street, London EC1M 5NA, UK. t: (44 171) 251 8034; f: 608 3149 *and* Euromonitor International, 111 West Washington Street, Suite 920, Chicago, IL 60602, USA. t: (1 312) 541 8024; 541 1567.

123. **International Marketing Data and Statistics (Year)**. a. £160. 'A massive compilation of hard-to-find up-to-the-minute statistics on all the key socio-economic, demographic and marketing parameters.' Data covered include: Economic Indicators; Finance and Banking; External Trade by Destination and Commodity. There is also a similar *European Marketing Data and Statistics (Year)* (a. £160).

124. **World Economic Factbook (Year)**. q. £155. Covers over 200 countries.

125. **World Marketing Data and Statistics on CD-ROM (Year)**. a. £695. A combination of data from the *International* and *European Marketing Data and Statistics.*

#28 Kogan Page 120 Pentonville Road, London N1 9JN, UK. t: (44 171) 278 0433; f: 837 6348.

126. **World Business and Economic Review (Year)**. a. £125. Contains political and economic analysis and statistics on 220 countries. Also available are *The Americas Review* and *The Europe Review.*

Others concentrate on the future:

#29 Capitol Publications 1101 King Street, Suite 444, Alexandria, VA 22313–2053, USA. t: (800) 327 7025/(1 703) 683 4100; f: (800) 645 4104/(1 703) 739 6490.

127. **Blue Chip Economic Indicators**. m. $498. 'What top economists are saying about the US outlook for the year ahead.' Current economic forecasts for top management, corporate planners, market research directors, economists, bankers, brokers and investors.

128. **Blue Chip Financial Forecasts**. m. $498. 'Top analysts' forecasts of US and foreign interest rates currency values and the factors that influence them.' Examples of the fifty 'Contributors to Domestic Survey' are: *Aubrey G Lanston*, *Banc One Corp*, *Chase Manhattan Bank*, *Federal National Mortgage Association*, *MMS International*, *Merrill Lynch*, *Mortgage Bankers Association*, *National Association of Realtors*, *Nomura Securities International*, *Prudential Insurance*, *Sanford C Bernstein*, *Standard & Poor's*, *Technical Data*, *US Chamber of Commerce*, and *Wells Fargo Bank*.

129. **Financial Times Currency Forecaster**. m. $695. 'Consensus forecasts of the worldwide currency and economic outlook.'

130. **Financial Times Global Investor**. m. $695. 'Worldwide forecasts of interest rates, equity indices, gold prices, currency and inflation.'

#30 Elsevier Advanced Technology PO Box 150, Kidlington, Oxford OX5 1AS, UK. t: (44 01865) 843656; f: 843971.

131. **Economic Forecasts: A Monthly Worldwide Survey**. m. £439. 'While many sources provide statistics, this journal is the only one to provide updated forecasts for the world's 25 major economies in one monthly reference, complete with authoritative commentary from some of the world's leading economic experts.'

#31 Political Risk Services 6320 Fly Road, Suite 102, PO Box 248, East Syracuse, NY 13057–0248, USA. t: (1 315) 431 0511; f: 431 0200.

132. **International Country Risk Guide**. l. $3,150. **cdrom**. 'Timely, accurate, complete – covering 130 countries worldwide . . . A *business-oriented risk model* gives you a detailed country-by-country breakdown of the comparative risks of investing time and money in each country. The ICRG model includes twenty-four indicators of financial, economic and political risk . . . A *wealth of data* is published every month, including such key indicators as trade balances and inflation rates, hard currency delays, official and parallel exchange rate differentials, total foreign debt, debt service ratios and much more.' A **diskette** version of the ICRG Tables is also available ($695).

#32 World Information Services Bank of America, Department 3015, 555 California Street, San Francisco, CA 94104, USA. t: (1 415) 622 1446; f: 622 0909.

133. **Country Data Forecasts**. l. $495. **online**. 'Provides detailed data tables showing the historical performance and five-year forecasts for 23 key economic measurements, including: population, economic growth, inflation, indebtedness, income per capita, size of the economy, trade performance, exchange rate.'

134. **Country Outlooks**. l. $495. **online**. 'Intelligence briefings that provide detailed economic information and financial forecasts for 30 key countries.'

135. **Country Risk Monitor**. l. $495. **online**. 'Ranks 80 countries for current and future business risk on the basis of a common set of economic and financial criteria, widely acknowledged as the most important country risk measuring tools (including): capacity to pay foreign debt, strength of trade performance, governmental fiscal responsibility, foreign indebtedness, involvement in international trade, income per capita.'

Some have a relatively focused customer market in mind:

#33 Esmerk Information Benham Valence, Newbury, Berkshire RG16 8LU, UK. t: (44 1635) 34867; f: 40212.

'Provides directors and key decision makers with a structured flow of intelligently tailored essential business and economic information to improve their vision of the international markets in which they trade. All information is tailored to individual needs. Information is culled from sources in more than 20 languages but delivered in abstract form in English from more than ten offices worldwide. The information is available in paper or electronic format on a daily or weekly basis.'

#34 SJ Rundt 130 E 63rd Street, New York, NY 10021, USA. t: (1 212) 838 0141.

136. **Financial Executive's Country Risk Alert**. 3/year. $450. Provides surveys and forecast information on international trade and currency matters, with specific risk evaluations for all countries.

137. **Rundt's World Business Intelligence**. w. $675. Covers international trade, security risk evaluations, political, financial, export and currency exchange forecasting for all countries.

Others have a relatively wide set of customer markets that they are aiming at:

#35 Economist Intelligence Unit 40 Duke Street, London W1A 1DW, UK. t: (71) 493 6711; f: (71) 491 2107. *Also* 215 Park Avenue South, New York, NY 10003, USA. t: (1 212) 460 0600; f: 995 8837.

"(EIU) is extending its electronic publishing activities with the launch of a new range of products. *EIU Electronic Publishing*, the Unit's new media division, will market the company's range of country, regional, industry and management information via online, CD-ROM, direct local area network (LAN) feed, fax and microform. A new service, *EIU Direct*, will feed regularly updated EIU business information directly into customers' local or wide area networks. Other online initiatives will include wider availability of EIU publications through online hosts FT PROFILE, MAID, DIALOG, and Mead Data Central, plus customised country monitoring services, delivered via Reuter Business Briefing, Global Report and Bloomberg. Partnerships have been established with CD-ROM publishers, resulting in the recently released five-set series of EIU regional business intelligence products on DIALOG OnDisc, while EIU's Country Reports, Country Forecasts and international business newsletters have been published on CD in co-operation with SilverPlatter Information."[66]

Here, as contrasts, are the sections *What EIU Information is Available* taken from the marketing publicity issued by EIU for each of the third-party hosts marketed in early 1995:

- *EIU OnLine with Dialog* [Knight-Ridder Information] 'Enables you to monitor, analyze and forecast market developments in 192 countries. It provides a one-stop guide to operating globally, with information on a wide range of management issues: economic and political trends, business conditions and regulations, financial techniques, organizational structures, labor developments, foreign trade opportunities, investment risks, government incentives, environmental concerns, corporate strategies and industry trends. The service contains the EIU's full database of economic and market statistics and forecasts.'

- *EIU OnLine with FT Profile* 'One-stop service for monitoring and analyzing country, industry and management developments around the world. It provides the latest analysis of economic and political trends, labor and trade conditions, business regulations, financial markets, environmental issues, and corporate strategies. The database also gives the latest trends and statistics for a range of industrial sectors, including tourism, consumer goods, commodities, and automotive markets.'
- *EIU OnLine with Global Report* 'Covers a wide range of economic data, analysis, and forecasts, including: important currency, interest rate stock and bond market consensus forecasts; country risk assessments, economic indicators and trends; and foreign exchange, trade and tax regulations. It also provides daily executive briefings covering the latest business developments in any of 192 countries.'
- *EIU OnLine with Mead Data Central* [Lexis/Nexis] 'You can monitor, analyze and forecast market developments in 44 countries . . . The database gives you access to EIU information on a broad spectrum of business topics, including economic and political trends, business conditions and regulations, financial techniques, organizational structures, labor developments, foreign trade opportunities, investment risks, government incentives, environmental concerns, corporate strategies and industry trends. The service contains the EIU's core economic and market data and forecasts.'
- *EIU OnLine with MAID* 'Allows you to monitor, analyze, and forecast developments in 192 countries. A broad spectrum of business topics is covered, including market conditions and forecasts, economic and political developments, trade opportunities, investment risks, environmental concerns, and trends and statistics for tourism, consumer goods, commodities and automotive markets.'
- *EIU OnLine with Reuter Business Briefing* 'You can answer questions for 33 countries on a wide range of economic, business, and political topics. This database includes the latest economic outlook, including GDP, interest rates, government spending, and inflation; summary EIU economic and financial data and forecasts; corporate taxes, including capital gains, dividend withholding, interest withholding and sales and excise taxes; and financial and trade regulations, including borrowing, hold accounts, incoming direct investment, leading, lagging, netting, and export and import controls. Many country profiles include consensus forecasts and other comparative data.'
- *EIU OnLine with The Bloomberg* 'EIU's Country Monitor on THE

BLOOMBERG terminal offers continuously updated information on economic and business conditions of some 74 countries as well as foreign exchange, tax and trade regulations in 25 major countries. You also receive monthly consensus currency forecasts from top international corporations and financial institutions.'

138. **EIU Business Intelligence Series**. **cdrom**. 'Contains all data and analysis from EIU's popular newsletters, as well as the complete Country Reports/Profiles and practical information for the top economies in each region from the following EIU reference publications: *Financing Foreign Operations* and *Investing, Licensing and Trading Conditions Abroad*. In addition, a topical EIU research report is included in each issue.'

139. **Business Europe**. w. £650. **online**. 'Briefing you on the latest business developments shaping your commercial future in Western Europe.'

140. **Crossborder Monitor**. w. £450. **online**. 'Designed to provide international executives with a global overview of fast-changing market developments requiring management attention.'

141. **Country Forecasts**. q. £360 per country. **online**. **cdrom**. 'Provides five-year macroeconomic forecasts for the world's top 55 economies.'

142. **Country Reports**. q. £160 per country. **online**. **cdrom**. 'Monitor and analyse recent political and economic developments, and give two-year outlooks for over 180 countries every quarter. In an easy-to-read format each report can be used as an introduction to a country or as a tool for keeping abreast of developments in major sectors . . . (Annual) **Country Profiles** can also be obtained as part of the EIU Reporting Service.'

143. **Country Risk Service**. q. £280 per country. **online**. 'Ratings for 82 highly indebted and developing economies . . . a tool designed to manage international investment portfolios.'

144. **European Trends**. q. £195. 'In-depth analysis of the critical, EC-wide trends that affect your business.'

145. **Financing Foreign Operations**. a. £85 per country. **online**. 'Offers a broad range of intelligence on financial opportunities around the world. By combining chapters on important supranational sources of funds with reports on capital sources, financial regulations and operating techniques in 45 countries, FFO provides the information needed to manage corporate finance on a global scale.'

146. **International Business Newsletters on Disc**. **cdrom**. m. 'The complete collection of the EIU's international newsletters . . . *Business Africa*, *Business Asia*, *Business China*, *Business Eastern Europe*, *Business Europe*, *Business Latin America*, *Business Middle East*, *Crossborder Monitor*.'

147. **Investing, Licensing and Trading Conditions Abroad**. a. £85 per country. **online**. 'Detailed information on operating conditions and practices, and the rules and regulations influencing them, in 63 of the world's markets, both major and exotic.'

148. **Western European Business Intelligence on Disc**. **cdrom**. m. 'Reports

on key regional markets in Belgium, France, Germany, Italy, Luxembourg, the Netherlands, Portugal, Spain, Switzerland, Turkey and the United Kingdom . . . *Country Reports/Profiles* . . . *Financing Foreign Operations* . . . *Investing, Licensing & Trading Conditions Abroad* . . . *Country Forecasts* . . . *European Trends* . . . You'll also receive full coverage from the EIU's specialized publications: *Business Europe* . . . *Crossborder Monitor* . . . *Global Outlook*.'

149. **World Commodity Forecasts**. 6/yr. $555. For investors, planners, analysts and businessmen; uses monitored trends to generate forecasts of spot prices and for the next 18 months of 27 commodities.

150. **World Market Atlas**. a. £295. 'Packed with 1,700 easy-to-use colour charts, graphs and maps, it shows you at a glance how 153 countries stack up against one another in terms of GDP, income per head, consumer spending and much more.'

151. **World Outlook (Year)**. a. 195. 'Forecasts the political and economic trends in more than 180 countries . . . Each country has a comprehensive 6–year series of macroeconomic indicators. Numerical GDP forecasts are given for all OECD economies and selected others.'

Lastly, some are aimed at a relatively specialist audience:

#36 Graceway Publishing Box 159 Sta.C, Flushing, New York, NY 11367, USA. t: (1 718) 463 3914; f: 544 9086.

152. **Journal of Business Forecasting Methods and Systems**. q. $55. Covers subjects such as how to prepare and use forecasts or set up a forecasting system, the problems that exist between forecasters and users and how they can be resolved, and experiences of different companies and individuals in the field. Gives forecasts of key economic variables in 47 countries.

153. **Quarterly Domestic & Global Forecasts of Key Economic Indicators**. q. $105. Provides one-year-ahead forecasts of real economic growth rate, inflation, and balance of payments for 47 countries plus interest and foreign exchange rates forecasts of 7 major countries. Also provides consensus forecasts of 13 key variables of the US economy, and for industry forecasts.

Others have a much more general audience in mind:

#37 The Economist Newspaper Limited 25 St James's Street, London SW1A 1HG, UK. t: (44 171) 830 7000; f: 839 4104. *Also* 111 West 57th Street, New York, NY 10019, USA. t: (1 212) 541 5730; f: 541 9378.

154. The **Economist**. w. £104. **online**. **cdrom**. £395. 'First published in September 1843 to take part in 'a severe contest between intelligence, which presses forward, and an unworthy, timid ignorance obstructing our progress' . . . One of the most authoritative and influential publications in the world . . . *Authoritative* (W)ritten for an audience of senior business,

political and financial decision-makers who value it for the accuracy of its incisive writing and lack of partisanship . . . *International* read in more than 180 countries . . . the only news or business publication with a truly international perspective. It is this that distinguishes The Economist from national newspapers and magazines which are mainly devoted to domestic news, written from an insular point of view . . . *Independent* . . . The editor is appointed by trustees who are free of commercial, political and proprietorial influence, while the paper is written anonymously because its collective voice and personality matter more than the identities of the individual journalists. This ensures a consistency of view which few other publications have matched.

The Economist's worldwide circulation has grown by 125% over the last 10 years and is now approaching 600,000 . . . *Reader Profile Highlights* Average Reading Time: 1 hour 40 minutes; University Degree: 81%; Average Household Income: US$159,000 pa; Top Management: 49% (*World Subscriber Survey 1994*).'

The financial information system

68. Having earlier broadly introduced the types of entities which trade, the types of transactions which they enter into, and the types of assets provided and received during such trade, it is now time to focus on the real concern of this book: the publicly available information sources which reveal data about the financial health of those entities – acting either as principals or as agents; financially interpreted data about the transactions which the entities enter into; and financial data related to the traded assets themselves. Where the traded assets represent *claims* on some third party – such as will often occur in secondary market trading – the entity financial data in which one is primarily interested frequently relates to the entity against whom the financial asset one would trade represents a claim; rather than to the entity presently holding the relevant asset of interest, and with whom one might be thinking of doing business.

69. We will start this discussion by recognizing that – as in any area of life – the information which becomes public relating to the phenomena which interest us, is only a relatively small subset of the totality of information which the relevant individuals and organizations are exchanging with each other. People as individuals, and as representatives of organizations, are constantly exchanging information with each other related to, in this case, their trading activities. Some of this information (eventually) becomes public. So, within, or alongside, the trading system – depending on the perspective one wishes to adopt – is what we might term a *trading information system*, ensuring the transmission between trading participants of the data, information and documents needed in the trading system itself. If such a trading information system did not exist, trade almost certainly could not take place: at the least it would take place much less cost/efficiently or cost/effectively (or both) than with such an information system in place. The 'trading information system' we are conceptualizing encompasses *all* of the information that needs to be exchanged between all of the individuals and organizations involved with each trading event: both principals and agents/auxiliaries.

70. One of the functions of this trading information system is to specify the amount of 'money' which will be exchanged between trading entities as a part of the transaction between them. Distinct from the financial system's intermediation role, there is a need for institutions within that system – especially 'banks' – to ensure the gathering, transmission, and receipt of money by and between the trading entities.

71. This money transmission system is needed to underpin the (primary and secondary) trading of real, but also of financial, assets: of equities and bonds; of futures, options and swaps; of mortgages and loans; and so on. In fact, as regards such financial asset trading, there will often (especially these days) be any number of 'micro-trades' involving different principals and agents in the paths between what we termed earlier ultimate surplus, and ultimate deficit, entities. But at the 'macro-trade' level, the purpose of the money transmision subset of the overall financial system is in the end for the first ultimate entity to be relieved of money and to receive in return a financial 'claim'; and for the second to receive money, but also at the same time a financial 'obligation'.

72. Without such a money transmission system or *payment system*[67] in place, trade of even minimal sophistication – whether of real or financial assets – just could not happen. However, critical as such a system is, its impact on the publicly available information corpus of finance is relatively small. If only for reasons of *bank secrecy*[68], in virtually every case when a specific payment, or – in the case of many transactions in securities – also an associated *clearance* and *settlement*[69] is made, no information on those individual transactions reaches the public domain. (Information on the trading event itself may be made public; but not via its associated payment, clearance and settlement system(s).) However, *payment, clearance and settlement* agencies will often publish statistical summaries of groups of transactions that they have recently channelled; and this information can be a useful indicator of activity in the relevant sectors of the economy:

(1) #38 Association for Payment Clearing Services Mercury

House, Triton Court, 14 Finsbury Square, London EC2A 1BR, UK. t: (44 171) 711 6200; f: 256 5527.

Oversees the operations of the *Cheque and Credit Clearing Company*, which operates the high volume paper clearings, *CHAPS and Town Clearing Company*, which operates the high value same-day clearings, and *BACS* which operates a bulk electronic clearing.

'Amongst the major responsibilities of APACS, in addition to overseeing the operations of the clearings mentioned above, are included: strategic studies and forecasting of payments matters and trends, formulating industry standards and maintaining comprehensive statistical data on money transmission activities. APACS also speaks for and lobbies on behalf of the UK payments industry and has become the recognised authority on all matters relating to money transmission and payment clearing activities in this country. Over the past two years, APACS has also become the focus for payments industry co-operative activity to combat plastic card fraud. This involves putting in place a range of anti-fraud measures and, for the longer term, examining appropriate developments in plastic card technologies.

Membership of a Clearing Company is open to any financial institution which can demonstrate its ability to meet fair, explicit and objective criteria. These criteria include:

(a) being subject to appropriate supervision (broadly speaking, this means banks and building societies operating in the UK, and European credit institutions);

(b) being able to meet the technical, operational and legal requirements of Membership;

(c) the maintenance of settlement account facilities at the Bank of England; and

(d) accounting for at least a certain volume of items passing through the given clearing (0.5% for CHAPS and Town and Cheque and Credit Clearing Companies and five million items per annum for BACS).'

Up to 1994, all the members were UK institutions – but 'from mid-1994, Credit Lyonnais SA and Deutsche Bank AG are expected to take up Membership of APACS and CHAPS and Town.'

155. **Clearing Statistics**. m. 'Details of the values & volumes of items through each of the clearing companies.'

156. **Sorting Code Numbers**. *Reed Information Services.*

157. **Standards Manual**. 'Available on a subscription basis. Subscribers are included on a mailing list and advised of changes to Standards as they are published.'

158. **Yearbook of Payment Statistics**. a. £15. Note that the 1990 Yearbook (£75) includes long run historical data.

(2) #39 Credit Card Research Group 2 Ridgmount Street, London WC1E 7AA, UK. t: (44 171) 436 9937; f: 580 0016.

159. **Card Expenditure Statistics**. m. £180. 'The value of credit and debit card expenditure each month broken down into ten sectors.'

(3) #40 Depository Trust Company 55 Water Street, New York, NY 10041, USA. t: (1 212) 898 1200; f: 898 3189.

Most corporate securities, as well as municipal bonds, are immobilised at the DTC. Depositories, in contrast to clearing corporations, immobilise physical securities and provide book-entry transfer and settlement services for their members.

(4) #41 ECU Banking Association [Association Bancaire pour L'ECU] Rue de la Paix 4, F-75002 Paris, France. t: (33 1) 44 86 04 20; 44 86 04 25. *Newsletter*.

Set up in 1986, principally to oversee a clearing system for ECUs. Membership is open to commercial banks which have their head office or a branch in one of the EU countries and which demonstrate sufficient interest in the development of ECU transactions. At the end of 1992, the system cleared about 6,500 transactions per day among 44 banks for an amount of about ECU 42 billion.

(5) #42 Electronic Funds Transfer Association 950 Herndon Parkway, Suite 390, Herndon, VA 22070, USA. t: (1 703) 435 9800; f: 435 7157.

Reports produced include: 'Consumer attitudes and perspectives on security at the ATM'; 'The business case for retail POS'; 'EBT in the United States'; 'EFT/POS in the supermarket environment'; 'ATM security in the 1990s.'

(6) #43 London Clearing House Roman Wall House, 1–2 Crutched Friars, London EC3N 2AN, UK. t: (44 171) 265 2000; f: 481 3462. *Marketing Department* t: (44 171) 265 2069.

'Clears trades executed on the following exchanges: *The International Petroleum Exchange* (IPE); *London Commodity Exchange* (LCE previously known as London Fox); *The London International Financial Futures and Options Exchange* (LIFFE); *The London Metal Exchange* (LME). When LCH registers a trade it becomes the central counterparty by novation; that is the buyer to every LCH Member seller and the seller to every LCH Member buyer. As central counterparty, LCH ensures the financial performance of trades through to, and including, delivery. This means that if a Member goes into default, LCH will continue to perform to all other Members with open contracts. At present volumes, LCH is providing this service for over 150 million contracts per year. (NB: LCH is not the counterparty to and has no involvement with the contract between client and broker.)

The financial integrity of London's futures and options markets is upheld by the regulatory structure governing the exchanges, LCH and Members, in addition to the comprehensive approach LCH takes to risk management across all its operations. This approach encompasses: Counterparty assessment; Margining; Position and price monitoring; Central banking; Delivery; Default management. In January 1993, LCH had 171 Members, the number of Members clearing for each Exchange being: LCE 55, IPE 45, LIFFE 116, LME 37.'

(7) #44 National Automated Clearing House Association 607 Herndon Parkway, Suite 200, Herndon, VA 22070, USA. t: (1 703) 742 9190; f: 787 0996.

Formulates and promulgates rules and standards for processing automated clearing house transactions throughout the USA. Also houses the *National Association for Check Safekeeping*.

(8) #45 New York Clearing House Association 100 Broad Street, New York, NY 10004, USA. t: (1 212) 612 9200; f: 612 9253.

Operates the *Clearing House Interbank Payments System* (CHIPS) 70 per cent of whose payments are dollar-denominated international payments. Like the Federal Reserve System's *Fedwire* system, CHIPS is a credit transfer system; unlike Fedwire, however, CHIPS nets payment transactions multilaterally and settles the net obligations at the end of the day. Also operates *ACH*, a low-value, batch payment system.

(9) #46 Options Clearing Corporation 440 South LaSalle Street, Suite 2400, Chicago, IL 60605–1050, USA. t: (1 312) 322 6222; f: 322 2593.

Clears and settles all listed options. (Futures contracts and options on futures are cleared and settled through clearing houses associated with the eleven US futures exchanges.)

73. Thus, we are conceptualizing our trading domain as consisting of three transport mechanisms, running in parallel (but actually in practice all wrapped up, each within the others). There is the trading system itself, trading assets, real or financial. There is that portion of the financial system whose function is to transport money. And there is what we have termed the trading information system, exchanging information between the trading entities. Such information includes, for instance, details of the principals and agents who would be involved with specific trades; the characteristics of the assets to be traded, at what prices; the arrangements for handling the money.[70] For many types of trade, such information will be encompassed within a specially written *contract*. In other cases, there will be an implied written contract.

74. Now, proportions of this 'trading information' are made publicly available. Most obviously, this occurs in situations where the trading participants need or wish to make a public market in the assets they would trade. Actually, as regards the trading of 'financial assets', the absolutely most complete and up-to-date information on what is on offer and by whom used by a prospective trader deciding whether to trade is usually only quasi-publicly available. That is, it is available in its most recent and complete form only to those formally registered to trade in the appropriate *financial market*: brokers, dealers, market makers. But for many organized markets these days, the rest of us – via the real-time, online information services – can have access to something that is close to that available to the traders themselves. We will give examples of such services in Chapter 8 of the book.

75. Surrounding these trading, payment, and trading information systems are the legal, economic and political systems applicable in the country – or countries – wherein the prospective traders are registered to trade.[71] Although the information sources produced and used in these latter systems are not the central focus of this book, they will occupy a great deal of our attention. We cannot make progress in understanding the whys and wherefores of the publicly available information corpus of finance unless we make an effort to understand the national and international legislative and regulatory processes; and the economic and political imperatives that guide those processes.

76. In particular, as has already been touched upon, the policies and practices of the *organizations* comprising the world's legal, economic and political systems are instrumental in determining:

- the characteristics of the organizational entities which are allowed to transact with each other (ie which are allowed, corporately, to exist);
- the nature of the transactions that each characterized entity is allowed, required and (economically) able to enter into;
- the nature of the information that is in turn allowed, required and able to be publicly generated about those entities and transactions.

77. At the risk of totally confusing the reader, we might note that we could have written a book which had as its prime focus the legal, economic and political organizations which exchange information with each other, the nature of those exchanges being subject to the exigencies of a financial environment! Clearly, the overall approach actually adopted here is just one of a number which could have been chosen to structure the panoply of information sources generated and used by those who practice and research in 'finance'.

78. In fact, it is worthwhile reminding ourselves that the constructs we have used such as 'activity', 'arrangement', 'environment', 'framework', 'imperative', 'system', are merely devices to try to help us make sense of a complex trading world. Although there would be agreement between individuals on the key elements that should be included in one or another construct (e.g. a nation's central bank could be said to be a component both of its 'financial system' and of its 'economic environment'), there would be disagreements at the margins. Further, the relative emphasis that any one individual (such as you, the reader) felt should be given to each specific element would be influenced by that individual's prior knowledge and expertise: that which they bring to the point at which 'new' (i.e. new to that individual), publicly available information is sought.

79. Finance, as most other subject areas covered in this Bowker-Saur series, consists of a number of professional sub-disciplines. Each has its own set of publicly available information sources used by its practitioners and researchers. Each specific set of sources will be well known by those who practice and research in the relevant sub-discipline. Indeed, as regards finance, it will already be apparent – if not already known – that effective practice and research is impossible without such a knowledge. This, simply because the prime 'material' of finance is not one or another chemical entity, or archaeological artefact, or historical source text, or musical score, or technological creation, or the earth, or the body, or the mind, or the spirit: it is **information** itself.[72] And where to find that information – whether it is an obscure tax rule, or a stock market indices value, or a credit rating for a bank, or a manual on mortgage securitization techniques, or a historical run of inflation figures, or the code of conduct for dealing in interest rate swaps, or a current yield for a Yankee bond, or the latest balance of payments data, or a recent working paper on multi-period information markets, or details of the new proposals for accounting for derivatives, or the value of a beta, and so on and so on – *has* to be known by those who work within the relevant sub-disciplines. Otherwise practice and research just is not possible. New finance professionals find out from old finance professionals the information sources that they must use.

80. So, we might ask, why a book like this? Perhaps for three reasons. First, those practising or researching in one sub-discipline of finance might value a list of sources that will give them an entrée to another.[73] Second, information and library professionals, and members of the information industry more generally who work with published 'finance' information, might appreciate from what follows how their work fits into the overall global trading system. Third, perusal of the book might help those who are not professionally involved with the finance discipline to relate to an area which often seems unnecessarily clouded in mystery. Of course, the details can be complex. But the broad framework which I have tried to reflect in the chapter arrangements which follow – of private and public entities trading financial (and real) assets with each other, managing and investing such money as they have, aided by one or another financial institution or market, with the whole subject to the ramifications of specific national and international legal, economic and political environments: that seems not. All readers of this book are participants in the world's trading and its associated financial systems: directly or indirectly we are all *investors*. The more that we understand about these systems, the better.

81. Returning then to the overall approach that we have chosen, entities are transacting assets, money and information within legal, economic and political environments. As it were at right angles to these flows, information appears in the public domain: about the entities, their assets and their transactions. We have so far implied two reasons why such releases of information might occur:

- It is *necessary* for the information to appear if (market-based) trade is to prosper.
- The information is *required* – by some external edict – to be released.

To these two can now be added a third reason:

- The entities involved with trade – principals, agents, or auxiliaries – have *chosen*, of themselves, publicly to release the information.

82. There is – as we have already alluded – a fourth reason why 'financial' (and other related) information about trade and trading entities becomes publicly available. This is where there has been – shall we say prosaically – an *inadvertent* escape of information. The trading entity or entities would not have wished such information to have been released; but somehow it was. Of course, what often happens is that the information inadvertently first reaches just one or a small number of people; and this only comes to light (if it does) when there is a subsequent unexpected price move in a relevant trading market. Often, this *insider dealing*[74] – illegal in the UK, USA and many (but by no means all) other countries – will trigger a 'press' statement (issued perhaps following pressure from the market authorities). Sometimes the authorities feel that it is prudent to suspend trading of the relevant assets for a period until things settle down.

83. However, the elements that we should – and will – discuss that apply to the 'inadvertent' public release of financial information seem no different from those which determine the positive release of such information. So we do not need specifically to concern ourselves further with the former area here – except in one respect. This is to remind ourselves that much of the information which is generated and used within 'finance' might better be said to be semi-publicly (or semi-privately) available, rather than truly available to the populace at large. This is certainly the case within the trading markets: but that is as much for regulatory and supervisory reasons, than from a desire to restrict information availability to a select group. However, the whole of 'finance' is characterized by collections of information that it has been necessary, required, or chosen to release beyond the individual or organizational entity; but with the information released only in fact being available at that time for perusal by a select group of people: at least in practice, if not in theory. We will expand a little on this important theme in Chapter 3. An important sub-set of this semi-public/semi-private information is information given *off-the-record*: for instance, to external financial analysts by corporations; or to lobby journalists by governments.

84. Summarizing then again, individuals and organizations *supply* information to the public *financial information system* (if we might commandeer that phrase) because they perceive or are told that there is a *demand* for such information. Elaborating on our earlier three-fold distinction, the information that it is purely *necessary* to release publicly for trade to take place or be facilitated is in fact a very small subset of the totality of 'finance' information available in the public arena (that is, once one discounts the 'required' and 'chosen' (and 'inadvertent') release of information). It comprises, simply, the (usually overtly contractual) specification of the asset to be traded, of its negotiating price, and of the identity of the trader who wishes to trade. (The trader may well be a broker acting on behalf of the current owner of the asset.) Note that it is not 'necessary' before initiating a trade to know anything about the well-being of the principals and agents with whom one might wish to deal; nor about any entity or entities against which the (financial) asset to be traded ultimately represents a 'claim'. It would be unusual for most of us to take 'pot luck' and trade in this way without some or all of this knowledge: but it can be done!

85. Where information is *required* to be made publicly available, it will often be because those specifying the requirement believe that there is, or will be, or ought to be, a demand for such information: for instance, by investors seeking protection for their investments. In specifying the details of the relevant disclosure or reporting requirements, the concern of the 'authorities' often is as much with the formal content and timing of entry into the public domain of the information required to be released, as it is with the actual requirement for disclosure/reporting. As is well known, the reporting requirements of most trading entities – both in the UK and the US – has grown tremendously over the last two to three decades. Whether this has led in the end to a fairer society (assuming that to be the ultimate objective), is debatable. (It certainly has led to a more bureaucratic society, as the following pages will testify!)

86. Finally, there is the trade-related information which is *chosen* to be released by trading entities. Much of this ultimately is *marketing and public relations* material which trading principals, agents, and claimant bodies hope will encourage (or less frequently discourage) trade of the assets with which they are involved (or implicated). As well as relating directly to the assets and their current owners, such published material frequently also will include information about the legal, economic and political environments within which the assets, or the entities against whom the assets represent claims, exist; or it is forecast that they might exist in the future. All this information is supplementary to the information which the trading principals, agents and claimant bodies are required, or it is necessary, to release into the public domain.

87. The largest body of truly publicly available 'finance' information which has been 'chosen' to be made public comes of course from the *commercial publishers*, and from the members of the *information industry*[75] more generally. Commercial publishers principally perform two – usually overlapping – roles in the public domain financial information system. First, they act as conduits, taking information generated by the various types of entity active in the financial system itself and making that information publicly available. Second, they try to add value to such information, offering some sort of commentary. The first is supplier driven: financial markets need to publish information to encourage trade to take place; companies will disclose their accounts, if only because they are legally required to do so; academics will want to publish their research so as to engage the attention of other academics and to further their careers; professional and trade bodies will desire to have their voices heard on behalf of their memberships; governments will wish to publicize their policies and precepts; and so on. The second type of activity is commercially driven – and is often intimately bound up with the workings of the advertising industry. Many publications perform the conduit and value-adding functions equally well: newspapers will report stock prices or company results at the same time as including assessments of what the figures mean. Commercially produced magazines and journals, as well as reproducing the data and articles and papers and other material submitted to them (subject to widely varying degrees of editorial/refereed control), will also frequently contain specially written or commissioned commentaries. The information contained in the offerings of the information industry does not *have* to be published (i.e. it is not 'needed' or 'required'); but if its availability sells 'copy', then it will be.

88. Individuals and organizations involved with trade thus supply information to the public domain because they need to, are required to, or they choose to. At the micro-level, these individuals and organizations may be the actual entities who would like to trade, are trading, or have traded financial (and real) assets. Alternatively, the information suppliers may be one or another agent or auxiliary who has assisted, is assisting, or would like to assist such principals in their trading activities. In their first release to the public of particular pieces of information, the principals and agents/auxiliaries may themselves be the 'publishers'. Or, instead, the services of commercial publishers may be used. Or both methods of *primary release* of the information may be used more or less simultaneously. Note the emphasis here on the primary release – or, as we shall term it later – looking from the outside on to the trading system – the *generation* – of trade-related information. This will prove to be significant. Also, let us remind ourselves of the related information transfer processes that take place, whereby summaries of groups of trade-related information – *statistics* – are publicly released in addition to, or instead of, the information relating to specific trades and trading entities.

89. All this is rather dry and theoretical! So let us be a little more practical. Contrasting the three key distinct types of trade-related data and statistics whose importance we stressed earlier:

- Information is statutorily required to be released by *corporations* to specially designated agencies with a form and content often determined by other agencies. That information is then made publicly available to all who wish to see it as soon as is feasible. The agencies to whom the information is disclosed do not themselves normally add value to the information; but there are a number of commercial organizations who do. The depository process was until the early 1990s predominantly a paper-based one; but the advent of systems such as the US Securities and Exchange Commission's *EDGAR* project is gradually turning this area too into a fundamentally electronically-based activity.
- On the other hand, the delivery of current data from the

financial markets into the public domain has for long been an electronically-based activity. Although some financial markets via their own computer systems make such data available for online searching by the general public (rather than just by those registered to trade in the appropriate market) most of the time the data is distributed by real-time data feeds to commercial vendors – who in turn make the data more generally available. The form and content of the data emanating from the various types of financial market (which, when compared to the form and content of the accounting data produced by corporations, is relatively uncomplicated) is determined by agreement between those who trade in each specific market (otherwise a market could hardly exist!). However, for many markets, the commercial vendors expend immense efforts adding value to the basic data they receive from the trading market players: this being one of the major competitive differences between them. Where a financial market is officially or quasi-officially regulated, audit and other historical data for each trade will be centrally collected; which information will frequently be publicly released subsequently in summary form.

- The commercial financial data vendors to whom we have just referred are increasingly one-stop shops giving access not only to current (and historical) financial market data; but also both to the accounting (and other) data disclosed by corporations, as well as to the financial data and economic statistics released by *governments and government agencies.* However, before releasing their data, the latter bodies as has already been noted take great trouble to translate the data they originally gather from trading entities (including from themselves) into data series which are internally and externally consistent. As well as being made available in electronic form, such series are also generally still published in a traditional paper-based format.

Forms of literature

90. It should by now be abundantly clear that answering the question of what 'financial' information relating to anticipated or progressing or completed trade between individuals, between organizations, and between individuals and organizations, becomes publicly available to whom, when, where, how, and why, is a little complicated! Further, if we are to attempt anything like a comprehensive introduction to the information sources of finance, the sources that 'publish' such overt trade-related information are only a proportion of those which we should illustrate in this text; as a perusal of this list of *forms of literature* will remind us:

- Abstracting and indexing journals
- Bibliographies
- Bills
- Card services
- Case studies
- Catalogues
- Codes
- Codes of conduct
- Command papers
- Committee reports
- Congressional papers
- Corporate accounts
- Corporate reports
- Conference proceedings
- Data series
- Decisions
- Dictionaries
- Directives
- Directories
- Discussion papers
- Dissertations
- Edited works
- Encyclopedias
- Forms
- Gazettes
- Handbooks
- Law reports
- Laws and statutes
- Looseleaf works
- Magazines
- Market research reports
- Monographs
- Newsletters
- Newspapers
- Official annual reports
- Parliamentary papers
- Press releases
- Prospectuses
- Regulations
- Research reports
- Scholarly journals
- Source guides
- Standards
- Statistical series
- Statutory instruments
- Textbooks
- Theses
- Trade journals
- Treaties
- Working papers

91. A small number of these forms are indeed used solely as vehicles to publish instances of the three key types of data and statistics we have highlighted. But the majority are used to carry other publicly available information germane to the financial system: of which the leading financial newspapers, such as the *Financial Times*,[76] and the *Wall Street Journal*,[77] are the ultimate print-on-paper based exemplars.

92. And that multifariousness is before we have properly introduced the electronically based artefacts. Some of these are physical artefacts, the portable data compilations – *databases* – on CD-ROM, diskette, magnetic tape, or which can be handheld.[78] Others are collections of digital information which can be directly interacted with only via the use of some sort of external telecommunication link: in batch access mode (very rare these days); or by direct online access – the remote data meanwhile either being updated periodically in what we shall later call *scheduled* mode; or updated in *real time.* Such a link can either be via a modem linked to one's personal workstation; or can be via one's organizational local area network.

93. Until a few years ago, it could be tedious technologically to engineer such links. But now of course we have the *Internet* and especially the *World Wide Web* to make the linking much much easier – at least in theory, if not in practice.
94. Then, finally, for completeness, we should remind ourselves of the *broadcast* 'radio' and 'television' services, which deliver financial – or more generally 'business' – news by cable, terrestrially from a transmitting station, or via satellite. In one sense, broadcast services are real-time services: if we wish to know the latest on, say, the 'Barings' crisis, we might 'switch on the news'. But, in another sense, they are not: one is dependent on the news actually being delivered at the time one switches on.
95. Given all these and a number of other varying aspects of the 'information sources in finance (and banking)' – such as their geographical coverage, hardly even mentioned so far – I would suggest that there are within this subject field, perhaps more than the usual issues of structure which need to be tackled if we are to allow those new to the field (the prime intended audience for this book) to gain an easy perspective.

Structural facets

96. In this book I have especially responded to four major structural facets to help us to cope with the diversity just outlined. Again, they might be conceptualized as choices of perspective which allow us at that time to concentrate on particular facets of the universe of published information sources, relegating other facets to the background for the time being.

(a) First, we have responded fully to the *electronic imperative* – which is now so pervasive in this field. In Chapter 8 we illustrate the sophistication of the commercial electronically based information systems which facilitate the flows of finance information from producer to user; and note how a relatively small number of members of the information industry have come to dominate those flows.
(b) Second, as will already be apparent, we are relatively preoccupied here with the commercial and especially non-commercial *information providers* who are active in the financial arena. We are as much interested in who supplies the information which appears in the public domain; as with what that information is. All of the serial information sources we cite are categorized by their providing entity. This approach complements the subject-based approach generally adopted in the many excellent source guides already available elsewhere.[79] It also facilitates direct recourse to those providers by the reader:

often essential in a field such as finance where information sources appear and disappear with disturbing frequency.

(c) Third, a crucial aspect that has only just been mentioned, we are careful to distinguish the *geographical focus* of the non-commercial organizations that we reference. Such a categorization takes precedence over the specific segment of the financial system that the organizations are concerned with: reflecting the overriding importance of legal jurisdiction in the practice of finance.

(d) Fourth, given the premium placed on *currency of information* within the financial system, the published information artefacts which we reference are almost wholly primary serials; the non-serial and non-primary sources that we cite being almost totally relegated to the *Notes* to each chapter.

97. The first two of these four organizing features reflect one of the global financial system's most crucial present tussles. This is between, on the one hand, those private organizations intent upon exploiting the continual computing and telecommunication advances to maximum commercial advantage; and, on the other hand, the non-commercial official and quasi-official organizations charged with trying to regulate and supervise the world's financial, and its associated financial information, flows.

98. Axiomatically, at the kernel of this tussle is indeed the question of who has access to what financially related information, when, where, how and why. Private trading individuals and organizations who have the means, will judge that it is worth their while to invest significant capital to try to ensure that they have to hand the most up-to-date, trade-related information possible and feasible (in addition to the information that they have to acquire – that is necessary – before trade can take place at all). They will also generally try to avoid publicly revealing details of their own financial health and intentions to those with whom they might wish to trade in the specific markets which interest them.

99. Meanwhile, governments and government appointed and recognized agencies will be determined by their laws, regulations and required procedures on trying to ensure:

(a) First, that the financially related information that society deems must be released by entities into the public domain – that is *required* – is as *true and fair* a reflection of the underlying phenomena that it describes as is possible and feasible.

(b) Second, that *sufficient* information is released to ensure an agreed level of *investor protection*.

(c) Third, that no one individual or organization, or specific group of individuals or organizations, is able to profit from any access to such disclosed information that they are able to secure, ahead of others.

100. Axiomatically also, then, the information sources generated and used by these opposing forces are bound to be somewhat complicated. Private individuals and organizations – aided and abetted by the players in the financial information industry – have much to gain from devising new or modified forms of trade which can circumvent the authorities' current complex of laws, regulations and required procedures (especially those relating to tax). Those authorities will, in turn, continually be amending the complex to try to ensure – ultimately – that the overall financial system meets national political, economic and social goals, as defined by the relevant legislature – whilst trying to be careful in a global financial system not to drive away business to more hospitable regulatory environments.

101. One key consequence of all this is that serious participants in the financial system (trading principals or agents/auxiliaries) make little or no use of conventional print-on-paper based public access libraries to find such publicly available information as they need to maximize their trading returns. The information needed will either be obtained electronically, direct from the work desk; or, if only available in print-on-paper (or other static) form, copies will be kept close by in the office, or within the participants' work group. Material not available in one of these two locales when needed will be obtained directly from the public or private organization producing the information; or from an intermediary agent or broker. It is almost always just not cost effective to spend valuable time visiting a distant publicly accessible library to obtain needed information: where, in any case, the information may well not be available – or, if available, be up to date.

102. In fact, we have currently a rather curious hybrid situation. Traditional libraries continue to buy – and thus publishers continue to publish – print-on-paper documents (and other physical information artefact compilations such as microforms, and now cdroms and diskettes) containing information on one or another segment of the financial system, the majority of which data – unavoidably – is out of date, sometimes woefully out of date, by the time the artefacts are available for perusal by the libraries' customers. Meanwhile, data that is truly up to date is being 'gathered' and 'displayed' by the real-time data providers; with those who have access to such systems never dreaming of relying on a comparable physical information artefact to provide the published information they need before making, for instance, a critical investment decision.

103. Naturally one would wish to stress that the general unavailability of much truly current published financial information within the majority of 'finance' libraries is not because of any incompetence on the part of those who manage those libraries! In a very real sense it is an early manifestation of the concept of the *virtual library*. Those intimately involved with trading systems have the technological and financial means almost to avoid using 'real' libraries altogether: instead going straight to those who generate and display information for the public domain. I will be suggesting at the end of the book that this process of transition from real libraries to virtual libraries as regards all non-historical published information of practical value to those who work in the financial system – and, indeed, much other published information used within that system – will be complete within the next ten years.
104. Actually, the question of the ease and speed of public information availability – important as it is to those of us charged at present with helping to facilitate that availability – pales into insignificance when we ask ourselves what real value any of the published sources of trade-related information traditionally found in libraries – and much indeed of what is publicly available in total – have in the investment process! I have in mind here, of course, the fact that virtually all of the financial information that it is 'required' to be released is retrospective information: it does not speak of what is happening now, at this very moment; but of what has happened previously – sometimes a relatively long time ago. Further, information that is 'chosen' to be released by trading entities, will often tend, naturally, to put the best gloss on the area discussed. There are stringent regulations in many advanced countries to try to prevent the release of positively misleading information; but these cannot be totally effective – and once one moves to an international dimemsion the whole becomes highly problematic:

> No matter what degree of international cooperation the authorities ultimately achieve, effective supervision faces severe limits, especially in an age of rapid financial innovation and increasing financial integration. Supervisors inevitably have much poorer information than the managers of the institutions they supervise. Moreover, they get the information with a time lag that is compounded by processing delays inherent in any bureaucratic structure. In most cases, if the managers of an institution want a particular risk profile, supervision and regulation cannot effectively keep them from attaining their objective.
>
> Many important international banks do not publicly disclose much information that is pertinent to evaluating safety and soundness. An indication of this problem is that in every country banks disclose much more information to the banking authorities than to the general public.

The limited information they do disclose is generally not comparable across banks within the country, much less across banks in different countries. This may be a useful area for public policy intervention, but international harmonization of accounting standards and disclosure policy would involve most of the difficulties that have impeded harmonization of meaningful, risk adjusted capital-asset ratios. It is not clear that efforts to harmonize disclosure would be more successful.

Nonetheless, pressure from the *Basle Committee* to raise capital adequacy ratios has led indirectly to some improvements in disclosure. In order to get the best possible price for new issues of equity and subordinated debt, some banks have voluntarily disclosed their hidden reserves. And security analysts continue to exert pressure for more and better-quality disclosure as they attempt to compare the profitability of firms in different countries. Rating agencies are also becoming an important force for improving disclosure practices as banks attempt to tap sources of capital outside their domestic markets.[80]

105. But there is a much more fundamental reason for one's sceptism of the real value of the sorts of financial information traditionally found in libraries – which relates to an issue that I promised to return to at the outset of this chapter: the notion of *efficient markets*. Brealey and Myers – writing from an academic viewpoint – are categorical:

> The patron saint of the Bolsa (stock exchange) in Barcelona, Spain, is Nuestra Senora de la Esperanza – Our Lady of Hope. She is the perfect patron, for we all hope for superior returns when we invest. But competition between investors will tend to produce an efficient market. In such a market, prices will rapidly impound any new information, and it will be very difficult to make consistently superior returns. We may indeed *hope*, but all we can rationally *expect* in an efficient market is that we shall obtain a return that is just sufficient to compensate us for the time value of money and for the risks we bear.
>
> The efficient-market hypothesis comes in three different flavors. The *weak form* of the hypothesis states that prices efficiently reflect all the information contained in the past series of stock prices. In this case it is impossible to earn superior returns simply by looking for patterns in stock prices – in other words, price changes are random. The semi-strong form of the hypothesis states that prices reflect all published information. That means it is impossible to make consistently superior returns by reading the newspaper, looking at the company's annual accounts, and so on. The strong form of the hypothesis states that stock prices effectively impound all available information. It tells us that inside information is hard to find because in pursuing it you are in competition with thousands, perhaps millions, of active, intelligent, and greedy investors. The best you can do in this case is to assume that securities are fairly priced and hope that one day Nuestra Senora will reward your humility.
>
> The concept of an efficient market is astonishingly simple and

remarkably well-supported by the facts. Less than twenty years ago any suggestion that security investment is a fair game was generally regarded as bizarre. Today it is not only widely accepted in business schools, but it also permeates investment practice and government policy toward the security markets.[81]

106. However, Essinger, writing from a more practical viewpoint, in a quite different type of book,[82] is perhaps not so sure. His excerpt usefully starts by defining the major characteristics of the two historically quite different approaches to the analysis of securities for investment purposes: 'fundamental analysis' and 'technical analysis':

Fundamental analysis is based upon the notion that one way of assessing how the price of an investment instrument is likely to change in the future is thoroughly to investigate the current and likely future performance and business activity of the company which issues the instrument, as well as the industry sector to which the company belongs. Fundamental analysis, which is mainly used when assessing the prices of equities, is the most 'obvious' type of analysis and until the 1970s was almost the only type of analysis used. Fundamental analysis might mean reading the company's accounts and performing sophisticated analysis on them. It might mean studying industry trends, or speaking to the company directly. As a result of such investigation, fundamental analysts decide on whether a share is 'underpriced' or 'overpriced'. If it is the former, the fundamental analysts will advise his clients to buy the share (or will buy it himself). If it is the latter, the recommendation will be to sell: the implication is that soon the market will realize that the share is under or overpriced, and then the market will catch up.

It is extremely important to realize that implicit in the rationale of fundamental analysis is the idea that the market for the company's shares is an imperfect market: a perfect market is one where all participants have access to the same information, while an imperfect market is one where not all participants have access to the same information.

Note that this does not mean in an imperfect market insider trading is permitted, or that no efforts will be taken by the particular stock exchange which runs the market that all price-sensitive information is disseminated to all participants the instant that it becomes available. The assumption is that insider information is not permitted, and that the information that is available is readily available. People who believe in the existence of imperfect markets believe that even when a market is fairly run by the exchange that operates it, there will still be what might be termed 'pockets of imperfection' which will give one dealer or investor the opportunity to make money at the expense of less well-informed participants. For example, a company's annual report – which is available to everybody – may say nothing about a detail such as the likely passage of overseas legislation which will give the company the opportunity to trade in a lucrative foreign market. This is the kind of detail which a fundamental analyst hopes to locate in order to obtain better information than his competitors.

Technical analysis is quite different from fundamental analysis; it is sometimes called chartism, although the term 'technical analysis' is usually preferred by its practitioners.[83] Technical analysis pays little or no attention to the intrinsic nature of the company or the industry sector, but instead concentrates on the previous pattern of price movements.

At first sight, this seems rather startling. Does it mean that technical analysts believe that the future performance of a share or other type of investment instrument – or the overall direction of the market – is principally dependent upon past performance? In fact this is exactly what technical analysts believe. They create charts of price changes and claim that they can perceive a pattern in these changes. From these patterns, which are analysed by a variety of methods (usually proprietary), they believe that the future price movements are indeed predictable.

Like fundamental analysts, technical analysts believe that they can obtain an edge over the rest of the market's participants. Again, there is the unspoken assumption by technical analysts that information in the market is not understood equally well by everyone – that the market is not informationally efficiently.

Note that technical analysts believe both that there are patterns in market prices and that some are able to understand and predict from those patterns better than others.

Like fundamental analysts, technical analysts do not claim to get their predictions right every time. They do acknowledge that there are surprises, and that their own preferred forms of analysis are sometimes wrong. But they believe that unexpected changes are only evidence of the basic unreliability of the market – an unreliability by which they claim they can profit through their forecasting methods.

It might reasonably be asked whether there can possibly be any truth in the notion that previous price performance (that is, fluctuation) can be any guide to future fluctuation. After all, even a layman might suppose that fluctuations on a financial market are no different from events such as tossing a coin or spinning a roulette wheel – examples of events which are known to produce random variables (i.e. the mathematical probability of any event occurring is distributed evenly among all the possible events). Events which produce random variables are of their nature unpredictable. So-called 'systems' for winning at bingo, roulette, lotteries or the football pools do not work. Probably the only reason why some people still believe that these systems do work is that the events themselves are sufficiently complex for the effectiveness of the system not to be obvious. But nobody has ever tried to sell a system for predicting whether a single tossed coin will fall heads or tails – simply because the chance of either happening is so obviously equal and a system would seem ludicrous.

However, technical analysts confronted with the above reasoning would not deny that events such as tossing a coin or spinning a roulette wheel produced random variables. Technical analysts indeed would argue that the above reasoning is irrelevant because price fluctuations on financial markets are not random: they would say, in effect, that the price fluctuations are the result of human actions, and that human actions are anything but random.

Certainly it is true that major price fluctuations occur when important news items break. A drop in the rate of inflation, for example, will bring confidence to the market, just as news of a worsening balance of payments will reduce confidence. These events will tend to increase and decrease market prices respectively. But it does not necessarily follow from this that trend in a market price, or price of an individual instrument, can be predicted. Nor is it only the layman who might believe that market price movements were probably random. There is an important school of thought among academic economists that market price fluctuations are themselves random variables.[84]

107. Essinger then goes on in his book to recommend what he terms 'quantitative analysis':

Quantitative analysis draws elements from both fundamental analysis and technical analysis. In that quantitative analysis looks very carefully at the expected returns from owning an investment instrument, and the risk of those returns actually occurring, it makes use of fundamental factors; and in that it involves the very important assumption that previous returns (and the risk of obtaining those returns) can be extrapolated into future expectations of returns and risks, then it might also be said to borrow some of the thinking of technical analysts. What is certainly true is that quantitative analysis claims to be a particularly useful tool for obtaining consistently good performance from a relatively large, diversified portfolio. Since obtaining such performance from a relatively large portfolio is precisely what the professional investment manager will probably want to do, quantitative analysis is playing an increasingly important role within the investment management industry. Its name derives from the fact that it focuses on *quantities* of return and risk for the investment instruments under investigation.[85]

108. Finally, Essinger, too, comes back to the underpinning of the 'efficient markets hypothesis':

Integral to the reasoning behind quantitative analysis is the *efficient markets hypothesis* (EMH). This hypothesis, which has gained much ground in the USA and is becoming increasingly widely accepted in other countries, holds that while it is impractical to suggest that markets are perfect since some participants will at any one time have information which may give them the opportunity to gain a shortlived edge over other participants, the prices in the market will none the less reflect all relevant available information.

The notion of the EMH has extremely important implications for investment managers. If the EMH is valid, then the entire notion that abnormal profits can be *consistently* made on a stock exchange is revealed as nothing more than superstition; someone might be lucky enough to make abnormal profits, on occasion, but this only indicates good fortune. There are no real opportunities for consistent profits within stock exchanges because all opportunities evaporate through the pricing mechanism, which 'absorbs' and rapidly evens out the portions of imperfection which have given one participant the opportunity to make abnormal profits.

Furthermore, if the EMH holds, it follows that the claims of fundamental analysts and technical analysts to try to beat the market are invalid. Indeed fundamental analysts and technical analysts might be said to help to make the markets more efficient through their constant vigilance.

No definitive answer is available to the question of whether or not the EMH is valid. Despite the considerable efforts of dealers, investors and their advisors to try to beat the stock markets – efforts which millions of people make every day around the world – far less is understood about how markets really work than might be expected. A great deal is understood about the more simple elements of the market, such as how the price of a particular equity is likely to change if the company involved announces higher profits than expected, but overall the dynamics of the precise fluctuations of a market and the prices of instruments on those markets appear to be too complex for any one theory to provide a complete explanation of them. An analogy can be drawn with the human body, where doctors and surgeons have considerable knowledge of how individual elements of the body function, but a far less adequate understanding of how all the elements of the body function together in a living person, which explains why ailments affecting the whole person, such as stress, are far less likely to yield to medical treatment than ailments affecting one particular part of the body.

None the less, the EMH is gaining increasing currency among academics and many market participants as *probably* the best available explanation of how financial markets behave. The supporters of the EMH would agree that fundamental analysis and technical analysis can be useful tools, to an extent, but that they are likely to produce as many losses as gains. The protagonists of EMH argue that the only way to obtain consistent returns from a market that is efficient is to diversify assets according to certain principles which indicate – principally by mathematical means – how return and risk might be maximized for a given asset allocation. Conducting an analysis of these return and risk factors, and allocating assets according to the analysis, is what constitutes quantitative analysis.[86]

109. In a last quote on this fascinating subject, we might turn to Rutterford's first-rate introduction to stock exchange investment:[87]

In a sense, the semi-strong form of the efficient markets hypothesis is the most interesting of the three forms. . . . There is widespread agreement that the weak form of the EMH holds and that the use of technical analysis *on its own* is most unlikely to enable anyone consistently to make excess profits.

However, belief in the validity of the semi-strong form in its fullest sense calls into question not just the activities of chartists but the investment strategy of the majority of investment analysts in the City – (performing) fundamental analysis. . . . Most investment analysts act as industry specialists, spending their time forecasting future earnings, dividends or returns (according to preference)[88] for the companies within their chosen sector. . . . They do this by studying economic forecasts, industry reports, visiting the company, analysing company accounts and statements and generally forming a view on the company's prospects. This view is usually translated into an estimate of what they believe to be the share's intrinsic or 'correct' value . . . which is then compared with the current share price, and generates a 'buy', 'sell' or 'hold' recommendation to clients.

There are over 1,900 members of the Society of Investment Analysts, and many more professional and amateur analysts who are non-members. There are approximately 2,000 UK company equity securities currently listed on the Stock Exchange, of which around 900 have a market capitalization of under 25 million. This leaves approximately 1,100 shares with a market capitalization of over 25 million to be analysed by *at least* 1,900 analysts. Each major British company will be 'followed' by a good many analysts, who have available to them the same public information, can make the same company visits, and presumably pore over the same company accounts. With this is mind, the semi-strong form of the EMH . . . becomes readily believable. Any new piece of information made public will be so quickly analysed and absorbed into a new market estimate of the company's value that an investor trading on each announcement, say, of unexpectedly good earnings will act too late to be able to make excess returns.

The implications of the semi-strong form of the EMH for fundamental analysis, if it closely reflects reality, are far-reaching . . . (It implies) that the best available indicator of a share's so-called intrinsic value is its current market price. So a fundamental analyst's search for undervalued shares within his sector using publicly available information is a waste of time. For example, a study of the intangible assets of companies could lead an analyst to believe that certain companies were undervalued and others overvalued. However, if the method of valuing intangible assets is publicly available in the notes to the accounts, other analysts will already have impounded whatever additional knowledge was contained in the notes into the share price. Not all analysts and investors need to have fully digested and analysed the details of the accounts. All that is required is for a sufficient number of analysts and their clients to have traded in the share with that knowledge. . . . The implication for those concerned with corporate disclosure and accounting standards is therefore that careful consideration should be applied to *what* information is disclosed rather than *how* it is disclosed, since each new item of information not previously available may improve the market's estimate of the share's worth.[89]

110. I have quoted at some length from those three texts, partly because they are excellent entrées to a crucial topic from functionally separate areas of finance; but also as an indication of the quality of the debate that can take place from quite different vantage points. There is a great literature out there waiting to be tapped!

The traditional finance library

111. Having set a framework of finance and finance-related information supply to the public domain, it is now time to try systematically to categorize the full range of vehicles used to make that information publicly available. Despite the *electronic imperative*, we will find it best to do this by first surveying the various types of traditional non-electronic 'static' information artefacts (such as printed books and journals and reports and so on). In Chapter 8, we will consider the quite dramatic effects that the widespread availability of sophisticated computing and telecommunications facilities has been having on our field.

112. Notwithstanding my broadside a moment ago against traditional libraries, let us imagine that you – the reader – have just entered a predominantly print-based library, which happens to contain a wide variety of publications 'about' finance. You have just started work in the field and you would like the 'librarian' to give you an introduction to finding your way around the variety of materials that are available. What might the librarian say?:

(a) *First*, we would hope that the librarian would say that what you see before you is only a subset of the total amount of 'relevant' material potentially available worldwide. Further, the material that is available outside of the library is increasingly very speedily accessible via electronic communication. This often can be done direct from the desk, rather than via the use of a librarian or other information professional intermediary. Indeed, the librarian should say that, for that reason, his or her (traditional) library – as a source of published 'finance' information – most probably will not be here in 10 years time (unless the library has significant archival aspirations).

(b) *Second*, in outlining the facets the librarian has used to organize the physical information artefacts in the library, the first that might well be mentioned would relate to the critical difference between *serial* and *non-serial* publications. As well as often needing to be physically shelved in different ways, the former would tend to be turned to when up-to-date material is needed; the latter for background (as in the text that you are reading now).

(c) *Third*, it would also be helpful to remind you that certain items in the library – both serial and non-serial – contain *secondary* material: these often only being used when an entrée to *primary* sources (people, organizations or published items) is needed.

(d) Next, it might be sensible, *fourth*, to make a distinction between those information artefacts used solely or primarily to trace *data*; and those used solely or primarily to trace – if not fiction! – some sort of *elaboration* of that data. We have been overwhelmingly preoccupied in this chapter so far with the finance system and its various environments as factual phenomena generating factual data (entity accounts, financial market data, economic and financial statistics). In Chapter 3, we will be surveying the types of *value-adding processes* that can be applied to such data.

(e) Having perhaps given you the impression that much supposedly value-added material is of dubious 'value' (such naturally having a minimal presence in the library!), no doubt the librarian, *fifth*, would rush to point out that many commentaries exist which *are* of real value: especially those which are the result of rigorous *scholarly research and study* (see Chapter 7).

(f) The academic associations, academic institutions, and research centres which involve themselves with such work are a subset of a wider network of non-profit making organizations, including – as well as the national and international official organizations – a large number of professional and trade bodies: many of which are of great importance – especially in their roles as self-regulatory agencies. The librarian would then wish to stress, *sixth*, that often the best – or sometimes only – way to find up-to-date publicly available information about certain aspects of finance is via the publications of, and then if needs be, personal contact with, such organizations.

(g) This would lead naturally, *seventh*, to a few words about the *grey literature* of finance. If the library was located within the private sector – for instance, within a bank, an insurance company, law firm or financial newspaper publishing company – then that library might well contain much notionally private finance-related literature. Such material would often have been obtained by a member of the firm acting in a personal capacity: who had then passed it on to the firm's library for safe keeping (and more general availability within the firm). Conversely, if the library was located within the public sector – being a national, public or academic library – then it would be unlikely to contain much (up-to-date) material of this type. We have already anticipated the discussion of this issue of semi-public/ semi-private information which occurs later.

(h) *Eight*, if the library had significant involvement with legal and regulatory source documents, the librarian would need to engage you in a quite separate and somewhat involved description of the peculiar nuances of such literature. This occurs here in Chapter 2.

(i) By this stage, *ninth*, your suspicions will have started to have been confirmed. On the one hand, the world's financial system generates a very large amount of highly specialized published material; on the other hand, it generates a mass of material aimed at the non-specialist: much of this is distributed free of charge (if you can manage to acquire it); much of it – if commercially available – is expensive to very expensive. The intellectual rigour of such material varies from very high to very low.

(j) Finally, *tenth*, as you perhaps brandish some such list of 'finance' forms of literature as the one given earlier in this text, the librarian might be tempted to try to explain how those forms relate to the facets he or she had just outlined. Perhaps five *broad groupings* would be characterized:

(1) First, a group of *general purpose tools* used to carry the full range of primary material. The *non-serials* among these ('books'):

Edited works
Monographs
Textbooks

in most libraries would be shelved in a classified sequence using one of the general library classification schemes; or perhaps a specialized scheme such as the *London Classification of Business Studies.*[90] The *serials*:

Magazines
Newsletters
Newspapers
Trade journals

would normally tend to be arranged on the shelves by title of serial (except perhaps in some larger libraries); but with the

Annual reports (official and corporate)
Market research reports

frequently being shelved by name of issuing body. These general purpose non-serials and serials carry within their covers both fact and commentary.

(2) Publications in a possible second broad grouping transport historical *factual data and statistics* – but with some members of the group extending such data and statistics into forecasts:

Corporate accounts
Data series
Statistical series

(3) The third grouping might comprise the material produced for and by the *legislative and regulatory system*. Some such material is designated differently in different jurisdictions:

United Kingdom

Command papers
Gazettes
Parliamentary papers
Statutory instruments

United States

Congressional papers
Codes
Forms

European Union

Decisions
Directives

In other cases the same designation is used:

Bills
Codes of conduct
Law reports
Laws and statutes
Prospectuses
Regulations
Standards
Treaties

(4) The fourth grouping could contain the forms of literature used in *scholarly processes*:

Case studies
Conference proceedings
Discussion papers

Dissertations
Research reports
Scholarly journals
Theses
Working papers

(5) Last and fifth, there are the various types of *non-primary material*. These might be classified into three sub-groups:

Reference works

Card services
Directories
Encyclopedias
Handbooks
Looseleaf works

Finding tools

Abstracting and indexing journals
Bibliographies
Catalogues

Guides to secondary material

Source guides

Tracing primary sources

113. There is a wealth of *non-primary sources* which can be used to find primary sources. We end this chapter with a list of major – and a number of minor – examples. After some paragraphs covering the more general tools, we list some subject-specific items. Where details of the serials cited in this book have not been obtained directly from their producer, I have normally obtained them from one of the prime reference guides to such forms of literature:

160. **Ulrich's International Periodicals Directory (Year)**. *RR Bowker*. a. $395. Five volumes. **cdrom**. q. £435. The 1994–95 edition 'contains information on more than 147,000 serials published throughout the world arranged under 967 subject headings'.

Other guides to serials include:

161. **Bacon's Newspaper/Magazine Directory**. *Bacon's Information*. a. $270. **cdrom**. $995 (includes *Bacon's Radio/TV/Cable Directory*). Two volumes. 'The best media guide for PR professionals, Bacon's is the most compehensive and accurate source of dailies, weeklies and magazines

with the most editorial contacts of any directory! Only Bacon's contains vital information on every US and Canadian daily, all US weeklies, plus over 9,900 business, trade and consumer magazines and newsletters, news services and syndicates.'

162. **Boston Spa Serials on CD-ROM**. *British Library Document Supply Centre.* s-a. £425. 'In addition to the Centre's own holdings . . . provides access to holdings in other important collections in the United Kingdom. Over 450,000 records.'

163. **Newsletters in Print**. *Gale Research.* **diskette**. 11,000 US/Canadian titles, arranged under 7 broad categories comprising over 30 specific subjects.

164. **Oxbridge Directory of Newsletters**. *Oxbridge Communications.* a. $395. 'More than 20,000 North American newsletters makes this the largest source of information on this growing, influential medium.'

165. **Periodical Title Abbreviations**. *Gale Research.* i. $325. 130,000 different abbreviations for periodical titles and selected monographs in all fields.

166. **Serials Directory**. *EBSCO.* a. £235. **cdrom**. a. £375. Includes information on over 140,000 international titles (journals, newspapers and monographic series).

167. **Standard Periodical Directory**. *Oxbridge Communications.* a. $495. **cdrom**. $695. '85,000 North American periodicals, including magazines, newsletters, newspapers, journals and directories.'

In addition to *EBSCO*, who produce also a commercial serials directory, other leading serials agents – such as *Blackwell's*, *Faxon* and *Swets* – also produce frequently revised directories of the serials which they distribute.

114. This organization aims to maintain a complete inventory of world-wide serials:

#47 International Serials Data System International Centre, 20 rue Bachamont, 75002 Paris, France. t: (33) 1 42 36 73 81; f: 40 26 32 43.

168. **ISSN Compact**. **cdrom**. q. £940. 'Records of more than 670,000 periodicals from 180 countries in 144 languages, with over 40,000 new entries and 60,000 updates per year.'

Tracing organizations

115. There are a number of directories which can be used to trace the details of organizations:

169. **Business Organizations, Agencies, and Publications Directory**. *Gale Research.* bi-a. **online**. Describes more than 25,000 US organizations, agencies, and publications of interest to US business researchers.

170. **Centres and Bureaux**. *CBD Research Limited*. i. £95. 2nd edition, 1993. '1,800 establishments in Britain serving a VERY wide range of interests.'

171 **Complete Guide to Associations in the UK**. *Searchline Publishing*. a. £65.

172. **Directory of British Associations & Associations in Ireland**. *CBD Research Limited*. i. £126. **cdrom**. 6,800 national organizations. 12th edition, 1994.

173. **Directory of European Industrial & Trade Associations**. *CBD Research Limited*. i. £127. 5th edition, 1991.

174. **Directory of Management Consultants in the UK**. *AP Information Services*. a. £79.50. 'Comprehensive details on over 1,750 consultancies from the major players through to the smaller highly specialised firms.'

175. **Encyclopedia of Associations**. *Gale Research*. s-a. £780. Three volumes. **online**. **cdrom**. **diskette**. 'The number one source for information on active associations, organisations, clubs and other non profit membership groups in virtually every field of human endeavour.' The electronic versions combine data from the US National, the US Regional, and the International print edition – giving access to details of a total of almost 90,000 associations.

176. **EU Trade and Professional Associations and their Information**. *Euroconfidentiel*. a. 100. Covers some 600 associations and their 8500 member companies or organizations.

177. **European Consultants Directory**. *Gale Research*. a. $225. Over 5,000 consultant organizations grouped by country, and by broad subject terms.

178. **European Directory of Management Consultants**. *AP Information Services*. a. £130. '2,500 consultancy firms throughout Western and Eastern Europe in every area of activity and industry.'

179. The (Year) **National Directory of Addresses and Telephone Numbers**. *Omnigraphics*. a. £69.95. Over 140,000 listings including: the top US businesses in 500 industries; over 8,000 federal, state and local government agencies; media and communications, including radio and TV; and business associations and organizations.

180. **National Trade and Professional Associations**. *Columbia Books*. a. $75. Compilation of over 7,500 trade associations, professional societies, and labour unions.

181. **Pan-European Associations**. *CBD Research LImited*. i. £60. 2nd edition, 1991.

182. **Trade Associations and Professional Bodies of the United Kingdom**. *Gale Research*. bi-a. Details of some 4000 associations and bodies.

183. **Yearbook of International Organizations (Year)**. *KG Saur*. a. $875. Three volumes. **cdrom**. Edited by the *Union of International Associations*.

'The Yearbook attempts to cover all 'international organizations", according to a broad range of criteria. It therefore includes many bodies which may be perceived, according to narrower definitions, as not being fully international or as not being of sufficient significance to merit inclusion. Such bodies are nevertheless included, so as to enable users to make their own evaluation in the light of their own criteria. For some users, these bodies may even be of greater interest . . . Users should be aware that the editors are subject to pressure from some international bodies to suppress certain categories of information. Reasons given for this pressure include:

- The body does not belong with 'international organizations' . . .
- The body is of 'no possible interest' to anyone else . . .
- Mention of the body, or of its normal relationships, attracts unwelcome attention . . .
- Mention of membership of the body may subject them to victimization . . .
- Organizations wish to avoid unsolicited mail (especially 'junk mail') . . .

In most cases, the editors resist these pressures; in some cases, the entry is reworded to respect the concern of the body in question. No entries have been eliminated as a result of such pressures.'

Tracing people

116. Tracing the people who work within organizations – when the name of the relevant organizations is not known – is frequently difficult. Data protection legislation – quite rightly – tends to limit the scope for using electronic database techniques. Professional and trade bodies often create directories of their members; but often also restrict (or try to restrict) distribution to the membership itself. Subject tools are notoriously partial and uneven – unless they have achieved the status, for instance, of directories like the UK's:

184. **Who's Who**. *A & C Black*. a. £80. With over 29,000 entries, it is an overview of international people from all walks of life.

117. Biographical tools relevant for those who work within finance include:

185. **Biography Index**. *HW Wilson*. m. **online**. **cdrom**. $1,095. Covers some 2,700 periodicals and nearly 2,000 books.

186. **Biography Master Index**. *Gale Research*. a. **online**. Indexes over 1,700 biographical dictionaries, including: *Standard & Poor's Register of Corporations, Directors and Executives*; *Dun & Bradstreet Reference Book of Corporate Management*; *Who's Who in Finance and Industry*; etc. Covers more than 3 million people encompassing 8 million citations.

187. **Business Media Directory**. *Bacon's Information*. a. $270. 'Covers

8,000 editors, beat reporters, columnists, frelancers and show producers at more than 1,000 top papers, magazines, radio and TV stations.'

188. **Consultants and Consulting Organizations Directory**. *Gale Research*. **diskette**. s-a. About 20,000 individuals and organizations in the USA available to act as consultants to business, industry and government.

189. **Current Biography**. *HW Wilson*. 11/year. $62. **cdrom**. $189/$129. There is also an annual *Current Biography Yearbook* ($62).

190. **Directory of Directors**. *Reed Information Services*. 'The 54,000 directors who control Britain's major companies are shown in volume 1, while volume 2 lists 15,000 companies and their 75,000 board members . . . For the first time many directors have included their year of birth . . . Our aim has been to compile the most accurate and comprehensive work of reference available. More than 70% of the entries shown have been updated since our last edition and 3,000 directors appear for the first time. We would like any director of a company with a paid-up capital of not less than £50,000 or a turnover in excess of £10 million who is not included, to inform the Editor of his/her appointment.'

191. **Duns Consultants Directory**. *Dun & Bradstreet International*. a. £329. 25,000 consulting firms in almost 200 separate specialities.

192. **Executive Speeches**. *Executive Speaker Company*. bi- m. $60. Features the full text of 10–20 speeches by executives. Includes quotations as well as listings of recently acquired speeches, books, & organization and agencies, that serve as information sources.

193. **Financial Planners and Planning Organizations Directory**. *Gale Research*. i. $195. More than 2,400 financial planners and 1,650 planning organizations are profiled in this directory.

194. **International Who's Who**. *Europa*. a. $260. Covers the world of leading men and women, both the famous and the less well-known. Bibliographical information about important figures from a wide variety of fields. Each entry gives nationality, date and place of birth, education, career details, present position, honours, awards, publications, current address, tel. no. and, wherever possible, personal interests.

195. **p180**. *PiMS UK Ltd*. **cdrom**. £1600. Access to 180,000 media contacts.

196. **Reference Book of Corporate Managements**. *Dun & Bradstreet International*. a. £649. Top executives in over 12,000 leading US corporations.

197. **Who's Who in European Business**. *Bowker-Saur*. i. £99. The top 5,000 business leaders in both Eastern and Western Europe.

198. **Who's Who in Finance and Industry**. *Marquis Who's Who*. a. $250. **cdrom** (as part of the *Complete Marquis Who's Who Plus*). Provides biographical coverage on more than 25,000 principal decision-makers and leaders. Data from this directory can also be searched within the One Source cdrom product *CD/Corporate: US Public Companies*.

199. **Who's Who in International Banking**. *Bowker-Saur*. i. £125. Provides

concise biographical and contact information on some 4,000 of today's leading bankers, including details about the entrant's education, career, civic interests, business and professional memberships, honours and awards, publications. Part 2 comprises a *Worldwide Banking Directory* 'spanning 130 territories and covering the world top 1000 banks, the European top 500, the American and the Asian top 200, the top 100 Latin American and the top 50 African banks'.

200. **Who's Who in Risk Capital (Year)**. *Initiative Europe*. a. £195. 'A biograhical directory of key investment executives. The book features over 1,000 individual entries from 300 companies in 19 countries.'

Tracing commercial information providers

118. There are a number of associations of commercial information providers who can provide useful leads for particular queries:

#48 American Business Press 675 3rd Avenue, Suite 415, New York, NY 10017, USA. t: (1 212) 661 6360; f: 370 0736.

#49 Association of Directory Publishers 105 Summer Street, Wrentham, MA 02093, USA. t: (1 508) 883 3688; f: 883 3717.

#50 Association of Information and Dissemination Services PO Box 8105, Athens, GA 30603, USA. t: (1 706) 542 6820; f: 542 0349.

#51 Audit Bureau of Circulation 207–209 High Street, Berkhamsted HP4 1AD, UK. t: (44 1442) 870800.

#52 Audit Bureau of Circulations 900 N Meacham Road, Schaumburg, IL 60173–4968, USA. t: (1 708) 605 0909; f: 605 0483.

'Formed in 1914 when advertisers, advertising agencies and publishers established ground rules for circulation auditing. ABC was created to enforce those rules and to provide audited circulation information to both the buyers and the sellers of advertised space . . . Every six months, ABC publisher members are required to file statements of their circulation which ABC issues as *Publisher's Statements* . . . For publishers who want to report substantial circulation changes, ABC can distribute an interim Publisher's Statement of circulation for the first three months within the regular six-month statement period . . . *Blue Books* . . . provide a compehensive reference collection of all Publisher's Statements issued for each filing period.'

201. **ABC Magazine Circulations**. m. **online**.

202. **ABC Newspaper Circulations**. m. **online**.

#53 BPA International 270 Madison Avenue, New York, NY 10016, USA. t: (1 212) 779 3200; f: 725 1721.

'Organization designed to verify the circulation data for the trade press and consumer magazines. Essentially, we perform a non-financial audit of subscriber demographics. . . . We are not a source for finance and banking but rather a source for advertising agencies trying to find the right subscriber audience for an advertiser's message.'

#54 Information Industry Association 555 New Jersey Avenue NW, Suite 800, Washington, DC 20001, USA. t: (1 202) 639 8262; f: 638 4403.

'Founded in 1968 . . . represents more than 550 companies involved in the creation, distribution, and use of information in print and digital formats . . . IIA's members range from entrepreneurial enterprises to Fortune 500 firms – from database publishers and information vendors to hardware manufacturers and software developers to telecommunication service providers and financial institutions. IIA's members are the leaders who have helped shape the industry as it exists today and are at the forefront of developing the new business environments of tomorrow. IIA is governed by its Board of Directors elected by the membership. Members participate through the Public Policy & Government Relations and Small & Emerging Business Councils, and six divisions and committees which address the market and media interests of member companies: Financial Information Services, Electronic Information Services, Optical Publishing, Voice Information Services, Directory Publishing, and Global Business Development.'

#55 Magazine Publishers of America 919 3rd Avenue, 22nd Floor, New York, NY 10022, USA. t: (1 212) 872 3700; f: 888 4217.

#56 National Federation of Abstracting & Information Services 1518 Walnut Street, Suite 307, Philadelphia, PA 19102, USA. t: (1 215) 893 1561; f: 893 1564.

'An international, not-for profit membership organization comprising more than 60 leading information producers, distributors, and corporate users of secondary information. Its purpose is to serve the world's information community through education, research and publication.'

203. **NFAIS Newsletter**. m. $110. News, features, and columns of interest to the abstracting and indexing community and the information industry, with member profiles and calendar listings.

204. **NFAIS Report Series**. 3/yr. $160. Research reports on critical issues of interest to the information industry, including global copyright issues, economics of database production, marketing guides, statistical information, human resources, and technological developments affecting the industry.

205. **NFAIS Yearbook of the Information Industry (Year)**. *Learned Information*. a. $50. Discusses the significant events that have influenced the information industry over the past year. Reviews critical issues, national and international policies. Features new technologies, with an emphasis on compact discs.

#57 New York Financial Writers' Association PO Box 21, Syosset, NY 11791, USA. t: (1 516) 921 7766; f: 921 5762.

'Founded in 1938 to raise the professional standards of financial journalism. Since then, business and financial news has moved from back among the stock tables to page one and has burgeoned throughout the broadcast media. The world's economic and financial system has become vastly more complex; its impact on everyday life has never been greater... Membership ... is open to business reporters, editors, and producers with newspapers, magazines, wire services, television, and radio in the New York metropolitan area with at least one year's professional experience. Approximately 100 news organizations are represented among the membership.'

#58 Newspaper Publishers Association 34 Southwark Bridge Road, London SE1 9EU, UK. t: (44 171) 928 6928; f: 928 2067.

#9 Periodical Publishers Association Imperial House, 15–19 Kingsway, London WC2B 6UN, UK. t: (44 171) 379 6268; f: 379 5661.

'The organisation of publishers of consumer, consumer specialist, business to business and professional magazines in the United Kingdom... The 200 or so publisher members produce more than 1,600 magazine titles which account for over 80 per cent by volume and value of magazine publishing in the UK.'

119. Publishers can be traced through:

206. **Complete Guide to Book Publishers in the UK**. *Searchline Publishing*. a. £65.

207. **Complete Guide to Magazine & Newspaper Publishers in the UK**. *Searchline Publishing*. a. £65.

208. **Directory of Publishing (Year)**. *Cassell* in association with *The Publishers Association* and *The Federation of European Publishers*. a. £115. Two volumes. 'The essential book trade directory'.

209. **Publishers Directory**. *Gale Research*. **diskette**. 18,000 currently active US and Canadian publishers and book distributors

210. **Publishers' International ISBN Directory**. *KG Saur*. a. $325. **cdrom**. Verified listings for publishers in 180 countries, indexed alphabetically, geographically and numerically by ISBN.

120. General media sources include:

211. **Bacon's International Media Directory**. *Bacon's Information*. a. $270. 'Comprehensive guide to over 23,000 trade, business and consumer magazines and newspapers throughout Western Europe.'

212. **Benn's Media**. *M-G Information Services*. a. £248. Three volumes: World, Europe and UK.

213. **Editors Media Directories**. *PR Newslink*. q. Volume 2: Business and Professional. £125.

214. **Gale Directory of Publications and Broadcast Media**. *Gale Research*. a. $290. **online**. s-a. Access both to print newsletters, magazines and directories as well as to radio and television stations and cable companies in one geographical sort.

215. **Guide to European Business Media**. *Lizard Limited*. s-a. £150. **diskette**. s-a. £400.

216. **Mediadisk PLUS**. *PR Newslink*. **diskette**. d. £1,980. 'Classified information on the entire UK media covering:

- National and regional daily newpapers
- Local weekly newspapers
- Trade journals
- Consumer magazines
- Radio and television stations and programmes
- London correspondents of foreign press
- A full list of editorial contacts
- Freelance journalists
- MPs

'Information includes addresses, telephone and fax numbers, frequency of publication, editorial policy, a publication profile and even type of photograph a publication will accept. Daily updates, by modem, ensure that changes in the UK media are integrated within the datanbase enabling the utmost precision when compiling media lists.'

Tracing information sources

121. First, some general business source guides:

217. **Bibliographic Index**. *HW Wilson*. 3/yr. **online**. **cdrom**. $395. Lists bibliographies with 50 or more citations published in books, pamphlets, or periodicals.

218. **Business Information Alert**. *Alert Publications*. 10/year. $152. **online**. The leading US-based journal for keeping up with new business information publications. Includes 'Subject guide to new business publications: 15–20 descriptive abstracts each issue; 5–8 critical reviews each issue'.

219. **Business Information Review**. *Headland Press*. q. £99. The leading UK-based journal of reviews and analysis of business information sources.

220. **Croner's A-Z of Business Information Sources**. *Croner Publications*. l. £114.80.

221. **Croner's European Business Information Sources**. *Croner Publications*. l. £109.75. 'Sources of information, advice and further contacts that can help you conduct your business across the national frontiers of the European states.'

222. **Directory of Business Information Resources**. *Grey House Publish-*

ing. a. $155. Associations, newsletters, magazines, trade shows. 8,000 entries, 800 pp.

223. **Encyclopedia of Business Information Sources**. *Gale Research*.

224. **European Business Intelligence Briefing**. *Headland Press*. 11/year. £129.

225. **Information Report**. *Washington Researchers*. m. **online**. Brief details of new US-based sources of business information; including studies, surveys, reports, directories, periodicals, databases. CD-ROMs, electronic bulletin boards etc. – including full ordering information and price (if any). Many sources listed are available free of charge, or at a very low cost.

226. **International Information Report**. *Washington Researchers*. **online**.

227. **What's New in Business Information**. *Headland Press*. 20/year. £129. Informative newsletter.

122. Turning now to specific forms of literature, there are a wide variety of print, cdrom and online sources that can be used to trace individual published items. We categorize these:

- Book reviews
- Books
- Conference proceedings and papers
- Market research reports
- Rankings
- Reference works
- Serial (and other) citations
- Statistics
- Theses and dissertations

BOOK REVIEWS

228. **Book Review Digest**. *HW Wilson*. 10/year. **online**. **cdrom**. $1,095. Covers about 6,500 English-language books per year.

229. **Book Review Index**. *Gale Research*. **online**. **cdrom**. Citations to reviews of books and new journals appearing in about 500 publications.

BOOKS

230. **Bibliographic Guide to Business and Economics**. *GK Hall*. a. $550. Three volumes. Covers books, reports, conference papers and miscellaneous publications in the New York Public Library, with additional entries covering all aspects of business and economics: history, population, demography, land-agriculture, industry, labour, transportation, communication, commerce, business administration, finance, foreign exchange, insurance, taxation, statistics.

231. **BookFind CD-Business & Law**. *Book Data*. **cdrom**. m. £750. Subset

of the the *BookFind-CD World Edition*, which covers over 2 million books.

232. **Books in Print (Year)**. *RR Bowker*. a. 10 vols. $425. **online**. **cdrom**. m. £875 (£1,195 for the version including *Book Reviews*). Covers English-language books currently published or distributed in the United States. The 1993–94 edition lists 1,153,000 titles from 41,000 United States publishers. There is also an **International Books in Print**, giving access to over 240,000 (1994) English-language titles published outside the US and UK.

233. **Boston Spa Books on CD-ROM**. *British Library Document Supply Centre*. **cdrom**. s-a. £425. 'Records of mainly English language books received at the Centre since 1980. The records include not only details of monographs but also theses, official publications, reports and translations. Approximately 650,000 records.'

234. **British MARC Quarterly**. *Library Corporation*. **cdrom**. q. $1,095.

235. **Cumulative Book Index**. *HW Wilson*. **online**. **cdrom**. $1,295.

236. **Global BookBank**. *Whitaker* and *RR Bowker* (and DW Thorpe). **cdrom**. m. £1,695. 'Combines the databases of the world book trade market leaders . . . Runs under the BRS software using the BookBank interface.' The Bowker version is marketed as the *Bowker-Whitaker Global Books in Print Plus*, and runs on the Plus System search software platform. The single 'Finder' disc offers approximately 2 million short format in-print and forthcoming bibliographical records from some 90,000 publishers throughout the world. There is also a two-disc 'Premium' service, with longer records.

237. **Harvard Business School Core Collection (Year)**. *Harvard Business School Press*. a. £55.95. 'Lists over 3,600 books – basic graduate textbooks, important business classics, up-to-date handbooks on principal management topics, and recent titles of general interest to the business reader – that Harvard Business School faculty, researchers, and students consider central to their work.'

238. **LaserCat**. *WLN*. **cdrom**. a. $1300. Over 4 million USMARC cataloguing records.

239. **LC MARC English**. *Library Corporation*. **cdrom**. w. $2,995. 'The complete de-duped Library of Congress English language MARC database . . . 3,747,300 records.'

240. **OCLC Online Union Catalog**. *OCLC*. **online**. 'The world's most comprehensive bibliography, with more than 28 million bibliographic records.' Also known as *WorldCat*.

241. **Whitaker's Books in Print (Year)**. *Whitaker*. a. Five volumes. **online**. **cdrom**. The 1994 edition contains details of about 600,000 titles from 22,000 publishers.

242. **WLN Database**. *WLN*. **online**. Contains more than 8 million MARC bibliographic records.

CONFERENCE PROCEEDINGS AND PAPERS

243. **Bibliographic Guide to Conference Publications**. *GK Hall*. a. $325. Indexes approximately 26,000 private and government conference publications including proceedings, reports, and summaries of conferences, meetings, and symposia in all fields.

244. **Boston Spa Conferences on CD-ROM**. *British Library Document Supply Centre*. q. £450. Over 300,000 records so far. There is a monthly print version; and the dataset is also available **online**.

245. **Directory of Published Proceedings**. *InterDok Corporation*. Series SSH: *Social Sciences/Humanities*. q. $365.

246. **PapersFirst**. *OCLC*. **online**. 'Index to individual papers presented at conferences, symposia, and proceedings worldwide.'

247. **ProceedingsFirst**. *OCLC*. **online**. 'Tables of contents for papers presented at worldwide conferences, professional meetings, and symposia.'

MARKET RESEARCH REPORTS

248. **FINDEX (Year)**. *Euromonitor Publications*. a. £275. **online**. 'The most complete guide to market research reports, studies and surveys. Details of around 9,900 market research reports . . . The **cdrom** *Market Research Locator* 'is the electronic equivalent of the printed publication . . . but with 17,000 market reports from over 700 international publishers, it is more than twice the size of the printed equivalent. It has recently been enhanced with additional European coverage, by covering more European publishers and more European markets.'

249. **Marketing Surveys Index**. *Marketing Strategies for Industry*. l. £385. **online**. 'The most efficient reliable and cost effective source of world wide market reports . . . More than 1000 publishers from around the world contribute to MSI.'

RANKINGS

250. **Business Rankings Annual (Year)**. *Gale Research*. a. $140. Includes for instance rankings for: accounting firms, banks and banking, brokers, corporations, financial institutions, insurance, investment activities, and stocks. Each entry includes a list of up to 10 items in the ranking.

251. **European Business Rankings**. *Gale Research*. 2,250 business statistics and rankings from thoughout Europe.

REFERENCE WORKS

252. **Current British Directories**. *CBD Research Limited*. i. £140. '4,100 directories published in Britain . . . 60 local publications . . . Index of over 1,150 publishers with full contact details & publications.' 12th edition, 1993.

253. **Current European Directories**. *CBD Research Limited*. i. £140. **cdrom**. Covers 3,000 directories: 3rd edition, 1994.

254. **Directories in Print**. *Gale Research*. a. **diskette**. 15,000 entries, for directories published in the USA and overseas.

255. **Guide to American Directories**. *Klein Publications*. bi-a. $85. Covers over 200 classifications of business, industry and the professions.

256. **Reference and Research Books News**. *Books News*. 8/yr. $40. Concise, subject-arranged reviews of new scholarly and reference books appropriate for academic and public libraries and librarians.

257. **Trade Directories of the World**. *Croner Publications*. l. $89.90.

SERIAL (AND OTHER) CITATIONS

258. **ABI/INFORM**. *UMI*. **online**. **cdrom**. m. Business and management database available in a choice of three editions: *Global* Over 1000 titles – including 350 non-US titles; *Research* Over 800 titles; *Select* Over 350 titles plus the most recent six months of the *Wall Street Journal*.

259. **ArticleFirst**. *OCLC*. **online**. 'Bibliographic citations that decribe items listed on the table of contents pages of more than 11,500 journals . . . Records contain OCLC library holdings, and many include abstracts.'

260. **BusinessNews**. *Individual*. **online**. d. Brief summaries of two week's worth of news items from *HeadsUp*, a service that provides access to news items gleaned from 300 wire services and other news sources, covering industry, business and company news.

261. **Business Periodicals Ondisc**. *UMI*. **cdrom**. Full images of the articles in nearly 450 business and management journals. 'A subscription includes the *ABI/Inform* database which serves as an index to the full text.'

262. **Business Periodicals Index**. *HW Wilson*. m. **online**. **cdrom**. $1,495. Covers about 350 periodicals, with since April 1993 daily indexing of the *Wall Street Journal* and the Business Section of the *New York Times* in the electronic version of the Index.

263. **ContentsFirst**. *OCLC*. **online**. 'Contains the complete table of contents pages and holdings information from more than 11,500 journals.'

264. **Current Contents**. *Institute for Scientific Information*. w. **online**. Citations, with abstracts from some 7000 journals across the whole of the humanities, social sciences and sciences.

265. **Globalbase**. *Infomat*. **online**. Almost a million summaries of articles taken from some 700 worldwide publications, over 90 per cent of which are published outside the USA.

266. **Institute of Management International Databases Plus.** *Bowker-Saur*. *cdrom*. q. £799. 'This is the largest, most comprehensive collection of multi-media resources on management.' Includes coverage of journals,

books, management working papers, short courses, audio-visual material, company practices, training packages, all primarily focussing on the UK.

267. **Magazine Index**. *Information Access Company*. **online**. Indexes 500 popular magazines, mainly published in North America. A separate file **Magazine ASAP** selectively provides the complete text for about 130 of the publications covered.

268. **Periodical Abstracts**. *UMI*. **cdrom**. m. Abstracts of articles in some 1,500 general serials with a rolling six months of the *Wall Street Journal* and the *New York Times*. Also available in other configurations.

269. **PROMT**. *Information Access Company*. **online**. Some 3 million citations with selected full texts covering international business literature.

270. **Research Index**. *Business Surveys*. l. £295. **online**.

271. **Social Sciences Index/Full Text**. *UMI*. **cdrom**. 'Instant access to the full image of over 200 periodicals in the Social Sciences field.'

272. **Social SciSearch**. *Institute for Scientific Information*. **online**.

273. **Trade & Industry Index**. *Information Access Company*. **online**. Provides indexing and selective abstracting of over 300 trade and industry journals, as well as comprehensive but selective coverage of business and trade information from nearly 1,200 additional publications. **Trade & Industry ASAP** provides selective complete text and indexing for over 200 of these journals, plus news releases from *PR Newswire*.

274. **Wilson Business Abstracts**. *HW Wilson*. m. **online**. **cdrom**. $2,495. Access to 350 leading English-language business magazines. Includes about 75,000 abstracts per year.

STATISTICS

275. **Current Index to Statistics: Applications, Methods and Theory**. *American Statistical Association* in association with the *Institute of Mathematical Statistics*. a. $75. Keyword index of articles from statistical journals and related publications, worldwide.

276. **Statistical Masterfile**. *Congressional Information Service*. **cdrom**. q. $10,045. 'Access to authoritative statistics from:

- The US Government: **American Statistics Index** (ASI) unlocks the world's largest and most prolific source of statistical data: the US government. Spanning the mid-1960s to the present, ASI covers every kind of statistical publication of general research value from more than 500 federal agencies.
- Across America: **Statistical Reference Index** offers precise access to statistical information from leading American sources outside the US government. SRI covers statistical publications of some 1,000 associations and institutes, businesses and commercial publishers, state government agencies, and independent and university research centers. SRI covers from 1981 to the present.

- Across the world: **Index to International Statistice** (IIS) covers statistics published by approximately 100 international intergovernmental organizations since 1983. Among these are the United Nations and its affiliated agencies, the European Community, the Organization for Economic Co-operation and Development, the Organization of American States, major commodity organizations and many other sources.'

ASI is also available for searching **online**.

277. **Statistics Sources (Year)**. *Gale Research*. a. Two volumes. 95,000 citations to over 2000 statistics sources, arranged in a single alphabetical sequence. Includes in addition sections covering: Selected Bibliography of Key Statistical Sources; Federal Statistical Telephone Contacts; Federal Statistical Data Bases. There are two Appendices: Source Publications; Sources of Nonpublished Statistical Data.

THESES AND DISSERTATIONS

278. **Dissertation Abstracts**. *UMI*. **online**. **cdrom**. Covers virtually every doctoral dissertation completed at accreditated institutions in the US. Some master's theses and foreign language dissertations are included. Abstracting and indexing of nearly 1,500,000 theses. There is also a *Dissertation Abstracts International*.

Tracing information professionals

123. The three main UK-based information science/library professional bodies – each of which has special interest groups concerned with the subject field of this text – are:

(a) **#60 Aslib** The Association for Information Management, Information House, 20–24 Old Street, London EC1V 9AP, UK. t: (44 171) 253 4488; f: 430 0514. e: pubs@aslib.demon.co.uk.

'Aslib . . . as the National Awareness Partner for the *IMPACT 2* (Information Market Policy Actions) Programme of the Commission of the European Union Directorate for General for Telecommunications, Information Market and Exploitation of Research (DG XIII), provides the latest information on the activities of IMPACT, the Commission and the European information market . . . The NAP network extends awareness of professional electronic information services throughout the Member States of the European Union and EFTA.'

279. **Aslib Directory of Information Sources in the United Kingdom**. i. (8th ed., 1994). £250. **cdrom** £285. 'With 8034 entries, completely revised and updated, plus a compendium of sources on the EU Single Market, a comprehensive list of acronyms and over 3000 index terms, this directory is an encyclopedia of UK information sources. . . . New features of the eight edition include a separate category for organizations holding trade and statistical information, of vital importance to business, and expanded

details of publications, particularly valuable for tracking newsletters and pamphlets which, as grey literature, are often extremely difficult to procure.

280. **Aslib Index to Theses**. *Learned Information*. q. £175. **cdrom**. 'The only authoritative and comprehensive bibliography of theses accepted for higher degrees by the Universities of Great Britain and Ireland.'

281. **Managing Information**. 10/year. £49. Collections of news, articles, book reviews – with an especial emphasis on the management of electronic information sources.

282. **Online and CD Notes**. 10/year. £85. News of developments in the electronic information industry.

(b) **#61 Institute of Information Scientists** 44–45 Museum Street, London WC1A 1LY, UK. t: (44 171) 631 8003; f: 430 1270. Special interest groups include:

- *City Information Group*
- *UK Online User Group*

(c) **#62 Library Association** 7 Ridgmount Street, London WC1E 7AE, UK. t: (44 171) 636 7543. *Library Association Publishing* f: 636 3627; e: lapublishing@la-hq.org.uk.

283. **Walford's Guide to Reference Material**. i. Three volumes. Volume 2 covers *Social and Historical Sciences, Philosophy and Religion*. (6th ed. 1994. 1,156 pp. £130.)

124. In the United States, the major organizations are:

#63 American Library Association 50 E Huron Street, Chicago, IL 60611–2795, USA. t: (1 800) 545 2433; f: (1 312) 944 2641.

#64 American Society for Information Science 8720 Georgia Avenue, Box 501, Silver Spring, MD 20910, USA. t: (1 301) 495 0900; f: 495 0810.

#65 Special Libraries Association 1700 Eighteenth Street NW, Washington, DC 20009–2508, USA. t: (1 202) 234 4700; f: 265 9317. e: sla1@capcon.net. *Newsletter*.

'The second largest library and information-related association in America and the third largest in the world.' The SLA has a *Business and Finance Division*.

284. **Guide to Special Issues and Indexes of Periodicals**. i. $56.

285. **Special Libraries**. q.

286. **Who's Who in Special Libraries (Year)**. a. $60.

125. There are a large number of specialist associations involved with one or another aspect of financial information provision. Two contrasting examples are:

#66 Reference Point Foundation Two University Plaza, Suite 414, Hackensack, NJ 07601, USA. t: (1 201) 996 1880; f: 996 1883.

'The Reference Point Foundation does not produce publications, but rather we promote the use of public access using computer technologies. One of the ways we accomplish that is though an online system called the *Information Exchange*, which is a nonprofit public utility for electronic dissemination of public information. Nonprofit information providers use the Information Exchange to distribute their publications, papers, research etc. Our major distribution channel is through the public library system.'

#67 Society of Competitive Intelligence Professionals 1700 Diagonal Road, Suite 520, Alexandria, VA 22314, USA. t: (1 703) 739 0696; f: 739 2524. *Newsletter*.

'*Competitive Intelligence* The process of ethically collecting, analyzing and disseminating accurate, relevant, specific, timely, foresighted and actionable intelligence regarding the implications of the business environment, competitors and the organization itself.'

126. Finally, information professionals within the UK and Europe can be traced via two reliable publications – both of which have subject indexes:

287. **Who's Who in the European Information World (Year)**. *TFPL Publishing*. a. £135.

288. **Who's Who in the UK Information World (Year)**. *TFPL Publishing*. a. £90. 'Information specialists, librarians and record managers from commercial organisations, national libraries, government departments, academic institutions, public libraries, charities, associations, research institutions etc.; lecturers in library and information science; information brokers and consultants; key individuals from information industry suppliers (on-line database providers/hosts, publishers, CD-ROM publishers, library suppliers/subscription agents, automated library systems).'

Subject specific tools

127. We will now list examples of a range of secondary and tertiary publications which can be used to answer more specific subject queries. These are classified into three sub-sections:

- Legal, economic and political environments
- Financial institutions and markets
- The electronic imperative

The first two are further categorized into sources which have an international, European, United Kingdom and United States dimension; the last into sources used primarily as reference works, and those used for current awareness.

LEGAL, ECONOMIC AND POLITICAL ENVIRONMENTS

• *International*

#68 International Association of Law Libraries PO Box 5709, Washington, DC 20016–1309, USA. t: (1 202) 662 6152; f: 778 6652.

'Founded in 1959, the IALL now has over 500 members in more than 50 countries on five continents . . . (It) is a worldwide association of librarians, libraries and other persons and institutions concerned with the acquisition and use of legal information emanating from sources other than their own jurisdictions. The IALL's basic purpose is to facilitate the work of librarians who acquire, process, and utilize foreign and international legal resources.'

Serials

289. **Accounting and Tax Database**. *UMI*. **online**. **cdrom**. 'Abstracts and indexing to over 300 key accounting, tax and financial management publications, plus selected articles from more than 800 additional newspapers, business journals and magazines.'

290. **Accounting Articles**. m. *Commerce Clearing House*. 'This service will alert you to key accounting developments across the world. It highlights current articles published in accounting, business and other publications covering many phases of accounting. Reports span articles from periodicals in the United States, Canada, the United Kingdom, Australia and Asia; published proceedings and papers delivered at accounting institutes; as well as pronouncements of the *American Institute of Certified Public Accountants* and Statements of the *Financial Accounting Standards Board*, the US *Governmental Accounting Standards Board* and the *International Federation of Accountants*.'

291. **Accounting Research Directory**. *Paul Chapman Publishing*. i. (3rd ed., 1994). £57.50. Database of accounting literature, covering seven journals: *Accounting Review*; *Accounting, Organizations and Society*; *Auditing: A Journal of Theory and Practice*; *Contemporary Accounting Research*; *Journal of Accounting & Economics*; *Journal of Accounting Research*; *Journal of Accounting, Auditing and Finance*.

292. **Butterworths International Law Directory**. *Reed Information Services*. 'Details more than 6,000 international law offices and their 14,000 lawyers in 140 countries, plus information on branches and areas of expertise.'

293. **Catalog of New Foreign and International Law Titles**. *Ward and Associates*. bi-m. $250.

294. **Index to Legal Periodicals**. *HW Wilson*. 11/year. $260. **online**. **cdrom**.

$1,495. 'Coverage of over 630 noted law journals, yearbooks, institutes, university publications, and law reviews published in the United States, Puerto Rico, Great Britain, Ireland, Canada, Australia and New Zealand . . . Broadened its scope to include monograph coverage in 1994.'

295. **Information Technology and the Law**. *Martinus Nijhoff Publishers.* s-a. $149.50. Comprehensive international bibliography of significant literature in the field of legal information science and computer law.

296. **International Directory of Government (Year)**. *Europa Publications.* i. £210. 'Details over 15,000 government ministries, departments, agencies, corporations and their connected bodies from every country in the world.'

297. **PAIS International**. *Public Affairs Information Service.* m. $540. **online**. **cdrom**. Almost 400,000 citations to literature across the social sciences with an emphasis on public affairs and policy.

298. **PTS Forecasts**. *Information Access Company.* **online**. Summaries of articles, with an emphasis on statistical forecasting data, culled from a wide range of trade, government and research publications

299. **Sage Public Administration Abstracts**. *Sage Publications.* q. £202. 'All aspects of public administration.'

300. **UNBIS Plus on CD-ROM**. **cdrom**. q. £1,995/£595. Published for and on behalf of the *United Nations* by *Chadwyck-Healey*. 'Much more than a bibliographic database of UN documents and publications. It includes citations to tens of thousands of non-UN publications acquired by the UN libraries in New York and Geneva and also contains – for the major UN organs – the full text of resolutions, voting information and citations to speeches.'

301. **World Agricultural Economics and Rural Sociology Abstracts**. *CAB International.* m. $661. **diskette**. **cdrom**. 'Aspects include: Agricultural economics . . . Supply, demand and prices . . . International trade . . . Finance and credit . . . Farm economics . . . Cooperatives.'

- *Europe*

#69 European Information Association c/o Central Library, St Peter's Square, Manchester M2 5PD, UK. t: (44 161) 228 3691; f: 236 6547. *Newsletter*.

Serials

302. **Directory of EC Information Sources**. *Euroconfidentiel.* a. £165. 'Since the first edition in 1989, the Directory of EC Information Sources has been regarded as an indispensable reference work and is to be found in the offices of decision makers worldwide . . . Now fondly known as "*the Bible*" amongst EC buffs.' The Directory contains the following Parts:

- The European Commission Information Source
- The European Parliament Information Source

- The EC's Other Institutions Sources of Information
- Foreign Representatives in Brussels
- Press Agencies and Journalists Specialising in EC News
- Consultants Specialising in Community Questions
- Lawyers and Legal Advisors Specialising in Community Questions
- Professional Organizations Sources of Information
- Postgraduate Degrees in European Integration

303. **EC Institutions' Yellow Pages**. *Euroconfidential*. a. 4,100 BEF. 'Details of key personnel in each of the major institutions: European Commission, European Parliament, Council, Economic and Social Committee, Court of Justice, European Investment Bank, Court of Auditors.'

304. **Euro Who's Who**. *Editions Delta*. 4,500 BEF. 'Includes biographies of the senior civil servants currently working within the European Communities (Council, Commission, European Parliament . . .) and within twenty other European governmental organizations . . . the chairmen and secretaries of the main non-governmental organizations and of the trade and professional associations set up at European level.'

305. **European Access**. *Chadwyck-Healey*. m. £130. An excellent tool for keeping up-to-date on developments in the European Union and Europe more generally.

306. **European Legal Journals Index**. *Legal Information Resources*. m. £333. Subsets are available on **diskette**. Includes articles relating to the legal developments concerning the Council of Europe, European Communities, and individual European countries – including Central and Eastern Europe – drawn from nearly 300 periodical titles.

307. **European References**. *Chadwyck-Healey*. **cdrom**. q. £700. 'Two of the foremost European Union bibliographic reference databases – *SCAD* (prepared by the EC Documentation Service) and *Spicers Centre for Europe* (prepared by Consultancy Europe Associates).'

308. **European Lobbyists Practical Guide**. *European Study Service*. a. 2,900 BEF. 'Professional associations engaged in lobbying . . . The Guide will prove invaluable to industrial and trading companies, banks, research firms, chambers of commerce, lawyers and consultants, as they will be able to see, at a glance, the organisation to contact.'

309. **Who's Who in European Institutions, Organizations and Enterprises: (Year)**. *Sutter's International Red Series*. a. £125.

310. **Who's Who in European Politics**. *Bowker-Saur*. i. £159. Covers over 8,000 politicians.

311. **Yearbook of the European Communities and of the other European Organizations**. *Editions Delta*. a. 5,900 BEF. 'An indispensable working tool for those needing accurate information on the structure and operation of the European Communities and on the bodies, whether private or public, which contribute to European integration: twenty other European governmental organizations: political, economic, scientific, technical and military (Council of Europe, WEU, CERN etc.); some 300 non-govern-

mental organizations . . . European university studies; European publications.'

• *United Kingdom*

#70 British and Irish Association of Law Librarians c/o 11 Lamintone Drive, Leamington Spa, Warwickshire, CV32 6SJ. t: (44 1926) 430000.

'Full membership is open to persons and institutions engaged in the provision or exploitation of law. Associate membership is open to individuals not so engaged, but who support the aims of the Association.'

312. The **Law Librarian**. *Sweet & Maxwell*. q. £38.

Serials

313. **Butterworths Law Directory**. *Reed Information Services*. 13,000 law firms and 40,000 solicitors in private practice. Over 6,000 barristers and their chambers, plus international law firms and other legal personnel.

314. **Councils, Committees & Boards**. *CBD Research Limited*. i. £110. '1,300 official and semi-official bodies in the UK . . . Index of chairmen'. 8th edition, 1993.

315. **Daily Law Reports Index**. *Legal Information Resources*. **diskette**. w. £450.

316. **Legal Articles Monthly**. *Legal Information Resources*. m. £144. 'Provides both tailor-made and ready-made current awareness in many different subject areas.'

317. **Legal Information Management Index**. *Legal Information Services*. bi-m. $118. Covers articles, bibliographies, surveys and critical reviews relating to legal information management and law librarianship.

318. **Legal Information Resources CD-ROM**. *Legal Information Resources*. **cdrom**. 3/year. £895. Covers all the company's databases, complete from their start dates.

319. **Legal Journals Index**. *Legal Information Resources*. m. £620. **diskette**. m. £450. Subsets are available on **diskette**. 'Indexes and briefly abstracts some 280 periodicals, published in the UK and covering the very wide scope of interest to lawyers.'

• *United States*

#71 American Association of Law Libraries 53 W Jackson Blvd, Chicago, IL 60604, USA. t: (1 312) 939 4764; f: 431 1097. *Occasional Papers* (e.g. 'Guidelines for cataloguing the files available through Lexis (June 1992)'. *Directory* (a. $100).

320. **Index to Foreign Legal Periodicals**. q. **online**. Produced with the *University of California Press*. Covers over 400 journals.

Serials

321. **Bernan Associates' Government Publications News**. *Bernan Associates.* 10/year.

322. **Best Lawyers in America**. *Woodward-White.* bi-a. $110. Lists approximately 12,000 of the best attorneys in the US as determined through a national poll of their peers.

323. **Bibliographic Guide to Government Publications**. *GK Hall.* a. $495. Covers all state, regional and federal government literature.

324. **Bimonthly Review of Law Books**. *Fred B Rothman.* bi-m. $80. Provides law librarians, legal academics and lawyers with reviews of contemporary legal topics.

325. **Bowne Digest for Corporate and Securities Lawyers**. *Brumberg Publications.* m. **online**. Abstracts of current articles from more than 280 legal periodicals.

326. (Year) **Capital Guide**. *Savings & Community Bankers of America.* a. $12. 'Names, phone numbers, and committee and subcommittee assignments of each House and Senate member. . . . Listings of federal agencies, executive departments and other government players who make a difference in the laws and policies affecting your institution. Banking, housing, real estate and related trade organisations are listed as well.'

327. **Capital Source**. *National Journal.* s-a. $80. **online**. Telephone directory of the Washington power structure, including government officials, trade associations, interest groups, political consultants and news media.

328. **CIS Federal Register Index**. *Congressional Information Service.* w. $675.

329. **CIS/Index to Publications of the United States Congress**. *Congressional Information Service.* m. $5,085 (with microfiche: $16,395). **online**. **cdrom** (*Congressional Masterfile 2 on CD-ROM*). q. $7,120. 'Congress is the single most important information-producing institution in the US. Its legislative acts are just the tip of an enormous iceberg. Behind every major law enacted – or even considered – lies months, often years, of intensive investigation and analysis. In addition, Congress continually monitors the activities of federal agencies and many matters of current interest. This takes place not on the floor of Congress, but in the offices and hearing rooms of its committees.

The 'working papers' that result from these efforts often represent the best information available on a given subject. After all, Congress not only has some of the nation's top experts on its staff, but has the authority to call witnesses from the public and private sectors, from around the country and throughout the world.

CIS developed its reference system to manage the hundreds of thousands of pages of information published each year by congessional committees. Cited as one of the 'landmarks in legal publishing' in the book of the same title, the *CIS/Index* has enduring research value not only for lawyers but for historians, political scientists, and researchers in a variety of other fields.

CIS editors systematically identify, collect, index, and analyze the publications of some 300 active House, Senate and joint committees and subcommittees. These publications include committee hearings and prints, reports, documents, and special publications.

330. **Congress in Print**. *Congressional Quarterly*. w. 'Catalog of everything published by Congress. Lists documents by subject and provides all needed ordering information.'

331. **Criminal Justice Abstracts**. *Willow Tree Press*. q. $150. **cdrom**. q. $395. 'Comprehensive coverage of the major journals in criminology and related disciplines, extensive coverage of books, and unparalleled access to reports from government and nongovernmental agencies.'

332. **Federal News Service**. *UMI*. **cdrom**. 'Full text transcripts of US government press briefings, speech interviews and statements.'

333. **Government Information Quarterly**. *Jai Press*. q.

334. **Government Reference Books**. *Libraries Unlimited*. bi.a. $65. Identifies key information resources from the printed matter issued by US government agencies. Arranged in four sections: general reference, social sciences, science and technology, and humanities.

335. **Law and Legal Information Directory**. *Gale Research*. bi-a. $320. Guide to law enforcement organizations and legal information in the US.

336. **Law Books and Serials in Print (Year)**. *RR Bowker*. a. £474. Three volumes. 'A multimedia sourcebook . . . With over 60,000 titles intended *exclusively* for legal professionals, this unmatched bibliography lists virtually every legal resource available in North America – books and serials, microfiche, audio and video cassettes, CD-ROM, software, and online databases . . . Includes descriptive annotations which provide expert guidance on selecting the right sources for every research need.'

337. **Law Firms Yellow Book**. *Monitor Leadership Directories*. s-a. $170. Covers more than 675 American Bar Association member law firms, lists more than 14,000 key individuals with a management role, departmental heads, managing partners of branch offices, and administrators of central and branch offices.

338. **Law Librarian's Bulletin Board**. *Legal Information Services*. 8/year. $36. Provides international coverage of news and developments in law libraries, government information, library organizations, industry news and job listings.

339. **Legal Publisher**. *JK Publishing*. m. $149. Contains information on new legal information books, magazines, newsletters, online services and related material.

340. **Legal Information Alert**. *Alert Publications*. 10/year. $159. **online**. 'Articles and book reviews of new legal information products written by practising law librarians.'

341. **Martindale-Hubbell Law Directory**. a. $645. Twenty-four volumes. 'For over a hundred years. lawyers, and every user of legal services in the US have looked to this Directory for information on their colleagues, as well as quick access to digests of laws. Now available as a powerful **cdrom** (q. $995), it contains over 800,000 lawyers and 50,000 law firms . . . (Also contains) portraits of the international community's 4,000 leading firms and their personnel.'

342. **Recent Titles in Law for the Subject Specialist**. *Ward and Associates.* bi-m. $630. Price covers 23 lists as a package. 'The only selection and reference tool which presents recent acquisitions of the nation's law libraries in each of 23 subject areas. Contributors include some 60 academic, bar, and law firm libraries . . . and the Library of Congress.' Subject areas include: banking, finance (including securities) and investment; taxation and estate planning; trade regulation and economics.

343. **Reports Required by Congress**. *Congressional Information Service.* q. $595 (index; with microfiche, $3795). **cdrom**. 'Access to federal department and agency reports required by law.'

344. **Washington Representatives (Year)**. *Columbia Books.* a. 'Who does what for whom in the nation's capital. A compilation of Washington representatives of the major national associations, labor unions and US companies, registered foreign agents, lobbyists, lawyers, law firms and special interest groups, together with their clients and areas of legislative and regulatory concern.'

345. **Who's Who in Congress**. *Congressional Quarterly.* bi.a.

FINANCIAL INSTITUTIONS AND MARKETS

- *International*

346. **GT Guide to World Equity Markets (Year)**. *Euromoney Publications* with *GT Management.* a. £100. Overview, 39 major country chapters plus sections on emerging markets and Eastern Europe. Each chapter follows a consistent format of ten major sections, including: Taxation and regulations affecting foreign investors; reporting requirements for companies listed on the stock exchanges, the level of protection given to shareholders, and the type of research facilities available to the foreign investor.

347. (Year) **Handbook of World Stock and Commodity Exchanges**. *Blackwell Business.* a. £250. 'Established itself as the definitive guide to stock, futures and options exchanges worldwide.'

348. **World Banking Abstracts**. *Blackwells.* bi-m. £345. Published in association with the *Institute of European Finance* and the *Chartered Institute of Bankers.* 'An invaluable reference source providing immediate access to 400 concise abstracts of key, contemporary articles of practical interest to banking and financial services managers . . . Over 400 journals and other publications are regularly surveyed by an expert team of banking and finance researchers. These periodicals include specialised research reports that are not widely available such as those from the US Federal

Reserve Banks, the EC research institutes and universities throughout the world, and English translated abstracts from leading foreign-language journals in banking and financial services . . . WBA has proved an important aid to a wide range of professionals, including bankers in all main banking functions, strategic planners, marketeers, regulators, finance, treasury specialists, accountants, consultants and trainers.'

349. **World Directory of Stock Exchanges**. *Bowker-Saur*. i. £195. 'Details on 108 stock exchanges in 54 countries. A wide range of information is given including:

- financial data and trading information
- a price index and tables to show how other stock exchanges are doing in your currency
- unique historical financial data
- the rules, chief participants and taxes
- full contact details for each exchange.'

- *Europe*

350. **European Business and Industry**. *Who's Who Edition*. a. Two volumes. I. *Biographies*; II. *Companies*.

- *United Kingdom*

351. **Banking Journals Index**. *Legal Information Resources*. **diskette**. m. £395. Covers about 70 primarily UK published journals.

352. **Insurance Journals Index**. *Legal Information Resources*. **diskette**. m. £450. Covers 100 journals on insurance, risk management and related topics. Contains information on insurance and reinsurance companies and brokers, cases, legislation, and new products pertinent to insurance.

353. **Oliver's Guide to the City of London**. *AP Information Services*. bi-a. £15. 'This unique business guide lists the key senior personnel by name, the addresses, business activities, telephone numbers and fax numbers for all companies in the City of London both alphabetically and by business sector.'

354. **Pensions Journals Index**. *Legal Information Resources*. **diskette**. m. £350. Covers over 45 pensions and employee benefits journals and newsletters. Contains references to articles, cases and legislation on occupational, personal and state retirement pensions, employee benefits, and pension fund management and investment.

- *United States*

355. **Banking Information Index**. *UMI*. q. $283.

356. **Banking Information Source Ondisc**. *UMI*. **cdrom**. 'Abstracts and indexing to articles from more than 300 core publications relevant to the financial services industry.'

357. **Finance Literature Database**. *McGraw-Hill*.

358. **III Data Base**. *Insurance Information Institute*. **online**. 'Selects and abstracts the most important materials being published by trade associations, the business, trade and consumer press and government agencies.'

359. **III Insurance Daily**. *Insurance Information Institute*. d. $7 per business day (Fax). **online**. 'At 8.30 a.m. each business day the III Insurance Daily, a compilation of abstracts on insurance-related topics from national and local papers, is distributed electronically to some 125 organizations which use it to expand their own information resources. . . . No newsletter covering the insurance industry is as comprehensive or as current as the Insurance Daily. Subscribers are the leading insurers in the U.S. as well as brokers, reinsurers, and law and consulting firms.'

360. **Insurance Periodicals Index**. *NILS Publishing Company*. a. $120. **online**. Published in association with the *Special Libraries Association: Insurance and Employee Benefits Division*. 'The industry's only comprehensive index to articles appearing in the insurance and employee benefits press. The Index covers articles, book reviews, statistical reports, new product information, letters to the editor and obituaries . . . Annually indexes more than 15,000 articles from over 30 major trade publications.'

THE ELECTRONIC IMPERATIVE

Reference works

361. **Business & Legal CD-ROMs in Print**. *Mecklermedia*. a. $55. 'Over 1700 CDROM products in business and law, including economics, patent information, taxation, finance, related government information and management.'

362. **Cd-rom Directory**. *TFPL Publishing*. a. £102. **cdrom**. s-a. £149. 'Definitive guide to all CD-ROM & multimedia CD titles published in the world, plus all companies involved in the industry.' Awarded the 1994 prize for the best printed directory by the *Directory Publishers Association*.

363. **CD-ROMS in Print**. *Mecklermedia*. a. $129.95. **cdrom**. 'Each of the 8,000 entries . . . includes a full description of the CD, key subjects covered, computer specifications, price, publisher, multimedia content,and much more. Contact information is given for each of the 3,800 publishing and distribution companies listed.'

364. **CompuServe Companion**. *Bibliodata*. a. $29.95. 'Newspapers, magazines and newsletters that are on CompuServe.'

365. **Directory of Law-Related CD-ROMs**. *Infosources Publishing*. a. $49. Provides detailed information on 450 CD-ROM products in the areas of law, legislation and regulation: includes publisher, search software and subject indexes. A *Supplement* is also available (3/year. $39).

366. **Gale Directory of Databases**. *Gale Research*. s-a. Three volumes. **online**. **cdrom**. **diskette**. Comprehensive coverage with detailed descriptions of some 9,000 databases in all subject fields available for searching

online; or delivered as cd-rom, diskette, magnetic tape or handheld products (or available for searching by batch access); or accessible via The Internet. The standard tool.

367. **European Multimedia Yearbook (Year)**. *Interactive Media Publications*. a. £101. "I'm absolutely bowled over with it. Anyone who doubted that there was a multimedia industry should rush out and buy it" (*Inside IT*).

368. **Fulltext Sources Online**. *BiblioData*. bi-a. $162. **online**. Covers some 5,000 'periodicals, newspapers, newsletters, newswires and TV/radio transcripts', reproduced on the following database vendors:

BRS
Burrelle's Broadcast Database
Data-Star
Datatimes
Dialog
Dow Jones News/Retrieval
FT Profile
G.Cam/EDD
Genios Wirschaftsdatenbanken
Info Globe
Infomart Online
Lexis/Nexis
NewsNet
Nikkei Telecom
QL Systems
Reuters
STN International
Westlaw

The publishers also offer *Custom Fulltext Sources Online*: a tailor-made version limited to and focused on specific vendors – with unlimited distribution rights within the subscribing organization.

369. **Information Industry Directory**. *Gale Research*. **diskette**. a. More than 30,000 organizations, systems and services worldwide involved in the production and distribution of information in electronic formats.

370. **Interactive Media International Newsletter**. *Interactive Media Publications*. m. £155.

371. **On INTERNET (Year)**. *Mecklermedia*. a. £24. 'An international guide to electronic journals, newsletters, texts, discussion lists and other resources on the Internet.'

372. **Online/CD-ROM Business Sourcebook**. *Headland Press*. a. £129. 'The only evaluative guide to electronic business databases. It is designed to indicate to the business user those databases which are likely to be of most use in searching for a particular category of information . . . The Sourcebook is unique in several ways:

- It deals with the full range of business databases in a single volume

- It emphasises UK and European services, while also covering the important files emanating from the USA and the rest of the world
- It evaluates databases, rather than merely describing them
- It is selective, presenting information on the most important databases
- It gives detailed analysis of the major host systems
- It includes diskette products and CD-ROMs, expanding the traditional definition of "online" databases
- It is completely updated each year to enable users to keep up-to-date.

The Sourcebook currently contains information on 80 hosts, eight major CD-ROM publishers and 1,289 electronic databases, including 302 on CD-ROM.' A valuable guide.

373. **National Directory of Bulletin Board Systems**. *Meckler*. a. $45.

374. **Newspapers Online**. *BiblioData*. a. $99. Covers 200 'local, regional, national and international daily newspapers online in full text and full coverage . . . Is a search tips book which helps those who need to search newspapers on major commercial systems figure out what is in the online file, and how to find it'.

375. **On Internet: An International Title and Subject Guide to Electronic Journals, Newsletters, Books and Discussion Lists on the Internet**. *Meckler*. a. $45.

376. The **RTFI Index**. *Waters Information Services*. l. 'Provides comprehensive information on every real-time market data service used by traders and investors around the world . . . A new update kit every six weeks or so containing the latest vendor profiles and new service analysis.' Another valuable guide.

Current awareness

377. **Advanced Searcher**. *Effective Technology Marketing*. bi-m. £88. 'Making sense of the database world.'

378. **Cable and Satellite Europe**. *21st Century Publications*. m. £70. 'The leading journal of international satellite and cable communications.'

379. **Cable and Satellite Yearbook**. *21st Century Publications*. a. £89. 'The annual directory of the industry.'

380. **CD-ROM Professional**. *Pemberton Press*. m. £95. 'More reviews, news and how-to articles than any other CD-ROM publication.'

381. **CD-ROM World**. *Meckler*. 11/year. $87.

382. **Counsel Connect**. *Counsel Connect*. m. The user's guide to Counsel Connect's electronic highway. Discusses issues relating to new and developing applications of e-mail and on-line technology in the legal profession, and reports on the Counsel Connect electronic service.

383. **CPA Technology Report**. *Harcourt Brace Professional Publishing*. m. $197. Articles on applications to business management, hardware, and

financial planning software, with a focus on Lotus 1–2–3, SuperCalc and Multiplan.

384. **Database**. *Online*. bi-m. $99. **online**.'The magazine of electronic database reviews.'

385. **Database Directory Service**. *Knowledge Industry Publications*. a. $395. Price includes supplement plus monthly *Data Base Alert* newsletter.

386. **Dealing With Technology**. *Waters Information Services*. bi-w. £425. 'We invite you to connect with the City's most powerful dealing room network – the network of IT professionals who rely upon *Dealing With Technology*. For years, technology trendsetters – from rocket scientist to CIO – in the City and on the Continent have read DWT for focused, in-depth news on the latest applications, platforms and competitive strategies in dealing room systems and proprietory execution. Today, as high-performance LANs and advanced workstations move from pilot to production, DWT remains the industry's foremost City-based newsletter for providing up-to-date business intelligence on dealing systems.

The key sources of market data and news are constantly changing – and the terms and conditions of user access are constantly being redefined. *Dealing With Technology* monitors the changes that affect your firm's strategy and applications – from exchange efforts to enforce permissioning of data feeds to the low profile maneuvers of interdealer brokers to the squabbling between Dow Jones and Reuters. In today's complex financial markets, no market data professional can afford to limit his or her attention to just one business area. Real-time information systems must meet the demands of global cross-market hedging and risk management. Whether it's bids and offers on a new instrument, a change in access policy, or a new third-party service, DWT will analyse and assess the announcements – not just quote the vendors.'

387. **Derivatives Engineering and Technology**. *Waters Information Services*. m. $495. Delivers behind-the-scenes reports on the latest software, systems, and networks supporting leading-edge financial engineering and risk management.

388. **Document Delivery World**. *Meckler*. 9/year. $39. 'The only magazine for document delivery professionals, librarians and end-users, covering a full range of information serching and document retrieval technologies.'

389. **Electronic Documents**. *Learned Information*. m. £96. 'Reducing the paper mountain by sharing text and images over electronic networks is the theme of this unique and timely publication.'

390. **Electronic Information Report**. *SIMBA Information*. w. $449. Newsletter.

391. **Electronic Marketplace Report**. *SIMBA Information*. bi-w. $432. Newsletter.

392. **Financial IT**. *Insurance Technology Group*. 44/year. £575.

393. **Financial Technology Bulletin**. *IBC Publishing*. m. £247. **online**.

394. **Financial Technology Review**. *Rand Publishing*. m. $96. Trade publication.

395. **Handbook of Digital Dealing Room Systems**. *Waters Information Services*. a. $695. Provides detailed information on the technology of digital trading room systems for financial markets.

396. **Information Today**. *Learned Information*. m. £45. 'The leading US monthly newspaper designed specifically for users and producers of electronic and optical information services . . . The ideal way to keep up to date with developments in the US information market.' Excellent value.

397. **Information World Review**. *Learned Information*. m. £24. **cdrom**. 'The only pan-European newspaper which focuses specifically on the information industry and is acknowledged, the world over, as the premier reference source for both users and producers of electronic information sources.' UK/European counterpart to *Information Today*.

398. **Inside Market Data**. *Waters Information Services*. bi-w. £495. **online**. Widely read news and comment on the real- time online data industry.

399. **Internet Connection**. *Bernan Associates*. m. $69. 'Your guide to government resources . . . The only newsletter devoted to finding free or low-cost information available from the US Government on the Internet.'

400. **Internet World**. *Mecklermedia*. m. $29. 'The only monthly newsstand magazine that focuses exclusively on the Internet.'

401. **Investment Management Technology**. *Waters Information Services*. bi-w. $595. Provides focused, in-depth coverage of the information technology demands of the institutional investor marketplace.

402. **Link Review of Interactive Services**. *Link Resources Corporation*. **online**.

403. **Link-Up**. *Learned Information*. bi-m. £46. **online**. 'For online users who need to get the most out of database searching and associated services . . . Each issue provides up-to- date coverage of the most exciting online services, the latest databases, the newest software, as well as updates on bulletin board systems and how to gain access to them. Stories on people, products and companies, as well as services and trends complement expert opinions about the world of online services and microcomputer communications.'

404. **Monitor**. *Learned Information*. m. £175. 'An analytical review of current events in electronic information.'

405. **Online**. *Online*. **online**. ie A leading US-based journal of reviews and news of the online database industry and its products and services entitled **Online** is produced by a company *Online* and is available for searching *online*! It is also produced in a print version (bi-m. $99).

406. **Online & CDROM Review**. *Learned Information*. bi- m. £82. 'Contains a unique blend of carefully refereed current research articles, international news round-ups and conference details.'

407. **Online Files Comparative Cost Analysis**. *Effective Technology Marketing*. q. £59. **diskette** £149. 'Are you paying too much online? Database search costs can vary up to 100% between different hosts.'

408. **Online Services: Review, Trends & Forecasts**. *SIMBA Information*. a. $795.

409. **Online/CD-ROM Business Information**. *Headland Press*. 11/year. £129. 'Independent tests and all the news of business databases.'

410. **Searcher**. *Learned Information*. 10/year. £50. 'The magazine for database professionals.'

411. **Television Business International**. *21st Century Publications*. 10/year. £50. 'The leading international magazine for the electronic entertainment industry . . . The most reliable source of news, comment and analysis of business trends across all national and international program and broadcast boundaries.'

412. **Television Business International Yearbook**. *21st Century Publications*. a. £150. 'The most comprehensive directory available of the world's television business . . . Up to date information on more than 160 television markets around the globe with statistical information on which channels lead the ratings, and the rules, regulations and business alliances that govern the market.'

Notes

(1) SMITH, G.D. and SYLLA, R. The transformation of financial capitalism: An essay on the history of American capital markets **Financial Markets, Institutions & Instruments** 2(2), May 1993, pp 6–7.

(2) WALMSLEY, J. **The foreign exchange and money markets guide**. *John Wiley*, 1992, p 4.

(3) McHUGH, F.P. An ethic of financial decision-making *IN* FROWEN, S.F. and McHUGH, F.P. eds. **Financial decision-making and moral responsibility**. *Macmillan*, 1995. 256 pp. 'These essays present the proceedings of a conference (held in 1992) at which financial policy-makers, bankers and academic economists debated with ethicians and theologians. In addition to a generalised discussion of the philosophy of economics and its relation to moral ideas, the papers address particular topics which include the role and responsibilities of central banks, inbuilt deficiencies of the financial system, moral conflicts in commercial and investment banking and in securities markets, problems of sovereignty and hegemony in the European monetary union, moral issues in international monetary relations, and the ethics of capital transfers to Eastern Europe and of financial liberalisation.'

cf PRINDL, A.R. and PRODHAN, B. eds. **The ACT guide to ethical conflicts in finance**. *Blackwell Finance*, 1994. 257 pp. Titles of chapters included in *Part III* 'Conflicts between holders of information' are: 'Information-sharing'; 'The ethics of insider trading'; 'What is really unethical about insider trading?'; 'The ethics of greenmail'; and 'How to avoid insider dealing'. An Appendix reprints the *Ethical Code of the Association of Corporate Treasurers.*

(4) As noted in the Preface, we will generally use the word 'finance' in such phrases as 'finance system' 'finance information system' and so on, as a shorthand for 'finance and banking', unless this would be misleading.

(5) GARDNER, M.J. and MILLS, D.L. **Managing financial institutions: An asset/liability approach**. 3rd ed. *Dryden Press*, 1994, pp 6– 7.

(6) SAMUELSON, P.A. and NORDHAUS, W.D. **Economics**. 14th ed. *McGraw-Hill*, 1992, pp 621–622.

(7) I have followed here the term preferred in the **System of National Accounts 1993** (p 90):

> Corporations may be described by different names: corporations, incorporated enterprises, public limited companies, public corporations, private companies, joint-stock companies, limited liability companies, limited liability partnerships, and so on. 'Corporation' is the preferred term used in the System for all these kinds of entities. A typical corporation may be described as: a legal entity, created for the purpose of producing goods or services for the market, that may be a source of profit or other financial gain to its owner(s); it is collectively owned by shareholders who have the authority to appoint directors responsible for its general management.

The *System of National Accounts* is a 'comprehensive, consistent and flexible set of macroeconomic accounts intended to meet the needs of government and private-sector analysts, policy makers and decision takers', prepared under the joint responsibility of five major international official organizations: United Nations, International Monetary Fund, Commission of the European Communities, Organisation for Economic Co-operation and Development, World Bank. We will quote from the publication describing the System at some length in the following. The volume presents an excellent structured approach to the financial system within a macroeconomic context.

System of national accounts 1993. Published jointly by: *Commission of the European Communities – Eurostat, International Monetary Fund, Organisation for Economic Co-operation and Development, United Nations* and *World Bank*, 1993. 711 pp. Prepared under the auspices of the Inter-Secretariat Working Group on National Accounts.

(8) BREALEY, R.A. and MYERS, S.C. **Principles of corporate finance**, 4th ed. *McGraw-Hill*, 1991, p 3.

(9) 'An instrument, such as a promissory note, which is recognised as legal evidence of a debt. A note is signed by the maker, called the borrower, promising to pay a certain sum of money on a specified date at a certain place of business, to a certain business, individual, or bank, called the lender.' (ROSENBERG, J.M. **Dictionary of banking**. *John Wiley*, 1993, p 243.)

(10) SECHREST, W.B. Global business and financial trends *IN* Norton J.J. and Auerback R.M. eds. **International finance in the 1990s**. *Blackwell*, 1993, pp 18, 30.

(11) We need not worry in this context what we might mean here by 'money' – except to note the difficulties of its definition: e.g. the composition of the money stock measure M1 used by the Federal Reserve reads: '(1) currency outside the US Treasury, Federal Reserve Banks, and the vaults of depository institutions, (2) travellers checks of nonbank issuers, (3) demand

deposits at all commercial banks other than those owed to depository institutions, the US government, and foreign banks and official institutions, less cash items in the process of collection and Federal Reserve float, and (4) other checkable deposits (OCDs), consisting of negotiable order of withdrawal (NOW) and automatic transfer service (ATS) accounts at depository institutions, credit union share draft accounts, and demand deposits at thrift institutions.' Similarly detailed definitions for M2, M3, L and Debt follow. (**Federal Reserve Bulletin**, 80 (11), November 1994, p A4)

(12) A *financial instrument* is cash, evidence of an ownership interest in an entity, or a contract that both:

a. Imposes on one entity a contractual obligation[1] (1) to deliver cash or another financial instrument[2] to a second entity or (2) to exchange other financial instruments on potentially unfavorable terms with the second entity

b. Conveys to that second entity a contractual right[3] (1) to receive cash or another financial instrument from the first entity or (2) to exchange other financial instruments on potentially favorable terms with the first entity.

That definition includes a variety of commonly recognized financial assets and financial liabilities, such as bonds, notes, loans, deposits, and trade receivables and payables. It also includes contracts that may not be recognized in financial statements at present – instruments that may be 'off-balance-sheet' – such as financial guarantees, letters of credit, loan commitments, obligations under operating leases, interest rate swaps and caps, and financial forward and option contracts.

The definition of a financial instrument *excludes* such contractual rights and obligations as prepaid expenses and deferred revenue, advances to suppliers, and most warranty obligations because their probable economic benefit or sacrifice entails the receipt or delivery of goods or services rather than financial assets or financial liabilities. The definition also excludes contracts to be settled by delivery of a commodity (other than foreign currency), such as bonds required to be settled in ounces of gold or barrels of oil rather than cash.

In addition, physical assets, such as inventories, real property, and equipment; a lessee's right to use physical assets; and intangibles, such as patents and goodwill, are all excluded by the definition of a financial instrument. Those assets could eventually lead to a receipt of cash; however, because no other entity has a present obligation to deliver cash, the entity has no present right to receive cash. The definition also excludes obligations for taxes and tort judgements. Those liabilities represent requirements to pay cash but do not arise from contracts; instead, such obligations are imposed by government or courts of law.

As with any definition that has consequences for accounting recognition and measurement, the breadth of the definition of a financial instrument is controversial.

[1] *Contractual obligations* encompass both those that are conditioned on the occurrence of a specified event and those that are not . . . For some financial instruments, the obligation is owed to or by a group of entities rather than a single entity.

[2] The use of the term *financial instrument* in this definition is recursive (because the term *financial instrument* is included in it), though it is not circular. The definition requires a chain of contractual obligations that ends with the delivery of cash or an ownership interest in an entity. Any number of obligations to deliver financial instruments can be links in a chain that qualifies a particular contract as a financial instrument.

[3] *Contractual rights* encompass both those that are conditioned on the occurrence of a specified event and those that are not . . . For some financial instruments, the right is held by or the obligation is due from a group of entities rather than a single entity.

(**An analysis of issues related to recognition and measurement of financial instruments**. *Financial Accounting Standards Board*, 1991, pp 1–2. Discussion Memorandum No 109–A.)

(13) The US Federal Reserve estimated a few years ago that only 4.9 per cent of international cash flows was linked to international trade.

(14) Gardner and Mills op cit pp 11–12.

(15) Gardner and Mills op cit p 10.

(16) **Encyclopedia of banking and finance**. 9th ed. *McGraw-Hill*, 1991, p 583.

(17) NEWMAN, P., MILGATE, M. and EATWELL, J. eds. **New Palgrave dictionary of money & finance**. *Macmillan Press*, 1992, v 2, p 508. This text (2,559 pp, £375, three volumes) was 'The first reference book ever to be awarded the Eccles Prize for Excellence in Economic Writing from Columbia Business School.'

(18) **Dictionary of finance**. *Oxford University Press*, 1993, pp 42, 250.

(19) JOHNSON, H.J. **Financial institutions and markets: A global perspective**. *McGraw-Hill*, 1993, pp 122–123.

(20) Also, note the differences in UK and US usage: for instance:

Most non-American speakers of English can easily understand terms such as 'accounts receivable', 'accounts payable' or 'sales'. However, in some cases, confusion is possible. For example:

United States	*United Kingdom*
Accounts payable	Creditors
Accounts receivable	Debtors
Amortization	Depreciation
Bylaws	Articles of association
Capital surplus	Share premium
Certificate of incorporation	Memorandum of association
Common stock	Ordinary shares
Constant dollar accounting	Current purchasing power
Current rate method	Closing rate method
Deferred income tax credits	Deferred tax
Fiscal year	Financial year
General price level adjusted	CPP
Income	Profit
Income statement	Profit and loss account
Inventories	Stocks
Leverage	Gearing
Notes	Bills
Paid-in surplus	Share premium
Par value	Nominal value
Pooling of interests	Merger accounting
Preferred stock	Preference shares
Property, plant and equipment	Fixed assets
Purchase accounting	Acquisition accounting
Real estate/property	Land
Sales	Turnover
Statement of financial position	Balance sheet
Stock	Shares
Stock dividend	Bonus issue (small)
Stockholders' equity	Shareholders' funds
Stock split	Bonus issue (large)
Treasury stock	Own shares

The most usual meaning of the UK terms 'stock' and 'shares' are translated

> in the US terms 'inventory' and 'stock' respectively. It would be unwise therefore to try to discuss with an American the use of FIFO for *stock* valuation. Worse, the US expression 'Treasury Stock' might be taken to mean gilt-edged (i.e. government) loan securities in the United Kingdom, whereas it actually means a corporation's own shares bought back and held in the corporate treasury. There is, of course, an institutional difference here. Although UK companies have been allowed to buy back their shares since 1981, such 'own shares' would not be seen on a balance sheet because they must be cancelled.

(NOBES, C. and PARKER, R. **Comparative international accounting**. 4th ed. *Prentice Hall*, 1995, pp 161–162).

(21) KOHN, M. **Financial institutions and markets**. *McGraw-Hill*, 1994. 868 pp.

(22) Kohn op cit p 10.

(23) Kohn op cit pp 10, 13, 14, 15, 23, 24.

(24)
> Agency problems arise when a principal hires an agent to perform certain tasks, yet the agent does not share the principal's objective. To align the agent's incentives with his own, the principal may use a variety of instruments, including cash bonuses, equity shares, promotions and dismissals. . . . The agency literature has distinguished between incentive problems caused by hidden action and those caused by hidden information. The former refer to situations where it is prohibitively costly for the principal to observe the agent's actions. Hidden information problems occur when the agent has better information that the principal regarding the desirability of certain actions. Influenced by earlier literature on insurance contracts, problems of hidden action and hidden information are frequently referred to as moral hazard and adverse selection, respectively. In many agency situations, of course, both these factors are present.

(REICHELSTEIN, S. Agency *IN* Newman, P., Milgate, M., and Eatwell, J. eds. **New Palgrave dictionary of money & finance**. *Macmillan Press*, 1992, v 1, p 23).

See also ASSOCIATION INTERNATIONALE DES JEUNES AVOCATS. **Commercial agency and distribution agreements**. 2nd ed. *Graham & Trotman*, 1993. 656 pp. Law and practice in the member states of the EC and EFTA.

(25) The **International Standard Classification of Occupations** (*International Labour Office*, 1990 [ISCO-88]) uses ten major groups at the top level of aggregation. It is surprising, when one thinks about it, how many different occupational roles frequently need to become involved in one or another aspect of trade. Using the ILO nomenclature, one could imagine the holders of jobs within all these occupations finding out some 'inside' trade-related information:

Major Group 1: Legislators, Senior Officials and Managers

1110 Legislators
1120 Senior government officials
1210 Directors and chief executives
1227 Production and operations department managers in business services
1231 Finance and administration department managers
1233 Sales and marketing department managers
1234 Advertising and public relations department managers
1236 Computing services department managers
1317 General managers in business services

Major Group 2: Professionals

2121 Mathematicians and related professionals
2122 Statisticians
2131 Computer systems designers and analysts
2132 Programmers
2411 Accountants
2421 Lawyers
2422 Judges
2431 Archivists and curators
2432 Librarians and related information professionals
2441 Economists

Major Group 3: Technicians and Associate Professionals

3121 Computer assistants
3122 Computer equipment operators

Minor Group 341: Finance and Sales Associate Professionals

Finance and sales associate professionals buy and sell financial instruments, different types of insurance, real estate, travel and other business services, deal on the foreign exchange, act as wholesale representatives or as buyers on behalf of organisations, or they appraise the value of commodities, real estate and other properties, and they sell these by auction.

Tasks performed usually include: analysing market trends for financial instruments, the foreign exchange, commodities and real estate and buying and selling on behalf of clients or on their own behalf; advising on and selling insurance coverage; ensuring proper recording of transfers of financial instruments and ownership of real estate . . . appraising the value of commodities, real estate or other property, or selling by auction.

3411 Securities and finance dealers and brokers[a]
3412 Insurance representatives
3413 Estate agents
3414 Travel consultants and organisers
3415 Technical and commercial sales representatives
3416 Buyers
3417 Appraisers, valuers and auctioneers
3421 Trade brokers
3422 Clearing and forwarding agents
3423 Employment agents and labour contractors
3431 Administrative secretaries and related associate professionals
3432 Legal and related business associate professionals
3433 Bookkeepers
3434 Statistical, mathematical and related associate professionals
3441 Customs and border inspectors
3442 Government tax and excise officials
3444 Government licensing officials
3450 Police inspectors and detectives

[a] 'A Broker by any Other Name . . . Depending on where you do business, you may find your broker known as: *Financial Consultant* at Merrill Lynch or Shearson Lehman Hutton; *Institutional Salesman* at Salomon Brothers; *Securities Salesperson* at Goldman Sachs; *Account Executive* at Drexel Burnham, Prudential-Bache or Dean Witter; *Investment Executive* at PaineWebber; or *Portfolio Salesman* at First Boston. Of the biggest brokerage houses, only Morgan Stanley calls a broker simply a *Broker*' (WURMAN, R.S., SIEGEL, A. and MORRIS, K.M. **The Wall Street Journal guide to understanding money & markets**. *AccessPress*, 1990, p 12). 'We may live in the information age, but much of the information we deal with every day is often perplexing. Perhaps most confusing of all is the world of finance. We're deluged with data, analyses and trends – often couched in jargon that makes our eyes glaze over. Do we know what M1, M2 and M3 represent or do they seem only the name of bus routes? What are bulls and bears, the Dow Jones Average, the consumer price index, junk bonds, futures contracts, Treasury notes, and

arbitrage?. . . . In the straightforward manner of a conversation, this guide explains the 'tools' of the financial arena – the terms, the charts, the tables.'

Major Group 4: Clerks

4111 Stenographers and typists
4112 Word processor and related operators
4113 Data entry operators
4115 Secretaries
4121 Accounting and bookkeeping clerks
4122 Statistical and finance clerks
4141 Library and filing clerks
4142 Mail carriers and sorting clerks
4143 Coding, proof-reading and related clerks
4211 Cashiers and ticket clerks
4212 Tellers and other counter clerks
4214 Pawnbrokers and money-lenders
4215 Debt-collectors and related workers
4221 Travel agency and related clerks
4222 Receptionists and information clerks
4223 Telephone switchboard operators

Major Group 7: Craft and Related Trades Workers

7341 Compositors, typesetters and related workers

As I shall comment again later in the text, no wonder information leaks out from time to time!

(26) GILMORE, W.C. ed. **International efforts to combat money laundering**. *Grotius Publications*, 1992. 356 pp.

BOSWORTH-DAVIES, R. **Money laundering**. *Chapman & Hall*, 1994. 320 pp. 'A practical guide to the new legislation.'

POWIS, R.E. **The money launderers**. *Probus*, 1992. 383 pp.

(27) PAGE, A.C. and FERGUSON, R.B. **Investor protection**. *Weidenfeld & Nicolson*, 1992, 384 pp. £18.99. 'Provides the first comprehensive, up-to-date account of the law governing the protection of investors in the United Kingdom.'

(28) **Comparative analysis of disclosure regimes**. *International Organisation of Securities Commissions*, 1991, p 2.

(29) GORDON, P.D. and GRAY, S.J. **European financial reporting: United Kingdom**. *Routledge* in association with the *Institute of Chartered Accountants in England and Wales*, 1994, p 20.

(30) cf Note (7). Henceforth here: 1993 SNA.

(31) 1993 SNA op cit p xxxiii.

(32) 1993 SNA op cit p xxxiv.

(33) 1993 SNA op cit p xlvii.

(34) 1993 SNA op cit p 1.

(35) 1993 SNA op cit p 1.

(36) ESTRIN, S. and LAIDLER, D. **Introduction to microeconomics**. 4th ed. *Harvester Wheatsheaf*, 1995. 505 pp. 'Economics is about scarcity. The word "scarcity" is used here in a special sense: it refers to a state of affairs in which, given the wants of society at any particular moment, the means available to satisfy them are not sufficient. If all desires cannot be totally

satisfied, then choices have to be made as to which of them are going to be satisfied, and to what extent. To say that economics is about scarcity then is also to say that it is about choice. . . . The scope of the scarcity problem as it faces society is enormous and complex. . . . It is not only at the social level that scarcity exists and choices have to be made. Individual economic agents face the same problem too. Such agents may be individuals, families, capitalist firms, co-operative enterprises or government departments. . . . Microeconomics is particularly concerned with the behaviour of individual economic agents.'

(37) 1993 SNA op cit pp 11–12.

(38) The SNA uses the notion of 'production' in a very wide sense – not just with reference to 'manufacturing':

> The activity of production is fundamental. In the System, production is understood to be a physical process, carried out under the responsibility, control and management of an institutional unit, in which labour and assets are used to transform inputs of goods and services into outputs of other goods and services. All goods and services produced as outputs must be such that they can be sold on markets or at least be capable of being provided by one unit to another, with or without charge. The system includes within the production boundary all production actually destined for the market, whether for sale or barter. It also includes all goods and services provided free to individual households or collectively to the community by government units or NPISHs (non-profit institutions serving households) (SNA 1993 op cit p 4).

(39) SNA 1993 op cit p 3.

(40) *Non-profit institutions* are legal or social entities created for the purpose of producing goods and services whose status does not permit them to be a source of income, profit or other financial gain for the units that establish, control or finance them. In practice, their productive activities are bound to generate either surpluses or deficits but any surpluses they happen to make cannot be appropriated by other institutional units. The articles of association by which they are established are drawn up in such a way that the institutional units which control or manage them are not entitled to a share in any profits or other income which they receive. For this reason, they are frequently exempted from various kinds of taxes.

Non-profit institutions serving households (NPISHs) consist of NPIs which provide goods or services to households free or at prices that are not economically significant. Two main types of NPISHs may be distinguished. The first type consists of NPISHs which are created by associations of persons to provide goods or, more often, services primarily for the benefit of the members themselves. The services are usually provided free, being financed by regular membership subscriptions or dues. They include NPISHs such as professional or learned societies, political parties, trade unions, consumers' associations, churches or religious societies, and social, cultural, recreational or sports clubs . . . In some communities, NPISHs may be found which do not possess any legal status or formal articles of association . . . The second type of NPISH consists of charities, relief or aid agencies that are created for philanthropic purposes and not to serve the interests of the members of the association controlling the NPISH.

(41) SNA 1993 op cit p 101.

(42) SNA 1993 op cit p 96.

(43) ISIC Rev 3 was published by the *Statistical Office of the United Nations* as Statistical Paper Series M No 4 Rev 3. 189 pp. $20. That Office also publishes a *Provisional Central Product Classification* and the *Standard International Trade Classification*. The UK's **Standard Industrial Classification**

of Economic Activities 1992 (HMSO) follows closely the ISIC classification (and the European Union's NACE classification). The major headings in *Section J: Financial Intermediation* of UK SIC are:

65	*FINANCIAL INTERMEDIATION, EXCEPT INSURANCE AND PENSION FUNDING*
65.1	Monetary intermediation
65.11	Central banking
65.12	Other monetary intermediation
65.12/1	Banks
65.12/2	Building societies
65.2	Other financial intermediation
65.21	Financial leasing
65.22	Other credit granting
65.22/1	Credit granting by non-deposit taking finance houses and other specialist consumer credit grantors
65.22/2	Factoring
65.22/3	Activities of mortgage finance companies
65.22/4	Other credit granting not elsewhere specified
65.23	Other financial intermediation not elsewhere classified
65.23/1	Activities of investment trusts
65.23/2	Activities of unit trusts and property unit trusts
65.23/3	Security dealing on own account
65.23/4	Activities of bank holding companies
65.23/5	Activities of venture and development capital companies
65.23/6	Financial intermediation not elsewhere specified
66	*INSURANCE AND PENSION FUNDING, EXCEPT COMPULSORY SOCIAL SECURITY*
66.0	Insurance and pension funding, except compulsory social security
66.01	Life insurance
66.02	Pension funding
66.03	Non-life insurance
67	*ACTIVITIES AUXILIARY TO FINANCIAL INTERMEDIATION*
67.1	Activities auxiliary to financial intermediation, except insurance and pension funding
67.11	Administration of financial markets
67.12	Security broking and fund management
67.12/1	Fund management activities
67.12/2	Security broking and related activities
67.13	Activities auxiliary to financial intermediation not elsewhere classified
67.2	Activities auxiliary to insurance and pension funding
67.20	Activities auxiliary to insurance and pension funding

(44) 1993 SNA op cit pp 97–98.

(45) In paragraph 11.

(46) 1993 SNA op cit p 97.

(47) 1993 SNA op cit p 98.

(48) 1993 SNA op cit pp 98–99.

(49) MURPHY, N.B. and ROGERS, R.C. Commercial banking *IN* ALTMAN, E.I. ed. **Handbook of financial markets and institutions**. 6th ed. *John Wiley*, 1987, pp 13.4–13.5. (This book includes an Appendix *Sources of financial and investment information*.)

(50) 1993 SNA op cit p 99.

(51) 1993 SNA op cit p 99.

(52) 1993 SNA op cit p 572.

(53) And we have not even mentioned such entities as hire purchase corporations, investment corporations, and other corporations engaged in the provision of personal finance or consumer credit; the problem of how to categorize holding corporations whose activities straddle the boundary between financial and non-financial corporations; where to classify bodies which regulate or supervise financial corporations; how to handle the tendency for non-financial corporations in some countries to raise funds themselves by selling their own obligations directly on the money or capital markets; what should happen when a central bank also engages in commercial banking; what to do about reinsurance; and so on and so on.

(54) 1993 SNA op cit p 244.

(55) **Derivatives: Practices and principles**. *Group of Thirty*, 1993, pp 29–30. Prepared by the *Global Derivatives Study Group*. See also:

FOX-ANDREWS, M. and MEADEN, N. **Derivatives markets and investment management**. *Prentice Hall/Woodhead-Faulkner*, 1995. 188 pp. 'The use of derivatives markets and instruments continues to be one of the fastest growing, and controversial, areas in the financial world. Investment products using these tools are pushing back the limits of new techniques and systems and are challenging global regulators. Investors seek reassurance and opportunity, as well as understanding and information. Litigation is on the increase. The collapse of Baring Brothers Bank in March 1995 has caused new storms about these markets. . . . We are not academics and this is not an academic book. We have tried to present a reasonably comprehensive overview of the current situation in this field. . . . Following from comments on our first book *Futures Fund Management* published in 1991, we have also put in some appendices with some quite basic general information about the industry. Hopefully this will help make the book of interest to both "professional" and "amateur" readers.'

ERRINGTON, C. **Financial engineering**. *Macmillan Publishers*, 1994. 303 pp. 'A handbook for managing the risk-reward relationship.'

KLEIN, R.A. and LEDERMAN, J. eds. **The handbook of derivatives & synthetics**. *Irwin Professional*, 1994, 900 pp. £72.50. 'The most comprehensive and up-to-date book on the fastest growing area in the financial markets. . . . Featuring more than 40 chapters written by the industry's leading experts from around the globe.'

(56) MARSHALL, J.F. and BANSAL, V.K. **Financial engineering: A complete guide to financial innovation**. *New York Institute of Finance*, 1992, pp 273–275.

(57) 1993 SNA op cit pp 586–587.

(58) KOHN op cit pp 455–456.

(59) There are a number of useful books on the interpretation of economic statistics:

ANDERSON, V. **Alternative economic indicators**. *Routledge*, 1991. £8.99. "This is a book sure to cause a stir among development economists, environmental activists and others looking for better signposts in an uncertain world" (Ian Miles).

NATIONAL RESEARCH COUNCIL: PANEL ON FOREIGN TRADE STATISTICS. **Behind the numbers: U.S. trade in the world economy**.

National Academy Press, 1992. 297 pp. Addresses the adequacy of existing data on US international transactions and addresses the issue of providing useful economic data better to inform public and private decision-makers. Includes an assessment of existing data for three areas of US international transactions – merchandising trade, international services transactions, and international capital flows – and presents recommendations for improving the data.

HILDEBRAND, G. **Business cycle indicators and measures: A complete guide to interpreting the key economic indicators**. *Irwin Professional*, 1992. 277 pp. '*What started out as curiosity turned into a quest*. Indicators are quoted frequently in the news and on television. Bond and stock prices, political action, optimism or pessimism seem to all be affected by the announcement of the status of particular indicators. An increased interest in predictive models started an inquiry to find out what indicators were, who they were developed by, why they were developed, where they had applicability, and how they are used. The investigation seemed simple enough, but on getting involved, it became apparent that the desired information was scattered among many different publications. Needed explanatory or basic publications were out of print. Much of the information was only available on microfiche. The constant back-and-forth between current and noncurrent publications reminded me of a rat trying to get out of a maze. This can be very discouraging to anyone desiring semi-immediate information. . . . The purpose of this handbook is to simplify an inquiry into (almost wholly US-based) business-cycle indicators by making an organized search for relevant information a less painful process.'

PLEETER, S. and WAY, P.K. **Economics in the news**. *Addison-Wesley*, 1993. 432 pp. News articles from *The Wall Street Journal*, *Newsweek*, *US News and World Report*, *Time*, *The New York Times*, *Business Week*, *The Washington Post*, and other periodicals are grouped into sections and analyzed with reference to contemporary economic issues.

PLOCEK, J.E. **Economic indicators: How America reads its financial health**. *New York Institute of Finance*, 1991. 396 pp. 'In the more than 12 years that I have been following economic and financial data, first as an employee of government agencies and then on Wall Street, its users (primarily participants in the financial markets, but also reporters, investors, and analysts) have become increasingly sophisticated. . . . But more education is necessary to overcome the rumors and truisms that often substitute for hard data even among the individuals whose livelihoods depend on these indicators. It is my hope that this book will contribute to the market's understanding of the factors underpinning economic indicators.'

SOMMERS, A.T. with BLAU, L.R. **The US economy demystified**. 3rd ed. *Lexington Books*, 1993. 190 pp. 'The meaning of US business statistics and what they portend for the future.'

FRUMKIN, N. **Guide to economic indicators**. 2nd ed. *ME Sharpe*, 1994. 272 pp. 'The first edition of this book was chosen as a *Choice* magazine Outstanding Academic Book.'

SANTOW, L.J. **Helping the Federal Reserve work smarter**. *ME Sharpe*, 1994. 160 pp. 'Leonard Santow is one of the preeminent Fed watchers of long standing. His insights will be helpful to both the aspiring practitioner as well as to those who are already very knowledgeable in this field' (Henry Kaufman).

SCHAEFER, H.G. **International economic trend analysis**. *Quorum Books*, 1995. 'American business leaders need a comprehensive understanding of the existing global economic and monetary system. . . . Based on key economic and financial indicators published weekly in *The Economist*, Schaefer integrates a discussion of established international economic concepts with actual economic and financial data, giving readers a system to evaluate current economic indicators and anticipate future trends.'

WEBB, R.I. **Macroeconomic information and financial trading**. *Blackwell Business*, 1994. 'The reaction of bond prices to the arrival of macroeconomic information provides a fascinating glimpse into the macroeconomic beliefs of traders and the way in which new information is incorporated into prices. This ground-breaking book challenges the assumption that these reactions represent rational responses to the arrival of relevant information in an internationally efficient capital market. Rather, it suggests that the often anomalous behaviour of economic reports is more indicative of a reaction to 'noise' (non-informational factors) than information.'

SCHULTZE, C.E. **Memos to the president: A guide through macroeconomics for the busy policymaker**. *Brookings Institution*, 1992. 334 pp. A construction of 29 memos from the Council for Economic Advisers to the President of the United States. The first four give general macro-economic background, the next fifteen run through the short-run cycle part of macroeconomic, the next nine deal with the long-run cycle, and the last summarizes the differences between the author's centrist views on macroeconomics and other prominent opinions.

STEIN, H. and FOSS, M. **The new illustrated guide to the American economy**. *AEI Press*, 1995. 250 pp. $14.95. "Here it is, the huge and puzzling American economy, neatly broken down into colorful charts. . . . But the usual brain-draining info clutter inundating the dismal science is made lively and informative in this surprising little book by the clear thinking authors" (*Wall Street Journal Magazine of Personal Business Smart Money*).

NIEMIRA, M.P. and ZUKOWSKI, G.F. **Trading the fundamentals: The trader's complete guide to interpreting economic indicators & monetary policy**. *Irwin Professional*, 1993. 300 pp. 'Explains the significance, reliability and market impact of 23 of the most widely followed economic indicators.'

(60) **Yearbook of International Organizations**, v 1, 1993/94, p 1310.

(61) **Measurement of international capital flows**. *IMF*, 1992. Final Report and Background Papers.

(62) WALMSLEY op cit p 40.

(63) DENNIS, G.E.J. **International financial flows: A statistical handbook**. *Graham & Trotman*, 1984. 365 pp.

(64) DENNIS op cit pp 135–136.

(65) DENNIS op cit pp 151–152.

(66) *What's New in Business Information*, January 1995.

(67) SUMMERS, B.J. ed. **The payment system: Design, management, and supervision**. *IMF*, 1994. 214 pp. $22.50; **Payment systems in the Group of Ten countries**. 4th ed. *BIS*, 1993. 549 pp. Prepared by the *Committee on Payment and Settlement Systems*. 'This fourth edition of the "Red Book" has been extensively revised. The coverage of different segments of each country's payment system has been broadened, statistical information has been

improved and presented in time series form, a special chapter on cross-border payment system arrangements has been added, and a comprehensive list of terms and abbreviations has been included. . . . In the future, the Committee on Payment and Settlement Systems will also publish separate country studies on payment systems in non-G-10 countries. This will be done in association with the central bank concerned. Such special editions are currently (December 1993) being prepared in collaboration with the *Reserve Bank of Australia*, the *Bank of Finland*, the *Central Bank of Norway*, and the *Central Bank of Iceland*.'

Payment systems in EC member countries. *Committee of Governors of the Central Banks of the Member States of the European Economic Community*, 1992. 337 pp. Prepared by an ad hoc Working Group on EC Payment Systems. Describes in detail payment systems in the twelve countries plus cross-border payment systems. Includes comparative tables: notes and coins in circulation; points of entry into the payment system; cash dispensers and ATMs; EFT/POS; use of payment cards; major interbank funds transfer systems in the European Community; use of payment instruments: all figures are for 1990.

RAYNER, S. **Payment cards in Europe: Product trends and market outlook**. *FT Management Reports*, 1993. £274. 'Examines the effects of strong national market differences on the provision of pan-European card schemes and looks at the likely impact of European harmonisation on the international card markets.'

(68) CAMPBELL, D. ed. **International bank secrecy**. *Sweet & Maxwell*, 1992. 31 jurisdictions.

(69) cf **Report to the Governor of the Bank of England**. *Task Force on Securities Settlement*, 1993. 37 pp.

Terms of Reference

1. In the light of the Stock Exchange's decision to suspend development of Taurus, to consider the best way forward for the development of securities settlement, share registration and share transfer in the UK and to identify possible alternatives to Taurus, having regard to speed of implementation, cost, ownership, governance and financing as well as system structure.
2. To recommend a preferred option and to make recommendations for managing its implementation.
3. To report to the Governor of the Bank of England by the end of June 1993 at the latest.

Membership of the Working Party – which was formed in March 1993 – included members of these organizations: Bank of England; London Stock Exchange; Securities and Investment Board; London Clearing House; Association of Private Client Investment Managers and Stockbrokers; Citibank NA; British Merchant Bankers Association Securities Trading Committee; HM Treasury; CIN Management Limited.

(70) In *countertrade* (or 'barter') it is possible for trade to take place without a parallel exchange of money – or, more generally, of something that can readily be turned into money. But most of the time in the world nowadays, people and organizations 'purchase' the (real) assets they need. 'A countertrade transaction, as it is normally understood, is an economic transaction in which one party supplies, or procures the supply of goods or other

economic value to the second party, and, in return, the first party agrees to purchase or procures to be purchased from the second party, or from a party designated by the second party, goods or other economic value, so as to achieve an agreed ratio between the reciprocal performances.' (Quoted in: MONTAGUE, A.A. Countertrade *IN* Norton J.J. and Auerback R.M. eds. **International finance in the 1990s: Challenges and opportunities**. *Blackwell*, 1993, p 276).

(71) And we must not forget tax havens: GRUNDY, M. **Grundy's tax havens – Offshore business centres: A world survey**. 6th ed. *Sweet & Maxwell*, 1993.

(72) GOODHART, C.A.E. **Money, information and uncertainty**. 2nd ed. *Macmillan Press*, 1989. 512 pp. 18.99. 'The book provides a comprehensive survey of monetary economics, with the first nine chapters concerned with micro issues, such as the role of, and demand for, money, the role and functions of banks and of the Central Bank; and the final nine chapters covering macro-economic issues, such as the transmission mechanism of monetary policy and international monetary problems.'

(73) But only to the foothills of that other sub-discipline: 'The tasks of saying what is known about some aspect of the world, of answering minute particular questions about public knowledge, and of saying that a new survey is accurate or an old survey is still accurate, all call for the same qualifications: those of the practitioner in the field that is responsible for the particular area of knowledge. The outsider is always free to assert his own judgement and to disagree with the insiders, and if enough outsiders disagree with the insiders, the insiders may lose their position as recognised producers of knowledge. But as long as the group retains its socially granted authority, those who recognise this authority will accept no other judgement as having weight, unless it is the judgement of a representative of a group having a more firmly established grant of authority' (WILSON, P. **Public knowledge, private ignorance: Toward a library and information policy**. *Greenwood Press*, 1977, p 23).

(74) HOPT, K.J. and WYMEERSCH, E. **European insider dealing**. *Butterworths*, 1991. Interprets and analyses the EC Insider Dealing Directive and gives a comprehensive account of the status of insider dealing legislation in member states.

BERGMANS, H. **Inside information and securities trading**. *Kluwer Academic Publishers*, 1991.

ASHE, M. and COUNSELL, L. **Insider trading**. 2nd ed. *Tolley*, 1993. 275 pp.

(75) cf DRAKE, W.J. ed. **The new information infrastructure: Strategies for US policy**. *Brookings Institution*, 1995. 300 pp.

(76) VAITILINGAM, R. **The Financial Times guide to using the financial pages**. *Pitman Publishing*, 1993. 216 pp. Clearly written guide in three Parts: I. *Identifying the players*: investors, companies, financial institutions, governments. II. *Interpreting the markets*: stocks and shares, indices and aggregates, international equities, trusts and funds, bonds and eurobonds, cash and currency, futures and options, primary products. III. *Understanding the economies*: UK economic indicators and surveys, the European economy.

(77) LEHMANN, M.B. **The Dow Jones-Irwin guide to using 'The Wall Street Journal'**. 3rd ed. *Dow Jones-Irwin*, 1990. 382 pp.

LEHMANN, M.B. **Real world applications: The Wall Street Journal work-**

book. 3rd ed. *Irwin*, 1994. 'Designed to help students analyze macro-economic-oriented articles from this important periodical and put its information to use.'

(78) I use here the terminology in a leading source guide to such databases: **Gale Directory of Databases**. *Gale Research*. s-a. Volume 2: CD-ROM, Diskette, Magnetic Tape, Handheld, and Batch Access Database Products. Volume 1 covers: Online Databases.

(79) For example:

SCHLESSINGER, B. ed. **The basic business library: Core resources**. 3rd ed. *Oryx Press*, 1994. 368 pp. $39.50. 'Annotated core list of nearly 200 prime information sources, plus a bibliography of approximately 300 other business sources.'

MEYER, A.D. and SWAGER, R.J. **A bibliography of selected topics in economic development literature**. *American Economic Development Council*, 1994. $45. 'References cover a broad spectrum of topics, including education, infrastructure, economic development programs, and financing.'

MacDONALD, B. **Broadcasting in the United Kingdom: A guide to information sources**. 2nd ed. *Mansell*, 1993. 334 pp.

LAVIN, M.R. **Business information: How to find it, how to use it**. 2nd ed. *Oryx Press*, 1992. 499 pp. $49.95. An excellent review of major US sources, with very helpful and detailed explanations of the nature of different types of business information. ('Recipient of the 1992 Business Reference Services Section/Gale Research Award for Excellence in Business Librarianship') The same publishes have produced an equally good international companion: PAGELL, R.A. and HALPERIN, M. **International business information: How to find it, how to use it**. *Oryx Press*, 1994. 384 pp. $74.95. 'All major business environments outside the US are covered in this comprehensive resource, including special coverage of the most recent sources on Eastern Europe, and Asia. Two prominent business librarians bring a wealth of electronic and print sources within easy reach of professional and student business researchers, business instructors, and reference and business librarians. The authors evaluate a wide range of materials and describe the best current sources for information about companies, industries, markets and finance.'

FISHER, W. ed. **Business journals of the United States**. *Greenwood Press*, 1991. £49.50.

Business Week's guide to global investments using electronic tools. *McGraw-Hill*, 1994. 448 pp. £30.95 (book/disc package). 'Discover on line information services that provide timely information needed to analyze individual companies and understand tax and legal issues on a global scale. Master the intricacies of investing in bonds, options and commodities. Track down the best sector and country funds, and discover the value of online trading and stock analysis.... This guide comes replete with coupons for free trial time on various online services'.

NICHOLS, S.J. **CD-ROM and online law databases**. *Aslib*, 1993. 149 pp. £26.

BRITTIN, M. **CD-ROM and online business statistical databases**. *Aslib*, 1993. 136 pp. £26.

FRIEDMAN, C. ed. **Commodity prices**. 3rd ed. *Gale*, 1991. 630 pp.

Encompassing over 14,700 listings of 10,400 products covered in nearly 200 different sources, this guide gives specific information to guide the user to the periodicals, yearbooks, online sources, and other services that list commodity prices. Also covers the related financial instruments.

RILEY, S.G. ed. **Corporate magazines of the United States**. *Greenwood Press*, 1992. 304 pp. £67.50.

POPOVICH, C.J. and COSTELLO, M.R. **Directory of business and financial information services**. 9th ed. *Special Libraries Association*, 1994. 471 pp. $75. 1249 abstracted titles from 370 publishers. 'Services' are defined as 'information distributed by individuals or companies which make a business of providing the general distribution of facts, statistics or news in a focused subject area for a specialized readership: offering continuous updates at least twice per year. Typically, this criterion applies to current awareness services in looseleaf format as well as newsletters including electronic access on a selective basis.'

NEWBY, G.B. **Directory of directories on the Internet: A guide to information sources**. *Meckler*, 1994. 153 pp. $29.50.

EVINGER, W.R. ed. **Directory of federal libraries**. 2nd ed. *Oryx Press*, 1993. 384 pp. $97.50.

EC Financial Services Guide. *American Chamber of Commerce in Belgium*, 1992. 157 pp. [Produced by the EC Committee of the Chamber.] Narrative summaries of key issues in the EC decision-making process, followed by a directory containing: key contacts within Community institutions with telephone numbers; overview of how financial markets function in each EC Member State, with details of ministerial and related agencies; review of current reform in the US financial sector; and details of US government personnel who are instrumental in the formation of the financial services market.

European databanks: A guide to official statistics. *Eurostat*, 1992. 91 pp. 'The number of databanks has risen sharply over the past few years, particularly in Europe.... In view of the large number of sources and data producers, it is not easy to obtain the information one requires.... With the assistance of some 30 national statistical offices and international organizations, over 80 databanks have been identified and presented.'

European markets: A guide to company and industry information sources. 4th ed. *Washington Researchers*. 1992. 551 pp.

European money and banking statistical methods: 1993. *Office for Official Publications of the European Communities*, 1993. 291 pp. 'Description of the compilation of banking and monetary statistics in the member states of the European Economic Community and the countries of the European Free Trade Association.'

European statistics: Official sources. *Eurostat*, 1992. 206 pp. 'The completion of the single European market and greater cooperation between the European Community, EFTA, and the countries of Central and Eastern Europe require an effective system of information on official statistics. Around 200 addresses are listed here . . . (including) the full addresses of the following bodies:

- Statistical offices of international and supranational organizations
- National statistical offices
- Regional statistical offices

- National ministries and central banks which publish statistics.

RAMSAY, A. **Eurostat Index**. 5th ed. *Capital Planning Information*, 1992. 45. 'Subject keyword index to the statistical series produced by the *Statistical Office of the European Communities*. . . . A bibliography lists publications useful to trace Eurostat titles.'

EVINGER, W.R. ed. **Federal statistical source: Where to find Agency experts and personnel**. 29th ed. *Oryx Press*, 1991. 176 pp. $37.50. 'The most direct route to the more than 4,000 individuals throughout the federal government who assemble and disseminate statistical information.'

Finance. *Reviews of United Kingdom Statistical Sources*, Volume XXI, 1987. *Pergamon Press* FOR *Royal Statistical Society* and *Economic and Social Research Council*. 495 pp. In two Parts: *Financial Data of Banks and Other Institutions* and *Life Assurance and Pension Funds*. 'The termination of ESRC support for the series leaves individual projects in a variety of different states and its effect on the coverage of financial statistics is that this volume represents only a part of the field with which it was intended to deal when originally planned.' Each part comprises a detailed analysis and classified arrangement of the statistical data elements present in respectively 35 and 112 sources.

Financial newswires: The real-time news agencies 1992/93. *Waters Information Services*, 1992. 208 pp. $2,995. Includes *Profiles* of: AFX, Bloomberg, Dow Jones, Extel Financial, Futures World News, Jiji Press, Knight-Ridder Financial News, Kyodo News Service, Market News Service, Munifacts/ Bond Buyer Wire, Nikkei, Reuters, VWD, and the Press Release Services Business Wire and PR Newswire.

VAITILINGAM, R. **The Financial Times guide to using the financial pages**. *Pitman Publishing*, 1993. 216 pp. Clearly written guide in three Parts: I. *Identifying the players*: investors, companies, financial institutions, governments. II. *Interpreting the markets*: stocks and shares, indices and aggregates, international equities, trusts and funds, bonds and eurobonds, cash and currency, futures and options, primary products. III. *Understanding the economies*: UK economic indicators and surveys, the European economy.

ESSINGER, J. **Global directory of financial information vendors**. *Business One Irwin*, 1994. 290 pp.

MAXYMUK, J. ed. **Government CD-ROMs: A practical guide to searching electronic documents databases**. *Mecklermedia*, 1993. 165 pp. $47.50. 'The variety of different search softwares, protocols, and information retrieval methods used in CD-ROM databases issued by the US Government has made the librarian's task of maintaining electronic collections all the more difficult. This volume attempts to classify and describe the different search procedures in detail and to bring order to the multiplicity of search softwares employed on government discs.'

KINDER, R. ed. **Government documents and reference services**. *Haworth Press*, 1991. 288 pp. £26.95.

I'M guide. *Commission of the European Communities*, 1994. 788 pp. £40. 'A directory of information products and services which are publicly available in Europe and which do not require specially dedicated equipment for access. This one-stop information tool has been assembled via a network of national correspondents organized by IMPACT.'

EAGLE, S. ed. **Information sources for the press and broadcast media**. *Bowker-Saur*, 1991. 220 pp. £39.

AUGER, C.P. **Information sources in grey literature**. 3rd ed. *Bowker-Saur*, 1993. 250 pp. 'Grey literature – publications with little or no general distribution.'

CUNNEW, R. **The insurance sourcebook**. *Longman* in association with the *Chartered Insurance Institute*. 1992. Detailed directory and guide to sources of information on and for insurance, including coverage of: official sources, associations, colleges and universities, commercial organizational sources (accountants, consultants, insurers and intermediaries, lawyers, market research providers, stockbrokers etc.), followed by subject classified listings of serials, reference books, and textbooks, and a section on computer-based services and libraries and information units.

SPICELAND, J.D. and AGRAWAL, S. **International guide to accounting journals**. 2nd ed. *Paul Chapman Publishing*, 1993. £39.95. 'The most comprehensive national and international guide to accounting journals available . . . . It covers over 300 journals in accounting and related areas, including 150 published in the USA and over 150 in 33 other countries.'

FLEMING, M.C. and NELLIS, J.G. **International statistics sources**. *Routledge*, 1995. Two volumes. '*Instat* provides a comprehensive subject guide to sources of international statistical data. Its essential purpose is to allow users to trace sources of international data on particular subjects easily and quickly. The attempt has been made to cover all international sources of statistical data published by both public and private bodies. Altogether, around 400 sources are included. Purely national sources, restricted to data for one country, are not covered. The publications indexed are, generally speaking, the latest editions available at the time of preparation of *Instat*: 1991 to mid-1994. No restriction has been imposed as to the range of subject matter included in *Instat*. It covers, therefore, not only the full range of economic, political, business and social statistics, but also statistics concerning many other areas of interest such as the environment, science and technology, defence and climate. The wide coverage area will be evident from the list of the 46 subject areas given in the Contents.' These subject areas include: commodities; development and aid; finance; income and wealth; international trade and finance; living costs and standards; national accounts; parliament and public affairs; prices; and taxation.

RESNICK, R. and TAYLOR, D. **The Internet business guide: Riding the Information Superhighway to profit**. *Sams Publishing*, 1994.

MOREHEAD, J. and FETZER, M. **Introduction to United States government information sources**. 4th ed. *Libraries Unlimited*, 1992. 474 pp. "In short, all those interested in US government publications or documents librarianship should have this book." (*Government Publications Review*).

BENTLEY, L.H. and KIESL, J. **Investment statistics locator**. *Oryx Press*, 1994. 320 pp. 'This new research tool is the quick and simple route to finding recurrently published charts and tables of statistical information. Nearly 75 periodicals that specialise in business, investment, and economic subjects and regularly publish statistics are indexed in this book. This index directs the user to periodicals that present the most current data, including international and electronic sources.'

SHULER, J. **Key guide to electronic resources: Government information**.

Meckler, 1993. 150 pp. $35. 'Comprehensive evaluative directory of electronic reference sources in the field of government-produced information.'

COX, J. **Keyguide to information sources in online and cd-rom database searching**. *Mansell*, 1991. 272 pp. £55.

BLACKMAN, J. **The legal researcher's Internet directory**. *Legal Research of New York*, 1994.

Proceedings of the financial information sources seminar. *Learned Information*, 1993. 176 pp. £48. 'Held during the 46th Conference of the International Federation for Information and Documentation, 26th October 1992. Organised by the Banking, Finance and Insurance Special Interest Group.'

BEYERLY, E. **Public international law: A guide to information sources**. *Mansell*, 1991. 352 pp.

CLINCH, P. **Legal information: What it is and where to find it**. *Aslib*, 1995. 50 pp. £12.

The market data industry 1992/93. *Waters Information Services*, 1993. 306 pp. 'This study of the real-time market data industry was undertaken with the belief that this multi-billion dollar industry deserved a more in-depth examination and quantitative analysis than was formerly available. The size, structure and major players in this industry have never been documented in any detail outside of the internal reports prepared by the strategic planning and marketing staffs of the market data vendors themselves. This information was previously not available in a public report.' Detailed *Vendor Profiles* are given for: Automatic Data Processing, Bloomberg, Bridge Information Systems, ILX Systems, Knight-Ridder, Quick Corp, Quotron Systems, Reuters Holdings, S&P Comstock, Telekurs, Telerate Systems, Topic, Track Data Corp. *Other Vendors* briefly profiled are: Beta Systems. Bonneville Market Information, CQG Inc, Commodity Market Services/Manifast, Fininfo, Future Source, IDM/Marts, PC Quote, SDIB, Shark/DBC, Star Data Systems.

POWELL, L.S. **Mortgage banking sourcebook**. 2nd ed. *Mortgage Bankers Association of America*, 1992, 105 pp. $35.00. A reference guide to information sources on the mortgage lending industry.

MILLER, A.C. and PUNSALAN, V.J. **Refereed and nonrefereed economic journals: A guide to publishing opportunities**. *Greenwood Press*, 1988. 252 pp.

TALLEY, P.L. **The savings and loan crisis: An annotated bibliography**. *Greenwood Press*. 1993. 192 pp. £49.50.

Sources of European economic and business information. 6th ed. *Gower*, 1995. 352 pp. £125. 'Completely revised and updated by the *British Library Business Information Research Service*. The aim of the directory is to provide a listing of the major sources of economic and business statistical information for 32 countries in Europe. Publications listed in the directory cover a wide range of economic topics, including economic conditions, socio-economic data, public finance, industry, business and commerce. They are published by a variety of bodies – international organizations, national statistical offices, government departments, specialist publishers, banks and financial institutions, professional and trade associations, etc.'

StatBase locator on disk: UNSTAT's guide to international computerized

statistical databases. *United Nations*, 1994. $20. 'An inventory of international statistical databases from which data are available in electronic formats. . . . Provides information on the organization, content, producing agency and means of access for each database. All fields of social and economic statistics with internationally-available data are covered for Statistical databases of all United Nations agencies, Eurostat (European Union) and OECD. *StatBase Locator on Disk* is self-contained, with user-friendly software for searching and retrieving database information.'

ROBINSON, J.S. **Tapping the government grapevine: The user-friendly guide to US government information sources**. *Oryx Press*, 1993. 240 pp. $34.50.

ENDRES, K.L. ed. **Trade, industrial and professional periodicals of the United States**. *Greenwood Press*, 1994. 496 pp. £89.95. 'Provides a view of the specialised business press. It includes profiles, arranged alphabetically, of about 70 periodicals, reflecting the diversity of the specialised business press.'

UNITED NATIONS CENTRE ON TRANSNATIONAL CORPORATIONS. **Transnational business information: A manual of needs and sources**. *United Nations*, 1991. 216 pp.

CLINCH, P. **Using a law library**. *Blackstone Press*, 1992. 264 pp. £12.50.

SEARS, J.L. and MOODY, M.K. **Using government information sources: Print and electronic**. 2nd ed. *Oryx Press*, 1994. 552 pp. $115. 'This RASD/American Library Association 'Outstanding Reference Source' explains the uses and accessibility of government information sources within the context of actual research.'

KROL, E. **The whole Internet: User's guide & catalog**. 2nd ed. *O'Reilly & Associates*, 1994.

ARMSTRONG, C.J. **World databases in business**. *Bowker-Saur*, 1994. 1500 pp. £165.

Volumes in the *World Bibliographic Series* from Clio Press (*ABC-Clio*) 'are aimed mainly at the English-speaker and each volume comprises a selective, critically annotated bibliography of the organization, or organizations, concerned: 300–1,000 entries; covers books, articles, theses, directories and databases; compiled by acknowledged authorities; includes an informative introduction and detailed indexes.' Volumes in the series include: BARATTA, J.P. **United Nations System**. *ABC-Clio*, 1994. 350 pp. £39.50; SALDA, A.C.M. **International Monetary Fund**. *ABC-Clio*, 1993. 334 pp. £36.25; SALDA, A.C.M. **World Bank**. *ABC-Clio*, 1994. 306 pp. £36.50; PAXTON, J. **European Communities**. *ABC-Clio*, 1992. 208 pp. £31.50.

(80) HERRING, R.J. and LITAN, R.E. **Financial regulation in the global economy**. *Brookings Institution*, 1995, pp 147–149.

(81) Brealey and Myers op cit pp 309–310.

(82) ESSINGER, J. **The investment manager's handbook**. *Chapman & Hall*, 1993. 440 pp. £55. Includes in Part Three of the Handbook the following information for 27 countries: the address and telephone number of the country's principal stock exchange(s); the country's principal regulatory authority for the securities industry; the prevailing national time difference from Greenwich Mean Time (GMT); the forms and types of securities issued within each country; the structure and regulation of the financial

markets in the country; information about the country's leading custodian banks.

(83) HEXTON, R. **Technical analysis in the international currency markets**. *Kogan Page*, 1993. 288 pp. £32.95. 'This book: will be the first totally devoted to international currency markets; is based on the author's own expert trading experiences. . . . Aimed mainly at the private investor, this book will also provide a useful reference book for the professional trader.'

HEXTON, R. **Technical analysis in the options markets: The effective use of computerised trading systems**. 2nd ed. *Kogan Page*, 1993. 256 pp. £29.95. 'Richard Hexton is chairman of the *London School of Investment* and a member of the *Society of Technical Analysts*.'

(84) ESSINGER op cit pp 28–30.

(85) ESSINGER op cit p 30.

(86) ESSINGER op cit pp 30–31.

(87) RUTTERFORD, J. **An introduction to stock exchange investment**. 2nd ed. *Macmillan Press*, 1993. 445 pp. £16.50. Based on the UK environment, with the chapters arranged in three main sections: evaluation of securities; investment strategy; international investment and investing institutions. 'The book therefore aims not only to provide an introduction to the world of investment, describing how the Stock Exchange works, the types of security quoted on it and the main types of investor, but also to explain the *principles* underlying Stock Exchange investment.'

(88) Rutterford notes that 'although dividends are actual cash flows and earnings are accounting figures, earnings are the more popular variable to forecast (despite their limitations as predictors)'.

(89) RUTTERFORD op cit pp 297–299.

(90) EDWARDS, H. **London Classification of Business Studies**. 3rd ed. *London Business School*, 1991. Mimeograph.

Further reading

CAVANAGH, J., WYSHAM, D. and ARRUDA, M. eds. **Beyond Bretton Woods: Alternatives to the global economic order**. *Pluto Press*, 1994. 320 pp. £12.95. Published in association with the *Transnational Institute*, Amsterdam.

BELLO, W. et al. **Dark victory: The United States, structural adjustment and global poverty**. *Pluto Press* for the *Transnational Institute*, 1994. 144 pp. DFI 35,30. 'Published in the year of the 50th anniversary of the IMF and the World Bank, Walden Bello offers a persuasive argument that re-colonisation of the Third World has been carried out through the agencies of the international banks, with disastrous consequences: reduction of social welfare, wage cuts, devaluation of local currencies etc.'

BAUMOL, W.J. and BLINDER, A.S. **Economics**. 6th ed. *Dryden Press*, 1994. 960 pp. £15.95. 'The finest edition yet in a book characterised by continuing innovation and excellence.'

BARRO, R. and GRILLI, V. **European macroeconomics**. *Macmillan Press*, 1994. 584 pp. £18.99.

BROWN, W. and HOGENDORN, J.S. **International economics**. *Addison-Wesley*, 1994. 600 pp.

KREININ, M.E. **International economics**. 7th ed. *Dryden Press*, 1995. 500 pp. £17.50. 'Provides a simplified but comprehensive analysis of international economic relations, with the fundamental objective of extracting maximum policy from a minimum number of theoretical constructs. It also features a flexible organization focusing on the study of international economics through international trade and international finance.'

EDWARDS, R.W. **International monetary collaboration**. 2nd ed. *Transnational Juris Publications*, 1994. $125. (Looseleaf – to be supplemented). 'The first edition . . . was awarded the *Certificate of Merit* by the American Society of International Law. . . . This revised and updated edition is the most comprehensive book written on the institutions and legal structure of international monetary relations, including the IMF, BIS, OECD, IBEC, FECOM, and more. Of particular merit is its analysis of the myriad developments in the European Community monetary system and the former socialist states of Eastern Europe.'

BERTHELEMY, J-C. and VOURC'H, A. **Debt relief and growth**. *OECD*, 1994. 192 pp. $24. 'Is the debt crisis over? This volume reminds us that, even if the severity of the crisis has been reduced for some of the most spectacular debtors, the problem persists for many of the others.'

VAN MEERHAEGHE, M.A.G. **International economic institutions**. 6th ed. *Kluwer Academic Publishers*, 1992. 398 pp. £110.75. Critical appraisal of the major institutions, including: IMF, World Bank, OECD, EU.

GREEN, S.L. **Macroeconomics: Analysis and application**. *Dryden Press*, 1993. 600 pp. $16.95. 'It goes beyond conventional discussions of monetary and fiscal policy in the applications section with separate chapters considering the effects of macroeconomic events on asset price determination business management decisions, social issues such as unemployment, poverty, income distribution and crime and personal issues such as retirement planning and employment opportunities.'

PORTER, T. **States, markets and regimes in global finance**. *Macmillan Press*, 1993. 200. £40.00. 'This book argues that international regulatory institutions become stronger when oligopolistic institutional arrangements decay and competitive pressures intensify. This is shown to be the case for global finance by careful studies of two inter-state institutions: the *Basle Committee on Banking Supervision* and the *International Organization of Securities Commissions*, and of the international banking and securities industries which they seek to regulate.'

BHAGWATI, J. **The world trading system at risk**. *Princeton University Press*, 1991. 156 pp. Based on the author's Harry Johnson Memorial Lecture at the Royal Society of Arts in London in 1990.

CHAPTER TWO

Legal, Economic and Political Environments

Exploring the legal arena

1. National legal, regulatory and supervisory frameworks are the single most important differential distinguishing one country's trading activity from another's. They determine the types of organizational entity which can flourish in each country, what services and products each type of entity can provide, how they will be taxed, and how the whole is regulated and supervised. The frameworks can thus have a decisive influence on national and especially international business competitiveness and ultimately, on each nation's relative economic success. The frameworks also determine – of particular relevance here – the flows of 'required' information from each trading entity into the public domain. They define what information must be produced, in what form and content, when, for whom . . . and why (the last if only by implication). They specify the bodies who will determine that form and content – which often it transpires are not the same bodies as those responsible for ensuring that the information is produced, and on time, in that defined form and content.

2. So the codes, directives, laws, regulations, rules, standards and treaties form the fourth key type of publicly available factual finance information which all finance professionals must learn to relate to: alongside the entity accounts, financial market data, and economic and financial statistics whose importance has been already emphasized.

3. Despite important differences between nations, in all market-based economies there are seven types of organization which play a more or less significant determining role in each nation's trading system:

- The legislature: where the laws and regulatory and supervisory frameworks are made and economic and political policies are forged. This is the Congress in the USA; it is the Parliament in the UK – but with the latter subject in many areas now to the decisions of the various bodies comprising the European Union.
- The executive: government and its departments.
- The judiciary: the courts where the laws are interpreted and upheld.
- The central bank: for instance, the Federal Reserve System in the USA, the Bank of England in the UK.
- The agencies: we use this term here, not in the rather specific senses sometimes used by the UK and US governments, but to denote a wide variety of 'official', 'quasi-official' and 'non-official' bodies which are not in themselves government departments, but are directly or indirectly mandated in some way by Parliament or Congress to provide specific services. Some in their operations will be virtually indistinguishable from government departments; others are private (and *privatized*) organizations.
- Certain professional and trade bodies to whom the law delegates self- regulatory and supervisory activities; or whom take it upon themselves (at least for a time) to perform these duties within a defined trading zone.
- The organized financial markets.

4. All of these bodies are producing information for the public domain as part of what earlier we described as the 'unfortunately rather convoluted, legal, regulatory and supervisory infrastructure'. In this chapter, we explore a little the nature of those infrastructure bodies which are operative in the UK, the USA, Europe, and internationally; and we give examples of some of the serial publications which the bodies produce. We also review instances of the many types of commercial serial publication which have arisen: each aiming at trying to unravel for a specific target audience at least some of the convolutions. Clearly, there is no sense in which the following is a comprehensive review of the totality of information sources which would be 'relevant' to (or 'admissible' in) particular legal situations. In any case, the manner in which legal professionals approach the solution of specific problems with which they are faced hardly comes over in what follows: for a start, 'precedent' – with its corollary of an exhaustive examination of prior writings – is of supreme importance in the legal systems of the UK and the USA. So this chapter is very much a layman's introduction to 'the law', in the sense that all of us involved with one or another aspect of trade and finance ought to know something about what the lawyers get up to (perhaps we leave too much to the lawyers?).[91] I cannot imagine that anyone with a real legally based problem to be solved would use this book as their sole guide: but, just in case, irrespective of the answer to my question of a moment ago – do not: consult a lawyer!

5. Having given that necessary disclaimer, we must be careful not to make the legal area at an information source level more complicated than it is. We might think of the complex of material as primarily divisible into four groups – which we will term colloquially:

- Works in progress
- The works
- Embellishments to the works
- Interpretations of the works

6. *Works in progress* is the law being made. Here is a good account of the position in the United Kingdom:[92]

> The legislative process has been described and analyzed in a number of academic works and legal text books. . . .[93] Statute law which is made in this country (so excluding European Community law . . .) is contained in two different basic sets of documents, made under differing authority, but with absolutely equal binding force as far as the citizens or bodies to which it applies are concerned. Primary legislation is contained in Acts of Parliament, enacted by the Queen in Parliament following passage by both Houses,[94] and not subject to challenge by the courts.[95] Delegated legislation is made by Ministers under powers given by Acts of Parliament; it is (nearly always) set out in the form of a statutory instrument which may or may not be subject to parliamentary proceedings. The exercise by a Minister of his power to make delegated legislation may be challenged in the courts.
>
> It is convenient to identify six stages in the legislative process for Government bills. The first stage is the *initiation of legislation*. Bills may be initiated for many reasons and may emerge from a range of sources . . . (including prior) political commitments; . . . ministerial responses to new political challenges or emergency situations; international requirements; proposals of the two Law Commissions; recommendations of Royal Commissions, select committees or other inquiry bodies; parliamentary debates; studies made within government departments; decisions made by courts or observations by judges drawing attention to some apparent defect of the law; and annual or other routine requirements (sometimes important, as in the Finance Bill).
>
> Once Ministers have agreed on the need for legislation, the second stage of the process – the *preparation of legislation* – can go ahead. . . .

At this stage there may be consultations with outside bodies affected by the proposed legislation or with various pressure or interest groups that wish to influence its content. These may be largely informal, or more formally require responses to Green Papers or other consultative documents. . . . This second stage has been well described as 'putting the bones on the skeleton'.

Approval for the inclusion of a bill in the Government's legislative programme has to be obtained from the Future Legislation Committee of the Cabinet. This approval gives the necessary authority for the third stage in the process, when the *drafting* of the bill is done. . . . When the drafting of the bill has been completed, the bill must be finally cleared by the Legislation Committee of the Cabinet before it is presented to Parliament and published.

Legislation now enters the fourth stage of the process, the *scrutiny and passage of bills by both Houses of Parliament.*[96] The majority of Government bills (23 out of 39 in session 1991–92) and especially most politically important or controversial bills, are introduced first into the Commons, and published. Each bill has a general debate on second reading; individual clauses and amendments may be debated in committee and on report; and it is read the third time and passed. The bill is then similarly scrutinised and passed by the Lords. Any amendments made by the Lords have to be agreed by the Commons before the bill can be presented for Royal Assent and become an Act of Parliament.

The fifth stage is the *publication* of Acts of Parliament by H.M. Stationery Office, on behalf of the Statutory Publications Office, as soon as possible after they have been given Royal Assent. . . . The Law Commission has a continuing programme of consolidation of previous statute law and each session a number of consolidation Acts are passed which do not change the law (though corrections of apparent errors and minor improvements may be allowed). . . . All the public Acts of each year are published in several volumes of Public General Acts and Measures.

When an Act is passed and published, the legislative process does not stop. Delegated legislation may be made under the Act. The new law has to be complied with; various bodies will be concerned with its enforcement; many people, and ultimately the courts, will be concerned with its interpretation. Our sixth stage is therefore *post-legislative review* in the light of experience.

The legislative process for the production and review of delegated legislation is somewhat different. This legislation springs from the requirements of primary legislation and not from independent policy choices. Its preparation and drafting (in the form of statutory instruments) is conditioned by the contents of the parent Act. The parliamentary processes, if there are any (some minor instruments are not subject to any formal parliamentary scrutiny) are quite different – either to approve a statutory instrument (the affirmative procedure) or to annul it (the negative procedure) – according to the terms of the parent Act.[97] Motions for annulment of statutory instruments are usually called 'prayers'. Delegated legislation is published separately from primary legislation. And review is encouraged by the fact that it is much easier to amend delegated legislation in the light of experience than it is to amend Acts of Parliament.

7. *The works* We use this phrase to describe the actual written primary and secondary – delegated – legislation itself, the situation in the USA, as compared to the UK, being complicated by the federal system of government:[98]

> The United States is a common-law jurisdiction with a federal system of government. Under the federal constitution each state has independent authority over all matters except those delegated to the federal government. Thus the term 'American law' is an umbrella term covering 51 different legal systems, one for each of the 50 states and one for the federal law. While this multiplicity of jurisdictions may have little impact on the law student, who encounters American law principally when it yields common-law precedents, when it comes to legal practice it takes on a deep significance. Each state has its own legislature and its own body of public, criminal and private law. Legal actions may be governed by state law only or by federal law only or perhaps by a combination of both. Jurisdictional conflicts can be a real problem.
>
> The sources of federal law are found in the Constitution, the Acts of Congress, federal rules and regulations, and in the decisions of the Supreme Court of the United States, the inferior federal courts, and administrative agencies. The sources of state law are found in each state's constitution as adopted by the electorate, the enactments of the legislature (and those enacted directly by referendum), and the written decisions of the highest court of appeal.[99]

8. *Embellishments to the works* are particularly important in the financial field. For the UK, this is well brought out in Guy Holborn's recent (and excellent) *Butterworth's Legal Research Guide.*[100] Holborn is especially good on relating what he terms *quasi-legislation*, to the formal officially delegated legislation itself:

> In the United Kingdom, as in most jurisdictions, there are two main classes of legislation. Primary legislation consists of the Acts – or statutes, the terms are interchangeable – passed by Parliament itself. The other class, usually published in the form of statutory instruments (SIs), is variously termed secondary, subsidiary, subordinate or delegated legislation. The last most accurately reflects its nature as this is legislation made under powers delegated by Parliament, typically to government ministers. It may (or may not) receive limited Parliamentary scrutiny, but Parliament itself does not have time, even if it were desirable in principle, to enact all the rules, regulations and matters of detail required in the administration of the modern state. . . . Unlike in many jurisdictions which have written constitutions and constitutional courts, the legality of primary legislation in the United Kingdom cannot be challenged in the courts. Only secondary legislation can be subject

to judicial review, if it is made in excess of its enabling powers (ultra vires).

There is one obvious proviso to the last proposition, which qualifies the traditional two-fold classification of legislation set out, namely the European dimension. European community legislation, although in a sense delegated legislation, does not fit neatly into either category and needs to be treated separately. Another category of material . . . is not strictly speaking legislation, in that it is not directly legally enforceable, but it nonetheless may have legal consequences. It is highly miscellaneous, but is compendiously described as quasi-legislation, codes of practice being perhaps the most commonly cited example.

From the wide range of other kinds of quasi-legislation, one particular example worth mentioning is extra-statutory concessions made by the Inland Revenue. Naturally enough these cannot override a statutory provision, but in practice a mass of detailed regulation of taxation is made in this way. Longmans publish a looseleaf *Inland Revenue Practices and Concessions* and recent information may be found in *Simon's Tax Intelligence.*

Other important materials are the rule books of the various Self-Regulatory Organisations (SROs), such as LAUTRO and FIMBRA, that are recognised under the Financial Services Act. They are published in printed form (usually by the SROs themselves) and may be reprinted in works such as the *Encyclopaedia of Financial Services Law.* But they are also available in an electronic version, C-Text, together with the Companies Acts and other related sources, supplied by Compliance. This is used by the bodies themselves and by some of the City law firms. It is regarded as being the most up-to-date source.

Other examples of quasi-legislative materials are . . . British Standards, Accounting Standards, the Rules and Regulations of the Stock Exchange, and the Stock Exchange *Admission of Securities to Listing.* The latter are partly delegated legislation . . . in that they are made under the Financial Services Act, but they are also partly made simply pursuant to its Deed of Settlement.

No particular rules can be laid down for finding and using quasi-legislation. The most important kinds are published by HMSO, but mostly it will be issued by government departments or the relevant bodies themselves.[101]

9. *Interpretation of the works* occurs primarily in the courts and results in what Holborn calls in the relevant chapter Case Law. This is where matters start to present some difficulties for the researcher: in two senses, for our purposes. First, here is Holborn again:

Finding and using legislation, as the last chapter indicated, may have its intricacies, but at least the material is reasonably finite. If you are looking for a statute in force, it is likely to be in the three or four shelves of books that comprise *Halsbury's Statutes.* Even the SIs, which seem to be published in daunting numbers, occupy only a few stacks in the law library. Law reports, on the other hand, represent a quantity of material of a different order of magnitude – only the largest law libraries contain anything approaching the complete corpus of published law reports. . . . The problem is compounded by the English common law doctrine that the force of a legal decision does not depend on it being reported.

It is worth looking briefly at how it is decided to report a case. The decision is in the hands of the editor of the series of law reports, not in the hands of the judge, though the judge, or indeed counsel, can suggest that a case is worth reporting. . . . Apart from *The Law Reports*, most law reporting is in the hands of competing commercial publishers. . . . Economic limitations can determine whether a case, particularly one of only specialist interest, sees the light of day. Conversely, some series may include cases which in truth add nothing new, but which are included to give the impression of better coverage than their rivals. New series of law reports continue to start up, while others cease publication.[102]

10. The other complication – for the outsider coming new to 'the law' – is the range of primary and delegated legislation which may be invoked in specific situations. For instance, if we examine the 'Table of statutes' listed at the outset of Cox's useful – and compendious – text,[103] as well as the expected:

Bank Charter Act 1844
Bank of England Act 1694
Banking Act 1987
Bills of Exchange Act 1882
Building Societies Act 1986 (and prior Acts for 1836, 1874 1894, 1939, 1962)
Cheques Act 1957
Companies Act 1985 (and the Acts for 1948 and 1989)
Consumer Credit Act 1974
Finance Act 1968
Finance (No 2) Act 1975
Financial Services Act 1986
Friendly Societies Act 1992
Income and Corporation Taxes Act 1988
Insolvency Act 1986
Insurance Companies Act 1982
Moneylenders Act 1927 (and for 1900)
Pawnbrokers Act 1960 (and for 1872)
Prevention of Fraud (Investments) Act 1958
Social Security Pensions Act 1975
Statute of Frauds (1677)

we find the on the surface perhaps less expected:

Betting and Gaming Duties Act 1981
Charitable Pawn Offices (Ireland) Act 1842

Criminal Justice Act 1988
Criminal Justice (International Cooperation) Act 1990
Criminal Justice (Scotland) Act 1987
Data Protection Act 1984
Drug Trafficking Offences Act 1986
Fraudulent Dispositions Act 1991 (Bahamas)
Glass-Steagall Act 1934 (USA)
International Companies Act 1982 (Malta)
International Business Companies (IBC) Act 1990 (Bahamas)
McFadden Act (USA)
Moneylenders' Act (Northern Ireland) 1933
Offshore Trust Act 1988 (Malta)
Pawnbrokers Act (Northern Ireland) 1954
Police and Criminal Evidence Act 1984
Prevention of Terrorism (Temporary Provisions) Act 1989
Reserve Forces (Safeguard of Employment) Act 1985
Securities Act 1933 (USA)

11. Fortunately, if one wishes simply to start to understand the legal situation as it applies to specific areas – such as 'the law relating to banking services' or 'the law of the investment markets' or the 'company structures' that are legally permissible – there will more often than not be a number of commercial texts to choose from, at varying levels of intellectual rigour and sophistication. Such books are strongly recommended as entrées to the relevant area of finance: not just to its legal aspects; but also as more general introductions. Lawyers have to try to be perfectly precise in what they write and say. Thus where – as so often in finance activity – there is uncertainty as to what exactly are the phenomena one needs to relate to, it is often best to turn first to a text originating within the law, rather than to a non-legal text. These legal texts can be refreshingly direct and even entertaining; as, for instance, in these excerpts from examples of UK texts covering the three topics just referred to:

(i) A variety of statutes define bank or a banker for particular purposes without actually explaining the term itself. For example, the Bills of Exchange Act 1882, s.2 states that a banker is 'someone who carries on the business of banking'. This is, to say the least, not very helpful. The same is also largely true of the Banking Act 1987, which talks in terms of 'authorised institutions' and not 'banks' as such. The Act's purpose is the regulation of deposit-taking and so it only deals specifically with 'banks' in so far as the use of the name 'bank' is restricted by the Bank of England to larger authorised institutions. Even then, overseas banks are exempt from this restriction. The Act tells us very little about the role and characteristics of a bank and it does not directly regulate the way in which banks carry out their business.[104]

(ii) An investment, like an elephant, is more easily recognised than defined. Its abstract meaning, namely the activity of investing, is the corollary of saving and the antithesis of consumption. If resources are invested, whether they are derived from unexpended income or the proceeds of selling or disposing of assets, they are used to acquire 'things' which are retained for a shorter or longer period in the expectation that while retained they will yield an income to the owner, or that they will eventually be disposed of at a price exceeding the cost of acquiring them, or that they will achieve both results.

In its concrete sense the word investment means the 'thing' or 'things' which are invested in. The difficulty then arises of defining those 'things' which are capable of being investments and differentiating them from other 'things' which are not so susceptible. The difficulty occurs because the character of a 'thing' as an investment does not depend on its physical qualities or the purposes to which it can be put, but on the purpose which the owner of it has in mind when he acquires it.[105]

(iii) *Every business is different, and every business is unique* Two platitudes – clichés – neither more than half true. In relation to leaders there was some research carried out a few years ago which concluded that their skills and personalities were enormously varied, but that they did share two qualities essential for their jobs. First, they had to be able to see just a little bit further than other people, and second, they had to know how they and their subordinates would perform under pressure. The researchers said that those leaders could buy-in the first, by surrounding themselves with seers – those who have *understanding*; it is a gift to the extent that it is derived from intuition, but the more vital part comes from experience and from the hard thought that experience should engender.

Which brings us to the first of our platitudes; while different businesses have distinguishing features, they share frameworks, have patterns of operations whose similarities are remarkable. Frameworks and patterns are capable of being understood. They are set partly by company law and accounting thought, partly by tax constraints, and to a large extent by the economic relationships between the directors of businesses, their customers and their suppliers – those who supply the necessary capital and labour among them. Knowledge of all the separate rules will get us some part of the way, knowledge of company law, of accounting, and of tax; but if we seek understanding, to be able to see what the future may be – can be – we need to be able to put all that knowledge together, to weave its strands into the right patterns.

Roget's Thesaurus offers some alternatives for platitude: twaddle, claptrap, bunkum, rubbish, balderdash, moonshine, fiddlestick, flummery, inanity, rot, tosh, bosh, havers, blethers, tripe, bilge, bull, hooey, hokum, boloney. But I do not think he was describing the attempt to understand the framework of business.[106]

12. Thus, there is certainly no need for the legal layman – at least in the first instance – to wade through masses of original source material when trying to engage the legal ramifications of the topic of concern. Indeed, as already implied, that could be positively misleading. Further, if the original sources need eventually to be referred to, it will usually be best to use a commercial annotated text, of which, again, there are large numbers of authoritative examples. For instance, *Butterworths Banking Law Handbook*[107] not only covers all of the relevant 'Statutes'; but also the 'Statutory Instruments', the 'Rules for the Conduct of Clearing', 'Bank of England Notices', and 'EEC Directives'.

13. Such a recommendation is especially applicable to the USA – even though in fact there the approach to 'the law' applicable in specific cases often differs significantly from that common in the UK:

> American lawyers regard legal research as involving a search for primary authorities applicable to the case in point. In some respects this contrasts with the English approach, in which the use of textbooks plays a large part and the aim is to arrive at a summarized statement of the legal position. America is a litigious society with a correspondingly large legal profession and the vast output of legal literature thereby generated is geared to the publication and indexing of primary sources. For the English reader this poses problems. There are relatively few introductory texts written from a broad practical viewpoint. The most commonly used keys to searching primary materials are subject and citation indexes, with our more familiar tables of cases and statutes less in evidence.[108]

14. However, as regards the USA (and, indeed, elsewhere), in addition to such introductory background texts as exist, there are a large number – a very large number – of commercially produced *legal serials* published, which supplement and update the background texts (to the extent that these exist). We will reference several hundred of these in a moment. Before that, we should summarize the overall approach adopted in this chapter. Its central core – coming after the next section – references the range of UK and US national official and quasi-official organizations concerned with the legal and regulatory frameworks of each country. A number of these organizations have of course economic, political and other remits in addition to their more specific concerns with legislative processes. In this they overlap with some matters already covered in Chapter 1, but from an international perspective. This central part of the chapter in fact references examples of the first five of the seven types of organization listed at the outset of the chapter (as playing a determining legal/regulatory/supervisory role in each country's trading and financial system). Following, after an interlude reviewing the notions of 'incorporation' and of 'financial accounting', we cover examples of the sixth type of organization, the professional and trade bodies. However, here we expand the coverage to include also consideration of European and international bodies, as well as those which have a UK or US focus. (Examples of the seventh type of organization – the financial markets – are given in Chapter 5). Some of the bodies which we reference in this section are concerned with trade and development matters. This allows a link to a number of official bodies concerned with that area (of which the *United Nations* will be the most conspicuous). We end the chapter with an overview of that unique body, the *European Union*.

Commercial serials

15. Although many of the serials referenced below are directly concerned with 'the law', it is convenient also to treat here serials which relate to taxation – and the *fiscal environment* more generally; to *accounting, auditing and reporting*; and to *bankruptcy and insolvency*. To a lesser degree, I have also thought it to be helpful to reference items focusing on areas which – while not central to the main thrust of this book – nevertheless need continually to be borne in mind: e.g. antitrust, competition, corporate law, credit, going public, mergers and acquisitions, and so on. These sorts of issues are applicable to financial corporations – just as they are applicable to corporations in general. It will be seen that many of the commercial information providers publish material relevant to several of these fields.

16. Four large publishing conglomerates are very active in this segment of the publishing market, all having a significant presence elsewhere in the finance commercial publishing system (as we shall see later). The first we consider, *Thomson Corporation*, upon examination turns out to own a remarkably wide range of companies active in one or another area of finance publishing. We take the Corporation as a good illustration of the significant concentration which has occurred, and continues to occur,[109] across this segment of the overall information industry. Using material from the 1994 Annual Report of Thomson (published in spring 1995), we find:

(1) #72 Thomson Corporation Suite 2706, Toronto Dominion Bank Tower, PO Box 24, Toronto-Dominion Centre, Toronto, Ontario, M5K 1A1, Canada. f: (1 416) 360 9912. *Also* The Metro Center, One Station Place, 6th Floor, Stamford, CT 06902, USA. f: (1 203) 328 9408 *and* The Quadrangle, PO Box 4YG, 180 Wardour Street, London W1A 4YG, UK. f: (44 171) 734 0561.

(**1**) *Thomson Corporation Publishing International* (TCPI) consists of four groups with over 16,000 employees:

- *International Thomson Publishing* provides media-diverse information products serving worldwide marketplaces mainly in the education, professional, reference and library fields (e.g.)

  Chapman & Hall
  Gale Research
  International Thomson Publishing
  Research Publications
  Routledge
  Wadsworth

- *Thomson Business Information* provides information, software and print products and services for the worldwide scientific, technical, intellectual property, construction, library, corporate, medical, automotive repair and casualty insurance marketplaces (e.g.)

  Information Access Company
  The Institute for Scientific Information

- *Thomson Corporation Publishing Limited* provides information services for the legal, professional and commercial marketplaces, principally in the UK, Scandinavia and Australasia (e.g.)

  Gee
  Law Book Company
  Legal Information Resources
  Professional Publishing
  Sweet & Maxwell

- *Thomson Regional Newspapers* is the largest publisher of regional newspapers in the UK.

TCPI provides 60,000 products, including 100 online services, 200 CD-ROM products, 45,000 books and directories, 6,500 software and 1,600 video/audio products, and 700 subscription-based journals.

(**2**) *Thomson Financial & Professional Publishing Group* has two business groups with over 8,000 employees:

- *Thomson Financial Services* provides quality financial and investment information, research, analysis and software products to worldwide financial and corporate communities (e.g.)

  American Banker/The Bond Buyer
  Asset Backed Securities Group
  AutEx
  CDA Investment Technologies
  Dalcomp
  DealWatch
  First Call
  Electronic Settlements Group
  ILX Systems

International Financing Review
The Investext Group
Muller Data
Municipal Market Data
Securities Data Company
Securities Data Publishing
Securities Information Center
Sheshunoff Information Services
Technical Data
Thomson BankWatch
Thomson Financial Publishing
Thomson Investment Software
Thomson Municipal Services
TradeView/Trade Route
Valorinform

- *Thomson Professional Publishing* provides primary, analytical and business information, in both print and electronic formats, to the legal, tax, accounting, human resources and regulatory marketplaces, mainly in North America (e.g.)

  Clark Boardman Callaghan
  Faulkner & Gray
  Lawyers Cooperative Publishing
  Research Institute of America
  Warren Gorham & Lamont

'Together they provide 3,300 individual products, including some 170 online services, 180 CD-ROM products, 40 software packages, 440 loose-leaf services, 175 newsletters and approximately 2,000 books and directories.'

17. A range of examples of legal and cognate subject area serials produced by *Thomson Corporation* companies follows here, classified by issuing entity:

(1) #73 American Banker Newsletters 1325 G Street NW, Suite 900, Washington, DC 20005, USA. t: (1 202) 347 2665; f: 347 1158.

413. **American Banker's Washington Watch**. w. $695. **online**. Analysis of the developing regulatory and legislative initiative affecting insured financial institutions. Covers events at the FDIC, the Federal Reserve Board, and the Office of the Comptroller of the Currency.

414. **Banking Attorney**. w. $725. **online**. Intensive analyses of legal issues, legal rules and litigation affecting depository institutions.

415. **Credit Union Accountant**. w. $675. **online**. Focuses on accounting policy changes for credit unions emanating from government agencies.

416. **Insurance Accountant**. w. $750. **online**. Regulatory, legislative, and accounting policy developments affecting the insurance industry's accounting practices. Covers all the relevant major developments within

the National Association of Insurance Commissioners, the AICPA, the FASB, the IRS, and the SEC, as well as relevant court cases impacting on insurance accounting.

417. **Insurance Regulator**. w. $750. **online**. Federal and state-by-state developments.

418. **International Bank Accountant**. w. $695. **online**. Accounting issues of interest to banks in the USA, Canada and Europe. Contains a USA ledger that summarizes events in the UK, France, Germany and Canada, as well as others on a periodic basis.

419. **International Banking Regulator**. w. $925. **online**. 'Designed for the people who run foreign banks that have US operations. Concentrates on the unique laws governing foreign banks and their effect on such processes as applying to opening or changing the status of a bank branch. Tracks the activities of foreign banks into areas such as securities and commercial paper. A monthly companion, *International Banking Report*, enhances the weekly with reports from the American Banker, Thomson BankWatch, and other newsletters regarding banking activities around the world.'

420. **LDC Debt Report**. w. $850. **online**. 'Economic, political, tax, and regulatory devlopments that affect emerging markets bond pricing and investment.'

421. **Mortgage Marketplace**. w. $750. **online**. 'The newsletter for the secondary mortgage markets. Covers political developments, regulatory changes and accounting issues affecting the secondary market.'

422. **NCUA Watch**. w. $675. **online**. Covers policy and expected policy, as well as actions such as lawsuits, pertaining to the activities of the National Credit Union Administration.

423. **Public Finance Watch**. w. $645. **online**. State and local insurance of public finance instruments and the market for those securities.

424. **Regulatory Compliance Watch**. w. $675. **online**. Covers the legal, regulatory, and legislative developments in Washington affecting the nation's banks, savings and loan institutions, and credit unions.

425. **Thrift Regulator**. w. $715. **online**. Concentrates on regulatory, congressional and judicial developments affecting the savings and loan industry.

(2) #74 Clark Boardman Callaghan 155 Pfingsten Road, Deerfield, IL 60015–9917, USA. t: (1 800) 323 1336; f: (1 708) 948 9340. *Also* c/o Sweet & Maxwell, South Quay Plaza, 183 Marsh Wall, London E14 9FT, UK. t: (44 171) 538 8686; f: 538 9508.

Note For all the following serials the price given is for the initial text, and all subsequent releases are 'charged on publication'. Here, as elsewhere, it is worthwhile making a comparison of the

UK and US prices charged for publications – where there is a choice of place of purchase.

426. **Acquisitions and Mergers**. l. £289. Three volumes.

427. **Analysis of Key SEC No-Action Letters (Year)**. a. £97.50. Focuses on what currently constitutes the 'common law' of the US Securities and Exchange Commission, and its implications for today's securities practice.

428. **Anderson on the Uniform Commercial Code**. i. £692. Eleven volumes.

429. **Annual Survey of Bankruptcy Law (Year)**. a. £135.

430. **Antitrust Law Handbook (Year)**. a. $79.50. Presents a comprehensive overview and update of American antitrust law and practice, featuring governing theory, substantive issues, procedural aspects, significant developments and trends and key cases.

431. **Antitrust Law Sourcebook (Year)**. a. $79.50. Offers a compilation of federal and state statutory and administrative materials regularly used by antitrust practitioners, and a plethora of information on antitrust enforcement in domestic and international arenas.

432. **Banking Crimes**. l. £96.

433. **Broker-Dealer Regulation**. l. £107.

434. **Commercial Asset-Based Financing**. l. £359. Four volumes.

435. **Commodities Regulation: Fraud, Manipulation and Other Crimes**. l. £180. Two volumes.

436. **Corporate Anti Takeover Defences (Year)**. a. £96.

437. **Corporate Dividends and Stock Repurchases**. l. £96.

438. **Couch on Insurance**. i. 1959. Thirty-three volumes.

439. **Creditor's Rights Handbook (Year)**. a. £85.

440. **Emerging Trends in Securities Law (Year)**. a. £81.

441. **Exempted Transactions under the Securities Act**. l. £489. Five volumes.

442. **Fletcher Cyclopedia of Corporations**. i. £1442. Thirty-six volumes.

443. **Going Public and the Public Corporation**. l. £356. Four volumes.

444. **Going Public Handbook (Year)**. a. £96.

445. **Herzog's Bankruptcy Forms and Practice**. l. £184. Two volumes.

446. **Insider Trading Regulation**. l. £107.

447. **Internal Revenue Manual: Abridged and Annotated**. q. $295. Three volumes. Provides a selected abridgement, supplemented with annotations, of the IRS's massive official *Internal Revenue Manual*.

448. **International Capital Markets and Securities Regulation**. l. £556. Six volumes.

449. **International Trade and US Antitrust Law**. l. £107.

450. **Investments Limited Partnership Handbook (Year)**. l. £107.

451. **Law of Transnational Business Transactions**. l. £276. Three volumes.

452. **Liability of Attorneys and Accountants for Securities Transactions**. a. $95. Explores potential attorney liability for disclosure advise to clients, preparation of disclosure documents, agreements, and closing documents, and creation of formal legal agreements.

453. **Limited Liability Company Handbook (Year)**. a. £97.

454. **Mertens Law of Federal Income Taxation: Treatise**. i. £751. Nineteen volumes.

455. **O'Neal's Close Corporations**. l. £168. Two volumes.

456. **Opinion Letters in Security Matters**. l. £289. Three volumes.

457. **Partnership Law for Securities Practitioners**. l. £107.

458. **Real Estate Investment Trusts Handbook (Year)**. a. £96.

459. **Regulation of Investment Advisers**. a. $95. Provides detailed explanations of SEC regulation requirements and procedures to help investment advisers avoid SEC violations.

460. **S Corporations: Federal Taxation**. l. £107.

461. **Section 16 of the Securities Exchange Act**. l. £180. Two volumes.

462. **Securities and Federal Corporate Law**. l. £556. Five volumes.

463. **Securities Law Handbook (Year)**. a. $105.

464. **Securities Law Review (Year)**. a. $85. Covers the latest developments in securities law.

465. **Securities Practice: Federal and State Enforcement**. l. £193. Two volumes.

466. **Securities Regulation Forms**. l. £356. Three volumes.

467. **Shareholder Derivative Actions**. l. £103.

468. **Shareholder Litigation**. l. £257. Three volumes.

469. **State and Local Government Debt Financing**. l. £257. Three volumes.

470. **Tax Aspects of Real Estate Investments**. l. £177. Two volumes.

471. **Uniform Commercial Code Reporting Service**. m. $782.50. Official text of the Code, focusing on sales of goods, leases, bankruptcy, secured transactions, product liabilities, warranties, consumer loans, debt collections, letters of credit, and damages.

472. **Venture Capital and Small Business Financings**. l. £489. Four volumes.

(3) #75 Faulkner & Gray 11 Penn Plaza, 17th Floor, New York, NY 10001, USA. t: (1 212) 967 7000; f: 967 7155.

473. **Accounting Technology**. m. **online**. Covers technology issues for the accounting profession, including hardware, software and office equipment.

474. **Accounting Today**. bi-w. $96. **online**. Reports news of the profession, emphasizing the people, organizations, technology, emerging issues and competitive strategies that influence the field's direction.

475. **Banking Law Review**. q. $125. Practical legal guidance for bankers and their attorneys. Provides in-depth coverage of landmark cases, critical legal issues in banking, new laws and regulations, and protective strategies.

476. **Bankruptcy Law Review**. q. $125. Presents interpretations, analysis and news.

477. **Consolidated Returns Tax Report**. m. $345. Provides new tax planning strategies for consolidated filing and important changes in the tax laws.

478. **Corporate Taxation**. bi-m. $175. Delivers practical articles and timely reporting of corporate tax developments.

479. **Journal of Taxation of Estates and Trusts**. q. $125. **online**. Covers new developments from the IRS, the Treasury, and the courts.

480. **Journal of Taxation of S Corporations**. q. $125. **online**.

481. **Practical Accountant**. m. $60. **online**. Forum covering every facet of accounting and taxes.

482. **Taxation of Mergers and Acquisitions**. m. $345. Offers sophisticated tax advice, analysis of tax developments, and expert planning advice.

(4) #76 Gee South Quay Plaza, 183 Marsh Wall, London E14 9FS, UK. t: (44 171) 538 5386; f: 538 8623.

483. **Auditor's Factbook**. l. 75.

484. **Financial Reporting & Disclosure Manual**. l. £85. With reference to the disclosure requirements of The Stock Exchange, The Accounting Standards Board, The Auditing Practices Board, and statutory requirements, covers all relevant areas, including: profit and loss accounts, balance sheets, cash flow statements, statements of accounting policy and auditors' reports and directors' reports.

485. **Income Tax Factbook**. l. £55.

486. **Mergers & Acquisitions**. l. £240. 'Unique source of information and guidance for every participant in M&A activity, whether working within a company – on either side of a proposed acquisition – or in an advisory capacity. All areas are covered in detail including management buy-ins, management buy-outs and consortium offers.'

487. **Mergers & Acquisitions in Europe**. l. £325. 'The most comprehensive source of information on continental cross-border activity . . . Critical areas covered include methods of acquisition, tax implications, accounting aspects, controls and competition rules.'

488. **Small Business Tax and Finance**. m. £85. 'Three client bulletins are issued each year which are exclusive four-page newsletters suitable for photocopying onto your own headed notepaper and sending to your clients.'

489. **Strategic Tax Planning**. l. £295. Designed by a team drawn from major law and accountancy practices as well as leading companies, for those involved in corporate taxation and in minimising the cost of tax to companies. Central theme is investment orientated, describing medium to long-term startegies for reducing the exposure to tax of business transactions.

490. **Tax Factbook**. l. £75. Single volume, updated six times per year, including coverage of income, corporation, and capital gains tax.

491. **Taxation Manual**. l. Includes checklists, suggested documentation for working papers, and specimen official forms and letters for principal tax claims and elections.

492. **VAT Factbook**. l. £85. Single volume, with regular updates. Includes: registration; the EC and VAT; international services.

493. **VAT Intelligence**. m. £140. Technical briefings; new information and publications from HM Customs and Excise and new EC directives; reports of each month's most important cases from the VAT Tribunals, the High Court, the European Court of Justice.

(5) #77 Research Institute of America 90 Fifth Avenue, New York, NY 10011, USA. t: (1 212) 645 4800; f: 337 4279.

494. **Federal Income Tax Regulations**. s-a. $52.

495. **Federal Tax Coordinator 2D**. l. $1,375. Thirty-five volumes. **online**. Provides analysis of federal tax law, including commentary and practical guidance, and official source materials. There is also a *Weekly Alert* ($175).

496. **Federal Tax Regulations**. l. $310. Five volumes. Presents full text of income tax regulations and details regulatory activity following tax reform legislation.

497. **Internal Revenue Code**. s-a. $32. Complete Internal Revenue Code.

498. **Official IRS Publications**. w./m. $260. Consists of more than 140 taxpayer information publications.

499. **RIA Internal Revenue Code and Regulations**. l. $275. Seven volumes. Presents the full text of the Internal Revenue Code and all final, temporary and proposed regulations.

500. **RIA Tax Guide**. l. $350. Two volumes. **cdrom**.

(6) #78 Sweet & Maxwell South Quay Plaza, 183 Marsh Wall, London, E14 9FT, UK. t: (44 171) 538 8686; f: 538 9508.

501. **British Tax Review**. bi-m. £120.00.

502. **Commercial Laws of Europe**. m. £405.00. 'Full-text reporting service of national and international legislation. Major enactments in Europe are reported in full, as are international conventions and treaties, implementation decrees, and EEC mainstream directives and regulations. All texts appear in English as well as in the original foreign language.'

503. **Common Market Law Reports**. w. $480. There is also an *Antitrust Supplement* (m.).

504. **EC Competition Law Handbook (Year)**. a. £60.00. "This Handbook is quite simply a must. Buy it!" (*European Business Law Review*).

505. **Encyclopedia of Competition Law**. l. £360.00/£198.00. Two volumes. Includes issues of the newsletter *In Competition*, also available separately (£95.00).

506. **Encyclopedia of Consumer Credit Law**. l. £330.00/£136.00. Two volumes.

507. **Encyclopedia of Financial Services Law**. l. £495.00/£395.00. Three volumes.

508. **Encyclopedia of Insurance Law**. l. £278.00.

509. **European Commercial Cases**. bi-m. £330. Major decisions of European national courts in certain areas of commercial law.

510. **European Competition Law Review**. bi-m. £205.00.

511. **European Current Law**. m. £330.00. Provides practitioners, research departments, academics and libraries with a comprehensive guide to legal developments thoughout Europe.

512. **European Journal of International Law**. q. £30.00.

513. **European Law Review**. bi-m. £245.00.

514. **Financial Services Brief**. 10/year. £95.00.

515. **Franchising: Law and Practice**. l. £125.00.

516. **Hoskin VAT Case Digest: UK and Community Law**. l. £240.00/£195.00. Three volumes.

517. **Housing Law Reports**. bi-m. £179.

518. **International Company and Commercial Law Review**. m. £335.00.

519. **International Insurance Law Review**. m. £335.00.

520. **Journal of Business Law**. bi-m. £120.00.

521. **Journal of International Banking Law**. m. £335.00.

522. **Law of Loans and Borrowing**. l. £150.00. 'Considers every aspect of

the subject from domestic mortgages and consumer credit to raising money on the quoted Eurobond market.'

523. **Law of Occupational Pension Schemes**. l. £180.00. Two volumes.

524. **Law of Transnational Business Transactions**. l. £283.00. Three volumes.

525. **Palmer's Company Law**. l. £360.00/£245.00. Five volumes. 'Included in the service is *Palmer's IN COMPANY* a monthly newsletter which provides subscribers with up to date commentary and analysis on company law cases and developments.' The Newsletter is also available separately (£70.00).

526. **Revenue**. 10/year. £65.00. Newsletter giving overview of developments in taxation matters, complementing Sweet & Maxwell's taxation loose-leaf services.

527. **Tax Avoidance**. l. £195.00.

528. **Weinberg and Blank on Take-Overs and Mergers**. l. £230.00. Two volumes.

(7) #79 Warren, Gorham & Lamont One Penn Plaza, New York, NY 10119, USA. t: (800) 950 1205; f: (1 212) 971 5240. *Also* c/o Sweet & Maxwell, South Quay Plaza, 183 Marsh Wall, London E14 9FT, UK. t: (44 171) 538 8686; f: 538 9508.

529. **Accounting and Auditing Disclosure Manual**. a. 'Is the only work of its kind to deliver all the requirements and examples you need to prepare fast, accurate financial statements and auditors' reports . . . The *Manual* has over 108 sections to help you minimize your risk of omitting key disclosures. It includes nearly 4,400 required and recommended disclosures . . . Contains 1,400 detailed examples.'

530. **Accounting & Auditing Update Service**. i: 35–40 issues per year. $256.50. 'This unique newsletter service provides straightforward analysis and interpretation of all new FASB and AICPA pronouncements *as they're issued*. Within two weeks of an original pronouncement, your interpretative *Technical Bulletin* will be sent to you.'

531. **Bank Auditing and Accounting Report**. m. $232.95. 'It keeps you up-to-date with the latest developments at the FASB, AICPA, SEC, OCC, FRB and FDIC.'

532. **Bank Income Tax Return Manual**. a. $150.

533. **Bank Officers Handbook of Commercial Banking Law**. a. $115.

534. **Banker's Letter of the Law**. m. $188.75. Alerts bank attorneys to the latest rulings involving federal and state banking issues. Cites specific cases and translates 'legalese' into everyday language.

535. **Banking Law Journal**. bi-m. $125.98. **online**. Covers every area of major interest to bankers and bank attorneys, with practical material for bank counsel use. There is also a *Banking Law Journal Digest* (a. $120).

536. **Bankruptcy Law Letter**. m. $147.25. Covers recent developments in bankruptcy law; includes involuntary position, adequate positions, automatic stay, use, sale, and lease of property.

537. **Bankruptcy Law Manual**. a. 'Cited in over 75 judicial opinions, and recently cited by the Supreme Court, this convenient, easy- to-use manual gives you practical, reliable guidelines you need to practice effectively in today's fast-moving bankruptcy field.'

538. **Consumer Credit & Truth in Lending Compliance Report**. m. $176.75. Focuses on the latest regulatory rulings and findings involving consumer lending and credit activity.

539. **Federal Banking Laws**. s-a. 'This one comprehensive volume serves as a federal statutory and regulatory reference for banking – so there's no need to search through multi-volume services when you need information in a hurry.'

540. **Federal Income Taxation of Banks and Financial Institutions**. a.

541. **Government Accounting and Auditing Update**. m. $161.25. Informs readers of changes in government accounting and financial reporting and how they affect their businesses.

542. **Internal Auditing Alert**. m. $200.45.

543. **Journal of Bank Taxation**. q. $141.50. **online**. 'Widely acknowledged as the leading publication for bank tax professionals.'

544. **Journal of Bankruptcy Law and Practice**. bi-m. $141.50.

545. **Journal of Corporate Taxation**. q. $225.95. Provides analysis and guidance for practitioners who must stay on top of all of the latest developments and their planning implications. Covers corporate reorganizations, compensation and fringe benefits, tax accounting, international developments, closely held corporations, and consolidated tax returns.

546. **Journal of International Taxation**. m. $262.25. **online**. 'Offers broad-based, in-depth coverage of United States taxation issues relating to international transactions as well as foreign taxation matters.'

547. **Journal of Partnership Taxation**. q. $141.50. **online**.

548. **Journal of Real Estate Taxation**. q. $130.00. **online**.

549. **Journal of S Corporation Taxation**. q. $141.50.

550. **Journal of Taxation**. m. **online**. 'The one publication no tax professional should be without.'

551. **Journal of Taxation of Exempt Organizations**. q. $157.25. **online**. Gives advice, strategies, and analysis of the current tax situation for nonprofit organizations.

552. **Journal of Taxation of Investment**. q. $225.95.

553. **Law of Bank Deposits, Collections and Credit Cards**. 3/year. 'Rou-

tinely cited by the courts, Barkley Clark's master reference is a single, convenient source that addresses virtually every question that can arise in relation to collections, credit cards, bank deposits and letters of credit.'

554. **Law of Electronic Fund Transfer Systems**. s-a.

555. **Lender Liability Law Report**. m. Articles analyze court decisions and new legislation. Provides suggestions for developing protective mechanisms for lenders and the means of defending borrowers suits.

556. **S Corporations**. l. Provides in-depth explanations, new ideas from experts in the field, updates on latest developments and official documents and relevant legislative history.

557. **SEC Compliance: Financial Reporting and Forms**. l. Five volumes. Contains the official text of the rules and forms required by the Securities and Exchange Commission along with explanations of periodic reporting forms, and coverage of other related developments.

558. **SEC Guidelines: Rules and Regulations (Year)**. a. $60.

559. **Securities Regulation**. l. $843. Five volumes. Covers US legislation and other topics affecting the securities trading industries.

560. **Securities Regulation Law Journal**. q. $173. Offers analysis and advice through articles and features by noted practitioners and scholars to help readers keep up with the constant changes in the law, rules, and regulations.

561. **Small Business Controller**. q. $153.15.

562. **Tax Law Review**. q. $177.20. **online**.

563. **Tax Planning for Corporate Acquisitions**. s-a.

564. **Tax Treaties**. l. £339.00. Three volumes. 'In-depth analysis and full official text of every treaty, supplementary treaty and protocol between the United States and foreign countries relating to income, gift and estate taxes. Also included are Senate Committee reports and reports of the Secretary of State explaining the background of the treaties and the meaning of each provision therein.'

565. **Taxation for Accountants**. m. $186.95. **online**.

566. **US International Taxation**. l. £300.00. Two volumes. 'An outstanding reference that provides authoritative, in-depth and practical analysis of the laws governing US taxation of US persons with foreign income and foreign persons with US income.'

567. **WGL Tax Audio Alert. audiocassette**. m. $224.75. Provides tax and tax law reports, analysis and commentary. Not available in printed format.

18. Three other major publishing conglomerates active in legal publishing are *Pearson*, *Reed Elsevier*, and *Wolters Kluwer*. Pearson has two significant presences in this area, *FT Law & Tax* (formerly largely trading under *Longman Law, Tax and Finance*), and *Tolley*; but it also publishers some relevant serials under the imprint *FT Newsletters*.

(1) #80 FT Law & Tax 21–27 Lamb's Conduit Street, London WC1N 3NJ, UK. t: (44 171) 242 2548; f: (71) 831 8119.

568. **Agency Law**. l. £155. 'Provides a much needed practical guide to this whole area of law.'

569. **Agricultural Law, Tax and Finance**. l. £160.

570. **Allied Dunbar Investment and Savings Handbook**. a. £21.

571. **Allied Dunbar Tax Handbook**. a. £21. Advice and information on the workings of income tax, capital gains tax, corporate tax, inheritance tax and value added tax.

572. **Busy Solicitors' Digest**. m. £59.

573. **Capital Tax Planning**. m. £149. 'Covers every aspect of Inheritance Tax and Capital Gains Tax management, plus estate planning and trusts.'

574. **Capital Taxes and Estate Planning in Europe**. l. £159.

575. **Charities: The Law and Practice**. l. £145.

576. **Company Lawyer**. 10/year. £190. Designed to keep readers up-to-date with developments in company and commercial law.

577. **Company Procedures Manual**. l. £139.

578. **Consumer Credit Control**. l. £365. Four volumes. 'All firms who supply goods and services on credit or hire, or arrange credit and hire facilities are affected by the extensive systems of credit and hire control under the Consumer Credit Act 1974. The work provides detailed and up-to-date guidance on the credit control system.'

579. **Dymond's Capital Taxes**. l. £299. Three volumes. 'The one source of advice and information that will solve virtually every inheritance tax problem.'

580. **Equipment Leasing**. l. £185.

581. **Harrison's Inland Revenue Index to Tax Cases**. l. £320. Three volumes. 'Access to over 3,000 reported judgements and related judicial decisions.'

582. **HM Customs & Excise Official VAT Guides**. l. £165. Three volumes. The explanatory guides issued by Customs and Excise, reproduced and fully indexed.

583. **Housing Law and Precedents**. l. £140.

584. **Inland Revenue Clearances**. l. £145.

585. **Inland Revenue Official Tax Guides**. l. £185. Two volumes. Reproduces the entire range of leaflets, pamphlets and booklets issued by the Inland Revenue.

586. **Inland Revenue Practices and Concessions**. l. £220. Two volumes. "This is a book which no-one involved in tax can afford to be without." (*Solicitors Journal*).

587. **Insolvency**. l. £299. Four volumes. 'Practical and authoritative information and comment on the whole area of corporate and personal insolvency.'

588. **Insolvency Intelligence**. 10/year. £149.

589. **International Banking and Financial Law**. m. £185. 'Nowadays, people simply do not have the time to wade through lofty journals to search out relevant information on the latest developments in international banking law and practice. What's needed is a straightforward, practical information service where the utmost thought has gone into presenting all the relevant facts and guidance in the clearest, most convenient way.'

590. **International Insurance Law and Regulation**. l. £195.

591. **International Tax Systems and Planning Techniques**. l. £230. 'Probably provide(s) more facts, figures and guidance for the successful management of a multi-national business operation than any other single publication.'

592. **International Trust Precedents**. l. £205. 'Provides a complete library of documents, with clear supporting commentary, to create effective trusts in key overseas jurisdictions.'

593. **Leasehold Law**. l. £275.

594. **Life Assurance Law and Practice**. l. £175.

595. **Local Government Finance: Law and Practice**. l. £165.

596. **National Insurance Contributions Handbook**. l. £149.

597. **Pensions: Law and Practice**. l. £290. Two volumes. 'This is the authoritative source of expert advice and practical information on the law, administration and taxation of company and personal pension schemes.'

598. **Practical Lending and Security Precedents**. l. £185. Two volumes. 'From standard provisions in modern mortgages to substantial syndicated term loan, all the essential documents needed to prepare loans and finance agreements.'

599. **Practical Tax Planning and Precedents**. l. £215. Three volumes. 'The opportunities to reduce or even eliminate the impact of taxation are set out and explained in this work.'

600. **Practical Trust Precedents**. l. £145. 'Contains all the material needed to create airtight trusts with allowances for flexibility to meet changing needs.'

601. **Property Law Bulletin**. 10/year. £145.

602. **Social Welfare Law**. l. £170.

603. **Solicitors Journal**. w. £99.

604. **Tax Case Analysis**. m. £265. 'Considers all important decided tax cases.'

605. **Taxation of Remuneration Packages**. l. £150.

606. **Touche Ross PAYE/P11D Handbook**. l. £165.

607. **Unit Trusts: The Law and Practice**. l. £350. Two volumes. 'Essential details of relevant statutes, statutory instruments, regulatory requirements and judicial decisions . . . Nothing of importance is overlooked in the works' exhaustive coverage of the rules and regulations governing the operation and management of unit trusts. . . . The duties and obligations of trustees and managers are explained, as are the rights and liabilities of unitholders.' Created by *Linklaters & Paines*.

608. **Use of Offshore Jurisdictions**. l. £199. 'Specialist guidance on how to take full advantage of the tax, financial and commercial benefits offered by offshore centres.' Created by *Nigel Harris & Partners*.

(2) #81 FT Newsletters Maple House, 149 Tottenham Court Road, London W1P 9LL, UK. t: (44 171) 896 2222; f: 896 2276. *Also* Financial Times, 14 East 60th Street, Penthouse, New York, NY 10022, USA. t: (1 212) 888 3469; f: 729 9598.

609. **Business Law Brief**. m. £335.00. **online**. 'Is a survey of international business law which ranges worldwide.'

610. **Financial Regulation Report**. 11/year. £405.00. **online**.

611. **World Accounting Report**. m. £350. **online**.

612. **World Tax Report**. m. £320.00. **online** 'Who reads Financial Times World Tax Report?: Finance directors and chief financial officers; Investment and merchant bankers; Legal and accounting tax advisers; Stockbrokers; Commercial bankers; Corporate treasurers; Government finance departments and revenue authorities.'

(3) #82 Tolley Publishing Company Tolley House, 2 Addiscombe Road, Croydon, Surrey CR9 5AF, UK. t: (44 181) 686 0115; f: 686 3155.

613. **Compliance Monitor**. m. £275. 'For compliance officers and their advisers, covering all aspects of financial services compliance (including): News of rulebook changes from SIB, the SROs and RPBs; Regulatory announcements by the Stock Exchange, Bank of England and the Treasury; Analysis of regulatory case law and EC Directives; New compliance areas such as the Charities Act 1992 and the regulation of pension schemes.'

614. **European Business Monitor**. m. £95.

615. **Insolvency Law & Practice**. bi-m. £130. Covers all areas of insolvency law and practice.

616. **Insurance Law & Practice**. q. £105. Covers all aspects of insurance law and practice.

617. **Taxation**. w. £95. 'Since 1927, this leading weekly journal has provided an unrivalled service of announcements, news and legal decisions for all those engaged in tax work. Includes expert comment and analysis, together with a forum for readers' queries, and reviews of higher court tax cases and VAT tribunal cases.'

618. **Tolley's Capital Allowances (Year)**. a. £29.95.

619. **Tolley's Capital Gains Tax (Year)**. a. £26.95.

620. **Tolley's Corporation Tax (Year)**. a. £25.95.

621. **Tolley's Income Tax (Year)**. a. £29.95.

622. **Tolley's Inheritance Tax (Year)**. a. £23.95.

623. **Tolley's Inheritance Tax Service**. l. £120/60.

624. **Tolley's Insolvency Law and Practice**. bi-m. £120.

625. **Tolley's Insolvency Service**. l. 'Major new looseleaf work (1994).'

626. **Tolley's Insurance Law & Practice**. q. £100.

627. **Tolley's Journal of International Franchising and Distribution Law**. q. £100.

628. **Tolley's National Insurance Contributions Legislation (Year)**. a. £21.95.

629. **Tolley's National Insurance Contributions (Year)**. a. £31.95.

630. **Tolley's Official Tax Statements (Year)**. a. £34.95. 'Contains the full text of all Inland Revenue Extra-Statutory Concessions and Statements of Practice, together with important Press Releases and CCAB/ICAEW Statements.'

631. **Tolley's Practical NIC**. m. £95. 'Providing guidance of every aspect of National Insurance planning and compliance for companies and individuals both in the UK and overseas.'

632. **Tolley's Practical Tax**. bi-w. £105.

633. **Tolley's Practical VAT**. m. £114.

634. **Tolley's Tax Cases (Year)**. a. £30.95. Brief reports of more than 2,500 court decisions relevant to UK tax legislation.

635. **Tolley's Tax Computations (Year)**. a. £33.95. 'Comprises over 460 worked examples.'

636. **Tolley's Tax Data (Year)**. a. £13.95. 'Draws together . . . a mass of factual information covering all the main UK taxes and related matters, which would otherwise take hours of research from a whole range of source material.'

637. **Tolley's Tax Guide (Year)**. a. £23.95. 'This practical work looks at

everyday situations, found in commercial and personal life, and explains all the relevant UK taxes which must be taken into consideration.'

638. **Tolley's Tax Legislation (Year)**. a. In three parts: *Income Tax, Corporation Tax, and Capital Gains Tax* £31.95 (two volumes); *Inheritance Tax* £14.95; *Value Added Tax* £21.95. 'Widely regarded as the most reliable available.'

639. **Tolley's Tax Office Directory (Year)**. a. £8.50. **diskette**. £50.00.

640. **Tolley's Tax Service**. l. £450/£195. Four volumes. Covers Income Tax, Corporation Tax and Capital Gains Tax.

641. **Tolley's Tax Tables (Year)**. a. £9.95. 'No other publication responds as quickly and effectively to your needs, providing pre-calculated tables for all the main UK taxes.'

642. **Tolley's Value Added Tax (Year)**. a. £26.95.

643. **Tolley's VAT Service**. l. £325/£180. Two volumes.

644. **Trust Law International**. q. £110. Offers extensive coverage of trust law both within the UK and internationally.

19. *Reed Elsevier* – the owners of the publishers of this book – also has within its stable the UK's *Butterworths*; and, in the USA, the recently renamed *Michie Butterworth*:

(1) #83 Butterworths Borough Green, Sevenoaks, Kent, TN15 8PH, UK. t: (44 1732) 884567; f: 884079.

645. **Audit Report**. m. £220.

646. **Bankruptcy Practice Deskbook**. l. $285. Three volumes. Incorporates the ongoing changes in the Bankruptcy Code, Rules, and case law developments in all states.

647. **Butterworth Tax Treaties**. a. £245.

648. **Butterworths Annual European Review**. a. £155.

649. **Butterworths Budget Tax Tables (Year)**. a. £4.95.

650. **Butterworths Company Law Service**. l. £235. Kept up-to-date by six service issues per year, and a bi-monthly bulletin reporting current developments. Subscribers also receive a copy of the latest edition of *Butterworths Company Law Handbook*, containing the full text of current companies legislation.

651. **Butterworths EC Brief**. w. $563. Covers in summary all proposed and enacted EC legislation, and all UK legislation implementing it, as well as decisions of the European Court, COM Documents and other official reports.

652. **Butterworths EC Legislation Implementator**. bi-a. £155. Guide to the implementation in the UK of EC Directives as well as an overview of implementation of key provisions in other Community Member States.

653. **Butterworths European Law Service**. l. A series of 31 titles, each comprising a *Legislation and Commentary Box* and a *Cases and Commentary Box*. Each title is updated six times per year with the full text of new and amended legislation and new cases with commentary where appropriate. There is also a cumulative fortnightly briefing service for each title listing new legislation, cases and articles. The titles include: Companies; Banking and Financial Services; Insurance; Taxation; International Trade and External Relations.

654. **Butterworths Journal of International Banking and Financial Law**. q. £385. Each issue contains a mixture of articles, international briefings, book reviews and an update service where top City of London firms report on the latest developments.

655. **Butterworths Merger Control Review**. q. £160. Newsletter providing expert coverage of all developments of significance in the application of UK and EC competition law.

656. **Butterworths Orange Tax Handbook (Year)**. a. £21. Legislation relating to inheritance tax, national insurance contributions, stamp duty and value added tax.

657. **Butterworths Tax Planning**. l. £250. Two-volume work recommending the most effective strategies to be adopted on corporate, personal and indirect taxation.

658. **Butterworths Tax Treaties**. l. £235. Contains the texts of all the current double tax agreements between the UK and other countries.

659. **Butterworths UK Tax Guide (Year)**. a. £17.95. Narrative reference text that deals with all the principal taxes, and is fully up- to-date with the provisions of each year's UK Finance Act.

660. **Butterworths Yellow Tax Handbook (Year)**. a. £21. Text of the legislation relating to income tax, capital gains tax and corporation tax, in an amended and updated form suitable for use in assessment.

661. **Encyclopaedia of Banking Law**. l. $790. Three volumes. Includes coverage of: UK statutory regulation of banking, banking and the EEC, the relationship between bank and customers, domestic banking operations, securities, and international banking operations – including extensive sections on assignments and loan syndication.

662. **European Communities Legislation: Current Status (Year)**. a. £495. Reference source to all Community secondary legislation published in the Official Journal of the European Communities since 1952, apart from those instruments solely concerned with the daily running of the Communities. Each annual volume supercedes the previous year's volume; and there are also cumulative quarterly supplements as well as a fornightly newsletter. The subscription also includes bi-annual copies of *Butterworths EC Legislation Implementator*.

663. **Financial Reporting and Accounting Service**. l. £195. Volume 1 is a comprehensive commentary about current best pratice, with an assess-

ment of the rules and regulations: updated twice per year. Volume 2 covers SSAPs, SORPs, FRSs, exposure drafts, technical releases, discussion papers etc.: updated at least three times per year.

664. **Financial Services: Law and Practice**. l. Price varies. Three volumes. Provides a comprehensive source of reference on the laws regulating UK investment business. Included are the full texts of the Financial Services Act 1986, and the SIB and SRO Rule Books, with commentary concentrating on the practical implications of the UK system of authorisation and regulation of investment business. Bi-monthly updates and a monthly bulletin of news and comment on prospective and recent legislation and important new cases.

665. **Goode's Consumer Credit Legislation**. l. £490. Two volumes. Comprehensive survey of all the legislation relating to consumer credit, including the full current text of the Consumer Credit Act 1974.

666. **International Agency and Distribution Agreements**. l. $425. Four volumes, the first of which analyses the issues involved in foreign commercial agreements. Annotated specimen forms are provided as an aid to drafting and there is an extensive bibliography. The other three volumes deal with the impact of national law on agency and distribution arrangements, including chapters on 56 countries contributed by experienced local practitioners.

667. **International Income Tax Rules of the United States**. l. $125.

668. **Is It In Force?**. a. £46. A concise guide to the exact commencement dates of all UK Acts of Parliament and General Synod Measures passed over the last quarter century.

669. **Joint Ventures with International Partners**. l. $200. Technical and legal examination of joint venture laws and practices; provides the 'ins' and 'outs' of forming joint ventures with overseas business entities.

670. **Law of the European Communities**. l. Four volumes; eight updating issues per year.

671. **Moores Rowland's Orange Tax Guide (Year)**. a. £30.95. Commentary on the tax legislation contained in *Butterworths Orange Tax Guide*.

672. **Moores Rowland's Yellow Tax Guide (Year)**. a. £30.95. Commentary on the tax legislation covered in *Butterworths Yellow Tax Guide*.

673. **New Law Journal**. w. **online**. Covers the entire legal spectrum, including the provision of legal services and legal practice.

674. **Simon's Tax Cases**. i. £150.

675. **Simon's Taxes**. l. £645. Ten loose-leaf volumes widely recognized as the leading authority on UK income tax, corporation tax and capital gains tax. Monthly updates.

676. **Simon's Weekly Tax Service**. w. £250. Comprises the *Intelligence* and the *Cases*. The former presents an outline of the week's developments, including detailed summaries of all cases decided, and the full texts

of statutory instruments and official press releases. Also covered are Parliamentary proceedings, double taxation agreements, and changes in Inland revenue concessions and practice.

677. **Tax Havens Encyclopaedia**. l. £150. Assembles material necessary to enable the tax praxctitioner to assess the relative advantages and disadvantages of various tax havens. Part 1 deals with the law and practice and anti-avoidance measures of the UK, USA, France, Germany, Canada, Australia and India; while Part 2 covers individual tax haven jurisdictions. Updated bi-annually.

678. **Tax Journal**. w. £112.

679. **Value Added Tax**. l. £215. Contains the text of the relevant Acts of Parliament, statutory instruments, EC Directives and Regulations. Relevant Customs and Excise press releases are included as well as Customs and Excise Notices and Leaflets.

Butterworths has a joint venture with *Compliance*:

(2) #84 Compliance Globe House, Lavender Park, West Byfleet, Surrey KT14 6ND, UK. t: (44 1932) 336203; f: 336206.

'One of the originators in providing legislation and regulations on computer systems for ease of access, currency and completeness of information. Our clients include some of the largest legal and advisory companies in the United Kingdom. We also supply over seven hundred security brokers with regulatory reporting systems . . . Following a joint venture with *Butterworths*, the legal publishers, we are able to offer a complete range of legal reference and guidance material. As a result of this union we have created an ambitious and exciting new product which will take legal and regulatory publishing on computer systems well into the next decade. . . . The product *books on screen* is the realisation of a design team made up of over forty firms of lawyers and financial advisers. . . . We have been overwhelmed by the positive feedback this product has created and it has already led to joint ventures with other countries that recognise the innovation of the product and its relevance to professional advisors all over the world.'

680. **COMPANY LAW Books on Screen**. **diskette**. m. Provides access to a range of Butterworths company law sourcebooks.

681. **TAX Books on Screen**. **diskette**. w. Includes:

- *Butterworths Orange and Yellow Tax Handbooks*
- *Moores Rowlands's Orange and Yellow Tax Guides*
- *Butterworths UK Tax Guide.*

Weekly updates contain all the latest developments in the major UK taxes based on *Simon's Weekly Tax Service.*

(3) #85 Michie Butterworth PO Box 7587, Charlottesville, VA 22906–7587, USA. t: (1 804) 972 7600. *Also* Butterworths, Halsbury

House, 35 Chancery Lane, London WC2A 1EL, UK. t: (44 171) 400 2500; f: 400 2482.

682. **Administrative Interpretations of the Uniform Consumer Credit Code**. l. $110.

683. **Annual Review of Banking Law**. a. $130.50. **online**. Covers national and international banking law developments.

684. **Banking Law in the United States**. a. $95. Reviews and analyses of the laws and regulations governing banking practice in the US.

685. **Blue Sky Compliance Manual**. l. $75. A state-by-state guide.

686. **ERISA and Benefits Law Journal**. q. $125.

687. **International Income Tax Rules of the United States**. l. $125. Describes international tax rules of the United States, concentrating on the tax rules that resolve potential conflicts between the US claims for tax revenue from transnational income and the claims of other national tax jurisdictions.

688. **International Personal Tax Planning Encyclopedia**. a. $175. Two volumes.

689. **Michie's Federal Law on Disc**. **cdrom**. $2500/$588. Comprehensive coverage of US Supreme Court and Federal Circuit cases.

690. **Securities Arbitration Procedure Manual**. l. Discusses issues encountered in a securities arbitration dispute, including evaluation of the merits of a case and its preparation and presentation to arbitration panels anywhere in the country.

691. **Securitization: Asset-Backed and Mortgage-Backed Securities**. a. $90. Covers all federal and state regulatory and tax provisions governing securitized transactions, including rules of accounting and rating agency requirements.

Also, Reed Elsevier now owns the online information service *Lexis/Nexis* – which it acquired late in 1994.

20. Mention of the latter prompts a reference to the major rival to that service – *WESTLAW* – which is operated by *West Publishing Corporation*:

(1) #86 West Publishing Corporation 620 Opperman Drive, Eagan, MN 55123–1396, USA. t: (1 612) 687 8000; f: 687 7302. *International Division* f: (1 612) 687 7849.

> 'West publications and services work together to make up the kind of total research system you won't find elsewhere. While other publications give you bits and pieces of the information you need, West books, WESTLAW, West's Desktop Practice Systems and West CD-ROM Libraries combine to give you the whole package. Every time you add another West source to your library, you increase the utility

and effectiveness of all your West references. With a library of interrelated tools from West, you'll save time, you'll save energy, and you'll find the information you need quickly and easily.

The universal *West Key Number System* of case law classification makes it possible to locate similar cases regardless of when or where they are decided. In addition, Cross References and Library References throughout the West System allow Reporters, Digests, encyclopedias, and statutes to function smoothly as integrated law-finding units. Then, when you add WESTLAW, the capability of your library increases greatly. Make Key Numbers and descriptive terms part of your computer search, and you have the answer in an instant.'

- *CD-ROM Topical Libraries* 'There are currently five West CD-ROM Topical Libraries available: Bankruptcy, Federal Securities, Federal Taxation, Government Contracts, and Military Justice . . . (The) Libraries typically include case law, digests, statutes and regulations, treatise work and other related material. To ensure that your legal research is current, West CD-ROM Topical Libraries are kept up-to-date (at no additional charge) by new discs or, for selected libraries, a combination of new discs and electronic updating.'
- *National Reporter System* 'Began in 1876, when a small pamphlet called 'The Syllabi' was published to provide prompt and reliable state court reports to lawyers and judges in Minnesota. Today, the system makes available reported cases from every state and federal court. It is credited with bringing order to legal research . . . Each case published in any unit of the National Reporter System is reviewed by lawyer-editors who prepare case synopses, write headnotes for each point of law, and classify each case by its points of law to make research faster and easier. The headnotes are also used in the *American West Digest System*, an important adjunct to the National Reporter System. Before an opinion is reported, its text is thoroughly reviewed. References to other decisions are checked and verified by West's experienced professionals. Each year, 70,000 case citiation errors are found and corrected. Then, to make the latest cases available as soon as possible, advance sheets are published on a regular, usually weekly, basis.'
- *Bankruptcy Reporter* 'Covers reported bankruptcy cases from the US Bankruptcy Courts, US District Courts, US Courts of Appeals, and the US Supreme Court. Service includes weekly advance sheets and bound volumes published as needed.'

692. **Corpus Juris Secundum**. i. $3365. One hundred and fifty- seven volumes.

693. **Federal Reporter 2d**. i. $25,238. Nine hundred and seventy- nine volumes.

694. **Federal Supplement**. i. $21,252.50. Eight hundred and four volumes.

695. **Federal Tax Regulations**. a. $240. Five volumes.

696. **Guide to American Law**. i. $1,244. Twelve volumes.

697. **Internal Revenue Code**. a. $72.50. Two volumes.

698. **Uniform Laws Annotated**. i. $2,077. Twenty-nine volumes. Master Edition.

699. **United States Code Annotated**. $2169. Two hundred and twenty-seven volumes including nine general indexes. **cdrom**. 'Has been the annotated statute service of choice for generations of American lawyers.'

21. As an aside, having just referenced some remarkably large US works of literature, we might note the comment of Logan, writing in the mid-1980s: 'The interlocking nature of American legal literature can be frustrating if, as is almost invariable, non-American law libraries stock only a limited range of series'. Logan then went on to suggest that: 'Access to retrieval systems such as LEXIS or WESTLAW may reduce this problem in the future'.[110]

By the time that Holborn was writing a brief introduction to United States law only some six or seven years later,[111] the use of one or the other of those database systems had become the normal starting point of US legal research:

> The complexity of United States legal literature is a consequence of the federal legal system: the researcher has to cope not only with the mass of federal law but also the law of each individual state. While the law may often be similar from state to state because their courts follow similar common law principles (disregarding the anomalous position in the mixed jurisdiction of Louisiana) and their legislatures may adopt model laws such as the Uniform Commercial Code, variations, sometimes quite radical ones, do occur . . .
>
> Acts of Congress are officially issued in loose form and bound volumes as *Statutes at Large* in the same way as Queen's Printer copies of Public General Acts, but for most purposes the preferable source is the *United States Code* which is a compilation by topic, each topic being called a 'title', of the main legislation in force. It comes in three versions, the official version published by the government printer, and two versions published by rival commercial publishers, *United States Code Annotated* (West) and *United States Code Service* (Lawyers' Co-operative). The latter two, because of their extensive annotations, are to be preferred. The bound volumes have pocket part supplements and are reissued from time to time. Subordinate legislation is published daily in the *Federal Register*, and is consolidated in the *Code of Federal Regulations*.
>
> Like the United States Code, the reports of the Supreme Court are available in an official series and two rival annotated commercially-published series . . . The sheer volume of American case law means that Lexis (or Westlaw) is unquestionably the best finding tool.

We will give some details of both those massive online database systems in Chapter 8. However, here, we will use the opportunity to reference:

(1) #87 National Archives and Records Administration 8th Street and Pennsylvania Avenue NW, Washington, DC 20408, USA. t: (1 202) 501 5525; f: 208 6256. The core publications listed below are issued by the Administration's *Office of the Federal Register* (t: (1 202) 523 5240; f: 523 6866).

The Office . . . maintains a free electronic bulletin board service *FREND* (Federal Register Electronic News Delivery), for public law numbers, Federal Register finding aids, and related information. To access by modem, phone 202–275–0920. In addition, the Federal Register's public inspection list and table of contents are also available on the National Archives' *Fax-on-Demand* system, phone 301–713–6905.'

700. **Code of Federal Regulations**. a. $829. **online**. **diskette**. $15,600. 'Annual codification of the general and permanent rules published in the *Federal Register*. The Code is divided into 50 titles that represent broad areas subject to Federal regulation.'

701. **Federal Register**. d. $490. **online**. **cdrom**. **diskette**. d. $19,500. 'Provides a uniform system for publishing Presidential documents, regulatory documents with general applicability and legal effect, purposed rules, notices and documents required to be published by statute.' The *Federal Register Index* 1993–1995 has also been issued on **diskette** ($78).

702. **United States Government Manual (Year)**. a. $23. **diskette**. $20. 'Provides comprehensive information on the agencies of the legislative, judicial and executive branches. . . . Also includes information on quasi-official agencies; international organizations in which the Unites States participates; and boards, commissions and committees. . . . The Manual is published as a special edition of the *Federal Register*.' (Much of the organizational annotation below is taken directly from this volume.)

703. **United States Statutes at Large**. a. $132. Annual compilation of *Slip Laws* – which are pamphlet prints of each public and private law enacted by Congress.

22. Returning to our consideration of large conglomerates active in legal publishing, the serials which we might cite here published by the last, *Wolters Kluwer* (ie they are in the English language and are UK, US, Europe, or internationally based), largely now appear under the badge *Kluwer Law International*, which company is – according to the 1994 Annual Report of the company – an: 'English-language publisher of European and international law, catering to libraries, academics and practitioners located worldwide. Kluwer Law International incorporates the publishing activities of the former imprints *Kluwer Law and Taxation*, *Graham & Trotman Law*, and *Martinus Nijhoff Publishers*'.

(1) #88 Kluwer Law International PO Box 85889, 2508 CN The Hague, The Netherlands. t: (31 70) 308 1500; f: 308 1515. *Also* 675 Massachusetts Avenue, Cambridge, MA 02139, USA. t: (1 617) 354 0140; f: 354 8595.

704. **Business Law Review**. 11/year. £242.

705. **Business Law in Europe**. l. $206. Provides comprehensive, up-to-date information on significant aspects of company, tax and labor law affecting business and investment decisions in the EC member states and Switzerland.

706. **Capital Markets Forum Yearbook**. a. £60. Volume 1, 1993 'offers a forum for debate and comment . . . under the auspices of the recently formed *Capital Markets Forum* of the IBA's (International Bar Association) Section on Business Law (establised as a private sector initiative).'

707. **Corporate Acquisitions and Mergers**. l. £265 Volume 1: UK; Volume 2: Continental Europe. Coverage of the legal, financial, tax and administrative issues affecting acquistions in Western European countries. Quarterly updates.

708. **Comparative Law of Monopolies**. l. £165. Three volumes. Examines the laws on restrictive agreements, monopolies and mergers in the jurisdictions of the USA, UK, Germany and the EC.

709. **Comparative Law Yearbook of International Business**. a. £73.00. A special issue *Financial Services in the New Europe* was produced in 1993 (£79.50).

710. **EEC Merger Control Reporter**. l. $858. Publishes all EC merger control decisions in the original language and in English translation. Also includes the basic EEC merger control legislation, coverage of other relevant decisions, and case notes.

711. **Encyclopedia of International Commercial Litigation**. l. £70. Each country section gives a general account of the structure of the courts and their jurisdiction and of civil litigation procedures, as well as the local legal profession, its specialist areas and how it charges, and the local judiciary. The procedural course through the courts of typical kinds of commercial litigation is then traced.

712. **European Accountancy Yearbook (Year)**. a. Includes profiles of 2000 major European accountancy firms in 22 countries and 5 tax havens, covering all of the EC and EFTA countries, together with details of corporate tax data, national accounting qualifications, and national institutes and associations.

713. **European Business Law Review**. 11/year. £242. Publishes short practical analyses of recent legal developments in European business law, including news on specific countries and coverage of EC directives, legislation, treaties, case notes and other related matters.

714. **European Financial Services Law**. m. £195. 'Provides compliance management within financial institutions, their legal advisers, and regulatory bodies, with a high quality, regular source of information on current developments in European law and regulation affecting the financial services industry.'

715. **International Business Series. Volume 1: Legal Aspects of Doing Business in Europe**. l. $260. Provides up-to-date references to the law and regulations of countries in Western and Central Europe, including tax and labour laws, and regulations governing imports, investment and expatriation of profits.

716. **International Business Series. Volume 6–7: Legal Aspects of Doing Business in North America**. l. $260. Provides up-to-date references to the laws and regulations of each of the 9 provinces of Canada, the 50 states of the USA and Puerto Rico, including tax and labour laws and regulations governing imports, investments and expatriation of profits.

717. **International Encyclopedia of Comparative Law**. i. Instalments have been published annually in recent years: 1993 brought *Instalment 28*: £124.00.

718. **International Encyclopaedia of Laws. Corporations and Partnerships**. l. $143. Publishers' studies of the law of public and private companies and partnerships in individual countries, from an international, comparative perspective, with discussion of EC company law and decisions of the European Court of Justice.

719. **International Encyclopaedia of Laws. Insurance Law**. l. $115. Covers national and international insurance law, including international organizations in the field of insurance, EC law with respect to private insurance, and discussions of the principles and practice of insurance law in different countries.

720. **Single European Market Reporter**. l. $200. Comprehensive practical guide to changes in European legislation as a result of the European Commission's Single European Market programme, including an overview of likely future developments, and discussion of strategic implications.

721. **Structuring Foreign Investment in US Real Estate**. l. $189. Provides detailed coverage of all major issues of interest to foreign individuals and corporations with US real estate holdings, including all special provisions of US income, gift and estate tax regulations. Also discusses tax and investment protection strategies.

722. **United States Income Tax Treaties**. l. $200. Comprehensive reference to the more than 40 bilateral US tax treaties in force, with expert commentary and analysis.

723. **United States Internal Revenue Service International Tax Compliance Information**. l. $300. Contains coursework designed by agents of the IRS. Provides insight into what IRS examiners have been taught to look for when reviewing international tax cases.

However, within the overall Wolters Kluwer worldwide operation, there is also currently marketed an imprint *Kluwer Publishing*:

(2) #89 Kluwer Publishing Croner House, London Road, Kingston upon Thames, Surrey KT2 6SR, UK. t: (44 181) 547 3333; f: 547 2637.

724. **Business Law Handbook**. l. £304.50. Two volumes. 'A complete guide to the law affecting business. This service was the first to bring together all aspects of the law in business and is deservedly still the leader in its field.'

725. **Insurance Contract Law**. l. £323.80. Two volumes. 'An award winning reference service providing clarity to the law and practice of insurance contracts.'

726. **Regulation of Insurance**. l. £297.60. Two volumes.

727. **Reinsurance Law**. l. £474.55. Two volumes.

which emanates from the same address as *Croner Publications*, a subsidiary of *Wolters Kluwer UK*.

(3) #90 Croner Publications Croner House, London Road, Kingston upon Thames, Surrey KT2 6SR, UK. t: (44 181) 547 3333; f: 547 2637.

728. **Guide to Corporation Tax**. l. £168.30. 'Designed to help the non-tax technician make sense of this complex subject, and prepare for the on-going changes in legislation.'

729. **VAT Information Service**. l. £254.90. Two volumes.

23. There are four other commercial publishing companies who have a major presence in this field: the first two also have a substantial UK presence, in addition to that in the USA:

(1) #91 Bureau of National Affairs 1231 25th Street, NW, Washington, DC 20037, USA. t: (1 202) 452 4200; f: 452 4610. *Also* BNA International, 17 Dartmouth Street, London SW1H 9BL, UK. t: (44 171) 222 8831; f: 222 5550.

730. **Antitrust & Trade Regulation Report**. l. $1,020. **online**. Comprehensive notification service on the latest judicial, legislative, administrative, and regulatory actions affecting restrictive trade practice law enforcement, in US federal, state and international contexts. Printed version updated weekly; online versions daily.

731. **BNA's Bankruptcy Law Reporter**. l. $844. **online**. Current developments in bankruptcy litigation, legislation and regulation. Printed version updated weekly; online daily.

732. **International Trade Reporter**. l. $2,607. **online**. 'A total resource for the detailed business information you need to compete and thrive in a

changing international marketplace. Find accurate reporting and cogent explanations of foreign and domestic trade regulation, legal actions, and import/export policy.'

733. **BNA International Business and Finance Daily**. **online**. No print version.

734. **BNA International Trade Daily**. **online**. Electronic only product.

735. **BNA Real Estate Investment Software**. **diskette**. 'Your most valuable tool for calculating the tax and cash-flow consequences of buying, selling, or holding real estate and related investments.'

736. **BNA's Banking Report**. l. $1,004. **online**. In-depth current notification of federal and industry challenges and changes to legislation, regulation, litigation, and policies, plus specific items on banks, legal actions, thrift news, economic developments and international finance. Printed version updated weekly; online daily.

737. **BNA's Bankruptcy Law Reporter**. w. $844. Notification service covering various areas of bankruptcy law.

738. **BNA's Corporate Counsel Weekly**. w. $562. 'Get the big picture of the legal challenges facing corporations today with this report on the whole spectrum of business law. It features concise, objective coverage of more areas of critical interest to coporate practitioners – in fewer pages – than any other resource available.' The **online** version is daily.

739. **Daily Report for Executives**. d. $5,642. **online**. 'The most inclusive resource available for on-time, on-target coverage of national and international legal and economic developments. . . . You'll be among the first – and often among the few – to start the day fully informed, ready to act on and influence governmental policies pivotal to your interests. The *Report* gives you immediate access to the same information that the nation's policymakers are using themselves to make daily decisions and long-term plans.' Issues are organized into these sections:

- *Regulation, Economics & Law*
- *Analysis & Reports*
- *Congressional & Presidential Activity*
- *Taxation, Budget & Accounting*
- *Tax Decisions & Rulings*
- *Text* Full text of major economic reports
- *Features* Weekly treatment of state tax issues
- *Economic Statistics*
- *Outlooks* Annual forecasts of what you can expect from Congress and the White House.

Each daily report averages 100 pages.

740. **Daily Tax Report**. d. $1,945. **online**. 'America's most comprehensive daily tax service – the definitive source for information on a full spectrum of issues in taxation, pensions, budget and accounting.'

741. **Securities Regulation & Law Report**. w. $1,016. **online**. d. Divided

into five sections: Federal Securities and Corporate Developments; State Developments; Commodities Regulation; Accounting and Disclosure; No-Action Letters (summaries of SEC releases). There is also an online *BNA Securities Law Daily*.

742. **Tax Management Financial Planning Journal**. m. $300. **online**. Provides coverage on the state of financial planning today, including new legislative, regulatory and economic developments.

743. **Tax Management IRS Practice and Policy Series**. m. $321. Comprehensive discussion of IRS practice from audits through collections. Covers IRS directories and industry specific handbooks that help facilitate dealings with the IRS.

744. **Tax Management International Journal**. m. $350. **online**. Review of current international tax, fiscal, and economic developments affecting worldwide business operations.

745. **Tax Management Portfolio Plus**. **cdrom**. m. $1,794. 'A unique analytical information and reference service on effective tax planning, written by practitioners for practitioners, covering virtually every critical tax topic.'

746. **Tax Management Primary Sources**. l. $1,000. Covers legislative history of the Internal Revenue Code.

747. **Tax Management Weekly Report**. w. $868. **online**. Reports developments affecting taxation and the tax aspects of accounting. Covers summaries of federal cases including the US Tax Court, synopses of IRS general counsel and technical advice memoranda, analysis of noteworthy IRS revenue ruling, procedures and private letter rulings, and status reports of Treasury Department actions on pending regulations.

748. **Tax Planning International**. l. $745. 'A global perspective on contemporary tax challenges and opportunities. This unique service offers reliable facts, figures, and interpretative insights on tax developments around the world.'

749. **United States Law Week**. w. $780. **online**. d. 'A selective overview of precedent-setting developments in all areas of the law, from all jurisdictions nationwide . . . plus comprehensive coverage of activity in the nation's highest court.'

- *BNA Online* 'BNA's electronic publishing division offers more than 80 electronic services in law, labor, business, finance, international developments, environment and tax – accessible through Lexis, Nexis, Westlaw, Dialog, Dialcom, and the Human Resource Information Network (HRIN). BNA Online also produces 21 specialised daily news services available only in electronic form, written by the editors of the corresponding weekly or biweekly BNA print services. These publications have no print counterparts.'
- *BNA PLUS* Provides free-of-charge customer support for all BNA subscribers. 'Our knowledgeable information specialists are ready to answer questions about any BNA publication and related topics.'

(2) #92 CCH CCH Editions, Telford Road, Bicester, Oxford OX6 0XD, UK. t: (44 1869) 253300; f: 974700 *and* CCH Incorporated, 4025 West Peterson Avenue, Chicago, IL 60646, USA. t: (1 312) 866 6000; f: 866 3895.

750. **Accountancy Law Reports**. m. $605. US.

751. **Accountants SEC Practice Manual**. l. Two volumes.

752. **Blue Sky Law Reports**. bi-w. $875.

753. **British Companies Legislation**. l. £21.50. Two volumes.

754. **British Company Law & Practice**. l. Two volumes.

755. **British International Tax Agreements**. l. Two volumes.

756. (Year) **British Master Tax Guide**. a. £22. **diskette**.

757. **British Tax Cases**. a. £189.

758. **British Tax Guide**. m. $460.

759. **British Tax Reporter and Tax Legislation**. l. Eleven volumes. 'Covers all United Kingdom direct taxes in a practical, accessible manner.'

760. **British VAT Guide**. l.

761. **Code and Regulations**. m. $330.

762. **Commodity Futures Law Reports**. bi-w. $705.

763. **Congressional Legislative Reporting**. i. Price varies.

764. **Consumer Credit Guide Reports**. l. $900. Five volumes. Covers federal and state consumers credit, and disclosure rules.

765. **EC Merger Control Monitor**. l. 'Provides key information for each merger referred to the European Commission.'

766. **Federal Banking Law Reports**. l. Six volumes. 'No single law or system controls the business of banking. Rather, there are a hundred different statutes and regulations which affect daily operations. The reporter keeps bankers in close touch, not only with the basic control measures, but also with unfolding developments, current interpretations and trends.'

767. **Federal Securities Law Reports**. l. $1,210. Eight volumes. 'Covers the federal laws administered by the US Securities and Exchange Commission regulating the issuance of and dealing in securities.'

768. **Federal Tax Articles**. m. $470.

769. **Federal Tax Manual With Monthly Reports**. l. $255.

770. **Global Franchising Alert**. m.

771. **Inheritance, Estate and Gift Tax Reports Federal-All States**. w. $1,010. Covers estate-gift tax on federal and state levels.

772. **International Income Taxation**. a. 'Principle code sections relating to the United States taxation of the income from international trade and investment.'

773. **International Offshore Financial Centres**. l. 'The general principles to be considered when contemplating using a third jurisdiction for international tax planning are first discussed in broad terms. How these principles relate to . . . (twenty-eight) . . . individual jurisdictions are then considered in detail.'

774. (Year) **International Tax Handbook**. a.

775. **International Tax Planning Manual**. l. Divided into *Corporations* (two volumes), *Expatriates & Migrants* (one volume), and *Real Estate Transactions* (one volume).

776. **IRS Letter Rulings**. w. $1,240. Reprints of the responses to tax queries of Inland Revenue decisions.

777. **SEC Accounting Rules**. l. £231. 'Contains Regulation S-X, Regulation S-K and the Securities and Exchange Commission's Codification of its Financial Reporting Policies and its series of financial rpeorting and enforcement releases – all arranged and organized for preparing financial statements required in registration and reporting forms.'

778. **SEC Docket**. l. 'Compilation of all releases officially issued by the Securities and Exchange Commission.'

779. **Secured Transactions Guide**. l. Five volumes.

780. **Shepard's Federal Securities Law Citations**. q. $360.

781. **Tax Court Reports**. w. $860.

782. **Tax Transactions Library**. l. $935.

783. **Taxes**. m. $140. **online**. This is the US version. There is also a UK version.

784. **Taxes on Parade**. w. $65.

785. **Trade Regulation Reporter**. l. Seven volumes. 'Specifically designed to assist lawyers and attorneys, retailers, trade associations, advertisers, and local and offshore businesses operate within the complicated trade regulation law.'

786. **US Federal Tax Forms**. l. Three volumes.

787. **US Federal Tax Guide**. l. Eight volumes.

788. **UK Financial Services Reporter**. l. Three volumes.'The commentary, written by a specialist team of authors under the general editorship of Dr Barry Rider, President of the *British Institute of Securities Laws*, guides the user through the maze of rules and regulations associated with the Financial Services Act.'

789. **US Income Tax Regulations**. a.

790. **US Master Tax Guide**. l. An annual hardback volume is also available.

791. **US Standard Federal Tax Reporter**. l. $1,610. Twenty-two volumes. **online**. 'Designed for the tax specialist who requires comprehensive coverage of the entire US federal income tax structure. It reports on law, regulations, court decisions, Tax Court case digests, IRS rulings, tax planning and new developments. The *Taxes on Parade* newsletter and Specials, which detail current legislation-in-progress are also included.'

792. (Year) **UK Tax Statutes and Statutory Instruments**. a. Two volumes. 'Reproduces the tax legislation, statutory instruments, extra- statutory concessions, Inland Revenue statements of practice and other official pronouncements.'

793. **US Tax Treaties**. l. Three volumes. 'The full text of income, estate and gift tax treaties entered into by the United States.'

(3) #93 Matthew Bender 11 Penn Plaza, New York, NY 10001, USA. t: (1 212) 967 7707; f: 967 1069. *International Division* 1275 Broadway, Albany, New York, NY 12204, USA. t: (1 518) 487 3000; f: 462 3788.

794. **Accounting for Banks**. i. $185. Discusses accounting principles applicable to banks within the framework of their operations.

795. **Antitrust Counseling and Litigation Techniques**. a. $650.

796. **Antitrust Laws and Trade Regulation**. $530. Two volumes.

797. **Bank Holding Company Compliance Manual**. l. $245. Guide to the day-to-day compliance responsibilities faced by bank holding company line officers.

798. **Banking Law**. l. $1,700. Twelve volumes. Operational guidance for bank officers, with analysis of statutory law and agency regulations.

799. **Banking Law Manual: Legal Guide to Commercial Banks, Thrift Institutions and Credit Unions**. l. $185. Examines the basic legal issues related to financial institutions and the regulatory framework within which they operate. Includes a comparative analysis of various types of financial institutions.

800. **Bender's Federal Tax Week**. w. $250.

801. **Collier Bankruptcy Cases**. bi-m. $710.

802. **Collier Bankruptcy Compensation Guide**. l. $195. Examines the Bankruptcy Code's provisions, case law, and current practice trends relevant to the compensation of attorneys, trustees and other professionals involved in bankruptcy cases. Contains substantive analysis as well as strategic and practical guidance.

803. **Collier Bankruptcy Manual**. l. $335. Three volumes. Provides substantive analysis necesary for handling a case under the Bankruptcy Code – keyed to the section numbers of the 1978 Code.

804. **Collier Handbook for Creditors' Committees**. a. Covers the role of Chapter 11 creditors' committees, fiduciary responsibilities and Chapter 11 plan negotiators.

805. **Collier Lending Institutions and the Bankruptcy Code**. l. $200. Practice-oriented guide to the impact of bankruptcy on lending transactions.

806. **Collier on Bankruptcy**. l. $2,360. Eleven volumes. Provides detailed discussion, by the leading bankruptcy authorities, of the Bankruptcy Code as amended. Includes coverage of the bankruptcy judges, United States trustees, and Family Farmer Bankruptcy Act of 1986.

807. **Collier Real Estate Transactions and the Bankruptcy Code**. l. $200. Practice-oriented guide to the impact of bankruptcy on real estate transactions, for both the general practitioner and the real estate specialist.

808. **Commercial Law Report**. m. $215.

809. **Commercial Loan Documentation Guide**. i. $120. Covers the full spectrum of loan documentation; includes forms, checklists and useful hints for both borrowers and lenders.

810. **SEC Financial Reporting: Annual Reports to Shareholders, Form 10–K, Quarterly Financial Reporting**. l. Presents basic guidelines to financial reporting in SEC disclosure reports. The focus is on 10–Ks and 10–Qs. Additional chapters discuss the special requirements of banks and insurance companies.

811. **Tax Havens of the World**. l. $250.

812. **Trust Department Administration and Operations**. i. $260. Covers every aspect of setting up a trust department, day-to-day administration, asset management, operations, marketing, and internal management.

(4) #94 Shepard's/McGraw-Hill 555 Middle Creek Parkway, Colorado Springs, CO 80921, USA. t: (1 719) 488 3000; f: 481 7448.

813. **Antitrust Adviser, 3–E**. i. $95. Pragmatic discussions of the Sherman Act, the Clayton Act, the Robinson-Patman Act and the Federal Trade Commission Act.

814. **Broker-Dealers and Securities Markets**. a. $95. Focuses on Securities and Exchange Commission rules, their various interpretations and their many relationships to the brokerage industry and regulatory process.

815. **Federal Income Taxation of Corporate Liquidations**. Provides the analytical framework needed to select and implement appropriate techniques for any corporate liquidation.

816. **Federal Information Disclosure, 2–E**. l. $195. Two volumes. Covers the disclosure of information from agency files under the *Freedom of Information Act*, the mechanics of suing the government for mandatory disclosure of this information, the 1974 *Privacy Act* and its significant impact on gathering information.

817. **Federal Tax Aspects of Bankruptcy**. Explains relevant tax laws and

the relationships between the Bankruptcy Act of 1980, the Bankruptcy Reform Act of 1978 and the Tax Reform Acts of 1984 and 1986.

818. **Federal Tax Planning**. a. $195. Three volumes. Provides details of tax planning, ranging from simple home ownership to more complicated activities such as leasing arrangements amomg family members, closely held corporations, divorces, and timber holdings.

819. **Franchising Adviser**. a. $95. Discusses all the key elements of a successful franchise system: trademark selection and registration, trade secret and copyright licensing, franchise agreements, including state and industry regulations.

820. **Fraud, Window Dressing and Negligence in Financial Statements**. a. $165. Two volumes. Advice to protect yourself and your clients from being victimized by false or negligently prepared financial statements.

821. **Guide to International Commerce Law**. Discusses laws relating to import and export of products and technology, distribution in the US and abroad and foreign investment, with emphasis on transactions and contracts between U.S. and foreign firms.

822. **Insurance Law Citations**. q. $660. Six volumes. Lists insurance law cases, with citations to cases decided by the US Supreme Court, lower federal courts and state courts.

823. **Insurance Litigation Reporter**. m. $320. Analyzes trends and summarizes recent litigation affecting insurance law.

824. **International Corporate Taxation**. a. $110. Examines the international tax consequences of transactions carried out by and occuring between corporations and their shareholders.

825. **International Individual Taxation**. a. $95. Highlights tax planning techniques for international income situations, reflecting all important laws and treaties since 1976, including the 1986 Tax Reform Act.

826. **Manual of Foreign Investment in the United States**. Provides analyses and practical commentary on antitrust restrictions on foreign direct investment, taxation of foreign investors, federal securities laws, US acquisitions by foreign investors and foreign investment in real property.

827. **Regulation of the Commodities Futures and Options Markets**. l. $195. Discusses the Commodity Exchange Act and CFTC regulations. Provides examples of day-to-day issues, in-depth analyses of law and regulations related to exchanges and market participants and off-exchange instruments.

828. **Securities Fraud and Commodities Fraud**. a. $490. Seven volumes. Covers misrepresentation, non-disclosure, manipulation, churning and insider trading.

829. **Shepard's Citations**. **online**. "Provides a comprehensive list of citations to a given case, statute or administrative decision. Includes analysis of the cited case, or other legal authority, covering the history

(eg affirmed, dismissed, superseded), treatment (eg critized, harmonized, overruled); and operation of orders (eg amended, revoked, revised). Jurisidictions covered are federal (eg United States Citations, Federal Citations), regional (eg Atlantic Reporter Citations, Southwestern Reporter Citations), state (eg California Citations, Michigan Citations), and topical (e.g. Federal Labor Law Citations, Bankruptcy Citations). Specific citator coverage for *LEXIS* and *WESTLAW* is different; the user must check each service to determine what citators are included in that service." (*Gale Directory of Databases*) Several print citation journal series are available.

830. **Shepard's Uniform Commercial Code Citations**. bi-m. $390.

24. Finally, in our examples of commercial serials concerned with one or another aspect of the legal, regulatory and supervisory environments of trade in financial assets, we cite some titles from publishers who have a smaller presence in this field. These we have divided into three groups: those primarily relating to the UK environment – often including also consideration of the European Union environment; those relating to the US environment; and those with an international focus: but as elsewhere, the division is not clear cut.

United Kingdom and Europe

(1) #95 Barry Rose Law Periodicals Little London, Chichester, West Sussex PO19 1PG, UK. t: (44 1243) 787841; f: 779278.

831. **Trading Law and Trading Law Reports**. bi-m. £69.75. Details various aspects of consumer trading law, competition, monopolies, mergers, international trade, credit trading and fair trading, including important trading law cases.

(2) #96 Centaur Communications St Giles House, 49– 50 Poland Street, London W1V 4AX, UK. t: (44 171) 439 4222; f: 439 0110

832. The **Lawyer**. w. £50. Circulation: 18,300. Covers legal news from law practices, commerce and industry, and the public sector. Contains features on various aspects of commercial law as well as management.

(3) #97 T & T Clark 59 George Street, Edinburgh EH2 2LQ, UK. t: (44 31) 225 4703; f: 220 4260.

833. **Times Law Reports**. m. £110. 'Universally acknowledged for their quality and authority and are authenticated for use as precedents in court . . . Cover every branch of law and come from a wide range of jurisdictions including the courts of England and Wales, Scotland, the European Court of Justice . . . and the International Court of Justice.'

(4) #98 Company Reporting 68 Dundas Street, Edinburgh EH3 6QZ, UK. t: (44 131) 558 1400; f: 556 0639.

834. **Company Reporting**. m. £358. Respected monthly review of UK financial reporting practice.

(5) #99 Dun & Bradstreet International Holmers Farm Way, High Wycombe, Buckinghamshire, HP12 4UL, UK. t: (44 1494) 422000; f: 422260. *Also* Dun & Bradstreet Information Services, 3 Sylvan Way, Parsipanny, NJ 07054–9947, USA. t: (1 201) 605 6000; f: 605 6930.

835. **D&B Securities Taxation**. a. £510. UK capital gains tax and income tax full service. There is also an *Overseas Income Tax Full Service* (540).

836. **Stubbs Gazette**. w. £295. UK tax news.

(6) #100 Eclipse Publications 18–20 Highbury Place, London N5 1QP, UK. t: (44 171) 354 5858; f: 359 4000.

837. **Occupational Pensions**. m. £99. Provides guidance on new legislation and changes to regulations. Includes comprehensive surveys on named organizations.

(7) #101 HLT Publications The Gatehouse, Ruck Lane, Horsmonden, Tonbridge, Kent TN12 8EA, UK. t: (44 1892) 723968; f: 724206.

HLT Textbooks 'are written to meet the needs of students taking examinations. . . . These textbooks are updated every year to take account of recent developments in the law.' Titles include: 'Commercial law: Sale of goods, commercial credit and agency' (£18.95); 'Company law' (£18.95); 'Contract law' (£16.95); 'Equity and trusts' (£16.95); 'European community law' (£17.95); and 'Law of international trade' (£18.95).

838. **Law Update (Year)**. a. £6.95. 'An annual review of the most recent developments in specific legal subject areas.'

(8) #102 IBC Publishing IBC House, Vickers Drive, Brooklands Industrial Park, Weybridge, Surrey KT13 0XS, UK. t: (44 1932) 354020; f: 353844 *and* 290 Eliot Street, Box 91004, Ashland, MA 017121–9104, USA. t: (1 508) 881 2800; f: 881 0982.

839. **Corporate Briefing**. 10/year. £145. 'The unique monthly newsletter that allows you to keep in touch with the many legal and regulatory developments that can affect the smooth running of your company.'

840. **Credit & Finance Law**. 10/year. £147. 'Briefing from experts for all those involved in credit transactions, bringing together legal developments affecting both consumer and commercial credit.'

841. **International Tax Digest**. bi-m. £257. **online**. Published in conjunction with *Ernst and Young International*.

842. **International Tax Report**. m. £315. 'Since its inception in 1972 . . . has become one of the most widely read tax publications.'

843. **Property Finance & Development**. m. £159.

844. **Trusts & Estates**. 10/year. £147. 'Since its launch in 1986 . . . has become the authoritative reference source on tax planning opportunities.'

(9) #103 ILI Infonorme London Information, Index House, Ascot, Berkshire SL5 7EU, UK. t: (44 1344) 23377; f: 291194.

845. **Eurolaw. cdrom**. 'The full text of European Union legislation and law (treaties, secondary and proposed legislation, case-law, national implementation and parliamentary questions). It includes briefings on the UK implementation prepared by the DTI.'

(10) #104 Jordan Publishing 21 St Thomas Street, Bristol BS1 6JS, UK. t: (44 117) 923 0600; f: 924 0586.

846. **Business Law and Practice**. a. £17.50.

847. **Commercial Law and Practice**. a. £17.50.

848. **International Corporate Procedures**. l. £250/£110. 'This important international loose-leaf encyclopaedia is an essential first point of reference for professional advisers to businesses around the world seeking to set up, run or obtain information about companies, partnerships, branches or joint ventures abroad. The work contains information on the principle forms of business enterprise in 57 of the world's major trading states and offshore financial centres, considering each form from three angles: formation and organisation, tax and accounting, and information availability.'

849. **Public Companies and the City**. a. £17.50.

(11) #105 Kogan Page 120 Pentonville Road, London N1 9JN, UK. t: (44 171) 278 0433; f: 837 6348.

850. **Tax Facts (Year)**. a. 8.99. 'Continues to provide an invaluable guide for everyone wanting to benefit from more effective tax planning.'

(12) #106 Legalese 28–33 Cato Street, London W1H 5HS, UK. t: (44 171) 396 9292; f: 396 9300.

851. **Legal Business**. 10/year. £450. Covers news of commercial law firms and their clients.

(13) #107 Lloyd's of London Press Sheepen Place, Colchester, Essex, CO3 3LP, UK. t: (44 1206) 772277; f: 772880. *Also* Legal Publishing Division, 27 Swinton Street, London WC1X 9NW, UK. t: (44 171) 833 8933; f: 833 5521 *and* 611 Broadway, Suite 308, New York, NY 10012, USA. t: (1 212) 529 9500; f: 529 9826.

852. **International Journal of Insurance Law**. q. £79.

853. **Lloyd's Law Reports**. m. £258.

854. **US Maritime Alert**. w. $435.

(14) #108 Monitor Press Rectory Road, Great Waldingfield, Sudbury, Suffolk CO10 0TL, UK. t: (44 1787) 378607; f: 880201.

855. **Commercial Leases**. m. £137. For professional property and investment managers, solicitors and chartered surveyors.

856. **Company Law Monitor**. m. £160. Addresses the practical implications of all the major relevant cases, statutes and regulations, including those from the European Economic Community for company lawyers and senior management.

857. **European Law Monitor**. m. £129.

858. **Financial Services Law Letter**. m. £152. Covers legislation and regulations affecting all those involved in the financial services industry.

859. **Housing Law Monitor**. m. £127.

860. **Insurance Law Monthly**. m. £134. Covers pending and new legislation and developments on insurance law.

861. **Pensions Today**. m. £165. For pension-fund managers, trustees, company secretaries, persons specialising in broking and insurance companies.

(15) #109 Technical Indexes Willoughby Road, Bracknell, Berkshire RG12 8DW, UK. t: (44 1344) 426311; f: 424971.

862. **Financial Services Compliance Data**. **cdrom**. m. 'For successful operation within the framework of the Financial Services Act 1986 and the rulebooks of each Self Regulating Organization (SRO) of the Securities and Investments Board (SIB), *every compliance officer needs rapid, straightforward access to relevant documents* . . . On just one disc . . . holds the full texts of the entire collection of SRO rulebooks . . . the SIB Rulebook, the Financial Services Act 1986 and other complete legislation with complementary material from HMSO and the Bank of England. Also available are the full texts of the Rules of the London Stock Exchange . . . Listings Rules . . . City Code . . . Money Laundering Regulations . . . The London Code of Conduct Regulations . . . Friendly Societies Acts of 1984 & 1992.'

(16) #110 Tuckers' Directories 355 Deansgate, Manchester M3 4LG, UK. t: (44 61) 832 5075; f: 833 9040.

863. **Tuckers' Directory of the Accountants 500**. a. 'The definitive guide to the UK's leading five hundred firms who employ accountants.'

(17) #111 VNU Business Publications VNU House, 32–34 Broadwick Street, London W1A 2HG, UK. t: (44 171) 439 4242; f: 437 4841.

864. **Accountancy Age**. w. £100. **online**. Coverage of events in the accounting world as well as of other news items likely to be of interest to accountants. Circulation: 62,202.

United States

(18) #112 A/N Group PO Box 895, Melville, NY 11747. t: (1 516) 549 4090; f: 385 9828.

865. **Small Business Tax Review**. m. **online**.

(19) #113 Alert Publications Partners 1401 Brickell Avenue, Suite 570, Miami, FL 33131, USA. t: (1 305) 530 0500; f: 530 9434.

866. **Money Laundering Alert**. m. $345. **online**. 'If you are a jeweler, boat dealer, car dealer, airplane dealer, accountant or lawyer you must know your reporting duties. The IRS conducts unannounced Form 8300 compliance checks nationwide. Penalties for intentional noncompliance now start at $25,000. Soon bankers may be responsible for knowing if and when their customers have filed Form 8300.'

(20) #114 American Lawyer Media 600 Third Avenue, 2nd Floor, New York, NY 10016. t: (1 212) 973 2800; f: 972 6258.

867. **American Lawyer**. 10/year. $595. **online**. 'With more news and insightful articles than any other legal publication.'

868. **Legal Times**. w. $475. **online**. Covers law, lobbying, and politics in Washington DC.

(21) #115 Andrews Publications 1646 West Chester Pike, PO Box 1000, Westtown, PA 19395. t: (800) 345 1101/(1 610) 399 6600; f: 399 6610.

Subscribers have unlimited use of an extensive database of documents from court cases across the country through *Andrews Document Access Service*. Also available is *Andrews Advisor*, a quarterly newsletter for law librarians.

869. **Andrews' Professional Liability Litigation Reporter**. m. $550. Focuses on the third party liability of attorneys, investment bankers, financial advisors, accountants and other professionals. The targeted actions involve allegations of securities law violations, breach of fiduciary duty, etc.

870. **Chapter 11 Update**. bi-w. $450. **online**. Monitors all the significant legal proceedings associated with the corporate reorganizations under Chapter 11 in bankruptcy courts nationwide.

871. **Commodities Litigation Reporter**. m. $750. Provides coverage of major reparations and enforcement actions involving the scope of the Commodity Exchange Act. Includes investor lawsuits alleging fraud, churning, breach of fiduciary duty, noncompetitive trading, price manipulation, unauthorized trading and other violations.

872. **Failed Bank and Thrift Litigation Reporter**. bi-w. $825. **online**. Follows developments in lawsuits over bank officers' fiduciary responsibilities, the liability of third party professionals such as accountants and

lawyers, and the liability of carriers who provide directors and officers insurance to failed institutions. The publication also targets failed bank actions involving allegations of securities fraud and violations of the Commodity Exchange Act.

873. **Failed Leveraged Buyout Litigation Reporter**. m. $700. Coverage of leveraged buyout and related business issues in bankruptcy, federal district and appellate courts. Topics covered include debt restructuring, initial bankruptcy filings, fraudulent conveyances, preferential transfers, various officer/director/advisor liability issues, tax and financing, reorganization and compensation matters.

874. **Insurance Industry Litigation Reporter**. bi-w. $825. **online**. Reports on developing issues in the field of insurance litigation.

875. **Lender Liability Litigation Reporter**. bi-w. $700. Covers the latest cases involving allegations of fraudulent banking practices on the parts of lenders and borrowers. Issues addressed include breach of fiduciary duty, contract violations, the Truth-in-Lending Act and the Comprehensive Environmental Response Compensation and Liability Act. Also covers cases in which the federal government has taken over a financial institution which may have violated borrowers' rights.

876. **National Bankruptcy Reporter**. w. $1,800. **online**. In depth coverage of bankruptcy filings of companies with assets in excess of $150,000. Information coming directly from an original court filing is reported before any radical changes are made.

877. **Pension Fund Litigation Reporter**. m. $650. Covers recent developments in suits against employee benefit plan administrators and trustees alleging violations of their fiduciary responsibilities. New legislation and regulations governing funding decisions are also covered.

878. **Securities Insider Trading Litigation Reporter**. bi-w. $1,250. 'The national journal of record reporting litigation concerning insider trading and other securities law abuses which adversely affect market stability.'

(22) #116 Beard Group Box 9867, Washington, DC 20016. t: (1 301) 951 6400; f: 951 3621.

879. **Turnarounds & Workouts**. bi-w. $354. News for people tracking distressed companies. A *Supplement* (m. $48) contains data and statistics for professionals on troubled companies in the USA and Canada.

(23) #117 Buraff Publications 1350 Connecticut Avenue NW, Suite 1000, Washington, DC 20036. t: (800) 333 1291; f: (1 202) 862 0999.

880. **Bank Bailout Litigation News**. w. $645. Washington-based lawyer-written newsletter on failed bank and thrift liquidation issues. Includes in-depth analyses of the latest cases in the transactional, professional liability and enforcement areas of failed banking law.

881. **Buraff's Litigation Reports: Bank Lawyer Liability**. bi-w. $745. 'Text

and analysis of RTC, FDIC, OTS, and related actions against bank lawyers.'

882. **International Securities Regulation Report**. bi-w. $795. **online**. Provides information on regulation of international securities trading, new trading links among markets, and cooperation among governments in enforcing securities law.

883. **Lender Liability News**. bi-w. $597. Liability issues facing lenders in all areas: fraud, breach of fiduciary duty, environmental cleanup. Covers litigation, legislation and regulation, and new industry practice (how lenders are reducing their exposure in negotiating, administrating and enforcing loan agreements).

(24) #118 Commodities Law Press Associates 40 Broad Street, 20th Floor, New York, NY 10004–2315. t: (1 212) 612 9545; f: 425 0266.

884. **Futures International Law Letter**. m. $285. Covers legal developments affecting commodity futures in US and world-wide.

(25) #119 Compass Data Systems 1174 E 2700 S, Suite 1, Salt Lake City, UT 84106. t: (1 801) 485 4005; f: 485 4032.

885. **FDIC Regulations**. **diskette**. bi-m. **cdrom**. bi-m. 'Complete 3 volume set of FDIC Law, Regulations and Related Acts.'

886. **Internal Revenue Code, Treasury Regulations & Taxpayer Publications**. **diskette**. q. **cdrom**. q.

887. **United States Supreme Court Cases**. **diskette**. q. **cdrom**. q. 'Full text of the US Supreme Court since 1981.'

(26) #120 Congressional Quarterly 1414 22nd Street NW, Washington, DC 20037. t: (800) 432 2250; f: 728 1863.

888. **Congressional Quarterly Service: Weekly Report**. w. $1349. **online**. Provides detailed reports on all major legislative action, the president's legislative proposals, statements and major speeches and analyses of the Supreme Court's decisions. Includes coverage of political and lobbying activities.

(27) #121 Counsellor Publications Box 19070, Alexandria, VA 22320. t: (1 703) 739 0489.

889. **Bankruptcy Counsellor**. bi-w. $345. Newsletter.

(28) #122 Counterpoint Publishing 84 Sherman Street, PO Box 928, Cambridge, MA 02140. t: (800) 998 4515/(1 617) 547 4515; f: 547 9064. e: info@counterpoint.com.

Provides products via CD-ROM, the Internet, Lotus Notes within Windows, Macintosh, FolioViews, World Wide Web, Gopher and E-Mail environments.

890. **Code of Federal Regulations via Internet**. m. $1,950. Available via World Wide Web or Gopher, in full or as individual titles: e.g. *17CFR Commodity & Security Exchanges* (m. $295).

891. **Compact Disc Code of Federal Regulations**. m. $1,950. 'The complete text of all 50 CFR titles.' Also available on **diskette**, either in full, or as individual titles: e.g. *12CFR Banks & Banking* (m. $295.)

892. **Compact Disk Federal Register. cdrom**. w. $1,950. 'Widely acclaimed as the most complete, accurate and timely electronic version of the Federal Register . . . It includes the complete text, tables, charts and graphics found in six months' of Federal Registers derived directly from the official US government tapes. All rules, proposed rules, notices and presidential documents are included.'

893. **Daily Federal Register via Modem**. d. $3,900. 'Automatic delivery of the full-text . . . on day of publication.' Price includes 'free script-writing, free high-speed modem and free communications software'. There is also a service which delivers in *Lotus Notes* format (d. $6,000); and one delivering via the *Internet* (d. $1,000).

894. **Federal Register/Code of Federal Regulations Tracker Service. online**. 'Keeping abreast of the daily Federal Register is made simple . . . (This) email based service allows you to receive notification of articles in the Federal Register that conform to your criteria. All you need is an email address through any service that has an *Internet* connection, including *America Online, AT&T Mail, Class, CompuServe, Delphi, MCI Mail, Netcom, Panix, Pipeline, Prodigy, The Microsoft Network*, or any Internet account worldwide. Each day Counterpoint's computer reads every article in the Federal Register and automatically notifies you of articles that you might want to read. You then just check the articles you want and they are sent to you automatically. No more using expensive online services or waiting for delayed paper copies. . . . Every proposed rule, final rule and notice from the more than 140 Executive Branch agencies is, by law, published in the daily *Federal Register*.'

(29) #123 Dorset Group 212 W 35th Street, 13th Floor, New York, NY 10001. t: (1 212) 563 4008; f: 564 8879.

895. **Bank Resolution Reporter**. bi-w. $295.

896. **Managing Mortgages**. m. $36. General management publication for mortgage brokers, wholesale lenders, and managers.

897. **Problem Asset Reporter**. bi-w. $398. **online**. Contains information on the latest activity, investments and dealmaking with the Resolution Trust Corporation.

(30) #124 Emerson Company 12356 Northup Way, Suite 103, Bellevue, WA 98005. t: (1 206) 869 0655; f: 869 0746.

898. **Directory of Accounting Firms Worldwide**. a. $295. **diskette**.

899. **Emerson's Auditor Change Report**. bi-m. $245. Tracks changes in

auditors at publicly held companies and auditors used in initial public offerings.

900. **Professional Services Review**. m. $295. Includes special features, and commentary on current events involving the 'Big 6' accounting-consulting firms.

(31) #125 Executive Enterprises Publications 22 West 21st Street, New York, NY 10010–6904. t: (1 212) 645 7880; f: 645 1160.

901. **Journal of Corporate Accounting and Finance**. q. $152. **online**. Provides advice on dealing with current issues. Examines corporate accounting practices and policies, and analyzes existing and proposed professional regulatory and tax law developments.

902. **Letters of Credit Report**. bi-m. $245. Bank guarantees and acceptances. For bankers, lawyers, and foreign correspondents on domestic and foreign legal developments impacting letters of credit, bank acceptances and guarantees.

(32) #126 Federal Legal Publications 157 Chambers Street, New York, NY 10007. t: (1 212) 619 4949.

903. **Antitrust Bulletin**. q. $85. **online**.

904. **Journal of Reprints for Antitrust Law & Economics**. s-a. $55.

(33) #127 William S Hein 1285 Main Street, Buffalo, NY 14209–1987. t: (1 716) 882 2600; f: 883 8100.

905. **Hein Checklist of Statutes**. s-a. $27.

(34) #128 Hudson Sawyer Professional Services Marketing 950 East Paces Ferry Road, Suite 2425, Atlanta, GA 30326–1119, USA. t: (800) 954 6462/(1 404) 264 9977; f: 264 9968.

906. **Big Six Evaluations**. a. $175. 'Fortune 1000 financial executives rate services of the Big Six firms . . . in 16 specific categories and on topical subjects; reports audit fees in relation to revenue and to assets.'

907. **Bowman's Accounting Report**. m. $215. 'The accounting profession's independent newsletter of record . . . Reports and analyses the news, trends, strategies and politics that affect accountants and their firms.'

(35) #129 Institutional Investor 488 Madison Avenue, New York, NY 10022. t: (1 212) 303 3300; f: 303 3527. *Also* Institutional Investor (Europe), 56 Kingsway, London, WC2B 6DX. t: (44 171) 430 0881; f: 404 5455.

908. **Bank Accounting and Finance**. q. $125. **online**. Peer research articles on all financial, legislative and corporate aspects of operating a bank.

(36) #130 Kiplinger Washington Editors Inc 1729 H Street NW, Washington, DC 20006–3938. t: (1 202) 887 6400; f: 331 1206.

909. **Kiplinger Tax Letter**. bi-w. $56. News focussing on tax issues and problems associated with personal or business management.

910. **Kiplinger Washington Letter**. w. $73. News, information, analyses and forecasts affecting personal lives and finances.

(37) #131 Law Reporters 1519 Connecticut Avenue NW, Suite 200, Washington, DC 20036. t: (1 202) 462 5755; f: 328 2430.

911. **Bank and Corporate Governance Law Reporter**. m. $1,650. 'Civil litigation, bank & corporate governance, mergers & acquisitions.'

912. **RICO Law Reporter**. m. $1,350. 'Civil litigation, RICO, commercial fraud.'

(38) #132 LRP Publications 747 Dresher Road, Horsham, PA 19044. t: (1 215) 784 0860; f: 784 0870.

913. **Consumer Bankruptcy News**. w. $255. Newsletter.

(39) #133 National Journal 1730 M Street NW, Suite 1100, Washington, DC 20036. t: (1 202) 857 1400; f: 833 8069.

914. **National Journal**. w. $837. **online**. 'The weekly on politics and government.'

(40) #134 National Underwriter Company 505 Gest Street, Cincinnati, OH 45203. t: (1 513) 721 2140; f: 721 0126.

915. **Advanced Sales Reference Service**. l. $428. Eight volumes. Federal and state tax information 'for the life insurance and planning professional'.

916. (Year) **Tax Facts 2**. a. $19.95. Covers 'Stocks, Bonds, Mutual Funds, Real Estate, Oil & Gas, Puts, Calls, Futures, Gold, Savings Deposits.' There is also a *Tax Facts 1* ($19.95) covering life insurance.

917. **TAXLINE**. m. $48. 'The reliable source for current, accurate information on the constantly changing tax scene.'

(41) #135 NILS Publishing Company 21625 Prairie Street, Chatsworth, CA 91313–5833. t: (800) 423 5910/(1 818) 998 8830; f: 718 8482.

For over 40 years, NILS Publishing Company has delivered the laws, regulations and other materials that affect the way an American insurance business operates. The National Insurance Law Service has been the industry's partner over those years, bringing insurance professionals the information they need to comply with the myriad of regulatory requirements that confront them.

In 1981, NILS began a project to convert all of that information into an electronic database.... The result was *INSURLAW*: a comprehensive online database that featured consistent and exhaustive indexing, extensive subject coding, and innovative cross-referencing information...

Unfortunately, online services cost more than most researchers are prepared to pay. Every time a researcher uses an online system, they incur telecommunication charges, connect charges, search charges, print charges . . . the list goes on and on. When research is limited to a single state, or just a few states, traditional book research has proved to be the more cost-effective approach. As a result, use of INSURLAW typically was reserved for those big, multi-state research questions that can be answered only by the powerful search capabilities that until now – only online provided . . .

While online services have introduced new ways of finding information, they lack some of the features that have made books effective sources of information for centuries. For example, online does not provide the familiar structure of a book (which can be helpful in finding information). . . . When you pick up a book for the first time, you expect to find a beginning, a middle and an end. You expect to see certain finding aids: tables of contents, headings and subheadings, and perhaps an index. You expect the book to be divided into logical parts, chapters, sections and other divisions. . . . Books are not without their drawbacks however. Anyone who has been charged with updating the looseleaf volumes of the National Insurance Law Service will tell you: It's a big job. In 1990 alone, a subscriber to the full library of Red Books received more than 700 separate updates and revisions. In these packages the received more than 75,000 new and revised pages. . . . Clearly, there was room to improve upon both online and printed sources.

In the mid-1980s, a new information technology appeared: CD-ROM . . . CD-ROM meant that NILS Publishing Company could develop an information service that combined the important structural and contextual features found in the Red Books of the National Insurance Law Service, and the search power of INSURLAW online . . . *INSource* is the name of a new family of CD-ROM information services.

918. **INSource: The Red Books on CD-ROM. cdrom**. $2,200/month for 11 months. 'The insurance laws, related laws, advance laws to insurance and related laws, insurance regulations for all 50 States, the District of Columbia, Puerto Rico, and the US Virgin Islands; and selected attorney general opinions, related regulations and other regulatory materials as available. Includes the Red Books Thesaurus.'

919. **Insurance & Liability Reporter**. bi-w. 'Do you receive information on important insurance and liability developments 8 weeks or more after decisions are published? The *Insurance & Liability Reporter* brings you news within 2 to 4 weeks. While other legal newsletters wait for advance sheets, the *Insurance & Liability Reporter* uses online legal services and a network of 64 US and Canadian law firms.'

920. **National Insurance Law Review**. q. $95. 'Current insurance law issues, discussed by the best legal minds in the US today . . . Important insurance articles from the most respected American law reviews, reprinted in their original, unabridged form.'

(42) #136 New Generation Research 225 Friend Street, Suite 801, Boston, MA 02114. t: (1 617) 573 9550; f: 573 9554.

921. **Bankruptcy DataSource**. m. $5,000. Provides information on all public companies in bankruptcy, in default or in financial distress, including creditors, committees, securities, plans of reorganisation and other major events.

922. (Year) **Bankruptcy Yearbook and Almanac**. a. $150. Comprehensive source published annually in March of each year.

923. **Turnaround Letter**. m. $195. Investment newsletter that follows distressed companies, bankruptcies and other turnaround opportunities.

(43) #137 New York Law Publishing Company 345 Park Avenue South, New York, NY 10010. t: (800) 888 8300, (1 212) 779 9200; f: 696 2047.

924. **Equipment Leasing Newsletter**. m. $275.

925. **Law Journal EXTRA!. online**. 'A breakthrough online information and communications service designed to meet the needs of the nation's legal community:

- *Late-Breaking News* 'Legal News Line provides up-to-the minute coverage of important legal stories from across the country via a customised news service compiled from a variety of sources, including the LJX editorial staff. . . . Stay abreast of the latest trends and issues in the business world or quickly scan the news of the day with business, financial and general news from *AP Online*, updated around the clock, from the Associated Press. . . . The *National Law Journal*, *Law Technology Product News* and the *New York Law Journal* Online . . . Government Releases: Read the latest announcements from various federal and state agencies even before they make the newspaper headlines.'
- *The Virtual Law Office – Legal Resources and More* 'Inside information on courts, judges, lawyers, government and more . . . Federal Decisions . . . Legal Intelligence Files . . . Lobbyists & Databases . . . Brief Banks.'
- *Internet Access: Easy to Use and Customized for Lawyers* 'You've heard about it, read about it, and may even have tried it. But what you haven't seen is this – Internet access that is not only easy to use, but specifically designed for lawyers. Using the award-winning *Pipeline* software, *Law Journal EXTRA!* links thousands of valuable Internet resources to over 30 practice area menus. Many of these critical resources – which previously were available to most lawyers only at a premium charge – are at your fingertips for a fraction of the cost that you would pay other commercial online services. . . . *Federal Agencies* Find the latest securities filings from the SEC's EDGAR database or view proposed regulations, news releases, legislation and other valuable resources from the EPA, the FCC, the Labor Department, the FDA, the FDIC and hundreds of other federal and state

government agencies.... *Specialized Resources*... the international law specialist can search virtually all treaties and view updates from the United Nations, NATO and the World Bank by clicking on "International Law".... *The Law Library* Instantly connect to the Library of Congress, search card catalogs from leading law libraries nationwide... *Full Internet Access*... Any Internet resources in the world, from White House documents to the Paris Metro map, can be easily retrieved. The software supports the major Internet functions including Gopher, World Wide Web, WAIS, Veronica, Archie, FTP and Telnet.'

- *Electronic Communications* 'Use the advanced communication tools... to link yourself to the world or communicate with colleagues and clients privately: *E-Mail*... *Online Discussion Groups*... *Real-Time Conferencing*... *Calendar of Events*.'

'*Law Journal EXTRA!* offers the highest quality information at the lowest rates of any major legal online service. Just remember 10. That's $10 per month subscription charge and $10 for each hour you use the service, a fraction of what other services charge.'

926. **National Law Journal**. w. $110. **online**. News and analyses of latest trends and developments in all areas of law. Circulation: 45,000.

(44) #138 Panel Publishers 36 West 44th Street, No 1316, New York, NY 10036–8102. t: (1 212) 790 2000; f: 302 5119.

927. **International Tax Journal**. q. $136. Articles, columns and tax notes pertaining to the international tax market.

928. **Journal of Pension Planning and Compliance**. q. $136. Technical articles on major issues confronting the pension community.

929. **Journal of Property Tax Management**. q. $136. Commentary on issues and legislation affecting property tax, property valuation and property appraisal.

(45) #139 Prentice Hall Law & Business 270 Sylvan Avenue, Englewood Cliffs, NJ 07632–2513. t: (1 201) 894 8484.

930. **Banking Policy Report**. bi-w. $345. **online**.

931. **DOJ Alert**. m. $225. **online**. Newsletter relating to the US *Department of Justice*.

932. **Federal Tax Guide**. l. $795. Analyzes the entire body of federal tax law. Provides practical 'how-to' aids and tips. Includes a *Tax Bulletin* (w.) and *Special Reports* (i).

933. **Federal Taxes 2nd**. l. $1,350. Seventeen volumes. Provides in one source complete explanation of federal taxes with analysis of all the official material. Subscribers to this service also receive a password to *PHINet*, Prentice Hall's menu-driven online tax information service.

(46) #140 SNL Securities 410 East Main Street, PO Box 2124, Charlottesville, VA 22902. t: (1 804) 977 1600; f: 977 4466.

934. **SNL Weekly ComplianceFax**. w. $97. 'What's going on at the Fed? the OTS? the FDIC? the OCC? the SEC? It's alphabet soup, and the *ComplianceFax* helps you digest all the activity at every agency each week.... What does the world's greatest deliberative body have up its collective sleeve? The *ComplicanceFax* takes the hot air out of congressional pronouncements and summarizes what you need to know.... Each week, an outside counsel takes an in-depth look at a timely compliance-related issue affecting your institution.... Keeps tabs on the issues affecting regulatory compliance in the banking industry... Be aware of compliance-related events slated for upcoming weeks... Find the release you need with the *ComplianceFax* index – a quick reference for agency releases, court documents, and congressional bills and testimony released during the past month.'

(47) #141 Washington Law Reporter Company 1001 Connecticut Avenue NW, Suite 238, Washington, DC 20036–5504. t: (1 202) 331 1700; f: 785 8476.

935. **Daily Washington Law Reporter**. d. $180. Newsletter.

(48) #142 Washington Regulatory Reporting Associates Box 356, Basye, VA 22810. t: (1 703) 856 2216.

936. **Antitrust Freedom of Information Log**. w. $335. **online**. Provides brief summaries of the *Freedom of Information Act* requests received at the Antitrust Division of the US Justice Department.

(49) #143 Washington Service Bureau 655 15th Street NW, Washington, DC 20005. t: (1 202) 508 0600; f: 508 0694. Also offer a *document supply service*.

937. **Bank Digest**. d. $715.

938. **CFTC Administrative Reporter**. l. $1,425.

939. **ERISA Citator**. l. $615.

940. **ERISA Update**. l. $985.

941. **Ethics in Government Reporter**. l. $650.

942. **Federal Ethics Report**. m. $195.

International

50) #144 CIFAR [Center for International Financial Analysis & Research] Princeton Service Center, 3490 US Route One, Princeton, NJ 08540, USA. t: (1 609) 520 9333; f: 520 0905.

943. **Global Register of the Leading International Accounting Firms**. i. $195. (1st ed., 1994) 'A comprehensive listing of client, partner and office

data on 28 leading international accounting firms in more than 150 countries.'

944. **International Accounting and Auditing Trends**. i. $345. (4th ed., 1994). 'A comprehensive review of global financial reporting practices, accounting standards and a competitive analysis of leading international accounting firms.'

(51) #145 DYP Group Bridge House, 181 Queen Victoria Street, London EC4V 4DD, UK. t: (44 171) 236 2175; f: 489 1487.

945. **Liability Risk & Insurance**. m. £220. Provides summaries of key legal cases and liability developments from around the world.

(52) #146 Euromoney Publications Nestor House, Playhouse Yard, London EC4V 5EX, UK. t: (44 171) 779 8888; f: 779 8818.

946. **International Corporate Law**. 10/year. £225. **online**.

947. **International Financial Law Review**. m. £365. **online**.

948. **International Law Firm Management**. bi-m. £250.

949. **International Tax Review**. 10/year. £315. **online**.

950. **Tax Developments Yearbook (Year)**. a. $75. '13 countries are covered from Latin America, Western Europe and Asia.'

(53) #147 Foreign Tax Law Publishers Box 2189, Ormond Beach, FL 32175– 2189, USA. t: (1 904) 253 5785; f: 257 3003.

951. **Tax and Commercial Laws of the World**. l. $2,300/$1,200. **diskette** $1,900/$1,000. 117 countries (but excluding the USA). Initial Set of 79 binders and 205 monographs *or* 120 PC-diskettes. Initial price includes all supplements, revised editions and new countries published, and a free subscription to the *Foreign Tax Law Bi-Weekly Bulletin* (bi-w. $125) for one year. Subsets of the whole are available.

(54) #148 Grotius Publications Cambridge University Press, Publishing Division, The Edinburgh Building, Shaftesbury Road, Cambridge CB2 2RU, UK. t: (44 223) 312393; f: 315052.

952. **International Law Reports**. i. £79.00 per volume. '*Volume 93* is devoted to decisions on the relations between European Community law, public international law and the laws of the various Member States of the European Community.'

(55) #149 Information Handling Services 15 Inverness Way E, Englewood, CO 80150, USA. t: (1 303) 790 0600; f: 397 2747.

953. **US Banking Library**. **cdrom**. 'Includes over 200,000 pages of US banking laws, regulations and documents, on one CD-ROM. The disc is updated monthly and daily *Federal Register* updates can be obtained online when required from the *IHS Bulletin Board* service.'

954. **Worldwide Standards**. **cdrom**. Includes coverage of standards from *British Standards Institution, European Legislation & Standards Service* (Eurofile), *International Organisation for Standardization, American National Standards Institute, Association for Information & Image Management, National Information Standards Organization.*

(56) #150 Lafferty Publications The Tower, IDA Centre, Pearse Street, Dublin 2, Ireland. t: (353 1) 671 8022; f: 671 8240. *Also* Diana House, 4th Floor, 33/34 Chiswell Street, London EC1Y 4SE, UK. t: (44 171) 782 0590; f: 782 0586 *and* 420 Lexington Avenue, Suite 1745, New York, NY 10170, USA. t: (1 212) 557 6726; f: 557 7266.

955. The **Accountant**. m. £249. 'The world's oldest accounting bulletin.'

956. **Corporate Accounting International**. 10/year. £499.

957. **European Accountant**. 10/year. £449.

958. **International Accounting Bulletin**. bi-w. £549.

(57) #151 Oceana Publications 75 Main Street, Dobbs Ferry, New York, NY 10522, USA. t: (1 914) 693 8100; f: 693 0402.

959. **Annual Survey of American Law**. a. Price varies. Focuses on developments and issues which affect the legal system in America.

960. **International Regulation of Finance and Investment**. l. $175.

961. **International Securities Regulation**. l. $525. Four volumes. 'With the globalization of financing and securities trading, lawyers in the . . . jurisdictions to be covered by these books will wonder how they could ever have gotten along without them' (*American Journal of International Law*).

962. **International Tax Treaties of All Nations. Series A**. l. $775. Fourteen volumes. Provides English language texts of all tax treaties in force between two or more nations.

963. **International Tax Treaties of All Nations. Series B**. $1,450. Twenty-six volumes. Tax treaties in force between two or more nations not yet published by the U.N.

964. **Law and Practice Under the GATT and Other Trading Arrangements**. l. $135.

965. **Money Laundering, Asset Forfeiture and International Financial Crimes**. bi-m. $300.

(58) #152 Transnational Juris Publications 1 Bridge Street, Irvington-on-Hudson, NY 10533, USA. t: (1 914) 591 4288; f: 591 2688.

966. **World Arbitration & Mediation Report**. m. $455. Covers arbitration and other alternatives to litigation in international commercial disputes.

(59) #153 John Wiley 605 Third Avenue, New York, NY

10158–0012, USA. t: (1 212) 850 6000; f: 850 6088 *and* Baffins Lane, Chichester, West Sussex, PO19 1UD, UK. t: (44 1243) 779777; f: 775878.

967. **International Accounting Summaries**. i. 'A guide for interpretation and comparison.' Produced in association with *Coopers & Lybrand (International)*.

968. (Year) **International Tax Summaries**. a. £89. 'Information on the tax systems in over 114 countries.' Produced in association with *Coopers & Lybrand (International Tax Network)*.

25. The reader will note an especial aspect of the legal and related publishing field: the use of copy prepared by commercial law and accounting firms. There is a similar practice in parts of the securities industry.

26. Thus, there are a very large number of commercial serials which focus on one or another aspect of the legal, regulatory and supervisory environments of finance activity. Many are direct competitors – covering the same or very similar facets of the overall field. Where there is competition, should one attempt to say which is 'the best' in each specific area? I would suggest 'No'. (It is hardly difficult to sample each specific area's candidates: just ring the publisher!) This particular writer certainly is not prepared to offer a view as to whether, for instance, *Butterworths Journal of International Banking and Financial Law* is 'better' than the FT Law & Tax *International Banking and Financial Law* is 'better' than the Sweet & Maxwell *Journal of International Banking Law*. Each will have its fans (otherwise it would not survive in the commercial marketplace); each will have particular strengths for particular purposes. And, in any case if one or another of those publications seemed at this time of writing to provide the most cost/effective service for specific segments of the overall market, you can be sure that the others would soon respond with 'new features'. After all, there are no technical problems in acquiring copies of the source material used to produce each publication. So the opportunities present elsewhere in the finance information arena to acquire a news 'scoop', or to display the acquired data/information to the customer more quickly than rival services, or to engage in some especially clever piece of data manipulation, are hardly present with legal publications.

The organizational framework

27. The source material used as input by the commercial serials sampled above arises from a range of legislative, regulatory and supervisory processes briefly alluded to at the start of this chapter. More specifically, the material is released to the public domain by one or another of a complex of official, quasi-official and self-regulatory organizations which exist within each national jurisdiction; within Europe (the European Union); and internationally. Focusing for the time being on the UK and the USA, we will now give examples of the major types of relevant information provider, contrasting practice in those two countries. We will concentrate especially in the next few paragraphs on the regulation and supervision of commercial banking, insurance and securities business.

28. Moving to our immediate task, as a highly simplified overview of what is, I am afraid, a rather large and dense amount of material (but, unfortunately, that's the way it is), we can write that both the UK and the USA have upper and lower legislatures, where one's particular interest is often in fact in the various Committee discussions and decisions prior to formal legislation, rather than in what happens on the floor of the House (or Senate). Both countries have central banks, each having critical regulatory and supervisory responsibilities for the respective financial systems: we follow the treatment of those with examples of other statutory bodies in each country which have distinct additional responsibilities for the players in the respective national financial systems.

29. Within the government departments, it is then appropriate to outline the structure of the entities primarily concerned respectively with revenue and finance (in the UK there is a separation of function; in the USA the functions are combined under the Department of the Treasury). At this point we also consider some other departments and formally designated agencies which have specific responsibilities with regard to banks and other depository institutions. As regards insurance, which is somewhat briefly considered next, in the UK the major body of relevance is the Department of Trade and Industry, though there are some other entities of interest; but for the USA – where insurance is predominantly state registered – we simply reference national bodies representative of state insurance officials. There has not been space here to do other than make tangential reference to US legal, regulatory and supervisory environments operative at a state, rather than at a federal level.

30. Moving to the securities industry, on the surface we have two similar bodies: the Securities and Investments Board in the UK, and the Securities and Exchange Commission in the USA. But the latter has a considerably wider remit than the former: with much that is regulated and supervised in the USA by the SEC, being in the UK regulated and supervised by the Department of Trade and Industry, Companies House, or the London Stock

Exchange. However, even though the SEC is of supreme importance, it does not have the playing field to itself; and it is possible to reference a number of other bodies in the USA concerned with one or another aspect of securities business regulation and supervision.

31. That will have completed our overview of the official and quasi-official regulatory and supervisory framework of banking, insurance and securities activity in the two countries. However, before we embark on the actual details, four further points will be made. *First*, there is of course a whole raft of bodies concerned with the technicalities of upholding and maintaining the law. It does not seem appropriate for the assumed audience for this book to do other than remind the reader of the sorts of organization that support those due processes. Some are generic entities; others are in being specifically with reference to financially related matters:

United Kingdom

(1) **#154 Crown Prosecution Service** Head Office, 50 Ludgate Hill, London EC4M 7EX. *Public Enquiry Point* t: (44 171) 273 8152.

- *Fraud Division* Investigation and prosecution of serious and complex fraud, other than cases which are referred to the *Serious Fraud Office*. Restraint and confiscation of the proceeds of drug trafficking and serious crime.

(2) **#155 Law Commission** Conquest House, 37–38 John Street, Theobald's Road, London WC1N 2BQ. t: (44 171) 411 1220; f: 411 1297. *Annual Report. Working Papers.*

Set up in 1965, under the Law Commission Act 1965, to take and keep under review all the law with which they are concerned with a view to its systematic development and reform, including in particular the codification of such law, the elimination of anomalies, the repeal of obsolete and unnecessary enactments, the reduction of the number of separate enactments, and generally the simplication and modernization of the law. The Commission's publications are available from *HMSO*, eg 'The law of trusts: Delegation by individual trustees' (HC 110, 1994, £8.25).

969. **Law Under Review: A Quarterly Bulletin of Law Reform Projects**. q.

(3) **#156 Serious Fraud Office** Elm House, 10–16 Elm Street, London WC1X 0BJ. t: (44 171) 239 7272; f: 837 1689.

Department for the investigation and prosecution of cases involving serious and complex fraud. The Criminal Justice Act 1987 provides its statutory basis.

United States

(4) #157 Administrative Office of the US Courts Thurgood Marshall Federal Judiciary Building, One Columbus Circle NE, Washington, DC 20544. *Annual Report.*

970. **Federal Judicial Workload Statistics**. q. Includes, for instance, information on number of bankruptcy filings by categories and by regions (but no financial information on the filers).

- *Bankruptcy Division* t: (1 202) 273 1900
- *Statistics Division* t: (1 202) 273 2240

(5) #158 Department of Justice 10th Street and Constitution Avenue NW, Washington, DC 20530. t: (1 202) 514 2000; f: 633 4371. *Freedom of Information* t: (1 202) 514 3642.

'As the largest law firm in the Nation, the Department of Justice serves as counsel for its citizens.'

- *Antitrust Division* t: (1 202) 514 2692; f: 514 8123. Responsible for promoting and maintaining competitive markets by enforcing the Federal antitrust laws.
- *Civil Division* t: (1 202) 514 3301. Represents the United States, its departments and agencies, members of Congress, Cabinet officers, and other Federal employees. Its litigation reflects the diversity of Government activities, involving, for example ... commercial issues such as contract disputes, banking, insurance, patents, fraud, and debt collection ... The *Commercial Litigation Branch* is responsible for litigation associated with the Government's diverse financial involvements. This litigation includes all monetary suits involving contracts, express or implied; actions to foreclose on Government mortgages and liens; bankruptcy and insolvency proceedings; and suits against guarantors and sureties.
- *Criminal Division* Develops, enforces and supervises the application of all Federal criminal laws, except those specifically assigned to other Divisions. Includes a *Fraud Section*, which conducts investigations and prosecutes about 100 fraud cases of national significance or great complexity annually; and a *Money Laundering Section*. The latter works with the law enforcement and regulatory agencies using an interagency, interdisciplinary and international approach.
- *Tax Division* t: (1 202) 514 2901; f: 514 2085. Represents the United States and its officers in all civil and criminal litigation arising under the internal revenue laws, other than proceedings in the *United States Tax Court*.
- *Office of Justice Programs* Established by the *Justice Assistance Act* of 1984 and reauthorized in 1992 to provide Federal leadership coordination and assistance needed to make the Nation's justice system more efficient and effective in preventing and controlling crime.
    - *Bureau of Justice Statistics* Responsible for collecting, analysing, publishing, and disseminating statistical information on crime, its

perpetrators and victims and the operation of the justice systems at all levels of government and internationally.

- *National Criminal Justice Reference Service* Clearinghouse of information and publications concerning Office of Justice Programs programs and other information of interest to the criminal justice community.
- *National Institute of Justice* Primary research and development agency of the Department.

971. **National Criminal Justice Database on CD-ROM**. a. $28. '120,000 bibliographic records for documents on criminal justice.'

(6) **#159 Executive Office for United States Trustees** Suite 700, 901 E Street NW, Washington, DC 20530. t: (1 202) 307 1391.

Formed under the Bankruptcy Act to run the United States Trustee Program. The trustees overall duty is the prevention of bankruptcy fraud. Specific duties include appointing people (lawyers, committees, trustees etc.), examining bankruptcy reports such as disclosure statements, approving rates of compensation for bankruptcy professionals, seeing that documents are filed on time, etc.

(7) **#160 Supreme Court of the United States** United States Supreme Court Building, 1 First Street NE, Washington, DC 20543. t: (1 202) 479 3000. *Public Information Office* t: (1 202) 479 3211.

(8) **#161 United States Court of International Trade** One Federal Plaza, New York, NY 10007. t: (1 212) 264 2814.

Has jurisdiction over any civil action arising from Federal laws governing import transactions.

(9) **#162 United States Tax Court** 400 Second Street NW, Washington, DC 20217. t: (1 202) 783 3238; f: 606 8704.

An independent judicial body.

972. **Tax Court Reports**. m. $29. **online**. Presents judicial decisions on points of law in cases heard in open court, for subsequent citation as precedent.

32. *Second*, we will remind the reader that the majority of the UK and US publications of the bodies we will cover in this section of the chapter appear in the catalogues of the two respective national official publications agencies. We will refer to those agencies here, noting especially their expanding involvements in the electronic dissemination of the material each handles. Obviously, each agency handles documents from many more relevant official and quasi-official bodies than those referenced below. On the other hand, the sorts of organizations we are interested in in this book do not funnel all of their published output through HMSO and GPO. We do not try to disentangle that aspect here: if the publication you need does not appear to be distributed by the appropriate national official publishing agency, contact the generating organization directly. We also reference here two bodies concerned with the press and public relations aspects of each government:

(1) #163 Central Office of Information Hercules Road, London SE1 7DU, UK. t: (44 171) 928 2345.

Acts as the publicity procurement Agency for Government departments, agencies and other public sector clients, on a repayment basis. . . . Each of the main government departments has its own information division, public relations branch or news department. These are normally staffed by professional information officers responsible for communicating their department's activities to the news media and the public – sometimes using publicity services provided by the COI. The *Reference Services* section of the Office compiles a useful series of introductory booklets *Aspects of Britain*: eg 'Financial Services' (1994).

973. **Britain (Year): An Official Handbook**. a. The Section *Economic Affairs* includes helpful introductory chapters on National Economy, Public Finance, and Finance and Other Service Industries. Each volume contains a list of the public Acts of Parliament passed in the last year.

974. **Hermes**. **online**. **cdrom**. Text of press releases issued by the Office.

(2) #164 HMSO St Crispins, Duke Street, Norwich NR3 1PD, UK. t: (44 1603) 622211; f: 695582. *Publications Centre* PO Box 276, London SW8 5DT, UK. t: (44 171) 873 0011; f: 873 8200. *HMSO Electronic Publishing* St Crispins, Duke Street, Norwich NR3 1PD, UK. t: (44 1603) 695498; f: 696501. In the *United States*: UNIPUB 4611–F Assembly Drive, Lanham, MD 20706–4391, USA. t: (800) 274 4888/(1 310) 459 7666; f: 459 0056.

Executive Agency and a Government Trading Fund. Its main operations are: the procurement and production of printing and the supply of stationery, furniture, office equipment and systems for Parliament, Government departments, local authorities, nationalized industries and other parts of the public service; and the publication and sale of printed material for these bodies and for international organizations. As publisher for Parliament and the Government, HMSO produces a wide range of publications for sale by its own bookshops and by agents in Britain and overseas.

975. **Civil Service Year Book**. a. £21. **cdrom**. a. £60. The official and comprehensive guide to UK government departments and agencies. Includes brief descriptions of the functions of each department, together with telephone/fax numbers and the names of key personnel. (Much of the organizational annotation below is taken directly from this volume.)

976. **Daily List**. d. 87. Covers international as well as national organizational output.

977. **Finance Act (Year). diskette**. a. £39.95. The full text version.

978. **HMSO Agency Catalogue**. a. £7.75. Covers the publications of international organizations for which HMSO is an agent, including UN, EC, OECD. The publications are also listed in the daily and monthly HMSO catalogues alongside UK domestic publications.

979. **HMSO in Print on Microfiche**. *HMSO*. bi-m. £109.50.

980. **HMSO Monthly Catalogue**. m. £17.50. There is also an *Annual Catalogue* (£12.75).

981. **List of Statutory Instruments together with the List of Statutory Rules of Northern Ireland for the Month of (Month)**. m. Annual cumulation also available.

982. **London Gazette**. d. £365. Includes *Company Law Official Notifications*. There are also *Belfast Gazette* and *Edinburgh Gazette*.

983. **SI-CD**. s-a. £850. Published by *HMSO* in collaboration with *Context*. Full text of all SIs issued from 1 January 1987 onwards; short form entries for items from 1980. 'Statutory Instruments set out the detailed provision, under the authority of enabling Acts of Parliament, which create the means for the Government to fine tune the legislative machine.'

984. **UKOP**. q. £950. Published by *HMSO* in collaboration with *Chadwyck-Healey*. Catalogue of United Kingdom Official Publications. 'Unrivalled coverage of United Kingdom official publications... enhanced by the presence of publications from major British, European and international organisations for which HMSO is an agent. UKOP now contains nearly 300,000 records from 1980 to date.'

(3) #165 United States Government Printing Office Superintendent of Documents, Washington, DC 20402–9325, USA. t: (1 202) 783 3238; f: 512 2250 (publications), 512 2233 (subscriptions). *Electronic Information Dissemination Services* t: (1 202) 512 1526.

- *Electronic Information Products: CD-ROM* 'This list is updated every 7–10 days. To obtain a new copy, call t: (1 202) 512 1530, f: 512 1262, send Internet e-mail to <help@eids05.eids.gpo.gov> or write to: Superintendent of Documents, Electronic Products Coordinator, PO BOX 37082, Washington, DC 20013–7082. This list can be downloaded free from the *Federal Bulletin Board* by logging in at (1 202) 512 1387 (8–N–1) and downloading CDROMLST.WP (WordPerfect 5.1) or CDROMLST.TXT (ASCII text – can be listed to the screen) from the FREE library. To download via anonymous FTP, ftp to: eids04.eids.gpo.gov (/gpo/access/info/products/cdromlst.txt). US and Canada only – to obtain through an automated return-fax service, dial from a fax or touch-tone phone: (202) 512 1716, choose option 4, option 4 again, and then request document 9001.'
- *Federal Bulletin Board* 'Enables Federal agencies to provide the public with immediate, self-service access to Government information in electronic form at reasonable rates or free through agency sponsor-

ship.' Over 7,000 files are available from more than 100 "Libraries" from over 25 Government Agencies, including: US Congress, General Accounting Office, Internal Revenue Service, etc. The Board carries files on a wide variety of subjects, such as: 1995 US Government Budget, GATT and NAFTA etc. Telnet: federal.bbs.gpo.gov 3001.

- *GPO Access* 'Get the *Official, Authentic* Version Via *GPO Access* on the Internet:

  - Complete – Full text and graphics of the *Federal Register*, *Congressional Record*, *US Code*, and other Federal databases
  - Timely – All updated by 6 am daily except for the *Congressional Record*, which is usually available by 11.00 am depending when Congress adjourns the previous day
  - Convenient – Access via Internet to a Wide Area Information Server (WAIS) at GPO. Customized local WAIS client software and free User Manual from GPO
  - Inexpensive – Just over $1 per day

'Databases include: *Federal Register Service*, *Congressional Record Service*, *Legislative Service*, *GAO Service*.' http://www.access.gpo.gov.

- *Guide to Government Information* 'This booklet is your guide to the more than 12,000 different books, peridocials, posters, pamphlets and subscription services available for sale from the Superintendent of Documents. Because it would be impractical to list all 12,000 publications in one catalogue, these publications are listed in more than 150 free subject catalogs. Each catalog, known as a "Subject Bibliography", is devoted to one broad are of interest, This Guide contains an alphabetical listing of Subject Bibliographies, followed by a more detailed index to the subject areas.'

The *Alphabetic Listing* in this Guide includes the topics: *Accounting and Auditing* (42); Annual Reports (118); Business (4); Census of Business (152); Census of Governments (156); Congress (201); Congressional Directory (228); Cost of Living (226); Directories (114); Economic Development (319); Economic Policy (204); Economy (The) (97); Electronic Information Products (314); Export/Import (317); Federal Government (141); Federal Trade Commission (100); *Financial Institutions* (128); General Accounting Office (250); Government Printing Office (244); *Insurance* (294); Intergovernmental Relations (211); Internal Revenue Cumulative Bulletins (66); International Trade (123); Libraries (150); National Institute of Standards and Technology (290); *Securities and Investments* (295); Small Business (307); Specifications and Standards (231); Statistics (273); Student Financial Aid (85); Tax Court Reports (67); *Taxes* (195); United States Code (197); United States Reports (25).

985. **GPO Sales Publications Reference File**. **magtape**. bi-w. $850. 'A guide to current publications offered for sale by the Superintendent of Documents arranged by GPO stock numbers; Superintendent of Documents classification numbers; and alphabetically by subjects, titles, agency series and report numbers, key words and phrases, and personal authors.'

986. **Monthly Catalog of United States Government Publications**. m. $199. **online**. **cdrom**. 'The most comprehensive listing of government publications issued by Federal departments and agencies.

(4) #166 Government Information Services 4301 Fairfax Drive, Suite 875, Arlington, VA 22203–1627, USA. t: (1 703) 528 1000; f: 528 6060.

987. **Federal Budget Report**. bi-w. $295. Analysis of congressional and presidential budget activities.

33. *Third*, a reference seems appropriate to the US *Freedom of Information Act*:

'The *Freedom of Information Act* (FOIA) gives private parties the right to obtain information that is in the possession of the government. The purpose of the FOIA is to prevent 'government in secret' by providing a mechanism for public disclosure of information in the possession of the government (including administrative agencies). The FOIA requires that each federal agency make available for public inspection and copying its opinion in decided cases, any statements of policy and interpretations not published in the *Federal Register*, and any administrative staff manuals that might affect the public. There are exceptions to the coverage of the FOIA, the reasons for most of which are obvious. Some of the most important of these exceptions are materials concerning national defense or foreign policy; trade secrets and commercial or financial information that businesses have given to agencies to comply with statutes or administrative regulation.'[112]

Some 'Freedom of Information' telephone contact numbers are given in the US entity entries below.

34. Last and *fourth*, although it is I trust helpful in this context to try to separate out below the major functions of each body referenced, clearly there is much overlap in responsibilities. Further, from a reporting point of view, there is also much duplication: with banks, insurance companies, securities firms and other related entities having to report what is often basically the same information to differing authorities. (But of course it is not quite the same: which makes the whole thing so tedious!) Much of this duplication arises because of the still continuing belief in the USA that the businesses of banking, securities and insurance should be kept commercially separate. This has not generally been the case in other countries, which contrast Dale[113] has covered well in his text. He describes recent history in the USA, Japan, UK, Canada, Germany, Switzerland and the EEC, being especially good at contrasting the differing approaches in the different jurisdictions. In the USA:

Policy is designed to compartmentalize risks within bank holding com-

> panies so as to prevent cross-infection between the bank and its related entities, using for this purpose elaborate firewalls that restrict a bank's ability to engage in intra-group financial transactions.

Whereas in the UK, for instance, apart from in one specific area of financial acitvity – gilt-edged trading – the underlying assumption behind the regulation of bank's general securities business appears to be that the risks are indivisible. Thus:

> The regulation of combined banking/securities businesses also calls for an appropriate allocation of responsibilities between regulatory agencies. In the UK, Parliament chose to divide statutory responsibility for regulating such conglomerates between the SIB and the Bank of England; the SIB being responsible for regulating businesses authorized to conduct securities/investment activities under Section 25 of the Financial Services Act of 1986, while the Bank is responsible for supervising the banking activities of those firms authorized to undertake such business under the Banking Act of 1987.

In a footnote, confirming the comment a moment ago, Dale adds:

> In practice, the division of regulatory responsibilities is more complex than this might suggest, given the proliferation of self-regulatory organizations (SROs) that operate within the statutory framework. A UK banking group may thus have to confront the following array of regulators:
>
> - The Bank of England's Banking Supervision Division regulates commercial banking activities.
> - The Bank's Wholesale Market Supervision Division regulates wholesale market transactions.
> - The Bank's Gilt-Edged Division regulates (separately capitalized) gilt operations.
> - The Securities and Futures Authority (SFA) regulates non-wholesale debt/interest rate operations, equity operations and financial and commodity futures and options operations.
> - The Investment Management Regulatory Organization (IMRO) regulates fund management operations.'

35. Overall, Dale concludes from his survey:

> The case for financial diversification, based on economies of scope and competitive equality, has prevailed over counter-arguments that emphasize potential conflicts of interest and the possible systemic risks associated with securities business undertaken within banking groups. Accordingly, national policymakers have been pressing for removal of the remaining barriers between banking and securities markets. Indeed, the EEC has now adopted the universal banking model as part of its 1992 financial liberalization programme, while Canada, the USA and Japan are either proposing or implementing major initatives aimed at expanding banks' securities powers. The likelihood is that before

> long the traditional distinction between commercial and investment banking will have disappeared throughout the industrialized world.

However, having reminded us at the outset of the fragile nature of banks:

> Banks possess a number of characteristics that can, taken together, give rise to contagious financial disorders. . . . In fulfilling their intermediary function, (they) operate on a relatively low capital base . . . (A) large proportion of their assets are not readily marketable and can be disposed of promptly (if at all) only at a significant discount of their book value. . . . A third feature of banks is their dependence on a precarious deposit/funding base which can be relied upon to sustain operations only so long as the bank concerned commands the confidence of financial markets. . . . Finally, the financial condition of a bank cannot be determined from its published statements. This is because key risk parameters such as the quality of the loan portfolio are not captured in the accounts and also because such information as may be available can be quickly out-dated by subsequent transactions (for instance, in the foreign exchange, futures and options markets). The lack of transparency means that sound banks can fall victim to market rumour and unsound banks can go undetected until it is too late.

All of this is potentially exacerbated by the internationalization of the financial services industry which has removed the 'protective bulkheads' separating one banking jurisdiction from another, leading to an increasing potential for cross-border contagion within the global banking system, Dale states that:

> The central question that has to be addressed is whether it is desirable from a prudential standpoint for banks to be permitted to engage freely in securities markets as is now happening on a global scale. . . . What emerges from the analysis is that securities activities are not inherently riskier or less risky than banking but that they do provide opportunities for additional risk-taking by aggressively managed institutions. Furthermore, it is a disturbing fact that where wider powers have been granted to deposit-taking firms these powers have tended to be used in a risk-enhancing manner.

36. Dale had already noted that:

> It is a paradoxical fact that as national banking systems have been deregulated to market forces, regulatory authorities, in their role as lender of last resort, have become more inclined to intervene in support of troubled banks and/or their depositors.

His survey of the regulatory arrangements for combined banking and securities businesses had demonstrated 'conflicting approaches adopted by the USA and the EEC, in particular, and the more general policy confusion that exists both within and between the major financial centres'. If we add to that, the fact that:

> The banking industry worldwide has been seriously weakened by a number of factors in a situtation where financial institutions are also having to adjust to revolutionary changes in information technology and a proliferation of innovative financial instruments.

it is not surprising that Dale concludes that:

> If policymakers are to conduct financial experiments it is desirable that they should do so on a limited scale so that any unforeseen destabilising consequences can be contained. . . . A principle declared objective of those who are responsible for these reforms is to ensure that financial institutions compete with one another on a level playing field. However, in the light of the arguments presented here there is a serious danger that the level playing surface may be no more than thin ice.

37. *The legislatures*

United Kingdom

(1) #167 House of Lords Parliament Office, House of Lords, Westminster, London SW1A 0PW. t: (44 171) 219 3000. *Library* t: (44 171) 219 5242. *Journal and Information Office* t: (44 171) 219 3107.

988. **House of Lords Hansard on CD-ROM**. **cdrom**. q. £500. Published by *HMSO* in collaboration with *Chadwyck-Healey*. The official report of the House of Lords.

Select Committees are standing committees consisting usually of about a dozen members of all parliamentary parties. They have very wide powers to call for evidence. Minutes of each Committee's proceedings are normally published as *House of Lords Papers*. An important House of Lords *Select Committee* is:

- *European Communities Committee* t: (44 171) 219 3326.

(2) #168 House of Commons Westminster, London SW1A 0AA. t: (44 171) 219 3000. *Library* Enquiries (other than from Members) t: (44 171) 219 4272.

989. **House of Commons Hansard on CD-ROM**. **cdrom**. q. £1,200. Published by *HMSO* in collaboration with *Chadwyck-Healey*. The official report of the House of Commons.

990. **House of Commons Weekly Information Bulletin**. w. £88.80.

Select Committees The key relevant Committees are listed here; but other committees can naturally become involved with financially related issues: e.g. the operation of pension funds has been covered by the *Social Security Committee*, and the Housing Corporation considered by the *Environment Committee*. Minutes of the Committees are normally published as *House of Commons Papers*.

- *European Legislation Committee* t: (44 171) 219 5467
- *Finance and Services* t: (44 171) 219 3270
- *Public Accounts* t: (44 171) 219 3273
- *Trade and Industry* t: (44 171) 219 5469
- *Treasury and Civil Service* t: (44 171) 219 3285.

There are also six versions of the:

- *Standing Committee on Statutory Instruments* t: (44 171) 219 3771.

991. **Parliament**. *Context*. **cdrom**. d. £480. 'Based on the long established *POLIS* database searched every day by MPs, peers and officials at the Palace of Westminster.' Includes coverage of:

- *Biographies of MPs*
- *International and foreign official publications*
- *Legislation – Acts and Statutory Instruments*
- *Official publications*
- *Parliamentary papers*
- *Parliamentary proceedings*
- *Parliamentary questions*

Two bodies in the United Kingdom to some degree perform the detailed monitoring functions of the US Congress *General Accounting Office* (which is referenced in a moment):

(3) #169 National Audit Office 157–197 Buckingham Palace Road, Victoria, London SW1W 9SP. t: (44 171) 798 7000; f: 828 3774. *Annual Report*.

The Comptroller and Auditor General is responsible for controlling receipts and issues from the Consolidated and National Loans Funds. His officers examine the accounts of government departments, certain public bodies and international organisations. He reports to Parliament on the economy, efficiency and effectiveness of public spending.

(4) #170 Audit Commission for Local Authorities and the National Health Service in England and Wales 1 Vincent Square, London SW1P 2PN. t: (44 171) 828 1212; f: 976 6187. The Commission's publications are either available from *HMSO*, or from the Commission themselves: Publications Section, Audit Support, Audit Commission, Nicholson House, Lime Kiln Close, Stoke Gifford, Bristol BS12 6SU. t: (44 117) 923 6757. *Annual Report*.

The Commission publishes a large number of relatively small guides, papers and reports: e.g. 'Who audits the auditors' (1994, free); 'Regular as clockwork: Raising the standard of local government financial accounting' (1993, £6); 'People, pay and performance: A management handbook for local government' (1995, £11) – as well as occasional more substantial items: e.g.'Fraud audit manual' (1994, £65).

'To be responsible for the appointment of auditors of the accounts of local authorities and health authorities and certain other public bodies in England and Wales. The Commission's role is to ensure the continued integrity of local government by ensuring money is legally spent for the purposes intended, and to help local authorities and health authorities to ensure that the services they decide to provide are run as economically, efficiently and effectively as possible.'

United States

(5) #171 Senate The Capitol, Washington, DC 20510. *Information*: t: (1 202) 224 3121.

Senate Committees Relevant Standing Committees include:

- *Committee on Agriculture, Nutrition and Forestry*
    - *Subcommittee on Agricultural Credit*
    - *Subcommittee on Agricultural Production and Stabilization of Prices*
- *Committee on Appropriations*
    - *Subcommittee on Treasury, Postal Service, and General Government*
- *Committee on Banking, Housing, and Urban Affairs* 534 Dirksen Office Building, Washington, DC 20510. t: (1 202) 224 7391; f: 224 5137.

To which Committee shall be referred all proposed legislation, messages, partitions, memorials and other matters relating to the following subjects:

1. Banks, banking and financial institutions
2. Control of prices of commodities, rents and services
3. Deposit insurance
4. Economic stabilization and defence production
5. Export and foreign trade promotion
6. Export controls
7. Federal monetary policy, including Federal Reserve System
8. Financial aid to commerce and industry
9. Issuance and redemption of notes
10. Money and credit, including currency and coinage
11. Nursing home construction
12. Public and private housing (including veterans' housing)
15. Renegotiation of government contracts
14. Urban development and urban mass transit

Such Committee shall also study and review, on a comprehensive basis, matters relating to international economic policy as it affects the United

States monetary affairs, credit, and financial institutions; economic growth, urban affairs and credit, and report from time to time.

- *Subcommittee on Economic Stabilization and Rural Development*
- *Subcommittee on International Finance and Monetary Policy*
- *Subcommittee on Securities*

- *Committee on the Budget*
- *Committee on Finance*
    - *Subcommittee on Deficits, Debt Management and Long-Term Economic Growth*
    - *Subcommittee on Energy and Agricultural Taxation*
    - *Subcommittee on International Trade*
    - *Subcommittee on Private Retirement Plans and Oversight of the Internal Revenue Service*
    - *Subcommittee on Social Security and Family Policy*
    - *Subcommittee on Taxation*
- *Committee on Foreign Relations*
    - *Subcommittee on International Economic Policy, Trade, Oceans and the Environment*
- *Committee on Governmental Affairs*

Includes:

- consideration of budget and accounting measures, other than appropriations except as provided in the Congressional Budget Act of 1974
- government information
- receiving and examining reports of Comptroller General of United States.

- *Permanent Subcommittee on Investigations*
- *Subcommittee on Regulation and Government Information*

- *Committee of the Judiciary*
    - *Subcommittee on Antitrust, Monopolies and Business Rights*
- *Committee on Small Business*
    - *Subcommittee on Competitiveness, Capital Formation and Economic Opportunity*

(6) **#172 House of Representatives** The Capitol, Washington, DC 20515. *Information* t: (1 202) 224 3121; *House Librarian* (1 202) 225 0462. w: http://www.house.gov.

House Committees Examples of important Standing Committees include:

- *Committee on Agriculture*
    - *Subcommittee on General Farm Commodities*

    - *Subcommittee on Environment, Credit and Rural Development*
- *Committee on Appropriations*
    - *Subcommittee on Foreign Operations, Export Financing and Related Programs*
    - *Subcommittee on Treasury, Postal Service and General Government*
- *Committee on Banking, Finance and Urban Affairs* 2129 Rayburn House Office Building, Washington DC 20515. t: (1 202) 225 4247; f: 225 6580.

Created in March 1865, when the House amended its rules to provide for the establishment of a *Committee on Banking and Currency.* The Committee's work has led to major legislation, and covers, for example:

- Banks and banking, including deposit insurance and federal monetary policy.
- Money and credit, including currency and the issuance of notes and redemption thereof; gold and silver, including the coinage thereof; valuation and revaluation of the dollar.
- Community development (including metropolitan and nonmetropolitan areas).
- Public and private housing.
- Economic stabilization, defense production, renegotiation, and control of the price of commodities, rents, and services.
- International finance.
- Financial aid to commerce and industry (other than trnasportation).
- International financial and monetary organizations.
- *Subcommittee on Consumer Credit and Insurance*
- *Subcommittee on Economic Growth and Credit Foundation*
- *Subcommittee on Financial Institutions Supervision, Regulation and Deposit Insurance*
- *Subcommittee on General Oversight, Investigations and the Resolution of Failed Financial Institutions*
- *Subcommittee on International Development, Finance, Trade and Monetary Policy*

- *Committee on the Budget*
- *Committee of Foreign Affairs*
    - *Subcommittee on Economic Policy, Trade and Environment*
- *Committee on Government Operations*
    - *Subcommittee on Commerce, Consumer and Monetary Affairs*

  Overseas the federal regulatory agencies, including the FDIC, NCUA, OTS and RTC.
- *Committee on the Judiciary*

992. **United States Code**. i. **cdrom**. $36. 'From the *Office of the Law*

Revision Counsel... The consolidated full- text of all 50 titles of the Federal Government's official compendium of US laws in effect.'

- *Subcommittee on Economic and Commercial Law*

- *Committee on Small Business*
    - *Subcommittee on Minority Enteprise, Finance and Urban Development*
    - *Subcommittee on Regulation, Business Opportunities and Technology*
- *Committee on Ways and Means*
    - *Subcommittee on Select Revenue Measures on Trade*

Joint Committees of the Senate and the House include:

- *Joint Economic Committee*
- *Joint Committee on the Library*
- *Joint Committee on Printing*
- *Joint Commitee on Taxation*
- *Bipartisan Committee on Entitlement and Tax Reform*

993. **Congressional Directory**. bi-a. **diskette**. $78. 'Presents short biographies of each member of the Senate and the House, listed by States and Districts, respectively. Includes additional data such as his/her committee memberships, terms of service, administrative assistant and/or secretary, room and telephone numbers. Also lists officials of the courts, the military establishments, and other Federal departments and agencies.'

994. **Congressional Record**. d. **online**. **diskette**. d. $13,260. Publishes the proceedings of Congress, The *Daily Digest*, printed in the back of each issue, summarises the proceedings of that day in each House, and before each of their Committees and Subcommittees.

995. **Daily Bill Digest**. d. **magtape**. d. $13,260. 'A compilation of bills reported and filed by the various Committees of the US Senate and House of Representatives.' Also available on **diskette** are the actual *Daily Bills*, issued as published (d. $13,260).

996. **Senate and House Reports**. i. **diskette**. $13,260. 'All reports issued by the various Committees of the US Senate and House of Representatives.'

Two other important bodies within the Congress system are:

(7) #173 Congressional Budget Office Ford House Office Building, Second and D Streets SW, Washington, DC 20515, t: (1 202) 226 2809.

Provides Congress with assessments of the economic impact of the Federal budget.

- *Office of Intergovernmental Relations* t: (1 202) 226 2600

997. **Annual Report on the Budget**. a.

(8) #174 General Accounting Office 441 G Street, NW, Washington, DC 20548–0001. t: (1 202) 512 3000.

Prime function of this influential body is to provide an independent audit of government agencies and programmes. Operates under the control of the *Comptroller General of the United States*, who is appointed by the President with the advice and consent of the Senate for a term of 15 years.

The Office offers a range of products to communicate the results of its work. The type of product depends on the assignments' objectives and the needs of the intended user. Product types include testimony, oral briefings, and written reports. All of GAO's unclassified reports are available to the public; however GAO will honor a requestor's desire to postpone release of a report for up to 30 days. The report will be made public automatically following the requestor's release or public disclosure of the contents.

A list of GAO reports issued or released during the previous month is furnished monthly to Congress, its Members, and Committees. Copies of GAO reports are also furnished to interested congressional parties; Federal, State, local and foreign governments; members of the press; college faculty, students and libraries; and nonprofit organizations.

Copies of unclassified reports are available from the US General Accounting Office, PO Box 6015, Gaithersburg, MD 20884–6015. Phone 202–512–6000. The first copy of each report is free; additional copies are $2 each . . . For further information, contact the *Office of Public Affairs*, General Accounting Office, 441 G Street NW, Washington, DC 20548. t: (1 202) 512 4800. Copies of GAO Reports are available **online** via Information Access Company's *PTS Newsletter* database.

998. **GAO Review**. q. $11.

And, finally, there is:

(9) #175 Library of Congress 101 Independence Avenue SE, Washington, DC 20540. t: (1 202) 707 5000. *Public Affairs Office* t: (1 202) 707 2905.

999. **LC MARC – Books. online**. Bibliographic and cataloguing information on over 4 million books published throughout the world since 1968.

- *Congressional Research Service* t: (1 202) 707 7904. Serves the public through its elected representatives in Congress . . . Provides objective, nonpartisan research, analysis, and informational support of the highest quality to assist Congress' legislative, oversight and representative functions. It also helps ensure an informed national legislature . . . Also maintains those parts of the Library of Congress' automated information system that covers legislative matters, including digests of all public bills and briefing papers on major legislative issues.

1000. **Congressional Research Reports. online**. Contains abstracts of all reports produced by the US *Congressional Research Service*.

- *National Serials Data Program*

1001. **New Serial Titles**. m. $395. Catalogue entries for newly published serials recorded at the Library.

38. Next, we consider the *central banks*, where it is convenient also to reference a number of other bodies with key regulatory/supervisory responsibilities for deposit-taking institutions:

United Kingdom

(1) #176 Bank of England Threadneedle Street, London EC2R 8AH. t: (44 171) 601 4444; f: 601 4771. *Working Papers* For example: 'A model of building society interest rate setting' (22); 'Deriving estimates of inflation expectations from the prices of UK government bonds' (23); 'Potential credit exposure on interest rate swaps' (25).

'The Governor thought that it would be useful to have a strategy weekend, away from the pressures of the office, where the Executive Directors and the Governors could discuss the structure of the Bank, and assess whether it was still suitable for the demands of a fast-changing world. We decided that, under the existing structure, not all Bank staff could relate their individual contributions to the core purposes of the Bank; the international work, in a separate division, was not plugged in to the mainstream work of the Bank; and, in all areas, the operational and analytical people needed to be closer together. We therefore agreed to organise the Bank into two 'wings', focusing on the bank's two main objectives – monetary stability, and financial stability – with a separate central services area that would serve both wings.'[114]

1002. **Bank of England Inflation Report**. q. £16. Seeks greater openness in explaining the basis of monetary policy. Analyses inflationary trends and pressures and examines the range of intermediate indicators that help gauge the future path of inflation. "There is no more important document in the whole panoply of monetary policy making than the Bank of England's Inflation Report" (*The Guardian*).

1003. **Bank of England Financial Indicators. online**. Almost 8,000 monthly, quarterly, and annual time series.

1004. **Bank of England Quarterly Bulletin**. q. £24. The prime source of statistical data on the UK monetary system. Each issue also includes reviews of recent economic and financial developments, research and analysis papers, and reprints of recent speeches by the Governor or other Bank officials.

- *Central Gilts Office* Computerized book-entry transfer and associated payment system for UK government stocks (gilt-edged stocks), established in 1986.
- *Central Moneymarkets Office* Book-entry transfer and payment system for sterling money market instruments, which began oper-

ations in 1990. (Until its introduction, messengers walked from office to office in the City of London, the risks of this well illustrated when £292 million of treasury bills and certificates of deposit were stolen at knife point.)

- *City Capital Markets Committee* Acts as a focal point within the City for views concerning current issues and future developments, including company law matters, which affect the domestic and international capital markets in the City. Consists of a Chairman appointed by the Governor of the Bank of England, and twelve other members serving in a personal capacity, appointed by the Chairman, but with the Governor's approval.
- *CREST* "Following the abandonment, in March 1993, of plans to replace the London Stock Exchange's *TALISMAN* system with *TAURUS* (an automated system to dematerialize UK equity and other quoted corporate securities and provide a full-book-entry transfer system for all stock movements), the CREST system is being developed by the Bank. This will provide stock accounts and book-entry transfer in UK corporate securities for those who are members. These are likely to include brokers, market makers, institutional investors and custodians. Individual investors will most likely have access through nominee facilities. Investors will be able to choose to retain stock certificates, and transactions involving certificates will also pass through the central CREST system. CREST will provide delivery-versus-payment based on existing funds transfer mechanisms. The new system is intended to go live in 1996 . . . Long-term ownership of the CREST system has yet to be determined."[115]
- *Deposit Protection Board* Set up in 1982 with funds derived from contributions by participating banks. It insures up to £20,000 per deposit and will pay out up to 75 per cent of the amount lost through bank failure. Multiple deposits can effectively increase that cover. In recent years the board has compensated for losses resulting from the failure of more than a dozen institutions.

Some other UK bodies broadly concerned with various aspects of the regulation and supervision of deposit-taking institutions, include:

(2) #177 Banking Appeals Tribunal 15 Bedford Avenue, London WC1B 3AS. t: (44 171) 631 4242.

Constituted under the *Banking Appeal Tribunal Regulations 1987* (SI 1987/1299) on an ad hoc basis to hear appeals against certain decisions of the Bank of England; e.g. regarding commercial bank authorization.

(3) #178 Office of the Banking Ombudsman 70 Gray's Inn Road, London WC1X 8NB. t: (44 171) 404 9944; f: 405 5052. (There is also an *Office of the Building Society Ombudsman.*)

Operates a scheme to resolve complaints against banks. The Ombudsman is appointed by, and is responsible to, an independent Council. Any member of the public who has received a banking service, even if not a bank customer, can submit a complaint. Sole traders, partnerships and clubs are covered, but not companies. The service is free. All the main high street banks in the UK are members of the scheme. The Ombudsman and the Council each year produce an *Annual Report* which describes the work of the past year, analyses the complaints received, and makes recommendations to the banks.

(4) #179 Building Societies Commission 15 Great Marlborough Street, London W1V 2LL. t: (44 171) 494 6677; f: 494 6677. *Prudential Notes*; *Guidance Notes*.

Established by the Building Societies Act of 1986 as the statutory body responsible for the supervision of building societies. Advises HM Treasury and other government departments on matters related to building societies.

(5) #180 Building Societies Appeals Tribunal 15 Bedford Avenue, London WC1B 3AS. t: (44 171) 631 4242.

Constituted on an ad hoc basis to hear appeals against certain decisions of the Building Societies Commission.

(6) #181 Friendly Societies Commission 15 Great Marlborough Street, London W1V 2LL. t: (44 171) 494 6548; f: 494 7016.

Established under the *Friendly Societies Act 1992* to make statutory instruments, to monitor and supervise friendly societies, and 'to police provisions of the Act which require a society either to conform to the "genus" friendly society, or to convert into a company and lose the name'.

(7) #182 Registry of Friendly Societies 15 Great Marlborough Street, London W1V 2LL. t: (44 171) 437 9992.

Serves three statutory bodies: the Building Societies Commission, the Central Office of the Registry of Friendly Societies and the Friendly Societies Commission, together with the Assistant Registrar of Friendly Societies for Scotland. The Central Office provides a public registry for mutual organisations registered under various Acts. It is responsible for the prudential supervision of friendly societies and credit unions. It advises HM Treasury and other government departments on matters related to Friendly Societies.

United States

(8) #183 Federal Reserve System 20th Street and Constitution Avenue, Washington, DC 20551. t: (1 202) 452 3462; f: 452 3819. *Freedom of Information* t: (1 202) 452 3684. A booklet *Public Information Materials* catalogues the majority of publications produced by the twelve Federal Reserve Banks and the Board of Governors of the System. These publications include a large number of introductory pamphlets aimed at audiences that differ in terms of academic level and technical knowledge, and most of which are listed as free of charge : e.g. *Open Market Operations*; *Treasury Auctions*; *Depository Institutions and Their Regulators*; and so on. The booklet does not include many of the occasional and technical reports distributed by the Reserve Banks and the Board of Governors. The latter are listed in *The Fed in Print*, produced by the Federal Reserve Bank of Philadelphia [see below]. A useful introduction is **The Federal Reserve System: Purposes and Functions**. 1985. 120 pp, available from the Board of Governors, currently being reissued in revised form (see Note 134).

The two major publishing operations within the System are the *Board of Governors*, and the twelve individual *Federal Reserve Banks*. But organizationally we should also note:

- *Federal Open Market Committee* The System's key monetary policy making body, comprised of the Board of Governors and the Reserve Bank presidents, 5 of whom serve as voting members on a rotating basis. Minutes of the Meetings of the Committee appear in the *Federal Reserve Bulletin*, 2–3 months after each Meeting. The Committee has designated the *Federal Reserve Bank of New York* as its agent in executing open market transactions.

and also the System's *Consumer Advisory Council*, *Federal Advisory Council*, and *Thrift Institutions Advisory Council*.

(a) *Board of Governors*

Comprises 7 members serving staggered 14–year terms, each appointed by the US President, and confirmed by the Senate. *Publications* Services, MS-138, Washington, DC 20551. t: (1 202) 452 3244; f: 728 5886. The April *Annual Report* reviews monetary policy and the state of the US economy for the year and reports on System operations. The February *Annual Report: Budget Review* reviews the budgets of the entire Federal Reserve System. There is also a *Finance and Economic Discussion Series*.

1005. **Federal Reserve Bulletin**. m. $25. **online**. Features articles on selected topics in economics, domestic and international business activity, and recent developments in the banking community and the Federal Reserve itself. The Bulletin reprints the full-text of Statements to the US Congress of its officials, together with the bi-annual *Monetary Policy Report to the Congress*. Of particular interest also is each month's section 'Legal Developments' which, amongst other matters, details the arguments for accepting, or rejecting, merger and acquisition proposals from banking institutions.

The Bulletin is notable for its extensive set of *Financial and Business Statistics*. Some 70 Tables are categorized in these sections:

- *Money Stock and Bank Credit*
- *Policy Instruments*
- *Federal Reserve Banks*
- *Monetary and Credit Aggregates*
- *Commercial Banking Institutions*
- *Weekly Reporting Commercial Banks*
- *Financial Markets*
- *Federal Finance*
- *Securities Markets and Corporate Finance*
- *Real Estate*
- *Consumer Instalment Credit*
- *Flow of Funds*
- *Domestic Nonfinancial Statistics*
- *International Statistics* Categorised as:
  Summary Statistics
  Reported by Banks in the United States
  Reported by Nonbanking Business Enterprises in the United States
  Securities Holdings and Transactions
  Interest and Exchange Rates

These regular Tables are supplemented by a series of Special Tables of quarterly data.

The Bulletin also publishes periodically an *Anticipated Schedule of Release Dates for Periodic Releases* of some 30 data sets.

The Board of Governors issue a large number of specialized statistical releases. Some of the releases are available to the public through the US *Department of Commerce* Economic Bulletin Board. These include, for instance:

- *Aggregate Reserves*
- *Factors Affecting Reserve Balances*
- *Money Stock*
- *Assets and Liabilities of Insured Domestically Chartered and Foreign Related Banking Institutions*
- *Foreign Exchange Rates*
- *Selected Interest Rates*
- *Industrial Production and Capacity Utilization*
- *Consumer Instalment Credit*
- *Flow of Funds*

Also published by the Board are:

1006. **Actions of the Board: Applications and Reports Received**. w. Released Friday, covering the week ended the previous Saturday.

1007. **Aggregate Summaries of Annual Surveys of Securities Credit Extension**. a. Published in February, with respect to the period to the end of the previous June.

1008. **Annual Statistical Digest**. a.

1009. **Balance Sheets for the US Economy**. s-a. Published in October and April: relates to the previous year.

1010. **Bank Holding Company Supervision Manual**. Prepared for use by Federal Reserve examiners in the supervision, regulation, and inspection of bank holding companies and their subsidiaries.

1011. **BankRoll II. online**. Descriptive and financial information culled from the financial reports submitted to the Board by about 8,500 US bank holding companies.

1012. **Debits and Deposit Turnover at Commercial Banks**. m. Released 12th of the month, covering activity in the previous month.

1013. **Federal Reserve Regulatory Service**. l. $200. Three-volume service containing all Board regulations as well as related statutes, interpretations, policy statements, rulings, and staff opinions. For those with a more specialized interest in the Board's regulations, parts of the service are published separately as handbooks pertaining to monetary policy, securities credit, consumer affairs, and the payment system. The content is updated monthly, and there are citation and subject indexes.

1014. **Finance Companies**. m. Available on the 5th working day of the month referring to the 2nd month previous.

1015. **Flow of Funds Account**. q. $960. **online**. **diskette**. Some 3,500 quarterly and annual time series on the sources and uses of funds in 50 sectors of the US economy. A new edition of the Board's *Guide to the Flow of Funds Accounts* was published in 1993, and lists each flow series in the Board's main flow of funds statistical release, describing how the series is derived from source material. The Guide also explains the relationship between the flow of funds accounts and the national income and product accounts and discusses the analytical uses of flow of funds data.

1016. **Geographical Distribution of Assets and Liabilities of Major Foreign Branches of US Banks**. 15th of March and each succeeding quarter, relating to the previous quarter.

1017. **List of Foreign Margin Stocks**. q. Foreign equity securities that meet the criteria in *Regulation T* (Credit by Brokers and Dealers). The *Federal Reserve Bulletin* publishes listings of additions and deletions to the List.

1018. **List of Marginable OTC Stocks**. q. Includes stocks traded over-the-counter in the United States that have been determined by the Board to be subject to the margin requirements under certain Federal Reserve regulations, as well as OTC stocks which have a National Market System, and for which transaction reports are required to be made pursuant to an effective transaction reporting plan. The *Federal Reserve Bulletin* publishes listings of additions and deletions to the List.

1019. **Loans and Securities at all Commercial Banks**. m. Available 3rd week of the month relating to the previous month's transactions. Similarly released is *Major Nondeposit Funds of Commercial Banks*.

1020. **Report on the Terms of Credit Card Plans**. s-a. March and August, referring to January and June respectively.

1021. **Selected Information on Insured US Commercial Banks Ranked by Assets**. Published by the *US National Technical Information Service*. Ranks approximately 2,600 insured banks with assets totalling $100 million or more in descending order by size of consolidated assets.

1022. **Selected Interest and Exchange Rates**. w. $30. Series of charts.

1023. **Staff Studies**. i. Studies and papers on economic and financial subjects that are of general interest. 1–2 Studies per year.

1024. **Survey of Terms of Bank Lending to Business**. Mid-month of March relating to February; and then every quarter similarly.

1025. **Research Library: Recent Acquisitions**. m. Published on the first of the month and free of charge.

(**b**) *Federal Reserve Banks* These are:

(i) *#184 Federal Reserve Bank of Atlanta* Public Information Department, 104 Marietta Street NW, Atlanta, GA 30303. t: (1 404) 521 8500; f: 521 8050. *Working Papers.*

1026. **Economic Review**. bi-m. **online**. New research and educational articles on macroeconomic, financial and international issues relevant to monetary policy. Studies of developments in financial markets and instruments, such as stock-market volatility and the success rates of de novo banks, are also presented.

1027. **Financial Update**. q. Newsletter featuring articles on developments in the financial services industry and the payments system.

(ii) *#185 Federal Reserve Bank of Boston* Research Library – D, PO Box 2076, Boston, MA 02106. t: (1 617) 973 3000; f: 973 5918. *Research Reports*; *Working Papers.*

1028. **Conference Series**. a. Papers and discussions at the Annual Conferences that have been held since 1969, comprising leading representatives from universities, government, business and finance. Each conference takes as its theme an important issue affecting economic policy: e.g. the 1991 Conference covered *The financial condition and regulation of insurance companies.*

1029. **New England Economic Review**. bi-m. Includes articles of broad economic interest: national, international and regional in scope.

(iii) *#186 Federal Reserve Bank of Chicago* Public Information Center, 230 South LaSalle Street, PO Box 834, Chicago, IL 60690–0834. t: (1 312) 322 5111; f: 322 5959.

1030. **Bank Structure and Competition**. a. Papers presented at the annual conferences sponsored by the Bank: typically each volume is some 600 pages long.

1031. **Economic Perspectives**. bi-m. Contains surveys and in-depth articles on banking, business, agricultural, and international sectors.

(iv) *#187 Federal Reserve Bank of Cleveland* Public Affairs Department, PO Box 6387, Cleveland, OH 44101–1387. t: (1 216) 579 2047; f: 579 2813. *Working Papers.* The Research Library of the Bank publishes an annual *Subject Index to Economic Publications* indexing all of its publications.

1032. **Economic Review**. q. **online**. Features research and analysis on monetary, economic, and banking topics of district and national interest.

(v) *#188 Federal Reserve Bank of Dallas* Public Affairs Department, 2200 North Pearl Street, Dallas, TX 75201. t: (1 214) 922 6000; 922 5268. *Working Papers.*

1033. **Economic Review**. bi-m. **online**. Contains articles on economic and financial topics at district, national and international levels.

1034. **Financial Industry Issues**. q. **online**. Newsletter presenting research about the financial industry in the eleventh district. There is also a *Financial Industry Studies* (bi-a) presenting research on economic and financial topics, with emphasis on the financial industry at regional, national and international levels.

1035. **Quarterly Survey of Agricultural Credit Conditions**. q.

1036. **Trade-Weighted Value of the Dollar Index**. m. Presents a measure of the trade-weighted value of the US dollar against 101 US trading partners. It also presents sub-indexes for specific countries and geographic areas.

(vi) *#189 Federal Reserve Bank of Kansas City* Public Affairs Department, 925 Grand Boulevard, Kansas City, MO 64198–0001. t: (1 816) 881 2683; f: 881 2569. *Symposium Series*; *Working Papers.*

1037. **Economic Review**. q. **online**. Written by the bank's economic research staff to be understood by the interested layman, although some articles are fairly technical.

(vii) *#190 Federal Reserve Bank of Minneapolis* Research Department, PO Box 291, 250 Marquette Avenue, Minneapolis, MN 55401– 0291. t: (1 612) 340 2446; f: 340 2545. *Staff Reports.*

1038. **Quarterly Review**. q. **online**. Economic research aimed at improving policymaking by the Federal Reserve System and other governmental authorities.

(viii) *#191 Federal Reserve Bank of New York* Public Information Department, 33 Liberty Street, New York, NY 10045. t: (1 212) 720 6134; f: 720 8028. *Research Papers.*

1039. **Quarterly Review**. q. **online**. Describes patterns and trends in banking, investment, and capital market activities. Includes regular reports: *Monetary Policy and Open Market Operations*; and *Treasury and Federal Reserve Foreign Exchange Operations*.

(ix) *#192 Federal Reserve Bank of Philadelphia* Publications Desk, Economic Research Department, PO Box 66, Philadelphia, PA 19105– 0066. t: (1 215) 574 6115; f: 574 3980.

1040. **Banking Legislation and Policy**. q. Newsletter summarizing and updating pending banking and financial legislation at both the federal and state (PA,NJ,DE) levels.

1041. **Business Review**. bi-m. **online**. Presents articles written by staff economists and dealing with economic policy, financial economics and banking, and regional economic issues.

1042. **Fed in Print**. bi-a. An index of articles, papers, reports, proceedings and monographs published by the Federal Reserve System.

1043. **Livingston Survey**. bi-a. Summarizes forecasts from business, government, and academic consultants. Started in 1946 by columnist Joseph A Livingston, it is the oldest continuous survey of economists' expectations. Published in June and December.

1044. **Survey of Professional Forecasters**. q. Short-term forecasts of major macroeconomic data, plus long-term forecasts of inflation.

(x) *#193 Federal Reserve Bank of Richmond* Public Services Department, PO Box 27622, Richmond, VA 23219. t: (1 804) 697 8111; f: 697 8044.

1045. **Cross Sections**. q. Reviews business conditions and economic developments.

1046. **Economic Quarterly**. q. **online**. Articles on monetary theory and policy, banking and finance.

(xi) *#194 Federal Reserve Bank of San Francisco* Public Information Department, PO Box 7702, San Francisco, CA 94120. t: (415) 974 2163; f: 974 2318.

1047. **Economic Review**. q. **online**. Contains detailed technical articles relating economic theory to current policy issues.

(xii) *#195 Federal Reserve Bank of St Louis* Public Information Office, PO Box 442, St Louis, MO 63166. t: (1 314) 444–8444; f: 444 8731.

1048. **International Economic Conditions**. 5/year. Reports selcted data pertaining to international transactions and economic developments.

1049. **Monetary Trends**. m. Features charts and tables of selected national monetary and federal budget data.

1050. **National Economic Trends**. m.

1051. **Review**. bi-m. **online**. Examines national and international economic developments, particularly their monetary aspects.

1052. **US Financial Data**. w. Provides charts and tables of selected monetary data.

- *Fedwire* Real-time gross settlement system, used principally for domestic payments. There is also a separate electronic, book-entry, government securities transfer facility. Fedwire links the twelve Federal Reserve Banks to participating institutions and several Federal government agencies. The Fed is in the process of implementing a new unified communications network, *FEDNET*, which will replace existing central and regional networks. FEDNET has been designed to provide improved contingency backup and security and to permit significant increases in network traffic. It will have the capability for transmission of voice and video, in addition to data.

39. Moving to various *government departments* in the UK and the USA involved with the execution of economic, monetary and fiscal policy and practice, we have:

United Kingdom

(1) #196 Board of Inland Revenue Somerset House, London WC2R 1LB. t: (44 171) 438 6622. *Annual Report.*

Administers and collects direct taxes – mainly income tax, corporation tax, capital gains tax, stamp duty and petroleum revenue tax, and advises the Chancellor of the Exchequer on policy questions involving them. The Department is organised under a series of accountable management units under the *Next Steps* programme.

1053. **HyperTax**. m. £650. Published by *HMSO* in collaboration with *CLS (UK)*. 'Based on:

- The Inland Revenue's tax legislation volumes, fully revised for each release
- Current Extra Statutory Concessions and Statements of Practice, and all press releases that affect interpretation of the legislation
- The latest versions of the Finance Bills
- Tax cases from 1860 to the present
- Commentary; Technical articles; Treaties; Tax periodicals; Tax form images'.

1054. **Inland Revenue Statistics (Year)**. a. £20. Published by the *Statistics and Economics Office.*

1055. **Tax Case Leaflets**. i. £58.

1056. **Tax Case Reports**. i. £42.

1057. **Taxes Acts (Year)**. £80. Six volumes. The income tax, corporation tax and capital gains tax enactments including the Finance Act, with tables of rates of tax, personal reliefs etc. cross references from former enactments, other legislation and statutory regulations etc. affecting the application of the taxes.

Major sections of relevance within the Inland Revenue are:

- *Company Tax Division* Policy on Corporation Tax (including Advance Corporation Tax); purchase of own shares; close companies; demergers; group relief and losses; industrial and provident societies. t: (44 171) 438 6390/6973
- *Financial Institutions Division* This Division has sections concerned with:
  - Technical advice on life assurance, general assurance. t: (44 171) 438 6572
  - Policy on financial concerns including banks; Lloyds; Stock Exchange; unit and investment trusts. t: (44 171) 438 7517
  - Technical advice on banks and financial concerns; Lloyds. t: (44 171) 438 7300
  - Technical advice on Stock Exchange; new financial instruments; Exchange differences.
  - Building societies, unit and investment trusts. t: (44 171) 438 6666/7617
  - Policy on taxation of interest received; relief for interest paid; unit and investment trusts; building societies. t: (44 171) 438 6218
- *International Division* Covers a wide range of policy issues, with sections dealing with:
  - Coordination of EC matters. t: (44 171) 438 6254
  - Policy on liaison with OECD; individual residence and domicile; non-resident trusts. t: (44 171) 438 6015
  - International cooperation on tax matters; policy on paying and collecting agents. t: (44 171) 438 6348
  - International organizations; diplomatic privilege; Cases IV and V of Schedule D and CATA. t: (44 171) 438 6654
  - Offshore funds. t: (44 171) 438 6370
  - Overseas tax comparisons. t: (44 171) 438 6429
  - Research, investigation and technical advice on agency; non-residents trading in the UK; company residence; controlled foreign companies; foreign partnerships. t: (44 171) 438 7610
  - Research, investigation and technical advice on international avoidance problems including transfer pricing and thin capitalization. t: (44 171) 438 7575/7627/6916
  - Policy on double taxation agreements (several units covering different countries)
- *Statistics and Economics Office* Forecasts of yields of Inland Revenue duties; estimation of costs of yields of tax changes; collection, presentation and analysis of statistics of economic or social value derived from the administration of Inland Revenue duties; economic advice:
  - Budgetary support and forecasting. t: (44 171) 438 6472

- Personal incomes. t: (44 171) 438 7195
- Company sector. t: (44 171) 438 6109
- Capital and wealth. t: (44 171) 438 6463
- Economics unit. t: (44 171) 438 6343
- Information technology. t: (44 1903) 509714

There is also the:

(i) #*197 Pension Schemes Office* Lynwood Road, Thames Ditton, Surrey KT7 0DP. t: (44 181) 398 4242.

' "It is amazing how many people forget that the Pension Schemes Office is part of the Inland Revenue". So said . . . (the) *Controller of the Pension Schemes Office* when addressing the NAPF Conference in May 1993. There have been strong indications since then that the Revenue's income-raising role has been elevated and that inspectors are now examining pension funds in much more depth, seeking out activities which are taxable. Awkward questions about your actuarial valuation results and compliance visits to ensure that you apply Inland Revenue limits correctly remain a remote threat. However, it seems both are on the increase.

From time to time, the Revenue appears blinking from the mountain of paper under which we try to keep it buried, it shakes itself and causes quakes throughout the pensions industry. It has been doing so recently and rumours are rife regarding its burrowing into two areas of pension fund activity – trading and sub-underwriting.

There was serious concern a few years ago, when it became known that a Special Office had been set up in Sheffield to investigate whether funds had been carrying out transactions which could be regarded as trading and which were not, therefore, covered by the tax exemption which relates to investment income.

The second issue which has been extensively reported relates to sub-underwriting of share issues. Section 592(3) of ICTA 1988 makes it clear that pension schemes are exempt from tax on sub-underwriting commissions if they are applied '*for the purposes of the scheme*'. However, the Revenue appears to be arguing that this applies only if underwriting is occasional and that if the scheme underwrites on a 'habitual' basis, the activity becomes trading and is taxable. Having had a first crack at this in the late 1980s and been seen off, the Revenue are having another go.

The Bank of England was concerned a few years ago when the Inland Revenue threatened to disrupt the market in relation to stock lending and to derivatives. In each case it persuaded the Inland Revenue to drop the issue and appropriate legislation followed. It will be interesting to see what happens this time."[116]

(2) #198 Revenue Adjudicator's Office 3rd Floor, Haymarket House, Haymarket, London SW1Y 4SP. t: (44 171) 930 2292; f: 930 2298. *Annual Report*.

Looks into complaints about the way that the *Inland Revenue* and the *Valuation Office Agency* have handled someone's affairs, and recommends how complaints should be settled.

(3) #199 Special Commissioners of Income Tax 15–19 Bedford Avenue, London WC1B 3AS. t: (44 171) 631 4242.

An independent appelate tribunal which hears appeals against certain decisions of the Inland Revenue.

(4) #200 Department for National Savings Charles House, 375 Kensington High Street, London W14 8SD. t: (44 171) 605 9300; f: 605 9438.

Offers a wide range of schemes for personal savers. The Director of Savings reports to Treasury Ministers.

(5) #201 HM Customs and Excise New King's Beam House, 22 Upper Ground, London SE1 9PJ. t: (44 171) 620 1313; f: 865 5005.

Responsible for collecting and administering Customs and Excise duties and Value Added Tax and advises the Chancellor of the Exchequer on any matters connected with them. The Department is also responsible for preventing and detecting the evasion of revenue laws. In addition, the Department undertakes certain agency work on behalf of other departments, including the compilation of United Kingdom overseas trade statistics.

1058. **HM Customs and Excise News Releases**. bi-w. £65. Distributed by the *Central Office of Information*.

1059. **HyperVAT**. m. 450. Published by *HMSO* in collaboration with *CLS (UK)*. 'Centres on HM Customs and Excise own consolidation of the *Value Added Tax Act 1983*. All relevant major amending legislation, incorporation Acts and SIs, is included.'

(6) #202 VAT and Duties Tribunals 15–19 Bedford Avenue, London WC1B 3AS. t: (44 171) 631 4242.

The Tribunals exist to hear appeals against decisions of the Commissioners of Customs and Excise.

(7) #203 HM Treasury Parliament Street, London SW1P 3AG. t: (44 171) 270 3000. *Enquiries* t: (44 171) 270 4870/270 4860. The UK Government's finance ministry. *Information Division* t: (44 171) 270 5238.

The Office of the Lord High Treasurer has been continuously in commission for well over 200 years: the Lord High Commissions of HM Treasury consist of the First Lord of the Treasury (who is also the Prime Minister), the Chancellor of the Exchequer and five junior Lords. This Board of Commissioners is assisted at present by the Chief Secretary, a Parliamentary Secretary who is the Chief Whip, a Financial Secretary, the Minister of State, an Economic Secretary and by the Permanent Secretary. The Prime Minister and First Lord is not primarily concerned in the day-to-day aspects of Treasury business. The Parliamentary Secretary and the Junior Lords are Government Whips in the House of Commons. The management of the Treasury devolves upon the Chancellor of the Exchequer and, under him, the Chief Secretary, the Financial Secretary, the Minister of State and the Economic Secretary.

The Chief Secretary is responsible for the control of public expenditure (including local authority and nationalized industry finance); nationalized industry pay; value for money in the public services (including Next Steps). The Financial Secretary discharges the traditional responsibility of the Treasury for the largely formal procedure for the voting of funds by Parliament. He also has responsibility for other Parliamentary financial business (public accounts committee, comptroller and auditor general, exchequer and audit acts); Inland Revenue taxes (other than oil taxation), general oversight of the Inland Revenue (excluding valuation office); Privatization and wider share ownership policy; European Community business including the Community budget and Economic and Monetary Union; Competition and deregulation policy.

The Minister of State has responsibility for monetary policy; Treasury responsibilities for the financial system, including banks, building societies and other financial institutions; Department for National Savings; Registry of Friendly Societies and National Investments and Loans Office; The Royal Mint. The Government Actuary's Department; the Government Centre for Information Systems; the Valuation Office; International Financial Issues and Institutions (other than EU); Industrial and Export Credit casework; Treasury interest in General Accounting issues; Treasury Bulletin and economic briefing; Official Statistics and the Central Statistical Office. All Treasury Ministers are concerned in tax matters.

Some major Treasury functional groups of relevance are:

- *Aid and Overseas Services Division* Aid to and financial relations with developing countries. Foreign and Commonwealth Office expenditure. t: (44 171) 270 4886
- *Banking and Mutuals Division* Legislative framework for potential supervision of banks; EC banking legislation; banking services law; payment systems; legislative framework for building societies, friendly societies, co-ops and industrial and provident societies. t: (44 171) 270 4493
- *Eastern European and Former Soviet Union Division* General policy advice and briefing on countries of Eastern Europe and the former Soviet Union. Economic advice on countries of Eastern Europe and the former Soviet Union. Assistance for Eastern Europe amd the former Soviet Union. t: (44 171) 270 4498
- *Economic Briefing Unit* General briefing and advice on UK economy. Coordination of briefing on matters of Treasury interest. t: (44 171) 270 5206/5207
- *European Community Division 1* EC finance and economic policy issues; single market issues; preparation for EC Finance Ministers meetings. International trade policy, including GATT. European Investment Bank. t: (44 171) 270 4432
- *European Community Division 2* EC future financing. UK net pay-

ments to EC institutions; EC budget revenue (own resources). t: (44 171) 270 4435

- *Export Finance Division* Export finance and credit policy; international debt rescheduling; financial relations with heavily indebted countries. t: (44 171) 270 4720
- *Fiscal Policy Group* Includes the Tax Policy Division and the Economics of Taxation and Social Security Division. t: (44 171) 270 5666
- *General Financial Issues Division* Money laundering legislation; city competitiveness; wider share ownership; wholesale markets; financial sanctions issues; tax matters affecting financial institutions; fraud; leasing, consumer credit; Trustee Investment Act. Bank of England; Royal Mint; currency and coinage. Economic advice on financial institutions and markets. t: (44 171) 270 4495
- *International Financial Institutions and Debt Division* International Monetary Fund; World Bank, Regional Development Banks; European Bank for Reconstruction and Development; Group of Seven Finance Ministers' meetings; Commonwealth Finance Ministers' meetings. t: (44 171) 270 5565
- *Monetary Group* Covers policy and analysis of foreign exchange markets and rates, the reserves and foreign exchange borrowing, and domestic funding. t: (44 171) 270 4591
- *Securities and Investment Services* Oversight of the regulations of the financial services sector and investor protection implementation; monitoring of the Financial Services Act 1986; regulation and implementation of EC Directives in the financial services area, and issues of market access. t: (44 171) 270 5278
- *World Economy Division* World economic prospects; economics of industrial countries; OECD; economic advice on general international economic issues, trade policy, international monetary systems and the EC. t: (44 171) 270 4700

1060. **Forecasts for the UK Economy**. m. £75. 'Please note that Forecasts for the UK Economy is a summary of published material reflecting the views of the forecasting organisations themselves and does not in any way provide new information on the Treasury's own views. It contains only a selection of forecasters, which is subject to review. No significance should be attached to the inclusion or exclusion of any particular forecasting organisation. HM Treasury accepts no responsibility for the accuracy of material published in this comparison.' The June 1994, issue, for example, compared the forecasts of 24 'City forecasters' published in May or June, and 16 'Non-City forecasters', published between April and June (apart from the OECD December forecast). There is also a November forecast from the Treasury itself, and a May forecast from the **Panel of Independent Forecasters** (the 'seven – now six – wise men'). As examples of ranges of specific forecasts in this June 1994 issue: GDP highest is 3.4, lowest is 1.9; Retail Price Index: highest 3.9, lowest 1.7; Public Sector Borrowing Requirement (1995–96) highest is 34.7 bn, lowest 15.1 bn.

(8) #204 National Debt Office National Investment and Loans

Office, 1 King Charles Street, London SW1A 2AP. t: (44 171) 270 3867; f: 270 3860.

Retains some of its original responsibilities for the reduction of the National Debt, but its principal function is managing the investment portfolios of certain public funds (including the funds of the National Insurance scheme and the National Savings Bank).

(9) #205 Office of the National Lottery PO Box 4465, London, SW1Y 5XL. t: (44 171) 240 4624; f: 240 1128/4710.

Set up under the National Lottery etc. Act 1993. Is responsible for the grant, variation and enforcement of Licenses to run the National Lottery.

(10) #206 PAYMASTER, Office of HM Paymaster General Sutherland House, Russell Way, Crawley, West Sussex RH10 1UH. t: (44 1293) 560999; f: 530942. *Annual Report.*

Provides banking, pensions and financial information services for the Government and public sector bodies.

(11) #207 Royal Mint Llantrisant, Pontyclun, Mid- Glamorgan, CF7 8YT. t: (44 1443) 222111; f: 228799. *Also* 7 Grosvenor Gardens, London SW1W 0BH. t: (44 171) 828 8724; f: 630 6592. *Annual Report.*

Responsible for the production of coin for the United Kingdom, and for overseas countries.

- *Royal Mint Advisory Committee on the Design of Coins, Medals, Seals and Decorations* The Committee meets under the Presidency of HRH Prince Philip, and its members include a nominee of the Royal Academy, a sculptor, two numismatists, and experts in lettering and heraldry. The members are appointed by HM The Queen, on the recommendation of the Chancellor of the Exchequer.

We might also refer here to:

(12) #208 Cabinet Office 70 Whitehall, London SW1A 2AS. t: (44 171) 270 1234.

Comprises the Cabinet secretariat, which supports Ministers collectively in the conduct of Cabinet business.

1061. **Government's Expenditure Plans (Years)**. a. £9.55.

1062. **Public Bodies (Year)**. a. £12. Provides brief details, including expenditure, about public bodies for which Ministers have a degree of accountability.

- *Efficiency Unit* To help Government departments improve the value for money of the resources that they use and to maintain the impetus in opening Central Government work to competition.

(i) *#209 Citizen's Charter Unit* Government Offices, Horse Guards

Road, London, SW1P 3AL. t: (44 171) 270 1838; f: 270 5824/6362/5968/6327.

Implement, develop and co-ordinate the Citizen's Charter initiative.

United States

(13) #210 Department of the Treasury 1500 Pennsylvania Avenue NW, Washington, DC 20220. t: (1 202) 622 2000. *Freedom of Information* t: (1 202) 622 0930. Examples of major Bureaux of the Department of importance in this context are:

(i) *#211 Bureau of the Public Debt* 999 E Street NW, Washington, DC 20239. t: (1 202) 219 3300; f: 219 3321.

Mission is to borrow the money needed to operate the Federal government and to account for the resulting public debt.

1063. **Daily Treasury Statement**. d. $401. Cash and debt operations of the United States Treasury.

1064. **Monthly Statement of the Public Debt of the United States**. m.

1065. **Tables of Redemption Values for U.S. Savings Bonds, Series E and Tables of Redemption Values for U.S. Savings Bonds, Series EE**.

(ii) *#212 Financial Management Service* 401 Fourteenth Street SW, Washington, DC 20227. t: (1 202) 287 0669.

Mission is to improve the quality of government financial management.

1066. **Financial Connection**. q.

1067. **Monthly Treasury Statement of Receipts and Outlays of the United States Government for Period from . . .** m.

1068. **Treasury Bulletin**. q.

(iii) *#213 Inter-American Development Bank* 1300 New York Avenue NW, Washington, DC 20577. t: (1 202) 623 1000; f: 623 3096.

(iv) *#214 Internal Revenue Service* 1111 Constitution Avenue NW, Washington, DC 20224. t: (1 202) 622 5164; f: 622 8653. *Freedom of Information* t: (1 202) 622 3546.

Responsible for administering and enforcing the internal revenue laws and related statutes.

1069. **Controller's Monthly Financial Report**. m.

1070. **Cumulative List of Organizations**. q. $48. Lists the names of tax-exempt organizations.

1071. **Internal Revenue Bulletin**. w. $144. **online**. Announces official IRS rulings, Treasury decisions, Executive Orders, legislation, and court decisions pertaining to internal revenue matters.

1072. **Internal Revenue Bulletin Index-Digest System**. i. In four parts: 1. *Income Tax* ($42); 2. *Estate and Gift Taxes* ($23); 3. *Employment Taxes* ($19); 4. *Excise Taxes* ($21).

1073. (Year) **IRS Federal Tax Forms. cdrom**. a. $69. 'Contains 1994 Federal tax forms with instructions as well as prior year tax products beginning with tax year 1991. All forms presented as Adobe Acrobat .PDF files, allowing facsimile screen display and printing. The Acrobat viewer is included on the disc. Windows is strongly recommended, although reduced functionality is available in DOS.'

1074. **IRS Research Bulletin**. a. $10. Serves as a major vehicle for communicating recent tax administration research to IRS executives and to the general public.

1075. **IRS Taxpayer Information Publications. magtape**. a. $78. 'Contains the text of publications that provide information on individual income tax returns.'

(a) *#215 Statistics of Income Division* 500 N Capitol Street NW, 5th Floor, Washington, DC 20224. t: (1 202) 874 0700; f: 874 0922.

'Since June 1992, over 282 files have been added to the SOI electronic bulletin board system and are available for access. They include data from recent *SOI Bulletin* publications for returns covering individuals, corporations, partnerships, sole proprietorships and estates . . . Internal Revenue Service (IRS) Statistics of Income (SOI) Bulletin Board announces since starting in June, 1992, we have received our 2500th caller on April 22, 1994.'

1076. **SOI Bulletin**. q. $25. 'A Quarterly Statistics of Income Report . . . The earliest published annual financial statistics obtained from the various types of tax and information returns filed, as well as information from periodic or special analytical studies of particular interest to students of the US tax system, tax policymakers and tax administrators. It also includes personal income and tax data by State and historical data for selected types of taxpayers, in addition to data on tax collections and refunds and on other tax-related items.'

(v) *#216 Office of the Comptroller of the Currency* 250 E Street SW, Washington, DC 20219. t: (1 202) 874 4900; f: 874 4950. *Publications* Comptroller of the Currency, PO Box 70004, Chicago, IL 60673–0004. Examples of complimentary publications available include: 'The changing shape of retail banking: Responding to customer needs'; 'Money laundering: A banker's guide to avoiding problems' – as well as the charged 'Banking laws for examiners' ($30), 'Banking regulations for examiners' ($60, four volumes), 'Risk-based capital model for bankers' (diskette, $20).

1077. **Comptroller's Handbook**. 'Contains policies and procedures for the examination of the commercial activities of national banks. Beginning in 1994, all additions to the Comptroller's Handbook ($90) were published in booklet form. These booklets are available separately for $6.00 each.'

1078. **CRA Report**. m. $25. 'List of *Community Reinvestment Act* ratings of national banks that have become public in the previous 30–day period. It also contains the full text of evaluations for banks rated less than "satisfactory".'

1079. **Interpretations and Actions**. i. $125. 'Includes legal staff interpretations, trust interpretative letters, securities letters, and bank accounting advisory series, which represent the informal views of the Comptroller's staff concerning the applications of banking law to contemplated activities or transactions. The publications also announce final enforcement actions against national banks and public evaluation and final decisions under the *Community Reinvestment Act*.'

1080. **OCC Bulletins**. i. $100. 'Issuances sent to all national banks and examiners. They provide information of continuing concern regarding OCC or OCC-supported policies and guidelines, and inform readers of pending regulation changes and other general information.'

1081. **Quarterly Journal**. q. $60. 'The journal of record for the most significant actions and policies of the Office . . . Includes policy statements, decisions on banking structure, selected speeches, testimony, material released in the interpretive letters series, summaries of enforcement actions, statistical data, and other information of interest in the administration of national banks . . . Four issues of the Quarterly Journal make up the OCC's *Annual Report*. The March issue contains the report of operations for the previous year.'

1082. **Weekly Bulletin**. w. $250. 'Report of all corporate decisions by the OCC nationwide . . . Applications, approvals or denials, and consummations are noted for new banks, mergers, consolidations, and purchases and assumptions that result in national banks. This publication also carries applications for operating subsidiaries, and branch and title changes, changes in controlling ownership, and other corporate changes for national banks. As a matter of convenience for parties interested in national bank corporate activities, the publication also releases the public CRA evaluations monthly.'

(vi) *#217 Office of Thrift Supervision* 1700 G Street NW, Washington, DC 20552. t: (1 202) 906 6000.

'Established as a bureau of the Treasury Department on August 9, 1989, and became operational in October of that year, as part of a major reorganization of the thrift regulatory structure mandated by the *Financial Institutions Reform, Recovery and Enforcement Act* (FIRREA).'

(vii) *#218 United States Mint* 633 Third Street NW, Washington, DC 20220. t: (1 202) 874 6000; f: 874 6282.

(viii) *£219 United States Savings Bond Division* 1111 Twentieth Street NW, Washington, DC 20226. t: (1 202) 634 5389.

Other important US regulatory/supervisory organizations include:

(14) #220 Federal Deposit Insurance Corporation 550 17th Street NW, Washington, DC 20429–9990. *FDIC Reading Room* t: (1 202) 898 8563; 898 6985. *Freedom of Information* t: (1 202) 898 7021. *Annual Report.*

'Created by Congress in 1933 to restore public confidence in the nation's banking system following a severe financial crisis. To maintain public confidence in banking institutions, the mission of the FDIC is to: Protect depositors' accounts; Promote sound banking practices; Reduce the disruptions caused by bank failures; Respond to a changing economy and banking system . . . The chief roles of the Division of Supervision (DOS) include examining approximately 7,000 state-chartered commercial banks that are not members of the *Federal Reserve System* and 600 state-chartered savings banks for safety and soundness and for compliance with consumer and civil rights laws . . . The FDIC is responsible each year for collecting and analyzing more than 47,000 quarterly Call Reports filed by state-chartered and national banks. The information collected is used by the FDIC, regulators and others interested in monitoring conditions at individual institutions. The FDIC also administers and enforces the registration and reporting provisions of the Securities and Exchange Act of 1934 for certain publicly traded institutions. At the end of 1993, 215 banks were registered with the FDIC, up from 213 one year earlier. Copies of reports filed are publicly available through DOS's disclosure unit.'

'Except where noted, publications are available free of charge':

1083. **Call Aggregation Tables**. q. $100. Ten volumes. 'Aggregate statistics on banks taken from call report data submitted to the FDIC.'

1084. **Call Reports**. q. $6 per report. 'Also known as *Reports of Condition and Income.* Short quarterly financial reports that contain balance sheets and income statements as well as some detailed schedule information for individual banks. All banks are required to submit call reports to the FDIC.'

1085. **Credit Manual: Division of Liquidation**. i. 'FDIC procedures for liquidating a failed bank. This manual is available to the public by filing a Freedom of Information Act request with the *Office of the Executive Secretary.*'

1086. **Data Book: Operating Banks and Branches**. a. 'A multi- volume set containing deposit information for all commercial banks, mutual savings banks, and domestic branches of foreign banks.'

1087. **Economic Trends**. q. 'Short overview of the US economy, focusing on statistics such as household spending, employment, and gross domestic product. Graphs show recent trends in real estate, finance, and commercial bank activity.'

1088. **Failed Bank Cost Analysis**. a. 'Report summarising the financial aspects of bank resolutions from 1985 to the present. Contains a list of failed banks as well as bank failure statistics organized by region, state, assets, transaction type, year, charter, and cost outlay.'

1089. **FDIC Banking Review**. i. 'Research articles on a wide range of financial topics of relevance to the FDIC and the banking industry.'

1090. **FDIC Consumer News**. q. 'Information on the latest regulatory developments and a wide range of topics of interest to consumers presented in a nontechnical manner.'

1091. **FDIC Enforcement Decisions and Orders**. *Prentice Hall Law and Business*. l. $410. Four volumes. 'The enforcement decisions of the FDIC, the full text of consent degrees entered into by the FDIC, and other orders and opinions . . . Although this set is not published by the FDIC, it is an important source of FDIC information.'

1092. **FDIC Investment Properties**. q. 'Selective listing of preliminary information on commercial properties, multi-family properties, hotels, motels, and land currently available for purchase from FDIC's Division of Liquidation . . . Asking prices begin at $250,000.'

1093. **FDIC Law, Regulations and Related Acts**. l. Three volumes.

1094. **Financial Institution Lists**. q. 'Lists of all FDIC-insured institutions.'

1095. **Merger Decisions**. a. 'Decisions made by the FDIC Board of Directors on bank mergers and bank absorptions resulting in state nonmember banks.'

1096. **Quarterly Banking Profile**. q. 'A statistical release of aggregate data on commercial bank performance and savings bank performance. A brief discussion of current trends in bank earnings, loans, and losses is included. Published within 75 days of the end of the reporting period, this report is the earliest release of industry-wide aggregate data.'

1097. **Statistics on Banking**. a. 'A statistical profile of the US banking industry. Includes the total number of banks and branches, and aggregate information on the assets, income and liabilities of insured banks.'

1098. **Survey of Real Estate Trends**. q.

1099. **Trust Assets of Financial Institutions**. a. 'Year-end data on trust assets for the 5,000 financial institutions with trust powers.'

1100. **Uniform Bank Performance Reports**. q. $40 per report. 'Reports created for each insured commercial bank and FDIC-insured savings bank which compare an individual institution with its peer group institutions. In a concise format, a UBPR shows the impact of management decisions and economic conditions on a bank's performance and balance-sheet composition. The UBPR is computer-generated from an FDIC database and contains several years worth of data presented in ratio, percentage, and dollar format. Banks are ranked in these reports according to their asset base.'

(i) *#221 Federal Financial Institutions Examination Council*

Inter-agency body established in 1978, whose purpose is to prescribe uniform principles, standards, and report forms for the federal examination of financial institutions and to promote coordination in other areas of supervision.

1101. **FFIEC Information Systems Handbook**. a. $25. 'Provides guidance for regulatory examiners in the examination of information systems operations in financial institutions and independent service bureaus. It also includes an overview of information systems concepts and practices, examples of sound information systems controls, and FFIEC examination work programs.'

(15) #222 National Credit Union Administration 1775 Duke Street, Alexandria, VA 22314–3428. t: (1 703) 518 6300; f: 518 6439. *Freedom of Information* t: (1 703) 518 6410.

Regulates all federally chartered credit unions. Administers the *National Share Insurance Fund*, which provides deposit insurance for federal credit unions and many state credit unions.

1102. **National Credit Union Administration Rules and Regulations**. l. $56.

(16) #223 Resolution Trust Corporation 801 17th Street NW, Washington, DC 20434. t: (1 202) 416 6900; f: 416 2580. *Freedom of Information* t: (1 202) 906 5896.

Responsible for managing and selling insolvent savings and loan institutions.

(17) #224 Thrift Depositor Protection Oversight Board 808 17th Street NW, 8th Floor, Washington, DC 20232. t: (1 202) 416 2650; f: 416 2610.

Cabinet-level panel that sets policy for the Resolution Trust Corporation. Membership comprises: Chairmen of the Federal Reserve and Federal Deposit Insurance Corporation, Secretary of the Treasury, Director of the Office of Thrift Supervision, President of the Resolution Trust Corporation, two independent Presidential appointees.

In addition, with reference to the State level, there are:

(18) #225 American Council of State Savings Supervisors PO Box 34175, Washington, DC 20043–4175. t: (1 202) 371 0666.

(19) #226 Conference of State Bank Supervisors 1015 18th Street, NW, Suite 1000, Washington, DC 20036–5275. t: (1 202) 296 2840; f: 296 1928.

(20) #227 National Association of State Credit Union Supervisors 1901 N Fort Myer Drive, Suite 201, Arlington, VA 22209. t: (1 703) 528 8351; f: 528 3248.

We also reference here related departments of the US *Executive Branch*:

(21) #228 Executive Office of the President 1600 Pennsylvania Avenue, Washington, DC 20500–0001. t: (1 202) 395 3000. *Publications Office* t: (1 202) 395 7332.

(i) *#229 Council of Economic Advisers* Old Executive Office Building, 17th Street and Pennsylvania Avenue NW, Washington, DC 20500–0001. t: (1 202) 395 5084; *Statistical Office* t: (1 202) 395 5062.

Established by the Employment Act of 1946 to provide economic analysis and advice to the President and thus to assist in the development and implementation of national economic policies. The Council also advises the President on other matters affecting the health and performance of the US economy.

1103. **Economic Indicators**. m. **online**.

1104. **Economic Report of the President**. a. **diskette**. a. $78. The short Report is followed by an extensive *Annual Report of the Council of Economic Advisers*, with chapters in recent reports for instance covering 'Monetary and Fiscal Policy in the Current Environment', 'Markets and Regulatory Reform', and 'Whither International Trade and Finance?'.

(ii) *#230 Office of Management and Budget* Executive Office Building, Washington, DC 20503. t: (1 202) 395 3080; f: 395 3746. *Office of Administration* t: (1 202) 395 7250.

Evaluates, formulates and coordinates management procedures and program objectives within and among Federal departments and agencies. It also controls the administration of the Federal budget, while routinely providing the President with recommendations regarding budget proposals and relevant legislative enactments. Responsible also for supervising the activities of federal statistical agencies.

1105. The **Budget of the United States Government**. a. **cdrom**. $24. **diskette**. $22. 'Includes the budget message of the President, the Office of Management and Budget's introduction to the new budget, and sections on investing in the future; acknowledging the inherited debt; managing for integrity and efficiency; and notes and appendices.'

1106. **Weekly Compilation of Presidential Documents**. w. **online**. **diskette**. w. $4,056. 'Makes available transcripts of the President's news conferences, messages to Congress, public speeches and statements and other presidential materials released by the White House.'

(iii) *#231 Office of the United States Trade Representative* 600 17th

Street NW, Winder Building, Washington, DC 20506. *Office of Public Affairs* t: (1 202) 395 3230; f: 395 3911.

Responsible for directing all trade negotiations of and formulating trade policy for the United States.

40. *Insurance* In the *United Kingdom*, the body primarily responsible, in addition to many other relevant duties – especially as regards company legislation – is:

(1) #232 Department of Trade and Industry Ashdown House, 123 Victoria Street, London, SW1E 6RB. t: (44 171) 215 5000; f: 828 3258. *Enterprise Initiative* t: (0800) 500 200. *Business in Europe* t: (44 117) 944 4888. *The Innovation Enquiry Line* t: (0800) 442 001. *Information Division* t: (44 171) 215 5000; f: 222 4382/233 7919.

1107. **Accounts (Year)**. a. Statements prepared pursuant to section 409 of the Insolvency Act of the sums received and paid by the Secretary of State for Trade and Industry under section 403, and of the sums credited and debited to the Investment Account by the National Debt Commissioners.

1108. **Companies in (Year)**. a.

1109. **Directory of Authorised Insolvency Practitioners. diskette**. a. £98. Those authorized to act in that capacity in Great Britain.

1110. **Insurance Annual Report (Year)**. a.

Major DTI functional sections of relevance are:

- *Companies Division*
    - *Branch 1* Law on directors. Fifth Company Law Directive. General company law policy. Corporate governance. Law on company formation, Partnership law. Thirteenth (Takeover) Directive. Review of the status of Companies House. t: (44 171) 215 3204; f: 215 3323
    - *Branch 2* Financial Reporting, including Company accounting, and EC Accounting Directives. Sponsorship of the accountancy profession; statutory audit requirements and regulation of auditors. t: (44 171) 215 3237; f: 215 3323
    - *Branch 3* Registration of company charges; the law relating to groups of companies; disclosure of interests in shares; European Company Statute; European Economic Interest Groupings. Financial assistance by companies for the acquisition of their own shares. t: (44 171) 215 3320; f: 215 3146.
    - *Branch 4* Accountancy advice. Accounting standards, UK, OECD and UN. t: (44 171) 215 3532.
    - *Branch 5* Review of Patent Office; Review of Companies House. t: (44 171) 215 3394; f: 215 3369.
- *Competitiveness Division* t: (44 171) 215 6935; f: 215 6984

  - *Branch 1* Factors influencing competitiveness. CD interest in related DTI policies. Relations with CBI, IoD and similar bodies. t: (44 171) 215 6929
  - *Branch 2* CD interest in the policies of other Government departments, including briefings for Cabinet and Cabinet Committees. Tax advice to DTI. t: (44 171) 215 6931
  - *Branch 3* New initiatives for improving performance of UK suppliers. t: (44 171) 215 8383

- *Deregulation Unit* t: (44 171) 215 6500; f: 215 6471

Responsible for driving forwards the Government's Deregulation Initiative across Whitehall, including in HM Treasury, HM Customs and Excise, Inland Revenue, and the Central Statistical Office departments, as well as promoting deregulation in the EC and liaison with DG XXIII. Provides secretariat for the *Advisory Panel on Deregulation*, which advises the Deregulation Unit on the impact of regulatory requirements on business and enterprise development: the Panel consists of a chairman and 11 other members, who are appointed by the Secretary of State for Trade and Industry, and are selected from the private sector for their expertise.

- *Economics and Statistics Division* f: (44 171) 828 3258

  - *Branch 1* Advice and briefing on macroeconomic policy in UK performance and the world economy. Reporting and briefing on the UK economy including pre-release briefing on statistics, assessments and forecasts. Advice on competitiveness issues including public expenditure and taxation, labour markets, finance for business and the transport infrastructure. Preparation of the weekly note and the stock brief on recent developments in the economy. t: (44 171) 215 6042
  - *Branch 2* Cross sectoral analysis and briefing including industrial modelling. Analysis and provision of UK overseas trade statistics, INTRASTAT and overseas direct investment. Development and maintenance of databases on Trade and Industry. Comparisons of other economic variables. Survey control and advice on statistical surveys, insolvency statistics, policy on industrial statistics, liaison with CSO, EC, OECD and other Departments, industry and external users. t: (44 171) 215 1922

- *Insurance Division* t: (44 171) 215 3104/3165; f: 215 3104/3165

  - *Branch 1* Authorization of insurance companies wishing to carry on business in the UK; supervision of UK authorized non-life insurance companies operating in the UK. Divisional training.
  - *Branch 2* Supervision of those companies not dealt with by Branch 1 (ie specialist life and London market companies); life insurance policy issues.
  - *Branch 3* International insurance questions. Negotiation and implementation of EC directives on insurance. Relations with other international bodies and non-EC overseas countries; Insurance intermediaries.

- *Branch 4* Co-ordination and sponsorship of the insurance industry and general policy issues not covered by Branch 2; complaints and enquiries from the public; supervision of Lloyd's; Terrorism insurance; receipt and processing of annual solvency returns from insurance companies and enquiries on annual returns regulations; divisional administration.

- *International Trade Policy Division* f: (44 171) 215 6767
  - *Branch 1* General trade policy. UK input to EC external trade policy. Article 113 Committee. GATT and WTO. Trade aspects of Economic Summits. Tariff issues. OECD.
  - *Branch 2* Trade in services; new trade issues including trade and environment; trade and labour standards; trade and competition. International investment policy. General commodity policy; general trade policy involving developing countries, including operation of EU's generalised system of preferences scheme.
  - *Branch 3* Import policy. External aspects of Single Market.

- *Investigations Division* t: (44 171) 215 6426; f: 215 6573

Investigations under the Companies Acts, The Financial Services Act 1986 and the Insurance Companies Act 1982.

Also associated with the Department are:

(i) *#233 British Overseas Trade Board* 66–74 Victoria Street, London SW1E 6SW. t: (44 171) 215 4919; f: 215 2853.

Formed in 1972 to direct and develop the Government export promotion advisory services. The Board is assisted by fourteen advisory groups covering specific areas.

(ii) *#234 Export Credits Guarantee Department* PO Box 2200, 2 Exchange Tower, Harbour Exchange Square, London E14 9GS. t: (44 171) 512 7000; f: 512 7649.

The UK's official credit insurer. As well as being responsible to the President of the Board of Trade, the Department is also – as part of its statutory mandate – answerable to the *Export Guarantees Advisory Council*, made up of leading bankers and businessmen, and with which the Department must consult prior to offering certain types of guarantee.

(iii) *#235 Insolvency Rules Committee* Room 704, Bridge Place, 88–89 Eccleston Square, London SW1V 1PT. t: (44 171) 215 0773.

The Lord Chancellor is to consult this Committee before making any rules under (a) Section 411 of the *Insolvency Act 1986* (company insolvency rules); and (b) Section 412 of the *Insolvency Act 1986* (individual insolvency rules).

(iv) *#236 Insolvency Service* 21 Bloomsbury Street, London WC1B 3QW. t: (44 171) 323 3090; f: 636 4709. *Enquiries* t: (44 171) 637 6568.

Insolvency policy including: EC questions; administration and investigation of compulsory insolvencies and prosecutions; disqualifications in all corporate insolvencies; regulation of insolvency practitioners; accounting and management of funds in insolvency cases.

1111. **Insolvency General Report for the Year (Year).** a.

(v) *#237 Simpler Trade Procedures Board*

'SITPRO carries out work on trade facilitation for the *Department of Trade and Industry* (identifying bottlenecks – imposed by governments or business – in the international trading process and proposing solutions). The Department is now reviewing this work, to determine its future direction and organisation. Anyone wishing to put views to the review team should contact . . .'

Other relevant UK bodies concerned with aspects of the insurance industry which might be referenced are:

(2) #238 Insurance Brokers Registration Council 15 St Helen's Place, London EC3A 6DS. t: (44 171) 588 4387; f: 638 7617. *Annual Report*. *Register* 'Names and particulars of all individuals (approximately 15,000) who have been registered as at 31 March 1994' (£55). *List* 'Names and principal place of business of bodies corporate (approximately 2,600) which are carrying on business as insurance brokers and have been enrolled as at 18 March 1994' (£20).

'Statutory body set up by Parliament to regulate insurance brokers.'

(3) #239 Insurance Ombudsman Bureau City Gate One, 135 Park Street, London, SE1 9EA. t: (44 171) 928 7600; f: 401 8700.

Founded in 1981 by a group of major insurance companies, but now has over 300 members. Covers disputes both between insurers and individual policyholders, and between individual investors and unit trust management companies.

In the *United States*, the regulation and supervision of insurance is largely state based:

(4) #240 National Association of Insurance Commissioners Suite 1100, 120 West 12th Street, Kansas City, MO 64105–1925. t: (1 816) 842 3600; f: 471 7004. *NAIC Publications* t: (1 816) 374 7259. *Newsletter*.

State officials who supervise insurance.

1112. **Accounting Practices and Procedures**. l. $300/$100. 'These loose-leaf manuals compile current statutory accounting practices and procedures prescribed or permitted by insurance regulatory authorities.'

1113. **Annual Statement Diskette Filing Specifications**. l. $200. For insurers filing their annual statements on diskette.

1114. **Directory to Assist Receivers of Insolvent Companies**. a. $25. 'Accountants, lawyers, reinsurance specialists and general consultants who are interested in helping insurance departments administer receiverships.'

1115. **Emerging Accounting Issues Working Group Subscription**. i. $60. Minutes of the Association's Working Group.

1116. **Financial Review of Alien Insurers**. a. $275. There is also a *Quarterly Listing of Alien Insurers*.

1117. **International Directory of Insurance Regulatory Officials**. s-a. $50. 'Lists chief regulatory officials, addresses, and phone and fax numbers for approximately 160 countries.'

1118. **Journal of Insurance Regulation**. q. $50. **online**. 'Essential to insurance professionals, regulators and academicians. It's your source for information to help you understand critical regulatory issues with authoritative insights not available anywhere else.'

1119. **Listing of Companies**. l. $150. 'Lists more than 5,000 property, life and fraternal insurers, as well as alien insurers and reinsurers included in the NAIC database.'

1120. **Model Laws, Regulations and Guidelines**. l. $250/200. 'Every NAIC model law, regulation and guideline ever published.'

1121. **Offshore Directory**. a. $50. 'Twelve offshore countries – Caribbean, Guernsey, Malta and the Isle of Man – provide the summaries of their insurance regulations.'

1122. **Schedule D Holdings**. **cdrom**. Lists every debt issue, preferred stock, and common stock held by every US insurance company that files with the NAIC. Covers more than 5,400 insurance companies.

1123. **Statistical Compilation**. a. Two volumes: Property/Casualty; Life/Health. $150 per volume. 'These publications respond to numerous requests from consumers and industry professionals for aggregated annual statement data for . . . insurance companies.' A *Statistical Handbook* is also published ($100) which 'explains the collection, compilation and reporting of insurance statistical information.'

(5) #241 National Conference of Insurance Legislators Box 217, Brookfield, WI 53008. t: (1 414) 782 6669; f: 782 9607. *Newsletter*.

41. Before we treat the third major area of financial institutional activity – securities – we will reference a small number of designated organizations concerned with an area closely related to that of insurance, that of *pensions*:

United Kingdom

(1) #242 Government Actuary's Department 22 Kingsway, London WC2B 6LE. t: (44 171) 242 6828; f: 831 6653.

Provides a consultancy service to departments and to the public sector, both in the United Kingdom and overseas. Advises on a wide range of actuarial issues including occupational and personal pensions, and the financial supervision of insurance companies and friendly societies.

(2) #243 Occupational Pensions Board PO Box 2EE, Newcastle-upon-Tyne, NE 99 2EE. t: (44 191) 225 6414; f: 225 6283.

Established in 1973 primarily to oversee occupational pension schemes. 'Our printed material (ie Memoranda and Announcements) is available free of charge to those organisations who satisfy the relevant criteria . . . Revised arrangements for the distribution of OPB memoranda were introduced in 1976 because of the need to reduce public expenditure . . . One copy of each memorandum was in future to be sent to each organisation on the existing distribution list which had a concern with occupational pensions . . . Other current recipients (and anyone wishing in future to be added to the list) could continue to receive a copy only if (i) they satisfied the OPB that they has a concern with occupational pensions which warranted their receiving the guidance given in the memoranda, and (ii) they did not otherwise have access to the memorandum.'

(3) #244 Pensions Ombudsman 11 Belgrave Road, London SW1V 1RB. t: (44 171) 834 9144; f: 821 0065.

Appointed by the Secretary of State for Social Security under the Social Security Act 1990: responsible to Parliament. Attempts to resolve disputes between individuals and their pension schemes. Funded by a statutory levy on pension schemes based on their numbers of members.

United States

(4) #245 Federal Retirement Thrift Investment Board 805 15th Street NW, Washington, DC 20005.

(5) #246 Financial Institutions Retirement Fund 5 Corporate Park Drive, White Plains, NY 10604. t: (1 914) 694 1300; f: 694 9384. *Annual Report*.

(6) #247 Pension Benefit Guaranty Corporation 2020 K Street, NW, Washington, DC 20006.

Government agency which monitors and regulates approximately 95,000 pension plans that cover nearly 40 million workers.

42. *Securities* As has already been noted, the SEC in the USA has a far wider remit than the SIB in the UK; and because the former body is so fundamental to the subject area of this book, but is also very well known, we allocate here only a relatively small amount of space to its operations:[117]

(1) #248 Securities and Investments Board Gavrelle House, 2–14 Bunhill Row, London EC1Y 8RA, UK. t: (44 171) 638 1240; f: 382 5900.

The designated agency under the *Financial Services Act 1986* (FSA) for regulating the activities of investment businesses in the UK.

"The first thing that strikes the reader of the FSA (apart from its complexity and length) is the broad terms in which much of it is couched. For example, if one looks up capital requirements under the Act all that one finds is the following:

The Secretary of State may make rules requiring persons authorised to carry on investment business by virtue of sections 25 or 31 above to have and maintain in respect of that business such financial resources as are required by the rules . . . and may make provision as to assets, liabilities and other matters to be taken into account in determining a person's financial resources for the purposes of the rules and the extent to which and the manner in which they are taken into account for that purpose.

This level of generality reflects the distinctive blend of statutory and self-regulation that characterises the UK system. The regulatory powers conferred by the Act are transferred to a designated agency called the Securities and Investments Board (SIB). The agency was required by the Act to stipulate a set of rules and regulations regarding the conduct and operation of investment businesses. However, unlike most regulators, it is not the primary function of this agency to regulate businesses directly (save in a few exceptional cases). Instead, the primary function of the agency is to certify a number of clubs (called Self-Regulating Organizations (SROs)) whose membership derives from different parts of the investment business. Certification requires acceptance by the agency of the rules of the clubs and the way the rules operate. The primary relevance of the agencies' rules is therefore to act as a benchmark or more accurately a minimum to which the rules of the clubs have to conform. The clubs do not have any direct powers under the Act except to sanction members who do not comply with their rules and ultimately to expel them. The importance of this stems from the fact that any business under the terms of the FSA has to be a member of a club (or, in the exceptional circumstances mentioned above, directly authorised by the agency). [Alternatively a firm may be a member of a recognised professional body (such as one of the accountancy associates) or authorized under the Insurance Companies or Friendly Societies Acts.] Therefore the operation of an investment business is inconsistent with rejection or expulsion from a club . . . The blend of statutory and self- regulation is thought to be more flexible than self-regulation (which is, for example, used to regulate take-overs in the United Kingdom). It can respond to the needs of investors and firms without requiring the ratification of Parliament but at the same time provides regulatory authorities with powers to force compliance and prosecute for fraud."[118]

1124. **SIB Full Subscription Service**. £240. 'A copy of each rules release, guidance release and formal consultation document published by SIB.'

1125. **SIB Press Notices**. £100. Copies of all SIB press notices.

(i) *#249 Investment Management Regulatory Organization* Broadwalk House, 6 Appold Street, London EC2A 2AA, UK. t: (44 171) 628 6022; f: 920 9285. *Directory of Members* (£25); *Register of Members* (15); *Statements of Recommended Practice* (£5 each). A *Full Subscription Service* (£150) includes: Rules Notices, Rules Releases plus all other IMRO Publications; Consultation Documents; IMRO Reporter; Policy Statements; Performance Indicators; Report & Accounts; Notice to Members. There is also a *Press Releases and Public Register* Service (£200).

1126. **IMRO Rule Book**. l. £160/£100.

(ii) *#250 Personal Investment Authority* 1 Canada Square, Canary Wharf, London E14 5AZ, UK. t: (44 171) 538 8860; f: 418 9300.

'The main body which regulates firms that sell investments to the public . . . The new regulator for the retail sector . . . SIB (Securities and Investments Board) set a deadline for FIMBRA (Financial Intermediaries, Managers and Brokers Regulatory Association) and LAUTRO (Life Assurance and Unit Trust Regulatory Organization) firms to apply to an alternative regulator, in most cases PIA, at 30 September 1994 . . . The sorts of investments covered by the PIA complaints arrangements include:

- life assurance (including endowment policies)
- personal pensions
- unit trusts
- personal equity plans (PEPs)
- guaranteed income bonds
- investment trust savings schemes
- offshore funds (eg gilt funds, bond funds)
- advice on and arranging dealing in shares
- management of a portfolio of investments
- broker funds
- advice on Business Expansion Schemes (BES) and Enterprise Investment Schemes
- advice on and arranging deals in traded options.'

1127. **PIA Press Releases**. i. £200.

1128. **PIA Rules and Updates**. l. £80. For £100 copies of *PIA News, Regulatory*, and *Euro Updates* are included.

(iii) *#251 Securities and Futures Authority* Cottons Centre, Cottons Lane, London SE1 2QB, UK. t: (44 171) 378 9000; f: 403 7569. Publications available to non-members of the SFA are: 'Rulebook' (£100); 'Rulebook Amendments' (£90); 'Board Notices' (£90); 'Membership Directory' (£15).

(2) #252 United States Securities and Exchange Commission 450 50th Street NW, Washington, DC 20549, USA. t: (1 202) 272 3100. *Freedom of Information* t: (1 202) 942 4320. The major US regulatory body for the securities business.

- *SEC Information Line* 'Instant information 24 hours a day, 7 days a week. Dial (1 202) 942 8088 and press the digit code which corresponds to the message you wish to hear:

GENERAL INFORMATION

10 • SEC Information Line Directory
15 • SEC Address and Business Hours
20 • SEC Organizational Structure
25 • Public Affairs
30 • Public Reference Room
33 • Publications

OFFICE OF CONSUMER AFFAIRS AND INFORMATION SERVICES

35 • Investor Inquiries
40 • Investor Complaints
45 • Freedom of Information Act Requirements
50 • Privacy Act Requests

DIVISION OF CORPORATION FINANCE

55 • Small Business Firms
60 • International Corporate Finance

DIVISION OF INVESTMENT MANAGEMENT

65 • Investment Adviser Registration
70 • Investment Company Registration
75 • Applications for Exemptive Relief
80 • Electronic Filing of Form N-SAR

DIVISION OF MARKET REGULATION

85 • Broker-Dealer Registration
90 • Lost and Stolen Securities
95 • Trading Suspensions'

1129. **SEC News Digest**. d. $840. Commission meeting notices; Administrative proceedings; proposed rule changes; SEC releases; list of form types registrations.

43. There are a range of other official, quasi-official, and self-regulatory bodies – especially in the United States – involved with the regulation and supervision of trade in financial assets, including:

United Kingdom

(1) #253 Investment Ombudsman 6 Frederick Place, London EC2R 8BT. t: (44 171) 796 3065.

(2) #254 Investors Compensation Scheme 2–14 Bunhill Row, London EC1Y 8RA. t: (44 171) 628 8820; f: 382 5901. *Annual Report.*

United States

(3) #255 Commodity Futures Trading Commission 2033 K Street NW, Washington, DC 20581. *Office of Public Affairs* t: (1 202) 254 8630; f: 254 3678. *Freedom of Information* t: (1 202) 254 3382. *Annual Report.*

'The Federal regulator and overseer of the trading of commodity futures and option contracts in the US. The agency's mission includes protecting customers who use these markets and monitoring the markets to detect and prevent commodity price distortions and market manipulations . . . Under the law, the CTFC is responsible for regulating exchange trading of futures contracts for a variety of foreign currencies, financial instruments such as Treasury bills and bonds, stock indices, foodstuffs, grains, industrial materials, livestock and related products. It is also charged with regulating leverage contracts, options on futures contracts, and options on physical commodities trading on commodity markets.'

(4) #256 Municipal Securities Rulemaking Board 1818 N Street NW, Suite 800, Washington, DC 20036. t: (1 202) 223 9347; f: 872 0347.

(5) £257 National Futures Association 200 West Madison, Suite 1600, Chicago, IL 60606–3447. t: (1 312) 781 1300; f: 781 1467. *Annual Review.*

'Congressionally authorized self-regulatory organization of the US futures industry.' Parties who are required to be a member of the Association are: Futures Commission Merchants, Commodity Pool Operators, Introducing Brokers, Commodity Trading Advisors, and Associated Persons. Exchanges, banks, and commodity business firms may join, but membership is not compulsory. Floor traders and floor brokers are not required to be members, because they are subject to exchange regulation. One must be a member of the NFA in order to do commodity-related business with the public. 'NFA maintains a database of disciplinary and registration information about the over 100,000 current and former US registrants. Information is provided without cost to interested parties and is also available to foreign regulators. In fact, the SFA has a direct access computer terminal in its own office.'

(6) #258 North American Securities Administrators Association One Massachusetts Avenue, NW, Suite 301, Washington, DC

20001. t: (1 202) 737 0900; f: 783 3571. The Association issues a wide variety of free or cheaply priced publications.

'The national voice of the 50 state agencies responsible for investor protection and the efficient functioning of the capital markets at grassroots level in the US . . . Overseeing the multi-trillion dollar investment marketplace in the United States is an enormous task that directly affects the financial well-being of millions of Americans and requires the close attention of the federal and 50 state governments.

The fundamental distinction between state and federal securities regulation is **when** fraud is stopped. Federal securities regulators generally lack the authority to halt unfair securities offerings and, as a result, rely on *after-the-fact* enforcement to deter future misconduct. The Securities and Exchange Commission's full disclosure approach requires small investors to pore over highly complex and legalistic documents in order to avoid abusive or fraudulent offerings. By contrast, the *front-end* licensing and registration activities of state securities agencies work to spot and stop fraud and abusive sales practices before the money of small investors is lost. It is in this way that state securities regulation serves as both a 'safety net' for small investors and a crucial complement to federal enforcement efforts.

The 'preventive medicine' philosophy of state securities regulation dates back more than two decades before the creation of the SEC. The first modern 'blue sky' securities law was adopted in 1911 by the state of Kansas. The term *blue sky* refers to speculative schemes that, in the words of a judge of that period, had no more substance than a 'square foot of Kansas blue sky'.

NASAA and the National Association of Securities Dealers jointly operate the *Central Registration Depository*, a 50–state computer link for coordinated agent registration and transfers . . . Now under development is the *State Registration Depository*, which would allow for the one-stop, paperless registration at the state level of securities offerings.

A pillar of NASAA's efforts to protect individual investors is an aggressive and innovative investor education program. The Association unveiled a toll-free *investor hotline* three weeks after the 'Black Monday' stock market crash. More than 15,000 individuals were assisted during the first six months of the Hotline's operation . . . NASAA periodically issues the *NASAA Investor Bulletin*.'

(7) #259 Securities Investor Protection Corporation 805 15th Street, NW, Suite 800, Washington, DC 20005–2207. t: (1 202) 371 8300; f: 371 6728.

Private corporation established by Congress to administer the *Securities Investor Protection Act* 'SIPC shall not be an agency or establishment of the United States Government . . . SIPC shall be a membership corporation the members of which shall be all persons registered as brokers or dealers (except those engaged exclusively in the distribution of mutual fund shares, the sale of variable annuities, the insurance business, furnishing investment advice to investment companies or insurance company separate accounts, and those whose principal business is conducted outside of the United States. Also excluded are government securities brokers and dealers who are registered as such under section 15(a)(1)(A) of the Securities Exchange Act of 1934.' (Section 3(a)(1)(A) & (2)(A))

44. For two areas of finance activity, there are several designated organizations in the *United States* which are without direct parallel in the United Kingdom:

Agriculture

(1) #260 Farm Credit Administration 1501 Farm Credit Drive, McLean, VA 22102–5090. t: (1 703) 883 4000; f: 734 5784. *Freedom of Information* t: (1 703) 883 4414. *Annual Report. Newsletter.*

Responsible for ensuring the safe and sound operation of the banks, associations, affiliated service organizations and other entities that comprise the *Farm Credit System.*

(2) #261 Farm Credit Council 50 F Street NW, Suite 900, Washington, DC 20001. t: (1 202) 626 8710; f: 626 8718.

(3) #262 Federal Agricultural Mortgage Corporation 919 18th Street NW, Suite 200, Washington, DC 20006. t: (1 202) 872 7700.

Mortgage financing

(4) #263 Department of Housing and Urban Development 451 7th Street SW, Washington, DC 20410. t: (1 202) 708 1422; f: 708 0209.

(i) *#264 Government National Mortgage Association* [Ginnie Mae] HUD Building, Room 6100, Washington, DC 20410. t: (1 202) 708 0926; f: 708 0490.

'Purpose is to support the Government's housing objectives by establishing secondary market facilities for residential mortgages; guaranteeing mortgage-backed securities composed of FHA-insured or VA-guaranteed mortgage loans that are issued by private lenders and guaranteed by GNMA with the full faith and credit of the United States; and through its mortgage-backed securities programs, increases the overall supply of credit available for housing by providing a vehicle for channeling funds from the securities market into the mortgage market.

"Banks and other mortgage lenders have long traded residential mortgages with investors and other lenders as a means of adding liquidity to their portfolios. Mortgages have a security rarely equalled in nongovernmental investments . . . The problem with mortgage trading is that every loan is unique – tailored specifically for a certain person, a certain property, a certain locality, and a certain rate. This has made for a general lack of liquidity and led to the immobilization of huge amounts of money tied up in mortgage investments. At the end of 1985, for instance, there was over $2.2 trillion of outstanding mortgage debt in the United States, or about $400 billion more than the entire U.S. national debt at that time.

The key to unlocking this financial treasure was supplied by the Government National Mortgage Association (GNMA) . . . Mortgage bankers can now assemble pools of similar mortgages, usually in multiples of $1 million, and submit them to GNMA. The association guarantees the pools and packages them into a 'pass-through' security which is then sold to investors in unit multiples of $25,000. The buyer becomes in effect a pro rata holder of numerous government guaranteed mortgages – either Veterans Administration guaranteed or Federal Housing administration insured . . . The mortgage banker, on the other hand, receives cash from the GNMA sale and can immediately start to make new mortgage commitments. The process seems to have created a situation with no losers.

Small wonder, then, that GNMA's success has been emulated. Outstanding GNMA securities rose from $250 million in 1970 to almost $400 billion by the end of 1990. Other government agencies as well as commercial interests also began issuing mortgage-backed securities, so that by the end of the third quarter, 1990 over $984 billion in mortgage pool securities were outstanding."[119]

(5) #265 Federal Home Loan Mortgage Corporation [Freddie Mae] 8200 Jones Branch Drive, McLean, VA 22102. t: (1 703) 903 2000; f: 903 2447. Government Sponsored Enterprise. *Annual Report*.

(6) #266 Federal Housing Finance Board 1777 F Street NW, Washington, DC 20006. t: (1 202) 408 2938; f: 408 1435.

Established in 1989 by the Federal Home Loan Bank Act, as amended by the Financial Institutions Reform, Recovery and Enforcement Act 1989 as an independent regulatory agency.

(7) #267 Federal National Mortgage Association [Fannie Mae] 3900 Wisconsin Avenue, NW, Washington, DC 20016. t: (1 202) 752 4422; f: 752 4933. Government Sponsored Enterprise. The *Office of Housing Research* (t: (1 202) 752 4933) have compiled a brochure 'Published Research: Indexed by Subject' (May 1994). *Annual Report*.

1130. **Housing Policy Debate**. q. $free. Stimulates thoughtful and insightful discussion on a broad range of housing issues, including public policy, home mortgage finance and international housing finance.

1131. **Journal of Housing Research**. s-a. $free. Provides an outlet for theoretical and emprical research on a broad range of housing issues, including housing policy, home mortgage finance and international housing finance.

45. Summarizing, after this introduction to some of the major players and their publications comprising the legal, regulatory and supervisory environments of UK and US banking, insurance and securities businesses, we might write that the broad array of types of body concerned with such processes are not dissimilar in the USA and the UK. In both jurisdictions, we have the justice system using and interpreting a corpus of primary legislation which is supplemented by the mass of delegated legislation supplemented by quasi-legislation (to use Holborn's term) issued by bodies such as: the Inland Revenue (UK) and the Internal Revenue (US); by the Bank of England and the Federal Reserve Bank; by the Securities and Investments Board (UK) and the Securities and Exchange Commission (US); by the London Stock Exchange and the New York Stock Exchange; and so on. Those obvious UK/US organizational parallels by no means extend throughout the whole of our concerns here. Also, the USA is much less prepared to allow the *self-regulation* of key areas than is the UK. But at the end of the day, in both countries, if the 'legal' information source sought is not a law/statute, then it must have been publicly 'generated' by a single prescribed organization: government department, public or private agency, professional or trade body. For many such organizations, the generated source will subsequently be 'displayed' by each country's official publication agencies (*HMSO* in the UK; *GPO* in the US). Otherwise, copies of the regulation or code or standard or whatever will be obtainable directly from the generating body itself; or via a (value-adding?) commercial information provider. The reader will have noted that the electronic imperative – as, for instance, currently exemplified by *The Internet* and *The World Wide Web* – is threatening to erode some of the value-adding ease of access to officially produced legal and regulatory documents, formally the sole province of the commercial publishers.

Incorporation

46. We noted earlier in our treatment of 1993 SNA how critical is the notion of 'in*corporation*'. Because the vast majority of published sources relating to the financial states of trading entities arise ultimately from the requirement for incorporated entities – *corporations* – to submit to specially designated agencies, reports and accounts prepared according to rules sanctioned in law, it is appropriate to delve further into this notion. Writing from a UK viewpoint:

> A legal person is anything recognized by law as having legal rights and duties. With one main exception, a legal person in this country is simply a person in the ordinary sense: a human being. In general, his or her

rights begin at birth and end at death and, subject to rules such as those of capacity (e.g. special rules to protect minors), the same rules apply to everyone.

In one important instance, English law also grants legal personality to an artificial person. This arises where a group of persons together form a *corporate* body of some sort. The corporate body can acquire a legal personality separate from that of its members, with some of the legal powers of a natural person. It can, for example, own property and make contracts, even with its own members, in its own name.[120]

47. Elaborating further, from a different text:

In the UK the law permits a range of different types of business organisation. At one end of the spectrum is the sole trader or one man unincorporated business: at the other, the massive public limited company whose business operations may have a significant effect on the entire economy. The principal types of business organisation in the UK are the sole trader, the partnership and the corporate association.

The *sole trader* is responsible for the conduct of the business and thus for the debts incurred. In general, there is no requirement for registration, disclosure of financial information or any other form of public accountability.

Under English law separate legal personality is not conferred on a *partnership*. Partners are collectively called a firm but the firm does not enjoy the separate legal status of a company. Under Scots law, a partnership does enjoy a legal personality separate from that of the partners. Thus the firm can enter into contracts in its own name and can sue and be sued in the same manner as a limited company. Ultimately, however, the partners in a Scottish firm are, in common with those in an English firm, responsible to the full extent of their personal assets for the debts and liabilities of the firm . . . The only regulatory control on the freedom to associate in partnership is that partnerships of more than twenty must incorporate unless they are solicitors, accountants, stockbrokers or other partnerships exempted by the Secretary of State.

The formation of a *company* results in the creation of a legal entity that enjoys a distinct status quite separate from its members. Once Parliament and the courts had clearly recognised the separate status of business corporations and bestowed the privilege of limited liability on its members, it quickly acquired popularity as a form of business association. . . . In practice, in the context of small businesses, directors often have to compromise the protection of limited liability. Creditors invariably seek personal guarantees from the directors before they will extend funds to a small business. Thus the director may obtain the protection of limited liability in dealings with trade creditors and consumers but not in respect of long term commitments with banks or other financial institutions. In many respects the attractiveness of corporate status lies in the greater flexibility in terms of financing operations, the additional marketability of shares, perpetual succession and majority rule.

A central theme of British company law is registration and disclosure.

> Since 1908 legislation has required companies to disclose progressively more financial information in published accounts and returns to the Registrar of Companies. Such disclosure is justified in terms of a vague notion that it represents the price of limited liability and a basic report to shareholders on a stewardship function by directors . . . The main argument in support of maintaining full disclosure of financial statements for all companies is that it helps maintain an efficient system of credit reporting and represents an index of corporate solvency.[121]

48. As that second extract indicated, in the UK it is common to equate the word *company* with that of the separate incorporated legal entity. In the USA, usage can be somewhat different, as Lavin (in his award-winning text) usefully summarizes:

> Most people use words like 'establishment', 'firm', 'corporation' and 'industry' interchangeably. Commonly used business terns have specialized economic or legal meanings. Properly speaking, an establishment is any single location of a business, while an enterprise is the company as a whole. An industry is the total group of industries engaged in a similar business activity. Banking and chemical manufacturing are examples of industries.
>
> The word 'company' is an inclusive term for any type of business organization. A company can be a proprietorship, a partnership, or a corporation. The sole proprietorship is the simplest and most common form of business organization. Any individual can form a proprietorship with little cost or effort . . . A partnership is an association of two or more people for the purpose of jointly owning a business. Registering a partnership is similar to filing a proprietary name, although the partners may wish to draft 'Articles of Copartnership' to specify their mutual rights and obligations.
>
> A corporation is a special type of company – an 'artificial legal being' created by state charter, endowed with special powers, and capable of surviving the deaths of its owners. Unlike a proprietorship or partnership, the corporation exists in the eyes of the law as an entity separate from the owners. In the United States, a business may incorporate in any one of the 50 states, regardless of where it resides . . . The Articles of Incorporation also authorise the number of shares of stock that can be issued; the owners receive these shares in proportion to their degree of ownership.
>
> Why incorporate? A major reason is the concept of limited liability. In theory, the owner of a corporation only risks the money put into the corporation; the owner's personal assets are protected from creditors, lawsuits, and other potential claims against the corporation. Incorporation also affords the business with additional means for financing growth. If a company wishes to sell stock as a means of raising capital, it must first incorporate. Not all corporations sell stock to the public; most U.S. corporations are privately held (also called closely held).
>
> Federal and state laws require that certain information on publicly held corporations must be divulged to the public. Other forms of business, including the private corporation, are under no such restric-

tions; in fact, most businesses guard information about themselves very carefully. Thus, publicly held corporations are generally simpler to investigate than other types of businesses.

Public companies constitute a tiny fraction of all firms in the United States, but they are responsible for most of the nation's business activity. But what does 'public' really mean? All such corporations sell stock to the general public, but this is a fairly vague statement. To say that a public company must have more than a certain number of stockholders doesn't capture the principle behind public ownership either. A better way to think about public companies is to consider how people become shareholders. Anyone who wishes to acquire stock in a public company may do so by purchasing shares on the open market. In private firms, the stockholders are typically the principals in the company – the founders, members of their families, key employees, and perhaps others who have a direct relationship with it. If a stockholder in a private company wishes to reduce his or her investment in the firm, the stock could be sold or transferred to anyone the owner chooses, but normally it would be offered to the existing stockholders. There is no ready marketplace for buying and selling shares of private companies.

A gray area separates the publicly owned company and the truly private entity. The government has created many exceptions to the broad definition of 'public', making the distinction between the two categories less than clear. For example, some firms may need to raise more capital than can be obtained from the immediate group of principals, yet don't wish to 'go public'. An alternative is to consult a business broker or investment banker who specializes in arranging company financing. Such a specialist may sell stock to a venture capital firm, a financial institution, or a small group of sophisticated investors. Depending on the transaction, such deals are called either private placements or limited offerings.[122]

49. The reader may have remembered from our earlier extensive review of the *System of National Accounts* that the System uses the designation *corporation* to denote a 'legal entity, created for the purpose of producing goods or services for the market, that may be a source of profit or other financial gain to its owner(s)'; and thus would include within that definition 'incorporated enterprises, public limited companies, public corporations, private companies, joint-stock companies, limited liability companies, limited liability partnerships, and so on'. Although we are especially concerned in this book with what Lavin above terms 'public companies', we must also note the importance of other types of organized legal entity to finance activity: such as those arising from the concepts of *mutuality* and *trusteeship*. Unfortunately, it has not been possible to pursue the legal information source ramifications of those and other similar related types of entities here.

Financial accounting

50. In both the UK and the USA, the financial accounting rules used by incorporated bodies to disclose their financial states are authorized by non-governmental agencies. That agency in the UK is the *Accounting Standards Board*, which operates within the framework of the *Financial Reporting Council* (FRC); and because also it is relatively a new body, it is worth exploring in some detail how it sees its role:

(1) #268 Financial Reporting Council Holborn Hall, 100 Gray's Inn Road, London, WC1X 8AL t: (44 171) 404 8818; f: 404 4497. Established in 1990, following the report of the *Review Committee on the Making of Accounting Standards* (the Dearing Report). In outline, the Council consists of:

- *Accounting Standards Board* 'Role is to make, amend and withdraw accounting standards . . . By the *Accounting Standards (Prescribed Body) Regulations* (SI 1990/1667) the Secretary of State for Trade and Industry prescribed the Accounting Standards Board for the purposes of section 256(1) of the *Companies Act 1985* with the effect that statements of standard accounting practice issued by the Board are "accounting standards" for the purposes of the accounting requirements of the Act.'
- *Urgent Issues Task Force* Subcommittee whose 'main role is to assist the Board in areas where an accounting standard or Companies Act provision exists, but where unsatisfactory or conflicting interpretations have developed or seem likely to develop'.
- *Financial Reporting Review Panel* 'The role of the Panel is to examine departures from the accounting requirements of the Companies Act 1985 and if necessary to seek an order from the court to remedy them. Its authority stems from *The Companies (Defective Accounts) (Authorised Persons) Order 1991 (SI 1991/13)* made by the Secretary of State for Trade and Industry which, from 1 February 1991, authorised the Panel for the purposes of section 245B of the Companies Act 1985 (which was inserted into that Act by the Companies Act 1989).'

Delving further:

'Although the FRC and its companion bodies have the strong support of Government, they are not government-controlled, but rather part of the private sector process of self-regulation and this is reflected in their constitutions, membership and financing. The *Department of Trade and Industry*, together with the *Northern Ireland Department of Economic Development* and the *National Audit Office*, provides around one-third of the FRC's finances, around one third coming from the *Consultative Committee of Accountancy Bodies* and the balance from the *London Stock Exchange* and the banking and investment communities.

The remit of the Council is to provide support to the operational bodies, the *Accounting Standards Board* and the *Financial Reporting Review Panel*, and to encourage good financial reporting generally. At its first meeting, in May 1990, the Council codified this role as being:

- To promote good financial reporting, and in that context from time to time make public reports on reporting standards. In that role it would from time to time make representations to Government on the current working of legislation and on any desirable development of it;
- To provide guidance to the Accounting Standards Board on work programmes and on broad policy issues;
- To verify that the new arrangements are conducted with efficiency and economy and that they are adequately funded.

The Council's constitution provides for it to publish an annual report reviewing the state of financial reporting and making known the views of the Council on accounting standards and practice. . . . The Council, through its then chairman, was one of the three initiators and sponsors of the *Committee on the Financial Aspects of Corporate Governance* (the Cadbury Committee) and four members of the Council were members of the Committee.

- *Accounting Standards Board* 'Unlike the former *Accounting Standards Committee*, the Accounting Standards Board is autonomous; it needs neither outside approval for its actions, nor approval from the company's directors. It is however the practice of the Board to consult widely on all its proposals . . . At its first Meeting the Board agreed to adopt the 22 extant *Statements of Standard Accounting Practice* (SSAPs) issued by the former Accounting Standards Committee or its predecessor. . . . The Board has also (in 1990) set out its policy in respect of the development of *Statements of Recommended Practice* (SORPs) . . . (but) while the principle of this approach will remain unaltered the Board has currently under development some modifications to its scrutiny mechanism.

The Board has indicated that its general aim in the making of accounting standards is to centre them as far as possible on principles rather than by the prescription of highly detailed rules. One of the Board's current tasks therefore, on which work is well advanced, is the development of a *Statement of Principles* as a framework within which consistent accounting standards can be formulated . . . The Board's policy is to consult widely on all its proposals, which are issued in a variety of forms. For some the proposal is first issued informally in *Discussion Draft* or *Discussion Paper* form. For all new proposals there is a formal *Exposure Draft* stage, the comments received on which are normally placed on public record. A list of the *Financial Reporting Standards* (the Board's term for accounting standards), Exposure Drafts, Discussion Papers, Discussion Drafts and other ASB publications issued to date is (available from the Board).'

- *Urgent Issues Task Force* 'The UITF operates in a broadly similar way to its USA and Canadian counterparts by seeking to reach a consensus on the issue under consideration. There are 15 voting members, of whom 11 constitute a quorum. The requirement for the achievement of consensus is that not more than two of the voting members or their alternated present at the meeting dissent. Unless the consensus thus established conflicts with the law, accounting standards, or the Board's policy or plans, the Board would expect it to be regarded as accepted practice in the area in question, and the intention is that it should be considered to be part of the corpus of practices forming the basis for what determines a true and fair view.

The urgent nature of the matters tackled by the UITF necessarily means that it is not possible for it to follow an extended consultation and due process procedure. The Board has therefore taken special measures to publicise the matters on the UITF's agenda, and *UITF Information Sheets* are now circulated to some 4,000 people, including the finance directors of all listed companies. The results of the UITF's deliberations on a subject, including the reaching of a consensus, are promulgated by means of periodically issued *UITF Abstracts.*'

- *Financial Reporting Review Panel* 'By agreement with the Department of Trade and Industry the normal ambit of the Panel is public and large private companies, the Department dealing with all other cases. . . . The Panel does not scrutinise on a routine basis all company accounts falling within its ambit. Instead it acts on matters drawn to its attention, either directly or indirectly.

In considering an individual case the Panel normally operates by means of a Group of five or more members drawn from the overall Panel membership constituted to deal with it. That Group is responsible for carrying out the functions of the Panel for that case; there is no collective involvement by the other Panel members. Groups normally aim to discharge their tasks by seeking voluntary agreement with the directors of a company on any necessary revisions to the accounts in question. (The Companies Act 1989 made possible the voluntary revision of accounts as well as their revision by court order). But if that approach fails and the Panel believes that revisions to the accounts are necessary it will seek a declaration from the court that the annual accounts of the company concerned do not comply with the requirements of the Companies Act 1985, and for an order requiring the directors of the company to prepare revised accounts.'[123]

51. Staying with the UK, Elliott and Elliott[124] have made an especial effort to produce an introductory volume that asks *why* the information that financial accountants produce should be measured and produced in specific forms. They point out that the search for a conceptual framework for financial reporting is being pursued in the USA, Australia, Canada and in the *International Accounting Standards Committee*, as well as in the UK by the Accounting Standards Board (as noted a moment ago):

(1) #269 International Accounting Standards Committee 167 Fleet Street, London EC4A 2ES, UK. t: (44 171) 353 0565; f: 353 0562.

Annual Review. The *IASC Publications Subscription Service* (£230) is 'the only way to keep up to date with international accounting standards'.

'Was formed in 1973 by an agreement of the leading professional bodies in ten countries. Now represents more than 100 accountancy bodies from 78 countries. Unlike many international organizations, governments do not belong to the IASC: it is a private-sector body with representatives from professional accounting organizations. 'The Committee has become the signal force worldwide to develop international financial accounting standards and seek their widest possible acceptance and use.'

1132. (Year) **Bound Volume of International Accounting Standards**. £30.

Elliott and Elliott point out that in each forum, the starting point of the investigation has been the same, ie: 'commencing with a consideration of the objectives of financial statements, qualitative characteristics of financial information, definition of the elements, and when these are to be recognised in the financial statements'.

The authors offer a helpful introductory review of work of this type in the UK; and their Summary to that chapter gives a useful overview of the whole area from the perspective of that jurisdiction:

> Directors and accountants are constrained by a mass of rules and regulations which govern the measurement, presentation and disclosure of financial information.
>
> Regulations are basically derived from three major sources. These are the legislature in the form of statutes, the accountancy profession in the form of standards, and the Stock Exchange in the form of obligations and listing requirements.
>
> There have been a number of reports relating to financial reporting in the UK, and in other countries. The preparation and presentation of financial statements continues to evolve. Serious steps are being taken to provide a conceptual framework and there is growing international agreement on the setting of standards.
>
> User needs have been accepted as paramount; qualitative characteristics of information have been specified; the elements of financial statements have been defined precisely; the presentation of financial information has been prescribed; and comparability between companies is seen as desirable.
>
> However, the intention remains to produce financial statements that present a true and fair view. This is not achieved by detailed rules and regulations and there will continue to be a need for the exercise of judgement. This opens the way for creative accounting practices that bring financial reporting and the accounting profession into disrepute. Strenuous efforts will continue to be needed from the auditors, the ASB, the Review Panel and the Financial Reporting Council to contain the use of unacceptable practices. The regulatory bodies show that they have every intention of accepting the challenge.

52. On the last point, it is of interest to refer the reader to a book which caused some considerable controversy in the UK when it was published ('the book they tried to ban').[125] To quote from the sleeve note:

> 'ACCOUNTING FOR GROWTH is a deliberate play on words: Was most of the growth in company profits during the 1980s due to the improved efficiency of British industry or was it generated from the manipulation of profits by creative accounting?
>
> TERRY SMITH strips away the camouflage of creative accounting to allow readers to examine company accounts afresh and decide whether profits are genuine and how strong a company's finances really are.
>
> Each of the creative accounting techniques examined is accompanied by examples from actual public company reports and accounts to enable readers to follow the techniques used and to perform their own analysis.
>
> THE TECHNIQUES EXAMINED INCLUDE:
>
> - Acquisition accounting
> - Capitalization of costs
> - Disposals – including deconsolidation on disposal
> - Brand accounting
> - Changes in depreciation
> - Deferred consideration
> - Convertibles with put options and MPS
> - Extraordinary and exceptional item
> - Off balance sheet finance
> - Pension fund accounting
> - Contingent liabilities
> - Currency mismatching

In the Acknowledgements in the book, Smith writes (the last sentence, surely, somewhat tongue in cheek!):

> I fully acknowledge that the comments expressed in this book are my opinions, and I am not suggesting that the practices analysed are illegal, or that they even contravene Generally Accepted Accounting Practice (also know as 'GAAP') or that the various companies and accountants mentioned did not have valid reasons for using these techniques. I am more interested in the impact of these practices upon the clarity of financial information than in whether or not they satisfy the letter of the law or regulation. I believe that it is in the public interest for these issues to be discussed. Finally, I wish to acknowledge the help of all those companies who gave permission for reproduction of parts of their Annual Report and Accounts to illustrate this book.

53. Given the difficulties in creating accounting data, the reader may wonder that anyone would care to rely on those figures. But:

> Protection by disclosure is one of the underlying principles of the (UK) Companies Act. The theory is that if members, creditors and the public can find out relevant information about a company they will do so and then conduct their affairs with it accordingly. It has however always been clear that disclosure alone is not sufficient protection and recently extensive new measures have been passed . . . Publicity nevertheless remains important and is achieved in four main ways:
>
> a. The requirement of official notification of certain matters in the Gazette;
>
> b. The registration of certain information at the Companies Registry;
>
> c. The compulsory maintenance of certain registers by the company; and
>
> d. The requirement to make an annual return and disclose the company's financial position in its published accounts and director's report.[126]

54. Those are the basic disclosure requirements for private incorporated enterprises in the UK. As we saw in the quotation from Lavin, private companies in the USA generally do not have to disclose their 'private' affairs. However, in both countries, if a corporation decides to *go public* – to raise capital by offering an *equity* stake to others (rather than by generating *debt* or using internally generated funds to expand the business) – the amount, detail and frequency of the information about the entity required to be submitted to the authorities increases substantially. In the UK, the financial accounts and reports that all incorporated companies must submit – whether or not they are public corporations – is lodged with *Companies House*. The reliability of the such submitted accounts will naturally be dependent on the reliability of the prior auditing process.

(1) #270 Companies House Crown Way, Cardiff CF4 3UZ, UK. t: (44 1222) 388588; f: 380900. *Enquiries* t: (44 1222) 380801. *London Search Room* Companies House, 55–71 City Road, London EC1Y 1BB, UK. t: (44 171) 253 9393; f: 608 0435.

'Has three main statutory functions:

- to incorporate and dissolve companies
- to register documents filed under the Companies Acts and related legislation
- to make information available to the public.

The main legislation governing Companies House's functions is the *Companies Act 1985*, as amended by the *Companies Act 1989*. This lays down the obligations of companies and their directors enjoying limited liability and the duties of the Registrar of Companies. It specifies information which companies must present to Companies House and which the Registrar must make available to the public.

To help people administering limited companies to meet their obligations and to help the public gain access to information, Companies House produces a series of publications.'

1133. **Companies House Direct**. **online**. Information on 1,000,000 live and 500,000 dissolved companies, as well as access to the *Directors Register*, which contains details of 4 million company director and secretary appointments.

55. UK publicly quoted companies in addition to their duties with regard to Companies House, must disclose an amount of much more detailed information to the Company Announcement's Office of the *London Stock Exchange*, which information is in turn made public via the Exchange's *Regulatory News Service* (which is referenced later).

56. Public corporations in the USA, when compared to the UK (and indeed the rest of the world) are subject to a considerably greater degree of detailed disclosure, under the auspices of the *Securities and Exchange Commission*. The corollary of the extensive and detailed corporate reporting requirements imposed by the SEC is that there is a much larger number of types of commercial publication – based on the data submitted – than is the case in the UK. We have already noted that the SEC has an extremely wide remit extending beyond concerns with financial accounting and disclosure matters to the much more demanding areas of securities and investment regulation: we should allow a little more to be said about its function in the US economy:

Mission 'Under the Securities Exchange Act of 1934, Congress created the Securities and Exchange Commission (SEC). The SEC is an independent, nonpartisan, quasi-judicial regulatory agency. The agency's mission is to administer the federal securities laws that seek to provide protection for investors. The purposes of these laws are to ensure that the securities markets are fair and honest and to provide the means to enforce the securities laws through sanctions where necessary.

Under the direction of the Chairman and Commissioners, the staff ensures that publicly held entities, broker-dealers in securities, investment companies and advisers, and other participants in the securities markets comply with federal securities laws. These laws were designed to facilitate informed investment analyses and decisions by the investing public, primarily by ensuring adequate disclosure of material information.'

The extensive 1993 *Annual Report* of the SEC lists its 'Key 1993 Results' under these headings:

- *Enforcement*
- *International Affairs*

- *Regulation of the Securities Markets*
- *Investment Companies and Advisers*
- *Full Disclosure*
- *Accounting and Auditing Matters*
- *Other Litigation and Legal Activities*
- *Economic Research and Analysis*
- *Policy Management and Administrative Support*

57. Although the Securities and Exchange Commission is actually empowered to write accounting standards, policy in practice is to delegate this task to the US *Financial Accounting Standards Board*; but matters are not straightforward:

> A volume of great length would be required to present a comprehensive description and analysis of financial accounting and reporting practices in North America . . . The United States is a federation of fifty individual states, each of which has its own legislative body with extensive powers to control business activity and levy taxes within its own boundaries. The right to practise as a public accountant is also conferred by the individual states and the requirements for conferring that right differ slightly from state to state; membership of the national body, the American Institute of Certified Public Accountants (AICPA), is not required as a condition for exercising the right to practise, and many practitioners elect not to become members.
>
> Laws governing transactions in securities were first introduced by individual states, beginning in Kansas in 1911. Such state laws became widespread; they are generally known as 'blue sky laws', after a quip to the effect that unscrupulous Kansas dealers were trying to sell the blue sky. They normally require registration of a proposal to offer securities for sale, and disclosure of information; in some cases they confer on a state official the right to refuse permission for the proposal to go ahead.
>
> The most important regulations for the control of dealings in securities are now enforced at the federal level of government under the Securities Act of 1933 and the Securities Exchange Act of 1934, which were passed after the financial crises of 1929 onwards. However, neither these statutes nor any others contain detailed provisions relating to financial accounting and reporting. The United States has no statutory requirements for accounting in a form that is comparable to the accounting sections of the UK Companies Acts. . . . The federal securities legislation established a Securities and Exchange Commission (SEC) to administer the securities regulations. The primary function of the SEC is to ensure that investors are furnished with information necessary for informed investment decisions. It requires publication and receives registration of prospectuses and periodic financial reports. It also has power to prescribe the methods to be followed in the preparation of financial reports and to prescribe the form and content of those reports.
>
> One vital point is that only the minority of US companies (about 12,000) are SEC-registered and have to obey its accounting and audit-

ing rules. Other companies have no compulsory audit or published financial reporting requirements, although many companies are required to publish audited accounts by their shareholders or lenders . . . A company must register with the SEC if it wishes there to be a market in its securities. Once registered, it has to publish accounts, file reports, have CPA audit, follow the Regulations, and comply with the Generally Accepted Accounting Principles (GAAP).[127]

(1) #271 Financial Accounting Standards Board 401 Merritt 7, PO Box 5116, Norwalk, CT 06856–5116, USA. t: (1 203) 847 0700; f: 849 9714. *Prepayments* FASB Order Department, PO Box 30816, Hartford, CT 06150, USA.

'*Statements of Financial Accounting Standards* establish new standards or amend those previously issued. *Statements of Financial Accounting Concepts* set forth fundamentals on which future financial accounting and reporting standards will be based. *Interpretations* clarify, explain, or elaborate on FASB Statements, Accounting Research Bulletins, or ASB Opinions. *Technical Bulletins* are staff documents that provide guidance on implementation and practice problems. *Exposure Drafts* are proposed Statements of Financial Accounting Standards or Concepts or proposed Interpretations issued for public comment prior to adoption. *Discussion Memorandums* and *Invitations to Comment* are documents issued on major projects as a basis for public comment, both in writing and, at times, at a public hearing. Proposed *Technical Bulletins* are issued for public comment prior to issuance of a final Bulletin. *Reports* are occasionally published based on work undertaken by the staff or by others in conjunction with the Board. This includes question-and-answer implementation guides. The newsletter *Status Report* carries news of developments in the standards-setting process and the status of technical projects.' The *Comprehensive Subscription Plan* ($220) gives copies of all these documents.

1134. **EITF Abstracts**. l. $292. Documentation of the *Emerging Issues Task Force*. (Combined with the task force issue summary packages and final minutes of each meeting the price is $578.)

1135. **Financial Accounting Research System. diskette**. q. $560/$495. Includes: Original Pronouncements; Current Text; Emerging Issues Task Force Abstracts; Implementation Guides; Comprehensive Topical Index.

1136. **Original Pronouncements and Current Text**. l. $441.

(2) #272 Governmental Accounting Standards Board *Prepayments* GASB Order Department, PO Box 30784, Hartford, CT 06150, USA. *Newsletter.*

'Established by FASB in 1984 to establish standards of financial accounting and reporting for state and local government entities.' *Comprehensive Subscription Plan* $120.

1137. **Governmental Accounting Research System. diskette**. $295/$260. 'Efficient and effective access to all the necessary governmental accounting literature. GARS has been demonstrated to show a significant reduction in research time. Using advanced search and retrieval software from *Folio Corporation* (the same software used by AICPA for its Electronic Research Products), GARS represents an important step in the research of governmental accounting issues.'

58. Lastly, we might note the existence of three bodies in the *United Kingdom* concerned with aspects of *competition* (*antitrust* tending in the *United States* to be dealt with more formally via the legal system):

(1) #273 Monopolies and Mergers Commission New Court, 48 Carey Street, London WC2A 2JT. t: (44 171) 324 1467; f: 324 1400. *Press and Information Adviser* t: (44 171) 324 1407.

Investigation of monopolies, mergers and other matters referred to the Commission under the Fair Trading Act 1973, the Competition Act 1980, and other Acts. "In accordance with section 83(3) and (3A) of the *Fair Trading Act 1973*, the Secretary of State has excluded from copies of the report, as laid before Parliament and as published, certain matters, publication of which appears to the Secretary of State to be against the public interest, or which he considers would not be in the public interest to disclose and which, in his opinion, would seriously and prejudicially affect certain interests. The omission is indicated by a note in the text."[128]

(2) #274 Office of Fair Trading Field House, Breams Buildings, London EC4A 1PR. t: (44 171) 242 2858; f: 269 8800. *Information Branch* t: (44 171) 242 2858; f: 269 8961 (liaison with the news media; production and marketing of consumer and trader information material).

Non-ministerial department whose principal objective is to promote and safeguard the economic interests of consumers. Administration of a number of Acts including the Consumer Credit Act 1974, the Competition Act 1980, and competition aspects of other legislation.

(3) #275 Panel on Takeovers and Mergers PO Box 226, The Stock Exchange Building, London EC2P 2JX. t: (44 171) 382 9026; f: 638 1554. *Annual Report*. Self-regulating organization.

1138. **City Code on Takeovers and Mergers**. l. £15.

1139. **Panel Statements**. i. £10.

The professional and trade bodies

59. It is not possible to overestimate the information providing importance of professional and trade bodies to the members of such bodies. Although many such organizations have a policy of restricting distribution of the information they generate to the organizations' membership, many do not. Further, even those associations who offer information services 'strictly for members only' will usually respond to serious queries with at least a lead of where to try elsewhere. This applies especially where the organization has a public advocacy role (and thus should try not to upset those outside the organization!). It is very difficult to get the balance right here, for many such bodies. On the one hand, the organizations need reasons for members to continue to pay their subscriptions (where membership is not a professional requirement). The quality and extent of the associations' information and library services can be one such reason. On the other hand, the organizations must continue to relate well to the 'general public' (and to attract new members). Many of the bodies attempt to resolve this dilemma by charging non- members (more) for such information/library services.

60. The professional and trade bodies which we reference in this particular chapter are divided into six groups – each group organized with regard to four geographical domains: United Kingdom, United States, Europe and International. The six groups are:

- The legal environment
- The economic and monetary environment
- The fiscal environment
- Accounting, auditing and reporting
- Bankruptcy and insolvency
- Trade and development

The last area, which is given only a limited indicative treatment here, allows a bridge to references to a sample of official organizations concerned with trade and development that have not found a place in the book so far. This will lead finally and appropriately to a section giving a brief overview of the *European Union*.

61. United Kingdom

The legal environment

(1) #276 Association of Pension Lawyers c/o The Honorary Secretary, 50 Stratton Street, London W1X 6NX. t: (44 171) 491 6766; f: 629 7900.

(2) #277 British Insurance Law Association c/o ARA Conference Services, 90 Bedford Court Mansions, Bedford Avenue, London WC1B 3AE. t: (44 171) 637 0333; f: 637 1893.

(3) #278 British Standards Institution Linford Wood, Milton Keynes MK14 6LE. t: (44 1908) 220022; f: 225080.

'Publishes British Standards which include British adoptions of international and European standards. Some of these cover areas such as financial transactions, banking procedures, identification cards and cost accounting. All British Standards and other BSI publications are listed in the:

1140. **BSI Standards Catalogue (Year)**. a.

'British Standards are also covered by the online catalogue *Standardline* which can be accessed via Fiz Technik and the CD-ROM *Perinorm* which in addition contains details of many foreign and international standards:

1141. **PERINORM Europe**. **cdrom**. m. £1300. 'The world's first bibliographic database of standards and technical regulations on compact disk ... National standards for Austria, France, Germany, Netherlands, Switzerland and the UK; European and international standards including ISO, IEC, CEN and CENELEC ... *PERINORM International* (£1710) contains (in addition) ... American standards, including ASTM, IEEE, UK and ANSI.'

(The database):

1142. **IHS International Standards and Specifications**. *Information Handling Services*. **online**.

Covers British Standards as well as a large number of US and other national and international standards. Full text standards in electronic format are available on:

1143. **Worldwide Standards Service on CD-ROM**. *Information Handling Services*. **cdrom**.

'BSI holds the secretariat for ISO 4217: Codes for the representation of currencies and funds. We are responsible for notifying the World Bank of changes in currency codes.'

(4) #279 Chartered Institute of Arbitrators International Arbitration Centre, 24 Angel Gate, City Road, London EC1V 2RS. t: (44 171) 837 4483; f: 837 4185.

1144. **Arbitration**. q. £67.

(5) #280 Law Society of England and Wales 50–52 Chancery Lane, London WC2A 1SX. t: (44 171) 242 1222; f: 405 9522.

1145. **Law Society's Gazette**. w. £70. **online**.

1146. **Law Society's Guardian Gazette**. m. £70. **online**.

(6) #281 Life Assurance Legal Society c/o Freeman Box Solicitors, 8 Bentinck Street, London W1M 6BJ. t: (44 171) 486 9041; f: 486 2552.

(7) #282 Society for Computers and Law 10 Hurle Crescent, Clifton, Bristol, BS8 2TA. t: (44 1272) 237393; f: 239305.

'To encourage and develop both IT for lawyers and IT related law . . . Membership is available to anyone involved or with an interest in IT and law and today its fast growing membership is approaching 2,000.'

1147. **Computers and Law**. bi-m.

The economic and monetary environment

(8) #283 Confederation of British Industry Centre Point, 103 New Oxford Street, London WC1A 1DU. t: (44 171) 379 7400; f: 240 1578.

1148. **CBI/Coopers & Lybrand financial services survey**. q. 'Covers a broad range of financial services activities including banking, insurance and building societies and securities houses. It offers a unique and up-to-date insight into the recent trends and future prospects for the majority of market sectors within financial services. Respondent organisations employ over half the workforce in the industry.'

The fiscal environment

(9) #284 Association of Her Majesty's Inspectors of Taxes and Senior Revenue Officials 2 Caxton Street, London SW1H 0QH. t: (44 171) 222 6242; f: 222 5926. e: ait@fdanews.demon.co.uk.

The trade union and professional association representing senior Inspectors of Taxes and other senior Inland Revenue employees: AIT is an independent section of *The Association of First Division Civil Servants*. The Association's publications are 'unavailable to non members'.

(10) #285 Institute of Taxation 12 Upper Belgrave Street, London SW1X 8BB. t: (44 171) 235 9381; f: 235 2562. The Institute sponsors the *Association of Taxation Technicians*.

1149. **Taxation Practitioner**. *Tolley*. m. £55.

Accounting, auditing and reporting

(11) #286 Association of Accounting Technicians 154 Clerkenwell Road, London EC1R 5AD. t: (44 171) 837 8600; f: 837 6970.

Founded in 1980 to provide a recognized qualification and a membership body for accounting support staff in accounting practice, industry and commerce and the public sector. Sponsored by the five major accountancy bodies in the UK.

(12) #287 Association of Authorised Public Accountants 10 Cornfield Road, Eastbourne, East Sussex, BN21 4QE. t: (44 1323) 410412; f: 733313.

'A Recognised Supervisory Body under the Provisions of the Companies Act 1989.'

(13) #288 Association of Cost & Executive Accountants Tower House, 141–149 Fonthill Road, London N4 3HF. t: (44 171) 272 3925; f: 281 5723.

Professional and examining body representing cost and executive accountants. 'The Association is the only accounting body which provides training to produce financial decision-makers and teaches management auditing.'

1150. **Executive Accountant**. q. £12. Official journal of the Association.

(14) #289 Auditing Practices Board PO Box 433, Moorgate Place, London EC2 2BJ. t: (44 171) 920 8650; f: 639 6009.

Established in 1991 by agreement between the six members of the *Consultative Committee of Accountancy Bodies*. Designed to lead the development of auditing practice in the UK so as to: establish higher standards of auditing; to meet the needs of users of financial information; to ensure public confidence in the auditing process.

(15) #290 Chartered Association of Certified Accountants 1 Woodside Place, Glasgow G3 7QF. t: (44 141) 331 1044. *Technical Department* 29 Lincoln's Inn Fields, London WC2A 3EE. t: (44 171) 242 6855; f: 831 8054.

1151. **Find. diskette**. £349. 'Financial Information Database . . . Complete with the SSAPs, FRSs, UITF abstracts, Statements of Accounting Standards and the Auditing Standards and Guidelines. By adding companies legislation, and further modules as they become available, Find builds into a complete computer based library allowing you to search for and cross reference a subject over many volumes.' Produced by the *Certified Accountants Educational Trust*.

(16) #291 Chartered Institute of Management Accountants 63 Portland Place, London W1N 4AB. t: (44 171) 637 2311; f: 631 5309. The Institute publishes in association with *Academic Press* an *Advanced Management Accounting & Finance Series* of short texts on specific topics, and with *Butterworth-Heinemann* a series of *CIMA Textbooks* and *CIMA Professional Handbooks*, as well as a substantial list of other books.

1152. **Management Accounting**. m. £30. **online**.

1153. **Management Accounting Research**. *Academic Press*. q. £105. 'Aims to serve as a vehicle for publishing original research in the field of management accounting. Such contributions will include case studies, scholarly papers, distinguished review articles, comments, and notes. The journal will also provide management accountants with comprehensive access to a variety of source material on management accounting topics via detailed abstracts and cumulative index of published material.'

(17) #292 Consultative Committee of Accountancy Bodies PO Box 433, Chartered Accountants Hall, Moorgate Place, London EC2P 2BJ. t: (44 171) 920 8100; f: 920 0547.

Established as a body to act in concert by: Chartered Association of Certified Accountants; Chartered Institute of Management Accountants; Chartered Institute of Public Finance and Accountancy; Institute of Chartered Accountants in Ireland; Institute of Chartered Accountants of England and Wales; Institute of Chartered Accountants of Scotland.

(18) #293 Institute of Chartered Accountants in England and Wales PO Box 433, Chartered Accountants' Hall, Moorgate Place, London EC2P 2BJ. t: (44 171) 628 7060; f: 628 1791. *Accountancy Books* is the publishing arm of the Institute, and publishes the majority of the serials cited below.

1154. **Accountancy**. m. **online**. Provides detailed coverage of the activities of the Institute, as well as a more general coverage of business activities.

1155. **Accountants Digests** 18/year. £230. Designed to provide an authoritative overview of the latest legislation, regulations, standards, and practice and financial management issues. Each issue is an in-depth analysis of one subject: e.g. *Banking Relationships* (1992); *Purchase of Own Shares* (1992); *Business Regulation and Financial Reporting in Germany* (1993); *Professional Liability of Practising Accountants* (1993).

1156. **Accounting and Business Research**. q. £75. Academic journal.

1157. **Accounting Standards (Year)**. a. £16.95. The accountant's authoritative source of reference on financial reporting.

1158. **Applying GAAP (Year): A Practical Guide to Financial Reporting**. a. £29.95. Designed as a clear and simple-to-understand guide to all UK accounting standards.

1159. **Auditing and Reporting (Year)**. a. £16.95. Includes all current UK Auditing Standards and Guidelines and Auditing Exposure Drafts, together with Institute statements on auditing and reporting.

1160. **Financial Reporting (Year)**. a. £59. A survey of UK reporting practice. Leading experts discuss topical and controversial issues in reporting practice, followed by an overview of current financial reporting practice, based on the financial reports of 300 major UK companies.

1161. **ICAEW Taxation Service**. *Gee*. l. £325. Major reference source on business and personal taxation. Quarterly updates, with each Autumn a complete revision covering all Finance Act and other provisions.

1162. **Implementing GAAS (Year): A Practical Guide to Auditing and**

Reporting. a. £29.95. 1993/4 was the first edition of this guide to GAAS (Generally Accepted Auditing Standards).

1163. **Institute of Chartered Accountants in England and Wales Directory of Firms (Year)**. *Macmillan Press*. a. £63. Over 13,500 entries, including details of specialization by industry/market.

1164. **Investment Business Compliance Manual**. l. £100/£70. Two supplements per year. Practical working manual to help set up and manage the systems required to ensure compliance under categories 1 and 2 of the Financial Services Act and the Institute's Regulations.

1165. **List of Members and Firms (Year)**. a. £38. Includes members of firms issued with Insolvency Licenses, and members authorized to carry on Investment Business under the Financial Services Act.

1166. **Practical Corporation Tax Manual (Year)**. a. £38.50.

1167. **SCAS & VSCAS Companies' Accounts Disclosure Checklist**. l. £80/ £65.

1168. **Tax Briefings**. l. £150. A series of 20 industry briefings, with each covering in 15–20 pages the major tax aspects. Coverage includes: insurance brokers, investment business, investment products, pension schemes, and stockbrokers.

1169. **Tax Digests**. m. £175. The latest legislation and its implications, technical developments and topical concerns.

1170. **Update**. m. £75. Designed to alert readers to forthcoming changes and the implications of new legislation, including: tax and tax cases; accounting and auditing developments; company law; financial information.

(19) #294 Institute of Company Accountants 40 Tyndalls Park Road, Bristol BS58 1PL. t: (44 117) 973 8261; f: 923 8292.

1171. **Company Accountant**. bi-m. £16.25.

(20) #295 Institute of Financial Accountants Burford House, 44 London Road, Sevenoaks, Kent TN13 1AS. t: (44 1732) 458080; f: 455848.

'Incorporated in 1916, the Institute was the first professional body to represent internal auditors . . . There are nearly 12,000 Fellows, Associates, Licentiates and Students in the Institute, and its second- tier body, the *International Association of Book-Keepers*, and representation now extends to more than 80 countries world-wide.'

1172. **Accounting World**. bi-m. £24.

(21) #296 Pensions Research Accountants Group c/o Membership Secretary (PRAG), Government Actuary's Department, 22 Kingsway, London WC2B 6LE.

'Independent research and discussion group for the development and exchange of ideas in the pensions field. Its efforts are concentrated mainly on the areas of reporting and accounting by pension schemes but it has also produced reports on other related matters. . . . The first, and probably the best known, publication of the Group was a report entitled "Financial Reports for Pension Funds". This report had a revolutionary effect on pension fund reporting and formed a blueprint for subsequent legislation and accounting practices. . . . The total membership is currently about 120 and is increasing all the time. The Group is always looking for new members since a constant stream of new ideas and enthusiasm is needed if PRAG is to continue to produce the high calibre reports for which it is renowned.' *PRAG Booklets* include: "Security of pension schemes" (£10); "Pension fund investments: Futures and options" (£25); "Investment performance for UK pension funds" (£12.50); "Pension fund surpluses" (£7.50); "Pension funds – Information needs of members and pensioners" (£2.50); "Pension scheme annual reports" (£7.50).

Bankruptcy and insolvency

(22) #297 Bankruptcy Association of Great Britain & Ireland 4 Johnson Close, Abraham Heights, Lancaster LA1 5EU. t: (1524) 64305; f: (1524) 844001.

(23) #298 Insolvency Practitioners Association Moor House, 119 London Wall, London EC2Y 5ET. t: (44 171) 374 4200; f: 588 7216.

'I regret that our information is just available to our members.'

(24) #299 Society of Practitioners of Insolvency 18–19 Long Lane, London EC1A 9HE. t: (44 171) 600 3375; f: 600 3602. *List of Members* (£100).

Trade and development

(25) #300 British Chambers of Commerce [Association of British Chambers of Commerce and Industry] 9 Tufton Street, London SW1P 3QB. t: (44 171) 222 1555; f: 799 2202.

'The coordinating, lobbying and representational arm of the Chambers of Commerce and Industry covering England, Wales, Scotland and Northern Ireland . . . As a member of a British Chamber you are part of a growing network of 95,000 UK businesses . . . Membership ranges from the sole trader to the multi-national. . . . UK Chambers are part of a European network of 800 Chambers; there are Chambers throughout the world. Those resources are at your disposal to help solve your problems.'

1173. **Business Briefing**. w. £94. 'Monitor of business statistics, news, regulations and information.'

1174. **Quarterly Economic Survey**. q. £200. 'Britain's most extensive business survey . . . drawn from a sample of over 7,000 companies in 15 regions.'

(i) *Chambernet UK* 22 Great Victoria Street, Belfast BT2 7BJ. t: (441 232) 312121; f: 312068. In association with *National Westminster Bank*.

1175. **Chambernet National Business Database. cdrom**. £1,800. 'Access to the British Chambers of Commerce high quality and previously unavailable national business database of company information. . . . Contains 83,000 business records and 143,000 named decision makers responsible for 19 key management functions.'

(26) #301 British Importers Confederation Rooms 309–315, 3rd Floor, Kemp House, 152–160 City Road, London EC1V 2NP. t: (44 171) 490 7262; f: 250 0965.

'The only British trade association established to protect and promote the interests of British importers irrespective of the goods traded . . . Its aim is to promote the freedom of British business to source internationally with the minimum of impedimenta, whilst providing a practical information and advice service to member companies, in an area of economic activity otherwise poorly served in this respect.' *BIC Information Circulars* 'are frequent information circulars disseminated to *BIC member companies only*, which update members on the latest developments in the trade and cover such matters as: changes in EEC regulations; DTI and HM Customs notices; trade policy developments; import trade opportunities; trade missions, seminars, new trade publications etc. *This valuable news circular is only available to member companies and organisations*'.

1176. **Directory of British Importers**. *Trade Research Publications*. a. £120. Two volumes. 4000 entries.

1177. **Importing Today**. *Setform*. bi-m. £22.

1178. **Worldtrade: A Practical Guide to Doing Business in Overseas Markets**. a. £21.50.'Information on: sourcing overseas, customs matters, transportation, trade finance, information systems and legal issues.'

(27) #302 British Invisibles Windsor House, 39 King Street, London EC2V 8DQ. t: (44 171) 600 1198; f: 606 4248. *Annual Report*. Regularly collates and publishes *statistics* on UK invisible earnings.

Formed 'to suggest, and where possible implement, measures for encouraging invisible earnings, both at home and abroad. Membership is representative of the principal contributors to Britain's invisible earnings, and BI has close links with government departments and the Bank of England. Approximately 90% of BI's funding comes from firms and institutions in the private sector of the economy'.

(28) #303 British International Freight Association Redfern

House, Browells Lane, Feltham, Middlesex TW13 7EP. t: (44 181) 844 2266; f: 890 5546. *Directory of Members* (£15).

(29) #304 British Trade and Investment Office 845 3rd Avenue, 11th Floor, New York, NY 10022, USA. t: (1 212) 745 0495; f: 745 0456.

(30) #305 Crown Agents St Nicholas House, St Nicholas Road, Sutton, Surrey SM1 1EL, UK. t: (44 181) 643 3311; f: 643 8232.

'We are a self-financing public body, and are independent of any commercial interest. We act with complete impartiality: our responsibility is to our clients alone – to safeguard their interests and to extract the best terms and conditions from suppliers and service organisations . . . On our clients' behalf we buy from manaufacturers and suppliers throughout the world, and take care of all the problem areas – specifications, sourcing, tendering, bid evaluation, negotiation, order administration, freighting, insurance and payment. All discounts and savings are passed on to clients . . . As well as working for UK government, we count among our clients governments and public sector bodies in over 120 countries, as well as the major national and international development and research organisations . . . Because we have no private shareholders our costs are low, consistent with our continuing need to develop our business along efficient and commercial lines . . . Our work in the development of banking and trade finance is practical and draws on our first-hand experience of what clients want to know and need to be able to do. Over 130 delegates attended our seventh *Round Table of the Small States Financial Forum* in Washington last September.'

(31) #306 TWIN 5–11 Worship Street, London EC2A 2BH. t: (44 171) 628 6878; f: 628 1859.

'*The Problem*: *TWIN* and *TWIN Trading* recognise that:

- the market tends to concentrate resources including information, and hence power, in the hands of a relatively small section of society
- those with most resources become market makers while others enter the market in positions of weakness
- profit for the few and growth for some thrive on the uncertainty, inequality and the vulnerability of those who have few productive assets or only their labour to sell
- atomised decision making within the market can produce long-term destructive consequences, for example on the environment.

The Solution: *TWIN* and *TWIN Trading* aim to be part of the solution by working together with small producer associations to:

- assist in overcoming obstacles to independent trade
- ensure more benefits of production remain in the hands of producers
- enable producers to implement social and economic development programmes from the extra income earned.'

1179. The **Network**. q. £10. 'Aims to keep networkers in touch and to provide appropriate and practical information on trade and technology issues.'

Official trade and development bodies

(32) #307 Overseas Development Administration 94 Victoria Street, London SW1E 5JL. t: (44 171) 917 7000; f: 917 0016. The *Library* (t: (441 355) 843163/3599/3246) contains material on aid and developing countries, with a separate *Statistics Library*: t: (44 355) 843272. *Newsletter*.

Deals with British development assistance to overseas countries. Includes capital aid on concessional terms provided directly to developing countries or through multilateral aid organizations, including the United Nations and its specialized agencies. The world is divided into about a dozen regions each of which is serviced by a separate department. Within the International Division there is also an *International Financial Institutions Department*: t: (44 171) 917 0605; f: 917 0219.

62. United States

The legal environment

(1) #308 American Arbitration Association 140 West 51st Street, New York, NY 10020–1203. t: (1 212) 484 4000; f: 307 4387.

Public-service, not-for-profit organization offering a broad range of dispute resolution services, including in banking, insurance, international trade, securities etc. The Association co-sponsors and houses the *World Arbitration Institute* (t: (1 212) 484 4117), which serves as a centre for information, publications and education in international commercial arbitration.

1180. **Arbitration & The Law (Year)**. *Transnational Juris Publications*. a. $65. 'Contains digests of all the most important cases, legislation, and rules of the previous year.'

1181. **Arbitration Journal**. q. $50. **online**.

(2) #309 American Bar Association 750 N Lake Shore Drive, Chicago, IL 60611. t: (1 312) 988 5000; f: 988 6281. To order publications by phone or to receive additional information, contact *Member Services*: t: (1 312) 988 5522.

The national organization of the US legal profession, founded in 1878, and now the largest voluntary professional organization in the world, with a membership of more than 350,000 – representing about half the lawyers in the United States. Membership is open to lawyers admitted to practice and in good standing before the bar of any state or territory of the USA.

1182. **ABA Journal**. m. $66. **online**. The Association's official journal. The editorial focus is primarily for lawyers in private law firms with a general practice. Circulation: 431,000.

1183. **Bibliography of American Bar Association's Publications. online**. Also online are descriptions of *Current ABA Research Projects.*

1184. **Washington Letter**. m. $30. From the *Governmental Affairs Office.* Newsletter reports on congressional activity affecting legislation of interest to lawyers and the organized bar.

1185. **Washington Summary**. w. (while Congress in session). $55. From the *Governmental Affairs Office.* Tracks legislation and federal regulations of interest to lawyers by abstracting the *Congressional Record* and the *Federal Register.*

Sections of the Association include:

- *Antitrust Law* The heart of the Section's activity lies in its more than 40 committees which cover antitrust exemptions, international trade, and the Robinson-Patman and Sherman Acts.

1186. **Antitrust**. 3/year. $30. **online**. Publishes articles on developments in antitrust law.

1187. **Antitrust Law Journal**. q. $30. **online**.

- *Business Law* More than 375 committees and subcommittees cover such topics as banking law, corporate law, futures regulation, and federal regulation of securities. [Questions on bankruptcy are to be addressed to the 'Section on Business Law' at the Chicago address: 750 N Lake Shore Drive, Chicago, IL 60611. t: (1 312) 988 5000.]

1188. **Business Law Today**. 6/year. $28.

1189. **Business Lawyer**. q. $28. **online**. Journal of business and financial law.

- *International Law and Practice* 'International Law News' is a quarterly newsletter available to Section members only.

1190. **International Lawyer**. q. $31. **online**. Directed to lawyers with an interest in the fields of international business transactions, public international law, and comparative law.

- *Real Property, Probate and Trust Law* Organized into two Divisions: the *Real Property Division* and the *Probate and Trust Division*.

1191. **Probate and Property**. 6/year. $34. For lawyers devoting a large part of their practice to real estate law or the laws dealing with wills, trusts, and estates.

1192. **Real Property, Probate and Trust Journal**. q. $28. Scholarly articles in the fields of estate planning, tax planning, and real property law.

- *Taxation Newsletter* (q. $20).

This Section is 'one of the nation's largest and most authoritative sources of up-to-the-minute information and expertise concerning every substantive area of tax law'.

1193. **Tax Lawyer**. q. $83. **online**. Journal of scholarly articles.

- *Tort and Insurance Practice* Analyzes developments in all branches of tort and insurance law and trial practice and offers concrete solutions.

1194. **Fidelity and Surety News**. q. $100. Provides a current digest of opinions about construction contract bonds, financial institution and other bonds, court bonds, and surety's rights.

1195. The **Brief**. q. $18.

1196. **Tort and Insurance Law Journal**. q. $100. **online**. Provides a current digest of opinions about construction contract bonds, financial institution and other bonds, court bonds, and surety's rights.

There is also:

- *Forum Commission on Franchising*

1197. **Franchise Law Journal**. q. $31. **online**. Legal trends in franchising.

The Association offers two computer-based services:

- *ABA/net* This service – offered in conjunction with *AT&T EasyLink Services* – provides access to a range of online services, including:
    - *Colleague Directory* Allows searching for other legal professionals across areas of speciality and geographic location
    - *Commercial Online Search Services* Access to both LEXIS/NEXIS and WESTLAW as well as to over 1000 other online databases
    - *Corporate 250 Program* Facilitates immediate exchange of time-sensitive documents and information
    - *Legal Conferences* Electronic forum for discussing topics of interest with colleagues, clients or vendors nationwide
    - *MVP (Maximum Value Products) Program* Unlimited use of state law material via the LEXIS/NEXIS service at one predictable monthly charge

- *AMBAR* Offers 'instant access to ABA facts', containing data on all Association units, including their publications, programs, activities, and products. Can be accessed directly through the online services *LEXIS/NEXIS* or *WESTLAW*; or by calling the AMBAR number in Chicago where an ABA staff member will conduct a key word search for the enquirer. In either case, the enquirer will 'learn the answer to the two most often asked questions: "Does the ABA have (name your subject)?" or "Is the ABA working on (name your subject)?" '.

(3) #310 American Corporate Counsel Association 1225 Connecticut Avenue NW, Suite 302, Washington, DC 20036. t: (1 202) 296 4522; f: 331 7454. *Newsletters.*

Produce a number of publications: e.g. 'Insider trading handbook: Model policies and procedures' ($60); 'Legal audits of multinational companies' ($25).

1198. **ACCA Docket**. **online**.

(4) #311 American Foreign Law Association c/o Whitman and Ransom, 200 Park Avenue, New York, NY 10166. t: (1 212) 351 3277; f: 351 3131.

1199. **American Journal of Comparative Law**.

(5) #312 American Legislative Exchange Council 214 Massachusetts Avenue NE, Suite 240, Washington, DC 20002. t: (1 202) 547 4646; f: 547 8142.

(6) #313 American National Standards Institute 11 W 42nd Street, New York, NY 10036. t: (1 212) 642 4900; f: 302 1286.

Non-profit organization which, among a wide range of standard-setting activities, sponsors industry standards for financial communications and transaction processing.

(7) #314 American Society of International Law 2223 Massachusetts Avenue NW, Washington, DC 20008–2864. t: (1 202) 939 6000; f: 797 7133. *Newsletter.*

Professional membership organization committed to promoting the study and use of law in international affairs. Founded in 1906, the Society serves as a forum, research centre and publisher for scholars, officials, practising lawyers, students and others from around the world.

1200. **American Journal of International Law**. q. $120. **online**. ' "Nobody working in international law can do without the *American Journal of International Law.* This view is held not only in the West but in the East as well." (*Frowein: Max Planck Institute for Comparative Public Law and International Law*). With almost 7000 subscribers worldwide, the *Journal* is indispensable for all professionals working in international law, economics, trade and foreign affairs.'

1201. **Basic Documents of International Economic Law**. q. **online**. Project of the Society's *International Economic Law Interest Group.* Originally published in 1990 by Commerce Clearing House, it includes coverage of the regulation of international trade, finance and foreign investment, and of regional economic organizations, and is now kept up-to-date online.

1202. **International Legal Materials**. bi-m. $170. **online**. Reproduces full-text documents in all areas of finance and banking, and has included important documents from the *Basle Committee, International Organiz-*

ation of Securities Commissions, regional economic organizations, multilateral development banks etc.

12039. **Proceedings of the International Meeting**. a. $60. **online**.

(8) #315 Association of Certified Fraud Examiners 716 West Avenue, Austin, TX 78701. t: (800) 245 3321, (0800) 962049 (uk)/ (1 512) 478 9070; f: 478 9297.

'The professional organization for fraud examiners. The mission of the Association is to reduce the incidence of fraud and white-collar crime, and to assist the Membership in its detection and deterrence. To accomplish its mission, the Association:

- Provides bona fide qualifications for Certified Fraud Examiners through administering the Uniform Examination for Certified Fraud Examiners;
- Sets high standards for admission, including demonstrated competence through mandatory continuing professional education;
- Requires Certified Fraud Examiners to adhere to a strict code of professional conduct and ethics and monitors adherence by Members;
- Serves as the international representative for Certified Fraud Examiners to business and government; and
- Provides leadership to inspire public confidence in the integrity, objectivity, and professionalism of Certified Fraud Examiners.'

1204. **Fraud Examiners Manual**. l. $249. Two volumes. **diskette**. $199.

(9) #316 Association of Commercial Finance Attorneys c/o Connecticut National Bank, 1 Corporate Center, 18th Floor MSN 712, Hartford, CT 06013. t: (1 203) 520 7094; f: 240 5077.

(10) #317 Association of Defense Trial Attorneys 600 Bank 1 Building, Peoria, IL 61602. t: (1 309) 676 0400; f: 676 3374.

(11) #318 Association of Life Insurance Counsel c/o Lincoln National Corporation, 200 E Berry Street, Fort Wayne, IN 46802. t: (1 219) 455 5582; f: 455 5403.

'The price for the Association's annual Proceedings is $40, but the Board will be considering a price increase in May.'

(12) #319 Association of Real Estate License Law Officials PO Box 129, Centerville, UT 84014. t: (1 801) 298 5572.

(13) #320 Association of Securities and Exchange Commission Alumni c/o Stroock & Stroock & Lavan, 1150 17th Street NW, Suite 600, Washington, DC 20036–4603. t: (1 202) 452 9250; f: 293 2293.

(14) #321 Banking Law Institute 22 W 21st Street, New York, NY 10010. t: (1 212) 645 7880; f: 675 4883.

(15) #322 Commercial Law League of America 175 West Jackson Boulevard, Suite 1541, Chicago, IL 60604–2703. t: (1 312) 431 1305; f: 431 1669.

1205. **Commercial Law Bulletin**. bi-m. **online**.

1206. **Commercial Law Journal**. q. $75. **online**. Discusses legal aspects of business.

(16) #323 Committee to Support the Antitrust Laws c/o Jonathan W Cuneo, 317 Massachusetts Avenue NE, Suite 300, Washington, DC 20003. t: (1 202) 789 3962; f: 789 1813.

(17) #324 Conference on Consumer Finance Law c/o Peterson & Ross, 200 E Randolph Drive, Suite 7300, Chicago, IL 60601. t: (1 312) 861 1400.

1207. **Consumer Finance Law Quarterly Report**. q. $50. **online**.

(18) #325 Customs and International Trade Bar Association Office of the President, One Astor Plaza, 1515 Broadway, New York, NY 10036. t: (1 212) 944 7900. *Newsletter*.

'In terms of function this Association is, I believe, a fairly standard Association of practicing attorneys which is characterised by the fact that its members are highly specialized in the fields of customs and international trade and its membership is therefore small. Membership requirements are only that one has to be admitted to the Bar and admitted to practice before the *United States Court of International Trade* which hears most actions in the subject speciality areas.'

1208. **Research Index: US International Trade Laws**. q. $450.

(19) #326 ERISA Industry Committee 1400 L Street NW, Suite 350, Washington, DC 20005. t: (1 202) 789 1400; f: 789 1120.

(20) #327 Federal Bar Association 1815 H Street NW, Suite 408, Washington, DC 20006–3697. t: (1 202) 638 0252; f: 775 0295.

'With over 200 titles available, the Federal Bar Association is one of the leading resources of not only the most up-to-date but also historical information on subjects ranging from administrative practice and government contracts to immigration and taxation. Chances are, if you're looking for a publication dealing with a specific area of federal law or practice, you'll find it in this catalog.'

1209. **Federal Bar News & Journal**. 10/year. $25. **online**.

1210. **Federal Lawyer**. m. $30. 'The Official Publication of The Federal Bar Association.' Volume 42, No 1, January 1995 was the 75th Anniversary Issue.

1211. **Insurance Tax Seminar**. a. $50.

1212. **Lawyers Job Bulletin Board**. m. $30.

1213. **Tax Law Conference**. a. $75.

(21) #328 Federation of Insurance and Corporate Counsel 302 Centre Lane, PO Box 11, Walpole, MA 02081–0111.

1214. **Federation of Insurance and Corporate Counsel Quarterly**. q. $26.

(22) #329 National Association for Law Placement 1666 Connecticut Avenue, Suite 325, Washington, DC 20009. t: (1 202) 667 1666; f: 265 6735.

(23) #330 National Association of Attorneys General 444 N Capitol Street, Suite 339, Washington, DC 20001. t: (1 202) 434 8000; f: 434 8008.

1215. **Antitrust Report**. bi-m. $145.

1216. **Financial Crimes Report**. bi-m. $100. 'Published under a grant from the *US Department of Justice*, reports on a variety of efforts to address profit-motivated crimes.'

(24) #331 National Association of Bond Lawyers 2000 Pennsylvania Avenue NW, Suite 9000, Washington, DC 20006. t: (1 202) 778 2244; f: 778 2201.

(25) #332 National Association of Securities and Commercial Law Attorneys 1301 K Street NW, E Tower, Suite 650. Washington, DC 20005. t: (1 202) 789 3963; f: 789 1813.

(26) #333 National Conference of Commissioners on Uniform State Laws 676 North St Clair Street, Suite 1700, Chicago, IL 60611. t: (1 312) 915 0195; f: 915 0187.

(27) #334 National Conference of State Legislatures 1560 Broadway, Suite 700, Denver, CO 80202. t: (1 303) 830 2054; f: 863 8003.

1217. **Fiscal Letter**. bi-m. $35. 'Prepared by and for state fiscal experts, it gives a national perspective on state issues. Regular features include recent state tax and budget actions, appropriations issues and tax reform measures.'

1218. **LegisBrief**. w. $79. 'Each issue . . . covers a pressing topic in state government, analyzes successful approaches taken, offers alternative courses of action and offers better understanding of important developments.' For example: 'Interstate banking and branching' (June 1994).

1219. **Legislative Finance Papers**. i. 'Comprehensive studies of state tax revenue and expenditure issues.'

1220. **State Legislatures**. m. $49. 'Unbiased insight on state issues and politics.'

(28) #335 National Society of Compliance Professionals PO Box 351, Lakeville, CT 06039. t: (1 203) 435 0843; f: 435 3005.

'Provides a support system for everyone in securities compliance . . . We are pleased by your interest and would also be pleased to be mentioned in your forthcoming book. However, I should point out that our regular publications, the *NSCP Currents* and the *HotLine Memo*, are sent to NSCP members as part of their membership benefits and are not, generally speaking, available to persons who are not members of NSCP. Perhaps you would care to mention this . . . For your information, the *Current* contains articles of interest to compliance professionals, and the *Hotline* keeps them informed of legislative and regulatory developments.'

(29) #336 National Standards Association 1200 Quince Orchard Blvd, Gaithersburg, MD 20878, USA. t: (1 301) 590 2300; f: 990 8378.

1221. **CSI Congressional Record Reporter**. d. Price varies.

1222. **CSI Federal Register**. d. Price varies.

(30) #337 Practising Law Institute 810 Seventh Avenue, New York, NY 10019. t: (1 212) 765 5700.

1223. **Annual Institute on Securities Regulation**. a. $85.

(31) #338 Real Estate Law Institute 303 W Cypress, PO Box 12528, San Antonio, TX 78212. t: (1 210) 225 2897; f: 225 8450.

The economic and monetary environment

(32) #339 American Business Conference 1730 K Street NW, Suite 1200, Washington, DC 20006. t: (1 202) 822 9300; f: 467 4070.

(33) #340 American Institute for Economic Research Division Street, Great Barrington, MA 01230. t: (1 413) 528 1216; f: 528 0103.

(34) #341 Business Council 888 17th Street, NW, No 506, Washington, DC 20006. t: (1 202) 298 7650; f: 785 0296.

(35) #342 Business Roundtable 200 Park Avenue, Suite 2222, New York, NY 10166. t: (1 212) 682 6370.

(36) #343 Concord Coalition 1025 Vermont Avenue NW, Suite 810, Washington, DC 20005. t: (800) 231 6800/(1 202) 737 1077.

'A grass roots movement to restore fiscal sanity to our nation. Mounting levels of federal debt threaten our economic vitality and darken the future of generations to come. We must put our nation back on a path to prosperity . . . Concord coalition chapters across America are sending a message to our elected officials that the American people are ready to make the tough choices necessary to restore our nation's economic vitality.'

(37) #344 Conference Board 845 Third Avenue, New York, NY 10022. *Customer Orders and Service Department* t: (1 212) 339 0345; f: 980 7014.

1224. **Across the Board. online**.

1225. **Chief Economist's Letter**.

1226. **Economic Road Maps**.

1227. **Economic Times**.

1228. **Global Business Briefing**.

1229. **International Economic Scoreboard**.

1230. **US Economic Outlook**.

- *Conference Board Europe* t: (32 2) 640 62 40; f: 640 67 35

(38) #345 Congressional Economic Leadership Institute 201 Massachusetts Avenue NE, Suite C8, Washington, DC 20002. t: (1 202) 546 5007; f: 546 7037.

(39) #346 Council on Competitiveness 1401 H Street NW, Suite 650, Washington, DC 20005. t: (1 202) 682 4292; f: 682 5150. *Newsletter*.

1231. **Competitiveness Index**. a. $10. 'US performance is compared with that of other Summit 7 countries in this annual assessment of America's competitive position. The Index addresses four key areas: investment, productivity, trade and standard of living.'

(40) #347 Exploratory Project for Economic Alternatives 1000 Connecticut Avenue NW, Suite 9, Washington, DC 20036. t: (1 202) 483 6667; f: 986 7938.

(41) #348 National Economic Association c/o University of Michigan, School of Business, Ann Arbor, MI 48109–1234. t: (1 313) 763 0121; f: 763 5688. For the promotion of blacks in the economic profession and the understanding of the economic problems confronting the black community.

1232. **Review of Black Political Economy**. q. $76.

(42) #349 National Economists Club PO Box 19281, Washington, DC 20036. t: (1 703) 532 9048; f: 534 2137.

(43) #350 OMB Watch 1742 Connecticut Avenue NW, Washington, DC 20009. t: (1 202) 234 8494; f: 234 8584. *Newsletter*.

'A nonprofit research, educational, and advocacy organization that monitors Executive Branch activities affecting nonprofit, public interest, and community groups. As the name implies, the White House *Office of Management and Budget* (OMB) is OMB Watch's main focus since OMB oversees nearly all governmental functions. Our goal is to encourage broad public participation in government decision-making to promote a more open and accountable government.'

1233. **Government Information Insider**. 'Covers issues regarding government information and regulation.'

(44) #351 Rebuild America Coalition 1301 Pennsylvania Avenue, Suite 501, Washington, DC 20004. t: (1 202) 393 2792; f: 737 9153.

(45) #352 Redeem Our Country PO Box 333, 1051 South Lemon Street, Suite E, Fullerton, CA 92632. t: (1 714) 871 2950; f: 871 5353.

'A national volunteer organization dedicated to abolishing the Federal Reserve System and fractional banking . . . (It) has a membership of over 35,000 and that could be expanded to a couple of million if we had the time, staff and money to do so.'

1234. **National Educator**. m. $20. 'The number one, non- affiliated, generally circulated, conservative, monthly tabloid newspaper in the nation . . . We believe in God, in the Constitution, in the Bill of Rights, the free enterprise system, the right to keep and bear arms, protection of the family and a strong national defense force. We are opposed to strong central government, a privately owned money system (the Federal Reserve), the Genocide Treaty, abortion, the welfare society, government-run public schools, the terror tactics of the IRS, excessive aid to Zionist Israel, Liberation Theology, "no win" wars and trade and loans to the communists. Our list of for and against is much longer.'

(46) #353 Women's Economic Round Table 866 United Nations Plaza, Suite 4052, New York, NY 10017. t: (1 212) 759 4360; f: 666 1625.

The fiscal environment

(47) #354 American College of Tax Counsel c/o University of Alabama, Tuscaloosa, AL 35487.

1235. **American Journal of Tax Policy**. s-a. $22. **online**.

(48) #355 American Tax Policy Institute PO Box 66115, 1050 Connecticut Avenue NW, Washington, DC 20036. t: (1 202) 457 8050; f: 429 4997.

(49) #356 Common Ground – USA 1475 Terrace View Lane, Plymouth, MN 55447. t: (1 612) 473 1235; f: 475 0190.

- *Georgist Registry*

(50) #357 The Fair Tax 11015 Cumpston Street, North Hollywood, CA 91610. t: (1 818) 763 1000; f: 769 7358.

(51) #358 Federation of Tax Administrators 444 N Capitol Street, Suite 348, Washington, DC 20001. t: (1 202) 624 5890; f: 624 7888.

(52) #359 Free the Eagle 666 Pennsylvania Avenue SE, Suite 402, Washington, DC 20004. t: (1 703) 257 4782; f: 257 4758.

(53) #360 FSC/DISC Tax Association 2975 W Chester Avenue, Purchase, NY 10577. t: (1 212) 370 3995; f: (1 914) 723 6270.

(54) #361 Henry George Foundation of America 2000 Century Plaza, Number 238, Columbia, MD 21044. t: (1 410) 740 1177; f: 740 3279.

(55) #362 Institute of Tax Consultants 7500 212th Street SW, Number 205, Edmonds, WA 98206. t: (1 206) 774 3521; f: 672 0461.

(56) #363 Multistate Tax Commission 444 N Capitol Street NW, Suite 425, Washington, DC 20001. t/f: (1 202) 624 8819.

1236. **Multistate Tax Commission Review**. i. $35 for four issues. 'Significant developments and policy issues in state taxation of multijurisdictional business activity.'

(57) #364 National Association of Enrolled Agents 200 Orchard Drive, Gaithersburg, MD 20878. t: (1 301) 212 9608; f: 990 1611.

Produce a variety of publications for 'professional practice management & promotion'.

(58) #365 National Association of Tax Practitioners 720 Association Drive, Appleton, WI 54914–1483. t: (1 414) 749 1040; f: 749 1062. *Newsletter*.

'Serving the needs of the tax preparation profession since 1979.'

1237. **Tax Practitioners Journal**. q. $30. Articles in the *Winter 1994/95* issue include: 'New tax increases on the horizon?'; 'Is tax preparer registration in the future?'; 'IRS cracks down on tax protest schemes'; and 'The future of electronic filing . . . As tax filing becomes more and more electronic, what changes and trends are being implemented to enhance the tax filing system?' Quoting from the last article: 'In 1994, approximately 13.5 million tax returns were filed electronically. By the year 2000, the IRS expects to receive 80 million returns from individuals and practitioners using this method . . . On-line services are another vehicle for reaching those who file their own returns. Subscribers to on-line services can file their tax returns conveniently and inexpensively from their own computers, Last year, *CompuServe* offered on-line electronic filing to its subscribers. Check with your local IRS electronic filing coordinator to learn which on-line services are available this year.'

(59) #366 National Tax Association – Tax Institute of America 5310 E Main Street, Suite 104, Columbus, OH 43213. t: (1 614) 864 1221; f: 864 1375.

1238. **National Tax Journal**. q. $80. **online**. Articles on taxation and public finance in the United States and foreign countries. The subscription includes the *Proceedings of the Annual Conference on Taxation* and copies of the quarterly *NTA Forum*.

(60) #367 Tax Analysts 6830 N Fairfax Drive, Arlington, VA 22213. t: (1 703) 533 4600; f: 533 4444.

'Nonprofit organization founded in 1970. Publications are our principal means of rendering public service. These publications provide forums for the discussion of a wide variety of tax ideas. By facilitating discussion, we seek to encourage development of fiscal systems that are fair, simple, and economically efficient . . . Our complete *Access Service* lets you order the full text of any document summarized in any of Tax Analysts' publications.'

1239. **Current Internal Revenue Code, Treasury Regulations, and IRS Publications. cdrom**. $299.

1240. **Daily Tax Highlights and Documents**. d. $1999.

1241. **Daily TaxFax**. d. $1629. Delivered by fax.

1242. **Exempt Organization Tax Review**. m. $499. Covers tax developments affecting nonprofit organizations and contains full-text documents of important court cases and rulings.

1243. **Highlights & Documents**. d. $1749. 'The nation's most comprehensive daily tax publication.'

1244. **Index Digest Bulletin**. bi-a. $99. 'Summaries of all letter rulings and technical advice memorandums released by the IRS during a six-month period.' There is also a complimentary *Full-Text IRS Letter Rulings* which also covers technical advice memorandums.

1245. **Insurance Tax Review**. m. $299. **online**.

1246. **IRS Letter Rulings and Technical Advice Memorandums**. w. $999. **cdrom**. $299. (1990 to present; 1980–1989 $199.)

1247. **IRS Revenue Rulings and Revenue Procedures. cdrom**. $299.

1248. **Letter Ruling Review**. m. $99. **online**. 'Discusses significant developments in recently issued IRS letter rulings and technical advice memorandums.'

1249. **State Tax Notes**. w. $749.

1250. **Tax Directory**. q. $249. **online**. Covers public and private sector personnel and organizations involved with tax in the US.

1251. **Tax Notes**. w. $1499. **online** 'The finest tax magazine published in the United States.' There is also a *Tax Notes Microfiche Database*, where 'each week, Tax Analysts places from 3,000 to 5,000 pages of full-text documentation'. ($1999).

1252. **Tax Notes International**. w. $749. **online**. There is also a *Tax Notes International Microfiche Database*. ($699).

1253. **Tax Notes Today**. **online**. d. "Updated daily, this is a US federal tax information database . . . The Monday issue also contains the *Internal Revenue Bulletin*" (*Bibliodata Fulltext Sources Online*).

1254. **Tax Practice**. w. $199. The *Tax Practice Microfiche Database* ($699) includes Court Petitions and Complaints.

1255. **Tax-Related Documents**. w. $499. 'A collection of unique and hard-to-find tax documents.'

1256. **TaxBase**. **diskette**. $247.50 per tax professsional in the firm. 'Comprehensive, electronic tax service that is delivered daily in Lotus Notes format. It consists of five databases: *Tax Notes Today*, *State Tax Notes*, *Tax Notes International*, *Petitions and Complaints*, and the *TaxBase Edition of Highlights & Documents*.'

1257. **US Tax Treaty Reference Library**. **microfiche**. 'By far the most comprehensive collection of US tax treaty documents.'

(61) #368 Tax Council 1801 K Street, NW, Suite 7202, Washington, DC 20006. t: (1 202) 822 8062; f: 466 3918.

'Nonprofit business-supported organization concerned with Federal Tax Policy.'

(62) #369 Tax Executives Institute 1001 Pennsylvania Avenue NW, Suite 320, Washington, DC 20004–2505. t: (1 202) 638 5601; f: 638 5607.

'The professional association of corporate tax executives . . . Members are responsible for tax affairs of more than 2,700 leading companies in the United States and Canada.'

1258. **Tax Executive**. bi-m. $105. **online**. 'Has approximately 5,800 subscribers. Approximately 5,000 are members of the *Tax Executives Institute* . . . Other paid subscribers are tax professionals engaged in accounting and law practices; university, law, or business libraries; and government officials and agencies.'

(63) #370 Tax Foundation 1250 H Street, NW, Suite 750, Washington, DC 20005–3908. t: (1 202) 783 2760; f: 783 4687.

Respected research organization having in membership individuals and business firms interested in federal, state, and local government fiscal matters.

1259. **Facts and Figures on Government Finance**. a. $55. 'The taxing and spending practices and fiscal activities of government at all levels.'

1260. **Special Reports**. bi-m. $50. 'Distributed to policy makers, tax and budget analysts, and corporate executives nationwide. Each issue provides an economic analysis of a topical issue, as written by Foundation economists.'

1261. **Tax Features**. m. $50. 'Each issue includes an article by a member of the Senate Finance Committee or House Ways and Means Committee.'

1262. (Year) **State Fiscal Prospects**. Examines the current fiscal situations and tax proposals for all 50 states.

(64) #371 Tax Reform Action Coalition 1725 K Street NW, Suite 710, Washington, DC 20006. t: (1 202) 872 0885; f: 785 0586.

Accounting, auditing and reporting

(65) #372 Accountants for the Public Interest 1012 14th Street, NW, Suite 906, Washington, DC 20005. t: (1 202) 347 1668; f: 347 1663.

1263. **API Account**. q. $35. Includes reports on national and affiliate volunteer activities, and on issues relating to volunteer accounting.

(66) #373 Accreditation Council for Accountancy and Taxation 1010 N Fairfax Street, Alexandria, VA 22314–1574. t: (1 703) 549 6400; f: 549 2984.

(67) #374 American Association of Attorney-Certified Public Accountants 24196 Alicia Parkway, Suite K, Mission Veijo, CA 92691. t: (1 714) 768 0336.

(68) #375 American Institute of Certified Public Accountants 1211 Avenue of the Americas, New York, NY 10036. t: (1 212) 575 6200. *Publications* Harborside Financial Center, 201 Plaza Three, Jersey City, NJ 07311–3811. t: (800) 862 4272; f: (1 201) 938 3329.

The national professional association of certified public accountants (accountants licensed to practice public accounting), an organization of about 300,000 members. AICPA produce or distribute a large number of publications, many of which are however 'available to AICPA members only'. Examples of those more generally available are:

1264. **AICPA Audit and Accounting Guides**. *CCH*. l. Three volumes. 'Reproduces updated versions of the many AICPA audit guides previously published as soft-covered books.'

1265. **AICPA Audit and Accounting Manual**. *CCH*. l. 'Developed by the American Institute of Certified Public Accountants as a single reference, containing practical suggestions for carrying out the varied technical tasks that make up an accountant's daily work.'

1266. **AICPA Financial Statement Preparation Manual**. l.

1267. **AICPA Professional Standards**. *CCH*. l. $149. **diskette**. $200. Contains all pronouncements and interpretations currently in effect.

1268. **AICPA Technical Practice Aids**. l. Two volumes. 'The more timely and important inquiries handled by the American Institute of Certified Public Accountants' Technical Information Service are reproduced here in question and answer format, organized by subject, and topically indexed for easy access. Also included are Statements of Position from the Institute's Accounting Standards and Auditing Standards Divisions, Issue Papers and Practice Bulletins.'

1269. **Audit and Accounting Guides Service**. l. $315. **diskette** $370. Keeps subscribers current on their particular industry or area, with timely updates, new audit and accounting pronouncements, and annual *Audit Risk Alerts*. The material for individual subject areas is available for separate purchase as paperbacks.

1270. **CD-NAARS**. **cdrom**. $2195. 'Now, combining the enormous storage capacity of optical disks with the powerful, easy-to-use search and retrieval software of Folio Corporation, the AICPA offers you its popular database on CD-ROM. It contains the searchable full text of financial statements, related notes, and auditor's reports, exactly as they are presented in over 4,000 annual reports to shareholders. But unlike on-line services, CD-NAARS lets you make unlimited searches without incurring the extra costs for time charges and multiple search fees.' NAARS (*National Automated Accounting Research System*) is also available as part of the *TOTAL On-Line and Accounting Library* on Lexis/Nexis.

1271. **CPA Client Bulletin**. m. **online**. Covers the range of topics a CPA would discuss with small business and tax clients.

1272. **CPA Letter**. 10/year. $40. **online**. A news report to members. Circulation: 290,000.

1273. **Index to Accounting and Auditing Technical Pronouncements**. **disk**. Indicates which statement, bulletin, guide, interpretation, government regulation should be taken into account for the full range of audit and accounting principles, practices and procedures.

1274. **Practising CPA**. m. **online**.

1275. **Journal of Accountancy**. m. $69. **online**. Reports on new developments, trends, management advisory services, taxation, education, professional subjects.

1276. **Tax Adviser**. m. $94. **online**. Reports and analyses of new tax developments and money-saving opportunities in tax planning and tax compliance.

(69) #376 American Society of Women Accountants 1755 Lynnfield Road, Suite 222, Memphis, TN 38119. t: (1 901) 680 0470; f: 680 0505

(70) #377 American Women's Society of Certified Public Account-

ants 401 N Michigan Avenue, Chicago, IL 60611. t: (1 312) 644 6610; f: 321 6869.

(71) #378 Association of Government Accountants 2200 Mount Vernon Avenue, Alexandria, VA 22301–1314. t: (1 703) 684 6931; f: 548 9367.

1277. **Government Accountants Journal**. q. $55. **online**.

(72) #379 BKR International 40 Exchange Place, Suite 1100, New York, NY 10005. t: (1 212) 809 5796; f: 809 5965.

'Organization comprised of accounting firms located in major cities . . . BKR products and services . . . are available only to members.'

(73) #380 Institute of Internal Auditors International Headquarters, 249 Maitland Avenue, Altamonte Springs, FL 32701–4201, USA. t: (1 407) 830 7600; f: 831 5171. *Also* IIA-United Kingdom, 13 Abbeville Mews, 88 Clapham Park Road, London SW4 7BX, UK.

'The primary international association for internal auditors. IIA members enjoy exclusive member resources such as *up-to-the-minute* information on current issues . . . top-notch professional development, certification, and *leading-edge research* . . . One out of every ten members of the Institute of Internal Auditors is a government auditor. . . . With nearly 50,000 members in more than 200 chapters and national institutes worldwide, you can extend your network of contacts through active participation at the chapter, district, or international levels as well as through involvement with international committees.' The Institute has a large range of books and other media publications; for instance: 'Government Auditing Standards – The hypertext version' (**diskette**. 1994. $30); 'The hunt for fraud: Prevention and detection techniques' (**multimedia package**. 1995. $625.); 'Internal auditing manual shell-on-disk' (**diskette** 1995. $495.); 'Electronic AAP' (**diskette**. 1994. $89).

1278. **Internal Auditor**. m. $60. **online**. 'The award-winning professional journal dedicated to serving the profession. Each issue presents a variety of articles, practical case studies, research, and advanced theories.'

(74) #381 Institute of Management Accountants 10 Paragon Drive, Montvale, NJ 07645. t: (1 201) 573 9000; f: 573 8185.

1279. **Management Accounting**. m. $125. **online**.

(75) #382 National Association of Black Accountants 7249A Hanover Parkway, Greenbelt, MD 20770. t: (1 301) 474 6222; f: 474 3114.

(76) #383 National Association of State Boards of Accountancy 380 Lexington Avenue, New York, NY 10168–0002. t: (1 212) 490 3868; f: 490 5841.

1280. **CPA Candidate Performance on the Uniform CPA Examinations**. bi-a. 162.50. 'Contains statistical reports for each of four examinations, including performance of first-time and repeat candidates by state and performance of candidates by school for each institution represented at the examination by five or more candidates.'

1281. **State Board Report**. m. $40. 'Digest of current developments affecting state accountancy regulation.'

(77) #384 National Conference of CPA Practitioners 3000 Marcus Avenue, Lake Success, NY 11042. t: (1 516) 488 5400; f: 488 5549.

(78) #385 National Society of Public Accountants 1010 N Fairfax Street, Alexandria, VA 22314. t: (1 703) 549 6400; f: 549 2984.

1282. **National Public Accountant**. m. $18. **online**. For accounting and tax practitioners.

Bankruptcy and insolvency

(79) #386 American Bankruptcy Institute 510 C Street NE, Washington DC 20002–5810. t: (1 202) 543 1234; f: 543 2762.

Founded on Capitol Hill in 1982, the Institute is 'the nation's leading multi-disciplinary, non-partisan organization devoted to education and research on bankruptcy issues'. Membership has grown to some 4000 professionals in all areas of the insolvency community including: bankruptcy judges, attorneys, trustees, accountants, appraisers, liquidators, real estate brokers, credit managers, turnaround and workout specialists, commercial lenders and investment bankers. In addition to the serials below, the Institute offers both members and non-members a variety of priced publications on bankruptcy issues, including *Legislative Materials* (bills, public laws, committee reports, hearing testimonies) and various other ABI Publications (e.g. meeting materials, legislative bulletins, statistical packets).

1283. **ABI Journal**. 10/year. $20. **online**.

1284. **American Bankruptcy Institute Law Review**. *LRP Publications*. bi-a. $48.50. **online**. Published in association with *St John's University School of Law*.

(80) #387 American College of Bankruptcy 510 C Street NE, Washington, DC 20002. t: (1 202) 544 1195; f: 543 2762.

(81) #388 National Association of Bankruptcy Trustees 3008 Milwood Avenue, Columbia, SC 29205. t: (1 803) 252 5646; f: 765 0860.

The Association's quarterly *Newsletter* discusses bankruptcy issues and ways to manage a bankruptcy practice more efficiently.

(82) #389 National Conference of Bankruptcy Judges 235 Secret Cove Drive, Lexington, SC 29072. t: (1 803) 957 6225.

1285. **American Bankruptcy Law Journal**. q. $56.50. **online**.

Trade and development

(83) #390 American Association of Exporters and Importers 11 West 42nd Street, 30th Floor, New York, NY 10036– 8002. t: (1 212) 944 2230; f: 382 2606.

(84) #391 American Chamber of Commerce Researchers Association c/o Greater Houston Partnership, 1100 Milam Building, 25th Floor, Houston, TX 77002–5507. t: (1 502) 897 2890; f: 894 9917.

1286. **ACCRA Cost of Living Index**. q. $100. Data for 280–310 urban areas. Includes a composite index, six component indexes and average rises for 59 goods or services items.

(85) #392 American Countertrade Association 121 S Meramec Avenue, Number 1102, St Louis, MO 63105–1725. t: (1 314) 727 5522; f: 727 8171.

(86) #393 American Economic Development Council 9801 West Higgins Road, Suite 540, Rosemont, IL 60018–4726. t: (1 708) 692 9944; f: 696 2990. *Membership Directory. Newsletter.*

'The largest, oldest and foremost international economic development association, serving more than 2,500 economic development professionals worldwide.'

1287. **Economic Development Review**. q. $48.

(87) #394 Bankers' Association for Foreign Trade 1600 M Street NW, Suite 700, Washington, DC 20036. t: (1 202) 452 0952; f: 452 0959. Members receive a series of discounts of published products and services.

(88) #395 Consumers for World Trade 2000 L Street NW, Washington, DC 20036. t: (1 202) 785 4835; f: 416 1734.

(89) #396 Cooperative Assistance Fund 655 15th Street NW, Site 375, Washington, DC 20005. t: (1 202) 833 8543; f: 393 2199.

(90) #397 Corporation for Enterprise Development 777 N Capital Street NE, Suite 801, Washington, DC 20002. t: (1 202) 408 9788; f: 408 9793.

'Seeks to promote economic vitality and opportunity for all, and especially for low-income populations and communites . . . CFED's clients and collaborators come from the broadest possible range, including policymakers and practitioners in local, state and federal government; private corporations; foundations; trade associations; labor unions; and non-profit organizations.'

1288. **Development Report Card for the States**. a. $70. 'Provides readers with a reliable set of economic indicators for benchmarking state growth and development . . . (C)harts each state's strengths and weaknesses over time and provides information for planning future economic growth strategies.'

(91) #398 Council of State Chambers of Commerce 122 C Street NW, Suite 330, Washington, DC 20001. t: (1 202) 484 5222.

(92) #399 Council on Foreign Relations 58 E 68th Street, New York, NY 10021. t: (1 212) 734 0400; f: 861 2759.

(93) #400 Emergency Committee for American Trade 1211 Connecticut Avenue, Washington, DC 20036. t: (1 202) 659 5147; f: 659 1347.

'An organization of the heads of about 60 large US firms with substantial overseas business interests. Their annual worldwide sales total ovr $1 trillion and they employ over 5 million persons. ECAT's purpose is to support measures that facilitate an expanding international economic system.'

Produce occasional publications: eg 'A new account of the critical role of US multinational companies in the US economy' (1993).

(94) #401 National Association of Development Companies 4301 N Fairfax Drive. Suite 860. Arlington, VA 22203. t: (1 703) 812 9000; f: 812 9008.

(95) #402 National Association of Development Organizations 444 North Capitol Street NW, Suite 630, Washington, DC 20001. t: (1 202) 624 7806; f: 624 8813. *Newsletter. Special Reports.*

'Promotes economic development in America's small cities and rural areas, and the *NADO Research Foundation* provides information and training for development professionals and local officials. Since its founding in 1967, NADO has been the nation's leading advocate for a regional approach to economic development.'

(96) #403 National Association of State Development Agencies 750 1st Street NE, Suite 710, Washington, DC 20002. t: (1 202) 898 1302; f: 898 1312.

(97) #404 National Customs Brokers and Forwarders Association of America One World Trade Center, Suite 1153, New York, NY 10048. t: (1 212) 432 0050; f: 432 5709. *Bulletin.*

'The trade association of customs brokers, international freight forwarders and international air cargo agents in the United States. Its membership includes brokers and forwarders in 33 affiliated associations throughout the nation.'

1289. **Who's Who of Customs Brokers & International Freight Forwarders**. a. $24.

(98) #405 National Congress for Community Economic Development 1875 Connecticut Avenue NW, Suite 524, Washington, DC 20009. t: (1 202) 234 5009; f: 234 4510. *Newsletters.*

'A national, nonprofit association of organizations engaged in the economic revitalization of distressed communities . . . NCCED offers a wide array of publications which provide critical information on community-based development.'

(99) #406 National Council for Urban Economic Development 1730 K Street NW, Suite 915, Washington, DC 20006. t: (1 202) 223 4735; f: 223 4745.

(100) #407 National Development Council 41 E 42nd Street, Suite 1500, New York, NY 10017. t: (1 212) 682 1106; f: 573 6118.

(101) #408 National Foreign Trade Council 1270 Avenue of the Americas, New York, NY 10020. t: (1 212) 399 7128; f: 399 7144.

(102) #409 Public Works and Economic Development Association Capitol Hill Office Building, 412 1st Street SE, Suite 60, Washington, DC 20003. t: (1 202) 488 1937; f: 863 9361.

(103) #410 Trickle Up Program 54 Riverside Drive, New York, NY 10024–6509. t: (1 212) 362 7958; f: 877 7464. e: 73444.557@compuserve.com.

'An independent, non-profit organization dedicated to creating new opportunities for employment and social well-being among the low-income populations of the world. Contributions to the *Trickle Up Program* are tax-deductible under Section 501(C)(3) of the Internal Revenue Code.'

Official trade and development bodies

(104) #411 Advisory Commission on Intergovernmental Relations 800 K Street NW, South Building, Suite 450, Washington, DC 20575. t: (1 202) 653 5650; f: 653 5429.

1290. **Changing Public Attitutes on Governments and Taxes**. a.

1291. **Significant Features of Fiscal Federalism**. a.

(105) #412 Agency for International Development 320 21st Street NW, Washington, DC 20523. t: (1 202) 647 1850; f: 647 0432.

Administers US foreign economic assistance programmes throughout the developing world. Development assistance is in the form of loans and grants.

1292. **US Overseas Loans and Grants and Assistance from International Organizations**. a.

(106) #413 Department of Agriculture Economic Research Service, Room 208, 1301 New York Avenue, NW Washington, DC 20005–4788. t: (1 202) 219 0512.

1293. **Agricultural Income and Finance**. q.

1294. **Foreign Agricultural Trade of the United States**. bi-m. $25. Contains quantity and value of US farm exports and imports, plus price trends.

1295. **Journal of Agricultural Economics Research**. q. $8. Discusses issues affecting the economics of agriculture, such as international trade in agricultural commodities. Covers a wide range of subjects in agricultural economics and methods of analysis.

1296. **World Agricultural Supply and Demand Estimates**. m. $20. Monthly forecasts of production, domestic use, stocks and exports for major crops of the U.S. and the world.

(107) #414 Export-Import Bank of the United States 811 Vermont Avenue NW, Washington, DC 20571. t: (1 202) 566 8990. *Freedom of Information* t: (1 202) 254 3382. *Annual Report*.

Facilitates and aids in financing exports of US goods and services. In contrast to certain other governments' programmes, Eximbank financing is, by statutory mandate, enjoined from supplanting private sources of export financing. Eximbank's role is to assist US exporters when such private financing is unavailable, and the bank's programmes are largely defined by that policy constraint on its operations.

(108) #415 Foreign Credit Insurance Association 40 Rector Street, 11th Floor, New York, NY 10006. t: (1 212) 306 5000; f: 513 4704.

Created by Eximbank and a group of private insurance companies in 1961 to help US exporters develop and expand their overseas sales by protecting them against loss should a foreign buyer default for political or commercial reasons.

(109) #416 Federal Trade Commission Pennsylvania Avenue at 6th NW, Washington, DC 20580–0001. t: (1 202) 326 2222; f: 326 2050. *Freedom of Information* t: (1 202) 326 2431. The Commission produces a monthly *Library Bulletin*. *Annual Report*.

In brief, the Commission is charged with keeping competition free and fair.

(110) #417 United States Council for International Business 1212 Avenue of the Americas, New York, NY 10036–1689. t: (1 212) 354 4480; f: 575 0327. *Annual Report*.

'Advances the global interests of American business both at home and abroad. It is the American affiliate of the *International Chamber of Commerce*, the *Business and Industry Advisory Committee to the OECD*, and the *International Organisation of Employers.* As such it officially represents US business positions in the main intergovernmental bodies, and vis-a-vis foreign business communities and their governments.' Its subgroups include those on: Banking and Commercial Practice, Economic and Financial Policy, European Community, Insurance, Multinational Enterprise and International Investment, and Taxation.

(111) #418 United States International Trade Commission 500 E Street SW, Washington, DC 20436. t: (1 202) 205 2000; f: 205 2798. *Freedom of Information* t: (1 202) 205 1802. *Annual Report.*

1297. **Operation of the Trade Agreements Program**. Highlights major American trade policy developments.

1298. **Quarterly Report to the Congress and the East-West Foreign Trade Board on Trade Between the United States and the Nonmarket Economy Countries**. Information and analysis on US trade with nonmarket economy countries.

63. Europe

The legal environment

(1) #419 Conseil des Barreaux de la Communauté Européene [Council of the Bars and Law Societies of the European Community] Rue Washington 40, B-1050 Brussels, Belgium. t: (32 2) 640 42 74; f: 647 79 41.

(2) #420 Fédération Internationale pour le Droit Européen [International Federation of European Law] Via Nicolo' Tartaglia 5, I-00197 Roma, Italy. t: (39 6) 808 15 56; f: 808 07 31.

The economic and monetary environment

(3) #421 Association for the Monetary Union of Europe 26 Rue de la Pépinière, 75008 Paris, France. t: (33 1) 45 22 33 84; f: 45 22 33 77. *Annual Report. Newsletter.*

'The Association was set up in 1987 at the suggestion of former French President Valéry Giscard d'Estaing and former German Chancellor Helmut Schmidt, as the voice of Europe's business community expressing the need for monetary stability and a single European currency. It does so by taking public positions on matters related to European Monetary Union, and by conducting research in order to clarify some of the issues in the public debate. Anxious to preserve its independence and political neutrality, the Association cooperates actively with public authorities, of which it is a respected partner. The Association also organizes seminars and publishes material in order to increase knowledge of EMU and the practical use of the emu . . . The Association operates through a small permanent secretariat in Paris, a prestigious Board of Directors meeting quarterly and different national working groups in the 12 EC countries . . . Membership is open to any business, company or professional organization, whether large or small, provided it shares the vision of Europe as a single zone of currency stability, with free movement of goods and services.'

The fiscal environment

(4) #422 Confédération Fiscale Européenne [European Tax Confederation] H Poppelsdorfer Allee 24, D-53115 Bonn; Postfach 1340, D-53003 Bonn, Germany. t: (49 228) 726 39 44; f: 726 39 52. *Biennial Report.*

1299. **European Taxation**. m. $570. *International Bureau of Fiscal Documentation.*

Accounting, auditing and reporting

(5) #423 Fédération des Experts Comptables Européens Rue de la Loi 83, 1040 Brussels, Belgium. t: (32 2) 231 05 55; f: 231 11 12. The Federation have carried out surveys, including: 'Analysis of European accounting and disclosure practices.' (£60); 'European survey of published accounts' (£50), both published by *Routledge.*

'The representative organisation for the accountancy profession in Europe.' Members are the national professional accountancy bodies, and there is a direct link to the *International Federation of Accountants.*

Bankruptcy and insolvency

(6) #424 Association Européenne des Praticiens des Procedures Collectives [European Insolvency Practitioners Association] 7 Russell Place, Nottingham NG1 5HJ, UK. t: (44 115) 924 0175; f: 924 0272. *Annual Congress*; *Newsletter.*

Founded in 1901 and registered in France. 'European organisation of insolvency professionals . . . Its members consist of lawyers and accountants who are insolvency practitioners. Other lawyers and accountants who are advisers to insolvency practitioners, together with bankers, judges, regulators and credit insurers, who are interested in the insolvency process, are associate members having no voting rights at general meetings. A major part of the work undertaken by members also includes the rehabilitation or reconstruction of troubled businesses. Members of AEPPC are individuals, and no partnership or body corporate is admitted to membership. . . . Each member is entitled to receive a summary of the practices and procedures relevant to insolvency laws of each European country on joining AEPPC.'

Trade and development

(7) #425 EDICOM 21 rue Tournefort, 75005 Paris, France. t: (33 1) 47 07 29 29; f: 47 07 31 29.

1300. **Electronic Trader**. 10/year. £75. 'EDI and Electronic Commerce in Europe.'

(8) #426 EU Committee of the American Chamber of Commerce in Belgium Avenue des Arts 50, Bte 5, 1040 Brussels, Belgium. t: (32 2) 513 68 92; f: 513 79 28. 'The key organization in Europe representing the views of European companies of American parentage.'

1301. **EC Information Handbook**. a. BEF 1500. 'Complete guide to the organizations involved in EC affairs and to contacts within the European institutions.'

(9) #427 EURODAD [European Network on Debt and Development] Square Ambiorix, 10, B-1040 Brussels, Belgium. t: (32 2) 732 70 07; f: 732 19 34.

'A network of non-governmental organisations (NGOs) in 16 European countries. It aims to coordinate the activities of NGOs working on the issues of debt and structural adjustment in developing countries in order to ensure that their views be brought to bear on decision-makers in Europe.'

1302. **Third World Debt in the 1990s**. q. 'Newsletter which can be received free of charge.'

64. International

The legal environment

(1) #428 Association Internationale de Droit des Assurances [International Association for Insurance Law] c/o Barlow Lyde & Gilbert, Beaufort House, 15 St Botolph Street, London EC3A 7NJ, UK. t: (44 171) 247 2277; f: 782 8509. *US Chapter* c/o Werner & Kennedy, 1633 Broadway, New York, NY 10019, USA. t: (1 212) 408 6900; f: 408 6950. *Information Bulletin*; *World Congress* (quadrennial).

'Purposes are to increase the study and knowledge of international and national insurance law and related matters and, to this end, to promote and develop collaboration between its members at an international level.'

(2) #429 International Bar Association 2 Harewood Place, Hanover Square, London W1R 9HB, UK. t: (44 171) 629 1206; f: 409 0456.

'A Federation of National Legal Associations and Individual Lawyers . . . It is composed of over 15,000 individual lawyer members in 163 countries and 142 Law Societies and Bar Associations together representing more than 2.5 million lawyers . . . The *Section on Business Law* (SBL) was established to promote an interchange of views amongst members of the IBA as to laws, practices, and procedures affecting business, financial and commercial activities throughout the world . . . Its 28 specialist Committees (e.g. Banking Law; Insurance; Insolvency and Creditors' Rights; Issues and Trading in Securities; Multinationals and Foreign Investment Policy; Capital Markets Forum; International Capital Markets Group) each cover a specific area of business law . . . The Section journal *International Business Lawyer* is sent free to members 11 times per year.'

(3) #430 International Juridicial Institute PO Box 96827, 2509 JE, The Hague, The Netherlands. t: (31 70) 346 09 74; f: 345 32 96.

'Provides lawyers, notaries, the judiciary, companies and private persons with legal advice in the form of documented reports. These reports discuss the appropriate rules of private and international and foreign law.'

(4) #431 International Law Association Charles Clore House, 17 Russell Square, London WC1B 5DR, UK. t: (44 171) 323 2978; f: 323 3580. *Conference Report* (bi-a.)

'The oldest such organization in the world, was founded in Brussels in 1873. It is a private membership organization whose objectives, under its Constitution, include "the study, elucidation and advancement of international law, public and private, the study of comparative law, the making of proposals for the solution of conflicts of law and for the unification of law, and the furthering of international understanding and goodwill". Membership of the Association, at present about 3800, is spread among 41 Branches in various countries of the world. *Committees* of the Association include:

- *International Commercial Arbitration*
- *International Monetary Law*
- *International Securities Regulation*
- *International Trade Law*
- *Legal Aspects of Sustainable Development*
- *Regional Economic Development Law.*'

(5) #432 International Organization for Standardization 1 Rue de Varembé, CH-1211 Geneva 20, Switzerland. t: (41 22) 749 01 11; f: 733 34 30.

Aims to promote the development of standardization and related activities in the world with a view to facilitating the international exchange of goods and services and to developing cooperation in the sphere of intellectual, scientific, technological and economic activity. Has close working relations with all the major international official organizations; and links with a very wide range of professional, trade and other bodies, including the *International Federation of Stock Exchanges*. The Organization has been instrumental in developing the *International Securities Identification Numbering* (ISIN) system.

(6) #433 International Organization of Supreme Audit Institutions A-1030, Vienna, Austria. t: (43 1) 711 71 8467; f: 712 94 25. *Occasional Papers.*

'By *supreme audit institution* is meant such public body of a state which, however designated, constituted or organized, exercises, by virtue of law, the highest public auditing function of that state.'

1303. **International Journal of Government Auditing**. q. $5. **online**. 'Printed and published in the United States at the *General Accounting Office*.'

(7) #434 International Society of Securities Administrators c/o Union Bank of Switzerland, PO Box 645, CH-8021, Zurich, Switzerland. t: (41 1) 235 7421; f: 234 2211. Has more than 1500 members worldwide. *Newsletter*.

1304. **ISSA Handbook (Year)**. a. $250. Three volumes. **diskette** $600. 'Extensive information on 39 of the world's major financial markets with regard to types of securities, structure and regulation of financial markets, securities trading, clearing, settlement and custody, taxes as well as laws and regulations.'

The economic and monetary environment

(8) #435 Club of Rome Secretariat General, 34 avenue d'Eylau, 75116 Paris, France. t: (33 1) 47 04 45 25; f: 47 04 45 23.

Has sponsored the production of a large number of books, including the very influential 'The Limits to Growth' (1972).

(9) #436 Group of Thirty 1990 M Street, NW, Suite 450, Washington, DC 20036, USA. t: (1 202) 331 2472; f: 785 9423.

Thirty bankers, consultants and academics sponsoring the production of a series of widely respected publications, examples of which are:

Special Reports

'Clearance and settlement systems: Status reports' (1992)
'Derivatives: Practices and principles' (1993) – including three appendices: I 'Working papers'; II 'Legal enforceability: Survey of nine jurisdictions'; III 'Survey of industry practice'

Occasional Papers

38 'Why now? Change and turmoil in US banking' (1992)

39 'EMU and the regions' (1992)
40 'The new trade agenda' (1992)
41 'The threat of managed trade to transforming economies' (1993)
42 'Tripolarism: Regional and global economic competition' (1993)
43 'The ten commandments of systemic reform' (1993)
44 'Global derivatives: Public sector responses' (1993)
45 'The impact of trade on OECD labor markets' (1994)
46 'In search of a level playing field: The implementation of the Basle Capital Accord in Japan and the United States' (1994)

(10) #437 Institute of International Finance 2000 Pennsylvania Avenue, NW, Suite 8500, Washington, DC 20006–1812, USA. t: (1 202) 857 3600; f: 775 1430.

'A unique association of leading financial institutions worldwide. In recent years, its public statements have had an acknowledged effect in the formulation of official views and policies. The Institute was created after senior international bankers joined officials from bank supervisory authorities, the IMF and the World Bank to discuss the international financial outlook at a meeting held in England in 1982. Thirty-eight leading banks in Europe, Japan and North America then decided to establish the Institute.

Membership in the Institute is open to any institution which has, or proposes to have within the immediate future, international exposure as a result of holding loans or equity in portfolio for its own risk. There are two categories of membership in the Institute: *full* membership is restricted to commercial banks; *associate* membership is open to investment banks, multinational and trading firms, export credit agencies and other institutions with cross-border interests . . . Our publications are only available to members under an annual membership fee . . . We do not publish for the public.'

1305. **Country Analysis.** 100/year. 'In-depth analysis of economic conditions and policies of individual countries . . . Full reports are produced shortly following country missions; updates are provided between missions . . . A *Monthly Economic Review* for some 20 selected countries includes the latest available data on key financial indicators, highlighting main trends graphically and providing a valuable bridge of information between regular country reporting.'

1306. **Country Database**. 'Includes economic data and projections of domestic economic performance, external trade, balance of payments, external debt and debt service as well as indicators of monetary, fiscal and exchange rate policies . . . Also made available to members on *diskette* for use on personal computers as well as **online** through a major worldwide database service.'

(11) #438 Offshore Group of Banking Supervisors PO Box 140, The Parade, St Helier, Jersey, JE4 8QZ, Channel Islands. t: (44 1534) 603400; f: 70755.

'Relatively informal gathering of nineteen offshore centres which meets on an annual basis. It does not produce any publications. However, details of the work of the Group are included in regular reviews of banking supervision carried out by the Basle Committee . . . The Offshore Group does not produce any printed or cdrom publications.'

(12) #439 World Economic Forum 53 Chemin des Hauts-Crêts, CH-1223 Cologny/Geneva, Switzerland. t: (41 22) 736 02 43; f: 786 27 44. *Annual Meeting. Annual Report.*

'The world's foremost institution integrating leaders from business, government and the sciences into a global partnership for economic and social progress. It is an international membership organization established as a foundation in Switzerland in 1971. It is independent, not-for-profit and impartial, tied to no political, partisan or regional interests.'

1307. **World Competitiveness Report**. Published in partnership with the *International Institute for Management Development (IMD)*, Lausanne. a. SFr 800. 'More than 370 statistical tables ranking countries' performance.'

1308. **World Link**. Published with *Euromoney Publications.* bi-m. £95.

The fiscal environment

(13) #440 Commonwealth Association of Tax Administrators c/o Commonweath Secretariat, Marlborough House, Pall Mall, London SW1Y 5HX, UK. t: (44 171) 747 6473; f: 930 0827. *Newsletter.*

'Provides a platform for Commonwealth tax administrators to meet and discuss problems of common concern and to develop closer links with each other . . . CATA has established very useful links with other international organizations and co-ordinates the activities of the *Council of Executive Secretaries of Tax Organizations.*'

(14) #441 International Bureau of Fiscal Documentation PO Box 20237, 1000 HE Amsterdam, The Netherlands. t: (31 20) 626 7726; f: 622 8658. *Also* IBFD Publications USA, 24 Hudson Street, Kinderhook, NY 12106, USA. t: (1 518) 758 2245; f: 758 2246. *Annual Report.*

'In the 56 years since its foundation, IBFD has grown into one of the most respected organizations studying and documenting international taxation systems and investment legislation. Clients, including Ministries of Finance, international corporations, legal and accountancy practices, banks, educational institutions and others, look to IBFD as a first-class source of information. As an independent, not-for-profit research foundation the information it offers is always objective and unbiased.'

Reference works

1309. **Corporate Taxation and Cross-Border Payments in OECD Countries. diskette**. 3/year. $515/$315.

1310. **EC Corporate Tax Law**. l. $745/$290. Two volumes.

1311. **European Tax Handbook (Year)**. a. $160. 'Details of corporate and individual taxation in over 30 major countries, plus EC information.'

1312. **European Taxation Database on CD-ROM**. **cdrom**. 3/year. $4,810/ $3,090.

1313. **Guide to the European VAT Directives**. l. $860/$400. Five volumes. 'Comprehensive analysis of all aspects of the EC's Directives on VAT.'

1314. **Guides to European Taxation**. l. $5,005/$2,525. Six volumes. There is also a *Supplementary Service to European Taxation* giving the 'Full text (in English) of almost every European tax treaty, tax system summaries and worldwide tax bibliography' ($1,660/$815).

1315. **International Guide to Mergers and Acquisitions**. l. $745/$315. Two volumes. 'Complete details of tax regulations, legislation and practice. Full outline of company law.'

1316. **International Guide to Partnerships**. l. $690. 'Complete guide to company and tax law applying to partnerships.'

1317. **Tax Treaties Database on CD-ROM**. **cdrom**. s-a. $3,090/$1,370.

1318. **Tax Treatment of Transfer Pricing**. l. $1,115/$430. Four volumes.

1319. **Taxation of Permanent Establishments**. l. $690/$175.

1320. **Taxation of Private Investment Income in OECD Countries**. **diskette**. 3/year. $515/$315.

Current awareness

1321. **Bulletin for International Fiscal Documentation**. m. $315.

1322. **International Transfer Pricing Journal**. 3/year. $260.

1323. **International VAT Monitor**. bi-m. $450.

1324. **Tax News Service**. w. $375. **online**. d. 'IBFD's acclaimed newsletter, reporting on news, trends, proposals, and changes in international taxation and investment. Over 200 countries are represented with comprehensive coverage of developments of international interest.'

(15) #442 International Fiscal Association World Trade Center, Beursplein 37, PO Box 30215, 3001 DE Rotterdam, The Netherlands. t: (31 10) 405 2990; f: 405 5031. *Yearbook*.

'The only non-governmental international organisation dealing with fiscal matters. It comprises taxpayers, their advisers, government officials and university professors and is therefore a unique forum for discussing international fiscal questions.'

1325. **Cahiers de Droit Fiscal International**. *Kluwer Academic Publishers*. i. Series started in 1939.

Accounting, auditing and reporting

(16) #443 International Federation of Accountants 114 West 47th Street, Suite 2410, New York, NY 10036, USA. t: (1 212) 302 5952; f: 302 5964.

Among other activities, develops and issues international auditing standards, which were accepted in 1992 for financial reporting in international financial markets.

1326. **IFAC Handbook Subscription Service**. $200. 'Accountancy is a global profession and international standards and developments are important to all accountants. Public practitioners, educators, accountants in industry and accountants in government need to be aware of what is happening elsewhere in the world . . . The Service provides:

- paperback bound volumes of all final pronouncements of IFAC (as of July 1st) and IASC – International Accounting Standards Committee (as of January 1st)
- timely mailings throughout the year, of all new IFAC pronouncements and exposure drafts, as well as studies/discussion papers
- the quarterly *IFAC Newsletter* which reports on technical activities, new publications, conferences and significant professional issues
- the *IFAC Annual Report*, and
- any other IFAC related documents (issued by eg the *International Capital Markets Group*)'.

(i) *#444 International Auditing Practices Committee*

Bankruptcy and insolvency

(17) #445 INSOL International c/o 71 Avenue Road, Ingatestone, Essex, CM4 9HB, UK. t: (44 1277) 353240; f: 353250. *Newsletter*.

'World wide federation of national associations of accountants and lawyers who specialise in the insolvency area . . . For the avoidance of doubt INSOL has not agreed to subscribe for any entry in your Directory.'

1327. **International Insolvency Review**. *Wiley Chancery Law*. s-a. £98. 'Journal of the *International Association of Insolvency Practitioners*.'

Trade and development

(18) #446 Organisation Mondiale du Commerce Centre William Rappard, 154 rue de Lausanne, 1211 Geneva 21, Switzerland. t: (41 22) 739 5111; f: 739 5458.

1328. **GATT Focus**. 10/yr. free. Covers current events and issues in international trade, member countries' efforts to resolve trade problems, and the Uruguay Round multilateral trade negotiations.

(19) #447 Bureau International des Tarifs Douaniers [International

Customs Tariffs Bureau] Rue de l'Association 38, B-1000 Brussels, Belgium. t: (32 2) 516 87 74; f: 218 30 25.

1329. **International Customs Journal**. 'Please note that, under the terms of the Convention of July 5th, 1890, which created the *International Customs Tariffs Bureau*, the latter is authorised to supply copies of the *International Customs Journal* only to the Governments of the Signatory States. These States take the measures necessary to the distribution, on their territory, of the copies of the afore-mentioned Journal to which they are entitled. In the case of your Country, the body to which that mission has been allocated is the . . . *Department of Trade and Industry*.'

(20) #448 Commonwealth Association for Development Export House, 168 Tower Bridge Road, London SE1 3LS, UK. t: (44 171) 357 7017; f: 357 7113. *Newsletter*.

(21) #449 Commonwealth Development Corporation 1 Bessborough Gardens, London SW1V 2JG, UK. t: (44 171) 828 4488; f: 828 6505. *Newsletter*.

'A British public corporation committed to promoting economic growth in developing countries. CDC invests in commercially viable development projects by making long-term loans and by subscribing equity. It also provides management and other support services.'

(22) #450 Commonwealth Secretariat Marlborough House, Pall Mall, London SW1Y 5HX, UK. t: (44 171) 839 3411; f: 930 0827.

1330. **International Development Policies**. q. £40. Review of the activities of international organizations.

(23) #451 Confederation of International Trading Houses Associations Adriaan Goekooplaan 5, 2517 JX The Hague, The Netherlands. t: (31 70) 354 68 11; f: 351 27 77.

'An organisation which represents and defends the interests of trading houses and their associations in Europe.'

(24) #452 International Chamber of Commerce [ICC] 38 Cours Albert 1er, F-75008 Paris, France. t: (33 1) 49 53 28 28; f: 49 53 29 42. *Annual Report*. *ICC United Kingdom* 14–15 Belgrave Square, London SW1X 8PS, UK. t: (44 171) 823 2811; f: 235 5447. *Annual Report*. *US Council* 1212 Avenue of the Americas, New York, NY 10036, USA. t: (1 212) 354 4480; f: 575 0327.

'The World Business Organisation . . . The International Chamber of Commerce exists, quite simply, to make it easier to do business internationally. As an independent, international business organisation, the ICC is unique in that:

- it draws its membership from the developed and developing world (over 7,500 companies and business associations in 140 countries

- its membership is cross-business and cross-sectoral
- it has first class consultative status with the United Nations, including the specialist UN agencies.'

ICC Commissions and Working Bodies include:

- *Banking Technique and Practice*
- *Financial Services*
- *Insurance*
- *International Commercial Practice*
- *International Trade Policy*
- *Law and Practice Relating to Competition*
- *Multinational Enterprises*
- *Investment*
- *Taxation*

1331. **Documentary Credits Insight**. q. $190. 'Contains analytical information and up-to-the-minute information from the same experts who drafted *UCP 500* (The ICC Uniform Customs and Practice for Documentary Credits: 1993). It also offers a country- by-country update on documentary credits from correspondents in more than 25 countries.'

1332. **Letter of Credit Update**. m. $495. For businessmen, bankers and lawyers. Covers legislative and judicial developments concerning letter of credit practices.

- *ICC Commercial Crime Services* t: (44 181) 591 3000; f: 594 2833. 'Sales of the CCS Special Report on "Prime bank instrument frauds" (£25) are exceeding expectations. A decision has now been made to update the report to include the problem of commodity frauds, largely because many of the new spate of sugar frauds are connected with the players behind "Prime Bank Instrument Frauds".
- *ICC PUBLISHING* The publishing subsidiary of ICC, which 'produces and sells, notably through the National Committees of the ICC and its American subsidiary – ICC Publishing Inc – the works from ICC Commissions and experts. It also offers guides and corporate handbooks on topics ranging from banking practice, international commercial arbitration, and joint ventures in the Eastern countries to advertising and telecommunications'. Examples of ICC publications are: 'Funds transfer in international banking' (290 FF); 'Bills of Exchange: a guide to legislation in European countries' (155 FF); 'ICC Uniform Rules for contract bonds' (55 FF); 'Competition law and information-based services' (350 FF); 'International contracts for sale of information services' (325 FF).

(25) #453 International Reciprocal Trade Association 9513 Beach Mill Road, Great Falls, VA 22066, USA. t: (1 703) 759 1473; f: 759 0792.

(26) #454 World Customs Organization rue de l'Industrie, 26–38, B-1040 Brussels, Belgium. t: (32 2) 508 42 11; f: 508 42 33.

'An intergovernmental organization with a mission to secure, through co- operation between governments, the highest degree of harmony and uniformity in all customs systems worldwide, in the interests of international trade . . . The *Harmonized Commodity Description and Coding System*, commonly referred to as the Harmonized System (HS), is a multipurpose nomenclature combining in a single integrated instrument the descriptions required for Customs tariffs, statistical nomenclatures, transport and other trade-related classifications. It comprises some 5,000 groups of goods each identified by a six-digit code and is provided with the necessary definitions and rules to ensure its uniform application.'

1333. **Harmonized System Commodity Data Base on CD-ROM**. **cdrom**. BF 9000. 'The most powerful tool to find the correct Harmonized System code for products traded internationally.'

(27) #455 World Trade Centers Association One World Trade Center, Suite 7701, New York, NY 10048, USA. t: (1 212) 432 2626; f: 488 0064.

'The World Trade Center concept brings together business and government agencies involved in foreign trade. Ideally a *World Trade Center* puts all the services associated with international trade under one roof. These services often include trade information and communications services, World Trade Center clubs, trade education programs, trade missions, and exhibit and display facilities.'

1334. **WCTA World Business Directory**. *Gale Research*. a. Descriptions of international businesses.

1335. **World Traders**. q.

- *World Trade Center Network* 'This electronic trading and communication service connects you to over 180 World Trade Centers – and to more than 3,000 of their clients and affiliates. . . . Offers or enquiries that you post on NETWORK's Bulletin Board can be read immediately in 140 countries . . . NETWORK's *Global Database* gives you the world's best online collection of business information at your fingertips. Using a simple menu and your own key words, you can access more than 150 databases covering over 50,000 sources of information, (including): Eight D&B databases; Three Moody's databases; Four Kompass databases; Three S&P databases; TRW US Business Credit Reports . . . The online charge is $10 US per hour (on a per minute basis). Charges for a search range from $3.45 to $11.50 US and charges for retrieving a single complete record range from $3.45 to $39.10 US depending on the database involved.'

Official trade and development bodies

(28) #456 UNITED NATIONS SYSTEM United Nations Plaza, New York, NY 10017, USA. t: (1 212) 963 1234; f: 758 2718.

The UN itself publishes and disseminates information on various subjects including business, economics, trade, international law; and it publishes a number of statistical series of relevance to finance. Their publications can be enquired about and purchased directly from the UN sales section in: *New York* (Sales Section, 2 United Nations Plaza, Room DC2–853, Dept 403, New York, NY 10017, USA. t: (1 212) 963– 8302; f: 963 3489); and *Geneva* (Sales Office and Bookshop, CH- 1211 Geneva 10, Switzerland. t: (41 22) 917 2614; f: 917 0027); from designated agencies (in the UK, *HMSO*), or through the normal channels. The *Directory of Selected Collections of United Nations System Publications* (1990) is a quick reference to libraries and information centres in 170 countries where publications of the UN system can be found. Included is a list of *UN Information Centres*, which include: 18 Buckingham Gate, London SW1E 6LB, UK. t: (44 171) 630 1981 *and* 1889 F Street NW, Washington, DC 20006, USA.

1336. **UNS/SABIR**. **cdrom**. i. £155. United Nations System/Selected Agencies Bibliographic Information Records. 'Contains over 195,000 bibliographic records describing the publications and documents of 32 organisations in the United Nations System. In most cases the records are selected from the library databases of the contributing organisations.'

Apart from a number of *Intergovernmental Organizations Related to the United Nations* which are considered elsewhere in this text, the other UN organizations that we cover primarily are ordered as in *Appendix III* 'Structure of the United Nations' in the 1993 edition of:

1337. **Yearbook of the United Nations**. *Martinus Nijhoff*. a. £78.00. Prepared by the *Department of Public Information*. 'Although the *Yearbook* is based on official sources, it is not an official record.'

Leaving aside within that Appendix the *Security Council* and the *International Court of Justice*, the bodies of relevance here come within the ambit either of the *General Assembly*, or of the *Economic and Social Council*, or of the *UN Secretariat*.

GENERAL ASSEMBLY The Assembly has four types of committees:

- *Main Committees* The six Main Committees include the *Economic and Financial Committee* and the *Administrative and Budgetary Committee.*
- *Procedural Committees*
- *Standing Committees* The two Standing Committees consist of experts appointed in their individual capacity for three-year terms:
    - *Advisory Committee on Administrative and Budgetary Questions*
    - *Committee on Contributions*
- *Subsidiary and Ad Hoc Bodies* These include:
    - *Board of Auditors*
    - *Committee on Information*

- *International Law Commission*
- *Investments Committee*
- *Joint Advisory Group on the International Trade Centre UNCTAD/GATT*
- *Panel of External Auditors*
- *United Nations Capital Development Fund*
- *United Nations Commission on International Trade Law* The Commission produces:

1338. **Yearbook (Year)**. a. £40.00.

The General Assembly's Subsidiary and Ad-Hoc bodies also include two more substantial bodies:

(i) *#457 United Nations Conference on Trade and Development* Palais des Nations, 1211 Geneva 10, Switzerland. t: (41 22) 907 1234; f: 907 0057. UNCTAD's *Reference Unit* produces a *Guide to UNCTAD Publications* and an *UNCTAD Statistical Pocket Book. Discussion Papers* (e.g. 'Financial liberalization: The key issues' (March 1993)).

1339. **Handbook of International Trade and Development Statistics (Year)**. a. £65.00.

1340. **Trade and Development Report (Year)**. a. £35.00.

1341. **UNCTAD Commodity Yearbook (Year)**. a. £55.00.

1342. **UNCTAD Review**. i. 'International journal which publishes scholarly articles on all aspects of international trade, finance and development.'

1343. **World Investment Report (Year)**. a. £35.00. 'Transnational corporations and integrated international production.'

- *Coordinating Committee on Multilateral Payments Arrangements and Monetary Cooperation among Developing Countries*
- *Division on Transnational Corporations and Investment* This produces:

1344. **Transnational Corporations**. 3/year. $35. 'Basic objective . . . is to publish articles that provide insights on the economic, legal, social and cultural impacts of transnational corporations in an increasingly global economy and the policy implications that arise therefrom. It focuses especially on political-economy issues related to transnational corporations.'

(ii) *#458 United Nations University* Public Affairs Section, 53–70, Jingumae 5–chome, Shibuya-ku, Tokyo 150, Japan. t: (81 3) 3499 2811; f: 3499 2828. e: mbox@hq.unu.edu.

'Autonomous body of the United Nations with academic freedom guaranteed by its Charter.'

There is also the directly related:

(iii) *#459 UNU World Institute for Development Economics Research* UNU/WIDER, Katajanokanlaituri 6 B, FIN-00160 Helsinki, Finland. t: (358 0) 693 841; f: 693 8548. *Research for Action Series*; *Study Group Series*; *Working Papers.*

'Concentrates on policy-oriented socio-economic research to solve urgent problems.' The Institute regularly co-publish monographs in association with commercial publishers.

1345. **World Economy Group Annual Report**. *MIT Press*. a.

ECONOMIC AND SOCIAL COUNCIL Promotes world cooperation on economic, social, cultural and humanitarian problems. The Council has a coordinating function between the UN and the specialized agencies. In addition to two regular sessional committees:

- *Economic Committee*
- *Social Committee*

the subsidiary bodies reporting to the Council consist of (a) Functional Commissions; (b) Regional Commissions; (c) Standing Commissions; (d) Expert Bodies.

(a) *Functional Commissions* The single Commission of this type of interest here is the:

- *Statistical Commission* "The *Economic and Social Council*, noting that the Statistical Commission has completed a fundamental review of the structure and operation of the international statistical system and, as a result, has made recommendations and decisions for strengthening the international statistical system, including the following:

(a) A more active *Working Group on International Statistical Programmes and Coordination* to monitor progress in coordination and cooperation within the international statistical system between sessions of the Statistical Commission;

(b) Strengthened statistical divisions of the United Nations regional commissions and strengthened regional conferences of national chief statisticians in all five regions in terms of their responsibilities for statistical development in their regions;

(c) More effective working relationships between the *Subcommittee on Statistical Activities of the Administrative Committee on Coordination* and the Statistical Commission and the Working Group;

(d) The establishment of six task forces as mechanisms for developing a more integrated work programme among international organizations in the following subject areas: national accounts, industrial and construction statistics, international trade statistics, finance statistics, price statistics, and environment statistics."[129]

(b) *Regional Commissions* There are five:

(iv) *#460 Economic Commission for Africa* Africa Hall, POB 3001, Addis Ababa, Ethiopia. t: (251 1) 517200; f: 514416.

1346. **African Socio-Economic Indicators (Year)**. a. £16.50.

1347. **African Statistical Yearbook (Year)**. a. £43.00.

- *Pan-African Documentation and Information Service* Established in 1980 to improve information handling and access amongst the members of the Commission.

(v) *#461 Economic Commission for Europe* Palais des Nations, 1211 Geneva 10, Switzerland. t: (41 22) 917 2893; f: 917 0036.

1348. **East-West Investment**. q. £48.00.

1349. **Economic Bulletin for Europe**. i. £43.00.

1350. **Economic Survey of Europe in (Year)**. a. £42.00.

- *Committee on the Development of Trade*
- *Conference of European Statisticians*

(vi) *#462 Economic Commission for Latin America and the Caribbean* (ECLAC) Casilla 179 D, Santiago, Chile. t: (56 2) 210 2000; f: 208 1946.

1351. **Economic Survey of Latin America and the Caribbean (Year)**. a. £40.00.

1352. **Statistical Yearbook for Latin America and the Caribbean**. a. £43.00.

(vii) *#463 Economic and Social Commission for Asia and the Pacific* (ESCAP) United Nations Building, Rajadamnern Avenue, Bangkok 10200, Thailand. t: (66 2) 288 1234; f: 288 1000.

1353. **Economic and Social Survey of Asia and the Pacific (Year)**. a. $50.

1354. **Statistical Indicators for Asia and the Pacific**. q. $60.00.

1355. **Statistical Yearbook for Asia and the Pacific (Year)**. a. $68.00.

- *Committee for Regional Economic Cooperation*
- *Committee on Statistics*
- *Statistical Institute for Asia and the Pacific* t: (81 3) 3357 8351.

(viii) *#464 Economic and Social Commission for Western Asia* PO Box 927115, Amman, Jordan. t: (962 6) 694351; f: 694981.

1356. **National Accounts Studies of the ESCWA Region**. a. $56. 'The 11th, 12th, 13th and the 14th issues include national accounts data on Palestine (West Bank and Gaza Strip), in addition to unified tables for the Republic of Yemen, following the unification of the People's Democratic Republic of Yemen and the Yemen Arab Republic.'

1357. **Statistical Abstract of the ESCWA Region**. a. $30. 'Available data for the preceding 10 years for each country of the ESCWA region are presented in statistical tables grouped into nine sections: 1–Population, 2–Social Statistics, 3–National Accounts, 4–Agriculture, Forestry and Fishing, 5–Industry, 6–Energy, 7–Foreign Trade, 8–Finance and Price Index Numbers, 9–Transport, Communication and Tourism.'

1358. **Survey of Economic and Social Developments in the ECSWA Region**. a. $42.

(c) *Standing Committees* Of importance are:

- *United Nations Commission on Transnational Corporations* t: (1 212) 963 1234; f: 758 2718.
- *United Nations Committee for Development Planning* t: (1 212) 963 4669; f: 963 4116.

(d) *Expert Bodies* These include two of direct interest here:

- *Ad Hoc Group of Experts on International Cooperation in Tax Matters*
- *Intergovernmental Working Group of Experts on International Standards of Accounting and Reporting* 'Reports to the Commission on Transnational Corporations, and consists of 34 members, elected for three-year terms by the Economic and Social Council according to a specific pattern of equitable geographical distribution. Each State elected appoints an expert with appropriate experience in accounting and reporting.'

SECRETARIAT The main body of interest is the:

- *Department of Economic and Social Information and Policy Analysis* whose *Statistical Division* (t: (1 212) 963 6170; f: 963 4116) oversees the publication of:

1359. **Commodity Trade Statistics**. bi-w. £135.00. 'Every year about 100 countries supply the . . . Division with their international trade statistics, detailed by commodity and partner country. These data are processed into a standard format with consistent coding and valuation and are then stored in a computerized data base system.'

1360. **International Trade Statistics Yearbook**. a. £85.00.

1361. **Monthly Bulletin of Statistics**. m. $450.

1362. **National Accounts Statistics**. a. $125. Comprises separate series: *Analysis of Main Aggregates*; *Main Aggregates and Detailed Tables.*

1363. **Statistical Yearbook (Year)**. a. $110. **cdrom**. a. $249. 'Statistical global compilation of population and manpower; national accounts; wages; prices and consumption; balance of payments; finance; health; education; culture; science and technology; development assistance; industrial property; agriculture; forestry and fishing; industrial production; energy; external trade; communication; transport; and international tourism.'

1364. **World Economic and Social Survey (Year)**. a. £42.00. 'This year, to signal our intention to integrate the treatment of the economic and social dimensions of development more fully, we have added the word "social" to the name of the *Survey*. It is our hope that the *Survey* will serve as a main background document for the discussions of the world economy that take place annually in the United Nations . . . The statistical annex contains standardized economic and financial data pertaining to the analytical groupings of countries that are the main focus of the discussions in the text and to the key parameters of the international economy.'

1365. **World Statistics in Brief: United Nations Statistical Pocketbook**. a. $7.50.

Finally, some other relevant serials produced by the United Nations are:

1366. **International Accounting and Reporting Issues**. a. £18.95.

1367. **International Tax Agreements**. i. Supplements to the main volume – which is no longer in print – on the status of international agreements.

1368. **Monthly Commodity Price Bulletin**. m. £75.00.

1369. **Treaty Series**. i. Treaties and International agreements registered or filed and recorded with the Secretariat of the UN.

1370. **World Investment Directory (Year)**. a. £43.00.

(29) #465 International Labour Office *ILO Publications* CH-1211 Geneva 22, Switzerland. t: (41 22) 799 61 11; f: 798 63 58. *Also* ILO Publications Center, 49 Sheridan Avenue, Albany, NY 12210, USA. t: (1 518) 436 9686; f: 436 7433.

'Founded in 1919 to advance the cause of social justice and, by so doing, to contribute to ensuring universal and lasting peace. A unique feature of its structure is that representatives of workers and employers take part with government representatives in the *International Labour Conference*, the Governing Body of the ILO and in many of its regional and other meetings.'

1371. **Bulletin of Labour Statistics**. q. $84. 'Articles on methodology and special topics, Trilingual tables of current statistics on employment, unemployment, hours of work, wages, consumer prices.'

1372. **International Labour Documentation**. 10/year. $80. **cdrom**. a. $850. 'Abstracting bulletin produced from the database *LABORDOC* . . . available for interactive and retropective **online** searching through several information hosts.'

1373. **International Labour Review**. bi-m. $64. 'A multidisciplinary review presenting the results of original research and comparative analyses of labour, social and economic issues . . . and reviews of recent books received or published by the ILO.'

1374. **Year Book of Labour Statistics**. a. $168. Contains essential statistical information for following the evolution of labour and of living and working conditions throughout the world.

(30) #466 World Trade Organization rue de Lausanne 154, CH-1211 Geneva 21, Switzerland. t: (41 22) 739 51 11; f: 731 42 06. WTO publications are also available from *HMSO Books* in the UK and from *UNIPUB* in the US.

"The Final Act of the *Uruguay Round* was signed in Marrakesh in April 1994, bringing to a conclusion the eighth and most ambitious set of multilateral trade negotiations. One hundred and twenty-five countries participated in the Round, which will reduce tariff and nontariff barriers to trade in goods, strengthen trade rules and extend multilateral rules to new areas – services and intellectual property – and establish the *World Trade Organization*."[130]

1375. **FOCUS**. 10/year. $free. 'Newsletter reporting on trade- related matters, including features on economic developments and major trade policy issues. It covers negotiations, dispute settlements and other activities of the Member States and the GATT Secretariat.'

1376. **International Trade (Year): Trends and Statistics**. a. SF 40. 'A comprehensive review of recent world trade developments, together with 120 pages of statistical tables and charts . . . The first edition of this annual publication will be available at the end of 1994.'

The European Union

65. There are so many excellent guides available to the European Union and its documentation that we will only give a brief summary of two aspects here: the institutions of the EU itself; and the main types of documentation those institutions produce. For the first, we will use as our 'text' Neill Nugent's authoritative book: 'Government and Politics of the European Union': highly recommended as an introduction to another potentially complex field.[131]

66. The major 'Institutions and Political Actors of the European Union' are arranged in six chapters by Nugent:

- *The Commission* 'Frequently portrayed as the civil service of the EU, the Commission is in reality both rather more, and rather less, than that: rather more in the sense that the Treaties, and political practice, have assigned to it much greater policy initiating and decision-making powers than national civil services, in theory at least, enjoy; rather less in that its role regarding policy implementation is greatly limited by virtue of the fact that it is agencies in member states which are charged with most of the EU's day-to-day administrative responsibilities.

The Commission is centrally involved in EU decision-making at all levels and on all fronts. With an array of power resources and policy instruments at its disposal – and strengthened by the frequent unwillingness or inability of other EU institutions to provide clear leadership – the Commission is at the very heart of the EU.'

- *The Council of Ministers* 'The Council of Ministers is the principal meeting place of the national governments and is the EU's main decision-making institution.'
- *The European Council* 'The main reason for the creation of the European Council was a growing feeling that the Community was failing to respond adequately or quickly enough to new and increasingly difficult challenges . . . A new focus of authority was seen as being required to try and make the Community more effective, both domestically and internationally. What was needed . . . was a body which would bring the Heads of Government together on a relatively informal basis to exchange ideas, to further mutual understanding at the highest political level, to give direction to policy development, and perhaps sometimes to break deadlocks and clear logjams. It was not anticipated that the leaders would concern themselves with details of policy.'
- *The European Parliament* 'Since it was first constituted . . . the European Parliament . . . has generally been regarded as a somewhat ineffective institution. It is a reputation which, today at least, is not entirely justified. For whilst it is true that the EP's constitutional powers aere not comparable with those of national legislatures, developments over the years have come to give it, in practice, a not inconsiderable influence in the EU system. As with national parliaments this influence is exercised in three main ways: through the legislative process, through the budgetary process, and through control of and supervision of the executive.'
- *European Union Law and the Court of Justice* 'An enforceable legal framework is the essential basis of decision-making and decision application in all democratic states. Although not itself a state, this also applies to the EU. It does so because the EU is more than merely another international organisation in which countries cooperate with one another on a voluntary basis for reasons of mutual benefit. Rather it is an organisation in which states have voluntarily surrendered their right, across a broad range of important sectors, to be independent in the determination and application of public policy.

An EU legal order is thus an essential condition of the EU's existence. The sources of that order are to be found in a number of places . . .

- *The Treaties* . . .
- *European Union legislation* . . .

The Treaties distinguish between different types of legislation . . .

- *Regulations* . . . A regulation is . . . Of "general application" . . . "Binding in its entirety . . . Directly applicable in all Member States"; that is, without the need for national implementing measures, it takes immediate legal effect right across the EU on the date specified in the regulation . . .

- *Directives* . . . A directive shall be binding, as to the result to be achieved, upon each Member State to which it is addressed, but shall leave to the national authorities the choice of form and method.
- *Decisions* . . . A decision shall be binding in its entirety upon those to whom it is addressed . . . It may be addressed to any or all member states, to undertakings, or to individuals. Many decisions are highly specific and are, in effect, administrative rather than legislative acts. Others are of a more general character and can be akin to regulations, or even, occasionally, directives.'

- *Other Institutions and Actors* eg *The Economic and Social Committee*; *The European Investment Bank*; *The Court of Auditors.*

67. An Appendix to Nugent's book is a short but valuable guide to *Further Reading*. Quoting from this:

The EU issues a vast amount of material, from brief information leaflets to weighty reports. Most of this material is available from the *Office for Official Publications of the European Communities* and/or directly from the appropriate EU institution . . . The Treaties establishing the European Union, and especially the *Treaty of European Union* together with the *Treaty Establishing the European Community*, should naturally be consulted by all those who wish to understand the nature and functioning of the EU.

The *Official Journal of the European Communities (OJ)* is issued on most weekdays and provides the authoritative record of decisions and activities of various kinds. It is divided into three series. The 'L' (Legislation) series is the vehicle for publication of EU legislation . . . The monthly *Bulletin of the European Communities* provides a general account of most significant developments . . . The *General Report of the Activities of the European Communities* is published annually and provides an excellent summary of both institutional and policy developments. Where necessary it can be supplemented by the annual reports that are also published by most of the institutions.

The most detailed analysis and information about EU policies is usually to be found in documentation produced by the Commission. Leaving aside one-off publications, this appears in three main forms. First, in serialised reports which are issued on a regular basis and which cover just about every aspect of EU affairs. . . . Second, an enormous amount of information is issued by the Statistical Office . . . All Statistical Office publications carry the *Eurostat* logo imprint. Third, there are Commission Documents (COMDOCS) which are made up principally of monitoring reports, policy reviews, and – most importantly – proposals for Council and EP (European Parliament) and Council legislation.

68. European institutions

(1) #467 EUROPEAN UNION

(i) *#468 EUR-OP* [Office for Official Publications of the European Communities] 2 rue Mercier, L-2985 Luxembourg. *General Information* t: (352) 2929 426 58/46 62 56; f: (352) 2929 42 763/ 46 90 49.

'The official publisher of all of the organs of the European Union, such as the European Parliament, the Council of Ministers, the European Commission, the Court of Justice, the Court of Auditors, the Economic and Social Committee, the European Centre for the Development of Vocational Training, the European Foundation for the Improvement of Living and Working Conditions, the European Investment Bank, and other Union Authorities such as the Agencies created during the course of 1994.

EUR-OP systematically publishes about 6000 monographs and around 110 periodicals a year, as well as an important number of CD-ROMs, databases, videos, etc., in 11 languages. Whatever needs to be known about the European Union can be found in EUR-OP's products. . . . *EUR-OP News* is a quarterly periodical in which the most recent EU publications on developments in EU policy are presented. It can be obtained free from EUR-OP.

EUR-OP has appointed some 50 sales agents to make sure that all EUR-OP's paper and audiovisual products can be easily obtained throughout the world. Following the principle of subsidiarity, all EUR-OP publications have to be purchased through these agents which are based near the citizen (in the UK: *HMSO Books* (Agency Section) HMSO Publications Centre, 51 Nine Elms Lane, London SW8 5DR. t: (44 171) 873 9090; f: 873 8463. In the USA: *UNIPUB* 4611–F Assembly Drive, Lanham, MD 20706–4391, USA. t: (800) 274 4888/(1 310) 459 7666; f: 459 0056.). Citizens living in countries in which EUR-OP has not yet appointed a sales agent can contact EUR-OP sales agent in Luxembourg. EUR-OP publications can also be ordered in every good bookshop. . . . *Eurobookshops* (in the UK these are the HMSO bookshops in Belfast, Birmingham, Bristol, Edinburgh, London, and Manchester), which display EUR-OP publications in a separate section of window, are obliged to keep a permanent stock of the most important EUR-OP publications and have access to a direct online ordering system for publications that are out of stock. The Eurobookshops' staff are trained to advise customers on EU affairs and publications and to direct them to the appropriate institutions and information sources.

Free-of-charge publications are not available at EUR-OP nor its sales agents, but have to be ordered directly at the author services or institutions that initiated the publication. To obtain the free-of-charge Commission publications, the citizen can apply to the Commission Office in his country. The *Commission Offices* in the Member States (eg European Commission Office in the United Kingdom, Jean Monnet House, 8 Storey's Gate, London SW1P 3AT, London, UK. t: (44 171) 973 1991/2; f: 973 1900/01) are run by DG X of the Commission which is responsible for informing the European citizen on all aspects of the Commission's activities. *Euro-Info Points*, which offer a display of free-of- charge information leaflets on the different aspects of EU policy, also have access to EU databases and a staff trained to answer questions of a general interest. Students, researchers and the public in general can consult all EUR-OP publications at one of the more then 700 *European Documentation Centres* (EDCs). EDCs, usually located in universities and large public libraries, can recieve the complete range of EU publications.'

Examples of these are:

1377. **Bulletin of the European Communities**. 10/year. £99.20. 'An official reference covering all spheres of Community activity.'

1378. **Completing the Internal Market of the European Community**. *Kluwer Law & Taxation Publishers*. l. 'The text in English of all Proposals for Directives, the Directives themselves, the Regulations, the Decisions, and the Recommendations which comprise the legislative programme for the creation of the Internal Market.'

1379. **Directory of Community Legislation in Force**. bi-a. $140. Two volumes. 'All EU legislation in force.'

1380. **Directory of European Community Trade and Professional Associations**. *Editions Delta*. a. 3,500 BEF. 'Official publication of the European Communities which lists European federations of associations of which the European Commission has official cognizance . . . For each of the 570 trade and professional associations . . . (there is) as well the list of the national member organizations with their addresses and telephone numbers. Thus, altogether some 6000 associations are included.'

1381. **ECU-EMS Information**. m. **online**.

1382. **European Union Press Releases**. **online**.

1383. **Official Journal of the European Communities**. d. **cdrom**. q. £260. 'The only daily in the world published in nine languages.' Three separate series:

- *L: Legislation* d. £280. Contains all the legislative acts and regulations whose publication is obligatory under EU treaties, as well as other acts.
- *C: Information and Notices* d. £400. **cdrom**. q. £650. Covers the complete range of Community information other than legislation.
- *S: Supplement to the Official Journal* d. 'Some 400 tenders issued by public institutions are published every day.'

The *Debates of the European Parliament*, which is a verbatim report of the Parliament's proceedings, appears at intervals of approximately one month as an annex to the Journal. There is also an *Index to the Official Journal of the European Communities*.

1384. **Panorama of EU Industry**. **cdrom**. 'An extensive review of the situation of the manufacturing industries and services in the EU. It provides analyses of industry structure, the current situation, trends in production, employment and trade, country comparisons of EU figures with the USA and Japan, and figures from 1983 to 1993 with forecasts for major sectors up to 1997.'

1385. **SCAD Bulletin**. w. £183.20. **online. cdrom**. q. 695. 'Analytical bulletin, mentioning the bibliographic references of the main Community acts, the publications of the European institutions and of articles from periodicals.' The subscription also covers the series *SCAD Bibliographies* and *SCAD Bibliographic Files*.

1386. **Single Market. cdrom**. q. £250. 'Draws on the three best source of information available: *Spearhead* – produced by the UK *Department of Trade and Industry*; *Info 92* – produced by the *Secretariat of the European Commission*; and *European Update* – produced by *Deloitte & Touche Europe Services*. Reflecting SINGLE MARKET's excellence, it was named the Best European Information Source (Electronic) by the UK *European Information Association* in 1992.'

EUR-OP continues to make strenuous efforts to allow its output to be accessed throughout the Union as speedily as possible:

- *Catalogues* 'All available traditional EUR-OP publications are listed in annual catalogues; a video catalogue contains the titles of existing audiovisual products and a regularly updated directory of public databases keeps customers informed on the various electronic products that have been produced by the EU institutions. All these catalogues can be obtained free of charge at EUR-OP and clients can request to be included in EUR-OP's mailing list for all future updates.'
- *CATEL* 'A bibliographic database that is used to search, select and order all the products of EUR-OP. EUR-OP's sales agents are connected to this database.'
- *Electronic products* 'A series of databases is there to help obtain whatever information you need – quickly, easily and in the language of your choice: EU law, press releases, references, public tenders, statistics etc. . . . In order to further facilitate access to these on-line services, the first part of EUR-OP's new system of *national gateway distributors* became operational in January 1995. These gateways will allow access to all information services provided by the European Commission *Eurobases* and to TED (*Tenders Electronic Daily*).'
- *Europe on Internet* 'With a view to providing EU citizens with clear, comprehensive and up-to-date information on the objectives, institutions and policies of the EU, DG X of the European Commission (responsible for information) is now linked to the world-wide information data base *Internet* (initially this service will be available in English only). The *EUROPA* server is a pilot project and contains general information on the EU, the Commission (tasks, compositions, speeches by the President or Commissioners, organisations, guide to document access), an "ABC" on EU policies providing access to broad public information emanating from the Directorate-Generals

and information on access to the Commission's databases such as I'M GUIDE, CORDIS, Eurobases, Eurostat, ISPO. It contains also information on EUR-OP and its services . . . Soon EUR-OP News or extracts of it will also be available . . . *http://www.cec.lu*.'

(ii) *#469 Eurobases* 200 rue de la Loi, 1049 Brussels, Belgium. t: (32 2) 295 0001/03; f: 296 0624. *Context* are Eurobases' UK Gateway Distribution Agency.

'At present EC databases are available to the public through a great number of commercial host organizations and also through the services of the European Communities' own hosts. Eurobases is the European Communities "commercially oriented host service" offering a unique selection of Community online information to a world-wide clientele.' EUR-OP's gateway distributors offer the following databanks:

1387. **ABEL**. 'Document delivery system: enables you to order on- line all EU legislation, proposals for new legislation and other information published in the *Official Journal*, via fax or letter.'

1388. **CELEX**. Official legal database of the EU, containing over 40 years of treaties, regulations, directives, and case law.

1389. **ECLAS**. 'Catalogue of the EU's main library in Brussels. This Library contains the central collections of *all* information and publications on the European Union from all 23 Directorates and 7 other EU-wide institutions. The database is nultilingual.'

1390. **EUROCRON**. 'Three statistical data sets covering the most important sectors of the social and economic climate in the EU, regional statistics and agricultural statistics.'

1391. **IDEA**. 'In the second half of 1994 a new database will be launched by *Eur-OP* (Office for Official Publications) and hosted experimentally on ECHO. . . . IDEA (*Interinstitutional Directory of European Administrations*) contains the directories of the following European institutions: *European Investment Bank*, *Court of Justice*, *Court of Auditors*, *European Commission*, *European Parliament*, *Council of the European Union*, *Economic and Social Committee.* When new EU institutions are added at a later stage, these will also be included. Information provided will include name and title, institution and function, languages spoken and contact details . . . This new interinstitutional database will contribute considerably towards improving the transparency of the work of the EU, as it will enable users to locate the official they need in order to obtain information on a particular area of European policy.'

1392. **INFO 92**. 'The state of the implementation of the single market and the social charter (description of the relevant directives), including the incorporation of Union directives into the national legislation of Member States.'

1393. **OIL**. 'Weekly indicative prices of petroleum products without duties and taxes.'

1394. **RAPID**. Full text of all documents issued by the *Spokesman's Service* – press releases, information memos, speeches and key documents.

1395. **SCAD**. 'Bibliographic database containing more than 190,000 titles of documents on EU policy.'

1396. **TED**. 'Containing invitations to tender, tender awards and other notices for public contracts not only from Member States but also from ACP countries, EFTA States, Japan and the USA.'

(iii) *#470 European Commission Host Organisation* [ECHO] B.P. 2373, L-1023 Luxembourg. t: (325) 34981 200; f: 34981 234.

'ECHO is happy to announce the launch of the new I'M – (Information Market) Europe World Wide Web service, which is to open on 1 September 1994. An initiative of *DG XIII-E (Information industry and market and language processing*) of the European Commission, the World Wide Web will provide information on the European Union and initiatives for the global information society.'

(iv) *#471 Information Market Observatory*

1397. **Information Market Guide**. 580 pp. £40. 'Information products and services which are publicly available in Europe and which do not require specially dedicated equipment to access. This one-stop information tool has been collected via a network of national correspondents organized by IMPACT.'

(v) *#472 Statistical Office of the European Communities* The Office's statistical series publishers are termed *Eurostat* Information Office, L-2920, Luxembourg. t: (352) 4301 34567; f: 43 64 64.

1398. **Basic Statistics of the European Community**. a. $14.

1399. **Comext**. **online**. **cdrom**. 11/year. 3000 EU. 'External statistics of the EU and its Member States.'

1400. **Consumer Price Index**.

1401. **Consumer Prices in the EEC**.

1402. **CRONOS**. **online**. **cdrom**. 900,000 time series of economic data.

1403. **Earnings in Agriculture**.

1404. **Earnings – Industry and Services**. s-a. $71.

1405. **EC External Trade Indices**.

1406. **Economic Accounts for Agriculture and Forestry**.

1407. **ECU-EMS Information**.

1408. **Eurocron**. **online**. Includes: *Eurostatistics* which 'comments on and publishes the main economic and social indicators needed to analyze short-term trends in the economic activity of the 12 Member States, the Community as a whole, and the USA and Japan'.

1409. **Europe in Figures**.

1410. **Eurostat-CD (Year). cdrom**. s-a. 1500 EU. 'Contains economic and social statistics, regional data, external trade data at product level and the nomenclatures used to classify the different data.'

1411. **Eurostatistics**. 11/year. Data for short-term economic analysis.

1412. **External Trade**. Divided into: Analytical Tables A-L, Imports and Exports; External Trade and Balance of Payments; External Trade Statistical Yearbook; External Trade, System of Generalised Tariff Preferences.

1413. **Family Budgets: Comparative Tables**.

1414. **General Government Accounts and Statistics**.

1415. **Government Financing of Research and Development**.

1416. **Money and Finance**. q. **online**. 'Outlines the financial statistics of the European Community, the United States of America and Japan. The time series cover the period from 1978 to 1989 and are annual, quarterly or monthly. There are three parts to the publication:

- Structural indicators covering financial accounts, money supply, public finance, the differences in interest rates, exchange rates, the position vis-à-vis the rest of the world and foreign reserves.
- Statistics on the European Monetary System
- The current indicators used in economic analysis; the consolidated balance sheets of credit institutions, money supply, public finance, interest rates and dividend yields, etc.'

1417. **National Accounts**. Divided into: ESA Aggregates; ESA Detailed Tables by Branch; ESA Detailed Tables by Sector; ESA Input-Output Tables.

1418. **Quarterly National Accounts ESA**. q. **online**. 'Comparison between those Member States which compile quarterly accounts, the United States of America and Japan.'

1419. **Results of the Business Survey Carried Out Among Managements in the Community**.

1420. **Sigma**. bi-m. 'The objective of Sigma, the bulletin of European statistics, is to provide up-to-date information, from a statistical viewpoint, on the progress of measures taken in the run-up towards European integration.'

The major bodies of the Union are:

(vi) *#473 Council of the European Union* Rue de la Loi 170, B-1048, Brussels, Belgium. t: (32 2) 234 6111; f: 234 7397.

(vii) *#474 Commission of the European Communities* Rue de la Loi 200, B-1049, Brussels, Belgium. t: (32 2) 235 1111. *Also* 8 Storey's Gate, London SW1P 3AT, UK. t: (44 171) 973 1992; f: 973 1900 *and* The Delegation of the European Commission to the United States, Public Enquiries Section, 2300 M Street NW, Washington, DC 20037, USA. t: (1 202) 862 9539; f: 429 1766. ('Provides information ONLY on the European Union. . . . We respond to requests ONLY from the United States.')

(viii) *#475 European Parliament* L-2929, Luxembourg. t: (352) 43001.

(ix) *#476 Court of Justice* L-2925, Luxembourg. t: (352) 43031; f: 4303 2500.

(x) *#477 Court of Auditors* 12 Rue Alcide De Gasperi, L-1615, Luxembourg. t: (352) 43981; f: 439342.

(xi) *#478 European Investment Bank* 100 Boulevard Konrad Adenauer, L-2950 Luxembourg. t: (352) 4379 1; f: 437704. *Also* 68 Pall Mall, London SW1Y 5ES, UK. t: (44 171) 839 3351; f: 930 9929. *Annual Report*; *Newsletter*.

'The EIB's main activity is to contribute concretely, by financing capital projects, to the balanced development of the Community, while adhering to the rules of strict banking management. . . . The EIB borrows the bulk of its resources on the capital markets – mainly through public bond issues – where it commands a prime position regularly endorsed by the "AAA" rating awarded to its securities. . . . The texts on European Union agreed at the Maastricht European Summit confirm and strengthen the EIB's role in promoting economic and social cohesion.'

(xii) *#479 European Monetary Institute* Kaiser Strasse, 29, D-60311, Frankfurt-am-Main, Germany. t: (49 69) 27 22 70; f: 27 22 72 27.

The main tasks of the new body, established with its own legal personality under Article 109f of the *Treaty of Economic Union* (the 'Maastricht Treaty'), and replacing the *Committee of Governors of the Central Banks of the Member States of the European Economic Community* and the *European Monetary Cooperation Fund*, are to strengthen the coordination of EU member states' monetary policies and to prepare for the transition to stage three of economic and monetary union (EMU) in the monetary field. The Institute took up its duties on 1 January 1994, becoming fully operational in Frankfurt in the autumn of that year.

(xiii) *#480 European Bank for Reconstruction and Development The Documentalist* One Exchange Square, London EC2A 2EH, UK. t: (44 171) 338 6000; f: 338 6100. *Publications* t: (44 171) 338 6541; f: 338 7544. *Working Papers*.

"The political and environmental missions of the Bank, its combination of public and private sector project lending and the fact that it is dedicated solely to the countries of Central and Eastern Europe, gave the Bank its niche among financial institutions. This is particularly important for the Bank given that its activities overlap with those of existing institutions such as the World Bank Group and the European Investment Bank. Indeed, when the proposal for the Bank was first raised, the necessity of another lending institution was widely questioned, not least by existing institutions".[132]

1421. **Economics of Transition**. *Oxford University Presss.* q. £160. 'Since the journal's launch in 1992, the study of transition has developed into a new field in economics, which reaches well beyond eastern Europe. Transition economics is also relevant to all countries engaged in an institutional or systemic transformation process.'

1422. **Finance Bulletin**. i. 'An occasional newsletter for the investment and financial community.'

1423. **Transition Report**. a. £25. 'Features a unique approach to the measurement of economic transition in eastern Europe and the former Soviet Union.'

(xiv) *#481 Economic and Social Committee* 2 rue Ravenstein, B-1000, Brussels, Belgium. t: (32 2) 519 9011; f: 513 4893.

(xv) *#482 European Seed Capital Fund Network* evca, Keibergpark, Minervastraat 6, Box 6, B-1930, Zaventem, Belgium. t: (32 2) 720 60 10; f: 725 30 36. *Newsletter.*

'It is without question that small- and medium-sized enterprises (SMEs) are of considerable importance to national and regional economies.... Yet it is these firms that experience the most difficulty in raising finance for start-up or expansion. Venture capital is not usually available for early-stage investments and traditional sources of finance, such as the banks, are not always willing to provide funds in any form for what is seen as a particularly risky sector of investment. Recognising this sitution, in 1989, the Commission of the European Communities launched a pilot *European Seed Capital Scheme*.... Twenty four funds were selected to participate in the pilot scheme (plus one more after German unification), there being at least one fund in each country of the European Union.... It was early realised that encouraging the creation of the funds was not in itself enough to reduce the risks and improve their viability.... The Commission, therefore, decided to provide help to the funds to assist them to share their experiences and to give them opportunities to develop their management skills.... The ESCFN was established to facilitate these tasks and the *European Venture Capital Association* was selected to manage these activities.'

(2) #483 Council of Europe *Publishing and Documentation Service* F-67075, Strasbourg Cedex, France. t: (33) 88 41 22 63; f: 88 41 27 80.

'Set up "to achieve a greater unity between its members for the purpose of safeguarding and realising the ideals and principles which are their common heritage and facilitating their economic and social progress". . . . At 10 February 1995 it is, with thirty-four member countries, the European organisation with the widest geographical representation.'

(3) #484 European Free Trade Association 9–11 rue de Varembé, CH-1211 Geneva 20, Switzerland. t: (41 22) 749 11 11; f: 740 15 22.

69. *Commercial serials* Examples of some of the commercial serials concerned with the European Union's activities end this Chapter:

(1) #485 Abacus Data Services Challenge House, 616 Mitcham Road, Croydon, Surrey, CR9 3AU, UK. t: (44 181) 683 6444; f: 683 6445.

1424. **European Trade Statistical Reports**. Officially appointed agents of the *Statistical Office of the European Communities* providing import or export data for all EU countries.

1425. **UK Trade Statistical Reports**. Quantity and value of any product imported to or exported from the UK: officially appointed agents of *HM Customs and Excise*. Also provide information on UK importers: by product, by importer, by post code.

(2) #486 Agence Europe Boulevard Saint-Lazare 10, B-1210, Brussels, Belgium. t: (32 2) 219 02 56; f: 217 65 97.

1426. **Economic Interpenetration**. d. 10,000 BF. 'Information concerning the setting up of companies, mergers, takeovers, concentrations, and transnational technical and financial agreements.'

1427. **Europe Daily Bulletin**. d. 47,000 BF. **online**. 'For the last 40 years, Agence Europe has been considered thoroughout the world as THE SOURCE (some call it "The Bible") of information on European economic and political integration.'

1428. **Weekly Selected Statistics**. w. 6,000 BF. 'Statistics concerning a broad variety of sectors, above all in the European community: production, trade, employment, population trends etc.'

(3) #487 Europe (London) 25 Frant Road, Tunbridge Wells, Kent TN2 5JT, UK. t: (44 1892) 533813; f: 544895.

1429. **Agra Europe**. w. 760 ($1,368). Covers European and world developments affecting the production and marketing of food and agricultural commodities.

(4) #488 Buraff Publications 714–716 Church Street, Alexandria, VA 22314, USA. t: (1 202) 862 0990.

1430. **EuroWatch**. bi-w. $797. 'News and analysis from European capitals and Washington DC on how US and other business interests are affected by the European Community's program to remove national barriers and create a "single market" for the trade and movement of goods, services, capital, labor.'

(5) #489 Consultancy Europe Associates Navigation House, 48/50 Millgate, Newark, Nottinghamshire, NG24 4TS, UK. t: (44 1636) 610620; f: 613289.

'We do not yet have a 1995 price list, as a major American company, *Congressional Quarterly*, has recently taken a 49% share in CEA and at the moment everything is still in a state of flux. The easiest things to deal with are: the CD-ROM of our *Spicers* database, which is published by *Context*... and the Briefings and guide books we publish with *Longmans*.... With regard to the information services which we run from the database, these range at the moment from £500 for a one-topic, monthly bulletin to £3500 for a local authority requiring specific bulletins for each of its 12 Directorates. We intend over the next few weeks to simplify our price structure so that we can offer a more flexible service, with information on current EU legislation available in either paper or electronic form and at intervals to suit the client (monthly, weekly or even daily).'

1431. **Europe's Money**. *Longman*. a. £45. 'An analytical guide to all items speifically itemised in the EU budget.'

(6) #490 Coopers & Lybrand: European Union Office Avenue de Tervuren 2, B-1040 Brussels, Belgium. t: (32 2) 741 0811; f: 733 6618.

1432. **EUROSCOPE**. **online**. Includes *EU Commentaries* 'a series of reports on individual subjects, ranging from Agriculture to VAT (and including Banking and Securities, Insurance and Monetary Union). Apart from detailing important policy and legislative related developments, the EC Commentaries also contain information on EU funding opportunities for business and on the progress of the Union's single market programme. Ranging from 40 to 200 pages long, all EU Commentaries are also available in hard copy format.' Also contains a series of bulletins published by *Europe Information Service*.

(5) #491 Context Grand Union House, 20 Kentish Town Road, London, NW1 9NR, UK. t: (44 171) 267 8989; f: 267 1133.

'A leading electronic publisher of law and official information. Context's coverage of European Union material is unsurpassed in depth and breadth. No other publisher matches the full range of *JUSTIS* CD-ROM and online titles. And even more United Kingdom sources are now available to Context's customers.... Context is pioneering the combination of CD-ROM and online technology. Many of the CD-ROM titles... are backed up by online updates.... Context have been appointed the UK Gateway Distribution Agency for *EUROBASES*, the EU's official databases.'

1433. **JUSTIS CELEX**. **cdrom**. 'Carries the complete (EU) CELEX database. In addition, certain missing texts of the documents stored on CELEX have been added.'

1434. **Official Press Releases**. **cdrom**. q. £500. Combines '*Hermes* – from the UK's *Central Office of Information*; and *Rapid* – from the Spokesman's Service of the *European Communities*.'

(7) #492 Croner Publications Croner House, London Road, Kingston upon Thames, Surrey KT2 6SR, UK. t: (44 181) 547 3333; f: 547 2637.

1435. **Croner's Europe**. l. £246.32. Two volumes. **diskette**. 'Provides those doing business in the European Union with up-to-date reliable information, in both loose-leaf and electronic formats.'

(8) #493 Deloitte & Touche Europe Services Rue Royale 326, 1210 Brussels, Belgium. t: (32 2) 219 56 96; f: 223 19 95.

1436. **EU and Eastern Europe Database**. w. BF 4,500 per report. **online**. Series of 45 'real-time' reports on EC and Central and Eastern Europe affairs. The reports provide an analysis and explanation of the developing business and economic environment in each Central and Eastern European country, and detailed evaluations of EC policy areas. The latter include layman's versions of all current and proposed EC legislation and policies. Also issued is a newsletter *European Update* (bi-m.)

(9) #494 ELLIS Publications PO Box 1059, 6201 BB Maastricht, The Netherlands. t: (31 4457) 2275; f: 2148.

1437. **EUROCAT**. **cdrom**. q. £450. 'A major advance in providing access to the record of the activities, policies and legislation of the EU. It helps demystify the complex documentary output of the EU's institutions and enables users to find the information they need more easily than ever before. (It) brings together over 490,000 records from the four databases of the *Office for Official Publications of the European Union*: *CATEL* The database used by the Office to produce its catalogues and to index the Official Journal; *ABEL* Tables of contents of the Official Journal L series; *CELEX* The official database of European Union law; and *SCAD* including records of actual legislation, preparatory acts, Commission Final Documents, European Parliament working papers and bibliographic records of publications distributed or published by the Office.' Co-published by *Chadwyck-Healey* and the European Union's *EUR-OP*.

1438. **OJCD**. **cdrom**. q. £695. 'Full text oriented CD-ROM covering legislation, proposed legislation, case law, parliamentary documents and information and notices as published in the Offcial Journal, European Court Records and other official documents and publications. It incorporates the *CELEX* database – the official legal database of the EU institutions – that provides, since 1952, the most complete coverage available of legislation, proposed legislation and case law . . . The combination of case law from the Official Journal C series and the European Court Reports, as well as documents from the Courts information office, is unique. Cases are covered from registration to judgement and finally to the removal from the Courts register.'

1439. **OJINDEX+. diskette**. 10/year. £260. 'A comprehensive and current access tool to the *Official Journal of the European Communities*, all COM final documents and *European Court of Justice* offset prints . . . It is the only index that covers the L and C series completely.'

1256. **SCAD+CD. cdrom**. q. £1250. 'The official bibliographic database of the European Communities. It contains abstracts from over 2,000 journals covering an extensive range of community activities as well as bibliographic entries for publications, documents and legislation produced by EC institutions.'

(10) #495 Eurocom Regent House, 76 Princess Street, Luton, Bedfordshire LU1 5AT, UK. t: (01 582) 452911; f: 483841.

1441. **Regional Development International**. m. £45. Reports on regional development programs, promotes inward, cross-border and indigenous investment projects. Helps overseas, mainland European and UK corporate investors.

(11) #496 Euroconfidentiel rue de Rixensart 18, B- 1332 Genval, Belgium. t: (32 2) 652 02 84; f: 653 01 80.

1442. **Access to European Union**. a. 2650 BEF. 'Covers the latest economic and legislative developments in all major industrial and commercial sectors. Written by an adviser at the European Commission, the publication contains over 1000 references to key Community texts and constitutes essential reading for anyone wanting to understand how Community policy shapes economic, political and social life in the Member States.'

(12) #497 Eurofi Eurofi House, 37 London Road, Newbury, Berkshire, RG14 1JL, UK. t: (44 1635) 31900; f: 37370.

1443. **Guide to European Community Grants and Loans**. a. £360. 'Comprises a basic core of detailed information on all the Community funds and indicates for each scheme: the main objectives – the legislative basis – who is eligible – the levels of funding – deadlines for applications – contact points within the EC.'

(13) #498 Europe Information Service 6 rue de Genè ve, B-1140 Brussels, Belgium. t: (32 2) 242 60 20; f: 242 95 49.

1444. **European Intelligence**. m. BEF 19,300. 'Features a monthly update on the completion of the Single Market: company law, free movement, standardisation etc.'

1445. **European Insight**. w. BEF 16,200. 'Brief information package covering EU-related events of the week.'

1446. **European Report**. bi-w. BEF 46,200. **online**. **cdrom**. 'EIS's flagship publication provides a regular and comprehensive overview of EU affairs.'

For instance, the 10 December 1994 issue contained items with the titles: 'EU Budget: Agreement on revising financial estimates'; 'Closer monetary cooperation between EU and new member states'; 'Commission withdraws pension fund Directive'; 'Structural Funds: ECU 4 billion approved for final round of industrial aid' and 'ECU 2.76 billion approved for fourth package of rural aid'; and ECU 1.2 billion approved for two Irish aid packages'; 'Data protection: Ministers overcome major obstacle to information society'; 'Farm Council: Agri-Monetary System, GATT key issues on December 12/13 Agenda'; 'GATT/WTO: WTO launch celebrations overshadowed by outstanding problems' in an issue of 110 pages.

1447. **Multinational Service**. m. BEF 32,000. 'Outlines the EU activities and decisions with respect to multinational corporations in Europe and worldwide.'

(14) #499 European Study Service Avenue Paola 43, B-1330 Rixensart, Belgium. t: (32 2) 653 90 19; f: 652 03 02.

1448. **Banking and Financial Services in the European Union**. q. BEF 11,900/6,000. Compiled by *Deloitte & Touche Europe Services*. '*A* Comprehensive details of all the initiatives (legislation, proposed legislation, major court cases) and programmes adopted by the European Union in the following fields: Capital Movements; Credit Institutions; Prudential Supervision; Protection of Consumers & Depositors; Insolvency; Securities; Mortgage Credit; Investment Services. *B* A business insight into progress in areas of particular interest both to the banking industry and to industrial and commercial companies alike: Taxation; Money Laundering; Pension Funds; Deposit-Guarantee Schemes; State-Backed Export Finance; Cross-Border Transactions; Computerised Data; UCITS; Stock Exchanges; Investor Compensation. *Exhaustive Annexes* Complete texts of all EU legislation relating to banking and financial services mentioned in the report. *Key Contacts* Names and addresses of professional associations, European Institutions' personnel involved in the fields of banking and financial services and other information providers.'

1449. (Year) **Guide to European Community Grants and Loans**. q. BEF 10,200. 'The definitive work on the subject.'

1450. **Insurance Industry in the European Union**. q. BEF 11,900/6,000.

(15) #500 Reed Reference Publishing 121 Chanlon Road, New Providence, NJ 07974, USA. t: (1 908) 464 6800; f: 665 3528. *Also* Maypole House, Maypole Road, East Grinstead, West Sussex, RH19 1HH, UK. t: (44 342) 330100; f: 330192.

'Alongside our publishing under the Bowker-Saur imprint we distribute titles from leading reference imprints RR Bowker, Martindale-Hubbell, Marquis Who's Who, National Register Publishing, KG Saur and DW Thorpe. Together as Reed Reference Publishing, we share an international commitment to excellence in the publication of reference information and databases.'

1451. **EC Grants and Loans Database. diskette**. q. £299. 'Provides the only searchable, up-to-date overview of financial support regulations published in the English language on floppy disk.'

Notes

(91) cf HOWARD, P.K. **The death of common sense: How law is suffocating America**. *Random House*, 1994. 206 pp.

(92) **Making the law**. *Hansard Society for Parliamentary Government*, 1992, pp 6–9. 'The Report of the Hansard Commission on the Legislative Process'.

(93) The extract footnotes: WALKLAND, S.A. **The legislative process in Great Britain**. *Allen & Unwin*, 1968; MIERS, D.R. and PAGE, A.P. **Legislation**. 2nd ed. *Sweet and Maxwell*, 1990; BENNION, F.A.R. **Statute law**. 3rd ed. *Longman*, 1990; and ZANDER, M. **The law-making process**. *Weidenfeld & Nicholson*, 1980.

(94) Unless passed by the Commons alone and presented for Royal Assent under the Parliament Acts 1911 and 1949.

(95) Except in respect of compliance with European Community law.

(96) The extract comments that the legislative proceedings in both Houses, and the relevant procedures, are summarised in: GRIFFITH, J.A.G. and RYLE, M. **Parliament**. *Sweet and Maxwell*, 1989, pp 227–244 and 480–490.

(97) See GRIFFITH and RYLE, op cit, pp 244–247 and 488–489.

(98) Even in the United Kingdom, there is, for instance, a separate Scottish Law.

(99) LOGAN R.G. United States of America law *IN* Logan, R.G. ed. **Information sources in law**. *Bowker-Saur*, 1986, p 272.

(100) HOLBORN, G. **Butterworths legal research guide**. *Butterworths*, 1993. 352 pp.

(101) HOLBORN op cit pp 39, 40, 103.

(102) HOLBORN op cit p 124.

(103) COX, D.W. **Banking and finance: Accounts, audit and practice**. *Butterworths*, 1993. 869 pp. 'This book is intended to be a thorough introduction to the banking and finance industries. It seeks to provide information on all major aspects of the subject, with coverage from pawnbroking and building societies, through retail banking and trade finance, to complex financial products. The breadth of coverage will enable the reader to appreciate the full spectrum of the financial service industry.'

(104) PALFREMAN, D. **Law relating to banking services**. 4th ed. *Pitman Publishing*, 1993, p 1. (M+E Handbooks) This introductory text, designed to be suitable for students taking the *Chartered Institute of Bankers*' Associateship examination, references the following Acts in addition to those already listed above from Cox's book: Bankers' Books Evidence Act, Bills of Sale Act 1978, Business Names Act 1985, Civil Evidence Act 1968, Civil Liability (Contribution) Act 1978, Company Directors Disqualification Act 1986, Company Securities (Insider Dealing) Act 1985, Criminal Law Act 1977,

Deeds of Arrangement Act 1914, Enduring Powers of Attorney Act 1985, Factors Act 1889, Interpretation Act 1986, Land Charges Act 1925 (and 1972), Land Registration Act 1925, Law of Property (Miscellaneous Provisions) Act 1989, Law of Property Act 1925, Law Reform (Contributory Negligence) Act 1945, Leasehold Reform Act 1967, Life Assurance Act 1774, Limitation Act 1980, Limited Partnership Act 1907, Marine Insurance Act 1906, Married Women's Property Act 1882, Matrimonial Homes Act 1983, Mental Health Act 1983, Minors' Contracts Act 1967, Misrepresentation Act 1967, Partnership Act 1890, Policies of Assurance Act 1867, Powers of Attorney Act 1971, Protection from Eviction Act 1977, Race Relations Act 1976, Rent Charges Act 1977, Sale of Goods Act 1979, Sex Discrimination Act 1975 (and for 1986), Stamp Act 1853, Suicide Act 1961, Supply of Goods and Services Act 1882, Taxes Management Act 1970, Theft Act 1968, Torts (Interference with Goods) Act 1977, Trustee Act 1925, Unfair Contract Terms Act 1977.

(105) PENNINGTON, R.R. **The law of the investment markets**. *Blackwell*, 1990, p 1.

(106) WAINMAN, D. **Company structures**. *Sweet & Maxwell*, 1995, p v. Subtitled: 'Law, tax and accounting for companies and groups growing and evolving'.

(107) McBAIN, G.S. ed. **Butterworths banking law handbook**. 2nd ed. *Butterworths*, 1993. 1,254 pp.

(108) LOGAN op cit p 273.

(109) For instance, to take some more obvious recent examples: Thomson itself made the major acquisition of Information Access Company in late 1994; at the same time Reed Elsevier was acquiring Lexis/Nexis. Not long before that, Pearson – who operate the Financial Times group of companies – had taken over Extel; and Reuters had taken Quotron. Just before this book went to press, Primark, the owners of Datastream, announced the purchase of Disclosure (and of I/B/E/S). These sorts of industry concentration will continue – subject to any antitrust/monopoly restraints.

(110) LOGAN op cit p 273.

(111) HOLBORN op cit p 209, who had cited earlier a more extensive UK published introductory guide by Logan (**United States legal research**. *Legal Information Resources*, 1990). A major introductory volume published in the USA in the early 1990s makes the same point in its preface 'This new edition . . . reflects a transition in the current state of American legal research. The computer is now an essential search tool but it has not replaced the traditional printed sources. Computerized research supplements but does not supplant the book. Many online sources are based on printed tools and incorporate their structure and logic. An understanding of books is therefore essential to effective use of the electronic media. Furthermore, despite the continued expansion of the two major computer services, large areas of printed material remain available only in books and microforms. The resulting symbiosis of the two methods pervades most of the Chapters that follow and shapes the actual practice of legal research today.' The chapters are: The research process; Court reports; Case-finding; Case-finding by computer; Statutes; Legislative history; Administrative law; Looseleaf services; Secondary materials; International law (subdivided into US sources and General sources); English and Commonwealth legal research; The Civil Law system. (COHEN, M.L. and OLSON, K.C. **Legal research in a nutshell**. 5th ed. *West Publishing*, 1992. 370 pp). See also:

Searching the Law. *Transnational Juris Publications*, 1993. $130. "The book is arranged very differently from the usual chapter-by-chapter exposition of the various types of research materials. It has broken down the field of law into its major components, and under each is a list of all the leading texts, journals, treatises, and bibliographies for a particular component. This very practical arrangement allows the book to be used by the law student, lawyer, paralegal, or the layman to solve legal research problems" (*International Journal of Legal Information*).

(112) CONRY, E.J., FERRERA, G.R. and FOX, K.H. **The legal environment of business**. *Allyn and Bacon*, 1993, pp 153–154.

(113) DALE, R. **International banking deregulation: The great banking experiment**. *Blackwell*, 1992.

(114) Interview with the former *Deputy Governor*, Spring 1994.

(115) **Payment Systems in Group of Ten Countries**, *Bank for International Settlements*, 1993, p. 411.

(116) **Primer** *Bacon & Woodrow* November 1994.

(117) GRAHAM, J.W. **The US Securities and Exchange Commission: A research and information guide**. *Garland Publishing*, 1993. 344 pp. Other volumes in the series *Research and Information Guides in Business, Industry and Economic Institutions* include:

- Franchising in business: A guide to information sources
- The informal economy: A research guide
- The World Bank Group: A guide to information sources
- Global countertrade: An annotated bibliography
- The New York Stock Exchange: A guide to information sources
- The American Stock Exchange: A research and information guide.

(118) MAYER, C. **The regulation of financial services: Lessons from the United Kingdom** *IN* DERMINE, J. ed. **European banking in the 1990s**. 2nd ed. *Blackwell Publishers*, 1993, pp 46–47.

(119) TEWELES, R.J., BRADLEY, E.S. and TEWELES, T.M. **The stock market**. 6th ed. *John Wiley*, 1992, pp. 52–53.

(120) MARSH, S.B. and SOULSBY, J. **Business law**. 5th ed. *McGraw-Hill*, 1992, p 51.

(121) SAVAGE, N. and BRADGATE, R. **Business law**. 2nd ed. *Butterworths*, 1993, pp 467, 468, 470.

(122) LAVIN, M.R. **Business information: How to find it, how to use it**. 2nd ed. *Oryx Press*, 1992, pp 114–5; 182–183.

(123) **State of financial reporting: A review**. *Financial Reporting Council*, 1991.

(124) ELLIOTT, B. and ELLIOTT, J. **Financial accounting and reporting**. *Prentice Hall*, 1993. 639 pp. A very clear US introduction to accounting and reporting is: PORTER, G.A. and NORTON, C.L. **Financial accounting: The impact on decision makers**. *Dryden Press*, 1995. 879 pp.

(125) SMITH. T. **Accounting for growth: Stripping the camouflage from company accounts**. *Century Business*, 1992. 226 pp.

(126) ABBOTT, K.R. **Company law.** 5th ed. *DP Publications*, 1993, p 209. A good basic introduction for the UK with a wide coverage.

(127) NOBES, C. and PARKER, R. **Comparative international accounting**. 4th ed. *Prentice Hall*, 1995, pp 145–147.

(128) **Historical on-line database services: A report on the supply in the UK of services which provide access to databases containing archival business and financial information**. *HMSO*, 1994, p iv. Cm 2554.

(129) *Yearbook of the United Nations* 47, 1993, p 1110.

(130) **International trade policies: The Uruguay Round and beyond.** *International Monetary Fund*, 1994, Volume II (Background Papers), p. 1. *Appendix II* of this document is a 'Summary of specific commitments in the financial services sector of selected countries' (United States, European Union, Japan, Brazil, India, and Korea).

(131) NUGENT, N. **Government and politics of the European Union**. 3rd ed. *Macmillan Press*, 1994. 400 pp. 12.99. "An excellent book with which it is difficult to find fault" (*West European Politics*); "this is by far the best teaching text on the European Community that I have come across." (*Journal of Common Market Studies*).

(132) WALKER, E. The EBRD **Capital Market Strategies** 1, July 1994, p 1.

Further reading

MUELLER, G.G., GERNON, H. and MEEK, G.K. **Accounting: An international perspective**. 3rd ed. *Irwin*, 1994. 200 pp. $27.95. 'Designed for the introductory accounting course. It supplements existing introductory accounting textbooks, which are largely void of international content, and is the only resource available for this purpose. The book provides a general, nontechnical overview of the subject matter of international accounting.' There is also an *Instructor's Manual*.

BROMWICH, M. and HOPWOOD, A. eds. **Accounting and the law**. *Prentice Hall* in association with *Institute of Chartered Accountants in England and Wales*, 1992

MARTIN, I. **Accounting in the foreign exchange market**. 2nd ed. *Butterworths*, 1993.

TORRES, F. and GIAVAZZI, F. eds. **Adjustment and growth in the European Monetary Union**. *Cambridge University Press* for *Centre for Economic Policy Research*, 1993. 388 pp. £37.50.

BURCH, D. **Aid, technology and export subsidies: Perspectives on the political economy of mixed credits**. *Avebury*, 1994. 150 pp. £32.50.

Analysis of the Bank Secrecy Act Regulations and the Money Laundering Control Act. *Savings & Community Bankers of America*, 1992. 281 pp. $205.95.

Bank audit manual. *American Institute of Certified Public Accountants*, 1992. 3 vols.

HALL, M.J.B. **Banking regulation and supervision: A comparative study of the UK, USA and Japan**. *Edward Elgar*, 1993. 279 pp.

BRYAN, L.L. **Bankrupt: Restoring the health and profitability of our banking system**. *Harper Business*, 1991. 314 pp.

BROWN, C., MALLETT, D. and TAYLOR, M. **Banks**. *Accountancy Books*, 1993. 552 pp. £65.00. Review of all UK accounting standards and statements of recommended practice which affect the banking industry, including: the impact of EC legislation; control of banking activity; 'money laundering'; the development of securitisation; the implications of the Bingham Report.

BEATTIE, V.A. and others. **Banks and bad debts: Accounting for loan losses in international banking**. *Wiley*, 1995. 214 pp. £45.00. 'Features a unique compendium, provided by *Price Waterhouse*, of up- to-date information describing the accounting and regulatory treatment of impaired loans in 14 major countries.'

BBA Accounting Guide. *British Bankers' Association*, 1992. £40. 'Guidance on how to comply with the new legislation affecting banks' annual accounts.'

BCCI affair: A Report. *US GPO*, 1992. 672 pp. $20. 'Reports on an investigation of the Bank of Credit and Commerce, International (BCCI) and how it was able to penetrate the United States banking system and conduct global financial crime. Includes information on how Federal agencies such as the State Department and the Central Intelligence Agency handle the special problems posed by BCCI.'

SANDERS, S. ed. **Bond market compliance: Regulation of London's euromarkets**. *IFR Books*, 1993. Coverage includes:

- *ISMA Regulation of the Secondary Market in International Securities*
  - ISMA market regulation
  - CRD rules for reporting dealers and IDBs
- *The Money Market Exemption*
  - s43 of the FSA and the ability to gain listed money market exemption
  - The London Code of Conduct – May 1992
  - Wholesale counterparties – practical implications for compliance
- *Financial Regulation*
  - SFA vs Bank of England regulation
  - Implications of financial regulation for corporate structures
- *SFA Membership and Registration*
- *Application of SFA's Conduct of Business Rules*
- *EC Developments*
  - Investment services and other directives in the investment sector; regulatory and structural implications
  - Money-laundering: international, EC and domestic initiatives; regulatory and structural implications.

KAY, J.A. and KING, M.A. **The British tax system**. 5th ed. *Oxford University Press*, 1990. 250 pp.

LIEBERMAN, J.K. and SIEDEL, G.J. **Business law and the legal environment**. 3rd ed. *Dryden Press*, 1992. 1,392 pp.

WALMSLEY, K. **Butterworths company law handbook**. 9th ed. *Butterworths*, 1993. 2,066 pp.

SABOLOT, D. ed. **Butterworths financial services law handbook**. *Butterworths*. 1993. 1,030 pp. 'Contains all the relevant primary and secondary legislation relating to this notoriously difficult legal area. Also includes a selection of the principal and generally applicable regulatory items.'

COURTNEY, B. **Butterworths trust taxation manual**. 3rd ed. *Butterworths*, 1993. 176 pp.

RYDER, F. and BUENO, A. **Byles on bills of exchange**. 26th ed. *Sweet & Maxwell*, 1988. £98.00. "As usual the last word on the subject of bills, cheques and promissory notes" (*Banker's Magazine*).

COX, C. and ROSS, H.J. **Capital gains tax on businesses**. *Sweet & Maxwell*, 1992. £50.00.

ZANDER, M. **Cases and materials on the English legal system**. 6th ed. *Weidenfeld & Nicolson*, 1992. 688 pp. £17.99. "This book needs no recommendation. The scope of its material is wide and deep, critical and constructive" (*New Law Journal*).

GOODHART, C.A.E. **The central bank and the financial system**. *Macmillan Press*, 1994. 310 pp. £13.99.

FRAZER, W. **The central banks: The international and European directions**. *Quorum Books*, 1994. 280 pp. £53.95. The principal central banks considered are the Bank of England, Federal Reserve, and Bundesbank.

Commercial real estate finance: A current guide to representing lenders and borrowers. *American Bar Association*, 1993. 448 pp. $69.95. From the *Real Property, Probate and Trust Law* Section. Includes discussions of traditional and new financing methods and how to use them, drafting provisions, and bankruptcy and tax issues.

ALEXANDER, D. ed. **Comparative international accounting**. *Dryden Press*, 1995. 512 pp. £17.50. Covers the five major geographical regions of the globe: Europe, North America, Australasia, Japan and the Pacific Basin, together with the developing countries. Economic, political, historical and cultural influences are examined by each contributor, as are the inter-relationships within a region and those relationships extending beyond it.

HOWELLS, G. **Consumer debt**. *Sweet & Maxwell*, 1993. £35.00.

Convention on bankruptcy law. *Europe Information Service*, 1994. BEF 10,000. 'After 25 years of negotiations, the EU Member States are at last about to put their signatures to a Convention on Insolvency Procedures.'

Coopers Accounting Comparisons. *Gee*. 1993. Comparisons of accounting and financial reporting requirements in 15 countries gathered into 5 volumes for UK/Europe: I. UK, France, Germany and the Netherlands; II. UK, Belgium, Italy and Spain;. III. UK, Denmark, Portugal and Greece; IV. UK, Luxembourg, Austria and Switzerland; V. UK, Norway, Sweden and Finland; *plus* 2 volumes for UK, Japan and UK, USA, Canada.

BROWN, C. and FRANKLIN, R. **Countertrade: Paying in goods and services**. *FT Law & Tax*, 1994. £100.

BROWN, L.N. **The Court of Justice of the European Communities**. 4th ed. *Sweet & Maxwell*, 1994, 350 pp. £22.00.

Credit union audit manual. *American Institute of Certified Public Accountants*, 1992. 2 vols.

EFFROS, R.C. ed. **Current legal issues affecting central banks**. *IMF*. Two volumes have been announced in a new series based on biennial IMF seminars held for central bank general counsels: Volume I was published in 1993; Volume II announced for 1994.

Digest of State accountancy laws and State Board regulations. *American Institute of Certified Public Accountants*, 1993. $25. Published in association with the *National Association of State Boards of Accountancy.* 'A compilation of state by state narrative summaries, tables and charts detailing the principal legal requirements that govern the licensing and regulation of professional accountants in the United States.'

JACK, R. **Documentary credits**. *Butterworths*, 1993. 410 pp. Documentary credits secure payment in international trade transactions. This book gives a comprehensive account of the workings of documentary credits in the context of English law and under international banking practice as applied in England. This new edition has been necessitated by a new and substantial revision of the ICC's Uniform Customs and Practice for Documentary Credits. "Anyone who has ever been confused by the complex interlocking relationships created by letters of credit can do no better than buy this book." (*Journal of International Banking Law*).

BAKER, P. **Double taxation conventions and international tax law**. 2nd ed. *Sweet & Maxwell*, 1994. 450 pp. £85.00.

ANDENAS, M. and KENYON-SLADE, S. **EC financial market regulation and company law**. *Sweet & Maxwell*, 1993.

SHERIDAN, M.B.G. and CAMERON, J.A. eds. **EC legal systems: An introductory guide**. *Butterworths*, 1992.

EC unification reports. *Admerca*, 1994. SFr 6,000. History, green paper, policies and issues, country analysis, impacts, measures for a range of industries, including banks/securities.

DUNN, J. **The economic limits to modern politics**. *Cambridge University Press*, 1992. 238 pp. £12.95.

EL-AGRAA, A.M. ed. **The economics of the European Community**. 4th ed. *Harvester Wheatsheaf*, 1994. £565 pp.

SHERIDAN, M.B.G. and CAMERON, J.A. eds. **EFTA legal systems: An introductory guide**. *Butterworths*.

EVANS, P. and WALSH, J. **The EIU guide to the new GATT**. *Economist Intelligence Unit*, 1994. 136 pp. The twenty-three chapters include: 'Agreement on trade in services'; 'Agreement on trade-related investment measures'; 'The impact on services'; 'The World Trade Organisation'.

Electronic banking and the law. 2nd ed. *IBC Publishing*, 1993. £69.

BUENO, A., HEDLEY, R. and STALLEBRASS, P. **Electronic transfers of funds**. *Sweet & Maxwell*, 1994.

INGMAN, T. **The English legal process**. 5th ed. *Blackstone Press*, 1994.

CANZONERI, M.B., GRILLI, V. and MASSON, P.R. eds. **Establishing a central bank: Issues in Europe and lessons from the U.S.** *Cambridge University Press*, 1992. 328 pp. £32.50. Papers from a conference held in 1991 sponsored by the *Centre for Economic Policy Research, Georgetown University: Centre for German and European Studies* and the *International Monetary Fund*.

ALEXANDER, F. and ARCHER, S. eds. **The European accounting guide**. 2nd ed. *Harcourt Brace Professional*, 1995. 1,200 pp. £57.95. 'The first complete survey of European accounting and financial reporting.'

GRETSCHMANN, K. ed. **Economic and monetary union: Implications for national policy-makers.** *Martinus Nijhoff*, 1993. 300 pp. £78.

SLOMAN, J. **Economics**. 2nd ed. *Harvester Wheatsheaf*, 1994. 960 pp. £16.95. 'The UK's bestselling introductory textbook.'

HUDEC, R.E. **Enforcing international trade law**. *Butterworths*, 1993. 500 pp. Legal history of the General Agreement on Tarrifs and Trade (GATT) from 1975 to date.

MINIKIN, R. **The ERM explained**. *Kogan Page*, 1993. 144 pp. £12.95. 'A straightforward guide to the exchange rate mechanism and the European currency debate.'

European Commercial Law Series. *Longman Law, Tax and Finance*, 1992–. Individual country volumes include coverage of: mergers and acquisitions, taxation and finance, and insolvency amongst a range of other topics.

SHAW, J. **European Community law**. *Macmillan Press*, 1993. 304 pp. £8.99.

GIOVANNINI, A. and MAYER, C. eds. **European financial integration**. *Cambridge University Press* for *Centre for Economic Policy Research*, 1992. 369 pp. £16.95.

DINAN, D. **Ever closer union? : An introduction to the European Community**. *Macmillan Press*, 1994. 512 pp. £12.99.

Exchange control policy. *OECD*, 1993. 90 pp. $18.

KRUGMAN, P. and MILLER, M. eds. **Exchange rate targets and currency bands**. *Cambridge University Press* for *Centre for Economic Policy Research*, 1992. 272 pp. £13.95. "This book has set the trend for a whole new area of research" (*Economic Journal*).

MILLER, P., REDDING, R. and BAHNSON, P. **The FASB: The people, the process, and the politics**. 3rd ed. *Irwin*, 1994. 192 pp. 'Provides a complete introduction to and description of the Financial Accounting Standards Board. The text describes why financial reporting exists, why GAAP are needed, and why the FASB was created.'

HERMAN, E. ed. **The federal budget: A guide to process and principal publications**. *Pierian Press*, 1991.

SCHICK, A. **The Federal budget: Politics, policy, process**. *Brookings Institution*, 1995. 240 pp. $15.95. "An up-to-date, clear explanation of the federal budget. . . . He has captured the politics of federal budgeting from the original lofty goals to the stark realities of today. . . . Anyone who wants to understand federal budgeting should read this book" (from reviews by members of Congress).

BANURI, T. and SCHOR, J.B. **Financial openness and national autonomy: Opportunities and constraints**. *Clarendon Press*, 1992. WIDER Study in Development Economics.

VITTAS, D. ed. **Financial regulation: Changing the rules of the game**. *World Bank*, 1992. 449 pp. Fourteen papers originating at a conference in Cambridge, Massachusetts, in 1990.

ALEXANDER, D.J.A. and BRITTON, A. **Financial reporting**. 3rd ed. *Chapman & Hall*, 1993. 648 pp. £19.99. In three parts: *Part I* The conceptual framework; *Part II* The legal framework; *Part III* The regulatory framework.

McGEE, A. **The financial services ombudsmen**. *Tolley*, 1992. 69 pp. £10.95.

BALDASSARRI, M. and ROBERTI, P. eds. **Fiscal problems in the Single-Market Europe**. *Macmillan Press*, 1994. 294 pp. £45.00.

TURCOM, R. **Foreign direct investment in the US**. *Sweet & Maxwell*, 1993. £95.00 'Eleven articles on areas of law directly relevant to a potential foreign investor.'

Foreign investment in US real estate: A comprehensive guide. *American Bar Association*, 1990. 1045 pp. Compiled by the *Real Property, Probate and Trust Law* Section. Provides an overview of US law for foreign investors, from the time the investor considers acquiring property to the time of liquidation. The book covers regulatory restrictions, taxes, financing, immigration and insolvency.

WILSON, A. **Friendly Societies: A guide to the new law**. *Butterworths*, 1993. 200 pp.

PARRY, H., REES, W. and BETTELHEIM, E. **Futures trading law and regulation**. *FT Law & Tax*, 1993. £79. Covers the contractual and fiscal framework, both in the UK and the EC; including off-exchange trading and the criminal law dimension.

DAVIES, D. **GATT: A practical guide**. *FT Law & Tax*, 1995. £125.

PETERSMANN, E-U. **The GATT world trade and legal system after the Uruguay Round**. *Transnational Juris Publications*, 1992. 250 pp. $95.

COLAS, B. **Global economic cooperation: A guide to agreements and organizations**. 2nd ed. *Kluwer Law and Taxation Publishers*, 1994. 560 pp. £46. "Aims at giving a complete and coherent picture of the global economic legal and institutional system. The agreements selected here – some 300 in total – cover those multilateral treaties which are open to all states, and which regulate trade, money, finance and environmental protection and facilitate the negotiation of international contracts and the enforcement of arbitral awards and judicial decisions. It is intended to serve the needs of scholars, international business lawyers, government officials and legislators working in this field, as well as those engaged in the operation of international trade. For the general reader, this book will prove a useful guide" (*International Chamber of Commerce*).

SWARY, I. and B. TOPF. **Global financial deregulation**. *Blackwell Business*, 1992.

GOTTSCHALK, J.A. **The global trade and investment handbook**. *Probus Publishing*, 1993. 675 pp. 'A country-by-country reference to business practices, regulations and laws.'

KASERMAN, D. and MAYO, J. **Government and business: The economics of antitrust and regulation**. *Dryden Press*, 1995. 656 pp. £41.

Government securities and debt management in the 1990s. *OECD*, 1993. 220 pp. $42. 'This volume is aimed at making the reader familiar with policy issues and techniques of government debt management. In addition, it provides a factual survey of debt instruments, selling techniques, the organisation of primary and secondary markets in government securities, and other relevant information on government debt management in OECD member countries.'

DALE, P. ed. **Guide to libraries and information units: In government departments and other organisations**. 31st ed. *British Library: Science Reference and Information Service*, 1993. 196 pp. £36. 700 entries. 'The best, most detailed directory of: UK government libraries; Libraries with authoritative collections on current affairs and subjects of topical concern (including public and official bodies, regulatory bodies, trade associations, charities, and other selected organisations).' Also available is a *Guide to libraries in Western Europe* (£36) and a *Guide to libraries in key UK companies* (£20).

MATHIJSEN, P.S.R.F. **A guide to European Community law**. 6th ed. *Sweet & Maxwell*, 1994, 470 pp. £26.00.

LEONARD, D. **Guide to the European Community**. *Economist Books*, 1993. 262 pp.

Guide to trust institution federal filings. *American Bankers Association*, 1990. A compilation of all of the federal reports that are required to be filed by trust institutions. 'The guide can serve as a checkpoint for trust institutions as they continue to pursue a valiant effort to submit all the appropriate tax filings and multitude of other required reports on time.'

BERNSTEIN, R. and WOOD, D. **Handbook of arbitration practice**. 2nd ed. *Sweet & Maxwell*, 1993. £92.00. "Nearest thing there is to a standard work in this field" (*Litigation*).

LYNCH, T.D. and MARTIN, L.L. **Handbook of comparative public budgeting and financial management**. *Marcel Dekker*, 1993. 328 pp. $140.

FRIEDMAN, B. and HAHN, F. eds. **Handbook of monetary economics**. *North-Holland*, 1990

RABIN, J. **Handbook of public budgeting**. *Marcel Dekker*, 1992. 760 pp. $195.

FRENCH, D. **How to cite legal authorities**. *Blackstone Press*, 1994. £15.

OAKES, R. **Insurance brokers: An industry accounting and auditing guide**. *Accountancy Books*, 1995. 352 pp. £55. 'The definite guide for brokers, their financial advisers, accountants and auditors.'

FONTAINE, M. ed. **Insurance contract law**. *Association Internationale de Droit des Assurances*. Developing collection of monographs. *Volume 1* (1990): Covers 15 European countries, Eastern and Western,including the UK; *Volume 2*: (1993): Covers 14 countries worldwide, including the USA.

RADEBAUGH, L.H. and GRAY, S.J. **International accounting and multinational enterprises**. 3rd ed. *John Wiley*, 1993. 582 pp. Includes a detailed treatment of attempts to classify accounting and reporting systems, an account of the pressure for international accounting harmonization and disclosure, together with a summary of multinational management perspectives on information disclosure and regulation. A cultural classification is used as the basis for discussion and analysis of accounting systems and practices in a selection of industrialized countries: the UK and the USA in the context of the Anglo-Saxon culture area, the Netherlands and Sweden as representatives of the Nordic countries, Germany and Switzerland as representatives of Germanic countries, France and Italy as representatives of the developed Latin countries, and Japan as a representative of the developed Asian countries.

ERNST & YOUNG. **International bank accounting**. 3rd ed. *Euromoney Publications*, 1994. $295.00. Two volumes. Detailed coverage of 16 countries, plus chapters on the European Community and the Middle East.

NORTON, W. **International banking regulation and supervision**. *Graham & Trotman*, 1994.

SEIDI-HOHENVELDERN, I. **International economic law**. 2nd ed. *Martinus Nijhoff Publishers*, 1992. 304 pp. £66.50.

International estate planning: Principles and strategies. *American Bar Association*, 1991. 937 pp. Prepared by the *Real Property, Probate and Trust Law* and the *International Law and Practice* Sections. Aids lawyers in understanding basic principles of international asset management, the complex taxation issues involved, jurisdictional variations and options, and government controls. Included are vehicles and strategies to preserve assets, step-by-step procedures for structuring the plan, avenues of protection, and case studies of jurisdictions closely linked to the USA.

NOBES. C. **International guide to interpreting company accounts: Overcoming disparities in national accounting procedures**. *FT Management Reports*, 1994. £225. 'The report examines the sheer scale of international accounting differences and identifies explanatory factors; analyses important topics for which valuation and measurement differ internationally on a comparative basis for nine major countries; studies the complex area of pension fund accounting across 21 countries; assesses the unusual features of financial reporting in nine major countries; details numerical comparative information for the UK and the US, in particular the calculation of "earnings" and "equity"; explains Japanese financial reporting and the influence of Germany and the US; describes the origins, working and influence of the *International Accounting Standards Committee*, and the contrast between International Accounting Standards and the current rules that apply in the US, UK, Japan and Germany; points out further difficulties for international analysis, including language problems; and proposes the construction of benchmarks for international comparison.'

NEXIA INTERNATIONAL. **The international handbook of corporate and personal taxes**. 2nd ed. *Chapman & Hall*, 1994. 688 pp. £50

NEXIA INTERNATIONAL. **The international handbook of corporate governance**. *Chapman & Hall*, 1995. 352 pp. £39.50.

NEXIA INTERNATIONAL. **The international handbook of financial reporting**. *Chapman & Hall*, 1993. 416 pp. £40. A dozen or so pages each designed to give an overall view for 34 countries of the framework within which financial statements are prepared.

International insurance industry guide. 5th ed. *Coopers & Lybrand*, 1993. £20. 'Particular attention to regulatory, taxation and accounting practices, and considerations in establishing an insurance operation.'

SHAW, M.N. **International law**. 3rd ed. *Grotius Publications*, 1991. 837 pp. £24.95. 'It sets the subject firmly in the context of world political events and brings out the importance of the many political, cultural and economic influences that affect international law.'

D'AMATO, A. **International law: Process and prospect**. 2nd ed. *Transnational Juris Publications*, 1993. 250 pp. $65. 'He grapples with questions at the core of the subject: does international law exist and is it real; how can the law of individual rights be accommodated in an international legal system that is apparently addressed to nations and not to individuals; and more.'

MEESSEN, K.M. **International law of export control**. *Graham & Trotman*, 1992. 208 pp. £48.

SORNARAJAH, M. **The international law on foreign investment**. *Grotius Publications*, 1994. 450 pp. £55.00. 'Foreign investment involves the transfer of tangible or intangible . . . (intellectual property rights, such as patents, copyright, know-how, etc) . . . assets from one country into another for the purpose of use in that country to generate wealth under the total or partial control of the owner of the assets. It is contrasted with portfolio investment where there is a movement of money for the purpose of buying shares in a company formed or functioning in another country, the distinguishing element being that, in portfolio investment, there is a divorce between management and control of the company and the share ownership in it.'

HOUTTE, H.v. **International trade and finance law**. *Sweet & Maxwell*, 1994. 600 pp. £120. 'The approach it takes is a very transnational one, and the book contains information on the completion of GATT.'

BUGG, R. and WHITEHEAD, G. **International trade and payments**. *Woodhead-Faulkner*, 1994. 219 pp. 'Practical introduction to the structure and regulation of international trade, how it is financed and how payments are made.'

HAY, P. **An introduction to US law**. 2nd ed. *Butterworths*, 1991.

POINTON, J. ed. **Issues in business taxation research**. *Avebury*, 1993. 190 pp. £35.00.

PORTWOOD, T. **Joint ventures under EEC Competition Law**. *Athlone Press*, 1995. 192 pp. £45. In the *European Community Law Series*.

Labourers in different vineyards? The banking regulators and the legal profession. *American Bar Association*, 1993. 314 pp. $15. Report of the ABA Working Group on Lawyers' Representation of Regulated Clients.

LASOK, D. and LASOK, K.P.E. **Law and institutions of the European Union**. 6th ed. *Butterworths*, 1994. 786 pp. 'To understand the nature of the law one must understand the nature of the society from which it emanates and which it purports to govern. We are used to the concepts of national and international law. The former is the law of a sovereign state and as such it governs the society comprised in a state that is a group of people living within a defined area under a government which has executive, legislative, judicial and administrative powers. International law, on the other hand, is the body of rules which governs relations between states and such international organizations as are set up and recognised by states as bearers of rights and duties. In exceptional situations individuals may be regarded as subjects of international law. As a body of rules international law is derived partly from custom and state practice, partly from the will of states expressed in treaties and partly generated by institutions (eg the United Nations Organization) set up by states and based on a treaty.

The object of this book is to define and analyze a nascent body of law which can be described as the law of the European Community. It is neither a national nor an international system of law in the accepted sense of these terms but a *sui generis* system emanating from the will to create a European Community. It reflects, of course, the nature of this design.' (From the *Preface to the first edition*, 1973.)

REDFERN, A. and HUNTER, M. **Law and practice of international commercial arbitration**. 2nd ed. *Sweet & Maxwell*, 1991. £130.00.

Legal aspects of privatisation. *Council of Europe*, 1993. 222 pp. Proceedings of the 21st Colloquy on European Law, Budapest, 15–17 October 1991.

McCARTY, F.W. and BAGBY, J.W. **The legal environment of business**. 2nd ed. *Irwin*, 1993. 816 pp. £44.95.

SHIHATA, I.F. **Legal treatment of foreign investment**. *Kluwer Academic Publishers*, 1993. £92.00.

RAYNER, K. **Listing securities in the United States and the United Kingdom**. *Graham & Trotman*. 268 pp. Comparative guide to the regulatory and accounting requirements.

HASLAM, S.M. and PEERLESS, S.G.G. **The London securities markets: organis-**

ation, regulation, auditing and financial reporting. *Accountancy Books*, 1990. 432 pp. £35.00. Comprehensive reference guide to the complex operations of the securities industry.

CLOUGH, M. **Mergers and acquisitions in the EC: A guide to the regulation of commercial activity**. *FT Management Reports*, 1994. £262. Includes an 'Overview of all Merger Regulation Decisions to End 1993'.

Model tax convention: Attribution of income to permanent establishments. *OECD*, 1994. 50 pp. $11. Issues in International Taxation: No. 5. 'The business profits article of the Model Tax Convention provides that the country where business income arises may tax a foreign enterprise on such income only if the enterprise has in that country a permanent establishment to which the income is attributable. This publication includes a discussion of the circumstances under which income is to be attributed to a permanent establishment for purposes of an income tax treaty, particularly where goods, services, or intangibles are transferred to or from the permanent establishment.'

BIRDS, J. **Modern insurance law**. 3rd ed. *Sweet & Maxwell*, 1993. 24.00.

QUIGLEY, J.M. and SMOLENSKY, E. eds. **Modern public finance**. *Harvard University Press*, 1994. 368 pp. £31.95. "These essays add up to a comprehensive, lucid and very up-to-date presentation of the state of the art in public finance theory, with the presentation done by those who truly are the authorities" (*Netzer, New York University*).

Modernizing the financial system: Recommendations for safer, more competitive banks. *US GPO*, 1991. 681 pp. $35. 'Provides recommendations to revitalize for taxpayers a banking system that is safe, sound, and competitive; a regulatory system that is strong, efficient, and streamlined; and a deposit insurance fund that is well-capitalized with industry funds. Also known as: *Federal Deposit Insurance System Study*.'

NOLLING, W. **Monetary policy in Europe after Maastrict**. *Macmillan Press*, 1993. 264 pp. £40.00.

ARESTIS, P. ed. **Money and banking: Issues for the Twenty-first century**. *Macmillan Press*, 1993. 336 pp. £45.00. Collection of essays.

FERRAN, M. **Mortgage securitisation: Legal aspects**. *Butterworths*, 1992.

National treatment for foreign-controlled enterprises. *OECD*, 1993. 185 pp.

COLLINS, S.M. and BOSWORTH, B.P. eds. **The new GATT: Implications for the United States**. *Brookings Institution*, 1995. 128 pp. $10.95.

The North American Free Trade Agreement: Its scope and implications for North American lawyers, businesses, and policymakers. *American Bar Association*, 1993. $75. Issued by the Standing Committee on *Continuing Education of the Bar*.

Obstacles to trade and competition. *OECD*, 1993. 112 pp. $30.

Origins and causes of the Savings and Loan debacle: A blueprint for reform. *US GPO*, 1993. 117 pp. $4.25. 'A Report to the President and Congress of the United States . . . Presents the findings, conclusions, and recommendations of the Commission regarding the savings and loan crisis and the measures needed to prevent the recurrence of such crises in the United States financial system.'

OAKLEY, A.J. **Parker and Mellows: The modern law of trusts**. 6th ed. *Sweet & Maxwell*, 1994. 570 pp. £27.50.

BENNETT, P. **Pension fund surpluses**. 2nd ed. *FT Law & Tax*, 1994. £79.

SELF, R. **The pension fund trustee handbook**. *Tolley*, 1993. 137 pp. £15.

NEVITT, G. **Pension schemes: An industry accounting and auditing guide**. *Accountancy Books*, 1995. £55. 'The legislative framework of the industry, including the interaction with the State scheme . . . The book incorporates all current legislation up to the *Pensions Act 1993*.'

WHITE, A. and PUNTER, J. **Pensions issues in mergers and acquisitions**. *FT Law & Tax*, 1993. £75.

MASSON, P.R. and TAYLOR, M.P. eds. **Policy issues in the operation of currency unions**. *Cambridge University Press*, 1993, 264 pp. £30.00. 'This book provides an overview as well as the latest research on currency unions – geographical areas throughout which a single currency circulates as the medium of exchange.'

ARTIS, M.J. ed. **Prest and Coppock's The UK economy**. 13th ed. *Weidenfeld & Nicolson*, 1992. 440 pp. £10.99. 'The most up-to-date, systematic and balanced assessment of British economic life.'

Professional accounting in foreign countries. *American Institute of Certified Public Accountants*. 'A series of volumes reviewing information on the business environment . . . professional accounting principles and practices . . . and auditing procedures as they currently exist in various foreign countries. Some 20 countries completed at the time of writing, each priced at $30'.

HYMAN, D.N. **Public finance**. 4th ed. *Dryden Press*, 1992. 650 pp. £46.50.

HENLEY, D., LIKIERMAN, A., PERRIN, J.R., LAPSLEY, I., EVANS, M. and WHITEOAK, J. **Public sector accounting and financial control**. 4th ed. *Chapman & Hall*, 1992. 336 pp. £18.50. 'The most authoritative text available on public sector accounting and finance in the UK.'

The regulation and prevention of economic crime internationally. *Kogan Page*, 1994. 250 pp. £40.00. 'Written at the behest of the British *Foreign Office*, presents international best practice in the control of economic crime. It will be an invaluable resource for both institutions in Eastern Europe and the developing world and for any international corporation or financial institution dealing in these areas. Furthermore, this definitive book is equally relevant to the developing world where a range of legislation and archaic practice is currently being rationalised under the auspices of the G7 nations, and where compliance with the new legislation will soon be mandatory.'

EDWARDS, F.R. and PATRICK, H.T. eds. **Regulating international financial markets: Issues and policies**. *Kluwer Academic Publishers*, 1992. 317 pp. Twenty-three papers, one previously published, presented at a conference in New York in 1990.

REISNER, R. and GRUSON, M. eds. **Regulation of foreign banks**. *Butterworths*, 1991. £92.50. Primarily covers the situation in the USA; but also includes detailed consideration of regulation within the EC, with chapters focusing on regulation in France, UK and Germany, as well as Japan.

WHITE, J. **Regulation of securities and futures dealing**. *Sweet & Maxwell*, 1992. £72.00. '(The author) is Head of the Conduct of Business Department at the (UK) *Securities and Futures Authority*.'

Regulatory reform, privatisation and competition policy. *OECD*, 1992. 134 pp. $31.

Resolving the Thrift crisis. *US GPO*, 1993. 109 pp. $7. Examines the underlying causes of the savings and loan crisis, and the progress of the cleanup through the end of 1992, with special attention given to the role of the Resolution Trust Corporation.

WHITEHOUSE, C. **Revenue law: Principles and practice**. 11th ed. *Butterworths*, 1995.

THOMPSON, A. **The Second Banking Directive**. *Butterworths*, 1991.

Spicers Guide to the EU Structural Funds and Initiatives. 2nd ed. *Longman*, 1994. £65. Published in association with *Consultancy Europe Associates*. "Excellent. The best guide to this complex subject area that we have seen" (*UK Department of Trade and Industry*).

GREENWAY, D. and WINTERS, A. eds. **Surveys in international trade**. *Blackwell Business*, 1994. 1,320 pp. 'Ten literature surveys in international trade covering both theory and policy.'

STEDMAN, G. **Takeovers**. *FT Law & Tax*, 1993. £79.

Tax information exchange between OECD member countries: A survey of current practices. *OECD*, 1994. 116 pp. $15.

WILLIAMS, D.W. **Tax on the international transfer of information**. *Longman Law, Tax and Finance*, 1991. Shows how the flow of information can be carried out in a tax efficient manner by complying, or negotiating with, the tax authorities. Provides the practitioner with examples of the different approaches of jurisdictions, demonstrating the contrasting techniques they employ, assessment of the various reporting requirements, details on customs duties, and how they apply to the inward and outward flows of information.

CARMICHAEL, K.S. and WOLSTENHOLME, P.H. **Taxation for Lloyd's underwriters**. 4th ed. *Butterworths*, 1993. 270 pp.

KNOESTER, A. ed. **Taxation in the United States and Europe**. *Macmillan Press*, 1994. 448 pp. £50. *Confederation of European Economic Associations* conference volume.

DAVIS, C. **Taxes Management Act: A practical guide to compliance**. *FT Law & Tax*, 1994. £65.

Taxing profits in a global economy: Domestic and international issues. *OECD*, 1992. 486 pp. $84.

MAAS, R.W. **Tolley's anti-avoidance provisions**. 2nd ed. *Tolley*, 1992. 632 pp. £49.50. 'Comprehensive review of statute and case law aimed at preventing the avoidance of the five main UK taxes.'

FINNEY, M.J. and DIXON, J.C. eds. **Tolley's international tax planning**. 2nd ed. *Tolley*, 1993. 1,400 pp. £85. Two volumes. 'Includes studies of the corporate tax compliance regimes in fifteen major states.'

JEFFERY, D. and others. **Tolley's tax compliance and investigations**. 3rd ed. *Tolley*, 1992. 424 pp. £34.95. 'The various investigation techniques and strategies of the Inland Revenue.'

Tolley's tax havens. 2nd ed. *Tolley*, 1993. 600 pp. £50. Covers 28 tax havens around the world.

DIXON, J.C. **Tolley's trading in Europe**. *Tolley*, 1992. £448 pp.

BALDWIN, R. **Towards an integrated Europe**. *Centre for Economic Policy Research*, 1994. 256 pp. £12.95.

GOLDIN, I., KNUDSEN, O. and MENSBRUGGHE, D.v.d. **Trade liberalisation:**

Global economic implications. *OECD*, 1993. 218 pp. $43. 'This joint World Bank-OECD Development Centre publication analyzes the potential gains from trade liberalisation and from different GATT agreements over the next decade.'

ERNST & YOUNG. **UK/US GAAP comparison**. 3rd ed. *Kogan Page*, 1994. 356 pp. £44.95. 'The only publication which compares and contrasts the requirements of UK and US Generally Accepted Accounting Practice.'

SCHACHTER, O. and JOYNER, C. **United Nations legal order**. *Grotius Publications*, 1994. £120. 'In these two volumes the eminent contributors provide an in depth analysis of the United Nations legal order, emphasising the problems of UN Charter interpretation.' The chapters include: 11. Economic relations and development; 24. Financial responsibilities of members.

HORIGUCHI, Y. **The United States economy: Performance and issues**. *IMF*, 1992. 599 pp.

HUFBAUER, G.C. **U.S. taxation of international income: Blueprint for reform**. *Institute for International Economics*, 1992. 276 pp.

PRICE WATERHOUSE. **VAT in the Single Market: The Price Waterhouse guide through the maze**. *Graham & Trotman*, 1993. 128 pp. £95.00.

FRASER, R. ed. **Western European economic organizations: A comprehensive guide**. *Longman Group*, 1992. 448 pp. 'Looks at the overall economic position in Western Europe both in the international and regional context and in terms of the political, economic and structural conditions of each of the 19 countries covered – defined as Austria, Belgium, Denmark, Finland, France, Germany, Greece, Iceland, Ireland, Italy, Liechtenstein, Luxembourg, the Netherlands, Norway, Portugal, Spain, Sweden, Switzerland and the United Kingdom.'

CAVES, R.E., JONES, R.W. and FRANKEL, J.A. **World trade and payments**. 6th ed. *HarperCollins*, 1993. 682 pp. £19.95. *Part I* The basic trade model; *Part II* International trade patterns and income distribution; *Part III* The theory and practice of commercial policy; *Part IV* Money, income and the balance of payment accounts.

CHAPTER THREE

Value-adding Processes

1. In this chapter, we will describe the simple map of information flows which underlies the structure of this book. During this exercise, we will focus particularly on the sorts of *value-adding information processes*[133] which occur within and around the trading system – allowing us to elaborate on and extend elements which we have already introduced in the previous two chapters.

2. In creating such a diagram, it is productive to choose a specific vantage point from which to view the totality of the value-adding information flows. There are all sorts of multi-dimensional information and other resource flows occurring in the world's trading and its associated financial systems. By choosing a specific lens to examine those flows – a purpose, if you will, for the picture we will create – we reduce the number of objects and processes which we must try to bring together: since many, which would be important if we chose another vantage point, can be left out of the map as of relatively minor importance.[134]

3. The lens which we will choose is one that might be used by the *investor*. Imagine that you are a person – working either for yourself, or for an institution – perusing the world outside and wondering where best to 'invest' some funds that you happen to have currently available. You are aware that there are a large number of publicly available information sources designed to help you in your task: perhaps you have perused one or another textbook of 'investment' which has a section or sections labelled *sources of investment information* – or some such.[135] But you would like a fuller understanding of how the various types of information source arise and their relationships to each other. What are the prime information flows? What value is aiming to be added by those who initiate such flows?

4. With such an 'investment' lens the initial broad outline of the map that we will develop is easily drawn (**see Figure 3.1**) – echoing the major thrust of this book so far. Entities trade, transferring assets, money and information between each other. Such trade can be facilitated by the assistance of one or more of the various types of financial institution and market: each acting either in an intermediating role or a financial asset handling role (or in a few cases in both roles). This trading system is subject to the exigencies of the relevant legal, economic and political environments. Of the total amount of information in this overall system, whether or not it has been transported between the trading and other entities who comprise it, or restricted to date to being held within the entities' individual organizational boundaries, a portion becomes publicly available. The portion of this information which can be related to an individual trading event may become public in anticipation of trade, while trade is taking place, after the trading event. Using our earlier terminology, the public availability of the information may be necessary, required, chosen, inadvertent or off-the-record (to the extent that the latter becomes 'on-the-record').

5. Although our focus here is on the flows of *information* within and outside of the trading system, it is difficult in real life – and ultimately unproductive – to try to disentangle the value-adding which specifically relates to information – especially publicly available information – from other types of value-adding occuring within that system. As has been noted or implied at several points in this book (starting with the very first sentence of its very first quotation), the trading of financial assets particularly is intimately entwined with the trading of information itself. So the map that we will draw contains just a slice of the totality of resource transfers occurring within the trading system 'orange'.

6. It is necessary to explore a little exactly what we might mean by the word 'information'. In a general sense, information, whether or not publicly available, can be conceptualized as being 'about' the phenomena characterized earlier as 'things' and 'processes'. Unfortunately, the word is frequently used in rather a vague sense; and it can mean different things to different people. So we need to explain the way that we propose now to use the term here.

7. I like the continuum: data . . . information . . . knowledge . . . wisdom.[136] Roughly, comprising *data* are the characters, digits, graphic elements, sound elements, motion elements which are able to be organized by the human being into meaningful chunks – or 'statements' – which we can call *information*. Such organization may need to be minimal – as on the financial trading floor, or in

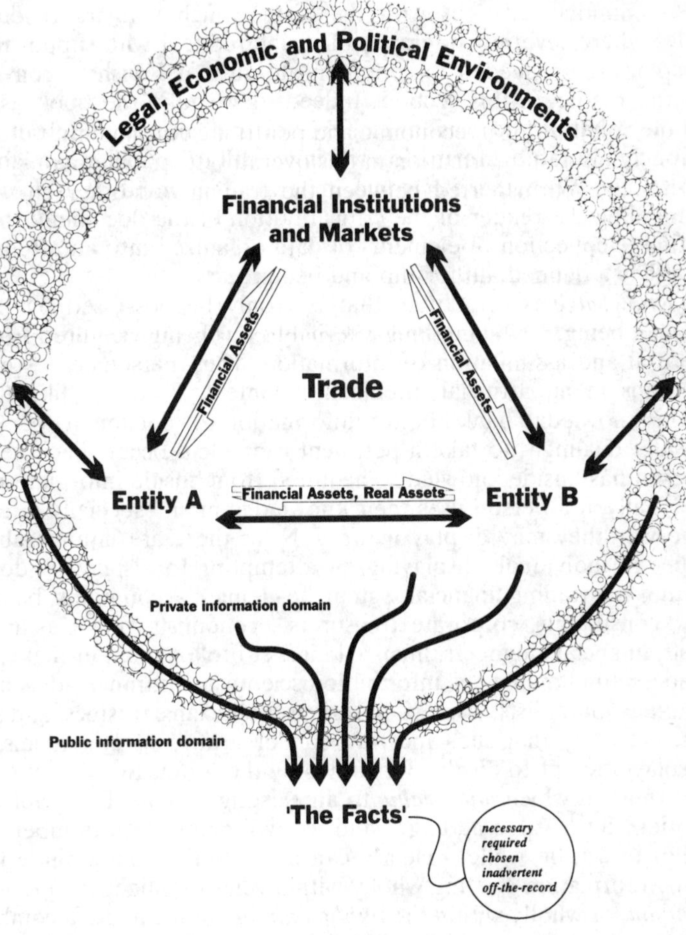
Legal, Economic and Political Environments
Financial Institutions
and Markets
Financial Assets
Financial Assets
Trade
Entity A
Financial Assets, Real Assets
Entity B
Private information domain
Public information domain
'The Facts'
necessary
required
chosen
inadvertent
off-the-record

Figure 3.1

the foreign exchange dealing room – for the data transmitted to be understood as information. In such environments, the 'rules' previously agreed by the traders provide all that is necessary for what in other environments would be thought to be unorganized data, to be recognized as information. Alternatively, the data organization may have to be quite elaborate for a full message to be communicated – as with the 'data' which you are reading now: where several paragraphs of structured text with supporting graphics seem needed to communicate all that I wish to convey to the reader in this section. Indeed, if we take the book as a whole, what we have is an example of that important subset of publicly available information which we call the publicly available *document*. With the electronic imperative in mind, it is worth reminding the reader of the critical notion of the document: that ultimate collection of elements of data organized into an artefact that has a defined authorship and pedigree.[137]

8. *Knowledge* is something that can only be possessed by the human being. It is something internal to our being, acquired from perusal and assimilation of information. Thus, personally, except perhaps in an artificial intelligence context, I do not like the term 'knowledge bank': better 'information (or document) bank'. Insider dealing – to take a pertinent example – occurs because a person has 'inside knowledge' acquired from 'inside information'.

9. Finally, if a person uses their knowledge in an especially effective way they may display *wisdom*. Now: there are innumerable types of individuals displaying, or attempting to display, wisdom within the trading/financial system: academics, accountants, bankers, consultants, corporate treasurers, economists, financial analysts, financial engineers, financial market brokers/market-makers/traders, fund managers, information scientists, insurance advisors/brokers, journalists, lawyers, librarians, politicians, trustees, and so on. One way that such individuals – or groups of individuals – display/attempt to display wisdom is by the production of data or information which *adds value* to an existing corpus of data/information. Such value-adding – and we will delineate a number of types in a little while – clearly can use as input source material data/information existing wholly within what we might the *private domain*; or wholly within the *public domain*; or it can use a combination of private and public data/information. In turn, the output of the value-adding process may be kept private; or it may be made public. Or the whole – or parts of the whole – of the value-adding process may take place in a semi-public (or semi-private) arena. If the person adding value uses private information to which they did not previously have access, that information may have been proferred by its owner or holder willingly; or it may have been (legally?) acquired by one or more of a number of techniques of (competitive) intelligence.[138]

10. The vast majority of those who use 'financial' information sources are normally unconcerned with these nuances of data/information origination and public availablity. For example, *corporate treasurers*, intent on automating the global treasury and faced with needing to consider all of these sub-systems:[139]

- Balance and transaction reporting
- Money transfer
- Transaction tracking and position reporting
- Transaction initiation (on-line dealing system)
- Transaction confirmation
- General ledger
- Communications
- Cash planning and forecasting
- Account reconciliation
- Multilateral netting
- Decision-support modules (analytical and hedge strategy)
- Market and rate information
- Dealer-support systems
- Letters of credit

hardly spends time and energy worrying about whether the data/information needed for each system has come from this or that source; or is totally 'private' or totally 'public' or something in between! They just need the optimal collection of data/information to do the job they are charged with doing, obtained in the most optimal way.

11. However, here, it is helpful to have those concerns as an aid to our presentation. In fact, we will find it best to suggest a sharp distinction between that data/information which is firmly within the private domain, as against that which is within the public domain. Ideally, we need a word for the latter: let us call this data/information *the facts*. Our prime interest then is in producing a picture which describes the range of financial 'facts' produced for the public arena, who produces those facts, how they cross the boundary between private and public availability, and what value-adding can be and is done to those facts once they are publicly available.

12. Actually, my reason for making this precise distinction between public and private is more than simply because it is presentationally convenient. As we shall elaborate on in a later section, what bedevils this subject field is the large amount of pertinent data and information which is known to certain investors, and to certain players more generally in the trading system, but not to others.

However, we cannot – must not – proceed on the basis that this is an economically/politically/socially desirable state of affairs! Thus the model that we will develop, sharply distinguishing private data/information from public data/information, is an ideal. Maybe the electronic imperative is gradually enabling society to realize that ideal.

13. So: in the model we have entities – in a trade role, in a trade-assisting role, in a trade-regulatory role – holding items of 'recorded'[140] data and information within their organizational boundaries; or transmitting such data/information 'privately' one to the other. Various private value- adding processes are taking place within the system. Some of this data/information – a relatively small proportion – become publicly available as 'facts'. Once so available, we are characterizing a further set of processes – no different from the value-adding processes occuring privately or semi- privately – whereby individuals, and individuals acting on behalf of organizations publicly 'add value' to these facts. Note that those adding value may well do this within both the private and the public domains: generally, that is the norm. Note also that by the time data or information appears in the public domain, an amount of value may already have been added to it since its original formulation.[141] This happens for instance where a newspaper or a news broadcast is the first publicly to report data/ information which they have received from another (totally private) source and have edited before its public release.

14. However, one of the most fundamental trends in recent years, facilitated by the electronic imperative, has been that investors and other participants in the financial/trading system are less and less content to use data/information to which someone else has already added value (or perhaps not, in their eyes, as the case might be!). On the other hand, players such as *Dow Jones* (producer of the *Wall Street Journal*), and *Pearson* (producer of the *Financial Times*), regard such value-adding as one of the prime competitive advantages which they bring to the information industry marketplace. What type of finance data/information value is added by whom, when and where, is thus turning out to be one of the key competitive questions for those who work in the finance publishing industry. In the old days, only a relatively few industry players had direct access to the data feeds, newswires and press releases which comprise the majority of the raw data/information used by the producers of the newspapers, magazines and electronic databases to produce 'copy'. Now, increasingly, we all do.

15. A further preliminary point regarding Figure 3.1, before we move on. The 'Financial Institutions and Markets', and the organizations comprising the 'Legal, Economic and Political Environments' are depicted in that figure respectively in their roles as facilitators and regulators of trade; rather than as trading entities in their own right – which all will be at some time. Where they are fulfilling the latter role (eg by trading in the money markets) we would characterize them in the model as instances of Entities A and B. The reader will be well aware of the potential for internal conflict in these differing roles of participant in trade, as against facilitator/regulator of trade.[142]

16. Developing our model further, we will now engage in four processes:

(a) First, we will remind ourselves of the 'facts' that – in this context – the 'investor' is keen to ascertain.
(b) Second, we will briefly revisit our earlier classifications of the world's entities (trading or otherwise) refining these to a form which is of value in this context.
(c) Third, we will explore the process of making the 'facts' produced by these various entities, publicly available. This will be particularly helpful when we come later to the electronic imperative.
(d) Fourth, we will then finally attempt to categorize the different types of value-adding process that occur using these 'facts' as input.

The facts

17. The most critical of these have earlier in the book been described as falling primarily into four groups, which can now be paraphrased:

- facts produced by *entities* acting in a trading mode;
- facts produced by the *markets* where those entities trade:
- facts culled from those entities by certain *authorities* which are subsequently made public (as such or summarized);
- the *rules* of trade issued by certain of the authorities.

18. Except in two respects, it does not seem necessary to elaborate on those statements. The remainder of this book is full of examples of published sources of such facts (and of sources which provide data or information which add value to the facts). The two respects relate, first, to the groupings of entities which we call *industries*; and, second, to the groupings of financial instruments we call *indices*. We will briefly treat both these notions with reference to one of a number of textbooks of 'Investment' which is especially appropriate for that purpose: Reilly and Norton's *Investments*.[143]

19. It is comforting, again, that the model that we are developing can straightforwardly be related to the authors' *Overview of the Investment Process.* This is seen as comprising three steps:[144]

- *Analysis of Alternative Economies and Securities Markets* Objective: Decide how to allocate investment funds among countries and within countries to Bonds, Stocks and Cash
- *Analysis of Alternative Industries* Objective: Based upon the Economic and Market Analysis, determine which industries will prosper and which industries will suffer on a global basis and within countries
- *Analysis of Individual Companies and Stocks* Objective: Following the selection of the best industries, determine which companies within these industries will prosper and which stocks are undervalued.

Very roughly, the first of these processes relates in this text to the information sources which we have listed relevant to national and international legal, economic and political environments; the second and third to the sorts of sources we will shortly give examples of in Chapter 4.

20. Reilly and Norton especially stress the order in which they feel that their three analyses should be carried out:

> Although you might agree with the logic of the three-step investment process, you might wonder how well this process works in selecting investments. Several academic studies have supported this technique. First, studies indicated that most changes in an individual firm's *earnings* could be attributed to changes for all firms and changes in the firm's industry, with the earnings changes by all firms being the more important. Although the relative influence of the general economy and the industry on company earnings varied among individual firms, the results consistently demonstrated the significant effects of the economic environment on firm earnings.
>
> Second, several studies have found a relationship between aggregate stock prices and various economic series such as employment, income or production. These results supported the view that there is a relationship between stock prices and economic expansions and contractions.
>
> Third, an analysis of the relationship between the *rates of return* for the aggregate stock market, alternative industries, and individual stocks showed that most of the changes in rates of return for individual stocks could be explained by changes in rates of return for the aggregate stock market and the stock's industry. Although the importance of the market effect tended to decline over time and the significance of the industry effect varied among industries, the combined market-industry effect on the individual firm's rate of return was still important.[145]

21. It is not appropriate in this text to explore the publicly available sources of industry information. Suffice it merely to note the broad categories Reilly and Norton identify at the end of their chapter

'Industry Analysis' under the heading *Sources of Industry Information*:[146]

1. Independent industry journals
2. Industry and trade associations
3. Government reports and statistics
4. Independent research organizations
5. Brokerage house research

22. Earlier in Reilly and Norton's text, there is an excellent introductory chapter 'Security-Market Indicator Series':

> A fair statement regarding *security-market indicator series* – especially those outside the United States – is that everybody taks about them, but few people understand them. Even those investors familiar with widely publicized stock-market series, sch as the Dow Jones Industrial Average (DJIA), usually know very little about indexes for the U.S. bond market or for non-U.S. stock markets such as Tokyo or London.[147]

23. Reilly and Norton are able in a score of pages first to summarize the differentiating factors which are used to construct the various types of market index available (the nature of the sample, the weighting of sample members, computational procedures). Then, second, they list and review examples of some forty 'stock-market indexes' (eg S&P 500 Composite; FT-Actuaries World Indexes; Morgan Stanley Capital International (MSCI) Indexes) and about a dozen 'bond market indexes (eg Lehman Brothers Aggregate; Salomon Brothers High-Yield) prominent in the marketplace.

24. A final note on 'facts': apart from the four types of facts listed earlier which entities within the private domain find it necessary or are required to generate for the public domain, there is a fifth group of data/information about the trading system which can be immensely relevant to the investor. We have already discussed how trading entities can 'choose' publicly to release data or information. There is also a second very important group of entities who choose to release such data or information – but these are entities which are outside of the trading system, as it were, looking in upon it. Such entities – analysts, journalists, researchers and so on – as people who are not involved or implicated in the trade in any way (to repeat an earlier phrase) – discover and publicly report data and information which is (voluntarily) released to them by those who *are* 'involved' or 'implicated'. This fifth category of data/information comprises an immense range: running, at one extreme, from the journalist reporting a natural disaster over the newswire; to, at the other, an academic researcher making a painstaking study of one or another aspect of the trading/financial system.

25. Important as this fifth type of data/information is (it is material garnered by those outside the trading system, rather than material proferred by those inside the system), it need not detain us long. For the purposes of developing our simple model, it does not seem to me to matter whether the information flowing from the private trading domain to the public domain has been 'pushed' or 'pulled' from the inside to the outside.

The entities producing the facts

26. There are then three major groupings within the trading system from whom – one way or another – facts of relevance to the investor reach the public domain. Summarizing the presentation earlier:

(1) *Trading entities* Members of the five categories of entity characterized by 1993 SNA are 'required' to produce 'accounts' of their past and current and often also planned trading situation. (Even households must submit tax returns.) These facts – to the extent that they are made publicly available – are normally delivered to the public domain via an official department, agency, or self-regulatory body: either being transmitted in their totality; or in a summarised form (as 'statistics').

(2) *Financial markets* These are the various types of public organized financial market fulfilling roles as (secondary) market trade facilitators. Primarily these markets help generate the data and information which is 'necessary' for efficient and effective trade to take place.

(3) *Institutions comprising the legal, economic and political environments of trade* These institutions produce two distinct types of facts for the public domain: economic and financial statistics; primary, secondary and quasi legislation. We should also include in this third group the financial markets when they are operating in a regulatory and supervisory role: both of trade of existing financial instruments; but also of the issue of new (primary) instruments.

27. In addition to these publicly available 'required' and 'necessary' facts generated from and for the trading system, there are the facts which are 'chosen' to be released by its players (pushed or pulled). There are also the 'facts' which become available 'inadvertently' (including those that had been originally presented as 'off-the-record').

Making the facts publicly available

28. Trying to think in a rather fundamental sense, it has seemed useful to distinguish what we might term the *generation* of data/information so that it is ready to be publicly perused, from the *display* of that data/information to its (potential) user, once it is at least notionally publicly available. This is of particular value in considering what we might call *time-critical data/information*: for instance, the sort which might well have a significant effect on financial market trading.

29. In fact, the generation of a large proportion of such time-critical data/information is planned in advance. At first sight, this may appear to be nonsense, given the seemingly continual flurries of frantic activity in the financial markets. Did the dealers know all along what was going to happen? The answer is 'no': they did not know what was going to happen: though they may well have guessed in advance, and thus when their guesses were confirmed, the data/information just generated was – as the phrase is – *discounted by the markets*. The dealers simply knew something was going to happen (for instance, the release of some company's results, or of some piece of economic data, or of commentary from a respected analyst); and they were ready to act – to buy or to sell – in case the facts did not match up to the anticipated facts. All of the major scheduled announcements are planned well in advance (the timings of many are listed in newspapers such as the *Financial Times* or the *Wall Street Journal*): if only to ensure that the relevant reporters are in the right place at the right time (where such intermediaries are needed). The time-critical element resides in converting the publicly generated data/information into publicly displayed data/information as speedily as possible.

30. Naturally, there is time-critical data/information which is propelled into the public domain without prior warning. This perhaps falls into two groups. First, there are the unanticipated economic and financial announcements: the sudden hike in interest rates; the takeover bid; and so on. Second, there are the major personal, political and environmental calamities: assassinations, declarations of war, earthquakes, etc. The first group are processed from generation to display much as the anticipated announcements – except that the trader is presumably not ready and waiting to act at quite the same level of concentration. In fact, as we have already mentioned, there are very strict rules as to how unanticipated corporate and official announcements must be made (the announcements naturally being unanticipated only by their recipient – not by those who are in some sense 'inside' the entity making the announcement).

31. With the second type of unexpected release of data/information, there is clearly an opportunity for one or another reporter to generate a *scoop*: maybe simply because he or she happens to be in the right place at the right time and is able therefore before the competition to generate the appropriate data/information ready for it to be converted into a displayed format.[148] One of the problems nowadays faced by newswire journalists is that there is such pressure to get the story on to the system ahead of the competition, that there is not time to write what they would feel would be a good piece. To some degree this is being coped with by the journalists posting a short message first summarizing the bare bones of the story; with a more carefully constructed elaboration following a little later.
32. There would seem to be just three prime methods of information generation, and four of display:

INFORMATION GENERATION

To recap, we are defining this as the process whereby data/information which is not publicly available is converted into a formal artefact – which is then in a format suitable for 'publication':

- *Spoken* statement: e.g. press conference (almost invariably accompanied by a press release).
- *Electronic* statement: e.g. financial market data-feed; video feed.
- *Printed* statement: e.g. author's manuscript.

INFORMATION DISPLAY

We have defined this as the process whereby generated data/information is placed in a position where it can directly be perused by a potential user of – or customer for – that data/information.

- *Broadcast* radio; television.
- *Real-time electronic* display: the real-time data services.
- *Scheduled electronic* display: the traditional interactive online search services.
- *Print-on-paper* (and other portable physical information artefacts: e.g. microform; CD-ROMs).

33. The generation of data/information and its display can effectively be simultaneous. Good examples would be: the broadcast of the Chancellor of the Exchequer's annual Budget speech in the UK Parliament; the real-time delivery of financial market data via electronic networks. A lively current development is the supply of video signals to personal workstations via the real-time financial data services. Personally, as an aside, I find this particularly interesting not because of the technological wizardry that has made it possible but more because it is a marrying of what we might perhaps call a 'serial' data display system to a 'parallel' data display system. Textual and numeric data displayed on the video display unit of a personal computer can be picked out from the totality of data directly available at that time with impunity. If we do not like what we see, we can 'in parallel' immediately and rapidly choose a second screen and then a third and so on until we are content; or we give up. Video, and especially audio, are in contrast essentially 'serial' media. The technology may allow us to pick out a 'video bite' or a 'sound bite'; but we then normally have to stay and watch or listen to that video or sound bite for some time before we can truly assess its relevance. We cannot at a glance determine its value – as we can with screen fulls of data and text (and compare the similar difference between voice-mail and electronic mail).

34. Most of the time there is a delay between the generation of data/information and its display. Thus how the interval between generation and display is policed is critical. There have been many instances reported where – in the time between generating data/information (e.g. producing a press release or copy for a newspaper or a magazine or a new or updated database) and that data/information actually being displayed, 'insiders' have 'illegally' made profitable use of the information.

Adding value to the facts

35. Our simple model can now be represented as in **Figure 3.2**. I have identified six types of value-adding process which can be applied to the financial – and, more generally, trading – 'facts', which have been generated for, and displayed in, the public domain. We will term these:

- *Composition*
- *Summary*
- *Comment*
- *Analysis*
- *Forecast*
- *Advice*

36. We use the word *composition* as the editor of a newspaper might do when he or she 'composes' an issue. Here the value-adding relates to the choice and positioning of the facts available to the editor. As has already been noted, many users of publicly available finance information are questioning whether they would

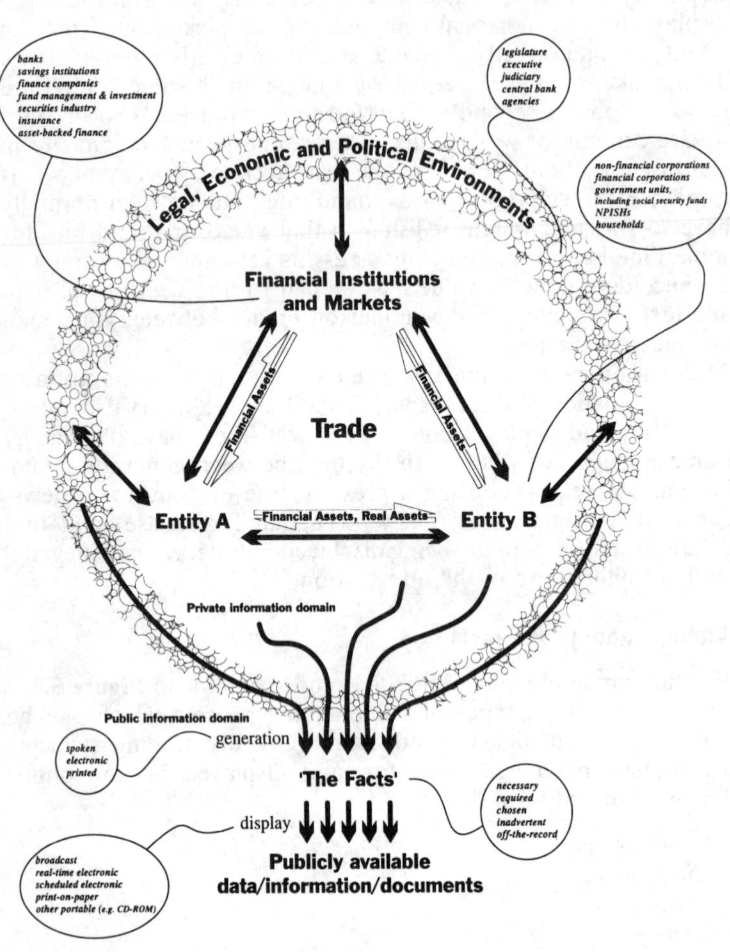
banks
savings institutions
finance companies
fund management & investment
securities industry
insurance
asset-backed finance
legislature
executive
judiciary
central bank
agencies
non-financial corporations
financial corporations
government units,
including social security funds
NPISHs
households
Legal, Economic and Political Environments
Financial Institutions and Markets
Financial Assets
Financial Assets
Trade
Entity A
Financial Assets, Real Assets
Entity B
Private information domain
Public information domain
generation
spoken
electronic
printed
'The Facts'
necessary
required
chosen
inadvertent
off-the-record
display
broadcast
real-time electronic
scheduled electronic
print-on-paper
other portable (e.g. CD-ROM)
Publicly available
data/information/documents

Figure 3.2

rather determine the choice of facts to be delivered to them – rather than have that determined by an editor. This has reminded me of some comments in an interview that Michael Bloomberg gave a year or two ago to a popular magazine:

> Only newspapers don't interest him. 'We deal in real-time information – by the time it appears in a newspaper it can be ten, twelve, eighteen hours old.' Unlike his terminal and its thousands of functions, newspapers can't be personalised – not yet anyway. 'The trouble with newspapers is that they print the same pages for everybody. The newspaper of the future will print the stories only you care about.'[149]

37. Very often, the facts as originally generated (eg in a press release) are summarized before they are displayed. We might define *summary* as an indicative or informative description of the main points of each generated chunk of data/information. Meanwhile, where space is tight, the overall 'editor' of the publication where the summary would appear will be deciding which stories to run for specific issues. This is a far from trivial task where there is competition amongst story providers for exposure. Thus the employment of *public relations* personnel by players and bystanders – each trying to ensure that 'their' story is prominently included – or even just included – in the leading newspapers, magazines, news broadcasts and so on.[150] Once it is decided to include a story, there is then the decision as to how much space or time to allocate to it. Some stories will not be summarized: for instance, the report will match the relevant press release more or less word for word. For others, choices will be made as to the points to be covered.

38. The ultimate in summary are the *non-primary publications*: examples of which we covered in an earlier chapter. We might write a few more words about the notion of 'primary' literature to extend the brief introduction given earlier. As it happens, and as earlier in the clarification of the distinction between primary and secondary securities issuers and owners, it transpires that we need to be careful here too in defining what we mean by the word 'primary'. Intuitively, newspapers would be classified conclusively as a primary form of literature: indexes to newspapers as examples of secondary forms. Yet, increasingly, newswire and financial market data feeds become available in real time on our personal computer workstations – not just to market professionals, but to all who can afford to subscribe. So that portion at least of the data/information which might comprise the following day's newspaper one might describe as 'secondary'.

39. In the law there is a quite different usage again of these troublesome terms primary and secondary. Using the English legal system as an example:

> Law books are commonly divided into two broad categories: *primary materials* and *secondary materials*. Put simply, this division distinguishes the law itself from commentaries on the law. Primary materials include the written sources of the law: Acts of Parliament, subordinate legislation, and reported decisions of the courts and tribunals. Secondary materials include all types of legal literature which are not formal records of law, such as encyclopedias, digests of cases, textbooks, journals, dictionaries, indexes and bibliographies.[151]

If we turn to economics, we have yet further scope for misunderstanding:

> As in many other fields of economics, international banking statistics may be reported at three levels. *Primary* sources represent the collection of data on international banking at the level of the individual bank or bank branch. Alternatively, *secondary* data sources refer to the aggregation by individual central banks of relevant data on international banking activity of banks within that particular country, perhaps including the overseas branches of banks whose parent offices are located at home. Finally, in *tertiary* sources, data are compiled across a certain group of countries to reflect as wide as possible a concept of global international financial intermediation.[152]

Terminological difficulties continue to abound!

40. I do not feel it necessary to write anything here about *comment*: we are all familiar with its various guises. *Analysis* – on the other hand – with its connotation of a much more rigorous and often numerically based examination of the 'facts', seems as though it might occupy a very large amount of our time. But, actually, it is not difficult as a concept: again, we all recognize the analytical process when we come across it. Where the problems arise with analysis, are in the details of the analytical technique(s) used, and whether that technique or those techniques was/were used in a proper manner. This can only be judged by a full understanding of the nature of the relevant techniques; and by a rigorous examination of the results of using such techniques. As with *forecasting*, there are no 'information source' problems that need to be rehearsed. It is just a case of finding the appropriate books, journal articles, reports and so on relevant to the task in hand.

41. There is, however, one particular type of analysis which we should dwell upon for a moment: the analytical output of *rating agencies*. Debt (and credit) ratings are an extremely important component of the capital raising process. To illustrate some of the potential complexities of the rating process, we reproduce here descriptions prepared early in the 1990s by the two leading *debt* *rating* services – Moody's and Standard & Poor's. These are the *Ratings Definitions* published by the first; and a quote from a booklet piece entitled *Role of Ratings* for the second:

(i) *Moody's Rating Definitions*

(a) *Short-term*

Moody's short-term debt ratings are opinions of the ability of issuers to repay punctually senior debt obligations which have an original maturity not exceeding one year. Obligations relying upon support mechanisms such as letters-of-credit and bonds of indemnity are excluded unless explicitly rated.

Moody's employs the following three designations, all judged to be investment grade, to indicate the relative repayment ability of rated issuers:

PRIME-1 Issuers rated Prime-1 (or supporting institutions) have a superior ability for repayment of senior short-term debt obligations. Prime-1 repayment ability will often be evidenced by many of the following characteristics:

- Leading market positions in well-established industries
- High rates of return on funds employed
- Conservative capitalization structure with moderate reliance on debt and ample asset protection
- Broad margins in earnings coverage of fixed financial charges and high internal cash generation
- Well-established access to a range of financial markets and assured sources of alternate liquidity

PRIME-2 Issuers rated Prime-2 (or supporting institutions) have strong ability for repayment of senior short-term debt obligations. This will normally be evidenced by many of the characteristics cited above but to a lesser degree. Earnings trends and coverage ratios, while down, may be more subject to variation. Capitalization characteristics, while still appropriate, may be more affected by external conditions. Ample alternate liquidity is maintained.

PRIME-3 Issuers rated Prime-3 (or supporting institutions) have an acceptable ability for repayment of senior short-term obligations. The effect of industry characteristics and market compositions may be more pronounced. Variability in earnings and profitability may result in changes in the level of debt protection measurements and may require relatively high financial leverage. Adequate alternate liquidity is maintained.

NOT PRIME Issuers rated Not Prime do not fall within any of the Prime Rating categories . . .

(b) *Long-term*

Aaa Bonds which are rated Aaa are judged to be of the best quality. They carry the smallest degree of investment risk and are generally referred to as 'gilt-edged'. Interest payments are protected by a large or by an exceptionally stable margin and principal is secure. While the various protective elements are likely to change, such changes as can be visualized are most unlikely to impair the fundamentally strong position of such issues.

Aa Bonds which are rated Aa are judged to be of high quality by all standards. Together with the Aaa group they comprise what are generally know as high-grade bonds. They are rated lower than the best bonds because margins of protection may not be as large as in Aaa securities or fluctuation of protective elements may be of greater amplitude or there may be other elements present which make the long-term risk appear somewhat larger than the Aaa securities.

A Bonds which are rated A possess many favourable investment attributes and are to be considered as upper-medium-grade obligations. Factors giving security to principal and interest are considered adequate, but elements may be present which suggest a susceptibility to impairment some time in the future.

Baa Bonds which are rated Baa are considered as medium-grade obligations (i.e. they are neither highly protected nor poorly secured). Interest payments and principal security appear adequate for the present but certain protective elements amy be lacking or may be characteristically unreliable over any great length of time. Such bonds lack outstanding investment characteristics and in fact have speculative characteristics as well.

Ba Bonds which are rated Ba are judged to have speculative elements; their future cannot be considered well assured. Often the protection of interest and principal payments may be very moderate and thereby not well safeguarded during both good and bad times over the future. Uncertainty of position characterizes bonds in this class.

B Bonds which are rated B generally lack characteristics of the desirable investment. Assurance of interest and principal payments or of maintenance of other terms of the contract over any long period of time may be small.

Caa Bonds which are rated Caa are of poor standing. Such issue may be in default or there may be present elements of danger with respect to principal or interest.

Ca Bonds which are rated Ca represent obligations which are speculative in a high degree. Such issues are often in default or have other marked short-comings.

C Bonds which are rated C are the lowest rated class of bonds, and issues so rated can be regarded as having extremely poor prospects of ever attaining any real investment standing.

Moody's ratings are opinions, not recommendations to buy or sell, and their accuracy is not guaranteed. A rating should be weighed solely as one factor in an investment decision and you should make your own study and evaluation of any issuer whose securities or debt obligations you consider buying or selling.

(ii) *Role of Ratings*

Over the years, S&P's ratings have achieved wide investor acceptance as easily usable tools for differentiating credit quality. Issuers range from public corporate utilities . . . (to) municipal issuers . . . (to) foreign governments . . . (to) foreign corporations. Issuers sell bonds with varying security pledges and seniority and also issue debt that is insured, structured, or complex in various other ways. Ratings published by S&P provide a single scale to compare among this array of different debt instruments.

The value of a rating emanates from validity of criteria and reliability of judgement and analysis of S&P's professional staff . . . The credibility of ratings also requires objectivity. S&P's objectivity results from not investing for its own account, not serving as an underwriter, financial advisor, or manager of funds, and being independent of the issuer's business.

S&P operates with no governmental mandate, subpoena powers, or any other official authority. As part of the media, it simply has a right to express its opinions in the form of letter symbols. Recognition as a rating agency relies on investors' willingness to accept its judgement.

To use credit ratings properly, one should first understand what a rating is and is not. The rating performs the isolated function of credit risk evaluation, which is one element of the entire investment decision-making process. . . . A credit rating is not a recommendation to purchase, or sell, or hold a particular security. A rating cannot constitute a recommendation as it does not take into consideration other factors, such as market price and risk preference of the investor. Moreover, because S&P receives confidential information from issuers, S&P believes it would be improper to recommend the purchase or sale of rated bonds. Rating agencies that do publish 'market' recommendations may forego management contact, relying exclusively on publicly available data.

A rating is not a general purpose evaluation of an issuer. For example, an issuer with an 'AA' rating on a particular obligation is not necessarily 'better than' an issuer with a 'BBB' rating, as the 'AA' rating may be based primarily on a specific security or third-party support underlying the obligation.

Although many probing questions are asked the issuer at various stages of the rating process, S&P does not perform an audit, nor does it attest to the authenticity of the information provided by the issuer and upon which the rating may be based. Ratings can be changed, withdrawn, or placed on CreditWatch as a result of changes in, or unavailability of, information.

Ratings do not create a fiduciary relationship between S&P and users of the ratings; there is no legal basis for the existence of such a relationship.

It is commonplace for companies to structure financing transactions to reflect S&P's credit criteria so they qualify for higher ratings. However, the actual structuring of a given issue is the function and responsibility of an issuer and its advisors. S&P is the recipient and user of materials prepared by those in a position to attest to such materials' accuracy and completeness. Although S&P will react to a proposed financing, publish papers outlining its criteria for that type of issue, and interpret and make evaluations available to an issuer, underwriter, bond counsel, or financial advisor, it does not function as an investment banker or financial advisor. Adoption of such a role ultimately would impair the objectivity and credibility that are vital to S&P's continued performance as an independent rating agency.

S&P's guidance also is sought on credit quality issues that might affect S&P's opinion of corporate creditworthiness. For example, companies solicit S&P's view on hybrid preferred stock, the sale of accounts receivable, or other innovative financing techniques before putting them into practice. Nor is it uncommon for debt issuers to undertake specific and sometimes significant actions for the sake of maintaining their ratings. For example, one large company faced a downgrade of its 'A-1' commercial paper rating owing to a growing component of short-term, floating-rate debt. To keep its rating, the company chose to restructure its debt maturity schedule in a way consistent with S&P's view of what was prudent.

Many companies go one step further and incorporate specific rating objectives as corporate goals. But S&P does not encourage companies to manage themselves with an eye toward a specific rating. The more appropriate approach is to operate for the good of the business as management sees it, and to let the rating follow. Ironically, managing for a very high rating can sometimes be inconsistent with the company's ultimate best interests, if it means being overly conservative and foregoing opportunities. Indeed, S&P questions whether linkage of a company's long-term financial strategy to a specific rating category makes sense.

42. Finally, the sixth of the value-adding processes we have identified: *advice*. The key characteristic of advice in the context of investment is that it is a *regulated* activity; for instance, using a UK example:

You probably won't find better financial advice Our reputation as leading financial advisers rests on our ability to keep ahead of changing economic conditions with market leading investment products and financial services. We also place enormous importance on providing the highest standards of thoroughly researched independent advice on a broad range of topics.

Allied to this, at *Chase de Vere*, we aim to translate the highly competitive and complex world of financial services into friendly, informal and easy to digest advice. Experience tells us that it is these factors that have helped to distinguish us from other investment advisers and given us the profile we now enjoy. Our technical research information is regularly used by the financial media. Information supplied by Chase de Vere is published each week in the *Sunday Times*, and the Saturday editions of the *Times*, *Daily Telegraph* and the *Independent* and each month, in *The International*, *Expat Investor*, *Moneywise*, etc.

Chase de Vere Investments is fully affiliated to all the major professional bodies, that supervise and control the financial services industry. In addition to the strict codes of conduct laid down by these bodies we have our own very stringent internal code and carry over £5,000,000 of Professional Indemnity Insurance underwritten at Lloyds of London. We only deal with secure, quality investment groups wth top performance records and/or market leading rates.

The Small Print It is a requirement under the Financial Services Act, in presenting the information contained within *Financial Outlook*, that the products and services are correctly described and represented. This is covered within the appropriate product literature. However, we are also obliged to include standard 'health warnings'. Although they may have varying degrees of relevance to the investments or services you are considering, we would recommend you read though them for your own protection. In the case of unit trusts or equity-linked investments, it should be noted that the value of the underlying investments and the income therefrom can fall as well as rise and you may get back less than you invested. Past performance is not necessarily an assurance for the future and should only be used as a guide. . . . All information contained in Financial Outlook is based on our understanding of present financial and tax legislation.

43. The requirement for the registration of those who offer financial (planning) *advice* exists also in the USA; and in most other trading nations.[153]

Public, semi-public and private information

44. Notwithstanding the apparent cornucopia of sources cited or implied in this text, in many ways they are the tip of the iceberg; and frequently a rather unimportant tip – for the day-to-day operation of the financial system. Further, even though current information for some areas of the system can perhaps be said to be publicly available, it is for most of us often only notionally so. There are two main reasons for this (aside from a reluctance or inability (or both) to pay the price charged for many publications and electronic services in this field). The first arises from the semi-public and private nature of significant portions of the world's trading system. The second from the highly competitive nature of much financial system activity, whereby there is advantage to be gained in only releasing the information one has gained to 'clients and colleagues'. We will illustrate these two themes in turn in the following paragraphs.

45. As has already been noted, a significant proportion of trade in financial assets is not carried out via formally organized and recognized markets – whether exchange based or over-the-counter. These private placements and private deals remain private – unless the trading entities choose for them to be reported: for example, by placing in the financial press so-called *tombstone advertisements.* Alternatively, the trades might be reported to a relevant professional or trade association, or to an agent in the relevant trading market who has assumed responsibility for collecting data from the market's participants – which information the organization subsequently makes available (often in summary form) to each of the participating entities. These sorts of processes are exceptionally important in providing feedback mechanisms to the trading entities on what is happening in the relevant market. Further, where a specific information provider can obtain the exclusive right to broadcast such data, this can give them considerable competitive advantage. (This was very important at one stage during the growth of the real-time electronic service Bloomberg.) Much of this type of private or semi-private data *does* find its way (eventually) into widely available publications (such as financial magazines and newspapers): but only as a matter of record, and frequently in abbreviated form.

46. Where there is a true information market, in the sense that there is a 'public' electronic exchange of data between all the participants who wish to make that specific market, if the market is specialized (as many financial markets are), there is no incentive to make the information exchanged available beyond those professionals registered to trade in the market itself. The data being exchanged could easily be viewed by those with access rights to the relevant pages of the appropriate real-time data vendor(s); and thus might be said to be 'publicly available'. But that is as far as the data dissemination will go – and one could argue need go (apart from for purposes of trade clearance and settlement, and of supervision and regulation of the specific market concerned – to the extent the latter exists).

47. However, as has already been touched upon, this whole area of real-time data exchange is one of great current development and innovation; and there is both excitement, and concern, at the shifting boundaries between information that is truly – and affordably – 'publicly available'; and that which is – in practice – only available to the chosen few. The 'excitement' (for those who are excited by such matters!) is captured in this advertisement by Bloomberg:

On-Line Trading in the Eurobond Market

> Innovation in the Eurobond market? That's nothing new. The Eurobond market has been the place where the most sophisticated investors, issuers and dealers meet with the latest financing and investment ideas. Innovation has been a hallmark of the Eurobond market's success because it has provided issuers and investors with more options and more ways to accomplish their financial goals. As a result, Eurobonds have been the securities with all the latest bells, whistles and warrants.
>
> With the Euromarket accustomed to innovation, it would seem unlikely that any fundamental change is possible. However, there is something essentially new for the Eurobond market: THE BLOOMBERG Electronic Trading Floor. Now traders can buy and sell Eurobonds with leading dealers without even picking up the telephone. Just scan screens of live bids and offers, and execute transactions with just a few keystrokes on THE BLOOMBERG keyboard.
>
> THE BLOOMBERG Electronic Trading Floor doesn't just change the way Eurobonds are traded. It enhances the entire analytical process of selecting, analyzing and reviewing the performance of securities. Imagine knowing the exact price at which you can buy a bond – before you spend any time analyzing it. And imagine having the right information to analyze trading potential:
>
> - live offering price to run option-adjusted spread analysis.
> - real trading levels from previous trading days as you graph historical yield spreads.
> - live tradeable prices to determine the current value of your portfolio, or its duration.
> - live tradeable prices for rich-cheap searches on your portfolio to identify bonds which should be sold.[154]

48. The 'concern' is reflected in a recent important and detailed report from the US Securities and Exchange Commission's Division of Market Regulation.[155] Perhaps the public at large should not be concerned that certain professionals with access to certain systems can obtain better trading prices and can trade with lesser overheads for, say, Eurobonds, than those professionals who do not have access to those systems. But where there is wide ownership of securities by the populace at large – as is the case with US equities – and at the same time:

> The market for major US equities has become somewhat dispersed among various competitors as users have sought alternatives to the NYSE, Amex and NASDAQ when these markets would not or could not meet their needs. The resulting increase in market competition has created a veritable 'menu' of systems in the equity markets.[156]

then questions on the degree of information equity are raised. It is felt to be wrong if the large professional firms in the equity market routinely can get better deals for themselves than everyone else.

49. Thus the prime conclusion of the SEC Division's Report reads:

> The Division believes that specific adjustments in four areas are needed to address equity market developments. First, the public dissemination of quotations and transactions can be improved to provide better execution for customers, stimulate competition between markets, and link activities of retail customers, institutional investors, and professional intermediaries. Second, better disclosure of certain order handling practices and soft dollars would ensure that professionals put their customers' interests first. For some dealer practices, disclosure may not be sufficient and the markets should set standards to ensure that customers are treated fairly. Third, to maintain a fair competitive environment, the regulatory responsibilities of the various markets and market participants should be rationally allocated, with care taken not to stifle the ability of alternative markets and services to emerge. Finally, unnecessary restrictions on access by investors, professionals, and issuers to the wide array of equity markets should be removed.[157]

50. That conclusion brings out well the key balance that must be sought between allowing unfettered competitive pressures to improve the efficiency and quality of market processes: yet at the same time ensuring that all who wish have both equitable market access, and an agreed degree of investor protection. One principle method that the authorities use in their attempt to strike and maintain that balance in formally organized markets is by requiring the disclosure of trading and of trading entity data/information. Much specific data/information of this type – that relating to a specific trade or to a specific entity – remains private to the authorities: though often, as we have noted, it will be collated by each market authority and published as soon as is feasible as *financial market statistics*.

51. We will now turn to illustrate the second area of valuable private or semi-private information. Beyond the actual trading and entity data that is collected and distributed, there is an immense volume of information made available by commercial organizations who are players in the financial system offering comment, analysis, forecasting – and *advice* – of one sort or another. Very well known are the *stockbroker newsletters* – many of which used to be obtainable free of charge by non- profit making organizations such as academic libraries. Nowadays, such newsletters are seen as a valuable component of the services offered by premium service brokers, and are normally only available in current form to the brokers' clients (but the financial newspapers and magazines will often note their recommendations). We might here refer in passing – because they are not covered elsewhere in this text – to the large number of similar, but commercially available, investment advice sheets that are published, especially in the United States.[158] Excerpts from three typical examples are:

(i) The **Addison Report**. Gives you: Stock, bond and commodity market overview; 30–40 stock recommendations each issue; mutual fund switch advice for stock, bond and gold funds; conservative and speculative monitored lists; objectives and mental stops for each stock recommended; quarterly special reports focusing on: technical analysis of the Dow Industrials, the Dow Utilities, and various stock groups; daily telephone hotline messages to keep you abreast of the market changes. . . . Keep informed every week with our Hotline messages. Recordings go 'on-line': Monday & Thursday by 8.30 AM E.T.; Tuesday, Wednesday & Friday by 7.30 AM E.T. The Monday and Thursday Hotlines will be three minute messages that analyze the technical and fundamental actions of the markets and give specific recommendations. Tuesday, Wednesday and Friday Hotlines will be one minute or less with brief updates, recommendations, or strategy changes. Additionally, when the Dow closes up or down by 40 points or more, a special three-minutes message will be made the following weekday morning by 8.30 AM E.T. Many newsletters charge extra for this service. WE PROVIDE THIS ADDITIONAL SERVICE AT NO EXTRA CHARGE!

(ii) **MPT Review**. The Nation's Number 1 Advisory Service (up over 1,092%) from 1985 through 1993 as rated by *The Hulbert Financial Digest* . . . The objective of Modern Portfolio Theory (MPT) is merely to achieve optimal returns with minimal risk. MPT became very popular in the 1970s as academia embraced it and started experimenting with various ways to calculate risk and return. After literally hundreds of academic articles and research papers on MPT, academia reached one major conclusion – the stock market is extremely efficient and it is almost impossible to outperform the stock market with MPT. This distressing news that you could never 'beat' the market was unthinkable in my opinion. At that time I was only 19, but I had already been studying successful mutual fund management styles and separately concluded that you could beat the market with a disciplined investment style that uncovered 'up and coming' stocks.

After building a database of approximately 300 OTC stocks, I started calculating Alphas (i.e. return independent of the market), Betas (i.e. market sensitivity), and Standard Deviations (i.e. volatility) . . . After three years of research proving that high Alpha stocks outperformed the market I became sold on MPT! I was still puzzled why academia came to an entirely different conclusion regarding the usefulness of MPT. After reading textbooks and various published articles, the reason became crystal clear – academia ignored Alpha. Inasmuch as Alpha calculates how much of a stock's return is independent of the market, Alpha is absolutely vital to identifying stocks that are likely to outperform the market. I had identified the secret ingredient that academia ignored!

(Today) no matter how good my Alphas, Betas and other MPT risk and return indicators are, I have concluded that the key to successful stock selection is simply extensive research and hard work. At Navellier & Associates, we perform extensive computer screening to uncover promising stocks. However, despite all the computer research we conduct, we must also manually perform fundamental analysis to identify the best stocks.

(iii) **Stockmarket Cycles**. Included with our regular subscription is a daily telephone update which features short term timing for the popular market averages as well as specific recommendations for stock index futures trading and commodity projections for bills, bonds and gold. . . . Stockmarket Cycles is proud to have achieved one of the best records in the industry. Here's how Mark Hulbert, an independent newsletter observer who monitors over 100 investment advisory services, has evaluated our timing:

'In the August 30, 1993 edition of *Forbes*, their annual mutual fund issue, Stockmarket Cycles was Number 1 in the country for specific mutual fund recommendations over the past six years through June 1993. . . . In its August 1991 ranking of market timers over a five-year period, the *Hulbert Financial Digest* shows Stockmarket Cycles fourth in the rankings. . . . In the August of 1990 . . . (it) has the Number 1 market timing record . . . *Forbes* Magazine, May 15, 1988 – Mark Hulbert names Peter Eliades "The most consistent mutual fund switcher".'

52. The reader will note the references to the *Hulbert Financial Digest* which is the major US – and frequently quoted – monitor of newsletter performance:

Each quarterly issue . . . reports the year up-to-date performance of close to 400 investment strategies recommended by over 130 financial newsletters. In addition, we compare the previous 60 months' performance of each portfolio to the *Wilshire 5000 Index* and also indicate the riskiness and clarity of the newsletter. In each January and July issue we report the *Long Term Performance Ratings*, as well as current data, for every year we've tracked each newsletter starting from June 1980. The non-quarterly issues provide detailed studies and analyses interpreting the ratings.

Hulbert (316 Commerce Street, Alexandria, VA 22314, USA. t: (1 703) 683 5905) also produces an *Introductory Booklet* explaining how best to use the Digest; a *Newsletter Directory*, containing the addresses, phone numbers, and prices of the newsletters tracked by the HFD; and a book *The Hulbert Guide to Financial Newsletters* (Dearborn Financial Publishing), which includes 'Scoreboards' ('numerous different scoreboards ranking the newsletters over varying periods of time'); 'Risk-Adjusted Rankings'; 'Mutual Fund

Newsletter Scoreboards'; 'Detailed Graphs and Commentary'; 'Directory' (including 'which newsletters manage money and/or have a telephone hot-line'). Hulbert also frequently contributes a column to the magazine *Forbes.*

53. At the other end of the spectrum are the privately produced *economic forecasts*, with these again, frequently, having a restricted distribution.[159] The US *Morgan Guaranty* is a good example here, currently producing:

a. **Corporate Credit Outlook – Financials, Industrials, Utilities**. w. 'Credit analyses of US investment-grade companies, industry developments, and regulations affecting issuer financial standings. The focus is on changing credit situations that could affect prices of fixed-income securities.'

b. **Emerging Markets Data Watch**. w. 'Economic intelligence and data forecasts for those active day-to-day in the financial markets of emerging market countries.'

c. **Emerging Markets Economic Outlook**. q. 'Economic forecasts and analyses of trends and poiicies of emerging market countries.'

d. **Emerging Markets Outlook**. w. 'Commentary on the market for emerging market instruments: Brady bonds; Euro-bonds; pre-Brady loans; local market instruments; foreign exchange. Includes market strategy commentary, investment strategy advice, relative value analytics, and returns for the Emerging Markets Bond Index, Latin Eurobond Index, and South African Bond Index. The first issue of each month is the most comprehensive.'

e. **European Bond Basis Outlook**. bi-w. 'Short- to intermediate- outlook for the major European bond futures basis markets.'

f. **European Market Outlook and Strategy**. bi-w. 'Summary of views and strategies for European fixed-income and currency markets by country and for Europe as a whole. Provides specific trade recommendations.'

g. **Fixed Income Cross Sector Report**. m. 'Market outlook and strategy for the US fixed-income market: Treasuries and STRIPs, agencies, corporates, assets-backeds, mortgage-backeds.'

h. **Global Data Watch**. w. 'Economic intelligence and data forecasts for those active day-to-day in the financial markets of industrial countries.

i. **Global Markets**. m. 'Intermediate-term outlook for main industrial-country markets, based on analyses and forecasts of JP Morgan strategists and researchers.'

j. **Global Options Analysis**. w. 'Weekly analysis of global bond and "swaption" markets, including analysis of implied and historical volatility. This includes specific trade recommendations.'

k. **Industrial Handbook**. s-a. 'Review of US industrials, covering approximately 150 corporations.'

l. **Portfolio Manager's Summary**. w. A review of the most recent company- and industry-specific reports and comments made by JP Morgan equity and high yield analysts, as well as a comprehensive list of equities currently recomended by those analysts.'

m. **Short-Duration Cross Sector Report**. m. 'Analysis of relative value in floating-rate and fixed-income securities which have maturities of five years of less. Commentary provided on value within each sector and across sectors.'

n. **US Economic Outlook**. bi-m. 'Quarterly forecasts and discussions of trends shaping growth and inflation.'

o. **US and European Bond Futures Rollover Outlook**. q. 'Outlook for major US, European, and Japanese bond futures calendar spreads going into futures expiration.'

p. **US Markets**. m. 'Intermediate-term outlook for US fixed income and foreign exchange markets, including implications of economic and policy outlook and cross-sector market strategy.'

q. **Volatility and US Payrolls**. m. 'Analysis of option volatilities prior to the monthly payroll reports, including historical payroll-day performance and current break-even price changes.'

r. **World Financial Markets**. bi-m. 'A discussion of current and prospective economic and financial conditions in the major industrial countries of the world, and typically, one or more feature stories on topics of broad economic, market and policy significance.'

s. **Yankee Handbook**. s-a. 'Guide to the Yankee market, covering over 100 issuers.'

The penultimate entry in that list – which we have already referred to in an earlier chapter – is a very good example of a publication which receives wide circulation and visibility: yet is not commercially available. There are thousands of valuable and valued similar publications produced by entities such as investment banks, stockbroker firms, accountancy firms and so on active in the global financial system.

54. This private or semi-private availability of potentially useful material extends further. For instance, an example of an organization producing economically related assessments in the UK, but which is not in the mainstream of such organizations, is *Trade Indemnity*:

> Has been in the business of credit risk management for 75 years. Today it is the UK's leading credit insurer, and has a major presence in the export and international markets. Trade Indemnity helps companies to manage risks and to survive the extremes of global economic cycles,

both in times of economic growth and of hard recession . . . As a service to clients, Trade Indemnity publishes:

Quarterly Business Review An analysis of the UK economy, bad debts and business failures coupled with an in depth study of sectors of UK industry and commerce.

Quarterly Export Survey Conducted in conjunction with *Export Times*, this survey assesses the confidence of UK exporters, the state of order books and the international credit risk outlook.

Quarterly Financial Trends Survey A unique source of information on the financial pressures affecting individual companies in the UK and the ways in which they are responding.

Trading Lines A quarterly newsletter on topical export issues for brokers, leading exporters and export influencers, covering topics such as risk assessment of foreign countries and companies, topical issues and problems facing exporters.

55. So there is a large amount of (value-added) financial and economic *data and information* of one type or another available in the semi-public arena. The other major area of restricted distribution literature relates to the *regulatory environment*. Two good exemplars of commercial organizations producing potentially valuable material from the UK would be *Clifford Chance* and *Bacon & Woodrow*:

(i) *Clifford Chance* 'A leading international law firm with offices in 19 cities throughout the world. We provide a comprehensive range of business and financial legal services . . . All our publications are available to clients and contacts free of charge. We reserve the right not to send the publications to our competitors, but otherwise we are happy to distribute as required on request to our *Publications Unit*.'

Apart from producing a number of guides and overviews to specific areas of finance, the company regularly issues over a dozen *Newsletters*, including

- EC Newsletter
- European Financial Services Newsletter
- European Competition Policy Review
- Legislative & Regulatory Review.

(ii) *Bacon & Woodrow* The 'largest independent actuarial consulting partnership in Europe with over 800 staff and partners'. The company is the UK member of *Woodrow Milliman*, an international network of actuarial and consulting firms represented in more than 90 offices in 21 countries. The company produce several publications for the finance community:

Boardroom Bulletin A quarterly newsletter for senior executives and directors on relevant pay and performance related reward issues;

Focus A newsletter produced by the firm's Insurance Division periodically examining key issues in the insurance and financial services industry in the UK, Europe and the rest of the world;

Analysis A detailed technical periodical reviewing developments and trends in the corporate occupational pension scheme sector;

Primer A quarterly review of trends in the financial markets designed for trustees of pension funds.

The company also formally publish each year jointly with *NTC Publications* a compact *Pensions Pocket Book* and a similar *Pay & Benefits Pocket Book*.

56. Summarizing the points made in this section, a remarkably large proportion of information of the type with which we are concerned in this text, once generated, is available first – or forever – only to certain restricted groups of people, and not to the public at large: it exists in a twilight zone half way between partial and full disclosure. **None of this material has been formally cited and indexed in this book**: to do so would not have been helpful. Indeed, many financial and other commercial institutions whom one knows regularly produce important sources which are widely used in practice within the financial system, have replied when contacted that such material is not generally available and should not be publicly referenced: for instance:

> I am writing to confirm that your assumptions are correct, [our US investment bank] would not want you to refer to any of its publications within your book *Information Sources in Finance and Banking*, as these are for private circulation only.
>
> I refer to your letter of . . . We produce NO information output which is distributed free of charge. All our output is for limited distribution to clients only.
>
> NO publications available to the public and make no reference to them in the book.

Often, such can be gleaned from the publication itself; for example:

> This material is for your private information, and we are not soliciting any action based upon it. Opinions expressed are our present opinions only. The material is based upon information which we consider reliable, but we do not represent it as accurate or complete and it should not be relied upon as such. We, or persons involved in the preparation or issuance of this material may, from time to time, have long or short positions in, and buy or sell securities, futures or options identical with or related to those mentioned herein . . . [investment bank] may have acted upon or used this research prior to or immediately following its publication.

57. People and organizations within the securities industry, professional and trade bodies involved with that industry, national and international official and quasi-official organizations are all gatherers and generators of data and information which only some time later – if at all – is formally and publicly displayed in a sense that the 'outsider' would recognize. Other examples of people and organizations who frequently have access to financially related data/information which the rest of us normally do not (at least at that time) would include credit and debt rating agencies, financial market analysts, consultants, market research companies, lobby correspondents, a whole raft of corporate 'advisors' – such as accountants, auditors, financial printers, registrars, trustees and so on – who in addition to the lawyers themselves are involved with the legal paraphernalia which accompanies much significant trade between entities, people in the know within the trading entities themselves (such as board members, corporate treasurers, secretaries), and of course the banks and other institutions (such as clearance and settlement agencies) who are charged with the transmission of financial assets from one entity to another once trade is under way. Perhaps it is no wonder that financial market sensitive information leaks out from time to time!
58. The complete version of the information flow map that we have developed is given in **Figure 3.3**. This anticipates the classifications we will use in one of the next four chapters: that concerned with the entities comprising the *Financial Institutions and Markets.* The other three chapters where sources are given illustrating the points made in this and previous chapters are: *Financial Management and Investment*, *Scholarly Research and Study* and *Corporations.* To the last we now move.

Notes

(133) cf TAYLOR, R.S. **Value-added processes in information systems**. *Ablex Publishing Corporation*, 1986. 257 pp.

(134) The corollary, of course, is that the information sources relevant to the areas of 'finance and banking' which are given minor prominence in the map, also themselves are also given here a relatively minor coverage. For instance, although we have naturally referred to the Bank of England and the Federal Reserve, the critical sources that those organizations produce are not given the attention that they would be if we adopted a different vantage point (eg a concern with information sources relevant to the optimal conduct of a country's economic and monetary policy and practice). So it is perhaps worth stressing that, for instance, the *Bank of England Quarterly Bulletin* and the monthly *Federal Reserve Bulletin* give superb up-to-date coverage of national (and international) developments of such macro-financial issues, as well as being full of useful articles and

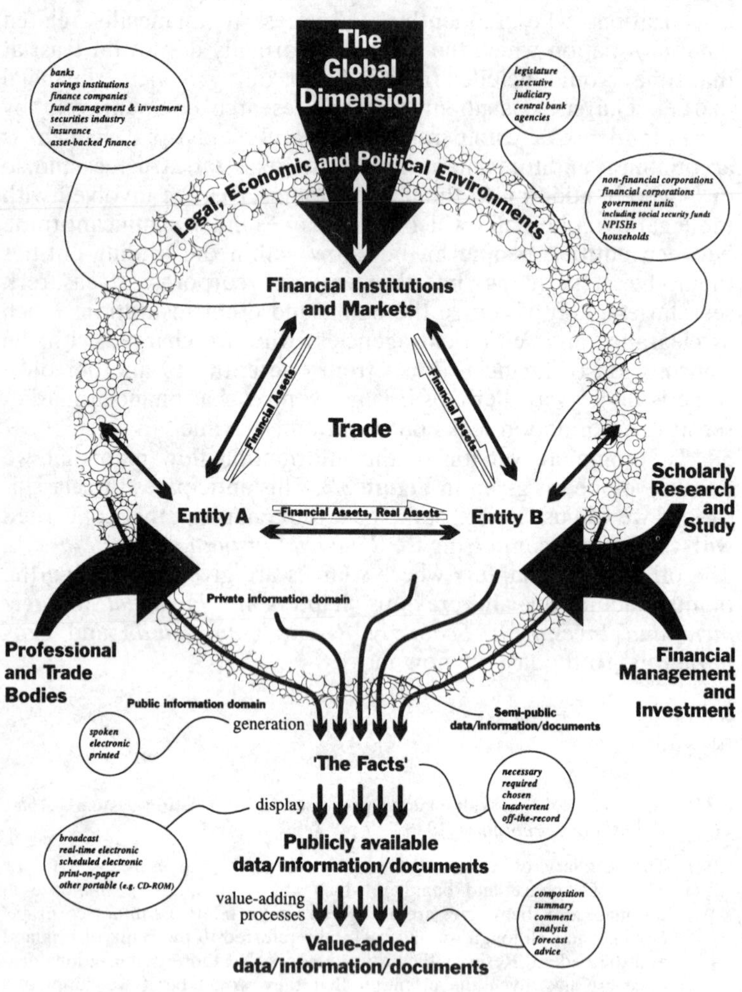
The Global Dimension
banks
savings institutions
finance companies
fund management & investment
securities industry
insurance
asset-backed finance
legislature
executive
judiciary
central bank
agencies
Legal, Economic and Political Environments
non-financial corporations
financial corporations
government units
including social security funds
NPISHs
households
Financial Institutions and Markets
Financial Assets
Financial Assets
Trade
Scholarly Research and Study
Entity A
Financial Assets, Real Assets
Entity B
Private information domain
Professional and Trade Bodies
Financial Management and Investment
Public information domain
generation
Semi-public data/information/documents
spoken
electronic
printed
'The Facts'
necessary
required
chosen
inadvertent
off-the-record
display
broadcast
real-time electronic
scheduled electronic
print-on-paper
other portable (e.g. CD-ROM)
Publicly available data/information/documents
value-adding processes
composition
summary
comment
analysis
forecast
advice
Value-added data/information/documents

Figure 3.3

notes on a remarkably wide range of 'relevant' subjects. For example, quoting from recent issues of the two journals:

(i) The Bank of England collects banking and related data for a variety of purposes – including the conduct of prudential supervision, the compilation of monetary, banking and similar financial statistics, and as a contribution to the national accounts and balance of payments statistics compiled by the Central Statistical Office. The aim is to collect the data as efficiently and economically as possible. This article briefly recounts developments since the start of the last review of banking statistics in 1987 and outlines the statistics currently available. It lists the main bids for new statistics of which the Bank is already aware, and invites comments from users on their existing and prospective needs.'[1]

(ii) The Federal Reserve Board on March 2, 1995, announced publication of a revised and updated paperback book that explains the structure and operations of the Federal Reserve System. This eighth edition of *Purposes and Functions* has been redesigned to appeal to a general audience and can supplement college-level classroom texts on the Federal Reserve's role in monetary policy and the global economy. The purpose of the book, first published in 1939, is to explain the structure, responsibilities, and operating techniques of the Federal Reserve System. The new edition reflects changes since the seventh edition was published in 1984 – changes in monetary and regulatory policies, in laws governing the Federal Reserve, and in the financial system.

Beginning with this issue of the Bulletin, the Legal Developments section will carry in the January, April, July, and October issues a quarterly index to orders issued or actions taken by the Board of Governors. The index will list the applicant, the merged or acquired bank or approved activity, the date of approval.[2]

[1] Banking statistics: recent and prospective developments. **Bank of England Quarterly Bulletin** 35(1), February 1995, pp 72–75.

[2] Announcements: Publication of eighth edition of *Purposes and Functions*; Publication of a new index for the legal developments section of the *Federal Reserve Bulletin*. **Federal Reserve Bulletin**. 81(4), April 1995, p 355.

(135) For example: JONES, C.P. **Investments: Analysis and management**. 4th ed. *John Wiley*, 1994 contains:

- *Appendix 6–A*: 'Finding and using bond information'; 'Sources of bond information'; 'Understanding published bond information';
- *Appendix 9–A*: 'Stock information'; 'Using stock information'; 'Reading common stock information';
- *Appendix 12–A* 'Published information about the economy – government publications';
- *Appendix 14–A*: 'Sources of information for common stocks'; 'The financial press; 'Corporate reports'; 'Brokerage firms'; 'Investment advisory services'; 'Investment advisory services and investment newsletters';
- *Appendix 19–A* 'Obtaining information on investment companies'; 'Reading investment company information'; 'Obtaining information about investment companies'.

(136) cf WALFORD, R.B. **Network system architecture**. *Addison-Wesley*, 1990, p 122.

(137) cf WILSON, P. **Two kinds of power: An essay on bibliographic control**. *University of California Press*, 1968. 155 pp.

(138) FULD, L.M. **The new competitor intelligence: The complete resource for finding, analysing, and using information about your competitors**. *John Wiley*. 1995. 482 pp.

(139) **Building the next-generation global treasury**. *Economist Intelligence Unit*, 1992, p 151. Research Report No. F-208.

(140) cf MEADOW, C.T. **Text information retrieval systems**. *Academic Press*, 1992. 302 pp. 'My intent in this book is to provide a comprehensive treatment of information retrieval covering all aspects of this complex field, emphasising operational systems rather than research, and constantly reminding the reader of the interrelationships among the users, the mechanical information retrieval system, and the databases... Information retrieval is a communication process. It involves an author, composer, artist, or other record originator and a reader, viewer, listener, or user of information. But these two principles are not in direct communication. A record is created for *later* use, and its use requires finding the record among large numbers of other records, all of which share attributes that caused them to be grouped together in the first place. In addition to the two principles in the communication, there are others who may be directly or indirectly involved: those who decide what aspects of a record should be represented in the computer-searchable database; those who transform, index, or encode the information in various ways to create the computer record; those who help the user perform a search; those who design and implement the computer software; and those who decide what services will be offered to users (what software, what databases, what prices).' See also: VICKERY, B. and VICKERY, A. **Information science in theory and practice**. *Butterworths*, 1987. 384 pp.

(141) One can easily be tempted into tedious pedantry here! For example, when the Chairman of the US Federal Reserve or the Governor of the Bank of England announces a purely factual change in some monetary instrument, they will almost always 'add value' to that factual announcement by explaining why the change was 'necessary'. Here we might argue that the supplementary comments are in turn 'facts', rather than simply a piece of value-adding. Certainly such statements will have been formulated wholly within the private domain.

(142) cf THOMPSON, D.F. **Ethics in Congress: From individual to institutional corruption**. *Brookings Institution*, 1995. 200 pp. $12.95. 'More members of Congress have been investigated and sanctioned for ethical misconduct in the past decade and a half than in the entire history of the institution. But individual members are probably less corrupt than they once were. Stricter ethics codes and closer scrutiny by the press and public have imposed standards no previous representatives have had to face.'

(143) REILLY, F.K. and NORTON, E. **Investments**. 4th ed. *Dryden Press*, 1995. 670 pp.

(144) REILLY and NORTON op cit p 244.

(145) REILLY and NORTON op cit p 246.

(146) REILLY and NORTON op cit p 440.

(147) REILLY and NORTON op cit p 120.

(148) The former editor of the magazine *The Economist*, Rupert Pennant-Rea, when interviewed after his appointment as Deputy Governor of the Bank of England, said that one of the most exhilarating moments of his life had

been posting a newswire scoop from Paris a full fifteen minutes ahead of the competition!

(149) BLACKHURST, C. Totally wired. **Gentlemen's Quarterly**, November 1993. On the last sentence in the quote, those information scientists who have grappled with the immense difficulties of persuading automated information retrieval systems to recall with an acceptable degree of precision exactly the text-based items relevant to the purpose needed, and to leave the rest in the system, may be understandably highly sceptical here! But at least in such a scenario the control of what is retrieved and what not from the global totality of news stories would potentially be in the hands of the customer (censorship permitting); rather than first being subjected to the whims of the media editors.

(150) JOHNSON, L. and BLACKSTONE, T. **The investor relations handbook.** *Investors Imprint*, 1990. 107 pp. 'This book is designed to help strip away the mystique with which the City deliberately surrounds itself. Much of what the circus of fund managers, stockbrokers, merchant bankers, and PR men do is simple.... We have tried in this publication to put their work in perspective, and help owners and managers take advantage of the Square Mile – instead of permitting the opposite, which is so frequently the case.'

ROSENBAUM, M.A. **Selling your story to Wall Street: The art & science of investor relations**. *Irwin Professional*, 1994. 300 pp. £28.50. 'The best book ever written on investor relations.'

(151) LOGAN op cit.

(152) DENNIS op cit.

(153) MacHARG, M.L. and KAMEDA, R.R.W. eds. **International survey of investment adviser regulation**. *Kluwer Law International*, 1994. 368 pp. £75.00. 'The primary purpose of this major reference work is to help shape the direction of investment management regulation . . . In view of the rapid pace of internationalisation of the world's securities markets, knowledge of regulatory schemes around the world is an absolute necessity for both legal practitioners and international money managers.'

(154) **Bloomberg: A Magazine for Bloomberg Users**. 3(7), July 1994, p 34.

(155) **Market 2000: An examination of current equity market developments**. *US Securities and Exchange Commission: Division of Market Regulation*. 1994. 86 pp plus seven *Analytical Studies* and seven *Appendixes* (Appendix VII being a 49–page *Bibliography*).

(156) Market 2000 op cit p 11.

(157) Market 2000 op cit p 16.

(158) A good introductory article is: SMITH, A. Stockbroker research. **Business Information Review** 8(2), October 1991, pp 3–13. 'Research is very costly and is justified by the dealing commissions that stockbrokers receive, although some securities firms charge a fee for their research. Another factor is that some brokerage houses take securities on to their own account and this can create a business pressure to emphasise that stock when dealing with clients. There are very few completely independent and impartial research services carrying out analyses and recommendations in the UK, presumably because of the prohibitive cost . . . In the USA, there are over 1,000 independent research firms and the practice of fund managers buying in research is common.'

(159) However, such forecasts are also produced by public sector academic and research institutes – and of course by governments themselves; and these forecasts by definition are firmly in the public domain and can be purchased. c.f. FILDES, R. ed. **World index of economic forecasts**. 4th ed. *Gower*, 1995. 125. 'Information on 230 organizations (in 58 countries), many new to this edition, while others from previous years have ceased forecasting and been removed . . . All sections are structured to incorporate profiles of macroeconomic and specialist forecasters; and surveys of business activities, investment plans and consumer purchasing . . . The book also includes an introduction which describes how forecasts are produced, together with their use and value to those with forecasting responsibilities in organizations.'

Further reading

ZIMMERMAN, J.L. **Accounting for decision making and control**. *Irwin*, 1995.

CUSHING, B.E. and ROMNEY, M.B. **Accounting information systems**. 6th ed. *Addison-Wesley*, 1994. 1136 pp. 'Integrates the traditional coverage of accounting systems with the coverage of contemporary information technology.'

WHITE, G.I., SONDHI, A.C. and FRIED, D. **The analysis and use of financial statements**. *John Wiley*, 1994.

BROWN, P.J. **Constructing & calculating bond indices: A guide to the EFFAS Standardized Rules**. *Irwin Professional*, 1993. 130 pp. £35. 'Explains how popular bond indices are constructed, the strengths and weaknesses of the indices and how they differ from one another.' (EFFAS is the *European Federation of Financial Analysts Societies*.)

SHAW, H. **Decision making: cases in financial and quantitative management**. *Elm Publications/Training*, 1994. 96 pp. £5.95. 'Forty case studies from beginner's level on small to medium sized businesses, with accounting ratios, prescribed formats for company accounts, glossary and DCF tables. A good text for students new to accounting and financial analysis.' Also available is a *Tutor's Manual*.

HOLDEN, K., PEEL, D. and THOMPSON, J. **Economic forecasting: An introduction**. *Cambridge University Press*, 1991. 223 pp. £11.95. 'It is the only text currently available which provides a comprehensive coverage of methods and applications in this fast-growing area.'

HENRY, S.G.B. and PATTERSON, K.D. **Economic modelling at the Bank of England**. *Chapman & Hall*, 1990. 288 pp. £55.

BOMHOFF, E.J. **Financial forecasting for business and economics**. *Academic Press*, 1994. 288 pp. £19.95. 'Until recently a formidable gap separated practical business economists, who forecast economic growth and exchange and interest rate fluctuations, from academic researchers. Academic journals focused on statistical techniques which were inappropriate for practical business forecasting. Economic theory, especially in the field of business cycle research, became more and more abstract and harder to apply. These twin developments drove many practitioners to technical analysis. Fortunately, the gap is being bridged. New scholarly research offers much more scope for useful forecasts of exchange rates and stock market indices.'

FOSTER, G. **Financial statement analysis**. 2nd ed. *Prentice Hall*, 1986. 625 pp.

PLUMMER, T. **Forecasting financial markets**. 2nd ed. *Kogan Page*, 1993. 272 pp. £30. "For those who simply want to understand what technical analysis is about this book is as clear-cut and easy to read an introduction as one could want" (*The Independent*).

BOWLIN, O.D. et al. **Guide to financial analysis**. 3rd ed. *McGraw-Hill*, 1994.

TYRAN, M.R. and WARD, M. **Handbook of business and financial ratios**. *Woodhead-Faulkner*, 1992. 352 pp. £19.95.

BRUCE, B.R. and EPSTEIN, C.B. eds. **The handbook of corporate earnings analysis**. *Irwin Professional*, 1994. 400 pp. £50. 'Earnings expectations drive the equity market. Even a casual reader of the financial press will note the many stories each day that attribute stock price movements to changes in analysts' forecasts or to earnings reports that differ significantly from analysts' expectations. This book explains how investors can profit from a deeper understanding of the relationship between earnings expectations and stock prices.'

BERLIN, H.M. **Handbook of financial market indexes, averages and indicators**. *Dow Jones Irwin*, 1990. 262 pp.

WARFIELD, G. **How to read and understand the financial press**. 2nd ed. *Harper Perennial*, 1994. 241 pp.

BRETT, M. **How to read the financial pages**. 4th ed. *Century Business*, 1995. 336 pp. £12.99. 'The business bestseller written for the layman – which the City buys as well.'

ANDREW, J. **How to understand the financial press**. 2nd ed. *Kogan Page*, 1993. 176 pp. £9.99.

HOLMES, G. and SUGDEN, A. **Interpreting company reports and accounts**. 4th ed. *Woodhead-Faulkner*, 1990. 219 pp.

HOGARTH, R.M. **Judgement and choice: The psychology of decision**. *John Wiley*, 1987. 311 pp. 'This book is written for an audience that consists of neither professional psychologists nor decision theorists. It is written for decision makers, people who manipulate their specialist knowledge in making choices, be it in industry, commerce, government service, medicine or indeed any other professional activity. Consequently the book is written at a non-technical level. . . . Many of the examples chosen for illustration actually concern business applications.'

REID, W. and MYDDLETON, D.R. **The meaning of company accounts**. 5th ed. *Gower*, 1992. 372 pp. £18.95.

TRIPPI, R.R. and TURBAN, E. eds. **Neural networks in finance and investing**. *Irwin Professional*, 1993. 513 pp. £57.50. 'Explains how neural networks draw conclusions from incomplete data, recognize patterns as they unfold and forecast price moves.'

SHIM, J.K., SIEGEL, J.G. and LIEW, C.J. **Strategic business forecasting: The complete guide to forecasting real-world company performance**. *Irwin Professional*, 1994. 350 pp. 40. 'Shows how to forecast virtually every aspect of corporate performance. The authors explain a variety of mathematical and statistical methods for forecasting and demonstrate how these techniques can be applied to real-world situations.'

CHAPTER FOUR

Corporations

1. There is just one sequence of *commercial information providers* in this chapter. There are a large number of *source guides* to 'company information' in the marketplace.[160]

2. Commercial information providers

(1) #501 American Banker Newsletters 1325 G Street NW, Suite 900, Washington, DC 20005, USA. t: (1 202) 347 2665; f: 347 1158.

1452. **Insiders' Chronicle**. w. $445. **online**. Buy/sell transactions of corporate officers, directors and beneficial owners, including transactions filed on SEC Form 4, 144 letter stock trades, 13D filings. *Insider Alert* highlights those companies that have been the target of repeated or especially heavy insider accumulation.

1453. **Private Placement Reporter**. w. $795. **online**. 'Covers the buying, selling and trading of unregistered securities. Talks about deals and pricing, covenent packages and spreads, and agents and investors.'

(2) #502 American Business Information 5711 South 86th Circle, PO Box 27347, Omaha, NE 68127, USA. t: (1 402) 592 9000; f: 331 1505.

Maintains a database of details of 10 million businesses, accessible via telephone/fax (*ABI NETWORK*) or online (*American Business Lists Online*). Since early 1994, ABI's database has included *Credit Rating Codes*:

'Our business information is compiled from 5,000 telephone directories, 10,000 annual reports, 150,000 press releases, Chamber of Commerce

Directories, SEC Records, major newspapers, and many other sources. And we make over . . . *14 million telephone calls* . . . every year to verify the accuracy of the database, validating addresses and enhancing each record with Owner or Manager's Name, Number of Employees, Suite Number, and other hard-to-find data. All this information is obtained by over 300 full-time researchers in Omaha. We are proud that we have the finest business database in the country.

When customers like you repeatedly told us that you needed a system to obtain credit indicators on businesses, we went to work. We developed *CREDIT RATING CODES* after years of painstaking analysis. We are using the demographic information of our database, historical performance data and other information. Our sophisticated computer programs develop predictive statistical models based on multivariate regression analysis to determine credit-worthiness of businesses. These proprietory scoring models have been used successfully in our own business, and, finally, we are able to offer credit rating information for the exclusive use of our customers.'

1454. **American Business Directory**. **online**. Brief details of some 11 million US companies. *Business America on CD-ROM* (s-a. $7500) is the portable version.

(3) #503 Argus Vickers 17 Battery Place, New York, NY 10004, USA. t: (1 212) 425 7500; f: 509 5408. *Also* American Equity Research Limited, Royex House, Aldermanbury Square, London EC2V 7HR, UK. t: (44 171) 606 0006; f: 606 0666.

1455. **Insider Options**. bi-w. 'Lists exercised options by corporate officials. Providing the company's name and address, the individual's name and title, shares obtained, price per share and current number of shares held.'

1456. **Investment Analysis and Update**. i. 'Concentrates on specific companies of current interest to investors. There are typically ten or more analyses published monthly.'

1457. **Investment Portfolio Guide**. m. '40-page review of the industries monitored by Argus.'

1458. **Portfolio Selector**. m. 'Presents Argus' top North American recommendations. The Director of Research . . . selects common equities arranged according to specific objectives: Income; Capital Gains & Income; Capital Gains – Investment Grade; Capital Gains – Risk-oriented, Large Cap; and Capital Gains – Risk-oriented, Small and Mid-Cap. Dividends, earnings estimates and key fundamental data are included, along with a brief comment on one company in each group. Accompanying the five portfolios is a Market Outlook Commentary, a Technical View and the Director's Choice – the featured 'buy' of the month. Published two weeks after the Portfolio Selector is our *Viewpoint*. *Viewpoint* defines Argus' investment policy according to economic, political and market developments, outlining strategies for investing in stocks and bonds.'

1459. **Transactions & Intentions**. 2/week. 'Report for all 144, 13d and 14d filings. 144's are filed by a corporate insider who wishes to sell a "restricted" or unregistered stock. A form is filed with the SEC at least 3 days prior to the sale of the security. 13d and 14d's are filed with SEC within 10 days after 5% of a target's stock is acquired.'

1460. **Weekly Insider Report**. w. 'Reporting and analysis of SEC Form 4s which consider equity purchases and sales by corporate insiders, such as officers, Vice Presidents, Directors etc. and owners of more than 10% of a US public company. A unique feature offered in the *Weekly Insider* is our "Sell-Buy" ratios. This highlights insider sentiment regarding the overall securities market . . . For our time sensitive investors we offer *InsiderFax*. Utilising common place technology the *Weekly Insider Report*, excluding the Company Index section, is faxed to a selected location every Tuesday, in addition to the mailed copy.'

(4) #504 CD-ROM Publishing Company 1 Great Scotland Yard, London SW1A 2HN, UK. t: (44 171) 839 2266; f: 839 6632. Wholly owned subsidiary of *Bureau van Dijk*, a consulting firm operating companies in Brussels and Paris since 1973.

1461. **AMADEUS**. **cdrom**. bi-m. 15000 EU plus 4000 EU for the Ownership Section. 'A Pan-European corporate database with detailed accounts and descriptive information on the top 125,000 companies in Europe, with financial analysis software.' Data provided by *Jordan Publishing*.

1462. **EMMA**. **cdrom**. q. £3,000 (including 12,000 credits for downloading or printing records). 'Contains reports on over 600,000 British companies with information on name, address, date of incorporation, company type, activity, directors, holding companies, turnover, net assets, pre-tax profit and number of employees. The data is assembled and compiled by *ICC Information Group*.'

1463. **FAME**. **cdrom**. m. £5,900 (top 110,000 companies); £3,900 (additional 100,000 companies). 'Detailed historical annual accounts and financial ratios for the 210,000 major public and private British companies plus descriptive information for 50,000 additional Holdings and Subsidiaries. . . . The data is compiled by *Jordan Publishing*. An online connection with the Jordans host in Bristol may be provided to access updated accounts.'

1464. **HALO**. **cdrom**. m. £5,900. 'Holdings, Accounts and Lines of Ownership . . . Contains detailed reports for all UK and Irish- registered companies quoted on the International Stock Exchange or with equity shares dealt on an OTC basis . . . The data is assembled and compiled by *Jordan Publishing* and *Hemmington Scott*.'

(5) #505 CIFAR [Center for International Financial Analysis & Research] Princeton Service Center, 3490 US Route One, Princeton, NJ 08540, USA. t: (1 609) 520 9333; f: 520 0905.

'Independent research group established in 1984 . . . Its continuously updated collection of annual reports and interim reports of 25,000 companies worldwide form the nucleus of the research efforts at CIFAR. Additionally, CIFAR regularly updates its extensive reference library on international accounting and capital markets information.'

1465. **Cfarbase**. **online**. **cdrom**. Covers 14,000 companies in 50 countries. 'More than 7 years of comparable standardized data on key financial and non-financial variables.' *CfarQuest* is 'an on-demand reference service utilizing CIFAR's vast analytical resources on companies and capital markets worldwide ... Up-to-date and comprehensive profiles on over 25,000 leading companies worldwide ... Ranking by industry, country, region or worldwide ... Available around the clock, 365 days per year.'

1466. **Global Company Handbook**. i. $495 (3rd ed., 1994). Analysis and rankings of the financial performance of 'the world's leading 12,000 companies'.

1467. **Global Company News Digest**. m. $395. Covers 5,000 companies: 'Over 100 leading worldwide newspapers and financial/business publications reviewed each month'.

(6) #506 Digital Directory Assistance 6931 Arlington Road, Suite 405, Bethesda, MD 20814–5231, USA. t: (1 301) 657 8548; f: 652 7810.

1468. **PhoneDisc**. **cdrom**. Four versions: *PowerFinder* $249; *Residential* $79; *Business* $79; *ComboPack* $129.

(7) #507 Disclosure 5161 River Road, Bethesda, MD 20816, USA. t: (1 301) 951 1300; f: 657 1962 *and* 26–31 Whiskin Street, London EC1R 0BP, UK. t: (44 171) 278 7848; f: 278 3898.

1469. **Compact D/SEC**. 'The **cdrom** version of the *Disclosure SEC Database* offers complete profiles for close to 11,000 public companies, including annual balance sheets, income statements, cash flow statements, quarterly financial statements and much, much more. ... Covers every company filing with the Securities and Exchange Commission, both domestic and foreign. The data is taken from 10K, 10Q, 8K and proxy reports.'

1470. **Compact D/'33**. **cdrom**. 'The first CD-ROM database to provide quick, round the clock access to every issue filed with the Securities and Exchange Commission on or after January 1, 1990. ... Covers all transactions, not just the underwritten public offerings, including poison pills, exchange offers, conversions, and more. In the past year, we've added close to 6,000 deals, more than any competitor.'

1471. **Disclosure/Spectrum Ownership Database**. **online**. q. Ownership data for 5,000 US companies.

1472. **EDGARPlus**. **online**. **magtape**. c. The *SEC Online* database supplemented with data acquired and processed via the US SEC's EDGAR project. Covers some 5,000 companies.

1473. **Fortune 500 on Disk**. **diskette**. a. Accounting and other data covering the two Fortune 500 US company rankings.

1474. **LaserD/International**. **cdrom**. 'An *image based product* which covers annual reports on over 14,500 companies from around the world . . . Think ahead. That's what we did when developing the incredible *Laser D II* system. By utilizing the fastest- growing user interface in the world, we give you the features you need today, like networking and multi-tasking. Along with the upward compatibility you'll need tommorow, It's one of the many reasons there's no other system quite like *Laser D II*. Reasons like EDGAR compatibility, with full text searching. A sophisticated print queue manager. Domestic and international document collections, to monitor global business connections. Integrated accounting software, to track usage and charge back research expenses to clients or other departments. Networking and faxing capabilities. *Laser D II* is the document retrieval system of the future. It's here today. And if you're in the business of public company research, you can't afford to be without it.'

1475. **SEC Online**. **online**. **cdrom**. Full text of documents filed by public companies with the US Securities and Exchange Commission. Covers all companies traded on the New York and American Exchanges as well as selected NMS/NASDAQ companies. Gives access to the actual, unedited text of these companies' 10Ks, 10Qs, 20Fs, Annual Reports, and Proxy Statements, including Amendments and Exhibits.

(8) #508 Dun & Bradstreet International Holmers Farm Way, High Wycombe, Buckinghamshire, HP12 4UL, UK. t: (44 1494) 422000; f: 422260 *and* **Dun & Bradstreet Information Services** 3 Sylvan Way, Parsipanny, NJ 07054–9947, USA. t: (1 201) 605 6000; f: 605 6930.

1476. **America's Corporate Families and International Affiliates**. a. £798. Two volumes. Covers about 15,000 US and foreign parents and some 70,000 subsidiaries.

1477. **British Business Rankings**. a. £150. 'The only published record of the relative position of Britain's 5,000 largest employers.'

1478. **CD/Business Locator**. **cdrom**. q. £950. Summary information on over 2 million UK companies, including those that have gone out of business during the last five years.

1479. **Corporate Financial Performance**. a. £195. Covers 50,000 UK businesses.

1480. **D&B Europa**. a. £438. Four volumes. **online**. **cdrom**. **diskette**. **magtape**. Company data from some 20 European countries, the number of companies covered (between about 60,000 and 120,000) and the level of detail varying between the various media used.

1481. **Dun & Bradstreet Reference Book of American Business**. bi- m. £945. Five volumes. Listings of approximately 3 million businesses.

1482. **Dun & Bradstreet United Kingdom**. **online**. m. Brief but wide-ranging information on over 425,000 actively trading companies.

1483. **Dun's Business Identification Service**. s-a. £795. Microfiche listing of more than 10 million US establishments.

1484. **Dun's Business Rankings**. a. £399. Ranks 8000 US businesses.

1485. **Dun's Business Update**. **online**. Bi-weekly updates on 600,000 US businesses.

1486. **Dun's Electronic Business Directory**. **online**. Current information on about 9 million US entities including some 700,000 banks, savings institutions and insurance companies; and over 1 million professionals in a wide variety of fields including the majority of those covered in this Book.

1487. **Dun's European Marketing Database. online**. A wide range of basic information on 2.7 million companies, data being obtained from D&B's offices and by questionnaires and telephone enquiries.

1488. **Dun's Financial Records Plus**. **online**. Summary balance sheet and income statements for about three quarter of a million US companies.

1489. **Dun's Reference Plus**. **cdrom**. Bi-monthly updating for four million US entities, including credit ratings.

1490. **European Market Guide**. s-a. £945. Two volumes. 'Over a quarter-of-a-million listings for 21 countries are provided in this two- volume credit reference guide for Northern and Southern Europe.'

1491. **Industry Norms and Key Business Ratios**. a. £215. 'Based on information contained in more than one million (UK) public and private financial statements, this statistical survey presents the most widely used ratios in business today.' Covers three years of data, but also available in a one-year coverage edition, and an edition excluding the 'industry norms' data.

1492. **International Dun's Business Identification Service**. s-a. £695. 'The most broadly based record in existence of international businesses, more than 2,000,000.'

1493. **International Dun's Market Identifiers**. **online**. Two and a half million private and public companies in about 150 countries.

1494. **International Risk & Payment Review**. m. £495. Covers over 100 countries, providing essential risk assessment for international traders.

1495. **Key British Enterprises**. a. (plus two updates). £495. Six volumes. **online**. **cdrom**. 'Covers the 50,000 largest actively trading companies in the UK . . . selected from Dun & Bradsreet's database of 1.4 million companies. Each qualified company is then sent a questionnaire to check and update the details we hold on them. Supplementary information is obtained from the appropriate Dun & Bradstreet *Business Information Report*, telephone interview and the company's annual report. Because the world of business is constantly changing, the companies listed in these volumes have different degrees of financial health. Inclusion in this directory, therefore, does not indicate endorsement of a company by Dun & Bradstreet.' *Volume 5* cross-references by trade names, export markets and directors' names (over 130,000 individuals); and *Volume 6* 'British Business Rankings', selects the 5,000 largest employers from the main volumes and ranks them by sales and employees, within county and within line of business. The *online* version includes, in addition, three years of financial accounts data.

1496. **Key Business Ratios**. a. £225. 'As well as providing 20 key business ratios – ranging from asset utility and financial status to employee productivity and profitability – for more than 370 UK industry groups, balance sheet and profit and loss averages are given for each of the last three financial years.'

1497. **Million Dollar Directory**. a. £895. Five volumes. **online**. **cdrom**. 'The most respected business reference source . . . information on 160,000 businesses – 90% of which are privately owned.' A *Top 50,000* version (£495) is also available.

1498. **Principal International Businesses**. a. £495. Lists a wide range of marketing facts and figures on the world's top 50,000 business firms in 133 countries.

1499. **Who Owns Whom: International**. a. £839. **online**. **cdrom**. Six volume series covering United Kingdom, Continetal Europe, North America, and Australasia and the Far East.

(9) #509 Earnings Guide Box 1, Horsham, West Sussex, RH12 3YY, UK. t: (44 1403) 791155; f: 791152.

1500. **Earnings Guide**. m. £270. **diskette**. w. £1,200. 'The monthly consensus of company earnings & profit forecasts . . . We check approximately 35,000 individual UK forecasts each month.'

(10) #510 ELC International 109 Uxbridge Road, Ealing, London W5 5TL, UK. t: (44 181) 566 2288; f: 566 4931.

1501. **Europe's Largest Companies**. **diskette**. q. £1,550. Financial information on 25,000 companies in Europe and Scandinavia, including key data on the financial services sector.

1502. **Europe's 15,000 Largest Companies**. a. £185. Lists of the top companies in 15 countries of Western Europe ranked by turnover, with tables of the largest banks and insurance companies ranked by assets.

1503. **UK's 10,000 Largest Companies**. a. £150. **diskette**. Ranked by sales, with separate listings of the largest banks, insurance companies, and financial companies, ranked by assets. For *updating*: 'We use various sources to update the database from which this title is published, principally registered accounts, telephone research and data supplied direct from the companies themselves.'

(11) #511 Euromoney Publications Nestor House, Playhouse Yard, London EC4V 5EX, UK. t: (44 171) 779 8888; f: 779 8818.

1504. The **European 5000**. a. Four volumes. 'With data supplied by *World-scope/Disclosure Partners* and with editorial contributed by *Price Water-house*, Euromoney's own researchers and a team of leading law firms, this major research work collects all the key financial and operating information relevant to the investor, financier, adviser or supplier. It is designed explictly to serve as an easy reference point for anyone needing to have a comprehensive and up-to-date profile of any of Europe's key companies. . . . Our aim has been to supply as much useful information as possible as the best possible price: The European 5000 is not going to be a substitute for on-line data but it is the obvious alternative.'

(12) #512 Euromonitor Publications 60–61 Britton Street, London EC1M 5NA, UK. t: (44 171) 251 1105; f: 251 0985. *Also* Euromonitor International, 111 West Washington Street, Suite 920, Chicago, IL 60602, USA. t: (1 312) 541 8024; 541 1567.

1505. **European Directory of Medium Sized Companies**. a. £275. Covers 4,000 companies in Western and Eastern Europe.

1506. **World's Major Companies**. a. £275. 'Brand new, thoroughly researched directory to the top companies across the globe. Euromonitor has contacted each of the 4,000 companies listed to compile detailed entries and to ensure that all the information is correct and fully up-to-date.

(13) #513 Financial Times Number One, Southwark Bridge, London SE1 9HL, UK. t: (44 171) 873 4090; f: 873 3197.

1507. **Financial Times FT 500**. a. **diskette**. 'Lists the 500 largest quoted companies in Europe, ranked by their size at the end of September each year. A second table does the same for UK companies listed on the London Stock Exchange . . . The key distinguishing feature of the FT 500 is that it ranks a company by its market capitalisation. That is the number of shares the company has in issue, multiplied by the market price of those shares. There are several ways to calculate a company's size and all of them have drawbacks. Many tables base size on turnover. But this approach does not allow a proper representation for banks and some other financial services companies and tends to exaggerate the importance of commodities trading businesses. Another approach is to rank companies by profits, but such a table will exclude large companies which have move temporarily into loss. Ranking by the number of a company's employees can also provide some insight into size, but it says nothing about the dynamism of the business. A table based on market capitalisation overcomes many of these problems.'

(14) #514 FT Information Fitzroy House, 13–17 Epworth Street, London EC2A 4DL, UK. t: (44 171) 825 8000; f: 825 7999. Now also markets products and services from *Extel Financial*.

1508. **European Handbook**. bi-a. £205. Two volumes. 'Includes up to three years of financial information on over 2,000 leading European companies.'

1509. **EXSTAT**. **online**. Financial information on approximately 3,500 UK companies.

1510. **Extel Financial Workstation**. **cdrom**. '*Company Research* provides access to the full *Extel Card* service, comprehensive daily company news and share prices for all companies.... For those who also subscribe to Extel's *Equity Research* service, an automatic link from Company to Equity is provided. Equity Research offers both graphic and tabular performance analysis on global securities... *Precendents Research* has been specifically designed for Corporate Financiers, Financial Institutions, Registrars or Listed Companies to provide information on all equity/debt offers and issues and Section C company announcements which occur within the UK domestic market including the Official List, Unlisted Securities Market, Rule 535 and Foreign UK Listed companies... *Bond Research* is an essential tool for all bond trading organisations for the following applications: Settlement, Dealing support, Syndication, New issue comparisons, and Research.'

1511. **Extel Foreign Exchange Rates Record**. l. 'A record of the daily, monthly and annual highs, lows and averages for 20 currencies against sterling and cross rated to the dollar and the ECU.'

1512. **Extel International Bonds Service**. l. 'Comprehensive record on over 12,000 international and Eurobonds from 79 countries.'

1513. **Extel Professional Advisers to New Issues**. a. 'All issues covered in the publication relate to securities where a London listing was sought. As many new issues are being offered through international underwriters, the book contains coverage of all lead underwriters irrespective of domicile.'

1514. **Extel Securities Taxation Services**. 'Extel Financial is the leading supplier of Capital Gains Tax and dividend and interest data to taxation practitioners and other financial advisers throughout the United Kingdom and the Republic of Ireland. Apart from the Inland Revenue offices... accountants, solicitors, stockbrokers and banks rely on Extel Financial for coverage of the thousands of capital events and dividend and interest information which they reuqire when updating portfolios and completing tax returns.'

1515. **Extel UK Dividend and Interest Record**. q. £180. 'A complete record of dividend and interest payments for income tax purposes.' There is also an *Extel International Dividend and Interest Record* (£640) covering 32,000 securities listed on 60 stock exchanges.

1516. **Financial Times Mergers and Acquisitions International**. m. **online**. There is also an *FT Mergers and Acquisitions News*.

15173. **International Securities Database**. **online**. 35,000 securities traded on non-US/Canada stock exchanges.

1518. **Major UK Companies Handbook**. bi-a. 'Five years of financial data on the major 750 companies quoted on the London Stock Exchange.'

1519. **Smaller Companies Handbook**. a. £165. Two volumes. 'Detailed corporate and financial information on 1500 smaller companies quoted on the Main and Unlisted Securities Markets.'

(15) #515 FT McCarthy The Old Silk Works, Beech Avenue, Warminster, Wiltshire BA12 8LX, UK. t: (44 1985) 215151; f: 217479

1520. **FT Stats Fiche**. Microfiche. £420.

1521. **McCarthy on CD-ROM**. m. Articles on companies and industries selected from about 70 newspapers and magazines.

1522. **McCarthy Press Cuttings**. l. Can be purchased as *UK Quoted* £3,190; *UK Unquoted* £1,100; *European* £1,100.

1523. **MIRAC Company Annual Reports**. Microfiche. £4,210.

(16) #516 Fulcrum Directories 254 Goswell Road, London EC1V 7EB, UK. t: (44 171) 253 0353; f: 490 0206.

1524. **Index of Nominees and their Beneficial Owners**. a. 'As in previous years, the information . . . is derived from the inspection of company documents in the public domain: the registers that UK public companies are statutorily obliged to maintain of the replies they have received to their enquiries under Section 212 of the Companies Act 1985. As most subscribers will already know, this is the part of the Act which gives a public company the right to ask shareholders to confirm the beneficial ownership of their shares. Unfortunately these registers often contain inaccuracies which, wherever possible, we have attempted to identify and remove from the current edition. We are always pleased to hear from subscribers who have spotted errors which have slipped through the net.'

(17) #517 Gale Research 835 Penobscot Building, Detroit, MI 48226–4094, USA. t: (1 313) 961 2242; f: 961 6815.

1525. **Companies International**. **cdrom**. a. £1,500. Combines two Gale Research directories, **Ward's Business Directory** (which is also available separately on **diskette**) and **World Business Directory**, which together provide information on some 250,000 US and international companies from 191 countries. Approximately 94 per cent of the US companies are privately owned.

(18) #518 Global Securities Information 627 E Street NW, Suite 300, Washington, DC 20004, USA. t: (1 202) 628 1155; f: 628 1133.

'A professional research organization based in Washington, DC which specializes in the real time dissemination of vital corporate information released at the *Securities and Exchange Commission* (the "SEC") and other government agencies that oversee financial markets. GSI provides you with the information you need to stay abreast of the securities markets by offering a variety of demand and subscription services. GSI provides a proactive stance on your behalf, while always acting as a confidential agent. GSI believes in constant communication, and going that extra step to ensure that each request is fulfilled with the personal touch you deserve.... Founded in 1988, GSI has built a reputation based on professional excellence throughout the corporate, legal and financial communities.... Each GSI team member goes through a rigorous training program which enables them to understand your needs.

Watch Services

- *Hourly Corporate Watch* 'Every day an experienced professional completes a thorough checklist in search of filings made by and/or on the registrant you specify: Two checks on the SEC's workload computer system; Two checks on the SEC's EDGAR computer system; Hourly checks of Merger & Acquisition filings (tender offers, tender offer responses and 13Ds); Hand checks of all filings in rotation, including: 33' Act registration statements, 8Ks, proxy statements, 144s and 3s and 4s.'
- *SEC Document Watch* 'A GSI research associate monitors the SEC computer and the SEC rotations on a continuous basis until the document you requested is filed.'
- *Custom Watch* 'You define the parameters of the watch.'
- *SEC Release Watch* An experienced GSI representative checks the SEC digest for upcoming issues and releases.'
- *Corporate Intelligence Watch* 'There are two types.... It makes sense to stay informed on a real time basis of any surprise filings made on your company or client by non-corporate/unaffiliated entities. When you institute an *Insurance Watch* you cover all the bases at the SEC. Although surprises may not be eliminated, you can be assured that in the event a filing is made on your company or client, you will be the first to know. We beat the "wire" and can get hard copy into your hands in minutes.... Filings include: 14Bs, PRE14Cs & DEF14Cs in the case of proxy contests; 13Gs filed by institutional investors; 13Ds filed on your company; 14D-1s filed by potential acquirors. *Corporate Competition Watch* Stay ahead of important financial and other material disclosures of publicly held competitors. We provide you with up to the minute notification of filings made at the SEC by and on the competitor(s) you designate ... The cost of Corporate Intelligence Watch is only $50.00 per month or $500 per year.'

Databases

- *Registration Database* 'Allows GSI research specialists to search thousands of registration statements ... Contains selected data from all original S-1, S-2, S-3, S-4, S-8, S-18, F-1. F-2, F-3, F-4, F-6, F-7, F-9, F-10, N-1A, N-2 and Schedule B registrations filed with the SEC from April 1988 to the present, and is updated daily.'
- *Tender Offer Database* 'Contains selected information from tender offers, self tender offers, buybacks and exchanges.'
- *Proxy Database* 'We can search by state of incorporation of the

registrant, industry of registrant and over 500 proposals put to a shareholder vote. . . . Based on a universe of 50,000 proxy statements.'

- *SEC Rule Making Database* 'To quickly and accurately locate the comment letters and corresponding SEC releases you need . . . RMD is based upon the SEC's official record of comment letters received and is supplemented by our staff. . . . We categorize each letter into one of the following groups: Self regulatory organizations; Corporations; Academic institutions; Accountants; Trade associations; Professional associations; Individuals; Institutional investors; Broker dealer/Investment advice; Law firms; Government entities; Other.'

Other Agencies

'Provides confidential and timely research, retrieval and watch services at government agencies:

- *Courts (Federal and State)*
- *Banking Agencies (Federal and State)* Office of Thrift Supervision; Resolution Trust Corporation; Federal Deposit Insurance Corporation; Federal Reserve Board; Office of the Comptroller of the Currency
- *Federal Agencies* Municipal Securities Rulemaking Board; Federal Trade Commission; Office of Management and Budget; Internal Revenue Service.'

(19) #519 Graham & Whiteside Tuition House, 5–6 Francis Grove, London SW19 4DT, UK. t: (44 181) 947 1011; f: 947 1163.

1526. **Major Companies of Europe**. a. £650. Three volumes.

1527. **Medium Companies of Europe**. a. £609. Three volumes.

(20) £520 Hemmington Scott City Innovation Centre, 26–31 Whiskin Street, London EC1R 0BP, UK. t: (44 171) 278 7769; f: 278 9808.

1528. **Company REFS**. m. £795. 'Indispensible information for active investors . . . The quickest and simplest way to find the shares that match YOUR criteria . . . Contains facts and figures you won't find in any other single publication. And they are all calculated for you from authoritative up-to-date data, every month.' *Volume 1* 'Tables of leaders and laggards plus other important indicators that help you identify at a glance which companies you wish to research in more detail: Sector listings; Directors' buying and selling transactions in the last six months; Chief Executive changes in the last 12 months; Consensus brokers' forecast changes; Results announced in the last month.' *Volume 2* 'Individual company entries for each and every UK stockmarket company . . . All UK registered companies with quoted equity shares (fully listed and USMs excluding investment trusts) – approximately 1600 in total . . . with fully comparable data on each, plus a range of ratios, statistics and forecasts which you cannot access from any other single source.'

1529. **Hambro Company Guide**. q. £99. **diskette**. m. £595. Covers all UK companies listed on the International Stock Exchange. Comprehensive summaries including five year's profit and loss data, graph of share price relative to FT All Share Index, gearing, return on capital employed, dividends, names of professional advisers etc. Separate listings of: Auditors and their Clients; Financial Adviser and their Clients; Financial PR Advisers and their Clients; Foreign Banks in London; Investment Managers; Registrars; Solicitors and their clients; Stockbrokers and their clients.

Available to subscribers of the Guide is a service *FAST Share.* In conjunction with *City Line* (a *Financial Times* service), this links directly to *SEAQ* to give real-time individual share price information, and a range of financial reports, including: UK Stock Market, UK Company News, Foreign Exchange and Currencies, Sterling Rates, Bullion Report, Base Metals, Wall Street Report, Tokyo Market Report, Far Eastern Round-up, European Round-up. The technology which makes FAST Share possible is based on using a multi-frequency telephone with computerised translation of SEAQ digital prices into human speech. Telephone calls are charged at 48p per minute (peak rate); 36p per minute (evenings and weekends).

1530. **Henderson Top 2000 Charities (Year)**. a. £89.50 (£45 to registered charities. 'At last – your complete guide to UK charities. That's right. Following months of concentrated research . . . the most extensive survey of charity finances ever undertaken in the UK. But that's not all. Uniquely, this new publication brings together the three parts of the charity finance equation: The charities; The corporate donors; The professional advisers . . . making this the only single source of information on the charity sector.'

1531. **Performance Rankings Guide**. s-a. £135. Two main sections: *Companies Section* 'An instant indication of a company's performance ranked against all stockmarket companies and ranked against companies within its sector.' *League Tables* 'How companies perform by 27 key financial criteria.'

1532. **Price Waterhouse Corporate Register**. bi-a. £150. 'The No. 1 Information Source on Decision Makers in UK Stockmarket Companies . . . The only contact book to focus exclusively on the people who run the UK's 2,100 quoted companies (fully listed, USM and OTC stockmarket companies) . . . Profiles 20,000 directors and senior executives, and lists their advisers.'

(21) #521 IBM IBM United Kingdom Limited, Alencon House, Alencon Link, Basingstoke, Hampshire RG21 1EJ, UK. *Also* PhoneLink plc, John Douglas House, 620 Woodchurch Road, Preston, Birkenhead L43 0TT, UK.

'IBM and *PhoneLink plc* are working in partnership with many of the UK's largest companies to provide an unparalleled business service which will appeal to every business that needs accurate, speedy and affordable information. For the first time users can have immediate access to a world of business information that will not only increase their efficiency, but the efficiency of the whole company. Tel-Me is the first true information application. It is easy to learn, can be used on almost any PC and is incredibly fast, all enquiries are fulfilled within 15 seconds.

When you need to research the financial profile of a company, or simply wish to obtain the best trading terms, what does that involve? Calls to credit reference agencies. Visits to Companies House. Thumbing through Annual Reports ... Tel-Me offers you all the available information at your own PC. Tapping within seconds into the *Infocheck* or *CCN* database, the Tel-Me Company Profiler provides immediate access for purposes of credit assessment and business analysis.

Need to scan the latest national or international news, or monitor changes in the City? ... Your news horizons are likely to be limited through years of experience of traditional media. With Tel-Me "News on Demand", the *Press Association* provides you with access to a vastly increased range of topics drawn from the world's leading sources. These are continuously updated 24 hours a day and can be used to isolate specific items of interest as well as allowing you to maintain a profile of your competitors. These news items are largely unedited, immediate, detailed and informative.

Tel-Me. Designed by PhoneLink plc and marketed by IBM.'

(22) #522 ICC Information Group *Credit Information Services* 16–26 Banner Street, London EC1Y 8QE, UK. t: (44 171) 251 4941; f: 251 4616. *ICC Business Ratios* Field House, 72 Oldfield Road, Hampton, Middlesex, TW12 2HQ, UK. t: (44 181) 783 0922; f: 783 1940.

'ICC understands the needs of today's businesses and the modern credit management function. It provides information in ways that match your own systems, in formats to suit managers as well as analysts and at cost-effective rates that allow access to all the information appropriate to your specific needs ... Credit information available includes the following:

- Corporate details and credit information on 1.2 million UK limited companies
- Comprehensive credit reports on over 700,000 currently trading companies
- Highly detailed analysis on the top 100,000 companies
- Adverse information on sole traders and partnerships.'

Other services offered by ICC include: Risk Analysis, Monitoring, International Information, Official Company Documentation. Information can be received online or via cd-rom, magnetic tape, system download or hard copy. Online/cdrom services include:

1533. **Broker 50**. **cdrom**. m. 'Instant access to company, industry and country research from leading UK and European stockbrokers and bank analysts.'

1534. **Credit Index CD-ROM**. m. 'Unique credit CD-ROM ... containing key credit information on 1.2 million UK Limited companies . . . (A)ccess to essential credit information on your suppliers and customers in a matter of minutes for as little as *£2.25 a report* (based on an annual usage of 4,000 reports).

1535. **ICC Company Directory**. **online**. **cdrom**. Basic reference data for 2.2 million companies registered in the UK, including companies dissolved since 1968.

1536. **ICC Company Financials**. **online**. **cdrom**.

1537. **ICC Full Text Company Reports**. **online**. **cdrom**.

1538. **ICC Sharewatch**. **online**. Covers shareholdings with more than one quarter of a percent of equity and reportable transactions by directors and shareholders holding 3 per cent or more for UK quoted companies. The data comes from the *Companies Registration Office*.

1539. **ICC Stockbroker Research**. **online**. Some 18,000 reports from 40 brokerage firms.

(23) #523 IDD Information Services Two World Trade Center, New York, NY 10048, USA. t: (1 212) 432 0045; f: 912 1457.

1540. **Mergers & Acquisitions**. bi-m. $325. 'Selected information in this publication has been provided by *Securities Data Company*, New Jersey, (1 201) 622 3100) and is the copywritten property of SDC. SDC obtains and gathers its information from sources it considers to be reliable; however, SDC does not guarantee the accuracy or completeness of the information hereunder, which is supplied on an "as is" basis, SDC makes no warranties, express or implied, including, specifically, any warranty of merchantability or fitness for a particular purpose as to such information. In no event shall SDC be liable for any damages, direct or indirect, consequential or compensatory, including, but not limited to, lost profits, even if SDC is on notice of the possibility of the same.'

1541. **Mergers & Acquisitions International**. bi-w. $595.

1542. **Mergers & Acquisitions Report**. w. $1,175. 'Newsletter providing exclusive briefing on every aspect of the world of M&A.'

(24) #524 Infocheck Group Godmersham Park, Godmersham, Canterbury, Kent, CT4 7DT, UK. t: (44 127) 813000; f: 813100.

1543. **Mergers & Acquisitions Database**. 'Holds over 10,000 UK and European deals dating back to 1985, covering divestments, leveraged buyouts, mergers and takeovers.'

(25) #525 Information America One Georgia Center, 600 W Peachtree Street, NW, Atlanta, GA 30308, USA. t: (1 404) 892 1800; f: 881 0278.

1544. **Bankruptcy Records**. **online**. 'Uncovers the availability of assets, discovers encumbrances, reveals potential financial complications and the financial status of parties. Filings are available for California, New Jersey and Texas, plus selected records for regions of Georgia and Pennsylvania.'

1545. **Business Finder**. **online**. 'Contains information on more than 15 million companies in the United States and 2 million in Canada; and over 1.25 million professionals. Profile information includes company or professional name and title, address, telephone number, type of business and SIC.'

1546. **People Finder**. **online**. 'Access to information on 111 million people, 92 million households, and 61 million phone numbers.'

1547. **SEC Filings**. **online**. 'Contains reports filed by over 6,000 public companies with the Securities and Exchange Commission. Includes 10Ks, 10Qs, annual reports, proxy statements and 20 Fs.'

1548. **Sleuth**. **online**. 'Search millions of state and county records simultaneously to find relationships between people and businesses that would be virtually impossible to determine by other methods. . . . Records searched include corporate and limited partnerships, state and county UCCs and liens, sales and use tax information, and assumed/fictitious names.'

- *DOX* 'When you need official copies of public documents from anywhere in the United States, *DOX* is the answer. IA professionals give you accurate and timely copies of public record filings and corporate certificates from any jurisdiction in the country. In most states, Secretary or Department of State documents can be ready in one day or less. For requests in local jurisdictions, orders can usually be completed in one to three days.'

(26) #526 International Executive Reports 717 D Street, NW, Suite 300, Washington, DC 20004, USA. t: (1 202) 628 6900; f: 628 6618.

1549. **World M&A Network**. q. $345. 'Companies for sale, companies seeking to purchase other companies, and sources of acquisition financing. Focuses on mid-market companies with revenues from $1 million to $100 million. The largest US service of its kind, it is useful for any company or individual around the world interested in buying or selling a company, and is particularly valuable for business brokers and investment banks. Most listings are in the United States, but there are also some from Canada, England, Japan and elsewhere. Over 1000 listings per issue.'

(27) #527 Information Access Company 362 Lakeside Drive, Foster City, CA 94404, USA. t: (1 415) 358 4643; f: 358 4759 *and* Watergate House, 13–15 York Buildings, London WC2N 6JU, UK. t: (44 71) 930 3933; f: 930 9190.

1550. **Company Intelligence**. **online**. **cdrom**. Covers over 100,000 of the largest public and private US companies, with directory data derived from *Ward's Business Directory of US Private and Public Companies* (which in turn derives its data on publicly traded firms from the *Disclosure Online* database). The online version also includes data on some 30,000 international companies provided by *Graham & Trotman*.

(28) #528 Investext Group Thomson Financial Services, 22 Pittsburgh Street, Boston, MA 02210, USA. t: (800) 662 7878/(1 617) 345 2704 *and* Thomson Financial Services, 11 New Fetter Lane, London EC4A 1JN, UK. t: (0800) 317 577/(44 171) 815 3860; f: 815 3857.

1551. **Investext. online**. 'We're pleased to announce that the Investext database has grown to become the world's *largest online source of European stockbroker research reports.* In fact, an average of 100 new European company and industry reports are added to Investext each business day. . . . The Investext database is the most comprehensive collection of its kind – offering over 600,000 stockbroker research reports authored by analysts at more than 310 investment banks and brokerage firms around the world. Approximately 50 percent of all reports added to Investext now focus on UK and European companies and industries.' *Pipeline* 'is the exclusive online database that lets you order the latest investment research reports within 24 hours after they are authorized for release . . . PIPELINE cites over 75,000 reports from Investext's in-house collection.'

1552. The **Research Bank. cdrom**. 'Investment research reports from over 250 of the world's leading investment banks, brokerage companies, and consulting firms.' The *European Edition* draws reports from over 100 investment banks in 16 European countries.

(29) #529 Jordan Publishing 21 St Thomas Street, Bristol BS1 6JS, UK. t: (44 117) 923 0600; f: 924 0586.

1553. **Best of British: The Top 20,000 Companies**. a. £225. Four volumes.

1554. **Britain's Top Foreign Owned Companies**. a. £190. Two volumes. Covers 2,500 companies. 'Ownership areas covered include the USA, Europe, Japan, Latin America, Australia, the Middle East and Africa.'

1555. **Britain's Top Privately Owned Companies**. a. £395. Five volumes.

1556. **JordanShare. diskette**. 'Comprehensive, low-cost subscription service which provides lists of all shareholders with holdings equal to or above 0.15% in the publicly quoted and USM companies . . . Completely updated beneficial owner data obtained in association with *Fulcrum Research Limited*, by utilising powers of s.212 of the Companies Act.'

1557. **JordanWatch. online**. 'Latest company names, registered office details and filing dates on all UK companies . . . Detailed financial profiles on the top major companies including profit and loss statements and balance sheet details presented in standard formats together with ratio and trend data . . . A regularly updated information service on newly formed companies including directors' names and home addresses.'

(30) #530 Market Guide 2001 Marcus Avenue, Suite 5200, Lake Success, NY 11042, USA. f: (1 516) 676 9240.

'The developer of a superior database containing text and financial and descriptive information on publicly traded companies. Our database covers 6,500 companies traded in the US, including many foreign companies trading here as ADRs or ADSs. The Market Guide database is currently distributed by most of the major information vendors in the US including:

- *Bloomberg Financial Markets, L.P.*
- *Bridge Trading Systems*
- *Charles Schwab & Co*
- *ILX*
- *Investext*
- *Lotus One Source*
- *Quotron*
- *Shark*
- *Telemet America*
- *Telescan*
- *Track Data*

Market Guide's main distinguishing feature is that it is the *only* analytic database that preserves the "as reported line item descriptions". When companies issue their financial statements, they use line item descriptions that best reflect their operations. . . . This "as reported line item presentation" of financial statements gives the user a better understanding of the company by allowing him to:

- Determine the relative importance and growth rates of different revenue streams
- Determine the impact that changes in the business environment may have on the operations of a company. For example, how will a two percent rise or fall in interest rates impact the company's profitability?
- Distinguish between fixed and variable expenses
- View the industry specific reporting practices of different companies
- More accurately assess the quality of assets.'

1558. **Market Guide Select OTC Stock Edition**. q. $345. 'Determine the merits of 800 promising OTC companies. The companies included in this book have been carefully *selected* from our database of over 6,000 companies. . . . Many of these companies are not yet followed by other sources. Discover them early and profit as Wall Street begins recognising their attractiveness.'

(31) #531 MarketPlace Information Corporation 460 Totten Pond Road, Waltham, MA 02154–1906, USA. t: (1 617) 672 9200; f: 672 9290.

1559. **MarketPlace Business**. **cdrom**. q. $849. 'Information on more than 8 million businesses in the US: that's 4 out of every 5 companies . . . MarketPlace data is supplied by the highly respected specialist in business information . . . *Dun & Bradstreet*. . . . Every year a staff of more than 1,300 professionals compile and update records through interviews, public documents, and directories. MarketPlace lists have an average deliverablity of 90–95%.' The price includes: current quarter's software and database; product documentation, 1 year free technical support; unlimited access to counts and summary statistics; unlimited ability to create and preview lists; meter and ability to 'download' up to $300 worth of data (3,000 meter credits) from the CD-ROM. *Desktop Marketer* is 'A newsletter for users and friends of MarketPlace Business'. The January 1995 issue contained a 'Head to Head' comparison with *SelectPhone* and *PhoneDisc*.

(32) #532 McGraw-Hill 1221 Avenue of the Americas, New York, NY 10020–1095, USA. t: (1 212) 512 2000; f: 208 1718. *Also* McGraw-Hill Book Company Europe, Shoppenhangers Road, Maidenhead, Berks, SL6 2QL, UK. t: (44 1628) 23432; f: 770224.

1560. **Business Week 1000 Multimedia CD-ROM**. a. £351.33. 'In the first-ever CD-ROM version of the *Business Week 1000*, you can sort and rank companies in any way you wish, delve into their history and financial records with Standard & Poor's company data, listen to executive's views on the issues of the day, and watch a corporate turnaround in action.'

1561. **Business Week's Guide to Mutual Funds**. a. £21.95. 'Provides current performance ratings on over 1500 mutual funds, plus guidance on how to invest safely and successfully.'

1562. **Standard & Poor's 500 Guide (Year)**. a. £16.95. Data on companies making up the S&P 500.

1563. **Standard & Poor's MidCap 400 Guide (Year)**. a. £16.95. Company profiles. 'The MidCap 400 is S&P's stock market index to many smaller, fast-growing companies that are not as well followed by the "Street".'

1564. **Standard & Poor's Stock and Bond Guide**. a. £17.95. 'Available through the book trade for the first time last year, this single-volume Standard & Poor's resource has quickly become the "standard" in its field. It gives everyone easy access to S&P's respected stock, bond, mutual fund, and variable annuity information – the facts, figures, analyses, performance data, and forecasts that have helped guide investment decisions for generations of savvy investors and professionals.'

(33) #533 Media General Financial Services PO Box 85333, Richmond, VA 23293–0001, USA; 301 E Grace Street, Richmond, VA 23219, USA. t: (1 804) 775 8000; f: 649 6097.

'Provides ready access to the most detailed, accurate, up-to-date business information available today . . . A leading financial data publisher that for twenty years has been meeting the information needs of the most demanding users. The company maintains one of the most comprehensive common stock databases, one of the largest mutual fund databases, and proprietory databases on the financial markets, industries and coporate bonds. MGFS data is widely available through *Dialog Information Services, Dow Jones News Retrieval Service* . . . and *Thomson Financial Networks*. MGFS, in conjunction with the *Associated Press*, provides stock data to 100 major metropolitan newspapers, and sells directly to trade publications. MGFS also sells financial data directly to end-users on diskettes, magnetic tape or hard copy . . . MGFS puts the latest, most valuable information where you need it. At your fingertips.

MGFS uses only audited company and SEC documents. Although our stock database offers many calculated ratios, we provide financial results on an "as reported" basis, with no massaging or re-classifying data. You decide how best to use the data in your analyses. . . . Our turnaround time for processing and updating information is among the best in the industry. For both quarterly and annual data, new information is input within several days of its receipt. . . . We continually monitor companies that are slow to report their information , watch for new listings on major exchanges, and we visit the SEC monthly to ensure timeliness and efficiency.'

1565. **Executive Stock Report**. w. 'Designed primarily for senior corporate management, it is particularly popular with investor relations professionals. . . . The subscriber supplies the list of stocks, and we supply a report which examines how your company is performing against its competition, based on a wide range of criteria.'

1566. **MegaInsight Common Stock Database**. **online**. $4,000. **cdrom**. $3500. 'Detailed financial statement data on over 8,000 public companies and 172 major industry groups . . . All financial data is fully adjusted for stock splits and dividends, includes two years of daily stock price information, and is presented on an "as reported" basis to preserve historical correlations.'

(34) #534 Moody's Investors Service 99 Church Street, New York, NY 10007, USA. t: (1 212) 553 0300; f: 553 4700. *Also Dun & Bradstreet International* Holmers Farm Way, High Wycombe, Buckinghamshire HP12 4UL, UK. t: (44 1494) 422000; f: 422260.

1567. **Moody's Company Data**. **cdrom**. m. 'Over 10,000 public companies. Innovative easy-to-use software for extraordinary search capability.' Also available: *Moody's Company Data with EDGAR*. **cdrom**. 'The best US public company database just got better! Now, exclusive, fully integrated access to SEC EDGAR filings . . . The entire SEC EDGAR submission, exactly as filed . . . No delays for phone connection, or cumbersome full-report downloads.'

1568. **Moody's Corporate News – International**. **online**. News on 5,000 International non-US companies. There is also a US version.

1569. **Moody's Dividend Record**. Twice weekly. £425.

1570. **Moody's Corporate Profiles**. **online**. Covers 5,000 US companies.

1571. **Moody's Annual Dividend Record**. a. 'Dividend data on over 17,000 securities.'

1572. **Moody's Handbook of Common and OTC Stocks**. q. £225. There is also a *Moody's Handbook of NASDAQ Stocks*.

1573. **Moody's Handbook of Dividend Achievers**. a. 'Profiles of more than 300 companies paying increasing dividends for at least 10 consecutive years.

1574. **Moody's Industrial Manual**. a. (plus a twice-weekly update). £1,250. Covers financial and operating data of every industrial corporation on the NYSE and ASE, plus over 500 on regional exchanges.

1575. **Moody's Industry Review**. bi-w. £449. 'Key financial data on the 4,000 firms listed on the New York and American stock exchanges, OTC and regional exchanges. Comparative statistics . . . key business ratios . . . rankings . . . return on capital.'

1576. **Moody's International Manual**. a. (plus weekly updates). £1,495. **cdrom**. Financial and business information on approximately 4,700 major corporations, sovereigns and their municipalities, and national and supranational institutions in 108 countries. Facts and figures selected for inclusion 'are for the most part based upon information obtained directly from corporations or from stockholders' reports and, in certain instances, Securities and Exchange Commission reports and registrations'.

1577. **Moody's OTC Industrial Manual**. a. (plus a twice-weekly update). £1,150. Covers over 3,200 OTC industrial companies traded on NASDAQ or over-the-counter.

1578. **Moody's OTC Unlisted Manual**. a. (plus a weekly update). £1,150. Covers financial facts and corporate data on over 2,000 companies not listed on the NASDAQ national market system.

1579. **Moody's Public Utility Manual**. a. (plus a weekly update). £1,250. Covers financial and operating data on all US public utilities.

1580. **Moody's Transportation Manual**. a. (plus a weekly update). £1,050.

1581. **Moody's USA Annual Dividend Record**. a. £80.

(35) #535 National Register Publishing 121 Chanlon Road, New Providence, NJ 07974, USA. t: (1 908) 464 6800; f: 665 3528. *Also* Maypole House, Maypole Road, East Grinstead, West Sussex RH19 1HH, UK. t: (44 342) 330100; f: 330192.

1582. **Corporate Affiliations Plus. cdrom**. q. £1,695. 'Consolidating the new **Directory of Corporate Affiliations**, the **International Directory of Corporate Affiliations**, and the **Directory of Leading Private Companies**, this CD-ROM can unravel the inextricable maze of today's corporate relationships. (It) reveals the links between some 16,000 major US domestic and internationally-based corporations and their 140,000 subsidiaries. . . . Complete financial and personnel profiles are also provided for each company, so you can use the database to extract basic data on sales, assets, liabilities and more . . . Includes information on up to 20 outside service firms for each company in the database.' Also available **online**.

(36) #536 Nelson Publications One Gateway Plaza, Port Chester, NY 10573, USA. t: (1 914) 937 8400; f: 937 8908.

1583. **Nelson's Directory of Investment Research**. a. $500. Two volumes. Lists of primarily US-based financial analysts cross-referenced to the companies and industries that they analyse. Covers some 5,000 US and 4,000 non-US companies.

1584. **Nelson's Earnings Outlook**. m. $240. Reports on consensus earnings per share estimates for over 3,000 stocks based on forecasts by analysts from approximately 200 investment firms worldwide; includes quarterly industry profiles.

1585. **Nelson's Guide to Institutional Research**. 10/year. $95.

(37) #537 OneSource Information Services 150 Cambridge Park Drive, Cambridge, MA 02140, USA. t: (800) 554 5501; f: (1 617) 441 7239 *and* Lotus Park, The Causeway, Staines, Middlesex, TW18 3AG, UK. t: (44 1784) 445702; f: 445033.

Produce a wide range of CD-ROMs with data sourced from a variety of leading suppliers; for instance:

1586. **CD/Europa**. **cdrom**. Sourced from *Dun & Bradstreet Corporation*.

1587. **CorpTech Profiles**. **Lotus Notes**. Sourced from *CorpTech*.

1588. **International Equities**. **cdrom**. Sourced from *I/B/E/S International*; *Morgan Stanley International*; *Worldscope*; *Worldscope Emerging Markets*; *World Market Review*.

1589. **International Public**. **cdrom**. Sourced from *Extel Financial*.

1590. **Investext Reports**. **Lotus Notes**. Sourced from *Investext Group*.

1591. **SEC Filings**. **cdrom**. Sourced from *SEC Online*.

1592. **SEC Text**. **Lotus Notes**. Sourced from *SEC Online*.

1593. **UK Private+**. **cdrom**. Sourced from *ICC Information Group*.

1594. **UK Small Companies**. **cdrom**. m. Details of 170,000 trading companies with a turnover or net worth below £300,000.

1595. **US Equities**. **cdrom**. Sourced from *BARRA*; *Ford Investor Services*; *I/B/E/S International*; *IDSI*; *Market Guide*; *S&P Compustat*; *Value Line Publishing*.

1596. **US Private+**. Sourced from *Information Access Company*; *Directory of Corporate Affiliations/US Private*; *Ward's Business Directory*.

1597. **US Private Profiles**. **Lotus Notes**. Sourced from *Ward's Business Directory*.

1598. **US Public**. **cdrom**. Sourced from *Dow Jones News/Retrieval*; *Information Access Company*; *Investext Group*; *Market Guide*; *Moody's Investors Service*; *UMI*; *Stock Price History*; *Who's Who in Finance & Industry*.

1599. **US Public Profiles**. **Lotus Notes**. Sourced from *Market Guide*.

1600. **Worldscope Profiles**. **Lotus Notes**. Sourced from *Worldscope*.

(38) #538 Reed Information Services Financial Publications, Windsor Court, East Grinstead Road, East Grinstead, West Sussex, RH19 1XA, UK. t: (44 342) 335962; f: 335977.

1601. **Kelly's Directory**. a. £155. **cdrom**. Classified list of over 80,000 UK businesses.

1602. **Kompass UK**. **online**. **cdrom**. 'Contains information on around 135,000 companies taken from the following major UK directories: *Kompass*; *Kelly's*; *Dial Industry*; *Directory of Directors*; *British Exports*.'

1603. **Kompass Europe**. **online**. **cdrom**. Covers some 350,000 companies across thirteen European countries. All data is taken from the relevant Kompass Register – which includes detailed coverage of the products and services offered by each company.

(39) #539 Reference Press 6448 Highway 290 East, Suite E-104, Austin, TX 78723, USA. t: (512) 454 7778; f: (512) 454 9401. *Also* c/o William Snyder Publishing Associates, 5 Five Mile Drive, Oxford OX2 8HT, UK. t/f: (44 865) 513186.

1604. **Hoover's Guide to Private Companies**. a. $49.95. Profiles the largest privately owned companies in the USA, including histories, financial data, and pertinent names and addresses.

1605. **Hoover's Handbook of World Business (Year)**. a. £26.95. "It's truly amazing that this wealth of information is available for such a terrific price" (*Morgan Directory Reviews*).

1606. **Hoover's Handbook of American Business (Year)**. a. £28.95. **online**. **cdrom**. £39.95. "You simply can't find more informaton on Corporate America in any other single source" (*Business Week*).

1607. **Hoover's Handbook of Emerging Companies**. a. $32.95. Profiles 250 growth companies, including high profile and lesser known companies. Contains financial data, an overview of operations and pertinent names and addresses.

1608. **Hoover's MasterList of Major US Companies (Year)**. a. £39.95. **cdrom**. £79.95. 'You'll find nearly 6,000 US companies represented:

- Every public company traded on the New York Stock Exchange, AMEX and NASDAQ Exchanges
- 500 of the leading and most influential private enterprises
- Hundreds of the fastest growing companies
- More than 150 foreign companies with US operations
- Companies included in the *Fortune* Industrial 500, *Fortune* Service 500, *Business Week* 1000, *Forbes* Private 400, and *Inc* 500.

Compare this directory to others costing hundreds, even thousands of pounds more, and you'll see why there's no other resource book available that gives you so much value for money.'

(40) #540 SDC Publishing 40 West 57th Street, 8th Floor, New York, NY 10019, USA. t: (1 212) 765 5311; f: 765 6123.

1609. **Buyouts**. bi-w. $495. **online**. 'Newsletter for management buyouts, leveraged acquisitions, and special situations.'

1610. **Directory of M&A Intermediaries**. a.

1611. **Merger Yearbook**. a. $395. Listing of acquisition announcements by industry, indexed by corporate and individual targets.

1612. **Mergers and Corporate Policy**. 50/yr. $825. Lists merger announcements by industry in each issue.

(41) #541 SMR Inc PO Box 7476, Boulder, CO 80302, USA. t:(1 303) 442 4121

1613. **Stock Charts**. w. $575. 'Regardless of investment goals, the process of deriving profits is common to all using the SMR Trading System:

- Receive stock/commodity chart publication on a weekly basis
- Update SMR Oscillator plotting figures on a daily basis
    - via Fax/Modem Service – includes 49-day moving average, open, range, close
    - via SMR Hotline – plotting figures only
- Analyze oscillator movement in conjunction with additional chart information
- Consult the SMR Stock/Commodity Trading Manual as to what type of buy or sell signal may have been generated by the new data
- Compare your results to SMR Direct signals (if received) or contact SMR
- Implement the signal.'

(42) #542 Standard & Poor's 25 Broadway, New York, NY 10004, USA. *Also* 18 Finsbury Circus, London EC2M 7BP, UK. t: (44 171) 826 3510.

1614. **Bond Guide**. m. Covers more than 6,000 corporate bonds, 600 convertibles plus 300 Canadian and international issues. A special feature, *Credit Watch*, focuses on fixed income issues under surveillance for possible ratings changes by S & P's analytical staff. Available in whole or in part on magnetic tape or electronically transmitted, which versions include a wide range of data items not included in the print version.

1615. **Daily Stock Price Record**. d. Covers NYSE, OTC and AMEX stocks.

1616. **Earnings Guide**. m. $135. Earnings forecasts contirbuted by 130 analysts.

1617. **Emerging and Special Situations**. m. **online**. 'Provides sound investment advice for investors seeking small-cap stocks with potential for superior capital gains.'

1618. **Global Vantage**. **online**. Comprehensive coverage of corporate financial and other data for corporations worldwide.

1619. **New Issues Institutional Research**. Facsimile delivered service for asset managers looking to boost their performance through the purchase of initial public offerings. Covers from 120 to 150 IPOs per year. Each includes a description of the offering, first day investment factors, concise investment appraisal, and a buy/flip/avoid opinion. The reports are designed to arrive before widespread, syndicate institutional research coverage occurs, with the advice coming without any corporate finance ties.

1620. **Outlook**. w. Identifies developments that affect stock performance and makes recommendations on when to buy, hold and sell.

1621. **Private Label Newsletters**. m. Provide banks, brokerage firms, pension plan operators and others with an inexpensive way to to build and maintain relationships with their clients. Includes *Market Month*, for the discount brokerage community, and newsletters with advice on 401k plans, trust management, tax planning, each of which are available for custom imprinting.

1622. **S&P MarketScope**. **online**. Continuously updated service providing comprehensive information on 5200 US corporations.

1623. **Standard & Poor's Corporate Descriptions plus News**. **online**. **cdrom**. Covers approximately 12,000 primarily US corporations, with some international coverage. There is a version without the News component.

1624. **Standard & Poor's Corporate FirstFacts**. **online**. Brief details of 10,000 publicly quoted companies on NYSE, AMEX, regional US stock exchanges and NASDAQ.

1625. **Standard & Poor's Dividend Record**. **online**. For 12,000 stocks quoted in the US and Canada.

1626. **Standard & Poor's Industry Financial Data**. **online**. Monthly, quarterly and annual time series for about 100 US industry groups.

1627. **Standard & Poor's Register – Corporate**. **online**. Descriptive information on over 50,000 mainly US public and private companies. There is a *Biographical* version of the database, profiling some 70,000 directors and executives.

1628. **Stock Reports**. l. 3 vols. Two-page reports on all companies listed on the New York Stock Exchange, the American Stock Exchange, and more than 1500 of the most active and widely-held companies whose securities are traded Over-The-Counter and on regional exchanges.

(43) #543 Tertiary Publications Brook House, Eriswell Crescent, Walton-on-Thames, Surrey, KT12 5DS, UK. t: (44 1932) 248358; f: 245569.

1629. **Directory of Nominees**. a. £75. 'Companies with the word "Nominees" as part of their registered name have been surveyed whilst companies or enterprises which act as nominees but do not bear this title have not been included. The Directory covers British registered companies only, with a few exceptions, and no attempt has been made to include those registered elsewhere, such as the Channel Islands.'

(44) #544 Thomas Publishing Company World Headquarters, Five Penn Plaza, New York, NY 10001, USA. t: (1 212) 290 7277; f: 290 7365. *Also* c/o Thomas Marketing and Distribution, 2 Leopold Avenue, London SW19 7ET, UK. t: (44 181) 395 4828; 395 4838.

1630. **Thomas Register of American Manufacturers**. a. £329. Twenty-seven volumes. **online**. **cdrom**. 'The most complete, most accurate and up-to-date reference to all North American Industry.'

(45) #545 Tudor House Publications Lonsdale House, 7/9 Lonsdale Gardens, Tunbridge Wells, Kent TN1 1NU, UK. t: (44 1892) 515454; f: 511547.

1631. **Acquisitions Monthly**. m. £255. 'Involved in European M & A? *Amdata* has the answers. In the fast-changing European M & A scene, the importance of up-to-date, accurate and easily accessible research material is becoming more vital to the day. The quality and precision of research required by professionals in this area has been provided for many years by Amdata, an established database produced by Acquisitions Monthly, the 'bible' of the M & A world – driven by unique software designed by Computasoft. Amdata is sourced from our exclusive network which records every small domestic deal and stake purchases in each country. Already found invaluable by the financial community including international banks, accountancy firms and management consultants, Amdata is the leading M & A acquisition database.'

(46) #546 Value Line Institutional Services 220 East 42nd Street, New York, NY 10017, USA. t: (1 212) 907 1500; f: 661 2807.

"Provides corporate customers with extensive financial and statistical data gathered by Value Line analysts. Products range from packaged databases and industry analysts' research to Custom Data Services, which enable clients to tailor their information needs exactly. The current Value Line services comprise *Value Line Data File, Value Line Estimates and Projections, Value Line Convertibles Securities File*, and *Value Line Industry Review*."[161]

(47) #547 The Wall Street Transcript 99 Wall Street, New York, NY 10005, USA. t: (1 212) 747 9500.

1632. **Wall Street Transcript**. w. 'The longest-lived secondary source of brokerage reports.' The Transcript appears *online* within 24 to 48 hours of publication.

(48) #548 Waterlow Company Services Classic House, 174–180

Old Street, London EC1V 9BP, UK. t: (44 171) 250 3350; f: 608 0867.

'Offers a comprehensive range of company searches designed to meet your deadlines, as well as your information needs. Information available for a UK Company Search will include:

- Registered Name
- Change of Name (if any)
- Registered Number
- Registered Address
- Certificates of Incorporation
- Memorandum & Articles of Association
- Mortgage Documents
- Accounts
- Annual Return
- Share Structure
- Receivership/Liquidation Documents (if any)

A *Company Search* gives you all the information you need to be legally satisfied of a company's existence, its owners and its officers, and will also give you considerable information concerning its financial health . . . Searches requested by 2pm will be sent out by first class post the same day. If you require the results quickly use either our Expedited 2 hour service or Urgent 4 hour service. The results can be sent by fax or courier.'

Notes

(160) Ruth Pagell and Michael Halperin's book **International business information: How to find it, how to use it** (*Oryx Press*, 1994), has an excellent series of Chapters on 'Accounting Standards and Practices', 'Company Information: Issues', 'Company Information: Directory Sources', 'Company Information: Financial Sources', 'Company Information: Electronic Sources', 'Corporate Affiliations and Corporate Change', together with some valuable Appendixes: 'Selecting a Company Directory – A Checklist', 'Glossary – Company Definitions', 'Synthesis of Accounting Standards in 48 Countries', 'Sample of UK and French Balance Sheets', and 'Disclosure Requirements of Major Stock Exchanges'. Other guides include:

ENGLISH, L. **CD-ROM and online business and company databases**. *Aslib*, 1994. 139 pp. £26. 'A selective list of the most well-known or useful company and business sources available, emphasising databases which are of broad potential interest.'

European companies: A guide to sources of information. 4th ed. *CBD Research Limited*, 1992. 220 pp. £80. 'For each country includes: Currency & languages used . . . Name of department responsible for registration of companies . . . Lists of the various legal forms of companies . . . Guides to the formation of companies . . . All stock exchanges with full address details . . . Credit reporting organisations . . . Directories of companies . . . Guides to company relationships eg 'Who Owns Whom'. . . Directories of directors & other business biographies . . . Finance directories covering banks, insurance companies etc . . . Newspapers, journals & magazines with company news . . . Databases of companies.'

SCOTT, J. **European company information**. *London Business School* in association with *Gale Research*, 1993. 318 pp.

How to find information about companies. *Washington Researchers.* Three volumes covering more than 9,000 sources of competitor intelligence: I. Organized by type of source; II. Organized by type of information; III. Organized by type of target company.

How to find information about divisions, subsidiaries and products. 3rd ed. *Washington Researchers.* 160 pp.

How to find information about private companies. 4th ed. *Washington Researchers.* 147 pp.

HALPERIN, M. and BELL, S.J. **Research guide to corporate acquisitions, mergers and other restructuring**. *Greenwood Press*, 1992. 232 pp. $44.95.

See also the appropriate sections of the more general sourceguides referenced in Note (79).

(161) FOSTER, P. **Online/CD-ROM Business Sourcebook 1995/96**. *Headland Press*, p 175

Further reading

BEGG, P.F.C. **Corporate acquisitions and mergers**. 3rd ed. *Graham & Trotman*, 1991. 'A practical guide to the legal, financial and administrative implications.'

ROCK, M.L., ROCK, R.H. and SIKORA, M. **The mergers & acquisitions handbook**. 2nd ed. *McGraw-Hill*, 1993. 608 pp. £65.95. 'Articles by more than 60 of the leading M&A practitioners, plus principles and techniques illustrated with Fortune 500 case studies.'

CHAPTER FIVE

Financial Institutions and Markets

The structure of this chapter is:

Organizations

International

- BANKS
- SAVINGS INSTITUTIONS
- FINANCE COMPANIES
- SECURITIES INDUSTRY
- INSURANCE
- ASSET-BACKED FINANCE

Organizations

Europe

- BANKS
- SAVINGS INSTITUTIONS
- FINANCE COMPANIES
- SECURITIES INDUSTRY
- FUND MANAGEMENT AND INVESTMENT
- INSURANCE
- ASSET-BACKED FINANCE

Organizations

United Kingdom

- BANKS
- SAVINGS INSTITUTIONS
- FINANCE COMPANIES
- SECURITIES INDUSTRY
- FUND MANAGEMENT AND INVESTMENT
- INSURANCE
- ASSET-BACKED FINANCE

Organizations

United States

- BANKS
- SAVINGS INSTITUTIONS
- FINANCE COMPANIES
- SECURITIES INDUSTRY
- FUND MANAGEMENT AND INVESTMENT
- INSURANCE
- ASSET-BACKED FINANCE

Commercial information providers

1. Organizations: International

Banks

(1) #549 International Centre for the Training of Bank Professionals Alain Van Bokstael, 7 rue du Général Foy, F-75008 Paris, France. t: (33 1) 42 94 61 00; f: 45 22 39 74.

(2) #550 International Monetary Conference

'Private membership organization for approximately 100 of the world's largest commercial banks. Its annual meeting discussions are off-the-record and closed to all but the members. As a policy of the organization listings in information resources publications are declined. We do not publish any materials. Some speech texts may be available at the close of each annual meeting in June, but must be requested in writing each time, since we do not maintain a mailing list for non-members.'

(3) #551 Women's World Banking 104 East 40th Street, New York, NY 10016, USA. t: (1 212) 768 8513; f: 768 8519.

Founded in 1979 'to promote and encourage the direct participation by women and their families in the full use of the economy, particularly by those women who have not generally had access to the full services of established financial institutions'.

Savings institutions

(4) #552 Confédération Internationale du Crédit Populaire [International Confederation of Popular Credit] Secretariat General, Le Ponant de Paris – 5, rue Leblanc, 75511 Paris Cedex 15, France, t: (33 1) 40 39 66 19; f: 40 39 60 60. *Bureau de Bruxelles* 40 rue de l'Industrie, 1040 Brussels, Belgium. t: (32 2) 513 39 52; f: 511 03 46.

International organization 'linking financial and banking institutions whose most specific aim is to favour the *growth*, in the largest sense of the word, *of small and medium-sized companies*, as well as of the middle-classes'. Fourteen countries are currently members: 'Austria, Belgium, Canada, France, Germany, Hungary, Italy, Morocco, Spain and Turkey are active members. Great Britain, Japan, the Netherlands and Switzerland have the status of a correspondent member.'

(5) #553 International Co-operative Alliance 15 route des Morillons, 1218 Grand-Saconnex, Geneva, Switzerland. t: (41 22) 798 41 21; f: 798 41 22. e: icageneva@gn.apc.org. *Annual Report* (CHF 10). *Directory* (CHF 40). *Newsletter* (CHF 25).

1633. **Review of International Co-operation**. 3/year. CHF 80. 'Keep informed of co-operative activities around the world.'

- *Co-op Network* "Offers information, expertise, technical assistance and related consultation to promote or support viable co-operative development in agriculture, housing, production, retailing amd wholesaling, and insurance and other financial services" (*Co-operative and Mutual Insurance Network*).

(6) #554 International Cooperative Banking Association c/o Co-operative Bank, 1 Balloon Street, PO Box 101, Manchester M60 4EP, UK. t: (44 161) 832 3456; f: 832 9707. *Journal* (a. £5).

'The details you have for the IBCA are correct up to September 1995, when a new President will be elected from another country where the Secretariat will also be domiciled. To date the name of the new President is unknown.'

(7) #555 International Savings Bank Institute Rue Albert-Gos 1–3, Postbox 355, CH-1211 Geneva 25, Switzerland. t: (41 22) 347 74 66; f: 346 73 56.

'Founded in 1924 . . . is a non-governmental body representing . . . 115 direct members in 83 countries, totally 2,800 savings banks. It is a centre for contacts and information for its members throughout the world. One of the ISBI's major aims is to improve the awareness of the importance of savings banks and to help promote the interests of its member institutions internationally.'

1634. **Savings Banks International**. q. SFr 60.

(8) #556 International Union of Housing Finance Institutions 111 East Wacker Drive, Chicago, IL 60601–4680, USA. t: (1 312) 946 8200; f: 946 8201. *Directory of Members* ($75).

'Originally founded in 1914, the Union now has over 350 members in 75 different countries. Full membership is open to building societies, savings associations, savings banks, commercial banks, mortgage banks and other institutions which provide housing loans. Other institutions interested in housing finance, including government and quasi-government bodies, mortgage insurers and academic institutions are eligible for associate membership.'

1635. **Housing Finance International**. Published in association with the *Housing Development Finance Corporation, India*. q. $125. The March 1994 issue, for example, contains the articles: 'The applicability of secondary mortgage markets to developing countries'; 'Simplicity versus complexity in the evolution of housing finance systems'; 'The French secondary mortgage market'; 'Mortgage securitisation in the UK: An emerging market?'; 'Challenge and change in the US mortgage market'.

1636. **Sourcebook**. bi-a. $45. 'A unique compendium of housing finance information from most of the countries that have formal housing finance systems.'

(9) #557 World Council of Credit Unions PO Box 2982, Madison, WI 53701–2982, USA. t: (1 608) 231 7130; f: 238 8020. *Annual Report. Newsletters.*

'At this time, there is no charge for receiving our publications.'

- *International Liaison Committee on Cooperative Thrift and Credit*

Finance companies

(10) #558 International Franchise Association 1350 New York Avenue NW, Suite 900, Washington, DC 20005, USA. t: (1 202) 628 8000; f: 628 0812.

'The Voice of Franchising.' The IFA has an extensive *Publications Catalog*.

1637. **Franchise Legal Digest**. q. $195. Reviews current domestic and international legal and legislative developments concerning franchising.

1638. **Franchise Opportunities Guide**. i. $15. 'A comprehensive listing of the world's leading franchise companies grouped by product or service with an alphabetical index, plus sources of legal advice, financial assistance, and more.'

1639. **Franchising World**. bi-m. $12. **online**. 'The latest know-how, trends and developments in the industry that accounts for more than one-third of all retail sales in the US.'

- *Franchise It!* 'A Windows program that can filter more than 1,000 franchises based upon multiple selection criteria, a benefit that can not be offered by the directories currently in print. These search criteria can include the type of business, equity capital requirements, IFA membership, number of franchises in operation (**diskette**. $49.95).

(11) #559 World Leasing Council c/o Leaseurope, avenue de Tervuren, 267 bte 9, B-1150, Brussels, Belgium. t: (32 2) 771 21 08; f: 770 75 96. *Statistics.*

'Informal organisation aiming to promote the creation of Leasing Associations, respectively grouping leasing companies on an international level in order: 1. To exchange experiences and to undertake specific tasks in the interest of its members. These specific tasks can cover . . . a world wide collection and distribution of information on leasing such as: insurance; legal problems; accounting matters; statistical data; import and export; cross-border leasing . . . 2. To establish a closer cooperation on a world level of all existing leasing company groupings . . . 3. To enable the strengthening of the position of the national leasing associations, leasing federations or the leasing industry as a whole in their contacts with national, international or supra-national authorities. For this reason the *WORLD LEASING COUNCIL* should act as a point of contact for international bodies such as OECD, Unidroit, IASC, etc. and maintain close cooperation with organisations who have proved to be effective in one way or another in the leasing sector, for example Management Centre Europe/America, London Business School, Leasing Digest, etc.'

Securities industry

(12) #560 Fédération Internationale des Bourses de Valeurs [International Federation of Stock Exchanges] 22 Boulevard de Courcelles, 75017 Paris, France. t: (33 1) 40 54 78 00; f: 47 54 94 22.

(i) *#561 International Capital Markets Group*

Founded in July 1989, as a cooperative arrangement between the *International Bar Association: Section on Business Law* (via the *Capital Markets Forum*), the *International Federation of Accountants* and the FIBV. It aims to consider developments in world capital markets, proposals for regulation of markets and, in general, matters which affect transnational investment and transnational acquisition of capital, promote investor confidence and enhancement of investor protection.

(13) #562 Gold Institute 1112 Sixteenth Street NW, Suite 240, Washington, DC 20036, USA. t: (1 202) 835 0185; f: 835 0155. *Annual Report*. *Newsletter* ($25).

'International association that includes miners, refiners, bullion suppliers, manufacturers of gold products, and wholesalers of gold investment products. Its mission is, therefore, to promote the common business interests of the gold industry as a whole by:

- Providing members with relevant, current statistical data and other information on the gold industry
- Providing members with early identification of changes in the operating climate for the industry
- Providing information and statistics on the gold industry to the media and the public
- Acting as a spokesperson for the industry.

1640. **Gold (Year)**. a. $110. 'Authoritative annual study of world gold markets.'

(14) #563 International Bond & Share Society 68 Viney Bank, Croydon CR0 9JT, UK. t: (0181) 657 7721; f: 657 0744.

1641. **International Bond and Share Society Journal**. q. $25.

(15) #564 International Brokers' Association c/o Midland Montagu Ltd, 10 Lower Thames Street, London EC3R 6AE, UK. t: (44 171) 260 4710; f: 260 4427.

(16) #565 International Cocoa Organization 22 Berners Street, London W1P 3DB, UK. t: (44 171) 637 3211; f: 631 0114. *Annual Report*

1642. **Quarterly Bulletin of Cocoa Statistics**. q. £40.

(17) #566 International Coffee Organization 22 Berners Street, London W1P 4DD, UK. t: (44 171) 580 8591; f: 580 6129.

(18) #567 International Cotton Advisory Committee 1629 K Street NW, Suite 702, Washington, DC 20006, USA. t: (1 202) 463 6660; f: 463 6950. e: secretariat@icac.org.

1643. **Cotton: Review of the World Situation**. bi-m. $135. By fax (m.) $230. 'Provides projections of world supply and demand by country and international cotton prices.' *ICAC documents on cdrom* includes all issues from May 1992 to March 1994 plus a range of other information, including the annual volumes of *Cotton: World Statistics* from 1924 to the present.

(19) #568 International Energy Agency 2 rue André Pascal, F-75775 Paris CEDEX 16, France. t: (33 1) 45 24 82 00; f: 45 24 99 88.

1644. **Energy Prices and Taxes**. a. FF 750. Contains a major international compilation of energy prices at all market levels: import prices, industry prices and consumer prices.

(20) #569 International Iron and Steel Institute rue Colonel Bourg

120, B-1040 Brussels, Belgium. t: (32 2) 735 9075; f: 735 8012. *Annual Report.*

1645. **World Steel in Figures**. a. Contains facts on employment, capital investment expenditure, iron ore production, scrap consumption, and the geographic distribution of production and consumption.

(21) #570 International Lead and Zinc Study Group Metro House, 58 St James's Street, London SW1A 1LD, UK. t: (44 171) 499 9373; f: 493 3725.

(22) #571 International Money Market Trading Association c/o First National Bank of Chicago, 90 Long Acre, London WC2E 9RB, UK. t: (44 171) 836 3434; f: 438 4295.

'Formerly the *International CD Market Trading Association* ... Has for many years provided an active forum for the principal traders in Euro $CDs and more recently UK ECU T'Bills to air views and discuss problems which arise in the market place from time to time. The Association also provides focal points for the authorities (eg British Bankers Association, Bank of England) to consult when standards are set or changes are made to the Regulatory Environment.' The Association has about two dozen Full Members and a similar number of Associate Members.

(23) #572 International Organization of Securities Commissions Tour de la Bourse, Postbox 171, 800 Victoria Square, 45th floor, Suite 4510, C-Montreal H4Z 1C8, Canada. t: (1 514) 875 8278; f: 875 2669. *Annual Report.*

The key organization for international co-operation by securities market authorities. Public Documents are made available after each of the Organization's *Annual Conferences.* Valuable reports produced include 'International Equity Offers' ($50) and 'Comparative Analysis of Disclosure Regimes' ($20). *Working Groups and Parties* include:

- Clearing and settlement
- Derivative markets
- Disclosure
- Enforcement and the exchange of information
- Multinational disclosure and accounting
- Regulation of market intermediaries
- Regulation of secondary markets

(24) #573 International Primary Market Association 1–3 College Hill, London EC4R 2RA, UK. t: (44 171) 248 0933; f: 489 9316. *Members and Recommendations Handbook* (£65 including updates).

'Established in 1984 as the trade association for leading underwriters both of debt for the public sector and of debt and equity for the corporate sector. IPMA's membership includes the leading banks and investment banks in Australia, Europe, Japan and North America. IPMA's Members underwrite and manage the overwhelming majority of new international capital market issues launched in Europe.

In the last five years, the increasingly popular *IPMA Screen Communications System* has greatly improved the process of syndicating new issues. The System enables a Lead Manager simultaneously to invite prospective members of the syndicate into the deal at the touch of a button and they in turn have the facility instantly to respond. Full details of the issue can be disseminated rapidly and in a clear standard format which virtually eliminates the scope for misunderstanding. The System provides a modern replacement to the traditional telephone invitations from the Lead Manager to prospective syndicate participants and their subsequent replies in second telephone calls. This process was not only expensive in terms of staff resources but could also take a considerable amount of time, during which market conditions could change so that prospective co-managers who telephoned later rather than sooner could be at a disadvantage. In addition, since the market has for some time been characterised by the need to undertake hedging operations, speed is of the essence.

The System is established as an industry standard in its own right and its technical excellence is widely – perhaps universally – praised.' Non-members listed as subscribing to the System include: *Bloomberg Financial Markets*; *Bloomberg Business News*; *IFR Publishing*; *MCM*; *Reuters*; and the *International Securities Market Association*.

(25) #574 International Rubber Study Group York House, Empire Way, Wembley, HA9 0PA, UK. t: (44 181) 903 7727; f: 903 2848.

1646. **Rubber Statistical Bulletin**. m. £93.

(26) #575 International Securities Market Association Rigistrasse 60, PO Box 169, CH-8033 Zurich, Switzerland. t: (41 1) 363 42 22; f: 363 77 72. *Also* Seven Limehouse, Docklands, London E14 9NQ, UK. t: (44 171) 538 5656; f: 538 4902 (*Subscriptions Department* f: (44 171) 538 9183). *Annual Report. Members' Register* (s-a. £70).

'A unique self-regulatory organization, developed by and on behalf of the very firms which constitute the international securities market. The members of ISMA are not individuals but international securities houses, currently comprising some 885 firms from 40 different countries. . . . In order to serve the interests on an orderly, well-functioning market, ISMA remains dedicated to independence from governmental and non-governmental pressures alike. In ISMA's opinion, this independence is an essential element in preserving the continued flow of international capital within an increasingly regulated environment. If the fundamental liberty of international cross-border trading is to be maintained, only sensible pragmatic self-regulation will be successful.

ISMA views the following as its major achievements since inception: The establishment of uniform market practices which now govern nearly all transactions in international securities between members . . . The edition of ISMA's statutes, by-laws, rules and recommendations in loose-leaf form, published in January 1992, now allows members and other interested parties to keep the "Rule Book" up-to-date cn a continuing basis ... The dissemination of accurate and timely market information and statistical services to members and non-members, through the provision of *daily electronic data* and via daily, weekly, fortnightly and annual *data-based publications* ... The promulgation of recommendations to issuing houses on new issue specifications and the format of international securities ... The approval by the UK Secretary of State for Trade and Industry (now HM Treasury) as the only International Securities Self-Regulating Organisation (ISSRO) for the purposes of the UK Financial Services Act ... The introduction of *TRAX*, and industry-wide transaction matching and reporting system embracing some 24,000 debt-related instruments and internationally traded equities ... The award of membership of the *International Council of Securities Associations* (ICSA), a forum for non-governmental regulatory organizations whose objective is to aid and encourage the sound growth of the international securities markets by promoting and encouraging harmonization in the procedures and regulation of those markets.

ISMA has been collecting and storing data and prospectuses concerning international securities since the inception of the bond market. This huge data resource forms the ultimate source material for a number of ISMA products and services. ... You can commission ISMA's data department to create your own tailor-made graphs, reports and charts. ... Furthermore, ISMA had installed a document image processing system which is used for the creation of a computerised image database for the thousands of prospectuses that the Association now holds. The system captures and stores large numbers of paper documents together with detailed indexing which makes access to documentation quick and easy. Prospectuses can be supplied by fax or by post on request. This *Prospectus Image Database* is a valuable source of capital market material from the market's representative body.'

1647. **Computer Updated International Database**. **online**. 'Addresses the growing demand for electronic information in an increasing number of international securities. Supplied as raw data with daily updates, CUPID offers subscribers the basis for the development of their own in-house information system.'

1648. **Daily Eurobond List**. d. £958.

1649. **International Bond Manual**. l. £683.20. 'Contains information on over 13,000 international securities ... All who use it consider it to be the bible of the international securities market ... Updates are despatched to subscribers every two weeks.'

1650. **ISMA Price Service**. **online**. 'Bid and offer prices on over 7000 bond issues on a daily basis. This data is supplied by the most active market makers and once received an average is calculated separately for the bid and offer side of each quotation for each security to produce a single consolidated price. This is an excellent indicator of the current market price for a particular issue ... Widely used by major information vendors such as Bloomberg, Datastream, Extel, Interactive Data, Quick, Reuters and Telekurs as well as the major market makers.'

1651. **Weekly Eurobond Guide**. w. £938. 'Closing quotations on over 7000 securities . . . The price information . . . is largely supplied by ISMA's reporting dealers.'

(27) #576 International Sugar Organization 1 Canada Square, Canary Wharf, London E14 5AA, UK. t: (44 171) 513 1144; f: 513 1146.

1652. **Statistical Bulletin**. m. £45.

(28) #577 International Swaps and Derivatives Association 1270 Avenue of the Americas, Suite 2118, Rockefeller Center, New York, NY 10020–1702, USA. t: (1 212) 332 1200; f: 332 1212.

"Monitors trading activity in swaps worldwide . . . Was formed in 1985 and in 1987 produced a standardised master agreement to cover cross-border OTC swap transactions. This standard form agreement was revised in 1992, and is widely used by practitioners. The benefit of the master agreement is that all swaps transacted under a single master agreement are generally considered to be a single transaction. This means that, in the event of the bankruptcy of one party, the receivers are unable to cherry-pick those individual contracts under which the bankrupt party is a net receiver, enforcing payment from parties to whom money may be owed on other contracts that are in default."[162]

(29) #578 International Tea Committee Sir John Lyon House, 5 High Timber Street, London EC4V 3NH, UK. t: (44 171) 248 4672; f: 248 3011.

'A small statistical bureau for the collection and publication of world tea statistics relating to acreage, production, imports, exports, quantities sold and prices realised at various auction centres etc.

1653. **Monthly Statistical Bulletin**. m. £150.

(30) #579 International Textile Manufacturers Federation Am Schanzengraben 29, Postfach, CH-8039 Zurich, Switzerland. t: (41 1) 201 7080; f: 201 7134.

1654. **International Cotton Industry Statistics**. a. SFr 100.

(31) #580 International Wheat Council One Canada Square, Canary Wharf, London E14 5AE, UK. t: (44 171) 513 1122; f: 712 0071.

'Membership of the Council gives governments access to a large amount of up-to-date information on market conditions. A new article in the 1986 *Convention* sets out the elements of the information system. This provides for regular reports, exchanges of information and special studies dealing with wheat, other grains and the principal grain products, focusing primarily on supply, demand and market conditions, developments in national policies and their effects on the international market, and matters concerning the improvement and expansion of trade, utilisation, storage and transportation, especially in developing countries.'

1655. **Food Aid Shipments**. a. £50. 'Report on cereals aid shipments by members of the *Food Aid Convention*.'

1656. **Grain Market Report**. 11/year. £250. 'Comprehensive facts and figures on the current world situation for wheat and coarse grains. Supplemented by analyses on matters of topical interest.'

(32) #581 International Wool Secretariat Wool House, Carlton Gardens, London SW1Y 5AE, UK. t: (44 171) 930 7300.

(33) #582 Iron and Steel Statistics Bureau Canterbury House, 2 Sydenham Road, Croydon CR9 2LZ, UK. t: (44 181) 686 9050; f: 680 8616.

1657. **International Steel Statistics Summary Tables**. a. £100. The tables cover production of iron and crude steel, imports and exports of finished steel products. There are available separate more detailed figures for major steel producing countries.

(34) #583 Organization of the Petroleum Exporting Countries Obere Donaustrasse 93, A-1020 Wien, Austria. t: (43 1) 21 11 20; f: 26 43 20.

1658. **OPEC Bulletin**. 10/year. Includes oil industry news, organization reports, market reviews, statistics, alternative energy news and surveys, OPEC publications and *Fund for International Development* news, new acquisitions for the OPEC library, and a calendar of events.

(35) #584 Silver Institute 1112 Sixteenth Street NW, Suite 240, Washington, DC 20036. t: (1 202) 835 0185; f: 835 0155. *Newsletter* ($25).

The mission of the Institute is to increase worldwide demand and to be the authoritative information source for silver.

1659. **World Silver Survey**. a. $45.

(36) #585 World Bureau of Metal Statistics 27a High Street, Ware, Hertfordshire, SG12 9BA, UK. t: (44 1920) 461274; f: 464258.

'Small UK based publishing organisation whose speciality is . . . the collection and dissemination of metal statistics.'

1660. **World Metal Statistics**. m. £900. 'Contains up to date information on aluminium, antimony, cadmium, copper, gold, lead, molybdenum, nickel, silver, tin and zinc.' Also produce *Quarterly* (£500), and *Annual* (£150) summaries.

(37) #586 World Federation of Diamond Bourses Pelikaanstraat, B02918 Antwerp, Belgium. t: (32 3) 232 7655.

(38) #587 World Gold Council Kings House, 10 Haymarket, London SW1Y 4BP, UK. t: (44 71) 930 5171; f: 839 6561.

'Non-profit association of around 70 gold producing companies from 13 countries. The Council's primary objective is to stimulate demand for gold by promoting its consumption in jewellery, investment and industrial uses.'

1661. **Gold Demand Trends**. q. 'This will publish data (from the final quarter of 1992) on the demand for gold during the preceding quarter with comments and charts. It will also include a review of central bank activities in the gold market and a general record of developments in the gold price.'

Insurance

(39) #588 Association Internationale de la Mutualité 8–10 rue de Hesse, CH-1204 Geneva, Switzerland. t: (41 22) 311 45 28; f: 311 45 41. *Newsletter*.

'Brings together the top executives and technical experts of independent health insurance and social benefit organisations from more than 20 countries . . . AIM's 35 members . . . are either national federations or individual organisations of national importance and all are not-for-profit.'

(40) #589 Association of International Life Offices Secretariat, PO Box 22, L-5201 Sandweiler, Luxembourg. t: (352) 44 26 59; f: 44 26 74.

'Although AILO produces a number of regular reports and surveys, these are made exclusively available to the Association's members. However, the Association remains at the disposition of anyone requiring details, whether they be directly concerned with AILO and its activities, or on the international insurance industry in general. This has been greatly facilitated by the establishment in November 1993, of a permanent Secretatiat . . . The main objectives of such a move was the centralisation of the various administrative functions . . . and to establish a central point of enquiry and communication for members, press and the general public.'

(41) #590 Bureau International des Producteurs d'Assurances & de Réassurances [International Association of Insurance and Reinsurance Intermediaries] Avenue Albert-Elisabeth 40, B-1200 Brussels, Belgium. t: (32 2) 735 60 48; f: 732 14 18.

'Non profit-making international organisation grouping professional associations of insurance intermediaries worldwide. It has presently a membership of 49 associations, established in 28 countries and representing some 250,000 insurance agents and brokers, employing in all about

1,500,000 people. . . . Being a world-wide organisation with a strong European base, BIPAR is the official spokesman of insurance intermediaries with a number of international bodies: European Communities, EFTA, GATT, UNCTAD, International Chamber of Commerce, UNICE, CEA, BEUC . . . Sorry, but all our publications are reserved for our member associations.'

(42) #591 Confederation of Insurance Trade Unions c/o National Union of Insurance Workers, 27 Old Gloucester Street, London WC1N 3AF, UK. t: (44 171) 405 6798.

(43) #592 International Actuarial Association Rue du Fossé-aux-Loups, 48, B-1000 Brussels, Belgium. t: (32 2) 213 69 76; f: 213 82 78.

'Founded in 1895 . . . Is a worldwide association which is professional, non-political and non-profit-making. Its aim is to serve as a *link* between actuaries and actuarial associations of various countries and to promote *research* into actuarial science and practice.'

- *ASTIN* [Actuarial Studies in Non-life Insurance] 'Promotes research into technical problems in general (non-life) insurance and reinsurance.'
- *AFIR* [Actuarial Approach for Financial Risks] 'Encourages research into actuarial problems encountered in the financial sector. Since its creation in 1988, this section has proved highly successful and enjoyed rapid growth.'

1662. **ASTIN Bulletin**. Jointly issued by AFIR and ASTIN, giving details of their activities and publishing 'highly scientific articles'.

(44) #593 International Association of Consulting Actuaries c/o 2175 Marine Drive, Apartment 607, Oakville, ON L6L 5S5, Canada. t: (1 416) 825 4046.

(45) #594 International Association of Mutual Insurance Companies Rue La Boetie 114, F-75008 Paris, France. t: (33 1) 42 25 59 37; f: 42 56 04 49. *Newsletter*.

'Created in 1963, has a membership of over 200 mutual insurance companies located in 27 countries.'

1663. **Mutuality**. s-a. Bulletin available in English, French, German and Spanish.

(46) #595 International Claim Association c/o 1710 First Avenue, Rock Island, IL 61201, USA. t: (1 309) 786 6481.

(47) #596 International Co-operative and Mutual Insurance Federation PO Box 21, Altrincham, Cheshire WA14 4PD, UK. t: (44 161) 929 5090; f: 929 5163. *Newsletter*.

'More than a hundred co-operative and mutual insurers . . . in nearly 50 countries.'

- *Cooperative Insurance Development Bureau*
- *International Cooperative Reinsurance Bureau*

(48) #597 International Credit Insurance Association Secretariat, Postfach 16, CH-7018 Flims-Waldhaus, Switzerland. t: (41 81) 39 36 39; f: 39 36 28. *Directory. Newsletter.*

'Provides its member companies with a forum for the exchange of ideas and information, in order to improve and develop their specialised services to the business world . . . *Credit Insurance* covers manufacturing, trading and service organisations against the risk of loss due to the insolvency of their customers.' The Association has members located in some 30 countries.

(49) #598 International Insurance Society Box 870223, Tuscaloosa, AL 35487–0223, USA. t: (1 205) 348 8974; f: 348 8973. *Newsletter.*

'Incorporated in 1965: "To facilitate international understanding, the transfer of ideas and innovations, and the development of personal networks across insurance markets through a joint effort of leading executives and academics on a worldwide basis" . . . We currently have approximately 1,100 individual members and 150 corporate members from over 80 nations.' The Society publishes a *Seminar and Proceedings Manual* each year in which appears the papers presented at its annual Seminar. 'We are distributing these on a complimentary basis to libraries . . . However, we do not as yet provide these to the general public.'

(50) #599 International Union of Aviation Insurers 6 Lovat Lane, London EC3R 8DT, UK. t: (44 171) 626 5314; f: 929 3534.

'We are an international trade association for aviation insurers. We gather information for distribution to our members . . . Our publications are produced for the sole benefit of our members.'

(51) #600 International Union of Credit and Investment Insurers [Berne Union] 17/18 Dover Street, London W1X 3PB, UK. t: (44 171) 409 2008; f: 495 6082.

'We read in the Book of Proverbs chapter 22, line 26 "be not one of those that are sureties for debts". If the advice of Solomon had been followed this booklet would never have been written, and the 40 members of the Berne Union, not to mention the much greater number of domestic credit insurance institutions, factors, forfaiters and the like, would never have come into existence.

State controlled organisations and private insurance companies covering political risks on behalf of the State constitute the membership of the Union, all participating as insurers and not as representatives of their

Governments. The Statutes of the Union provide that its purposes shall be to work for:

- the international acceptance of sound principles of export credit insurance and the establishment and maintenance of discipline in the terms of credit for international trade; and
- international co-operation in encouraging a favourable investment climate and in developing and maintaining sound principles of foreign investment insurance.'

(52) #601 LIMRA Life Insurance Marketing and Research Association, PO Box 208, Hartford, CT 06141–0208, USA. t: (1 203) 677 0033; f: 678 0187 *and* LIMRA International/Europe, 34 Clarendon Road, Watford, Hertfordshire, ED1 1JJ, UK. t: (44 1923) 226178; f: 236561.

'Supports and enhances the marketing function of its member countries around the world through original research, products and services. By conducting more than 100 surveys and studies, LIMRA compiles data on virtually every facet of the insurance industry.' The Association produces and markets a very wide range of published products and services, both in the US and internationally.

1664. **LIMRA's Marketfacts**. bi-m. $95. **online**. 'Features articles by leading life, health, and/or multiple-line insurance and financial services executives who have successfully solved marketing problems. LIMRA researchers and industry marketing experts tell how to spot the marketing opportunities of the future and how a company can capitalize on its unique chracteristics to find its own niche.'

(53) #602 LOMA Life Office Management Association, 5770 Powers Ferry Road, Atlanta, GA 30327–4308, USA. t: (1 404) 951 1770. *Publications* t: (1 404) 984 3780; f: 984 0441. *Newsletters.*

'An international associaiton of over 850 life/health insurance and financial services companies, LOMA has been a well-established, reliable partner and invaluable resource for the industry since 1924. LOMA helps its members stay ahead of the competition, and improve their management and operations, though quality products, services, training and education.' The Association produces an extensive Products & Services Catalog.

1665. **Resource**. m. $36. 'One of the main reasons that LOMA publishes *Resource* magazine is to provide a source of valuable information that member companies can use to more effectively manage their operations.' Circulation: 25,000.

Asset-backed finance

(54) #603 International Assets Valuation Standards Committee *Executive Headquarters* 15 Delisle Avenue, Toronto, Ontario, MV4 1SB, Canada. t: (1 416) 922 3999; f: 922 3589. *International Bureau*

12 Great George Street, London SW1P 3AD, UK. t: (44 171) 222 7000; f: 222 9430.

'Asset valuation has its roots in classical and contemporary economics. Valuation principles and techniques were established, and in the main were similar, in many countries prior to the 1940s. However, recognition of valuation as a profession developed after the 1940s . . . During the 1960s and 1970s several national valuation bodies developed and promulgated Standards of Professional Practice for their members. . . . As these movements continued it became apparent that international financial developments and the globalization of markets reached the stage that international valuation standards were sorely, needed . . . The International Assets Valuation Standards Committee (TIAVSC) was formed in 1981.

The principal TIAVSC objective is to formulate and publish, in the public interest, valuation Standards and procedural guidance for the valuation of assets for use in financial statements, and to promote their worldwide acceptance and observance. The second objective is to harmonize Standards among the world's states, and to make disclosures of differences in standards statements and/or applications of Standards as they occur. It is a particular goal of TIAVSC that international valuation Standards be recognised in statements of international accounting and other reporting standards . . . Members work with controlling and regulatory authorities, both statutory and voluntary, and societies of other professional bodies . . . Liaison with the *International Accounting Standards Committee*, *International Federation of Accountants*, *International Auditing Practices Committee*, and *International Organization of Securities Commissions* is especially important to TIAVSC activities. . . . TIAVSC was granted Roster status with the *United Nations Economic and Social Council* in May 1985.'

(55) #604 International Association of Assessing Officers 130 E Randolph Street, Suite 850, Chicago, IL 60601–6217, USA. t: (1 312) 819 6100; f: 819 6149.

'Mission is to provide leadership in accurate property valuation, property tax administration, and tax policy throughout the world.'

1666. **Assessment Journal**. bi-m. $200. Includes the *Assessment and Valuation Legal Reporter*, formerly published separately.

1667. **IAAO Membership Directory**. a. $400. 'All recipients of the directory must sign an agreement not use it or allow it to be used for creating commercial mailing lists.'

(56) #605 International Association of Corporate Real Estate Executives 440 Columbia Drive, Suite 100, West Palm Beach, FL 33409, USA. t: (800) 726 8111/(1 407) 683 8111; f: (1 407) 697 4853.

(57) #606 International Real Estate Federation 23 Avenue Bosquet, 75007 Paris, France. t: (33 1) 45 50 45 49; f: 45 50 42 00. Compuserve Address 100564,625. *Newsletter. Special Reports* (eg 'International real estate markets, property legislation and professional practice')

'*FIABCI* is the French acronym for the International Real Estate Federation. Based in Paris, the Federation is a worldwide organisation of professionals dedicated to the development of global real estate as an ethical, profitable and dynamic industry working to meet the real estate needs of the international community.' FIABCI's *Documentation Centre* 'receives information from the four corners of the globe on all matters related to real estate. This wealth of knowledge is made available to members through the Federation's publications, and through direct consultation.' The annual *Directory* (FF 2,200) 'contains the names, addresses and areas of specialisation of all FIABCI members classified by country (6,000 members from 51 countries – approximately 400 pages).'

(58) #607 International Society of Appraisers 500 North Michigan Avenue, Suite 1400, Chicago, IL 60611, USA. t: (1 312) 661 1700; f: 661 0769.

2. Organizations: Europe

(1) #608 European Financial Management and Marketing Association 16 Rue d'Aguesseau, 75008 Paris, France. t: (33 1) 47 42 52 72; f: 47 42 56 76. *Newsletter. Press Review.*

'Founded in 1971. Since its creation, it has constantly worked to encourage dialogue and advance its members ideas in all the fields of financial management and marketing. Its current membership is formed by more than 140 European financial institutions or groups of financial institutions. *Two thirds of the 50 largest establishments in Europe are members of EFMA*. In addition to these members from 15 different European countries, EFMA has associate members throughout the world: North and South America, the Far East, the Middle East and the Maghreb. EFMA works not only *beyond geographical frontiers* but *also bridges the divisions between professions*, bringing together banks of all types and categories, insurance companies, specialised credit establishments and financial subsidiaries of industrial and retailing groups . . . EFMA's *Documentation Centre* is considered by the profession as the best in the field. Access, entirely free of charge, is strictly reserved to members. They may choose to consult the publications by visiting the centre or asking for the documents in their research area to be sent to them. Bibliographical supplements, lists of indexed articles and the *Doc'Info bulletin* are sent to members several times a year to keep them informed on additions to the library.'

(2) #609 European Group of Financial Institutions Rue Defacqz 125, 1050 Brussels, Belgium. t: (32 2) 534 5813; f: 534 50 44.

European Economic Interest Group

(3) #610 Union of the Finance-Personnel in Europe c/o Rheinweg 33, D-5300 Bonn 1, Germany. t: (49 228) 23 00 31; f: 23 70 29.

Confederation of national finance trade unions in Europe.

Banks

(4) #611 Fédération Bancaire de la Communauté Européene [Banking Federation of the European Union] 10 rue Montoyer, B-1040, Brussels, Belgium. t: (32 2) 508 3711; f: 511 2328. *Annual Report.*

Representatives of national banking professional associations within Europe, including all the member countries of the proposed European Economic Area. Committees of the Federation include: Payment Systems Steering Group; Legal Committee; Fiscal Committee; Banking Supervision Committee; Accounts Committee; Consumer Affairs Committee; Mortgage Credit Committee; Communications Committee; Financial Markets Committee; Payment Systems Committee; Telecommunications Committee.

(5) #612 European Association of Cooperative Banks [Groupement Européen des Banques Coopératives] Rue de la Science 23–25, Boite 9, B-1040 Brussels, Belgium. t: (32 2) 230 11 24/230 14 19; f: 230 06 49. *Annual Report.*

Created in 1970 'both to strengthen collaboration between European cooperative banking groups as well as to chart a course of action aimed at defending these institutions' professional interests on a European-wide scale'. The membership of over 25 organizations comprises cooperative banking groups from both within and outside the European Union. The Association is one of the three main representative organizations in the European credit sector, and is officially recognized as such by the EU, alongside those organizations representing commercial and savings banks. 'European savings and credit cooperatives, characterised in the past by their preponderance in the agricultural, SME and craft-industry sectors, have today developed into universal banks, providing both their corporate and personal members and clients with a comprehansive range of modern financial services. With a total of more than 50 million members and clients, they rank among some of Europe's most prestigious banking groups . . . We do not, as a professional banking entity, issue either printed or electronic matter on a regular basis.'

Savings institutions

(6) #613 European Federation of Building Societies D-5300 Bonn 1, Postfach 14 29, Buschstrasse 32, Germany. t: (49 2 28) 20 44 10; f: 20 44 22.

(7) #614 European Savings Bank Group Avenue de la Renaissance 12, B-1040 Brussels, Belgium. t: (32 2) 739 16 11; f: 736 09 55.

Finance companies

(8) #615 Eurofinas [European Federation of Finance House Associations] Avenue de Tervuren 267, B-1150 Brussels, Belgium. t: (32 2) 778 05 60; f: 778 05 79. *Annual Report.*

(9) #616 Europafactoring [European Federation of Factoring Associations] Avenue de Tervuren 267, 1150 Brussels, Belgium. t: (32 2) 771 21 08; f: 770 75 96.

(10) #617 European Venture Capital Association evca, Keibergpark, Minervastraat 6, Box 6, 1930 Zaventem, Belgium. t: (32 2) 715 00 20; f: 725 30 36.

'Mission is to promote the European venture capital industry globally to facilitate pan-European private equity investment in unquoted companies via a range of services. evca's strategy is to focus on core activities of key importance and of pan-European relevance to the venture capital industry. This includes such tasks as setting professional standards, gathering and publishing comprehensive Europe-wide statistics and analysis and facilitating the exchange of information and opportunities for our members throughout Europe . . . evca now represents over 200 leading venture capital companies in Europe and 100 Associate members including law practices, professional advisory firms and banks.' *Special Papers* (e.g. 'The evca performance measurement principles' (1994); 'An introductory guide to US initial public offerings for European venture-backed companies' (1994)).

1668. **evca Yearbook**. a. ECU50. 'Unique reference book, distributed and sold worldwide, which presents the results of an annual survey of venture capital in Europe.'

1669. **Newsline/Press Summary**. m. ECU250.

(11) #618 Leaseurope [European Federation of Equipment Leasing Company Associations] avenue de Tervuren 267 Bte 9, B-1150 Brussels, Belgium. t: (32 2) 771 21 08; f: 770 75 96.

Securities industry

(12) #619 European Managed Futures Association International House, 1 St Katherine's Way, London E1 9UN, UK. t: (44 171) 265 3688; f: 481 8485. *Newsletter.*

'EMFA was launched in September 1990 in Montreux, when, after months of preliminary work and consultations, it appeared necessary to create in Europe an association in its own rights to represent the fast growing industry of *Managed Futures* and to promote Managed Futures as a new asset class. EMFA has gone from strength to strength and with 115 corporate members, is now recognised as the umbrella organisation representing Managed Futures in Europe. . . . Full members can be any person whose business involves transactions in futures and options and whose place of business is Europe. Associate members can be any person whose business involves offering legal, accountancy or other professional services, and those who are not resident in Europe.'

1670. **EMFA Yearbook**. a. £35. 'The first directory of this kind worldwide and although it covers primarily the European aspects of the managed futures industry, it has not limited its coverage to the European region . . . (It) includes articles and features on . . . European traders and funds statistics . . . International regulatory update . . . List of all European managed futures funds . . . Listing of the US *Managed Futures Association*'s members . . . The directory contains 160 pages and approximately 700 names of participants in the managed futures industry.'

(13) #620 Federation of European Stock Exchanges Rue du Midi 2, 5ieme Etage, 1000 Brussels, Belgium. t: (32 2) 513 05 18; f: 512 49 05. *Directory.*

1671. **European Stock Exchange Statistics**. m. Covers equity, bond and derivative markets.

Fund management and investment

(14) #621 Fédération Européenne des Fonds et Sociétés d'Investissement [European Federation of Investment Funds and Companies] Square de Meeus 20, B-1040 Brussels, Belgium. t: (32 2) 513 39 69; f: 513 26 43.

'We do not have any publications available to the general public.'

(15) #622 European Federation for Retirement Provision Rue des Pierres, 29 Steenstrat, B-1000 Brussels, Belgium. t: (32 2) 502 54 66; f: 502 74 77.

Insurance

(16) #623 Association of European Cooperative and Mutual Insurers Galilée Building, Avenue Galilée 5 – Bte 19, B-1030 Brussels, Belgium. t: (32 2) 250 94 99; f: 250 96 00.

'Established in 1978 in response to the need to anticipate the internationalisation of insurance and the coming of the Single European Market. With the inception of the Single European Market on 1 January 1993, the Association opened its membership to all insurers of the solidarity economy . . . Unfortunately, our publications are not distributed outside.'

(17) #624 Comité Européen des Assurances [European Insurance Committee] 3 bis, rue de la Chaussée d'Antin, F 75009 Paris, France. t: (33 1) 44 83 11 83; f: 47 70 03 75. *Annual Report.*

'Set up in 1953 . . . is the Federation of National Associations of insurance companies in European countries with a market economy (25 members)' Produces various Papers (e.g. 'European Insurance Employment Statistics 1993' June 1994), reports and submissions to the EU.

1672. **CEA Info**. m. FFr 350. Reports developments in the EU and in the markets of the national associations which are members of the CEA.

(18) #625 Groupe Consultatif des Associations D'Actuaires des Pays des Communautés Européennes [Consultative Group of Associations of Actuaries in the Countries of the EC] c/o Napier House, 4 Worcester Street, Oxford OX1 2AW, UK. t: (44 1865) 794144; f: 794164.

Asset-backed finance

(19) #626 Confédération Européene des Administrateurs de Biens Chaussée Waterloo 715 Boite 30, B-1180 Brussels, Belgium. t: (32 2) 344 48 60; f: 347 64 24.

(20) #627 EU Mortgage Federation Avenue de la Joyeuse Entrée 14/2, B-1040 Brussels, Belgium. t: (32 2) 230 25 51; f: 230 64 11. *Annual Report.*

'Founded in 1967 on the initiative of the Belgian and Dutch associations, the EC Mortgage Federation brings together European institutions (credit institutions, financial institutions, building societies, insurance companies) whose main activity is granting housing, industrial and agricultural credit . . . Contrary to the majority of professional European organisations, the Mortgage Federation represents both public institutions and private commercial or non-commercial companies.' The Federation have published a range of studies, e.g.: 'Securitisation of mortgage backed securities in the EC' (1992, BEF 250); 'The main refinancing instruments' (1992, BEF 500); 'Mortgage banks and the mortgage bond in Europe'

(1993, BEF 2,960); 'Hypostat: A decade of mortgage statistics' (1994, BEF 1,500).

1673. **Directory of European Community Mortgage Lenders**. i. BEF 2,500. 'The result of the first major survey of the mortgage sector in the Community.'

1674. **Directory of European Community Mortgage Lenders**. a. BEF 2,500.

1675. **Mortgage Banks and the Mortgage Bond in Europe**. l. BEF 2,960.

(21) #628 European Group of Valuers of Fixed Assets Avenue Araucaria 31, B-1020 Brussels, Belgium. t: (32 2) 268 5555.

66. Organizations: United Kingdom

Banks

(1) #629 American Banking & Securities Association of London 28 High Hurst Close, Newick, East Sussex, BN8 4NJ. t: (44 82) 572 3304.

(2) #630 Banking Information Service 10 Lombard Street, London EC3V 9AT. t: (44 171) 626 9386; f: 283 9655.

Specialist education unit funded by the commercial banks whose three overall aims are: to create and maintain positive links between the banking community and its future customers and staff who are still in education; to develop, through the Careers Service and Bankers in Schools Service, a guidance and filtering system for future recruits; to encourage the integration into the curriculum of provision for Economic and Industrial Understanding, and especially the management of personal and business finance. The Service produces a large number of teaching and careers information resources – which are described and illustrated in the *Brochure* 'A comprehensive guide to educational resources'.

(3) #631 Banking, Insurance and Finance Union Sheffield House, 1b Amity Grove, London SW20 0LG. t: (44 81) 946 9151.

Trade union.

(4) #632 British Bankers' Association 10 Lombard Street, London EC3V 9EL. t: (44 171) 623 4001; f: 283 7037. The *British Bankers' Press & Information Office* provides information on banking to the press and the public. t: (44 71) 626 8486.

'The trade association for banks authorised by the Bank of England to take deposits in the UK . . . Representing over 300 member banks from over 60 countries.' Examples taken from the Association's 1992/93 *Annual Report* show the range of its involvements:

- *Banking Regulation & Supervision* UK Banking Regulation (e.g. BCCI affair); Implementation of the Second Banking Coordination Directive; Solvency Ratio Directive; US Regulation (e.g. proposed subsidiarisation requirement from the US Treasury and Federal Reserve Board for non-US banks doing business in the US).
- *Legal, Lending & Operational Affairs* Export Finance; Loan Guarantee Scheme.
- *Accounting & Taxation* UK Accounting Regime (e.g. proposals from the Accounting Standards Board); Statements of Recommended Practice; VAT (e.g. implementation of EC single market legislation); SAYE Share Option Bonus Scheme.
- *Foreign Exchange & Money Markets* Money Markets: Market Standards (e.g. improved distribution of the 'BBA Interest Settlement Rate' through Knight-Ridder and Reuters as well as Telerate, broadened its use as the market standard); Commercial Paper Guidelines; Cross-Border Payments (e.g. publication of the European industry guidelines on remote payments).
- 'The BBA has also played its part in encouraging best practice in the international markets operating in London. The BBA's *guidelines, standardised documentation* and *terms of agreement* are now used in the London market for certificates of deposit, forward rate agreements (*FRBBA*), interest rate swaps (*BBAIRS*) and synthetic agreements for forward exchange (*SAFEBBA*) master terms. This year we also introduced London market guidelines on commercial paper, working with the Association of Corporate Treasurers, and the international currency option market's ICOM terms, with the Foreign Exchange Committee of New York and the Tokyo Market Practices Committee.'
- *Small Businesses & Consumer Affairs* EC Consumer Directives; Banking Relationships with Small Businesses; Banking Ombudsman & Small Businesses.
- *Investment Regulation & Securities Markets* Investment Services Directive; Securities Markets (e.g. replacement of the TAURUS system); Regulation of Retail Investment; Revised UCIT's Directive (unit and investment trusts).
- *Employment & Staff Matters* Bank Staff (e.g. co-operative exercise with the police, unions, the Health & Safety Executive and victim support groups on the prevention of violence to staff).
- *Statistics* Statistical Data: Revised definitions of data for reporting purposes which enhanced their utility for banks; e.g. on mortgage lending by banks, and distinctions between retail and wholesale deposits.
- *Crime Prevention* EC Money Laundering Directive; Terrorism & Insurance; Fraud: The BBA's Fraud Intelligence Unit extended its database and intelligence gathering activities, as well as providing workshops and in-house sessions for member banks.

1676. **Abstract of Banking Statistics**. a. £15. 'The BBA has a sizeable statistical unit which collects data on a wide range of banking activities. The information collected is considered to be a valuable primary source by government, economists, journalists and other economic and financial commentators. Some of the information is published in regular news releases.'

1677. **Statements of Recommended Practice**. i. Statements for the banking industry produced from time to time by the Association. 'Established SORPs have the approval of the Accounting Standards Board; exposure drafts are consultative documents, as yet not established or recognised by the Accounting Standards Board.'

(5) #633 London Investment Banking Association 6 Frederick's Place, London EC2R 8BT. t: (44 171) 796 3606; f: 796 4345.

'The principal trade association in the United Kingdom for firms active in the merchant banking and securities industries.' The Association is very active in all aspects of the industries, and has a number of specialist committees. However, its sole publication is its *Annual Report*. Previously known as the *British Merchant Banking and Securities Houses Association*.

(6) #634 Chartered Institute of Bankers 10 Lombard Street, London EC3V 9AS. t: (44 171) 623 3531; f: 283 1510.

The major UK professional body for banking, founded in 1879 with a current membership of 95,000. The *Chartered Building Societies Institute* merged with this Institute in 1993.

No. of staff 93 Full time; 10 Part time.

Affiliated organisations within Europe: European Bank Training Network; International Foundation for Computer-based Education in Banking and Finance.

Publications

1678. **Banking World**. m. £56. **online**.

Yearly programme of publishing through subsidiary *Bankers Books*; Local Centre News; Education News.

Member profile 'Worldwide membership served by 96 UK local centres and 7 overseas local centres in Bermuda, Cyprus, Gibraltar, Hong Kong, Malta, Mauritius and Sri Lanka. Membership covers employees from more than 4,000 banks and other financial institutions, in over 150 countries.'[163]

(7) #635 Foreign Banks and Securities Houses Association 5 Laurence Pountney Lane, London EC4R 0BS. t: (44 171) 621 9557; f: 220 7116. *Annual Report*.

'Our "publications" are generally in-house, being intended for our membership, and relate to fundamental, even mundane, operational problems . . . Intended for wider circulation, is . . . "A review of software in the City of London" . . . prepared and published in conjunction with *Terence Chapman Associates* . . . who hold the marketing rights (1992)'. Over 200 members.

Savings institutions

(8) #636 Association of British Credit Unions Unit 307, Westminster Business Square, 339 Kennington Lane, London SE11 5QY. t: (44 171) 582 2626; f: 587 1774.

A representative body for credit unions in the UK providing a range of support services. The Association produces a number of promotional brochures.

(9) #637 Building Societies Association 3 Savile Row, London W1X 1AF. t: (44 171) 437 0655; f: 734 6416. *Publications* Enquiries to *BSA/CML Bookshop* (t: (44 171) 437 0655; f: 287 0109) which also handles publications of the *#638 Council of Mortgage Lenders*.

1679. **Building Societies Act 1986 Practice Manual**. l. £900.00/£350.00.

1680. **Building Societies Yearbook (Year)**. *Franey Publishers*. a. £60.00. 'Provides balance sheets of member societies, details of directors and senior managers and key statistics on societies and housing finance generally . . . Incorporates the *Council of Mortgage Lenders Yearbook*'.

1681. **Building Society Annual Account Data (Year)**. a. £40.00. **diskette** £100.00. Features data drawn from the published reports and accounts of building societies.

1682. **Building Society Annual Accounts Manual**. l. £115.00.

1683. **Building Society Taxation Manual**. l. £180.00.

1684. **European Community Mortage Bulletin**. bi-m.

1685. **Housing Finance**. q. £60.00.

1686. **Housing Finance Fact Book (Year)**. a. £20.00.

1687. **Housing Legislation Manual**. l. £85.00/£50.00.

1688. **MIRAS Lenders Manual**. l. £200.00/£120.00.

1689. **Monthly Statistics Digest**. m. £48.00. 'Provides all the information provided in the BSA's monthly figures press release on mortgage lending and savings.'

1690. **Mortgage Monthly**. m. £12.00.

1691. **Mortgage Weekly**. w. £250.00. Digest of news stories covering the housing and mortgage markets and the organizations that operate them.

(10) #639 National Conference of Friendly Societies Royex House, Aldermanbury Square, London EC2V 7HR. t: (44 171) 606 1881; f: 606 0794. *Newsletter*.

'The trade association of registered friendly societies other than collecting friendly societies. Their trade association is the *Association of Collecting Friendly Societies*.'

Finance companies

(11) #640 Association of British Factors & Discounters 1 Northumberland Avenue, Trafalgar Square, London WC2N 5BW. t: (44 171) 930 9112; f: 839 2858. *Annual Report.*

Exists to promote factoring and discounting to a wide public of users, potential users, trade associations, professional bodies and government. The Association comprises twelve of the UK's largest factoring firms representing over 90 per cent of the market for factoring and discounting services, and accounting in 1991 for a sales volume of £14.2 billion.

(12) #641 British Venture Capital Association Essex House, 12–13 Essex Street, London WC2R 3AA. t: (44 171) 240 3846; f: 240 3849.

'The representative body for the venture and development capital industry in the UK . . . (It) represents every major source of venture capital in the UK. The Association (1993/94) has 117 full members, 99 associate members and 3 honorary members. All members are active in making long-term equity investments, primarily in unquoted companies. They include independent firms with institutional funds under management, wholly owned subsidiaries or divisions of larger financial institutions and venture capital organisations wholly funded either directly or indirectly from Government sources.

Associates fall into two categories: financial organisations who invest in venture capital, but only as a minor part of their overall activities; and professional advisers who have experience in dealing with various aspects of the venture capital industry.' These members and associates are all listed in:

1692. **British Venture Capital Association Directory (Year)**. a.

The Association also publishes:

1693. **Report of Investment Activity**. a. £30. 'Aggregate information (accompanied by analysis) on the investment activity of BVCA full members by financing stage, industry sector and region together with details on independent funds raised.'

(13) #642 Consumer Credit Association of the United Kingdom Queen's House, Queen's Road, Chester CH1 3BQ. t/f: (44 1244) 312044.

1510. **CCA News**. bi-m. £24. In-house magazine for members of the largest UK Trade Association for the unsecured lending industry.

(14) #643 Consumer Credit Trade Association Tennyson House, 159–163 Great Portland Street, London W1N 5FD. t: (44 171) 636 7564; f: 323 0096.

1695. **Consumer Credit**. £15. Covers news of relevance to credit grantors' and consumers' rights, protection and related topics.

(15) #644 Finance & Leasing Association 18 Upper Grosvenor Street, London W1X 9PB. t: (44 171) 491 2783; f: 629 0396.

'The major UK representative body for the finance and leasing industry.'

(16) #645 National Consumer Credit Federation 98/100 Holme Lane, Sheffield S6 4JW. t/f: (44 114) 234 8101.

(17) #646 National Pawnbrokers Association 1 Bell Yard, London WC2A 2JP. t: (44 171) 242 1114; f: 405 4266. *Newsletter.*

'Founded in 1892 to provide a central organisation to promote and safeguard the interests of pawnbrokers.'

Securities industry

(18) #647 Association of Private Client Investment Managers and Stockbrokers 112 Middlesex Street, London E1 7HY. t: (44 71) 247 7080; f: 377 0939. *Annual Report.*

Formed in 1990 to represent the views and concerns of private client investment managers and stockbrokers to government departments, the Securities and Investments Board and other regulatory authorities in order to further the making of investments on behalf of private clients.

(19) #648 Federation of Commodity Associations Gafta House, 6 Chapel Court, Rivington Street, London EC2A 3DQ, UK. t: (44 171) 814 9666; f: 814 8383. *Bulletin.*

Founded in 1943. 'An EC-recognised organisation made up of Members from Associations, Federations, organisations and companies involved in the commodity trades. Direct representation can be made through the FCA to the Commission. . . . The administration of the Secretariat for the FCA is carried out by the *Grain and Feed Trade Association*.'

(20) #649 Futures and Options Association Roman Wall House, 1–2 Crutched Friars, London EC3N 2AN. t: (44 171) 488 4610; f: 696 9562.

(21) #650 Gilt-Edged Market Makers Association The London Stock Exchange, Old Broad Street, London EC2N 1HP. t: (44 171) 797 1197; f: 334 8958.

Members are firms dealing in government securities.

(22) #651 Institutional Fund Managers Association 31–45 Gresham Street, London EC2V 7DN. t: (44 171) 600 3914; f: 600 3895. *Annual Report.*

'To represent the interests of UK based institutional fund managers. IFMA will consult on behalf of its members with regulatory organisations, trade associations, Government and other bodies in the UK, the European Community and internationally, to ensure that the industry's concerns are made known and taken into account. IFMA's other objectives include: becoming the leading national source of information about institutional fund management; providing a forum of discussion for its members; and encouraging the maintenance of high professional standards.' *Standing Subcommittees of the Executive Committee* include:

- Regulation & Taxation
- Europe & International
- Practice
- Education & Training
- Accounting Standards Working Group
- Securities Settlement Working Group
- Fund Management Data Working Group
- Pensions and Custody Working Group

1696. **Fund Management Survey (Year)**. a. 'Based on a quesionnaire sent to our members earlier this year. The information in the survey covers a significant part of the fund management industry in the UK, and . . . contains data on assets under management, the importance of overseas clients, the different types of institutional portfolios managed, staffing levels and fund managers' contribution to the balance of payments . . . Although information is readily available on certain aspects of fund management, comprehensive data remains difficult to come by. Funds under management can only be obtained by adding the totals for individual management companies or by deriving a figure from the asset holdings of fund managers' main clients – pension funds, insurance companies and unit and investment trusts. Official statistics on fund managers' overseas earnings are available only from 1990.'

(23) #652 International Petroleum Exchange of London International House, 1 St Katharine's Way, London E1 9UN. t: (44 171) 481 0643; f: 481 8485. *Also* 10 East 40th Street, Suite 4210, New York, NY 10016, USA. t: (1 212) 213 3200; f: 213 8855.

1697. **Daily Futures and Options Reports**. d. £250. 'Detail opening and closing prices, highs and lows, trading volumes and other vital data for IPE futures and options contracts . . . Reports may be delivered by facsimile, on the condition that they shall not be duplicated or otherwise circulated without the Exchange's prior consent.'

(24) #653 Joint Exchanges Committee 28/29 Threadneedle Street, London EC2R 8BA. t: (44 171) 283 1345; f: 588 3624.

'Committee of the Chairmen and Chief Executives of each of the London futures and options exchanges.'

(25) #654 London Bullion Market Association 6 Frederick's Place, London EC2R 8BT. t: (44 171) 796 3067; f: 796 4345. *Newsletter.*

'Formally incorporated in 1987 . . . Membership is open to those companies and other organisations which are actively engaged in trading, refining, melting, assaying, transporting and/or vaulting gold and/or silver within or for persons in the United Kingdom and is made up of two classes: Market Maker Member and Ordinary Member.'

(26) #655 London Commodity Exchange 1 Commodity Quay, St Katharine Docks, London E1 9AX. t: (44 171) 481 2080; f: 702 9923.

"In June 1987, the exchange changed its marketing name to *London FOX, the Futures and Options Exchange.* In January 1991, the exchange merged with the *Baltic Futures Exchange*, a move which enabled the exchange to broaden its product base substantially. In June 1993, following a major restructuring of management and organization, the exchange reverted to its original trading name of the London Commodity Exchange. The LCE's method of trading is primarily open outcry, although white sugar futures and options are traded on an automated trading system." (BATTLEY, N. ed. **The world's futures & options markets**. *Probus Publishing*, 1993, pp 147–8).

(i) *#656 CMS* Commodity Market Services, 1 Commodity Quay, St Katherine Docks, London E1 9AX, UK. t: (44 171) 702 0202; f: 488 4256.

'The *CMS FutureView* system is a windows based, real-time price reporting terminal, providing worldwide coverage of real-time prices from the Commodity and Financial Futures markets as well as FX coverage from leading London Banks.'

(27) #657 London Discount Market Association 39 Cornhill, London EC3V 3NU. t: (44 171) 623 1020; f: 220 7620.

Membership comprises the houses with discount accounts at the Bank of England.

(28) #658 London International Financial Futures and Options Exchange Cannon Bridge, London EC4R 3XX. t: (44 171) 623 0444; f: 588 3624. *Also* LIFFE USA, 74 Trinity Place, Suite 2002, New York, NY 10006–2101, USA. t: (800) 647 9979/(1 212) 385 1515; f: 385 1721.

'Created by the merger, in March 1992, of the *London International Financial Futures Exchange* and the *London Traded Options Market*, LIFFE is Europe's exchange – and on a global scale the third largest in the world – devoted to financial futures and options.' LIFFE produces a number of 'Publications for private investors or private client brokers'; 'Risk management and accounting publications'; and 'Specialist publications for institutional investors' – as well as Contract brochures for: Government bond products; Short term interest rate products; Equity and index products. 'LIFFE reserves the right to charge for any of its publications or to limit the number of copies being mailed out.'

(29) #659 London Metal Exchange 56 Leadenhall Street, London EC3A 2BJ. t: (44 171) 264 5555; f: 680 0505.

'The world centre for base metal trading . . . of the main industrially used non-ferous metals – namely, copper, primary aluminium, aluminium alloy, lead, nickel, tin and zinc . . . As a *Recognised Investment Exchange* . . . (its) function is to provide an efficient and orderly market which fully complies with relevant sections of Schedule IV of the *Financial Services Act 1986*, other relevant rules and guidance issued by SIB and other relevant UK, EC, US and other authorities, where appropriate. The primary roles of the Exchange are to:

- provide a market where participants, primarily from non-ferrous base metals related industries, have, *inter alia*, the opportunity to hedge against risks arising from base metals price fluctuations
- provide reference prices for the worldwide pricing of activities relating to non-ferrous base metals
- provide for appropriately located storage facilities to enable market participants to make or take physical delivery of approved brands of non-ferrous base metals.

The LME is not a cash cleared market, its unique floor and inter-office trading procedure is combined with a clearing system operating between principals based on bank guarantees and other forms of collateral. Both floor and inter-office trading are covered by a matching system run by the *London Clearing House*, whose role is to act as a central counterparty to trades executed between clearing members and thereby reduce risk and settlement costs. Another advanced electronic system keeps watch over prices bid, offered and traded, so as to provide ready data on market activity to the world.

Hedging, a form of insurance, is the *raison d'être* for any commodity market. . . . Metal passes through a number of processing stages before it reaches the finished product. Between each stage there can be a considerable time lapse which reduces a company's ability to match physical purchases with its physical sales, resulting in risk exposure to possible changes in market price. To guard against such changes, it is prudent to hedge each physical transaction by entering into an offsetting forward contract on the Exchange.

Simple options contracts for metals were traded in London even before the establishment of the Exchange. Indeed, some say that trading of options goes back as far back as the trading of metals. But it was not until 1987 that the LME introduced *traded options* as official Exchange contracts. Options contracts give trade hedgers and investors a more flexible alternative to futures as a means of trading on the Exchange.

All LME contracts assume an eventual delivery of physical metal on the prompt date. In the main this does not happen as the vast majority of LME business is for trade hedging, whereby most LME contracts are cancelled out by equal and opposite buy/sell back contracts. . . . All futures markets, including the London Metal Exchange, cater for speculation amongst their services. Indeed, speculators play an important role in futures trading, as they bring liquidity into the market, often taking up the risk that the trade hedger is trying to avoid. Speculation is, however, a high-risk venture which can result in spectacular profits and losses alike.

It should only be undertaken by professional investors or institutions who have sufficent capital to withstand putting a portion of it at risk.'

Based on turnover figures from January-December 1994 at average settlement prices for the period, trade at the London Metal Exchange was some *US $9 billion per day.*

(30) #660 London Stock Exchange [International Stock Exchange of the United Kingdom and the Republic of Ireland] London EC2N 1HP, UK. t: (44 171) 797 1000; f: 588 3504.

"The venerable London Stock Exchange ranks behind the TSE, NYSE, and NASDAQ in trading volume. In an effort to make its image more current, the exchange changed its name to the *International Stock Exchange* in the late 1980s. The change was ignored by virtually everyone except those who wrote promotional brochures for the exchange. That is unfortunate because the exchange had become probably the most international of all exchanges. The trading volume of some other European equities is actually greater in London than it is in the home country."[164]

1698. **Member Firms of the London Stock Exchange**. a. £15.

1699. **Quality of Markets Monthly Fact Sheet**. m. £53.

1700. **Stock Exchange Official Yearbook (Year)**. *Macmillan Press.* a. £199. 'Authoritative source of information on the 3600+ companies quoted on the London Stock Exchange.'

1701. **Stock Exchange Quarterly**. q. £79.

1702. **Who's Who in the City (Year)**. Published under licence by *Macmillan Press.* a. £95. '14,000 key figures in the UK financial community.'

(i) *#661 Regulatory News Service*

'Service for the receipt, validation and publication of regulated announcements provided by companies in compliance with the *Continuing Obligations of Listing* ... The Exchange's *Yellow Book*:

1703. **Listing Rules**. l. £20/£10. There is also a *Commentary of The Listing Rules and tables of destination and derivation.*

sets out the Continuing Obligations of listed companies regarding the notification of information.

RNS is designed to ensure that regulated announcements, particularly those which might reasonably be expected to have a material effect on market activity and prices of securities, are validated and communicated promptly to the market through the RNS subscriber network.

The key features of RNS are:

- A computerised system to validate the authenticity of all regulated announcements.
- A telephone confirmation of release service, confirming publication of an announcement by RNS to the issuer (or authorised agent).

- The simultaneous publication of regulated announcements by computer-readable feed to all RNS subscribers.
- Each announcement consists of two elements: a headline, containing the company name and type of announcement, prepared by the Exchange; and the full text of the announcement as prepared by the company.'

(ii) *£662 SEAQ International*

(31) #663 OMLX: The London Securities and Derivatives Exchange 107 Cannon Street, London EC4N 5AD. t: (44 171) 283 0678; f: 815 850

(32) #664 Securities Institute Centurion House, 24 Monument Street, London EC3R 8AJ. t: (44 171) 626 3191; f: 626 3062. Formed in 1992.

'The Stock Exchange has abolished individual membership . . . The new professional body for individual practitioners in the securities industry as a whole is the Securities Institute . . . In the first two years of the Institute's life, there have been around 8,000 membership applications. New applications are coming from practitioners in fund management, the derivative markets, corporate finance, compliance and administration . . . The only *guaranteed* way to reach the Institute's members who comprise the heart of Britain's securities industry is through the *Securities & Investment Review*.

Securities Institute Services Limited (t: (44 171) 626 3052; f: 283 0712) publishes a wide range of study workbooks and manuals. Some provide the documentation needed to support courses, and others are designed to cover the syllabus material of Institute qualifications . . . Titles include: "The regulatory environment"; "Introduction to securities and investment"; "UK securities settlement: Basics of Talisman"; "Introduction to futures and options"; "Global custody" . . . Forthcoming: "Unit trust administration"; "Bond settlement"; "Emerging markets"; "PEP administration".'

1704. **Securities & Investment Review**. *Silverdart*. m. £95.

Fund management and investment

(33) #665 Association of Investment Trust Companies Durrant House, 8–13 Chiswell Street, London EC1Y 4YY. t: (44 171) 588 5347; f: 638 1803.

'The trade association representing investment trusts. Formed in response to problems in the fixed-interest securities markets during the depression of the 1930s, the AITC is an unincorporated association whose main purpose is the promotion, protection and advancement of the common interests of its Members and their shareholders. Membership is available to companies which are closed-ended, listed on a recognised stock exchange and taxed as investment companies, and which manage a portfolio of mainly marketable shares and securities. . . . AITC represents over 250 Investment Trust Companies, with assets exceeding £40 billion . . . AITC compiles authoritative statistical information about its membership and publishes a *Monthly Information Service* which surveys the performance of Member companies. . . . As you may not be entirely familiar with all the terms associated with investment trusts, we also produce this *User's Guide* which explains the technicalities in simple language.'

1705. **Investment Trust Directory**. bi-a. £25. 'Vital information on investment trusts . . . If you're looking for investment trusts which concentrate on income or capital growth, or invest in certain geographical or industrial areas, the nineteen categories containing 250 investment trusts will help you find them . . . We've also included articles and statistics to give you a better picture of the investment trust industry as a whole.'

(34) #666 Association of Pensioner Trustees c/o Suntrust Ltd, PO Box 290, Bristol BS99 7SL. t: (44 117) 942 6911; f: 942 0441. *Newsletter.*

'Formed in 1979 (and) recognised as the official body representing the interests and aspirations of pensioner trustees and their clients. The Association's members are drawn from all sides of the business and financial community. They include banks, insurance companies, actuaries, solicitors, insurance brokers, accountants and benefit consultants. Before approval is granted to a small self-administered pension scheme the Inland Revenue insist that at least one of the trustees should be a pensioner trustee – that is, a trustee approved and recognised by the *Pension Schemes Office* of the Inland Revenue.'

(35) #667 Association of Unit Trusts and Investment Funds 65 Kingsway, London WC2B 6TD. t: (44 171) 831 0898; f: 831 9975. Available free of charge are: *Unit Trust Industry Sales Statistics* (m.); *PEP Sales Statistics* (q.); *Performance Charts* (m.).

1706. **Unit Trust Review and Directory (Year)**. *Professional Business Information*. a. £325.

1707. **Unit Trust Yearbook (Year)**. *FT Management Reports*. a. £120.

(36) #668 National Association of Pension Funds 12–18 Grosvenor Gardens, London SW1W 0DH. t: (44 171) 730 0585; f: 730 2595.

'Comprises:

1200 Fund Members

- Companies, firms and other organisations which provide pensions for their employees – including most of the largest employees in the private and public sectors – and
- Corporate trustees where a group of employers has established an "industry-wide" occupational pension scheme or an individual

employer has set up a subsidiary trustee company to administer its pension scheme.

350 Other Members

- Companies or firms providing professional services to pension funds such as consultancy, actuarial, legal, administration or investment services.'

1708. **NAPF Annual Survey of Occupational Pension Schemes**. a. £96. 'A unique source of up-to-date information on the vital statistics and benefit structures of occupational pension schemes in the UK.'

1709. **NAPF Pensions Legislation Service**. *Butterworths*. l. £190. Two volumes. 'Designed to bring all relevant current legislation in two convenient loose-leaf volumes.'

1710. **NAPF Yearbook**. a. £50. Lists the 'Fund Members' and the 'Other Members'.

(37) #669 Pension Trustees Forum 1 Queen Anne's Gate. London SW1H 9BT. t: (44 171) 233 0206; f: (44 114) 275 0998. *Newsletter*.

Association of pension fund trustees.

(38) #670 Pensions Management Institute 4–10 Artillery Lane, London E1 7LS. t: (44 171) 247 1452; f: 375 0603. *Newsletter*.

'Founded in 1976 to promote professionalism amongst those working in the field of pensions. Today, it is acknowledged as the Institute for pensions professionals.'

1711. **Ivanhoe Guide to Pensions Management (Year)**. *Charles Letts*. a. £9.95. 'Authoritative analysis of the profession . . . aimed at students seeking information on career opportunities and at the general reader.'

(39) #671 Society of Pension Consultants Ludgate House, Ludgate Circus, London EC4A 2AB. t: (44 171) 353 1688; f: 353 9296. *Newsletter*.

Corporate membership organization.

Insurance

(40) #672 All-Party Parliamentary Group on Insurance and Financial Services c/o Post Magazine, 58 Fleet Street, London EC4Y 1JU. t: (44 171) 353 4881; f: 583 6069.

Founded in 1991, and includes about a score of members. An *All-Party Group* is "an unofficial group consisting exclusively of MPs and Peers which acts as a focus of cross-party discussion of a particular topic – for example, cycling, penal affairs or science. The term "registered group" is used for groups which admit outsiders as members as well as MPs and Peers."[165]

(41) #673 Association of British Insurers 51 Gresham Street, London EC2V 7HQ. t: (44 171) 600 3333; f: 696 8999.

Trade association for insurance companies, with some 450 members transacting all classes of insurance business. Members account for over 90 per cent of the worldwide business of the UK insurance company market. Statistical and computing services are provided to member companies and ABI also represents its members to the public, government and other outside bodies. The Association's *Public Affairs Department* provides a large number of introductory leaflets to different aspects of insurance.

1712. **ABI Statistical Service**. £117.50. Includes:

- *Insurance Statistics* a. Summary figures on long-term and general business insurance, investments, balance of payments and related figures from other sources such as the Family Expenditure Survey and other Government publications.
- *Long-Term Business Statistics.* a. Most series are given for a five-year period.
- *Quarterly New Long-Term Business* q.
- *Sources of New Premium Income.* a.
- *UK Market Statistics.* a. Estimate of total premium income of UK insurance industry. Figures include all companies authorised in the UK, Lloyds, Mutual Clubs and Associations and Friendly Societies.
- *Catalogue of Statistical Sources.* First section gives details of all known sources of statistical information about UK insurance and insurers. Second section is a series of appendices giving statistical information mentioned earlier in the catalogue. Both sections are updated at regular intervals.
- *British Insurers' International Committee* 'The Joint Committee of the Association of British Insurers, Lloyd's, the International Group of P&I Clubs and the British Insurance (Atomic Energy) Committee. The BIIC is also the National Association member of the Comité Européen des Assurances.' *Bulletin*.

(42) #674 Association of Consulting Actuaries 1 Wardrobe Place, London EC4V 5AH. t: (44 171) 236 5514; f: 236 1889. *Annual Report*; *Membership List*.

'Draws its membership from individual consulting actuaries working in over 50 consulting firms ... The major part of the members' work is as advisers to UK pension funds with assets approaching £350 billion and a total membership of over 11 million ... A particularly important area in which our members are active in advice is in connection with mergers and acquisitions, and the subsequent rationalisation of the pension arrangements already created by the companies concerned. It is not always appreciated that the sums at stake in negotiations of this kind can be very substantial, compared with the purchase considerations.'

(43) #675 British Insurance and Investment Brokers' Association

14 Bevis Marks, London EC3A 7NT. t: (44 171) 623 9043; f: 626 9676.

Formed to represent both insurance brokers and independent financial advisers.

1713. **The Broker**. *Lloyd's of London Press.* q. £12. 'Provides news and views important to the insurance broking market.'

1714. **Directory of Investment Brokers**. a. £35.

- *United Kingdom Credit Insurance Brokers' Committee*

(44) #676 Chartered Institute of Loss Adjusters Manfield House, 376 Strand, London WC2R 0LR. t: (44 171) 836 6482; f: 836 0340.

(45) #677 Chartered Insurance Institute 20 Aldermanbury, London EC2V 7HY. t: (44 171) 606 3835; f: 726 0131. *Annual Report*; *Occasional Papers.*

'Primary objective is to promote efficiency and improvement in the practice of insurance among members engaged or employed in that activity. It does this by providing a wide range of educational and training activities, and by setting high standards of ethical behaviour. In addition to this, it provides a host of services from which members derive substantial benefit. . . . The CII Library . . . holds one of the largest collections of insurance books in the world as well as a range of audio and video cassettes, periodicals and journals. . . . It publishes an annual insurance reading list. . . . It also publishes detailed bibliographies on specific subjects. Updates to these lists appear in the CII Journal.'

1715. **CII Journal**. bi-m. £18. Provides information on CII activities and articles on matters of interest to insurance people.

Directly or indirectly associated with the Institute are:

- *College of Insurance* 'Provides an extensive range of introductory and technical courses and a programme of conferences and seminars.'
- *Insurance Institute of London* 'A local institute of the Chartered Insurance Institute. Membership is available to those engaged or employed in insurance.'

1716. **Journal of the Insurance Institute of London**. a. £5.

- *Society of Fellows* Founded in 1986.

1717. **Journal of the Society of Fellows**. s-a. £10. Contains articles about insurance, the law, and marketing as they pertain to insurance, reinsurance, and financial services at the postgraduate level.

- *Society of Financial Advisers* 'Marketing financial services in the 1990s is a highly demanding and complex business requiring wide ranging knowledge and skills. The public increasingly expects financial advisers to be educated to a recognised professional level and by law financial advisers must now offer 'best advice' to their clients. The

Securities and Investments Board and other regulatory authorities are also pressing for higher educational and ethical standards. That is why the Chartered Insurance Institute has responded to the urgent need for a professional body within the industry by establishing the Society of Financial Advisers.'

- *Society of Technicians in Insurance*
- *Worshipful Company of Insurers* About 420 members, of which some 350 are Liverymen.

(46) #678 Corporation of Insurance and Financial Advisors 174 High Street, Guildford, Surrey GU1 3HW. t: (44 1483) 39121; f: 301847. *Newsletter* (£1.50 per issue).

'Initially formed in 1968 to combat the spate of rogue mortgage broking, the Corporation . . . has steadily grown to national proportions and is now the foremost body whose members specialise in the Financial Services Industry.'

(47) #679 Faculty of Actuaries 23 St Andrew Square, Edinburgh EH2 1AQ. t: (44 131) 220 4555; f: 220 2280.

1718. **Transactions of the Faculty of Actuaries**. 2–3/year. £9/issue.

(48) #680 Institute of Actuaries Staple Inn Hall, High Holborn, London WC1V 7QJ. t: (44 171) 242 0106; f: 405 2482. *Library* Napier House, 4 Worcester Street, Oxford OX1 2AW. t: (44 1865) 794144; f: 794094. *Occasional Publications*

Founded in 1948. 'Life insurance is still the principal sphere of occupation of actuaries . . . but a growing number are becoming concerned with the application of statistical theory to the problems of general insurance (fire, accident, marine, etc.). In recent years there had been a rapid increase in the number of actuaries in whole-time consulting practice, largely as a result of the great extension of privately invested pensions schemes . . . The Stock Exchange and other fields of investment provide obvious outlets for actuarial expertise, particularly with the rapid growth of institutional investment.'

1719. **Journal of the Institute of Actuaries**. *Alden Press*. 3/year.

- *Staple Inn Actuarial Society*

(49) #681 Institute of Insurance Brokers Higham Business Centre, IIB House, Midland Road, Higham Ferrers, Northants, NN10 8DW. t: (44 1933) 410003; f: 410020. *Newsletter*.

Brokers registered under the *Insurance Brokers (Registration) Act 1977*.

1720. **Insurance Broker**. q. £12.

(50) #9682 Institute of London Underwriters 49 Leadenhall Street, London EC3A 2BE. t: (44 171) 488 2424; f: 702 3010. *Annual Report*.

'Those of us who have survived the past five years have come through one of the worst periods ever for marine insurers. Losses have been on an unprecedented scale and, sadly, some underwriters are still only now realising the true cost of business written in the late 1980s and early 1990s . . . You will have noted in the press in recent months that a number of initiatives are under way in the market to seek better ways of maintaining London's prime position in the world's insurance market. I give no secrets away when I say that the ILU, the *London Insurance and Reinsurance Market Association* (LIRMA) and the ABI (*Association of British Insurers*) now liaise regularly in order to present a more cohesive company market, while *Lloyd's, Lloyd's Insurance Brokers' Committee*, the ILU and LIRMA are also discussing ways of marketing London as a single market and streamlining market practices.'

(51) #683 Institute of Public Loss Assessors 14 Red Lion Street, Chesham, Buckinghamshire, HP5 1HB. t: (01 494) 782342; f: 774928.

'To provide a Professional Corporate Body for the protection of all the interests of those engaged in the Service of the Public as Public Loss Assessors . . . We do not publish any books regarding our products or services, partly due to the fact that the Office of Fair Trading made it very difficult for us to provide any financial information to potential clients.'

(52) #684 Insurance Industry Training Council Churchill Court, 90 Kippington Road, Sevenoaks, Kent TN13 2LL. t: (44 1732) 741124; f: 741231.

(53) #685 Insurance Technology Trade Association c/o Ivy Cottage, Newtown Common, Newbury, Berkshire RG15 9DE. t: (44 1635) 45391; f: 522910.

(54) #686 Life Insurance Association Citadel House, Chorleywood, Rickmansworth, Herts, WD3 5PF. t: (44 1923) 285333; f: 285395.

'The Association for Professional Financial Advisers . . . Founded in 1972 to foster professionalism in *your* industry. It campaigns for professional standards and recognition for all financial advisers – in other words *your* success, standing and competence. We offer

- Representation
- Professional Qualifications
- Continuing Professional Development
- Support Services.'

(55) #687 Lloyd's Aviation Underwriters' Association Lloyd's Building, Lime Street, London EC3M 7DQ. t: (44 171) 327 4045; f: 327 4711.

(56) #688 Lloyd's Motor Underwriters' Association Irongate

House, Dukes Place, London EC3A 7LP. t: (44 171) 626 7006; f: 929 1224.

(57) #689 Lloyd's of London One Lime Street, London EC3M 7HA. *Public Affairs* t: (44 171) 623 7100; f: 626 2389. *Information Centre* t: (44 171) 623 7100; f: 327 5599.

'Lloyd's is an insurance market unique in the world. Almost anything can be insured there . . . This business flows from all parts of the world and represents an income of some £25 million in premiums each working day. Lloyd's is not a company. It has no shareholders and accepts no corporate liability for risks insured there. Lloyd's is a society of underwriters, all of whom accept insurance risks for their personal profit or loss and are liable to the full extent of their private wealth to meet their insurance commitments' (*Brochure* 9/91).

"Suddenly, in the 1990s, everything turned sour. The vast expansion of the market in the past two decades hid serious conflicts of interest and declining standards of underwriting, and also a terrible legacy from latent asbestos and pollution risks. Instead of profits, Lloyd's faced ruinous losses which threatened to bankrupt thousands of its Names who had joined on the basis of unlimited liability and now discovered what this meant. When times were good, the occasional chicanery and the odd underwriting disaster went unnoticed. But as the losses grew larger and larger, "Utmost good faith" seemed to have disappeared in the cauldron of a perverted market riddled with insider dealing."[166]

(58) #690 Lloyd's Underwriters' Association Lloyd's Building, 1 Lime Street, London EC3M 7DQ. t: (44 171 626) 9420; f: 327 4443.

'This Association is a trade association acting solely for the marine underwriters at Lloyd's and, as such, is not in a position to supply any publications of any type.'

(59) #691 Lloyd's Underwriters' Non-Marine Association 6th Floor, Chesterfield House, 26–28 Fenchurch Street, London EC3M 3DQ. t: (44 171) 623 9191; f: 623 9390.

Listed publications are: 'Overseas taxes' (£40); 'Red book' (Two volumes, 50 per volume); 'UK policy book' (£100); 'USA/Canada policy book' (£100).

(60) #692 London Insurance and Reinsurance Market Association London Underwriting Centre, 3 Minster Court, Mincing Lane, London EC3R 7DD. t: (44 171) 617 4444; f: 617 4440.

Issues various publications, including the Seminar Papers and Reports from the biennial *International Reinsurance Seminars*

1721. **Reinsurance Statistics (Years)**. a. £30. 'London Company market figures.'

(61) #693 London Processing Centre Trinity Road, Folkestone, Kent, CT20 2RJ. t: (44 1303) 850111; f: 252 858.

'LPC is now a joint procesing centre for the *Institute of London Underwriters* (ILU) and the *London Insurance and Reinsurance Market Association* (LIRMA).'

(62) #694 Mutual Insurance Companies Association c/o The NFU Mutual & Avon Group, Tiddington Road, Stratford on Avon, CV37 7BJ. t: (44 1789) 204211; f: 202886.

(63) #695 National Union of Insurance Workers 27 Old Gloucester Street, London WC1N 3AF. t: (44 171) 405 6798; f: 404 8150.

(64) #696 The 150 Association c/o The Honorary Secretary, Eagle Star Insurance, London Commercial Centre, 82/84 Fenchurch Street, London EC3M 4ES. t: (44 171) 929 1111.

Asset-backed finance

(65) #697 Association of Mortgage Lenders PO Box 22, Honiton, Devon, EX14 0YT. t: (44 1404) 43563; f: 43091.

'In the competitive mortgage market, the centralised lenders, which can be defined as those lenders which attract business primarily from brokers and life companies and which raise finance from the wholesale money markets, see a need to have a trade body to represent their interests. While most mortgage representation is handled through the Council of Mortgage Lenders upon whose Executive Committee the AML has five representatives, there are nonetheless pertinent mortgage matters which largely reflect on centralised lenders alone.' The 1992/3 Report listed 20 members.

(66) #698 Association of Property Unit Trusts 155 Bishopsgate, Ninth Floor, London EC2M 3XY. t: (44 171) 628 6000; f: 214 1630.

The 1994 *Year Book* 'provides details of the 22 members of the Association whose assets amount to approximately £2 billion, and which span the UK, Continental Europe and North America'.

(67) #699 British Property Federation 35 Catherine Place, London SW1E 6DY. t: (44 171) 828 0111; f: 834 3442.

'The trade association of the property industry . . . Membership includes: property development companies, property investment companies, banks, insurance companies, pension funds . . . By putting forward considered and well argued views, the BPF has gained recognition as the authoritative voice of the property industry.'

(68) #700 ISVA 3 Cadogan Gate, London SW1X 0AS. t: (44 171) 235 2282; f: 235 4390. *Membership Directory* (£55, published by *Macmillan Press*).

'The professional Society for Valuers and Auctioneers.' The Society publishes a range of books.

(69) #701 Royal Institution of Chartered Surveyors 12 Great George Street, London SW1P 3AD. t: (44 171) 222 7000; f: 222 9430.

1538. **Royal Institution of Chartered Surveyors Directory (Year)**. *Macmillan Press*. a. £86.00. Two volumes: List of members, and geographical directory.

- *Building Cost Information Service*

4. Organizations: United States

(1) #702 Association of Financial Services Holding Companies 888 17th Street, NW, Suite 312, Washington, DC 20006. t: (1 202) 223 6575; f: 331 3836.

(2) #703 Financial Institutions Marketing Association 401 N Michigan Avenue, Chicago, IL 60611–4267. t: (1 312) 644 6610; f: 321 6869.

'Our members are financial services executives who feel that their performance would be enhanced by improving their marketing expertise. And because our members represent all sectors of the financial services marketplace – banks, savings institutions and credit unions – they constitute a valuable market for firms, like yours, that provide services that can help them . . . *The FIMA Bookshelf* Everything today's marketer should have on the bookshelf!'

(3) #704 Financial Managers Society 8 South Michigan Avenue, Suite 500, Chicago, IL 60603–9805. t: (800) 275 4367/(1 312) 578 1300; f: 578 1308.

'A professional society for Financial Managers of financial institutions such as thrifts, savings & loans, banks and credit unions. Our members include CFOs, treasurers, controllers, internal auditors, DP managers and operating officers. Our current membership is over 2,100 individuals.'

1723. **Financial Institutions Internal Audit Manual**. a. $465. 'In eight parts: I. The function of internal auditing in financial institutions; II. Lending; III. Retail Operations; IV. Financial Audits; V. Trust; VI. Corporate; VII. Compliance; VIII. Information Management.'

1724. **FMS Update**. bi-w. $305. 'Covers the latest accounting and regulatory information, as well as current news and trends related to financial institutions. Two important regular grids are *Regulatory Checklist* (pending regulations from FDIC, Federal Reserve Board, OCC, and OTS) and *Accounting Issues Report* (priorities from AICPA, EITF, FASB, FDIC, FFIEC, FRB, OCC, OTS and SEC).'

(4) #705 Financial Services Volunteer Corps 425 Lexington Avenue, New York, NY 10017–3909. t: (1 212) 455 7200; f: 983 9847.

(5) #706 Financial Women's Association of New York 215 Park Avenue S, Suite 2010, New York, NY 10003. t: (1 212) 533 2141; f: 982 3008.

(6) #707 National Association of Credit Card Merchants 217 N Seacrest Boulevard, Box 400, Boynton Beach, FL 33425. t: (1 407) 737 8500; f: 737 5800.

'Provides over 3500 companies and banks with manuals, a monthly newsletter, fraud-blocker databases and consulting services – all focused on credit card problems.'

1725. **Directory of All Prison and Jail Addresses and Zip Codes**. l. $505.50. **diskette**. $1515. 'Federal, state, county, municipal . . . You'll never know that the order coming from or going to "Suite 444, 123 Main Street" is really an inmate in Cell 444, State Prison, 123 Main Street unless you screen all orders against (this Directory).'

1726. **Directory of Mail Drop Addresses and Zip Codes**. l. $605.50. **diskette**. $2535.

Banks

(7) #708 American Bankers Association 1120 Connecticut Avenue NW, Washington, DC 20077–5760. *Customer Service* t: (800) 338 0626/(1 202) 663 5087; f: 663 7543.

'ABA members are committed to shaping the future of banking, managing change and positioning their industry to succeed in an increasingly competitive financial services industry . . . ABA's banker leadership and staff deal in depth with all the issues affecting the industry, including the condition of the industry, compliance and the regulatory burden, credit unions, housing, marketing, taxation, legal accounting, agriculture, trust, securities, economics and postal issues. In cooperation with state bankers associations, ABA's nationwide grassroots network can be quickly mobilized to communicate with Congress, the federal government and the general public on matters critical to the entire industry.

Your financial institution must do everything it can to avoid hiring those who have been convicted of *any* criminal offence involving acts of dishonesty or breach of trust. . . . Now you can fulfill these legal obligations by using the most thorough and reliable program available: *The ABA Fingerprint Service.* Through this unique service, administered by the ABA in association with the FBI, your institution simply submits fingerprint cards and vital statistics of each newly hired employee to the ABA. . . . (And the Bureau finds a criminal record or "hit" on approximately *eight percent of all cards submitted*!).

ABA offers more than 400 different products, from books and periodicals to information services and sophisticated software. We also sponsor dozens of national conferences and schools, and present more than 1,000 courses through our educational arm, the *American Institute of Banking.*'

1727. **ABA Bank Compliance**. q. $295. Provides information on legislative and regulatory changes, what they mean for banks, and how to satisfy new requirements. The quarterly issues are supplemented by monthly issues of the *Legislative and Regulatory Advisory*, and of the *Executive Update*, giving 'a concise and efficient "brief" of important changes and activities, proposed and finalised, on all legislative and regulatory matters'.

1728. **ABA Bank Security**. m. $210. 'The ideal resource for keeping up with the latest news and trends in physical security, internal/external crimes, and information security . . . Plus you'll get thorough analyses and tips for prevention following every news piece . . . insights from leading industry consultants . . . and input from the staff of relevant federal agencies *that you can't find anywhere else!*'

1729. **ABA Bankers News**. bi-w. $96. 'For everyone in your bank – especially CEOs, managers and compliance officers.'

1730. **ABA Banking Journal**. *Simmons-Boardman Publishing Corporation*. m. $25. **online**. Provides a current look at trends, products and developments in financial services.

1731. **ABA Directory of Trust Banking**. *Polk*. a. $295.

1732. **ABA Key to Routing Numbers**. s-a. $59. 'Official list of all US routing and transit numbers includes all financial institutions – banks, savings and loans, and credit unions – with their routing numbers and city and state locations (over 60,000 entries).'

1733. **ABA Management Update of Personal Trust & Private Banking**. bi-m. $200. Compendium of articles written by industry leaders, academicians, and management consultants, providing information on management issues, industry trends, and reports on innovative bank programs in trust and private banking.

1734. (Year) **Bank Card Industry Report**. a. $895. 'Features dozens of tables and graphs on bank card activities, segmented by bank size and type of card offered. Plus, the industry's only cumulative analysis of five years of VISA and MasterCard statistics, as well as in-depth analyses.'

1735. **Bank Directors Briefing**. m. Newsletter offered only through bank CEOs. 'Nearly 1,000 banks like yours now subscribe, to help their board members stay abreast of what's happening in banking.'

1736. (Year) **Bank Insurance Survey**. a. $135. 'Compare the limits, premiums and deductibles of your bank's most critical insurance policies with those of other banks of the same asset size – and with the entire banking industry. Hundreds of banks contributed to the survey, along with the *FBI* and the *Surety Association of America*.'

1737. **Bank Operations Bulletin**. m. $150. Provides current information on the multitude of industry developments and changes in regulations, operational techniques, systems and procedures, and standards.

1738. **Bank Personnel News**. m. $150. Reports on developments in banking, private industry, and the Equal Employment Opportunity Commission, National Labor Relations Board, Congress, the federal courts, and other government agencies.

1739. (Year) **Check Fraud Survey**. a. $97. 'Help you spot trends in check fraud losses, discover how your bank compares with your competitors, and find ways to reduce losses. Based on a nationwide survey conducted by ABA.'

1740. **Commercial Lending Review**. *Institutional Investor*. q. $105. **online**. 'Practical commercial lending guidance and how-to techniques in credit and financial analysis.'

1741. **Consumer Credit Delinquency Bulletin**. q. $160. Features graphs and tables reporting monthly consumer loan delinquency rates and average dollar amounts on both a national and a state-by-state basis, for ten types of loan: personal, home equity, home improvement, automobile (direct and indirect), bank card, cheque credit etc.

1742. **D-Linq. diskette**. m. 'ABA's Delinquency Database Service . . . brings you month-end year-end delinqency ratios by state and loan category.'

1743. **Employee Benefits Quarterly**. q. $200. Designed for Employee Benefits Trust Professionals. Provides information on pension and tax law changes, DOL and IRS regulations, court rulings, liability developments, and reporting and participant recordkeeping requirements. In addition, covers emerging issues, such as global custody and fiduciary environmental liability.

1744. **Federal Advertising and Marketing Law Guide**. l. $295/$220. All relevant federal laws and regulations for bank marketing and advertising culled from more than a dozen sources.

1745. **Financial Services Industry Trends**. bi-m. $200. 'Helps you confront the difficult industry challenges bankers face today in trust operations and securities processing: risk management . . . shortened settlement cycle . . . changing regulations . . . mutual fund processing . . . system conversions and upgrades . . . depository developments . . . globalization of the securities markets . . . training and staff development . . . and more!'

1746. (Year) **Home Equity Lines of Credit Report**. a. $253. Includes types of collateral that bankers hold, typical duration and repayment schedules, and loan-to-value ratios; statistics on the number of banks offering home equity lines of credit, the number of dollars they have loaned, and their profitability.

1747. (Year) **Instalment Credit Report**. a. $269. Comprehensive data on instalment loans, segmented by bank size, and including tables, graphs and charts covering areas such as financing terms, loan delinquencies and losses, and expense elements.

1748. **ISO Register**. l. $225. 'Sanctioned by the *International Organization for Standardization* (ISO) and maintained by ABA, this Register is the official list of unique credit and debit card Issuer Identification Numbers (IINs) throughout the world . . . Available only to issuers listed in the Register.'

1749. **Journal of Agricultural Lending**. q. $90.

1750. **Payment Systems Strategies**. q. $245. 'A quarterly monograph on assessing and implementing retail delivery systems.'

1751. **Retail Banking Digest**. bi-m. $200. 'One-stop source for all the vital news and views you need in the consumer banking industry.'

1752. **Retail Banking Report**. a. $180. Enables comparison of a bank's retail performance, operations, and marketing with those of commercial banks nationwide.

1753. **Securities Processing Digest**. q. $200. 'An Operations Guide to Investment Instruments & Procedures'. Each issue contains complete descriptive and operational information on one of the nonstandard securities, like CMOs or Auction Rate Securities. Contains 'information you cannot get from any other single source'.

1754. **Statistical Information on the Financial Services Industry**. a. $150. The 1993 edition covered 1982 to 1992/3. 'Compilation of text, tables and graphs describing the banking industry and other sectors of the Financial Services Industry . . . It provides a thorough analysis of the structure, status and changes in markets for financial products and services, plus new information on demographic and financial services market data, and consumer attitudes and trends.'

1755. **Trust & Financial Advisor**. q. $245. 'Provides technical information on fiduciary law, tax law, financial planning, and investment management. Each issue will also: Profile a leader in the trust industry; Give you important updates on ABA trust programs, schools, training products – and the ICB *Certified Trust and Financial Advisor* (CTFA) program; Feature a networking section where you can find information about recent promotions and other news concerning CTFAs and graduates of the *National Graduate Trust School*.'

1756. **Trust Letter**. m. $210. Provides current information on national legislation and regulation that impact trust and investment businesses.

- *ABA Center for Bank Training* 'Founded in 1993 . . . works as a partner to support the in-house training needs of ABA member banks and Service Member companies.'
- *ABA Education Foundation* 'Fiscal illiteracy affects everyone, from consumers to the bankers who serve them. Now you can join industry peers who are fighting the problem of fiscal illiteracy through consumer education . . . Through programs like the Foundation-spon-

sored *Personal Economics Program* . . . volunteers from across the country work with educators to teach people in their communities – youngsters, teens and adults – about banks, banking services, and personal financial management.'

- *Accredited Standards Committee, X9 On Financial Services* This Committee is 'comprised of major banks, retailers, suppliers, government agencies, trade associations and vendors . . . X9 is the industry leader in pooling technical expertise to develop accepted standards for all facets of the financial arena.' Copies of the standards are available from the *Washington Publishing Company.*

1757. The **Standard**. q. $112. 'Keep up to date on the standards area . . . The Standard is fast becoming the reference of choice for everyone connected with bank operations.'

- *American Financial Skylink* Satellite educational TV network. 'As a subscriber, you'll receive two hours of banking specific programming every week. And, because you record the programs from your satellite dish, they're available to you and your staff whenever you need them.'
- *American Institute of Banking* The largest industry-sponsored adult education program in the world. Charged with fulfilling the mission of the ABA by providing banking-specific educational and training programmes. It is a nationwide organization of more than 400 ABA-chartered chapters and study groups. Nearly 200,000 bankers annually enroll in AIB programs.
- *Bank Marketing Association* Affiliate of ABA and a 'leading provider of marketing education, information and training to the financial services industry . . . When you join BMA you . . . get priority treatment (and discounts) at BMA's *Information Center*, where you can access real-life marketing plans and programs, actual samples of brochures, survey and job descriptions, competitive insights, statistics and demographic information – and much more.'

1758. **Analysis of (Year) Bank Marketing Expenditures**. a. $130. Covers bank spendings on advertising, public relations, sales promotion, training and research.

1759. **Bank Marketing**. m. $60. **online**. Explores all aspects of retail and corporate bank marketing. Feature articles include informative how-tos, banker-written case histories, and updates on "hot topics" in bank marketing.

- *Center for Banking Information* t: (1 202) 663 5221; f: 828 4535. 'No matter what your connection with the banking industry, ABA's Center for Banking Information (CBI) is your first source for answers and information. Your request will be processed with the utmost care and timeliness, and it will be held in confidence. Our complimentary *Ready Reference* service is ready for any questions, and our friendly and knowledgeable staff knows just where to look . . . either by quickly scanning the files, or conducting a thorough data search for you.

You'll also want to know about our financial database service – the *Banking Information Source* (BIS), now being administered by University Microfilms Inc. (*UMI*). UMI, a leader in information technology, promises bankers like you even better access to the research expertise you've relied on over the years. UMI is combining ABA's old *Banking Literature Index* (BLI) and BMA's *Financial Industry Information Service* (FINIS) into a more powerful database, and adding a CD-ROM format and full-text search capabilities.

As an ABA member, however, you can still call on CBI staff to serve all your information needs, including database searches. You may also access these databases at the Center, whose other services include quick reference calls, *FYI Research Kits* (... a collection of recent banking articles, book chapters, perhaps a brochure about a new publication or meeting – to help you gain an overview of areas of special interest to you ($65 each)...), delivery of timely articles, book rentals, and more. CBI is *your* information center, and you can call or stop in anytime. In addition to our electronic capabilities, you'll also find theses from the *Stonier Graduate School of Banking*, more than 900 banking-related periodicals, and over 70,000 books on banking and the financial arena, including a fine banking law collection.'

- *Center for Community Development* 'Designed to help the banking industry increase its lending to minorities and low- and moderate-income communities.'
- *Center for Legal and Regultory Compliance* 'As the definition of "compliance" has expanded, and compliance responsibilities cut across so many functional areas of the bank, ABA has responded by establishing the Centre ... to serve your bank even more effectively by:
    - Coordinating ABA's compliance initiatives in one area, to reflect the central significance of compliance in banking, as well as our strong and focused commitment to facilitating and strengthening your bank's compliance efforts
    - Positioning the Center as the singular, primary resource within the banking industry for dealing with compliance issues, expanding the breadth of our scope beyond traditional areas, and providing greater depth in our level of resources products and staff expertise
    - Targeting our efforts to the broad range of individuals within the bank for whom compliance responsibilities exist, so that we can meet the specific and varied needs of all the relevant executive, professional and support staff.'
- *Corporate Trust Associates* 'As a member ... you'll enjoy these benefits: Recognition as a professional in the national organization that speaks for the entire corporate trust industry; *Network News*, the newsletter (three issues per year) that gives you details on legislation, regulation, regional developments, major court cases, tax issues and other matters essential to your job; *CT Membership Directory*, published annually, provides the names, addresses and phone numbers of

every CT Banker and Affiliate Member . . . The *Certified Corporate Trust Specialist* (CCTSTM) program is designed to recognize the knowledge and expertise you have accumulated over the years by managing account relationships or operations functions. To earn the CCTS designation, you must pass a rigorous examination on the core subjects of corporate trust, account administration and management, and systems and operations.'

- *CUSIP* [Committee on Uniform Securities Identification Procedures] 'The acknowledged industry standard for proper identification and description of corporate, municipal, government, mortgage-backed, private placement and Canadian and Mexican numbers. CUSIP is a system of universally accepted nine-character codes that allows you to: expedite transactions . . . automate front and back office operations . . . reduce clerical errors . . . speed deliveries and transfers . . . lower your programming and storage costs . . . print out results of "searches" . . . and more.'

CUSIP products and services produced by the *CUSIP Service Bureau* include:

1760. **CUSIP Corporate Directory and Updating Service**. 'Provides CUSIP numbers and standard descriptions on all corporate issues and issuers (municipals excluded).'

1761. **CUSIP Digest of Changes**. 'Affords quick access to information on capital changes, mergers, acquisitions, and other corporate changes.'

1762. **CUSIP International-CINS**. 'The *International Securities Identification Directory* (ISID) is an alphabetical compilation of more than 200,000 non-North American securities. Each is listed with its nine-character CUSIP of CINS (CUSIP International Numbering System) and is cross-referenced to most major National Security Identification Numbers.'

1763. **CUSIP Master Directory and Updating Service**. 'The only printed source of nine-character identification numbers and standard descriptions on over two million domestic and Canadian securities. The Directory gives you a uniform number and description that is used in all phases of securities dealings.'

1764. **CUSIP Mortgage-Backed Services**. 'Contains all outstanding mortgage-backed issues and pre-assignment of new issues issued by the various federal agencies: GNMA, FNMA, FMAC.'

1765. **CUSIP-PPNs**. 'The only source for private placement numbers (PPNs), containing information on more than 90,000 privately-placed issues held by the insurance industry.'

- *Community Bankers Council* 'ABA is committed to meeting the needs of banks of *all* sizes. And, because our membership includes a large number of community banks, we offer a full range of products and services specially designed to help you . . . Meeting *your* specific needs as a community banker is the major focus of the Community Bankers Council.'

- *Corporation for American Banking* For-profit subsidiary offering special products and services to help enhance fee income and cut costs.
- *Stonier Graduate School of Banking* Held at the *University of Delaware*. 'The preeminent graduate banking school, and the only banking school sponsored by the ABA.'

(i) #*709 Institute of Certified Bankers* Suite 600, 1120 Connecticut Avenue, NW, Washington, DC 20036.

National nonprofit association of certified professionals in the financial services industry. 'The *Certified Regulatory Compliance Manager* (CRCM) option enables you to become part of the nation's leading group of bank compliance managers. You'll have the attention and respect of management and your peers. And you'll get ongoing benefits to keep you on top of changes that affect your bank's compliance program. The rewards of certification are abundant, but the requirements are rigorous, including a comprehensive certification examination. To prepare for it, you may use ABA's award-winning *CRCM Examination Student Handbook* ($190).

Due to recent changes in the *Bank Protection Act* (Regulation P), security officers are now held personally responsible for establishing and monitoring a formal security program in financial institutions. But, when you become a *Certified Financial Services Security Professional*... both you and your bank can be certain you are fully competent in all areas regulated by the Bank Protection Act. The CFSSP designation tells management that it can rely on you.'

(8) #710 American Association of Bank Directors 4719 Hampden Lane, Suite 300, Bethesda, MD 20814. t: (1 301) 951 0583; f: 654 1733. *Newsletter*. ($15).

1766. **Directors Handbook**. l. $295/$125. 'Updated quarterly . . . contains information you must know to fulfill your fiduciary responsibilities, meet the business judgement rule, and protect yourself against lawsuits.'

1767. (Year) **Survey of Bank and Savings Institution Boards of Directors**. a. $75. 'Survey sent to 1,000 randomly-selected chairmen of bank and savings institution boards of directors. It was designed to develop data on current board structures and committees, causes of board resignations, director compensation and benefits, director indemnification and insurance, and board edutcation programs.'

(9) #711 American Society of Bank Directors PO Box 2739, Alexandria, VA 22301–0739. t: (1 703) 683 3030.

(10) #712 Bank Administration Institute One North Franklin Street, Chicago, IL 60606. t: (1 312) 553 4600; f: 683 2426.

1768. **Bank Fraud**. m. $189.

1769. **Bank Management**. m. $59. **online**.

(11) #713 Bankers' Round Table 805 Fifteenth Street NW, Washington, DC 20005. t: (1 202) 289 4322; f: 785 2605. *Research Reports.*

'Promotes the business of banking and encourages the development of sound banking and financial policies and practices. Membership... is reserved for the 125 largest banking companies in the US. The senior executives of those companies serve as representatives to the Roundtable.'

(12) #714 Consumer Bankers Association 1000 Wilson Blvd, Suite 3012, Arlington, VA 22209–3908. t: (1 703) 276 1750; f: 528 1290.

'The Association for Retail Banks and Thrift Institutions.'

1770. **Compliance Examinations Update**. *Warren Gorham Lamont*. bi-m. $278. Update service written by two lawyers covers the latest compliace violations in the industry. Offers helpful curing techniques to protect a compliance program.

(13) #715 Independent Bankers Association of America Washington Office, One Thomas Circle, NW, Suite 950, Washington, DC 20005–5802. t: (1 202) 659 8111; f: 659 9216.

'The IBAA is the only national trade association which exclusively represents the interests of the nation's community financial institutions... IBAA's *Corporate Associate Membership* program was established as a means for companies and firms to effectively market their products and services to community banks.

During the past year, we successfully fought off one of the greatest challenges to community banking, our diversified financial system and to Main Street America. The administration's radical financial consolidation and concentration legislative proposals would have wrought the most sweeping changes in our nation's financial system in our lifetimes. The proposals were aimed at consolidating the financial services industry and restructuring our economy by permitting commercial firms to own banks. The administration proposals for so-called financial reform would have cut consumers' deposit insurance, undercutting your ability to gather deposits in your community and, in turn, make the loans that are necessary for your community's long-term economic growth. Other aspects of the administration proposal would have opened the door to the common ownership of banks and securities firms (repeal of Glass-Steagall), mandated nationwide interstate insurance branching with no role for individual states in the matter and implemented regulatory restructuring that would have centralized regulatory and supervisory power in the U.S. Treasury.

Collectively, the administration plan posed one of the biggest threats to the economic well-being of Main Street, USA, in this half-century. Early on, IBAA, representing the nation's community bankers, recognised this threat and began systematically and strategically responding to it... The Congress rejected all of the administration's reform proposals' (From the *1991 Annual Report*).

1771. **Independent Banker**. m. $25. Circulation of 10,000.

(14) #716 Institute of International Bankers 299 Park Avenue, 38th Floor, New York, NY 10171. t: (1 212) 421 1611; f: 421 1119.

Trade association engaged in lobbying on behalf of foreign banks doing business in the USA.

(15) #717 National Association for Bank Cost & Management Accounting PO Box 458, Northbrook, IL 60065–0458. t: (1 708) 272 4233; f: 272 6445.

1772. **Journal of Bank Cost & Management Accounting**. 3/year. $75. **online**. Covers issues affecting cost and management accounting in the financial services industry.

(16) #718 National Association of Urban Bankers 1010 Wayne Avenue, Suite 1210, Silver Spring, MD 20910. t: (1 301) 589 2141; f: 495 2914.

(17) #719 National Independent Bank Equipment and Systems Association 1411 Peterson, Park Ridge, IL 60068. t: (1 708) 825 8419; f: 825 8445.

(18) #720 Robert Morris Associates [The Association of Bank Loan and Credit Officers] One Liberty Place, Suite 2300, Philadelphia, PA 19103–7398. t: (1 215) 851 9100; f: 851 9206.

Seeks to improve the principles and practice of commercial lending and credit functions, loan administration and asset management in commercial banks. RMA publishes a range of manuals and guides, eg: 'The business of banking for bank directors' (1994, $20); 'A credit risk-rating system: Tool for managing credit risk' (1994, $45); 'Bankruptcy concepts: A desk reference for lenders' (1994, $55); 'Know your customer: A guide to finding information sources' (1992, $24); 'Yes you can exchange commercial credit information: Some regulations you need to know about' (1993, $5).

1773. **Annual Statement Studies**. a. $110. 'When it comes to making a credit decision, you can go by your instincts . . . Or you can go by this book . . . For more than 70 years, thousands of commercial lending and credit professionals have used the *Statement Studies* regularly to assist them in reaching sound loan decisions. It provides composite balance sheets and income data on industries of all types with which you can easily compare the data of your specific borrowing customer, client or prospect . . . (It) includes data for 409 different industries, identified by titles and SIC numbers. This information is a result of data supplied from financial statements of borrowing customers of RMA member banks.'

1774. **Commercial Lending Newsletter**. m. $35. Presents articles on commercial lending-related topics, including loan officer productivity, management issues, statistical data and problem loans.

1775. **Credit Information Exchange Directory**. a. $25. 'The names, phone numbers, and addresses of more than 1,500 bankers who are directly involved in the exchange of commercial credit information.'

1776. **Journal of Commercial Lending**. m. $49.50. 'The only monthly publication devoted exclusively to commercial lending and credit.'

(19) #721 United States Council on International Banking c/o 1 World Trade Center, Suite 1963, New York, NY 10048. t: (1 212) 466 3352; f: 432 0544.

Banks involved in international operations.

Savings institutions

(20) #722 American League of Financial Institutions 1709 New York Avenue, NW, Suite 201, Washington, DC 20006. t: (1 202) 628 5624.

Federal and state chartered minority savings and loan associations in twenty-five states and the District of Columbia.

(21) #723 Credit Union Executives Society 6410 Enterprise Lane, Suite 300, Madison, WI 53719–1143; PO Box 14167, Madison, WI 53714–0167. t: (1 608) 271 2664; f: 271 2303.

'*Reinventing Ourselves by Reinventing CUES* It's been a year since the Credit Union Executives Society (CUES) announced its decision to refocus its efforts on the professional development needs of senior credit union executives. Since that time, CUES board members and professional staff have moved quickly to develop plans for what will soon become the most comprehensive career enhancement opportunities in the credit union movement – CUES Executive Development Programs . . . There are many challenges ahead for the credit union movement. We must continually reinvent ourselves as professionals and as leaders if we – and our credit unions – are to experience continued success into the 21st century' (*1994 Summer/Fall CUES Catalog*).

1777. **Credit Union Management**. m. $60. **online**. 'The award-winning monthly publication with management, marketing and operations information for your entire credit union management staff.'

1778. **Credit Union Director**. q. $38.

- *Financial Marketing Association*
- *Financial Supplies Forum* 'The critical networking link between CUES members and suppliers of credit union products and services. Membership benefits include *CUES Membership Directory* listing 3,000+ CUES members, along with FSF member firms.'

(22) #724 CUNA & Affiliates PO Box 431, Madison, WI 53701–0431. t: (1 608) 231 4000; f: 231 4370.

'As a national resource for the credit union movement, CUNA and Affiliates provides products and services specifically tailored for leagues and credit unions. Information services, education and training, governmental affairs, financial services and research and planning are all available through affiliation with the Credit Union System.'

1779. **Credit Union Executive**. bi-m. $99. **online**.

1780. **Credit Union Magazine**. m. $30. Circulation: 47,500.

1781. **Credit Union Directors Newsletter**. m. $58.

1782. **Credit Union Manager Newsletter**. bi-w. $120.

1783. **Credit Union Newswatch**. w. $100.

(23) #725 National Association of Federal Credit Unions 3138 N Tenth Street, Arlington, VA 22201. t: (800) 336 4644/(1 703) 522 4770; f: 524 1082.

Formed in 1967 to represent federally chartered credit unions, and liaise with relevant regulatory agencies. 'As soon as major credit union regulations are proposed or issued as final, NAFCU's regulatory staff attorneys study them and write analyses explaining their potential or actual impact on credit unions. As soon as these analyses are complete, they're published along with the verbatim copies of the regs in *Regulatory Alerts* and *Final Regulations*.'

1784. **Federal Credit Union**. bi-m. $99. 'Insightful analysis through in-depth coverage of the latest events and major trends in Washington that affect credit unions.'

1785. **Update**. w. $299. 'Award-winning weekly newsletter . . . Concise, complete summary of the important events from Washington that affect credit unions.'

(24) #726 National Credit Union Management Association 4989 Rebel Trail, NW, Atlanta, GA 30327. t: (1 404) 255 6828; f: 851 1752.

'Established in 1949 for the purpose of providing management and leadership training for the Chief Financial Officer and their elected corporate directors. Membership in NCUMA has an asset threshold of ten million dollars. We currently have a list of 5,500 credit unions in the United States and 1,100 in Canada. Our publications have historically included an *Annual Statistical Analysis of US Credit Unions*, produced in conjunction with two major universities; manuals on statutory compliance with federal regulations, specifically in the area of Human Resource Management, and a monthly *Credit Union Employment and Labor Law Newsletter*.'

(25) #727 Savings & Community Bankers of America 900 19th Street, NW, Suite 400, Washington, DC 20006. t: (1 202) 857 3100; f: 296 8716.

'The national trade association for savings and community financial institutions.' *Directory of Members* (available from *Thomson Financial Publishing*).

1786. **Advisor**. m. $185. 'Provides your security officers with up-to-the-minute advice on the techniques used by criminals and methods for preventing crimes.' Including: Loan frauds; Money Laundering; Bank Secrecy Act liabilities; etc.

1787. **Corporate Finance Letter**. m. $395. Focuses on the structuring and management of consumer loans: For chief financial officers and managers.

1788. **Directors & Trustees Digest**. m. $50.

1789. **Economic Outlook**. m. $170.

1790. **Federal Guide**. l. $815. Comprehensive coverage of laws, regulations, policy statements, advisory opinions, interpretations for *Office of Thrift Supervision*; *Federal Deposit Insurance Corporation*; *Comptroller of the Currency*; *Federal Reserve Board*; *Resolution Trust Corporation*; etc.

1791. **Regulatory Report**. m. $430.

1792. **Savings & Community Banker**. m. $50. **online**.

1793. **Special Management Bulletin**. i. $130.

1794. **Supervisory Service**. l. $525. 'A standard reference to the fundamental laws and regulations governing savings institutions.'

1795. **Tax Insight**. m. $295.

1796. **Thomson Savings Directory**. *Thomson Financial Publishing*. s-a. $159. 'A one-stop, all-in-one guide to complete details on the entire savings industry. Besides being updated twice a year, the Directory is also supplemented by the *Registrar's Alert*, a leaflet that is mailed to subscribers when significant changes occur to the industry.'

1797. **Trustees & Directors Handbook**. l. $150. 'To keep your board members informed and up-to-date on their crucial corporate governance roles.'

1798. **Washington Perspective**. w. $350.

(26) #728 United States League of Savings Institutions 111 E Wacker Drive, Chicago, IL 60601–4680. t: (1 312) 644 3100; f: 644 9358.

1799. **Savings Institutions**. m. $36. **online**. Publication of interest to management and supervisory personnel at savings institutions.

1800. **Savings Institutions Sourcebook**. a.

Finance companies

(27) #729 American Financial Services Association 919 18th Street, NW, 3rd Floor, Washington, DC 20006. t: (1 202) 296 5544; f: 223 0321.

'Organized in 1916 . . . represents more than 450 companies operating more than 10,000 offices engaged in the extension of consumer credit throughout the United States.'

1801. **Consumer Finance Bulletin**. m. $95.

- *Consumer Credit Education Foundation*

(28) #730 Equipment Leasing Association of America 1300 North 17th Street, Suite 1010, Arlington, VA 22209. t: (1 703) 527 8655; f: 527 2649.

'Represents over 850 member companies to the business community, government, and the business media . . . EIA members include: independent leasing companies (38 per cent), bank leasing companies (19 per cent), financial service companies (12 per cent), captive leasing subsidiaries of manufacturing companies (10 per cent), lease brokers or packagers (6 per cent), and investment bankers (4 per cent). Another eight per cent represent the legal and accounting profession.'

1802. **Equipment Leasing Today**. 10/year. $100.

1803. **Leasing Buyer's Guide**. **diskette**. a. $150. 'Nationwide listings of key resources for the leasing industry including funding sources, accountants, appraisers, remarketers, insurance specialists, executive recruiters, and attorneys.'

1804. **State Tax Manual**. a. $155.

1805. **Who's Who in Equipment Leasing**. a. $350.

(29) #731 National Venture Capital Association 1655 N Fort Myer Drive, Suite 700, Arlington, VA 22209. t: (1 703) 351 5269; f: 351 5268. *Annual Report*; *Membership Directory*.

Founded in 1973 and comprised of over 200 professional venture capital companies.

Securities industry

(30) #732 American Stock Exchange 86 Trinity Place, New York, NY 10006–1881. *Publication Services*: t: (1 212) 306 1386; f: 306 1372. *Also* 2 London Wall Buildings, London Wall, London EC2M 5SY, UK. t: (44 171) 628 5982; f: 628 3220.

1806. **American Stock Exchange Company Guide**. $50. Manual of listing requirements, policies, procedures for corporation executives, attorneys, accountants. Periodic updates included.

1807. **American Stock Exchange Stocks, Bonds, Options and Derivatives Symbol Book**. q. The official list of Amex securities.

1808. **Amex Fact Book**. a. $15. Summarizes equity and options trading statistics, but also includes the address, telephone number and industry of every Amex company at year-end.

1809. **Electronic Symbol Book**. m. $500. ASCII electronic listing of Amex stocks, bonds and equity-based derivative securities on floppy diskette. Published as of the last business day of the month. Available from the *Market Data Services Division*: (1 212) 306 1349.

1810. **New on the Amex**. i. Two-page reports on recently listed companies. Each provides a business description and the financial profile of a new issue on the Exchange. Available only to investment professionals from *Amex Investor Relations*: (1 212) 306 1691. There is a sister *New on the ECM* of recently listed *Emerging Company Marketplace* companies, and also an *ECM Updates* service, both available under the same conditions.

1811. **Short Interest Report**. m. ASCII format floppy disc product containing the short interest positions in all stocks and equity products (e.g. warrants, rights, preferred stocks etc.), available from the *Market Reports Department*: (1 212) 306 1529. The reports are compiled from data submitted by member organizations.

1812. **Stocks, Bonds, Options and Derivatives**. q. List of Amex-traded equities, bonds, and derivatives, available from the *Amex Dividends and Rulings Department*: (1 212) 306 1469.

1813. **Weekly Bulletin**. w. $20. News of membership changes, notices, new and supplemental listings, listing removals, subscription offerings, dividends, and stockholder meetings. Contact the *Registration Department*: (1 212) 306 1442.

(31) #733 Chicago Board of Trade Market & Product Development, 141 W Jackson Boulevard, Suite 2210, Chicago, IL 60604–2994. t: (1 312) 435 3558; f: 341 3168. *European Office* 52–54 Gracechurch Street, London EC3V 0EH, UK. t: (44 171) 929 0021; f: 929 0558.

Produce a large number of introductory *Leaflets* (e.g. 'US Treasury Futures', 'Flexible Treasury Options on US Treasury Bond and Note Futures'), *Booklets* (e.g. 'Commodity Trading Manual Home Study Workbook', 'Using Interest Rate Futures in Portfolio Management', 'CBOT Financial Instruments Guide', 'Treasury Futures for Institutional Investors') and *Books* (e.g. 'Commodity Trading Manual'). The *Market Information Department* (435 3633) provides CBOT and MidAmerica Commodity Exchange commodity prices, volume numbers, cash prices and seat prices; *Market Data Services* historical price information on computer diskettes.

1814. **CBOT Databank. diskette**. Historical data on all futures and options contracts.

1815. **CBOT Research Symposium Proceedings**. q. 'Research papers and commentaries presented at the Chicago Board of Trade's four research seminars held each year.'

1816. **CBOT Statistical Annual. diskette**. a. 'Daily record of CBOT futures prices.'

1817. **Commodity Futures Trading: Bibliographies**. a. $4. 'Important writings on futures trading from books, general and trade periodicals, professional journals, and academic theses.'

(32) #734 Chicago Board Options Exchange 400 South LaSalle Street, Chicago, IL 60605. t: (800) OPTIONS/(1 312) 786 7442; f: 786 7367. *Also* Toll-free from the UK: (0800 89 2299).

'Welcome to the *End User Computing Data Sales Department*. We compile an array of trading data to assist you with your research and market analysis while reducing your research time and costs . . . (We) offer data on the following:

- Options on over 290 stocks
- LEAPS Long-Term AnticiPation Securities (Long-term options) are listed on 37 large, well-known companies.
- S&P 100 Index (OEX) and S&P 500 Index (SPX) Short-term Options, OEX and SPX LEAPS and OEX and SPX CAPS
- Long-term and Short-term Interest Rate Options.'

Educational Materials and Literature available from the CBOE includes:

1818. **CBOE Market Statistics**. a. 'Statistical information on all products traded at the Chicago Board Options Exchange for the most current year.'

1819. **Options Bibliography**. i. '1991 revised. Compilation of information written about exchange-traded options from 1973 to 1990.'

1820. **Options Reference Manual: A Guide for Institutional Investors**. i. $25. '1991 revised. Provides an overview of the most common administrative, operational and procedural questions that arise when institutional investors consider listed options.

(33) #735 Chicago Mercantile Exchange *Office Services Department* 30 S Wacker Drive, Chicago, IL 60606–7499. t: (1 312) 930 8210; f: 466 4410. *Also* Pinnacle House, 23–26 St Dunstan's Hill, London EC3R 8Hl, UK. t: (44 171) 623 2550; f: 623 2565. *Annual Report*.

'Making the complexities of futures and futures options markets understandable is a primary goal of the Chicago Mercantile Exchange. The CME has produced a library of materials explaining various aspects of futures and options markets, individual commodity futures and options contracts and how they operate in our economic marketplace.' Examples are: 'Bibliography and information source list' ($3); 'An introduction to futures & options' ($10); 'GLOBEX executive summary' ($free); 'An introduction to interbank foreign exchange and Rolling Spot' ($0.50); 'Russell 2000 Index Futures & Options' ($0.50). The CME also market videotapes: e.g. 'The financial marketplace' ($25); 'Institutional trading strategies' ($10); 'Technical analysis' (Six tapes: $350).

1821. **CME Rule Book**. l. $75.

1822. **Daily Bulletin**. d. Two parts: *Domestic* $840; *Foreign* $1268. Each part can be subscribed to in one or more of four sections: Agricultural Products; Currency Products; Interest Rate Products; Equity Products.

1823. **Special Executive Reports**. v. $150.

(34) #736 Coffee, Sugar & Cocoa Exchange 4 World Trade Center, New York, NY 10048, USA. t: (1 212) 938 2800; f: 524 9863.

(35) #737 Corporate Transfer Agents Association PO Box 2000, Rahway, NJ 07065. t: (1 212) 612 5845.

(36) #738 Depository Trust Company 55 Water Street, New York, NY 10041. t: (1 212) 898 1200; f: 898 3189.

Most corporate securities, as well as municipal bonds, are immobilized at the DTC. Depositories, in contrast to clearing corporations, immobilize physical securities and provide book-entry transfer and settlement services for their members.

(i) *#739 National Securities Clearing Corporation* t: (1 212) 412 8400

(37) #740 Emerging Markets Traders Association 63 Wall Street, 20th Floor, New York, NY 10005. t: (1 212) 293 5000; f: 293 5039.

'The documentation produced by EMTA is generally made available to the marketplace free of charge. There are, however, fees charged to participate in our automated trade confirmation and matching system and multilateral netting facility.'

(38) #741 Forex USA c/o Bank Polska, Kasa Obiekisa, 470 Park Avenue South, New York, NY 10016. t: (1 212) 725 8834; f: 213 2971.

Members are foreign exchange traders and dealers.

(39) #742 Futures Industry Association 2001 Pennsylvania Avenue, NW, Suite 600, Washington, DC 20006–1807. t: (1 202) 466 5460; f: 296 3184.

1824. **Futures Industry**. bi-m. $24.

(i) *#743 Futures Industry Institute* t: (1 202) 223 1528; f: 296 3184.

'Now you have access to data you never had access to before . . . For the first time, one source for a futures and options database is available to futures industry professionals and academics, and other researchers. Available data include: Tick data on US and selected non-US futures and options; Daily data on US and selected non-US futures . . . Over two dozen worldwide exchanges are contributing data to this project.'

1825. **Futures and Options Fact Book**. q. $140. **diskette**. $140. 'The most comprehensive guide to world futures trading available.'

(40) #744 Managed Futures Association 540 Cowper Street, Suite 101, Palo Alto, CA 94301. t: (1 415) 325 4500; f: 325 4944. *Newsletter.*

'Established March 1991 as a joint effort by the Directors of the *Managed Futures Trade Association* and the *National Association of Futures Trading Advisors* . . . Dedicated to protecting and advancing the broad interests of its members by representing the industry to regulatory and legislative governing bodies and to the investing public.

With members worldwide, the MFA represents the full spectrum of the managed futures industry. Comprising our diverse membership are: Commodity Trading Advisors, Commodity Pool Operators, Futures Commission Merchants, Introducing Brokers, Associated Persons, Account Executives, and futures exchanges, as well as those who provide products and services to the managed futures industry.'

1826. **Derivatives**. q. $25.

1827. **MFA Journal Encore**. bi-a. $25. 'Reporting of current issues in the managed futures industry.'

(41) #745 Midwest Stock Exchange [Chicago Stock Exchange] 440 South LaSalle Street, Chicago, IL 60605. t: (1 312) 663 2222; f: 663 2396.

1828. **Chicago Stock Exchange Guide**. *CCH*. m. $395.

(i) *#746 Mortgage-Backed Securities Corporation*

Compares and nets trades in mortgage-backed securities.

(42) #747 Minneapolis Grain Exchange 130 Grain Exchange, Minneapolis, MN 55415. t: (1 612) 338 6212; f: 339 1155.

(43) #748 NASDAQ 1735 K Street, NW, Washington, DC 20006. t: (1 202) 728 8039; f: 785 1804 *and* 33 Whitehall Street, 10th Floor, New York, NY 10004. t: (1 212) 858 4000; f: 858 3980. *Also* NASDAQ International, 43 London Wall, London EC2M 5TB, UK. t: (44 171) 374 6969; f: 374 4488. *Publications* National Association of Securities Dealers, NASD MediaSource, PO Box 9403, Gaithersburg, MD 20898–9403, USA. t: (1 301) 590 6578; f: 590 6368.

'In two decades, Nasdaq has transformed securities trading into a 21st century industry. With its international network of computers and telecommunications Nasdaq has moved beyond the limitations of a centralised trading floor and become the best-performing major stock market in the world. The core of Nasdaq's success is its competing market makers. They do more than trade a company's stock, they sponsor it – discussing it with investors and their advisors and issuing reports on the companies in which they make markets. That's what brings the world's top companies to Nasdaq. And there are more US and non-US companies on Nasdaq than on all the other US stock markets combined – more than 4,000 in total. Nasdaq is now the second largest stock market in the US and accounts for more than half of all equity shares traded in the US every day.

Nasdaq provides you with three ways of keeping track of your stocks. The first is *Informm*, an on-line trading information database that allows you to receive current and historical data about your company's stock on your own personal computer . . . As well as watching daily trading activity through Informm, you will receive a monthly written *Summary of Activity*, giving daily trading figures for your stock, a summary of the monthly trading totals, and a list of the active market makers in your stock. Nasdaq will also send you *customized reports*, including a record of trading activity for your stock, a peer comparison and analysis of liquidity and volatility. The *Nasdaq Financial Executives Journal* is published once a quarter, and focuses on a particular investor relations topic. It includes interviews with industry experts, case studies and company strategies. The Journal is also provided as a summary on an audio cassette, which includes live interviews.

Nasdaq regularly produces *Investor Handbooks* to increase knowledge and interest in Nasdaq stocks. The books are published in conjunction with *Moody's Investors Service*, and distributed among the broker community . . . The *Nasdaq Annual Report Showcase* is produced as a special advertising section placed in *The Economist* magazine where investors can read a short description of Nasdaq-listed companies and then order the annual reports they want free of charge . . . Once a quarter Nasdaq publishes the *Nasdaq International Magazine*, which provides an informed look at news items of international interest, with a round-up of the world's press and features on managing growth, market analysis and country reports.

The Nasdaq Stock Market, Inc, is a wholly-owned subsidiary of the NASD (*#749 National Association of Securities Dealers*, Member Firm Registration Services, PO Box 9403, Gaithersburg, MD 20893–9403), the nation's largest self-regulatory organization for the securities industry. The NASD carries out its regulatory responsibilities through member education, on-site compliance examinations of member firms, automated market surveillance, testing and registration of securities personnel, and review of member advertising and underwriting arrangements. The NASD also provides a forum for investors and members to arbitrate disputes.'

1829. **NASD Notices to Members**. m. $225. 'Newsletter informing subscribers about regulatory and other NASD developments, including actions taken at bimonthly Board of Governors meetings. Requests for member votes and comments are disseminated through *Notices to Members*.'

1830. **NASD Regulatory & Compliance Alert**. q. $80. 'Newsletter dealing with NASD, federal, and state compliance developments and updates on NASD regulatory policy.'

1831. (Year) **Nasdaq Fact Book & Company Directory**. a. $20. 'Data on the performance of Nasdaq securities, statistics on The Nasdaq Stock Market, as a whole, and directory information for each Nasdaq company.'

1832. **Subscriber Bulletin**. bi-m. $80. 'Developments in The Nasdaq Stock Market, The PORTAL Market, OTC Bulletin Board service, and Nasdaq International with emphasis on new trading technologies and regulations and enhancements to the Nasdaq system.'

(44) #750 New York Cotton Exchange 4 World Trade Center, New York, NY 10048. t: (1 212) 938 2702; f: 488 8135.

(45) #751 NYMEX New York Mercantile Exchange, 4 World Trade Center, New York, NY 10048. t: (1 212) 938 4910; f: 432 6286. *Also* 35 Piccadilly, London W1V 9PB, UK. t: (44 71) 734 7282.

'When it comes to physical commodity futures, your best opportunities are still in the land of opportunity . . . The US. Europe. The Far East. In a global financial community, they're next door neighbors. In the physical commodity market. one stands apart. The US – home of the New York Mercantile Exchange.

When NYMEX merged with *COMEX*, each exchange brought powerful resources to the union. The combination of these resources gives the energy and metals market tremendous advantages – increased market research and development, more advance technological support, and virtually around-the-clock hedging and investment opportunities with *NYMEX ACCESS*, our after-hours global electronic trading system.

Just as important, every trade is free of counterparty credit risk, and is monitored by the most diligent regulatory system in the world. Our clearing members include some of the most respected names in the banking and financial industries.'

(46) #752 New York Stock Exchange 11 Wall Street, New York, NY 10005. t: (1 212) 656 6537; f: 656 5748.

1833. **New York Stock Exchange Fact Book**. a. $10. 'A summary of various statistical series issued by NYSE with additional relevant data originated by other organizations.' An Appendix to the Fact Book summarizes the *Publications* produced by NYSE.

(47) #753 Philadelphia Stock Exchange 1900 Market Street, Philadelphia, PA 19103–3584. t: (1 215) 496 5000; f: 496 5653. *Also* 12th Floor, Moor House, 119 London Wall, London EC2Y 5ET, UK. t: (44 171) 606 2348; f: 606 3548. *Annual Report*.

The *Publications Catalog* from *PHLX* ('Since 1790 – A Market Without Walls') contains a variety of free of charge 'Reading Materials' on Equities; Options (eg 'Taxes and options: A guide for the individual investor'; 'The Options Clearing Corporation – An overview' ('This booklet outlines the functions of The Options Clearing Corporation and its subsidiary, The Intermarket Clearing Corporation. It includes sections on their structure, clearance and settlement processing')); Equity Options; Index Options (eg 'Index option statistics'); Currency Options (eg 'Understanding currency options'); 'European Office Newsletter'; 'a monthly publication focusing on issues related to the currency option market. Particular emphasis of topics of interest to the European market participants; distributed to interested persons in Europe); Currency Futures.

(48) #754 Public Securities Association 40 Broad Street, 12th Floor, New York, NY 10004. t: (1 212) 809 7000; f: 797 3895. *Newsletter.*

Banks and dealers that underwrite, trade and sell US government and federal agency securities, municipal securities, mortgage-backed securities, and money market securities.

(49) #755 Securities Industry Association 120 Broadway, 35th Floor, New York, NY 10271. t: (1 212) 608 1500; f: 608 1604.

Investment bankers, securities underwriters, and dealers in stocks and bonds.

1834. **Foreign Activity Report**. q. $60. Tracks purchases and sales of US securities by foreign investors.

1835. **Securities Industry Data Bank. online**. q. Income and balance sheet data compiled from the *Financial and Operational Combined Uniform Single* (FOCUS) reports submitted by securities firms to the SEC.

1836. **Securities Industry Trends**. m. $96. Information on economic developments affecting securities firms. Includes profitability and financial statements of the securities industry.

1837. **Securities Industry Yearbook**. a. $115. Lists association members with descriptions of their activities.

1838. **SIA Washington Report**. bi-m. $25. Informs members of pertinent legislative and regulatory developments in Washington.

1839. **Who's Who in the Securities Industry**. *Economist Publishing Company*. a. $18. Published for the Association's annual convention.

(50) #756 Securities Information Center Operations Manager, PO Box 296, Wellesley Hills, MA 02181. t: (1 617) 235 8270.

Operates the *Lost and Stolen Securities Program.*

(51) #757 Security Traders Association 1 World Trade Center, Suite 4511, New York, NY 10048. t: (1 212) 514 0484; f: 321 3449.

(52) #758 Wall Street Planning Group c/o Chase Manhattan Bank, 28th Floor, 1 Chase Manhattan Plaza, New York, NY 10018. t: (1 212) 552 7735; f: 968 0075.

Fund management and investment

(53) #759 American Society of Pension Actuaries 4350 N Fairfax Drive, Suite 820, Arlington, VA 22203. t: (1 703) 516 9300; f: 516 9308.

(54) #760 Association of Independent Trust Companies 401 N Michigan Avenue, Chicago, IL 60611. t: (1 312) 644 6610; f: 321 6869.

(55) #761 Association of Private Pension & Welfare Plans 1212 New York Avenue NW, Suite 1250, Washington, DC 20005–3987. t: (1 202) 289 6700.

(56) #762 Investment Company Institute 1401 H Street, NW, Twelfth Floor, Washington, DC 20005. t: (1 202) 326 5800; f: 326 5985. *Newsletter*.

Formed in 1940 for open-end and closed-end investment companies registered under the *Investment Company Act 1940*. About 2,000 members.

1840. **FUNDamentals**. i. 'Data reference memos from the ICI Research Department which summarise the main findings from research published at ICI or other published sources. Issues of FUNDamentals are produced several times per year on topics of interest to members.' e.g. 'America's Top Wealthholders' (November 1993); 'Shareholders' Perceptions of Investment Risk' (January 1994).

1841. **Guide to Mutual Funds**. a. $5.00. Includes listing of over 2,700 mutual funds, as well as introductory text.

1842. **Mutual Fund Fact Book**. a. $15.00. Industry trends and statistics. Presents facts and figures on the mutual fund industry, including trends in sales and assets, and includes basic explanation of mutual funds, history, development, etc.

1843. **Trends in Mutual Fund Activities**. m. $120.00. Shows industry sales, exchange, redemptions, assets, cash holdings and portfolio transactions for the current month, previous month and comparable periods of the previous year.

1844. **Perspective on Mutual Fund Activity (Year)**. a. $30. 'This report (Summer 1993) provides an in-depth analysis of the motivating forces behind last year's stagnant economy and the continued growth of the mutual fund industry. It explores the vigorous activity in the fund industry as well as other developments and trends such as investors' growing appetite for foreign investment. An examination of financial intermediaries explores their impact in the capital markets and the key role mutual funds play as providers of capital for businesses, municipalities, and lenders. The final section of this edition looks at another source for future growth for the industry as it examines a relatively new distribution opportunity for mutual funds, selling through banks.'

(57) #763 Mutual Fund Educational Alliance 1900 Erie Street, Suite 120, Kansas City, MI 64116. t: (1 816) 471 1454; f: 471 5446.

'*The Association of No-Load Funds.* We are a non-profit trade organization which strives to educate the public on mutual fund investing and the benefits of direct-marketed mutual funds, or those funds which have no sales or costly broker's fees associated with them.'

1845. **Investor's Guide to Low-Cost Mutual Funds**. a. $5.00. **online**. Includes over 650 funds.

(58) #764 National Association of Investment Companies 1111 14th Street NW, Suite 700, Washington, DC 20005. t: (1 202) 289 4336; f: 289 4329.

(59) #765 National Association of Small Business Investment Companies 1199 N Fairfax Street, Suite 200, Alexandria, VA 22314. t: (1 703) 683 1601; f: 683 1605.

(60) #766 National Investment Company Service Association 850 Boylston Street, Suite 407A, Chestnut Hill, MA 02167. t: (1 617) 277 1855; f: 277 1588.

(61) #767 Pension Real Estate Association 95 Glastonbury Road, Glastonbury, CT 06033. t: (1 203) 657 2612; f: 659 4784.

Insurance

(62) #768 ACORD 1 Blue Hill Plaza, 15th Floor, PO Box 1529, Pearl River, NY 10965–8529. t: (1 914) 620 1700; f: 620 3600.

(63) #769 Alliance of American Insurers 1501 Woodfield Road, Suite 400 West, Schaumburg, IL 60173–4980. t: (1 708) 330 8500; f: 330 8602.

Produces and sells a number of generally short publications: e.g. *Insurance Department Directory* ($35.00), which lists the principal insurance department personnel of each state, indicating their responsibilities, and giving telephone and fax numbers where available; *Household Insurance Expenditures in 1991* ($10.00), which is 'the only analysis ever done summarizing actual household reports on how much families pay for insurance coverage'.

(64) #770 All Nations 1 Nationwide Plaza, Columbus, OH 43216. t: (1 614) 249 6344; f: 249 3090.

(65) #771 American Academy of Actuaries 1720 I Street NW, 7th

Floor, Washington, DC 20006. t: (1 202) 223 8196; f: 872 1948. *Yearbook.*

Founded in 1985 to bring into one professional organization all qualified actuaries in the United States. Professional recognition as an actuary in the United States (and Canada) is achieved by passing a series of ten examinations administered by the *Society of Actuaries* and the *Casualty Actuarial Society.*

(i) #772 *Actuarial Standards Board*

Established in 1988 to promulgate standards of practice and compliance guidelines for the actuarial profession. The Board is a separate entity from the Academy, but draws upon Academy staff and financial support to accomplish its work.

1846. **Contingencies**. bi-m. $24. Reports on and analyses actuarial trends in insurance and business.

1847. (Year) **Issues Digest**. a. Summary of the major issues with which the Academy is involved, especially its government relations activities.

(66) #773 American Agents Association PO Box 7079, Hilton Head Island, SC 29938. t: (1 803) 785 2808; f: 785 9068.

(67) #774 American Association of Insurance Management Consultants c/o Paige Proctor Consulting, 410 North Prairie Street, PO Box 3517, Bloomington, JL 61701. t: (1 309) 828 8851; f: 829 2919.

Purpose is 'to serve as a networking organization for North American based insurance consultants to exchange ideas on various fields of expertise. In addition, once a year the group assembles for a Convention for the presentation of papers on subjects of importance to the North American insurance marketplace ... Our organization does not publish any materials that would qualify as regular periodicals.'

(68) #775 American Association of Managing General Agents 9140 Ward Parkway, Kansas City, Missouri 64114. t: (1 816) 444 3500; f: 444 0330.

Founded in 1926 as a national trade association of insurance managing offices with contractual authority to perform managerial functions on behalf of insurors through the American agency system. The *AAMGA University* provides a course of study designed expressly for insurance wholesalers. Membership in the Association is 'highly selective': there are approximately 250 member agencies as well as 150 companies who are associate members. AAMGA member firms write more than $5 billion in premiums annually. 'Unfortunately, AAMGA's directory and newsletter are available to members only. I am unable to send you any publications.'

(69) #776 American Council of Life Insurance 1001 Pennsylvania

Avenue, NW, Washington, DC 20004–2599. t: (202) 624 2000; f: 624 2319.

'The leading advocacy and public information trade association for the life insurance industry in the United States. Comprised of more than 620 member companies, representing 95 percent of the life insurance in force in the United States and 95 per cent of pensions with life insurance companies, the Council represents the industry in a broad spectrum of legislative and regulatory matters at federal, state and municipal levels of government. It also serves as a major source of information regarding the legal, investment and actuarial aspects of the life insurance, pension and annuity business.'

1848. **Investment Bulletin**. q. $60. Survey of mortgage commitments on commercial properties.

1849. **Life Insurance Fact Book**. bi-a. Free of charge.

- *Center for Corporate Public Involvement*

(70) #777 American Institute for Chartered Property Casualty Underwriters 720 Providence Road, PO Box 3016, Malvern, PA 19355–0716. t: (1 215) 644 2100; f: 251 9995.

(71) #778 American Institute of Marine Underwriters 14 Wall Street, 8th Floor, New York, NY 10005–2145. t: (1 212) 233 0550; f: 227 5102.

The membership includes some 120 marine insurance companies representing 90 per cent of the US marine insurance market.

(72) #779 American Insurance Association 1130 Connecticut Avenue NW, Suite 1000, Washington, DC 20036. t: (1 202) 828 7100; f: 293 1219.

National trade association representing property-casualty insurance companies. 'AIA's 220 property-casualty insurers provide insurance to businesses and individuals throughout the United States. Together they control more than $137 billion in assets and annually underwrite more than $56 billion in direct written insurance premiums. Affiliated with 79,000 independent insurance agents nationwide, a substantial portion of the companies' business is commercial liability insurance . . . In addition, AIA member companies employ approximately 145,000 individuals and contribute $1.6 billion in taxes and fees to state government revenues each year.' *AIA Law Publications* are a series of loose-leaf summaries of current law for all 50 states.

1850. **State Taxation Manual**. l. $130. 'State-by-state descriptions of specific taxes, fees, and assessments levied on property/casualty insurance companies.'

(73) #780 American Society of CLU & ChFC 270 S Bryn Mawr

Avenue, Bryn Mawr, PA 19010–2195. t: (1 610) 526 2513; f: 526 2538.

'As the premier association for professional development in the field of insurance and financial services, the American Society represents over 35,000 members who have earned or are working toward their Chartered Life Underwriter or Chartered Financial Consultant designations from The American College in Bryn Mawr, Pennsylvania. Through education, experience and high ethical standards, American Society members have earned the public's trust and confidence in areas that include retirement, estate and financial planning, tax strategies, investments, wealth accumulation and life and health insurance.'

1851. **Focus: A Quarterly Digest of Insurance & Financial Strategies**. q. $129. Audio tapes and listener's guides.

1852. **Journal of the American Society of CLU & ChFC**. bi-m. $32. **online**.

1853. **Keeping Current**. q. $129. 'For more than 20 years, this quarterly audio tape and syllabus subscription has won respect for its ability to keep practitioners informed of tax, legislative and other developments.'

(74) #781 Associated Risk Managers International 702 Colorado Street, Number 200, Austin, TX 78701. t: (1 512) 479 6886; f: 479 0577.

(75) #782 Captive Insurance Companies Association 655 Third Avenue, New York, NY 10017. t: (1 212) 687 4501; f: 986 9716.

'The recognised authoritative organization which promotes captive insurance companies, regardless of domicile or structure, as viable alternatives available to optimize risk transfer and risk funding.'

(76) #783 Conference of Consulting Actuaries 1110 W Lake Cook Road, Suite 235, Buffalo Grove, IL 60089–1968, USA. t: (1 708) 419 9090; f: 419 9091.

'Advances the practice of actuarial consulting by serving the professional needs of consulting actuaries and by promoting members' views within the actuarial profession.'

1854. The **Proceedings (Year)**. a. $95. Contains research papers authored by CCA members and others and transcripts presented at Annual Meetings.

(77) #784 Consumer Credit Insurance Association 542 South Dearborn Street, Suite 400, Chicago, IL 60605. t: (1 312) 939 2242; f: 939 8247.

'CCIA is a trade organization; as such, our publications are developed for member company use. CCIA does not generally make available its publications to non-members (although certain publications may be shared on an ad hoc basis).'

(78) #785 Council of Insurance Agents and Brokers 316 Pennsylvania Avenue SE, Suite 400, Washington, DC 20003. t: (1 202) 547 6616; f: 546 0597.

(79) #786 CPCU Society 720 Providence Road, PO Box 3009, Malvern, PA 19355. t: (1 215) 251 CPCU; f: 251 2761.

For professionally qualified members of the *American Institute for Chartered Property Casualty Underwriters.* Membership 23,000.

(80) #787 Health Insurance Association of America 1025 Connecticut Avenue NW, Suite 1200, Washington, DC 20036. t: (1 202) 223 7780.

(81) #788 Independent Insurance Agents of America 127 S Peyton Street, Alexandria, VA 22314. t: (1 703) 683 4422; f: 683 7556.

'The nation's oldest and largest non-profit, trade association representing the business interests of individual agents and their employees. Members offer all types of insurance, from property and casualty to life and health . . . Through IIAA's government affairs office, located on Capitol Hill, IIAA informs its members on a wide range of legislative issues that affect independent insurance agents' day-to-day businesses. In addition to advising members, the government affairs office plays an active role in tracking legislation and has an extensive lobbying effort. In fact, IIAA was named one of the top ten lobbying organizations in Washington by *Fortune* magazine.'

1855. **Independent Agent**. m. $24.00.

(82) #789 Inland Marine Underwriters Association 111 Broadway, Mew York, NY 10006. t: (1 212) 23 7958.

'Since its creation in 1931 . . . has dedicated itself to serve as the collective voice of the US inland marine insurance association. With the support of over 370 member companies, IMUA advocates the interests of the US inland marine industry before regulatory bodies . . . IMUA achieves comprehensive communications with underwriters and the public through an array of publications, including educational seminar transcripts, an *Overview of Trends and Developments* (a fact book issued every two years), *IMPACT* quarterly newsletter, and periodic news releases to the trade and general press.'

(83) #790 Insurance Accounting and Systems Association PO Box 51340, Durham, NC 27717. t: (1 919) 489 0991; f: 489 1994.

'The world's largest member-company insurance organization, IASA serves health care, life, property-liability and reinsurance companies. It promotes through cooperative effort, the study and development of modern practices and procedures applicable to insurance accounting and systems.' A number of publications are prepared for the membership.

(84) #791 Insurance Education Foundation 3601 Vincennes Road,

PO Box 68700, Indianapolis, IN 46268–0700. t: (1 317) 876 6046; f: 879 8408. *Newsletter.*

'Established in 1988 with a mission "to educate Main Street America about how insurance works". Working from the premise that it is easier to build positive attitudes than reverse negative ones, the initial focus of IEF to accomplish this mission has been the development of programs specifically directed toward high school students.'

(85) #792 Insurance Information Institute 110 William Street, New York, NY 10038. *Publications Service Center* t: (1 908) 225 2727; f: 732 1916.

'The mission of the Insurance Information Institute (III) is to improve public understanding of insurance – what it does and how it works. For more than 30 years, the III has provided definitive and credible insurance information. Today the III is recognised by the media, governments, regulatory organizations, universities and the public as a primary source of information, analysis, and referral concerning insurance . . . The Institute does not lobby. Its central function is to provide accurate and timely information on insurance subjects.'

1856. **III Data Base. online**. 'Selects and abstracts the most important materials being published by trade associations, the business, trade and consumer press and government agencies.'

1857. **Insurance Daily**. d. $7/day. Summaries of articles relating to the property and casualty insurance industry.

1858. (Year) **Insurance Facts**. a. $22.50. Comprehensive statistical yearbook about the property-liability insurance business.

1859. **Insurance Issues Update**. l. $75.00. "Excellent! Very well researched and professionally written. We avidly look forward to each new envelope of updates."

1860. **Insurance Pulse**. a. $35. 'Widely acclaimed annual survey of public opinion on economic and insurance matters of concern to the property/casualty business.'

(86) #793 Insurance Institute of America 720 Providence Road, Malvern, PA 19355. t: (1 610) 644 2100; f: 251 9995.

Educational and certification institute.

(87) #794 Insurance Research Council 1200 Harger Road, Suite 310, Oak Brook, IL 60521. t: (1 708) 572 1177; f: 672 9856.

Conducts surveys on property/liability insurance issues. 'We also sell data bases from our research studies; special discounted rates are offered to academicians.'

1861. **PAM (Year)**. a. $10. *Public Attitude Monitor Series.* Annual surveys of US households, measuring public attitudes on a variety of topics related to risk and insurance.

(88) #795 Insurance Services Office 7 World Trade Center, New York, NY 10048–1199. t: (1 212) 898 6000; f: 898 5525.

'I am writing to you in response to your recent enquiry regarding the use of some of our publications for your book ... We regret to inform you that we will be unable to confirm your request, due to the fact that ISO's materials cannot be used outside the United States for writing insurance.'

(89) #796 Life Insurers Conference The Pavilion, Suite 301, 5770 Powers Ferry Road NW, Atlanta, GA 30327. t: (1 404) 933 9954; f: 933 9956.

'An association of life insurance companies which serve the basic life and health insurance needs of the American public through the *Home Service* system and other distribution methods ... *Pre-Need Funeral Insurance.* Approximately one-fifth of LIC members are either entirely or partially in the business of providing life insurance for "final expenses".'

(90) #797 Life Underwriter Training Council 7625 Wisconsin Avenue, Bethesda, MD 20814. t: (1 301) 913 5882; f: 913 0123.

(91) #798 Mortgage Insurance Companies of America 727 15th Street NW, 12th Floor, Washington, DC 20005. t: (1 202) 393 5566; f: 393 5557. *Fact Book and Membership Directory.*

(92) #799 National Association of Independent Insurers 2600 River Road, Des Plaines, IL 60018–3286. t: (1 708) 297 7800; f: 297 5064.

'Non-profit trade group representing the interests of more than 500 property-casualty insurance companies in the US. Our member companies write more than a third of the automobile insurance in the US and a quarter of the homeowners' coverage. In addition, they provide almost $14 billion of coverage (about 15 per cent of the total market) in commercial lines, such as trucking, taxi fleets, workers' compensation and multi-peril protection for businesses ... We pledge ... to collect and compile statistical information related to the insurance industry, and to provide on a membership or other basis statistical services to property, casualty or surety companies.'

(93) #800 National Association of Insurance Brokers 1300 Eye Street NW, Suite 900E, Washington, DC 20005. t: (1 202) 628 6700; 628 6707.

'An organization of 35 companies, which administer the majority of the coverage in the $110–billion commercial property-casualty market in the U.S. and conduct major operations around the world.' The organization produces several publications about the industry.

(94) #801 National Association of Insurance Women (International) PO Box 4410, Tulsa, OK 74159. t: (1 918) 744 5195; f: 743 1968.

(95) #802 National Association of Independent Life Brokerage Agencies 1735 N Lynn Street, Suite 950, Arlington, VA 22209–2022. t: (1 703) 524 2302; f: 524 2303.

(96) #803 National Association of Life Underwriters 1922 F Street, NW, Washington, DC 20006–4305. t: (1 202) 331 6000; f: 835 9607.

1862. **Federal Legislative Reports**. l. $50.

1863. **Life Association News**. m. $6. **online**. Circulation: 144,000.

1864. **State Legislative Reports**. l. $50.

- *Political Action Committee*

(i) *#804 Association for Advanced Life Underwriting*

AALU has the primary responsibility within the overall NALU legislative program for: business insurance; estate planning; non-qualified retirement plans; qualified retirement plans. It is an association 'with an exclusive, limited membership made up of the 1,500 top people in advanced life underwriting. Because the association has limited membership, approved applicants are placed on a waiting list ... As a benefit, those on the waiting list receive the *Washington Report* to help them become familiar with the organization ... (The Report) is written by AALU's counsel based on recent legislative developments, judicial or administrative decisions from various agencies. It's an excellent way to stay ahead and to add value to your marketing skills.'

(ii) *#805 General Agents and Managers Association* t: (1 202) 331 6088; f: 785 5712. *Newsletter* (bi-m, $20)

'The only national organization dedicated to serving the professional and personal needs and interests of field management in the life insurance and related financial services industry.'

(97) #806 National Association of Mutual Insurance Companies 3601 Vincennes Road, PO Box 68700, Indianapolis, IN 46268. t: (1 317) 875 5250; f: 879 8408.

(98) #807 National Association of Professional Insurance Agents 400 N Washington Street, Alexandria, VA 22314. t: (1 703) 836 9340; f: 836 1279.

1865. **Professional Agent**. m. Established in 1931.

(99) #808 National Council of Self-Insurers 10 S Riverside Plaza, Suie 1530, Chicago, IL 60606. t: (1 312) 454 5110; f: 454 6166.

(100) #809 National Council on Compensation Insurance 750 Park of Commerce Drive, Boca Raton, FL 33487. t: (1 407) 997 1000; f: 997 4233.

(101) #810 Property Loss Research Bureau 1501 Woodfield Road, Suite 400 West, Schaumburg, IL 60173–4978. t: (1 708) 330 8650; f: 330 8657.

'Thank you for your interest in our organization. However, the Property Loss Research Bureau is a not-for-profit trade association of insurance companies and our Bylaws prohibit distribution of our publications outside of the membership.'

(102) #811 Reinsurance Association of America 1819 L Street, NW, 7th Floor, Washington, DC 20036–3818. t: (1 202) 293 3335.

(103) #812 Risk and Insurance Management Society 655 Third Avenue, New York, NY 10017. t: (1 212) 286 9292; f: 986 9715.

1866. **Insurance Availability Survey**. a. $50. 'Annual survey (since 1986) of RIMS member organizations. Evaluates market conditions for ten lines of commercial insurance.'

1867. **Risk Management**. m. $54. 'Covers the risk management/employee benefits scene worldwide.'

(i) *#813 International Federation of Risk and Insurance Management Associations*

(104) #814 Self-Insurance Institute of America PO Box 15466, Santa Ana, CA 92705. t: (1 714) 261 2553; f: 261 2594.

'A national (some international members) trade association of the self-insurance industry.'

1868. **Self-Insurer**. m. $110. Published by the *Self-Insurers Publishing Corporation*.

(105) #815 Society of Actuaries 475 N Martingale Road, Suite 800, Schaumburg, IL 60173–2226. t: (1 708) 706 3500; f: 706 3599. *Prepayments* PO Box 95668, Chicago, IL 60694.

Founded in 1949 by the amalgamation of the *Actuarial Society of America* (1889) and the *American Institute of Actuaries* (1909). The international research and examination organization for actuaries working in the life and health insurance, employee benefits, and pension fields.

1869. **Actuarial Research Clearing House**. $40.

1870. **Actuary**. $15.

1871. **Record**. q. $60. Contains the proceedings of spring and annual meetings of the SOA, including session discussions.

1872. **Statistics for Pension Actuaries**. $25.

1873. **Transactions (General)**. a. $55. Presents formal and scholarly papers contributed by SOA members.

(i) *#816 Conference of Actuaries in Public Practice*

(106) #817 Society of Chartered Property & Casualty Underwriters 720 Providence Road, Box 3009, Malvern, PA 19355. t: (1 610) 251 2728; f: 251 2761. *Newsletter* (Circulation: 23,000).

(107) #818 Surety Association of America 100 Wood Avenue S, Iselin, NJ 08830. t: (1 908) 494 7600; f: 494 7609.

(108) #819 Women Life Underwriters Confederation 17 S High Street, Suite 1200, Columbs, OH 43215. t: (800) 776 3008; f: (1 614) 221 1989.

Asset-backed finance

(109) #820 American Association of Certified Appraisers 800 Compton Road, Suite 10, Cincinnati, OH 45231. t: (1 513) 729 1400; f: 729 1401.

Originated in 1976: began granting designations in 1977. Since 1987, the Association has officially subscribed to the *Uniform Standards of Professional Appraisal Practice* as promulgated by the *Appraisal Foundation*.

(110) #821 American Land Title Association 1828 L Street NW, Suite 705, Washington, DC 20036. t: (1 202) 296 3671; f: 223 5843.

(111) #822 American Society of Appraisers PO Box 17265, Washington, DC 20041. t: (1 703) 478 2228; f: 742 8471.

International non-profit independent organization, established to provide 'an effective profession-wide affiliation working cooperatively for elevation of the standards of the appraisal profession'. Represented by some 6,500 members in 82 Chapters throughout the US, with members in a further 30 countries. Convenes annually in June the *International Appraisal Conference*. Has developed programs to produce 'Experienced, Tested, Certified, Designated' appraisers for businesses, real property, gems and jewelry, machinery and equipment, personal property, and so on.

1874. **Business Valuation Review**. q. $50. Provides information about the valuation of businesses, professional practices, corporate stock, and tangible/intangible assets. Updates of the *Bibliography of Business Valuation Literature* are published annually.

1875. **Journal of Appraisal Review and Management**. bi-a. $25.

1876. **Valuation**. bi-a. $10.00. Official journal of the Society.

(112) #823 Appraisal Institute 875 N Michigan Avenue, Suite 2400,

Chicago, IL 60611–1980. t: (1 312) 335 4100. *Publications* can be ordered from: PO Box 10956, Chicago, IL 60610–0956. t: (1 312) 733 2979; f: 733 3107.

'The world's leading organization of real estate appraisers.'

1877. **Appraisal Journal**. q. $35. **online**. 'The most prestigious publication of the appraisal profession.'

1878. **Appraiser News**. m. $25.

1879. **MarketSource**. q. $150. Data, trends and forecasts in single, family, multifamily, office, retail, and industrial property markets.

(113) #824 Appraisers Association of America 60 E 42nd Street, Suite 2505, New York, NY 10165. t: (1 212) 867 9775.

(114) #825 Association of Foreign Investors in US Real Estate 700 Thirteenth Street NW, Suite 950, Washington, DC 20005. t: (1 202) 434 4510; f: 434 4509.

'All publications produced by the Association are for the benefit of its membership and are not sold.'

(115) #826 Commercial Finance Association 225 West 34th Street, Suite 1815, New York, NY 10122. t: (1 212) 594 3490; f: 564 6053. *Annual Report.*

'Organized in 1943 and functions as the trade association for the asset-backed financial services industry.'

1880. **Compendium of Commercial Finance Law**. l. $350/$275. Four volumes. 'For asset-based lenders, factors, banks and other institutions engaged in secured transactions. It covers federal tax lien filing, selected federal statutes and regulations, interest statutes, corporate guarantees and secret liens, including a new section on environmental liens.'

1881. **Secured Lender**. bi-m. $48. **online**. 'Magazine of the Asset-Backed Financial Services Industry.'

(116) #827 Commercial-Investment Real Estate Institute 430 N Michigan Avenue, Chicago, IL 60611–4092. t: (1 312) 321 4470; f: 321 4530.

1882. **Commercial Investment Real Estate Journal**. q. $32. Practical information for professionals on all aspects of commercial real estate.

(117) #828 Institute of Business Appraisers PO Box 1447, Boynton Beach, FL 33425. t: (1 407) 732 3202; f: 732 4304.

(118) #829 Mortgage Bankers Association of America 1125 Fifteenth Street, NW, Washington, DC 20005–2766. t: (1 202) 861 6500; f: 466 2479.

'For over 2,300 mortgage bankers, brokers, commercial banks, thrifts, credit unions, investors, insurance companies and others, membership in the Mortgage Bankers Association of America makes good business sense. Membership in MBA provides professionals, like yourself, with the tools you need to make your company a leader in the real estate finance industry.' *Legislative/Regulatory Hotline* (1 202) 785 8420. *FNMA/FHLMC/GNMA Yields* 1 900 773 2020: Flat fee $1 per call, 24 hour Recorded Rate Message.

1883. **Financial Statements and Operating Ratios for the Mortgage Banking Industry**. a. $100.00. 'This reference report is the only one of its kind.' Published 2–3 years in arrears.

1884. **Mortgage Banking**. m. $40.00. **online** 'The only national monthly magazine devoted exclusively to real estate finance.'

1885. **National Delinquency Survey**. q. $60.00. With **disc** $140.00. 'The recognised source of information on mortgage delinquency and foreclosure rates. Based on a sample of over 15 million mortgage loans serviced by mortgage companies, commercial banks and thrifts . . . Quarterly issues are also available on spreadsheet formatted discs . . . *Customized NDS Reports* (q. $500.00) To get a true comparison of your portfolio with the industry average, the NDS results need to be reweighted to conform to the distribution of your portfolio across states and loan types . . . You send us information on your portfolio on diskette (we will provide the necessary software) and we will send you quarterly NDS results customized to your portfolio.'

1886. **Real Estate Finance Today**. bi-w. $85. 'In an independent readership survey, *Real Estate Finance Today* was ranked the best source for current industry news over six competing trade publications. It is the only major trade publication written out of Washington, D.C. assuring you complete up-to-the-minute coverage of the legislative and regulatory issues affecting real estate finance.'

1887. **Regulatory Compliance Manual**. l. $150.00/$75.00. 'The book is a handy reference for loan originators, underwriters, servicers, and others involved with RESPA; TIL; ECOA; CRA; HMDA; Flood Insurance; the Fair Collection Practices Act; and the Fair Credit Reporting Act.' Annual update.

1888. **Weekly Survey of Mortgage Interest Rates and Applications Volumes**. w. $300.00. Fax service.

(119) #830 National Association of Home Builders 1201 15th Street NW, Washington, DC 20005, USA. *Home Builder Bookstore* t: (800) 223 2665/(1 202) 822 0463; f: 822 0391.

1889. **Housing Market Statistics**. m. $105. Compilation of national and regional statistics on housing related indicators.

(120) #831 National Association of Independent Fee Appraisers 7501 Murdoch, St. Louis, MO 63119. t: (1 314) 781 6688; f: 781 2872.

1890. **Appraisal Review**. q.

(121) #832 National Association of Industrial and Office Properties Woodland Park, 2201 Cooperative Way, Herndon, VA 22071. t: (1 703) 904 7100; f: 904 7942.

'Our mission is to provide developers and owners of industrial, office and related commercial real estate with effective support and guidance to create, protect and enhance property values. We are a forum for all professionals who strive to improve the quality of America's workplaces.' The Association produces a wide range of *audio cassette tapes*, e.g.: 'The outlook for pension fund investment in real estate'; 'The future of REITs'; 'New directions in financing'; 'Foreign capital sources'; 'Trends in securitization'. ($15.95 per tape)

(122) #833 National Association of Mortgage Brokers 706 E Bell Road, Suite 101, Phoenix, AR 85022. t: (1 602) 992 6181; f: 493 8711.

'Not-for-profit professional society incorporated in 1973 which provides educational, legislative and networking services to residential and commercial Mortgage Brokers across the nation ... NAMB collects and disseminates statistical information and data relating to Mortgage Brokers and their profession.'

1891. **National Mortgage Broker**. m. $59.95.

(123) #834 National Association of Real Estate Appraisers 8363 East Evans Road, Scottsdale, AZ 85260–3614. t: (1 602) 948 8000; f: 998 8022. *Newsletter.*

'Currently we have approximately 13,000 members internationally, consisting of Certified Real Estate Appraisers (CREA), Certified Commercial Real Estate Appraisers (CRRA), Registered Professional Members (RPM), and our Affiliate Members ... The *Code of Professional Ethics and Uniform Standards of Professional Appraisal Practice*, to which a member must adhere, gives the industry the assurance it needs when accepting an appraisal report from an NAREA designated member ... The Association's publishing arm produces over seventy publications.'

(124) #835 National Association of Real Estate Brokers 1629 K Street NW, Suite 306, Washington, DC 20006. t: (1 202) 785 4477; f: 785 1244.

(125) #836 National Association of Real Estate Editors 3101 N Central Avenue, Number 560, Phoenix, AZ 85012. f: (1 602) 265 1699.

(126) #837 National Association of Real Estate Investment Trusts 1129 Twentieth Street NW, Suite 305, Washington, DC 20036. t: (1 202) 785 8717; f: 785 8723.

'Created in 1960 to serve as the official source of information for the REIT industry. Current industry assets total in excess of $60 billion.'

1894. **Compendium: Federal Taxation of REITs**. l. $500/$50. 'Compilation of proposed and enacted federal legislation, Treasury Department rulings, both private and published, affecting tax treatment of REITs.'

1895. **REIT Handbook**. a. $695. 'The complete guide to the real estate investment trust industry.'

(127) #838 National Association of Realtors 430 N Michigan Avenue, Chicago, IL 60611, USA. t: (1 312) 329 8458; f: 329 5978.

1896. **Real Estate Today**. 10/year. $25. **online**. Serves as a forum of ideas, opinions, and practical applications in all areas of residential, commercial-investment, and brokerage-management real estate. Also covers association activities and interests. Circulation: 775,855.

(i) *#839 Counselors of Real Estate*

1897. **Real Estate Issues**. s-a. $27. **online**. Offers in-depth articles by leading authors on the restructuring of the real estate industry.

(128) #840 National Association of Review Appraisers and Mortgage Underwriters 8383 East Evans Road, Scottsdale, AR 85260–3614. t: (1 602) 998 3000; f: 998 8022.

'The purpose of NARA/MU is to establish and improve Professionalism and Competency in the field of Appraisal Review and to offer a Professional Designation to qualified individuals.'

(129) #841 National Council of Exchangors 13410 E Cypress Forest Drive, Houston, TX 77070–4009. t: (1 713) 849 8411.

(130) #842 National Second Mortgage Association 8300 Utica Avenue, Suite 173, Rancho Cucamomga, CA 91730. t: (800) 342 1121; f: (1 909) 941 8248. *Newsletter*.

'Dedicated to the home equity lending professional. Founded in 1974, it is the leader in serving the home equity lending professional. The Association is comprised of representatives from major banks, bank holding companies, national and regional consumer finance companies, savings associations, small to mid-sized mortgage lenders, mortgage bankers and a full array of mortgage product and service providers.'

(131) #843 National Society for Real Estate Finance 2300 M Street NW, Suite 800, Washington, DC 20037. t: (1 202) 973 2801; f: 293 3083.

5. Commercial information provides

(1) #844 AI Research Corporation 2003 St Julien Court, Mountain View, CA 94043, USA. t: (1 415) 852 9140; f: 852 9522.

1896. **VenCap Data Quest**. **diskette**. q. $159.95. 'The quickest and easiest way to find venture capital sources! A comprehensive computerized database directory guide to venture capital funding sources . . . Over 395 venture capital firms with more than 550 venture capital sources.'

(2) #845 American Banker 1 State Street Plaza, New York, NY 10004, USA. t: (1 212) 943 6700.

1897. **American Banker**. d. $712. **online**. **cdrom**. 'In-depth daily news, analysis, and statistical tables covering the latest banking developments – from mutual fund activities to the state of the home mortgage market.'

(3) #846 American Banker Newsletters 1325 G Street NW, Suite 900, Washington, DC 20005, USA. t: (1 202) 347 2665; f: 347 1158. Some of these titles are marketed under the imprint *American Banker Bond Buyer*.

1898. **Asset Sales Reports**. w. $1,250. **online**. 'Covers loan sales and asset securitization in the US and all types of asset- and mortgage-backed securities outside the US. Reports on industry developments and trends, closing prices and yields on actively traded asset-backed securities. Interviews market leaders. Provides insights into the restructuring of asset-backed securities, reflecting current thinking in investor recourse and credit enhancement.'

1899. **Bank Mutual Fund Report**. w. $995. **online**. 'Scrutinizes the marketing and sale of investment products by banks, including mutual funds, annuities and related products. Covers the big players, reports on interesting deals, alerts readers to legal and regulatory threats, and profiles significant figures in the industry.'

1900. The **Bond Buyer**. d. $1,897. **online**. News articles, data, and other information on every aspect of the tax-exempt bond market. Included is essential data on planned bond issues, results of bond sales, IRS rulings, complete records of municipal authorities' borrowings, and detailed news stories on such subjects as corporate bonds, government securities, and financial futures.

1901. **CFO Alert**. w. $695. 'The newsletter for the chief financial officer of a financial services company. Warns the CFOs about accounting and regulatory changes and gauges their potential effect on firms. Profiles CFOs. Examines technological issues that will affect financial institutions as well as CFOs procurement choices. Keeps CFOs reminded of issues through a ledger and a calendar.'

1902. **Guarantor**. w. $995. 'The only weekly that provides an inside view of credit enhancement, from letters of credit to secondary market insurance.'

1903. **High Yield Report**. w. $795. **online**. 'Junk bonds, real estate, workouts, bankruptcies, and distressed securities covered directly and succinctly – with no garbage.'

(4) #847 AP Information Services Roman House, 296 Golders Green Road, London NW11 9PZ, UK. t: (44 181) 455 4550; f: 455 6381.

1904. **Pension Funds and their Advisers (Year)**. a. 87.50. Covers pension funds of all companies and organizations in the UK with over 500 employees, together with details of major European and North American funds. A statistical section indicates how and where the major funds invest their assets. Also listed are financial and property advisers, actuaries, pension fund consulatants, insurance companies and other advisers.

(5) #848 Argus Business 6151 Powers Ferry Road NW, Atlanta, GA 30339–2941, USA. t: (1 404) 955 2500; f: 955 0400.

1905. **Commercial Real Estate Investor Directory**. a. $79.95.

1906. **Directory of Trust Institutions**. a.

1907. **National Real Estate Investor**. m. $72. **online**. Covers the development, investment, financing and management of commercial real estate and its allied fields. Subscription includes *Directory*.

1908. **Pension World**. m. $68. **online**. For employee benefits plan sponsors and investment managers. Covers major areas affected by US investment: vehicles, practices and performance, employee benefit plan design and administration, and legislative developments and concerns. Alternative title: *Pension Management*.

1909. **Trusts & Estates**. m. $78. Subscription includes *Directory*. For trust and investment officers of banks, underwriters, and lawyers.

(6) #849 Argus Vickers 17 Battery Place, New York, NY 10004, USA. t: (1 212) 425 7500; f: 509 5408. *Also* American Equity Research Limited, Royex House, Aldermanbury Square, London EC2V 7HR, UK. t: (44 171) 606 0006; f: 606 0666.

1910. **Bond Traders Guide**. q. **online**. 'Contains US corporate and convertible debt holdings, with a separate section listing preferred stock holders. Containing information from over 5,500 institutional portfolios – more than 3,000 of which are not required to file with the SEC – it is compiled from quarterly and annual reports. Institutional coverage includes investment companies, major bank trusts, money managers, pension funds, mutual funds, colleges and insurance companies.'

1911. **Directory of Institutional Investors**. 'Contains a detailed list of over 6,500 institutional investors world-wide.'

1912. **Stock Traders Guide**. q. 'Lists alphabetically the holders of over 12,000 global equities . . . These institutions include mutual funds, unit trusts, investment trusts, banks, insurance companies, money managers and college endowment funds.'

(7) #850 Armstrong Information Third Floor, Brigade House, Parsons Green, London SW6 4TH, UK. t: (44 171) 736 7111; f: 371 7806.

1913. **Banking and Financial Training**. 10/year. £245. 'The only journal reporting on international training news, products and techniques specifically in the financial sector.' The March 1995 issue listed five pages of courses and conferences including those from the *International Center for Monetary and Banking Studies* in Geneva and the *International Foundation for Computer Based Education in Banking and Finance.*

1914. **Back Office Focus**. 10/year. £395.

(8) #851 Asset International 125 Greenwich Avenue, Greenwich, CT 06830, USA. t: (1 203) 629 5014; f: (203) 629 5024.

1915. **Global Custodian**. q. $80. 'Covers developments thoughout the world in global investing, market structure and regulation, product and technology development. September issue features exclusive supplement rating global custody services.'

1916. **International Investors Directory**. a. $350. Six volumes: International Securities Firms; International Investment Managers; Global Custodians/Subcustodians/Securities Lending; International Stock Exchanges and Central Depositories; Global Depository Receipts; International Indices and Index Derivatives.

1917. **Plan Sponsor**. 10/year. $150. 'The monthly magazine for users of investment services. Covers issues, events and other developments of concern to the $5 trillion pension plan sponsor community.'

(9) #852 Babson-United Investment Advisors 101 Prescott Street, Wellesley Hills, MA 02181–3319, USA. t: (1 617) 235 0900; f: 235 9450.

1918. **United Mutual Fund Selector**. bi-w. $124. Statistical information on mutual funds.

(10) #853 Bank Director PO Box 3468, Brentwood, TN 37024, USA. t: (1 615) 371 0406; f: 371 0899.

1919. **Bank Director**. q. $130. 'Started three years ago (in 1991) by a director for the purpose of keeping directors informed, to show how effective banks cope in today's environment.' Each issue includes a *Resources* Section: 'The following listings are intended to help bank directors locate information that can make them more effective. Many of the materials listed here are available in public and university libraries.'

(11) #854 Bank News 912 Baltimore Avenue, Kansas City, MO 64105–1784, USA. t: (1 816) 421 7941; f: 472 0397.

1920. **Bank News**. m. Founded in 1901.

(12) #855 Bauer Group PO Drawer 145510, Coral Gables, FL 33114–5510, USA. (1 800) 388 6686; f: (1 305) 441 0691.

'Research firm that processes and analyzes the quarterly financial data of all US banks and thrifts and semi-annual financial data of all US credit unions as reported to their corresponding regulators.

The rating of financial institutions has evolved from their rating as *investments* by securities firms. By these standards, Bank "X" with less capital but with a higher return on equity (ROE) would receive a higher rating than Bank "Y" with more capital but a smaller ROE. Bank "X" is maximising its return on equity . . . (In contrast) we concentrate on a bank's capital or rather its ability to retain capital (the reverse of capital depletion) not its relative profitability. Of course, profitability is required for a bank to get a high rating, but *capital is king*.

We employ conservative measures that take into account present performance and future projected performance. This is a controversial area that draws considerable criticism from poorly performing banks. "How can you project continued negative performance just because we've had problems in the past?", they ask. Our response is simple. "History being a good teacher, we prefer to err on the side of caution." Despite our conservatism many banks continue to produce stellar performances quarter after quarter. These institutions are proud of their performance and want to tell you so. They participate in a program that lets them *sponsor your enquiry* – they pay us to give you their rating, FREE. This sponsorship in no way affects the institution's rating.'

Bauer produce a wide range of reports on single institutions, through regional to federal coverage, along with coverage of specialist areas such as interbank liabilities and thrifts under RTC supervision.

1921. **Quarterly Report on All US Banks**. q. $350.

1922. **Analysis of Premiums Paid in RTC Resolutions**. w. $475.

1923. **Jumbo Rate News**. w. $415. 'The weekly commentary, record & analysis of the jumbo CD market . . . The *Omnibus Banking Bill*, signed into law, December 19, 1991, restricts institutions from soliciting CD funds nationwide through CD brokers. As of June 16, 1992, only credit-worthy institutions are authorized to solicit brokered CD deposits nationwide. These institutions have historically used our CD publications to generate deposits . . . All the institutions we survey are pre-screened and analyzed, credit-worthy, federally insured banks and thrifts. Institutions that list their rates pay no fee. However, to qualify for our weekly survey, they must submit current, detailed financial reports which must meet our stringent financial criteria.'

1924. **Rate Watch**. m. $99. 'Newsletter for financial advisors, accountants, bankers and prudent investors that emphasizes SAFETY-FIRST CD investments.'

1925. **Semi-Annual Report on All US Credit Unions**. bi-a. $350.

1926. **Quarterly Report on All US Thrifts**. q. $250.

(13) #856 BCA Publications 3463 Peel Street, Montreal, Quebec, H3A 1W7, Canada. t: (1 514) 499 9550; f: 843 1763.

1927. **Bank Credit Analyst**. m. $695. Independent monthly forecast and analysis of trends in major US investment markets, with particular emphasis on equities, business conditions, inflationary trends, interest rates, gold and the dollar. 'The forecasting approach is based on the principle that an expanding base of liquidity and non-inflationary credit creation lead to a favorable environment for sustainable economic expansion and therefore a healthy climate for stocks and bonds. Excessive credit creation leads to accelerating price inflation, balance of payments difficulties and adverse pressure on the currency, making for an unhealthy investment and economic climate and therefore creating the need for alternative investment and business strategies.'

1928. **BCA Interest Rate Forecast**. m. $645. Independent monthly forecast and analysis of trends in US interest rates and fixed-income markets. 'The forecasting is eclectic. While the publication focuses on the fundamental developments that determine interest rates, attention also is paid to technical market trends.'

1929. **Emerging Markets Analyst**. $595. The Service comprises: *Monthly Bulletin* Topical events in emerging markets and updates of investment strategy in these markets; *Country Quarterlies* Country forecasts for each emerging market combining fundamental factors, cyclical analysis and technical indicators; *Annual Backgrounders* Basic facts on the economy, politics and stock markets of each country covered. The markets of fourteen countries are regularly covered in full: Argentina, Brazil, Chile, China, Greece, Indonesia, Malaysia, Mexico, Portugal, South Korea, Taiwan, Thailand, Turkey, Venezuela; the developing markets of other countries are covered in less detail.

1930. **Forexcast**. w. $2,500. FAX service providing forecasts of intermediate-term currency trends, a background overview, specific currency comments and relevant charts.

1931. **International Bank Credit Analyst**. m. $595. 'Provides a forecast and analysis for the principal countries of interest rates, equity markets, gold and commodity prices, economic trends and currency movements.'

(14) #857 Bernstein Research Sanford C Bernstein, 767 Fifth Avenue, New York, NY 10153, USA. t: (1 212) 756 4599; f: 756 4462.

1748. **Banking Quarterly**. q. $1,800. Analysis of the US banking industry.

(15) #858 AM Best Company Ambest Road, Oldwick, NJ 08858, USA. t: (1 908) 439 2200; f: 439 3296.

'*Best's Ratings* possess a unique degree of reliability and credibility. AM Best maintains one of the world's largest insurance financial databases, backed by nearly a century of experience exclusively in this unique field. Best is an objective third-party source of information and ratings on thousands of foreign and domestic insurers.'

1933. **Best's Agents Guide**. a. $455. 'Concise profile information on nearly 1,600 insurers, including current *Best's Ratings* and *Financial Size Categories* and the latest two years of *Best's Profitability, Leverage and Liquidity Tests.*'

1934. **Best's Aggregates and Averages**. a. *Life/Health* $95. *Property/Casualty* $295. '400 pages of statistics on individual companies, insurer groups, individual lines of business, peer groupings, and the industry as a whole.'

1935. **Best's Casualty Loss Reserve Development Series**. l. a. $600. 'Ten years of data taken from *Schedule P* from up to 200 of the largest property/casualty companies.'

1936. **Best's Company Reports**. $15 per company. 'All the financial facts and operating results you need on life/health, property/casualty, and international companies that interest you.'

1937. **Best's Directory of Recommended Insurance Attorneys and Adjusters**. a. $460. Two volumes. **cdrom**. '5,200 law firms and 1,200 adjusting offices recommended by insurance companies and verified by AM Best.'

1938. **Best's Experience by State (By Line)**. **cdrom**. *Life/Health* ($3,900, 5 years); *Property/Casualty* ($9,000, 5 years). 'Shows premium and loss experience for over 2,200 property/casualty companies . . . (and) 1,100 Life and Accident and Health insurance companies.'

1939. **Best's Insurance Reports**. 'The classic industry reference'. Editions include: *Property/Casualty* 2,400 companies (a. $990; **cdrom**. a. $2,860); *Life/Health* 1,600 companies (a. $990; **cdrom**. a. $2,860); *International* 1,100 companies in 63 countries (a. $990).

1940. **Best's Intelligencer**. m. $375. 'Provides a synopsis of approved Commercial and Personal Lines policy rates and form revisions filed by insurance companies with state insurance departments.'

1941. **Best's Key Rating Guide**. a. *Life/Health* ($455, **diskette** $600); *Property/Casualty* ($455, **diskette** $600). 'Allows you to monitor the results of insurers around the year.'

1942. **Best's Market Guide**. a. $1,485. Three volumes: *Stocks*; *Bonds*; *Muni Bonds*. 'Provides details of the investment portfolio activity and holdings of over 1,900 life/health and property/casualty companies taken from *Schedule D* of those companies' annual statements. This data is invaluable to investment firms, financial analysts, investment officers within insurance companies, and financial consultants who need to track insurance investment activity.'

1943. **Best's Quantitative Analysis Report**. a. *Life/Health* ($35); *Property/Casualty* ($35). 'Fundamental quantitative information and analysis to evaluate an individual company's financial strength.'

1944. **Best's Review**. m. **online**. 'The *Property/Casualty* ($21) and *Life/Health* ($21) editions . . . are published and read by more than 250,000 high-caliber agents and brokers and insurance company managers.' Regular columns include: Reports on companies; Automation review; Executive changes; Market developments; Month in brief; Company reports index.

1945. **Best's Underwriting Guide**. l. $500/$100. Four volumes. 'Ideal training tool for beginning underwriters and a proven evaluation tool for more experienced personnel . . . Detailed descriptions of more than 460 commercial risk classifications.' There is also a *Best's Underwriting Newsletter* (m. $49).

1946. **BestWeek**. w. 'Published in two editions (*Property/Casualty* ($425) and *Life/Health* ($425)), this weekly report provides detailed, timely coverage of important facets of today's insurance industry. Financial news and legislative and regulatory activity are reported each week, along with commentary on key industry issues. Rating changes are provided through a supplement called *Best's Rating Monitor*; statistical studies such as 5-Year Assets Rankings are included regularly.' A compilation *Best's Insurance News on CD-ROM* appears quarterly ($500).

(16) #859 BKB Publications 150 Nassau Street, Suite 2030, New York, NY 10038, USA. t: (1 212) 267 7707; f: 267 7726.

1947. **Cheklist**. q. $25.'For executives in the check-cashing industry.'

1948. **Credit Union News**. bi-w. $95.

1949. **Today's Pawnbroker**. q. $25.

(17) #860 Blay's Guides Blay's House, Churchfield Road, Chalfont St Peter, Bucks, SL9 9EW, UK. t: (44 1753) 880484; f: 880238.

1950. **Blay's MortgageMatch**. **diskette**. w. £499. 'The best value no non-sense sourcing system for residential mortgages . . . holds all the essential details you need on around 1500 mortgage schemes.' Also available is a *Blay's MortgageMatch Commercial* (£296) devoted to loans for commercial property.

1951. **Factoring Database**. **diskette**. s-a. £115. 'The background, analysis and services available in the Factoring & Invoice Discounting field.'

1952. **Leasing Database**. **diskette**. q. £155. 'Providing critical information on the many institutions offering leasing facilities, this database helps advisers find the right leasing comapny for their client's business.'

1953. **Venture Capital Database**. **diskette**. q. £195. 'Covers nearly 200 venture capital organisations.'

(18) #861 Brock Associates 2050 West Good Hope Road, Milwaukee, Wisconsin 53209, USA. t: (1 414) 351 5500; f: 351 3140.

1954. **Brock Report**. w. $355. 'Aimed to help producers analyze commodity markets.'

(19) #862 Buckley Press 244/249 Temple Chambers, Temple Avenue, London EC4Y 0DT, UK. t: (44 71) 583 3030; f: 353 6867.

1955. **Insurance Directory (Year)**. a. £269. Four volumes: I. Insurance Companies; II. Brokers & Intermediaries; III. Statistics; IV. London Market. "Probably our single most valuable source of market data" (*Miller Knight*).

1956. **Post Magazine**. w. £85. **online**. 'Essential reading for all those involved in life or general business.'

1957. **Reinsurance Magazine**. m. £55. **online**.

1958. **Stone & Cox Life Assurance Handbook**. l. £85.50.

1959. **Stone & Cox Individual Pensions Handbook**. l. £85.50.

(20) #863 Callahan & Associates 1001 Connecticut Avenue NW, Suite 1022, Washington, DC 20036, USA. t: (1 202) 223 3920; f: 223 1311.

1960. **Callahan's Credit Union Report**. q. $149.

1961. **Credit Union Directory**. a. $135.

1962. **Credit Union Yearbook**. a. $250.

1963. **Quarterly Reports**. q. $195.

(21) #864 CAPS Combined Actuarial Performance Services Ltd, 11 Albion Street, Leeds LS1 5ES, UK. t: (44 113) 246 0416; f: 242 1041.

1964. **Annual Review of UK Pooled Pension Funds (Year)**. a. £240.

1965. **Pension Fund Investment Performance**. a. £250.

1966. **Quarterly Survey of UK Pooled Pension Funds**. q. £370.00. **diskette** 1100.00.

(22) #865 CD-ROM Publishing Company 1 Great Scotland Yard, London SW1A 2HN, UK. t: (44 171) 839 2266; f: 839 6632. Wholly owned subsidiary of **Bureau van Dijk**, a consulting firm operating companies in Brussels and Paris since 1973.

1967. **EURA-CD**. **cdrom**. m. $15,450. 'A financial database on 8,900 World Banks with financial analysis software . . . Up to 5 years detailed spreadsheet information on: the top 5,700 European banks; the top 1,050 North American banks; all the 185 Japanese commercial and sogo banks; more than 1,850 other major banks; the top 50 securities firms in the world; the leading 20 international banking and financial organizations . . . Details on ownership (shareholders and banking subsidiaries) on the 4,000 major banks worldwide . . . 2 years of Reuters full text articles related to banks and financial organisations, extracted from the *TEXTLINE* database with online access to the most recent news . . . *Moody's Ratings*, *Capital Intelli-*

gence Reports, BREE Ratings and Reports. EURA-CD is updated monthly. More current information is available through weekly update diskettes or online access to *EURABANK* (*Sleigh Corporation*) and *REUTERS TEXTBASE.*'

(23) #866 CDA Investment Technologies 3265 Meridian Parkway, Suite 130, Fort Lauderdale, FL 33331, USA. t: (800) 243 2324/(1 305) 384 1500; f: 384 1540.

1968. **Mutual Fund Charts**. Graphic displays of the total return of over 1,500 mutual funds, overall market indicators and CDA-developed mutual fund groups, over a 10 year period based on initial investment of $1,000. Includes discussion of final market values, broken down into principal, income and capital gains components.

1969. **Mutual Fund Report**. Analyzes the performance, risk posture, and percentile rankings of more than 1,500 funds.

1970. **Spectrum International**. Institutional holdings and ownership information on worldwide securities. Covers over 6,100 equities domiciled in 35 countries outside the US, and over 1,800 institutional trusts and funds in 13 countries worldwide.

(24) #867 Chart Analysis 7 Swallow Street, London W1R 7HD, UK. t: (44 171) 439 4961; f: 439 4966. Current *Chart Libraries* are:

1971. **Commodities**. w. 835. 'Over 33 different UK and US commodities and metals plus financial and stock exchange futures.'

1972. **Currency & Financial Futures**. w. £1,195. 'Thorough coverage of the foreign exchange and financial futures markets . . . 73 pages of comprehensive, easy to use charts, both line & bar and point & figure . . . Two pages of interpretations, plus preferred buy and sell recommendations.'

1973. **European Point & Figure Library**. w. £1,035. 'Over 400 charts of leading European shares.'

1974. **International Point & Figure Library**. w. £1,425. 'Covers leading shares of Pacific Basin, North American and South African stock markets.'

1975. **UK Point & Figure Library**. w. £1,315. 'Over 470 charts of UK listed shares.'

Also published is:

1976. **FullerMoney**. m. £172. 'The global strategy investment letter for international investors covering: World stockmarkets; Interest rates & bonds; Currencies; Commodities.'

(25) #868 Chartcraft 30 Church Street, POB 2046, New Rochelle, NY 10801, USA. t: (1 914) 632 0422; f: 632 0335.

'The nationally famous Chartcraft organization offers these eight objectives for every investor:

- Keep his own stocks under constant supervision
- Spot "buy formations" and signals in stocks and industry groups
- Watch for "sell signals" in other stocks or groups
- Formulate price objectives
- Be forewarned of resistance areas
- Foresee support areas
- Monitor the overtrend of the market, DJIA, etc
- Possess a visual history of every NYSE, ASE and popular OTC stock, along with many technical indicators, industry groups, mutual funds, options etc.

The Chartcraft *Point & Figure Method* can help the investor attain these eight important objectives because it is adaptable to many applications.'

1977. **Bi-Weekly Investors Intelligence**. bi-w. $184. 'A less technical, easy to read market letter, quoted in every *Barron's* and *Investors Daily* . . . It features our exclusive "Sentiment Index of Advisory Services" and Overbought/Oversold Index plus comments from leading professionals.'

1978. **Bi-Weekly Technical Indicator Review**. bi-w. $99. 'Covers all popular market indexes and indicators through P&F charts . . . Includes access to our TELEPHONE HOTLINE!'

1979. **Weekly Breakout Service**. w. $168. 'Chartbook containing P&F charts of all NYSE stocks with new BREAKOUTS! . . . Each chart is ANNOTATED by the editors of Chartcraft and includes Bullish/Bearish price objectives, 30–wk moving average, yield and P/E. Charts are also marked with current relative strength signal, a critical tool for stock selection. If you like P&F charts but don't have time for upkeep, this is for you!'

1980. **Weekly Futures Service**. w. $256.

1981. **Weekly Options Service**. w. $168.

1982. **Weekly Mutual Funds Breakouts**. w. $154.

1983. **Weekly Service on NYSE/ASE**. w. $256.

(26) #869 Christopher Resources 34 N White Street, Box 488, Frankfort, IL 60423–0488, USA. t: (1 815) 485 8399; f: 485 2499.

1984. **Complete Commodity Futures Directory Database**. **diskette**. $2,400 licence fee. 'All registered commodity futures and options professionals in the United States . . . The data is updated daily and a *Free* diskette is mailed within six (6) months. The data is licensed for a minimum of one (1) year and the licensee fee *remains the same* after the first year. The entire database is *ZIP̈* (CASS certified) which significantly reduces your postage costs and increases the accurancy of your mail delivery.'

1985. The **Complete Commodity Futures Directory**. 'Always current . . . printed electronically when ordered.' $195. 'Over 9,000 futures industry professionals and 1,800 service firms & exchanges. 85 *Specialized Industry Categories* e.g. Accountants/Compliance Services . . . Back Office

Consultants . . . Charting Equipment/Tools, Charting Services, Clearinghouses . . . Commodity Discount Brokerage Firms . . . Computer Voice Systems, Computerized Trading Services . . . Credit Reporting Services, Directories . . . Educational Institutions . . . Expert Witness . . . Financial Planning . . . Fund Administrators, Fund Indexes, Futures Grain Services, Government Regulators, Hedging Services, Hotlines, Index Services, Information Services . . . Journals, Magazines . . . Managed Account Reporting Services . . . News Services, Newsletters, Newspapers . . . Offshore Fund Services, Offshore Incorporation Services, Option Services, Organizations, Pension Fund Consultants . . . Price Reporting . . . Publishers . . . Seminar Services, Technical Trading Services . . . Trend Services, Weather Services.'

(27) #870 CIFAR [Center for International Financial Analysis & Research] Princeton Service Center, 3490 US Route One, Princeton, NJ 08540, USA. t: (1 609) 520 9333; f: 520 0905.

1986. **Global Bond Guide**. m. $295. Analyzes bond prices, default risks and yields of 3,000 corporate bonds worldwide. Includes 'more than 10 Global corporate bond indices uniquely created by CIFAR'.

1987. **Global Financial Report on Financial Services & Brokerage Firms**. m. $295.

1988. **Global Financial Report on International Banks**. m. $395. Report analyzing financial and non-financial data of the leading banks worldwide.

1989. **Global Financial Services Monthly**. m. 'Report analyzing key news, financial data and stock prices of the leading banks, insurance and other financial service companies.'

1990. **Global Investment Quarterly**. q. 'A unique investment quarterly analyzing global capital market trends, benchmarks and risk/return relationships in over 50 capital markets.'

(28) #871 City Research Group Lector Court, 151–153 Farringdon Road, London EC1R 3AD, UK. t: (44 171) 833 1681; f: 278 5981.

Make available the results of certain syndicated market research studies:

'The following (examples of) studies are available for purchase now. Most are annual programmes where the 1994 is available now, with the 1995 study available during the year. Fee ranges indicate the minimum fee for purchase of the core programme in England & Wales and the likely maximum cost for the core programme and all special subject modules for Great Britain:

- *Middle Market Corporate Banking* based on 1,600 hour long personal face-to-face interviews and 7,500 telephone interviews with finance directors and other senior executives responsible for choosing and using banks in companies across Great Britain with annual sales between £1m and £250m. Fees from £25,500 to £63,000 + VAT depending on markets covered and special subject modules taken.

- *Professional Sector Banking* based on 750 hour-long personal face-to-face interviews and 3,000 telepone interviews with partners in firms of accountants and solicitors across Great Britain choosing and using banks for their practice or client accounts. Fees from £18,000 to £42,000 + VAT depending on markets covered and special subject modules taken.
- *Share Registration* based on 600 telephone interviews with company secretaries in quoted companies across Great Britain choosing and using firms of registrars to manage their share registers. Fees from £8,250 + VAT for basic study to £11,000 + VAT including special subject module.
- *Survey of Independent Financial Advisers* based on 400 hour-long structured personal face-to-face interviews and 50 depth interviews with IFAs choosing and using life insurance companies for regular and single premium life and pensions business across Great Britain. Fee of £11,175 + VAT or £11,300 including VAT on special report.'

(29) #872 Claritas 53 Brown Road, Ithaca, NY 14850–1262, USA. t: (1 607) 257 5757; f: 266 0425.

'Claritas provides precision tools: the specific information, expertise, services and delivery options you need to make the most effective marketing decisions. We make it possible to integrate demographics, specialized data, customer data, geography, mapping and marketing experience into the process called *Precision Marketing*. Claritas developed Precision Marketing because we believe that data *connections* are just as important as data *collections*. We don't just guarantee the industry's most accurate, updated information, we also bring you the expertise and service that help you make critical connections to new markets, to new customers and to the trends that move the markets.

Through years of changing market conditions – booms, recessions, rising or falling inflation – sound information helps financial marketers make sound decisions. The financial databases we offer are built on the cornerstone of reliable data sources, in-depth research and proven proprietory methodologies. Claritas is proud to field the nation's largest syndicated database of consumer financial behaviour, *The Market Audit*. Our dedication to quality is reflected in our tradition of innovative products and services for the financial industry.'

(30) #873 Commerce Publishing Company 330 N Fourth Street, St Louis, MO 63102–2036, USA. t: (1 314) 421 5445.

1991. **American Agent and Broker**. m. $24. **online**. Provides sales management information to help multi-line insurance agents serve their clients better.

(31) #874 Commodity Research Bureau Suite 1820, 30 South Wacker Drive, Chicago, IL 60606, USA.

1992. The **Blue Line**. d.

1993. **Commodity Chart Service**. d.

1994. **Commodity Year Book Statistical Abstract Service**. 3/year.

1995. **CRB Commodity Index Report**. w.

1996. **CRB Commodity Yearbook**. a. 55. 'Dubbed the 'Bible' by market analysts and practitioners, the Knight Ridder CRB Commodity Yearbook has been published since 1939, providing a comprehensive source of valuable information on practically every commodity, from alcohol to zinc.

1997. **CRB Futures Chart Service**. w.

1998. **Electronic Futures Trend Analyzer**. d.

1999. **Final Markets**. d.

2000. **Futures Market Service**. w. $150. Provides a synopsis update about 36 major markets. Analyzes the week's most active commodity or futures-related conditions.

2001. **Knight-Ridder News Summaries**. d.

(32) #875 Computer Petroleum Corporation 510 World Trade Center, 30 E 7th Street, Suite 510, St Paul, MN 55101–4901, USA. t: (1 612) 225 9550; f: 298 0291.

2002. **Petroleum Industry News**. **online**. $24.95/per month delivered over *DTN Satellite System*, comprising: Market Monitor; Heard at the Street; Regional Market Summary.

(33) #876 Consensus Research International 8 St Johns Hill, London SW11 1SA, UK. t: (44 171) 738 1222; f: 738 1271.

'Principal activity . . . comprises ad hoc market research, viz surveys designed to the information needs of individual client companies and carried out on a confidential basis. Our particular interest is in financial, professional and business markets . . . Our other activities comprise research consultancy and information services, the latter drawing on published and unpublished sources, and comprising desk research and market intelligence bulletins for the financial services and IT sectors. Our principal work targeted at a wider audience (ie for purchase or subscription) includes:

- *Annual Broker Survey* "Evaluation of broking houses" analysis and research, conducted amongst the UK's largest publicly quoted companies; also covering other key issues. (£80)
- *Consumer Finance Market Segmentation* Unique attitudinal segmentation of the consumer market for financial services, established in the mid-1980s.
- *General Insurance Market: Consumer Segmentation*
- *Unit Trust Survey* 'Quarterly survey of awareness, behaviour and attitudes . . . Two quarters of the year, the survey covers the unitholder market, and two quarters, the intermediaries.'

(34) #877 Datamonitor Europe 106 Baker Street, London W1M 1LA, UK. t: (44 171) 625 8548; f: 625 5080.

'Independent strategic management consultancy which specialises in analysing company and market dynamics. Over the last decade the company has become the market leader in providing high quality data and analysis to the financial services sector . . . Datamonitor's portfolio of financial services reports is the product of a unique research process developed over a number of years . . . Throughout the year we conduct over 4000 telephone interviews with industry executives in order that we can continually update our extensive global industry databases, ensuring that any information you receive from us will be as up-to-date as possible . . .' Examples from the list of some 120 *Financial Services Sector Market Reports* scheduled to be produced in 1994/1995 are:

- **Financial Services for Housewives**. June 1994. 250 pp. $1,450.
- **Independent Financial Advisers**. August 1994. 200 pp. $1,995
- **UK Retail Banking**. August 1994. 400 pp. $1,450.
- **Corporate Pensions and Employee Benefits**. October 1994. 600 pp. $1,450.
- **Global Insurance Markets**. December 1994. 300 pp. $1,995.
- **Telephone Financial Services**. December 1994. 400 pp. $1,995.
- **Money Transmission Mechanisms: The Move Towards Cashless Payments**. January 1995. 320 pp. $1,995.
- **Stockbrokers**. January 1995. 500 pp. $2,900. Two volumes.
- **The Effect and Implications of Disclosure in Financial Services**. January 1995. 250 pp. $1,450.
- **Health Insurance**. February 1995. 300 pp. $1,450.
- **Offshore Funds**. April 1995. 250 pp. $1,450.
- **US Retail Banking**. April 1995. 500 pp. $1,995.
- **Global Derivatives Markets**. June 1995. 300 pp. $4,150

(35) #878 Dolan Media Suite 2180, Metropolitan Centre, 333 S Seventh Street, Minneapolis, MN 55402, USA. t: (1 612) 321 0561; f: 321 0563.

2003. **Finance and Commerce Daily Newspaper**. d. $119.

(36) #879 Duff & Phelps Credit Rating 55 E Monroe Street, Suite 3500, Chicago, IL 60603, USA. t: (1 312) 368 3100; f: 263 4064.

The *Financial Service* covers 'Finance, Banks, Brokerage, Insurance' and includes:

- *Credit Analysis Handbook* (q.)
- *Credit Decisions/Credit Comments* (w.)
- *Credit Rating Guide* (m.)
- *Comparative Statistics* (q.)
- *Analyst Contact Listing* (s-a.)
- *Banking Insights* (i.)

Database Electronic Rating Access is available on *Bloomberg* and provides press releases and rating changes as well as a *Municipal Service* and an *Emerging Markets Service.* Other individual publications include:

- *Asset Backed Monitor* (q.)
- *Insurance Claims Paying Ability Guide* (q.)

(37) #880 Dun & Bradstreet International Holmers Farm Way, High Wycombe, Buckinghamshire, HP12 4UL, UK. t: (44 1494) 422000; f: 422260 *and* **Dun & Bradstreet Information Services** 3 Sylvan Way, Parsipanny, NJ 07054–9947, USA. t: (1 201) 605 6000; f: 605 6930.

2004. **ERISA: The Red Book of Pension Funds**. a. £425. USA. 'Focussing on the top 25,000, this directory lists companies that report a minimum of $1.8 million in total net pension plan assets.' Includes a statistics section.

(38) #881 Dunn and Hargitt 22 North Second Street, Box 1100, Lafayette, IN 47902–9989, USA. t: (1 317) 423 2624; f: 423 4495.

2005. **Dunn & Hargitt Commodity Service**. w. $275.

(39) #882 DYP Group Bridge House, 181 Queen Victoria Street, London EC4V 4DD, UK. t: (44 171) 236 2175; f: 489 1487.

Reference works

2006. **European Insurance Yearbook (Year)**. a. £120.

2007. **Lloyd's Market (Year) Yearbook**. a. £95.

2008. **London Market Yearbook (Year)**. a. £100.

2009. **UK Brokers Yearbook (Year)**. a. £120.

2010. **World Reinsurers Yearbook (Year)**. a. £120.

Current awareness

2011. **European Insurance Market**. bi-w. £305.

2012. **Financial Reinsurance & Futures Newsletter**. m. £285. Covers the technicalities of the financial reinsurance sector and how it can affect other insurance companies.

2013. **Information Technology in Insurance**. m. £195.

2014. **Insurance & Reinsurance Solvency Report**. w. £355.

2015. **Life Assurance Market**. m. £180.

2016. **London Market Newsletter**. w. £355.

2017. **Marine & Aviation Insurance Report**. m. £305.

2018. **Reinsurance Market Report**. bi-w. £280.

(40) #883 EMAP Business Publications 33–39 Bowling Green Lane, London EC1R 0DA, UK. t: (44 171) 837 1212; f: 833 8072.

2019. **Insurance Age**. m. **online**.

2020. **Review**. m. Covers reinsurance.

(41) #884 Euromoney Publications Nestor House, Playhouse Yard, London EC4V 5EX, UK. t: (44 171) 779 8888; f: 779 8818.

Reference works

2021. **Airfinance Annual (Year)**. a. £95. 'The only reference book and directory to cover all aspects of commercial aircraft financing.'

2022. **Bondware**. **diskette**. 'Comprehensive database on the international bond and equity markets . . . Contains information on over 26,000 securities issued since 1980. These include every form of international bond or equity: straight bonds, equity warrant bonds convertibles, floating rate notes, international equity offerings, synthetic bonds, covered warrants and other derivative products . . . No other data source can match the detail that we provide.'

2023. (Year) **Brokers 1000**. a. £170. 'This is a unique global directory of brokers that supplies contact details, key personnel, products traded and areas of specialisation for the world's leading equity, debt and derivative broking firms.'

2024. **Capital Markets Handbook (Year)**. a. £95. 'Profiles 22 of the world's leading capital markets, along with a unique Capital Markets Directory giving contact details and key personnel for over 3,000 institutions worldwide. No other book gives the breadth or depth of analysis that this fully researched multi-contributor text can: the ideal information source for trader, banker, borrower or adviser.'

2025. **Cedel Euromoney Directory**. a.

2026. **Dow Jones Telerate Bank Register (Year)**. a. £170. 'The definitive bank directory.'

2027. **Equityware**. **diskette**. 'Complete database on the international equity market since 1983.'

2028. **Goldman Sachs Foreign Exchange Handbook (Year)**. a. £135. Two volumes. 'The first volume profiles all the key currencies . . . The second volume contains a unique directory of FX specialists, covering all the main markets, detailing over 2,500 institutions and providing contact details for over 35,000 FX personnel.'

2029. **International Investment Management Directory (Year)**. a. £155. 'Describing the investment strategy of over 1,000 firms, this is the first ever comprehensive worldwide directory of investment management companies.'

2030. **Loanware**. **diskette**. 'Comprehensive database on the global syndicated loan market from 1980.'

2031. **Noteware**. **diskette**. 'Database on the Euro-commercial paper and

Euronote market, covering such intruments as Note Issuance Facilities, MOFs, Sterling commercial paper programmes, Certificates of Deposit and Medium-term Notes.'

2032. **Offshore Finance Yearbook (Year)**. a. £130. 'A unique directory of 400 companies active in the offshore finance market.'

2033. **Paribas Derivatives Handbook (Year)**. a. £140. 'The directory includes full contact details and key personnel for over 2,000 institutions active in the derivatives markets worldwide, plus an invaluable contact directory for all derivatives exchanges.'

2034. **Project Finance Yearbook (Year)**. a. £95. 'Includes an extensive directory of over 600 companies providing finance and advice.'

2035. **Shipping Finance Annual (Year)**. a. £95.

2036. **World Leasing Yearbook (Year)**. a. £110. 'Has established itself as the industry standard.'

Current comment

2037. **Airfinance Journal**. 11/year. £245.

2038. **Asset Finance & Leasing Digest**. 10/year. £185. **online**. 'The only international magazine supplying worldwide coverage of the leasing and asset finance market, ranging from project finance and big ticket leasing to all aspects of the small ticket market.'

2039. **Capital Markets Guide**. m. £1,625. 'A listing of all deals captured by the Euromoney database.'

2040. **Corporate Cover**. 11/year. £75. 'The only specialist commercial insurance and risk management magazine produced for the information needs of the European insurance buyer and comercial broker.'

2041. **Corporate Finance**. m. £235. 'The leading international journal of financing techniques, M & A and risk management for corporate treasury and financial executives, and their advisers.'

2042. **Euromoney**. m. £165. **online**. **cdrom**. 'The leading monthly magazine, essential for everyone involved with capital markets and international finance . . . Over 160,000 people worldwide regard Euromoney as the leading source of information on international finance.'

2043. **Euroweek**. w. £1,550. **online**. 'Detailed coverage of new financings, trends and developments.'

2044. **Global Investor**. 10/year. £195. 'Covers all aspects of global and cross-border investment by fund managers, pension funds, insurance companies and other institutional investors.'

2045. **ICB Magazine**. bi-m. £105. 'The only magazine covering the banks' transaction and information processing services, from global custody and cash management to cross-border payments.'

2046. **ICB Newsletter**. m. £395. 'Dedicated to covering the banks' transaction processing related business, including interbank payments and clearing risks, SWIFT related topics and securities custody services.'

2047. **ICB Settlements Report**. q. £225. 'The monitor of worldwide transaction standards . . . devoted entirely to international securities clearing and settlement.'

2048. **International Bond Investor**. q. £95. 'The only magazine devoted to the international fixed-income investor.'

2049. **International Securities Lending**. q. £95.

2050. **Project and Trade Finance**. m. £320.

2051. **Reactions**. m. £165. 'The magazine with the highest audited circulation of the world's insurance and reinsurance markets.'

2052. **Treasury Manager**. m. £485. 'Provides independent information on currency forecasting and interest rate movements in both major and minor markets – each month providing hedged recommendations and features by market experts on the latest derivative products. It also compiles exchange and interest rate forecasts from over 40 leading analysts.'

(42) #885 Evaluation Associates 200 Connecticut Avenue, Suite 700, Norwalk, CT 06854, USA. t: (1 203) 855 2273; f: 855 2301.

2053. **International Manager Profiles**. $1,750.

2054. **Investment Manager Profiles**. $2,975. Three volumes. Also includes: Statistical Summaries (s-a.); Flash Reports & Data Base Charts (q.); Market Indices (m.).

2055. **Real Estate Manager Profiles**. $2,200.

(43) #886 Faulkner & Gray 11 Penn Plaza, 17th Floor, New York, NY 10001, USA. t: (1 212) 967 7000; f: 967 7155.

2056. **Bank Network News**. bi-w. $395. **online**. 'The leading source of news and analysis on the EFT industry.'

2057. **Bank Technology News**. 10/year. **online**.

2058. **CardFAX**. $695. **online**. 'At least four times a week, Card FAX delivers late-breaking card-related news items and advisories *directly to your FAX machine*. Days, weeks, sometimes months before they're reported in the press!'

2059. **Card Industry Directory**. a. $345. 'In-depth card industry profiles: Top 250 credit card issuers; Top 350 debit card issuers; Top 40 retailer programmes; Top 75 EFT networks; Top 50 card processors; Top 25 merchant banks; Guide to 3,500 card industry executives; Guide to 700 card industry vendors.'

2060. **Checks & Checking**. m. $295. 'The insider's report on checks & the checking business.'

2061. **Credit Card News**. bi-w. $375. **online**. 'Serving the nationwide credit card industry with data, information and insight.'

2062. **Credit Card Management**. m. $128. **online**. Covers all aspects of the industry.

2063. **EFT Network Data Book**. a. $95.

2064. **POS News**. 14/year. $295. **online**. 'Newsletter of retail electronic payments.'

2065. **Private Banking Report**. Contains the latest new trends, data and analyses of the affluent banking market.

2066. **United States Banker**. m. $48. **online**. Founded in 1891. Circulation: 39,000.

(44) #887 Federal Filings 601 Pennsylvania Avenue NW, South Building, Suite 700, Washington, DC 20004–2061, USA. t: (1 202) 393 7400.

2067. **Daily Bankruptcy Review**. d. Faxed news from Chapter 11 proceedings nationwide.

2068. **Daily Energy Investor**. d. Faxed coverage of key regulatory and legislative developments that impact investments in the natural gas, electric utility and oil industries.

2069. **FedFilings Investment Research**. 20/year. 'Independent, fundamental research reports on US equities.'

2070. **High Yield Weekly**. w. 'Exclusive news on more than 2000 high yield issuers.'

2071. **Mutual Fund Advance**. Twice-weekly. 'Advance word on new and amended funds filed at the SEC'

2072. **REIT Investor**. Twice-weekly. 'Tracks IPOs, including all amendments, shelf offerings, and institutional investment activity filed with the Securities and Exchange Commission. Targeted to attorneys, accountants, fund managers, equity analysts, investors, and real estate professionals.'

2073. **13F Advance**. 200/year. 'Timely news and analysis on the quarterly holdings of more than 50 of the most successful US money managers.'

(45) #888 Financial Information Inc (FII) 30 Montgomery Street, Jersey City, NJ 07302, USA. t: (1 201) 332 5400; f: 432 9779.

'*What We Do* We provide Financial Action and Transfer Services to the securities operations of banks, brokers, mutual fund and money managers throughout the United States and Canada. Our expert staff searches for and reports on any and all activities that may affect a security – purchase offers, redemptions, mergers, tender offers, put options, bankruptcies, new issues, liquidations, agent changes – and more. We then verify this information and deliver complete and accurate data to your operations center – either online or in print – on a daily basis. In short, we provide your firm with the up-to-date information you need to properly advise your client.

Best Source Network in the Industry Through the years we've compiled a vast network of information sources and established solid relationships within the financial community. This network is, without a doubt, the best source of information in the industry. It includes on-line transmissions; local dailies from major U.S. and Canadian cities; U.S. and Canadian Stock Exchange notices; agent, company and public relations firm releases; and daily clipping services. Each day our experienced staff of researchers and editors pore over this information searching for the latest news that will affect your firm's holdings.

All items are checked and verified and any inconsistencies or ambiguities are fully researched. The resulting data contains the most complete, accurate and timely information impacting your clients' securities. Our extensive research eliminates your need to research – freeing up your staff to concentrate on other important tasks . . . At FII, securities information is all we do and we do it better than anyone else.'

FII services include:

- *CUSIP On-Line Inquiry System* 'Access all data, including weekly updates, available in the CUSIP Master Directory
- *Daily Card (Reorganization) Service* 'Any and all corporate activity which affects publicly traded securities. The coverage includes stock splits, name changes, rights offers, mergers, purchase/exchange offers, tender offers, bankruptcies, recapitalizations.'
- *Daily Called Bond Service* 'Timely and reliable data on municipal and corporate redemptions . . . FII is on the mailing lists of over 500 Redemption Agents, so FII receives notices from agents at the same time as the registered holders . . . This is the only service to receive an automated feed from *Fiduciary Communications Company, Inc*, the company that provides agent-certified daily notices from more than 330 trustees to national newspapers on a daily basis. FII receivers this on-line transmission the night before publication, enabling FII to publish these transactions the same day as they appear in the newspaper. . . . FII uses more sources of information in the U.S. and Canada than any other vendor.'
- *Daily Transfer On-Line Inquiry System* 'Subscribers to the *Financial Stock Guide* and *Municipal Bond Guides* can access the information contained in these books, updated daily, with a personal computer.'
- *Financial Data Management System* 'PC-based software package provides the ability to download and process FII's Financial Actions . . . International Corporate Actions and Pricing . . . Retired CMO and MBS Securities Services.'
- *International Corporate Actions and Pricing* 'International data on dividends, capital changes, bid and mergers, company news and pricing on a daily basis. This information is gathered by two of the world's leading international data vendors: *Valorinform* based in Switzerland and *Extel Financial* based in the United Kingdom.'
- *Put Option Service* 'Information on optional puts, retention options

and options to convert the interest rate. This service also covers secondary options for municipal bonds, corporate bonds, and international securities and CMO's.'

- *Retired Collateralized Mortgage Obligation & Mortgage Backed Securities Service* 'This information is gathered and prepared by the *Asset Backed Securities Group* . . . This service will notify clients of CMO and MBS issues that are retired prior to the securities' last payment date on both agency-backed and most private-backed issues.'
- *Warrant Service* 'The only service in the industry dedicated to tracking warrant issues.'

(46) #889 Financial Intelligence & Research 12–14 Derwent Yard, London W5 4TW, UK. t: (44 181) 579 1091; f: 566 1789.

'By far the largest analyst of the UK Insurance Market with annual fees in excess of £1m from its UK Insurance Market Data & Analysis Services. Based in West London, we employ 30+ full-time staff with a range of skills including: actuarial, accounting, financial analysis, systems design, software development and systems support. Our current activities include:

- Supplier of the DTI's internal DTI Return validation and compliance system
- Supplier of Syndicate and Names Evaluation Systems to Lloyd's Members Agents accounting for over 50% of Market capacity
- Supplier of Bespoke Analysis to various recent Lloyd's Market Committees
- Analyst to the *Association of Lloyd's Members*, providing several annual publications each with circulations over 10,000
- We supply an international client base with UK Insurance Company analysis, both paper and computer based
- We are the leading supplier of DTI Returns Validation, Capture and Generation systems to UK insurers
- Bespoke software for internal information requirements.'

2074. **Insight**. **diskette**. '*Insight 1*, the Solvency and Class Underwriting System, contains extracted data from Forms 10–28 of the DTI Returns for over 250 Non-Life Insurance Companies. *Insight 2* is a 'Windows' based DTI Returns Library and Analysis tool, containing all data from Forms 10–28 and 31–35 of the DTI Returns for 78 key Non-Life Insurance Companies. All data is carefully validated to our exacting standards.'

2075. **Lloyd's Brokers**. a. £365. Financial status and performance.

2076. **Lloyd's Underwriting Agents**. a. £365. Financial status and performance

2077. **UK Insurance Companies: General Business**. a. £790. *Volume I* Solvency & Underwriting Performance; *Volume II* Class Underwriting Analysis.

2088. **UK Insurance Market: Corporate Profile Service**. l. 'An in-depth Corporate & Financial Analysis of one page per Company, cumulated alphabetically into one volume, presented in a purpose-designed binder and regularly updated. There are separate CORPORATE PROFILE services – one for each of the following sectors:

- *UK Insurers & Reinsurers* (240)
- *Lloyd's Brokers* (220)
- *Lloyd's Holding Companies* (150)
- *Lloyd's Underwriting Agents* (200)

All data is derived from filed Statutory and Regulatory Returns.'

2079. **UK Insurer Security Rating Service**. a. £545. *Volume I* 220 UK Life Offices; *Volume II* 220 UK General Business Insurers; *Volume III* Lloyd's Motor Syndicates. 'Security and Financial Strength Rating on over 400 UK Insurers, each supported by 4 pages of narrative & analysis.

- The *widest coverage* of any UK Market Rating Service available
- Chosen by *BIIBA* as the rating service of choice for their members
- The *highest quality* of research, analysis and presentation
- The only rating service to analyse Claims Reserves Development by Risk Group, by year of origin – *The Professional Analysis*
- *Value for Money* due to the wide usage of the ISAS service no other rating service offers better value for money

Based on a notional price per rating, ISAS costs less than half the price of comparable services.'

(47) #890 Financial Rates PO Box 088888, North Palm Beach, FL 33408–9919, USA. t: (407) 627 7330; f: (407) 627 7335.

2080. **Bank Advertising News**. w. $298. The latest creative marketing techniques and promotions by banks, thrifts, credit unions, and their agencies.

2081. **Bank Rate Monitor**. w. $495. Summarizes current deposit and loan rates set by banks and thrifts.

(48) #891 FINSTAT Fitzroy House, 13–17 Epworth House, London EC2A 4DL, UK. t: (44 171) 825 8227; f: 825 8039.

'The best investment decisions all rely on getting the right information at the right time from the best possible source. And in today's financial markets, the most authoritative source is the *Financial Times*. However, the Financial Times is more than just a newspaper. FINSTAT has been created to deliver vital statistical data from over 18 years of FT archives instantly, comprehensively and in a form that suits you. FINSTAT is for the finance professionals. . . . It gives you access to statistical information on a range of investments, including equities, gilts, unit trusts, insurance funds, offshore funds and investment trusts, as well as the FT indices, dividends, currency information . . . and more. FINSTAT data is delivered daily by electronic mail, weekly or monthly on disk and in printed form.

The *Electronic Data Feed* delivers prices and related information directly from the Financial Times to your computer to update a wide range of financial software applications and in-house systems . . . Most major software companies are compatible with FINSTAT's EDF because of its proven authority, reliability and simplicity. Their products include applications for:

- *Portfolio valuations*
- *Graphical analysis*
- *CGT and personal tax returns*
- *Technical analysis*
- *Index tracking*

The *FT-Actuaries Indices* have been produced and published by the Financial Times since 1962. The FT-Actuaries All-Share Index and its relevant sector indices represent the financial professional's benchmarks for the level of the UK market. . . . FINSTAT has recognised the need among fund managers and financial analysts to have access to the greatest possible detail of this information in an easy-to-manage electronic format. To meet this need FINSTAT has developed a range of electronic datafeeds which can be swiftly and easily incorporated into a spreadsheet or database environment. . . . The information includes:

- names of constituent stocks, along with their industry sectors
- constituent companies' share prices, yields and price earnings ratios
- number of shares in issue
- details of capital changes
- denominator levels
- market capitalisation changes

These are the actual statistics used in the calculation of the Index and represent a unique Financial Times resource.'

(49) #892 Firstmark 34 Juniper Lane, Newton Center, MA 02159, USA. t: (800) 729 2600/(1 617) 965 7989; f: 965 8510.

'We/ve *selected* the most comprehensive . . . Business databases available for use as mailing lists, PC databases or reports and we *support* more formats than anyone in the business . . . FIRSTMARK turns around 95% of all jobs within 48 hours – or immediately through our *Instant Database* modem service . . . You pay only for the data you receive. . . . There is no additional charge for individual selects or formatting into almost any major database, spreadsheet, or word-processor.

The *FIRSTMARK Financial Institutions Database* contains: 227,000 names of individual officers in US banks; 11,339 headquarter banks; 69,800 branches with manager's name; 2,297 savings and loan associations with senior officers' names.'

(50) #893 Franey Publishers South Quay Plaza, 183 Marsh Wall, London E14 9FS, UK. t: (44 171) 538 5386; f: 538 8624.

2082. **Mortgage Finance Gazette**. w. £44.20. **online**.

2083. **Who's Who in Mortgage Finance**. a. £49.50.

(51) #894 FT Magazines Greystoke Place, Fetter Lane, London EC4A 1ND, UK. t: (44 171) 405 6999; f: 2412 0263.

2084. **Banker**. m. £110. **online**.

(52) #895 FT Management Reports Maple House, 149 Tottenham Court Road, London W1P 9LL, UK. t: (44 171) 896 2222; f: 896 2399. *Also* Financial Times, 14 East 60th Street, Penthouse, New York, NY 10022, USA. t: (1 212) 888 3469; f: 729 9598.

2085. **Who Owns What in World Banking (Year)**. a. £192. 'Indispensable guide to the subsidiary and affiliated banking interests of over 200 of the world's largest banks including multinational and consortium banks.'

(53) #896 FT Newsletters Maple House, 149 Tottenham Court Road, London W1P 9LL, UK. t: (44 171) 896 2222; f: 896 2276. *Also* Financial Times, 14 East 60th Street, Penthouse, New York, NY 10022, USA. t: (1 212) 888 3469; f: 729 9598.

2086. **Credit Ratings in Emerging Markets**. q. £550.

2087. **Credit Ratings International**. q. £600. 'A unique information service, providing the ratings assigned by the world's most influential credit rating agencies to over 6000 issuers of internationally traded debt. Benchmark ratings of both short- and long-term paper are included, with different agencies' ratings of the same issuer presented side by side for ease of comparison. Multiple ratings of individual issuers are aggregated into the unique *FT-CRI Composite Index*. The *Agencies* whose ratings are included are all recognised by national authorities for regulatory purposes. They include:

- *Duff & Phelps, Chicago*
- *Fitch Investors Service, New York*
- *IBCA, London*
- *Moody's Investors Service, New York*
- *Standard & Poor's Corporation, New York*

as well as agencies from Canada, France and Japan.'

2088. **Euromarket Report**. w. **online**.

2089. **International Banking Report**. **online**.

2090. **World Insurance Report**. bi-w. £565. **online**. International service for the world's insurance and reinsurance management.

(54) #897 Greenwich Associates 8 Greenwich Office Park, Greenwich, CT 06831–5195, USA. t: (1 203) 629 1200; f: 629 1229.

'In the 21 years since we began with a set of ideals – and an original concept for a new service for senior management – to build a leading professional firm, we have enjoyed a remarkable acceptance in the major financial markets of the world. Now in 60 major markets for professional financial services, we serve virtually all the leaders. As senior executives rely increasingly on our experience, information and judgement, we appreciate the sober reponsibility that goes with our influence and gladly accept the requisite discipline as individual professionals and as a firm.

Three crucial components combine together in the value-added services we deliver as clients:

- *Relationships* The trust and confidence – and shared understanding – that comes over time from years and years of working productively and successfully together on important matters of strategy, tactics, and policy.
- *Experience* The accumulation of that deep understanding of the essential nature and dynamics of important competitive markets and of the organizations that compete in them that enables our consultants to give advice on which clients can always rely.
- *Research* The extensive, systematic, objective, and accurate information gathered from well-informed sources and presented promptly and in convenient form so our consultants and clients can put it to vigorous good use in making decisions and taking action. . . . Each year, 40,000 executives join in our interviews in 9 different languages in 20 countries. We invest nearly $500,000 *every year* in providing these busy executives with information they can use profitably in doing their jobs. Our *GREENWICH REPORTS* are sent to them as part of our 'thank you' for sharing with us their knowledge, experience, and judgement – upon which all our services depend. Full of solid factual information on what is really going on, with interesting and thought-provoking analysis and commentary, these reports are widely recognized as *the* authoritative source of the most important developments in the world's financial markets.

While most widely known for our extensive, continuous research – which is so clearly a powerfully differentiating factor – we believe our consultants' experience and expertise are even more important. And we *know* our long, long-term relationships with our clients are crucial. To us, our clients *are* the firm.'

(55) #898 Hanover Publishers 200 West 57th Street, New York, NY 10019, USA. t: (1 212) 399 1084; f: 245 1973.

2091. **Bankers Monthly**. m. Founded in 1883.

(56) #899 Harvard Business School Publishing 60 Harvard Way, Boston, MA 02163, USA. t: (1 617) 495 6700; f: 496 8066. *Also* c/o McGraw-Hill Book Company Europe, Shoppenhangers Lane, Maidenhead, Berkshire, SL6 2QL, UK. t: (44 1628) 23432; f: 770224.

2092. **Finance (Year)**. a. £16.50. 'Provides in-depth profiles of a wide range of firms that offer attractive financial services career opportunities, from the powerful Wall Stret giants to regional firms and boutique investment banks. . . . Also included are a mailing list of recruiting contacts of these companies, a selective bibliography of relevant books and directories compiled by the Career Resources Library at the Harvard Business School, and a useful glossary of investment banking and finance terms.'

(57) #900 Ibbotson Associates 225 North Michigan Avenue, Suite 700, Chicago, IL 60601–7676, USA. t: (1 312) 616 1620; f: 616 0404.

2093. **Stocks, Bonds, Bills and Inflation (Year)**. a. 'This book is a history of the returns on the capital markets in the United States from 1926 to the present.'

(58) #901 IBC Publishing IBC House, Vickers Drive, Brooklands Industrial Park, Weybridge, Surrey KT13 0XS, UK. t: (44 1932) 354020; f: 353844 *and* **IBC/Donoghue** 290 Eliot Street, PO Box 9104, Ashland, MA 017121–9104, USA. t: (1 508) 881 2800; f: 881 0982.

2094. **Banking Technology**. 10/year. £115. **online**. 'For almost a decade, nearly 60,000 senior executives in the finance sector have come to rely on *Banking Technology* as the most reliable source of information available to them . . . Has established itself as the global authority on financial systems with financial institutions and systems suppliers worldwide . . . No other publication reaches as many international financial operations executives in so targeted a manner.'

2095. **Bond Fund Report**. w. $1,095. Provides 30-day SEC yields, distribution rate, average duration, average maturity, and cash position for more than 700 bond funds. Features commentary, charts and summary data.

2096. **Cash Management News**. 10/year. £247. **online**. 'Details of new products and services, regular reviews, case studies and solutions to cash and treasury management problems.'

2097. **EDI Update**. 10/year. £247. 'Unique newsletter providing senior executives with informed, objective analysis in a clear, non-technical style.'

2098. **Financial Marketing Update**. m. £223. 'The only monthly newsletter that specifically deals with marketing across the whole of the financial sector.'

2099. **Financial Technology International Bulletin**. m. £269. 'Regarded as the world-wide authoritative digest of financial technology news.'

2100. **Insurance Systems Bulletin**. m. £269. **online**. 'Latest market developments relating to the impact of IT in insurance markets across the world.'

2101. **Money Fund Directory**. a. $29.95. Provides names, addresses, telephone numbers and ten-year performance history for more than 700 money market funds.

2102. **Money Fund Report**. w. $1,195. For investment professionals and bankers who compete with money funds. Reports on money fund portfolio holdings, 7–day and 30–day yields, and average maturities. Covers 950–plus taxable and tax-free money funds registered in the US and digests summary data for distinct groups of funds, from no-risk US Treasury funds to more aggressive funds that buy non-prime paper. 'The *only* complete statistical review of *every* money fund ... Since 1975, the required reference for money managers ... CEOs ... fixed income traders ... trust officers ... portfolio managers ... corporate treasurers and CFOs ... pension fund managers ... financial analysts ... anyone who needs to be current on monet market funds.'

2103. **Money Market Insight**. m. $595. Provides the investment professional with a statistical summary on over 860 taxable and tax-free money funds and reports on trends in short term investing with in-depth analysis of the fixed income market.

2104. **Mutual Funds Almanac**. 'Reference guide including performance data, toll-free telephone numbers and addresses for more than 1900 mutual funds.'

2105. **Quarterly Report on Money Fund Performance**. q. $425. **diskette**. q. $825. Provides expense ratios and other information for a comparative analysis of money fund performance.

2106. **Property Finance & Development**. m. 159. 'Expert insight and analysis of trends and developments in the UK market.'

(59) #902 IBCA Eldon House, 2 Eldon Street, London EC2M 7LS, UK. t: (44 171) 417 4222; f: 417 4242. *Also* 420 Lexington Avenue, Suite 609, New York, NY 10170, USA. t: (1 212) 687 1507; f: 687 1570.

'Established in 1978, IBCA is a leading international credit rating agency based in London, with offices in New York, Paris, Madrid, Barcelona and Tokyo. Independent and privately-owned, IBCA was created in response to the growing need for objective, carefully researched credit analysis of banks in different countries of the world. IBCA was the first credit rating agency to issue credit reports on international banks, and today offers the most extensive banking coverage available from any source. IBCA is recognised by subscribers throughout the world as an authority on international banks and banking systems. In 1988, we began expanding our coverage to include industrial and comercial corporations as well. Currently, we provide authoritative, objective and carefully researched credit analysis of more than 300 banks and financial institutions in 25 countries, and nearly 100 corporations in Europe.

We provide our ratings and reports to over 800 leading corporations and financial institutions worldwide. Among them are the treasury, credit and research departments of major banks, central banks, government agencies, investment houses, institutional investors and corporations.

IBCA is recognised by the US Securities and Exchange Commission as a Nationally Recognised Statistical Rating Organisation, by the Securities and Futures Authority in the UK and the Société des Bourses Françaises in France. We are also recognised in the US by the National Association of Insurance Commissioners.

Since receiving recognition from the regulatory authorities in the United States and Europe, IBCA has been asked by a growing number of issuers to rate their securities, which we do on request.'

2107. **Bank Rating Review Service**. q. £4,000. 'Rating Reviews book containing one page summaries on over 300 banks . . . Access to analysts who specialise in countries covered . . . Immediate notification of rating changes . . . Quarterly & Monthly book available on disc: additional cost £1000.'

2108. **Database Service**. **diskette**. m. £10,000. Financial data (but no ratings) on 3,500 banks in 90 countries. 'Implementation of the European Union's Banks Accounting Directive has meant a change in the data format for a large number of banks in the database. Also, we are working on a Windows version of the database which will be available on CD-ROM for the CD enthusiasts among you, towards the end of the year (1994).'

2109. **International Bank Rating Service**. £12,000. **cdrom**. £15,000. '*Non-US Banks*: Individual rating reports on over 300 banks . . . Reports on banking systems and prudential regulations of 25 (mainly OECD) countries . . . *US Banks* Individual rating reports on approx 45 US banks' holding companies & subsidiaries . . . Individual reports & ratings on largest 8 US investment banks.'

(60) #903 IDD Information Services Two World Trade Center, New York, NY 10048, USA. t: (1 212) 432 0045; f: 912 1457.

2110. **Bank Loan Report**. w. $3,200. **online**. 'Newsletter exclusively reporting major loans being made to US corporations.'

2111. **Bank Systems & Equipment**. m.

2112. **Directors & Boards**. q. $195. 'Journal for top management; members, directors and advisors of boards. A forum for discussion and analysis of trends, strategies etc.'

2113. **Corporate Finance: The IDD Review of Investment Banking**. s-a. $95. 'Contains complete information on financing activity for the past six months.'

2114. **Corporate Syndicate Personnel Directory**. s-a. $95. 'Lists syndicate managers and active syndicate personnel.'

2115. **Eliot Sharp's Financing News**. d. $4,600. 'Update on securities filings, new offerings, availability of new issues and changes in offering schedules.'

2116. **Going Public: The IPO Reporter**. w. $1,195. 'Lists new public offerings, analyzes market trends and indexes aftermarket performance of the top 100 IPOs.'

2117. **Insurance Software Review**. bi-m.

2118. **Investment Dealers' Digest**. w. $495. 'Securities issues in registration, muni and corporate finance data, Wall St news.'

2119. **Mortgage-Backed Securities Letter**. w. $1,595. **online**. 'Newsletter identifying major buyers and sellers of mortgage-backed securities.'

2120. **Mutual Fund Directory**. s-a. $275. 'Indexes load funds, no-load funds, institutional sales funds, contractual name changes/mergers, and much more.' There is also a *Bankers Edition* ($275).

2121. **Private Equity Week**. w. $780.

2122. **Private Placement Letter**. w. $995. 'Newsletter summarizing all recent private placements and summarizing market activity.'

2123. **Securities Traders' Monthly**. m.

2124. **Wall Street Computer Review**. m.

(61) #904 IFR Securities Data 11 New Fetter Lane, London EC4A 1JN, UK. t: (44 171) 815 3800; f: 815 3857.

2125. **Bondholder**. w. £2,650.

2126. **BlockDATA Online**. 'IFR Securities Data and *AutEx* have teamed up to provide online access to the only source for competitive intelligence concerning block trading activity – information that's critical to your marketing effort. Who's the number one broker in telecommunications stocks? What's your firm's share of advertised trading volume in ADRs? Who's trading a specific security?'

2127. **Capital Market Strategies**. q. £295.

2128. **Equities International**. w. 'Reports on developments in the international equity market which affect cross-border investors, banks and corporations.'

2129. **IFR Corporate Eye**. **online**. 'Screen-based swaps and funding service . . . Provides 24–hour coverage of the activities of the global corporate debt and arbitrage markets. It is available exclusively on *Telerate*.'

2130. **IFR Omnibase**. **diskette**. 'The most comprehensive database for International Capital Markets information. This is a custom designed, MS Windows application, allowing users to query, report and analyse any combination of capital markets information simultaneously.' There is also available an *IFR Bondbase* and an *IFR Equibase*, as well as an *IFR Notebase* ('covering the market in Euronotes, syndicated loans, sterling commercial paper and CDs') and an *IFR Bidbase* ('Information on cross-border mergers and acquisitions').

2131. **IFR Vigil**. **online**. '24–hour screen-based news service, available exclusively on *Telerate*. Providing news, data, pricing and comment on the Euromarkets and international bond and equity markets. IFR Vigil is designed for intermediaries, dealers, investors and borrowers.'

2132. **International Financing Review**. w. 'Every week . . . reports, analyses and interprets key developments in the international capital markets:

- Primary syndication details on all Eurobonds
- In-depth articles on new financial instruments and funding techniques
- League tables
- Features on risk management, futures, options and swaps
- News on people and markets – who is making the news, who is moving where, and the rumours in the markets.

Founded in 1973 . . . (it) is read in 67 countries by traders, loan syndication managers, corporate finance specialists, investment managers and treasurers . . . International Financing Review is the most accurate and well-informed observer of the international Euromarkets. Each edition draws on special reports from IFR correspondents around the world and is edited by a totally independent team of experienced financial journalists.'

2133. **Journal of the International Securities Market**. m.

(62) #905 Initiative Europe 69 Bondway, London SW8 1SQ, UK. t: (44 171) 735 9838; f: 820 0802.

2134. **Europe Buyout Monitor**. bi-m. £455. 'Meets the information needs of equity investors, professional advisors, and players such as mezzanine providers and specialist buyout houses.'

2135. **Initiative Europe Monitor**. bi-m. £475. 'News of Europe's venture capital markets . . . Incisive analysis includes: overview of funds being raised; summary of recent deals; market news.'

2136. **Review of Institutional Investors**. Joining Fee £8,500. 'Providing unique information on UK and Continental European investors in private equity funds, based on three years' research . . . Used by both active fundraisers and as a business development tool to identify the next generation of institutional investors.'

2137. **Unquote**. bi-w. £275. 'In August 1992, Initiative Europe launched *Unquote*, a fortnightly newsletter focusing on the UK venture capital industry. We spotted the need for concise, accurate reporting on the everyday activities of this fast changing industry. Nearly two years later, people involved in every aspect of venture capital, from advising to investing and fund-raising, have come to regard it as essential reading.'

(63) #906 Inside Mortgage Finance Publications PO Box 42387, Washington, DC 20015, USA. t: (1 301) 951 1240; f: 656 1709.

2138. **CRA/HMDA Update**. m. $395. 'Focuses on the new *Community Reinvestment Act* (CRA) and *Home Mortgage Disclosure Act* (HMDA) environment of the 1990s.'

2139. **CRA Rating Finder**. **diskette**. m. $250. 'Features 17,000+ ratings for banks and thrifts.'

2140. **Inside Mortgage Finance**. w. $595. 'Complete coverage and analysis of market trends and developments affecting residential mortgage finance. Quarterly ranking of top mortgage originators and servicers in the US. Emphasis on legislative and regulatory changes impacting mortgage lending and mortgage servicing as well as mortgage products. Comprehensive coverage of Fannie Mae, Freddie Mae, HUD, FHA, Ginnae Mae, and VA. Includes extensive data and statistics on mortgage rates, terms, volume, and secondary market activity.'

2141. **Inside Mortgage Securities**. w. $795. 'Complete coverage of the mortgage-related securities market and secondary mortgage market including regulatory and market developments. Includes extensive data on all mortgage-related securities as well as rankings of issuers and underwriters. Complete coverage of private-label MBS, Fannie Mae, Freddie Mae, Ginnie Mae, CMO, and commercial MBS and HEL security markets.'

2142. **MBS Deal Tracker. diskette**. m/q. $900. 'In response to numerous requests, *Inside Mortgage Securities* is now making its various mortgage securities databases available electronically to subscribers. With the new service ... you can easily track all new offerings of private-label MBSs, agency-back CMOs/REMICs, commercial MBSs, HEL-backed securities, and Ginnie Mae MBSs by issuer. The data files will be updated either monthly or quarterly and distributed on diskette (Lotus 1–2–3™ .wk3 files) ... The first distribution covers all deals done in the first quarter of 1994 ... (The service) is only available to *Inside Mortgage Securities* subscribers.'

2143. **Mortgage Lender Directory**. a. $250. **diskette**. a. $500. 'Features more than 4000 lenders that either originate, service or hold 1–4 family residential mortgages. The directory, compiled from government data on mortgage companies, thrifts and commercial banks, includes addresses and phone numbers for most firms as well as pertinent mortgage information.'

2144. **Mortgage Market Statistical Annual**. a. $295. 'A compilation of all the mortgage-related statistics from the newsletters *Inside Mortgage Finance* and *Inside Mortgage Securities* in one convenient, easy-to-use book.' Several rankings, including of 'top mortgage security issuers and underwriters'.

2145. **Seller/Servicer Update**. m. $395. 'Report on all mortgage seller and servicer notices issued by Fannie Mae, Freddie Mac, Ginnie Mae, FHA and VA – as well as private conduits and private mortgage insurance companies. Also included are summaries of all Federal Register announcements and legislation related to mortgage lending.'

2146. **Top 500 MBS Investor Database for (Year)**. **diskette**. a. $500. 'Complete database of the top 500 thrift, the top 500 commercial banks, and the top 500 federal credit unions in terms of their mortgage-related securities holdings ... The data, contained in Lotus 1–2–3™ .wk3 files, are derived from mid-year 1993 financial reports filed with the *Office of*

Thrift Supervision, the *Federal Deposit Insurance Corporation*, and the *National Credit Union Administration*.'

(64) #907 Institutional Investor 488 Madison Avenue, New York, NY 10022, USA. t: (1 212) 303 3300; f: 303 3527. *Also* Institutional Investor (Europe), 56 Kingsway, London WC2B 6DX, UK. t: (44 71) 430 0881; f: 404 5455.

2147. **Annuals on CD**. **cdrom**. $5,000. 'Imaging product which gives you instant access to the annual reports of around 7,000 banks worldwide.'

2148. **Bank Accounting & Finance**. q. $130. 'Designed to keep banking professionals and investors involved in the banking industry up-to-date on the latest accounting rulings, strategies for risk management and other financial reporting issues.'

2149. **Bank Letter**. w. $1,295. **online**.

2150. **Bank***stat*. **cdrom**. w. $15,000. 'Ready-analysed financials and imaged annual reports for around 7,000 banks . . . Since November 1993, Bank-Stat is now able to carry many additional types of qualitative risk information on the same CD-ROMs as the financial analysis. These include . . . Thomson BankWatch full reports and ratings, Moody's ratings, Financial Times Who owns Whom, Institutional Investor Country ratings. . . . Our expertise lies in understanding the accounting principles of banks around the world. We maintain separate accounting policies and data entry formats for each country and, if necessary, each type of institution within each country. . . . With over 240 users, **Bank***stat* is the most widely used credit risk analysis system in the world.'

2151. **BondWeek**. w. $1,470. **online**. Covers the taxable debt markets: treasuries, foreign sovereigns, mortgages, and investment grade and high-yield corporates. 'Only BondWeek talks to the major institutional investors to scope out their investment strategies.'

2152. **Corporate Financing Week**. w. $1,295. **online**. Coverage of all aspects of corporate capital raising, M & A and investment banking. Includes financial innovations, trans, private placements, LBOs, venture capital, accounting and regulatory issues, plus people moves.

2153. **Derivatives Week**. w. $1,295. **online**. 'Get the only weekly comprehensive coverage of who's using derivatives and how. With stories from London, Tokyo and New York, it provides competitive intelligence and reports on the instruments linked to equities, interest rates, commodities and currencies.' Includes each issue a page *Learning Curve*, the 'tutorial for new or potential users of derivatives', which 'is now accepting submissions from industry professionals'.

2154. **Foreign Exchange Letter**. w. $1,995.

2155. **Global Money Management**. bi-w. $1,295. Covers the international fund management industry.

2156. **Goldman Sachs Directory of Global Securities Lending and Repo**

(Year). a. 'Lists the firms that provide their services worldwide, indicating products offered, markets served, names of key contacts, and direct telephone and fax numbers.'

2157. **Institutional Investor**. m. $375. **online**. Produced in both a *US Edition* and an *International Edition*.

2158. **Journal of Derivatives**. q. $195. 'Brings together the most important developments in both derivatives theory and practice.'

2159. **Journal of Fixed Income**. q. $195. 'The one and only publication dedicated exclusively to fixed-income investments.'

2160. **Journal of Investing**. q. $175. 'Written *by* leading investment practitioners *for* leading investment practitioners.'

2161. **Journal of Portfolio Management**. q. $225. **online**. 'Provides in-depth, technical exploration of the most provocative theories in portfolio management.'

2162. **Money Management Letter**. bi-w. $1,295. **online**. Covers the business of US pension fund investment managers. Reports on which funds are hiring new money managers and why, what new strategies and products are being used, personnel changes that shift market power, and trends in master trust and custodial services.

2163. **Portfolio Letter**. w. $1,295. **online**. 'The only weekly newsletter that talks not just to analysts, but to major institutional investors.'

2164. **Real Estate Finance**. q. $110. 'Features articles written by leading real estate professionals, as well as case studies of actual financing deals. Regular coverage of taxation, appraisal, accounting and the law will ensure that you won't miss anything in these key areas.'

2165. **Wall Street Letter**. w. $1,450. **online**. Newsweekly for investment banking and brokerage community. Coverage includes the big firms as well as a number of smaller regional brokerage, mutual fund companies and firms providing services to the brokerage industry.

(65) #908 Insurance Marketing and Management 525 Broadway Street, Suite 300, PO Box 2440, Santa Monica, CA 90407–2440, USA. t: (1 310) 458 3222; f: 395 9018.

'The largest insurance and financial services marketing organization in North America, providing some 200 products, services, and publications to more than 7,000 subscribers. In 1993, insurance agencies throughout the United States distributed 3.6 million copies of the nine IMMS newsletters to customers and prospects . . . Some 3,000 agencies and brokerages enjoy the multiple benefits of *IMMS MEMBERSHIP*. . . . *IMMS SILVER MEMBERSHIP* offers an enhanced version of the membership program. . . . Silver Members receive a CD-ROM disc packed with the equivalent of more than 30,000 pages of quality information.'

2166. **IMMS Weekly Marketeer**. w. 'The most widely read weekly news and marketing bulletin in the industry.'

(66) #909 Insurance Publications 10709 Barkley, Suite 3, Overland Park, KS 66211, USA. t: (800) 762 3387; f: (1 913) 383 1247.

2167. **Broker World**. m. $6. Contains information pertinent to independent life and health insurance agents and brokers.

(67) #910 Insurance Publishing & Printing Company 7 Stourbridge Road, Lye, Stourbridge, West Midlands, DY9 7DG, UK. t: (44 1384) 895228; f: 893666.

2168. **Insurance Brokers' Monthly & Insurance Adviser**. m. £31. **online**.

(68) #911 Insurance Technology Group Suite 206, 16 Brune Street, London E1 7NW, UK. t: (44 171) 247 4213; f: 247 6866.

2169. **Insurance Technology Report**. m. £275. 'Sixteen pages of insurance technology news, features and reports – including two pages of international insurance systems news.' The subscription also includes *The Index of Insurance Systems Suppliers*, and *The Insurance Technology Report Bulletins*.

(69) #912 International Insider Publishing Company Ludgate House, 107 Fleet Street, London EC4A 2AB, UK. t: (44 171) 353 7314; f: 353 0017.

2170. **Bondwatch**. **online**. £250/month for unlimited access (on *Reuters*).

2171. **Daily Data Guide**. **online**. £797. 'Includes a daily fax sent between 6–7 pm London time showing all new international issues in the Eurobond Market shown on *Screen Insider* IIIA-Z/IIJA-Z pages on Reuter during that day.'

2172. **International Insider**. w. £450. 'The best private intelligence source on the Euromarkets . . . Hand delivered in many countries.'

(70) #913 International Insurance Monitor Box 9001, Mount Vernon, NY 10552, USA. t: (1 914) 699 2020.

2173. **International Insurance Monitor**. m. $25. **online**.

(71) #914 International Money Marketing St Giles House, 50 Poland Street, London W1V 4AX, UK. t: (44 171) 287 5678; f: 287 1536.

2174. **Offshore Trust Yearbook (Year)**. 'The essential guide to trustee and corporate developments, contracts and services in the world's principal offshore jurisdictions.'

(72) #915 Investext Group Thomson Financial Services, 22 Pittsburgh Street, Boston, MA 02210, USA. t: (800) 662 7878/(1 617) 345 2704 *and* Thomson Financial Services, 11 New Fetter Lane, London EC4A 1JN, UK. t: (0800) 317 577/(44 171) 815 3860; f: 815 3857.

2175. **BondText Muni**. **online**. 'Detailed and in-depth analysis of debt issued by states, cities, countries, and towns.'

2176. **MarkIntel**. **online**. 'Access to research from 21 of the world's leading consulting and market research firms.' Includes: *Datamonitor*; *Euromonitor*; *Find/SVP*; *Market Share Reporter*. 'Effective 10 December 1994, you can search the MarkIntel database on the *I/PLUS Direct* service FREE OF CONNECT CHARGES. There are also no subscription fees, and no per-line charge. You only pay for the data you choose to display, download, or order for delivery.' *Market Intelligence Monthly* provides details of a selection of reports added to the MarkIntel databases.

(73) #916 Investment Research of Cambridge 28 Panton Street, Cambridge CB2 1DH, UK. t: (44 1223) 356251; f: 329806.

2177. **Cambridge Futures Charts**. w. £515.

2178. **Currency Service**. w. £810.

2179. **Daily Fax Services**. d. £1,950 each service. Three services: Currency, Futures, Equity.

2180. **Global Trends**. m. £425. Weekly long-term charts, analysis and commentary covering major currencies, commodities and financial instruments.

2181. **Monthly Chart Book: European Equities**. m. £520.

2182. **Traded Options Service**. bi-w. £495. Daily high/low/close charts with volumes and indicators along with a summary of the technical status and interpretations.

(74) #917 Irwin Professional 1333 Burr Ridge Parkway, Burr Ridge, IL 60521, USA. t: (1 708) 789 4000; f: 789 6933 *and* 11 Millers Yard, Mill Lane, Cambridge CB2 1RQ, UK. t: (44 1223) 322018; f: 61149. Formerly known as *Probus*.

2183. The **Bond Markets (Year)**. i. 'A desktop reference to world debt market performance and analysis.' The Chapters are: Review of (Year); Economic and Monetary Activity; Mutual Funds, Market Returns, and the Money Market; US Government Securities; Mortgage-Backed Securities and Asset-Backed Securities; Corporate and Municipal Bonds; International Bonds; Derivative Securities.

(75) #918 ISD/Shaw 1150 Eighteenth Street NW, Washington, DC 20036, USA. t: (1 202) 296 5240; f: 452 6816.

'Advisors to financial services firms.'

2184. **Financial Services Alert**. w. $525. **online**. $1,325. By fax: $1,525.

2185. **Financial Services Regulation and Legislation**. bi-w. $1,250.

(76) #919 JR Publishing Box 6654, McLean, VA 22196, USA. t: (1 703) 532 2235.

2186. **Federal & State Insurance Week**. w. $347. **online**.

(77) #920 Key Note Publications Field House, 72 Oldfield Road, Hampton, Middlesex, TW12 2HQ, UK. t: (44 181) 783 0755; f: 783 1940.

2187. **Market Reports**. a. £185 per report. **online**. **cdrom**. 'The ideal way to gain an in-depth marketing analysis of a specific UK market sector.' Sectors covered include: Building Societies; Charities; Credit & Other Finance Cards; Debt Management & Factoring; Equipment Leasing; Insurance Broking; Mortgage Finance; Retail Banking.

2188. **Market Reviews**. i. £375 per review. 'To keep you abreast of developments and opportunities across an entire industry.' Current relevant titles are: 'Corporate Services in the UK'; 'UK Insurance Market'; 'Personal Finance in the UK'.

(78) #921 Kluwer Publishing Croner House, London Road, Kingston upon Thames, Surrey, KT2 6SR, UK. t: (44 181) 547 3333; f: 547 2637.

2189. **Handbook of Insurance**. l. £234.10. Two volumes. 'For many years the HANDBOOK OF INSURANCE has been acknowledged as the 'insurance bible' providing an unparalleled reference work for anyone involved in the insurance business.'

2190. **Insurance Register (Year)**. a. £106.70. 'The Insurance Register is made definitive by strict adherence to a set of criteria applied to each type of company during the initial research procedure prior to the revision of the directory:

- *Insurance and Reinsurance Companies* The Department of Trade and Industry's *Insurance Annual Report* for 1992 lists 823 legal entities authorised to transact a class or classes of business. Every company from this Report is listed in either the *Company Information*, *Exclusions*, or *Companies in Run-Off* sections.
- *Brokers* authorised to transact business at Lloyd's are listed, together with their principal underwriting subsidiaries. "Other Brokers" have been selected from the membership list of the British Insurance and Investment Brokers Association (BIIBA). For these companies, the term "Broker" has been applied to those registered with the Insurance Brokers Registration Council (IBRC) on or before 12 February 1993. Broking firms falling outside this clssification have been classified "intermediaries".
- *Underwriting Agents* We aim to include Lloyd's Underwriting Agents and those from the company market.
- *Loss Adjusters* Companies listed under this category employ at least one member of the Chartered Institute of Loss Adjusters.'

2191. **Insuring Foreign Risks**. l. £269.45. 'A unique guide, giving essential information on the diverse insurance facts and figures in over 200 countries and states world-wide. With insurance legislation and regulations constantly changing, instant access to up-to-date information from one reliable source is invaluable to the international insurance professional and UK organisation opening up new companies overseas.'

(79) #922 LACE Financial Corporation 118 North Court Street, Frederick, MD 21701, USA.

2192. **Quarterly Bank, Savings & Loan Rating Service**. q. $309.95. Features comprehensive coverage of over 16,000 financial services, including information on assets, income, liquidity, asset quality, and capital earnings.

(80) #923 Lafferty Publications The Tower, IDA Centre, Pearse Street, Dublin 2, Ireland. t: (353 1) 671 8022; f: 671 8240. *Also* Diana House, 4th Floor, 33–34 Chiswell Street, London EC1Y 4SE, UK. t: (44 171) 782 0590; f: 782 0586 *and* 420 Lexington Avenue, Suite 1745, New York, NY 10170, USA. t: (1 212) 557 6726; f: 557 7266.

2193. **Bank Annual Reports (Year) World Survey**. a. £549. 'An analysis of the Annual Reports of 100 of the world's largest banks – drawn from 28 countries.'

2194. **Bank Marketing International**. 10/year. £479.

2195. **Cards International**. bi-w. £579. 'Covers the global cards industry, from debit and credit cards to smart and private-label cards. It reports on international issues such as pricing, security, fraud, technology and legislation.'

2196. **Electronic Payments International**. 10/year. £499.

2197. **European Banker**. m. £299.

2198. **Funds International**. m. £499. 'Will provide superior intelligence on the world marketable collective investment funds. It is written specifically for senior management in investment funds and related industries.'

2199. **Insurance Industry International**. 10/year. £499.

2200. **Life Insurance International**. 10/year. £499.

2201. **Private Banker International**. 10/year. £499.

2202. **Real Banking Profitability (Year)**. a. £399. Using data collected by *IBCA*.

2203. **Retail Banker International**. bi-w. £579. 'Encompasses the whole consumer financial services sector, including retail banking products, cards, life insurance, mortgages and mutual funds.'

(81) #924 Lloyd's List International 1 Singer Street, London EC2A 4LQ, UK. t: (44 171) 250 1500; f: 250 0998.

2204. **Broker**. q. 12.

(82) #925 Lloyd's of London Press Sheepen Place, Colchester,

Essex, CO3 3LP, UK. t: (44 1206) 772277; f: 772880. *Also* Legal Publishing Division, 27 Swinton Street, London WC1X 9NW, UK. t: (44 171) 833 8933; f: 833 5521 *and* 611 Broadway, Suite 308, New York, NY 10012, USA. t: (1 212) 529 9500; f: 529 9826.

2205. **Lloyd's Casualty Week**. w. £310.

2206. **Lloyd's Insurance International**. m. $325. **online**. Offers in-depth coverage of world news as it relates to the insurance industry. Includes timely developments in insurance and reinsurance including property, casualty, aviation, fire, automotive, professional and product liability, accident and natural disasters.

2207. **Lloyd's List International**. d. £465. **online**. Covers shipping, insurance, energy, transportation amd finance, with special reports on selected business topics.

2208. **Lloyd's Shipping Economist**. m. £462.

(83) #926 Longman Group UK Longman House, Burnt Mill, Harlow, Essex, CM20 2JE, UK. t: (44 1279) 426721; f: 431059.

2209. **Financial Times World Insurance Yearbook**. a. £147.40.

(84) #927 MACE Management Accountancy & Computer Education, Brenfield House, Bolney Road, Ansty, West Sussex RH17 5AW, UK. t: (44 1444) 459151; f: 454061.

Specializes in the analysis of vertical information technology markets. Recent reports include:

- **Information technology in the UK banks**. 8th ed. January 1995. 225 pp. £195.
- **Information technology in the UK building societies & the Council of Mortgage Lenders**. 6th ed. November 1993. 211 pp. £195.
- **Information systems in the UK insurance industry**. 5th ed. February 1994. 217 pp. £195.
- **Information systems in the UK financial & commodity exchanges**. January 1993. 205 pp. £160.
- **Information systems in the banks of Europe**. May 1993. 299 pp. £295. Two volumes.
- **Information technology in the UK other financial institutions**. 2nd ed. November 1994. 264 pp. £195. 'This MACE vertical market report covers all financial institutions *NOT* included in the MACE reports on Banks, Building Societies, Insurance Organizations and Stock Exchanges. The remaining institutions are the following:
    - Credit Card Organisations
    - Credit Card Guarantee Operations
    - Credit Unions
    - Discount Houses
    - Factoring Services
    - Multi-Function Finance Houses

- Finance Corporations
- Investment Trusts
- Leasing & Hire Purchase Finance Houses
- The National Savings Movement
- Pension Funds
- Unit Trusts.'

(85) #928 Managed Account Reports 220 Fifth Avenue, 19th Floor, New York, NY 10001–7781, USA. t: (1 212) 213 6202; f: 213 1870. *Also* Park House, Park Terrace, Worcester Park, Surrey, KT4 7HY, UK. t: (44 171) 827 9977; f: 827 5236.

'The Global Source for Managed Futures . . . Every month, MANAGED ACCOUNT REPORTS provides in-depth reports of trading advisors, monthly performance data on over 170 private pools and all publicly offered futures funds, as well as important educational research and current development material to help you better understand what to look for in determining the true performance of account managers.'

2210. **MAR**. m. $299. 'Be the first to know about the latest developments in managed derivatives investments worldwide . . . Each month you'll receive:

- 32 pages of independent, timely and reliable advice
- Fastbreaking news and insights on worldwide developments
- Features examining controversial issues
- Sneak preview of upcoming funds
- In-depth qualitative and quantitative research tapping three extensive databases
- Comprehensive performance data on funds and pools
- Easy-to-use, advertising-free format.'

2211. **MAR Hedge**. m. $245. 'In January this year (1994) Managed Account Reports launched a new monthly publication covering performance measurement data for hedge funds. With the widespread recent publicity about these highly leveraged funds and their influence on the mainstream financial markets it is hard to separate the facts from the hype. MAR Hedge is packed full of the latest news from the industry, profiles of hedge fund managers and funds of funds, performance tables and fund rankings.' The *MAR Hedge Database* is also available on **diskette** (m. $6,000).

2212. **MAR's Quarterly Performance Reports**. q. $299. 'Analyzes each trading advisor's program in detail. Over 35 quantitative indicators are shown for each advisor as well as qualitative information. More than 400 trading advisors and programs are covered. Each quarter approximately 30 new trading advisors/programs are generally added.'

(86) #929 M-G Information Services Riverbank House, Angel Lane, Tonbridge, Kent, TN19 1SE, UK. t: (44 1732) 362666; f: 367301.

2213. **Crawford's Directory of City Connections**. a. £239.50 (with quarterly update service). "If you want to know which merchant bank, solicitor, or even PR company advises Bloggings & Co, you have a single reference. Alternatively, you may want to know what other clients solicitors Sharp Sharp and Bent have before hiring them for a tricky action. CRAWFORD's cross-referencing gives the answer" (*The Guardian*).

(87) #930 M2 Communications Reptile House, 20 Heathfield Road, Coventry, CV5 8BT, UK. t: (44 1203) 717 417; f: 717 418. e: info@m2.com.

2214. **Card Systems**. m. £449. 'A timely global digest of exclusive business intelligence for the credit, debit and smart card systems user, integrator and distributor. Banking and financial trading and transactional systems are also covered with a special relevance to this dynamic market sector.'

(88) #931 MAPS Market Assessment Publications, 4 Crinan Street, King's Cross, London N1 9UE, UK. t: (44 171) 278 2662; f: 833 2124.

'MAPS Reports lead in the field of strategic market intelligence. MAPS Reports are written by experienced marketing professionals and analysts to make a serious contribution to the understanding of market structures and dynamics . . . MAPS Reports are structured for easy access and comprehension. Every major topic is treated as a discrete Sector within which there are component Markets. The *Sector Report* is compiled as a broad introduction to the total sector, showing the structure of component markets, how they interact with each other, and the latest trends and market developments. *Market Reports* provide the market data and detailed analysis addressing, where appropriate, the following menu of issues and topics:

- Market Definition
- Strategic Overview
- Consumer Dynamics
- Supplier Profile
- Distribution
- Future Prospects
- Sources

Reports published in 1994 included:

- *Card/Phone Banking* Phone Services; Machine Services; Charge Cards; Credit Cards; Direct Debit & Switch Cards; Storecards
- *Selling Financial Services* Insurance Composites; Independent Intermediaries; Banks; Building Societies
- *Housing & Financing* Housing Stock, Build & Pricing Trends; Building Society Mortgages; Bank Mortgages; Securitised Mortgages/PEP Mortgages; Second Mortgages; Housing as an Investment
- *Insurance* Life; Property & Contents; Personal Effects; Motor; Travel; Permanent Health Insurance; Private Medical Insurance

- *Insurance & Investment* Pensions; School Fees; Endowment Assurance; Mortgages
- *Investment and Savings* Stocks & Shares; Gilts; Life Insurance; Personal Equity Plans; Personal Pensions; Unit Trusts/Investment Trusts; Tessas; National Savings.'

MAPS Reports are available on **cdrom**, and are accessible **online**.

(89) #932 McGraw-Hill 1221 Avenue of the Americas, New York, NY 10020–1095, USA. t: (1 212) 512 2000; f: 208 1718. *Also* McGraw-Hill Book Company Europe, Shoppenhangers Road, Maidenhead, Berks, SL6 2QL, UK. t: (44 1628) 23432; f: 770224.

2215. **Securities Week**. w. $1,310. **online**. Contains news and analysis of the securities industry, futures and options industries.

(90) #933 Media General Financial Services PO Box 85333, Richmond, VA 23293–0001, USA; 301 E Grace Street, Richmond, VA 23219, USA. t: (1 804) 775 8000; f: 649 6097.

2216. **Media General Corporate Bonds Database**. **online**. Provides three years of daily price and volume data.

2217. **Media General Mutual Funds Database**. **online**. 'Covers more than 1,800 stock and bond funds.'

2218. **Mutual Funds Performance Report**. **online**.

(91) #934 Metal Bulletin Futures and Options World Division, Park House, Park Terrace, Worcester Park, KT4 7HY, UK. t: (44 171) 827 9977; f: (44 181) 337 8943.

2219. **Derivatives in Fund Management**. bi-m. £125. Issue 1: November 1993. 'For the growing band of specialists in the institutional fund management community.'

2220. **Futures and Options World**. m. £95. 'For global financial & commodity derivatives markets.'

2221. **(Year) – The Year in Numbers**. a. £139. 'The definitive review of the year ... An editorial review of the year ... Monthly volume and open interest figures for over 350 of the most actively traded contracts – illustrated with graphs and comparisons with 1993 performance ... A comparison of key contracts across exchanges ... Comparison of total volume on US exchanges as opposed to the rest of the world over the last 5 years ... Total trading DTB vs LIFFE vs MATIF over the last 5 years ... A worldwide league table of the fastest growing contracts.'

(92) #935 Michie Butterworth PO Box 7587, Charlottesville, VA 22906–7587, USA. t: (1 804) 972 7600. *Also* Butterworths, Halsbury House, 35 Chancery Lane, London WC2A 1EL, UK. t: (44 171) 400 2500; f: 400 2482.

2222. **Commercial Paper and Payment Systems**. l. $150. Discusses traditional payment systems while analyzing the role of new, alternative methods as they complement or compete with historical modes of payment.

(93) #936 Micropal Limited Commonwealth House, 2 Chalkhill Road, London W6 8DW, UK. t: (44 181) 741 4100; f: 741 0939 *and* Micropal Inc, 31 Milk Street, Suite 1002, Boston, MA 02109, USA. t: (1 617) 451 1585; f: 451 9565.

2223. (Year) **Directory of Emerging Market Funds**. a. £1,000.

2224. **Emerging Market Fund Monitor**. m. £650. 'It is the only publication with a comprehensive guide and detailed information on Emerging Markets world-wide. Each issue contains comprehensive performance for equity and debt funds (open and closed ended).'

2225. **Full UK Equities Listing**. **diskette**. £1,000.

2226. **Offshore Funds**. £275. **diskette**. £1,750.

2227. **Quarterly Roundup of Emerging Markets**. q. £1,350. 'Covers important economic, political, and policy changes affecting more than 50 stock and bond markets world-wide, offering independent forecasts.'

2228. **UK Authorised Pension Funds**. £120.

2229. **UK Authorised Unit Trusts**. £120. **diskette**. £1,000.

2230. **UK Broker Managed Funds**. **diskette**. £500.

2231. **UK Group Pension Funds and Exempt Unit Trusts**. **diskette**. £500.

2232. **UK Investment Trusts**. £120. **diskette**. £500.

2233. **UK Life Insurance Funds**. £120.

2234. **UK Unit Linked Individual Pension Funds**. **diskette**. £600.

2235. **UK Unit Linked Life Funds**. **diskette**. £600.

(94) #937 Miller Freeman 1515 Broadway, New York, NY 10036, USA. t: (1 212) 869 1300.

2236. **Bank Systems + Technology**. m. $65. **online**. 'For officers in operations and systems management.'

2237. **Financial Trader**. bi-m. $38. 'Innovative strategies for global markets.'

2238. **Insurance + Technology**. m. $48. **online**. Articles on information strategies for insurance management.

2239. **Wall Street & Technology**. m. $65. **online**. 'Business strategies for the financial industry.'

(95) #938 Money Market Directories Box 1608, Charlottesville, VA 22902, USA. t: (800) 446 2810, (1 804) 977 1450; f: (1 804) 979 9962.

2240. **Consultant Compendium**. a. $695. 'The only authoritative source on pension investment consultants.'

2241. **Directory of Registered Investment Advisors (Year) with the Securities and Exchange Commission**. a. $295. Includes a title index of some 1200 investment newsletters produced by the Advisors listed.

2242. **Money Market Directory of Pension Funds and their Investment Managers**. a. $895. 'Profiles over 30,000 pension funds, asset managers, and service suppliers nationwide.'

2243. **Pensionscope Datasystems. diskette**. 'Provides the most comprehensive database available on the pension and investment industries.'

(96) #939 Moneyfacts Publications Laundry Loke, North Walsham, Norfolk, NR28 0BD, UK. t: (44 1692) 500765; f: 500865.

2244. **Bank Directory (Year)**. a. £29.95. 'Covers all banks authorised to operate in the UK, Channel Islands, and Isle of Man.'

2245. **Building Society Directory (Year)**. a. £19.95. 'Covers all UK building societies and includes and index of merged societies.'

2246. **Business Moneyfacts**. q. £59. 'The First Quarter 1995 issue briefly covered over 40 types of information including: Average Earnings, Base Rates, Chambers of Commerce, Commercial Finance Trade Bodies, Credit Insurance, Derivatives, Foreign Money Transmission, Forfaiting, Hotel Cards, Loan Schemes, Pension Fund Accounts, Source of Financial Help, Telephone Charge Cards, Venture Capital.'

2247. **Daily Updates Fax Service**. d. 'For instant *Daily Updates* on Mortgages, Savings, Annuities and Guaranteed Income Bonds, all you need is a fax machine. Simply pick up the handset on your fax machine, dial the number of the Fax Service you require and press the START button when prompted . . . The Fax Service you have selected will then come through on your machine . . . Available 24 hours a day.'

2248. **Moneyfacts**. m. £38.50. 'The leading guide to the savings, investment and mortgage rates offered by UK building societies and banks.'

(97) #940 Moody's Investors Service 99 Church Street, New York, NY 10007, USA. t: (1 212) 553 0300; f: 553 4700. *Also* **Dun & Bradstreet International** Holmers Farm Way, High Wycombe, Buckinghamshire, HP12 4UL, UK. t: (44 1494) 422000; f: 422260.

2249. **Moody's Bank and Finance Manual**. a. (plus twice-weekly update). £1,250. Full financial and operating data on 14,000 institutions in the USA.

2250. **Moody's Bond Record**. m. £225. 'Comprehensive, fact-filled guide to 56,000 fixed-income issues.' Includes Moody's ratings.

2251. **Moody's Bond Survey**. w. £1,250. Includes buy/sell recommendations.

2252. **Moody's Municipal and Government Manual**. a. (plus weekly update). Covers over 15,000 bond-issuing municipalities and government agencies. *Moody's Municipal and Government News* updates changes in Moody's ratings and new bond descriptions, financial statistics and audit reports, plus news affecting issues rated and covered in the manual.

2253. **Unit Investment Trusts Service Manuals**. Provides information on over 10,000 Unit Investment Trusts, including multi-state series.

2254. **Unit Investment Trusts Weekly Reports**. Provides current interest-principal payment data on over 13,000 series.

Moody's *Credit Research* services (bank, corporate, insurance, structured finance, etc.) is handled in the UK through: 51 Eastcheap, London EC3M 1LB. t: (44 171) 621 9068; f: 220 7295. *Rating Desk* t: (44 171) 772 5454. An example of such a service is:

- *Bank Credit Research* 'Designed to meet the credit analysis needs of investors in short- and long-term bank financing instruments and deposit obligations.' The service includes:
  - In-depth reports
  - Credit opinions: financial institutions
  - Real-time notification of rating actions as they are released by fax or Bloomberg
  - Industry studies
  - Special comments
  - Sovereign credit reports
  - Monthly rating lists
  - Statistical handbook

An example of a publication produced by the Service is:

2255. **Global Ratings Guide**. m. **online**. 'Moody's ratings provide the international capital markets with a globally consistent framework for comparing the credit quality of rated debt securities. The rating system permits a comparison of rated debt obligations regardless of the currency of the obligation, country of the issuer, or the industry in which the issuer operates.' This publication also provides: *Bank and Bank Holding Company Ratings*; *Bank Ratings by Country*; *Mutual Fund Ratings*; *Securities Industry Ratings*; *Insurance Industry Ratings*; *Insurance Financial Strength Ratings*.

(98) #941 Morningstar 225 West Wacker Drive, Chicago, IL 60606, USA. t: (1 312) 696 6000; f: 696 6001.

2256. **Closed End 250 Sourcebook**. a. $35. Provides performance data, rankings, portfolio information and written analysis for over 250 closed end funds.

2257. **Five Star Investor**. m. $79. 'Don't expect to find a convential investment newsletter . . . We created this publication because we know that you don't trust gimmicky articles like 'How to turn $500 into $500,000 in two weeks'. Nor are you apt to follow blindly the advice of a self-appointed investment guru . . . And that's why we made 5–Star Investor so dramatically different from traditional investment letters. This publication helps you build and manage your own winning mutual-fund portfolio. . . . More than half of each issue is devoted to our hand-picked mutual-fund universe, the Morningstar 500.'

2258. **Morningstar 500 Sourcebook**. a. $35.

2259. **Morningstar Closed End Funds**. l. $195.

2260. **Morningstar Mutual Funds**. l. $395. Provides comprehensive information, including performance data, ratings, portfolio listings, and written analyses on 1240 mutual funds. Features commentaries on various fund-related subjects.

2261. **Morningstar No Load Funds**. l. $145.

2262. **Mutual Fund Performance Report**. m. $195. Contains performance data, rankings and statistics for over 2,000 mutual funds.

2263. **Mutual Funds Ondisc. cdrom**. $795. Compares, analyzes and tracks over 2,400 mutual funds and produces customized reports and graphs.

2264. **Variable Annuity/Life Performance Report**. m. $195.

(99) #942 Mortgage Commentary Publications PO Box 28315, Washington, DC 20038–8315, USA. t: (1 202) 347 2665; f: 737 0860.

2265. **Mortgage Marketplace**. w.

(100) #943 National Quotation Bureau 150 Commerce Road, Cedar Grove, NJ 07009–1208, USA. t: (1 201) 239 6100; f: 239 0080.

- *Interdealer quotation system* '(The) Bureau is a recognised (by regulatory agencies) interdealer quotation system . . . An over-the-counter and third market, market maker listing service. Market makers list the securities that they want to make and/or are offering for sale. Currently, we have 352 market makers with 13,078 positions and 3,792 securities listing. This service is only available to registered security brokers and dealers.'

2266. **Pink Sheets & Yellow Sheets**. d. 'The complete OTC market picture at a glance . . . NQB's exclusive over-the-counter interdealer quotation system brings together buyers and sellers of equities (Pink Sheets) and taxable bonds (Yellow Sheets) with market makers at the point of sale. Only financial institutions, and registered brokers or dealers, may buy the Pink Sheets and Yellow Sheets. Only market makers who are registered brokers or dealers can be listed in the Pink Sheets and Yellow Sheets . . . Printed copy is delivered by the opening of the next trading day . . . Electronic copy is available through a number of terminal vendors including: Automatic Data Processing, Quotron, Reuters, Track Data and others.'

- *Library Research Service* 'Designed for legal firms, corporations, brokers, dealers, individual investors, research analysts, investment professionals, banks and insurance companies . . . Provides stock and bond prices for:
    - Legal and regulatory purposes
    - Portfolio evaluation
    - Tax planning
    - Estate planning
    - Corporate intelligence
    - Corporate reporting
    - Research analysis

Prices are available from prior to 1950 right up to today. We prepare reports for securities by inside bid and ask, range, last bid, last ask or closing price – usually the same day. We can send your reports by mail or FAX

NQB's research library contains all the securities listed for trading on the New York Stock Exchange, American Stock Exchange, Regional Stock Exchanges, NASDAQ and non-NASDAQ Pink Sheet securities. We also make available stocks, rights, warrants, units, mutual funds and options.'

- *Pricing service* 'Sold through wholesale vendors that provide value added electronic delivery. Coverage includes: NASDAQ, Bulletin Board, and unique NQB over-the-counter securities. It is available through: Muller Data, Interactive Data Corporation, Telekurs, PC Quote and Merrill Lynch. We are working with several prospective wholesalers including Bloomberg.'

2267. **National Bond Summary**. m. Covers 17,000 bonds in a similar format to the *National Stock Summary*.

2268. **National Stock Summary**. m. Covers 39,000 equities; current reference to 40,000 companies and 13,000 month-end market prices; and historic reference to 15 years of capital changes and other corporate actions. 'Even if a company in which you're interested has changed its name or is no longer traded, you'll be able to locate it.'

2269. **OTC Market Report**. w. 'For senior corporate officers, and corporate communications and public relations professionals, this weekly one-page sheet keeps you up to speed on vital information concerning the stock market's perception of your firm. . . . Can also keep you current on the financial community's view of your industry, and inform you of significant events impacting your competitors.'

2270. **National Quotation Bureau Pink Sheets**. d.

(101) #944 National Underwriter Company 505 Gest Street, Cincinnati, OH 45203, USA. t: (1 513) 721 2140; f: 721 0126.

2271. **FC&S Bulletins**. l. $550. Six volumes. **diskette**. 'Put the best back-up team in the business to work for you! . . . Standard policy forms; Coverages offered by individual companies; Court decisions on policy provisions; Anwers to real-life questions from today's insuarnce practitioners.' The six volumes are: *Casualty-Surety*; *Fire-Marine*; *Personal Lines*; *Companies & Coverages*; *Guide to Policies* (two volumes).

2272. **National Underwriter**. w. $156 (both editions). **online**. 'For nearly 100 years . . . has covered the *entire* industry. Both National Underwriter editions (*Life & Health/Financial Services*; *Property & Casualty/Risk & Benefits Management*) provide you with:

- Product news and trends that are shaping the marketplace
- Innovations that are changing today's companies and distribution systems
- News that affects how insurance professionals will do their jobs in the future
- Legislative and regulatory developments from Washington and the states
- Financial news and statistical information
- Complete, unbiased independent news coverage – timely, valuable information of the insurance industry as a whole, not just one or two segments.'

2273. **RF&S Bulletins**. l. $299. Two volumes. 'Risk Funding and Self-Insurance . . . Self-insurance is no longer a concept of the future – it's here now!'

(102) #945 Nelson Publications One Gateway Plaza, Port Chester, NY 10573, USA. t: (1 914) 937 8400; f: 937 8908.

2274. **Nelson's Directory of Plan Sponsors**. a. $475. Profiles the investments of more than 10,000 sponsors of pension and endowment funds.

2275. **Nelson's Guide to Pension Fund Consultants (Year)**. a. $250 Provides descriptions of more than 350 professional consulting firms serving sponsors of employee benefit funds, foundations, and endowments.

(103) #946 NOP Corporate and Financial 1&2 Berners Street, London W1P 4DR, UK. t: (44 171) 612 0181; f: 612 0222.

'We run the *Financial Research Survey* (FRS), a continuous monitor of personal financial holdings based on 60,000 interviews a year with consumers. We also run the *Business Start-Ups Survey*, based on interviews with businesses that have been trading for less than one year.'

(104) #947 NTC Publications Farm Road, Henley-on-Thames, Oxfordshire, RG9 1EJ, UK. t: (44 1491) 411000; f: 571188.

2276. **Insurance Pocket Book (Year)**. a. £26. '45,000 insurance facts concentrated into a handy pocket-sized volume . . . As well as providing a comprehensive and detailed statistical profile of the UK insurance business, the guide also contains valuable data on major overseas insurance markets, including the Life and General markets of Belgium, France, Germany, Italy, Netherlands, Spain, Australia, Japan and the USA. Published in association with *Tillinghast*, a leading international insurance and management consultancy.'

2277. **Pensions Pocket Book (Year)**. Published in association with *Bacon & Woodrow*. a. £17.50. Twenty sections, including: Background to Pension Schemes; Legal Framework to Pensions; Disclosure of Pension Scheme Information; The Financial Services Act and Pension Schemes; Accounting for Pension Costs.

(105) #948 Oceana Publications 75 Main Street, Dobbs Ferry, New York, NY 10522, USA. t: (1 914) 693 8100; f: 693 0402.

2278. **Payment Systems of the World**. l. $175.

(106) #949 OneSource Information Services 150 Cambridge Park Drive, Cambridge, MA 02140, USA. t: (800) 554 5501; f: (1 617) 441 7239 *and* Lotus Park, The Causeway, Staines, Middlesex, TW18 3AG, UK. t: (44 1784) 445702; f: 445033.

'A leading provider of business and financial information on compact disc . . . OneSource products offer a strategic advantage when used to support equity and fixed-income investment research, portfolio management, corporate finance and valuation strategies, credit analysis, and industry and competitive research. This information is collected from respected leading databases and is available by subscription that can be tailored to individual subscriber's needs and budgets. Complete compatibility with Microsoft, Excel, Lotus 1–2–3 amd other popular spreadsheet and word processing software, along with network access and support, add an extra element of convenience and versatility.'

2279. **American Banker**. **Lotus Notes**. Sourced from *American Banker*.

2280. **Articles**. **Lotus Notes**. Sourced from *Information Access Company*.

2281. **US Banks**. **cdrom**. 'Covers all federally insured institutions including commercial banks, bank holding companies, savings and loans, savings banks and branches.' Sourced from: *Sheshunoff Information Services*.

2282. **US Insurance**. **cdrom**. 'Information on US insurance companies including statutory financial information, claims-paying ability ratings and qualified solvency ratings.' Sourced from *Duff & Phelps Credit Rating*; *Laughlin Analytics*; *National Association of Insurance Commissioners*; *Standard & Poor's Insurance Rating Services*.

(107) #950 Oryx Press 4041 N Central Avenue, Suite 700, Phoenix, AZ 85012–3397, USA. t: (1 602) 265 2651; f: 265 6250. *Also* c/o Eurospan Group, 3 Henrietta Street, Covent Garden, London WC2E 8LU, UK. t: (44 171) 240 0856; f: 379 0609.

2283. **Pratt's Guide to Venture Capital Sources**. a. $225. Provides detailed profiles of more than 800 active U.S. and Canadian venture capital firms, with addresses, telephone and fax numbers, contact names, investment amounts, industry and project preferences, and capital under management.

(108) #951 Oster Communications 219 Parkade, Cedar Falls, IA 50613–2752, USA. t: (1 312) 977 0999; f: 977 1042.

2284. **Futures**. m. $39. 'News, analysis and strategies for derivatives traders & money managers.'

(109) #952 Petroleum Intelligence Weekly 575 Broadway, 4th Floor, New York, NY 10012, USA. t: (1 212) 941 5500; f: 941 5509. *Also* 8/14 Verculum Street, London WC1X 8LZ, UK. t: (44 171) 404 8810; f: 430 9908.

2285. **Petroleum Intelligence Weekly**. w. $1,475; via fax $2,950; with *Oil Market Flash* $2,450; via fax $3,925. 'Recognized as the "bible" of the industry . . . PIW's accuracy has made it a must-read for top-level oil executives, the financial community, government leaders, and those who want the best source of timely, accurate news, and original insights.'

(110) #953 Phillips Business Information 7811 Montrose Road, Potomac, MD 20854–3363, USA. t: (1 301) 340 2100; f: 424 7261.

2286. **Bank Automation News**. bi-w. $495. **online**. 'Keen analysis of the news, trends, issues and equipment in the branch and platform automation arena.'

2287. **Bank Securities Report**. bi-w. $595. **online**. 'Find out marketing strategies that can increase your market share.'

2288. **Card News**. bi-w. $495. **online**. 'Every other week, thousands of card executives consult Card News for a complete analysis of the entire transaction card industry.'

2289. **Corporate EFT Report**. bi-w. $595. **online**. 'As a Washington, D.C. based publication, Corporate EFT Report is uniquely qualified to give readers comprehensive coverage and exclusive analysis on regulatory issues as they occur.'

2290. **EFT Report**. bi-w. $495. **online**. 'Inside each issue is the latest word on ATM's, security, mergers, EBT, POS debit and much more!'

2291. **Financial Services Report**. bi-w. $795. **online**. Strategic information for the financial executive. Covers the latest legal, regulatory and business developments in the banking and financial services industries.

2292. **Item Processing Report**. bi-w. $495. **online**. 'Devoted solely to the remittance and check processing arena.'

2293. **Securities Marketing News**. **online**.

(111) #954 Polk RL Polk & Company Inc, Bank Services Division, PO Box 305100, 2001 Elm Hill Pike, Nashville, TN 37230, USA. t: (800) 827 2265/(1 615) 889 3350; f: 885 3081.

2294. **Polk Financial Institutions Directory**. s-a. $225. Covers North America.

2295. **Polk World Bank Directory**. a. $225.

2296. **Polk World Banking Profile: 2000 Major Banks of the World**. a. $425.

(112) #955 Privatisation International Suite 404, Butlers Wharf Business Centre, 45 Curlew Street, London SE1 2ND, UK. t: (44 71) 378 1620; f: 403 7876.

2297. **Privatisation International**. m. £325. 'Report on privatisation and project financing worldwide.'

2298. **Privatisation Yearbook**. a. £95.

(113) #956 RAM Research Corporation Box 1700, Frederick, MD 21702, USA. t: (1 301) 695 4660; f: 695 0160.

2299. **RAM Research Bankcard Update**. m. $695. Covers pricing and marketing trends and data on the bank credit card industry.

(114) #957 Rapaport Diamond Corporation 15 West 47th Street, New York, NY 10036, USA. t: (1 212) 354 0575; f: 840 0243.

2300. **Rapaport Diamond Report**. w. $220. 'Well known in the jewelry trade as the primary source of diamond price information . . . *RapNet* is our most advanced information and trading service. It is our way of linking the diamond, gem and jewelry trade together to form an electronic community where information and business is shared by all . . . RapNet provides a broad range of information. Naturally, the latest news and diamond prices are available instantly . . . You ask questions and receive answers from other members . . . Membership is limited to bona-fide members of the diamond or jewelry trade that have valid resale tax exemption certificates . . . RapNet does not in any way warrant either the accuracy of any information presented by the Service, the credit worthiness, representations, or honesty of any member.'

(115) #958 Reed Information Services Financial Publications, Windsor Court, East Grinstead Road, East Grinstead, West Sussex, RH19 1XA, UK. t: (44 342) 335962; f: 335977.

2301. The **Bankers' Almanac**. bi-a. **online**: **cdrom**: Four volumes. 'A directory of over 4,000 major international banks and their 168,000 branches worldwide. Also including over 23,000 other authorised banks.' Appendices include: *Lawyers Active in Banking Law*; *Associations, Institutions Etc.*; *Coins and Notes of the World*. The cdrom version includes 4 years' consolidated accounts for some 3,000 banks prepared by *IBCA*, with their Ratings where allocated.

2302. **Bankers' Almanac World Ranking**. a. 'The top 3000 international banks ranked by total assets.'

(116) #959 Risk Magazine 104–112 Marylebone Lane, London W1M 5FU, UK. t: (44 171) 487 5326; f: 486 0879.

2303. **Emerging Markets Investor**. m. £199.

2304. **Risk**. m. Leading review of risk-based financing techniques.

2305. **RISKDATA**. m/q. End-of-day swap prices for (variable) periods back to 1987 for 12 currencies. Supplied on **disc**; update by modem delivery. Optional graphics database. Data supplied by *Data Analysis Risk Technology (DART) Ltd*, based on prices provided by *Intercapital Brokers Ltd*.

(117) #960 Risk & Insurance Research Group 4 Henrietta Street, Covent Garden, London WC2E 8PS, UK. t: (44 171) 836 0614; f: 379 8335.

'Formed to meet the need for an independent organisation to undertake research and consultancy in risk and insurance.'

2306. **Captive Insurance Company Review**. m. £285. 'Technical news briefing on alternative risk financing.'

2307. **International Broker**. m. £255. 'Market review for insurance brokers.'

2308. **International Insurance Report**. m. £255. *Who Should Read It* 'The insurance buyers of corporations which have an international spread of risks; The major direct insurers and brokers providing a global service to major buyers; The reinsurers who need to know what is happening on the economic, legislative and tax front in the countries in which they are operating, as well as about local changes in tariffs, pricing and new covers etc.'

2309. **Worldwide Insurance Abstracts**. m. £265. 'Comprehensive digest of news, articles, facts and figures culled from sources all over the world. Its purpose is to act as a monthly "executive summary" in the fields of insurance, reinsurance and risk management.'

(118) #961 Rough Notes 1200 North Meridian Street, PO Box 564, Indianapolis, IN 46206, USA. t: (800) 428 4384/(1 317) 634 1541; f: (800) 321 1909/ (1 317) 634 1041.

2310. **Life & Health Insurance Sales**. m. $25. **online**.

2311. **Marketplace Search**. **diskette**. q. $79.95. 'Special risks. Hard to place coverages. Sure, they're a part of the business, but finding the right provider in your area could consume a lot of time and energy – until *Rough Notes* offered *Marketplace Search* in the fall of 1992.'

2312. **Policy, Form and Manual Analyses**. l. $330/$175. Three volumes. **diskette**. bi-m. $249.95. 'Reference tool used by agents, trainers, underwriters and claims prsonnel to answer tough questions about insurance issues. More than 300 policy forms and endorsements commonly used by property and casualty companies are analysed in easy to understand language.'

2313. **Rough Notes**. m. $25. 'Starting 117 years ago . . . has provided agents with the information and insights they need . . . *Rough Notes* tackles the tough issues like: Foreign ownership; Government intervention; marketing plans of insurers; producer management . . . (E)very month: Marketing Agency of the Month; Critical Issue Reports; Court Decisions and their effect on the industry; Risk Management assessments.'

(119) #962 Securities Data Publishing 40 West 57th Street, 11th Floor, New York, NY 10019, USA. t: (1 212) 765 5311; f: 765 6123.

2314. **Bank Insurance Marketing**.

2315. **Corporate Venturing Quarterly**.

2316. **UK Venture Capital Journal**. **online**.

2317. **Venture Capital Journal**. **online**. 'The only financial analyst of small business investment companies and venture capital companies.'

(120) #963 Seatrade Publications 42–48 North Station Road, Colchester CO1 1RB, UK. t: (44 206) 45121; f: 45190.

2318. **City of London Directory & Livery Companies Guide**. a. £17.50. 'A unique reference book listing all Liverymen of the City of London Companies by name and address, providing also an up-to-date guide to the City.'

(121) #964 Searchline Publishing Bull Lane, Chislehurst, Kent, BR7 6NY, UK. t: (44 181) 295 0739; f: 467 3180.

2319. **Bank Information Sheets**. l. £135.

2320. **Complete Guide to Banks in the UK & Who's Who**. a. £65.

2321. **Complete Guide to Financial Advisers in the UK**. a. £65.

2322. **Complete Guide to Leasing, Factoring, Invoice Discounting & Trade Financing Companies in the UK**. a. £65.

2323. **Complete Guide to Sources of Commercial Mortgages**. a. £65.

2324. **Complete Guide to Sources of Finance for Property Developers/ Investors**. a. £65.

2325. **Complete Guide to Venture Capital Companies in the UK (Year)**. a. £65. Covers 150 companies.

(122) #965 Sheshunoff Information Services 505 Barton Springs Road, Suite 1100, Austin, TX 78704, USA. t: (1 512) 472 2244; f: 476 1251.

2326. **Bank Database**. **cdrom**. q. 'An interactive historical database covering all federally insured banks and savings banks . . . Full balance sheet and income statement data, Sheshunoff Ratings, subcategory items and subtotals. Nonfinancial data includes city, state, county, MSA, certificate nos., holding company name and nos., minority ownership, phone and fax nos., number of branches, officers' names and titles.'

2327. **Bank Holding Company Database. cdrom**. q. 'An interactive historical database covering all federally insured bank holding companies . . . Full balance sheet and income statement data, Sheshunoff Ratings, subcategory items and subtotals. Nonfinancial data includes city, state, county, MSA, holding company nos., minority ownership, phone and fax nos., bank subsidiary names and certificate nos., number of branches, officers' names and titles.'

2328. **S&L Database. cdrom**. q. 'An interactive historical database covering all federally insured savings & loans . . . Full balance sheet and income statement data, Sheshunoff's Ratings, subcategory items and subtotals. Nonfinancial data includes city, state, county, MSA, certificate nos., holding company name and nos., minority ownership, phone and fax nos., number of branches, officers' names and titles.'

(123) #966 Sleigh Corporation PO Box 591, Franklin Lakes, NJ 07417, USA. t: (1 201) 405 1800; f: 405 1785.

'Since its inception in 1976, *EURASTAR* has been the world's leading electronic publisher of financial information on banks across the globe . . . The *EURABANK* database is constantly growing . . . today its coverage approaches 10,000 financial institutions located throughout the world! EURABANK contains a maximum of five years of annual data and, where applicable, five periods of interim data. The recently improved World format contains 1000 data items, thus allowing the specifics of all countries to be addressed. EURABANK relies principally upon local-language annual reports for its data. Where these reports are not available, official publications and other public sources are used, but are then superceded upon receipt of the annual reports . . . At EURASTAR, every effort is made to ensure that we gather only the most reliable sources.'

Delivery Options include:

- *Compact Disk* 'In the latter part of 1994, Sleigh Corporation joined forces with *OneSource Information Service* to produce a Windows-based CD-ROM product. The resulting product, *OneSource International Banks*, is the only bank information service on compact disk to provide up to five years of detailed financial information on nearly 10,000 banks throughout the world!'
- *Dial-Up* 'Individual banks, $25; Up to 199 banks, $20.00 per bank; 200 banks and over, $15.00 per bank.'
- *Diskette* 'Individual banks, $35; Up to 199 banks, $30.00 per bank; 200 banks and over, $25.00 per bank.'
- *Hard-Copy* 'Spreadsheet information on individual banks: $75.00 per bank'

2329. **EURABANK Top 2500. diskette**. Updates throughout the year. $7,000. The top 2,500 banks in the world.

(124) #967 SNL Securities 410 East Main Street, PO Box 2124, Charlottesville, VA 22902, USA. t: (1 804) 977 1600; f: 977 4466.

'A database and publishing company that focuses on banks, thrifts and specialized financial services companies. . . . Founded in 1987, SNL Securities has become the recognized authority for information on financial institutions. Subscribers, regulatory agencies, and national publications including *American Banker, Barron's, The New York Times* and *The Wall Street Journal* rely on our publications and databases for accurate and comprehensive financial, market and corporate information.

Every day our analysts track the industry and capture relevant news, merger activity, market data, and dividend and earnings anouncements for all 1,100 publicly traded financial institutions. When earnings announcements are released, our analysts contact each institution and obtain detailed financial data. The information is immediately added to SNL's databases. The speed with which we collect data, coupled with our extensive network of sources, allows us to offer the most comprehensive data available on the financial industry. Subscribers get immediate access to information, months before incomplete data is available from other sources. Our subscribers, the media, and regulatory agencies rely on us to provide error-free information.'

2330. **Bank MergerFax**. w. $1,700. Summaries and data on bank mergers, faxed over the weekend for Monday morning delivery.

2331. **Bank Mergers & Acquisitions**. m. $795. Analyzes and interprets the consolidation of the banking industry.

2332. **Bank Performance Report**. q. $995. 'Customized for your institution . . . The most timely, comprehensive, graphical and statistical report available – Produced moths before the Federal Reserve releases call report data!'

2333. **Branch Migration DataSource**. 'Provides current bank and thrift branch ownership data which can be viewed at the branch, institution or holding company level.'

2334. **Financial Services M&A Insider**. m. 'Not only reports on the terms and pricing ratios of all deals, it also goes to great lengths to uncover specific market and ownership changes that can tip off the next deal.'

2335. **Financial Services Quarterly**. q. $696. 'This is the only comprehensive reference guide available on specialized financial services companies including finance companies, mortgage bankers, GSEs, investment advisors, REITs, and securities brokers/dealers.' There is also a *Financial Services Daily*: 'All the important events of the previous day are delivered to your desk each morning.'

2336. **Monthly Market Report**. m. $495. 'The authoritative journal covering the thrift industry.'

2337. **Mortgage Bank Weekly**. w. Fax newsletter.

2338. **REIT Properties Listing**. 'Features over 6,000 real property investments owned by all publicly traded REITs . . . The only source that provides property ownership data along with key statistics and financial data.'

2339. **REIT Weekly**. w. Fax newsletter.

2340. **SNL Executive Compensation Review (Year)**. a. $550. 'A comprehensive review of executive compensation levels, stock option plans, directors' compensation, and other benefit programs at banks and thrifts.'

2341. **SNL Mortgage Bank Weekly**. w. $295.

2342. **SNL Quarterly Bank Digest**. q. $699. 'Get all the information you need on every bank and bank holding company in the country. One thousand pages packed with detailed GAAP financials – taken from 10Qs and annual reports – plus up-to-the minute market information, released months before regulatory data becomes available. Includes a detailed two-page report for each of the 400 publicly traded commercial banks and financials on all.' The *Bank Securities Monthly* – available separately for $395 – updates the quartery report.

2343. **SNL Quarterly Thrift Digest**. q. $695. 'Access information instantly on every S & L and savings bank in the country – public, private and mutual.' There is also a *Monthly Market Report* update available for a further $300 per annum.

(125) #968 Standard & Poor's 25 Broadway, New York, NY 10004, USA. t: (1 212) 208 8650; f: 412 0299.

2344. **Mutual Fund ProFiles**. In conjunction with *Lipper Analytical Services*. q. Covers over 750 equity-orientated, balanced, and long-term taxable fixed income funds: both Load and No-Load. Each issue provides Lipper's market phase rating, which measures relative performances in current and previous market cycles. Brief tabular listings are provided for an additional 350 smaller taxable funds and 400 municipal bond funds.

2345. **S&P Review of Banking & Financial Services. online**.

2346. **S&P Review of Securities & Commodities Regulation. online**.

2347. **S&P's Emerging & Special Situations. online**.

2348. **Security Dealers of North America**. s-a. $515. Lists more than 5,000 main offices and more than 7,500 branches of security dealers in North America; includes the names and addresses of more than 45,000 key executives, trade organizations, stock exchange symbols, and state securities administrators.

2349. **Standard & Poor's Called Bond Record**.

2350. **Standard & Poor's Commercial Paper Ratings Guide**.

2351. **Standard & Poor's Daily News. online**.

2352. **Standard & Poor's Financial Institutions Ratings**.

2353. **Standard and Poor's Directory of Bond Agents**.

2354. **Standard & Poor's Statistical Service**.

2354. **Standard & Poor's Daily Stock Price Record: NASDAQ**. q. Gives the daily prices for all stocks traded on the NASDAQ and compiles their averages.

2356. **Stock Price and Ratio Indexes**.

(126) #969 Standard & Poor's Insurance Rating Services 25 Broadway, New York, NY 10004, USA. t: (1 212) 208 1555; f: 412 0352.

2357. **S&P's Insurance Book**. l. £2,250. 'Monthly service delivers S&P rating updates and keeps you in touch directly with S&P analysts, plus in-depth analyses and bulletins on over 900 life/health, property/casualty, reinsurance and bond insurers.'

2358. **S&P's Insurer Solvency Review**. a. $145 per edition. 'Contains the qualified solvency ratings and claims-paying ability ratings you need to evaluate the financial condition of over 3,000 insurers. Life/health and property/casualty editions.'

2359. **S&P's Insurance Digest**. $245.

(127) #970 Standard & Poor's Ratings Group Garden House, Finsbury Circus, London EC2M 7BP, UK. t: (44 171) 826 3800.

2360. **CreditWire On-Line Service**. 'On-line, real-time news, ratings, rating actions and summary analysis. Choice of Corporate, Structured or Municipal Finance services on *Bloomberg* or your PC at $6,100 (per annum).'

2361. **Commercial Paper Ratings Guide**. m. $1,585. 'Ratings and analysis for commercial paper programs with immediate fax notification of ratings changes and announcements.'

2362. **Credit Analysis Reference Disk**. **cdrom**. m. $10,500. 'Includes the latest 12 months of S&P analysis, current ratings and 3 years of S&P news.'

2363. **CreditStats**. s-a. $375. 'Ratios and statistics by industry and by rating.'

2364. **CreditWeek**. w. $2,025. **cdrom** q. $2,925. 'Timely coverage and analysis including *CreditWatch* and *Rating Updates*.'

2365. **CreditWeek International**. m. $550. 'In-depth coverage and analysis of corporate, structured, sovereign and supranational issuers.'

2366. **CreditWeek Municipal**. w. $1,800. 'Features extensive rating analysis, changes and new ratings.'

2367. **Financial Companies Rating Service**. q. $1,150. 'Includes ratings, analysis and financial statistics.'

2368. **Financial Institutions Rating Service**. m. $3,582. 'Includes ratings, analysis and financial statistics . . . and immediate fax notification of rating changes and announcements.'

2369. **High Yield Quarterly**. q. $1,050. 'Complete source of credit information including analysis and ratings outlook on S&P rated high yield and preferred stock.'

2370. **Municipal Ratings Handbook**. m. $1,050. 'Features list of issues, ratings and CUSIPs.'

2371. **Put Bond Handbook**. q. $475. 'Complete source for credit quality and structural information on over 1,500 put bonds.'

2372. **Qualified Institutional Buyers Directory**. s-a. $475. 'Directory of QIBs eligible to purchase (unregistered) securities under Rule 144A.'

2373. **Ratings Handbook**. w. $275. 'Single comprehensive directory on issues and issuers rated by S&P.' *Ratings Handbook Plus* ($550) includes the Ratings Handbook with CUSIPs and up-to-minute voice interaction via telephone.'

2374. **Sovereign Reports**. q. $1,500. 'Comprehensive sovereign and supranational coverage including country reports, economic statistics and comparative ratios, commentary.'

2375. **Structured Finance**. q. $1,215. 'Ratings and analysis on structured debt issues and immediate notification of ratings changes and announcements.'

(128) #971 Thomson Financial Publishing 4709 West Golf Road, Skokie, IL 60076–1253, USA. t: (1 708) 676 9600; f: 933 8101.

2376. **American Bank Directory**. s-a. $299. Three volumes.

2377. **American Financial Directory**. s-a. $499. Five volumes. 'Listings for commercial banks, savings and loan associations, major credit unions, multi-bank and one-bank holding companies, and more.'

2378. **Bond Buyer's Municipal Marketplace**. s-a. $225. 'Commonly referred to as the Red Book . . . is the industry's #1 resource for the most current information on who's who, who's where, and how to reach them fast.' Also includes the latest municipal bond industry rankings.

2379. **RT Access. diskette**. q. 'The fastest, easiest way to match a financial institution to its routing number . . . Complete contact and funds transfer information, including names, addresses, return item phone numbers, Fedwire status, ACH capability, correspondents, and more.'

2380. **Thomson Bank Directory**. s-a. $499. Four volumes. 'The most highly-respected and widely-used industry resource for more than 117 years . . . Comprehensive, accurate and timely information on the more than 70,000 banks and branches worldwide . . . Includes *The Guide to Bank Holding Companies*, which includes up-to-date credit ratings from *Thomson BankWatch*, and *The Financial Services Guide*, a roster of corporate and interbank business services.' *Thomson Global DataBank* is the electronic version, available on **diskette** or **magtape** ($2,470).

2381. **Thomson Credit Union Directory**. a. $145.

2382. **Thomson Savings Directory**. s-a. $250.

(129) #972 Thomson Municipal Services/The Bond Buyer 395 Hudson Street, New York, NY 10014, USA. t: (1 212) 807 5954; f: 989 9281

2383. **Munifacts. online**. 'The most successful companies in the municipal bond business rely on *Munifacts News*. Munifacts provides up-to-the-second and in-depth municipal, corporate, government news and regional coverage; dealers offerings; a full suite of fixed income analytics; third-party services, and access to *The Bond Buyer*'s municipal database, *Muniview*.'

(130) #973 Tillinghast Financial Center, Suite 600, 695 East Main Street, Stamford, CT 06901, USA. t: (1 203) 326 5400.

2384. **Captive Insurance Company Directory (Year)**. a. $175. Also published is *Captive Insurance Company Reports* (m.).

(131) #974 Two-Ten Communications Communications House, 210 Old Street, London EC1V 9UN, UK. t: (44 171) 490 8111; f: 490 1255.

2385. **Briton's Index: Financial Institutions**. 3/year. £228. 'Over 488 pages of detailed information. Lists:

- Banks – UK & overseas incorporated
- 125 Venture Capital Companies – types of finance, max/min investment, specialisation
- Pensions – self-investing, company & local government. Fund values
- 270 Trusts – investment & units. Nature of trust, country focus & value
- Building societies, Insurance/Assurance companies and Charities
- Business & Professional bodies, chambers of commerce, information & research, government departments, regulatory organisations
- 7,600 named contacts, indexed by institutions and title
- 2,460 main entries.'

2386. **Briton's Index: Investment Research Analysts**. 3/year. £228. 'The most comprehensive Directory of stockbroker analysts available today. It is the essential starting point for any Investor Relations or Financial PR campaign . . . It is the result of continuous monitoring of City moves by a dedicated team of experienced researchers.'

(132) #975 United Communications Group 11300 Rockville Pike, Suite 1100, Rockville, MD 20852, USA. t: (1 301) 816 8950; f: 816 8945.

2387. **Credit Union Information Service**. bi-w. $337. 'Gives plain-English information to credit union managers on the most pressing challenges of the day, especially lending, regulations, examinations, membership expansion and services, and investments.'

2388. The **FERC Report**. bi-w. $346. 'Provides up-to-the-minute information to bank presidents and compliance officers on increasing profits and protecting the bank's safety and soundness. FERC stands for *Financial Enforcement Regulation and Compliance*.'

(133) #976 Value Line Publishing Inc 220 E 42nd Street, 6th Floor, New York, NY 10017, USA. t: (1 212) 907 1500; f: 818 9683.

2389. **Convertibles Survey**. $706.

2390. **Fund Survey**. $530.

2391. **Investment Survey**. w. $940.

2392. **Options Survey**. w. $600. 'The all in one service for listed options'. Divided in two parts: Part A – The Strategist contains feature articles, news briefs, option statistics and specific options recommendations; Part B – The Evaluation Section lists Value Line's evaluation and rank for future performance on over 15,000 options, along with deltas, volatilities, theoretical prices, and tickers.

2393. **OTC Special Situations**. $420.

(134) #977 Venture Capital Report Boston Road, Henley on Thames, RG9 1DY, UK. t: (44 1491) 579999; f: 579825.

2394. **Venture Capital Report**. 'Provides a service linking investors with entrpreneurial start-up and expanding companies.'

2395. **Venture Capital Report Guide to Venture Capital in the UK & Europe**. a. £106. 'The Bible of the venture capital industry ... Definitive directory of how and where to raise risk capital in the UK and Europe.'

(135) #978 VNU Business Publications VNU House, 32–34 Broadwick Street, London W1A 2HG, UK. t: (44 171) 439 4242; f: 437 4841.

2396. **Finance Director**. m. £45. 'Aimed at the most senior financial decision makers in UK business.'

(136) #979 The Wall Street Digest One Sarasota Tower, Sarasota, FL 34236, USA. t: (1 813) 954 5500; f: 364 8447.

2397. **Mutual Fund Advisor**. m. 'The top performing mutual funds.'

2398. **Wall Street Digest**. m. $150.

(137) #980 Warren, Gorham & Lamont One Penn Plaza, New York, NY 10119, USA. t: (800) 950 1205; f: (1 212) 971 5240. *Also* c/o Sweet & Maxwell, South Quay Plaza, 183 Marsh Wall, London E14 9FT, UK. t: (44 171) 538 8686; f: 538 9508.

2399. **Bank Asset/Liability Management**. m. $183.75. For bankers concerned with balancing an asset and liability portfolio. Helps bankers reduce exposure to interest rate volatility.

2400. **Bank Directors Report**. m. Newsletter.

2401. **Bank Technology Report**. m.

2402. **Bankers Magazine**. bi-m. $212.95. Established in 1846.

2403. **Clark's Bank Deposits and Payments Monthly**. m. $145.

2404. **Clark's Secured Transactions Monthly**. m. $125. Provides 'how-to' guidance on drafting air-tight lending agreements.

2405. **Modern Securities Transfers**. a. 'The classic authority on all legal aspects of securities transfers.'

2406. **Mortgage and Real Estate Executives Report**. bi-w. $140.00.

2407. **Mutual Funds Current Performance & Dividend Record**.

2408. **Real Estate Finance Journal**. q. $115. Provides analysis of current real estate financing events and issues, giving forecasts on important regulatory trends.

2409. **Thorndike Encyclopedia of Banking and Financial Tables (Supplement)**.

2410. **Truth-in-Lending Manual**. s-a.

2411. **Wiesenberger Panorama**. Provides key statistics on virtually every mutual fund registered in the USA. Displays assets, performance, expense ratio special services, year of origin, sales and redemption charges, hidden loads, investment policy, dividend policies and investment minimums.

2412. **Wiesenberger – Current Performance and Dividend Report**. Provides short term performance analysis on more than 900 funds and 280 money market funds.

2413. **Wiesenberger Mutual Fund Investment Analyzer**. q. Charting service for equity funds.

(138) #981 Wasendorf & Son 802 Main Street, Cedar Falls, Iowa 50613, USA. t: (800) 553 1711; f: (1 319) 277 0880.

2414. **Futures & Options Factors**. w. $228. 'The Futures Portfolio Advisor . . . This publication is strictly the opinion and conjecture of Russell R Wasendorf and is intended solely for informative purposes and is not to be construed, under any circumstances, by implication or otherwise, as an offer to sell or a solicitation to buy or trade in any commodities or securities herein named. Information is obtained from sources believed to be reliable, but is in no way guaranteed. No guarantee of any kind is implied or possible where projections of future conditions is attempted . . . *Risk Disclosure* Hypothetical or simulated performance results have certain inherent limitations. Unlike any actual performance record, simulated results do not represent actual trading. Also, since the trades have not actually been executed, the results may have under-or-over compensated for the impact, if any, of certain market factors, such as lack of liquidity. Simulated trading programs in general are also subject to the fact that they are designed with the benefit of hindsight. No representation is being made that any account will or is likely to achieve profits or losses similar to those shown.'

2415. **Pocket Charts**. w. $52. 'Coverage of the 40 most actively traded commodities.'

(139) #982 Waters Information Services Circulation Department, 57/59 Neal Street, London WC2H 9PJ, UK. t: (44 171) 240 2090; f: 240 2076 *and* PO Box 2248, Binghampton, NY 13902–2248, USA. t: (1 607) 770 9242; f: 770 9435.

2416. **FX Week**. **online**.

2417. **Trading Systems Technology**. bi-w. £595. **online**.

2418. **Wall Street Network News**. **online**.

(140) #983 Weiss Research PO Box 2923, West Palm Beach, FL 33402, USA. t: (800) 783 5330; f: (1 612) 895 5526.

2419. **Irving's Interest Rate Speculator**. $5,000. August 3, 1993: 'Interest sensitive options offer you the most extraordinary leverage you've ever seen. Even better, it's leverage that's only on ONE side. Your maximum risk is your initial investment. It's impossible to get the margin calls and forced liquidations that plague futures contracts and other leveraged investments. You can lose your entire initial investment – but never a penny more . . . With these options, you can be wrong again and again. Then all you have to do is hit just one right . . . If interest rates go up only half as much as under Carter, you can turn $1,000 into $375,000 . . . I am restricting my new service to a maximum of 1,000 subsribers. This is absolutely essential for two reasons. First, I want to make sure that we answer every single one of your questions. Second is the liquidity of the market. I want to make sure you get good fills on your buys and sells. So I have given firm instructions to return all checks beyond 1,000 subscribers.'

(141) #984 John Wiley 605 Third Avenue, New York, NY 10158–0012, USA. t: (1 212) 850 6000; f: 850 6088 *and* Baffins Lane, Chichester, West Sussex, PO19 1UD, UK. t: (44 243) 779777; f: 775878.

2420. **CRB Commodity Yearbook**. a. See *Commodity Research Bureau*.

2421. **Who's Who in Venture Capital**. a.

(142) #985 World Reports Limited 108 Horseferry Road, London SW1P 2EF, UK. t: (44 171) 222 3836; f: 233 0185. *Also* Suite 1209, 280 Madison Avenue, New York, NY 10016–0802, USA. t: (1 212) 599 4560; f: 599 4561.

2422. **Interest Rate Service**. q. $950.

2423. **International Currency Review**. q. $465.

2424. **London Currency Report**. q. $950.

2425. **Offshore Centres Report**. 10/year. $175.

Notes

(162) INGLIS-TAYLOR, A. **Dictionary of derivatives**. *Macmillan*, 1995, p 70.

(163) **Trade Associations and Professional Bodies of the United Kingdom**. 13th ed. *Gale Research*, 1995, p 235.

(164) TEWELES, R.J., BRADLEY, E.S. and TEWELES, T.M. **The stock market**. 6th ed. *John Wiley*, 1992, pp. 234–235.

(165) **Dod's Parliamentary Companion 1995**. *Dod's Parliamentary Companion*, 1995, p 742. 'Now in its 163rd year . . . Is the United Kingdom's most authoritative political reference book . . . Dod's Parliamentary Companion is essential for effective communication with Government, the Civil Service and the European Union.'

(166) RAPHAEL, A. **Ultimate risk**. *Bantam Press*, 1994, p 2.

Further reading

KOCH, T.W. **Bank management**. 3rd ed. *Dryden Press*, 1995. 800 pp. £46. 'This modern introduction to the management of commercial banks helps students learn to apply financial concepts to a variety of credit, investment, and funding decisions. Excellent coverage focuses on the current and future problems faced by banks in a changing regulatory environment.'

ESSINGER, J. **Banking technology as a competitive weapon**. 2nd ed. *FT Management Reports*, 1994. £260.

DUFEY, G. and GIDDY, I.H. **Cases in international finance**. 2nd ed. *Addison-Wesley*, 1993. 292 pp.

ANDERSON, S.C. and BORN, J.A. **Closed-end investment companies**. *Kluwer*, 1992. 139 pp.

BERRY, R.H., CRUM, R.C. and WARING, A. **Corporate performance evaluation in bank lending decisions**. *CIMA Publications*, 1993. 100 pp. £14.95.

BAIN, A.D. **The economics of the financial system**. 2nd ed. *Blackwell Business*, 1992. 320 pp. 'Analysis of the roles played by financial institutions and markets in the working of the UK economy.'

SCHWARTZ, R.A. **The equity markets handbook: Characteristics, analyses and strategies**. *HarperBusiness*, 1991. 752 pp. £45. 'Shows how disparate forces such as microeconomics, institutional market makers, traders, exchanges, regulations and the interplay of various markets themselves, come together to make the equity markets what they are . . . Offers complete coverage of the American and New York stock exchanges, over-the-counter markets, trading systems, secondary markets and the securities industry.'

DERMINE, J. ed. **European banking in the 1990s**. 2nd ed. *Blackwell Publishers*, 1993. 486 pp. Discusses France, Italy, Spain, Portugal, Switzerland and Germany, but with wider coverage than its title suggests, for example, including two chapters each on 'The Regulation of Financial Markets in Europe' and on 'European Equity Markets and Investment Banking'. Each chapter is followed by a critical comment from other authorities.

EUROPEAN BOND COMMISSION. **The European bond markets**. *Kogan Page*, 1990. 656 pp. £50. 'An overview and analysis for issuers and investors.'

European financial centres. No. 5: UK. *Economist Publications*, 1991.

COPELAND, L. and LYBECK, J. **European financial markets**. *Addison-Wesley*, 1993. 300 pp. 'This book is the first to integrate economic theory at a macro level with the institutional changes that will take place in the 1990s under the influence of the single European Act/White Paper.'

COPELAND, L. **Exchange rates and international finance**. 2nd ed. *Addison-Wesley*, 1994. 448 pp.

Factoring in the UK. *BCR Publishing*, 1993. £285. 'The first comprehensive Report & Guide to the UK factoring industry.'

KOGUCHI, K. and FORESTIERI, G. **Financial conglomerates**. *OECD*, 1993. 124 pp. 'The financial services industry can be conceived both as a single market for rather similar products and services, and as a number of relatively autonomous sectors with their specific history, products, institutions and official regulation. Developments in the 1980s have significantly narrowed earlier differences in product and institutional structures, and various financial services have become much closer substitutes for each other. At the same time, financial institutions have become exposed to new forms of competition as traditional lines of demarcation have become increasingly blurred. Given this new scope for competition, it has become particularly important for financial intermediaries to re-assess their overall business strategies so as to be able to meet the shifting demands of their clients and to seek new profitable business opportunities.'

DAIGLER, R.T. **Financial futures markets: Concepts, evidence and applications**. *HarperCollins*, 1993. 464 pp. £25.

KIDWELL, D.S., PETERSON, R.L. and BLACKWELL, D. **Financial institutions, markets and money**. 5th ed. *Dryden Press*, 1993. 700 pp. £17.95.

RIVETT, P. and SPEAK, P. eds. **The financial jungle: a guide to financial instruments**. 2nd ed. *IFR Publishing* FOR *Coopers & Lybrand*. 1991. 684 pp. 'The intention of this book is to enable the reader to enhance his understanding of the many different financial instruments which are now available for the raising of finance or for the management of risk.' Comprises a general introduction, and four main chapters (debt instruments, asset backed securities, equity and equity linked instruments, and hedging instruments), each of which ends with a summary of the accounting and taxation regimes in 18 European countries. An index lists the acronyms and titles of almost 400 financial instruments, ranging from Accreting (or Drawdown) Swap through Bunny Bonds, Flip Flop Notes, Long Straddle, Naked Warrants, Purgatory and Hell Bond, Seasonal Caps, Titrisation, Wedding Warrants, to Zero Coupon Swap.

CUMMINS., J.D. **Financial management of life insurance companies**. *Kluwer Academic Publishers*, 1993. £46.50.

COOPER, S.K. and FRASER, D.R. **The financial marketplace**. 4th ed. *Addison-Wesley*, 1993. 718 pp.

CAMPBELL, D. **Financial services in the new Europe**. *Graham & Trotman*, 1993. 376 pp. Special issue of *Comparative Law Yearbook of International Business*.

GENTLE, C. **The financial services industry: Corporate reorganization and regional economic development**. *Avebury*, 1993. 368 pp. £45.00.

ESSINGER, J. **Financial technology: Effective cost management**. *FT Management Reports*, 1994. £215.

HICKS, A. **Foreign exchange options: An international guide to options trading and practice**. *Woodhead Publishing*, 1993.

DNES, A. **Franchising: A case study approach**. *Avebury*, 1992. 336 pp. £37.50. Analysis of international franchising practices (i.e. allowing others to use a trade name to operate a satellite firm in return for a fee).

VAUGHAN, E.J. **Fundamentals of risk and insurance**. 6th ed. *John Wiley*, 1992. 766 pp. 'My intent from the beginning has been to create a text that is consumer-oriented. The main emphasis is on the insurance product and the use of insurance within the risk management framework. The traditional fields of life insurance, health insurance, property and liability insurance, and social insurance are treated in terms of their relationship to the wide range of insurable risks to which the individual and the business firm are exposed.'

BARTH, J.R., BRUMBAUGH, R.D. and LITAN, R.E. **The future of American banking**. *ME Sharpe*, 1992. 207 pp.

PIERCE, J.L. **The future of banking**. *Yale University Press*, 1991. 163 pp.

The future of money management in America. *Bernstein Research*, 1993, 85 pp. $1,000.

BROWN, M.M. ed. **Global offerings of securities: Access to the world equity capital markets**. *Kluwer Law International*, 1994. 108 pp. £60.00.

CLARKE, N. **Guide to eurobonds: A comprehensive analysis for issuers and practitioners**. *Economist Publications*, 1990. 206 pp. 'The subject of eurobonds is esoteric, that is, it is intelligible only to the initiated. The mystique that for too long has surrounded the subject has relegated the market in many people's minds to the realms of the inaccessible. Commentators themselves cannot repress their awe of the prestigious issuers or of the large sums raised in a single offering. Nor can they conceal their suspicions of the mass of anonymous investors that subscribe to eurobond issues of their slight doubts about the absence of regulation which has allowed the market to flourish and become the leading international debt securities market. Yet eurobonds are a relatively straightforward debt instrument and, thanks to the gradual deregulation of domestic financial markets, they are within the reach of a fast increasing number of issuers and investors worldwide. This book aims to dispel the myths about, and make intelligible the nature of, these instruments and the large variety of derivative products, currency sectors and investor markets that they encompass.'

GEISST, C.R. **A guide to financial institutions**. 2nd ed. *Macmillan*, 1993. 151 pp. The chapters are: International financial institutions; Commercial banking; Investment banking; Building associations; Life insurance companies and pension funds; American federal agencies; Deregulation and change in the 1980s.

MENDELSOHN, M. **The guide to franchising**. 5th ed. *Cassell*, 1992.

BECHHOEFER, 1. ed. **Guide to real estate and mortgage banking software**. *Real Estate Solutions*, 1993. 600 pp. $60.00.

CAPIE, F.H. **History of banking**. *Pickering & Chatto*, 1993. Ten volumes.

MACLENNAN, D. and GIBB, K. eds. **Housing finance and subsidies in Britain: Reviewing and moving forward**. *Avebury*, 1993, 240 pp. £35.00.

BRENNER, L. **The Insurance Information Institute's Handbook for Reporters**. *Insurance Information Institute*, 1993, 148 pp. $22.50.

DATTATREYA, R.E., VENKATESH, R.E.S. and VENKATESH, V.E. **Interest rate & currency swaps**. *Irwin Professional*, 1994. 232 pp. £45. 'Explains how swaps work and how they can be applied in to a variety of situations.'

GRABBE, J.O. **International financial markets**. 2nd ed. *Elsevier*, 1991. 421 pp. 'Standard economics courses, although labeled 'international finance' are really courses in open-economy macroeconomics whose principal focus is optimal monetary and fiscal policy in an open economy. These courses seem to imply that government policy is the major issue of importance in international finance.... In these courses financial markets are often so stylized that an average student with a practical orientation may be tempted into market segmentation: he or she comes to believe that there is economic theory and there is the real world, and never the twain shall meet.... Many descriptive institutional accounts of the international financial markets are also available, but these sometimes suffer from too much institutional detail and not enough theory.... In between these two extremes are standard financial management courses oriented toward multinational corporations or international banking. Such courses discuss international financial markets in connection with other management issues, but their scope is too broad for a proper treatment of financial markets as *markets*.... This book attempts to delineate the basic rules of the game in each of the three major international financial markets [foreign exchange markets, eurocurrency markets, international bond markets] and to convey to the student an intuitive feel for market dynamics.'

DUFFY, G. and GIDDY, I.H. **The international money market**. 2nd ed. *Prentice Hall International*, 1994. An excellent text.

CHANCE, D.M. **An introduction to derivatives**. 3rd ed. *Dryden Press*. 625 pp. Very good clear introduction.

BOVAIRD, C. **Introduction to venture capital finance**. *Longman Group*, 1990. 280 pp. 'The venture capital industry in the United Kingdom is the second largest in the world, after that of the United States. Relative to the size of the UK economy, the amount of venture capital available makes the industry the most highly developed in the world. All this has come about in the last fifteen years, prior to which there was no venture capital 'industry' to speak of.'

ADAMSON, M. and MALES, E. **IT in consumer financial services: The trend towards customer orientation**. *FT Management Reports*, 1994. £235. Includes chapters on: Retail banking; Life insurance; General insurance; Unit trusts; Plastic cards.

SMITH, A. **International financial markets: The performance of Britain and its rivals**. *Cambridge University Press* for *National Institute of Social and Economic Research*, 1992. 208 pp. £24.95.

DRAPER, P. with STEVENS, J. **The investment trust industry in the UK**. *Avebury*, 1989. 192 pp. £42.50.

REUVID, J. ed. **London's financial institutions and services**. *Kogan Page*, 1995. 300 pp. £30. 'Aimed at international bankers, investors, corporations and global traders, it presents the City's current and future role, describes its structure, and profiles its services and institutions in an authoritative yet accessible way.'

HAYES, S.L. and MEERSCHWAM, D.M. **Managing financial institutions**. *Dryden Press*, 1993. 420 pp. £19.95. Selection of cases.

COBHAM, D. ed. **Markets and dealers: The economics of the London financial markets**. *Longman*, 1992. 190 pp. £13.99.

COYLE, R.J. ed. **The McGraw-Hill handbook of American Depository Receipts**. *McGraw-Hill*, 1993. 450 pp. £48. 'This first-of-its- kind handbook pools the expertise of such distinguished firms as Credit Lyonnais, Standard & Poor's, NASD, KPMG Peat Marwick, Morgan Guaranty, and Smith Barney to create a definitive reference on ADRs for professionals and sophisticated investors.'

Microstructure of world trading markets. *Kluwer Academic Publishers*, 1993. 154 pp. £51.75. Reprinted from the *Journal of Financial Services Research*, Volume 6, Number 4, 1993. A valuable introductory collection of papers: especially interesting in this context is the Paper *Automated securities trading* emanating from the US Securities and Exchange Commission and the National Association of Securities Dealers:

'Technological developments have permitted rapid changes in the structures of securities trading markets. These changes call for a reevaluation of regulatory regimes. For example, because divergent market structures competing for order flow may fall within different regulatory structures, the proper allocation of regulatory costs should be weighed. Because of the open access by all investors to all markets that technology permits, regulators need to examine the level of oversight necessary to ensure the protection of investors. Because of existing statutory limits, automated systems pose particular problems in the U.S. regarding the appropriate levels of regulation for non-intermediated trading and cross-border systems that are regulated by overseas authority. On another topic, automation facilitates increased transparency. In turn, transparency promotes investor protection, encourages market liquidity, and fosters the efficiency of securities markets by facilitating price discovery and open competition, thus reducing the effects of fragmentation. In the end, because it enhances the efficiency of the market's price discovery function and liquidity, transparency contributes to the efficient allocation of scarce capital among competing demands for that capital. Finally, regulators should participate in the review of automated systems integrity, especially in the areas of capacity, security and disaster recovery.'

STIGUM, M. **The money market**. 3rd ed. *Dow Jones-Irwin*, 1989.

MAYER, T., DUESENBERRY, J.S. and ALIBER, R.Z. **Money, banking and the economy**. *Norton*, 1993. 574 pp.

The mortgage banking industry. *Bernstein Research*, 1993. 146 pp. $750. Market research study.

DAVIDSON, A.S. and HERSKOVITZ, M.D. **Mortgage-backed securities: Investment analysis & advanced valuation techniques**. *Irwin Professional*, 1993. 300 pp. £55. 'A blueprint for the analysis and valuation of mortgage-backed securities . . . To come to grips with the complexity of MBSs, a number of analytical approaches have been developed – none of which are appropriate for every situation. In this groundbreaking book, the authors identify the advantages and disadvantages of each approach and show investors how to develop an analytical method that is tailored to their own investment objectives.'

FABOZZI, F.J. and MODIGLIANI, F. **Mortgages and mortgage-backed securities markets**. *Harvard Business School Press*, 1992. 300 pp. $39.95.

DUNNING, J.H. **Multinational enterprises and the global economy**. *Addison-Wesley*, 1994. 687 pp. 'The most comprehensive and far-reaching study ever to be published on the interaction between the transborder activities of corporations and the Nation States in which they operate.'

DAVIS, E.P. **Pension funds: Retirement-income security, and capital markets: An international perspective**. *Clarendon Press*, 1995. 337 pp. 'Whereas in 1900 there were 500 million people over 60 in the world, by 2030, as a consequence of lower fertility and the diffusion of medical advances, there will be 1.4 billion. A quarter will be very old and two-thirds women. The issue of population ageing at such a rate poses economic problems of considerable magnitude, on a global scale. . . . This book offers an overview of the economic issues relating to one possible approach to population ageing – namely, the development of funded pension schemes to complement social security, as they have arisen in the industrial countries. The raw material for the analysis is a combination of the economic theory of pension funds and experience regarding social security, as well as the structure, regulation, and performance of pension funds in twelve OECD countries and two developing countries, using information available up to the time of writing – mid-1994. The countries studied are the USA, the UK, the Netherlands, Switzerland, Sweden, Denmark, Japan, Canada, Germany, Australia, France, and Italy, together with Chile and Singapore. The definition of pension funds employed is of financial intermediaries, usually sponsored by non-financial companies, which collect and invest funds on a pooled basis for eventual repayment to members in pensions.'

BROWN, G., DAVIES, R., DRAPER, P. and POPE, P. **Performance measurement for pension fund trustees**. *CIMA Publications*, 1994. 112 pp. £16.95.

Principles of banking. *American Bankers Association*, 1994. 260 pp. $49. 'Long recognised as the *standard introduction* to the banking industry.' *Instructor's Manual* $30; *The world of banking* videotape $345.

BOYDELL, S. and CLAYTON, P. **Property as an investment medium: Its role in the institutional portfolio**. *FT Management Reports*, 1993.

BRUEGGEMAN, W. and FISHER, J.D. **Real estate finance and investments**. 9th ed. *Irwin*, 1993. 832 pp. £45.95.

KAUFMAN, G.C. ed. **Reforming financial institutions in the United States**. *Kluwer Academic Publishers*, 1994. 208 pp. £59.75.

FERRIS, K. and JONES, M. **The Reuter guide to official interest rates**. *Irwin Professional*, 1994. 200 pp. £40. 'Covering 20 industrialized countries . . . provides a thorough explanation of how official interest rates are set, how central banks control money markets and the relationship between official rates and market rates.'

Saving for credit: The future for credit unions in Britain. *National Consumer Council*, 1994. 60 pp. The report of a working party convened by the National Consumer Council and funded by the *Joseph Rowntree Foundation*. 'Fifteen years ago the Credit Union Act gave credit unions in Britain their own legal framework. Numbers have risen impressively since the mid-eighties and there are now some four hundred, based in neighbourhoods, workplaces and churches across the country. . . . Despite this, credit unions remain on the margins. Less than half of one per cent of people in Britain are members.'

REDDY, M.T. **Securities operations: A guide to operations and information systems in the securities industry**. 2nd ed. *Prentice Hall*, 1995. 626 pp.

BENSTON, G. **The separation of commercial and investment banking**. *Macmillan Press*, 1990.

SUTCLIFFE, C.M.S. **Stock index futures: Theories and international evidence**. *Chapman & Hall*, 1993. 432 pp. £27.50. 'The primary aim of this book is to analyse the market from the point of view of a user, and the orientation is away from broad economic questions concerning the welfare effects of the existence of futures markets.'

PRATTEN, C. **The stock market**. *Cambridge University Press*, 1993. 220 pp. £27.95. 'Explains the instability of stock market prices. It describes and assesses theories of the determination of the level of, and fluctuations in, share prices. The practices of fund managers who now dominate activity on the stock market are analyzed and related to Keynes's theories. Keynes's analysis of the stock market was at the heart of his explanation of economic instability and it is apt to reassess his theory at a time when economic instability is greater than at any time since the 1930s. The book provides a wealth of information about the operations of the stock market and returns on investment.'

CLAURETIE, T.M. and WEBB, J.R. **Theory and practice of real estate finance**. *Dryden Press*, 1993. 700 pp. £23.95.

LUCA, C. **Trading in the global currency markets**. *Prentice Hall*, 1995. 567 pp. 'This book introduces you to all the significant aspects of foreign exchange in a practical manner, to best answer your typical questions, such as: Why do we trade currencies?; Who are the players?; What currencies do we trade?; What makes them move?; What instruments can we trade?; How can we use them?; How can we forecast currency behaviour?; How do we access the pertinent information? . . . There are no miracle answers, of course – at least not in this book. In fact, I generally shy away from rules of thumb. The only solid answer I favor is, 'It depends.'. What you will learn is what makes the market move and the traders tick.'

DYMSKI, G.A., EPSTEIN, G. and POLLIN, R. eds. **Transforming the US financial system: Equity and efficiency for the 21st Century**. *ME Sharpe*, 1993. 385 pp. $24.95.

Trends in the life intermediary market: 1988–1993. *Taylor Nelson AGB*, 1993. £995. 'The *Investment and Insurance Monitor* (IIM) is a continuous syndicated survey . . . among a sample of FIMBRA and IMRO members and measures business activity, confidence, suppliers used and possibly most important, main suppliers used. Several well-known life offices are not covered by IIM because they rely exclusively on their own sales forces and/or tied agents. But at the other extreme, ten major companies channel 80% or more of their business through Independent Financial Advisers (IFAs), three of them using IFAs exclusively.'

BUCKLE, M. and THOMPSON, J.L. **The United Kingdom financial system in transition: Theory and practice**. *Manchester University Press*, 1992. 312 pp.

MERCER, Z.C. **Valuing financial institutions**. *Business One Irwin*, 1992. 645 pp. Handbook on the financial analysis and valuation of banks and thrifts.

CHAPTER SIX

Financial Management and Investment

The structure of this chapter is:

Organizations

International

Europe

United Kingdom

- CORPORATE FINANCE AND TREASURY
- CREDIT MANAGEMENT
- FINANCIAL ANALYSIS
- FINANCIAL PLANNING AND ADVICE
- INVESTMENT
- PUBLIC FINANCE

United States

- CORPORATE FINANCE AND TREASURY
- CREDIT MANAGEMENT
- FINANCIAL ANALYSIS
- FINANCIAL PLANNING AND ADVICE
- INVESTMENT
- PUBLIC FINANCE

Commercial information providers

Financial management

Investment

1. Organizations: International

(1) #986 ACME – The Association of Management Consulting Firms 521 Fifth Avenue, New York, NY 10175–3598, USA. t: (1 212) 697 9693; f: 949 6571.

'The leading international association of firms engaged in the practice of consulting to management.'

(2) #987 Associated Credit Bureaus 1090 Vermont Avenue, NW, Suite 200, Washington, DC 20005, USA. t: (1 202) 371 0910; f: 371 0134.

An international association of credit rating agencies.

(3) #988 Financial Women International 500 N Michigan Avenue, Suite 1400, Chicago, IL 60611, USA. t: (1 312) 661 1700; f: 661 0769.

(4) #989 International Association for Financial Planning Two Concourse Parkway, Suite 800, Atlanta, GA 30328, USA. t: (1 404) 395 1605; f: 668 7758.

'*What is the IAFP?*

- the association for those persons giving advice regarding the achievement of financial objectives, and those who support them, for the ultimate benefit of the consumer
- the oldest (founded 1969) and largest organization of its type in the world
- members either work with clients in the areas of personal and/or corporate financial advice or provide services and products to those who do
- the only industry-wide organization which provides an exchange of knowledge and experience among all discliplines within the financial services industry.'

Who Are IAFP Members?

- Current membership: over 11,000
- 113 chapters
- members if all 50 states
- internationally, members in 22 countries.
- must have no record of any serious regulatory disciplinary action or felony conviction

- must subscribe to IAFP Code of Professional Ethics
- licensed to sell insurance (life, health, variable annuities), and/or securities
- registered as an investment adviser with the SEC

What is a Financial Advisor?

- A financial advisor is any person who, for compensation, provides advice to a client regarding strategies and actions to achieve financial goals based on an analysis of the personal and financial condition, resources and capabilities of the client. The IAFP suggests consumers ask questions about the planner's background, experience, education, methods of compensation, qualifications, professional affiliations and references. The IAFP also recommends consumers meet with a minimum of three financial planners before choosing one.'

2426. **Financial Planning**. m. $48.

(5) #990 International Association of Credit Card Investigators International Office, 1620 Grant Avenue, Novato, CA 94945, USA. t: (1 415) 897 8800; f: 898 0798. *Newsletter.*

'Gives professional investigators national and international investigative capabilities to establish effective card and travelers' cheque security programs. Members work to eradicate fraudulent card and travelers' cheque use, to promote a complete exchange of criminal intelligence, and to apprehend and prosecute lawbreakers.' 3500 worldwide members. 'As one of our member benefits we publish a quarterly newsletter which unfortunately is not distributed to the public.'

(6) #991 International Association of Financial Executives Institutes c/o Studio Valentina, Vio Cibrario 27, 10143 Torino, Italy. t: (39 11) 437 4558; f: 437 4318. *Annual Report. Newsletter.*

'Our publications are not sold to the public, but only distributed among the Association members. Founded in 1969 . . . Its aims are:

- to build and improve mutual understanding internationally among financial executives through the exchange of financial information, experience and ideas;
- to provide a basis for international cooperation among financial executives towards making financial systems and regulations more uniform, compatible and harmonious world-wide;
- to promote ethical considerations in the practice of financial management.

As IAFEI concludes its first quarter century of activity, it includes through its member institutes some 25,000 highly qualified financial executives in 21 countries, with Ecuador and several other countries currently expressing interest in joining, as well. IAFEI, as a powerful force in the financial community, is now recognized and respected in accounting, financial and governemental circles around the world. It stands poised for dramatic future professional participation.'

(7) #992 International Association of Investors in the Social Economy rue d'Arion 40, B-1040, Brussels, Belgium. t: (32 2) 230 30 57; f: 230 37 64.

'To foster and support the development of financial organisations, which invest:

- in enterprises of an ethical, ecological, cultural, and self-managing nature, including women's enterprises, and enterprises run by ethnic minorities;
- in enterprises whose aims encompass the needs of disabled people, healthier living, peace and the Third World; and
- in enterprises working within the social economy generally.

INAISE members do not fit into the traditional framework of financial institutions. The activities of INAISE members extend beyond the pure lending sphere. They also include donations, risk capital, guarantees, insurance, and consultancy. Pure financial trading activities are not their objective. INAISE bankers generally try to go beyond anonymous and technical banking. They involve the depositor and the investor in the loan policy of the bank.'

2427. **INAISE Newsletter**. q. BEF 450.

(8) #993 International Credit Association 243 North Lindbergh Boulevard, PO Box 419057, St Louis, MO 63141–1757, USA. t: (1 314) 991 3030; f: 991 3029. *Newsletters.*

'Established in 1912 to meet the needs of credit managers in the retail field. As the credit industry expanded, ICA's focus grew to cover all facets of the credit industry. Today, ICA represents approximately 9,000 credit executives located predominantly in the United States, but also in Canada, Europe, and the Pacific Rim.'

2428. **Credit World**. bi-m. $50. **online**. 'The official publication of the *International Credit Association*.'

2429. **Who's Who of Credit Management**. a. $100. 'A valuable reference for locating credit executives in the United States and Canada . . . Approximately 1,250 firm names and addresses.'

(i) *#994 Society of Certified Credit Executives* t: (L 414) 991 3030; f: 991 3029.

The professional certifying division of the ICA.

(9) #995 International Foundation of Employee Benefit Plans 18700 W Bluemound Road, PO Box 69, Brookfield, WI 53008–0069, USA. t: (800) 466 2366, (1 414) 786 6700; f: 786 2990. *Newsletters.*

'The foremost educational association in the employee benefits field . . . Continually examines the latest issues and trends in the employee benefits field, and publishes in-depth reports, studies, survey results, periodicals and books for both the benefits professional and the general consumer.'

2430. **Employee Benefits Journal**. q. $60.

2431. **INFOSOURCE**. **online**. 'The only *DIALOG* database devoted exclusively to employee benefits . . . It contains over 55,000 article summaries from more than 350 English language periodicals and newsletters, and is supplemented by research reports and books. Approximately 500 new summaries are added each month . . . Articles from over 80% of the journals indexed are available through the *EMPLOYEE BENEFITS INFOSOURCE Document Delivery Service* . . . A new edition of the . . . *INFOSOURCE Thesaurus* . . . contains more than 1,000 subject terms, plus cross-references.'

(i) *#996 International Society of Certified Employee Benefit Specialists* t: (1 414) 786 8771; f: 786 8650.

(10) #997 International Risk Management Institute 12222 Merit Drive, Suite 1660, Dallas, TX 75251–2217, USA. t: (1 214) 960 7693; f: 960 6037.

'Provides technical information to agents, brokers, consultants, underwriters, claims adjusters, risk managers, and legal professionals. IRMI publications concentrate solely on commercial lines, property/casualty insurance, and risk management. IRMI staff editors, research analysts, and advisors have the insurance and risk management education, training and experience needed to provide you with authoritative, state-of-the-art information. We believe, as I hope you will, that our publications are among the best available . . . Our overriding editorial policy is to stay out of the ivory tower and give you practical information you can use.'

2432. **CGL Reporter**. l. $180. 'Whether you're a producer, claims adjuster, underwriter, risk manager, or lawyer, you face some of the greatest challenges known to mankind – interpreting, explaining, and litigating commercial general liability policies! To navigate through the complex obscurities created by complex CGL policy wordings and conflicting court interpretations, you need an expert reference of prior legal cases – you need the *CGL Reporter*!'

2433. **Commercial Auto Insurance**. l. $240.

2434. **Commercial Liability Insurance**. l. $269. 'Endorsed by the *Independent Insurance Agents of America*.'

2435. **Commercial Property Insurance**. l. $250.

2436. **Manual of Rules, Classifications, and Interpretations for Workers Compensation Insurance**. l. $189.

2437. **Professional Liability Insurance**. l. $242.

2438. **Risk Financing**. l. $210. 'Easy-to-use-and-understand reference explaining all the various funding options for workers compensation (as well as general liability, professional liability, and auto liability) . . . Risk managers have relied on it since 1983 to help evaluate and arrange sophisticated risk financing programs.'

2439. **Risk Report**. m. $159. 'Written by highly qualified risk management, insurance, and legal practitioners from throughout the United States, these reports provide practical tips, techniques, and information to assist you in implementing the best possible risk management and insurance programs.'

(11) #998 International Society of Financiers POB 18508, Asheville, NC 28814, USA. t: (1 708) 252 5907; f: 251 5061.

'An elite peer group of *established* lenders, investors, brokers and consultants. All are involved with major domestic or international financial projects and transactions . . . Annual dues are $1000. And as you can see ISF is not for Amateurs! You'll be with the movers and *doers* with a storehouse full of 'inside' comnnections to share . . . A specialized world demands expertise and the brighter of us have discovered that someone, somewhere out there, has exactly the kind of information you need – to complete a transaction, or fund a project.

But just having the "price of admission" doesn't make anyone eligible to join. To become a member of this Society you *MUST* be a full-time professional in your field . . . Over the years, we noticed with horror, the deterioration of professionalism in our industry. Many business and financial digests, journals and financial opportunity advertisements had many published contacts, totally incapable of "doing the deal!" . . . So in July, 1979, the *International Society of Financiers* came into existence . . . ISF membership is now recognized and accepted internationally as the mark of a real, qualified professional . . . *The International Financiers* is a monthly newsletter created for the *exclusive* use of ISF members. It's not for sale, there are no subscriptions and "look see" sample issues are *NEVER* sent to anyone under any circumstances because nothing is in code.'

(12) #999 LIC International – League International for Creditors Roemerstrasse 56, D 51491 Overath, Germany. t: (49 2204) 71189; f: 71608. *Newsletter*.

'An association of independent debt-collecting, credit-reporting and law firms, including some credit insurances and factoring firms, located around the world. A number of these firms are confidential partners with Embassies and Consulates. Its 3,750 staff are skilled professionals. More than a quarter of a century of experience has molded LIC into what it is today: an organization of experts.'

(13) #1000 Organization for International Investment 1747 Pennsylvania Avenue NW, Suite 704, Washington, DC 20006, USA. t: (1 202) 659 1903; f: 659 2293.

2. Organizations: Europe

(1) #1001 Association Européene des Assurés de l'Industrie [European Risk Management Association] Quai d'Ougnée 14, 4102 Ougrée, Belgium. t: (32 41) 30 68 28; f: 30 68 47.

'A federation of risk management associations in Belgium . . . France . . . The Netherlands . . . Italy . . . Germany . . . Spain . . . United Kingdom . . . Switzerland . . . and Denmark. Their collective membership represents the major industrial and commercial companies in their respective countries.'

(2) #1002 European Federation of Financial Analysts Societies 39 Rue Saint-Lazare, 75009 Paris, France. t: (33 1) 44 53 91 26; f: 44 53 91 27.

'Established in 1962 as a Federation of national societies of investment analysts and securities managers . . . The Federation was founded by five national societies, and as of early 1992 it counted sixteen. National societies are members of the Federation, which counts approximately 10,000 persons . . . The responsibility for a number of EFFAS activities is delegated to specific commissions or to individuals, i.e. officers of EFFAS:

- *Commission on Accounting* Created in the late 1960s in order to help compare corporate accounts in the different European countries. The Commission devotes an increasing part of its time to discussions with accounting standards bodies, notably the *International Accounting Standards Committee*. The Commission also participates in the work of the *Accounting Advisory Forum of the European Communities*, set up in 1990 by the *Commission of the European Community*.
- *Commission on Bonds* Dates back to 1976. With more than sixty individual members from thirteen countries drawn from the research departments of major financial institutions, it aims at:
    - raising the standard of analysis of European bond markets
    - giving out information on these markets

Its first Guide to the **European Bond Markets** (640 pages) was published in November 1988, thereby materializing the outcome of the Commission's work. A second glossary of terms in six languages was published in 1989. The **European Futures and Options Markets** (1,100 pages) was published in early 1991.

- *Commission of the Award for the Best European Financial Report*
- *Commission on European Stock Markets*
- *Commission on Training and Qualification and Accreditation Board*
- *Commission on Ethics*
- *Commission on East European Countries*

The creation of an additional commission on *data standardisation* is currently under consideration.'

(i) *#1003 International Coordinating Committee of Financial Ana-*

lysts Associations Can be contacted via the European Federation. Its delegates are elected from the following professional organizations:

- *Asian Securities' Analysts Council*
- *Association for Investment Management and Research*
- *European Federation of Financial Analysts Societies*
- *Brazilian Association of Capital Market Analysts*
- *Investment Analysts' Society of South Africa*

(3) #1004 European Federation of Financial Executives Institutes Steenvelt 20 Boite 1, B-1180 Brussels, Belgium. t/f: (32 2) 332 32 47.

3. Organizations: United Kingdom

(1) #1005 Financial Executives' Group PO Box 433, Moorgate Place, London EC2P 2BJ. t: (44 171) 920 8516; f: 920 9611.

Founded in 1990: now has a membership of some 500.

Corporate finance and treasury

(2) #1006 Association of Corporate Treasurers 12 Devereux Court, London WC2R 3JJ. t: (44 171) 936 2354; f: 936 4685.

The Association publishes or sponsors a number of background texts on aspects of corporate treasury and has an extensive conference programme. 'Since its inauguration in May 1979, the Association of Corporate Treasurers has elected to membership more than eighteen hundred and fifty finance directors and corporate treasurers drawn mainly from leading UK companies. Admission to membership is dependent on the education and experince of the individuals concerned and upon the nature and responsibility of the appointments they hold and have held. The Association's examinations set high standards for corporate treasury and related knowledge . . . (The Association) is the only body in the UK concentrating exclusively on this important subject and setting professional standards for enrolment examination and election. . . . It is an independent body, governed by a Council of members whose work is supported by a number of active voluntary committees.'

2440. **ACT Manual of Corporate Finance and Treasury Management**. *Gee*. l. £185. Covers all aspects of the treasury and corporate finance functions, with sections on: Equity, Debt, Hybrids, Risk Management, Cash Management, Financial Organisation, Financial Markets, Regulation and Taxation Issues, and Occupational Pensions.

2441. **Treasurer**. *Silverdart*. 11/year. £120.

2442. The **Treasurer's Handbook**. a. £125. Sponsored by the *Royal Bank* *of Scotland*. 'The *Treasury Services* section is unsurpassed as a guide to who does what and where in over 500 UK financial service organisations. The 78 page *Cash Management* section . . . now helping you to do business in twenty three countries worldwide. Beneficial for anyone with cash-flows in foreign markets. The *Comparative Credit Ratings* are of enormous benefit for banks and corporates in helping you establish the security of your trading partners and the capacity of potential funding sources . . . (Also included are) *Key Financial Market Formulae and Tables* for Treasurers . . . (and) *Technical Guidance* for Treasurers . . . The Treasurer's Handbook is compiled by us and information is collated from many banks and official sources. We believe that there is no better deskside companion.'

(3) #1007 Centre for Interfirm Comparison Capital House, 48 Andover Road, Winchester, Hampshire, SO23 7BH. t: (44 1962) 844144; f: 843180.

'Independent company established in 1959 by the *British Institute of Management* in association with the *British Productivity Council* . . . Helps businesses of every kind to improve their profitability and productivity by providing expertise in performance measurement and financial control . . . All work we do is confidential to those participating; we do not have any published material available.'

(4) #1008 Institute of Chartered Secretaries & Administrators 16 Park Crescent, London W1N 4AH. t: (44 171) 580 4741; f: 323 1132.

'Founded in London in 1891 in order to establish and enhance the status of company secretaries, and define the standards of professional conduct to which members should aspire . . . The professional forum for 44,000 members and 23,000 students in 100 countries.'

2443. **Company Secretarial Practice**. *ICSA Publishing*. l. £165/£100. 'The most highly respected and authoritative manual in the field . . . The breadth of coverage offered . . . is unparalleled, containing essential knowledge on key topics such as:

- the registration and re-registration of companies
- capital
- public issues
- the registration of members
- dividends
- debentures and loan stock
- redemption and repurchase of shares and loan stock
- the role of the director
- the role of the company secretary
- auditors
- accounts, reports and circulars
- meetings
- take-overs and mergers

- receivers.'

2444. **Company Secretary**. m. £70.

2445. **Private Company Secretary's Manual**. l. £88/£50.

(5) #1009 Institute of Legal Cashiers and Administrators 1st Floor, 136 Well Hall Road, Eltham, London SE9 6SN. t: (44 181) 294 2021; f: 294 2006.

'The country's premier professional body dedicated to the education, support and promotion of specialist financial and administrative personnel working within the legal community.'

2446. **Legal Abacus**. q. £15. In association with the *Institute of Legal Accountants of Ireland*.

Credit management

(6) #1010 Association of Insurance & Risk Managers in Industry and Commerce 6 Lloyd's Avenue, London EC3N 3AX. t: (44 171) 480 7610; f: 702 3752.

(7) #1011 Credit Protection Association CPA House, 350 King Street, London W6 0RX. t: (44 181) 846 0000; f: 741 7459. *Newsletter*.

'Established in 1914 to offer Companies, Partnerships, and other organisations professional advice, assistance and action in controlling their customers' and clients' credit.'

2447. **MONIT**. **online**. 'Brings credit management into the age of the electronic office . . . At the touch of a button, MONIT (Members' On-line Notification and Information Terminal) users can initiate either CPA's proven overdue account recovery service and/or the dishonoured cheque recovery service and gain access to a rich database of information on over a million UK companies . . . MONIT provides members with connection to a comprehensive Companies House database.'

(8) #1012 Institute of Credit Management The Water Mill, Station Road, South Luffenham, Oakham, LE15 8NB. t: (44 1780) 721888; f: 721333. The *ICM Bookshop* sells a wide range of publications relevant to credit management.

'The Institute (ICM) was founded in 1939, has about 7,500 members and is the largest organisation in Europe for those engaged in the credit profession. ICM members hold important appointments in most sectors of industry and commerce where they are engaged in:

- liaising with the finance and marketing functions with the aim of optimising the contribution to profits of credit management
- formulating corporate credit policy
- assessing and reporting the creditworthiness of potential customers

whether trade or individual consumers, including the risk involved in any one sales outlet or market
- deciding the terms on which business should be allowed to UK and overseas customers
- collecting payments to agreed terms
- taking such action as is needed to collect sums due when a customer fails to meet the agreed terms of business
- processing sales accounting records.

People in credit management sum up these tasks by defining the role of the profession as "the executive control of the investment of funds in the accounts receivable asset".'

2448. **Credit Management**. m. £50.

(9) #1013 Institute of Risk Management Lloyd's Avenue House, 6 Lloyd's Avenue, London EC3N 3AX. t: (44 171) 709 9808; f: 709 0716. *Newsletter*.

'The profession is multi-disciplinary. It concerns itself with the identification, measurement, control, financing and transfer of risks which threaten life, property and the continued viability of enterprises. It is thus concerned with such diverse specialist areas as safety and health, fire engineering, security, insurance, legal liability exposures and risk financing. Whilst it has not historically entered areas of financial or trading risks many of the skills required are applicable in a variety of commercial applications. Political risks, currency fluctuation losses and risks arising from acquisition and sale of companies are all increasingly addressed by risk managers . . . The creation of the *Institute of Risk Management* in 1986 marked a major step towards greater professionalism in risk management and the promotion of excellence.'

2449. **Foresight**. *Risk & Insurance Research Group*. m. £235. 'The risk mangement professional is besieged with "information" from a plethora of news sources – the trade insurance press, brokers, insurers, etc. *Foresight* aims to help him not only by focusing on those market developments which are important to him but by providing an independent assessment of them from the risk management perspective.'

Financial analysis

(10) #1014 Institute of Investment Management and Research 211/213 High Street, Bromley, Kent, BR1 1NY. t: (44 181) 464 0811; f: 313 0587.

Formed to achieve, foster and maintain (by examination or otherwise) high standards of professional ability and practice in investment analysis, portfolio management and related disciplines.

2450. **Professional Investor**. 10/year.

Financial planning and advice

(11) #1015 IFA Promotion 28 Greville Street, London EC1N 8SU. t: (44 171) 831 4027; f: 331 4920.

(12) #1016 Independent Financial Adviser Association Page House, 164 West Wycombe Road, High Wycombe HP12 3AE. t: (44 1494) 443900; f: 474299.

(13) #1017 Institute of Financial Planning Hereford House, East Street, Hereford HR1 2LU, UK. t: (44 1432) 274891; f: 264861.

Formed in 1986. 'The activities of the Institute are directed towards improving the quality of financial advice given to members of the public. To achieve this the Institute has developed an examination (Financial Planning Examination), which is of degree standard, and professional in the way professional examinations are set by the ICAEW, the CIB, IoT and The Law Society. Certain members of the Institute who are appropriately qualified are admitted by Council to The Registry of Financial Planning Practitioners. Those on The Registry are considered suitably able to provide financial planning advice, and may be recommended to the public.'

2451. **Financial Planning**. q. £10.

(14) #1018 Management Consultancies Association 11 West Halkin Street, London SW1X 8JL. t: (44 171) 235 3897; f: 235 0825.

(15) #1019 Money Advice Association 1st Floor, Gresham House, 24 Holborn Viaduct, London EC1A 2BN. t: (44 171) 236 3566; f: 329 1579. *Newsletter*.

'Services we provide direct to our members are training, information exchange, seminars, and an Annual Conference with workshops and fringe meetings.'

(16) #1020 National Federation of Independent Financial Advisers c/o Portfolio Limited, Goodison House, 57 Wolborough Street, Newton Abbot TQ12 1JQ. t: (44 1626) 62164; f: 332413. *Newsletter*.

Investment

(17) #1021 Investor Relations Society 2nd Floor Executive Suite, One Bedford Street, London WC2E 9HD. t: (44 171) 379 1763; f: 240 1320. *Newsletter*.

Formed in 1980. 'Members comprise senior executives with management responsibilities for investor relations, including specialists in Public Affairs, Finance Directors and Company Secretaries . . . The purpose of investor relations is to help the financial community and investing public to evaluate a company. Its role is to provide comprehensive information for independent assessment and not actively to promote the purchase or sale of a company's shares. No audience is privileged in investor relations. Employees, shareholders and potential investors have equal status in terms of the listing agreement with the Stock Exchange. Identical information should therefore be available and given simultaneously to all audiences, including employees investment analysts and the media . . . The emergence of a global market in securities has made this obligation international as well as domestic.'

(18) #1022 ProShare (UK) Library Chambers, 13/14 Basinghall Street, London EC2V 5BQ. t: (44 171) 600 0984; f: 600 0947.

'If you find it difficult to track down the sort of independent advice you would like to help you make those vital investment decisions you need look no further. Launched in October 1992, The Proshare Association is the *only* substantial organisation set up to meet the demands of private investors. Membership costs just £30 per annum (£40 overseas) – a fraction of the cost of your daily newspaper – and gives you a wealth of user-friendly, unbiased information on stockmarket related topics . . . You get *The ProShare Bulletin* The monthly magazine . . . covering new issues; stockmarket reports; investment clubs; features by top financial journalists; sector analysis; news on company events and seminars . . . *Guide to Information Sources*: A comprehensive evaluation of all key investment information sources for the private investor . . . etc. etc. Proshare is supported by the Government, the London Stock Exchange and a wide range of industrial and commercial companies.'

Public finance

(19) #1023 Chartered Institute of Public Finance and Accountancy 3 Robert Street, London WC2N 6BH. t: (44 171) 895 8823; f: 895 8825.

2452. **Public Finance**. w. £93.

(i) *#1024 Centre for the Study of Regulated Industries*

Research Centre primarily concerned with the UK privatized utilities. *Discussion Papers*; *Regulatory Briefs*; *Regulatory Reviews*; *Research Reports*; *Seminar & Conference Series*; *Statistics Series*; *Technical Papers*.

(ii) *#1025 Public Finance Foundation*

'The independent research arm of CIPFA. The Foundation provides an impartial forum for debate and the exchange of ideas on public expenditure and related aspects of public finance, and on the management and administration of public services.'

2453. **Public Money & Management**. *Blackwell Publishers*. q. £111.50.

(20) #1026 Institute of Revenues Rating and Valuation 41 Doughty Street, London WC1N 2LF. t: (44 171) 831 3505; f: 831 2048.

2454. **Annotated Rating & Community Charge Legislation**. i. £290. 'All legislation pertaining to non-domestic rates and residual community charges.'

2455. **Benefit**. 10/year. £195. 'For those working in locally administered benefits.'

2456. **Non-Domestic Rating Legislation Database**. **diskette**. i. £346.63. 'All non-domestic rating legislation . . . relevant to the new national system introduced on 1 April 1990.'

4. Organizations: United States

(1) #1027 Financial Executives Institute 10 Madison Avenue, PO Box 1938, Morristown, NJ 07962–1938. t: (1 201) 898 4600; f: 898 4649. *Newsletters.*

'Joining FEI means being part of an influential network of peers, both nationally and within your local business community, who hold policy-making positions in finance. Your contacts will include 14,000 FEI Members who are the key decision makers at more than 7,000 corporations, including almost all the 1,000 largest corporations in America . . . From its inception in 1931, FEI has ensured its members a voice before legislative and regulatory bodies, and continues to serve a vital role as an advocate of the corporate financial executive's views on important issues . . . FEI's Washington office monitors legislation affecting business and represents you in areas, such as:

- Internal Controls
- Corporate Taxation
- Pension Investment
- Employee Benefits
- Health Care Reform
- Procurement Policy
- International Trade

Active membership is available to you if you perform the duties of a financial executive and your employing company meets the size criteria. You must participate in the formulation of policies for the operation of the enterprise and in the administration of chief components of financial functions:

- Accounting and Control
- Treasury and Finance
- Planning and Business Development
- Management of Retirement Funds and Investments
- Tax Administration
- Risk Management
- Information Systems
- Internal Audit

The Chief Financial Officer of any SEC registered company is eligible for membership regardless of company size.

2457. **Financial Executive**. bi-m. $50. 'Publication with an emphasis on technical content and business trend analysis.'

(i) *#1028 Financial Executives Research Foundation*

'A nonprofit educational organization ... the research affiliate of Financial Executives Institute ... The Foundation conducts research and publishes informative material in the field of business management, with particular emphasis on the practice of financial management and its evolving role.'

Corporate finance and treasury

(2) #1029 American Payroll Association 30 East 33rd Street, New York, NY 10016–5386. t: (1 212) 686 2030; f: 686 2789.

'A non-profit professional association for individuals engaged in payroll management, i.e. wage and employment tax withholding, reporting and depositing and all other automated and manual processes involved in paying employees. Founded in 1982, the APA provides payroll and employment tax-related educational programs, publications and professional support. The APA also represents its more than 11,000 members in the legislative and regulatory arenas on both state and federal levels.'

2458. **APA Guide to Payroll Practice and Management**. l. $119. 'A thoroughly researched training manual for use by any payroll department ... For each topic covered, (the Guide) lists page references for all of the major payroll information services guides (*The Bureau of National Affairs, CCH, Research Institute of America*) and the IRS Codes and Regulations.'

2459. **APA Basic Guide to Payroll**. l. $112.95. 'The original book on payroll – it is the best-selling payroll text in the country with more than 15,000 copies being sold each year.'

2460. **Payroll Currently**. bi-w. $247. 'Helps keep your organization in compliance with the most recent tax regulations and free from the costly penalties and interest payments that result from noncompliance.'

(3) #1030 Association for Corporate Growth 4350 DiPaolo Cener, Suite C, Dearlove Road, Glenview, IL 60025. t: (1 704) 699 1331; f: 699 1703.

(4) £1031 Association for Global Business Box 1381, Harrisonburg, VA 22801. t: (1 703) 433 7403; f: 568 3299.

2461. **Journal of Global Business**. s-a. $40. 'Aims to provide opportunities for the exchange of professsional ideas, to enhance research in the field of international business and global concerns, and to create a general awareness of significant accomplishments in the area of global enterprises.'

(5) #1031 Association of Publicly Traded Companies 1101 Connecticut Avenue NW, Suite 700, Washington, DC 20036. t: (1 202) 857 1114; f: 223 4579.

Companies that issue stock into public capital markets.

(6) #1033 Center for Entrepreneurial Management 180 Varick Street, Penthouse Suite, New York, NY 10014. t: (1 212) 633 0060; f: 633 0063.

(7) #1034 Entrepreneurship Institute 3592 Corporate Drive, Suite 101, Columbus, OH 43231. t: (1 614) 895 1153; f: 895 1473.

'The most successful non-profit educational organization designed to assist and encourage entrepreneurship and business growth.'

(8) #1035 IMAP/INTERMAC Merger & Acquisition Professionals, 60 Revere Drive, Suite 500, Northbrook, IL 60062. t: (1 708) 480 9037; f: 480 9282.

'Thank you for the interest you have expressed in our organization. Our two previous organizations – the *Institute of Merger and Acquisition Professionals* (IMAP) and the *International Association of Merger and Acquisition Consultants* (INTERMAC) – have recently consummated a merger. The interim name of the new organization is IMAP/INTERMAC.'

(9) #1036 Institute of Management and Administration 29 West 35th Street, 5th Floor, New York, NY 10001–2299. t: (1 212) 244 0360; f: 564 0465.

'Information Services for Professionals.' Produce a range of *newsletters* including:

2462. The **Cash Flow Enhancement Report**. m. $219.

2463. **Defined Contribution Plan Investing Report**. m. $843.

2464. **Report on Managing 401(K) Plans**. m. $219.

2465. **Report of Reducing Benefits Costs**. m. $219.

2466. **Report of Salary Surveys**. m. $219.

(10) #1037 Institute of Real Estate Management 430 N Michigan Avenue, Chicago, IL 60611. t: (1 312) 329 6000; f: 661 0217.

(11) #1038 Investment Program Association 607 14th Street NW, Suite 1000, Washington, DC 20005. t: (1 202) 775 9750; f: 331 8446.

Works to preserve limited partnerships and real estate investment trusts as a form of investment and a source of new capital for the economy.

(12) #1039 Joint Industry Group 818 Connecticut Avenue NW, 12th Floor, Washington, DC 20006. t: (1 202) 466 5490; f: 872 8696.

(13) #1040 National Association of Purchasing Management 2055 E Centennial Circle, PO Box 22160, Tempe, AZ 85285–2160. t: (1 602) 752 6276; f: 752 7890.

(14) #1041 National Federation of Independent Business *NFIB Education Foundation* Suite 700, Publications, 600 Maryland Avenue SW, Washington, DC 20024. t: (1 202) 554 9000; f: 484 1567.

'The Foundation's mission is to support NFIB by producing research – the "intellectual ammunition" – necessary to document the important role small and independent businesses play in the American economy.'

2467. **Small Business Economic Trends**. m. $150. 'One of the oldest authoritative reports on small business economic conditions. The report is based on a random sample survey of NFIB members regarding their views on Optimism, Credit Conditions, Prices, Employee Compensation, Sales, Earnings, Inventories, Capital Expenditures, Single Most Important Problem, and Regional Conditions.'

(15) #1042 National Institute of Pensions Administration 145 W 1st Street, Suite A, Tustin, CA 92680. t: (1 714) 731 3524; f: 731 1284.

(16) #1043 Profit Sharing Council of America 10 S Riverside, Number 1460, Chicago, IL 60606. t: (1 312) 441 8550; f: 441 8559.

- *Profit Sharing Research Foundation*

(17) #1044 Society of Financial Examiners 4101 Lake Boone, Suite 201, Raleigh, NC 27607. t: (800) 962 2384; f: (1 919) 787 4916.

(18) #1045 Treasury Management Association 7315 Wisconsin Avenue, Suite 1250W, Bethesda, MD 20814. t: (1 301) 907 2862; f: 907 2864.

'The principal organization representing private sector treasury professionals. The TMA supports the treasury management profession through continuing education, professional certification, publication, industry standards and government relations.'

(19) #1046 Turnaround Management Association 230 North Michigan Avenue, Suite 1310, Chicago, IL 60601. t: (1 312) 857 7734; f: 857 7739. *Directory* ($295). *Newsletter*.

'The only international organization serving the corporate revitalization community. There has been growing public awareness and recognition of the special skills needed to effectively and competently render assistance to companies in financial trouble and those constituencies affected by the company's difficulties . . . The corporate renewal profession is comprised of business executives, managers, consultants, attorneys, accountants, commercial bankers, investment bankers, investors, venture capitalists, executive recruiters, appraisers and liquidators, who are experienced and specialize in working with companies to preserve value and save jobs . . . Who can you trust to save your company? Look to a Certified Turnaround Professional. Through this professional designation the Corporate Renewal industry follows in the footsteps of other professions that have established stringent criteria that create a benchmark of practical experience, knowledge, and ethical integrity . . . This program is administered by the *#1047 Association of Certified Turnaround Professionals* (ACTP), an independent certifying body founded by the TMA. A comprehensive body of knowledge has been compiled by a faculty comprised of academics and professionals in the field, which is administered by *Northwestern University*.'

Credit management

(20) #1048 American Collectors Association PO Box 39106, Minneaolis, MN 55439–0106. t: (1 612) 926 6547; f: 926 1624.

'Debt collectors are financial specialists who help return billions of dollars to the United States economy every year through their debt collection services. They also help consumers build and retain favorable credit reputations and help businesses design credit policies to minimize bad debts. An international trade association of debt collectors, established in 1939, with members in the US and over 50 other countries in the world. The membership, of more than 3,500, includes sole proprietorships, partnerships, and corporations, ranging from one-person offices to firms employing more than 500 employees.'

2468. **Collector**. m. $50. 'Reports regulatory action of the *Federal Trade Commission*, yearly buyers guides for collection software and skiptracing services, what the future holds for the collection industry and other vital topics concerning consumer credit and collections.'

2469. **Corporate Collector Currents**. bi-w. $100. 'Concise, one-page rundown of legislation, court cases and trends in the collection industry.'

2470. **Cred-Alert**. m. $36. 'Focuses on legislation that affects creditor's remedies, important court decisions, regulatory decisions, and any new developments in the credit industry that affects the collection of past due accounts.'

(i) *#1049 American Commercial Collectors Association* t: (1 612) 925 0760; f: 926 1624.

A trade association of approximately 200 collection specialists, being 'the largest organization of commercial collectors in the world'. The newsletter of the Association, *Scope*, is 'only available to members'.

(21) #1050 Bankcard Holders of America 524 Branch Drive, Salem, VA 24153. t: (1 703) 389 5445.

Founded in 1980 as a private non-profit consumer organization dedicated to consumer credit education and advocacy. 'It is the first and only consumer group dealing exclusively with issues of importance to credit card holders. The association is funded by membership dues and publication sales, and receives no government or foundation support. It is not a lobbying organization, and is independent of any bank, credit card company, or financial institution.' A number of leaflets are produced by the association: e.g. 'Understanding Credit Bureaus'.

(22) #1051 Credit Professionals International 50 Crestwood Executive Center, Suite 301, St Louis, MO 63126. t: (1 314) 842 6280; f: 842 6310. *Newsletter.*

'More than 9,000 members in over 350 clubs in the United States and Canada . . . Purposes: To develop a closer contact among those working in the credit industry. To maintain friendly relationships between credit departments of various firms and business represented by the members and local credit bureaus. To stimulate education in the practice and procedure of credit.'

(23) #1052 National Association of Credit Management 8815 Centre Park Drive, Suite 200, Columbia, MD 21045–2117. t: (1 410) 740 5560; f: 740 5574.

'Founded June 23, 1896 in Toledo, Ohio, by 82 business credit executives. Membership has grown from 600 at the end of 1896 to more than 39,000 today . . . NACM are business credit grantors in manufacturing, wholesaling, service industries and financial institutions. Those members are served by 65 autonomous affiliated state and regional associations throughout the country.'

- *Credit Research Foundation of the NACM* 'Chartered in 1949, is a member supported research and education organization dedicated to developing and enhancing the skills, talents, knowledge and leadership qualities of credit and financial executives . . . Publishes a number of studies and analytical reports on topics of significant importance to the credit practitioner.'
- *International Credit Executives* 'Designed specifically for credit and financial executives who are responsible for the credit and collections functions of their companies' overseas affiliates and who are responsible for overseas receivables in general.'
- *National Institute of Credit* 'Oldest and broadest based educational activity of NACM, conducting its activities to give widest coverage to persons with different educational and business backgrounds.'

2471. **Business Credit**. m. $33. **online**. For corporate credit and financial professionals. Circulation: 37,000.

2472. **Credit Manual of Commercial Laws**. a. $79.50. 'The bible in credit and commercial law.'

2473. **Digest of Commercial Laws of the World**. *Oceana Publications* Compilation of commercial laws for countries of the world.

(i) *#1053 FCIB-NACM Corporation* 520 Eighth Avenue, New York, NY 10018. t: (1 212) 947 5368; f: 465 8360.

The international arm of the National Association of Credit Management.

'The premier international association of managers responsible for worldwide export financing, credit, treasury, and international subsidiary management . . . FCIB's *Hotline* provides members with valuable and timely information on a wide range of specific subjects in international finance, credit and treasury management. Seasoned professionals participate in the hotline service sharing their areas of expertise directly with other members in helping solve international problems. FCIB provides extensive country risk reports along with political risk and economic forecasts for its members. FCIB provides a worldwide credit reporting service enabling members to order credit reports at minimum costs while choosing the service to best meet their requirements. An on-line international credit reporting service is provided in cooperation with *Owens On-Line* through an electronic gateway provided by *Global Scan*.'

(24) #1054 National Consumer Credit Consultants 2840 W Arthur Avenue, Chicago, IL 60645–5222. t: (1 312) 465 0090. For profit organization.

(25) #1055 National Foundation for Consumer Credit 8611 2nd Avenue, Suite 100, Silver Spring, MD 20910. t: (1 301) 589 5600; f: 495 5623.

(26) #1056 National Recovery and Collection Association c/o BB & T, PO Box 500, Wilson, NC 27893. t: (1 919) 399 4226; f: 399 4712.

(27) #1057 Society of Risk Management Consultants 300 Park Avenue, New York, NY 10022. t: (800) 765 SRMC, (1 212) 572 6246.

'Although a number of its members have authored various publications, the Society, as an entity, neither publishes nor sells any publications to the public at large. That notwithstanding, a number of our members have an active practice with respect to banking and other financial institutions and might serve as a resource for your readers.'

Financial analysis

(28) #1058 Association for Investment Management and Research 5 Boar's Head Lane, PO Box 3668, Charlottesville, VA 22903. t: (800) 247 8132/(1 804) 980 3668; f: 980 9755. *Publications* PBD,

PO Box 6996, Alpharetta, GA 30239–6996. t: (800) 789 AIMR/(1 404) 442 8631; f: 442 8631 (except for subscriptions, which are ordered through AIMR Information Central: t: (800) 247 8132/(1 804) 980 3668; f: 980 9755.)

Nonprofit professional organization of investment practitioners. Its mission is to maintain a permanent professional organization with the highest possible ethical, professional, and educational standards within the broadly defined investment management and research community. Founded in 1990 as a result of the combination of the *Financial Analysts Federation* and *The Institute of Chartered Financial Analysts.* The Association produces a range of books, monographs and seminar proceedings, e.g.: 'Analysts' earnings forecast accuracy in Japan and the United States' (1994, $20); 'Managed futures and their role in investment portfolios' (1994, $30). 'AIMR makes its membership list of nearly 25,000 available for purchase to approved individuals and companies wishing to promote products and services. The list may be segmented in various ways.' *Newsletter.*

2474. **CFA Digest**. q. $40. Selections of abstracts of articles from the major academic and practitioner journals in investment, finance, economics, and other fields of interest to investment analysts and managers.

2475. **Financial Analysts' Journal**. bi-m. $150. **online**. 'Now in its 50th year . . . Edited with the practitioner in mind . . . Includes articles describing research in the fields of portfolio management, asset allocation, global investing, and security analysis. It also contains book reviews, short pieces on technical topics, and a column on "What Practitioners Need to Know About".'

(i) *#1059 International Society of Financial Analysts*

Established in 1985 'to help investment professionals from around the world meet the challenges of global investing'.

2476. **ISFA Digest**. 3/year. $50. Abstracts of articles pertaining to global investment from journals and magazines published in several countries.

(ii) *#1060 New York Society of Security Analysts* t: (1 212) 912 9249.

(iii) *#1061 Research Foundation of the Institute of Chartered Financial Analysts* t: (1 804) 980 364; f: 980 3634.

'Its mission is to identify, fund, and publish high-quality research that expands the body of useful and relevant knowledge available to practitioners in understanding and applying this knowledge; and to contribute to the investment management community's effectiveness in serving clients.'

(29) #1062 Fixed Income Analysts Society 170 Old Country Road, Suite 509, Mineola, NY 11501. t: (1 516) 739 3414; f: 739 3803.

Financial planning and advice

(30) #1063 Association of Investment Management Sales Executives 1211 Connecticut Avenue NW, Suite 812, Washington, DC 20036. t: (1 202) 296 3560.

(31) #1064 Co-Op America 1859 M Street NW, Suite 700, Washington, DC 20036. t: (1 202) 872 5307; f: 331 8166.

'Provides the economic strategies, organizing power, and practical tools for businesses and individuals to address today's social and environmental problems.' The *Socially Responsible Financial Planning Guide* helps people make financial decisions that are both 'value-added' and meet personal financial needs and goals.

(32) #1065 ESOP Association 1726 M Street NW, Suite 501, Washington, DC 20036. t: (1 202) 293 2971; f: 293 7568.

'The only non-profit trade association dedicated to employee ownership through ESOPs.'

2477. **Legislative, Regulatory and Case Law Developments: The Year in Review**. a. $75. 'A compilation of judicial decisions, legislative proposals and statutes, and formal regulatory guidance from the *Internal Revenue Service, Department of Labor*, and other agencies . . . an essential reference guide for professional ESOP advisers.'

(33) #1066 Institute of Certified Financial Planners 7600 E Eastman, Suite 301, Denver, CO 80231. t: (1 303) 751 7600; f: 751 1037. *Newsletter.*

'The nation's leading membership association for financial planning professionals. We provide benefits to thousands of Certified Financial Planner licensees, CFP candidates and other professionals with an active involvement in financial planning.

A *Certified Financial Planner* licensee is a professional who has achieved an advanced level of education in financial planning, meets stringent experience requirements and ascribes to high ethical standards . . . To earn the CFP mark, candidates must study and successfully complete a demanding examination process covering six key disciplines . . . CFP professionals possess specialized expertise in retirement planning, portfolio management, tax planning, insurance, estate planning and employee benefit planning. While the CFP designation is at the core of their vocation, many hold other professional designations, such as *Certified Public Accountant* (CPA), *Chartered Life Underwriter* (CLU), *Chartered Financial Consultant* (ChFC), and *Chartered Financial Analyst* (CFA) to name a few. Many are also licensed in other allied professions such as securities, law, insurance and real estate. CFP licensees and candidates have an average of twelve years experience in the financial services industry.'

2478. **Journal of Financial Planning**. q. $54. 'A leading source of research and strategies affecting financial planners and their clients.'

(34) #1067 National Association of Personal Financial Advisers 1130 West Lake Cook Road, Suite 150, Buffalo Grove, IL 60089–1974. *Newsletter.*

'The forum for fee-only financial advisors.'

2479. **NAPFA Advisor**. m. $60. 'From time to time, NAPFA Advisor publishes articles on technical subjects. These are offered in the spirit of one non-specialist helping other non-specialists. NAPFA makes no claim as to the accuracy or the timeliness of such advice.' The May 1995 issue introduced a New Feature: *Online Financial Resources* . . . 'Now that more than 100 NAPFA members are using online services – including CompuServe, America Online, Prodigy, and local Internet providers – we all need to share our resources.'

(35) #1068 National Center for Financial Education PO Box EA-34070, San Diego, CA 92163–4070. t: (1 619) 232 8811.

Investment

(36) #1069 American Association of Individual Investors 625 North Michigan Avenue, Chicago, Illinois 60611–3110. t: (1 312) 280 0170; f: 280 9883.

Not-for-profit corporation formed in 1978 for the purpose of assisting individuals in becoming effective managers of their own assets through programmes of education, information and research.

2480. **AAII Journal**. 10/year. 'Articles in the Journal always focus on how *you* can improve *your* results. While some articles cover the latest findings of academic research, there are also articles by experienced practitioners such as Peter Lynch, John Bogle, T. Boone Pickens, Robert Stovall, Ken Gregory and Mark Hulbert.'

2481. **Individual Investor's Guide to No-Load Mutual Funds**. a. In-depth analysis of over 600 funds with discussion of the process of selecting the best funds for specific situations. Quarterly updating service.

(37) #1070 Bond Investors Association 6175 NW 153 Street, Suite 229, Miami Lakes, FL 33014. t: (1 305) 557 1832; f: 557 1454. *Newsletter.*

'Non-profit organization providing bondholders the information they need to protect their capital and better manage their bond investments . . . The Association also provides members with a called bonds and ratings decline notification service for the bonds they hold . . . BIA provides daily updates on over 1500 bond issues in default for the *Bloomberg News Network* . . . Maintains a database of information on over 8,000 municipal and 1,500 corporate bonds in default. We are able to provide customized research reports on these issues on an individual basis.'

2482. **BIG BOND BOOK: The Directory of Below Investment Grade Corporate Bonds**. In conjunction with *Bloomberg Financial Markets* and *Houlihan Lukey Howard & Zukin Investment Management*. a. 'Details over 4,000 bond issuers.'

2483. **Defaulted Bonds Newsletter**. m. $295. 'Designed to update investors and holders in defaulted bonds who find the usual sources of information to be less than adequate.'

2484. **High Yield Securities Journal**. m. $99. 'Independent advice for bond & preferred stock investors.'

(38) #1071 Council of Institutional Investors 1616 P Street NW, Suite 350, Washington, DC 20036. t: (1 202) 745 0800; f: 745 0801.

Members include employee benefit plans, non-profit foundations, and non-profit endowment funds.

(39) #1072 Council on Economic Priorities 30 Irving Place, New York, NY 10003–2386. t: (1 212) 420 1133; f: 420 0988. *Research Reports* (m. $48).

'Independent, non-profit research organization founded 25 years ago to promote corporate social responsibility. Today our research also encompasses such timely issues as defense conversion, the environment and socially responsible investing.'

- *Transnational Corporations* 'Produces up to 60 case studies analyzing the impact of transnational corporations in developing countries. In conjunction with *New Consumer*, CEP's counterpart in the UK, the project will focus on exemplary corporate practices.'
- *SCREEN* 'Designed to meet investors' demands for information about corporate social responsibility issues. SCREEN monitors the social performance of leading companies for clients such as stock brokers, investment managers, pension plans, foundations, and socially screened funds.'

'CEP is supported by private foundations, individual donors and our worldwide membership.'

(40) #1073 Independent Investors Forum 1128 East Bluff Drive, Penn Yan, NY 14527. t/f: (1 315) 536 7895.

2485. **Independent Investors Forum. online**. 'The first computer accessed, interactive investment advisory service . . . An investment advisory forum that provides recommendations on stocks, bonds, options, short sales, and a variety of other investment opportunities dealing mostly with U.S. companies, but including several overseas firms, particularly in the U.K., Latin America, and the Pacific Rim. Data sources include the usual financial reports, Dow Jones, Standard & Poor's, company bulletins, plus several online and hard copy sources not usually covered by financial analysts. These sources include numerous trade and scientific publications as well as direct interviews with company officers and employees.

(A) unique feature of IIF is its discussion format. Rather than being a one-way transmission of analysis and recommendations on purchase or sale of securities, IIF is really an ongoing discussion where interested investors can carry on a dialogue at their leisure . . . The discussion format is unique to IIF and occurs through investor input on message boards and real time discussions, held primarily on the national service, known as *America Online*.'

(41) #1074 Investment Education Institute 1515 E 11 Mile Road, Royal Oak, MI 48067. t: (1 810) 583 6242.

2486. **Better Investing**. m. $20. 'The world's unique investment education publication . . . Its monthly "Stock to Study" selections have beaten the Dow Jones Industrials in 21 of 29 five-year periods since publication started in 1951 . . . Ten leading columnists . . . Only consumers financial publication with an all financial analyst editorial board. Five are Chartered Financial Analysts.'

2487. **Investor Advisory Service**. m. $125. Stock recommendations.

(42) #1075 Investor Responsibility Research Center 1755 Massachusetts Avenue NW, Suite 600, Washington, DC 20036. t: (1 202) 234 7500; f: 332 7500. *Annual Report*.

'Compiles and impartially analyzes information on the activities of corporations and institutional investors, on efforts to influence such activities, and on related public policies.'

2488. **Global Shareholder**. q. $100. Reports on US regulations affecting foreign proxies, shareholder rights, developments in Asia, Europe, and Australia, how American investors handle voting at non-US companies and the latest activist efforts to press overseas corporations on corporate governance and social issues.

(43) #1076 Mutual Fund Educational Alliance 1900 Erie Stret, Suite 120, Kansas City, MO 64116. t: (1 816) 471 1454; f: 471 5446.

'The Association of No-Load Funds . . . Trade association of direct-marketed funds whose members are committed to educating the individual investor.'

2489. **Investor's Guide to Low-Cost Mutual Funds**. s-a. $14. 'The most comprehensive guide to no-load and low-load funds available . . . Provides performance results and important information on more than 800 of the nation's leading mutual funds.'

(44) #1077 National Association of Investors Corporation 1515 East Eleven Mile Road, Royal Oak, MI 48067. t: (1 810) 583 6242; f: 583 4880.

'Investment education for individual investors and investment clubs . . .

Non-profit, volunteer organization operated by and for the benefit of its member clubs. It is independent of any company, broker or stock exchange . . . An annual sampling of NAIC member portfolios over the last 29 years shows that the average portfolio earned more than the Standard and Poor's 500 Index in all but seven years. Some individuals have built modest monthly investments of $10 or $20 into accounts worth over $200,000.' *Investors Manual* (Investment Club Edition; Individual Investors Edition); *First-Time Investor Manual*; *Accounting Manual*.

(45) #1078 National Investor Relations Institute PO Box 96040, Washington, DC 20090–6040. t: (1 703) 506 3570; f: 506 3571.

'Founded in 1969 as a professional association of corporate officers and investor relations consultants responsible for communication between corporate management, the investing public and the financial community.

Investor Relations Defined A corporate marketing activity combining the disciplines of communication and finance, and providing present and potential investors with an accurate portrayal of a company's performance and prospects. Conducted effectively, investor relations can have a positive effect on a company's total value relative to that of the overall market and a company's cost of capital (adopted in 1988)'.

2490. **Investor Relations Update**. m. $125.

(46) #1079 Social Investment Forum 430 1st Avenue N, Number 290, Minneapolis, MN 55401. t: (1 612) 333 8338.

Public finance

(47) £1080 Association for Public Policy Analysis and Management PO Box 18766, Washington, DC 20036. t: (1 202) 857 8788; f: 466 3982.

(48) #1081 Association of Local Housing Finance Agencies 1101 Connecticut Avenue NW, Suite 700, Washington, DC 20036. t: (1 202) 857 1197; f: 223 4579.

(49) #1082 Government Accountability Project 810 1st Street NE, Suite 630, Washington, DC 20002–3633. t: (1 202) 408 0034; f: 408 9855.

(50) #1083 Government Finance Officers Association 180 North Michigan Avenue, Suite 800, Chicago, IL 60601. t: (1 312) 977 9700; f: 977 4806. *Newsletter*.

'The leading professional association serving the interests of government finance practitioners. Through its programs and services the GFOA works to enhance and promote the professional management of goverment financial resources.'

2491. **Government Finance Review**. bi-m. $30. **online**.

2492. **Pensions & Benefits Update**. bi-m. $50.

2493. **Public Investor**. m. $85. 'Reports and analyses major economic, political and market events affecting public-sector investment officers.'

(51) #1084 Municipal Treasurers Association of the US and Canada 1229 Nineteenth Street NW, Washington, DC 20036. t: (1 202) 833 1017; f: 833 0375.

(52) #1085 National Association of County Treasurers and Finance Officers c/o National Association of Counties, 440 1st Street NW, 8th Floor, Washington, DC 20001. t: (1 202) 393 6226; f: 393 2630.

(53) #1086 National Association of Estate Planning Councils 1130 Lake Cook Road, Suite 150, Buffalo Grove, IL 60089. t: (1 708) 537 7722; f: 537 7740.

(54) #1087 National Association of State Auditors, Comptrollers, and Treasurers 2401 Regency Road, Lexington, KY 40503. t: (1 606) 276 1147: f: 278 0507.

(55) #1088 National Association of State Budget Officers Hall of States, 400 N Capitol Street NW, Number 299, Washington, DC 20001. t: (1 202) 624 5382; f: 624 7745.

(56) #1089 National Association of State Retirement Administrators PO Box 66794, Baton Rouge, LA 70896–6794. t: (1 702) 882 6500; f: 882 1045.

(57) #1090 National Council for Public-Private Partnerships 1010 Massachusetts Avenue NW, Suite 350, Washington, DC 20001–5402. t: (1 202) 467 6800; f: 467 6312. *Newsletter.*

'A nexus for the brightest ideas and best innovators in the partnership arena. Whether from city halls or boardrooms, our members bring to the table an unmatched dedication to providing the most productive and cost-effective public services in these areas: Provision of Public Services . . . New Infrastructure Development . . . Joint Public-Private Ventures . . . While membership is the best way to utilize The Council's resources, our headquarters . . . provides these services to the general public:

- *Consulting Services* The Council can provide a team of Sponsor Members on a paid consultant basis to lend their experience and expertise to your public-private partnership project or study
- *Information DataBase* Free information regarding partnerships are available from our extensive Information Exchange DataBase.'

(58) #1091 National Treasury Employees Union 901 E Street NW, Suite 600, Washington, DC 20004–2037. t: (1 202) 783 4444; f: 783 4085.

'There is no price list for NTEU publications. None are sold. All publications are produced for the benefit of our members and are provided to them at no cost.'

Commercial information providers

Financial management

Note: This and the following paragraph are an extremely limited list simply reminding the reader of the sorts of commercial publication available.

(1) #1092 Accountancy Books PO Box 620, Central Milton Keynes MK9 2JX, UK. t: (44 1908) 248000; f: 248001. Part of the *Accountancy Business Group*, the commercial division of the *Institute of Chartered Accountants in England and Wales.*

2494. **Financial Management Manual**. l. £130. 'A first reference source on the daunting range of issues facing today's financial manager, controller or director. The text includes worked examples and checklists to help answer both immediate and longer term financial and general management questions.'

2495. **Treasury Today**. m. £148.

(2) #1093 Argus Business 6151 Powers Ferry Road NW, Atlanta, GA 30339–2941, USA. t: (1 404) 955 2500; f: 955 0400.

2496. **Corporate Cashflow Magazine**. m. $78. **online**.

(3) #1094 Benefits & Compensation International East Wing, Fourth Floor, Hope House, 45 Great Peter Street, London SW1P 3LT, UK. t: (44 171) 222 0288; f: 799 2163.

2497. **Benefits & Compensation International**. 10/year. £225. 'The established forum of opinion for those responsible for total remuneration internationally, with an emphasis on pension planning including asset management. The magazine covers benefit plan design and remuneration trends worldwide, group life assurance, social security and retirement issues.'

(4) #1095 Bureau of National Affairs 1231 25th Street, NW, Washington, DC 20037, USA. t: (1 202) 452 4200; f: 452 4610. *Also* BNA International, 17 Dartmouth Street, London SW1H 9BL, UK. t: (44 171) 222 8831; f: 222 5550.

2498. **Tax Management Compensation Planning Journal**. m. $327. **online**. Reviews major employee benefit plans in use as well as developments in retirement, profit sharing, welfare plans, stock options, and other employee compensation arrangements.

(5) #1096 Centaur Communications St Giles House, 50 Poland Street, London W1X 4AX, UK. t: (44 171) 439 4222; f: 734 1120.

2499. **Corporate Money**. w. £255.

2500. **International Money Marketing**. m. £70.

2501. **Money Marketing**. m. £50.

2502. **Unit Trust Index**. m. £40.

(6) #1097 Chief Executive Publishing 233 Park Avenue S, New York, NY 10003, USA. t: (1 212) 979 4810; f: 979 7431.

2503. **Chief Executive**. 9/year. $95. **online**. Offers opinion written by and for CEO's in the US and abroad. Covers management, financial or business strategy, marketing, economic and public policy issues.

(7) #1098 Clark Boardman Callaghan 155 Pfingsten Road, Deerfield, IL 60015–9917, USA. t: (1 800) 323 1336; f: (1 708) 948 9340. *Also* c/o Sweet & Maxwell, South Quay Plaza, 183 Marsh Wall, London E14 9FT, UK. t: (44 171) 538 8686; f: 538 9508.

2504. **Corporate Communications Handbook**. a. $125. 'A guide to press releases and other informal disclosure for public corporations.'

(8) #1099 Croner Publications Croner House, London Road, Kingston upon Thames, Surrey KT2 6SR, UK. t: (44 181) 547 3333; f: 547 2637.

2505. **Guide to Credit Management**. l. £183.60. 'An essential tool for cashflow management for businesses of all sizes.'

2506. **Pay and Benefits Sourcebook**. l. £194.25. 'Provides a first starting point of reference for anyone determining pay policy . . . Regular updates keep the information right up-to-date, and as a subscriber you will also receive *Pay and Benefits Briefing* (bi-w.).'

(9) #1100 DP Publications Company Box 7130, Fairfax Station, VA 22039, USA. t: (1 703) 425 1322; f: 425 7911.

2507. **Executive Compensation Reports**. bi-w. $395. 'Exclusively devoted to reporting on compensation practices at over 1,000 corporations . . . Your cost-effective access to compensation information and trends based on actual documentation retrieved by us from the *Securities & Exchange Commission*. The intelligence we present to you is NOT based on nebulous surveys or arm chair puffery. It is a data base information service providing professionals like you with *hard, company-specific data* to reinforce your own firm's compensation decisions.'

(10) #1101 Economist Newspaper Group 253 Summer Street, Boston, MA 02210, USA. t: (1 617) 345 9700; f: 951 4090.

2508. **CFO: The Magazine for Chief Executives**. m. **online**. Circulation: 460,000.

(11) #1102 Financial World 1328 Broadway, Third Floor, New York, NY 10001–2116, USA. t: (1 212) 594 5030; f: 629 0021. *Also* c/o Media Partners, 1 Lambton Place, London W11 2SH, UK. t: (44 171) 221 5462; f: 229 0795.

2509. **Corporate Finance**. q. $115.

2510. **FW**. bi-w. $78. 'Biweekly magazine covering business and finance with an emphasis on corporations around the world. The publication goes beyond simply reporting business news. Financial World specialises in analyses that reveal the future of corporations . . . Financial World recognises that all strategic decisions are, in fact, financial decisions that have long-term implications. Our editors analyze corporate decisions of today and inform our readers of the consequences for tomorrow.'

(12) #1103 FT Law & Tax 21–27 Lamb's Conduit Street, London WC1N 3NJ, UK. t: (44 171) 242 2548; f: (71) 831 8119.

2511. **Financial Management Handbook**. l. £195. Two volumes. 'The complete guide to business finance.'

2512. **Moneyguide: The Handbook of Personal Finance**. l. £99.

(13) #1104 Gee South Quay Plaza, 183 Marsh Wall, London E14 9FS, UK. t: (44 171) 538 5386; f: 538 8623.

2513. **Financial Factbook**. l. £115. Two volumes. "Comprehensive collection of wide range of up-to-date statistical and reference material – easy to access and right level of detail . . . Provides answers to questions/problems which would otherwise have to be dealt with through phone calls or hours of sifting through books" (*Customer Comment*).

2514. **Practical Financial Management**. l. £120. Two volumes. 'Gives financial managers and executives down-to-earth guidance on all aspects of managing a business.'

2515. **Sources of Grants and Aid for Business**. l. £135. 'Comprehensive coverage of all available grants – UK, EC and corporate sources.'

(14) #1105 Hoke Communications 224 Seventh Street, Garden City, NY 11530–5771, USA. t: (1 516) 746 6700; f: 294 8141.

2516. **Fund Raising Management**. m. $94.

(15) #1106 IBC Publishing IBC House, Vickers Drive, Brooklands Industrial Park, Weybridge, Surrey KT13 0XS, UK. t: (44 1932) 354020; f: 353844 *and* **IBC/Donoghue** 290 Eliot Street, PO Box 9104, Ashland, MA 017121–9104, USA. t: (1 508) 881 2800; f: 881 0982.

2517. **Corporate Briefing**. 10/year. £135.

2518. **Treasury Manager**. m. 'Award-winning, monthly newsletter delivering in-depth coverage of news and trends to fast track treasury professionals.'

(16) #1107 Kluwer Publishing Croner House, London Road, Kingston upon Thames, Surrey KT2 6SR, UK. t: (44 181) 547 3333; f: 547 2637.

2519. **Effective Remuneration**. l. £168.25. 'A complete reference source for tax effective remuneration.'

2520. **Handbook of Risk Management**. l. £331.45. Two volumes. 'The definitive guide for anyone responsible for managing their company's risks.'

2521. **Handbook on Pensions**. l. £277.75. Two volumes. 'The complete reference source on all aspects of pension scheme provision and administration.'

2522. **Personal Financial Management**. l. £201.85. 'A unique all-in-one information guide to enable financial advisors to give the best advice.'

(17) #1108 NTC Publications Farm Road, Henley-on-Thames, Oxfordshire RG9 1EJ, UK. t: (44 1491) 411000; f: 571188.

2523. **Lifestyle Pocket Book (Year)**. a. £24. "I cannot commend too highly . . . gives a comprehensive statistical profile of British consumption habits and shopping habits: hobbies, interests and activities; holidays; media usage; personal finance and many other 'lifestyle' statistics . . . everything in the book is clearly dated and sourced" (*Business Information Review*).

2524. **Pay & Benefits Pocket Book (Year)**. a. £19.95. Published with *Bacon & Woodrow*.'The essential facts for dealing with personnel and pay.'

2525. **Personal Pensions Handbook & Unit-Linked Survey (Year)**. a. £27.50. 'Produced with the leading actuaries *Bacon & Woodrow*, an indispensable guide that describes the background, basic principles and technical considerations of personal pension provision. It also includes the latest survey providing detailed analyses of managed funds judged according to quantitative performance criteria.'

(18) #1109 Newman Books 32 Vauxhall Bridge Road, London SW1V 2SS, UK. t: (44 171) 973 6402; f: 233 5057.

2526. **Municipal Year Book (Year)**. a. £155. Two volumes. 'The only comprehensive guide to local and central government, and to the public services.'

(19) #1110 Reward Group Reward House, Diamond Way, Stone Business Park, Stone, Staffordshire ST15 0SD, UK. t: (44 1785) 813566; f: 817007.

'The premier data source on employee pay and benefits and cost of living information in the UK. We have an unrivalled, continuously updated salary database, and publish the widest range of salary surveys in the country... Today, Reward has over 9,000 satisfied customers, including many of the UK's largest and most exacting organisations'.

2527. **Cost of Living Survey**. s-a. £290. 'Provides all the information you require to compare costs throughout the UK... 267 prices collected for 120 items in over 100 locations.'

2528. **Directors Rewards**. a. £395. 'The largest survey of Director's pay in the UK, provides detailed information on pay, bonuses, fees and benefits for Chairman, Managing Director, and a wide range of functional Directors' posts, all analysed by company turnover and number of employees.' Produced in association with the *Institute of Directors.*

(20) #1111 Warren, Gorham & Lamont One Penn Plaza, New York, NY 10119, USA. t: (800) 950 1205; f: (1 212) 971 5240. *Also* c/o Sweet & Maxwell, South Quay Plaza, 183 Marsh Wall, London E14 9FT, UK. t: (44 171) 538 8686; f: 538 9508.

2529. **Journal of Cost Management**. q.

Investment

(1) #1112 Babson-United Investment Advisors 101 Prescott Street, Wellesley Hills, MA 02181–3319, USA. t: (1 617) 235 0900; f: 235 9450.

2530. **United & Babson Investment Report**. w. $268. '*EACH WEEK ON THE FRONT PAGE* there is a terse and timely summary of the current business and investment climate at a glance. *First the good news* (Reading Time: 8 seconds):... See the answers to questions like these: Is productivity up? Are interest rates down? Is the trade deficit shrinking? Are consumer prices holding steady?. *Then the Bad News* (Reading Time: 8 seconds):... See answers to questions like these: Has the inflationary cycle started over? What about housing starts? Are retail and manufacturers' inventories up? Is unemployment on the rise? Where do composite economic indicators stand? *And what it all means?* (Reading Time: 12 seconds): Here is how our senior editors, economists, planners and securities analysts see the near and longer term probablities – based on the latest weekly data evaluated within hours of press time, and visually referenced by the *Barometer & Business Index*... *THE INSIDE COVERS*... summarize the current views of other economic authorities on the stock market, bonds, money, interest rates, commodities, production, trade, foreign affairs and business in general... *THE INSIDE PAGES* present business, financial and economic news – plus special studies and specific investment recommmendations... and on *THE BACK COVER*... It is reserved for ideas, observations and opinions.'

(2) #1113 EF Baumer 401 Shatto Place, Los Angeles, CA 90020, USA. t: (1 213) 386 2111; f: 386 6470.

2531. **Dollar$Sense**. q. 'The Dollar$Sense Money Mangement Program is sponsored by leading financial institutions – i.e. US commercial and mutual savings banks, savings and loan associations (savings societies) and credit unions – nationally . . . Readership by financial institution customers nationwide is now over five hundred thousand each quarter. We recently printed our 36 millionth copy . . . In one major readership study, Dollar$Sense was selected by readers as the most helpful source in managing their money over *Modern Maturity, Money, The Wall Street Journal* and *Wall Street Week*.'

(3) #1114 Charterhouse Communications Third Floor, 4–8 Tabernacle Street, London EC2A 4LU, UK. t: (44 171) 638 1916; f: 638 3128.

2532. **What Investment**. m. £30. Circulation: 35,000

2533. **What Mortgage**. m. £23.60.

(4) #1115 Cornhill Publications 2 Goodge Street, London W1P 1FE, UK. t: (44 171) 240 1515.

2534. **Global Investment Management**. q. £72.

(5) #1116 Crain Communications 1400 Woodbridge, Detroit, MI 48207, USA. t: (1 313) 446 6000; f: 446 0347.

2535. **Business Insurance**. w. $80. **online**. News magazine for corporate, risk, employee benefit and financial executives. Circulation: 50,000.

2536. **Pensions & Investments**. bi-w. $165. **online**. The newspaper of corporate and institutional investing.

2537. **Pensions & Investments Performance Evaluation Reports**. q. $849.

(6) #1117 DAL Investment Company Russ Building, Suite 662, 235 Montgomery Street, San Francisco, CA 94104, USA. t: (1 415) 986 7979; f: 986 1595.

2538. ****NoLoad Fund*X**. m. $119. 'For over 17 years . . . has provided mutual fund investors with timely and essential fund performance information . . . The reliable information provided . . . performance data on over 700 noload and load mutual funds . . . makes it a valuable investment tool. A subscriber writes . . . "I've read all publications and yours is the best. You've distilled all the essential decision making information into a simple easy-to-read format. Your letter provides me with fact, not puffery".'

(7) #1118 Dow Jones 200 Liberty Street, New York, NY 10281–1099, USA.

2539. **Barron's-The Dow Jones Business and Financial Weekly**. w. $186.

"Published by the same people who bring you *The Wall Street Journal*. I would recommend *Barron's* for your library shelf. It often has far meatier articles than does the *Journal*, and it covers all industries. Its company profiles are among the best written and most valuable around, and its Quarterly Mutual Fund Record is a standard source. Written for educated businesspeople, *Barron's* explores its subjects in depth, assuming that its readers are already familiar with the superficial news – as might be provided in the *Journal*. It regularly offers stock and bond prices and Mutual Funds and Annual Reports Roundups."[167]

2540. **Smart Money**. New joint venture with *The Hearst Corporation*.

(8) #1119 EMAP Business Publications 33–39 Bowling Green Lane, London EC1R 0DA, UK. t: (44 171) 837 1212; f: 833 8072.

2541. **Planned Savings**. m. £55.

(9) #1120 FAMC First American Monetary Consultants, Norwest Bank Building, 3500 JFK Parkway, Fort Collins, CO 80525, USA. t: (800) 336 7000/(1 303) 223 4962; f: 223 4996.

2542. **Monetary and Economic Review**. m. $150. 'Offers valuable information to our readers on preserving and protecting their financial assets. Regular features include news and insights on the economy, investment strategies, tax strategies, the political scene, an exposé of the serious erosion of personal and religious freedoms in this country . . . A premium quality publication which combines the expertise of our staff economists and monetary consultants with that of nationally recognized guest columnists.'

(10) #1121 Fleet Street Publications IBC House, Vickers Drive, Brooklands Industrial Park, Weybridge, Surrey, KT13 0XS, UK. t: (44 1932) 354020.

2543. **Fleet Street Letter**. w. £45. 'Has been published for over 50 years, longer than any other investment newsletter. During this period it has built its reputaiton as one of the UK's leading stock-market tip sheets.'

(11) #1122 FT Business Magazines Greystoke Place, Fetter Lane, London EC4A 1ND, UK. t: (44 171) 405 6969; f: 242 0263.

2544. **Investors Chronicle**. w. £84. **online**. '*Warning* The price of stock market investments and the income derived from them can go down as well as up. They may also have poor marketability (ie prove difficult to buy and sell) . . . And remember that circumstances may change after our recommendations are published.'

(12) #1123 Global Finance Joint Venture 11 W 19th Street, New York, NY 10038, USA. t: (1 212) 337 5900; f: 337 5055.

2545. **Global Finance**. m. Aimed at corporate executives and institutional investors, covers current issues and major trends in international finance.

(13) #1124 Institute for Econometric Research 3471 N Federal Highway, Fort Lauderdale, FL 33306, USA. f: (1 305) 563 9003.

2546. **Investor's Digest**. m. $60. A digest of stock market advice and recommendations condensed from hundreds of Wall Street analysts.

(14) #1125 Investor's Daily 1941 Armacost Avenue, Los Angeles, CA 90025, USA. t: (1 213) 207 1832.

2547. **Investor's Daily**. d. **online**.

(15) #1126 Kiplinger Washington Editors Inc 1729 H Street NW, Washington, DC 20006–3938, USA. t: (1 202) 887 6400; f: 331 1206.

2548. **Kiplinger's Personal Finance Magazine**. m. $19.95. **online**. 'Ideas on saving, investing, taxes, major purchases . . . advancing one's career, buying a home . . . education, health and travel.' Circulation: 1,350,000.

2549. **Kiplinger's Retirement Report**. m. $59.95. 'The latest information about taxes, Social Security, health care, pensions, investments.'

Note

(167) FULD op cit p 131.

Further reading

BRIGHAM, E.F. and GAPENSKI L.C. **Cases in financial management**. *Dryden Press*, 1993. 304 pp. £28. 'These cases focus reader attention on analysis and interpretation rather than 'number crunching' techniques. Instructors may choose between directed and non-directed cases, or a blend of the two. Directed cases include questions which assist the student in working through the issues. Non-directed versions replace the questions with a guidance paragraph, so the cases require more original thinking and problem- solving from the student.'

DONALDSON, A. ed. **Companion to treasury management**. 2nd ed. *Blackwell Publishers*, 1993. Published in association with the Association.

EDWARDS, B. **Credit management handbook**. 3rd ed. *Gower*, 1990. 584 pp. £55. 'Contains contributions from no fewer than twenty-three authors, each of them an acknowledged expert on a particular aspect of credit management. The result is the most comprehensive single volume on the subject now available.'

LOFTHOUSE, S. **Equity investment management: How to select stocks and markets**. *John Wiley*, 1994. 375 pp. 'This book is written for investment professionals and students taking professional examinations. It is equity-orientated and discusses how to:

- analyse stocks
- analyse markets
- construct a portfolio

Apart from the 'How I Made My Second Billion' type of book, investment books fall mainly into two categories: (a) the academically rigorous and mathematically demanding textbook; (b) the elementary textbook which explains the basics such as how to calculate a yield and the merits of buying gilts at the post-office. UK investment professionals tend to ignore the first type of book and have read the second. Yet most want to know more than the second type of book has to offer. This book attempts to satisfy that demand.' Includes a 20–page *Bibliography*.

GARNER, D.R., OWEN, R.R. and CONWAY, R.P. **The Ernst & Young guide to financing for growth**. *John Wiley*, 1994. 361 pp. 'When most owners and entrepreneurs need growth capital they think 'bank'. But with the explosive growth of financial markets, there are now as many ways to raise capital as there are to spend it . . . This new edition . . . has been updated and expanded to include all the latest on state, federal, and international financing programs, all the new SEC reporting requirements, and more.' Includes coverage of: Going public; Borrowing; Generating extra cash; Private placement; Leasing; Venture capital.

DOUKAS, J. and MATHUR, I. eds. **European equity markets and corporate financial decision**. *International Business Press*, 1993. 249 pp. Previously published as *Journal of Multinational Financial Management* 3 (3/4), 1993.

VENEDIKIAN, H.M. and WARFIELD, G.A. **Export-import financing**. 3rd ed. *John Wiley*, 1992. 469 pp. 'Directed to the problems of those concerned with financing and otherwise facilitating United States exports and imports. As such, it is designed to provide guidance and orientation to international traders, corporate officers, bankers, and students of foreign commerce and banking.'

DOWNES, J. and GOODMAN, J.E. **Finance and investment handbook**. 3rd ed. *Barron's Educational Series*, 1990.

BRIGHAM, E.F. and GAPENSKI, L.C. **Financial management**. 7th ed. *Dryden Press*, 1993. 1152 pp. £16.95. 'The only text that presents a balance of financial theory and applications.'

DEMIRAG, I. and GODDARD, S. **Financial management for international business**. *McGraw-Hill*, 1994. 390 pp.

BALLING, M. **Financial management in the new Europe**. *Blackwell Publishers*, 1993. 248 pp. $29.95. 'Topics covered include: a survey of EC measures concerning corporate finance; investment patterns and decisions in a single European market; European financial institutions and markets; capital structure decisions; stockholder relations, investor information and dividend policy; volatilities and exposures in markets for stocks, bonds and foreign exchange; mergers and acquisitions; tax laws, tax treaties and tax management.' Winner of the *International Financial Management Association* Copenhagen Award for 1993.

BRIGHAM, E.F. **Fundamentals of financial management**. 6th ed. *Dryden Press*, 1992. 928 pp. £16.50.

HIRT, G.A. and BLOCK, S.B. **Fundamentals of investment management**. 4th ed. *Irwin*, 1993. 816 pp. £24.95.

DOBSON, G. **The global investor**. *Irwin Professional*, 1994. 300 pp. £47.50. 'Opportunities, risks and realities for institutional investors in the world's markets. *Appendices* include: Withholding tax rates; Representative indices in world markets; Some key data providers.'

AGGARWAL, R. **Global portfolio diversification**. *Academic Press*, 1993. 378 pp. £40.00.

RUTTERFORD, J. and MONTGOMERIE, R.R. eds. **Handbook of UK corporate finance**. 2nd ed. *Butterworths*, 1992.

O'NEIL, W.J. **How to make money in stocks**. 2nd ed. *McGraw-Hill*, 1994. 248 pp. £9.95. 'A winning system in good times or bad ... William J O'Neil is a mutual fund manager, investment adviser, publisher of the acclaimed *Investor's Business Daily*, and seminar leader.'

DOUGLASS, S.M. **Institutional investor's guide to managed futures programs**. *McGraw-Hill*, 1994. 256 pp. £51.95. 'Where can the country's 400,000 money and portfolio managers turn to enhance returns, gain new exposures in profitable asset classes, and reduce investment risk? ... (This book) systematically explains the nuances and complexities of today's hottest investment opportunities-futures funds and managed futures programs which actively manage a portion of an institutional investor's portfolio ... The guide fully examines basic fund structures, addresses tax planning and regulatory issues, and forecasts the growth of global futures markets and funds.'

DANIELS, J.D. and RADEBAUGH, L.H. **International business: environments and operations**. 6th ed. *Addison-Wesley*, 1994. 768 pp.

CLARK, E. LEVASSEUR and ROUSSEAU, P. **International finance**. *Chapman & Hall*, 1993. 736 pp. £19.99. 'Anyone looking for an approach to international finance that differs from that found in conventional North American texts will find this major book a real alternative.'

SOLNIK, B. **International investments**. 2nd ed. *Addison-Wesley*, 1991. 404 pp. Designed to provide the concepts, techniques and institutional information needed for successful international investment.

ROSS, D. **International treasury management**. 2nd ed. *Woodhead-Faulkner*, 1990.

BUCKLEY, P.J. and GHAURI, P. **The internationalisation of the firm**. *Academic Press*, 1992, 556 pp. £16.95. Reader of seminal articles on international business with particular reference to the experience of large European and American multinationals in Europe, Japan and the developing countries.

HORNGREN, C.T., SUNDEM, G.L. with SELTO, F.H. **Introduction to management accounting**. 9th ed. *Prentice-Hall*, 1993.

SHAUGNESSY, J.P. **Invest like the best**. *McGraw-Hill*. 1993. 336 pp. 'Unlock your computer to unlock the secrets of the top money managers ... This book and disc shows more than 380,000 computerised investors how to use their personal computers to emulate Wall Street's wizards. Unlike other books that merely describe the general methods of top managers, *Invest Like the Best* actually reduces those strategies to the core successful variables that experts use to pinpoint and select top stocks.'

AMLING, F. and DROMS, W.G. **Investment fundamentals**. *Dryden Press*, 1993. 650 pp. £37.50.

FRIDSON, M.S. **Investment illusions: A savvy Wall Street pro explodes popular misconceptions about the markets**. *John Wiley*, 1993. 230 pp. 'Many books about stocks and bonds appear every year. Almost nobody gets rich by following their so-called 'proven methods' for beating the market. Still, the stream of investment advice continues unabated. Surely, the readers of these volumes must notice that they're failing to become independently wealthy, but somehow they never abandon hope of discovering the magic formula. Their disenchantment applies only to the latest messiah whose 'amazingly simple system' has failed to work miracles. Thanks to this perennial optimism, a comparatively easy method exists for writing a well-received investment book. First, you promise spectacular results to those who follow your rules. Then, be purposefully vague about what the rules are. This simple device will prevent anyone from proving whether your system works or not. Readers won't feel cheated, provided your prose is sufficiently witty. And if wit is not your strong suit, you can indulge in denunciations of the two-bit politicians who are destroying the economy. Be sure, as well, to throw in some psychobabble and a few self-help nostrums. Finally, promote the book through television appearances in which you establish yourself as an unforgettable character (irrepressible punster, condescending oracle, unkempt genius, etc.). Alternatively, you might write an investment book that actually imparts useful information . . . Pick it up and browse if you ever catch yourself thinking that investment success is the product of anything other than disciplined thought and intensive effort.'

SEARS, R.S. and TRENNEPOHL, G.L. **Investment management**. *Dryden Press*, 1993. 992 pp. £33.50.

MAYO, H.B. **Investments**. 4th ed. *Dryden Press*, 1993. 816 pp. £45.50. 'Excellent introductory textbook.'

GRAY, B. **Investors Chronicle beginners' guide to investment**. *Century Business*, 1991. 432 pp. £12.99.

CHANDLER, B. **Managed futures: An investor's guide**. *John Wiley*, 1994. 225 pp. Published in association with *Managed Derivatives Magazine*.

GARRISON, R. **Managerial accounting**. 7th ed. *Irwin*, 1994.

MAHER, M.W., STICKNEY, C.P. and WEIL, R.L. **Managerial accounting**. 5th ed. *Dryden Press*, 1994. 891 pp. £17.95. 'This classic textbook's conceptual approach helps prepare students to focus on concepts and managerial uses of financial information, as opposed to the techniques of cost accounting.'

WESTON, F.J. and COPELAND, T.E. **Managerial finance**. 9th ed. *Dryden Press*, 1992. 950 pp. £15.95.

TULLER, L.W. **The McGraw-Hill handbook of global trade and investment financing**. *McGraw-Hill*, 1992. 535 pp. Chapters include: Development Banks and Bilateral Financing Sources; Countertrade; United States Government-Supported Export Trade Finance; plus a series of Chapters on financing trade and investment in various regions of the world. Appendixes include: Associations, Bureaus, and Agencies for International Trade; Foreign Credit Agencies Providing Credit Reports.

EITEMAN, D.K., STONEHILL, A.I. and MOFFET, M.H. **Multinational business finance**. 6th ed. *Addison-Wesley*, 1992. 680 pp.

BUCKLEY, A. **Multinational finance**. 2nd ed. *Prentice Hall*, 1992. 708 pp.

SHAPIRO, A.C. **Multinational financial management**. 4th ed. *Allyn and Bacon*, 1992.

CHORAFAS, D.N. and STEINMANN, H. **Off-balance sheet financial instruments**. *Probus Publishing*, 1994. 519 pp. 'Maximising profitability and managing risk in financial services.'

EMERY, D.R. and FINNERTY, J.D. **Principles of finance with corporate applications**. *West Publishing*, 1991. 898 pp.

STERN, J. and CHEW, D. eds. **Revolution in corporate finance**. 2nd ed. *Blackwell Publishers*, 1992.

ALLEN, D. **Strategic financial decisions**. *CIMA Publications*, 1994. 192 pp. 16.95.

ALLEN, D. **Strategic financial management: Managing for long-term economic success**. *FT Management Reports*, 1994. £229.

CHAPTER SEVEN

Scholarly Research and Study

The structure of this chapter is:[168]

Organizations

International

Europe

United Kingdom

- ACADEMIC ASSOCIATIONS
- ACADEMIC INSTITUTIONS
- RESEARCH CENTRES

United States

- ACADEMIC ASSOCIATIONS
- ACADEMIC INSTITUTIONS
- RESEARCH CENTRES

Commercial information providers

1. Organizations: International

(1) #1127 Association Internationale pour l'Etude de l'Economie de l'Assurance [Geneva Association; International Association for the Study of Insurance Economics] 18 Chemin Rieu, Geneva, Switzerland. t: (41 22) 347 09 38; f: 347 20 78.

Information Letter (Summaries of research activity); *Newsletter* (Liaison and information bulletin to promote contacts at university level in the field of risk and insurance economics). The *Research Programme on the Service Economy* and the *Research Programme on Social Security, Insurance, Savings and Employment* provides information on research and publications in these areas.

2550. **GENEVA Papers on Risk and Insurance: Theory**. *Kluwer Academic Publishers.* bi-a. $93.50. There is also an *Issues and Practice* version.

(2) #1128 Econometric Society c/o Department of Economics, Northwestern University, Evanston, IL 60208–2600, USA. t: (1 708) 491 3615.

'An international society for the advancement of economic theory in its relation to statistics and mathematics. The Society operates as a completely disinterested, scientific organization, without political, social, financial, or nationalistic bias.'

2551. **Econometrica**. *Blackwells.* bi-m. £96. (In 1989) 'ranked in a virtual tie for first among "core" economics journals, and in second place in citations from all journals.'

(3) #1129 International Association for Research in Income and Wealth c/o Department of Economics, New York University, 269 Mercer Street, Room 700, New York, NY 10003, USA. t: (1 212) 924 4386; f: 366 5067.

Founded in 1947. 'Its major objectives are: the furthering of research on national and economic and social accounting, including the development of concepts and definitions for the measurement and analysis of income and wealth; the development and further integration of systems of economic and social statistics; and related problems of statistical methodology . . . This is accomplished by holding biennial general conferences, by the circulation of scholarly papers, and by the publication of a quarterly journal.'

2552. **Review of Income and Wealth**. q. $100. Covers national and social accounting; microdata analysis of issues related to income and wealth; development and integration of micro and macro systems of economic, financial and social statistics; international comparisons of productivity, income and wealth; and related problems of measurement and statistical methodology.

(4) #1130 International Association of Business Forecasting c/o St Mary's University, One Camino Santa Maria, San Antonio, TX 78228–8607, USA. t: (1 210) 436 3705; f: 431 2115. *Newsletter.*

'Dedicated to:

- Enhancing the professional status of users and preparers of business forecasts.

- Promoting an understanding and appreciation for the work of professional forecasters among business managers.
- Encouraging research in the areas of forecasting methods and systems, and planning.'

(5) #1131 International Association of Financial Engineers c/o Department of Economics and Finance, St John's University, 8000 Utopia Parkway, Jamaica, NY 11439, USA. t: (1 718) 990 6161 ext 7381; f: 990 1868.

'• *Financial Engineering* The development and creative application of financial technology to solve financial problems and exploit financial opportunities.
- *Mission* The International Association of Financial Engineers is a world-wide non-profit membership organization devoted to networking industry practitioners and academicians working in the field of financial engineering.
- *Networking* Regional units of the Association around the globe sponsor periodic dinner meetings where members get together to discuss the latest developments in the field and hear from leading figures in business and academe; (e.g.) Chicago, Frankfurt, London, New York City, San Francisco, Tokyo, Toronto, Zurich.
- *The People* The leadership of the Association is drawn from across the business and academic spectrum; Senior Fellows include: Markowitz, Melamed, Miller, Modigliani, Samuelson, Scholes, Sharpe . . . Robert Merton (Harvard University) received the Association's first *Financial Engineer of the Year* award in December 1993, in recognition of his many contributions to the development of financial theory and, in particular, for his formative role in the development of continous time finance . . . The *ad hoc committee on Academic Curriculum* completed its work during the Fall (1993) and recommended a "core body of knowledge".'

2553. **Journal of Financial Engineering**. q. $180. Volume 1, Number 1 was June 1992.

(6) #1132 International Center for Monetary and Banking Studies [Centre International d'Etudes Monetaires et Bancaires] Avenue de la Paix 11A, CH-1211 Geneva 21, Switzerland. t: (41 22) 734 95 48; f: 733 3853.

'Created in 1973 as an independent, non-profit foundation, placed under the supervision of the Swiss *Federal Department of the Interior*. The Center is devoted to the scientific study of international monetary, financial, and banking issues. In pursuing this aim, the Center relies on the collaboration of specialists from central banks, international organizations, the private sector and the academic community.

Over the past decade, ICMB has built a solid reputation by successfully training excutives from over 800 institutions and 72 countries worldwide in the latest financial management techniques. A highly renowned international faculty enables participants to build sophisticated skills, while international audiences from varied institutions promote the sharing of ideas and experiences.' Courses scheduled for 1995 include:

- *Modern security analysis for practitioners*
- *Neural networks in capital markets*
- *Forecasting techniques in financial markets*
- *Bond portfolio and interest-rate risk management*
- *Options: Valuation, hedging and portfolio applications*
- *Equity portfolio management*'

(7) #1133 International Economic Association [Association Internationale des Sciences Economiques] 23 rue Campagne Première, 75014 Paris, France. t: (33 1) 43 27 91 44; f: 42 79 92 16. *Newsletter*.

Founded in 1949 on the recommendation of UNESCO. Aims to initiate or coordinate measures of international collaboration designed to assist the advancement of economic knowledge; secure and develop personal contacts between economists of different countries, by organizing round-table discussions and conferences; encourage provision of international media for the dissemination of economic thought and knowledge.

2554. **International Economic Association Conference Volumes**. *Macmillan Press*. i. 'The complete set of the first fifty volumes of conferences held by the International Economic Association is published by Macmillan as a tribute to the conferences and congresses held by the IEA since its inception in 1948 (1950). This is a unique chance to obtain the complete library edition of invaluable contributions to the history of world economics . . . Since 1979, Macmillan have published over 50 new volumes, continuing the tradition and the high standards of the first 50 volumes.'

(8) #1134 International Institute of Forecasters c/o CTIP, The Maxwell School, Syracuse University, Syracuse, NY 13244, USA. t: (1 315) 443 4661; f: 443 1075. *Newsletter*.

'To foster generation, distribution and knowledge on forecasting to academics and practitioners throughout the world. In 1993 the IIF had 478 members from 37 countries, a 34% increase over the previous year.'

2555. **International Journal of Forecasting**. *Elsevier Science*. 4/yr. Dfl.453. Publishes papers covering all aspects of forecasting.

(9) #1135 International Institute of Investment and Merchant Banking 1000 Thomas Jefferson Street NW, Suite 600, Washington, DC 20007, USA. t: (1 202) 965 6565; f: 965 4839.

(10) #1136 International Institute of Public Finance c/o Saar University, PO Box 15 11 50, 66041 Saarbrücken, Germany. t: (49 681) 302 3653; f: 302 4369.

'Founded in Paris 1937 and has since become an important academic institution in the field of public finance and public economics . . . Membership in the IIPF has grown steadily and now stands at approximately 950 members from more than sixty countries.' The Proceedings of each *Annual Congress* of the Institute are published (eg 'Public Finance and Irregular Activities' (49th Session, Berlin 1993; DM 100).)

(11) #1137 International Statistical Institute 428 Prinses Beatrixlaan, PO Box 950, 2270 AZ Voorburg, The Netherlands. t: (31 70) 337 5737; f: 386 0025. e: isi@cs.vu.nl. *Newsletter*.

'One of the oldest scientific associations functioning in the modern world. It was established in 1885 . . . The ISI is composed of some 1700 individual members who are the world's leading statisticians . . . This reservoir of expertise is supplemented by that of the members of the Institute's Sections . . . In total there are about 5000 members.'

2556. **Directory of Official Statistical Agencies**. a. $10.

2557. **Directory of Statistical Societies**. a. $10.

2558. **International Statistical Review**. 3/year. $58.

(i) *#1138 International Association for Official Statistics*

(12) #1139 Transnational Institute Paulus Potterstraat 20, 1071 DA Amsterdam, The Netherlands. t: (31 20) 662 66 08; f: 675 71 76.

'A decentralised fellowship of scholars, researchers and writers from the Third World, the US and Europe committed to critical and bold analysis of North-South issues, particularly those concerning conflict, poverty, and marginalisation.'

2. Organizations: Europe

(1) #1140 Association d'Instituts Européens de Conjoncture Economique [Association of European Conjuncture Institutes] c/o Institut de Recherches Economiques et Sociales, Place Montesquieu, 3 – 1348 Louvain-la-Neuve, Belgium. t: (32 10) 473426; f: 473945.

'This organization is in principle open to independent European Institutes involved in surveying economic conditions and developments and short-term economic forecasting. The association does not accept membership of bodies which are directly involved either in conducting economic policies or in representing economic interests. The proceedings and working papers of the organization are intended for internal use, and are only publicised with the agreement of their authors.'

(2) #1141 Centre for European Policy Studies rue Ducale 33, B-1000 Brussels, Belgium. t: (32 2) 513 40 88; f: 511 59 60.

(3) #1142 European Accounting Association c/o EIASM Rue d'Egmont 13, B-1050 Brussels, Belgium. t: (32 2) 511 9116.

2559. **European Accounting Review**. *Routledge*. 3/year. 86.

(4) #1143 European Association of Law and Economics c/o Institute for Transnational Legal Research, Postbus 616, 6200 MD Maastricht, The Netherlands. t: (31 43) 883060; f: 259091. *Newsletter*.

'The *Law and Economics* movement represents the most important intellectual challenge within legal scholarship in recent decades. Economic concepts are applied to explain and clarify legal issues, not only with respect to market law, anti-trust and tax law where the link between the legal and the economic disciplines is obvious, but also with respect to a wide gamut of non-market activities, ranging from liability issues to family matters and crime. *Law and Economics* has influenced legislation and case law. Many academic journals publish articles in the field, and *Law and Economics* has become an integral part of legal and economic education at the most prestigious universities in the US like Chicago, Yale, Harvard, Stanford and Berkeley. The European Association of Law and Economics (EALE) is the institutional response to the increasing importance of the economic analysis of law in Europe. The EALE was founded in 1984.'

(5) #1144 European Economic Association c/o Office of the Secretary, Van Evenstraat 2B, 3000 Leuven, Belgium. t: (32 16) 28 30 70; f: 28 33 61. *Newsletter*.

'International scientific body, with membership open to all persons involved or interested in economics . . . The Association's first objective of firmly establishing its existence was reached in 1986. Within a few months, some 900 economists from all over Europe (and from a number of non-European countries as well) agreed to become founding members . . . At present the membership stands well above 1700 . . . The *Annual Congress* . . . is a main event among the Association's activities . . . The plenary lectures and invited papers are published in the *Papers and Proceedings* issue of the *European Economic Review* appearing in March-April of the year following the Congress.'

2560. **European Economic Review**. *Elsevier Science*. m. $876.

(6) #1145 European Finance Association Rue d'Egmont 13, B-1050 Brussels, Belgium. t: (32 2) 511 91 16; f: (32 2) 512 19 29.

'The 1995 membership fee is 1,000 Belgian francs, which allows you to receive the *Newsletter* (s-a.).'

(7) #1146 Institut Européen d'Administration Publique [European Institute of Public Administration] OL Vrouweplein 22, PO Box 1229, 6201 BE Maastricht, The Netherlands. t: (31 43) 29 62 22; f: 29 62 96. *Newsletter*.

'The only independent institute of public policy and administration with a European mission of public service, linked to the EU, providing a variety of services to national administrations and institutions from the EU in support of their tasks and responsibilities related to *European integration*. The general aim of the Institute is to make a practical contribution to the European unification process by way of applied research, training, consultancy and publications on the institutions, decision-making processes and policies of the EU, and public management and law.' The Institute has produced a variety of non-serial publications including: *Guide to European Information* which aims 'to help those working daily or occasionally in the field of European affairs both inside and outside the European Union, to trace and use European Documents'. (1994. 50 pp, NLG 30).

3. Organizations: United Kingdom

Academic associations

(1) #1147 British Accounting Association c/o Professor J Dickinson, King Alfred's College, Winchester, SO22 4NR. t: (44 1962) 841515.

2561. **British Accounting Review**. *Academic Press*. q. £114. 'Forum for communication throughout the world between members of the academic and professional community concerned with the research and teaching, at degree level and above, of accounting, finance and cognate disciplines.'

2562. **British Accounting Review Research Register**. *Academic Press*. bi-a. Published in association with the *Institute of Chartered Accountants in England and Wales*. 'Includes the lecturing specialisms, research interests and publications of 1,357 academic staff in Accounting and Finance throughout the British Isles, across 101 universities, polytechnics and colleges.'

(2) #1148 Economists in Insurance Group (London) c/o Planning Group, Lloyd's of London, One Lime Street, London EC3M 7HA. t: (44 171) 327 5041; f: 327 5599.

(3) #1149 Hansard Society of Parliamentary Government St Philips Building North, Sheffield Street, London WC2A 2EX. t: (44 171) 955 7478; f: 955 7492.

'The principle objective of the Hansard Society, which was founded in 1944, is to promote knowledge of and interest in Parliamentary Government. Its work ranges over research, commissions on topical issues and an active schools programme.'

2563. **Parliament and Government Pocket Book (Year)**. *NTC Publications*. a. £16.95. 'A unique source of information on the UK and EU

Parliaments, their spending of public money, and the public's attitude to them.'

2564. **Parliamentary Affairs**. *Oxford University Press*. q. £52.

(4) #1150 Royal Economic Society c/o 32 The Grove, Brookmans Park, Hatfield, Hertfordshire AL9 7RN. t: (44 707) 653269.

2565. **Economic Journal**. *Blackwells*. bi-m. £95.

(5) #1151 Royal Statistical Society 25 Enford Street, London W1H 2BH. t: (44 171) 723 5882; f: 706 1710.

2566. **Applied Statistics**. *Blackwells*. q. £46.50. Journal of the Royal Statistical Society: Series C.

2567. **Journal of the Royal Statistical Society**. *Blackwells*. *Series A*. 3/year. £46.50; *Series B*. q. £46.50.

2568. **Statistician**. *Blackwells*. q. £125. Journal of the Royal Statistical Society: Series D.

(6) #1152 Society of Business Economists 11 Bay Tree Walk, Watford, Hertfordshire WD1 3RX. t: (0923) 37287.

2569. **Business Economist**. 3/yr. £22. Developments in the UK, overseas and world economics. Issues in applied economic theory and analysis of individual industries.

Academic institutions

(7) #1153 City University Northampton Square, London EC1V 0HB. t: (44 71) 477 8000; f: 477 8560. *City University Business School* Frobisher Crescent, Barbican Centre, London EC2Y 8HB. t: (44 71) 477 8000; f: 477 8880.

The research interests of the University's Department of Banking and Finance 'focus on monetary economics, monetary history, financial markets, international finance and regulation of banking systems'. In addition, several specialised research centres are designated:

- *Actuarial Research Centre* t: (44 171) 8470; f: 8572. 'Received substantial financial support from the insurance industry and the actuarial profession . . . The main research activities are concerned with stochastic modelling in life insurance and pensions (considering asset allocation, bonus policy, solvency); actuarial models in non life insurance (focusing on premium rating, reserving, solvency); mortality and morbidity models (including estimation and graduation of rates, multiple state models, data analytical issues). An important new development has been the establishment of a project on stochastic investment models and their actuarial applications.'
- *Centre for Insurance and Investment Studies* Funded mainly by the *Association of British Insurers.*

- *Centre for Internal Auditing* t: (44 171) 477 8651; f: 477 8880. 'Established in 1987 to act as a focal point for teaching and research into internal auditing and related disciplines such as computing, accounting and management studies.' *Working Papers.*
- *International Centre for Shipping, Trade and Finance*
- *NatWest Centre for Franchise Research*
- *Property Investment Research Centre* t: (44 171) 477 8208; f: 477 8573. *Discussion Papers.*

(8) #1154 London Business School Sussex Place, Regent's Park, London NW1 4SA. t: (44 171) 262 5050; f: 724 7875. http://www.lbs.lon.ac.uk gives full details of all the school's publications.

- *Centre for Economic Forecasting*

2570. **Economic Outlook**. *Blackwells.* q. £300. Forecast of the world economy combining a unique blend of analysis of the main trends with detailed figures on output, employment, inflation and other countries variables.

- *Institute of Finance and Accounting*

2571. **London Share Price Database**. 'Provides long-term historic stock market data for nearly 6000 UK shares over the thirty eight year period from 1955 to date. The database has been compiled by the London Business School from multiple sources including the Stock Exchange Daily Official List, The Stock Exchange Weekly Intelligence, the Stock Exchange Yearbook, the Financial Times, Moodies and Extel cards, Moodies/Stubbs Taxation Service, the Extel Annual Dividend and Capital Gains Tax Services, Frederick Mathieson's List of Quoted Securities, and Extel's EXSHARE service.'

2572. **Risk Measurement Service**. q. £320. 'Each issue contains:

- Risk measure and other key data for some 2,000 British shares, including every UK stock listed on the London Stock Exchange and the Unlisted Securities Market, and for all industrial sectors.
- An explanation of what these measures mean and how they can be used effectively
- Industry-level information for each sector and for every FT-Actuaries classification
- Highlight tables showing the best and worst performers and the highest and lowest risk shares each quarter.'

- *London Business School Information Service* t: (44 171) 723 3404; f: 706 1897. e: infoserve@lbs.lon.ac.uk. Fee-based information service.

(9) #1155 London School of Economics and Political Science Houghton Street, London, WC2A 2AE.

- *Centre for Economic Performance* t: (44 171) 955 7284; f: 955 7595. 'A non-profit organisation studying the reasons for economic success among firms and nations. It is an ESRC research centre.' *Discussion*

Papers e.g. 'International trade and scale economies: A new analysis' (1994); 'Monetary union or else?' (1995).

- *Financial Markets Group* t: (44 171) 955 7891; f: 242 1006. 'Launched in 1987. Its principal objective is to pursue basic research into the nature of financial markets and their links with the flow of savings and investment in the domestic and international economy . . . The research programme of the Group is divided into the following major areas:
    - The Efficiency of Financial Markets and Asset Price Behaviour
    - The Structure of Securities Markets
    - Corporate Finance
    - Regulation
    - Taxation, Saving and Portfolio Behaviour
    - Growth and Fluctuations

The research output of the Group is first published in the Financial Markets Group *Discussion Paper Series* . . . The Group also publish a quarterly *Review* which contains summaries of recent Discussion and Special Papers, seminars and conferences in a form which is non-technical.'

- *Suntory-Toyota International Centre for Economics and Related Disciplines* t: (44 171) 955 6698; f: 242 2357. *Newsletter. Occasional Papers. Discussion Papers* (a series of Lists including: 'Development Economics Research Programme'; 'Programme of Research into Economic Transformation and Public Finance').

(10) #1156 University of Cambridge The Old Schools, Trinity Lane, Cambridge CB2 1TN. t: (44 1223) 337733; f: 332332.

- *Department of Applied Economics* Some recent *DAE Working Papers* are: 'An empirical investigation of US bank deposit guarantees' (9402); 'Modelling UK mortgage defaults using a hazard approach based on American options' (9408); 'Information flows in the foreign exchange market' (9412).
- *Department of Land Economy*

(11) #1157 University of Exeter Northcote House, The Queen's Drive, Exeter, Devon, EX4 4QJ. t: (44 1392) 263263; f: 263108.

- *Centre for European Legal Studies*
- *Centre for European Studies* t: (44 1392) 264490; f: 264515.
- *Centre for Research in Finance and Accounting*

(12) #1158 University of Lancaster University House, Lancaster LA1 4YW. t: (44 1524) 65201; f: 594294.

- *Corporate Finance Reporting Group*
- *International Centre for Research in Accounting*

(13) #1159 University of Leicester University Road, Leicester LE1 7RH. t: (116) 252 2522; f: 252 2200.

- *Public Sector Economics Research Centre*

(14) #1160 University of London: Birkbeck College 7–15 Gresse Street, London W1P 2LL. t: (44 171) 631 6403; f: 631 6416.

- *Department of Economics* Recent *Discusssion Papers in Economics* include: 'A theory of tradable price caps' (1994); 'The savings-investment association' (1994).

(15) #1161 University of London: Queen Mary and Westfield College Mile End Road, London E1 4NS. t: (44 171) 975 5555; f: 975 5500.

- *Centre for Commercial Law Studies* t: (44 171) 975 5124; f: (44 181) 980 1079. 'The Centre has become a national and international focus for advanced teaching and research in commercial and business law. Through collaborating closely with the professions and with commerce in its activities, it offers a strong range of specialist expertise.'

(16) #1162 University of Loughborough Ashby Road, Loughborough, Leicestershire LE11 3TU. t: (44 1509) 263171.

- *Banking Centre* t: (44 1509) 223118; f: 233142. *Research Monographs* (e.g. 'The economics of bank charges for personal customers' (1993)); *Research Papers* (e.g. 'The future of banking: Is banking a declining industry?' (1994)).

(17) #1163 University of Nottingham School of Management and Finance, Portland Building, University of Nottingham, University Park, Nottingham NG7 2RD. t: (44 115) 951 5493/5494; f: 951 5503.

- *Centre for Management Buy-Out Research* Maintains a database of over 6,500 UK and European buy-outs and buy-ins. The Centre publishes the results of regular statistical and specialist survey research on buy-out markets.

(18) #1164 University of Reading Whiteknights, Reading RG6 2AE.

- *Centre for European Property Research* t: (44 1734) 318175; f: 318172.
- *ISMA Centre for Education and Research in Securities Markets*

(19) #1165 University of Strathclyde 141 St James Road, Glasgow G4 0LT. t: (44 141) 552 4400; f: 552 1757.

- *European Policies Research Centre* 'EPRC Ltd is a company associated with Strathclyde University, and has been in the forefront of the provision of business development information for over ten years . . . EPRC has firmly established a reputation as a leading supplier of business information. It is the combination of expert information – gathered efficiently, analysed sensibly and presented clearly – with sophisticated yet easy-to-use retrieval systems which has made EPRC information services widely sought after throughout Europe.' *Discussion Papers.*

2573. **AIMS. online**. 'Grants and financial support for UK business'.

2574. **EUROLOC. online**. 'Presents information on grants and incentives throughout Europe . . . Divided into three sections: A. *Financial Assistance for Business in Europe.* B. *News.* C. *Incentive Statistics* (the number of awards made, their average value, the breakdown of awards to different industry sectors or to different regions).'

2575. **European Community Funding for Business Development**. *Kogan Page.* i. (2nd ed. 1993). "A serious methodical study across a whole range of available programmes" (*Daily Telegraph*).

2576. **European Regional Incentives (Year)**. *Bowker-Saur.* a. £69. 'Provides a current and comprehensive review of all regional grants and other aid offered to industry and business in each of the 12 EC countries and Sweden. Full details, as well as authoritative analysis of trends, are given for approximately 35 schemes, which involve grants to businesses annually worth around 10 billion. "Widely acknowledged to be the definitive guide to this complex subject" (*European Information Service*).'

2577. **Government Funding for United Kingdom Business**. *Kogan Page.* a. £50. "An excellent reference source . . . it is likely to be worth its weight in gold to most business people" (*Accountant*).

2578. **STARS. online**. 'Contains detailed, structured and up-to-date information on the regulatory environment for business in the UK. (The database) also monitors new developments, both domestically and in the form of the Single European Market legislation . . . Divided into four sections: A. *Rules and Regulations for UK Business* Contains detailed information on some 150 laws, regulations, and codes of practice relevant to business in the UK. These cover eight distinct areas of business activity, including: Company law; Taxation; Importing and Exporting; and Consumer Law and Marketing. B. *Single European Market Legislation* Legislation relating to UK busienss is increasingly being affected by the mass of proposals, directives and regulations issued by the European Commission . . . The information in this file allows users to identify which European Commission proposals, directives and regulations are relevant to them. C. *Sources of Business Information and Advice* Details over 350 sources of business advice and assistance such as trade associations, professional bodies, development organisations, research centres, importing/exporting bodies, and industry-related services. D. *News* . . . Every day EPRC staff scrutinise parliamentary papers, trade magazines, journals and newspapers as well as literature from government departments and advisory groups. In addition, close contacts are maintained with relevant administering bodies. In this way, key information concerning the business regulatory environment is identified and used to update the information on STARS.'

(20) #1166 University of Sussex Sussex House, Falmer, Brighton BN1 9RH. t: (44 1273) 606755; f: 678335.

- *Institute of Development Studies* t: (44 1273) 606261; f: 691647. *Annual Report*. Produces *Discussion Papers, Research Reports*, and *Working Papers*, as well as sponsoring the commercial publication of a wide range of books.

2579. **IDS Bulletin**. q. £37. Recent papers have included: 'Knowledge is power? The use and abuse of information in development'; 'Towards democratic governance'; 'Fifty years on: The UN and economic and social development'.

- *International Economics Research Centre* Examples from their series *Discussion Papers in Economics* are 'Capital-asset ratios, deposit insurance and bank risk' (02/93); 'Common volatility in the foreign exchange market' (04/93).

(21) #1167 University of Wales Bangor, Gwynedd, Wales LL57 2DG. t: (44 1248) 382277; f: 364160.

- *Institute of European Finance* 'The purpose of the *IEF Research Papers in Banking and Finance* is to act as a general vehicle for the reporting of research and the discussion of issues in the institutional aspects of banking, insurance and finance. The authors are members of the Institute of European Finance and associates in universities and financial institutions throughout the world. Two special features are translations of journal articles that have appeared in languages other than English and invited papers from eminent authors.'

(22) #1168 University of Warwick Coventry CV4 7AL. t: (44 1203) 523523; f: 461606.

- *ESRC Macroeconomic Modelling Bureau* t: (44 1203) 523276; f: 523032. 'Objectives are to increase accessibility of macroeconomic models of the UK economy, to improve knowledge of their properties and performance, and to carry out comparative research. The current portfolio includes the models of the *London Business School*, the *National Institute of Economic and Social Research, Her Majesty's Treasury*, the *Bank of England*, and *Oxford Economic Forecasting*. The Bureau regularly publishes reviews and analysis of models and forecasts, and references to its research findings commonly appear in the media. It has become a recognised international authority on comparative assessment of macroeconomic models and its facilities represent a unique research resource.' *Discussion Papers*.
- *Financial Options Research Centre* 'Established in 1989 to bridge the gap betwewen leading academic work on financial markets and the needs of practitioners, particularly those concerned with derivative instruments and risk management. Recent *Pre-prints* are: "Option prices as predictors of stock prices: Intraday adjustments to information releases" (94/45); "A comparison of models for pricing interest rate derivative securities" (94/47).'

Research centres

(23) #1169 Adam Smith Institute 23 Great Smith Street, London SW1P 3BL. t: (44 171) 222 4995; f: 222 7544.

(24) #1170 British Institute of International and Comparative Law Charles Clore House, 17 Russell Square, London WC1B 5DR. t: (44 171) 636 5802; f: 323 2016. *Report. Newsletter.*

'Independent self-governing institute. Its objects are to conduct research, discussion and publication on public and private international law, comparative law and EC law . . . Membership is open to individuals, firms and corporations without restrictions on nationality. It is drawn from the judiciary, academic and practising lawyers, as well as lawyers engaged in government, commerce and industry in this country and abroad.'

2580. **Bulletin of Legal Developments**. bi-w. £95. 'Up-to-the-minute information service on developments in law all over the world . . . Nine out of the top ten law firms in the UK subscribe to the Bulletin of Legal Developments . . . Isn't it time you did too?'

2581. **Common Market Law Review**. *Kluwer Academic Publishers.* bi-m. Dfl 779. Published in association with the *Europa Institute*, University of Leiden, The Netherlands.

2582. **International and Comparative Law Quarterly**. q. £65.

(25) #1171 British–North American Committee British–North American Research Assocation, Grosvenor Gardens House, 35–37 Grosvenor Gardens, London SW1W 0BS. t: (44 171) 828 6644; f: 828 5830. *Also* c/o National Planning Association, 1424 16th Street, NW, Suite 700, Washington, DC 20036, USA. t: (1 202) 265 7685; f: 797 5516.

Produces various series of research papers: e.g. ROSE, H. 'The changing world of finance and its problems' (1993, 6); BALL, J. 'The world economy: Trends and prospects for the next decade' (1994, 10).

(26) #1172 Centre for Economic Policy Research 25–28 Old Burlington Street, London W1X 1LB. t: (44 171) 734 9110; f: 734 8760.

Established in 1983 to promote independent analysis and public discussion of open economies and the relations among them. It is pluralist and non-partisan, bringing economic research to bear on the analysis of medium- and long-run policy questions. A *Centre for Economic Policy Research International Foundation* is based in the United States. The *Bulletin* reviews the current activities of the Centre, and summmaries its extensive series of *Discussion Papers.*

2583. **Economic Policy: A European Forum**. *Cambridge University Press.* bi-a. 49. Published also for the *Maison des Sciences de l'Homme*, in association with the *European Economic Association*.

- *European Science Foundation Network in Financial Markets* 'In November 1988 the *European Science Foundation* (ESF) approved the formation of a Network in Financial Markets. This is the twelfth network to be approved by the ESF and the third in the area of the social sciences. A central objective of the Network in Financial Markets is to encourage the emergence of a community of academics working in finance in Europe. The Centre for Economic Policy Research is acting as the administrative centre of the Network . . . Network activities include:
    - A register of European researchers in financial economics
    - The Network *Newsletter*
    - A series of workshops
    - An annual summer symposium
    - Exchanges of scholars
    - Data banks on European financial statistics
    - Activities designed to encourage young scholars

The *ESF Network Working Papers* are available from CEPR (e.g. "No. 36: Private information and the design of securities". October 1993) . . . I should point out that ESF funding for the Network ends this Summer (1994) and the Network will continue its activities within CEPR's Financial Economics programme. This is a new programme area, resulting from the splitting of our Applied Macroeconomic programme in to Financial Economics and Industrial Organization as a result of the growth of activities in these areas.'

(27) #1173 Centre for the Study of Financial Innovation 18 Curzon Street, London W1Y 2AD. t: (44 171) 493 0173.

(28) #1174 CTI Centre for Accounting Finance and Management School of Information Systems, University of East Anglia, Norwich NR4 7TJ. t: (44 1603) 592312; f: 593343. e: cti-afm@sys.uea.ac.uk.

One of a number of subject area Centres supported by the UK higher education funding system as part of an initiative to promote the effective use of computers in teaching in higher education.

(29) #1175 CTI Centre for Computing in Economics Department of Economics, University of Bristol, 8 Woodland Road, Bristol BS8 1TN. t: (44 117) 928 8478; f: 928 8577. e: cticce@bristol.ac.uk.

Publications include: 'Resources for economists on the Internet' (by Bill Goffe: edited by the Centre) (December 1993, 21 pp); 'A guide to UK-based networked information resources for social scientists (May 1994, 25 pp).

2584. **WoPCAS: Working Papers Current Awareness Service**. **online**. 'Applications are invited from economists in all fields of research and study to join a new electronic mailing list which is being set up . . . in conjunction with the *University of Warwick* library service. The WoPCAS service provides lists of new working paper titles deposited with Warwick University library . . . in your electronic mail box . . . The list is only available to registered members. Registration involves a subscriber completing a declaration covering the use of the information received through the WoPCAS service . . . There is no charge for subscriptions.'

(30) #1176 European Economics and Financial Centre PO Box 2498, London W2 4LE. t: (44 171) 229 0402; f: 221 5118.

(31) #1177 Institute for Fiscal Studies 7 Ridgmount Street, London WC1E 7AE. t: (44 171) 636 3784; f: 323 4780. e: postbox@ifs.org.uk.

'One of Britain's pre-eminient micro-economic research centres, providing rigorous and independent commentary on taxation and government policy.' *Commentaries* e.g. 'Harmonising the fringes of national insurance and income tax' (1993, £6); UK household cost-of-living indices: 1979–1992' (1994, £6); 'The distribution of wealth in the UK' (1994, £6). *Report Series* e.g. 'The taxation of private pensions' (1993, £10); 'Pensions policy in the UK' (1994, £12.50); 'Local sales taxation' (1995, £10). *Working Papers.*

2585. **Fiscal Studies**. q. £63.80. **online**.

(32) #1178 Institute for Public Policy Research 30–32 Southampton Street, London WC2E 7RA. t: (44 171) 379 9400; f: 497 0373.

Independent charity whose purpose is to contribute to public understanding of social, economic and political questions through research, discussion and publication. Established in 1988 by leading figures in the academic, business and trade union community to provide an alternative to the free market think tanks. "The Institute for Public Policy Research could do for a Labour government what the Adam Smith Institute, the Centre for Policy Studies, and the Institute of Economic Affairs have done for the Conservatives" (*The Times*).

2586. **New Economy**. *Dryden Press.* q. £95. 'The overriding aim of *New Economy* is to challenge orthodoxy, to encourage new, innovative policy thinking and to illustrate the alternatives to pure free market economics.'

(33) #1179 Institute of Economic Affairs 2 Lord North Street, London SW1P 3LB. t: (44 171) 799 3745; f: 799 2137.

Produce a wide range of publications in various series, including: *Current Controversies* e.g. 'Do we need the IMF and the World Bank?' (1994); 'The road to monetary union revisited' (1994); 'Central bank independence: What it is and What will it do for us? (1993); *Hobart Papers* e.g. 'The end of macro-economics?' (1994); *Occasional Papers* e.g. 'Finance: Villain or scapegoat? (1994); *Research Monographs* e.g. 'Overseas investments, capital gains and the balance of payments (1992).

(34) #1180 National Institute of Economic and Social Research 2

Dean Trench Street, London SW1P 3HE. t: (44 171) 222 7665; f: 222 1435.

Independent non-profit-making body, whose object is to increase knowledge of the social and economic conditions of contemporary society. The Institute's *Discussion Papers* 'range over the whole field of macro and micro economics including studies in the field of European integration, productivity and industrial policy and macroeconomic simulations.'

2587. **National Institute Economic Review**. q. £80. **online**.

(35) #1181 New Economics Foundation 1st Floor, Vine Court, 112–116 Whitechapel Road, London, E1 1JE. t: (44 171) 377 5696; f: 377 5720. *Newsletter*.

'Works through research and campaigning, to develop economic tools for a more just and sustainable economy that meets human and environmental needs. We work with a range of other organisations, supported by our membership of 2000 concerned and active individuals.'

(36) #1182 Overseas Development Institute Regent's College, Inner Circle, Regent's Park, London NW1 4NS. t: (44 171) 487 7413; f: 487 7590.

'Founded in 1960 as an independent centre for development research and a forum for discussion. The Institute is engaged in policy-related research on a wide range of issues which affect economic relations between the North and South, and which influence social and economic policies within developing countries.' *Briefing Papers* e.g. 'Aid and political reform'; 'China's economic reforms'. *Working Papers* e.g. 'The informal financial sector: How does it operate and who are the customers?' (1992, £4); 'IMF lending: The empirical evidence' (1993, £4).

2588. **ODI Index to Development Literature**. bi-m. £20. 'Covers the selected contents of over 300 journals, working papers and research reports.'

(37) #1183 Policy Studies Institute 100 Park Village East, London NW1 3SR. t: (44 171) 387 2171; f: 388 0914.

'Britain's leading independent research organisation undertaking studies of economic, industrial and social policy; and the workings of political institutions. PSI is a registered charity, run on a non-profit basis, and is not associated with any political party, pressure group or commercial interest.'

2589. **Policy Studies**. *Carfax Publishing*. q. £68.

2590. **PSI Research Results**. *Carfax Publishing*. q. £45.

(38) #1184 Royal Institute of International Affairs 10 St James's Square, London SW1Y 4LE. t: (44 171) 957 5700; f: 957 5710.

Established in 1920 to promote the study and understanding of all aspects of international affairs.

2591. **International Affairs**. *Cambridge University Press.* q. £51. 'Britain's leading analytical journal of contemporary world affairs.'

2592. **World Today**. m. £30. 'For those who prefer knowledge over opinion . . . Written by the experts: read by the experts.'

4. Organizations: United States

Academic associations

(1) #1185 Academy of Legal Studies in Business c/o Executive Secretary, Department of Finance, 120 Upham Hall, Miami University, Oxford OH 45056. *Newsletter.*

Founded in 1923 to promote and encourage excellence in teaching, research and scholarship in undergraduate and graduate business law programmes and courses in schools of business. Eligible for anyone to join; but usually members are faculty in Schools of Business. Currently about 1000 members.

2593. **American Business Law Journal**. q. $24.

(2) #1186 Academy of Political Science 475 Riverside Drive, Suite 1274, New York, NY 10115–1274. t: (1 212) 870 2500; f: 870 2202.

'Among the many institutions, boards, committees and think tanks devoted to exploration and exposition of public policy, the *Academy of Political Science* stands distinctively in a niche of its own. The Academy's cachet derives partly from its maturity as an institution – it has been fulfilling its mandate since 1880. More important than longevity is the depth and breadth of intellectual competence the Academy's members bring to their chosen fields. Finally there is the assurance that *Political Science Quarterly* (published since 1886) and other publications of the Academy are not shaped by ideological or partisan considerations.'

2594. **Political Science Quarterly**. q. $146. 'The most widely read and accessible scholary journal covering government politics and policy, both international and domestic . . . PSQ is read by members of Congress and the executive branch, by state and local officials, by newspaper, magazine and TV editors and columnists, lawyers, and business leaders, as well as by political scientists, historians and economists.'

(3) #1187 American Academy of Political and Social Science 3937 Chestnut Street, Philadelphia, PA 19104. t: (1 215) 386 4594; f: 386 4630.

2595. **Annals of the American Academy of Political and Social Science**. 8/year. £120. 'The principal forum for problems and policy issues affecting America and the world community.'

(4) #1188 American Accounting Association 5717 Bessie Drive, Sarasota, FL 34233–2399. t: (1 813) 921 7747; f: 923 4093.

The major academic association for accountants, promoting education and research in accounting. Founded in 1916. The Association's *Annual Meeting* is held at various locations, attracting some 2,000 participants. The *American Taxation Association* is a Section of the Association. Publications series include: *Accounting Research Series* e.g. 'Market microstructure and capital market information content research' (1992, $15); *Accounting Education Series* e.g. 'A framework for the development of accounting education research' (1988, $12.00), which has an accompanying separate computerized database to assist in locating references in both the accounting literature and related fields ($40.00). A variety of miscellaneous publications are issued by the Association or its Sections from time to time.

2596. **Accounting Education News**. bi-m. $30. **online**.

2597. **Accounting Horizons**. q. $60. **online**.

2598. **Accounting Review**. q. $90.

2599. **Issues in Accounting Education**. s-a. $30. **online**.

Journals published by *Sections* of the Association include:

2600. **Auditing: A Journal of Practice & Theory**. s-a. $25. **online**.

2601. **Behavioral Research in Accounting**. a. $20.

2602. **Journal of Information Systems**. s-a. $30.

2603. **Journal of the American Taxation Association**. s-a. $20. **online**.

2604. **Journal of Management Accounting Research**. a. $15.

(5) #1189 American Agricultural Economics Association c/o Secretary-Treasurer, 80 Heady Hall, Iowa State University, Ames, IA 50011–1070. t: (1 515) 294 8700; f: 294 1234.

2605. **American Journal of Agricultural Economics**. 5/yr. $90.

(6) #1190 American Economic Association 2014 Broadway, Suite 305, Nashville, TN 37203. t: (1 615) 322 2595; f: 343 7590. *Journal of Economic Literature* 4615 Fifth Avenue, Pittsburg, PA 15213–3661. t: (1 412) 268 3869; f: 268 6810.

Organized in 1885; incorporated in 1923.

'The purposes of the Association as stated in the charter are:

1. The encouragement of economic research, especially the historical and statistical study of the actual conditions of industrial life.

2. The issue of publications on economic subjects.

3. The encouragement of perfect freedom of economic discussion. The

Association as such will take no partisan attitude, nor will it commit its members to any position on practical economic questions.

'Today the membership is approximately 20,800. In addition, approximately 5,600 libraries, institutions, and firms subscribe to the quarterly publications of the Association. Over 50% of the AEA membership is associated with academic institutions, 35% with business and industry, and the remainder largely with federal, state and local government agencies.'

The *Non-member subscription* for Institutions (libraries, businesses etc) – currently of $130 – includes a subscription to:

2606. **American Economic Review**. q. plus an annual *Papers and Proceedings.*

2607. **Journal of Economic Literature**. q. Each issue includes: an annotated list of new books classified by subject, a subject index of articles in current periodicals, selected abstracts of the more significant articles arranged by subject, and tables of contents for current issues of economics journals. There is an introductory section of longer critical book reviews. The **cdrom EconLit** is compiled from the Journal of Economic Literature and the **Index of Economic Articles**. It covers articles in over 300 journals, plus monographs and theses. Almost all of the articles are in English or have English summaries.

2608. **Journal of Economic Perspectives**. q. Provides economists with accessible articles that report on and critique recent research findings, and evaluate public policy initiatives.Includes *Recommendations for Further Reading* listing readings especially useful to teachers of undergraduate economics as well as other articles that are of broader cultural interest. In general, the articles chosen are expository or integrative and not focussed on original research.

2609. **EconLit**. **cdrom**. q. $1,595. 'Consists of the *Journal of Economic Literature*, the *Index of Economic Articles*, and Cambridge University Press's *Abstracts of Working Papers in Economics*.' Also available **online**.

(7) #1191 American Finance Association c/o Stern School of Business, New York University, 44 West Fourth Street, Suite 9–190, New York, NY 10012. t: (1 212) 998 0370.

2610. **Journal of Finance**. 5/year. $72. **online**.

(8) #1192 American Law Institute 4025 Chestnut Street, Philadelphia, PA 19104. t: (1 215) 243 1600; f: 243 1664.

(9) #1193 American Political Science Association 1527 New Hampshire Avenue NW, Washington, DC 20036. t: (1 202) 483 2512; f: 483 2657.

(10) #1194 American Real Estate and Urban Economics Association c/o School of Business, Indiana University, Room 428, Bloomington, IN 47401.

2611. **AREUE Journal**. *Learned Hands*. q. $70.

(11) #1195 American Real Estate Society c/o Real Estate Research Center, Department of Finance, UC 592A, James J Nance College of Business, Cleveland State University, Cleveland, OH 44115. t: (1 216) 687 4716; f: 687 9354.

Incorporated in 1985. 'Society of and for high-level practicing professionals and real estate professors at colleges and universities throughout the United States and the world.' *Newsletter* (bi-a.) jointly with the *International Association of Corporate Real Estate Executives*. An *International Real Estate Society* and a *European Real Estate Society* are in process of being formed at the time of writing. 'All publications are available through membership only.'

2612. **Capital Markets Report**. q.

2613. **Journal of Real Estate Literature**. s-a. Divided into eight sections: Review articles; Computer applications and software; Case studies; Book reviews; Data sets; Doctoral dissertations; Working papers; Indexing/abstracts of current journals.

2614. **Journal of Real Estate Portfolio Management**. s-a.

2615. **Journal of Real Estate Research**. q.

2616. **Real Estate Research Issues**. a.

(12) #1196 American Risk and Insurance Association c/o School of Business, California State University, 6000 J Street, Sacramento, CA 95819–6088.

2617. **Journal of Risk and Insurance**. q. $75.00. **online**. Presents scholarly articles on theory and practice relevant to insurance and related areas.

(13) #1197 American Statistical Association 1429 Duke Street, Alexandria, VA 22314–3402. t: (1 703) 684 1221; f: 684 2037.

'Since 1839 ASA has been providing members with up-to-date, useful information about statistics – from new methodologies and applications to professional development and opportunities. Today, ASA membership extends beyond statisticians and academicians to include thousands of economists, business executives, research directors, government officials, scientists, and other professionals who understand the practical value of statistical methods.' The Association publishes the annual *Current Index to Statistics: Applications, Methods and Theory*. Its Sections include *Business & Economic Statistics* and *Government Statistics*. Papers presented at the Association's *Annual Meeting*, given by members of each Section, are published.

2618. **Amstat News**. 11/year. $40. Newsletter.

2619. **Journal of Business and Economic Statistics**. q. $72. Articles dealing with applied problems in business and economic statistics.

2620. **Journal of the American Statistical Association**. q. $210. Articles on theoretical and applied aspects of statistics.

(14) #1198 Association for Business and Economic Research Box 6025, Morgantown, WV 26506–6025. t: (1 304) 293 7534.

2621. **University Research in Business and Economics: A Bibliography of (Year) Publications**. a. $25. Listing of publications of business and economic research organizations at colleges and universities, with emphasis on the US.

(15) #1199 Association for Comparative Economic Studies c/o Department of Economics, Queens College of CUNY, Flushing, NY 11367. t: (1 718) 997 5461; f: 997 5535.

2622. **Journal of Comparative Economics**. *Academic Press*. bi-m. $226. Research areas include: empirical analyses displaying appropriate sensitivity to the problems of comparing data generated by different economic systems; institutional descriptions accompanied by analyses of the interaction of institutions with the system.

(16) #1200 Association of American Law Schools 1201 Connecticut Avenue NW, Suite 800, Washington, DC 20036. t: (1 202) 296 8851; f: 296 8869.

(17) #1201 Eastern Finance Association c/o School of Business, Georgia Southern University, L-B 8151, Stesboro, GA 30458.

2623. **Financial Review**. q. $50. In association with *Midwest Finance Association* (c/o Department of Accounting and Finance, Rochester Institute of Technology, PO Box 9887, Rochester, NY 14623–0887).

(18) #1202 Financial Management Association c/o College of Business Administration, University of South Florida, Tampa, FL 33620–5500. t: (813) 974 2084; f: 974 3318.

2624. **Financial Management**. q. $109

(19) #1203 Foundation for Accounting Education Pam-Am Building, 200 Park Avenue, New York, NY 10166. t: (1 212) 973 8300. *Newsletter*.

(20) #1204 Foundation for Credit Education Box 239, 692 Brandywine Road, Nazareth, PA 18064. t: (1 610) 759 5367; f: 759 0406.

(21) #1205 Foundation for Economic Education 30 South Broadway, Irvington-on-Hudson, New York, NY 10533. t: (1 914) 591 7230; f: 591 8910.

'Ever since 1946 . . . has been promoting an understanding and acceptance of the free market, private property, limited government way of life and the moral and intellectual principles which form the basis of the free society. FEE's spirit is uplifting, reassuring, and contagious: it has inspired the creation of numerous similar organizations at home and abroad. The task of defending individual freedom is a continual duty. The monthly issues of *The Freeman*, our FEE seminars, and the books in this catalogue help serve that end.'

(22) #1206 Foundation for Research in International Banking and Finance c/o Graduate School of Management, University of California at Riverside, Riverside, CA 92521. t: (1 714) 832 0710.

Organizes annual symposia.

2625. **Recent Developments in International Banking and Finance**. a. Price varies.

(23) #1207 Governmental Research Association c/o Samford University, 315 Samford Road, Birmingham, AL 35229–7017. t: (1 205) 870 2482; f: 870 2654.

'Founded in 1914 . . . The national organization of individuals professionally engaged in governmental research.'

2626. **GRA Reporter**. q. $40. Includes a bibliography of publications by governmental research agencies.'

2627. **Professional Directory of Who's Who in Governmental Research**. i. $40.

(24) #1208 Institute of Financial Education 111 East Wacker Drive, Chicago, IL 60601–4389. t: (1 312) 946 8800.

'Has been a leader in providing high quality education, training and information services to the financial services community for over 70 years . . . (It) offers information in a variety of different formats. Classes are offered through independent study, in-house or chapter programs where available. All of our textbooks, manuals and training materials can be purchased independently as well.'

(25) #1209 Institute of Mathematical Statistics Business Office, 3401 Investment Boulevard, Suite 7, Hayward, CA 94545–3819. t: (1 510) 783 8141; f: 783 4131. e: IMS@stat.berkeley.edu.

2628. **Annals of Applied Probability**. q. $90.

2629. **Annals of Statistics**. bi-m. $150.

2630. **Annals of Probability**. q. $130.

2631. **Current Index to Statistics**. a. $75. **diskette**. 'Provides subject and author indexes to articles on statistical theory, methodology, and applications and to articles in the field of probability. Includes complete coverage of articles appearing in over ninety journals . . . and coverage of statistics and probability articles selected from many other journals.'

2632. **Journal of Computational and Graphical Statistics**. q. $95. Jointly with the *American Statistical Association* and the *Interface Foundation of North America.*

2633. **Statistical Science**. bi-m. $95.

(26) #1210 International Economics and Finance Society c/o Department of Economics, University of Oklahoma, Norman, OK 73019. t: (1 405) 325 5501.

(27) #1211 National Association of Business Economists 1233 20th Street NW, Suite 505, Washington, DC 20036. t: (1 202) 463 6223; f: 463 6239. *Newsletter*.

'The Objectives . . . are to:

- Provide a forum for the discussion of common interests and concerns of the members
- Keep members on the cutting edge of economic analysis and thought through an active seminar and publication program
- Promote actively the value of economics to business leaders, policy makers and the general population
- Maintain a role as macroeconomic forecasters while developing and promoting skills in microeconomics
- Support educational programs in our nation's schools to demonstrate the value of economics as a discipline
- Develop and offer programs of professional training to enhance the skills of our members
- Strengthen members ties' internationally with business economic professionals and associations in recognition of the global interdependence of the world economy
- Advance programs to enhance the measurement of economic activity acknowledging that accurate measurement is fundamental to sound economic analysis.'

2634. **Business Economics**. q. $40. **online**. 'Professional journal . . . featuring outstanding articles on applied economics, including: macro and micro economics; monetary and fiscal policy; short and long term business forecasting; interest rates; international economics; industry studies; deregulation; statistics; changing technology and book reviews.'

(28) #1212 Society of Government Economists c/o Bicentennial Building, Room 4103, Bureau of Labor Statistics, 600 E Street, NW, Washington, DC 20212. t: (1 202) 272 2610. *Bulletin* (aimed at economists employed by governments or interested in economic policy issues).

(29) #1213 Southern Economic Association c/o University of North Carolina at Chapel Hill Southern Economic Association, 300 Hanes Hall, CB 3340, Chapel Hill, NC 27514. t: (1 919) 966 5261.

2635. **Southern Economic Journal**. s-m. $57. Theoretical and empirical research in economics addressed primarily to teachers, researchers, and other professionals in business, economics, and related fields.

(30) #1214 Union for Radical Political Economics University of California, Riverside, Department of Economics, Riverside, CA 92521. t: (1 909) 787 3538; f: 787 5685.

(31) #1215 Western Economic Association International 7400 Center Avenue, Ste. 109, Huntington Beach, CA 92647. t: (1 714) 898 3222.

2636. **Contemporary Policy Issues**. q. $100.

2637. **Economic Inquiry**. 4/yr. $135.

Academic institutions

(32) #1216 Case Western Reserve University School of Law, 11075, East Boulevard, Cleveland, OH 44106–7148. t: (1 703) 549 9222; f: 836 3195.

2638. **Case Western Reserve Journal of International Law**. 3/year. $20. **online**.

2639. **Case Western Reserve Law Review**. q. $25. **online**.

(33) #1217 Cleveland State University University Center, Cleveland, OH 44115. t: (1 216) 687 4732; f: 687 9354.

- *Center for the Study of Real Estate Brokerage and Markets*

(34) #1218 Columbia University: Graduate School of Business Uris Hall, New York, NY 10027. t: (1 212) 280 4420; f: 280 8706.

2640. **Columbia Journal of World Business**. *JAI Press*. q. $125.

- *Center for International Business Cycle Research* 'Concerned with innovations in economic measurement methodology as applied to business cycles, inflation and financial markets in the United States and other industrial nations. Our research goals are to improve the timeliness, scope, and forecasting capabilities of economic indicators and to expand understanding of the fundamental economic relationships within and between the world's industrial markets.

CIBCR produces the weekly leading index which appears regularly in *Business Week* magazine. In addition, we produce the Long- Leading Index and Short-Leading Index of US economic activity, the Leading Index of Employment, the Leading Index of Inflation, the Daily Inflation Index, and Leading Indexes of the Services and Financial Service Industries. We compile and analyze leading indexes for eleven countries which are published by the Conference Board in its *International Economic Scoreboard*. We also designed the Daily Industrial Materials Price Index that is published by the *Journal of Commerce*.'

2641. **Business Cycle Database. diskette**. m. $2500/$1800. 'Provides access to over 500 economic series covering aa industrial economies (96 international series are unavailable from any other source).'

2642. **Early Economic Outlook**. d. $4500. 'Fax service that communicates our latest forecast developments directly to you. EEO's analysis comes from over seventy of CIBCR's proprietory indexes.'

2643. **LITMUS**. m. $12,000. '*Leading Indicator Timing Model for Use in Securities* . . . Provides the subscriber with a timely system of proprietory Long Leading indexes that anticipate major cyclical moves in the stock markets of the US, Japan, Germany, the UK, France and Australia . . . CIBCR publishes *LITMUS* every month with intermittent Buy and Sell signals flashed by FAX along with a complete analysis. All of the market analysis in *LITMUS* remains reserved for subscribers exclusively.'

- *Center for the Study of Futures Markets*

2644. **Journal of Futures Markets**. *John Wiley*. q. $638. Topics include financial futures, commodity forecasting techniques, corporate hedging strategies, tax and accounting implications of hedging, analysis of commodity trading systems. Includes *Futures Bibliography* in each issue.

- *Parker School of Foreign and Comparative Law*

2645. **Columbia Journal of Transnational Law**. 3/year. $30. **online**. Covers issues in public and private international law, comparative law and foreign law, for legal practitioners and scholars of the law.

(35) #1219 Cornell University Law School, Myron Taylor Hall, Ithaca, NY 14853. t: (1 607) 255 3387.

2646. **Cornell International Law Journal**. 3/year. $25. **online**.

2647. **Cornell Law Review**. bi-m. $35. **online**.

Department of Agricultural Economics t: (1 607) 255 4534; f: 255 9984.

2648. **Agricultural Finance Review**. a. Provides a forum for research and discussion of issues in agricultural finance.

(36) #1220 Fordham University School of Law, Lincoln Center, 140 West 62nd Street, Room 118, New York, NY 10023. t: (1 212) 636 6876; f: 636 6899.

2649. **Fordham International Law Journal**. q. $30. **online**.

2650. **Fordham Law Review**. bi-m. $35. **online**.

(37) #1221 Georgetown University Law Center, 600 New Jersey Avenue NW, Washington, DC 20001. t: (1 202) 662 9468.

2651. **Georgetown Law Journal**. bi-m. $35. **online**.

(38) #1222 Harvard University 1350 Massachusetts Avenue, Cambridge, MA 02138. t: (1 617) 495 1000; f: 496 5321.

- *Department of Economics*

2652. **Quarterly Journal of Economics**. *MIT Press*. q. $95. 'The oldest professional journal of economics in the English language.'

2653. **Review of Economics and Statistics**. *Elsevier Science*. q. $165.

- *Harvard Business School* Harvard Business School Publishing 60 Harvard Way, Boston, MA 02163–1098, USA. t: (1 617) 495 6700; f: 496 8066.

2654. **Harvard Business Review**. bi-m. $75. Publishes research and case studies on issues in corporate strategies, management, finance, regulatory policy, technology, international trends, and related subjects.

- *Harvard Law School*

2655. **Harvard International Law Journal**. s-a. $24. **online**.

2656. **Harvard Journal of Law and Public Policy**. 3/year. $32.50. **online**.

2657. **Harvard Law Review**. 8/year. $40. **online**.

- *Kennedy School of Government*

(39) #1223 Indiana University Graduate School of Business, Bloomington, IN 47405. t: (1 812) 855 6342.

2658. **Business Horizons**. *JAI Press*. bi-m. $110.

(40) #1224 New York University 70 Washington Square South, New York, NY 10012. t: (1 212) 998 1212; f: 995 4040.

- *Ross Institute*

2659. **Journal of Accounting, Auditing & Finance**. *Greenwood Press*. q. $95.

- *Salomon Brothers Center* Publications include: *Monograph Series*; *Newsletter*; *Occasional Papers*; *Working Papers*.

2660. **Financial Markets, Institutions and Instruments**. *Blackwells*. 5/year. $125.

2661. **Journal of International Financial Management and Accounting**. *Blackwells*. 3/year. £75.

- *School of Continuing Education in Law and Taxation*
- *School of Law*

2662. **Tax Law Review**. *Warren Gorham Lamont*. q. $107.75.

(41) #1225 Northwestern University: Kellogg Graduate School of Management 2001 Sheridan Road, Evanston, Illinois 60208.

- *Banking Research Center*

2663. **Journal of Financial Intermediation**. *Academic Press*. q. $150. Responds to the explosion of interest among academics in the design of financial contracts and institutions, spurred primarily by the development of information economics and option pricing.

(42) #1226 Ohio State University 1945 North High Street, Columbus, Ohio 43210–1172.

- *Department of Economics*

2664. **Journal of Money, Credit and Banking**. *Ohio State University Press.* q. $70. **online**. Reports major findings in the study of financial institutions, financial markets, monetary and fiscal policy, credit markets, money and banking.

(43) #1227 Princeton University Department of Economics, Fisher Hall, Princeton, NJ 08544–1021. t: (1 609) 258 4048.

- *International Finance Section*

2665. **Essays in International Finance**. i. $35.

(44) #1228 Stanford University Stanford Law School, Crown Quadrangle, Stamford, CA 94305–8610. t: (1 415) 723 3210.

2666. **Stanford Journal of International Law**. s-a. $22. **online**.

2667. **Stanford Law Review**. bi-m. $35. **online**. Articles and notes with conclusions on the interdisciplinary study of law.

(45) #1229 University of Chicago 5801 South Ellis Avenue, Chicago, IL 60637.

- *Graduate School of Business: Center for Research in Security Prices* t: (1 312) 702 7467; f: 753 4797.

Offer the extensive *CRSP Data Files* containing over 25 million data items covering US stock and bond prices.

- *Institute of Professional Accounting*

2668. **Journal of Accounting Research**. bi-a. $73.

- *Law School* t: (1 312) 702 9832; f: 702 0730.

2669. **Journal of Law and Economics**. *University of Chicago Press.* s-a. $41. Focuses on the influence of regulation and legal institutions on the operation of economic systems, especially the behavior of markets and the impact of governmental institutions on markets.

2670. **University of Chicago Law Review**. q. $30.

- *Research Center in Economic Development and Cultural Change*

(46) #1230 University of Florida Accounting Research Center, Gainesville, Florida 32611. t: (1 904) 392 0155.

2671 **Journal of Accounting Literature**. a. $20. **online**.

(47) #1231 University of Illinois at Urbana-Champaign Commerce West, 1206 South Sixth Street, Champaign, Illinois 61820.

- *Bureau of Economic and Business Research*
- *Center for International Education and Research in Accounting*

2672. **International Journal of Accounting: Education and Research**. *Springer Verlag*. q. 98.80.

(48) #1232 University of New Hampshire Durham, NH 03824. t: (1 603) 862 3369; f: 862 4468.

- *Center for Venture Research*

(49) #1233 University of New Orleans Lake Front, College of Business Administration, Business and Economic Research Division, New Orleans, LA 70148. t: (1 504) 286 6240; f: 286 6094.

2673. **Review of Financial Economics**. s-a. $25.

(50) #1234 University of Pennsylvania 3718 Locust Walk, University of Pennsylvania, Philadelphia, PA 19104–6297, USA.

- *Economics Department*

2674. **International Economic Review**. q. $150. Published in association with *Osaka University Institute of Social and Economic Research Association*.

- *Wharton School of Finance and Commerce*
- *Economics Research Unit*
- *Pensions Research Council*
- *S S Huebner Foundation for Insurance*

2675. **Huebner Foundation Monographs**. Presents scholarly research studies in risk and insurance.

(51) #1235 University of Virginia Darden Graduate School of Business Administration Charlottesville, VA 22906–6550.

- *Center for International Banking Studies* f: 1 804 924 4859.
- *Darden Educational Materials Services* t: (1 804) 924 3009; f: 924 4859.

2676. **Darden Case Bibliography (Year)**. a. 'The 1994–95 edition . . . contains entries for more than 1,000 cases, case series, and technical notes.' About 250 of these are contained in the 'Finance' subject section.[169]

(52) #1236 University of Washington DJ-10, Seattle, WA 98195. t: (1 206) 543 4598; f: 543 6872.

- *School of Business Administration*

2677. **Journal of Financial and Quantitative Analysis**. q. $85.

(53) #1237 Virginia Polytechnic Institute College of Business,

Department of Finance, Backsburg, VA 24061–0221. t: (1 703) 231 7699; f: 231 4706.

2678. **Journal of Financial Research**. q. $80. Published in association with the *Southwestern Finance Association*.

(54) #1238 Yale University School of Law, 401A Yale Station, New Haven, CT 06520. t: (1 203) 432 4861; f: 432 2592.

2679. **Yale Journal on Regulation**. s-a. $25. **online**. Forum for research and debate on regulatory policy and its impact on the public and private sectors.

2680. **Yale Law Journal**. 8/year. $36. **online**.

Research centres

(55) #1239 American Enterprise Institute for Public Policy Research 1150 17th Street NW, Washington, DC 20036. *AEI Press* t: (1 202) 862 5800; f: 862 7178 (and in the UK c/o *Eurospan*).

'One of America's leading "think tanks" . . . Home to several of the nation's most distinguished scholars . . . AEI's motto is "Competition of ideas is fundamental to a free society".'

(56) #1240 Brookings Institution 1775 Massachusetts Avenue NW, Washington, DC 20036. t: (1 202) 797 6000. *Marketing Department* t: (800) 275 1447/(1 202) 797 6258; f: 797 6004. e: bibooks@brook.edu.

Private, non-partisan organization founded in 1916, and devoted to research, education, and publication in economics, government, foreign policy and the social sciences generally. *Occasional Papers*.

2681. **Brookings Papers on Economic Activity**. 3/year. $70. "Timely, readable, high-powered analyses of current policies and economic trends while they are still fresh enough to be acted upon" (*Business Week*).

2682. **Brookings Review**. q. $17.95. **online**. '*The* quarterly magazine on the economic, political, and foreign policy issues of the day. Each issue provides provocative articles by seasoned professionals who know the ins-and-outs of Washington and the international scene.'

(57) #1241 Cato Institute 1000 Massachusetts Avenue NW, Washington, DC 20001–5403. t: (1 202) 842 0200; f: 842 3490.

(58) #1242 Center for Governmental Research 37 S Washington Street, Rochester, NY 14608. t: (1 716) 325 6360; f: 325 2612.

(59) #1243 Center for Policy Alternatives 1875 Connecticut Avenue NW, Suite 710, Washington, DC 20009. t: (1 202) 387 6030; f: 986 2539. *Newsletter*.

'Connects innovative people and ideas to build a new economy that is inclusive, sustainable and just. CPA's constituency of elected officials and activists promotes pragmatic public policy change that supports families, strengthens communities, conserves resources for future generations and enhances democratic participation by every citizen.'

2683. **ETI Update**. q. $65. 'Report on Economically Targeted Investment activity nationwide.'

(60) #1244 Center for Public Dialogue 10615 Brunswick Avenue, Kensington, MD 20895. t: (1 301) 933 3535.

(61) #1245 Center for the Defense of Free Enterprise Liberty Park, 12500 NE 10th Place, Bellevue, WA 98005. t: (1 206) 455 5038; f: 451 3959

(62) #1246 Committee for Economic Development 477 Madison Avenue, New York, NY 10022. t: (1 212) 688 2063; f: 758 9068 *and* 2000 L Street NW, Suite 700, Washington, DC 20036. t: (1 202) 296 5860; f: 223 0776. *Annual Report.*

'Devoted to policy research and the implementation of its recommendations by the public and private sectors. CED is unique among business-oriented organizations. Its 250 Trustees – mostly heads of major corporations and university presidents – personally select the issues to be studied. They formulate and vote on policy recommendations and speak out forcefully for their adoption by business and government.'

(63) #1247 Council for European Studies Box 44, Schermerhorn Hall, Columbia University, New York, NY 10027. t: (1 212) 854 4172; f: 749 0397.

(64) #1248 Economic Policy Institute 1730 Rhode Island Avenue NW, Suite 200, Washington, DC 20036. t: (1 202) 775 8810; f: 775 0819.

'To broaden the debate over economic policy to better serve the needs of America's working people through research and public education . . . Established 1986 . . . 35 Washington staff, including 10 PhD level economists; national network of over 200 university-based researchers; budget of $3 million . . . EPI's publications address important economic issues, analyze pressing problems facing the US economy, and propose new policies.' *Working Papers.*

(65) #1249 Employee Benefit Research Institute 2121 K Street NW, Suite 600, Washington, DC 20037. t: (1 202) 659 0670; f: 775 6312.

2684. **Quarterly Pension Investment Report**. q. Data on assets in the private and public pension system and the performance of pension investments.

(66) #1250 Entrepreneurial Leadership Center Bellevue College, 1000 Galvin Road S, Belleue, NE 68005. t: (1 402) 291 8100; f: 293 3819.

(67) #1251 Foreign Policy Association 729 Seventh Avenue, New York, NY 10019. t: (1 212) 764 4050; f: 302 6123.

(68) #1252 Foundation for Public Affairs 1019 19th Street NW, 2nd Floor, Washington, DC 20036. t: (1 202) 872 1750; f: 835 8343. *Newsletter.*

There is a sister organization, the *Public Affairs Council* at the same address (t: (1 202) 872 1790), which produces a range of books, audiotapes and videotapes to 'help with creating, implementing and improving public affairs programs'.

(69) #1253 Foundation for the Private Sector 3372 Cortese Drive, Los Alamitos, CA 90720. t/f: (1 213) 596 8898.

(70) #1254 Heritage Foundation 214 Massachusetts Avenue NE, Washington, DC 20002. t: (1 202) 546 4400; f: 546 8328.

(71) #1255 Hudson Institute Herman Kahn Center, 5395 Emerson Way, PO Box 26–919, Indianapolis, IN 46226. t: (1 317) 545 1000; f: 545 9639.

(72) #1256 Independent Institute 134 98th Avenue, Oakland, CA 95603. t: (1 510) 632 1366; f: 568 6040.

(73) #1257 Institute for Contemporary Studies 720 Market Street, 4th Floor, San Francisco, CA 94102. t: (1 415) 981 5353; f: 986 4878.

'Nonprofit, nonpartisan research institute founded in 1972. Through its imprint, *ICS Press*, the Institute has published some of the most influential, innovative, and readable books on public issues . . . ICS sponsors a variety of publications on a wide range of governance issues, including the key areas of entrepreneurship, the environment, education, governance and leadership, social policy, and international economic development.'

- *International Center for Economic Growth* 'An affiliate of the Institute for Contemporary Studies . . . Founded in 1985 to promote economic growth and human development in developing and post-socialist countries. The mission of ICEG is to strengthen local economic policy institutes as leaders in debates on institutional and policy reform in countries worldwide. To this end, ICEG works with a network of more than 310 correspondent institutes in more than 112 countries.' The Center produces a detailed *Publications Catalog. Newsletter.*
- *International Center for Self-Governance* 'Dedicated to promoting self-governing and entrepreneurial ways of life.'

(74) #1258 Institute for International Economics 11 Dupont Circle NW, Washington, DC 20036–1207. t: (1 202) 328 9000; f: 328 5432.

Private non-partisan nonprofit research institution for the study and discussion of international economics policy. The Institute's extensive list of books are distributed outside of the USA and Canada by *Longman Group*: e.g. 'The United States as a debtor country' (1994); 'The future of the world trading system' (1994); 'Equilibrium exchange rates' (1994); 'International monetary policymaking in the United States, Germany and Japan' (1993); 'The effects of foreign exchange intervention' (1993).

2685. **International Economic Insights**. bi-m. $60. Short articles, reviews of developments, book reviews etc. aiming to advance the economic policy debate by providing timely and provocative new thinking from all parts of the world.

(75) #1259 Institute for Monetary Freedom 958 Janet Lane, Lafayette, CA 94549. t: (1 510) 284 7565.

(76) #1260 Institute for Policy Studies 1601 Connecticut Avenue NW, Washington, DC 20009. t: (1 202) 234 9382; f: 387 7915. *Newsletter*.

'The end of the Cold War, along with the election of a Democratic Administration and Congress, has opened up dramatic new opportunities for change. New ways of thinking, new institutions, new political alliances, and new national policies are being born. Many of the ideas that IPS has been pushing for a generation – deep defense cuts, support for UN peacekeeping, economic conversion, progressive tax reform, responsible trade, national health care, guaranteed employment – are now being seriously debated on Capitol Hill. There is a greater receptivity in Washington to IPS ideas than ever before' (*30th Anniversary Brochure*, 1993).

(77) #1261 Institute for Socioeconomic Studies Airport Road and New King Street, White Plains, NY 10604. t: (1 914) 428 7400; f: 946 5663.

(78) #1262 Institute of World Affairs 375 Twin Lakes Road, Salisbury, CT 06068. t: (1 203) 824 5135; f: 824 7884.

(79) #1263 National Academy of Social Insurance 1776 Massachusetts Avenue NW, Suite 615, Washington, DC 20036–1904. t: (1 202) 452 8097; f: 452 8111.

(80) #1264 National Bureau of Economic Research 1050 Massachusetts Avenue, Cambridge, MA 02138–5398. *Publications Department* t: (1 617) 868 3900; f: 868 2742.

Private, non-profit research organization founded in 1920 and devoted to objective quantitative analysis of the American economy. *Working Papers* Major priced series producing about 300 titles annually ($1,300). The *NBER Digest* (m. $free) 'summarises four or five new NBER studies in a non-technical style'; the *NBER Reporter* ($20) 'provides abstracts of current NBER Working Papers as well as reviews of broad areas of NBER research. The Reporter also includes summaries of recent NBER conferences . . . A complete list of NBER Working Papers and Reprints can be accessed on the Internet by using our gopher at nber.harvard.edu.'

2686. **Macroeconomics Annual (Year)**. *MIT Press.* a. $35.

2687. **Tax Policy and the Economy**. *MIT Press.* a. $28.95.

(81) #1265 National Committee on Public Employee Pension Systems 1221 Connecticut Avenue NW, Washington, DC 20036. t: (1 202) 293 3960; f: 293 7614.

(82) #1266 Princeton Research Institute Western Management Center, Box 2702, Scottsdale, AZ 85252–2072. t: (1 609) 0305.

2688. **Corporate Growth**. m. $198. Covers all aspects of mergers, acquisitions, divestitures, corporate growth and development worldwide.

(83) #1267 Reason Foundation 3415 S Sepulveda Boulevard, Suite 400, Los Angeles, CA 90034. t: (1 310) 391 2245; f: 391 4395.

'National public-policy research organization with a practical, market-based approach and an outside-Washington perspective.'

2689. **Reason**. 11/year. $32.45. 'Explore the ideas and issues of individual liberty.'

- *Privatization Center*

2690. **Privatization (Year)**. a. $35. 'Covers contracting, infrastructure, and asset-sales in domestic and international privatization.'

2691. **Privatization Watch**. m. $135.

(84) #1268 Society for the Advancement of Economic Theory c/o Department of Economics, University of Illinois, 330 Commerce West Building, 1206 S 6th Street, Champaign, IL 61820–6271. t: (1 217) 333 0120; f: 244 6678.

2692. **Economic Theory**. bi-m. $69.

(85) #1269 Urban Institute 2100 M Street, NW, Washington, DC 20037. t: (1 202) 857 8702.

2693. **Policy Bites**. bi-m. free. Comments on economic and social issues.

(86) #1270 US Public Interest Research Group 215 Pennsylvania Avenue SE, Washington, DC 20003. t: (1 202) 546 9707; f: 546 2461.

5. Commercial information providers

(1) #1271 AB Academic Publishers PO Box 42, Bicester, Oxon OX6 7NW, UK. t/f: (01 869) 320949.

2694. **Journal of Interdisciplinary Economics**. 4/yr. £89.

(2) #1272 Academic Press 525 B Street, Suite 1900, San Diego, CA 92101–4495, USA. (800) 894 3434/(1 619) 699 6742; f: 699 6715 *and* 24–28 Oval Road, London, NW1 7DX, UK. t: (44 171) 267 4466; f: 482 2293.

2695. **Cambridge Journal of Economics**. 6/year. £155. Managed by the *Cambridge Political Economy Society*. Aims to provide a forum for neo-classical approaches to economics, following the tradition of Marx, Kalecki and Keynes. Strong emphasis on the provision and use of empirical evidence and on the formulation of economic policies. Includes commentaries on current affairs.

2696. **Contributions to Political Economy**. a. £155. Published for the *Cambridge Political Economy Society*. Includes reviews of important books published during the year.

2697. **Critical Perspectives on Accounting**. bi-m. £150. Aims to provide a forum for the growing number of accounting researchers and practitioners who realize that conventional theory and practice is ill-suited to the challenges of the modern environment, and that accounting practices and corporate behaviour are inextricably connected with many allocative, distributive, social and ecological problems of our era. Research areas include: financial accounting's role in the processes of international capital formation, including its impact on stock market stability and international banking activities; accounting's adjudicative function in international exchanges, such as that of the Third World debt.

2698. **Journal of Economic Theory**. bi-m. $710. 'One of the nine core journals in economics and ranks fourth among this core in the most recent survey of impact-adjusted citations. Among all journals in economics, the journal is seventh in impact-adjusted citations per character.' Includes regular sections of notes, comments, and letters to the editor.

2699. **Journal of Housing Economics**. q. $127. Research areas include: public policy; finance; international studies; law and regulation.

2700. **Journal of Urban Economics**. bi-m. $326. 'The leading journal for articles that illustrate empirical, theoretical, positive, and normative approaches to urban economics.'

(3) #1273 Blackwells 108 Cowley Road, Oxford OX4 1JF, UK. t: (44 865) 791100; f: 791347. *Also*: 238 Main Street, Cambridge, MA 02142, USA. t: (617) 547 7110; f: (617) 547 0789. (Includes the imprints: *Basil Blackwell*, *Blackwell Business*, *Blackwell Finance*, *Blackwell Publishers*).

2701. **Bulletin of Economic Research**. q. £84. **online**. 'Each volume includes a specially commissioned book review, taking the form of a consumer's guide to graduate/undergraduate texts in a specialist area.'

2702. **Corporate Governance: An International Review**. q. £95. "Corporate governance is fast becoming one of the key business issues of our times . . . this journal is splendidly timely and crucially important . . . it will open up the whole topic for informed debate" (*Charles Handy*).

2703. **Economica**. q. £37.

2704. **European Financial Management**. 3/year. £115.

2705. **Financial Accountability & Management**. q. £56. Aims to advance academic understanding, professional practice and policy debate in respect of the efficient, effective and indeed equitable conduct of financial accountability and management in governments, public services and charities.

2706. **Journal of Business Finance and Accounting**. 8/year. £159.

2707. **Journal of Common Market Studies**. 5/year. £109. **online**. Includes an *Annual Review* published in September.

2708. **Journal of Economic Surveys**. q. £69. 'Enables the busy economist to keep track of developments in all areas of economics.'

2709. **Journal of International Financial Management and Accounting**. 3/year. $120.

2710. **Journal of Time Series Analysis**. bi-m. £193.

2711. **Manchester School of Economic and Social Studies**. 5/year. £67.

2712. **Mathematical Finance**. q. $165. Established to investigate the interface between mathematics and finance. Financial theory, financial engineering, and related mathematical and statistical techniques are examples of suitable topics. The mathematics, which need not be at an advanced level, must be interesting and carefully presented in a rigorous manner.

2713. **Metroeconomica**. 3/year. £59.

2714. **Oxford Bulletin of Economics & Statistics**. q. £68. **online**.

2715. **Review of Economic Studies**. q. £68.

2716. **Review of International Economics**. 3/year. £84.

2717. **World Economy**. bi-m. £155. Includes summary of news and events.

(4) #1274 Butterworth-Heinemann Linacre House, Jordan Hill, Oxford OX2 8DP, UK. t: (44 1865) 310366; f: 310898. *Also* 313 Washington Street, Newton, MA 02158, USA. t: (1 617) 928 2500; f: 928 2620.

2718. **Economic Modelling**. q. £230. 'Fills a major gap in the economics literature, providing a single source of both theoretical and applied papers on economic modelling.'

2719. **Futures**. 10/year. £265. 'Generally recognised as the world's leading journal covering forecasting, planning and futures studies.'

2720. **International Review of Law and Economics**. q. $225. Research on the interface between economics and law including legal institutions, jurisprudence, legal history and political-legal theory.

2721. **Journal of International Money and Finance**. bi-m. £225.

(5) #1275 Cambridge University Press Publishing Division, The Edinburgh Building, Shaftesbury Road, Cambridge CB2 2RU, UK. t: (44 1223) 312393; f: 315052.

2722. **Journal of Public Policy**. 3/year. £62. 'Relates the world of social science ideas to the problems that face governments in advanced industrial society. The concerns of public policy are political, economic and social.'

(6) #1276 Carfax Publishing Company PO Box 25, Abingdon, Oxfordshire OX14 3UE, UK. t: (44 1235) 521154; f: 553559. *Also* PO Box 2025, Dunnellon, FL 33430–2025, USA. f: (1 904) 489 6996.

2723. **Communist Economies and Economic Transformation**. q. £158.

2724. **Development in Practice**. q. £115.

2725. **Economic Systems Research**. q. £212.

2726. **International Journal of the Economics of Business**. 3/year. £86.

2727. **International Yearbook of Law, Computers & Technology**. a. £104.

2728. **Journal of Applied Statistics**. bi-m. £232.

(7) #1277 Causeway Press PO Box 13, Ormskirk, Lancashire L39 5HP, UK. t: (01695) 576048; f: 570714.

2729. **Developments in Economics**. a. £37.50. 'An annual review ... Designed for both teachers and students in secondary and higher education ... Designed to be photocopied. Copyright is waived in respect of photocopying within the purchaser's institution.'

2730. **Developments in Politics**. a. £37.50.

(8) #1278 Chapman & Hall 2–6 Boundary Row, London SE1 8HN, UK. t: (44 171 865 0066; f: 522 9623. *Also* 115 5th Avenue, New York, NY 10003, USA. t: (1 212) 244 6412; f: 268 9964.

2731. **Accounting Education**. q. £125.

2732. **Applied Economics**. m. £575. **online**. Contains articles encouraging economic analysis to problems in the private and public sector.

2733. **Applied Economics Letters**. m. £130. Publishes short accounts of new and original research within two months of receipt.

2734. **Applied Financial Economics**. bi-m. £172. Provides an international forum to link the research community with financial institutes and markets.

2735. **Applied Mathematical Finance**. q. £130. Volume 2, 1995.

2736. **European Journal of Finance**. q. £130. Volume 1, 1995.

(9) #1279 Columbia Law Review Association 435 West 116th Street, New York, NY 10027, USA. t: (1 212) 854 4398.

2737. **Columbia Law Review**. m. $40. **online**.

(10) #1280 Elsevier Science PO Box 211, 1000 AE Amsterdam, The Netherlands. t: (31 20) 580 3911; f: 580 3598.

2738. **Accounting, Management and Information Technologies**. q. £195.

2739. **Accounting, Organisations and Society**. 8 issues/annum. £515.

2740. **Agricultural Economics**. 8/yr. DFl730. Provides a focal point for the publication of work on research, extension and out-reach, consulting, advising, entrepreneurship, administration and teaching, in the areas of agricultural economics.

2741. **Carnegie-Rochester Conference Series on Public Policy**. bi-a. DFl290. Reviews selected policy problems and issues confronting policy makers.

2742. **Economics Letters**. m. $755.

2743. **European Journal of Political Economy**. q. DFl600.

2744. **Journal of Accounting and Economics**. bi-m. $466.

2745. **Journal of Accounting and Public Policy**. q. $205. Publishes articles exploring the interaction of accounting with a wide range of disciplines including economics, public administration, political science, social psychology, policy science, and the law.

2746. **Journal of Accounting Education**. q. $200. Prepared with the *James Madison University: School of Accounting*.

2747. **Journal of Banking and Finance**. bi-m. $541.

2748. **Journal of Business Venturing**. 6/yr. $238. Details research on entrepreneurship, either as independent start-ups or within existing corporations.

2749. **Journal of Corporate Finance**. q. $168.

2750. **Journal of Development Economics**. bi-m. $559. Publishes papers relating to all aspects of economic development – from immediate policy concerns to structural problems of underdevelopment. The emphasis is on quantitative or analytical work, which is relevant as well as intellectually stimulating. *Book reviews*.

2751. **Journal of Econometrics**. bi-w. $1,003.

2752. **Journal of Economic Behavior and Organization**. m. $628.

2753. **Journal of Economic Dynamics and Control**. bi-m. $464.

2754. **Journal of Empirical Finance**. q. DFl306.

2755. **Journal of Financial Economics**. bi-m. $381.

2756. **Journal of International Economics**. m. $429.

2757. **Journal of Monetary Economics**. bi-m. $590.

2758. **Journal of Public Economics**. m. $745.

(11) #1281 Haworth Press 10 Alice Street, Binghamton, NY 13904–1580, USA. t: (800) 342 9678; f: (1 607) 722 6362. *Also* c/o Eurospan Group, 3 Henrietta Street, Covent Garden, London WC2E 8LU, UK. t: (44 171) 240 0856; f: 379 0609. (Includes the imprint *International Business Press*)

2759. **Journal of Business & Finance Librarianship**. q. $40. 'Devoted entirely to providing useful articles to information professionals who are involved with, or have an interest in, the creation, organization, dissemination, retrieval, and use of business information. The journal covers the business information needs of special libraries, academic libraries, and public libraries – as well as information services and centers outside of the traditional library setting.' Recent articles include: 'A selected guide to foreign trade statistical sources'; 'Free bank letters as sources of economic and financial information'; 'Corporate annual reports and the information needs of individual investors'; 'Government electronic bulletin boards'.

2760. **Journal of International Financial Markets, Institutions & Money**. q. $75.

2761. **Journal of Multinational Financial Management**. q. $75.

(12) #1282 International Library Law Book Publishers 101 Lakeforest Boulevard, Suite 270, Gaithersburg, MD 20877, USA. t: (1 301) 990 7755; f: 990 7642.

2762. **Banking Law Anthology**. a. $149.95. Selected best US law review articles, printed in their entirety, in the field of banking, selected from over 900 American law review journals.

(13) #1283 JAI Press 55 Old Post Road – No 2, PO Box 1678, Greenwich, CT 06836–1678, USA. t: (1 203) 661 7602; f: 661 0792 *and* The Courtyard, 28 High Street, Hampton Hill, Middlesex, TW12 1PD, UK. t: (44 181) 943 9296; f: 943 9317.

2763. **Accounting Education**. s-a. $95. New for 1996.

2764. **Advances in Accounting**. a. $73.25.

2765. **Advances in Accounting Information Systems**. a. $73.25.

2766. **Advances in Econometrics**. i. $73.25.

2767. **Advances in Futures and Options Research**. i. $73.25.

2768. **Advances in Investment Analysis and Portfolio Management**. i. $73.25.

2769. **Advances in Management Accounting**. a. $73.25.

2770. **Advances in Public Interest Accounting**. a. $73.25.

2771. **Advances in Quantitative Analysis of Finance and Accounting**. i. $157.50.

2772. **Advances in Taxation**. a. $73.25.

2773. **Financial Services Review**. s-a. $150.

2774. **Global Finance Journal**. s-a. $135.

2775. **International Review of Economics and Finance**. q. $135.

2776. **International Review of Financial Analysis**. 3/year. $125.

2777. **Journal of International Accounting Auditing & Taxation**. s-a. $140.

2778. **Journal of Small Business Finance**. 3/year. $125. Focuses on the financial, economic, and accounting aspects of small firms.

2779. **North American Journal of Economics and Finance**. s-a. $135. Published for the *North American Economics and Finance Association*.

2780. **Quarterly Review of Economics and Finance**. bi-m. $175. The Journal of the *Midwest Economic Association* published in cooperation with the *Bureau of Economic and Business Research, University of Illinois.*

2781. **Research in Accounting Regulation**. a. $73.25.

2782. **Research on Economic Inequality**. i. $73.25.

2783. **Research in Finance**. a. $73.25.

2784. **Research in Financial Services**. i. $73.25.

2785. **Research in Governmental and Nonprofit Accounting**. a. $73.25.

2786. **Research in International Business and Finance**. i. $73.25.

2787. **Research in Law and Economics**. a. $73.25.

2788. **Research in Real Estate**. a. $73.25.

(14) #1284 Journal of Applied Business Research B 620760, Littleton, CO 80162, USA. t: (1 303) 972 6604. f: 978 0413.

2789. **Journal of Applied Business Research**. q. $186. Publishes articles in the areas of accounting, economics, finance, information management, management and marketing.

(15) #1285 Kluwer Academic Publishers Group Marketing Department, Spuiboulevard 50, PO B 989, 3300 AZ Dordrecht,

The Netherlands. t: (31 78) 33 42 94; f: 33 42 54. *Also* Order Department, PO B 358, Accord Station, Hingham, MA 02018–0358, USA. t: (1 617) 871 6600; f: 871 6528.

2790. **Economics of Planning**. 3/year. $132.50. 'An international journal devoted to the study of comparative economics.'

2791. **European Journal of Law and Economics**. q. $179.50. Publishes analytical studies of the impact of legal interventions into economic processes by legislators, courts and regulatory agencies, with an emphasis on the EC and EC law.

2792. **Financial and Monetary Policy Studies**. DFl460.50.

2793. **International Tax and Public Finance**. 3/year. $265. Peer-reviewed journal, but including in each issue a section *International Tax Watch*.

2794. **Journal of Financial Services Research**. q. $192.50.

2795. **Journal of Real Estate Finance and Economics**. bi-m. $272.00.

2796. **Journal of Regulatory Economics**. q. $182.50. Publishes articles on the analysis of regulatory theories and institutions and on the practical aspects of regulation, including natural monopoly, deregulation, and new policy instruments.

2797. **Journal of Risk and Uncertainty**. bi-m. $282.00.

2798. **Open Economies Review**. q. $185.00. 'The topics covered... include, but are not limited to, models and applications of (1) trade flows, (2) commercial policy, (3) adjustment mechanism to external imbalances, (4) exchange rate movements, (5) alternative monetary regimes, (6) real and financial integration, (7) monetary union, (8) economic development, and (9) external debt.'

2799. **Policy Sciences**. q. $173.50. 'An international journal devoted to the improvement of policy making.'

2800. **Public Choice**. 16/year. DFl1,120. 'Deals with the intersection between economics and political science . . . Remains central in its chosen role of introducing the two groups to each other, and allowing them to explain themselves through the medium of its pages.'

2801. **Review of Accounting Studies**. q. DFl416.

2802. **Review of Derivatives Research**. q. DFl416. 'The rapid growth of derivatives research combined with the current absence of a *rigorous* research journal catering to the area of derivatives, and the long lead-times in the existing academic journals, underlines the need for *Review of Derivatives Research*... The *Review* has a double-blind refereeing process. In contrast to the delays in the decision making and publication processes of many current journals, the *Review* will provide authors with an initial decision within nine weeks of receipt of the manuscript and a goal of publication within six months after acceptance. Finally, a section of the journal is available for rapid publication of 'hot' issues in the market, small technical pieces, and timely essays related to pending legislation and policy.'

2803. **Review of Quantitative Finance and Accounting**. q. $198.00.

(16) #1286 Marcel Dekker 270 Madison Avenue, New York, NY 10016, USA. t: (800) 228 1160/(1 212) 696 9000; f: 685 4540.

2804. **Econometric Reviews**. q. $395.

2805. **International Journal of Public Administration**. m. $925.

(17) #1287 ME Sharpe 80 Business Park Drive, Armonk, NY 10504, USA. t: (1 914) 273 1800; f: 273 2106.

2806. **Challenge**. bi-m. $76. 'Who reads Challenge?

- Thousands of leading decision makers in the highest reaches of media, government, business, finance, think tanks, and academic institutions
- *Business Week*, *The New York Times*, *The Wall Street Journal*, *Barron's*, *Fortune*, and other prestigious publications, who draw on Challenge in their feature, lead, and editorial columns
- Academics, students specializing in economics, and other interested in clear analysis and groundbreaking insight into the realities underlying worldwide economic performance.'

2807. **Journal of Post Keynesian Economics**. q. $100.

(18) #1288 MIT Press 55 Hayward Street, Cambridge, MA 02142–1399, USA. t: (800) 356 0343/(1 617) 625 8569; f: 625 6660; e: mitpress-order-inq@mit-edu. *Also* Fitzroy House, 11 Chenies Street, London WC1E 7ET, UK. t: (44 171) 306 0603.

2808. **International Organization**. **online**. q. $85. Published for *The 10 Foundation*. 'Its actual scope is much broader than its title may suggest. The journal presents seminal articles not only on international institutions and cooperation but also on economic policy issues, security policies, and other aspects of international relations and foreign policy. Topics covered recently include:

- trade policies and GATT
- banking, debt and monetary affairs
- European integration
- economic development and adjustment
- international capital movements.'

2809. **Journal of Economics and Management Strategy**. q. $88.

(19) #1289 Oxford University Press Walton Street, Oxford OX2 6DP, UK. t: (44 1865) 267907; f: 267773.

2810. **Journal of Law, Economics, and Organization**. s-a. $43. Interdisciplinary journal integrating legal-economic scholarship with other social science disciplines. Promotes an understanding of complex social phenomena by examining such matters from a legal, economic, and organizational perspective.

2811. **Oxford Economic Papers**. q. $138.

2812. **Oxford Journal of Legal Studies**. q. 66. Examines the theory and issues arising from the relationship of law to other disciplines, with an emphasis on legal philosophy and socio-legal matters.

2813. **Oxford Review of Economic Policy**. q. $176.

2814. **Review of Financial Studies**. q. $160. Published with the *Society for Financial Studies.*

2815. **Statute Law Review**. 3/year. £64. Provides a forum for the consideration of the legislative process, the use of legislation as an instrument of public policy, and the drafting and interpretation of legislation.

2816. **Structural Change and Economic Dynamics**. s-a. $108.

(20) #1290 Routledge 11 New Fetter Lane, London EC4P 4EE, UK. t: (44 171) 583 9855; f: 815 0418. *Also* 29 West 35th Street, New York, NY 10001, USA. t: (1 212) 244 3336; f: 563 2269.

2817. **Accounting, Business and Financial History**. 3/yr. £46. Analyzes past developments in business and finance history; explains structure and practices; and aims to create a platform for solving current problems and predicting future developments.

2818. **Journal of Economic Methodology**. bi-a. £55.

2819. **Review of International Political Economy**. 3/year. £65.

(21) #1291 Sage Publications 2455 Teller Road, Thousand Oaks, CA 91320, USA. t: (1 805) 499 0721; f: 499 0871 *and* 6 Bonhill Street, London EC2A 4PU, UK. t: (44 171) 374 0645; f: 374 8741.

2820. **American Politics Quarterly**. q. £109. 'Promotes research into US political behaviour – including urban, state and national policies, as well as pressing social problems requiring political solutions.'

2821. **Comparative Political Studies**. q. £113.

2822. **Economic and Industrial Democracy**. q. £130. 'Covers aspects of industrial democracy, from the practical problems of democratic management to wide-ranging social, political and economic analysis.'

2823. **Economic Development Quarterly**. q. £115. 'Reports the latest research programmes, policies and trends in the USA.'

2824. **International Review of Administrative Sciences**. q. £125. 'The Journal of the *International Institute of Administrative Sciences* . . . Publishes comparative studies and national monographs on international administration, national civil services, controls on central government, administrative reform, public finance and the history of administration.'

2825. **Public Finance Quarterly**. q. £137. 'Studies the theory, policy and institutions related to the public sector of the economy.'

(22) #1292 Stern Stewart Management Services 40 West 57th Street, New York, NY 10019, USA. t: (1 212) 261 0600.

'A corporate finance advisory firm specialising in corporate valuation and restructuring.'

2826. **Bank of America Journal of Applied Corporate Finance**. q. $95.

(23) #1293 University of Chicago Press Journals Division, 5720 South Woodlawn Avenue, Chicago, IL 60637, USA. t: (1 312) 753 3347; f: 753 0811.

2827. **Journal of Business**. q. $52. **online**.

2828. **Journal of Political Economy**. bi-m. $109.

(24) #1294 John Wiley 605 Third Avenue, New York, NY 10158–0012, USA. t: (1 212) 850 6000; f: 850 6088 *and* Baffins Lane, Chichester, West Sussex, PO19 1UD, UK. t: (44 243) 779777; f: 775878.

2829. **International Journal of Finance & Economics**. q. 'A new forum for academics, professionals and policy makers with interests in new ideas, techniques and skills within international finance . . . Whilst maintaining the high standards of a fully refereed academic journal with technical, empirical and theoretical material, IJFE articles will also be accessible to non-specialists, policy-makers and practitioners. Each paper will be prefaced by a non-technical summary of up to 500 words . . . Will concern itself with such issues as exchange rates, balance of payments, financial institutions, risk analysis, international banking and portfolio management, financial market regulation, Third World Debt, European monetary union, the financial aspects of transition economies, financial instruments and international financial policy coordination. IJFE is aimed at researchers and graduate students in:

- International Economics
- International Finance
- Financial Economics
- International Political Economy
- Financial Analysts in Investment Banks and Other Financial Institutions
- Policy Markers and Corporate Treasurers.'

2830. **International Journal of Intelligent Systems in Accounting, Finance & Management**. q. $175. Publishes original material concerned with all aspects of intelligent systems in business-based applications with an aim of providing a forum for advancing theory and application of intelligent systems in business theory.

2831. **Journal of Applied Econometrics**. q. $345.

Notes

(168) A first-rate appreciation of the scholarly publication system of finance can be gained from: BREALEY, R. and EDWARDS, H. eds. **A bibliography of finance**. *MIT Press*, 1991. 822 pp. $90.

'This bibliography is about finance. That may sound straightforward but the boundaries of the subject are ill-defined and we were continuously obliged to make arbitrary rulings lest we encroach on such adjoining kingdoms as accounting, law and monetary economics. As a result we have provided less comprehensive coverage of topics such as these that lie on the borders of our subject. While we could never make up our minds where the subject stopped, at least we felt confident that articles which are written by financial economists and published in finance journals are probably about finance and these therefore form the core of this book.

Since usefulness seems more important than neatness, we have also included a small number of works that are not directly about finance but that are frequently referenced by finance authors. For example, we have included Keynes's General Theory (together with the chapter numbers of Keynes's criticisms of the stock market). We have also included a number of papers about information asymmetry and signalling equilibria as well as some of the more frequently referenced works on statistics and econometrics.

Our second main criterion for inclusion was that the work should be concerned with issues of lasting importance and this in turn means that it should be analytical rather than just descriptive. We sought to avoid obtruding our own opinions about a publications quality. Thus in the case of the major finance journals, such as the Journal of Finance and Journal of Financial Economics, we have included essentially all articles. But particularly where we were concerned with the professional journals we could not avoid making many, somewhat arbitrary, judgements as to the possible interest in the article. In such cases a recent publication date was more likely to ensure inclusion.

We have not limited our selection to the publications of any one country nor was our interest restricted to the capital markets of any one country. However, with minor exceptions all works are in the English language or, if this was not the original language of publication, they are available in translated form.

Our final criterion was that the work should be published. This means that we have excluded inter alia working papers and doctoral papers. Again there are a handful of occasions where we broke our own rules and included an unpublished but seminal paper such as Treynor's unpublished paper on the capital asset pricing model.

Some brief statistics may be of interest. The bibliography contains 12,037 entries. Approximately 120 periodicals are represented.' (From the *Introduction*.)

(169) The organization in Europe which handles most case studies (including those of IMD, Insead and London Business School) is the *European Case Clearing House*, Cranfield University, Cranfield, Bedford MK43 0AL.

CHAPTER EIGHT

The Electronic Imperative

1. I believe that we are at last currently witnessing a process – (especially) within the subject field we are concerned with here – which will quite soon lead to the demise of those shared collections of publicly available physical information artefacts which we call *libraries*: at the least, it will for all those who practice within the finance (and banking) disciplines. This is all part of a historical trend which has long been anticipated; as, for instance, in this piece written ten years ago:

> Immense resources world-wide are being invested in improving the way that society communicates, and this will mean radical changes for libraries, irrespective of whether individual librarians think the changes are for good or for bad. Libraries are trapped between publishers and readers. If those two groups find that some new mode of document or information delivery is more beneficial to them than present modes, then the new mode will prevail. Certainly within business, market forces will determine the outcome (and why not?).
>
> But no one knows the exact nature and timing of the changes to come. Let us hazard a few guesses. We will continue to read most complete documents as print-on-paper at least until the turn of the century. But as it becomes economic for publishers – and that is the overriding consideration – there will be a move towards supplying copies of documents on demand, via telecommunication networks, rather than by post from a warehouse store. When the time comes, libraries will have to acquire, or have access to, appropriate equipment (eg facsimile equipment) in order to receive the transmitted documents.
>
> Because it will be so easy and quick to obtain copies of documents from publishers, libraries will then purchase proportionately fewer documents in anticipation of demand, and more when demand materialises. Such a change on its own would not necessarily threaten the

continued viability of libraries. But the change will occur against a continuing reduction in their budget support (both in the private and public sectors). Thus many (small) libraries will survive only if they are able to develop services other than the delivery of copies of documents from stock, and are able to charge for these services. It may be that some (large) libraries will maintain their own store of machine-held documents (eg on digital optical discs) as an alternative to accessing publishers' stores; but I am doubtful that this will become significant.

On the future of libraries as suppliers of information, I would be surprised if all business-related documents used solely to retrieve numeric or primarily numeric information were not fully electronic within ten years, with other documents used solely to retrieve information (ie bibliographic tools) following suit within 20 years. Prediction of exact time-scale is, however, very difficult. In the mid-1970s we were told that viewdata systems such as PRESTEL would very shortly make newspapers disappear; they show no sign of doing so for a while yet. On the other hand, there were predictions in the 1940s and 1950s that fewer than 20 computers would eventually satisfy the world's need and that there was no large market for photocopiers! A general rule seems to be that it takes much longer than one would expect at first sight for people to change to a radically new way of doing things; but once the change starts in earnest, it spreads very quickly.

The provision of an online service by a host requires a very large investment, which has meant that hardly any of the hosts listed above have made any profits to date. We should also see quite shortly a decrease in the total number of hosts, with those that remain offering services of greater added value when compared with traditional publication methods. Add to this that very soon virtually all business library users will have purchased for other purposes the equipment needed for online and, suddenly, we will find that users are no longer visiting our libraries to retrieve information: they are getting it online.

Even if the quantum leap from paper-based to electronic information delivery – when it comes – means that many business library collections disappear, there will still be a need for information intermediaries. But distinct from now, those intermediaries will have to be prepared to offer advice, rather than neutral information. Physical collections of documents can be difficult, time-consuming and confusing for the non-librarian to use (though we would hope that librarians continually strive to make them less so). Thus there are roles at present for people whose function is 'merely' to indicate where in published literature the answer to a particular query might be found, rather than to give the inquirer the exact answer required. But once any piece of publicly available information can be retrieved by anyone at the touch of a button, the role of the librarian as a transparent information intermediary will disappear.[170]

2. Of course, we have by no means yet reached the state where 'any piece of publicly available information can be retrieved by anyone at the touch of a button'. But – for those who have the financial wherewithal – I would suggest that we will reach that situation by the end of the current decade. This is not to write that the participants in the financial system and their parent organizations will cease to use print-on-paper as a convenient means of *private* perusal, transport and storage of the publicly available information (and data) that they need to use.[171] Nor that the transport of 'published information' will be necessarily a wholly electronic process. Substantial documents, especially those whose subject matter benefits from a sophisticated physical appearance, will still naturally be produced and bound as print-on-paper artefacts. Printed newspapers, newsletters and magazines will be purchased by individuals and groups and browsed through as now as a means of keeping broadly up-to-date about what is going on. But on the relatively rare occasions when *specific* (historical) data, information, or documents are needed and are not already available in one's personal or workgroup 'library', they will be identified and requested online: then to be speedily delivered to the 'office' by courier, when online delivery of a digital version is not possible or acceptable.

3. There are three related imperatives driving this process along. First, all participants in the financial industry have on their desks increasingly sophisticated multi-tasking personal computer workstations connected to high bandwidth local- and wide-area telecommunication networks. This infrastructure – once there – can easily and at a low marginal cost be used to transmit publicly available as well as privately needed data, information and documents between networked entities.

4. Second, there can be an economic incentive for information providers to supply their information[172] electronically; since generally the intellectual property laws do not allow customers to copy without prior permission 'for research or private study' the information held within electronic artefacts, as they do under many circumstances with print-on-paper artefacts. (But this is an area of great current debate.) Further, where publishers (or agents such as online search or document delivery services acting on the publishers' behalfs) choose to withhold on a central database system the information they are making public, those publishers and agents are then able automatically to monitor and price each user retrieval of that information.

5. Print-on-paper (and microform) static artefacts can be picked up and moved, shelved in and loaned from cooperative stores such as libraries. Crucially, once the artefacts have been acquired and, as appropriate, paid for (ie once there is some notion of *ownership*), the information that the artefacts contain can be perused as needed over and over again without any further payment to the copyright owner. And the information is still there for the next person to use similarly – and so on and so on until it is obsolete in that situation. Economically, the information is *non-depletable.*

6. We might try to place the currently important dynamic medium *CD-ROM* (and other portable dynamic products) within the context of those comments. Many people have argued that there is no difference in principle between taking a print copy for personal use from a CD-ROM (or other portable) version of a publication (held, for example in a local library), as against from its equivalent in print. However, the publishers advising those framing our intellectual property laws are generally taking a different view. This may well partly be because portable optical/magnetic based compilations have a fundamentally different potential as media for transferring information from publisher to user. Left as stand-alone artefacts, and used simply to print out the information they contain, they are little different from static information products. Hardware and software is needed to enable user perusal of their information, before its output. The data retrieval and manipulation capabilities that the software provides can enable a more cost-effective acquisition by the user of the information he or she needs, than would be the case with a static medium. But that information, as with print and microform products, is fixed: until the product is manually replaced or updated.

7. However, one can frequently arrange for access to many portable optical/magnetic based compilations to be via local (and wide) area networks. Also, the information that they contain can be processed inhouse to produce other (value-added?) products (which the compilations' publishers then fear their customers may well be tempted to sell on). Thus, as information products, portable electronic databases straddle the boundary between dynamic and static information artefacts. In recognition of this, we might note the development of hybrid CD-ROM/online products. For instance, in some offerings, users can search the information that has been delivered on the latest issue of the portable product, locally and offline. Then, if appropriate, they are able automatically to log on to a remote more up-to-date version of the same database, and search just that database portion which has been generated by the producer since the local CD itself was mastered. In an alternative arrangement, source producers will automatically update locally held files of data – say, overnight: with the result that the information that the user is searching inhouse is never more than a day out of synchronization with the information held centrally.

8. Nevertheless, despite these and other refinements, this writer's view is that the popularity, particularly, of CD-ROM products among librarians is primarily and often solely not due to their effectiveness as artefacts for transferring published information from producer to user. (CD-ROMs are inherently relatively slow file servers – especially when networked over more than a small number of users.) It is simply because of their negligible marginal cost of use. In cases where it is possible for centrally held datasets to offer the similar unlimited use for a flat fee that is common with CD-ROM products, these will normally be preferred because they will usually be more up-to-date: especially, of course, if they are *real-time* online systems. The online systems will also often have more sophisticated search and retrieval software facilities than the CD-ROM products (though admittedly until recently, this often in many cases was not the case). The reader will note that I am assuming in this discussion that the telecommunication costs of connecting to a central database system will be a relatively small proportion of the *total* cost (i.e. including intermediary and customer time) of using that system. The upshot of all these comments is that in this book CD-ROMs (and other portable optical/magnetic products) have been conceptualized primarily as alternatives to print-on-paper (and microform) static information products; rather than as alternatives to (central) online database systems.

9. Many publishers distribute versions of their publications on CD-ROM; but two leading third party distributors, with examples of their products relevant to the finance area listed, are:

(1) #1295 Chadwyck-Healey The Quorum, Barnwell Road, Cambridge CB5 8SW, UK. t: (44 1223) 215512; f: 215514. e: mail@chadwyck.co.uk. *Also* 1101 King Street, Alexandria, VA 22314, USA. t: (800) 752 0515/(1 703) 683 4890; f: 683 7589.

- *British National Bibliography*
- *Economist*
- *EUROCAT*
- *Financial Times*
- *FT McCarthy*
- *Guardian*
- *House of Commons Hansard*
- *House of Lords Hansard*
- *Independent*
- *IntEc: The Index to International Economics, Development and Finance*
- *ISSN Compact*
- *Leadership Directories*
- *McCarthy*

- *Official Journal of the European Union*
- *SCAD*
- *Telegraph*
- *Times/Sunday Times*
- *UKOP*
- *UNBIS Plus*

(2) #1296 SilverPlatter Information 100 River Ridge Drive, Norwood, MA 02062–5026, USA. t: (1 617) 769 2599; f: 769 8763. *Also* 10 Barley Mow Passage, Chiswick, London W4 4PH, UK. t: (0800) 262 096/(44 181) 995 8242; f: 995 5159. e: info@silverplatter.com. w: http://www.silverplatter.com.

- *ABI/INFORM*
- *Book Review Digest*
- *Burrelle's Media Directory*
- *Business Periodicals Index*
- *Choice*
- *Corporate & Industrial News from Reuters*
- *Criminal Justice Abstracts*
- *Cumulative Book Index*
- *Dissertation Abstracts*
- *EconLit*
- *EIU Country Forecasts*
- *EIU Country Reports*
- *EIU International Business Newsletters*
- *Encyclopedia of Associations*
- *F&S Index plus Text*
- *Findex*
- *Gale Directory of Databases*
- *GPO*
- *Index to Foreign Legal Periodicals*
- *Index to Legal Periodicals*
- *Investext*
- *Newspaper Abstracts*
- *NTIS*
- *PAIS International*
- *SEC Online*
- *SEC-10K*
- *Social Sciences Index*
- *System for Information on Grey Literature*
- *UK Corporations*
- *Wilson Business Abstracts*
- *World Agricultural Economics and Rural Sociology Abstracts*

10. The third imperative driving along the wholesale transition to a paperless publication system for current practically useful finance information is the competition between the players in the financial information industry.

The financial information industry

11. The factors important in this competition can be introduced by the following excerpts from the 1993 Corporate Annual Reports of seven large players in this field (five US-headquartered, two UK) – all published in the Spring of 1994 (except for Bloomberg, a private company, where the information is taken from a broadsheet issued by the company at that time, and from a market research report published shortly before):

(I) *BLOOMBERG L.P.*

"No other vendor offered information and analytics in a seamless fashion the way Bloomberg did. While Telerate's exclusive agreement with inter-dealer broker Cantor Fitzgerald Securities Corp. gave it data that rivalled Bloomberg's bond prices from primary dealer Merrill Lynch, its system had been set up to provide pages of prices, not graphics, and its analytical products were weak. Knight-Ridder's MoneyCenter provided some analytics, but its database and charting software were not as strong as Bloomberg's. Even mighty Reuters could not rival Bloomberg's breadth and flexibility. It faced many technical obstacles in building a historical database for Decision 2000, Reuter's so-called 'Bloomberg killer' ".[173]

Bloomberg Financial Markets is a global, multimedia distributor of information services, combining news, data and analysis for global financial markets and businesses. Bloomberg provides real-time pricing, data, history, analytics and electronic communications 24 hours a day, 365 days a year through 37,000 proprietary terminals used by over 135,000 financial professionals in 62 countries worldwide.

The company has established a unique position within the financial services industry by providing a broad range of functions combined into a single "package" that represents substantial value, while at the same time addressing the demand for investment performance and efficiency in increasingly complex global markets and exchanges. Through an unparalleled combination of information and analytics, Bloomberg Financial Markets has quickly built a worldwide customer base of issuers, financial intermediaries and institutional investors.

Bloomberg's core business is *THE BLOOMBERG*, the fastest growing real-time financial information network, which links together the world's leading financial professionals. THE BLOOMBERG provides pricing capabilities with inside dealer quotes from the largest market makers, and it is the definitive source of indicative data for all securities, statistics, indices and research. THE BLOOMBERG covers all key global securities markets, including Equities, Money Markets, Currencies, Municipals, Corporate/Euro/Sovereign Bonds, Commodities, Mortgage-Backed Securities, Derivative Products and Governments. BLOOMBERG users also have the ability to consider alternatives and evaluate complex scenarios through THE BLOOMBERG's unique analytical capabilities.

At no additional cost, THE BLOOMBERG offers *BLOOMBERG Business News*. BLOOMBERG Business News has 250 reporters and editors in 45 bureaus worldwide that provide around-the-clock coverage of the world's governments, corporations, industries and all financial markets. BLOOMBERG Business News stories are fully integrated into THE BLOOMBERG'S Newsminder Monitors so that users are instantly alerted to developments in all stock and bond markets.

Bloomberg offers several additional products and services that draw upon the resources of Bloomberg Financial Markets:

- *BLOOMBERG Magazine* An award-winning magazine that complements THE BLOOMBERG with sophisticated insight in everything from securities products and current business to industry analyses and career management.
- *BLOOMBERG Forum* Through an executive interview at THE BLOOMBERG Forum, corporate officials and influential newsmakers deliver important news via a bundled array of services.
- *BLOOMBERG Business News* Appears weekday mornings on public television stations throughout the US.
- *BLOOMBERG Direct TV* Appears on a revolutionary satellite service expected to reach one million homes and selected cable systems by 1995.
- *BLOOMBERG News Radio AM 1130.*
- *BLOOMBERG Energy Newsletters.*

Headquartered in New York, Bloomberg Financial Markets has offices in 10 major cities across North America, Europe and Asia and news bureaus in 45 additional locations. The company is privately owned with Merrill Lynch holding a non-increasable 30% interest. Bllomberg Financial Markets is backed by two data support centers in the US and Great Britain, nine data collection centers and over sixteen hundred dedicated professionals worldwide'(*Company Profile: April 1994*).

(II) *DOW JONES* – TOTAL OPERATING REVENUE FOR 1993: $1.93 BILLION.

'Although 1993 was an uncertain time for the world economy and our industry, Dow Jones had a year of strong and satisfying growth. Dow Jones employees continued to demonstrate their ability to manage and grow the company's businesses in a tough and highly competitive environment – by raising revenues while controlling costs and still investing in new products and new technologies for the future.

Substantial progress was made in developing new products to serve customers better. SmartMoney, Dow Jones' new personal finance magazine published in partnership with Hearst Corp., went monthly last fall, ahead of initial schedule . . . We started a magazine in Europe called Central European Economic Review, which is inserted in The Wall Street Journal Europe on a quarterly basis. Dow Jones also began working with American City Business Journals Inc. to launch a monthly magazine called Biz, aimed at 500,000 chief executives or owners of the country's fastest-growing small businesses.

Information Services added significant new data to Dow Jones Telerate, such as Cantor Fitzgerald Securities Corp's U.S. Treasury prices for odd-lot securities and exclusive foreign exchange information from M.W.Marshall & Co. and Exco International, two major brokers in the global foreign exchange and money markets.

Business Information Services announced Personal Journal, a first-stage electronic Wall Street Journal that will be available this year bundled with Microsoft Corp.'s Microsoft At Work operating system. Business Information Services also moved to improve its full-text retrieval services and this year will be adding content of the New York Times to Dow Jones News/Retrieval.

Multimedia efforts produced the Dow Jones Investor Network, a video business-news service delivered to customers' computer terminals, which includes exclusive video interviews with business leaders and live coverage of major corporate announcements and events. We look forward to more exciting products, including the Telerate Windows workstation, The Wall Street Journal Interactive Edition and the multimedia unit's interactive video and text service, now being developed in collaboration with Nynex Corp.

As these products indicate, we again are assuming it will not be the external environment, but rather our own internal effort and enterprise, that will produce revenue and profit gains.

Finally, a few reflections on our industry. At Dow Jones we view all the recent industry passion for interactivity, multimedia, convergence and so on with a good deal of confidence. This is not some 'Brave New World' to us. Dow Jones has been providing interactive electronic information for more than two decades. Roughly half our company's revenue and profits already come from selling electronic information. And our business publications are uniquely suited to such distribution.

Moreover, Dow Jones and its products, like business information services and television programming, will only benefit from emerging, converging and multiplying distribution channels. Most importantly, however, Dow Jones believes that the greatest asset and value in the communications industry is content: exclusive content that is essential to a cohesive global community of customers; proprietary content carrying brand names that signify premier quality and command premium value. That is what Dow Jones is all about.'

(III) *DUN & BRADSTREET* – TOTAL OPERATING REVENUE FOR 1993: $4.71 BILLION.

'Our customers need answers – answers that deliver a better understanding of markets, where those markets are going and how to get there faster than the competition. In an increasingly complex world, Dun & Bradstreet is giving customers what they want – the insight necessary to succeed.

Dun & Bradstreet counts among its customers the leaders in today's global business community. These progressive companies are managing unprecedented change driven by globalization, advancing technology and shifting market demand. And they are radically redefining modern business in the process. What sets these companies apart is their use of information as the competitive weapon. By leveraging technology and transforming data into strategic decisions, these leadership corporations consistently and successfully position themselves at the forefront of market trends. We know, because these same companies are increasingly utilizing D&B information to enhance their competitive advantage.

We believe these businesses offer a glimpse into the way virtually all successful companies will be doing business in the 21st century. We see a world in which information drives business decisions at every level, from the shop foreman of a small growing business to the strategic planners of the world's largest multinationals. In tommorow's businesses, translating information into tactical and strategic decisions will be the differentiating competitive advantage.

D&B is uniquely positioned to make this view of the future a reality. Our new decision-support services provide customers with real business insights, not just data. Our global reach gives access to worldwide markets.

D&B's strategy builds on our strengths and is tightly focused on these goals:

- Invest for the future via new products, geographical expansion and acquisitions.
- Target high-growth market segments, including decision-support services.
- Be technology driven.
- Build on our core markets.
- Proactively develop products in advance of customer demand.
- Leverage competitive advantage and synergies across our businesses.'

(IV) *KNIGHT-RIDDER* – TOTAL OPERATING REVENUE FOR 1993: $2.45 BILLION.

'Exciting and positive things happened to your company in 1993. We start 1994 with solid earnings momentum in an improving economic environment . . . We made several acquisitions that we think will be very beneficial. We introduced new products. We invested in several potentially rewarding companies. And early in 1994, we announced a potentially important alliance with Bell Atlantic. All this reflects our ongoing strategy to grow our core businesses and make Knight-Ridder a profitable competitor on the information superhighway.

Business Information Services All three BIS operating groups performed well during the year. The largest of the three groups, *Dialog*, advanced its global growth strategy with two key moves – the purchase of Data-Star, Europe's leading archival information service, based in Bern, Switzerland, and laying the groundwork for the formation of a joint venture with Southam Electronic Publishing to create a strong archival information service for Canada called Infomart DIALOG. Dialog also made strategic investments in two very promising companies – Individual Inc, and Personal Library Software, Inc. Dialog launched a multiyear program to migrate its technology from mainframes to a distributed client/

server architecture. And in an important move that will reduce costs and improve customer service, Dialog decided to convert from a Dialog-maintained network to British Telecom's Global Network Services.

Knight-Ridder Financial (KRF) benefited from excellent worldwide growth of its MoneyCenter for Windows and ProfitCenter products. In December, in a move that will greatly strengthen its Asian operations, KRF acquired Equinet in Australia and the Dateline Asia-Pacific Database in Hong Kong. In Europe, KRF acquired 100% of the Spanish financial news service EFECOM, now known as KRF/Iberia. The *Journal of Commerce* had excellent results in print and electronic products.

Early in 1994, BIS purchased *Technimetrics*, a leading publisher of investor relations information.

We are building an increasingly valuable shareholder asset in BIS . . . Distribution of business information is, by its very nature, a global undertaking. Ultimately, it is our goal to realise solid double-digit operating margins in BIS. In the meantime, our growing expertise in collecting, transmitting and selling electronic information will be increasingly valuable in developing successful products for the emerging superhighway.

The past year was an unprecedented period for new ventures and alliances as we pursue our fundamental strategic objective of remaining an indispensable supplier of news, information and advertising in our markets. In addition to the numerous moves by the BIS Division, we announced in early 1994 an agreement with Bell Atlantic Video Services to develop the long-term role of news, information and advertising on the interactive, multimedia Stargazer system. This strategic alliance with one of America's major Regional Bell Operating Companies is an important step in developing new information and news services.

In Philadelphia, we announced the formation of KR Video Inc, which will begin producing local news for the Philadelphia television market in mid-1994. This venture and our work with Bell Atlantic will complement our efforts to deliver news and information over online services. In cooperation with America Online, we launched Mercury Center in San Jose. The Mercury News became the first newspaper to integrate its electronic online service with the daily newspaper. The Detroit Free Press entered a similar agreement with CompuServe in January 1994.

A period of major transition in the global information business has begun. We believe we are well positioned to emerge stronger than ever in this new era. Solid operating margins at our newspapers will provide us with substantial cash flow and investment capital. We are in good markets. We are stepping up our investments in new businesses that have good prospects of financial success in the years ahead. And BIS operations will continue to strengthen.

Knight-Ridder is changing faster than ever, adapting to the new realities of the information industry. We are delivering news and information 24 hours a day, around the globe, from doorstep to desktop. And we're getting better at it every day.'

(v) *MCGRAW-HILL* – TOTAL OPERATING REVENUE FOR 1993: $2.20 BILLION.

'Expanding globally. Enhancing capabilities. Inventing the future. Focusing on customers. These are McGraw-Hill's strategies for growth, and you'll find them at work in every part of the company. Our employees are finding opportunities to expand our businesses globally. They are providing information in innovative ways by using the latest advances in technology. Our employees are literally inventing the company's future by developing products and services that fulfil customer needs. To be where our customers are, to know their information needs, to create and then deliver the best products and services possible in the forms that they want: Those strategies have been our heritage and are the source of our new growth.

McGraw-Hill's best growth prospects are increasingly in countries outside the US, where the information needs of professionals in business, government, industry and education are growing rapidly. By penetrating local markets with products that are new or in a variety of languages, McGraw-Hill has helped its customers participate more fully in the global economy.

Standard & Poor's is a large contributor to McGraw-Hill's global growth. Having opened offices in Toronto and Mexico City in 1993, S&P Ratings now performs both domestic and cross-border debt-rating activities for clients in 10 world capital markets. These clients – taking advantage of S&P's reputation for analytical expertise and impartiality, long-term relationships with key market participants and exceptional analytical staff – have come to recognise the value of an S&P rating. McGraw-Hill's electronic products in currency, treasury, commodity and securities markets have also won many overseas customers. US brokerages have long benefitted from S&P Marketscope's real-time financial information service, for example. Recognizing a need for similar coverage of Western Europe's securities markets, S&P launched MarketScope Europe in 1993 to provide investment professionals there with comprehensive coverage of of events that affect share prices on stock exchanges throughout Europe.

Creating products in local languages is another avenue to global growth. MMS International is known for its reliable analysis of worldwide debt and currency markets. It developed its first local-language service – real-time analysis of the yen currency market in Japanese – in 1992, and added a currency market service in Chinese in 1993.

Of McGraw-Hill's three dozen magazines, many either carry International in the title or are published in a foreign language. The largest, Business Week, has worldwide English-language circulation of more than one million – some 115,000 in its Business Week International edition. Worldwide, 200 editors and reporters produce editions in English and three local languages. Nine of its 24 editorial bureaus are outside the US.

At McGraw-Hill, improving products is foremost. The company continually looks for ways to use technology so customers get information faster or in more detail; for ways to customize information to meet a specific need; and for opportunities to use information already collected. By enhancing the value of products, McGraw-Hill more successfully meets the information needs of its customers. Shepard's, for example, has compiled more than 260 million citations that trace the history of court decisions at the state and federal levels. Traditionally, citations were published exclusively in books. Today, they are in an electronic database, which is accessed to develop Shepard's print products and those created for fax, online and CD-ROM delivery – the ways customers increasingly prefer. In 1993, Shepard's added a new capability: collecting US Federal Court of Appeals and Supreme Court decisions electronically, further speeding the publishing and distribution process.

S&P services also flow directly to subscribers who, more and more, need real-time information that comes in one convenient product. By integrating several databases, S&P created S&P Research Reports, which allow customers to find out virtually everything S&P says about a particular company. Through S&P Reports On-Demand, every investor with a fax and touch-tone phone now can have easy access to the same information McGraw-Hill sells Wall Street traders and analysts, including Stock Reports, Industry Reports and Price Charts.

McGraw-Hill has always excelled in creating information products to satisfy customer needs – ideally positioning it to invent the future. Today, editorial expertise, strategic partnerships and quality information supply shape and energy to McGraw-Hill's product-development process . . . Company-wide teams of employees develop new product ideas and distribution channels. And employees from different business units regularly propose and launch new products that take advantage of the strengths of each. In 1993, the first joint effort between Professional Publishing and S&P Equity Services extended distribution of the S&P Stock and Bond Guide for the first time to shelves of America's bookstores . . . McGraw-Hill spurs product development through alliances with partners in key businesses. In 1993, McGraw-Hill became the largest stockholder in Liberty Brokerage, the country's second-largest interdealer broker for US Treasury securities; the move positions McGraw-Hill as a leading provider of fixed-income securities prices and information to the government securities brokerage business.

Some of the best new products germinate from already existing ones. The S&P 500, for example, has long been the benchmark of investment performance. In recent years, S&P developed the S&P MidCap 400 and the S&P/Barra indexes for growth and value. In 1993, S&P introduced an instrument that allows investors to own a security representing a share of the S&P 500 – called S&P Depositary Receipts, known as SPDRS or Spiders. More than 51 million Spiders were traded in 1993. McGraw-Hill licenses S&P intellectual property to financial institutions and collects a fee on each trade involving instruments based on its indexes. Developing new products and getting them quickly to market is a McGraw-Hill tradition, and an important way the company invents its future.'

(VI) *PEARSON* – TOTAL OPERATING REVENUE FOR 1993: £1.28 BILLION (EXCLUDING 0.55 BILLION DISCONTINUED OPERATIONS).

'1993 marks a turning-point in the history of Pearson. In June we took the decision to concentrate our resources on our media and entertainment businesses and by December Camco and Royal Doulton had become independent public companies. The thinking behind these moves is that as a media company we have great opportunities for deploying our brands and copyrights in expanding and overlapping media markets. These are developing rapidly and the skills of the centre in attracting, managing and motivating talented people need to be concentrated on helping to build these creative businesses.

Our operating companies' strongest capabilities are in the creation and development of brands and intellectual property, whether it's the Financial Times or Beatrix Potter, and we intend to supply our products to our customers in any way they want, be it on paper or to their computer and television screens. We are concentrating as far as possible on providing specialised products that our customers feel that they must have, or very much want to have, and although it is vital for us to understand the technology and availability of the delivery systems, we do not feel it is necessary to own them. We expect to develop new markets within our chosen information, education and entertainment fields, but we do not aim to develop new technologies. Whilst continuing to build on the written word, we are pursuing our strategy of putting more resources into screen-based businesses and during the year acquired Thames Television and Extel.

Thames is our first wholly-owned television production and distribution business and will play a central role in the development of Pearson television. Our investment in BSkyB is beginning to live up to our expectations, but until the rules applying to television ownership in this country are changed substantially, major development of our television interests here is effectively stymied. This is not all bad. For whilst we seek and expect a change in the law, we are pursuing attractive possibilities overseas and particularly in Asia, where we anyway wish to invest more over the next decade.

Extel considerably enhances the electronic services of the Financial Times. In addition to the old established Extel information cards, Extel provides a range of screen-based material and is developing its business in continental Europe and in Asia.

To sum up our strategy; we are focusing our attention on four major areas of development. First, we are continuing to select and invest in intellectual property and brand-driven markets. These include business news, professional publishing and training, consumer publishing, education, television entertainment and theme parks. Secondly, we are looking to invest further in Asia, where our publishing companies have already established bridgeheads for Pearson and where we are investing an increasing amount of executive time. Thirdly, we will be developing the links between our operating companies and, fourthly, we will move increasingly into the area of interactive multimedia, where we are positioning ourselves to take advantage of the opportunities that will develop.

The Pearson culture is a pillar of the strategy and has provided continuity and stability over many years. The culture embraces long-term perspective, fairness, honesty and quality. It has made Pearson an attractive company to sell a business to, to be a partner with and to work for. Preserving this culture is vital in our transition to a media company.'

(VII) *REUTERS* – TOTAL OPERATING REVENUE FOR 1993: £1.87 BILLION.

'Reuters prospered in 1993 because the tide in its markets flowed in its favour. The company was well-prepared to take advantage of this. It did many things to strengthen its business for the longer term, in addition to producing good current results . . . Reuters principal objectives continue to be to help all customers alike to improve their own performance through more and better information and to give better value year by year through advances in technology, product development, economies of scale and internal efficiencies.

We enter 1994 in a confident mood. Products have been re-fashioned. Pricing is keener. We expect to sell more, because the conditions in financial markets are simultaneously favourable in developed centres, and in emerging markets like China, East Europe and Latin America.

The largest population of dealing room terminals worldwide is in the equities market, where we have room to increase our share substantially. This is the reason for some of our recent acquisitions, including Quotron in the US (still at the letter of intent stage). We have enhanced our equities product line by adding price history and background details on thousands of companies in our database. We are still missing some historical information in the fixed income market which we neglected to collect and store in the past. A two-year programme to improve competitiveness in this market segment was launched in 1993. In foreign exchange, our main innovation will be an all-digital video news service on a window on the Reuter Terminal, due to be launched around mid-1994.

We retain our faith in the future of electronic trading. Instinet, fortifying itself by acquisition, has done particularly well in equities and expanded its global trading and analytical capabilities. Our new foreign exchange matching product, Dealing 2000 phase 2, is building liquidity all the time. GLOBEX, trading futures and options, has been successful in the Paris market but has so far failed to attract liquidity in Chicago. We hope to change the arrangements we have made with the Chicago exchanges.

Critical to all these ventures is our ability to keep close to our customers. We achieve this by maintaining stable prices and constantly adding new features to products without charge. We provide help desks all over the world which instantly respond to queries. We are concentrating our efforts on user-friendly design, recognising that we need to improve the ease of use of our products. We are adapting to the open world, in which we offer hardware, display software and data separately, rather than forcing these three bundled elements down the customer's throat. Many clients prefer to integrate information products on to networks and hardware they have already put in place.

We aim to use our cash to tap revenue streams in new markets. We have made a start in various new fields such as medical information. The message of multimedia is that the computer is going to change our lives more than we realised. There will be segments of every major industry that will use the power of information to improve performance. Each one may present us with a business opportunity. We shall be selective, though, because investments based solely on the lure of technology tend not to work. The investments we make are for the longer term.'

12. Those seven conglomerates are not of course the only major players active in displaying financial data, information and documents electronically to their customers. But they are all – to varying degrees – responding to seven major imperatives operating on the overall marketplace:

(i) The move to *real-time* generation and display of data, information and documents captured from financial and economic data, newswire and broadcast feeds. To deliver in real-time you have to gather in real-time.
(ii) The need for the vendors to *add value* to data/information delivered by those feeds on its way to the customer. There can be a conflict between currency and value: it takes time to add value.
(iii) The requirement for *seamless integration* with the customers' desktop/local area network technological environment – including the ability to customize and to carry all types of media.
(iv) The need to maximize the global *coverage* of current data/information/documents – but with the customer being able to decide which subsets of the whole actually to subscribe to.
(v) Seamless online retrieval of *historical data/information/documents*, as and when needed.
(vi) The attempt to obtain and retain *exclusivity* of data/information/documents or of the means of adding value to those artefacts: or both.
(vii) *Customer support* Excellent training, documentation, help desk facilities, etc. – and a general 'feel good about doing business with these guys'.

13. Personally, I find it difficult to conceive that we will not eventually end up with two or three mega industry players providing online – in real-time – virtually all of the finance professionals' financial data/information/document needs. This is what is happening in, for instance, the supporting broadcasting/computing/telecommunications industries; and, in quite different industries where 'one-stop-shops' are advantageous to the customer: eg the food retailing industry. Of course, there will always be a role for 'corner shops' to start up, flourish for a time, and then perhaps die – as the large players absorb or mimic their temporary competitive advantage (or alliances are formed). However, I suggest that it will be into the next century before we reach this situation of 2–3 players dominating the finance publishing industry (which 2–3?): and naturally the whole will be crucially dependent on the anti-trust/monopoly environment that will operate. There are indeed quite different market segments at the present time. For instance, the published 'information' needs of the market trader are quite different from those of the economic forecaster working in the City or on Wall Street and are quite different from those of the independent financial planner: and so on. But these needs are *overlapping*: and thus whoever forges the truly multi-functional workstation environment able to retrieve and add value to any type of publicly available data/information/document publicly generated anywhere in the world must surely win the ultimate prize. The customers of my library do not wish to use Reuters for this, and Datastream for that, and Knight-Ridder for the other, and so on and so on: they do it because it is not yet possible to retrieve all that they need via one service organized with a data architecture that makes the experience truly seamless and totally effective for the task in hand: and in real-time. But they will, sometime fairly soon! Do you – the reader – agree? (answers, on a postcard . . .!)

14. Meanwhile, we have a significant number of market segments continuing to function much as they always have done over the last 5–10–15–20 years. Although as we have just noted there is much overlap in types of products and services offered, it seems that the public online electronic database market currently falls into these ten groupings:

(i) Real-time data services
(ii) Historical data services
(iii) Credit rating services
(iv) Newswire services
(v) Full text news services
(vi) Scheduled online services
(vii) Consumer online services
(viii) Portable data systems
(ix) Gateway systems
(x) Document supply services

Note that we do not include a separate section here for the *broadcast* services; for example:

(1) #1297 CNN International CNN House, 10–22 Rathbone Place, London W1P 1DF, UK. t: (44 171) 637 6700; f: 637 6768 *and* One CNN Center, PO B 105366, Atlanta, Georgia 30303, USA. t: (1 404) 827 1500.

'The world's only 24-hour global news and information network.' Transcripts of several CNN programs are available online, including:

2832. **CNN News Transcripts**. **online**. d.

Although the broadcast services are important as purveyors of publicly available data and information relevant to the trading system, of even more importance is the incorporation of the radio and television feeds provided by such services into the real-time data services as provided by Bloomberg, Dow Jones Telerate, Reuters, and so on. Such developments can be pursued by the reader by perusal of these and other services engaged in *multimedia* development. There are also a number of electronic transcripts of broadcasts produced. The BBC offers its own:

(2) #1298 BBC Monitoring Caversham Park, Reading RG4 8TZ, UK. t: (44 1734) 472742; f: 463823.

2833. **BBC Summary of World Broadcasts**. d. **online** 'Unique document providing accurate, daily coverage of international political and economic affairs . . . Summaries of broadcasts and news bulletins or, in the case of important speeches and events, the complete text are published without additional comment or interpretation so you can be sure the information you receive is impartial. We also credit the source of each item so you can judge the validity of it yourself . . . The *SWB Dial-in Service* allows you unlimited access to the news on the day it happens . . . You can access the information as often as you like, each issue stays on the database for 30 days . . . **NEWSFILE** is the 24 hour newswire service of the BBC World Service . . . which we customize to the specific requirements of each customer . . . (and which) unlike other newswire services is extensive and free of editorial interpretation and bias. We reproduce the news as actually broadcast by radio, TV and government agencies from around the globe. Unlime any other news service our products are *immediate, concise, accurate and impartial*.'

2834. **World Broadcasting Information**. m.

which is available on a variety of hosts services. The transcripts of other services are also offered directly via the generic online hosts (as with CNN); or online as a specialist service, as in the well-known:

(3) #1299 Burrelle's Information Services 75 East Northfield Road, Livingston, NJ 07039–9873, USA. t: (800) 631 1160/(1 201) 992 6600; f: 992 5122.

2835. **Burrelle's Broadcast Database**. **online**. d.

or vendored on CD-ROM, as here:

2836. **Broadcast News**. *Research Publications International*. **cdrom**. q. £995. 'Over 34,000 full-text transcripts per year taken from over 60 different programmes on the following American television and radio networks: CNN, NPR, ABC News, and PBS.'

15. In the following pages, we profile examples of companies operating in each of the ten market segments we will explore in more detail, culled from brochures issued by the respective companies in the last year or so:

(i) Real-time data services

The market is dominated by Dow Jones/Telerate, Reuters – and now – Bloomberg; but with a number of other companies having a significant presence in specific areas – if not (yet . . . or still?) across the board: eg ADP, Bridge, Knight-Ridder Financial, S&P MarketScope, Telekurs, as well as a number of companies within the Thomson conglomerate. Following are, however, details of seven smaller niche players, each of whom – at the time of review – advertised particular strengths:

(1) #1300 A-T Financial Information 20 Exchange Place, 44th Floor, New York, NY 10005, USA t: (1 212) 344 2330 *and* Bastion House, 9th Floor, 140 London Wall, London EC2M 5NT, UK. t: (44 171) 600 6565; f: 600 2838.

'Creates technology to get integrated financial data and analytical tools into the hands of trading and investment professionals, faster than ever. Our software, the *A-T Financial Information System*, is targeted to a broad spectrum of financial institutions, providing the fastest real-time information in the industry, in a native MS-Windows, fault-tolerant environment. Since our technology is built to operate on PC-LANs, the A-T Financial Information System works more efficiently and inexpensively than packages tied to the expensive mainframe world.

A privately-held company with users throughout the United States and Europe, A-T Financial Information, Inc. is run by founders/managers who have decades of experience in securities trading, corporate finance and software development for the financial services industry. Our programmers have been developing applications in Windows since our founding in 1987. All of our software is written in-house so we can quickly develop new versions.

The A-T Financial Information System will satisfy all your trading and investing needs in real-time, quicker than the competition can . . . How do we achieve this? . . . Our software does not rely on expensive mainframe systems, which chew up valuable time in delivering data to you. The software processes multiple data and news feeds in IBM-compatible PC servers and 'bundles' them into an integrated stream of intelligent information on equities, bonds, foreign exchange, futures and options and other market movements, in real-time. We provide more detailed data from a variety of sources and do it faster than anyone else. We give you the fastest Dynamic Data Exchange (DDE) link in the industry, for Microsoft Excel spreadsheets or any other Windows application supporting DDE, so you can further analyze earnings, dividend and descriptive data. These critical analytics calculate the spread between selected equities and bonds, determine net asset value, evaluate portfolios and manipulate data any way you wish.'

A-T Financial Information advertise feeds from the following data providers:

- *Crossmar*
- *Dow Jones/Telerate*
- *Knight-Ridder*
- *NASDAQ Level II*
- *PC Quote*
- *Reuters*
- *S&P Comstock*
- *Telekurs*

The company also offers a service *TopStory News Retrieval* which 'provides your users with lightning-fast headlines and stories from a number of news feeds'. These include:

- *Dow Jones Broad Tape*
- *Dow Jones Canadian Wire*
- *Dow Jones Capital Markets*
- *Dow Jones Economic Wire*
- *Dow Jones European Corporation Reports*
- *Dow Jones Federal Filings*
- *Dow Jones Financial Wire*
- *Dow Jones Petroleum Markets Wire*
- *Dow Jones Press Releases*
- *Dow Jones Professional Investor Report*
- *Futures World News*
- *Knight-Ridder News*
- *Reuters North American Equities News Service*
- *S&P MarketScope Alerts*
- *The Wall Street Journal*

(2) #1301 Beta Systems 350 North Sunny Slope Road, Brookfield, WI 53005, USA. t: (1 414) 789 9000; f: 789 4858.

'Integrated real-time securities processing system. It supports most brokerage activities, including:

- Quotes, including news, stockwatch, research
- Sales Support, including customer book, security, inventory data
- Order entry, including switch and order match

- Trading/Inventory, including positions, P&L, cost of carry, exposure
- Operations, including P&S, cashiering, margin, dividend
- Accounting, including general ledger and accounts payable.

We think we have a superior product and The BETA System can truly make a difference . . . Presently (Fall 1993) we are connected to over 6000 terminals, and process upwards to 25,000 trades a day. We are connected to all the self-regulatory organizations and exchanges.'

BETAQUOTES 'Complete market data system used by thousands of stock brokers across the country. Information from all major exchanges, Dow Jones and Reuters, and third-party database providers is available . . . *BETAQUOTES3270* is another version of our product which provides quote information to users on their existing (IBM) 3270 network. It also provides *Dow Jones News Service* and *S&P Marketscope* as additional services.'

(3) #1302 Cognotec Europe House, World Trade Centre, East Smithfield, London E1 9AA, UK. t: (44 171) 702 1320; f: 702 1565.

'Real time treasury information service designed for corporations who have foreign exchange and/or money market exposure and need to manage their risk . . . News is gathered and displayed in real time from the Press Association, Knight-Ridder and VWD . . . Foreign Exchange and Stock Market reports from around the globe are taken from the News Brokers division of *International Financial News Services* . . . You can (also) access the Bank of England information database. Dow Jones and FTSE indices are also included. All the system information is provided in an easy to view full colour (viewdata) page format which can be downloaded into spread sheets and hard copies can be produced as required.'

(4) #1303 Data Broadcasting Corporation 1900 South Norfolk Street, PO B 5979, San Mateo, CA 94402–0979, USA. t: (1 415) 571 1800; f: 571 8507.

'Track the market tick by tick with real-time quotes from every major US exchange. Signal gives you unlimited real-time last sale quotes from the NYSE, AMEX, NASDAQ, OPRA (all options exchanges), CBT, CME . . . You get access to more than 65,000 issues – stocks, options, futures, money market funds and mutual funds . . . Track the market on your PC or Mac with your choice of more than 130 third party investment software programs . . . far more than any other quote service can offer you. All the leading packages work with Signal – DollarLink, MasterChartist, Aspen Graphics, MetaStock, TradeStation, and many more.

Choose the Signal receiver with the best reception for you:

- *FM Reception* 'Available in most major metropolitan areas in North America.'
- *Cable Reception* 'If your local cable system carries CNBC or C-SPAN, you can get Signal data via cable.'

- *Satellite Reception* 'With a satellite antenna you can get direct satellite reception throughout most of the North American continent.'

(5) **#1304 E*TRADE** America's Electronic Brokerage, 480 California Avenue, Palo Alto, CA 94306, USA. t: (800) STOCKS5/(1 415) 326 2700; f: 324 3578. e: 76703.2064@compuserve.com.

'Offers you online trading and one of the deepest discount commissions at the low price of only $19.95 per OTC trade . . . Our highly automated brokerage system sypports world-wide personal computer or touch tone access *AnyTime, AnyWhere, AnyWay.* You can place your orders 24 hours a day, making it possible for you to use the system when it is most convenient for you. Enter your orders via PC, later check or alter them via the *Tele*Master* Touch-tone system, and still later review the results at your convenience. As soon as your orders execute, your updated portfolio and an execution message will be waiting for you when you sign on next . . . *E*TRADE*'s system gives you instant access to the latest business news, security quotes, market data, company announcements and analysis information . . . *E*TRADE Securities* clears its transactions on a fully-disclosed basis through *Herzog, Heine, Geduld, Inc,* member of the New York Stock Exchange. Herzog is a leading market maker in NASDAQ securities . . . some say the *largest* market-maker.

If you desire, by paying monthly exchange fees you may receive Last Sale prices through *E*TRADE.* The 'Last Sale' price is the very last price at which the security traded and is transmitted to you instantly. Last Sale subscribers receive Last Sale prices from all exchanges including non-delayed Bid/Ask quotes from NASDAQ – that is, the current Bid and the Ask quoted by NASDAQ in National Market System and Over-The-Counter stocks. In accord with the regulations of the various Exchanges, the fees for Last Sale prices depend upon whether you are considered a 'Nonprofessional' subscriber . . . If you do not subscribe for Last Sale prices there is no exchange fee and you will receive prices delayed at least 15 minutes. Everyone receives the same 'Closing Prices' delayed at least 15 minutes.

The *New York Stock Exchange* requires a special form on which you warrant that you are a Nonprofessional subscriber. There are substantial penalties associated with misrepresentation. To qualify as a Nonprofessional, you must certify that you are a person who is neither:

(a) registered or qualified with the Securities and Exchange Commission ('SEC'), the Commodities Futures Trading Commission, any state securities agency, any securities exchange or association, or any commodities or futures contract market or association,

(b) engaged as an 'investment advisor' as that term is defined in Section 201(11) of the Investment Advisors Act of 1940 (whether or not registered or qualified under that Act), nor

(c) employed by a bank or other organization exempt from registration under Federal and/or State securities laws to perform functions that would require him/her to be so registered or qualified if he/she were to perform such functions for an organization not so exempt.'

*E*TRADE* receives securities data from the NYSE, AMEX, NASDAQ, CBOE, CHICAGO, PACIFIC, PHILADELPHIA, BOSTON and CINCINNATI Exchanges, and commodity information from the CBOT, CMERC and NY FUTURES Exchanges. News comes from *Comtex*.

(6) #1305 EuroAmerican Group 162 Queen Victoria Street, London. EC4V 4BS, UK. t: (44 171) 329 3377; f: 329 4508. *Also* 50 Broad Street, Suite 516, New York, NY 10004, USA. t: (1 212) 269 6686; f: 943 5750.

'*Satquote* has been specially designed to bring down the costs of financial information. Whether you need real-time prices on Stocks, Options, Futures or Foreign Exchange, Satquote is without doubt, the most cost effective provider of this information, on the market today.

EuroAmerican Group approached the development of Satquote with the trade in mind. In order to deliver traders fast, affordable information EuroAmerican Group approached the problem by a two-fold solution – Hardware and Software. In the mid 80s EuroAmerican Group foresaw the immense power of the Personal Computer but realised its limitations and decided to build on this by integrating the transputer card, the hardware solution. Thus a computer within a computer was created. This technology gives Satquote its incredible speed which the competition simply cannot match. Satellite technology using the broadcast system was pioneered by EAG in Europe. This allows traders to instantly access information. The competition's request based systems are by definition slower. With Satquote your PC is the host of all realtime information, not some distant mainframe. Therefore when you access Satquote, the information is there immediately. You see the information you want. Satquote's software solution was to make access easy and uncomplicated. There are no complicated manuals or directories to wrestle with, just a few simple key strokes that can be mastered within half an hour.

Satquote's main focus has been on exchange traded products and it delivers quotes at lighting speed accurately and reliably on equities, bonds, derivatives and commodity markets around the globe.

In addition to delivering exchange quoted products, Satquote has one of the finest global treasury feeds supplied by *Global Treasury Services*, a subsidiary of Citicorp which covers over twenty-five primary banks.

Satquote has chosen four news services to allow individuals the flexibility to choose the service that suits their supply and market place:

- *AFX News*
- *Futures World News*
- *Market News*
- *PR NewsWire*'

(7) #1306 Shark Information Systems 120 Wall Street, New York, NY 10005, USA. t: (1 212) 208 7700. *Also* 17 Epworth Street, London EC2A 4DL, UK. t: (44 171) 895 1772.

'The need was astoundingly evident. Every other quote system around was created in a simpler, slower era. *Before* the arrival of the personal computer. *Before* traders began looking at the critical *relationships* in their portfolios: between assets and groups of assets; between assets owned and assets in the marketplace. *Before* deregulation of the phone company changed forever all electronic delivery.

Our objective, then, was crystal clear. To build from scratch the fastest, most advanced, real time quote system. Putting at your command the enormity of technology available; our Shark would have no fins! Thus, when you dissect a Shark, you'll find fault tolerant mainframes, high-speed data transmission and complete network control. The result is a whole different animal. Shark does whatever the competition does – but with blinding speed, leaving the others in its wake.

Then, Shark moves into uncharted waters: providing information so instantly it actually *redefines the meaning of a quote*. It enables you to examine in hundreds of ways the relationships *between* assets – based upon your own strategy. Shark analyzes, pulverizes and harmonizes every conceivable chunk of market data you could need.

With other systems you can miss opportunity. Shark sniffs out opportunity and makes it *visible*. Opportunities that would have gone unnoticed, would have sped by too swiftly for you to act on. And isn't that what it's all about?'

(ii) Historical data services

This is a very important area: here are profiles of about a dozen companies active historically with particular types of financial or economic data and statistics. (Some also supply data or information in *real-time*: but often this is not quite 'real-time' – the quotes or whatever being delayed, say, by fifteen minutes.) Other prominent historical data players involved especially with economic data include *DRI/McGraw-Hill*, *FAME Information Services*, *Reuters Information Services (Canada)*, and *The WEFA Group*. Many of the services which concentrate on providing historic time series also supply copies of their data to the real-time data providers as *third-parties*. Many also offer their data offline in differing forms and formats – examples of which are referenced elsewhere in this Book.

(8) #1307 Argus Vickers 17 Battery Place, New York, NY 10004, USA. t: (1 212) 425 7500; f: 509 5408. *Also* American Equity Research Limited, Royex House, Aldermanbury Square, London EC2V 7HR, UK. t: (44 171) 606 0006; f: 606 0666.

'Since 1934, Argus has provided independent research which supports their analysts Buy, Hold and Sell recommendations. Company coverage is targeted at 'Blue Chip', Utilities and Special Situations equities. Two unique sections of this service are the Director of Research's *Portfolio*

Selector, which contains five actual portfolios each with a specific investment strategy, and a facility to build a customised portfolio by scanning the database, inputting up to 25 different investment criteria. The Economists at Argus also play an important part in providing economic opinions and forecasts, market and industry comments.

Our pricing is not complex . . . We package our research dependent upon the clients requirements. Clients that have full consultation with our analysts and receive publications will be charged in the region of £2000 per month. Clients that have the Newsletters that we research and are written by us are charged between £12,000 and £50,000 per year. An individual report for a company is £35.'

Argus use the full range of communication techniques to deliver their research to customers: print, facsimile, telephone, online, diskette, magnetic tape, and – soon – cdrom. Some examples are:

(i) *Facsimile*

- *Argus Action Facts – AM & PM* 'Sent prior to the New York market opening and at midday EST (17.00 hrs GMT) offers a review of current market activity, with comments, recommendations and earnings for selected stocks.'
- *Argus Alert* 'In addition, Argus sends faxes as needed about important and timely information, such as rating changes, interest rate updates and changes in recommended asset allocations.'
- *Argus Market Watch* 'Faxed before the New York Stock Market opens, provides a snapshot of the global markets with *Today's Market View*. The *Daily Spotlight*, a headline article with an accompanying graph about the US economy, is based upon the latest economic information released by the US Government and other sources, The *Market Outlook* and the *Statistics Diary* lists the latest and closing prices for global indices, exchange rates, long bond yields and one day and five day Call/Put ratios. *Stockpicker's Corner* provides the stock pick of the day.'

(ii) *Telephone*

- *Argus Interactive Conference Call-In* 'Focusing on timely and hot topics an interactive telephone conference is scheduled with customers and Argus analysts.'
- *CallARGUS* 'A daily two minute taped message that gives updates and interpretations of the latest developments affecting any of the stocks followed by Argus analysts.'
- *Consultation* 'Customers are encouraged to call Argus analysts for personal consultation about investment topics and to discuss issues relating to an Argus publication or fax.'
- *Insider Alert* 'Has been designed to offer investors a fast pro-active connection to US corporate insider trading. An 'insider' is deemed to be a company officer, director, vice president etc. When insider filings (form 4s) indicate an above average activity or unusual buying trend, you will be notified by telephone.'

(iii) *Online*

- 'The Argus Group On-line is accesible via any personal computer with a modem. This menu-driven system, offers services from *Argus Research Corporation*, *Business Wire*, *Market Guide*, *Star Services*, *Vickers Stock Research*. This exceptional mix of financial data serves Institutional Broker's trading desks, Corporate Finance areas, Libraries and M&A departments, Retail Brokers sales and research departments, Portfolio and Money Managers and Investor Relations teams.'

(9) #1308 CDA Investment Technologies 3265 Meridian Parkway, Suite 130, Fort Lauderdale, FL 33331, USA. t: (800) 243 2324/(1 305) 384 1500; f: 384 1540.

'*CDA/Investnet* is the most comprehensive source of insider trading data in the world. We collect our data directly from the various filings shown below that are required by the Securities and Exchange Commission, FDIC and OTS:

- *Form 3* Initial Statement of Ownership
- *Form 4* Statement of Changes in Beneficial Ownership
- *Form 144* Intention to Sell Restricted Securities

Over 12,000 companies, including many pink sheets are included in this database . . . Insider trading activity is available in a variety of formats: our own on-line system . . . magnetic tape, direct transmissions and copies of actual filings.'

- *Insider Trading Monitor* 'A user-friendly on-line system designed to meet your needs. Its updated daily so as to provide you with the most timely information possible. All you need is a PC with a modem . . . Once connected you'll be able to search our database by company or by insider name. Our flexible system design allows you to select an individual and find what companies he or she is a director of. You can also list all the transactions that have been filed for that individual (purchases, sales, gifts etc.) . . . Available for a $50 annual fee. Connect time is billed at $1.00 per minuts with a $35 minimum in any month where there is activity.'
- *CDA Bullseye Investor Relations Services* 'A powerful group of analytical and planning tools for investor relations professionals; providing all the information required to develop, track, and evaluate an effective investor relations program. Most Fortune 500 companies, as well as leading consulting firms, rely on Bullseye IR Services for focused information on institutional investors. Clients benefit from sophisticated applications, high quality technical support, and access to the most comprehensive, timely, and accurate information available anywhere.'
- *CDA/Spectrum* 'The leading provider of ownership information with more than 9000 US and 9,300 International equities covered . . . For the first time in the UK you can access the information by the delivery method suitable to your needs:

- Through your *Quote Screen* for the essentials at speed
- *Online* for searching and reporting to satisfy more complex and sophisticated needs
- On *Tape* or *Diskette* to customise and build your own applications
- *Publications* for reference and historical lookups.'

(10) #1309 CSI Commodity Systems Inc, 200 W Palmetto Park Road, Boca Raton, FL 33432, USA. t: (1 407) 392 8663; f: 392 1379.

'CSI is the industry's most respected source for data on futures, securities, indices and options. Traders and market professionals rely on CSI for timely, accurate data, delivered via modem or on diskettes. In today's global economy, every trader needs access to major world markets to balance risk. The international scope of the CSI data base makes CSI the one-stop servuce for savvy investors in the US and abroad. The CSI data base includes ... Securities ... Mutual funds ... Stock indices ... Futures ... Cash ... Futures Options.'

(11) #1310 DAIS Group 31 West 52nd Street, 10th Floor, New York, NY 10019, USA. t: (1 212) 246 7400; f: 246 2890.

'As financial instruments become more complex, the markets more volatile, and global investment opportunities more accessible, there is an increasing need for quality data and powerful decision support tools to help you refine your investment management process. The DAIS Group, a research division of the Franklin-Templeton worldwide organization, has been meeting this important need by providing *state-of-the-art investment technology* services to investment professionals with an emphasis on *stock selection models*, *value added analytics*, and *risk control tools*.

The DAIS system gives you access to proprietory and third party databases, robust quantitative models and sophisticated decision support software ... DAIS maintains a library of over 60 databases that cover a broad scope of domestic and international equity data. The databases range from *fundamentals* and *consensus earnings estimates* to quantitative stock *rankings* developed by DAIS and other leading researchers. The databases cover over 17,000 global securities with up to 10 years of historical data. Data is updated on a regular basis, in many cases daily, helping you stay on top of market trends. The DAIS system provides flexible analytic tools such as *screening* and *report writing* to assure full use of this extensive array of data. DAIS also offers the ability to maintain your own proprietory databases for custom calculations (eg composite rankings or earnings estimates) that can easily be merged with the existing data and analytics.'

Third-party databases listed by DAIS include:

- *Earnings Estimates* First Call; I/B/E/S; Value Line; Zachs
- *Fundamentals* Compustat; Ford; Value Line
- *Global* Armour Cash Flow; Global Columbine; International I/B/E/S; MSCI World Index Tracker.

'Each database is fully integrated with every other database. This means that users can run reports, screens or data downloads with a combination of data from various sources. This integration gives the user complete flexibility in data handling and analysis. The databases which users can access depends upon their level of DAIS services and their subscriptions to third-party research services and data vendors.

Pricing is completely dependent on the group of services purchased and is discussed on a case by case basis. Fees begin at $10,000 and run upwards of $100,000.'

(12) #1311 Datastream 58–64 City Road, London EC1Y 2AL, UK. t: (44 171) 250 3000; f: 253 0171 *and* 120 Wall Street, 15th Floor, New York, NY 10005, USA. t: (1 804) 4000; f: 804 4001.

'A US $100 million business, providing financial information services to the securities industry worldwide. Established in 1964, Datastream now serves 1,500 customer organisations throughout the investment community, in 40 countries across four continents. Datastream has the best data in the business and easy-to-use powerful applications. It comes straight to your desk, backed up by customer support to put you first . . . Datastream's corporate mission is straightforward. To be the best in financial information services . . . From stocks to bonds, indices to corporate financials, FX to economics, Datastream is the information choice that gives you the edge.'

As of May 1994, Datastream provided access to 33,667 series of worldwide equity prices, plus indices data and I/B/E/S forecasts; 11,605 sets of company accounts data; 32,891 sets of national economic data series from around the world, plus data from OECD and IMF; 22,762 series of unit trust data; 68,326 runs of bond data; and extensive series of futures and options data.

We are fully aware of the conflicting pressures affecting our customers concerning their need for more data while facing cost constraints. One of our major service enhancements in 1994 was the significant increase in data coverage, amounting to over 150 million data items. This included coverage from many emerging markets and extended coverage in others. Throughout 1995 we will continue enhancing our databases, applications, delivery mechanisms and customer service to meet and provide the best possible quality and value for money.'

The major types of data facility available via Datastream are categorised in the company's *1995 Summary of Programs* as:

- *Equities* 'You can use the programs in this section for information on: A single company or equity . . . An industry group/sector . . . A Datastream equity list (eg All Dutch equities) . . . Your own restricted list . . . Your own portfolio . . . Real time prices are provided for the following countries: Austria, Belgium, France, Germany, Italy, Netherlands, Spain, Switzerland and the UK.'
- *Company Accounts* 'Datastream holds company accounts data on companies worldwide, using standardised codings to provide a common definition at an international level. Key account items are

common to all companies covered, so enabling swift comparisons across companies and markets.'

- *Bonds* 'Bonds is a general term applied to all types of debt securities, for example, Governments, index-linked, convertibles, floating rate notes and miscelleneous fixed income issues. Datastream also classifies bond and equity warrants and convertible securities under this term. Use the programs in this section for information on: A single bond issue . . . A privately created bond . . . A Datastream bond list (eg UK index-linked gilts) . . . Your own restricted list . . . Your own portfolios . . . Real time prices are provided for the following countries: Austria, Belgium, France, Germany, Italy, Netherlands, Spain, Switzerland, UK (government bonds only).'
- *Futures & Options* 'You can use the 201's (programs) in this section for information on options contracts traded on exchanges in London (LIFFE), France (MATIF and MONEP), Germany (DTB), Netherlands (EOE), Switzerland (SOFFEX), Austria (OTOB), and liquid contracts in the United States (CME, PHLX, CBOT, CBOE and AMEX). Use the 250's (programs) for information on commodity and financial futures traded on exchanges in London, Europe, North America, Sydney and the Far East.'
- *Markets & News* 'These programs enable you to retrieve a range of information which provides useful background for your research on securities, and news about Datastream services. In general, the programs provide: Stock market indices; Interest rates; Exchange rates; Commodities information; Real-time information on UK companies; Intra-day share price movements; Intra-day market movements; Rights issues; Interest and exchange rates quoted in London; International market, company and general news; Major rises and falls on European exchanges; News about Datastream services.'
- *Economics* 'Key economic indicators are currently available for 30 countries relating to economic growth, employment, wages, prices, external trade, debt, and other significant information about a country's economy.'
- *Graphs & Reports* 'A *time series* is a series of values recorded consistently for a single item, at a given frequency over a period of time, normally at specified dates . . . The Datastream *Graphics Service* enables you to display and analyse a range of charts . . . These include: Line chart . . . Bar chart . . . Correlation and scatter chart . . . Pie chart . . . Horizontal bar chart . . . Flexible Format chart.'
- *Data Channel* 'Download data to other software packages, such as *Excel* and *Lotus 1–2–3*.'
- *Customised Data* '*Lists* enable you to research a large number of instruments at once . . . *Expressions* enable you to manipulate data . . . *Functions* are special Datastream codes that perform statistical calculations . . . *Programmable pages (Minder)* . . . build, store and display your own formatted screen. These programs work for any series and will display real time data: Datastream has real time links with many major exchanges and banks. Leave your page of stocks

displayed and press ENTER at any time during the day to refresh the screen to get the latest values.'

- *Portfolio Valuations* 'A range of portfolio valuation services, designed to meet the needs of multi-currency porfolios, across any investment complexion ... These services can be fully integrated with investment accounting services, so that a single data entry updates portfolios for both accounting and valuation purposes.'
- *Investment Accounting* 'Double-entry accounting and management information system for security and currency investments ... There are nine parts to the system: Capital Gains Tax System; Fundline (to download information from the Datastream mainframe to your PC); Income System; Investment Ledger; Money Market Ledger; Maturities Diary; Settlement System; Soft Dealing System; Stock Certificate Control System.'
- *Portfolio Performance* 'Enables institutional investors to measure their portfolios ... Calculations are based upon formulae approved by the United Kingdom *Society of Investment Analysts.*'

A new service introduced in 1995 is:

- *Marksman* 'The new company identification tool ... giving access to a database of over 400,000 private and public European companies. Data available includes company accounts, activities, profiles, news and market data ... Designed to fit the business practices of the M&A/Corporate Finance professional.'

(13) #1312 Ford Investor Services 11722 Sorrento Valley Road, Suite 1, San Diego, CA 92121, USA. t: (1 619) 755 1327; f: 455 6316.

- *Develop and test investment models with Ford's historical research data base* 'No look-ahead bias (At the end of each month from December, 1970, to present, you get the known, publicly available data on each company *as of that date*) ... No survivorship bias (You get data on companies no longer in existence) ... No restatement bias ... Affordable, easy-to-use ... You choose access mode (If you elect to use Ford's software, the data base can reside on Ford's mainframe or on your PC ... Or, you can receive the entire data base in a text file for use with your own software).
- *Use Ford's current data base for investment selection* Accurate, timely data (You receive fundamental data ... on a universe that includes all the equities an institutional investor can reasonably consider for his portfolio) ... Outstanding performance ... Used by industry leaders (Ford's 200 plus institutional clients manage 1.5 trillion dollars in aggregate) ... Your choice of software.
- *Get into global investing with Ford's international equity data base* Global valuation (Only from Ford can you receive fundamental data *plus* evaluations (projected growth rate, normal EPS, quality rating etc.) *plus* Ford's valuation model results on 6,500 global equities) ... Affordable, easy to use.'

(14) #1313 Haver Analytics 60 East 42nd Street, Suite 620, New York, NY 10017, USA. t: (1 212) 986 9300; f: 986 5857.

'Specializes in databases and software products for economic analysis and business decision-making. Our 50+ databases contain more than one million time series and are continually growing to meet the needs of our clients. Databases are updated shortly after release of data. CPI, PPI and GDP are available by 9 am on the day of release. Longer press releases such as the Employment Sitution are available within one hour of release.'

Sources of the Haver data include:

- *Survey of Current Business* (US Bureau of Economic Analysis)
- *Employment and Earnings* (US Bureau of Labor Statistics)
- *Flow of Funds* (Federal Reserve Board)
- *Survey of Mortgage Lending Activity* (US Department of Housing and Urban Development)
- *Stock Price Indices* (Standard & Poor's)
- *International Financial Statistics* (International Monetary Fund)
- *Debt Tables* (World Bank)
- *National Accounts* (United Nations)
- *Main Economic Indicators* (Organisation for Economic Co-operation and Development)

Haver Analytics offers its data online though *GE Information Services.* Once a user number is validated you pay for the resources you use each month when you extract data. These charges are divided into two types: cost of the data series . . . and costs associated with getting the data (computer connect time and computer resource units). Database subscriptions eliminate data access fees but do not include computer charges . . . There is a monthly invoice minimum of $50. Computer usage charges, data access fees and data directory charges will be applied against this amount.'

(15) #1314 I/B/E/S International Inc [Institutional Brokers Estimate System] 345 Hudson Street, New York, NY 10014, USA. t: (1 212) 243 3335; f: 727 1386. *Also* Epworth House, 25 City Road, London EC1Y 1AA, UK. t: (44 171) 496 1600; f: 588 8787.

'Global financial information provider best known as the premier source of earnings expectations data. As of June, 1994, the I/B/E/S database covers 14,500 companies in 42 countries with a total market value of $13.3 trillion – the practical universe of equity investment opportunities. Wherever you invest, I/B/E/S puts information at your service.

At present, I/B/E/S Inc. provides approximately 250,000 earnings per share estimates from 6,200 securities analysts at nearly 750 institutional research firms worldwide. These analysts contribute the data voluntarily because:

- They get I/B/E/S consensus data at no charge in return
- They receive a form of free publicity as a contributor to I/B/E/S

- Because their customers and followers ask them to contribute to I/B/E/S.

I/B/E/S' staff of 40 dedicated research analysts and systems professionals work around the clock to transform the data into the world's most comprehensive, reliable, convenient, and timely source of earnings expectations information. *Since accuracy is of paramount importance to realize the beneficial effects of the database, I/B/E/S takes the lead by proactively contacting the analysts on a daily basis to confirm that the published forecasts are precise and the most current.* I/B/E/S provides clients with the most current data on a frequency basis that meets their individual requirements. For the extremely active investor, intra-day broadcasts are available.

I/B/E/S professionals have an impressive track-record of working successfully with investors of virtually every style and size and will confidently work with your organization to provide applicable information at the appropriate frequency with pricing that will accommodate your budget. Data delivery options include:

- *I/B/E/S Express* Daily analyst detail via modem, right to your PC, with powerful manipulation software
- *I/B/E/S Global Aggregates* The power of earnings expectation information aggregated for use in asset allocation, cross-border valuation, index investing, and derivatives trading
- *I/B/E/S Alert* Summary data via dial-in to the I/B/E/S system
- *I/B/E/S Daily Fax* Earnings report data, new estimates, and earnings surprise
- *Summary Data Book* Consensus estimates, via printed report
- *Detail Report* Analyst-by-analyst estimates, via printed report
- *Earnings Estimate Monitor* Weekly revisions, via printed report
- *I/B/E/S Plus* Custom-designed reports based on customer specifications

I/B/E/S data are also available via more than 30 electronic sources and quote services including: Bloomberg, Bridge, FNN Shark, Quotron, Telerate, Lotus, DAIS, Vestek, FactSet, Datastream, CompuServe, Randall-Helms, S&P Compustat, Fame Software, IDC, Gould Research, and Ford Investor Services.'

2837. **Earnings Expectations Research**. i. Annotated bibliography. The fourth edition, published in 1992, covered 281 papers. The fifth edition will be published early in 1996 and 'will be sent to 1,000 of the top investment managers world-wide'.

(16) #1315 IDD Information Services Two World Trade Center, New York, NY 10048, USA. t: (1 212) 432 0045; f: 912 1457.

Since 1935, *Investment Dealers' Digest* (IDD) has investigated, chronicled, analyzed and regularly anticipated every major move on Wall Street. *IDD Information Services* serves the global financial marketplace by integrating a compehensive portfolio of domestic and international financial databases with powerful financial analysis software . . . IDD has long been regarded as the premier chronicler of Wall Street by investment and commercial bankers, major business publications and media organizations around the world. IDD's data is frequently used by such respected reporting organizations as *The Wall Street Journal. The New York Times, The Financial Times, Dow Jones Newswire, CNBC/FNN, The Economist*, and other prominent business publications worldwide.

IDD provides the financial marketplace with all industry-standard databases including its own proprietory *Tradeline* databases. For years, Tradeline has earned a reputation for delivering the most consistently accurate securities data in the business. *This is no accident.*

How to Select an Historical Quote Vendor . . . Ask them if they . . .

- *have experience in providing historical pricing information?* Tradeline has been providing historical pricing information to leading investment institutions, publications, and professionals for 20 years. We are the industry standard!
- *cover a large number of North American common and preferred stocks, warrants, convertible bonds, units, corporate debt, mutual funds, certificates, indices, puts, calls, convertible preferred, US government or agency debt and more?* Tradeline covers both active and inactive issues!
- *offer in-depth pricing, dividend, and capital change information?* Tradeline tracks over 70 issue specific fundamental and pricing related data items including EPS, shares outstanding, daily percent price change, and many more!
- *account for 20 years of stock splits, cash distributions and equivalents or both for total return information?* Tradeline allows you the flexibility to report 20 years of both adjusted and unadjusted pricing information for any reference date!
- *allows you to screen for issues based upon user specified variables such as percent price change, EPS, annual dividends, BETAs etc.?* Tradeline allows you to screen for issues based upon 36 different investment criteria. You can also define your own ranges and create custom reports!
- *provide the ability to download reports and pricing data to multiple report formats?* With Tradeline you can download to Metastock, Text and PRN formats!
- *follow a stock through its lifetime?* Tradeline links issues that undergo name changes, mergers & acquisitions, spin-offs and exchange changes. Inactive equities are held for indefinitely!
- *check their data against multiple sources?* Tradeline data is validated daily by comparing it to information found in *The Wall Street Journal, Standard & Poor's*, the *CUSIP Directory*, a real time feed, and through direct exchanges with various companies and exchanges!
- *cross validate their pricing to test an option against its underlying security?* Tradeline checks every option against Black-Scholes to insure its accuracy!
- *confirm unquoted issues, name changes, mergers & acquisitions, exchange changes, cash distributions, and duplicate Tickers!* Tradeline

data analysts will call the necessary exchanges and or companies to get the information or an explanation!'

Apart from the printed products referenced elsewhere in this Directory, IDD's services include:

- *IDD Benchmark* A voice response fax-delivered financial information service, developed in partnership with the Voice and Imaging Services Group of *PR Newswire.*
- *IDD Plus for Windows* 'A new integrated financial data management system which significantly improves the way financial professionals retrieve, screen and publish financial data. This new interactive system now integrates important financial information *seamlessly* from different sources for fast, simultaneous access to industry-standard, IDD proprietory and private client databases.

While all financial organizations require updated financial data to evaluate existing and new opportunities, everybody looks at numbers *differently.* There are hundreds of investment and commercial banking institutions vying for the business of a finite number of prospects. Every CFO has special financial data criteria unique to his or her company. Bankers must respond quickly and effectively to client business as well as industry market trends.

The IDD Plus system not only gives you and your company *total control* over data collection and output. It offers tremendous flexibility and operating features which allow you to customize reports, graphs or entire presentations. *Never before has such power been put into your hands* . . . IDD Plus for Windows is more than just another data retrieval product – *it's a new concept* – an authoring system that enables you to use predefined default settings; set your own defaults from our extensive on-screen menu list; or even create your own ticker symbol/data item sorting and retrieval protocols. This program gives you precision control and ease-of-use that simply hasn't been possible with systems of the past. You no longer *have to be a brain surgeon* to create customized retrieval settings that go beyond standard database system defaults.'

IDD Plus for Windows 'runs on all popular LAN systems. All of IDD's databases are available on-line directly from IDD's mainframe, or they can be installed in-house on your company's VAX/VMS, IBM/VM or UNIX system'.

Databases available include IDD's own:

- *Tradeline* 'Daily pricing, dividends and splits dating back 20 years, and descriptive information on over 200,000 North American securities and indices.'
- *Tradeline International* 'Daily pricing, dividends and splits dating back 7 years, and descriptive information on over 50,000 non-North American equities, indices and exchange rates as well as data from the third-parties: *Disclosure*; *I/B/E/S International*; *S&P Compustat*; *Value Line Publishing.*'

(17) #1316 Interactive Data Corporation Marketing & Sales, 14 Wall Street, 12th Floor, New York, NY 10005, USA. t: (1 212) 306 6999; f: 306 6962. *Also* Sales Department, 17/29 Sun Street, 3rd Floor, London EC2M 2PS, UK. t: (44 171) 375 1900; f: 253 3929.

'Serves major financial institutions and corporations world-wide. In North America, customers include major banks, brokerage firms, investment managers, and stock exchanges, including:

- 41 of the top 50 banks
- 41 of the top 50 brokerage houses
- 28 of the top 50 insurance companies
- 47 of the top 50 money management firms

In addition to distributing data directly to customers for their own use, Interactive Data is the data source for over 70 information providers . . . We have a number of product lines that allow access to this information, but I have singled out our PC server product *RemotePlus*. We have users who use this in both research and investment management applications . . . Unlike data services designed to download files or to provide terminal access, RemotePlus works from within your applications, retrieving information into your programs for immediate use. Using a software interface based on SQL (Structured Query Language), RemotePlus gives you consistent access to an enormous range of current and historical securities information.'

Interactive Data is a host in its own right, providing online access to data from half-a-dozen other US and UK database producers, as well as to their own data compilations:

'Financial data are available on more than 65,000 North American equity securities, as well as numerous North American government and municipal securities, and over 90,000 securities traded outside North America. Data are updated daily, monthly, quarterly or annually as new information becomes available. A wide range of database management and applications software is also offered to retrieve, manipulate, screen, download and analyze Interactive's and customer's data.

Delivery mechanisms available to suit individual customer's needs include direct mainframe-to-mainframe transmission, on-line telecommunication to a microcomputer or terminal, and computer tape delivered to the customer by courier or mail. Services are distributed directly to end-user customers and by direct sales distributors of value-added applications and other data delivery companies.

Interactive's services mainly target the banking, brokerage, insurance, mutual fund and money manager customer segments. End users include operations managers, money managers, portfolio managers, research analysts and pension fund sponsors.

Interactive receives the data from public sources, under license agreements from other organizations which collect data and creates its own evaluations for delivery to customers. Although certain licenses are important to the business, Interactive believes that it could continue to conduct the business without these licenses, although at a greater expense. Interactive has three or four main competitors in each of its business lines. The principal areas of competition are in quality of service, primarily accuracy, quantity of data, coverage, and price, and in the case of software, functionality.'

(18) #1317 MCM McCarthy, Crisanti & Maffei, 71 Broadway, New York, NY 10006, USA. t: (1 212) 509 5800; f: 509 7389 *and* 7 Holyrood Street, London SE1 2EL, UK. t: (44 171) 378 7273; f: 357 7959.

- *CorporateWatch* 'The new issues market is intensely competitive, demanding information that is both timely and accurate. CorporateWatch from MCM gives you the edge you need, providing the most rapidly disseminated information available on new issue debt, equity and private placements, all with an unparalleled degree of accuracy. CorporateWatch is unique. With exclusive information sources nurtured for over ten years, no one comes close to delivering such quality information. It is what you, the dealer demand. And it is only available from MCM.'
- *Currency Watch* 'This unique *Telerate*-based service provides continual Fundamental and Technical currency market analysis, daily and medium term, Regional market briefings, plus a series of Fundamental and Technical studies designed to highlight market trends and topical events.'
- *MoneyWatch* 'US government and agency securities are traded 24 hours a day, and the US economy impacts all of the world's financial markets, all of the time. This complex global market makes great demands on traders, who need to have at their fingertips a comprehensive source of analysis and advice. MoneyWatch from MCM provides Fundamental analysis and Technical trading strategies for US Treasury, Agency and money market securities, insights into US Federal Reserve Policy, Treasury operations and key global developments, plus timely forecasts and analysis of US economic data releases . . . This combination . . . makes MoneyWatch the definitive US government securities service.'
- *YieldWatch* 'European and Asia Pacific fixed income bonds and futures (including US T-bonds).'

(19) #1318 Multinational Computer Models 333 Fairfield Road, Fairfield, NJ 07004–1930, USA. t: (1 201) 575 8333; f: 575 8474. *Also* The Eclipse, 5 Bath Road, Slough, Berkshire SL1 3UA, UK. t: (44 1753) 536234; f: 570388.

'A leading provider of global treasury and risk management systems for currencies, commodities and interest rates. Over 100 of the US Fortune 500 companies and numerous other corporations both foreign and domestic, currently utilize MCM systems.' The company normally supply data only to users of their treasury management software; but from time to time they will supply sets of data to universities and other research organisations. The data they handle includes a wide global coverage of:

- Daily and monthly currency rates
- Daily and monthly interest rates
- Macro-economic data
- Commodity prices.'

(20) #1319 Telescan 10550 Richmond Avenue, Suite 250, Houston, TX 77042–5019, USA. t: (1 713) 952 1060.

'The art and science of making money: If you're serious, you start with Telescan . . . Telescan is well known in investment circles. The reason is very simple: The Telescan System is a proven and reliable investment tool that helps investors make profitable investment decisions. It works consistently well for individual investors, professional brokers, and money managers. And it will work for you . . .

Telescan is the nation's premiere provider of investment software, with over 30,000 satisfied users to prove it. We offer:

- The lowest cost for information in the industry, including a $45 unlimited use plan available after 6.00 pm and on weekends. Database access is available via a toll free number from 98% of US cities.
- An on-line historical database dating back nearly 20 years with technical and fundamental data on all stocks, mutual funds, options, indexes, industry groups, plus news from 12 major news wires around the world.
- Software specifically designed with ease-of-use in mind, and toll-free customer support from 8.30 am – 10.00 pm central for when you do have a question.'

(iii) Credit rating services

(21) #1320 CCN Credit Systems Consumer Enquiries, PO Box 40, Nottingham NG7 2SW, UK. t: (44 115) 986 8172.

- *Total Data 2000* 'The UK's premier business information service, providing the most complete on-line information resource for credit and financial management. It has been developed by the country's largest information service organisation, with over 165 years' experience in the collection and analysis of commercial information . . . CCN's massive data centres hold the largest credit information databases in the UK:
    - Every Limited Company in the UK, including 800,000 actively trading, and up to 10 years of full financial data – the most in-depth history available.
    - Over 1.7 million firms on our Small Business Register, the largest credit database of non-limited companies in existence.
    - More than four million directorships and company secretaries on the unique Directors Database, including personal details and records of past and present involvements.

- Millions of trade experiences on the Commercial CAIS database, giving current and historical trade payment behaviour.
- Details of every commercial and consumer County Court Judgement (CCJ) during the last six years.
- Complete Electoral Roll information on over 43 million individuals and 24 million households.
- Access for ordering International Business Reports from over 170 countries worldwide.

Total Data On-Line is modular by design. You choose the type of information you need to make a decision, enter the system at the appropriate level and determine which search options are most suited for your needs.

- *CCN Credit Systems* 'The leading provider of information and bureau processing to the consumer credit industry. The company processes over half of the UK's consumer credit enquiries, and holds the largest file of consumer credit referencing information in the UK.'

(22) #1321 Dun & Bradstreet Corporate Credit Services 1 Diamond Hill Road, Murray Hill, NJ 07974, USA. t: (1 908) 665 5000; f: 665 5803 *and* Dun & Bradstreet International, Holmers Farm Way, High Wycombe, Buckinghamshire, HP12 4UL, UK. t: (44 1494) 422000; f: 422260.

The following is paraphrased from recent D&B marketing literature and the SEC 10–K Report for the year 1993:

'D&B's key reports are positioned to provide different levels of information for different levels of risk, making it simple to choose the service to suit your particular needs:

- *D&B Compact Report* Concise information of your trading partners
- *D&B Monitoring* Early warning in the circumstances of your customers
- *D&B Payment Trend Report* A company's payment habits and trends over a 2 year period
- *D&B Risk Analysis* Through a series of comparisons, this analytical tool identifies your company's total risk exposure, including expected slow payment and bad debt, and provides a clear understanding of the strengths and weaknesses of your customer base.
- *D&B Select* Select any combination of individual modules to suit specific business transactions.
- *D&B Report* The core product.
- *D&B Comprehensive Report* The most extensive, which can contain all of these elements:

  Identification
  Evaluation:
    D&B Rating
    Maximum credit recommendation
    Payment performance
    Trend

D&B Rating comparison within industry sector
Summary:
- Employees
- Capital
- Sales
- Profit/loss
- Net worth
- Line of business

Public notice information:
- Legal public filings (e.g. County Court Judgements, winding-up petitions etc.)

Bankers
Principals:
- Name/title
- Personal details
- Current/previous directorships

Financial statement
Financial comparisons (3 years)
Performance ratios
Payment habits
Corporate structure
History and operations
Press cuttings
Management comment

In the USA, D&B provides its customers with access to a database containing information on more than 10 million US businesses. . . . Value-added solutions are provided through Specialized Industry Services (Credit Advisory System, Dun's Underwriting Guide, Bankers Advisory Service), Business Development Services, Analytical Services and Monitoring Services. Customers can receive information in printed formats, by fax, by telephone by DunsDial access and delivery system, through DunsPrint's online service, by touch-tone telephone from DunsVoice (a computer-generated voice system developed by DunsGate), or by being directly linked by computer via the DunsLink access and delivery system.

Subscribers to Credit Services (approximately 70,000 customers with more than 82,000 contracts in force throughout the US) use this information in making decisions to extend credit, underwrite insurance, evaluate purchases, and make other financial and risk assessment decisions. Credit Services' largest customers are major manaufacturers and wholesalers, insurance companies, banks and other credit and financial institutions . . . (However) D&B Express Service, accessible via an 800 number, provides companies that have an occasional need for business information with Business Information Reports and other products on specific companies . . . Credit Services is believed to be the largest commercial credit reporting agency in the world, but faces competition from in-house operations of businesses and other general and specialized credit reporting services.'

Dun & Bradstreet offer a very wide range of online, cdrom and diskette services – apart from the print products, examples of which were referenced earlier – including:

2838. **CD/Credit Register**. **cdrom**. m. £3,000 (giving 600 single company retrievals). Covers a quarter of a million UK companies.

2839. **Dun's Credit Guide**. **online**. Credit guideline on US trading companies.

2840. **Dun's Family Tree Service**. **online**. Tree relationships for some 200,000 corporations.

2841. **Dun's Legal Search**. **online**. Public record legal actions affecting US businesses.

2842. **Dun's Reference Plus**. **cdrom**. bi-m. Covers 4 million US businesses.

2843. **Dun's Underwriting Guide**. **online**. Aims to provide financial information that could affect underwriting decisions for some 9 million US companies.

2844. **DunsPrint Worldwide**. **online**. D&B Business Information Reports for approximately 16 million businesses worldwide.

2845. **Industry Norms & Key Business Ratios**. **diskette**. Covers some 800 US industries, including banks, securities, insurance and so on.

2846. **Payment Analysis Report**. **online**. Contains commercial credit information on a specific business. Includes the *D&B Rating*, which reflects the credit and financial strength of a business, and the *Paydex Score*, a numerical score of the company's past payment performance.

(23) #1322 Equifax Europe The Information Technology Centre, 3 New Augustus Street, Bradford BD1 5LL, UK. t: (44 1274) 759759; f: 759777. *Also* Equifax Inc, 1600 Peachtree Street NW, Atlanta, GA 30309, USA. t: (1 404) 885 8000; f: 888 5043.

'The world's leading supplier of consumer information . . . We are part of Equifax Inc, the leading supplier of consumer decision-support information to the finance, insurance, utility, healthcare and retailing industries. Established in 1899, Equifax is a $1.2 billion corporation . . . Access to our information, services and products is available to all organisations from the largest multi-national corporation to a sole trader and can be easily achieved via a modem, direct line, or CPU to CPU connection for instant decisions at point of sale.'

Equifax's *Credit Services – Consumer Data* include:

- *Electoral Roll* 44 million voters; Current & previous residency; Records since 1983
- *File Information* County Court Judgements; Sequestrations/Bankruptcies; Credit Search Enquiries
- *Credit Commitments* Bounced Cheque Details; Shows Tracing Activity taking place; Shows Debt Collection Actvity taking place

- *WESCORE* The first generic bureau score in this country, which summarises bureau data and predicts credit stress
- *EPIC2* Forecasts the probability for recovery of debts by litigation
- *WESTRACE* Provides a method of tracing people who may have moved away without notification
- *Neighbours* Up to 4 neighbours adjacent to problem address: Name and address provided

Commercial Information Services include:

- *Full Company Search* Includes full registration details, other trading addresses, directors' information, Consumer Credit Licence details, public record/gazette information (including appointment of receivers, liquidators, administrators and County Court Judgements), mortgages and charges, three years' accounts, financial analysis, capital structure and subscriber supplied information (including previous searches), credit transaction, payment details, account collections and commercial payments recorded by other subscribers.
- *Directors' Search* Details of directors including shareholdings, address and other directorship
- *Credit Reports* Include bank details, credit and trade references, details of principals, summary of operations, number of employees, registered number/business index number, registered office, trading styles, trading addresses, capital structure, information dates, details of land and buildngs, mortgages and charges, history of subject, financial summary and summary of public record/gazette information.

(24) #1323 TRW Business Credit Services 505 City Parkway West, Orange, CA 92668, USA. t: (1 714) 385 7000; f: 385 7121.

'Maintains a data base on 10 million US businesses, crossing all industries. Our data base is comprised of accounts receivable and financial data contributed monthly or quarterly, via tape or diskette, by our customers and other data contributors. Additionally we support our data base with public record and legal data, and with purchased data from third party sources . . . The strength to our methodology is that a TRW Business Profile, our primary business credit report, indicates not only a company's ability to pay, but their willingness to pay.' Other services include:

- *Small Business Advisory Report* Provides personal credit information on small business proprietors when that information is necessary in making a business credit decision.
- *TRW Trade Payment Guide* Providing summary information on up to 3 million businesses nationwide.
- *TRW International Reports* Comprehensive business credit reports on European and Canadian businesses, derived from *Creitreform* and *Creditel*, the leading vendors of business credit information in Europe and Canada, respectively.
- *TRW Intelliscore Services* Uses advanced statistical modelling, incorporating your own credit parameters, to deliver a credit risk score with supporting data on the companies the customer enquires upon.'

(iv) Newswire services

The first two services are designed primarily to help clients deliver information to the marketplace, rather than retrieve information from it.

(25) #1324 PR Newslink 9–10 Great Sutton Street, London EC1V 0BX, UK. t: (44 171) 251 9000; f: 251 3738.

- *Financial Results & Company Announcements* 'PR Newslink have a direct link with the *London Stock Exchange* for the submission of company announcements. Clients can transmit the text of an announcement to PR Newslink by modem or fax and have it transmitted directly to the Companies Announcements Office electronically in minutes. The speed and security of the electronic system of submitting information is preferred by the London Stock Exchange. Both the validation and preparation processes are faster, enabling announcements to be published quickly into the public domain. Immediately the announcement is released by the Stock Exchange, PR Newslink can fax or bike your press release or financial report to the media for same day coverage.
- *FAXLINK – multi broadcast distribution by fax* Simply send PR Newslink one copy of your Press release, by fax, bike or *Mediadisk PLUS* along with your press list. FAXLINK will then generate personalised fax header sheets automatically for each of the named editorial contacts chosen. Using over 100 lines, FAXLINK will have your story to each editor in just a few minutes. A two page story can typically be faxed to 200 Editorial and City contacts in under 15 minutes.'

(26) #1325 PR Newswire 806 Plaza Three, Jersey City, NJ 07311–3801, USA. t: (1 212) 832 9400; f: 596 1419.

'The acknowledged leader in the distribution of corporate, association and institutional information to the media and the financial community. Since founding the industry over 40 years ago, PRN has been its innovating force, providing a constant stream of enhanced newswire and fax services to professional communicators.'

(i) *Wire Services* These include:

- *National Newslines* 'The most comprehensive national circuit available . . . Provides access to thousands of newspapers, magazines, wire services and broadcast points across the US.' There are also (US) *Regional Newslines* and *State and Local Newslines.* 'The *Investors Research Wire* (IRW), which is transmitted to more than 100,000 terminals in the worldwide financial community, is included with all domestic Newslines at no additional charge.'

(ii) *Facsimile Services* For example:

- *Stocks On-Call* 'Stores all releases of public companies for 72 hours and provide access to investors, money managers, media and the public through a toll-free number'.

- *Company News On-Call* 'Provides immediate access to *all* of your company's news releases. It's the fastest, most effective and cost-efficient way of fulfilling requests after your release has been transmitted.'
- *Quarterlies On-Call* 'Public companies can save time and money by putting their quarterly report summary to shareholders on PR Newswire's Quarterlies On-Call service. The information is accessible 24 hours a day, 7 days a week through a toll-free number which can be publicized in the annual report, company literature or simply given to callers through the investor relations office.'

(iii) *Database Services*

'Every release that is transmitted by PR Newswire is stored in nearly 100 US and international databases and online services including *Lexis/Nexis*, *America Online*, *Dow Jones News/Retrieval*, *CompuServe* and *Dialog*. Since PR Newswire is recognized as the leading source of business information, these services are accessed daily by individual investors, analysts, academics and researchers.'

(27) #1326 AP-Dow Jones News Services 12 Norwich Street, London EC4A 1BP, UK. t: (44 171) 353 0480; f: 936 2348.

A joint venture between Associated Press and Dow Jones that provides international economic, business and financial news: founded 25 years ago and now delivers to 26,000 terminals in 63 countries. In addition to two broad international newswires, AP-Dow Jones offers specialized products dedicated to the coverage of European equities, banking and foreign-exchange and petroleum markets.

- *Bankers Report* 'Specialized news from international money and capital markets . . . Will quickly tell you about: Money market regulations; Foreign exchange markets; Interest rate changes; Economic indicators and trends; World events and political developments; Key bond, commodity and equity market news.'
- *Capital Markets Report* 'Sharply focused, market oriented news service with separate and exclusive reporting on all major sectors of the fixed-income and financial futures markets. And because CMR comes from *Dow Jones*, the foremost supplier of business and financial information worldwide, it's a news source you can trust. Rumors are reported because they affect the markets, but they are always carefully segregated from facts.

A primary focus . . . is keeping a eye on the Federal Reserve. Each day, the Report advises subscribers whether the Fed is expected to step into the market . . . the instant it does step in . . . and how the market reacts to what it does or doesn't do. In addition, CMR provides a full package of Fed data each Thursday and Friday – the moment it is released – and follows up with expert commentary and analysis, plus views from key Fed watchers on what the monetary authorities are doing and what they are likely to do.'

- *Economic Report* 'In-depth coverage of the world's currency markets, plus the main stories from the equities, commodities, financial futures and capital markets.'
- *European Corporate Report* 'News for traders, analysts and investors in the European stock markets.'
- *Financial Wire* 'Corporate and equities-market news from around the globe, Incorporates the *Dow Jones Broadtape*, the leading source of information affecting the US stock markets . . . You can count on AP-Dow Jones Financial Wire to quickly tell you about: Hot stocks; Economic indicators; World events; Stock splits; Mergers and acquisitions activity; Political developments; Bond and forex action. In addition, you'll receive stock market statistics, Dow Jones Averages and other leading international indexes, exclusive interviews with CEOs, and look-ahead analyses.'
- *Foreign Exchange Report* 'Focused news on developments that move the international foreign exchange markets . . . Including: Foreign exchange and interest rates; Major political, legislative, economic and financial news likely to influence the flow of money; Key economic indicators from major industrialised countries and many developing nations; Central bank activities; A daily and weekly calendar of events likely to affect money markets; Expert foreign exchange commentary throughout the business day.'
- *Professional Investor Report* 'Market-driven alerts on unusual U.S. stock trading activity, with fast follow-up articles that probe what's behind the alerts.'
- *International Petroleum Report* 'Fast, reliable information on oil prices and availability.'

(28) #1327 Associated Press 50 Rockefeller Plaza, New York, NY 10020, USA. t: (1 212) 621 1585; f: 621 5488.

'The Associated Press is the backbone of the world's information system. Every day, more than one billion people depend on AP news. With more than 3,000 staffers working out of 233 bureaus, with contributions from more than 1,500 member newspapers and 6,000 radio and television stations, AP covers local, state, national and international news like no one else can . . . No other news organization can match AP's breadth of coverage . . . The newest generation of AP Information Services delivers industry-specific news and information from all AP state news reports, as well as national and international news.

Here's how the *AP ALERT* services are created. Using a level of artificial intelligence, proprietory AP software continuously scan all of AP's national, internatioanl and state news wires. On a typical day the *AP ALERT* compouter reviews as many as 10,000 state, national and international news stories, selecting those that are relevant to a particular industry or subject. *No commercial reseller or news retailer offers this depth of AP copy.* The computer doesn't simply search for keywords or phrases. It studies the context of the words and matches them for relevance to the appropriate topic. A mathematical score is calculated for every item to determine the probability that the news story is pertinent to the topic area. This way, the system doesn't deliver stories about the "health" of the economy to the Medical/Health service, for instance. The computer also alerts our editors to AP stories that "might" be relevant to your industry. These stories are directed to a special queue where they are individually reviewed by editors to determine their relevance. Decisions made at this level are recorded by the software, enabling it to learn what to do when it encounters similar stories in the future.'

(29) #1328 Business Wire 1185 Avenue of the Americas, 3rd Floor, New York, NY 10036, USA. t: (1 212) 575 8822; f: 575 1854.

'An international relations wire service, distributing *full text* corporate news releases to the media and investment community worldwide. More than 12,000 organizations rely upon Business Wire for accurate and simultaneous distribution of their news releases. Business Wire, founded in 1961, is a privately held company headquartered in San Francisco, CA. There are 16 offices in the United States and affiliates in Paris and Tokyo. Business Wire news releases are delivered to the media and investment community via the AP Satnet phone line network and via Mainstream Data's FM service. Business Wire's fulltext news releases are also carried on many leading electronic databases and stock quote vendors.'

Business Wire is available online via, or as part of:

- *America Online*
- *Argus Research Corporation*
- *Bridge Information Systems*
- *Business Dateline*
- *CMA*
- *Comtex*
- *CompuServe*
- *Connect*
- *Corporate Data Exchange*
- *Delphi*
- *Dialog*
- *Dow Jones News/Retrieval*
- *Federal Filings*
- *First Call*
- *ITT Dialcom*
- *Lexis/Nexis*
- *NewsNet*
- *Reuter Company Newsyear*
- *Reuter Textline*
- *Summit Communications*
- *Track Data*
- *X*Press Information Systems*

(30) #1329 Comtex Scientific Corporation 4900 Seminary Road,

Suite 800, Alexandria, VA 22311, USA. t: (1 703) 820 2000; f: 820 2005.

'A leading value-added integrator of hundreds of information sources for electronic redistribution of news and information . . . Comtex is uniquely positioned within the information industry as the 'information factory' that integrates hundreds of the world's top information sources into customized, market-defined products.

Traditional technologies simply cannot keep pace with today's information pipelines. That's why, in June 1993, Comtex contracted with a company specialising in the development of highly sophisticated information filtering technology to create Comtex's artificial intelligence (AI) engine. The technology provides us with the ability to take in more information – 60,000 stories a day – and filter the data based on content rather than keywords.

Comtext is working to become the leading information provider to the redistribution marketplace. We service business and consumer on-lines, financial redistributors, software redistributors, bulletin boards, interactive television. CD ROM publishers, and wireless markets, to name a few. We will continue to deliver information products to new channels of distribution and new technologies on the immediate horizon.

We provide the largest 'one-stop-shop' for redistributors of information . . . We will determine pricing once we have determined your needs for information. Pricing is dependent on which products you choose and whether you will be reselling to others.'

Current News Sources listed by Comtex, apart from their own *Comtex Newsroom*, include:

- *American Banker*
- *BusinessWire*
- *Futures World News*
- *Insider Trading Monitor*
- *Inter Press Service*
- *Knight-Ridder/Tribune Business News*
- *Knight-Ridder Wire Services*
- *NewsNet*
- *PR Newswire*
- *Spy Wire*
- *States News Service*
- *US Newswire*

(31) #1330 Desktop Data 1601 Trapelo Road, Waltham, MA 02154, USA. t: (800) 255 3343; f: (1 617) 890 1565. *Also* Donnelley House, 25 Worship Street, London EC2A 2DX, UK. t: (44 171) 256 9133; f: 330 1519.

'With a few clicks of the mouse, individuals in your organization can effectively track all the news that will directly impact your business. That's because *NewsEDGE* monitors over 260 sources for you all day long and organizes a full-text indexed database of all the up-to-the-second news stories . . . You just tell NewsEDGE what to look for, and when relevant news breaks, you're immediately notified . . . In addition to real-time news wires, NewsEDGE offers newspapers, magazines and newsletters, providing the broadest range of timely sources and relevant information for all parts of your organization.

What started four years ago as a news solution for low-end, standalone PCs, has now evolved into a robust, client-server application that delivers thousands of news stories each day to hundreds of LAN-based users, all from a single NewsEDGE server. What's revolutionary is how NewsEDGE does all this on your existing networks and hardware . . . no matter what networks, user interfaces, and other applications you choose to run.

This revolutionary news delivery system is also revolutionary in price. We've reconstructed the way information can be purchased by enterprises with hundreds of electronically connected users. Instead of charges based on time on-line or amount of information used, NewsEDGE charges a fixed and predictable per user fee, maximising the way an organization can effectively control information costs.

Today, over 300 corporations, financial institutions, and government agencies worldwide are using NewsEDGE . . . These organizations have empowered their executives, marketing directors, sales managers, communications professionals, analysts, traders, lending officers, financial professionals, and others with comprehensive, up-to-the second information right at their desktops.'

(32) #1331 Federal Filings 601 Pennsylvania Avenue NW, South Building, Suite 700, Washington, DC 20004–2061, USA. t: (1 202) 393 7400.

'The core of our service is the *Federal Filings Business Newswire* (FFBN). It is from FFBN that all of the other services are derived and each service is a targetted segment of FFBN . . . We have a permanent presence in the SEC, read everything filed, and are often first out with the news, ahead, for instance, of Dow Jones themselves, and of Reuters . . . The staff features dozens of seasoned reporters and securities analysts – many with advanced business and legal degrees – who have earned a superior command of the markets they serve. Their mission is to bypass the more generic financial wires and uncover news which goes to the core of targeted, fundamental investing.'

- *Federal Filings Business Newswire* 'A broad-based financial news service providing real-time proprietory corporate news and fundamental equity-based investment research. The service includes indepth coverage of quarterly, interim, projected and pro forma financial data on more than 3,500 public companies and features intelligent tracking of insider, institutional and major shareholder activity. News concentrations include high yield, distressed, bankrupt, M&A, merger arbitrage, corporate finance, convertibles, energy regulation and research, and FDA drug hearings.' There are also: *High Yield Newswire*; *Convertibles Newswire.*

- *NewsManager for Windows* 'The best software for all Dow Jones newswires. It filters real-time news into customized windows, searches historical information, and color-codes headlines based on proprietory codes developed by Dow Jones and Federal Filings to classify industries, market sectors, news subjects, product lines and geographical regions.'
- *Document Retrieval* 'Fax, mail or over-night delivery of all SEC filings; select filings fron the DOT, FCC, FERC, ICC, OTS; as well as economic indicators.

Prices for these services are as follows: Federal Filings Business Newswire, $1,500/month; High Yield Newswire, $1,000/month.'

(33) #1332 Individual 84 Sherman Street, Cambridge, MA 02140, USA. t: (800) 766 4224/(1 617) 354 2230; f: 864 4066.

'Opportunity doesn't knock. It just hides in the news . . . Start the day with *First!* . . . Your Knowledge Agent . . . First! goes right to the source . . . First! doesn't wait for the news to show up in a trade magazine or business section. It goes to where the news begins: the wires and industry sources used by the business pages and the trade press . . . First! lets you spread the power of knowledge . . . Less data . . . more knowledge . . . No muss and no fuss . . . The difference is *SMART*.

What's our secret? No one else has SMART (System for Manipulation and Retrieval of Text) an advanced expert system technology under exclusive license to INDIVIDUAL Inc. SMART is the product of 20 years of research and development by one of the pioneers of text processing, Cornell's Dr Gerard Salton . . . Unlike conventional search tools and query languages, SMART recognizes topics and concepts, not word strings. SMART doesn't just spew out every mention of a major company just because you used the name as a keyword, and does not miss the one crucial reference because you forgot to include the company's common short name in your search. Instead, it compares multiple stories about the same events and then picks the best of the stories that get to the heart of the matter.'

Sources used by *First!* include:

- *American Banker*
- *Bond Buyer*
- *Business Wire*
- *Commerce Business Daily*
- *Federal Register*
- *Financial Times*
- *Financial Times Newsletters*
- *Inter Press Service*
- *Knight-Ridder Financial News*
- *Knight-Ridder/Tribune Business News*
- *Phillips Business Information Magazines*
- *PR Newswire*
- *Reuters Newswires*
- *Stock Quotes (AMEX, NASDAQ, NYSE).*

(v) Full text news services

(34) #1333 DataTimes 14000 Quail Springs Parkway, Suite 450, Oklahoma City, OK 73134, USA. t: (1 405) 751 6400: f: 755 8028.

Early in 1995, announced the availability of the new service:

- *EyeQ* 'Incorporates online retrieval from more than 5200 information sources, same-day and real-time news tracking, and on-demand 10–to 12–page corporate profiles created and delivered via fax, mail, or courier.'
- *Avenue Technologies* 'Will produce the reports using proprietory software that scans more than 5000 different journals and news sources, with the information then packaged into pre-formatted and presentation-quality reports. Profile reports will be available on more than 20,000 publicly traded companies in the US and internationally, and more than 12,000 US-based private companies.'

"DataTimes is breaking away from the rest of the online industry with the ultimate online package – combining price, product and packaging. The competition will be running as fast as they can to catch up. My prediction is, it's going to take off like a rocket."[174]

(35) #1334 Information Access Company 362 Lakeside Drive, Foster City, CA 94404, USA. t: (800) 227 8431.

Why Reference Systems are Not Like Pork Bellies 'Today, some database providers would have you believe that all reference systems are alike. A commodity. And that you should buy on price alone. Don't believe it for a second. There are huge diferences that you should know about before you buy. For information on how to shop for and critically compare reference systems, call 1–800–227–8431 ext 5300. And ask for a free copy of '*The Complete Guide to Evaluating and Selecting Reference Systems*'. Because buying a reference system should be based on information – not speculation.'

The Library Market 'Gathering information from the academic, business, legal, health, computer, and general reference areas, Information Access Company provides the most widely used and recognised databases in the library industry. The company provides two dozen databases for microform, CD-ROM, and wide area distribution delivery . . . Currently, CD-ROM represents the most popular form of delivery, and provides access to the entire *InfoTrac* family of index/abstract, full text, and multi-source databases. Wide area distribution, the fastest growing method, gives libraries three separate options for delivery. Libraries choose to load magnetic tapes of data on their own mainframe system, or access data through systems provided by OPAC vendors, or access data directly through the Information Access Center in Medford, Mass.

Besides the delivery options . . . libraries also have a wide array of choices in the types of databases they use. The first, the *index/abstract product*, is the heart of the product line. Index/abstract databases – such as *Magazine Index*, *Business Index*, *Legal Index* – contain thousands of citations and short abstracts to popular, general interest, scholarly, business, and specialized magazines, journals, and newspapers . . . The second form, the *full text product*, works in conjunction with its corresponding index/abstract database. Upon entering a search term, the user not only generates a list of indexes, but also pulls up the full text of designated articles, providing a full reference source to accompany the citation. These include *Magazine ASAP, Expanded Academic ASAP*, and *Business ASAP*. The third form, the *multi-source product*, provides a one-stop reference solution, encompassing directories, reference books, dictionaries, and pamphlets to produce a multi-faceted approach to research. *General BusinessFile* and *Health Reference Center* are two multi-source products which have answered health and business related questions for thousands of patrons.

The Corporate Market 'For over twenty years, corporate searchers have made Information Access Company their first stop for online business information. These databases cover business and industry, management, computers, technology, legal, health, marketing, international business, and general interest topics with detailed sources that no other information provider can offer. The rich content of these sources includes trade publications, industry newsletters, business journals, newswires, newspapers, research reports, government publications, and specialized economic, professional, and scholarly periodicals.

Twelve commercial online services, including *DIALOG, Mead Data Central*, and *Dow Jones News/Retrieval*, give these index/abstract and full text files worldwide availability . . . The databases' extensive international content and source coverage, with 1800 leading worldwide publications spanning fifty countries, heightens the international appeal of these products.'

(36) #1335 Reuters Business Information 85 Fleet Street, London EC4P 4AJ, UK. t: (44 171) 250 1122; f: 324 4527.

How can Reuters help you be better informed? . . . Reuters has been in the business of information for longer than most, and always at the cutting edge of innovation. Our new products continue the tradition of using technology to bring people and information together. Business information products do this simply, by providing a superb combination of information sources which are amazingly easy to get into and use, and, most importantly of all, are cost-effective. The *Business Information* products access a press database which contains a carefully chosen and comprehensive range of over 600 publications. Key broadsheet and business newswires from the UK, Europe and around the world; newswires, providing the very latest business and political updates, and a wide selection of magazines and trade journals. All these, combined with market price data, give an unparalleled coverage of the business world.

Letting you get at all this information is a graphical user interface based on Windows. Its simple design can turn novice to expert in less than ten minutes. With nothing more than a few clicks of a mouse, Business Information products open up a new world of information to anyone in business, and help you to find the edge you need to succeed.'

Three services are marketed under the Reuters Business Information umbrella – *Reuter Business Briefing*, *Reuter EU Briefing*, and *Reuter Insurance Briefing* – as noted in this excerpt from the Newsletter *Information At Work* issued in early 1995 'for customers of Reuters Business Information':

'If you use the Reuter Briefing services (*Business Briefing*, *Insurance Briefing*, *EU Briefing*) Current News offers instant access to up-to-the-second news from around the world. Complementing the five-year archive of publications which forms the core of the Briefing services, Current News enables you to follow events as they unfold, and to read stories that may not be reported in newspapers until the following day.

All Briefing users have access to news from *Reuters*. Reuters offers perhaps the definitive source of global breaking news, with a 140–year tradition of fast, accurate, and objective reporting. Stories, from journalists based in 75 countries, are normally available within seconds of being filed, and are categorised into four sections: *Economic*, *Political*, *General*, and *Sport*.

Customers of Reuter Insurance Briefing can see the Reuter news split into two specialised categories: *Risk*, which deals with items relating to political and economic risk; and *Insurance*, which covers corporate and industrial insurance news. Insurance Briefing also gives exclusive direct access to the *Lloyd's Information Casualty Wire*, which provides worldwide information on marine, non-marine, and aviation casualties, as well as port conditions, weather hazards and labour disputes.

Business Briefing additionally offers access to the *Regulatory News Service* (RNS). RNS is the *London Stock Exchange*'s method of distributing statutory company announcements. It carries the full-text of items such as results, bid and offer documents, and acquisition announcements. Reuter Business Alert can also access the Reuters and RNS parts of Current News, ensuring the latest information is delivered automatically to Business Alert users.'

(vi) Scheduled online services

The three main general business hosts are: Dow Jones News/Retrieval, FT Profile, and Knight-Ridder Information (Data-Star/Dialog) and it is instructive to classify the databases offered by the largest – Knight-Ridder – as of late 1994. Because there is so much data and information offered by Knight-Ridder Information, it is easy to become overwhelmed! But once the information is categorized into broad categories (I use primarily the chapter framework of this book), then the whole becomes more understandable. The classification used is:

(I) DATA

(II) NEWS

- *General newswires*
- *Specialist newswires*
- *Fulltext newsletter services*
- *Full text newspapers*

(III) LEGAL, ECONOMIC AND POLITICAL ENVIRONMENTS

- *International*
- *Europe*
- *United Kingdom*
- *United States*

(IV) CORPORATIONS

- *American Business Information*
- *Dun & Bradstreet Corporation*
- *ICC Information Group*
- *Infocheck Group*
- *Jordans*
- *McGraw-Hill*
- *Media General Financial Services*
- *Pearson*
- *Prentice-Hall Legal and Financial*
- *Primark*
- *Reed Elsevier*
- *Thomas Publishing Company*
- *Thomson Corporation*
- *TRW Business Credit Services*

(V) FINANCIAL INSTITUTIONS AND MARKETS

- *Market research*
- *Newspapers*

(VI) INDEXES AND GUIDES

- *Organizations*
- *People*
- *Electronic imperative*
- *By form of literature*
- *By subject*

(i) DATA

Knight-Ridder MoneyCenter

(ii) NEWS

- *General newswires*

Agence France Presse English Wire
AP News
Knight Ridder/Tribune Business News
Reuters
UPI News

- *Specialist newswires*

BNA Daily News
Business Wire
Federal News Service
Newswire ASAP
PR Newswire

- *Fulltext newsletter services*

Magazine ASAP/Magazine Database
McGraw-Hill Publications Online
Predicasts: Newsletters/PTS Newsletter Database
Newsearch
Reuter Textline/Textline Global News
Trade & Industry ASAP/Trade and Industry Database

- *Full text newspapers*

Financial Times
Independent
Times/Sunday Times (London)
USA Today

(iii) LEGAL, ECONOMIC AND POLITICAL ENVIRONMENTS

- *International*

Country Report Service
EconBase: Time Series and Forecasts
EIU Business International
Predicasts: Forecasts
PTS International Forecasts
Quest Economics Database
Tradeline

- *Europe*

CELEX
DRT European Business Reports
Spicers Centre for Europe – European Community Law

- *United Kingdom*

Spearhead – UK Analysis of EC Law

- *United States*

CIS
Commerce Business Daily
Federal Register
Federal Register Abstracts
GPO Monthly Catalog
GPO Publications Reference File
Journal of Commerce
Predicasts: US Time Series
PTS US Forecasts
PTS US Time Series
Tax Notes Today

(iv) CORPORATIONS

- *American Business Information*

American Business Directory
American Business 20 Plus Companies

- *Dun & Bradstreet Corporation*

D&B – Dun's Business Update
D&B – Dun's Electronic Business Directory
D&B – Dun's Financial Records Plus
D&B – Dun's Market Identifiers
D&B – European Dun's Market Identifiers
D&B – International Dun's Market Identifiers
D&B – Million Dollar Directory
Dun & Bradstreet Marketing Information on European Companies
Dun's Market Identifiers
Key British Enterprises Financial Performance
Moody's Corporate News – International
Moody's Corporate News – US
Moody's Corporate Profiles
Who Owns Whom

- *ICC Information Group*

ICC British Company Annual Reports
ICC British Company Directory
ICC British Company Financial Datasheets
ICC Directory of UK Companies
ICC Full-text UK Company Reports
ICC International Business Research
ICC Stockbroker Research
ICC UK Financial Datasheets

- *Infocheck Group*

INFOCHECK

- *Jordans*

JordanWatch – UK Companies

- *McGraw-Hill*

Standard & Poor's Corporate Descriptions plus News
Standard & Poor's Daily News
Standard & Poor's Register – Biographical
Standard & Poor's Register – Corporate

- *Media General Financial Services*

Media General Plus

- *Pearson*

Extel Cards
Extel International Financial Cards
Extel International News Cards
FT Mergers and Acquisitions

- *Prentice-Hall Legal and Financial*

M & A Filings

- *Primark*

Disclosure
Disclosure Database
Disclosure/Spectrum Ownership
SEC Online

- *Reed Elsevier*

Corporate Affiliations
Kompass Europe
Kompass UK

- *Thomas Publishing Company*

Thomas Register Online

- *Thomson Corporation*

Company Intelligence
Insider Trading Monitor
INVESTEXT
Predicasts: Annual Reports

- *TRW Business Credit Services*

TRW Business Credit Profiles

(v) FINANCIAL INSTITUTIONS AND MARKETS

- *Market research*

Consumer Reports
Datamonitor Market Reports
Euromonitor Market Direction
FT Reports – Finance, Insurance
ICC Keynotes Market Analysis

- *Newspapers*

American Banker
Bond Buyer

(vi) INDEXES AND GUIDES

- *Organizations*

Encyclopedia of Associations
Research Centers and Services Directory

- *People*

Biography Master Index

- *Electronic imperative*

Bibliodata: Full Text Sources Online
Directory of Online and Portable Databases

- *By form of literature*

ASI
Book Review Index
Books In Print
British Books In Print
Current Contents Search
Dissertation Abstracts Online
FINDEX
Gale Directory of Publications and Broadcast Media
IHS International Standards and Specifications
LC MARC – Books
Magazine Index
National Newspaper Index
Newspaper & Periodical Abstracts
Social SciSearch – Social Science Citation Index
Ulrich's International Periodicals Directory
US National Newspaper Index

- *By subject*

ABI/INFORM
Accounting & Tax Database
Congressional Records Abstracts
Economic Literature Index

FINIS: Financial Industry Information Service
Infomat International Business
Insurance Periodicals Index
Legal Resource Index
Management and Marketing Abstracts
Management Contents
National Technical Information Service
National Criminal Justice Reference Service
PAIS International
Predicasts: Indexes/PTS F & S Index/PTS Prompt
SVB Banking, Economy, Management
Trade & Industry Index
US Political Science Documents

Not all of these published products are referenced elsewhere in this book; but most of them are.

The main legal hosts are:

(37) #1336 Lexis/Nexis 9443 Springboro Pike, Miamisburg, OH 45342, USA. t: (1 513) 865 7607; f: 865 6949.

'Mead Data Central developed the LEXIS service in 1973, it was the world's first online legal research service. Six years later, MDC launched the NEXIS service, which now contains a vast array of news and business information sources from around the world. More than 650,000 active users have access to the LEXIS/NEXIS services. An average of 2.5 million documents are added each week to the more than 322 million documents online. The LEXIS/NEXIS services have grown to include:

- Over 2,300 continuously updated, full-text news and business information sources including newspapers, wire services, magazines, major news sources from around the world
- Financial statements and reports on public and private companies worldwide
- Investment analyst reports from prestigious brokerage firms around the world
- Cases, statutes and other legal materials from the EC, the UK (including Northern Ireland), France, Canada, Australia, New Zealand, the Irish Republic, China, the Commonwealth of Independent States, and the US
- The full text of 1.5 million patents filed with the US Patent Office since 1975
- Analytical surveys of countries and regions prepared by government and private organizations.'

(38) #1337 WESTLAW 620 Opperman Drive, Eagan, MN 55123, USA. t: (1 612) 687 7000; f: 687 7302.

WESTLAW has a gateway to the *Knight-Ridder* service, which significantly increases its database coverage. WESTLAW – as does Lexis profiled above – organizes its sources into a series of 'Libraries', the majority of which cover the relevant United States laws, regulations, codes, etc. and federal and state court decisions – as well as commentary and analysis reproduced from appropriate journals and newsletters. The WESTLAW Libraries most relevant to the financial system are:

- Antitrust and Trade Regulation Library
- Bankruptcy Library
- Business Organizations Library
- Commercial Law & Contracts Library
- Delaware Corporation Law Library
- Federal International Law – Treasury Decisions Data Base
- Federal Law Library
- Insurance Library
- International Law Library
- Pension & Retirement Benefits Library
- Real Property Library
- Securities and Blue Sky Laws Library
- Taxation Library

In addition there is a *Finance & Banking Library*, which:

"Contains the complete text of US federal and state court decisions, statutes and regulations, administrative law publications, specialized files, and texts and periodicals dealing with banking and financial services, including customer and institutional transactions, truth-in-lending laws, and consumer credit. Includes relevant decisions made by the US Supreme Court (1790 to date), US Court of Appeals (1891 to date) and US District Courts (1789 to date); related statutes and regulations from the US Code (current), the Federal Register (1980 to date), and the US Code of Federal Regulations (current); Comptroller General Decisions (1921 to date); Federal Deposit Insurance Corporation Materials (1979 to date); Federal Home Loan Bank Board Materials (1964 to 1989); the Federal Reserve Bulletin (1980 to date); the Federal Reserve Regulatory Service (current); the Office of the Comptroller of the Currency Banking Bulletins (1961 to date), the Office of the Comptroller of the Currency Banking Circulars (1968 to date), the Office of the Comptroller of the Currency Interpretative Letters (1977 to date), the Office of the Comptroller of the Currency Quarterly Journal (1962 to date); the Office of Thrift Supervision Regulatory Bulletins, Thrift Bulletins, and Legal Alert Memos (1988 to date), and the Office of Thrift Supervision and Resolution Trust Corporation News Releases (August 1989 to date); relevant case laws for all 50 states and the District of Columbia; such specialized files as the BNA Financial Services Database (comprising BNA's Banking Report and Securities and Regulation & Law Report), BNA Banking Daily, BNA International Finance Daily, BNA Headlines, and DataMerge's Financial Sources Handbook; topical highlights; and relevant law reviews, texts, and bar journals."[175]

Some other relevant niche scheduled hosts are briefly described here: though one of them, *MAID*, is positioning itself to try to join the very large players:

(39) #1338 CBD Search Services 21525 Ridgetop Circle, Suite 200, Sterling, VA 20166–6510, USA. t: (800) CBD 4551/(1 703) 450 1882; f: 450 1961.

'When the paper *Commerce Business Daily* just doesn't meet your needs . . . Bidding for government contracts is dynamic. With ever-increasing competition and complexity in the process, you must make use of all effective resources. You can't afford to overlook a potential bid. You want the CBD on a timely basis. And wading through the paper CBD is a chore. The answer: Take *ACTION*!

Of the electronic CBD services available, only ACTION gives you all of the following (and at no extra charge!):

- The full CBD daily
- Ability to perform unlimited bid request searches
- Your own search software included
- Network compatible
- Choose from Microsoft Windows, Microsoft DOS or Macintosh version
- Provide a summary Table of Contents that the printed CBD does not contain
- Add your own electronic notes
- Electronic highlighter pen included
- Mouse supported but not required
- Electronic bookmarks
- Built-in thesaurus
- Automatic daily or repetitive search profiles
- Word processor exporting and easy printing
- Available by 3.00 p.m. Eastern time the day *before* the issue date of the paper edition
- No additional software is required: ACTION is complete
- No connect time charges
- No keyword search match charges
- No other hidden charges that will nickel and dime you into frustration . . .

With *ACTION-CBD SEARCH* you receive the entire CBD by downloading from our system or by choosing FTP transfer or EMAIL via the Internet . . . (It) costs $745 per year for a single user . . . *CBDCheap* is a service for those organizations who only want to see notices from specific CBD categories . . . The Cost is $60/year per Section ($75/year per Section for Internet delivery) plus a $50 setup fee.'

(40) #1339 LegiTech 1029 J Street, Suite 450, Sacramento, CA 95814, USA. t: (1 916) 447 1886; f: 447 1109.

- *Washington On-Line* 'Accurate and timely tracking of Bill introductions, actions and calendars. Follow the progress of every Bill from introduction to the Oval Office . . . The weekly *Congressional Digest* keeps you in touch with political nuance and maneuvering. Learn why some bills move quickly while others are bottled up. Stay on top of Confirmation and Special Investigative Hearings . . . Budget one annual subscription fee and get the access you want. Choose Unlimited Access or Hourly Rate . . . Make the electronic revolution work for you.'

(41) #1340 Lloyd's Maritime Information Services One Singer Street, London EC2A 4LQ, UK. t: (44 171) 490 1720; f: 250 3142. *Also* 1200 Summer Street, Stamford, CT 06905, USA. t: (1 203) 359 8383; f: 358 0437. A joint venture company owned by *Lloyd's Register* and *Lloyd's of London Press.*

'*Shipping Information Services* is the division within the Company with particular responsibility for the sales and marketing of data . . . Information is recorded . . . related to the "birth, life and death" of known propelled seagoing merchant ships, their owners, reported movements, casualties, and charter fixtures . . . Lloyd's Agents are situated in some 1800 ports throughout the world and regularly report to Lloyd's of London Press on the movements of ships, together with maritime and aviation casualties and other significant events . . . Other sources of authoritative information include government departments and agencies, port authorities, classification societies, ship owners, shipbuilders, and maritime organisations . . . *AS+ For Windows* is a "PC Management Information system, incorporating the Vessels, Owners and Newbuildings of the world fleet, from the Lloyd's databases" . . . The *SEADATA* On-Line Maritime Information System "provides the most timely, compehensive and validated maritime information currently available from a single source".'

(42) #1341 MAID Maid House, 18 Dufferin Street, London EC1Y 8PD, UK. t: (44 171) 253 6900; f: 253 0060 *and* 352 Park Avenue S, New York, NY 10010–1709, USA. t: (1 212) 447 6900; f: 447 0060.

'The largest single source of news, research and corporate information. If you can't find what you're looking for in MAID, it probably doesn't exist . . . One screen – total control. Unless you know how to use it, even the most powerful tool is valueless. That's why we've spent 8 years designing a highly sophisticated, immensely powerful system that can be mastered in less than 10 minites. Whether you're a complete technophobe or a computer whiz. MAID's simplicity is due to the unique WorldSearch Screen, our own invention. Nobody else has it. In fact, nobody else has anything like it.

If you can read the WorldSearch screen, you can operate MAID, it's that simple. WorldSearch makes it easy to find what you want – even if it is the proverbial needle in a haystack. You can search by company, brand, product, country, name, phrase or even a single word. WorldSearch makes it possible to move between Newsline, Companyline and Researchline. All you have to do is hit a button.

Newsline plugs you into 10 million articles from 4,000 newspapers, magazines, journals and news wires in 190 countries. You can source items back as far as 10 years and articles are translated into English from 17 different languages.

Companyline gives you access to 4.7 million corporate financial statements, SIC listings and organisation records from all over the globe.

Researchline houses over 50,000 market research reports, although that number grows every day. Quality reports come from around the world.

"Market Analysis and Information Database Inc (a worldwide provider of business information services to Fortune 1000 companies; formerly known as M.A.I.D.) has formed *Profound Inc* (655 Madison Avenue, New York, NY 10022, USA. t: (1 212) 750 6900; f: 750 0660), an independent subsidiary . . . to "market its online database to a broader array of potential customers . . . There is a clarion call from companies of every size and stature for online business intelligence systems that are as easy to use as consumer online services" . . . Following this announcement, Profound signed a technology and marketing agreement with *Adobe Systems* to integrate Adobe Acrobat technology into the user interface, as well as capturing all market research, news and company profiles in Adobe's *Portable Document Format* (PDF), an open file format that preserves the appearance of documents across all major computer platforms and printers. This software will allow users to view and print exact replicas of original documents, including all graphics, illustrations and color . . . An economical pricing structure offers access to Profound basic Membership Services for $19.95 per month plus $6.95 per hour online time. This provides a *Custom Alert* service that displays news headlines and report titles, and continuously updated newswires, and market and country snapshots. *Extended Services* (i.e. viewing the full text of articles, reports and special market and country briefings) are available for additional cost."[176]

(43) #1342 OCLC 6565 Frantz Road, Dublin, OH 43107–3395, USA. t: (800) 848 5878; f: (1 614) 764 6096 *and* OCLC Europe, 7th Floor, Tricorn House, 51–53 Hagley Road, Edgbaston, Birmingham B16 8TP, UK. t: (44 121) 456 4656; f: 456 4680.

'Nonprofit computer service and research organization whose participants include more than 17,000 libraries in the US and 51 other countries and territories. OCLC systems help libraries locate, acquire, catalog and lend library materials . . . *FirstSearch* offers end users searching . . . and *EPIC* offers trained professionals low-cost searching.' OCLC has considerably expanded its online coverage in recent years; and, apart from its own databases:

- *ArticleFirst*
- *ContentsFirst*
- *OCLC Online Union Catalog*
- *PapersFirst*
- *ProceedingsFirst*
- *WorldCat*

it now hosts a wide range of third party databases, including:

- *ABI/Inform*
- *Biography Index*
- *Book Data*
- *BusinessNews*
- *Business Organizations, Agencies and Publications Directory*
- *Business Perodicals Index*
- *Cumulative Book Index*
- *Disclosure Corporate Snapshots*
- *Dissertation Abstracts*
- *Findex*
- *GPO Monthly Catalog*
- *Index to Legal Periodicals*
- *Newspaper Abstracts*
- *PAIS*
- *Wilson Business Abstracts*
- *Worldscope Global*

(vii) CONSUMER ONLINE SERVICES

The three major competitors – each carrying significant amounts of financial information at a relatively low cost – are:

(44) #1343 America Online 8619 Westwood Center Drive, Vienna, VA 22182, USA. t: (800) 227 6364/(1 703) 448 8700.

(45) £1344 Prodigy Services Company 445 Hamilton Avenue, White Plains, NY 10601, USA. t: (1 913) 993 8000.

and the service which we will profile:

(46) #1345 CompuServe 1 Redcliff Street, PO Box 676, Bristol BS99 1YN, UK. t: (800) 289378/(44 117) 976 0681.

- CompuServe: the world's leading online information service with almost 3 million members
- Over 2,000 services covering almost every subject under the sun
- Accessible via a local call in most major European cities
- Worldwide e-mail links to over 20 million addresses – from Internet to cc:Mail
- Over 800 leading software and hardware companies – from Apple to Zenith – providing support
- Stock quotes from the major exchanges around the world
- Latest news and sports action. Global and local weather reports
- The very best travel information – including AA Roadwatch and international airline schedules.

Premium Services are all the products which can't be made available free (*Basic Services*) or on a price-per-minute basis (*Extended Services*). These products deliver extremely valuable information which is charged for on a *per transaction* or *per report* basis.

- *Executive News Service* Create your own folders from the world's major newswires including 'PA' News and Reuters.
- *UK Company Library* Access to the world's most respected sources of business information such as Dun & Bradstreet, ICC, Infocheck, JordanWatch and Key British Enterprises company financial reports.
- *UK Newspaper Library* Database of full-text articles from leading newspapers including The Daily Telegraph and Sunday Telegraph, The European, The Financial Times, Today, The Guardian, The Times and Sunday Times, The Independent and Independent on Sunday.

CompuServe offers access to a remarkably wide range of databases, given one's perception of the host as primarily targetting itself to the consumer market. For instance, all of these are listed as being available via this host, directly or indirectly:

- *AP Datastream*
- *AP Online*
- *BusinessWire*
- *Citibase*
- *Compustat*
- *Corporate Affiliations Online*
- *Current Market Snapshot*
- *Daily Comment*
- *Disclosure SEC Database*
- *Dun's Electronic Business Directory*
- *Dun's Market Identifiers*
- *ExecuGrid*
- *FundWatch*
- *Futures Focus*
- *Global Report*
- *I/B/E/S United States Database*
- *Independent Insurance*
- *International Securities Database*
- *International Stocks Database*
- *Investext*
- *Investor's Forum*
- *Investor's Guide and Mutual Fund Directory*
- *IRS Publications*
- *Lexis/Nexis Forum*
- *Market Briefings*
- *MJK Commodities Database*
- *MMS Currency*
- *MMS Economic and Foreign Exchange Survey*
- *MMS Treasury*
- *MMS Weekly Market Analysis*
- *Money Magazine Financial Information Center*
- *NAIC Forum*
- *News-a-Tron Market Reports*
- *NewsGrid*
- *OTC NewsAlert*

- *RateGram Online*
- *Reuter Financial Report*
- *S&P MarketScope*
- *S&P Online*
- *Thomas Register Online*
- *Tickerscreen*
- *Trendvest Ratings*
- *TRW Business Credit Profiles*
- *US Government Publications*
- *UPI News*
- *Value Line Annual Reports*
- *Value Line DataFile*
- *Value Line Estimates and Projections File*
- *Value Line Qaurterly Reports*
- *Washington Post*

(viii) PORTABLE DATA SYSTEMS

Two good examples of what now is possible from hand-held systems – one from the UK and one from the US – are:

(47) #1346 Futures Pager 19–21 Great Tower Street, London, EC3R 5AQ, UK. t: (44 171) 895 9400; f: 895 8676.

'The UK's leading supplier of portable financial information . . . Futures Pager is the choice of the City. Dealers at 28 of London's largest 30 banks (*Euromoney* survey June 1993) use it to monitor up to 100 contracts traded in nine global financial centers . . . Delivers a comprehensive and reliable service which includes:

- Currencies, Futures, Interest Rates and Indices, updated every 2 minutes, 24 hours a day
- Major Government statistics and key Financial News
- Prices and News direct from REUTERS, the world's No 1 financial and news reporting service
- Optional enhancements such as Commodities, Daily highs, lows and traded volumes; Limit Alerts and Personal Paging and Directus.

The current costs are a £300 deposit and then £85/month for the 'Financial, Forex Indices & History' services. This price includes all Exchange fees and equipment costs and there are no additional connection of installation costs.'

(48) #1347 IDD Information Services Two World Trade Center, New York, NY 10048, USA. t: (1 212) 432 0045; f: 912 1457.

- *Tradeline Pocket Stock Guide* 'Put Wall Street in your shirt pocket . . . Stock performance information – anytime, anywhere . . . An electronic source of in-depth historical information on almost 6,000 New York, American and NASDAQ stocks, and over 120 leading market indices . . . Instantly evaluate an important investment recommendation the minute you hear it, go that extra mile for a client by providing instant information, or just catch up on your research while at home with your family . . . No more fumbling through bulky paper guides or newspapers, no more expensive on-line subscriptions, and no more complicated PC hookups. Information and screening capabilities normally available only on a PC are now available at your fingertips . . . And since financial information is constantly changing, periodic updates will be available on a subscription basis.

The Tradeline Pocket Stock Guide is one of the newest *Digital Books* available for the *Franklin Digital Book System*. Each Unit holds two Digital Books, containing up to 45Mb of data per book – that's equivalent to over 40,000 pages of information.' (The unit measures 5″ x 3″ x 1/2″ and weighs 4.6 ounces. 5 line 40 x 160 continuous pixel display.)

(ix) GATEWAY SYSTEMS

A UK example is BT:

(49) #1348 BT Business Information Systems Network House, Brindley Way, Hemel Hempstead, Herts HP3 8BR, UK. t: (0800) 200 700.

'Subscribe to BT's *Business Information Services* and you won't need to employ expensive outside agencies to find the facts and figures you need. Now everything you require – from customer contact details to credit analysis, from companies' profit and loss accounts to market sector reports, from directorships held to business news and analysis – can be accessed in seconds, using an ordinary PC. BT can offer you all this information from a single source – and you can access it from anywhere in the UK, from the comfort of your own office, or anywhere else where there is a PC and a telephone line . . . the portfolio includes many of the leading suppliers of business information, all included with your subscription and available with one telephone call, one password and one bill.'

Hosts accessible via this gateway include:

- *CCN Business Information*
- *Dun & Bradstreet International Risk Management Services*
- *Electronic Yellow Pages*
- *FT Profile*
- *ICC Information Group*
- *Infocheck*
- *Jordans*
- *New Prestel*
- *Reed Information Services*
- *Reuter Textline*

(x) DOCUMENT SUPPLY SERVICES

This is currently a very active arena, with competitive suppliers originating from various parts of the overall sector:

(50) #1349 British Library Document Supply Centre Boston Spa, Wetherby, West Yorkshire LS23 7BQ, UK. t: (44 1937) 546000.

'Provides more than 14,500 industrial, public, government and academic customers with the documents they need for research, information and education. Every two seconds it lends or photocopies documents from its stock of 7,000,000 books, journals, reports and theses, covering almost every subject in any language. It is the largest, fastest, most comprehensive and most efficient service of its kind in the world.

Because of recent interpretations of US copyright law and following legal advice about its photocopying services to the USA, the British Library has held discussions with the *Association of American Publishers* (AAP) on the photocopy service provided by BLDSC to US customers. The Library has decided to withdraw its royalty free photocopy service from the US and will in future provide only its royalty paid *Copyright Cleared Service* to US customers. At the same time the Library will be making arrangements with the UK Copyright Licensing Agency and the US Copyright Clearance Center for royalties in respect of this service to be paid to US publishers according to rates that publishers themselves set individually.

The British Library also discussed with AAP members the issue of electrocopying rights and after a meeting on 9 July (1993) AAP President Nicholas Velioes said: 'It is to the benefits of all parties, whether publishers, libraries or users to anticipate the opportunities presented by the new technologies. In cooperating with publishers from the outset the British Library is certainly moving into the future in a manner consistent with Copyright Law and serving the interests of all parties' (*Document Supply News*, September 1993, p. 2).

- *Inside Information*. A service offering access to the contents pages of over 10,000 of the most frequently requested journal titles held at the Centre. Can be searched **online** via Internet connection to the University of Bath's online service. (The file is also available on **cdrom**, as is a file *Inside Conferences*, containing details of conference papers from the 15,000 conference publications collected by the Centre.)'

(51) #1350 Capitol Publications 1101 King Street, Suite 444, Alexandria, VA 22313–2053, USA. t: (800) 327 7025/(1 703) 683 4100; f: (800) 645 4104/(1 703) 739 6490.

'Provides its subscribers with a quarterly listing of important federal documents that cover a broad range of issues . . . This miniature sample of the *Document Retrieval Master List* is designed to show you a few of the government publications that are available rapidly and efficiently through this service. Most of the documents listed here also may be obtained from various government offices for little or no charge.'

(52) #1351 Congressional Information Service 4520 East-West Highway, Suite 800, Bethesda, MD 20814–3389, USA. t: (800) 638 8380/(1 301) 654 1550; f: 654 4033. e: info@cispubs.com

'With CIS's *Government Documents on Demand*, anyone can easily obtain virtually any publication identified in the *CIS/Index* to congressional publications and legislative histories (since 1970) and of the *American Statistics Index* to federal statistical publications (since the early 1960s). Unlike dealing with the government, with CIS needed publications are always in stock.'

(53) #1352 Disclosure 5161 River Road, Bethesda, MD 20816, USA. t: (1 301) 951 1300; f: 657 1962 *and* 26–31 Whiskin Street, London EC1R 0BP, UK. t: (44 171) 278 7848; f: 278 3898. gale2 has 'Disclosure First.

- *Original Glossy Annual Reports from Anywhere in the World* '30 January 1995 . . . Between now and April, some 25,000 annual reports will be issued by firms throughout the world – and virtually any of them can be delivered to your desk within days of publication on the strength of a single phone call. With 100,000 documents collected from more than 60 countries, often in sets going back 3 years of more, international corporate information specialist Disclosure now owns the world's largest library of original annual reports. Despite the huge growth in CD-ROM and electronic delivery of public company documents, in which it is a world leader, Disclosure is finding an increasing demand for the "real thing". The Original preserves the image and integrity of the company and is useful for presentations. An annual report for any international public company, for any year back to 1990 or further costs £19.'

(54) #1353 Legal Information Resources Elphin House, 1 New Road, Mytholmroyd, Hebden Bridge, West Yorkshire, HX7 5DZ, UK. t: (44 1422) 886277; f: 886250.

'*DocDel* gives you rapid access to material from our library of some 600 journals, under our licence from the Copyright Licensing Agency Ltd, with delivery by fax, DX or post.'

(55) #1354 Reed Information Services Financial Publications, Windsor Court, East Grinstead Road, East Grinstead, West Sussex, RH19 1XA, UK. t: (44 1342) 335962; f: 335977.

Annual Accounts Express Delivery 'As the publishers of the world's leading source of information on international banks, we maintain a comprehensive library of over 3,000 Annual Reports from banks in over 150 countries . . . You will receive the accounts you want by return or fax . . . £25 (UK) or $40 (Overseas) for each set of Accounts.'

(56) #1355 SNL Document Retrieval 410 East Main Street, PO Box 2104, Charlottesville, VA 22902, USA. t: (800) 969 4121/(1 804) 977 4121; f: 971 2060 *and* 601 Indiana Avenue NW, Suite 503, Washington, DC 20004, USA. t: (1 202) 347 2724; f: 347 5278.

- *Specialists in Financial Institution Documents* 'When you need quick, reliable delivery of documents for banks, thrifts, or other financial services companies, you need SNL Document Retrieval . . . (It) is your direct link to Washington's regulatory environment. It is the only service bureau with operations solely devoted to providing information on the banking, thrift and financial services industries. We employ an experienced staff of information specialists who are capable of assisting clients ranging from the experienced banker to the individual investor.'
- *Document Retrieval Services* 'SNL Document Retrieval maintains an extensive in-house library containing 10Qs, annual reports, 10Ks and proxies for every publicly traded bank, thrift and non-bank financial services institution in the country. Our internal resources also include regulatory documents from federal banking agencies, congressional banking committee testimony, branch purchase applications and approval, and most merger agreements. Our vast, internal resources mean that almost all of the documents you need are available on-demand. When they are not, SNL Document Retrieval draws upon its inside knowledge of the regulatory agencies (including the OTS, FDIC, RTC, OCC, SEC and Federal Reserve), in order to quickly track down hard-to-find documents and information).'
- *Watch Services* 'Need to be informed of filings by investors or competitors? Need timely access to vital documents as they are released? Then our Watch Service is right for you . . . (We) will put any bank, thrift or other financial services institution "on watch" and immediately dispatch any documents you request, via fax or overnight delivery, as they are filed.'
- *Conversion Watch Services* 'For investors, attorneys and underwriters who need to know which mutual thrifts:
- Are the most attractive and likely conversion candidates
- Have announced intentions to convert
- Have filed applications to convert
- Have had their conversion applications approved

All this data is available – with same day fax notification – for every savings institution regulated by the Office of Thrift Supervision. (State-chartered banks are covered on a best-effort basis.)'

(57) #1356 Swets Subscription Service PO Box 830/2160 SZ Lisse, The Netherlands. t: (31 2521) 35111; f: 15888.

SwetScan is an electronic scanning service offering the contents page information of 14,000 scholarly and research journals immediately after publication of the titles – made available on paper, diskette, tape or on-line through the *DataSwets* worldwide information and communication system. *SwetDoc* offers the supply of a copy of any article found in the SwetScan contents pages.

(58) #1357 UMI 300 North Zeeb Road, PO Box 1346, Ann Arbor, MI 48106–1346, USA. t: (1 313) 761 4700; 665 5022. *Also* White Swan House, Godstone, Surrey RH9 8LW, UK. t: (44 1883) 744123; f: 744024. e: umi@ipiumi.demon.co.uk.

- *Document Delivery* 'UMI's *Article Clearinghouse* and *The Information Store* have joined forces to provide a document delivery service which makes available full issues of magazines and journals plus individual articles. All magazines and journals are copyright cleared and a choice of delivery options, including electronic delivery, is offered. Over 14,500 journals, 7,000 newspapers, and 1,200,000 doctoral dissertations are available in the Article Clearinghouse collection, including documents from the following UMI CD-ROM databases: Accounting and Tax Database; ABI/INFORM; Banking Information Source . . . Newspaper Abstracts, Periodical Abstracts.'
- *ProQuest Power Pages* 'The name of the network configuration for UMI's scanned image databases. This automated document delivery system offers a choice of configurations to streamline the information retrieval process by providing a faster, more convenient means of accessing a broad range of materials. Researchers can locate thousands of citations from a wide range of subject areas – quickly and easily. A single source will provide them with access to articles from hundreds of publications and allow them to retrieve an article facsimile at their own location or another of their choice within minutes. PowerPages works with a variety of network platforms and library automated systems . . . *PowerPages Components* ProQuest Network IMAGEserver software (NIS); CD-ROM jukebox; ProQuest Remote Image PRINTserver software; ProQuest Image FAXserver software.'

(59) #1358 UnCover Company 3801 East Florida Avenue, Suite 200, Denver, CO 80210, USA. t: (1 303) 758 3030; f: 758 5946; e: database.carl.org. *Also* c/o BH Blackwell, Hythe Bridge Street, Oxford OX1 2ET, UK. t: (44 1865) 261362; f: 261314 *and* c/o Readmore, 22 Cortlandt Street, New York, NY 10007–3194, USA. t: (800) 221 3306.

'UnCover is quite simply the largest on-line information source of its kind. The UnCover database contains over 4,000,000 articles drawn from over 13,000 journals . . . Using a computer, and appropriate communications hardware and software, you can access UnCover and search for articles on particular topics, by particular authors, or from particular journals. Once you have identified and requested an article of interest, it will be delivered to you, by fax, in twenty four hours or less.

(i) *UnCover Reveal* Users who have entered profiles on the system which include an e-mail address will be able to create a list of journal titles which are of interest to them. When UnCover checks in the next issue of any of those listed titles, the system will automatically send a copy of the table of contents information to the profiler's e-mail address . . . The recipient may respond via e-mail with an order for an article by replying to the message.'

(ii) *UnCover SOS* 'Allows you to order documents from over 16,000 periodicals indexed in the UnCover database. Uncover SOS (Single-Order-Source) staff will use UnCover to locate the citations you send us and order your articles for you. Articles will be sent to you via fax, usually within 24 hours and often much sooner. The charge per article for the Uncover SOS service is $10.00, plus copyright royalty fee. Orders sent outside the US and Canada will have a fax surcharge added.'

(60) #1359 Working Papers in Economics and Management University of Warwick Library, Coventry CV4 7AL, UK. t: (44 1203) 523523; f: 524211. e: w.papers@libris.lib.warwick.ac.uk.

'The aim is to develop a collection as comprehensive as possible in the areas of economics and management, and in other services of interest to researchers in economics and management. Items are obtained by donation, exchange and purchase. After four years, the Papers are deposited at the *British Library.* The collection contains about 25,000 items. 6,500 items are currently being received per annum, from about 700 institutions . . . A loan service operates within the UK by means of BLLD forms. For overseas clients, a photocopying service is offered, subject to copyright, using a system of pre-paid vouchers.' Access to bibliographic information about the collection can be gained via a range of e-mail, online, cdrom (and print) services.

16. I trust that the reader now appreciates the immense range of activity taking place revolving around the electronic distribution of publicly available financial data, information and documents to those who need such material. However, to end the book, I return to my earlier contention that – eventually – all the activity above will crystallize within two to three large real-time hosts. When one reads what was already available from one strong candidate for such a role in 1993, it is difficult to believe otherwise. The example is *Reuters* and I have taken the information from a variety of material issued by the company at that time:

Reuters real-time based services are gradually being merged into a seamless whole based on the concept of the *Reuter Terminal*. This is a sophisticated workstation which enables the customer to display Reuter data in a way that best suits their individual needs and preferences. The terminal comes equipped with Microsoft Windows, allowing several applications to be run at the same time, each in its own window. The windows can be sized and moved to suit customer requirements. Fonts can be sized and styled, either as a default for the whole screen, or for specific windows. The latter is particularly useful in busy screens, where users can emphasise the contents of some windows using bold, italic or a larger type face.

Using a mouse, fields of data can be copied from the Reuter Terminal into applications such as Microsoft Excel, where they will continue to be updated in real-time. A Japanese language version of the Terminal is available.

Reuter Terminal Graphics enables the customer to plot five types of chart (Tick/Line, Bar Chart, Candlestick, Volume, and Open Interest). Over a dozen Studies can be added to any data series displayed to provide analytical enhancement, including: moving averages; weighted close, RSI, moving average convergence/divergence; stochastics (fast or slow); and so on. A Toolbar feature rapidly zooms in on individual graph windows and changes the time period, chart type or instrument displayed. Up to six real-time and historical charts or studies can be displayed simultaneously and saved for instant retrieval. Every financial instrument available via the Reuter Terminal is given a *Reuter Instrument Code*: e.g. GBP= for spot sterling, F for Ford Motor Company. The codes are used to retrieve the data required.

Increasingly, customers can mix and match the real-time and also historically based services that they need access to; but for marketing purposes, Reuters presents its most advanced information services as a series of '2000' products. Each of these services is available via the Reuter Terminal, or as a datafeed direct to the customers internal network from Reuters own *Integrated Data Network*, which links Reuter data and news centres and customer sites worldwide. Within customer organizations, local-area network server-based versions of the Reuter products are being introduced.

Examples of '2000' series products are:

(i) *News 2000.* A system for delivering news on the Reuter Terminal. It provides an efficient, instantly updated display of latest news, together with a simple means of finding news on specific subjects of interest. Key features of News 2000 are:

- *Display of Latest News* A specially designed window displays all the latest news headlines and alerts and allows easy review of earlier news. It can be called up just by typing the code A.
- *Display of News Stories* The full text of stories can be accessed from headlines with a single action. Stories are displayed in a pop-up window to avoid disturbing the underlying screen.
- *Searching for News* Simple codes give access to news headlines by subject, providing a quick and accurate means of finding news. For example, US gives access to all news about the United States, ECI gives news on economic indicators. Market reports and other regularly issued stories can be called up directly into pop-up windows by their own codes.
- *Customized News* Customers can combine codes to search precisely for the news they require. These code combinations can be saved so that news of special interest can be called up at any time. The main categories of code are: Countries, Products, Topics, Industries, Commodities, Companies and Reports. Use of all these initially gives a set of headlines, with the exception of Reports, which takes the user

straight to a story in a pop-up window. The Countries codes are those of the International Standards Organisation (ISO). These are the same as the first two letters of the SWIFT code for each country's currency. Examples of product codes would be GB/O for UK gilt outlook, CHAT/ for London debt market talk. Topic codes would for instance be CEN for central bank intervention, ODD for 'human interest'. The code for news on individual companies is the Reuter Instrument Code; but corporate news can also be accessed by industry. The 20,000 or so companies quoted worldwide have been categorised under the Morgan Stanley International classification into 38 categories. Examples of commodities codes would be WOO for wool, and RUB for rubber news.

Finally, News 2000 has a range of regional and national news products, giving detailed local coverage, as optional extras.

(ii) *Securities 2000* Prices for over 100,000 instruments world-wide, including equities, options, index futures, corporate bonds and equity-linked debt. Prices are sourced from over a hundred exchanges and, for the over-the-counter markets, from some 1,200 individual contributors. This real-time data is supplemented by a range of historical data. Time and Sales displays for North American equity and equity option instruments provide a definitive audit trail of trades, cancellations and corrections, and can be used to monitor trends and determine market sentiment.

(iii) *Treasury 2000* Live prices, fed directly from the world's exchanges and contributed by leading institutions, are provided for: foreign exchange; money markets and treasury debt; sovereign and corporate debt; mortgage-backed and equity-linked securities; associated futures, options and OTC derivatives.

(iv) *Money 2000* Provides cash market data from almost 3,000 of the world's financial institutions supplemented with exchange traded financial futures and options information, giving wide coverage of: spot foreign exchange; forwards and deposits; treasury markets; forward rate agreements; OTC currency options; financial futures and options; spot crosses; money markets; synthetic agreements for forward exchange (SAFE) settlements; interest rate swaps. Reuters offer a number of specialist add-on services, of which these examples are of particular relevance to money and treasury dealings: *Capital Management* An independent consultancy service specialising in technical analysis of foreign exchange markets; *Prophesy* Real-time feed of US Treasury bills, notes and bonds traded in the interdealer broker market; *IDEA* Independent economic and market think-tank with extensive contacts among global economic policy makers; *MMS Market Analyses* Treasury, currency, European, UK, yen, Asia/Pacific, Canadian. Money 2000 dealers also have access to a wide range of national and international news and comment pages: including to *News 2000*.

Building on these basic information services, Reuters offer more specialised analytical tools. *Reuter Technical Analysis* is a high-performance, graphics-driven system for technical analysts in the foreign exchange, futures and commodity markets. *Decision 2000* is a sophisticated analytics system for traders and portfolio managers in the capital markets. It can assess the values of individual fixed-income instruments and optimise the values of portfolios based on them. Reuters also offers multi-user information systems for trading rooms and similar applications, which bring together information flows in digital or video format: these flows can include internal data and third-party data, as well as Reuter originated data. The systems of this type include *Triarch 2000*, an advanced digital information management system for medium to large dealing rooms. Another popular product is *Prism*, labelled as the world's most widely installed video switching system. In 1992, Reuters acquired *Visnews*, the world's largest international television news agency. Video images are being made available to Reuter Terminal users. In the dealing area, a two-phased introduction of Reuters latest foreign exchange transaction product, *Dealing 2000*, began in 1989. Its PC-based workstation uses artificial intelligence and advanced software to enhance users' dealing capabilities, enabling them, for example, to conduct four simultaneous 'conversations' with parties anywhere in the world. The second phase of Dealing 2000 adds a computerised matching facility, allowing automatic conclusion of trades between dealing banks when their buying and selling prices coincide.

Other services offered by Reuters include *INSTINET*, a real-time international electronic trading network for equities; and *GLOBEX*, an automated trading product for futures markets, designed to operate outside the regular trading hours of open-outcry markets. Reuters also create *Textline*, a full-text database of newspapers and magazines, available for searching on these online hosts: Data-Star, Dialog, FT Profile, Lexis/Nexis and Maid, as well as via BT Business Information Services.

17. In the Spring of 1993, Reuters acquired *American Real-Time Services* (ARTS), a company which had developed proprietory software that integrates market news and data from a variety of vendors, and runs on a range of client hardware, including desktop computers, workstations, and local area and wide area network servers. The major features advertised of the *ARTS System 4* mid-1993 – nicely summarize the key parameters with which the real-time (and other) data and information vendors are grappling:

- Outstanding information, accuracy and speed.
- Outstanding reliability.
- Outstanding flexibility in:

  Networking
  User Presentation
  Application Support
  Computer Platforms.

- One platform for integration of all applications.
- Easy to use.
- Complete Reuter global information inventory.

- Superior information quality as compared with vendors such as ADP, Quotron and ILX.
- Fully standards-based open architecture system.
- Flexible delivery of information via satellite or terrestial phone lines. Compatible with IP, X.25, SNA 3270, remote dial-in SLIP and asynchronous and bisynchronous communications.
- 3270 emulation service and/or use existing 3270 network for access order entry/processing systems.
- Robust redundancy available for system components inclusing automatic and/or manual switching of market data servers.
- Industry-leading remote diagnostics and servicing.
- Application program interface for support of proprietory applications.
- Market minder pages: Variable 'smart' user-configured screens monitor user-selected securities, news sources, tickers and data elements.
- Full-page quote screens: Dynamically updated quote screens for: Equities, Equity Options, Futures, Futures Options, Listed Corporate and Government Bonds, Mutual Funds, Indexes, Index Options and Statistics, and Fundamental Information.
- Option Series: Full Option Series Display, including LEAPS, by Expiration Date and Strike Price, Single-page Display of Calls and Puts, including Bid/Ask, Last Trade and Volume, and Open Interest. Bond, Futures, and Futures Options Series are also available. Familiar OPRA symbology and Reuter global symbology recognized.
- Time Series and Quotes Log: 10 day trade retrieval for Trades and Quotes including Time, Price and Market, Composite and Market Ticks, Opens, Highs and Lows, Trade Volume (Confirmed by Exchange) and Cumulative Volume. All Trade and Quote Condition Codes supported. Search by time, market, volume.
- Market Statistics: Displays for all major trading indexes and market averages.
- Reuter News: Headlines and chained text, 100 Day News Retrieval by Industry Groups, Topic, Market and Named Item Codes and Symbols. NewsEdge interoperability.
- Dow Jones News: Headlines and story text, 90 Day News Retrieval. Professional Investor Report, Capital Markets Report, The Wall Street Journal full text, Federal Filings, PR Newswire, BusinessWire. All Dow Jones News services provided via Dow Jones Composite Feed.
- ARTS Private Pages: Internal information system for inventory, research, etc. Entitlements, easy remote data entry – e.g. laptops, PCs etc. Popular word processors and other devices are used for editing.
- Third Party Data: S&P MarketScope, CDA Spectrum, Zach's, MMS, others.
- Graphics and Historical Data: Charting and formula processor capabilities are provided by the ARTS basic system product as well as through add-on packages. All world markets and instrument types.
- Spreadsheet links.

In summary:

'ARTS System 4 is designed to address a central business issue – enhancing productivity. By presenting *multiple data sources* in a single environment, System 4 enables users to see the specific news and information they need to make *effective decisions.* Quick and easy access to critical data is just one benefit of the system. ARTS System 4 fully supports several windows environments, allowing the user to plug easy-to-read text and numerics into a spreadsheet or use five- to ten-year historical pricing data to drive *high-powered* analytics and graphics.

Comprehensive information and the tools to manage it empower you to prospect smarter and service customers better, ARTS System 4's flexible functionality and ease of use lets you select, organize and display the mix of news, market data and analytics you need to be most productive.

ARTS System 4 is based on industry standards with *open connectivity* to any LAN environment – it works on a PC, dumb terminal, high-end UNIX workstation or a combination of hardware. That *flexibility* also means that System 4 is compatible with off-the-shelf or proprietory applications software. Hardware, software, news and data sources – you decide what you need and System 4 delivers.

And we respond quickly. As your needs change, we can adapt your system immediately, on-line, 24 hours a day. System 4's entitlement server enables us to *customise information* from keystation to keystation. Data feeds or applications can be added or subtracted at the flick of a switch.

To ensure this *seamless delivery* of information, System 4 boasts the industry's most efficient remote servicing. Unique self- diagnostic capabilities electronically anticipate – and avoid – system failure before it happens. As an added safeguard, System 4's triple redundancy feature gives you automatic backup without interruption.

System 4 is your window to Reuter information. No other equity information provider can match the power and reach of Reuters . . . Reuters is the *only* provider of complete *real-time* global coverage of 160 international stock, futures and options exchanges, inter-bank rates and debt, as well as news on equity, debt and money markets . . . For the most complete global news coverage, Reuter News keeps you up-to-date, moment to moment. Reuters is consistently ahead of the competition in delivering corporate, economic and political news to North American subscribers . . . And Reuters has more stories on large companies and covers more small cap stocks than any other *news provider*.

In addition to the full line of Reuter news and information products, System 4 integrates multiple services from *third-party vendors.* Pick and choose from an impressive list of news sources that includes DowJones News Service, The Wall Street Journal, Professional Investor Report, PR Newswire and Businesswire. For market data, create your own picture of markets of interest by selecting from S&P MarketScope, GOVPX, CDA Spectrum and a host of others.'

18. . . . but then, I suppose that there is always *The Internet*!

Notes

(170) LESTER, R. The impact of information technology. *IN*: CAMPBELL, M.J. **Manual of business library practice**. 2nd ed. *Clive Bingley*, 1985, pp 196–198.

(171) Note reports such as: 'Journalists and information staff at the BBC World Service would rather use press cuttings than online services . . . (The Service's) library, which handled nearly 42,000 enquiries in 1992, provides access to FT Profile, NEXIS and Blaise-Line . . . Journalists preferred press cuttings because they included pictures and were more up-to-date. Information assistants found press cuttings quicker and easier to use than online. They criticized online sources for their limited browsing facilities and lack of older and very current material. Despite these reservations, information staff believed that using online services increased their professional status' (**Online and CD Notes**, Jan/Feb 1994, p. 10).

(172) To avoid repetition, for the remainder of this chapter, I shall often just use the word 'information' as a shorthand for what we distinguished in Chapter 3, *Value-Adding Processes* to be 'data, information and documents'.

(173) **The Market data industry 1992/93**. *Waters Information Services*, 1993, p 84.

(174) **Information today**, January 1995.

(175) This description is taken from the **Gale directory of online databases**.

(176) **Database**, March 1995.

Further reading

CHORAFAS, D.N. and STEINMANN, H. **Database mining**. *Lafferty Publications*, 1994. 'Exploiting marketing databases in the financial industry.'

CRONIN, M.J. **Doing business on the Internet**. *Van Nostrand Reinhold*, 1994. 250 pp. $29.95.

Economics of online publishing: Strategies for making money online. *SIMBA Information*, 1995. $1,150. 'The new online marketplace: Where are the opportunities? . . . Choosing a business strategy & online vendor: Risks & rewards . . . Defining an online presence: Leveraging your current business . . . Becoming a content provider: Learning from other players (includes 15 detailed financial profiles of major consumer and business-to-business online vendors, including *America Online*, *CompuServe*, *Dialog*, *Dow Jones News/Retrieval*, *Lexis/Nexis*, *Prodigy*, *Telescan*, and *UNET 2*) . . . Online advertising & marketing: The new wave . . . The Internet: Is it for you?' Includes case studies of *Time Inc Magazine Group*, *Capital Cities/ABC*, *The New York Times Company*, *News Corporation*, *The Washington Post Company*, *The New York Law Journal*.

BREMNER, J.P. **Guide to database distribution**. 2nd ed. *National Federation of Abstracting and Information Services*. $175. 'Reviews the process of licensing machine-readable databases and addresses the important issues involved in negotiating database agreements, including intellectual property protection in the light of recent important copyright cases.'

MONOPOLIES AND MERGERS COMMISSION. **Historical on-line database services**. *HMSO*, 1994. Cm 2554.

READ, D. **The power of news: The history of Reuters: 1849–1989**. *Oxford University Press*, 1992. 431 pp.

Index to Organizations

Please note this index covers non-commercial organizations only.

#1185 **Academy of Legal Studies in Business**
#1186 **Academy of Political Science**
#372 **Accountants for the Public Interest**
#373 **Accreditation Council for Accountancy and Taxation**
#986 **ACME – The Association of Management Consulting Firms**
#768 **ACORD**
#772 *Actuarial Standards Board*
#1169 **Adam Smith Institute**
#157 **Administrative Office of the US Courts**
#411 **Advisory Commission on Intergovernmental Relations**
#412 **Agency for International Development**
#672 **All-Party Parliamentary Group on Insurance and Financial Services**
#769 **Alliance of American Insurers**
#770 **AllNations**
#771 **American Academy of Actuaries**
#1187 **American Academy of Political and Social Science**
#1188 **American Accounting Association**
#773 **American Agents Association**
#1189 **American Agricultural Economics Association**
#308 **American Arbitration Association**
#374 **American Association of Attorney-Certified Public Accountants**
#710 **American Association of Bank Directors**
#820 **American Association of Certified Appraisers**

#390 American Association of Exporters and Importers
#1069 American Association of Individual Investors
#774 American Association of Insurance Management Consultants
#71 American Association of Law Libraries
#775 American Association of Managing General Agents
#708 American Bankers Association
#629 American Banking & Securities Association of London
#386 American Bankruptcy Institute
#309 American Bar Association
#339 American Business Conference
#48 American Business Press
#391 American Chamber of Commerce Researchers Association
#1048 American Collectors Association
#387 American College of Bankruptcy
#354 American College of Tax Counsel
#1049 American Commercial Collectors Association
#310 American Corporate Counsel Association
#776 American Council of Life Insurance
#225 American Council of State Savings Supervisors
#392 American Countertrade Association
#1190 American Economic Association
#393 American Economic Development Council
#1239 American Enterprise Institute for Public Policy Research
#1191 American Finance Association
#729 American Financial Services Association
#311 American Foreign Law Association
#777 American Institute for Chartered Property Casualty Underwriters
#340 American Institute for Economic Research
#375 American Institute of Certified Public Accountants
#778 American Institute of Marine Underwriters
#779 American Insurance Association
#821 American Land Title Association
#1192 American Law Institute
#722 American League of Financial Institutions
#312 American Legislative Exchange Council
#63 American Library Association
#313 American National Standards Institute
#1029 American Payroll Association
#1193 American Political Science Association
#1194 American Real Estate and Urban Economics Association
#1195 American Real Estate Society
#1196 American Risk and Insurance Association

#64 American Society for Information Science
#822 American Society of Appraisers
#711 American Society of Bank Directors
#780 American Society of CLU & ChFC
#314 American Society of International Law
#759 American Society of Pension Actuaries
#376 American Society of Women Accountants
#1197 American Statistical Association
#732 American Stock Exchange
#355 American Tax Policy Institute
#377 American Women's Society of Certified Public Accountants
#823 Appraisal Institute
#824 Appraisers Association of America
#60 Aslib
#987 Associated Credit Bureaus
#781 Associated Risk Managers International
#40 Association Bancaire pour L'ECU
#1140 Association d'Instituts Européens de Conjoncture Economique
#1001 Association Europééne des Assurés de l'Industrie
#424 Association Européenne des Praticiens des Procedures Collectives
#804 Association for Advanced Life Underwriting
#1198 Association for Business and Economic Research
#1199 Association for Comparative Economic Studies
#1030 Association for Corporate Growth
#1031 Association for Global Business
#1058 Association for Investment Management and Research
#38 Association for Payment Clearing Services
#1080 Association for Public Policy Analysis and Management
#421 Association for the Monetary Union of Europe
#428 Association Internationale de Droit des Assurances
#588 Association Internationale de la Mutualité
#1133 Association Internationale des Sciences Economiques
#1127 Association Internationale pour l'Etude de l'Economie de l'Assurance
#286 Association of Accounting Technicians
#1200 Association of American Law Schools
#287 Association of Authorised Public Accountants
#720 Association of Bank Loan and Credit Officers
#300 Association of British Chambers of Commerce and Industry
#636 Association of British Credit Unions
#640 Association of British Factors & Discounters

#673 Association of British Insurers
#315 Association of Certified Fraud Examiners
#1047 Association of Certified Turnaround Professionals
#316 Association of Commercial Finance Attorneys
#674 Association of Consulting Actuaries
#1006 Association of Corporate Treasurers
#288 Association of Cost & Executive Accountants
#317 Association of Defense Trial Attorneys
#49 Association of Directory Publishers
#1140 Association of European Conjuncture Institutes
#623 Association of European Cooperative and Mutual Insurers
#702 Association of Financial Services Holding Companies
#825 Association of Foreign Investors in US Real Estate
#378 Association of Government Accountants
#284 Association of Her Majesty's Inspectors of Taxes and Senior Revenue
#760 Association of Independent Trust Companies
#50 Association of Information and Dissemination Services
#1010 Association of Insurance & Risk Managers in Industry and Commerce
#589 Association of International Life Offices
#1063 Association of Investment Management Sales Executives
#665 Association of Investment Trust Companies
#318 Association of Life Insurance Counsel
#1081 Association of Local Housing Finance Agencies
#697 Association of Mortgage Lenders
#276 Association of Pension Lawyers
#666 Association of Pensioner Trustees
#647 Association of Private Client Investment Managers and Stockbrokers
#761 Association of Private Pension & Welfare Plans
#698 Association of Property Unit Trusts
#1031 Association of Publicly Traded Companies
#319 Association of Real Estate License Law Officials
#320 Association of Securities and Exchange Commission Alumni
#667 Association of Unit Trusts and Investment Funds
#51 Audit Bureau of Circulation
#52 Audit Bureau of Circulations
#170 Audit Commission for Local Authorities and the National Health Service
#289 Auditing Practices Board
#712 Bank Administration Institute
#1 Bank for International Settlements

#176 Bank of England
#1050 Bankcard Holders of America
#394 Bankers' Association for Foreign Trade
#713 Bankers' Round Table
#177 Banking Appeals Tribunal
#611 Banking Federation of the European Union
#630 Banking Information Service
#631 Banking, Insurance and Finance Union
#321 Banking Law Institute
#297 Bankruptcy Association of Great Britain & Ireland
#600 Berne Union
#379 BKR International
#196 Board of Inland Revenue
#1070 Bond Investors Association
#53 BPA International
#1147 British Accounting Association
#70 British and Irish Association of Law Librarians
#632 British Bankers' Association
#300 British Chambers of Commerce
#301 British Importers Confederation
#1170 British Institute of International and Comparative Law
#675 British Insurance and Investment Brokers' Association
#277 British Insurance Law Association
#303 British International Freight Association
#302 British Invisibles
#1171 British-North American Committee
#233 British Overseas Trade Board
#699 British Property Federation
#278 British Standards Institution
#304 British Trade and Investment Office
#641 British Venture Capital Association
#1240 Brookings Institution
#180 Building Societies Appeals Tribunal
#637 Building Societies Association
#179 Building Societies Commission
#590 Bureau International des Producteurs d'Assurances & de Réassurances
#447 Bureau International des Tarifs Douaniers
#11 Bureau of Economic Analysis
#10 Bureau of the Census
#211 Bureau of the Public Debt
#4 Business and Industry Advisory Committee to the OECD
#341 Business Council
#342 Business Roundtable
#208 Cabinet Office

#782 Captive Insurance Companies Association
#1216 Case Western Reserve University
#1241 Cato Institute
#1033 Center for Entrepreneurial Management
#1242 Center for Governmental Research
#1243 Center for Policy Alternatives
#1244 Center for Public Dialogue
#1245 Center for the Defense of Free Enterprise
#163 Central Office of Information
#8 Central Statistical Office
#1172 Centre for Economic Policy Research
#1141 Centre for European Policy Studies
#1007 Centre for Interfirm Comparison
#1173 Centre for the Study of Financial Innovation
#1024 Centre for the Study of Regulated Industries
#1132 Centre International d'Etudes Monetaires et Bancaires
#290 Chartered Association of Certified Accountants
#279 Chartered Institute of Arbitrators
#634 Chartered Institute of Bankers
#676 Chartered Institute of Loss Adjusters
#291 Chartered Institute of Management Accountants
#1023 Chartered Institute of Public Finance and Accountancy
#677 Chartered Insurance Institute
#733 Chicago Board of Trade
#734 Chicago Board Options Exchange
#735 Chicago Mercantile Exchange
#745 Chicago Stock Exchange
#209 Citizen's Charter Unit
#1153 City University
#1217 Cleveland State University
#435 Club of Rome
#656 CMS
#1064 Co-Op America
#736 Coffee, Sugar & Cocoa Exchange
#1218 Columbia University: Graduate School of Business
#624 Comité Européen des Assurances
#826 Commercial Finance Association
#322 Commercial Law League of America
#827 Commercial-Investment Real Estate Institute
#474 Commission of the European Communities
#1246 Committee for Economic Development
#323 Committee to Support the Antitrust Laws
#255 Commodity Futures Trading Commission
#356 Common Ground – USA
#448 Commonwealth Association for Development

#440 Commonwealth Association of Tax Administrators
#449 Commonwealth Development Corporation
#450 Commonwealth Secretariat
#270 Companies House
#343 Concord Coalition
#283 Confederation of British Industry
#591 Confederation of Insurance Trade Unions
#451 Confederation of International Trading Houses Associations
#626 Confédération Europèene des Administrateurs de Biens
#422 Confédération Fiscale Européenne
#552 Confédération Internationale du Crédit Populaire
#344 Conference Board
#816 Conference of Actuaries in Public Practice
#783 Conference of Consulting Actuaries
#226 Conference of State Bank Supervisors
#324 Conference on Consumer Finance Law
#173 Congressional Budget Office
#345 Congressional Economic Leadership Institute
#419 Conseil des Barreaux de la Communauté Européene
#292 Consultative Committee of Accountancy Bodies
#625 Consultative Group of Associations of Actuaries in the Countries of the EC
#714 Consumer Bankers Association
#642 Consumer Credit Association of the United Kingdom
#784 Consumer Credit Insurance Association
#643 Consumer Credit Trade Association
#395 Consumers for World Trade
#396 Cooperative Assistance Fund
#1219 Cornell University
#737 Corporate Transfer Agents Association
#397 Corporation for Enterprise Development
#678 Corporation of Insurance and Financial Advisors
#1247 Council for European Studies
#229 Council of Economic Advisers
#483 Council of Europe
#1071 Council of Institutional Investors
#785 Council of Insurance Agents and Brokers
#638 Council of Mortgage Lenders
#398 Council of State Chambers of Commerce
#419 Council of the Bars and Law Societies of the European Community
#473 Council of the European Union
#346 Council on Competitiveness
#1072 Council on Economic Priorities

#399 Council on Foreign Relations
#839 Counselors of Real Estate
#477 Court of Auditors
#476 Court of Justice
#786 CPCU Society
#39 Credit Card Research Group
#1051 Credit Professionals International
#1011 Credit Protection Association
#723 Credit Union Executives Society
#305 Crown Agents
#154 Crown Prosecution Service
#1174 CTI Centre for Accounting Finance and Management
#1175 CTI Centre for Computing in Economics
#724 CUNA & Affiliates
#325 Customs and International Trade Bar Association
#200 Department for National Savings
#413 Department of Agriculture
#9 Department of Commerce
#263 Department of Housing and Urban Development
#158 Department of Justice
#210 Department of the Treasury
#232 Department of Trade and Industry
#738 Depository Trust Company
#1201 Eastern Finance Association
#1128 Econometric Society
#463 Economic and Social Commission for Asia and the Pacific
#464 Economic and Social Commission for Western Asia
#481 Economic and Social Committee
#460 Economic Commission for Africa
#461 Economic Commission for Europe
#462 Economic Commission for Latin America and the Caribbean
#13 Economic Development Administration
#1248 Economic Policy Institute
#1148 Economists in Insurance Group (London)
#40 ECU Banking Association
#425 EDICOM
#41 Electronic Banking Economics Society
#42 Electronic Funds Transfer Association
#400 Emergency Committee for American Trade
#740 Emerging Markets Traders Association
#1249 Employee Benefit Research Institute
#1250 Entrepreneurial Leadership Center
#1034 Entrepreneurship Institute
#730 Equipment Leasing Association of America

#326 ERISA Industry Committee
#1065 ESOP Association
#426 EU Committee of the American Chamber of Commerce in Belgium
#627 EU Mortgage Federation
#468 EUR-OP
#469 Eurobases
#427 EURODAD
#615 Eurofinas
#616 Europafactoring
#1142 European Accounting Association
#612 European Association of Cooperative Banks
#1143 European Association of Law and Economics
#480 European Bank for Reconstruction and Development
#470 European Commission Host Organisation
#1144 European Economic Association
#1176 European Economics and Financial Centre
#622 European Federation for Retirement Provision
#613 European Federation of Building Societies
#618 European Federation of Equipment Leasing Company Associations
#616 European Federation of Factoring Associations
#615 European Federation of Finance House Associations
#1002 European Federation of Financial Analysts Societies
#1004 European Federation of Financial Executives Institutes
#621 European Federation of Investment Funds and Companies
#1145 European Finance Association
#608 European Financial Management and Marketing Association
#484 European Free Trade Association
#609 European Group of Financial Institutions
#628 European Group of Valuers of Fixed Assets
#69 European Information Association
#424 European Insolvency Practitioners Association
#1146 European Institute of Public Administration
#624 European Insurance Committee
#478 European Investment Bank
#619 European Managed Futures Association
#479 European Monetary Institute
#427 European Network on Debt and Development
#475 European Parliament
#1001 European Risk Management Association
#614 European Savings Bank Group
#482 European Seed Capital Fund Network

#422 European Tax Confederation
#617 European Venture Capital Association
#467 EUROPEAN UNION
#159 Executive Office for United States Trustees
#228 Executive Office of the President
#347 Exploratory Project for Economic Alternatives
#234 Export Credits Guarantee Department
#414 Export-Import Bank of the United States
#679 Faculty of Actuaries
#260 Farm Credit Administration
#261 Farm Credit Council
#1053 FCIB-NACM Corporation
#262 Federal Agricultural Mortgage Corporation
#327 Federal Bar Association
#220 Federal Deposit Insurance Corporation
#221 Federal Financial Institutions Examination Council
#265 Federal Home Loan Mortgage Corporation
#266 Federal Housing Finance Board
#267 Federal National Mortgage Association
#184 Federal Reserve Bank of Atlanta
#185 Federal Reserve Bank of Boston
#186 Federal Reserve Bank of Chicago
#187 Federal Reserve Bank of Cleveland
#188 Federal Reserve Bank of Dallas
#189 Federal Reserve Bank of Kansas City
#190 Federal Reserve Bank of Minneapolis
#191 Federal Reserve Bank of New York
#192 Federal Reserve Bank of Philadelphia
#193 Federal Reserve Bank of Richmond
#194 Federal Reserve Bank of San Francisco
#195 Federal Reserve Bank of St Louis
#183 Federal Reserve System
#245 Federal Retirement Thrift Investment Board
#416 Federal Trade Commission
#648 Federation of Commodity Associations
#620 Federation of European Stock Exchanges
#328 Federation of Insurance and Corporate Counsel
#358 Federation of Tax Administrators
#611 Fédération Bancaire de la Communauté Européene
#423 Fédération des Experts Comptables Européens
#621 Fédération Européenne des Fonds et Sociétés d'Investissement
#560 Fédération Internationale des Bourses de Valeurs
#420 Fédération Internationale pour le Droit Européen
#644 Finance & Leasing Association

#271 Financial Accounting Standards Board
#1027 Financial Executives Institute
#1028 Financial Executives Research Foundation
#1005 Financial Executives' Group
#703 Financial Institutions Marketing Association
#246 Financial Institutions Retirement Fund
#1202 Financial Management Association
#212 Financial Management Service
#704 Financial Managers Society
#268 Financial Reporting Council
#705 Financial Services Volunteer Corps
#988 Financial Women International
#706 Financial Women's Association of New York
#1062 Fixed Income Analysts Society
#1220 Fordham University
#635 Foreign Banks and Securities Houses Association
#415 Foreign Credit Insurance Association
#1251 Foreign Policy Association
#741 Forex USA
#1203 Foundation for Accounting Education
#1204 Foundation for Credit Education
#1205 Foundation for Economic Education
#1252 Foundation for Public Affairs
#1206 Foundation for Research in International Banking and Finance
#1253 Foundation for the Private Sector
#359 Free the Eagle
#181 Friendly Societies Commission
#360 FSC/DISC Tax Association
#649 Futures and Options Association
#742 Futures Industry Association
#743 Futures Industry Institute
#174 General Accounting Office
#805 General Agents and Managers Association
#1127 Geneva Association
#1221 Georgetown University
#650 Gilt-Edged Market Makers Association
#562 Gold Institute
#1082 Government Accountability Project
#242 Government Actuary's Department
#1083 Government Finance Officers Association
#166 Government Information Services
#264 Government National Mortgage Association
#272 Governmental Accounting Standards Board
#1207 Governmental Research Association

#436 Group of Thirty
#625 Groupe Consultatif des Associations D'Actuaires des Pays . . .
#612 Groupement Européen des Banques Coopératives
#1149 Hansard Society of Parliamentary Government
#1222 Harvard University
#787 Health Insurance Association of America
#361 Henry George Foundation of America
#1254 Heritage Foundation
#201 HM Customs and Excise
#203 HM Treasury
#164 HMSO
#168 House of Commons
#167 House of Lords
#172 House of Representatives
#1255 Hudson Institute
#452 ICC
#1015 IFA Promotion
#1035 IMAP/INTERMAC
#715 Independent Bankers Association of America
#1016 Independent Financial Adviser Association
#1256 Independent Institute
#788 Independent Insurance Agents of America
#1073 Independent Investors Forum
#1223 Indiana University
#54 Information Industry Association
#471 Information Market Observatory
#789 Inland Marine Underwriters Association
#445 INSOL International
#298 Insolvency Practitioners Association
#235 Insolvency Rules Committee
#236 Insolvency Service
#1146 Institut Européen d'Administration Publique
#1257 Institute for Contemporary Studies
#1177 Institute for Fiscal Studies
#1258 Institute for International Economics
#1259 Institute for Monetary Freedom
#1260 Institute for Policy Studies
#1178 Institute for Public Policy Research
#1261 Institute for Socioeconomic Studies
#680 Institute of Actuaries
#828 Institute of Business Appraisers
#709 Institute of Certified Bankers
#1066 Institute of Certified Financial Planners
#293 Institute of Chartered Accountants in England and Wales

#1008 Institute of Chartered Secretaries & Administrators
#294 Institute of Company Accountants
#1012 Institute of Credit Management
#1179 Institute of Economic Affairs
#295 Institute of Financial Accountants
#1208 Institute of Financial Education
#1017 Institute of Financial Planning
#61 Institute of Information Scientists
#681 Institute of Insurance Brokers
#380 Institute of Internal Auditors
#716 Institute of International Bankers
#437 Institute of International Finance
#1014 Institute of Investment Management and Research
#1009 Institute of Legal Cashiers and Administrators
#682 Institute of London Underwriters
#381 Institute of Management Accountants
#1036 Institute of Management and Administration
#1209 Institute of Mathematical Statistics
#683 Institute of Public Loss Assessors
#1037 Institute of Real Estate Management
#1026 Institute of Revenues Rating and Valuation
#1013 Institute of Risk Management
#362 Institute of Tax Consultants
#285 Institute of Taxation
#1262 Institute of World Affairs
#651 Institutional Fund Managers Association
#790 Insurance Accounting and Systems Association
#238 Insurance Brokers Registration Council
#791 Insurance Education Foundation
#684 Insurance Industry Training Council
#792 Insurance Information Institute
#793 Insurance Institute of America
#239 Insurance Ombudsman Bureau
#794 Insurance Research Council
#795 Insurance Services Office
#685 Insurance Technology Trade Association
#213 Inter-American Development Bank
#214 Internal Revenue Service
#269 International Accounting Standards Committee
#592 International Actuarial Association
#603 International Assets Valuation Standards Committee
#989 International Association for Financial Planning
#428 International Association for Insurance Law
#1138 International Association for Official Statistics

#1129 International Association for Research in Income and Wealth
#1127 International Association for the Study of Insurance Economics
#604 International Association of Assessing Officers
#1130 International Association of Business Forecasting
#593 International Association of Consulting Actuaries
#605 International Association of Corporate Real Estate Executives
#990 International Association of Credit Card Investigators
#1131 International Association of Financial Engineers
#991 International Association of Financial Executives Institutes
#590 International Association of Insurance and Reinsurance Intermediaries
#992 International Association of Investors in the Social Economy
#68 International Association of Law Libraries
#594 International Association of Mutual Insurance Companies
#444 International Auditing Practices Committee
#5 International Bank for Reconstruction and Development
#429 International Bar Association
#563 International Bond & Share Society
#564 International Brokers' Association
#441 International Bureau of Fiscal Documentation
#561 International Capital Markets Group
#1132 International Center for Monetary and Banking Studies
#6 International Centre for Settlement of Investment Disputes
#549 International Centre for the Training of Bank Professionals
#452 International Chamber of Commerce
#595 International Claim Association
#553 International Co-operative Alliance
#596 International Co-operative and Mutual Insurance Federation
#565 International Cocoa Organization
#566 International Coffee Organization
#552 International Confederation of Popular Credit
#554 International Cooperative Banking Association
#1003 International Coordinating Committee of Financial Analysts Associations
#567 International Cotton Advisory Committee
#993 International Credit Association
#597 International Credit Insurance Association

#447 International Customs Tariffs Bureau
#1133 International Economic Association
#1210 International Economics and Finance Society
#568 International Energy Agency
#443 International Federation of Accountants
#420 International Federation of European Law
#813 International Federation of Risk and Insurance Management Associations
#560 International Federation of Stock Exchanges
#7 International Finance Corporation
#442 International Fiscal Association
#995 International Foundation of Employee Benefit Plans
#558 International Franchise Association
#1134 International Institute of Forecasters
#1135 International Institute of Investment and Merchant Banking
#1136 International Institute of Public Finance
#598 International Insurance Society
#569 International Iron and Steel Institute
#430 International Juridicial Institute
#465 International Labour Office
#431 International Law Association
#570 International Lead and Zinc Study Group
#550 International Monetary Conference
#2 International Monetary Fund
#571 International Money Market Trading Association
#432 International Organization for Standardization
#572 International Organization of Securities Commissions
#433 International Organization of Supreme Audit Institutions
#652 International Petroleum Exchange of London
#573 International Primary Market Association
#606 International Real Estate Federation
#453 International Reciprocal Trade Association
#997 International Risk Management Institute
#574 International Rubber Study Group
#555 International Savings Bank Institute
#575 International Securities Market Association
#47 International Serials Data System
#607 International Society of Appraisers
#996 International Society of Certified Employee Benefit Specialists
#1059 International Society of Financial Analysts
#998 International Society of Financiers
#434 International Society of Securities Administrators
#1137 International Statistical Institute

#660 International Stock Exchange of the United Kingdom and the Republic . . .
#576 **International Sugar Organization**
#577 **International Swaps and Derivatives Association**
#578 **International Tea Committee**
#579 **International Textile Manufacturers Federation**
#14 International Trade Administration
#599 **International Union of Aviation Insurers**
#600 **International Union of Credit and Investment Insurers**
#556 **International Union of Housing Finance Institutions**
#580 **International Wheat Council**
#581 **International Wool Secretariat**
#762 **Investment Company Institute**
#1074 **Investment Education Institute**
#249 Investment Management Regulatory Organization
#253 **Investment Ombudsman**
#1038 **Investment Program Association**
#1021 **Investor Relations Society**
#1075 **Investor Responsibility Research Center**
#254 **Investors Compensation Scheme**
#582 **Iron and Steel Statistics Bureau**
#700 **ISVA**
#653 **Joint Exchanges Committee**
#1039 **Joint Industry Group**
#155 **Law Commission**
#280 **Law Society of England and Wales**
#618 **Leaseurope**
#62 **Library Association**
#175 **Library of Congress**
#999 **LIC International – League International for Creditors**
#281 **Life Assurance Legal Society**
#686 **Life Insurance Association**
#796 **Life Insurers Conference**
#797 **Life Underwriter Training Council**
#601 **LIMRA**
#687 **Lloyd's Aviation Underwriters' Association**
#688 **Lloyd's Motor Underwriters' Association**
#689 **Lloyd's of London**
#690 **Lloyd's Underwriters' Association**
#691 **Lloyd's Underwriters' Non-Marine Association**
#602 **LOMA**
#654 **London Bullion Market Association**
#1154 **London Business School**
#43 **London Clearing House**
#655 **London Commodity Exchange**

#657 London Discount Market Association
#692 London Insurance and Reinsurance Market Association
#658 London International Financial Futures and Options Exchange
#633 London Investment Banking Association
#659 London Metal Exchange
#693 London Processing Centre
#1155 London School of Economics and Political Science
#660 London Stock Exchange
#55 Magazine Publishers of America
#744 Managed Futures Association
#1018 Management Consultancies Association
#745 Midwest Stock Exchange
#747 Minneapolis Grain Exchange
#1019 Money Advice Association
#273 Monopolies and Mergers Commission
#829 Mortgage Bankers Association of America
#798 Mortgage Insurance Companies of America
#746 Mortgage-Backed Securities Corporation
#363 Multistate Tax Commission
#256 Municipal Securities Rulemaking Board
#1084 Municipal Treasurers Association of the US and Canada
#763 Mutual Fund Educational Alliance
#1076 Mutual Fund Educational Alliance
#694 Mutual Insurance Companies Association
#748 NASDAQ
#1263 National Academy of Social Insurance
#87 National Archives and Records Administration
#717 National Association for Bank Cost & Management Accounting
#329 National Association for Law Placement
#330 National Association of Attorneys General
#388 National Association of Bankruptcy Trustees
#382 National Association of Black Accountants
#331 National Association of Bond Lawyers
#1211 National Association of Business Economists
#1085 National Association of County Treasurers and Finance Officers
#707 National Association of Credit Card Merchants
#1052 National Association of Credit Management
#401 National Association of Development Companies
#402 National Association of Development Organizations
#364 National Association of Enrolled Agents
#1086 National Association of Estate Planning Councils
#725 National Association of Federal Credit Unions

#830 National Association of Home Builders
#831 National Association of Independent Fee Appraisers
#799 National Association of Independent Insurers
#802 National Association of Independent Life Brokerage Agencies
#832 National Association of Industrial and Office Properties
#800 National Association of Insurance Brokers
#240 National Association of Insurance Commissioners
#801 National Association of Insurance Women (International)
#764 National Association of Investment Companies
#1077 National Association of Investors Corporation
#803 National Association of Life Underwriters
#833 National Association of Mortgage Brokers
#806 National Association of Mutual Insurance Companies
#668 National Association of Pension Funds
#1067 National Association of Personal Financial Advisers
#807 National Association of Professional Insurance Agents
#1040 National Association of Purchasing Management
#834 National Association of Real Estate Appraisers
#835 National Association of Real Estate Brokers
#836 National Association of Real Estate Editors
#837 National Association of Real Estate Investment Trusts
#838 National Association of Realtors
#840 National Association of Review Appraisers and Mortgage Underwriters
#332 National Association of Securities and Commercial Law Attorneys
#749 National Association of Securities Dealers
#765 National Association of Small Business Investment Companies
#1087 National Association of State Auditors, Comptrollers, and Treasurers
#383 National Association of State Boards of Accountancy
#1088 National Association of State Budget Officers
#227 National Association of State Credit Union Supervisors
#403 National Association of State Development Agencies
#1089 National Association of State Retirement Administrators
#365 National Association of Tax Practitioners
#718 National Association of Urban Bankers
#169 National Audit Office
#44 National Automated Clearing House Association
#1264 National Bureau of Economic Research
#1068 National Center for Financial Education
#1265 National Committee on Public Employee Pension Systems

#389 National Conference of Bankruptcy Judges
#333 National Conference of Commissioners on Uniform State Laws
#384 National Conference of CPA Practitioners
#639 National Conference of Friendly Societies
#241 National Conference of Insurance Legislators
#334 National Conference of State Legislatures
#405 National Congress for Community Economic Development
#1054 National Consumer Credit Consultants
#645 National Consumer Credit Federation
#1090 National Council for Public-Private Partnerships
#406 National Council for Urban Economic Development
#841 National Council of Exchangors
#808 National Council of Self-Insurers
#809 National Council on Compensation Insurance
#222 National Credit Union Administration
#726 National Credit Union Management Association
#404 National Customs Brokers and Forwarders Association of America
#204 National Debt Office
#407 National Development Council
#348 National Economic Association
#349 National Economists Club
#56 National Federation of Abstracting & Information Services
#1041 National Federation of Independent Business
#1020 National Federation of Independent Financial Advisers
#408 National Foreign Trade Council
#1055 National Foundation for Consumer Credit
#257 National Futures Association
#719 National Independent Bank Equipment and Systems Association
#1180 National Institute of Economic and Social Research
#1042 National Institute of Pensions Administration
#766 National Investment Company Service Association
#1078 National Investor Relations Institute
#646 National Pawnbrokers Association
#1056 National Recovery and Collection Association
#842 National Second Mortgage Association
#739 National Securities Clearing Corporation
#843 National Society for Real Estate Finance
#335 National Society of Compliance Professionals
#385 National Society of Public Accountants
#336 National Standards Association

#366 **National Tax Association – Tax Institute of America**
#15 *National Technical Information Service*
#1091 **National Treasury Employees Union**
#695 **National Union of Insurance Workers**
#731 **National Venture Capital Association**
#1181 **New Economics Foundation**
#45 **New York Clearing House Association**
#750 **New York Cotton Exchange**
#57 **New York Financial Writers' Association**
#1060 *New York Society of Security Analysts*
#752 **New York Stock Exchange**
#1224 **New York University**
#58 **Newspaper Publishers Association**
#258 **North American Securities Administrators Association**
#1225 **Northwestern University: Kellogg Graduate School of Management**
#751 **NYMEX**
#243 **Occupational Pensions Board**
#468 Office for Official Publications of the European Communities
#12 *Office of Business Analysis*
#274 **Office of Fair Trading**
#230 *Office of Management and Budget*
#178 **Office of the Banking Ombudsman**
#216 *Office of the Comptroller of the Currency*
#205 **Office of the National Lottery**
#231 *Office of the United States Trade Representative*
#217 *Office of Thrift Supervision*
#438 **Offshore Group of Banking Supervisors**
#1226 **Ohio State University**
#350 **OMB Watch**
#663 **OMLX: The London Securities and Derivatives Exchange**
#46 **Options Clearing Corporation**
#3 **Organisation for Economic Co-operation and Development**
#446 **Organisation Mondiale du Commerce**
#1000 **Organization for International Investment**
#583 **Organization of the Petroleum Exporting Countries**
#307 **Overseas Development Administration**
#1182 **Overseas Development Institute**
#275 **Panel on Takeovers and Mergers**
#206 **PAYMASTER, Office of HM Paymaster General**
#247 **Pension Benefit Guaranty Corporation**
#767 **Pension Real Estate Association**
#197 *Pension Schemes Office*

#669 Pension Trustees Forum
#670 Pensions Management Institute
#244 Pensions Ombudsman
#296 Pensions Research Accountants Group
#59 Periodical Publishers Association
#250 Personal Investment Authority
#753 Philadelphia Stock Exchange
#1183 Policy Studies Institute
#337 Practising Law Institute
#1266 Princeton Research Institute
#1227 Princeton University
#1043 Profit Sharing Council of America
#810 Property Loss Research Bureau
#1022 ProShare (UK)
#1025 Public Finance Foundation
#754 Public Securities Association
#409 Public Works and Economic Development Association
#338 Real Estate Law Institute
#1267 Reason Foundation
#351 Rebuild America Coalition
#352 Redeem Our Country
#66 Reference Point Foundation
#182 Registry of Friendly Societies
#661 Regulatory News Service
#811 Reinsurance Association of America
#1061 Research Foundation of the Institute of Chartered Financial Analysts
#223 Resolution Trust Corporation
#198 Revenue Adjudicator's Office
#812 Risk and Insurance Management Society
#720 Robert Morris Associates
#1150 Royal Economic Society
#1184 Royal Institute of International Affairs
#701 Royal Institution of Chartered Surveyors
#207 Royal Mint
#1151 Royal Statistical Society
#727 Savings & Community Bankers of America
#662 SEAQ International
#251 Securities and Futures Authority
#248 Securities and Investments Board
#755 Securities Industry Association
#756 Securities Information Center
#664 Securities Institute
#259 Securities Investor Protection Corporation
#757 Security Traders Association

#814 Self-Insurance Institute of America
#171 Senate
#156 Serious Fraud Office
#584 Silver Institute
#237 Simpler Trade Procedures Board
#1079 Social Investment Forum
#282 Society for Computers and Law
#1268 Society for the Advancement of Economic Theory
#815 Society of Actuaries
#1152 Society of Business Economists
#994 Society of Certified Credit Executives
#817 Society of Chartered Property & Casualty Underwriters
#67 Society of Competitive Intelligence Professionals
#1044 Society of Financial Examiners
#1212 Society of Government Economists
#671 Society of Pension Consultants
#299 Society of Practitioners of Insolvency
#1057 Society of Risk Management Consultants
#1213 Southern Economic Association
#199 Special Commissioners of Income Tax
#65 Special Libraries Association
#1228 Stanford University
#472 Statistical Office of the European Communities
#215 Statistics of Income Division
#160 Supreme Court of the United States
#818 Surety Association of America
#367 Tax Analysts
#368 Tax Council
#369 Tax Executives Institute
#370 Tax Foundation
#371 Tax Reform Action Coalition
#696 The 150 Association
#357 The Fair Tax
#224 Thrift Depositor Protection Oversight Board
#1139 Transnational Institute
#1045 Treasury Management Association
#410 Trickle Up Program
#1046 Turnaround Management Association
#306 TWIN
#1214 Union for Radical Political Economics
#610 Union of the Finance-Personnel in Europe
#457 United Nations Conference on Trade and Development
#458 United Nations University
#417 United States Council for International Business
#721 United States Council on International Banking

#161 United States Court of International Trade
#165 United States Government Printing Office
#418 United States International Trade Commission
#728 United States League of Savings Institutions
#218 United States Mint
#219 United States Savings Bond Division
#252 United States Securities and Exchange Commission
#162 United States Tax Court
#456 UNITED NATIONS SYSTEM
#1156 University of Cambridge
#1229 University of Chicago
#1157 University of Exeter
#1230 University of Florida
#1231 University of Illinois at Urbana-Champaign
#1158 University of Lancaster
#1159 University of Leicester
#1160 University of London: Birkbeck College
#1161 University of London: Queen Mary and Westfield College
#1162 University of Loughborough
#1232 University of New Hampshire
#1233 University of New Orleans
#1163 University of Nottingham
#1234 University of Pennsylvania
#1164 University of Reading
#1165 University of Strathclyde
#1166 University of Sussex
#1235 University of Virginia
#1167 University of Wales
#1168 University of Warwick
#1236 University of Washington
#459 UNU World Institute for Development Economics Research
#1269 Urban Institute
#1270 US Public Interest Research Group
#202 VAT and Duties Tribunals
#1237 Virginia Polytechnic Institute
#758 Wall Street Planning Group
#1215 Western Economic Association International
#819 Women Life Underwriters Confederation
#353 Women's Economic Round Table
#551 Women's World Banking
#5 World Bank
#585 World Bureau of Metal Statistics
#557 World Council of Credit Unions
#454 World Customs Organization

#439 **World Economic Forum**
#586 **World Federation of Diamond Bourses**
#587 **World Gold Council**
#559 **World Leasing Council**
#455 **World Trade Centers Association**
#466 **World Trade Organization**
#1238 **Yale University**

Index to Serials

2480 AAII Journal
1727 ABA Bank Compliance
1728 ABA Bank Security
1729 ABA Bankers News
1730 ABA Banking Journal
1731 ABA Directory of Trust Banking
1182 ABA Journal
1732 ABA Key to Routing Numbers
1733 ABA Management Update of Personal Trust & Private Banking
201 ABC Magazine Circulations
202 ABC Newspaper Circulations
1387 ABEL
258 ABI/INFORM
1283 ABI Journal
1712 ABI Statistical Service
1676 Abstract of Banking Statistics
1198 ACCA Docket
1442 Access to European Union
1154 Accountancy
864 Accountancy Age
750 Accountancy Law Reports
955 Accountant, The
1155 Accountants Digests
751 Accountants SEC Practice Manual
529 Accounting & Auditing Disclosure Manual
530 Accounting & Auditing Update Service
289 Accounting & Tax Database

1156 Accounting and Business Research
290 Accounting Articles
2817 Accounting, Business and Financial History
2596 Accounting Education News
2731 Accounting Education [Chapman & Hall]
2763 Accounting Education [JAI Press]
794 Accounting for Banks
2597 Accounting Horizons
2738 Accounting, Management and Information Technologies
2739 Accounting, Organizations and Society
1112 Accounting Practices and Procedures
291 Accounting Research Directory
2598 Accounting Review
1157 Accounting Standards (Year)
473 Accounting Technology
474 Accounting Today
1172 Accounting World
1107 Accounts (Year)
1286 ACCRA Cost of Living Index
426 Acquisitions and Mergers
1631 Acquisitions Monthly
1224 Across the Board
2440 ACT Manual of Corporate Finance and Treasury Management
1006 Actions of the Board: Applications and Reports Received
1869 Actuarial Research Clearing House
1870 Actuary
682 Administrative Interpretations of the Uniform Consumer Credit Code
915 Advanced Sales Reference Service
377 Advanced Searcher
2764 Advances in Accounting
2765 Advances in Accounting Information Systems
2766 Advances in Econometrics
2767 Advances in Futures and Options Research
2768 Advances in Investment Analysis and Portfolio Management
2769 Advances in Management Accounting
2770 Advances in Public Interest Accounting
2771 Advances in Quantitative Analysis of Finance and Accounting
2772 Advances in Taxation
1786 Advisor
1346 African Socio-Economic Indicators (Year)
1347 African Statistical Yearbook (Year)

568 Agency Law
1007 Aggregate Summaries of Annual Surveys of Securities Credit Extension
1429 Agra Europe
2740 Agricultural Economics
2648 Agricultural Finance Review
1293 Agricultural Income and Finance
569 Agricultural Law, Tax and Finance
1264 AICPA Audit and Accounting Guides
1265 AICPA Audit and Accounting Manual
1266 AICPA Financial Statement Preparation Manual
1267 AICPA Professsional Standards
1268 AICPA Technical Practice Aids
2573 AIMS
2021 Airfinance Annual (Year)
2037 Airfinance Journal
570 Allied Dunbar Investment and Savings Handbook
571 Allied Dunbar Tax Handbook
1461 AMADEUS
1476 America's Corporate Families and International Affiliates
1991 American Agent and Broker
2376 American Bank Directory
1897 American Banker
2279 American Banker [OneSource Information Services]
413 American Banker's Washington Watch
1284 American Bankruptcy Institute Law Review
1285 American Bankruptcy Law Journal
1454 American Business Directory
2593 American Business Law Journal
2606 American Economic Review
2377 American Financial Directory
2605 American Journal of Agricultural Economics
1199 American Journal of Comparative Law
1200 American Journal of International Law
1235 American Journal of Tax Policy
867 American Lawyer
2820 American Politics Quarterly
1806 American Stock Exchange Company Guide
1807 American Stock Exchange Stocks, Bonds, Options and Derivatives
1808 Amex Fact Book
2618 Amstat News
1758 Analysis of (Year) Bank Marketing Expenditures
427 Analysis of Key SEC No-Action Letters (Year)
1922 Analysis of Premiums Paid in RTC Resolutions

428 Anderson on the Uniform Commercial Code
869 Andrews' Professional Liability Litigation Reporter
2628 Annals of Applied Probability
2630 Annals of Probability
2629 Annals of Statistics
2595 Annals of the American Academy of Political and Social Science
2454 Annotated Rating & Community Charge Legislation
70 Annual Abstract of Statistics
1223 Annual Institute on Securities Regulation
18 Annual Labour Force Statistics
6 Annual Report on Exchange Arrangements and Exchange Restrictions
997 Annual Report on the Budget
683 Annual Review of Banking Law
1964 Annual Review of UK Pooled Pension Funds (Year)
1113 Annual Statement Diskette Filing Specifications
1773 Annual Statement Studies
1008 Annual Statistical Digest
959 Annual Survey of American Law
429 Annual Survey of Bankruptcy Law (Year)
2147 Annuals on CD
1186 Antitrust
730 Antitrust & Trade Regulation Report
813 Antitrust Adviser, 3–E
903 Antitrust Bulletin
795 Antitrust Counseling and Litigation Techniques
936 Antitrust Freedom of Information Log
430 Antitrust Law Handbook (Year)
1187 Antitrust Law Journal
431 Antitrust Law Sourcebook (Year)
796 Antitrust Laws and Trade Regulation
1215 Antitrust Report
2458 APA Basic Guide to Payroll
2459 APA Guide to Payroll Practice and Management
1263 API Account
2732 Applied Economics
2733 Applied Economics Letters
2734 Applied Financial Economics
2735 Applied Mathematical Finance
2566 Applied Statistics
1158 Applying GAAP (Year): A Practical Guide to Financial Reporting
1877 Appraisal Journal
1890 Appraisal Review

1878 Appraiser News
1144 Arbitration
1180 Arbitration & The Law (Year)
1181 Arbitration Journal
2611 AREUE Journal
259 ArticleFirst
2280 Articles
279 Aslib Directory of Information Sources in the United Kingdom
280 Aslib Index to Theses
1666 Assessment Journal
2038 Asset Finance & Leasing Digest
1898 Asset Sales Reports
86 Assets and Liabilities of Finance Houses and Other Credit Companies
1662 ASTIN Bulletin
1269 Audit and Accounting Guides Service
645 Audit Report
1159 Auditing and Reporting (Year)
2600 Auditing: A Journal of Practice & Theory
483 Auditor's Factbook
1914 Back Office Focus
211 Bacon's International Media Directory
161 Bacon's Newspaper/Magazine Directory
7 Balance of Payments Statistics Yearbook
1009 Balance Sheets for the US Economy
19 Balances of Payments of OECD Countries
908 Bank Accounting & Finance
2080 Bank Advertising News
911 Bank and Corporate Governance Law Reporter
2193 Bank Annual Reports (Year) World Survey
2399 Bank Asset/Liability Management
531 Bank Auditing and Accounting Report
2286 Bank Automation News
880 Bank Bailout Litigation News
1734 Bank Card Industry Report
1927 Bank Credit Analyst
2326 Bank Database
937 Bank Digest
1919 Bank Director
1735 Bank Directors Briefing
2400 Bank Directors Report
2244 Bank Directory (Year)
1768 Bank Fraud
797 Bank Holding Company Compliance Manual

2327 Bank Holding Company Database
1010 Bank Holding Company Supervision Manual
532 Bank Income Tax Return Manual
2319 Bank Information Sheets
2314 Bank Insurance Marketing
1736 Bank Insurance Survey
2149 Bank Letter
2110 Bank Loan Report
1769 Bank Management
1759 Bank Marketing
2194 Bank Marketing International
2330 Bank MergerFax
2331 Bank Mergers & Acquisitions
1899 Bank Mutual Fund Report
2056 Bank Network News
1920 Bank News
2826 Bank of America Journal of Applied Corporate Finance
1003 Bank of England Financial Indicators
1002 Bank of England Inflation Report
1004 Bank of England Quarterly Bulletin
533 Bank Officers Handbook of Commercial Banking Law
1737 Bank Operations Bulletin
2332 Bank Performance Report
1738 Bank Personnel News
20 Bank Profitability: Financial Statements of Banks (Years)
2081 Bank Rate Monitor
2107 Bank Rating Review Service
895 Bank Resolution Reporter
2287 Bank Securities Report
1030 Bank Structure and Competition
2236 Bank Systems + Technology
2111 Bank Systems & Equipment
2057 Bank Technology News
2401 Bank Technology Report
2084 Banker
534 Banker's Letter of the Law
2402 Bankers Magazine
2091 Bankers Monthly
2301 Bankers' Almanac
2302 Bankers' Almanac World Ranking
1448 Banking and Financial Services in the European Union
1913 Banking and Financial Training
414 Banking Attorney
432 Banking Crimes
355 Banking Information Index

356 Banking Information Source Ondisc
351 Banking Journals Index
798 Banking Law
2762 Banking Law Anthology
684 Banking Law in the United States
535 Banking Law Journal
799 Banking Law Manual: Legal Guide to Commercial Banks, Thrift Institutions and Credit Unions
475 Banking Law Review
1040 Banking Legislation and Policy
930 Banking Policy Report
1932 Banking Quarterly
2094 Banking Technology
1678 Banking World
1011 BankRoll II
889 Bankruptcy Counsellor
921 Bankruptcy DataSource
536 Bankruptcy Law Letter
537 Bankruptcy Law Manual
476 Bankruptcy Law Review
646 Bankruptcy Practice Deskbook
1544 Bankruptcy Records
922 Bankruptcy Yearbook and Almanac
2150 Bankstat
2539 Barron's-The Dow Jones Business and Financial Weekly
1201 Basic Documents of International Economic Law
1398 Basic Statistics of the European Community
2833 BBC Summary of World Broadcasts
1928 BCA Interest Rate Forecast
2601 Behavioral Research in Accounting
800 Bender's Federal Tax Week
2455 Benefit
2497 Benefits & Compensation International
212 Benn's Media
321 Bernan Associates' Government Publications News
322 Best Lawyers in America
1553 Best of British: The Top 20,000 Companies
1933 Best's Agents Guide
1934 Best's Aggregates and Averages
1935 Best's Casualty Loss Reserve Development Series
1936 Best's Company Reports
1937 Best's Directory of Recommended Insurance Attorneys and Adjusters
1938 Best's Experience by State (By Line)
1939 Best's Insurance Reports

1940 Best's Intelligencer
1941 Best's Key Rating Guide
1942 Best's Market Guide
1943 Best's Quantitative Analysis Report
1944 Best's Review
1945 Best's Underwriting Guide
1946 BestWeek
2486 Better Investing
1977 Bi-Weekly Investors Intelligence
1978 Bi-Weekly Technical Indicator Review
230 Bibliographic Guide to Business and Economics
243 Bibliographic Guide to Conference Publications
323 Bibliographic Guide to Government Publications
217 Bibliographic Index
1183 Bibliography of American Bar Association's Publications
906 Big Six Evaluations
2482 BIG BOND BOOK: The Directory of Below Investment Grade Corporate Bonds
324 Bimonthly Review of Law Books
185 Biography Index
186 Biography Master Index
1950 Blay's MortgageMatch
2126 BlockDATA Online
127 Blue Chip Economic Indicators
128 Blue Chip Financial Forecasts
1992 Blue Line
685 Blue Sky Compliance Manual
752 Blue Sky Law Reports
731 BNA Antitrust Database
734 BNA International Business and Finance Daily
735 BNA International Trade Daily
736 BNA Real Estate Investment Software
737 BNA's Banking Report
732 BNA's Bankruptcy Law Reporter
738 BNA's Corporate Counsel Weekly
1900 Bond Buyer
2378 Bond Buyer's Municipal Marketplace
2095 Bond Fund Report
1614 Bond Guide
2183 Bond Markets (Year), The
1910 Bond Traders Guide
2125 Bondholder
2175 BondText Muni
2022 Bondware
2170 Bondwatch

2151 BondWeek
228 Book Review Digest
229 Book Review Index
231 BookFind CD-Business & Law
232 Books in Print (Year)
233 Boston Spa Books on CD-ROM
244 Boston Spa Conferences on CD-ROM
162 Boston Spa Serials on CD-ROM
1132 Bound Volume of International Accounting Standards
236 Bowker-Whitaker Global Books in Print Plus
907 Bowman's Accounting Report
325 Bowne Digest for Corporate and Securities Lawyers
2333 Branch Migration DataSource
1195 Brief, The
973 Britain (Year): An Official Handbook
1554 Britain's Top Foreign Owned Companies
1555 Britain's Top Privately Owned Companies
2561 British Accounting Review
2562 British Accounting Review Research Register
1477 British Business Rankings
753 British Companies Legislation
754 British Company Law & Practice
755 British International Tax Agreements
234 British MARC Quarterly
756 British Master Tax Guide
757 British Tax Cases
758 British Tax Guide
759 British Tax Reporter and Tax Legislation
501 British Tax Review
760 British VAT Guide
1692 British Venture Capital Association Directory (Year)
2385 Briton's Index: Financial Institutions
2386 Briton's Index: Investment Research Analysts
2836 Broadcast News
1954 Brock Report
1533 Broker 50
433 Broker-Dealer Regulation
814 Broker-Dealers and Securities Markets
1713 Broker, The [British Insurance and Investment Brokers' Association]
2204 Broker, The [Lloyd's List International]
2167 Broker World
2023 Brokers 1000
2681 Brookings Papers on Economic Activity
2682 Brookings Review

1140 BSI Standards Catalogue (Year)
1105 Budget of the United States Government
1679 Building Societies Act 1986 Practice Manual
1680 Building Societies Yearbook (Year)
1681 Building Society Annual Account Data (Year)
1682 Building Society Annual Accounts Manual
2245 Building Society Directory (Year)
1683 Building Society Taxation Manual
1321 Bulletin for International Fiscal Documentation
2701 Bulletin of Economic Research
1371 Bulletin of Labour Statistics
2580 Bulletin of Legal Developments
1377 Bulletin of the European Communities
881 Buraff's Litigation Reports: Bank Lawyer Liability
2835 Burrelle's Broadcast Database
361 Business & Legal CD-ROMs in Print
1173 Business Briefing
2471 Business Credit
2641 Business Cycle Database
2634 Business Economics
2569 Business Economist
139 Business Europe
1545 Business Finder
2658 Business Horizons
97 Business Indicators
218 Business Information Alert
219 Business Information Review
2535 Business Insurance
846 Business Law and Practice
609 Business Law Brief
724 Business Law Handbook
705 Business Law in Europe
704 Business Law Review
1188 Business Law Today
1189 Business Lawyer
187 Business Media Directory
2246 Business Moneyfacts
169 Business Organizations, Agencies, and Publications Directory
262 Business Periodicals Index
261 Business Periodicals Ondisc
250 Business Rankings Annual (Year)
1041 Business Review
21 Business Sector Data Base
1874 Business Valuation Review

1560 Business Week 1000 Multimedia CD-ROM
260 BusinessNews
572 Busy Solicitors' Digest
647 Butterworth Tax Treaties
648 Butterworths Annual European Review
649 Butterworths Budget Tax Tables (Year)
650 Butterworths Company Law Service
651 Butterworths EC Brief
652 Butterworths EC Legislation Implementator
653 Butterworths European Law Service
292 Butterworths International Law Directory
654 Butterworths Journal of International Banking and Financial Law
313 Butterworths Law Directory
655 Butterworths Merger Control Review
656 Butterworths Orange Tax Handbook (Year)
657 Butterworths Tax Planning
658 Butterworths Tax Treaties
659 Butterworths UK Tax Guide (Year)
660 Butterworths Yellow Tax Handbook (Year)
1609 Buyouts
378 Cable and Satellite Europe
379 Cable and Satellite Yearbook
1325 Cahiers de Droit Fiscal International
1083 Call Aggregation Tables
1084 Call Reports
1960 Callahan's Credit Union Report
2177 Cambridge Futures Charts
2695 Cambridge Journal of Economics
326 Capital Guide
2127 Capital Market Strategies
706 Capital Markets Forum Yearbook
2039 Capital Markets Guide
2024 Capital Markets Handbook (Year)
2612 Capital Markets Report
327 Capital Source
573 Capital Tax Planning
574 Capital Taxes and Estate Planning in Europe
2384 Captive Insurance Company Directory (Year)
2306 Captive Insurance Company Review
159 Card Expenditure Statistics
2059 Card Industry Directory
2288 Card News
2214 Card Systems
2058 CardFAX

2195 Cards International
2741 Carnegie-Rochester Conference Series on Public Policy
2638 Case Western Reserve Journal of International Law
2639 Case Western Reserve Law Review
2462 Cash Flow Enhancement Report, The
2096 Cash Management News
293 Catalog of New Foreign and International Law Titles
1148 CBI/Coopers & Lybrand financial services survey
1818 CBOE Market Statistics
1814 CBOT Databank
1815 CBOT Research Symposium Proceedings
1816 CBOT Statistical Annual
1694 CCA News
362 Cd-rom Directory
1478 CD/Business Locator
2838 CD/Credit Register
1586 CD/Europa
1270 CD-NAARS
380 CD-ROM Professional
381 CD-ROM World
363 CD-ROMS in Print
1672 CEA Info
2025 Cedel Euromoney Directory
1388 CELEX
1 Central Bank Survey of Foreign Exchange Market Activity
170 Centres and Bureaux
2474 CFA Digest
1465 Cfarbase
1901 CFO Alert
2508 CFO: The Magazine for Chief Executives
938 CFTC Administrative Reporter
2432 CGL Reporter
2806 Challenge
1175 Chambernet National Business Database
1290 Changing Public Attitutes on Governments and Taxes
870 Chapter 11 Update
575 Charities: The Law and Practice
1739 Check Fraud Survey
2060 Checks & Checking
1947 Cheklist
1828 Chicago Stock Exchange Guide
1225 Chief Economist's Letter
2503 Chief Executive
1715 CII Journal
328 CIS Federal Register Index

329 CIS/Index to Publications of the United States Congress
1138 City Code on Takeovers and Mergers
2318 City of London Directory & Livery Companies Guide
975 Civil Service Year Book
2403 Clark's Bank Deposits and Payments Monthly
2404 Clark's Secured Transactions Monthly
155 Clearing Statistics
2256 Closed End 250 Sourcebook
1821 CME Rule Book
2832 CNN News Transcripts
761 Code and Regulations
700 Code of Federal Regulations
890 Code of Federal Regulations via Internet
22 Code of Liberalisation of Capital Movements
23 Code of Liberalisation of Current Invisible Operations
2468 Collector
801 Collier Bankruptcy Cases
802 Collier Bankruptcy Compensation Guide
803 Collier Bankruptcy Manual
804 Collier Handbook for Creditors' Committees
805 Collier Lending Institutions and the Bankruptcy Code
806 Collier on Bankruptcy
807 Collier Real Estate Transactions and the Bankruptcy Code
2645 Columbia Journal of Transnational Law
2640 Columbia Journal of World Business
2737 Columbia Law Review
1399 Comext
87 Commerce Business Daily
434 Commercial Asset-Based Financing
2433 Commercial Auto Insurance
1882 Commercial Investment Real Estate Journal
847 Commercial Law and Practice
1205 Commercial Law Bulletin
1206 Commercial Law Journal
808 Commercial Law Report
502 Commercial Laws of Europe
855 Commercial Leases
1774 Commercial Lending Newsletter
1740 Commercial Lending Review
2434 Commercial Liability Insurance
809 Commercial Loan Documentation Guide
2222 Commercial Paper and Payment Systems
2361 Commercial Paper Ratings Guide
2435 Commercial Property Insurance
1905 Commercial Real Estate Investor Directory

1971 Commodities
871 Commodities Litigation Reporter
435 Commodities Regulation: Fraud, Manipulation and Other Crimes
1993 Commodity Chart Service
762 Commodity Futures Law Reports
1817 Commodity Futures Trading: Bibliographies
54 Commodity Markets and the Developing Countries
1359 Commodity Trade Statistics
1994 Commodity Year Book Statistical Abstract Service
503 Common Market Law Reports
2581 Common Market Law Review
2723 Communist Economies and Economic Transformation
1469 Compact D/'33
1470 Compact D/SEC
891 Compact Disc Code of Federal Regulations
892 Compact Disk Federal Register
1133 Companies House Direct
1108 Companies in (Year)
1525 Companies International
1171 Company Accountant
1550 Company Intelligence
856 Company Law Monitor
576 Company Lawyer
577 Company Procedures Manual
1528 Company REFS
834 Company Reporting
2443 Company Secretarial Practice
2444 Company Secretary
680 COMPANY LAW Books on Screen
708 Comparative Law of Monopolies
709 Comparative Law Yearbook of International Business
2821 Comparative Political Studies
1880 Compendium of Commercial Finance Law
1892 Compendium: Federal Taxation of REITs
24 Competition Policy in OECD Countries (Years)
1231 Competitiveness Index
1985 Complete Commodity Futures Directory
1984 Complete Commodity Futures Directory Database
171 Complete Guide to Associations in the UK
2320 Complete Guide to Banks in the UK & Who's Who
206 Complete Guide to Book Publishers in the UK
2321 Complete Guide to Financial Advisers in the UK
2322 Complete Guide to Leasing, Factoring, Invoice Discounting & Trade Financing Companies in the UK

207 Complete Guide to Magazine & Newspaper Publishers in the UK
2323 Complete Guide to Sources of Commercial Mortgages
2324 Complete Guide to Sources of Finance for Property Developers/Investors
2325 Complete Guide to Venture Capital Companies in the UK (Year)
1378 Completing the Internal Market of the European Community
1770 Compliance Examinations Update
613 Compliance Monitor
1077 Comptroller's Handbook
364 CompuServe Companion
1647 Computer Updated International Database
1147 Computers and Law
1028 Conference Series [Federal Reserve Bank of Boston]
330 Congress in Print
993 Congressional Directory
763 Congressional Legislative Reporting
888 Congressional Quarterly Service: Weekly Report
994 Congressional Record
1000 Congressional Research Reports
477 Consolidated Returns Tax Report
2240 Consultant Compendium
188 Consultants and Consulting Organizations Directory
913 Consumer Bankruptcy News
1695 Consumer Credit
538 Consumer Credit & Truth in Lending Compliance Report
578 Consumer Credit Control
1741 Consumer Credit Delinquency Bulletin
764 Consumer Credit Guide Reports
1801 Consumer Finance Bulletin
1207 Consumer Finance Law Quarterly Report
1400 Consumer Price Index
1401 Consumer Prices in the EEC
2636 Contemporary Policy Issues
263 ContentsFirst
1846 Contingencies
2696 Contributions to Political Economy
1069 Controller's Monthly Financial Report
2389 Convertibles Survey
2646 Cornell International Law Journal
2647 Cornell Law Review
956 Corporate Accounting International
707 Corporate Acquisitions and Mergers

1582 Corporate Affiliations Plus
436 Corporate Anti Takeover Defences (Year)
839 Corporate Briefing
2496 Corporate Cashflow Magazine
2469 Corporate Collector Currents
2504 Corporate Communications Handbook
2040 Corporate Cover
437 Corporate Dividends and Stock Repurchases
2289 Corporate EFT Report
1787 Corporate Finance Letter
2041 Corporate Finance [Euromoney Publications]
2509 Corporate Finance [Financial World]
2113 Corporate Finance: The IDD Review of Investment Banking
1479 Corporate Financial Performance
2152 Corporate Financing Week
2702 Corporate Governance: An International Review
2688 Corporate Growth
2499 Corporate Money
2114 Corporate Syndicate Personnel Directory
478 Corporate Taxation
1309 Corporate Taxation and Cross-Border Payments in OECD Countries
2315 Corporate Venturing Quarterly
1587 CorpTech Profiles
692 Corpus Juris Secundum
2527 Cost of Living Survey
1643 Cotton: Review of the World Situation
438 Couch on Insurance
314 Councils, Committees & Boards
382 Counsel Connect
1305 Country Analysis
133 Country Data Forecasts
1306 Country Database
141 Country Forecasts
134 Country Outlooks
142 Country Reports
135 Country Risk Monitor
143 Country Risk Service
1280 CPA Candidate Performance on the Uniform CPA Examinations
1271 CPA Client Bulletin
1272 CPA Letter
383 CPA Technology Report
2139 CRA/HMDA Update

2138 CRA Rating Finder
1078 CRA Report
2213 Crawford's Directory of City Connections
1995 CRB Commodity Index Report
1996 CRB Commodity Yearbook
1997 CRB Futures Chart Service
2470 Cred-Alert
840 Credit & Finance Law
2362 Credit Analysis Reference Disk
2062 Credit Card Management
2061 Credit Card News
1534 Credit Index CD-ROM
1775 Credit Information Exchange Directory
2448 Credit Management
2472 Credit Manual of Commercial Laws
1085 Credit Manual: Division of Liquidation
2086 Credit Ratings in Emerging Markets
2087 Credit Ratings International
415 Credit Union Accountant
1778 Credit Union Director
1781 Credit Union Directors Newsletter
1961 Credit Union Directory
1779 Credit Union Executive
2387 Credit Union Information Service
1780 Credit Union Magazine
1777 Credit Union Management
1782 Credit Union Manager Newsletter
1948 Credit Union News
1783 Credit Union Newswatch
1962 Credit Union Yearbook
2428 Credit World
25 Creditor Reporting System: Individual Financial Transactions
439 Creditor's Rights Handbook (Year)
2363 CreditStats
2364 CreditWeek
2365 CreditWeek International
2366 CreditWeek Municipal
2360 CreditWire On-Line Service
331 Criminal Justice Abstracts
2697 Critical Perspectives on Accounting
220 Croner's A-Z of Business Information Sources
1435 Croner's Europe
221 Croner's European Business Information Sources
1402 CRONOS

1045 Cross Sections
140 Crossborder Monitor
1221 CSI Congressional Record Reporter
1222 CSI Federal Register
71 CSO Macro-Economic Data Bank
235 Cumulative Book Index
1070 Cumulative List of Organizations
1972 Currency & Financial Futures
2178 Currency Service
189 Current Biography
252 Current British Directories
264 Current Contents
253 Current European Directories
2631 Current Index to Statistics
275 Current Index to Statistics: Applications, Methods and Theory
1239 Current Internal Revenue Code, Treasury Regulations, and IRS Publications
1760 CUSIP Corporate Directory and Updating Service
1761 CUSIP Digest of Changes
1762 CUSIP International-CINS
1763 CUSIP Master Directory and Updating Service
1764 CUSIP Mortgage-Backed Services
1765 CUSIP-PPNs
1742 D-Linq
1480 D&B Europa
835 D&B Securities Taxation
2067 Daily Bankruptcy Review
995 Daily Bill Digest
1822 Daily Bulletin
2171 Daily Data Guide
2068 Daily Energy Investor
1648 Daily Eurobond List
2179 Daily Fax Services
893 Daily Federal Register via Modem
1697 Daily Futures and Options Reports
315 Daily Law Reports Index
976 Daily List
739 Daily Report for Executives
1615 Daily Stock Price Record
1240 Daily Tax Highlights and Documents
740 Daily Tax Report
1241 Daily TaxFax
1063 Daily Treasury Statement
2247 Daily Updates Fax Service

935 Daily Washington Law Reporter
2676 Darden Case Bibliography (Year)
1086 Data Book: Operating Banks and Branches
384 Database
385 Database Directory Service
2108 Database Service
386 Dealing With Technology
1012 Debits and Deposit Turnover at Commercial Banks
2483 Defaulted Bonds Newsletter
2463 Defined Contribution Plan Investing Report
1826 Derivatives
387 Derivatives Engineering and Technology
2219 Derivatives in Fund Management
2153 Derivatives Week
90 Detailed Wealth by Industry
26 Development Co-operation
2724 Development in Practice
1288 Development Report Card for the States
2729 Developments in Economics
2730 Developments in Politics
2473 Digest of Commercial Laws of the World
8 Direction of Trade Statistics
254 Directories in Print
2112 Directors & Boards
1788 Directors & Trustees Digest
1766 Directors Handbook
2528 Directors Rewards
898 Directory of Accounting Firms Worldwide
1725 Directory of All Prison and Jail Addresses and Zip Codes
1109 Directory of Authorised Insolvency Practitioners
172 Directory of British Associations & Associations in Ireland
1176 Directory of British Importers
222 Directory of Business Information Resources
1379 Directory of Community Legislation in Force
190 Directory of Directors
302 Directory of EC Information Sources
2223 Directory of Emerging Market Funds
1673 Directory of European Community Mortgage Lenders
1380 Directory of European Community Trade and Professional Associations
173 Directory of European Industrial & Trade Associations
1911 Directory of Institutional Investors
1714 Directory of Investment Brokers
365 Directory of Law-Related CD-ROMs
1610 Directory of M&A Intermediaries

1726 Directory of Mail Drop Addresses and Zip Codes
174 Directory of Management Consultants in the UK
1629 Directory of Nominees
2556 Directory of Official Statistical Agencies
245 Directory of Published Proceedings
208 Directory of Publishing (Year)
2241 Directory of Registered Investment Advisors (Year) with the Securities and Exchange Commission
2557 Directory of Statistical Societies
1906 Directory of Trust Institutions
1114 Directory to Assist Receivers of Insolvent Companies
1471 Disclosure/Spectrum Ownership Database
278 Dissertation Abstracts
388 Document Delivery World
1331 Documentary Credits Insight
931 DOJ Alert
2531 Dollar$Sense
2026 Dow Jones Telerate Bank Register (Year)
1481 Dun & Bradstreet Reference Book of American Business
1482 Dun & Bradstreet United Kingdom
1483 Dun's Business Identification Service
1484 Dun's Business Rankings
1485 Dun's Business Update
2839 Dun's Credit Guide
1486 Dun's Electronic Business Directory
1487 Dun's European Marketing Database
2840 Dun's Family Tree Service
1488 Dun's Financial Records Plus
2841 Dun's Legal Search
1489 Dun's Reference Plus
2843 Dun's Underwriting Guide
2005 Dunn & Hargitt Commodity Service
191 Duns Consultants Directory
2844 DunsPrint Worldwide
579 Dymond's Capital Taxes
2642 Early Economic Outlook
2837 Earnings Expectations Research
1500 Earnings Guide [Earnings Guide]
1616 Earnings Guide [Standard & Poor's]
1404 Earnings in Agriculture
1403 Earnings – Industry and Services
1348 East-West Investment
504 EC Competition Law Handbook (Year)
1310 EC Corporate Tax Law
1405 EC External Trade Indices

1451 EC Grants and Loans Database
1301 EC Information Handbook
303 EC Institutions' Yellow Pages
765 EC Merger Control Monitor
1389 ECLAS
2609 EconLit
2804 Econometric Reviews
2551 Econometrica
1406 Economic Accounts for Agriculture and Forestry
2822 Economic and Industrial Democracy
1353 Economic and Social Survey of Asia and the Pacific (Year)
1349 Economic Bulletin for Europe
114 Economic Chartbook
2823 Economic Development Quarterly
1287 Economic Development Review
131 Economic Forecasts: A Monthly Worldwide Survey
1103 Economic Indicators
2637 Economic Inquiry
1426 Economic Interpenetration
2565 Economic Journal
2718 Economic Modelling
2570 Economic Outlook [London Business School]
1789 Economic Outlook [Savings & Community Bankers of America]
1031 Economic Perspectives
2583 Economic Policy: A European Forum
1046 Economic Quarterly
1104 Economic Report of the President
1026 Economic Review [Federal Reserve Bank of Atlanta]
1032 Economic Review [Federal Reserve Bank of Cleveland]
1033 Economic Review [Federal Reserve Bank of Dallas]
1037 Economic Review [Federal Reserve Bank of Kansas City]
1047 Economic Review [Federal Reserve Bank of San Francisco]
11 Economic Reviews [International Monetary Fund]
1226 Economic Road Maps
1350 Economic Survey of Europe in (Year)
1351 Economic Survey of Latin America and the Caribbean (Year)
2725 Economic Systems Research
2692 Economic Theory
1227 Economic Times
72 Economic Trends [Central Statistical Office]
1087 Economic Trends [Federal Deposit Insurance Corporation]
2703 Economica
2742 Economics Letters

2790 Economics of Planning
1421 Economics of Transition
154 Economist, The
105 Economy at a Glance
1381 ECU-EMS Information
1472 EDGARPlus
2097 EDI Update
213 Editors Media Directories
710 EEC Merger Control Reporter
2519 Effective Remuneration
2063 EFT Network Data Book
2290 EFT Report
1134 EITF Abstracts
138 EIU Business Intelligence Series
389 Electronic Documents
1998 Electronic Futures Trend Analyzer
390 Electronic Information Report
391 Electronic Marketplace Report
2196 Electronic Payments International
1809 Electronic Symbol Book
1300 Electronic Trader
2115 Eliot Sharp's Financing News
1115 Emerging Accounting Issues Working Group Subscription
1617 Emerging and Special Situations
2224 Emerging Market Fund Monitor
1929 Emerging Markets Analyst
68 Emerging Markets Data Base
2303 Emerging Markets Investor
69 Emerging Stock Markets Factbook (Year)
440 Emerging Trends in Securities Law (Year)
899 Emerson's Auditor Change Report
1670 EMFA Yearbook
1462 EMMA
2430 Employee Benefits Journal
1743 Employee Benefits Quarterly
661 Encyclopaedia of Banking Law
175 Encyclopedia of Associations
223 Encyclopedia of Business Information Sources
505 Encyclopedia of Competition Law
506 Encyclopedia of Consumer Credit Law
507 Encyclopedia of Financial Services Law
508 Encyclopedia of Insurance Law
711 Encyclopedia of International Commercial Litigation
1644 Energy Prices and Taxes
580 Equipment Leasing

924 Equipment Leasing Newsletter
1802 Equipment Leasing Today
2128 Equities International
2027 Equityware
686 ERISA and Benefits Law Journal
939 ERISA Citator
940 ERISA Update
2004 ERISA: The Red Book of Pension Funds
2665 Essays in International Finance
941 Ethics in Government Reporter
2683 ETI Update
1436 EU and Eastern Europe Database
176 EU Trade and Professional Associations and their Information
1967 EURA-CD
2329 EURABANK Top 2500
304 Euro Who's Who
1437 EUROCAT
1390 EUROCRON
845 Eurolaw
2574 EUROLOC
2088 Euromarket Report
2042 Euromoney
110 Europa World Year Book (Year)
2134 Europe Buyout Monitor
1427 Europe Daily Bulletin
1409 Europe in Figures
1501 Europe's 15,000 Largest Companies
1502 Europe's Largest Companies
1431 Europe's Money
1504 European 5000
305 European Access
712 European Accountancy Yearbook (Year)
957 European Accountant
2559 European Accounting Review
2197 European Banker
350 European Business and Industry
224 European Business Intelligence Briefing
713 European Business Law Review
614 European Business Monitor
251 European Business Rankings
509 European Commercial Cases
662 European Communities Legislation: Current Status (Year)
2575 European Community Funding for Business Development
1684 European Community Mortage Bulletin

510 European Competition Law Review
177 European Consultants Directory
511 European Current Law
178 European Directory of Management Consultants
1505 European Directory of Medium Sized Companies
2560 European Economic Review
2704 European Financial Management
714 European Financial Services Law
1508 European Handbook
1445 European Insight
2011 European Insurance Market
2006 European Insurance Yearbook (Year)
1444 European Intelligence
2736 European Journal of Finance
512 European Journal of International Law
2791 European Journal of Law and Economics
2743 European Journal of Political Economy
857 European Law Monitor
513 European Law Review
306 European Legal Journals Index
308 European Lobbyists Practical Guide
1490 European Market Guide
123 European Marketing Data and Statistics (Year)
367 European Multimedia Yearbook (Year)
1973 European Point & Figure Library
307 European References
2576 European Regional Incentives (Year)
1446 European Report
1671 European Stock Exchange Statistics
1311 European Tax Handbook (Year)
1299 European Taxation
1312 European Taxation Database on CD-ROM
1424 European Trade Statistical Reports
144 European Trends
1382 European Union Press Releases
1432 EUROSCOPE
1410 Eurostat-CD (Year)
98 EUROSTAT-CD
1411 Eurostatistics
1430 EuroWatch
2043 Euroweek
115 Evans-Novak Political Report
1668 evca Yearbook
1150 Executive Accountant
2507 Executive Compensation Reports

192 Executive Speeches
1565 Executive Stock Report
1242 Exempt Organization Tax Review
441 Exempted Transactions under the Securities Act
1509 EXSTAT
1510 Extel Financial Workstation
1511 Extel Foreign Exchange Rates Record
1512 Extel International Bonds Service
1513 Extel Professional Advisers to New Issues
1514 Extel Securities Taxation Services
1515 Extel UK Dividend and Interest Record
27 External Debt Statistics
1412 External Trade
1951 Factoring Database
1259 Facts and Figures on Government Finance
872 Failed Bank and Thrift Litigation Reporter
1088 Failed Bank Cost Analysis
873 Failed Leveraged Buyout Litigation Reporter
1463 FAME
1413 Family Budgets: Comparative Tables
2271 FC&S Bulletins
1089 FDIC Banking Review
1090 FDIC Consumer News
1091 FDIC Enforcement Decisions and Orders
1092 FDIC Investment Properties
1093 FDIC Law, Regulations and Related Acts
885 FDIC Regulations
1042 Fed in Print
2186 Federal & State Insurance Week
1744 Federal Advertising and Marketing Law Guide
766 Federal Banking Law Reports
539 Federal Banking Laws
1209 Federal Bar News & Journal
987 Federal Budget Report
1784 Federal Credit Union
942 Federal Ethics Report
1790 Federal Guide
494 Federal Income Tax Regulations
540 Federal Income Taxation of Banks and Financial Institutions
815 Federal Income Taxation of Corporate Liquidations
816 Federal Information Disclosure, 2–E
970 Federal Judicial Workload Statistics
1210 Federal Lawyer
1862 Federal Legislative Reports

332 Federal News Service
701 Federal Register
894 Federal Register/Code of Federal Regulations Tracker Service
693 Federal Reporter 2d
1005 Federal Reserve Bulletin
1013 Federal Reserve Regulatory Service
116 Federal Reserve Releases
767 Federal Securities Law Reports
694 Federal Supplement
768 Federal Tax Articles
817 Federal Tax Aspects of Bankruptcy
495 Federal Tax Coordinator 2D
932 Federal Tax Guide
769 Federal Tax Manual With Monthly Reports
818 Federal Tax Planning
496 Federal Tax Regulations [Research Institute of America]
695 Federal Tax Regulations [West Publishing Corporation]
933 Federal Taxes 2nd
1214 Federation of Insurance and Corporate Counsel Quarterly
2069 FedFilings Investment Research
2388 FERC Report, The
1101 FFIEC Information Systems Handbook
1194 Fidelity and Surety News
1999 Final Markets
2092 Finance (Year)
12 Finance & Development
977 Finance Act (Year)
2003 Finance and Commerce Daily Newspaper
1422 Finance Bulletin
1014 Finance Companies
2396 Finance Director
357 Finance Literature Database
2705 Financial Accountability & Management
1135 Financial Accounting Research System
2475 Financial Analysts' Journal
2792 Financial and Monetary Policy Studies
2367 Financial Companies Rating Service
1066 Financial Connection
1216 Financial Crimes Report
2457 Financial Executive
136 Financial Executive's Country Risk Alert
2513 Financial Factbook
55 Financial Flows and the Developing Countries
1034 Financial Industry Issues

1094 Financial Institution Lists
1723 Financial Institutions Internal Audit Manual
2368 Financial Institutions Rating Service
392 Financial IT
2624 Financial Management
2511 Financial Management Handbook
2494 Financial Management Manual
28 Financial Market Trends
2098 Financial Marketing Update
2660 Financial Markets, Institutions and Instruments
193 Financial Planners and Planning Organizations Directory
2451 Financial Planning [Institute of Financial Planning]
2426 Financial Planning [International Association for Financial Planning]
610 Financial Regulation Report
2012 Financial Reinsurance & Futures Newsletter
1160 Financial Reporting (Year)
484 Financial Reporting & Disclosure Manual
663 Financial Reporting and Accounting Service
2623 Financial Review
1116 Financial Review of Alien Insurers
2184 Financial Services Alert
514 Financial Services Brief
862 Financial Services Compliance Data
1745 Financial Services Industry Trends
858 Financial Services Law Letter
2334 Financial Services M&A Insider
2335 Financial Services Quarterly
2185 Financial Services Regulation and Legislation
2291 Financial Services Report
2773 Financial Services Review
664 Financial Services: Law and Practice
1883 Financial Statements and Operating Ratios for the Mortgage Banking Industry
73 Financial Statistics
393 Financial Technology Bulletin
2099 Financial Technology International Bulletin
394 Financial Technology Review
129 Financial Times Currency Forecaster
1507 Financial Times FT 500
130 Financial Times Global Investor
1516 Financial Times Mergers and Acquisitions International
2209 Financial Times World Insurance Yearbook
2237 Financial Trader
1027 Financial Update

29 Financing and External Debt of Developing Countries
145 Financing Foreign Operations
1151 Find
248 FINDEX (Year)
1217 Fiscal Letter
2585 Fiscal Studies
2257 Five Star Investor
2543 Fleet Street Letter
442 Fletcher Cyclopedia of Corporations
1015 Flow of Funds Account
30 Flows and Stocks of Fixed Capital
1724 FMS Update
1375 FOCUS
1851 Focus: A Quarterly Digest of Insurance & Financial Strategies
1655 Food Aid Shipments
2649 Fordham International Law Journal
2650 Fordham Law Review
1060 Forecasts for the UK Economy
1834 Foreign Activity Report
1294 Foreign Agricultural Trade of the United States
91 Foreign Direct Investment in the United States
2154 Foreign Exchange Letter
31 Foreign Trade
32 Foreign Trade by Commodities
2449 Foresight
1930 Forexcast
1473 Fortune 500 on Disk
1197 Franchise Law Journal
1637 Franchise Legal Digest
1638 Franchise Opportunities Guide
819 Franchising Adviser
1639 Franchising World
515 Franchising: Law and Practice
1204 Fraud Examiners Manual
820 Fraud, Window Dressing and Negligence in Financial Statements
113 Freedom in the World
1520 FT Stats Fiche
2225 Full UK Equities Listing
1976 FullerMoney
368 Fulltext Sources Online
1696 Fund Management Survey (Year)
2516 Fund Raising Management
2390 Fund Survey

1840 FUNDamentals
2198 Funds International
2414 Futures & Options Factors
1825 Futures and Options Fact Book
2220 Futures and Options World
1824 Futures Industry
884 Futures International Law Letter
2000 Futures Market Service
2719 Futures [Butterworth-Heinemann]
2284 Futures [Oster Communications]
2510 FW
2416 FX Week
366 Gale Directory of Databases
214 Gale Directory of Publications and Broadcast Media
998 GAO Review
1328 GATT Focus
1414 General Government Accounts and Statistics
2550 GENEVA Papers on Risk and Insurance: Theory
1016 Geographical Distribution of Assets and Liabilities of Major Foreign . . .
33 Geographical Distribution of Financial Flows to Developing Countries
2651 Georgetown Law Journal
1986 Global Bond Guide
236 Global BookBank
1228 Global Business Briefing
1466 Global Company Handbook
1467 Global Company News Digest
1915 Global Custodian
56 Global Economic Prospects and the Developing Countries
2545 Global Finance
2774 Global Finance Journal
1987 Global Financial Report on Financial Services & Brokerage Firms
1988 Global Financial Report on International Banks
1989 Global Financial Services Monthly
770 Global Franchising Alert
2534 Global Investment Management
1990 Global Investment Quarterly
2044 Global Investor
2155 Global Money Management
57 Global Outlook and the Developing Countries
2255 Global Ratings Guide
943 Global Register of the Leading International Accounting Firms

2488 Global Shareholder
2180 Global Trends
1618 Global Vantage
265 Globalbase
109 GlobalVision
443 Going Public and the Public Corporation
444 Going Public Handbook (Year)
2116 Going Public: The IPO Reporter
1640 Gold (Year)
1661 Gold Demand Trends
2156 Goldman Sachs Directory of Global Securities Lending . . .
2028 Goldman Sachs Foreign Exchange Handbook (Year)
665 Goode's Consumer Credit Legislation
1277 Government Accountants Journal
541 Government Accounting and Auditing Update
2491 Government Finance Review
9 Government Finance Statistics Yearbook
1415 Government Financing of Research and Development
2577 Government Funding for United Kingdom Business
1233 Government Information Insider
333 Government Information Quarterly
334 Government Reference Books
1061 Government's Expenditure Plans (Years)
1137 Governmental Accounting Research System
985 GPO Sales Publications Reference File
2626 GRA Reporter
1656 Grain Market Report
346 GT Guide to World Equity Markets (Year)
1902 Guarantor
255 Guide to American Directories
696 Guide to American Law
728 Guide to Corporation Tax
2505 Guide to Credit Management
215 Guide to European Business Media
1443 Guide to European Community Grants and Loans
821 Guide to International Commerce Law
1841 Guide to Mutual Funds
284 Guide to Special Issues and Indexes of Periodicals
79 Guide to the Classification of Overseas Trade Statistics
1313 Guide to the European VAT Directives
1314 Guides to European Taxation
1464 HALO
1529 Hambro Company Guide
395 Handbook of Digital Dealing Room Systems
2189 Handbook of Insurance

1339 Handbook of International Trade and Development Statistics (Year)
2520 Handbook of Risk Management
347 Handbook of World Stock and Commodity Exchanges
2521 Handbook on Pensions
1333 Harmonized System Commodity Data Base on CD-ROM
581 Harrison's Inland Revenue Index to Tax Cases
2654 Harvard Business Review
237 Harvard Business School Core Collection (Year)
2655 Harvard International Law Journal
2656 Harvard Journal of Law and Public Policy
2657 Harvard Law Review
905 Hein Checklist of Statutes
1530 Henderson Top 1000 Charities (Year)
974 Hermes
445 Herzog's Bankruptcy Forms and Practice
2369 High Yield Quarterly
1903 High Yield Report
2484 High Yield Securities Journal
2070 High Yield Weekly
1243 Highlights & Documents
117 Highlights of Budget Deficit Financing
582 HM Customs & Excise Official VAT Guides
1058 HM Customs and Excise News Releases
978 HMSO Agency Catalogue
979 HMSO in Print on Microfiche
980 HMSO Monthly Catalogue
1746 Home Equity Lines of Credit Report
1604 Hoover's Guide to Private Companies
1606 Hoover's Handbook of American Business (Year)
1607 Hoover's Handbook of Emerging Companies
1605 Hoover's Handbook of World Business (Year)
1608 Hoover's MasterList of Major US Companies (Year)
516 Hoskin VAT Case Digest: UK and Community Law
989 House of Commons Hansard on CD-ROM
990 House of Commons Weekly Information Bulletin
988 House of Lords Hansard on CD-ROM
74 Housing and Construction Statistics
1685 Housing Finance
1686 Housing Finance Fact Book (Year)
1635 Housing Finance International
583 Housing Law and Precedents
859 Housing Law Monitor
517 Housing Law Reports
1687 Housing Legislation Manual

1889 Housing Market Statistics
1130 Housing Policy Debate
2675 Huebner Foundation Monographs
1053 HyperTax
1059 HyperVAT
1667 IAAO Membership Directory
1161 ICAEW Taxation Service
2045 ICB Magazine
2046 ICB Newsletter
2047 ICB Settlements Report
1535 ICC Company Directory
1536 ICC Company Financials
1537 ICC Full Text Company Reports
1538 ICC Sharewatch
1539 ICC Stockbroker Research
65 ICSID Review: Foreign Investment Law Journal
1391 IDEA
2579 IDS Bulletin
1326 IFAC Handbook Subscription Service
2129 IFR Corporate Eye
2130 IFR Omnibase
2131 IFR Vigil
1142 IHS International Standards and Specifications
358 III Data Base
359 III Insurance Daily
13 IMF Survey
2166 IMMS Weekly Marketeer
1162 Implementing GAAS (Year): A Practical Guide to Auditing and Reporting
1177 Importing Today
1126 IMRO Rule Book
2427 INAISE Newsletter
485 Income Tax Factbook
1855 Independent Agent
1771 Independent Banker
2485 Independent Investors Forum
1244 Index Digest Bulletin
1524 Index of Nominees and their Beneficial Owners
1273 Index to Accounting and Auditing Technical Pronouncements
320 Index to Foreign Legal Periodicals
294 Index to Legal Periodicals
34 Indicators of Industrial Activity
2481 Individual Investor's Guide to No-Load Mutual Funds
1491 Industry Norms and Key Business Ratios

1392 INFO 92
369 Information Industry Directory
1397 Information Market Guide
225 Information Report
295 Information Technology and the Law
2013 Information Technology in Insurance
396 Information Today
397 Information World Review
2431 INFOSOURCE
771 Inheritance, Estate and Gift Tax Reports Federal-All States
2135 Initiative Europe Monitor
584 Inland Revenue Clearances
585 Inland Revenue Official Tax Guides
586 Inland Revenue Practices and Concessions
1054 Inland Revenue Statistics
398 Inside Market Data
2140 Inside Mortgage Finance
2141 Inside Mortgage Securities
1455 Insider Options
446 Insider Trading Regulation
1452 Insiders' Chronicle
2074 Insight
587 Insolvency
1111 Insolvency General Report for the Year (Year)
588 Insolvency Intelligence
615 Insolvency Law & Practice
918 INSource: The Red Books on CD-ROM
1747 Instalment Credit Report
1163 Institute of Chartered Accountants in England and Wales Directory of . . .
266 Institute of Management International Databases Plus
2157 Institutional Investor
2238 Insurance + Technology
919 Insurance & Liability Reporter
2014 Insurance & Reinsurance Solvency Report
416 Insurance Accountant
2019 Insurance Age
1110 Insurance Annual Report (Year)
1866 Insurance Availability Survey
1720 Insurance Broker
2168 Insurance Brokers' Monthly & Insurance Adviser
80 Insurance Companies' and Pension Funds' Investment
725 Insurance Contract Law
1955 Insurance Directory (Year)
1858 Insurance Facts

1450 Insurance Industry in the European Union
2199 Insurance Industry International
874 Insurance Industry Litigation Reporter
1859 Insurance Issues Update
352 Insurance Journals Index
616 Insurance Law & Practice
822 Insurance Law Citations
860 Insurance Law Monthly
823 Insurance Litigation Reporter
360 Insurance Periodicals Index
2276 Insurance Pocket Book (Year)
1860 Insurance Pulse
2190 Insurance Register (Year)
417 Insurance Regulator
2117 Insurance Software Review
35 Insurance Statistics Yearbook (Years)
2100 Insurance Systems Bulletin
1245 Insurance Tax Review
1211 Insurance Tax Seminar
2169 Insurance Technology Report
2191 Insuring Foreign Risks
370 Interactive Media International Newsletter
2422 Interest Rate Service
542 Internal Auditing Alert
1278 Internal Auditor
1071 Internal Revenue Bulletin
1072 Internal Revenue Bulletin Index-Digest System
886 Internal Revenue Code, Treasury Regulations & Taxpayer Publications
497 Internal Revenue Code [Research Institute of America]
697 Internal Revenue Code [West Publishing Corporation]
447 Internal Revenue Manual: Abridged and Annotated
944 International Accounting and Auditing Trends
1366 International Accounting and Reporting Issues
958 International Accounting Bulletin
967 International Accounting Summaries
2591 International Affairs
666 International Agency and Distribution Agreements
2582 International and Comparative Law Quarterly
418 International Bank Accountant
1931 International Bank Credit Analyst
2109 International Bank Rating Service
589 International Banking and Financial Law
3 International Banking and Financial Market Developments
419 International Banking Regulator

2089 International Banking Report
1641 International Bond and Share Society Journal
2048 International Bond Investor
1649 International Bond Manual
2307 International Broker
146 International Business Newsletters on Disc
716 International Business Series: Legal Aspects of Doing Business in North America
715 International Business Series: Legal Aspects of Doing Business in Europe
14 International Capital Markets
448 International Capital Markets and Securities Regulation
518 International Company and Commercial Law Review
946 International Corporate Law
848 International Corporate Procedures
824 International Corporate Taxation
1654 International Cotton Industry Statistics
132 International Country Risk Guide
2423 International Currency Review
1329 International Customs Journal
1330 International Development Policies
36 International Direct Investment Statistics Yearbook (Year)
296 International Directory of Government (Year)
1117 International Directory of Insurance Regulatory Officials
1492 International Dun's Business Identification Service
1493 International Dun's Market Identifiers
2554 International Economic Association Conference Volumes
1048 International Economic Conditions
2685 International Economic Insights
2674 International Economic Review
1229 International Economic Scoreboard
717 International Encyclopaedia of Comparative Law
718 International Encyclopaedia of Laws. Corporations and Partners
719 International Encyclopaedia of Laws. Insurance Law
1588 International Equities
947 International Financial Law Review
15 International Financial Statistics
99 International Financial Statistics on CD-ROM
2132 International Financing Review
1315 International Guide to Mergers and Acquisitions
1316 International Guide to Partnerships
687 International Income Tax Rules of the United States
772 International Income Taxation
825 International Individual Taxation

226 International Information Report
2172 International Insider
1327 International Insolvency Review
590 International Insurance Law and Regulation
519 International Insurance Law Review
2173 International Insurance Monitor
2308 International Insurance Report
2029 International Investment Management Directory (Year)
1916 International Investors Directory
2672 International Journal of Accounting: Education and Research
2829 International Journal of Finance & Economics
2555 International Journal of Forecasting
1303 International Journal of Government Auditing
852 International Journal of Insurance Law
2830 International Journal of Intelligent Systems in Accounting . . .
2805 International Journal of Public Administration
2726 International Journal of the Economics of Business
1372 International Labour Documentation
1373 International Labour Review
948 International Law Firm Management
952 International Law Reports
1190 International Lawyer
1202 International Legal Materials
2053 International Manager Profiles
123 International Marketing Data and Statistics (Year)
2500 International Money Marketing
773 International Offshore Financial Centres
2808 International Organization
688 International Personal Tax Planning Encyclopedia
1974 International Point & Figure Library
1589 International Public
960 International Regulation of Finance and Investment
106 International Reports
2824 International Review of Administrative Sciences
2775 International Review of Economics and Finance
2776 International Review of Financial Analysis
2720 International Review of Law and Economics
1494 International Risk & Payment Review
37 International Sectoral Data Base
1517 International Securities Database
2049 International Securities Lending
961 International Securities Regulation
882 International Securities Regulation Report

2558 International Statistical Review
100 International Statistical Yearbook on CD-ROM
1657 International Steel Statistics Summary Tables
1367 International Tax Agreements
2793 International Tax and Public Finance
841 International Tax Digest
774 International Tax Handbook
927 International Tax Journal
775 International Tax Planning Manual
842 International Tax Report
949 International Tax Review
968 International Tax Summaries
591 International Tax Systems and Planning Techniques
962 International Tax Treaties of All Nations. Series A
963 International Tax Treaties of All Nations. Series B
1376 International Trade (Year): Trends and Statistics
449 International Trade and US Antitrust Law
733 International Trade Reporter
1360 International Trade Statistics Yearbook
1322 International Transfer Pricing Journal
592 International Trust Precedents
1323 International VAT Monitor
194 International Who's Who
2727 International Yearbook of Law, Computers & Technology
399 Internet Connection
400 Internet World
1079 Interpretations and Actions
1551 Investext
1590 Investext Reports
147 Investing, Licensing and Trading Conditions Abroad
1456 Investment Analysis and Update
1848 Investment Bulletin
1164 Investment Business Compliance Manual
2118 Investment Dealers' Digest
66 Investment Laws of the World
401 Investment Management Technology
2054 Investment Manager Profiles
1457 Investment Portfolio Guide
2391 Investment Survey
67 Investment Treaties
1705 Investment Trust Directory
450 Investments Limited Partnership Handbook (Year)
2487 Investor Advisory Service
2490 Investor Relations Update
2547 Investor's Daily

2546 Investor's Digest
1845 Investor's Guide to Low-Cost Mutual Funds
2544 Investors Chronicle
1073 IRS Federal Tax Forms
776 IRS Letter Rulings
1246 IRS Letter Rulings and Technical Advice Memorandums
1074 IRS Research Bulletin
1247 IRS Revenue Rulings and Revenue Procedures
1075 IRS Taxpayer Information Publications
2419 Irving's Interest Rate Speculator
668 Is It In Force?
2476 ISFA Digest
1650 ISMA Price Service
1748 ISO Register
1304 ISSA Handbook (Year)
168 ISSN Compact
1847 Issues Digest
2599 Issues in Accounting Education
2292 Item Processing Report
1711 Ivanhoe Guide to Pensions Management (Year)
669 Joint Ventures with International Partners
1556 JordanShare
1557 JordanWatch
1275 Journal of Accountancy
2744 Journal of Accounting and Economics
2745 Journal of Accounting and Public Policy
2659 Journal of Accounting, Auditing & Finance
2746 Journal of Accounting Education
2671 Journal of Accounting Literature
2668 Journal of Accounting Research
1295 Journal of Agricultural Economics Research
1749 Journal of Agricultural Lending
2789 Journal of Applied Business Research
2831 Journal of Applied Econometrics
2728 Journal of Applied Statistics
1875 Journal of Appraisal Review and Management
1772 Journal of Bank Cost & Management Accounting
543 Journal of Bank Taxation
2747 Journal of Banking and Finance
544 Journal of Bankruptcy Law and Practice
2827 Journal of Business
2759 Journal of Business & Finance Librarianship
2619 Journal of Business and Economic Statistics
2706 Journal of Business Finance and Accounting
152 Journal of Business Forecasting Methods and Systems

520 Journal of Business Law
2748 Journal of Business Venturing
1776 Journal of Commercial Lending
2707 Journal of Common Market Studies
2622 Journal of Comparative Economics
2632 Journal of Computational and Graphical Statistics
901 Journal of Corporate Accounting and Finance
2749 Journal of Corporate Finance
545 Journal of Corporate Taxation
2529 Journal of Cost Management
2158 Journal of Derivatives
2750 Journal of Development Economics
2751 Journal of Econometrics
2752 Journal of Economic Behavior and Organization
2753 Journal of Economic Dynamics and Control
2607 Journal of Economic Literature
2818 Journal of Economic Methodology
2608 Journal of Economic Perspectives
2708 Journal of Economic Surveys
2698 Journal of Economic Theory
2809 Journal of Economics and Management Strategy
2754 Journal of Empirical Finance
2610 Journal of Finance
2677 Journal of Financial and Quantitative Analysis
2755 Journal of Financial Economics
2553 Journal of Financial Engineering
2663 Journal of Financial Intermediation
2478 Journal of Financial Planning
2678 Journal of Financial Research
2794 Journal of Financial Services Research
2159 Journal of Fixed Income
2644 Journal of Futures Markets
2461 Journal of Global Business
2699 Journal of Housing Economics
1131 Journal of Housing Research
2602 Journal of Information Systems
1118 Journal of Insurance Regulation
2694 Journal of Interdiciplinary Economics
2777 Journal of International Accounting Auditing & Taxation
521 Journal of International Banking Law
2756 Journal of International Economics
2661 Journal of International Financial Management and Accounting
2760 Journal of International Financial Markets, Institutions & Money

2721 Journal of International Money and Finance
546 Journal of International Taxation
2160 Journal of Investing
2669 Journal of Law and Economics
2810 Journal of Law, Economics, and Organization
2604 Journal of Management Accounting Research
2757 Journal of Monetary Economics
2664 Journal of Money, Credit and Banking
2761 Journal of Multinational Financial Management
547 Journal of Partnership Taxation
928 Journal of Pension Planning and Compliance
2828 Journal of Political Economy
2161 Journal of Portfolio Management
2807 Journal of Post Keynesian Economics
929 Journal of Property Tax Management
2758 Journal of Public Economics
2722 Journal of Public Policy
2795 Journal of Real Estate Finance and Economics
2613 Journal of Real Estate Literature
2614 Journal of Real Estate Portfolio Management
2615 Journal of Real Estate Research
548 Journal of Real Estate Taxation
2796 Journal of Regulatory Economics
904 Journal of Reprints for Antitrust Law & Economics
2617 Journal of Risk and Insurance
2797 Journal of Risk and Uncertainty
549 Journal of S Corporation Taxation
2778 Journal of Small Business Finance
550 Journal of Taxation
479 Journal of Taxation of Estates and Trusts
551 Journal of Taxation of Exempt Organizations
552 Journal of Taxation of Investment
480 Journal of Taxation of S Corporations
1852 Journal of the American Society of CLU & ChFC
2620 Journal of the American Statistical Association
2603 Journal of the American Taxation Association
1719 Journal of the Institute of Actuaries
1716 Journal of the Insurance Institute of London
2133 Journal of the International Securities Market
2567 Journal of the Royal Statistical Society
1717 Journal of the Society of Fellows
2710 Journal of Time Series Analysis
2700 Journal of Urban Economics
1923 Jumbo Rate News
1433 JUSTIS CELEX

1853 Keeping Current
1601 Kelly's Directory
1495 Key British Enterprises
1496 Key Business Ratios
909 Kiplinger Tax Letter
910 Kiplinger Washington Letter
2548 Kiplinger's Personal Finance Magazine
2549 Kiplinger's Retirement Report
2001 Knight-Ridder News Summaries
1602 Kompass Europe
1603 Kompass UK
238 LaserCat
1474 LaserD/International
335 Law and Legal Information Directory
964 Law and Practice Under the GATT and Other Trading Arrangements
336 Law Books and Serials in Print (Year)
337 Law Firms Yellow Book
925 Law Journal EXTRA!
312 Law Librarian
338 Law Librarian's Bulletin Board
553 Law of Bank Deposits, Collections and Credit Cards
554 Law of Electronic Fund Transfer Systems
522 Law of Loans and Borrowing
523 Law of Occupational Pension Schemes
670 Law of the European Communities
451 Law of Transnational Business Transactions
524 Law of Transnational Business Transactions
1145 Law Society's Gazette
1146 Law Society's Guardian Gazette
969 Law Under Review: A Quarterly Bulletin of Law Reform Projects
838 Law Update (Year)
832 Lawyer, The
1212 Lawyers Job Bulletin Board
999 LC MARC – Books
239 LC MARC English
420 LDC Debt Report
593 Leasehold Law
1803 Leasing Buyer's Guide
1952 Leasing Database
2446 Legal Abacus
316 Legal Articles Monthly
851 Legal Business
340 Legal Information Alert

317 Legal Information Management Index
318 Legal Information Resources CD-ROM
319 Legal Journals Index
339 Legal Publisher
868 Legal Times
1218 LegisBrief
1219 Legislative Finance Papers
2477 Legislative, Regulatory and Case Law Developments: The Year in Review
555 Lender Liability Law Report
875 Lender Liability Litigation Reporter
883 Lender Liability News
1332 Letter of Credit Update
1248 Letter Ruling Review
902 Letters of Credit Report
452 Liability of Attorneys and Accountants for Securities Transactions
945 Liability Risk & Insurance
2310 Life & Health Insurance Sales
1863 Life Association News
594 Life Assurance Law and Practice
2015 Life Assurance Market
1849 Life Insurance Fact Book
2200 Life Insurance International
2523 Lifestyle Pocket Book (Year)
453 Limited Liability Company Handbook (Year)
1664 LIMRA's Marketfacts
402 Link Review of Interactive Services
403 Link-Up
1017 List of Foreign Margin Stocks
1018 List of Marginable OTC Stocks
1165 List of Members and Firms (Year)
981 List of Statutory Instruments together with the List of Statutory Rules . . .
1119 Listing of Companies
1703 Listing Rules
2643 LITMUS
1043 Livingston Survey
2075 Lloyd's Brokers
2205 Lloyd's Casualty Week
2206 Lloyd's Insurance International
853 Lloyd's Law Reports
2207 Lloyd's List International
2007 Lloyd's Market (Year) Yearbook
2208 Lloyd's Shipping Economist

2076 Lloyd's Underwriting Agents
1019 Loans and Securities at all Commercial Banks
2030 Loanware
595 Local Government Finance: Law and Practice
2424 London Currency Report
982 London Gazette
2016 London Market Newsletter
2008 London Market Yearbook (Year)
2571 London Share Price Database
2686 Macroeconomics Annual (Year)
267 Magazine Index
38 Main Economic Indicators
1526 Major Companies of Europe
1518 Major UK Companies Handbook
1153 Management Accounting Research
1152 Management Accounting [Chartered Institute of Management Accounting]
1279 Management Accounting [Institute of Management Accountants]
281 Managing Information
896 Managing Mortgages
2711 Manchester School of Economic and Social Studies
826 Manual of Foreign Investment in the United States
2436 Manual of Rules, Classifications, and Interpretations for Workers . . .
2210 MAR
2211 MAR Hedge
2212 MAR's Quarterly Performance Reports
2017 Marine & Aviation Insurance Report
1558 Market Guide Select OTC Stock Edition
2187 Market Reports
2188 Market Reviews
249 Marketing Surveys Index
2311 Marketplace Search
1559 MarketPlace Business
1879 MarketSource
2176 MarkIntel
341 Martindale-Hubbell Law Directory
2712 Mathematical Finance
4 Maturity, Sectoral and Nationality Distribution of International . . .
2142 MBS Deal Tracker
1521 McCarthy on CD-ROM
1522 McCarthy Press Cuttings
2216 Media General Corporate Bonds Database

2217 Media General Mutual Funds Database
216 Mediadisk PLUS
1527 Medium Companies of Europe
1566 MegaInsight Common Stock Database
1698 Member Firms of the London Stock Exchange
1095 Merger Decisions
1611 Merger Yearbook
1543 Mergers & Acquisitions Database
487 Mergers & Acquisitions in Europe
1541 Mergers & Acquisitions International
1542 Mergers & Acquisitions Report
486 Mergers & Acquisitions [Gee]
1540 Mergers & Acquisitions [IDD Information Services]
1612 Mergers and Corporate Policy
454 Mertens Law of Federal Income Taxation: Treatise
2713 Metroeconomica
1827 MFA Journal Encore
689 Michie's Federal Law on Disc
1497 Million Dollar Directory
1523 MIRAC Company Annual Reports
1688 MIRAS Lenders Manual
1120 Model Laws, Regulations and Guidelines
2405 Modern Securities Transfers
2542 Monetary and Economic Review
118 Monetary Policy Scorecard
1049 Monetary Trends
1416 Money and Finance
2101 Money Fund Directory
2102 Money Fund Report
866 Money Laundering Alert
965 Money Laundering, Asset Forfeiture and International Financial
2162 Money Management Letter
2242 Money Market Directory of Pension Funds and their Investment Managers
2103 Money Market Insight
2501 Money Marketing
2248 Moneyfacts
2512 Moneyguide: The Handbook of Personal Finance
2447 MONIT
404 Monitor
1361 Monthly Bulletin of Statistics
986 Monthly Catalog of United States Government Publications
2181 Monthly Chart Book: European Equities

1368 Monthly Commodity Price Bulletin
75 Monthly Digest of Statistics
2336 Monthly Market Report
1064 Monthly Statement of the Public Debt of the United States
1653 Monthly Statistical Bulletin
1689 Monthly Statistics Digest
1067 Monthly Treasury Statement of Receipts and Outlays of the United States
1571 Moody's Annual Dividend Record
2249 Moody's Bank and Finance Manual
2250 Moody's Bond Record
2251 Moody's Bond Survey
1567 Moody's Company Data
1568 Moody's Corporate News – International
1570 Moody's Corporate Profiles
1569 Moody's Dividend Record
1572 Moody's Handbook of Common and OTC Stocks
1573 Moody's Handbook of Dividend Achievers
1574 Moody's Industrial Manual
1575 Moody's Industry Review
1576 Moody's International Manual
2252 Moody's Municipal and Government Manual
1577 Moody's OTC Industrial Manual
1578 Moody's OTC Unlisted Manual
1579 Moody's Public Utility Manual
1580 Moody's Transportation Manual
1581 Moody's USA Annual Dividend Record
671 Moores Rowland's Orange Tax Guide (Year)
672 Moores Rowland's Yellow Tax Guide (Year)
2258 Morningstar 500 Sourcebook
2259 Morningstar Closed End Funds
2260 Morningstar Mutual Funds
2261 Morningstar No Load Funds
2406 Mortgage and Real Estate Executives Report
2119 Mortgage-Backed Securities Letter
2337 Mortgage Bank Weekly
1884 Mortgage Banking
1675 Mortgage Banks and the Mortgage Bond in Europe
2082 Mortgage Finance Gazette
2143 Mortgage Lender Directory
2144 Mortgage Market Statistical Annual
421 Mortgage Marketplace [American Banker Newsletters]
2265 Mortgage Marketplace [Mortgage Commentary Publications]
1690 Mortgage Monthly

1691 Mortgage Weekly
1447 Multinational Service
1236 Multistate Tax Commission Review
2370 Municipal Ratings Handbook
2526 Municipal Year Book (Year)
2383 Munifacts
2071 Mutual Fund Advance
2397 Mutual Fund Advisor
1968 Mutual Fund Charts
2120 Mutual Fund Directory
1842 Mutual Fund Fact Book
2262 Mutual Fund Performance Report
2344 Mutual Fund ProFiles
1969 Mutual Fund Report
2104 Mutual Funds Almanac
2407 Mutual Funds Current Performance & Dividend Record
2263 Mutual Funds Ondisc
2218 Mutual Funds Performance Report
1663 Mutuality
1708 NAPF Annual Survey of Occupational Pension Schemes
1709 NAPF Pensions Legislation Service
1710 NAPF Yearbook
2479 NAPFA Advisor
1829 NASD Notices to Members
1830 NASD Regulatory & Compliance Alert
1831 Nasdaq Fact Book & Company Directory
1417 National Accounts
39 National Accounts of OECD Countries (Years)
1362 National Accounts Statistics
1356 National Accounts Studies of the ESCWA Region
876 National Bankruptcy Reporter
2267 National Bond Summary
1102 National Credit Union Administration Rules and Regulations
971 National Criminal Justice Database on CD-ROM
1885 National Delinquency Survey
179 National Directory of Addresses and Telephone Numbers
373 National Directory of Bulletin Board Systems
94 National Economic, Social and Environmental Data Bank
1050 National Economic Trends
1234 National Educator
2587 National Institute Economic Review
596 National Insurance Contributions Handbook
920 National Insurance Law Review
914 National Journal

926 National Law Journal
1891 National Mortgage Broker
1282 National Public Accountant
2270 National Quotation Bureau Pink Sheets
1907 National Real Estate Investor
2268 National Stock Summary
1238 National Tax Journal
180 National Trade and Professional Associations
93 National Trade Data Bank
2272 National Underwriter
422 NCUA Watch
1583 Nelson's Directory of Investment Research
2274 Nelson's Directory of Plan Sponsors
1584 Nelson's Earnings Outlook
1585 Nelson's Guide to Institutional Research
2275 Nelson's Guide to Pension Fund Consultants (Year)
1179 Network, The
2586 New Economy
1029 New England Economic Review
1619 New Issues Institutional Research
673 New Law Journal
1810 New on the Amex
1001 New Serial Titles
1833 New York Stock Exchange Fact Book
163 Newsletters in Print
1669 Newsline/Press Summary
374 Newspapers Online
203 NFAIS Newsletter
204 NFAIS Report Series
205 NFAIS Yearbook of the Information Industry (Year)
2538 **NoLoad Fund*X
2456 Non-Domestic Rating Legislation Database
2779 North American Journal of Economics and Finance
2031 Noteware
96 NTIS Alerts
455 O'Neal's Close Corporations
1080 OCC Bulletins
837 Occupational Pensions
240 OCLC Online Union Catalog
2588 ODI Index to Development Literature
40 OECD Economic Outlook
41 OECD Economic Outlook: Historical Statistics
42 OECD Economic Studies
43 OECD Economic Surveys
44 OECD Financial Statistics

45 OECD Observer
47 OECD Reviews on Foreign Direct Investment
46 OECD STAN DataBase
101 OECD Statistical Compendium on CD-ROM
48 OECD Working Papers
498 Official IRS Publications
1383 Official Journal of the European Communities
1434 Official Press Releases
2425 Offshore Centres Report
1121 Offshore Directory
2032 Offshore Finance Yearbook (Year)
2226 Offshore Funds
2174 Offshore Trust Yearbook (Year)
1393 OIL
1438 OJCD
1439 OJINDEX+
353 Oliver's Guide to the City of London
371 On INTERNET (Year)
375 On Internet: An International Title and Subject Guide to Electronic Journals, Newsletters, Books and Discussion Lists on the Internet
405 Online
406 Online & CDROM Review
282 Online and CD Notes
409 Online/CD-ROM Business Information
372 Online/CD-ROM Business Sourcebook
407 Online Files Comparative Cost Analysis
408 Online Services: Review, Trends & Forecasts
1658 OPEC Bulletin
2798 Open Economies Review
1297 Operation of the Trade Agreements Program
456 Opinion Letters in Security Matters
1819 Options Bibliography
1820 Options Reference Manual: A Guide for Institutional Investors
2392 Options Survey
1136 Original Pronouncements and Current Text
2269 OTC Market Report
2393 OTC Special Situations
1620 Outlook
81 Overseas Trade Statistics of the United Kingdom
82 Overseas Transactions
164 Oxbridge Directory of Newsletters
2714 Oxford Bulletin of Economics & Statistics
2811 Oxford Economic Papers

2812 Oxford Journal of Legal Studies
2813 Oxford Review of Economic Policy
195 p180
297 PAIS International
525 Palmer's Company Law
1861 PAM (Year)
181 Pan-European Associations
1139 Panel Statements
1384 Panorama of EU Industry
246 PapersFirst
2033 Paribas Derivatives Handbook (Year)
991 Parliament
2563 Parliament and Government Pocket Book (Year)
2564 Parliamentary Affairs
457 Partnership Law for Securities Practitioners
2524 Pay & Benefits Pocket Book (Year)
2506 Pay and Benefits Sourcebook
2846 Payment Analysis Report
2278 Payment Systems of the World
1750 Payment Systems Strategies
2460 Payroll Currently
1965 Pension Fund Investment Performance
877 Pension Fund Litigation Reporter
1904 Pension Funds and their Advisers (Year)
1908 Pension World
2492 Pensions & Benefits Update
2536 Pensions & Investments
2537 Pensions & Investments Performance Evaluation Reports
354 Pensions Journals Index
2277 Pensions Pocket Book (Year)
861 Pensions Today
597 Pensions: Law and Practice
2243 Pensionscope Datasystems
1546 People Finder
1531 Performance Rankings Guide
1141 PERINORM Europe
268 Periodical Abstracts
165 Periodical Title Abbreviations
2522 Personal Financial Management
2525 Personal Pensions Handbook & Unit-Linked Survey (Year)
1844 Perspective on Mutual Fund Activity (Year)
2002 Petroleum Industry News
2285 Petroleum Intelligence Weekly
1468 PhoneDisc
1127 PIA Press Releases

1128 PIA Rules and Updates
2266 Pink Sheets & Yellow Sheets
1917 Plan Sponsor
2541 Planned Savings
2415 Pocket Charts
2693 Policy Bites
2312 Policy, Form and Manual Analyses
2799 Policy Sciences
2589 Policy Studies
991 POLIS
2594 Political Science Quarterly
2294 Polk Financial Institutions Directory
2295 Polk World Bank Directory
2296 Polk World Banking Profile: 2000 Major Banks of the World
2163 Portfolio Letter
1458 Portfolio Selector
2064 POS News
1956 Post Magazine
119 Potomac Portfolio Perspective
481 Practical Accountant
1166 Practical Corporation Tax Manual (Year)
2514 Practical Financial Management
598 Practical Lending and Security Precedents
599 Practical Tax Planning and Precedents
600 Practical Trust Precedents
1274 Practising CPA
2283 Pratt's Guide to Venture Capital Sources
83 Price Index Numbers for Current Cost Accounting
1532 Price Waterhouse Corporate Register
1498 Principal International Businesses
2201 Private Banker International
2065 Private Banking Report
2445 Private Company Secretary's Manual
2121 Private Equity Week
1621 Private Label Newsletters
2122 Private Placement Letter
1453 Private Placement Reporter
2297 Privatisation International
2298 Privatisation Yearbook
2690 Privatization (Year)
2691 Privatization Watch
1191 Probate and Property
897 Problem Asset Reporter
1854 Proceedings (Year), The

1203 Proceedings of the International Meeting
247 ProceedingsFirst
84 Producer Price Indices
1865 Professional Agent
2627 Professional Directory of Who's Who in Governmental Research
2450 Professional Investor
2437 Professional Liability Insurance
900 Professional Services Review
2050 Project and Trade Finance
2034 Project Finance Yearbook (Year)
269 PROMT
843 Property Finance & Development
601 Property Law Bulletin
2590 PSI Research Results
298 PTS Forecasts
1062 Public Bodies (Year)
2800 Public Choice
849 Public Companies and the City
2452 Public Finance
2825 Public Finance Quarterly
423 Public Finance Watch
2493 Public Investor
49 Public Management Developments
2453 Public Money & Management
209 Publishers Directory
210 Publishers' International ISBN Directory
2371 Put Bond Handbook
2372 Qualified Institutional Buyers Directory
1699 Quality of Markets Monthly Fact Sheet
2192 Quarterly Bank, Savings & Loan Rating Service
1096 Quarterly Banking Profile
1642 Quarterly Bulletin of Cocoa Statistics
153 Quarterly Domestic & Global Forecasts of Key Economic Indicators
1174 Quarterly Economic Survey
2652 Quarterly Journal of Economics
1081 Quarterly Journal [Office of the Comptroller of the Currency]
51 Quarterly Labour Force Statistics
50 Quarterly National Accounts
1418 Quarterly National Accounts ESA
2684 Quarterly Pension Investment Report
1921 Quarterly Report on All US Banks
1926 Quarterly Report on All US Thrifts

2105 Quarterly Report on Money Fund Performance
1298 Quarterly Report to the Congress and the East-West Foreign Trade Board ...
1963 Quarterly Reports [Callahan & Associates]
2780 Quarterly Review of Economics and Finance
1038 Quarterly Review [Federal Reserve Bank of Minneapolis]
1039 Quarterly Review [Federal Reserve Bank of New York]
2227 Quarterly Roundup of Emerging Markets
1035 Quarterly Survey of Agricultural Credit Conditions
1966 Quarterly Survey of UK Pooled Pension Funds
104 Quest Economics Database
2299 RAM Research Bankcard Update
2300 Rapaport Diamond Report
1394 RAPID
1924 Rate Watch
2373 Ratings Handbook
2051 Reactions
2202 Real Banking Profitability (Year)
2164 Real Estate Finance
2408 Real Estate Finance Journal
1886 Real Estate Finance Today
458 Real Estate Investment Trusts Handbook (Year)
1895 Real Estate Issues
2055 Real Estate Manager Profiles
2616 Real Estate Research Issues
1894 Real Estate Today
1192 Real Property, Probate and Trust Journal
2689 Reason
2625 Recent Developments in International Banking and Finance
342 Recent Titles in Law for the Subject Specialist
1871 Record, The
256 Reference and Research Books News
196 Reference Book of Corporate Managements
1441 Regional Development International
108 Regional Economic Projection Series
726 Regulation of Insurance
459 Regulation of Investment Advisers
827 Regulation of the Commodities Futures and Options Markets
1887 Regulatory Compliance Manual
424 Regulatory Compliance Watch
1791 Regulatory Report
727 Reinsurance Law
1957 Reinsurance Magazine

2018 Reinsurance Market Report
1721 Reinsurance Statistics (Years)
1893 REIT Handbook
2072 REIT Investor
2338 REIT Properties Listing
2339 REIT Weekly
1693 Report of Investment Activity
2465 Report of Reducing Benefits Costs
2466 Report of Salary Surveys
2464 Report on Managing 401(K) Plans
1020 Report on the Terms of Credit Card Plans
343 Reports Required by Congress
1552 Research Bank
2781 Research in Accounting Regulation
2783 Research in Finance
2784 Research in Financial Services
2785 Research in Governmental and Nonprofit Accounting
2786 Research in International Business and Finance
2787 Research in Law and Economics
2788 Research in Real Estate
270 Research Index
1208 Research Index: US International Trade Laws
1025 Research Library: Recent Acquisitions
2782 Research on Economic Inequality
1665 Resource
1419 Results of the Business Survey Carried Out Among Managements . . .
2203 Retail Banker International
1751 Retail Banking Digest
1752 Retail Banking Report
85 Retail Price Index
526 Revenue
52 Revenue Statistics of OECD Member Countries (Years)
2801 Review of Accounting Studies
1232 Review of Black Political Economy
2802 Review of Derivatives Research
2715 Review of Economic Studies
2653 Review of Economics and Statistics
2673 Review of Financial Economics
2814 Review of Financial Studies
2552 Review of Income and Wealth
2136 Review of Institutional Investors
1633 Review of International Co-operation
2716 Review of International Economics
2819 Review of International Political Economy

2803 Review of Quantitative Finance and Accounting
2020 Review [EMAP Business Publications]
1051 Review [Federal Reserve Bank of St Louis]
2273 RF&S Bulletins
499 RIA Internal Revenue Code and Regulations
500 RIA Tax Guide
912 RICO Law Reporter
2304 Risk
2438 Risk Financing
1867 Risk Management
2572 Risk Measurement Service
2439 Risk Report
2305 RISKDATA
2313 Rough Notes
1722 Royal Institution of Chartered Surveyors Directory (Year)
2379 RT Access
376 RTFI Index
1646 Rubber Statistical Bulletin
137 Rundt's World Business Intelligence
556 S Corporations
460 S Corporations: Federal Taxation
2328 S&L Database
1622 S&P MarketScope
2345 S&P Review of Banking & Financial Services
2346 S&P Review of Securities & Commodities Regulation
2347 S&P's Emerging & Special Situations
2357 S&P's Insurance Book
2359 S&P's Insurance Digest
2358 S&P's Insurer Solvency Review
299 Sage Public Administration Abstracts
1792 Savings & Community Banker
1634 Savings Banks International
1799 Savings Institutions
1800 Savings Institutions Sourcebook
1395 SCAD
1385 SCAD Bulletin
1440 SCAD+CD
1167 SCAS & VSCAS Companies' Accounts Disclosure Checklist
1122 Schedule D Holdings
410 Searcher
777 SEC Accounting Rules
557 SEC Compliance: Financial Reporting and Forms
778 SEC Docket
1547 SEC Filings [Information America]

1591 SEC Filings [OneSource Information Services]
810 SEC Financial Reporting: Annual Reports to Shareholders, Form . . .
558 SEC Guidelines: Rules and Regulations (Year)
1129 SEC News Digest
1475 SEC Online
1592 SEC Text
461 Section 16 of the Securities Exchange Act
1881 Secured Lender
779 Secured Transactions Guide
1704 Securities & Investment Review
462 Securities and Federal Corporate Law
690 Securities Arbitration Procedure Manual
828 Securities Fraud and Commodities Fraud
1835 Securities Industry Data Bank
1836 Securities Industry Trends
1837 Securities Industry Yearbook
878 Securities Insider Trading Litigation Reporter
463 Securities Law Handbook (Year)
464 Securities Law Review (Year)
2293 Securities Marketing News
465 Securities Practice: Federal and State Enforcement
1753 Securities Processing Digest
559 Securities Regulation
741 Securities Regulation & Law Report
466 Securities Regulation Forms
560 Securities Regulation Law Journal
2123 Securities Traders' Monthly
2215 Securities Week
691 Securitization: Asset-Backed and Mortgage-Backed Securities
2348 Security Dealers of North America
1021 Selected Information on Insured US Commercial Banks Ranked by Assets
1022 Selected Interest and Exchange Rates
1868 Self-Insurer
2145 Seller/Servicer Update
1925 Semi-Annual Report on All US Credit Unions
996 Senate and House Reports
166 Serials Directory
53 Services: Statistics on International Transactions (Years)
467 Shareholder Derivative Actions
468 Shareholder Litigation
829 Shepard's Citations
780 Shepard's Federal Securities Law Citations

830 Shepard's Uniform Commercial Code Citations
2035 Shipping Finance Annual (Year)
1811 Short Interest Report
102 Short-Term Economic Indicators on Diskettes
983 SI-CD
1838 SIA Washington Report
1124 SIB Full Subscription Service
1125 SIB Press Notices
1420 Sigma
1291 Significant Features of Fiscal Federalism
674 Simon's Tax Cases
675 Simon's Taxes
676 Simon's Weekly Tax Service
720 Single European Market Reporter
1386 Single Market
1548 Sleuth
561 Small Business Controller
2467 Small Business Economic Trends
488 Small Business Tax and Finance
865 Small Business Tax Review
1519 Smaller Companies Handbook
2540 Smart Money
2340 SNL Executive Compensation Review (Year)
2341 SNL Mortgage Bank Weekly
2342 SNL Quarterly Bank Digest
2343 SNL Quarterly Thrift Digest
934 SNL Weekly ComplianceFax
58 Social Indicators of Development
271 Social Sciences Index/Full Text
272 Social SciSearch
602 Social Welfare Law
1076 SOI Bulletin
603 Solicitors Journal
156 Sorting Code Numbers
1636 Sourcebook
2515 Sources of Grants and Aid for Business
2635 Southern Economic Journal
2374 Sovereign Reports
1823 Special Executive Reports
285 Special Libraries
1793 Special Management Bulletin
1260 Special Reports
1970 Spectrum International
16 Staff Papers [International Monetary Fund]
1023 Staff Studies

1562 Standard & Poor's 500 Guide (Year)
2349 Standard & Poor's Called Bond Record
2350 Standard & Poor's Commercial Paper Ratings Guide
1623 Standard & Poor's Corporate Descriptions plus News
1624 Standard & Poor's Corporate FirstFacts
2351 Standard & Poor's Daily News
2355 Standard & Poor's Daily Stock Price Record: NASDAQ
2353 Standard & Poor's Directory of Bond Agents
1625 Standard & Poor's Dividend Record
2352 Standard & Poor's Financial Institutions Ratings
1626 Standard & Poor's Industry Financial Data
1563 Standard & Poor's MidCap 400 Guide (Year)
1627 Standard & Poor's Register – Corporate
2354 Standard & Poor's Statistical Service
1564 Standard & Poor's Stock and Bond Guide
167 Standard Periodical Directory
1757 Standard, The
157 Standards Manual
2666 Stanford Journal of International Law
2667 Stanford Law Review
2578 STARS
469 State and Local Government Debt Financing
1281 State Board Report
1262 State Fiscal Prospects
1864 State Legislative Reports
1220 State Legislatures
1804 State Tax Manual
1249 State Tax Notes
1850 State Taxation Manual
1677 Statements of Recommended Practice
1357 Statistical Abstract of the ESCWA Region
88 Statistical Abstract of the United States
1652 Statistical Bulletin
1123 Statistical Compilation
1354 Statistical Indicators for Asia and the Pacific
1754 Statistical Information on the Financial Services Industry
276 Statistical Masterfile
76 Statistical News
2633 Statistical Science
120 Statistical Services
1363 Statistical Yearbook (Year)
1355 Statistical Yearbook for Asia and the Pacific (Year)
1352 Statistical Yearbook for Latin America amd the Caribbean
2568 Statistician
1872 Statistics for Pension Actuaries

1097 Statistics on Banking
2 Statistics on External Indebtedness
5 Statistics on Payment Systems in the Group of Ten Countries
277 Statistics Sources (Year)
2815 Statute Law Review
1613 Stock Charts
1700 Stock Exchange Official Yearbook (Year)
1701 Stock Exchange Quarterly
2356 Stock Price and Ratio Indexes
1628 Stock Reports
1912 Stock Traders Guide
2093 Stocks, Bonds, Bills and Inflation (Year)
1812 Stocks, Bonds, Options and Derivatives
1959 Stone & Cox Individual Pensions Handbook
1958 Stone & Cox Life Assurance Handbook
489 Strategic Tax Planning
2816 Structural Change and Economic Dynamics
2375 Structured Finance
721 Structuring Foreign Investment in US Real Estate
836 Stubbs Gazette
1832 Subscriber Bulletin
10 Summary Proceedings [International Monetary Fund]
1794 Supervisory Service
1767 Survey of Bank and Savings Institution Boards of Directors
89 Survey of Current Business
1358 Survey of Economic and Social Developments in the ECSWA Region
1044 Survey of Professional Forecasters
1098 Survey of Real Estate Trends
1024 Survey of Terms of Bank Lending to Business
1065 Tables of Redemption Values for US Savings Bonds
1276 Tax Adviser
951 Tax and Commercial Laws of the World
470 Tax Aspects of Real Estate Investments
527 Tax Avoidance
1168 Tax Briefings
604 Tax Case Analysis
1055 Tax Case Leaflets
1056 Tax Case Reports
781 Tax Court Decisions
972 Tax Court Reports
950 Tax Developments Yearbook (Year)
1169 Tax Digests
1250 Tax Directory

1258 Tax Executive
490 Tax Factbook
850 Tax Facts (Year)
916 Tax Facts 2
1261 Tax Features
677 Tax Havens Encyclopaedia
811 Tax Havens of the World
1795 Tax Insight
678 Tax Journal
1213 Tax Law Conference
562 Tax Law Review
1193 Tax Lawyer
2498 Tax Management Compensation Planning Journal
742 Tax Management Financial Planning Journal
744 Tax Management International Journal
743 Tax Management IRS Practice and Policy Series
745 Tax Management Portfolio Plus
746 Tax Management Primary Sources
747 Tax Management Weekly Report
1324 Tax News Service
1251 Tax Notes
1252 Tax Notes International
1253 Tax Notes Today
563 Tax Planning for Corporate Acquisitions
748 Tax Planning International
2687 Tax Policy and the Economy
1254 Tax Practice
1237 Tax Practitioners Journal
1255 Tax-Related Documents
782 Tax Transactions Library
564 Tax Treaties
1317 Tax Treaties Database on CD-ROM
1318 Tax Treatment of Transfer Pricing
681 TAX Books on Screen
617 Taxation
565 Taxation for Accountants
491 Taxation Manual
482 Taxation of Mergers and Acquisitions
1319 Taxation of Permanent Establishments
1320 Taxation of Private Investment Income in OECD Countries
605 Taxation of Remuneration Packages
1149 Taxation Practitioner
1256 TaxBase
783 Taxes
1057 Taxes Acts (Year)

784 Taxes on Parade
917 TAXLINE
1396 TED
411 Television Business International
412 Television Business International Yearbook
1302 Third World Debt in the 1990s
2073 13F Advance
1630 Thomas Register of American Manufacturers
2380 Thomson Bank Directory
2381 Thomson Credit Union Directory
1796 Thomson Savings Directory
2409 Thorndike Encyclopedia of Banking and Financial Tables (Supplement)
425 Thrift Regulator
833 Times Law Reports
1949 Today's Pawnbroker
618 Tolley's Capital Allowances (Year)
619 Tolley's Capital Gains Tax (Year)
620 Tolley's Corporation Tax (Year)
621 Tolley's Income Tax (Year)
622 Tolley's Inheritance Tax (Year)
623 Tolley's Inheritance Tax Service
624 Tolley's Insolvency Law and Practice
625 Tolley's Insolvency Service
626 Tolley's Insurance Law & Practice
627 Tolley's Journal of International Franchising and Distribution
629 Tolley's National Insurance Contributions (Year)
628 Tolley's National Insurance Contributions Legislation (Year)
630 Tolley's Official Tax Statements (Year)
631 Tolley's Practical NIC
632 Tolley's Practical Tax
633 Tolley's Practical VAT
634 Tolley's Tax Cases (Year)
635 Tolley's Tax Computations (Year)
636 Tolley's Tax Data (Year)
637 Tolley's Tax Guide (Year)
638 Tolley's Tax Legislation (Year)
639 Tolley's Tax Office Directory (Year)
640 Tolley's Tax Service
641 Tolley's Tax Tables (Year)
642 Tolley's Value Added Tax (Year)
643 Tolley's VAT Service
2146 Top 500 MBS Investor Database for (Year)

1196 Tort and Insurance Law Journal
606 Touche Ross PAYE/P11D Handbook
273 Trade & Industry Index
1340 Trade and Development Report (Year)
182 Trade Associations and Professional Bodies of the United Kingdom
257 Trade Directories of the World
785 Trade Regulation Reporter
1036 Trade-Weighted Value of the Dollar Index
2182 Traded Options Service
831 Trading Law and Trading Law Reports
2417 Trading Systems Technology
1873 Transactions (General)
1459 Transactions & Intentions
1718 Transactions of the Faculty of Actuaries
1423 Transition Report
1344 Transnational Corporations
2441 Treasurer
2442 Treasurer's Handbook, The
1068 Treasury Bulletin
2052 Treasury Manager [Euromoney Publications]
2518 Treasury Manager [IBC Publishing]
2495 Treasury Today
1369 Treaty Series
59 Trends in Developing Economies
1843 Trends in Mutual Fund Activities
1755 Trust & Financial Advisor
1099 Trust Assets of Financial Institutions
812 Trust Department Administration and Operations
644 Trust Law International
1756 Trust Letter
1797 Trustees & Directors Handbook
1909 Trusts & Estates [Argus Business]
844 Trusts & Estates [IBC Publishing]
2410 Truth-in-Lending Manual
863 Tuckers' Directory of the Accountants 500
923 Turnaround Letter
879 Turnarounds & Workouts
2228 UK Authorised Pension Funds
2229 UK Authorised Unit Trusts
2230 UK Broker Managed Funds
2009 UK Brokers Yearbook (Year)
788 UK Financial Services Reporter
2231 UK Group Pension Funds and Exempt Unit Trusts
2077 UK Insurance Companies: General Business

2078 UK Insurance Market: Corporate Profile Service
2079 UK Insurer Security Rating Service
2232 UK Investment Trusts
2233 UK Life Insurance Funds
1975 UK Point & Figure Library
1593 UK Private+
1594 UK Small Companies
792 UK Tax Statutes and Statutory Instruments
1425 UK Trade Statistical Reports
2234 UK Unit Linked Individual Pension Funds
2235 UK Unit Linked Life Funds
2316 UK Venture Capital Journal
1503 UK's 10,000 Largest Companies
984 UKOP
160 Ulrich's International Periodicals Directory (Year)
300 UNBIS Plus on CD-ROM
1341 UNCTAD Commodity Yearbook (Year)
1342 UNCTAD Review
1100 Uniform Bank Performance Reports
471 Uniform Commercial Code Reporting Service
698 Uniform Laws Annotated
2253 Unit Investment Trusts Service Manuals
2254 Unit Investment Trusts Weekly Reports
2502 Unit Trust Index
1706 Unit Trust Review and Directory (Year)
1707 Unit Trust Yearbook (Year)
607 Unit Trusts: The Law and Practice
2530 United & Babson Investment Report
77 United Kingdom Balance of Payments
78 United Kingdom National Accounts
1918 United Mutual Fund Selector
103 United Nations Statistics on CD-ROM
2066 United States Banker
992 United States Code
699 United States Code Annotated
702 United States Government Manual (Year)
722 United States Income Tax Treaties
723 United States Internal Revenue Service International Tax Compliance Information
749 United States Law Week
703 United States Statutes at Large
887 United States Supreme Court Cases
2670 University of Chicago Law Review
2621 University Research in Business and Economics: A Bibliography

2137 Unquote
1336 UNS/SABIR
1170 Update [Institute of Chartered Accountants in England and Wales]
1785 Update [National Association of Federal Credit Unions]
953 US Banking Library
2281 US Banks
92 US Direct Investment Abroad
1230 US Economic Outlook
1595 US Equities
786 US Federal Tax Forms
787 US Federal Tax Guide
1052 US Financial Data
789 US Income Tax Regulations
95 US Industrial Outlook
2282 US Insurance
566 US International Taxation
854 US Maritime Alert
790 US Master Tax Guide
1292 US Overseas Loans and Grants and Assistance from International
1597 US Private Profiles
1596 US Private+
1598 US Public
1599 US Public Profiles
121 US Quarterly Balance of Payments
791 US Standard Federal Tax Reporter
793 US Tax Treaties
1257 US Tax Treaty Reference Library
111 USA and Canada (Year)
608 Use of Offshore Jurisdictions
1876 Valuation
679 Value Added Tax
2264 Variable Annuity/Life Performance Report
492 VAT Factbook
729 VAT Information Service
493 VAT Intelligence
1896 VenCap Data Quest
472 Venture Capital and Small Business Financings
1953 Venture Capital Database
2317 Venture Capital Journal
2394 Venture Capital Report
2395 Venture Capital Report Guide to Venture Capital in the UK & Europe
283 Walford's Guide to Reference Material

2124 Wall Street Computer Review
2398 Wall Street Digest
2165 Wall Street Letter
2418 Wall Street Network News
1632 Wall Street Transcript
1184 Washington Letter
1798 Washington Perspective
344 Washington Representatives (Year)
122 Washington Service Calendar
1185 Washington Summary
1334 WCTA World Business Directory
1979 Weekly Breakout Service
1813 Weekly Bulletin [American Stock Exchange]
1082 Weekly Bulletin [Office of the Comptroller of the Currency]
1106 Weekly Compilation of Presidential Documents
1651 Weekly Eurobond Guide
1980 Weekly Futures Service
1460 Weekly Insider Report
1982 Weekly Mutual Funds Breakouts
1981 Weekly Options Service
1428 Weekly Selected Statistics
1983 Weekly Service on NYSE/ASE
1888 Weekly Survey of Mortgage Interest Rates and Applications Volumes
528 Weinberg and Blank on Take-Overs and Mergers
112 Western Europe (Year)
148 Western European Business Intelligence on Disc
567 WGL Tax Audio Alert
2532 What Investment
2533 What Mortgage
227 What's New in Business Information
241 Whitaker's Books in Print (Year)
2085 Who Owns What in World Banking (Year)
1499 Who Owns Whom: International
184 Who's Who
345 Who's Who in Congress
1805 Who's Who in Equipment Leasing
197 Who's Who in European Business
309 Who's Who in European Institutions, Organizations and Enterprises: (Year)
310 Who's Who in European Politics
198 Who's Who in Finance and Industry
199 Who's Who in International Banking

2083 Who's Who in Mortgage Finance
200 Who's Who in Risk Capital (Year)
286 Who's Who in Special Libraries (Year)
1702 Who's Who in the City (Year)
287 Who's Who in the European Information World (Year)
1839 Who's Who in the Securities Industry
288 Who's Who in the UK Information World (Year)
2421 Who's Who in Venture Capital
2429 Who's Who of Credit Management
1289 Who's Who of Customs Brokers & International Freight Forwarders
2412 Wiesenberger – Current Performance and Dividend Report
2413 Wiesenberger Mutual Fund Investment Analyzer
2411 Wiesenberger Panorama
107 Wiley Business Intelligence Reports
274 Wilson Business Abstracts
242 WLN Database
2584 WoPCAS: Working Papers Current Awareness Service
611 World Accounting Report
301 World Agricultural Economics and Rural Sociology Abstracts
1296 World Agricultural Supply and Demand Estimates
966 World Arbitration & Mediation Report
60 World Bank Group Directory
348 World Banking Abstracts
2834 World Broadcasting Information
126 World Business and Economic Review (Year)
149 World Commodity Forecasts
1307 World Competitiveness Report
61 World Debt Tables
62 World Development Indicators
63 World Development Report
349 World Directory of Stock Exchanges
1364 World Economic and Social Survey (Year)
124 World Economic Factbook (Year)
17 World Economic Outlook
2717 World Economy
1345 World Economy Group Annual Report
2090 World Insurance Report
1370 World Investment Directory (Year)
1343 World Investment Report (Year)
2036 World Leasing Yearbook (Year)
1308 World Link
1549 World M&A Network
150 World Market Atlas

125 World Marketing Data and Statistics on CD-ROM (Year)
1660 World Metal Statistics
151 World Outlook (Year)
2010 World Reinsurers Yearbook (Year)
1659 World Silver Survey
1365 World Statistics in Brief: United Nations Statistical Pocketbook
1645 World Steel in Figures
64 World Tables
612 World Tax Report
2592 World Today
1335 World Traders
1506 World's Major Companies
1600 Worldscope Profiles
1178 Worldtrade: A Practical Guide to Doing Business in Overseas Ma
2309 Worldwide Insurance Abstracts
954 Worldwide Standards
1143 Worldwide Standards Service on CD-ROM
2679 Yale Journal on Regulation
2680 Yale Law Journal
1374 Year Book of Labour Statistics
2221 Year in Numbers, The
1338 Yearbook (Year) [United Nations Commission on International Trade Law]
183 Yearbook of International Organizations (Year)
158 Yearbook of Payment Statistics
311 Yearbook of the European Communities and of the other European Organizations
1337 Yearbook of the United Nations